Encyclopedia of CRIMINOLOGY

Volume 1

Encyclopedia of CRIMINOLOGY

Volume 1
A-G

Richard A. Wright
J. Mitchell Miller
Editors

ROUTLEDGE
New York • London

Published in 2005 by

Routledge
An Imprint of the Taylor & Francis Group
270 Madison Avenue
New York, NY 10016

Published in Great Britain by
Routledge
An Imprint of the Taylor & Francis Group
2 Park Square
Milton Park, Abingdon
Oxon, OX14 4RN, U.K.

Routledge is an imprint of the Taylor & Francis Group

10 9 8 7 6 5 4 3 2 1

Library of Congress Cataloging-in-Publication Data

Encyclopedia of criminology/Richard A. Wright, editor, J. Mitchell Miller, editor.
p. cm.
Includes bibliographical references and index.
ISBN 1-57958-387-3 (set: alk. paper) — ISBN 1-57958-465-9 (vol. 1: alk. paper) — ISBN 1-57958-466-7 (vol. 2: alk. paper) — ISBN 1-57958-467-5 (vol. 3: alk. paper) 1. Criminology—Encyclopedias. I. Wright, Richard A. (Richard Alan), 1953- II. Miller, J. Mitchell.

HV6017.E5295 2005
364'.03—dc22 2004004861

Advisory Board Members

DEDICATION

To Richard A. Wright, an outstanding scholar, colleague, and friend

Contents

Alphabetical List of Entries

Thematic List of Entries

Cross-Cultural and Global Crime and Justice

History of Criminology

History of Legal and Criminal Justice Traditions

The Justice System

Measures of Crime

Professional Issues

Prominent Figures in Criminology and Criminal Justice

Theories of Criminal Behavior

Types of Criminal Behavior

Victimization

Introduction

Crime and the threat of victimization are inescapable realities of contemporary society. Crime is so commonplace that prevention and security measures are viewed as natural and necessary precautions in both public and private life. A considerable and growing percentage of public resources are allocated for juvenile delinquency prevention initiatives, law enforcement training and technology, corrections, substance abuse treatment and numerous other aspects of criminal justice. Crime has also spawned privatized security, loss prevention, investigation, and rehabilitation industries, indicators of a socially embedded problem that cannot be altogether remedied by public efforts.

Since the terrorist acts of September 11, 2001, the lines between criminal justice and military concerns have become more intertwined and have forced even greater resource commitment, as well as reconsideration of public and personal safety in everyday activities. Crime clearly impacts our daily lives by affecting the routine choices we make, including everything from where we live and how and with whom we interact to how freely we move and whether we must protect our personal property. Crime is so ordinary and widespread that we have become somewhat desensitized to less than sensational acts. It also, somewhat ironically, seems to simultaneously scare and mesmerize us. Entertainment media throughout the popular culture depict acts of greed and violence as glamorous and even heroic. Children play the popular video game True Crime wherein they assume a criminal role and steal, shoot and flee while parents watch quasi-reality policing shows in which law enforcement gets the better of crooks. These shows are largely overshadowed, however, by a general proliferation of crime glamorization in movies, music videos, and much of youth and urban subculture.

The scientific treatment of crime has also burgeoned during the last three decades, evident, in part, by the separation of criminology from sociology and the emergence of criminal justice as an independent academic discipline. While many criminologists continue to be trained in the sociological tradition, criminology and criminal justice departments today include psychologists, political scientists, lawyers, economists, and geographers. Moreover, research specific to crime and delinquency is routinely conducted in a number of other fields of study throughout the behavioral and health sciences, such as nursing, social work, public health, child and family studies, and medicine. The multifaceted and overlapping nature of crime has generated an enormous amount of scholarly research on a vast range of topics both within and across these concerned disciplines. The extant knowledge base also reflects multiple sources, that is, different methodological approaches and research designs featuring surveys, experiments, program evaluation, ethnography and edge ethnography, content and document analyses, the news media, social constructionism, and socio-legal and historical research.

The Encyclopedia of Criminology presents contributions that reflect the field's multidisciplinary composition and its theoretical and methodological plurality. The primary objective is to provide a comprehensive, digestible, and authoritative overview of traditional and contemporary topics that comprise criminology in a single reference publication. Previously focused primarily on theoretical concerns, criminology today is broadly oriented, from continued attention to the causes of crime, their interrelationships, and exploration of criminal processes to the address of crime, typically approached along the three prongs of the criminal justice system, law enforcement, the courts, and corrections.

The Encyclopedia of Criminology provides quick reference to definitive essays that span the scope of the discipline for interested individuals as well as students and scholars. The individual entries are linked to other related entries of interest by a thorough system of cross-referencing and blind entries that facilitate information searches through identifying synonymous and similar entry terms. The entries were selected so as to fully cover the following major substantive areas:

History of Criminology (9)

Important early developments and innovations in criminological theory and research and major justice systems events that impacted policy and practice are presented and discussed in social and cultural context. The influence of these events on the evolution of criminology as an academic discipline is addressed and provides an overview of criminology's rich history.

History of Legal and Criminal Justice Traditions (15)

The social, cultural, and historical origins of specific practices, why they emerged and the functions they served, and their influence on contemporary legal practice are presented in these essays.

Criminal Law (61)

The importance of legal concepts and principles for criminal justice in the United States and abroad are considered across these entries that relate the origination of laws, their evolution, and current status and impact within the criminal justice system. Fundamental legal concepts and principles are also related to larger social problems and policy issues, particularly important governmental actions and court cases.

Types of Criminal Behavior (124)

The major forms of criminal activity are addressed in these entries. Discussion speaks to the history of laws relating to the offense, the current, accepted legal definitions, up-to-date statistics pertaining to the extent of the behavior and known trends, and significant measurement issues. The correlates of each behavior are identified and associated theories are considered. Also, the policy initiatives taken to prevent these offenses and punish offenders are examined.

Correlates of Criminal Behavior (30)

Examination of the various factors that cause or are associated with crime. The important research on each correlate is reviewed and considered in terms of its implications for the criminological knowledge base, crime control policy, and criminal justice practice.

Victimization (8)

This relatively new specialization area is addressed through entries that present the leading theories and empirical research on victims of crime. The entries together comprise an epidemiology of victimization including its extent, frequency and trends. Attention is devoted to how research and public interest has resulted in new laws and changes in governmental policies. Victimization is considered in comparative context across these essays and leading issues in victimization research and advocacy are identified and critiqued.

Measures of Crime (15)

These entries provide an overview of how crime is calculated and rated. The major concepts and data-gathering techniques associated with each measure are reviewed and leading utilizations are noted. The development (timing and reasons) of measures, their import for criminological theory testing and revision, and controversies concerning their strengths and weaknesses are discussed.

Theories of Criminal Behavior (49)

The various theoretical traditions and specific explanations of crime are reviewed by a multidisciplinary approach, including positivistic, sociological, biological, psychological, and integrated perspectives. Pioneering scholars and works of each tradition are reviewed through presentation of leading assumptions and concepts and empirical support for each theory is assessed. The historical and contemporary policy and practice implications of the theories are also noted.

The Justice System (121)

This group of essays examines the major components, processes, and agencies that comprise the criminal and juvenile justice systems. The primary aspects of law enforcement, the courts, and corrections are reviewed. Comprehensive appraisal of system components features definitional synopsis, functions, and jurisdictional issues. Also included are the historical development and policy relevancy of each topic.

Cross-Cultural and Global Crime and Justice (45)

These essays examine the extent and types of criminal behavior, as well as crime control responses, in specific nations and larger areas of the world in both contemporary and historical context. In addition to relating the most common and serious crimes found in different countries, underlying cultural and religious influences on deviance and crime are considered in comparative and ethnocentric terms. Crime control policy efforts are identified, assessed and related to other social institutions of the region, such as religion, education, family, the media and the economy.

Professional Issues (8)

This broad group of articles examines important topics relating to criminal justice practice and criminology. The occupational entries are definitive in nature, but also provide practical information for students considering various criminal justice careers. The qualifications, scope of responsibilities and activities, salaries, and current levels of opportunity are identified. Other essays address resources and educational programs in criminal law, criminology, and criminal justice.

Prominent Figures in Criminology and Criminal Justice (44)

The major contributions of pioneers and other influential figures throughout the development of criminology and criminal justice are summarized. Brief biographies are presented and provide a background for understanding how major accomplishments such as important works, programs, and policies shaped the field. The enduring legacies of these entrants are also remembered.

J. Mitchell Miller,
Editor

Acknowledgments

The production of this set was a demanding, lengthy, and eventful undertaking. Many of the contributors are aware of its rather circuitous route to publication. The project began in 2000 by Fitzroy-Dearborn with Richard A. Wright of Chicago State University as editor, but was delayed in its early stages of development during 2001 when transitioned to Routledge. It was postponed again, tragically, later that year with the sudden passing of Richard Wright. A few months later, I assumed the editor's role and, along with the advisory board and the staff at Routledge Reference, began to contact the existing contributors with news of plans for completion and requests for entry updates to ensure currency of coverage. The project's renewal involved updating and expanding the entry list, selecting expert contributors, and working closely with the developmental editors. With a few thousand emails and a couple of hundred telephone calls later, the project assumed its final shape.

Of course, the contributors deserve many thanks; without their work and expertise the project would not have been possible. Editing the work provided many opportunities to interact with an incredible collection of scholars whose work here is evidence of how truly extensive criminology is today. The role of editor provided occasions to renew old friendships and meet many new colleagues from whom I have learned a great deal about my chosen profession. Working with the advisory board enabled opportunities to network and deliberate with many of criminology's leading contemporary figures and their participation both bolstered the quality of the *Encyclopedia* and was personally rewarding. In addition to conceptualizing the project, selecting specific entry topics, and identifying authoritative contributors, the advisory board served by authoring several entries, reviewing numerous manuscripts, and providing feedback to authors. They proved to be an exceptionally giving and hardworking group of colleagues for whose assistance and knowledge I am thankful.

Mark Georgiev, sponsoring editor at Routledge Reference, involved me as the coeditor of this project on the referral of Claude Teweles. For this I am grateful. Mark O'Malley and Joshua Pasternak of Routledge did an excellent job of keeping the project on track and facilitating numerous logistical issues as well as communicating with the several hundred contributors, particularly during the periods of uncertainty the project unavoidably experienced. Their guidance and focus made the project's scope seem less overwhelming and their professionalism throughout the process is greatly appreciated. Special thanks is also due to the University of South Carolina graduate students who worked on the project, Jennifer Tatum, John Shutt, Holly Ventura, and Jessica

McGowan. They provided momentum in numerous ways; correspondence, proofreading, facilitating contracts, library searches, cross-referencing and numerous other tasks essential to completion.

This *Encyclopedia of Criminology* marks the last major work started by my dear friend Richard Wright, so it seems fitting to remember him here. I recall when Richard was selected to edit the project and the high level of enthusiasm he displayed during its initial phases. Richard was remarkably broad in his interests and scholarship, a generalist whose writing touched the majority of specialization areas within the discipline. His breadth of knowledge, meticulous scholarship, and experience made him a natural choice for editing an encyclopedia surveying an academic discipline. So it was with his expectation of high standards in mind that the project was developed. I am confident that he would have been proud of the final product.

Abductions *See* **Kidnapping**

See **Kidnapping**

Abortion

When the U.S. Supreme Court legalized abortion with the decision in *Roe v. Wade* (410 U.S. 113, 93 S. Ct 705, 35 L. Ed 2d 147, 1973), there was the thought that this controversial subject would become marginalized. This appears to have been an error. The latest figures indicate that there is less support for abortion, primarily because of the controversy over partial birth abortions. Is the freedom for women to decide when and under what conditions they become mothers the most precious of all freedoms? Is abortion an issue that affects only women? Is it an issue of privacy? Or can the states intrude into the affairs and personal decisions of their citizens?

There are significant constitutional issues at stake in the judicial bias against women. One is the issue of privacy; the other is that of the Fourteenth Amendment right to due process and equal treatment. Does a woman have the right to autonomy over her body, or does the issue go further? What compelling reason is there for the Supreme Court to continue to listen to arguments regarding a woman's right to privacy? A review of all the cases regarding the issue of abortion is included.

There continues to be public debate regarding women's rights to privacy in state courts and legislatures as well as in the Supreme Court. In the 21st century we may see reproductive rights as the focus of the constitutional right to privacy. In the case of *Roe*, the Supreme Court indicated that a fetus is not a person and, therefore, not entitled to rights as protected under the constitution. However, the *Roe* decision did not give women the right to privacy at any time; rather, it applied a sliding scale.

Reproductive freedom has joined other rights such as freedom of speech or assembly. There are those who feel that women's role as the most basic means of production will remain the source of their second-class status if outside forces continue to either restrict or compel that production. In the words of Justice Miller, in the case of *Bradwell v. State of Illinois* (83 U.S. 130, 1872), "[t]he paramount destiny and mission of woman are to fulfill the noble and benign offices of wife and mother. This is the law of the Creator."

The freedom for women to decide when to become a mother and under what conditions are issues of great concern. Should states be prevented from intruding into the affairs and personal decisions of their citizens? The Supreme Court has held that laws prohibiting abortion are unconstitutional. In *Roe v. Wade* (1973), the Court held that "no state shall impose criminal penalties on the obtaining of a safe abortion in the first trimester of pregnancy." A woman cannot, under *Roe*, be charged criminally with obtaining an abortion, but there are administrative regulations and legal penalties that prevent her from doing so.

In December 1971, the Supreme Court heard a case (*Roe v. Wade*) brought to it by an unmarried pregnant woman who complained that the Texas statute permitting abortions only when necessary to save the life of the mother was unconstitutional. What was held in *Roe* was that a state may not, during the first trimester of pregnancy, interfere with or regulate the decision of a woman and her doctor to terminate the pregnancy by abortion; that from the end of the first trimester until the fetus became viable (usually about 24–28 weeks), a state may regulate abortions only to the extent that the regulation relates to the protection of the mother's health; and that only after the point of viability may a state prohibit abortion, except when necessary to save the mother's life. The Court further permitted the state to prohibit anyone but a licensed physician from performing an abortion.

The Court *did not accept* the argument that a woman has a constitutional right to have an abortion whenever she wants one and that the state has no business at all interfering with her decision. Rather, the Court established a sliding scale that balanced the right of the woman against the right of the state to interfere with the decision; it would have to prove that it had a compelling interest in doing so. During the first 3 months of pregnancy, when continuing the pregnancy is more dangerous than ending it, the Court found that no such compelling interest existed for overriding the *private* decision of a woman and her doctor. When abortion becomes a more serious procedure, the Court found that the state's interest in the matter increases enough to justify its imposition of regulations necessary to ensure that the mother's health is safeguarded. In the last trimester of the pregnancy, the Court found that the state's interest in the health and well-being of the mother as well as in the potential life of the fetus is sufficient to outweigh the mother's right of privacy except when her life is at stake.

The Court stated:

> This right of privacy ... is broad enough to encompass a woman's decision whether or not to terminate her pregnancy. The detriment that the State would impose upon the pregnant woman is apparent.
>
> Specific and direct harm medically diagnosable even in early pregnancy may be involved. Maternity, or additional offspring, may force upon the woman a distressful future. Psychological harm may be imminent. Mental and physical health may be taxed by child care. There is also the distress, for all concerned, associated with the unwanted child, and there is the problem of bringing a child into a family already unable, psychologically and otherwise to care for it. In other cases as in this one, the additional difficulties and continuing stigma of unwed motherhood may be involved. All these are factors the woman and her responsible physician will consider in consultation.

The Court continued by indicating in *Roe* that the right to terminate her pregnancy at whatever time was not acceptable by the Court. The court further indicated that the right to privacy was not absolute.

With regard to the argument presented that the fetus is a person, the Court went on to comment:

> [I]n nearly all ... instances [in which the word "person" is used in the Constitution] the use of the word is such that it has application only postnatally. None indicates, with any assurance, that it has any possible prenatal application. All this together with our observation ... that through the major portion of the nineteenth century prevailing legal practices were far freer than they are today, persuades us that the word *person* as used in the fourteenth amendment, does *not* include the unborn. ...

In answering the question of when life begins, the Court further stated:

> It should be sufficient to note ... the wide divergence of thinking on this most sensitive and difficult question.
>
> In areas other than criminal abortion, the law has been reluctant to endorse any theory that life as we recognize it, begins before live birth or to accord legal rights to the unborn except in narrowly defined situations and except when the rights are contingent upon live birth. In short, the unborn have never been recognized in the law as persons in the whole sense.
>
> We repeat ... that the State does have an important and legitimate interest in preserving and protecting the health of the pregnant woman. ... And that it has still another important and legitimate interest in protecting the potentiality of human life.

At the same time that the Supreme Court had decided the *Roe* case, it decided a second case—that of *Doe v. Bolton* (410 U.S. 179, 93 S. Ct. 739, 35 L. Ed. 2d 201, 1973), which involved a Georgia abortion statute that set forth several conditions that were to be fulfilled prior to a woman obtaining an abortion. These included a statement by the attending physician that an abortion was justified with the concurrence of at least two other Georgia licensed physicians; the abortion was to be performed in a hospital licensed by the state board of health as well as accredited by the Joint Commission on Accreditation of Hospitals; there was to be advance approval by an abortion committee of not less than three members of the hospital staff; and the woman had to reside in the state of Georgia. The Court held that these provisions *were overly restrictive, thereby treating abortion differently from comparable medical procedures*, and therefore, violating the constitutional rights of a woman to have an abortion. Since *Roe*, several states have passed laws that require the husband of a pregnant woman or the parents of a single mother to give their consent prior to having an abortion. Both of these requirements were struck down by the Supreme Court in *Planned Parenthood of Central Missouri v. Danforth* (428 U.S. 52, 1976).

Two other important issues bearing on the ability of women to obtain abortions are the right of hospitals to refuse to perform abortions and the right of Medicaid to refuse to pay for nontherapeutic abortions. In the case of *Nyberg v. City of Virginia* (667 F.2d 754 [CA 8 1982], dsmmd 462 U.S. 1125, 1983), a federal court of appeals concluded that a public hospital may not refuse to perform abortions:

> It would be a non sequitur to say that the abortion decision is an election to be made by the physician and his patient without interference by the State and then allow the State, through its public hospitals, to effectively bar the physician and his patient without interference by the State from using State facilities to perform the operation.

Theoretically, private hospitals may refuse to perform abortions, but it is not always easy to determine when a hospital is private. One needs to review whether it leases its facilities from the state government, whether it is extensively regulated by the state, whether it has received tax advantages, whether it has received public monies for hospital construction, and whether it is part of a general state plan for providing hospital services.

Under the decision in *Roe v. Norton* (408 F.Supp. 660, 1973), the Court concluded that federal Medicaid provisions prohibit federal reimbursement for abortion expenses unless a determination has been made that the abortion was medically necessary. The Court held that the government is not required by the Constitution to pay for any medical service, but once it does decide to do so, it must not unduly disadvantage those who exercise a constitutional right. Of late, laws have been passed that no birth-control clinic that receives funding from the federal government may give government information dealing with abortion. However, this has not stopped those who are against abortion from using whatever tactics are necessary to prevent such information from being disseminated, including that of bombing abortion clinics.

There have been cases—such as in the state of Idaho—that have attempted to make physicians criminally liable for performing abortions rather than lay the responsibility on the mother. Under the Idaho proposal, a man who had committed date rape, a term describing sexual assault by an acquaintance (although a rape regardless is a rape), could conceivably force the woman to carry the child.

Further decisions have been made affecting the woman's right to choose. For example, in the case of *Bellotti v. Baird* (443 U.S. 622, 99 S. Ct. 3035, 61 L.Ed. 2d 797, 1979), the Court had voted by a majority vote of 8-1 that a state may require a pregnant unmarried minor to obtain parental consent for an abortion if it also offers an alternative procedure. In the case of *Harris v. McRae* (448 U.S. 297, 100 S. Ct 2671, 65 L. Ed. 2d 784, 1980), the Court upheld by a margin of 5-4 the Hyde Amendment, which denies federal reimbursement for Medicaid abortions. And in the case of *City of Akron v. Center for Reproductive Health, Inc.* (462 U.S. 416, 103 S.Ct 2481, 76 L. Ed. 2d 687, 1983), the Court voted 6-3 that states cannot mandate what doctors tell abortion patients or require that abortions for women more than 3 months pregnant be performed in a hospital. In *Thornburgh v. American College of Obstetrics and Gynecologists* (476 U.S. 747, 106 S.Ct. 2169, 90 L.Ed. 2d 779, 1986), the Court voted 5-4 that states may not require doctors to tell women about risks of abortion and possible alternatives or dictate procedures to third-trimester abortions.

In the case of Ohio, upholding a law that required a minor to notify one parent before obtaining an abortion, Justice Kennedy wrote that "it is both rational and fair for the State to conclude that, in most instances, the family will strive to give a lonely or even terrified minor advice that is both compassionate and mature." However, Justice Blackmun, who was the senior author of *Roe*, wrote in what has been described as a stinging dissent that Kennedy and his adherents were guilty of "selective blindness" to the reality that "not all children in our country were fortunate enough to be members of loving families. For too many young pregnant women parental involvement in this intimate decision threatens harm, rather than promises of comfort." He ended by stating that "... a minor needs no statute to seek the support of loving parents. ... If that compassionate support is lacking, an unwanted pregnancy is a poor way to generate it." And in *Webster v. Reproductive Health Services* (492 U.S. 490, 109 S.Ct 3040, 106 L.Ed. 2d 410, 1989), the Court upheld 5-4 Missouri's law barring the use of public facilities or public employees in performing abortions, and requiring physicians to test for the viability of any fetus believed to be more than 20 weeks old.

Debate over these and other issues has spawned extensive litigation and put the Court in the position of reviewing medical and operational practices beyond its competence. We, therefore, believe that the time has come for the court to abandon its efforts to impose a comprehensive solution to the abortion question. Under the constitution, legislative bodies cannot impose irrational constraints on a woman's procreative choice. But, within those broad confines, the appropriate scope of abortion regulation should be left with the people and to the political processes the people have devised to govern their affairs.

The Court stated that Missouri had placed no obstacles in the path of those women seeking abortions. Rather, the state simply chose not to encourage or assist abortions in any respect.

In the case of *Rust v. Sullivan* (114 L.Ed. 233, 1991), the Court upheld by 5-4 the federal government's ban on abortion counseling in federally funded family-planning clinics. In the case of *Planned Parenthood of Southeastern Pennsylvania v. Casey* (505 U.S. 822, 1992), the court decided against the constitutionality of a law passed in Pennsylvania.

Informed Consent

At least 24 hours before the abortion, except in emergencies, the physician must tell the woman:

- The nature of the proposed procedure or treatment and the risks and alternatives.
- The probable gestational age of the unborn child.
- The medical risks associated with carrying her child to term.
- That government materials are available that list agencies offering alternatives to abortion.
- That medical assistance and benefits may be available for prenatal care, childbirth, and neonatal care.

Parental Consent

If the woman is under 18 and not supporting herself, her parents must be informed of the impending procedure. If both parents or guardians refuse to consent, or if the woman elects not to seek the consent, judicial authorities where the applicant resides or where the abortion is sought shall ... authorize ... the abortion if the court determines that the pregnant woman is mature and capable of giving informed consent.

Spousal Notice

No physician shall perform an abortion on a married woman ... without a signed statement ... that the woman has notified her spouse.

Exceptions

- Her spouse is not the father of the child.
- Her spouse, after diligent effort, could not be located.
- The pregnancy is the result of spousal sexual assault ... that has been reported to a law enforcement agency.
- The woman has reason to believe that notifying her spouse is likely to result in bodily injury.

Reporting

Each abortion must be reported to the state on forms that do not identify the woman but do include, among other items:

- The number of a woman's prior pregnancies and prior abortions.
- Whether the abortion was performed on a married woman and if her spouse was notified.

The Constitution has been interpreted in many cases to protect the woman from arbitrary, gender-based discrimination by the government, yet the struggle continues. Cases continue to be heard by the courts.

In *Akron v. Akron* and in *Hodgson v. Minnesota* (110 S. Ct 2926, 1990), Justice Sandra Day O'Connor has taken the middle ground as articulated in her dissenting opinion in these two cases, where she stated that the right to an abortion is a "limited fundamental right" that may not be "unduly burdened" in the absence of a compelling government interest, but may be burdened less severely upon a rational basis (947 F.2d at 689–691).

What is noteworthy with regard to the cases involving abortion is that the motivation of a woman becomes entirely irrelevant in determining whether such a right is fundamental. To date, the decision in *Roe* stands, but limitations have been placed, as evidenced in the case of *Planned Parenthood of Southeastern Pennsylvania v. Casey* (1992) where the Court upheld state restraints on a woman's right to choose an abortion freely. Here, the Court allows states to impose conditions on women seeking an abortion—an "informed consent" provision that includes a lecture to women in an effort to "educate" them about alternative choices to abortion, as well as a 24-hour waiting period to "think it over."

The decisions of the court have given the state considerable leeway that can make abortions costlier and more difficult to obtain. Such requirements by the state certainly continue to prove difficult for the poor woman who lives or works far from abortion clinics. Even a waiting period as short as 24 hours will force some women who cannot afford to stay overnight to make two trips to the clinic.

In the case of *Hill v. Colorado* (2000 W: 826733) the Court upheld a Colorado statute banning protesting or counseling efforts within 100 feet of health care facilities or 8 feet of their clients. Whereas in the case of *Stenberg v. Carhart* (2000), the Court struck down Nebraska's partial birth abortion ban. The Court held that Nebraska's statute criminalizing the performance of "partial birth abortion[s]" violates the Federal Constitution, as interpreted in *Casey* and *Roe.* Here, the Nebraska law at issue was the prohibition of any "partial birth abortion" unless that procedure was necessary to save the mother's life. It defines "partial birth abortions" as a procedure in which the doctor "partially delivers vaginally a living unborn child before killing the ... child," and defines the latter phrase to mean "intentionally delivering into the vagina a living unborn child, or a substantial portion thereof, for the purpose of performing a procedure that the [abortionist] knows will kill the ... child and does kill the ... child." Violation of this law was designated as a felony and provides for the automatic revocation of a convicted doctor's state license to practice medicine.

On January 22, 1993, President Clinton, in office only 2 days, revoked a rule adopted in the Reagan administration that prohibited doctors and nurses in federal family-planning programs from counseling women on abortion. On January 22, 2001, on his third day in office, President George W. Bush signed an order overturning the Clinton administration's policy of giving federal aid to overseas family-planning groups that offer abortion counseling. In addition, the Abortion Pill RU-486 was approved on September 28, 2000.

A kind of late-abortion referred to as partial birth abortion has been in the news of late. States have passed legislation to ban this procedure, calling it immoral. Such legislation was vetoed by President Clinton, but on March 13, 2003 the Senate voted to ban partial birth abortions. The House voted to pass the bill as well.

In a statement issued by the president, "I applaud the House for passing legislation banning partial birth abortions. Passage of this in legislation is a shared priority that will help build a culture of life in America. I urge Congress to resolve any differences and send the final bill as soon as possible so that I can sign it into law" (www.whitehouse.gov/news/releases/2003). And so it goes.

This bill makes it illegal for doctors to commit what is referred to as an overt act of killing the partly delivered child unless the mother suffers from some preexisting conditions where a full-term pregnancy will endanger her life. No sooner had the ink dried on the legislation, the courts stepped in and put a stay on it, pending further judicial arguments. This bill was a strong victory for those opposing abortions. The procedure, rarely used, is noted for its symbolism and politics. Women have become the focus of political action once again. This is an issue fought in Congress since 1995, that will continue to be fought. The bill, although providing an exemption from the ban in cases where the procedure is necessary to save a woman's life, does not provide any exemption to protect her life—an issue necessary to pass constitutional muster.

It has been over 70 years since Margaret Sanger, according to Ellen Chesler, "claimed that science would make women 'the owner, the mistress of her self.'" The spirit of Sanger's words lives on: that battles were fought and won in prior years does not mean that these decisions will remain. Battles won will still be fought.

Roslyn Muraskin

References and Further Reading

Chesler, E. RU-486: We need prudence not politics. *The New York Times*, Aug. 2, 1992.

Muraskin, R., *It's a Crime: Women and Justice*, 3rd ed., Prentice Hall, Upper Saddle River, NJ, 2003.

Abuse

See **Child Abuse; Domestic Assault; Elder Abuse; Same-Sex Domestic Violence**

Accident as a Defense to Criminal Liability

In order to commit a crime, the law generally requires the presence of the following two elements: a physical act or omission (known as the *actus reus*) and criminal intent (known as *mens rea*). A person may use the defense of "accident" to demonstrate that the *actus reus* was not voluntary and thus negate criminal liability. Although some crimes are defined as "strict liability" crimes, meaning that a person is liable regardless of their intent, these crimes still require an *actus reus*, and thus, accident defenses might be available for such crimes.

An act must be voluntary in order to constitute a criminal act. The act must have been committed with one of the following levels of mental intent: intentionally, knowingly, recklessly, or negligently. Thus, persons must either have intended to commit the particular act knowing that the result might occur from their intended actions, or at least have been reckless or negligent in allowing a physical act to occur. For example, persons commit intentional acts when they swing their arms to strike another. A man also commits a physical act if he swings his arms while dancing and strikes someone unintentionally. Although the person in that situation did not intend to harm anyone else or even to touch another person, it is clear that the person intended to swing his arms, and the person should have known that someone else could have been nearby who could have been harmed. However, a person suffering from a medical condition that causes seizures would not have intended any act if he suffered a seizure and accidentally struck someone while falling to the ground. Such a situation might be considered accidental and the person could most likely use the "accident" defense to avoid being criminally liable.

Not every accident will constitute a defense to a crime. One example of an accidental action that might otherwise be considered a crime would be the following scenario: a man driving down the highway has a heart attack and his car veers out of his designated lane of travel and into another vehicle, killing the driver of the second car. Although crashing into another person's car is normally considered a criminal act, and in such cases a person generally could be charged with some degree of homicide, in this case an argument can be made that the person did not voluntarily cause the crash and had no mental state in which he could have planned to do so.

However, what if the person who suffered the heart attack knew that he had a heart condition, had been prescribed medication that would help his condition, and refused to take the medicine? Or what if the person's doctor had informed him that he could suffer a heart attack while driving and the person did not heed the doctor's warning and drove anyway? In each of these cases, an argument can be made that the accident was not out of the person's control and that by making the voluntary decision to drive while he was aware that he may suffer a heart attack or to not take his medicine, the person was responsible for the accident. Similarly, a person who is driving when he is tired should know that he might fall asleep and causc harm to others, and such a person could not successfully use an accident defense.

Accident defenses have been successfully used by persons with medical conditions, including epilepsy and sleepwalking. Controversy exists over whether a person could claim to be in a hypnotic state and thus have "accidentally" committed a crime. In that case, an argument could be made that the person was not acting out of his own volition; on the other hand, an argument exists that a hypnotist cannot force someone to do something that the person would not otherwise agree to do. Additionally, an argument could be made that a hypnotized person's actions were voluntary if he volunteered to be hypnotized, although there might be some argument as to what suggestions he thought the hypnotist was going to give him.

An act that takes place while someone is intoxicated is generally not considered an "accident," as long as the intoxication is the direct or indirect cause of the crime. The reason behind this is that, assuming that the person purposefully drank alcohol, he should have assumed he could have become intoxicated and thus will be considered to have intended his actions. A defense similar to that of an accident defense may be used if a person becomes intoxicated involuntarily. For example, a person might be forced to ingest an intoxicating substance against his will or might drink something that he has good reason to believe is a nonalcoholic beverage when in fact it contains alcohol. Those facts may be sufficient to constitute a criminal defense as the person did not intend to become intoxicated and was unable to control his actions while in a state of intoxication.

Accident is available as a defense to crimes primarily because one of the purposes of criminal laws is to deter persons from committing crimes, and there can be no deterrence when someone is doing something accidentally. However, in situations where the act can be traced back to some negligence on the actor's part, such as the epileptic who fails to take his medicine, has a seizure, and harms someone by falling on them, punishing the actor may deter others in a similar situation from failing to take their medication, thereby eliminating the possibility of harm to others. Thus, punishing such a person might serve the purpose of deterrence. Another related defense is the "insanity defense" accepted by some states, where a person might argue that he committed a crime without knowing or intending it owing to a mental condition.

People v. Freeman, 142 P.2d 435 (Cal. App. 1943) is a case in which a person claimed accident as a defense to a crime. In that case, the defendant was charged with reckless driving when the car he was driving collided with another vehicle, killing one of the other car's occupants and severely injuring another. The defendant's sole defense was that he was unconscious when the accident took place, as he was having an epileptic seizure. On appeal, the court determined that this defense would constitute a valid "accident" defense and that the jury should be instructed so as to be able to find the defendant not guilty if they determined he had no knowledge of his crime at the time he committed it as a result of an epileptic seizure.

TINA M. FRYLING

References and Further Reading

Anderson, T.M. and Gardner, T.J., *Criminal Law*, 7th ed., Wadsworth Publishing Co., Belmont, CA, 2000.

Dressler, J., *Understanding Criminal Law*, 3rd ed., Lexis Publishing Co., Miamisburg, OH, 2001.

Loewy, A.H., *Criminal Law in a Nutshell*, 3rd ed., West Publishing Co., Saint Paul, MN, 2000.

See also **Defenses to Criminal Liability: Justifications and Excuses**

Accomplices, Aiding, and Abetting

Accomplices, aiders, or abettors are persons, other than the primary perpetrator, involved in the commission of crime. Their involvement may be before, during, or after the actual crime is committed. The assignment of criminal liability to participants in a criminal enterprise became known as the "doctrine of complicity." Under ancient Gothic and Roman law, as well as English common law, all persons who were accomplices, or aided and abetted in the commission of crime, received the same punishment as the principal perpetrator of the offense (Erlich, 1959; Radzinowicz, 1957).

However, as English common law evolved, distinctions between parties of crime began to emerge. Blackstone, the English legal scholar, suggests that such distinctions became necessary to avoid punishing accomplices as harshly as the principal perpetrator (Erlich, 1959). By the late 18th century, over 200 English crimes were punishable by death (Gardner and Anderson, 2003). The gravity of punishment caused courts to seek lesser punishment alternatives for accomplices who may not have directly participated in the commission of an offense. It was believed that having degrees of guilt, coupled with lesser punishment, would persuade persons not to act as principal perpetrators of crime (Erlich, 1959).

Under later common law, accomplices were distinguished from principals by creating four categories of parties to crime. Attached to these categories were different levels of criminal liability and punishment. Parties to crime were first divided between principals and accessories. Principal in the first degree is defined as the perpetrator who actually commits a crime. Second-degree principals included aiders and abettors present during the commission of the crime such as lookouts or getaway drivers. Accessories were divided between those involved before or after the commission of the crime, known as the "fact." Accessory before-the-fact is a person not present during the crime but who has aided in the planning or procurement of supplies to support the criminal event. Accessory after-the-fact is an abettor that gives aid or harbors a person known to have committed a crime.

In addition to separating principals and accessories, common law rules prohibited the prosecution of accomplices until after the first-degree principal was convicted. This doctrine arose to prevent the execution of an accomplice until after it was confirmed that the primary perpetrator had committed the offense. Once the first-degree principal had been convicted, prosecution of accessories could follow (Pollock and Maitland, 1923).

After the Revolutionary War, American criminal law adopted the English common law distinctions between parties to crime. However, these differences began to fade until many modern statutes assign criminal liability separated between principals and accessory after-the-fact. Principals include common law first and second-degree principals and accessory before-the-fact. Accessory after-the-fact is assigned lesser criminal liability and is treated as a separate category (Samaha, 1999).

In combining traditional common law distinctions between accomplices, the *Model Penal Code* (Model Penal Code, §2.6 1980) describes liability for the conduct of another as "a person is guilty of an offense if it is committed by his own conduct or the conduct of another person for which he is legally accountable, or both." Legal accountability is explained as "(a) acting with the kind of culpability [criminal mental state] that is sufficient for the commission of the offense, he causes an innocent or irresponsible person to engage in such conduct; or (b) he is made accountable for the conduct of such person by the Code or by the law defining the offense; or (c) he is an accomplice of such other person in the commission of the offense." The *Model Penal Code* defines an accomplice as "a person is an accomplice of another person in the commission of an offense if: (a) with the purpose of promoting or facilitating the commission of the offense, he (i) solicits such other person to commit it; or (ii) aids or agrees or attempts to aid such other person in planning or committing it; or

(iii) having a legal duty to prevent the commission of the offense, fails to make proper effort to do so; or (b) his conduct is expressly declared by law to establish his complicity" (Model Penal Code, §2.06 1 & 3 1980). Hence, modern statutes define an accomplice as a person who either solicits the commission of an offense, aids in its commission, or fails to prevent a crime knowing it is about to occur (Klotter, 1994).

Modern statutes require the proof of both criminal act and mental state to prosecute principals and accomplices. Ordinarily, accomplice acts involve such behaviors as inducing others to commit crime, procuring instruments of crime, serving as a lookout or getaway driver, or encouraging or failing to warn a victim. After-the-fact accomplice acts include harboring or sheltering fugitives, hindering prosecution, obstructing justice, or facilitating escape.

Another consideration involving the accomplice criminal act is the issue of "mere presence." This rule holds that persons present during a crime are typically held accountable as criminal accomplices *only* if they have a legal duty, offer words of encouragement, or engage in actions that support or infer their participation in furtherance of the crime. Therefore, simply being present during the commission of a crime, in the absence of words or actions encouraging the offense, is usually not sufficient to satisfy the accomplice criminal act requirement (Klotter, 1994).

Most courts attach criminal mental state liability for accomplices based on their criminal intent or specific purpose to aid another or commit a criminal offense. Reckless or negligent mental states can be applied to criminal responsibility if accomplice aiding and abetting enable the person to foresee the outcome of the criminal conduct (Samaha, 1999). Fewer courts have suggested that the accomplices' knowledge of the criminal intent is required to assign liability. Although common law collapsed all parties before and after the crime together as principals, modern statutes view complicity after-the-fact as lesser offenses such as obstruction of justice or harboring.

American jurisprudence applied complicity principles from both English common law and Blackstone's interpretation of parties to crime. Contemporary criminal statutes consider participants in crimes as having the same criminal liability if they are involved before or during the criminal event and satisfy the required act and mental state to constitute an offense. Some statutes treat accessories after the crime with lesser liability because they were not involved in the planning, procurement, or commission of the offense.

William P. Bloss

References and Further Reading

Erlich, J.W., *Erlich's Blackstone*, Nourse Publishing Co., San Carlos, CA, 1959.

Gardner, T. and Anderson, T., *Criminal Law*, 8th ed., West/Wadsworth, Belmont, CA, 2003.

Klotter, J., *Criminal Law*, 4th ed., Anderson Publishing, Cincinnati, OH, 1994.

Model Penal Code, American Law Institute, 1980.

Pollock, F. and Maitland, F., *The History of English Law, before the Time of Edward I*, 2nd ed., Vol. II, Cambridge University Press, Cambridge, 1923.

Radzinowicz, L., *A History of English Criminal Law and its Administration from 1750*, Vol. 2, Macmillan Company, New York, 1957.

Samaha, J., *Criminal Law*, 6th ed., West/Wadsworth, Belmont, CA, 1999.

See also **Conspiracy to Commit Crime; English Legal Traditions (Common Law)**

Acid

See **Lysergic Acid Diethylamide (LSD)**

Acquired Immune Deficiency Syndrome (AIDS) and the Law

Since the diagnosis in 1981 of the first case of what later became known as acquired immune deficiency syndrome (AIDS), this epidemic has emerged as one of the most significant public health threats of the early 21st century. By 2001, the United Nations estimated that 36 million people were infected worldwide with human immunodeficiency virus (HIV), the virus that causes AIDS, and 22 million had died. HIV/AIDS presents profound questions about the use of criminal laws to respond to infectious disease outbreaks.

Prosecution of individuals for acts posing a risk of HIV transmission was made possible by several scientific advances early in the epidemic. In 1984, HIV was first identified as the blood-borne virus that causes AIDS, and by 1985, a blood test was developed to identify those infected. At the same time, medical authorities established that HIV is transmitted by blood and certain body fluids (in particular, semen or vaginal fluids). The primary modes of knowing transmission are the exchange of bodily fluids during sexual contact and the sharing of syringes by injecting drug users, although prosecutions have focused almost exclusively on sexual transmission. In order to prove guilt in such cases, prosecutors must prove that the accused engaged in behavior posing a risk of transmission when the accused is aware of both his or her infection and the risk of transmission presented by his or her behavior. Although there have been relatively few such cases prosecuted, they are often highly publicized.

In such cases, traditional common law or statutory crimes can be prosecuted. Attempted homicide has been prosecuted, which unlike homicide, does not require the death of the victim and proof that transmission from the accused caused death (in most cases, the accused is unlikely to survive the victim). More frequently, assault or related offenses in which sexual contact is alleged to pose the risk of bodily injury are prosecuted. Charges have also been brought for reckless endangerment. Additionally, many jurisdictions have communicable disease control statutes that criminalize behavior posing a risk of transmitting sexually transmitted diseases, such as AIDS. Since the beginning of the epidemic, many jurisdictions have also adopted statutes that specifically prohibit behavior posing a risk of HIV transmission.

For prosecution of most of these offenses, it is not necessary to prove that HIV transmission did in fact occur. The Supreme Court of Canada, for example, ruled in *R v. Cuerrier* (1998) that because of the *serious risk* of bodily harm, failure of a person with HIV to disclose his or her HIV infection before engaging in unprotected sexual contact constituted an assault. The Court noted, however, that the consent of the partner to forms of sexual contact posing a risk of HIV infection was a defense to an assault charge.

In some cases, it is not necessary to prove that it was even possible for transmission to occur. In a case involving a prison inmate with HIV who bit a prison guard, a conviction for attempted murder was affirmed in 1993 by the New Jersey Superior Court on the basis that proof that HIV can be transmitted by a human bite is not required (saliva, without being mixed with blood, does not transmit HIV); it is sufficient to convict based on evidence that the accused subjectively believed his actions could transmit HIV.

Consideration of criminal sanctions must take into account the highly stigmatizing effect of HIV/AIDS. Society frequently views those infected as morally blameworthy and thus deserving discriminatory and unfair treatment and social ostracization. This attitude has been particularly prevalent in industrialized countries in which HIV/AIDS has been associated with socially unpopular groups: gay men, intravenous drug users, and prostitutes. This scapegoating of persons with HIV/AIDS was described in seminal works by Cindy Patton (1985) and Dennis Altman (1986), and, more recently, by William A. Rushing (1995) and Stephanie Kane (1998). Prosecution of individuals with HIV/AIDS can be seen as both an extension of such attitudes and as reinforcing social condemnation, not just of the individual accused, but of all infected persons.

Persons with or suspected of having HIV/AIDS are at risk as victims of criminal harassment or assault-type offenses, either because of the disease status itself or because of the perception that they are homosexual. Many U.S. jurisdictions have addressed this issue by adopting "hate crime" laws that punish crimes motivated by hatred based on the victim's disability (HIV/AIDS) or sexual orientation.

Many public health experts have condemned widespread use of criminal laws as a response to HIV/AIDS as both ineffective and counterproductive. Historically, attempts to control sexually transmitted diseases by means of coercive measures such as criminal prosecutions have proven unsuccessful, as demonstrated by Allan M. Brandt (1987). Fear of criminal prosecution may deter individuals with HIV risk from seeking testing to determine their own status. Indeed, in some cases, prosecutors have relied on records from medical clinics as evidence establishing that the accused knew he or she was HIV infected.

Criminal prosecutions have also been brought against government, pharmaceutical company, and blood collection agency officials who were alleged to have been responsible for transmission of HIV through blood transfusions and the distribution of infected blood products used to treat hemophilia. Thousands of blood transfusion recipients and persons with hemophilia were infected with HIV, and, in some cases, because they were unaware of their infection, they transmitted HIV to their sexual partners or to their children during pregnancy and birth. Such cases have been prosecuted in countries including Denmark, France, Germany, Japan, and Switzerland. In France, a national scandal emerged in 1991 that ultimately resulted in criminal charges against high-ranking officials, including the former Prime Minister. In 1997, blood supply safety concerns resulted in the conviction of two former laboratory managers at the New York Blood Center, an independent blood supplier, for conspiring to tamper with government-required HIV screening tests.

Sentencing issues arise in cases in which a defendant has HIV/AIDS. In some cases, sentencing judges have shown lenience in sentencing such defendants, although several courts have ruled that sentencing an individual to a term in prison that is likely to exceed the defendant's life expectancy is legal. Thus, in effect, a sentence of a significant term of years is a life sentence for an individual with IIIV illness, particularly given the inadequacy of health care in many prison systems.

In the U.S., increasing numbers of persons who inject drugs are infected with HIV and, as a result, they pass the virus to their sexual partners or to their children during pregnancy and childbirth. As a result, criminal laws that prohibit access to sterile syringes have been identified as barriers to HIV prevention (Gostin et al., 1997; Burris, 1996). Although the U.S. Congress withholds federal funds for programs such as syringe exchanges, in which addicts obtain new, clean syringes in exchange for used ones, many states and localities have removed criminal penalties contained in drug paraphernalia laws and support syringe-exchange programs as an important HIV prevention outreach effort to the drug addicted.

David W. Webber

Further Reading

Altman, D., *AIDS in the Mind of America: The Social, Political, and Psychological Impact of a New Epidemic*, Anchor Press/Doubleday, Garden City, New York, 1986.

Brandt, A.M., *No Magic Bullet: A Social History of Venereal Disease in the United States Since 1880*, Oxford University Press, New York, 1987.

Brandt, A.M., AIDS in historical perspective: Four lessons from the history of sexually transmitted diseases, *American Journal of Public Health*, 78, 367, 1988.

Burris, S., The legal strategies used in operating syringe exchange programs in the United States, *American Journal of Public Health*, 86, 1163, 1996.

Dalton, H.L., Criminal law, in *AIDS Law Today: A New Guide for the Public*, Scott Burris, Ed., Yale University Press, New Haven, Connecticut, and London, 1993.

Elliott, R., *After Cuerrier: Canadian Criminal Law and the Non-Disclosure of HIV-Positive Status*, Canadian HIV/AIDS Legal Network, Montreal, Quebec, 1999.

Elliott, R., *Criminal Law and HIV/AIDS: Final Report*, Canadian HIV/AIDS Legal Network and the Canadian AIDS Society, Montreal, Quebec, 1997.

Gostin, L.O., et al., Prevention of HIV/AIDS and Other Blood-Borne Diseases among Injection Drug Users: A National Survey on the Regulation of Syringes and Needles, *Journal of the American Medical Association*, 277, 53, 1997.

Jackson, M.H., The criminalization of HIV, in *AIDS Agenda: Emerging Issues in Civil Rights*, Nan D. Hunter and William B. Rubenstein, Eds., The New Press, New York, 1992.

Kane, S., *AIDS Alibis: Sex, Drugs, and Crime in the Americas*, Temple University Press, Philadelphia, Pennsylvania, 1998.

McColgin, D.L. and Elizabeth, T.H., Criminal Law, in *AIDS and the Law*, 3rd ed., David, W. W., Ed., John Wiley & Sons/Aspen Law Publications, New York, 1997, and Suppl. 2001.

Patton, C., *Sex and Germs: The Politics of AIDS*, South End Press, Boston, 1985.

Richards, D.A.J., Human rights, public health, and the idea of moral plague, in *In Time of Plague: The History and Social Consequences of Lethal Epidemic Disease*, Arien M., Ed., New York University Press, New York, 1991.

Rushing, W.A., *The AIDS Epidemic: Social Dimensions of an Infectious Disease,* Westview Press, Boulder, Colorado, and Oxford, 1995.

See also **Prostitution: Extent, Correlates, and Forms**

Actus Reus (The Criminal Act)

Ask a criminal lawyer what a crime is and you may well get a fairly bland response. A crime is a breach of the criminal law. But pursue your theme, and ask how you can identify such a breach from a given set of facts, and your respondent may be a little more expansive. For the purpose of analysis, all crimes are capable of being broken down into units, often referred to by authors as elements. If you like, these are the "set of ingredients" (Reed and Seago, *Criminal Law,* 1999, 16) which when put together make up the crime.

Think of murder; furthermore, think of the definition of that crime, which exists in the author's home jurisdiction of England and Wales. What set of ingredients constitutes murder? To begin with there needs to be a killing, or, as the textbooks say, the causing of death of a person in being. If, in the street, I bump into somebody, who, as a result, falls over, strikes her head on the curb, and dies, that is surely not murder—the law of England and Wales restricts murder to deaths caused with an intention either to kill or to cause grievous bodily harm. Moreover, even if a killing is done intentionally, it might not be murder. Perhaps, I have killed you in self-defense; perhaps we are in a jurisdiction with capital punishment and I am your executioner—there may be something that renders my (albeit intentional) killing of you lawful and thus not murder. Perhaps we are soldiers at war—a killing can only be murder if done, to use the persistent archaic phrase, "Under the Queen's Peace."

Look at the elements of murder outlined above. They can be divided, broadly speaking, into two kinds: those elements that concern the state of mind of the offender and those that do not. Criminal lawyers have historically referred to the former kind as the *mens rea* (literally, *guilty mind*) elements. Thus, the *mens rea* for murder is an intention to kill or to cause grievous bodily harm. The remaining elements can be referred to as the *actus reus* elements. Literally, *actus reus* translates into *guilty act.* Indeed, to conceive the *actus reus* as the guilty act that makes up a crime is correct, but it is also arguably incomplete.

In murder, we can see that the elements of the crime have to do with matters other than the state of mind of the offender and comprise more than mere acts. For sure, there must be an action. However, we can see that the crime of murder requires that a particular result (death) be brought about. Furthermore, it is not always the case that the bringing about of that result (even intentionally) is murder. For a killing to be murder, it must take place under particular circumstances, that is, it must be unlawful and it must be under the Queen's Peace.

This analysis can be applied, more or less, to all crimes. So in summary, we might say that the *actus reus* of a crime is the prohibited actions, producing the prohibited result, and conducted under the prohibited circumstances.

Now, we know what the *actus reus* is, we might want to ask what it actually means. What is its significance? One response is that the general requirement in criminal law of a prohibited act reflects what one might call a liberal skepticism toward the criminalization of mere thought. Simply thinking nefarious thoughts, however reprehensible others may find those thoughts, is not criminalized until (1) the thinker acts upon those thoughts and (2) in such a way as to breach a specific provision of criminal law. There is a similar reluctance to criminalize merely on account of a person's status, however unpleasant others may view that status. Indeed, the Supreme Court has suggested that there are constitutional limitations on the ability of states to criminalize persons on account of their status rather than their conduct. On this issue, compare the decisions in *Robinson v. California* (370 U.S. 660, 1962) (criminalization of the status of drug addiction was unconstitutional) and *Powell v. Texas* (392 US 514, 1968) (criminalization of public drunkenness of a chronic alcoholic could be constitutional because it was not the mere status of alcoholism which was being criminalized).

A further response to the question of the significance of the notion of *actus reus* is that the idea of an act connotes behavior that is done, that is, behavior which is voluntary. A defendant whose conduct is involuntary commits no offense, because there is no act. See, for example, the decision in *Martin v. State* (17 So.2d 427, 1944) where the defendant's conviction for "appearing" drunk in public was reversed because he was forcibly taken from his home to a public place by the police—there was thus no act of "appearance."

It should be noted that in some circumstances, the *actus reus* elements of an offense can be satisfied by a failure *to act.* While the general rule is "no act—no *actus reus*—no crime," where the law imposes a *duty to act*, a failure to do so can equate to a positive action and thus form the basis for criminal liability. For example, consider the decision in *Jones v. US* (308 F.2d 307, 1962), which suggests that a manslaughter conviction can arise from a failure to provide nourishment to a child who dies as a result, provided that the defendant has a duty to feed the child.

By way of conclusion, let us go back to where we started, and note that the elements of a crime are simply devices that help us to determine whether a given offense has been committed or not. They are in that sense, analytical tools, rather than freestanding concepts. What exists, or does not exist, is the complete offense. If all the elements are present—offense; if even a single element is missing—no offense.

BEN FITZPATRICK

References and Further Reading

Ashworth, A., *Principles of Criminal Law*, 3rd ed., Oxford University Press, Oxford and New York, 1999.

Dressler, J., *Understanding Criminal Law*, 3rd ed., Matthew Bender, New York, 2001.

Fletcher, G.P., *Rethinking Criminal Law*, Little Brown and Company, Boston, MA, 1978.

Kadish, S.H. and Stephen, J.S., *Criminal Law and its Processes*, 7th ed., Aspen, New York, NY, 2001.

Lacey, N. and Wells, C., *Reconstructing Criminal Law: Critical Perspectives on Crime and the Criminal Process*, 2nd ed., Butterworths, London, 1998.

LaFave, W.R. and Austin, W.S., Jr., *Criminal Law*, 2nd ed., Minn West Pub. Co., St. Paul, MN, 1986 and Suppl. 1999.

Reed, A. and Seago, P., *Criminal Law*, Sweet and Maxwell, London, 1999.

Simester, A.P. and Sullivan, G.R., *Criminal Law: Theory and Doctrine*, Oxford and Portland, OR, Hart, 2000.

Smith, J.C., *Smith and Hogan: Criminal Law,* 9th ed., Butterworths, London, 1999.

Williams, G., *Criminal Law: The General Part,* 2nd ed., Stevens, London, 1961.

Wilson, W., *Criminal Law: Doctrine and Theory,* Longman, London and New York, 1998.

See also **Elements of Crime; *Mens Rea***

Adler, Freda

In 1971, Freda Adler graduated from the University of Pennsylvania with a Ph.D. in sociology after successfully defending her dissertation entitled "The Female Offender in Philadelphia" and so officially began her distinguished career in criminology and criminal justice. Adler is a prolific and widely published researcher who has published hundreds of scholarly works in the form of books, research articles, monographs, technical reports, proceedings, book chapters, and law reviews. Her eminent career spans more than 30 years, and Adler is considered a pioneer in the field of criminology.

Freda Adler's scholarship can be characterized into several major areas: deinstitutionalization, drug abuse (addiction and crime, treatment issues), gender bias, the study of female criminality, women in criminal justice, international and comparative studies, forms of social control, maritime crime (e.g., insurance fraud, terrorism at sea), judicial training, and criminological theory. However, Adler is renowned for her groundbreaking and revolutionary scholarship focusing on female criminality.

Adler is the author of *Sisters in Crime* (1975). In this book she discusses the status of women in general and focuses in particular on female offenders. Her book is a study of the nature and extent of the changing patterns of female criminality and female delinquency in the U.S. Until Adler's pioneering study, criminologists focused almost exclusively on male offenders, relying on data that only examined male criminality and focusing on theories that only attempted to explain why boys and men broke the law. Predominantly, the field of criminology was made up of men, and these men studied and wrote about male delinquency and criminality. Adler's work was the main impetus for including gender into future discussions on the causes of criminality and for the continued focus of criminologists on female criminality.

Adler advocates the liberation thesis of criminality. In the liberation thesis, as girls are raised more like boys and when the same opportunities are present for both genders, girls will become more like boys in every way, including criminality. Adler conceived the notion that female criminality is a product of the changing social roles of women in society. Adler reports in her book *Sister in Crime* that females were not only committing more crimes but also engaging in traditionally male offenses. She notes staggering increases in female arrests for more traditional male offenses including burglary (up 168%), robbery (up 277%), embezzlement (up 280%), and larceny (up over 300%). She ties these apparent remarkable shifts in female criminality to the changing gender roles in American society. Adler concludes that many of the differences found in male and female criminality are rapidly decreasing. She attributes the narrowing of gender differences in criminality to be the result of changes in traditional sex roles, greater equality for women, and an increase in the female labor force.

Adler's work and that of others paved the way for contemporary theories of female criminality. Such explanations as economic marginalization, power-control theory, liberal feminism, radical feminism, Marxist feminism, and socialist feminism have their roots in Adler's pioneering work, for it was she who shifted the focus from the exclusive study of male criminality to include female criminality in the mix.

Throughout her distinguished career, Adler has held significant organizational leadership positions. Most notable and familiar is her role as the 47th president of the American Society of Criminology (ASC; 1994–1995). The ASC is the oldest professional society of criminologists in the U.S. Her legacy to the ASC includes her contributions made during her term as president. Adler is credited with establishing a new ASC National Policy Committee in direct response to U.S. Attorney Janet Reno's request for researchers to share their research findings with policy makers. Second, Adler developed a new Statewide Policy Committee within the ASC with contact persons in every state of the Union. Third, under Adler's leadership, the ASC became a full member of the Consortium of Social Science Associations.

Moreover, Adler has considerable editorial experience. Editorial responsibilities are time consuming and often tedious; however, without such commitment, the dissemination of knowledge and the growth of a discipline might be stifled. Adler has done more than her fair share in this important area of scholarly contribution. She has served (or is currently continuing her service) on the editorial boards of four prestigious and prominent journals: *Criminology, An Interdisciplinary Journal* (1971–1973; 1997–1998), *Social Pathology, a Journal of Reviews* (1993–), *Women and Criminal Justice* (1995–), and *The American Sociologist* (1997). In addition, she is the editor of *Advances in Criminological Theory* (1989–present). Her editorial responsibilities and duties also include serving the role of associate editor (*LAE Journal,* 1977–1982), editorial consultant (*Journal of Criminal Law and Criminology,* 1982–), board member, advisory board (*The Justice Professional,* 1996–), and consulting editor (*Journal of Research in Crime and Delinquency,* 1977–1982; *Criminology: An Interdisciplinary Journal,* 1978–1985; *Journal of Criminal Justice,* 1978–1985; *American Sociologist,* 1980–1985; *Justice Quarterly,* 1984).

Adler is active even today and very much involved in the field of criminology and criminal justice. Adler is an adviser to many governments, including Poland, Finland, Brazil, Guam, the Philippines, Egypt, Kuwait, Australia, Costa Rica, and the U.S. She is also a consultant to the United Nations.

Adler has been honored with many prominent awards. She is the recipient of the prestigious Herbert Bloch Award. This award, sponsored by the American Society of Criminology, recognizes outstanding service contributions to the ASC and to the professional interest of criminology. In 1994, Adler was named an ASC fellow. This honorary title is in recognition of scholarly contributions to the discipline (criminology and criminal justice), career development of other criminologists, and contribution to ASC organizational activities.

Currently, Freda Adler is a distinguished professor of criminal justice at Rutgers University, where she continues to teach, advise, and mentor both female and male students. For a 1-year period, Adler was the acting dean of the School of Criminal Justice at Rutgers University.

LAURA J. MORIARTY

Biography

Born in Philadelphia, Pennsylvania, November 21, 1934; daughter of David R. Schaffer and Lucia Green (De Wolfson). Educated at the University of Pennsylvania, B.A., 1956; M.A., 1968; and Ph.D. in sociology, 1971. Instructor in psychiatry, Temple University School of Medicine, 1971; assistant professor of psychiatry and research director of the Section on Drug and Alcohol Abuse, Medical College of Pennsylvania, 1972–1974; associate professor of criminal justice, Rutgers University, Newark, 1974–1978; visiting fellow, Yale University, 1976; professor of criminal justice, Rutgers University, Newark, 1978–1984; distinguished professor of criminal justice, Rutgers University, Newark, 1984–present.

Selected Works

Sisters in Crime, 1975.
The Criminology of Deviant Women (edited with Rita J. Adler), 1979.
The Incidence of Female Criminality in the Contemporary World (edited), 1981.
Nations Not Obsessed with Crime, 1983.
Outlaws of the Ocean: The Complete Book of Contemporary Crime on the High Seas (with Gerhard O.W. Mueller), 1985.
Criminal Justice (with Gerhard O.W.M. and Laufer, W.S.), 1994.
Criminology (with Gerhard O.W.M. and Laufer, W.S.), 1991; 4th ed., 2001.

References and Further Reading

Faith, K., An Interview with Freda Adler, *The Critical Criminologist* 5, no. 1, 1993.
Flynn, E.E. and Freda, A., A Portrait of a Pioneer, *Women and Criminal Justice* 10, no. 1, 1998.

See also **Feminist Theories of Criminal Behavior**

Administrative Law

Administrative agencies fall into two broad categories, social welfare agencies and regulatory agencies. A citizen can find himself the subject of an administrative dispute resulting from a deprivation of a "benefit" or "entitlement" provided citizens based on certain prerequisites. These social welfare disputes generally involve a citizen and an agency such as the Social Security Administration or Veterans Administration. Formal hearings are often required because of due process guarantees contained in the Fourteenth Amendment.

When such hearings are necessary, the citizen challenges the agency or an agency ruling as it pertains specifically to that citizen.

When dealing with regulatory agencies, the disputes that arise may involve an individual citizen, but will more often than not involve an industry or enterprise. Should groups or individuals oppose a potential regulation or change in a regulation, they would make their opposition known through a formal hearing process in front of an administrative law judge who would conduct an inquiry very much like a civil trial.

The objective of the hearing for a recipient seeking Social Security benefits would be to determine that citizen's eligibility for the benefit. The objective of the hearing involving a regulation or regulation change would be to determine the impact and viability of passing such a regulation. Both administrative agencies would seek an administrative court ruling but the impact of the ruling would be very different in terms of the persons affected.

When we speak of administrative courts, it is important to remember the different kinds of administrative agencies that have been created and what the court is expected to accomplish in regard to an agency's conduct (e.g., determining benefits, license eligibility, or promulgating industry-wide rules). The entity responsible for resolving disputes that arise from agency decisions, protection, rules, or regulations is the administrative court and the persons presiding over these tribunals are known as administrative law judges.

The constitutional system within the U.S. assigns law-making authority to the legislature, law enforcement authority to the executive branch of government, and the interpretation of the law to the judiciary. Administrative agencies do not fit directly into any of the three branches as described by the Constitution. Practical necessities of modern government demand that the law-making authority of the legislature and the decision making of the judiciary be delegated. The Constitution provides that "All legislative power herein granted shall be vested in a Congress of the United States" (Article I, Section 1). It also gave Congress the authority "To make all laws which shall be necessary and proper" (Article I, Section 8). It is this law-making authority that Congress has chosen to delegate to various agencies that were created to address particular issues and for a particular purpose. Congress creates an agency by legislative enactment. The empowering statute has much to do with the nature of the responsibilities being delegated to the agency. Beginning in the 20th century, Congress dramatically extended the delegation of power based on the need to create agencies that would provide continuous expert supervision, specialization, and systematic and uniform regulation within a highly complex and diverse society. Additionally, Congress has limited time and resources to address a growing popular need for service, rule making, rate setting, and policy decisions. These statutes are referred to as enabling statutes and are intended to define the duties and limitations of an agency in performing delegated legislative and quasi-judicial functions.

In delegating authority to agencies, Congress must provide sufficient standards to guide agencies in the administration of the delegated authority. The U.S. Supreme Court has allowed significant latitude in delegating duties to created agencies as long as the enabling statute includes sufficient standards to avoid a capricious and discriminatory exercise of authority. In dealing with the technical world of the 20th century, delegations have been broad deferring to the expertise of specialists in making rules and administering agencies designed to address technical issues of technical enterprises. Absent cases involving personal rights or the regulation of professions, the courts will view the delegation most favorably in support of the legislation. Congress may delegate its rule-making authority if that delegation is accompanied by sufficient standards to guide in the exercise of that authority. In delegating authority, Congress must concern itself with three issues regarding that delegation:

1. what powers may an administrative agency be given,
2. what are the reaches of that power, and
3. what limits are placed on that power (Schwartz, 1976).

Administrative adjudications are the equivalent of a civil court trial; parties may present evidence, may examine and cross-examine witnesses, and make opening and closing arguments to the Administrative Judge or Agency Official. Parties to administrative hearings may involve: (1) benefit claimants (welfare, veteran, aid to dependent children—should a benefit be denied, a hearing may be required); (2) licensees (utility companies, radio and television stations, doctors and lawyers); and (3) recipients of services (if a state railroad authority such as the Texas Railroad Commission or the Federal Railroad Administration were to increase shipping rates, all persons from shippers and railroad employees to recipients of shipped goods may have a recognizable interest in the outcome of a hearing pertaining to the increase in rates).

Most disputes arising from administrative action are resolved informally. An agency is not required to provide disputants with a formal hearing (trial) unless the statute creating and empowering the agency specifically requires formal hearings. Should the empowering statute require trials, it becomes necessary for judges to resolve disputes. In administrative trials the parties are not entitled to a jury; all evidence to be submitted, arguments to be made, and briefs written will be evaluated by the presiding judge.

The common law rule that the moving party (that initiates the litigation) has the burden of proof is generally applicable to administrative hearings. As in civil suits the amount of proof necessary to establish the moving party's position is proof based on a "preponderance of the evidence." The burden of proof in a criminal trial is proof beyond a reasonable doubt. Proof beyond a reasonable doubt is often referred to as virtual certainty or 99% certainty, whereas a preponderance of the evidence is 51% certainty.

In most administrative trials property is an issue. Recognizing that less protection need be provided to the litigants in suits dealing with money and property, a lesser standard of proof based on a preponderance of the evidence is acceptable.

Occasionally, liberty interests may be involved in an administrative trial as in an Immigration and Naturalization deportation proceeding. The U.S. Supreme Court has imposed a more rigorous standard in cases where issues of personal security or liberty are involved. In such cases, the administrative burden of proof rises to "clear and convincing" evidence (*Woodby v. Immigration and Naturalization Service* (385 U.S. 276, 1966). Clear and convincing proof falls somewhere between 51% certainty as required by a preponderance of the evidence, and 99% certainty as required by proof beyond a reasonable doubt, further from the former, closer to the latter.

The Administrative Trial

As in all litigation, a series of formal and informal rules have evolved governing the conduct of a trial. When the "trier of fact" is to be a jury, more formality is required to keep objectionable evidence and testimony from tainting the jury's decision. When the trier of fact is a judge, less formality is required because of the judge's ability to evaluate all types of evidence without affecting his or her objectivity. Administrative trials do not deal with the constraints necessary to protect juries in that persons appearing before administrative judges are not entitled to a jury trial. All administrative trials are *en banc* (before the judge). All rules of procedure are relaxed and the pursuit of truth by the judge is given a much wider breadth than in most trials. The objectives of the administrative judge include: (1) management of the hearing; (2) development of an accurate record of the proceedings; (3) objective assessment of testimony and submitted evidence; and (4) a statement of facts and conclusions of law relied upon for arriving at the final decision (Cooper, 2000, 213).

The administrative agency involved in the dispute will be represented by counsel. The Administrative Procedures Act allows the benefit of counsel or substitute representation for any litigant in administrative trials, but agencies are not required to appoint counsel. (*Lassiter v. Department of Social Services*, 452 U.S. 18, 1981). The administrative trial is less adversarial in nature than the criminal trial; resolution rather than winning is the ultimate goal. Administrative law judges expend effort to encourage disputants to seek arbitration or alternative dispute resolution.

One of the distinctive characteristics of many administrative trials is the practice of substituting written evidence for oral testimony. Many disputes deal with substantial quantities of written materials that can be examined and evaluated by an objective reader without assistance or interpretation. When written evidence is introduced it is also made available prior to trial during the discovery process so that the involved parties may also prepare written comments and submit them to the court. Witnesses who appear, if any do appear, are most often experts testifying on their interpretation of the documentation in question. Cross-examination is not necessary because the opposing side has the opportunity to present expert witnesses to put forth its interpretation of the documents in question. For example, if a disability dispute were to be decided by an administrative law judge, the issue may simply be one of medical record interpretation. Both sides would proffer expert medical witnesses to provide an interpretation of the existing medical records with the judge ultimately reading the records, assessing the expert's interpretations, and coming to an independent conclusion. The need for cross-examination in this type of trial is limited to challenging the experts' credentials; expert interpretation is challenged when the opposing expert opinion is offered. Written evidence has been relied upon most successfully in rate or price control proceedings, where economic and expert analysis rather than "eye witness" testimony provides the majority of testimony. Cross-examination is provided for in the Administrative Procedure Act in those instances where "... a full and true disclosure of facts" is required (APA 5 USCA §556(d)).

The APA requires that all agency decisions be part of a record and include a statement of findings of fact and conclusions of law and the support for each. The findings must be issued in writing even though the administrative law judge may have rendered an oral decision. The requirement that findings of fact and conclusions of law be supported by written reasons upon which findings and conclusions of law were based is to explain why the facts and conclusions reached by the court led it to the decision it rendered. These written decisions may be used as a precedent by other administrative courts and provide a record for judicial review. Appeal of decisions by administrative courts is generally to the agency head. The Doctrine of Exhaustion of Remedies prevents a premature suit in courts of general jurisdiction. Before a suit may be filed in a court of law many agencies require that the administrative due process provided for by statute be pursed to its completion before a cause of action vests that can be heard by a civil court. In some instances, the exhaustion of the administrative process allows a cause of action to be raised in federal court in a §1983 lawsuit alleging a Fourteenth Amendment due process violation. Section 1983 lawsuits are a creature of Congress. In 1970, the U. S. Congress passed a Civil Rights Act giving citizens the right to sue their state and state representatives for constitutional violations. The two fundamental elements of a §1983 lawsuit are: (1) Action by a state representative under the color of law and (2) The deprivation of a constitutional right.

In some instances, appeal from an agency may not require relitigating the dispute. If the statute empowering the agency provides for judicial review, the decision of the administrative court and the review of the administrative agency head can be appealed directly to a federal court of appeals. This appeal process is referred to as judicial review. In addition to specific language granting judicial review, the statute will also provide a deadline within which review must be initiated. The time limit varies from 30 to 90 days but is strictly enforced.

Most administrative decisions are never appealed. Those cases that are appealed, are often returned to the agency for findings clarification. The doctrine of nonreviewability when applied makes certain kinds of administrative decisions not subject to judicial appeal (review). Section 702 of the APA provides in part: "A person suffering legal wrong because of agency action, or adversely affected or aggrieved by agency action ... is entitled to agency review" Section 701 says that agency review is not available except when review is prohibited by statute or the decision is based on agency discretion.

When judicial review is warranted and permitted, the Court will examine the record of the administrative proceeding to determine if any of the following errors have occurred:

1. Has the agency exceeded the authority granted to it?
2. Were the parties afforded necessary due process?
3. Was the decision rendered an abuse of discretion?
4. Was the record supported by substantial evidence?
5. Was the action of the agency constitutional?

Reviewing courts can neither replace the agency nor its administrators as the "experts" in the area over which the agency has authority. The court also may not turn a blind eye to all administrative decisions by presuming that all agency decisions conform to their grant of authority. The five questions above allow reviewing courts to examine the conduct of the administrative agencies and the administrative courts while still deferring to agency expertise. Judicial review provides the balance between the deference accorded administrators and administrative courts and the restraints and circumstances under which they must operate (Cooper, 2000, 251).

RONALD BECKER

References and Further Reading

Cooper, P.J., 2000. *Public Law and Public Administration*, FE Peacock, Itasca, MN.

Schwartz, B., 1976. *Administrative Law*, Little Brown and Company, Boston, MA.

See also **Clemency and Pardons**

Adultery and Fornication

Several points come to mind when discussing adultery and fornication. First among these, however, is the fact that both must be clearly defined. Adultery is simply conjugal infidelity, meaning that a person who is married has sexual activity with another person other than the person to whom they are married (Anderson, 2001; Melody, 2003). Fornication, on the other hand, is any and all sexual activity conducted between persons not married to one another (Anderson, 2001; Melody, 2003). Most societies have taboos against adultery, particularly for women. In ancient times in a number of cultures adultery was largely a crime that applied to female spouses who were unfaithful, while remaining silent or even condoning such activity among men (Anderson, 2001; Melody, 2003).

During the Greco-Roman period, stringent laws against adultery existed, yet these laws continuously discriminated against the wife (Melody, 2003). The ancient idea that the wife was the property of the husband was the rationale behind this. In the early Roman law, there was no such thing as the crime of adultery on the part of a husband toward his wife (Melody, 2003). Further still, adultery was not considered a crime unless one of the parties was a married woman. Throughout Roman history, husbands have been documented to take advantage of, and benefit from, this legal immunity.

In the Mosaic Law, as in the Roman law, adultery meant only the carnal intercourse of a wife with a man who was not her husband (Melody, 2003). The intercourse of a married man with a single woman, on the other hand, was not counted as adultery, but as fornication. Further, penalties for the crime of adultery were quite severe, with both the adulterer (man committing adultery) and the adulteress (woman committing adultery) being put to death if they were caught. Further, the issue of men having legal impunity from punishment for adultery was completely undermined in the later Christian law, where both husbands and wives were required to maintain faithfulness (Melody, 2003). The requirement of mutual fidelity from both the husband and wife is implied in numerous scriptures of the Christian sect, particularly that of the Christian Sacrament (Melody, 2003). Despite this apparent requirement, some nations have not always maintained equity between husbands and wives when considering criminal responsibility (Melody, 2003). For instance, in 1857 the English Parliament passed a law by which a husband could obtain a divorce due to his wife's commission of adultery, but the wife, on the other hand, could take similar action against her adulterous husband only when his infidelity had been determined to have a sufficient level of cruelty attached to it so as to cause some form of grievous loss or public humiliation (Melody, 2003). This view of adultery was similarly passed along to the early New England colonies, whereas in Massachusetts the adultery of the wife, but not the husband, was sufficient ground for divorce (Melody, 2003).

But this brings to surface another critical point when discussing these actions: whether or not these acts are necessarily criminal. In fact, in most industrialized countries neither of these phenomena is considered criminal in nature (MacKay, 2001). However, in other cultures, particularly those nations that operate under Islamic justice, or Shari'a, such acts may indeed be considered criminal. But the basis for adultery's criminal definition has less to do with sexual infidelity than it does with economics and property ownership (Kalu, 2003). Indeed, many ancient cultures (and even some modern cultures) held women to be the chattel of the men to which they were legally connected (Kalu, 2003; Melody, 2003). Thus, wives were the property of their husbands. Similarly, women and particularly daughters, were property of their fathers and were a source of future dowry incentives. If daughters fornicated with other men this reduced their "value" under these systems and reduced the amount of dowry that the father could receive. Thus, adultery and fornication were largely based on property and economic "damage" done to husbands and fathers.

The key point to note is that regardless of whether the acts of adultery and fornication are criminal, they are almost always associated with beliefs based on religion and morality. However, this is ironic because though most people may claim to hold these acts as being inappropriate behavior, the amount of infidelity (adultery) and casual sexual activity (fornication) is being reported at increasing rates; and this is true in almost all the industrialized nations (MacKay, 2001). In fact, recent research, particularly within the field of psychology, is finding telling evidence of a universal tendency toward promiscuity or infidelity (Abraham et al., 2001; MacKay, 2001). This is important because the research is demonstrating with ever-convincing evidence that such actions may be genetically wired for men and women, regardless of cultural differences.

Despite this, however, most societies have prohibitions against adultery (MacKay, 2001). And, regardless of whether adultery (as opposed to fornication) is considered a crime, it is still currently considered an injustice that is committed against the spouse who is betrayed (Anderson, 2001). In modern times, of course, there is no such distinction with divorce being granted on the ground of adultery for both women and men. Still, the notion of adultery being an injustice is still held as a personal injury that is grievable through the civil court process, thus confirming the injurious nature of this activity, regardless of whether such activity is considered deviant (Anderson, 2001; Melody, 2003). The movement from criminal to civil jurisdiction is important for the infraction of adultery. For in early societies, the "sin" of adultery may have been considered a crime, particularly against the given religious institution. But, in modern nations such as the U.S. or those in Europe, distinctions between governmental decisions and religious beliefs are reinforced (with the exception of perhaps the Vatican). This means that adultery (and of course fornication, which is an even lesser offense in most places throughout the world) is less and less likely to be considered criminal. Yet, the civil notion of such actions being an injury against a person or a violation of a contract is similarly in a particular state of flux. This is because modern nations are moving toward increasingly open interpretations of sexuality and the resulting obligations between consenting sex partners (MacKay, 2001).

On an informal level, research consistently shows that despite general public condemnation of adultery, the action is committed with a great degree of frequency (Anderson, 2001; Garber, 2002; Melody, 2003). Thus, cultural attitudes have shaped, and will continue to shape, views and definitions of adultery, with the end result being that such activity ceases to be an issue of grievance in marriages that are considered "open" to outside sex partners or where such marriages are simply those of convenience (Anderson, 2001; MacKay, 2001). In either case, both the terms adultery and fornication are used to denote moral regulation of sexual activity. Although the rationale for such sexual regulation may vary, the two terms, when taken together, hold that sexual activity among unmarried participants is an action to be considered morally inappropriate. Whether such viewpoints on sexual activity will maintain continued support is frequently a matter of open and heated debate in numerous social and cultural circles throughout the world.

Robert D. Hanser

References and Further Reading

Abraham, W.T., Cramer, R.E., Fernandez, A.M., and Mahler, E. (2001). Infidelity, race, and gender: An evolutionary perspective on asymmetries in subjective distress to violations-of-trust. *Current Psychology, 20*(4), 337–348.

Anderson, K. (2001). *Adultery.* Richardson, TX: Probe Ministries International.

Garber, F. (2002). *Men, Women Get Equally Jealous: But Given a Choice, Infidelity is Worse for Men.* Available at http://webmd.lycos.com/content/article/52/49935.htm. WebMD Inc.

Janus, S., and Janus, C. (1993). *The Janus Report on Sexual Behavior.* New York, NY: John Wiley and Sons.

Kalu, O.U. (2003). Safiyya and Adamah: Punishing adultery with Sharia stones in twenty-first century Nigeria. *African Affairs, 102*(408), 389–408.

MacKay, J. (2001). Global sex: Sexuality and sexual practices around the world. *Sexual and Relationship Therapy, 16*(1), 71–82.

Melody, J.W. (2003). *The Catholic Encyclopedia, Volume I.* New York, NY: Robert Appleton Company. Available at http://www.newadvent.org/cathen/01163a.htm.

African Indigenous Justice System

Indigenous African societies had a well-defined and effective system of social and political control, prior to their contact with the outside world. Some of the indigenous institutions of social and political control have been replaced with state institutions of social and political control. Other indigenous institutions survived colonial subjugation and co-exist with and complement colonial institutions of social control. Like the former European colonial authorities, modern African states tend to monopolize power, authority, and social control mechanisms. Nonetheless, the indigenous institutions of social and political control remain relevant to people, especially in the rural areas, where the majority of the people reside.

There are therefore, two justice systems operating in contemporary African societies. One is the state administered justice system modeled on the Western judicial systems. The other is based on African value systems and administered through the indigenous justice institutions. African National constitutions generally recognize and approve the operations of the indigenous justice systems, provided their practices are not "repugnant to justice, equity and good conscience."

Broadly, indigenous African societies can be classified into two groups: (1) those with a centralized and hierarchical political authority and judicial institutions, and (2) those with a decentralized political authority. Societies in the first group are distinguishable by social and economic inequality and ethnic heterogeneity. The political superior, known variously as the "Paramount Chief" or the "King-in-Council" according to Elias (1962), has considerable power and authority extending over large territories. The use of organized force in enforcing conformity was common. Societies in the second group were less centralized, relatively egalitarian, and judicial and political authority was exercised through the Council of Elders. Communities in this group are usually homogenous, autonomous, and occupy smaller territories, making it feasible for direct and participatory democracy.

Litigants are free to pick and choose either of the justice systems—state or indigenous justice—that meets their needs. Although both justice systems wield considerable authority and their powers to enforce their decisions are perceived as legitimate, the dominant powers of the state are not in doubt. State courts retain the power and right to review and overturn decisions of the indigenous courts. State courts reinforce the powers and legitimacy of the indigenous courts by delegating cases to the indigenous courts. Further, decisions and opinions of indigenous court judges are admissible in state courts, especially on matters that pertain to the litigants' cultural practices.

The generality of African families are polygynous and extended. The African extended family consists of the husband, his wife or wives, their children and other relatives, often relatives of the husband who live in the same household or compound. Sometimes the spouses' parents live in the same home. Even where the elderly parents of the spouses do not live with the extended family, they can, in time of old age or terminal illness, move in with the family. Further, the adult married children of the spouses who live separately from the family are considered members of the extended family. They have certain rights as well as responsibilities that derive from their membership of the extended family. For example, in times of divorce or other crisis, married children of the spouses can return with their children and live either temporarily or permanently with the extended family.

Conflict is endemic in many African communities. Factors that contribute to conflict include polygynous marriages, extended families, the sharing of social amenities in the communities and the fact that some of the communities are close-knit. Allowing conflicts to protract is dangerous and counterproductive. Strenuous efforts are, therefore, made to find a lasting, peaceful, and acceptable resolution to a conflict as soon as possible. African societies have established and acceptable cultural approaches to addressing conflicts, as well as the way that third parties are expected to intervene. For example, rules about how long one has to wait to begin speaking after someone else has finished during mediation, are inculcated early in the people. People are taught early not to take laws into their hands and to recognize, respect, and patronize the various channels of conflict resolution.

Many African judicial processes are "process oriented." The goal is on achieving peaceful resolutions of disputes rather than on adherence to rules. Uchendu (1965) observes that social justice is more important than adherence to strict rules. Readjusting social relations, community harmony, and equilibrium is the goal of justice. A fair and just judgment must take into account a wider range of facts and interests, including that of the community, without necessarily compromising the facts of the matter.

In traditional African societies, according to Gyekye (1996) and Motala (1989), the individual's right to food and shelter was respected and protected. Everyone had access to land, as land was owned both privately and communally. The mainstay of most African economy was agriculture. Everyone was encouraged to work, and idleness carried a social stigma.

African religion is human centered (Mbiti, 1970). This human centeredness is an indication that the human being is paramount in value and is an end in itself. Morally speaking, the human being is the foundation of values. That human beings are at the center of the universe, does not suggest that other animals, plants, and all of nature are expendable. The maintenance of an equilibrium, harmony with other life forms, are essential for human survival (Kamalu, 1990).

The judgment and processes of African indigenous justice systems are shaped by restorative and transformative principles and communitarian values. As such, all the parties with a stake in the conflict are involved in the definition of harm and are actively involved in the search for solutions. Primary stakeholders to a conflict include the victim, the offender, their families and friends, witnesses, and their community members. Restorative justice processes recognize and respect the basic human needs of the victim, the offender, and the community. Essentially, there is an acknowledgement that victims of crime, their families, and the community are harmed and need restoration and healing. The quality and effectiveness of justice are measured through the well-being of victims and the community.

African indigenous justice systems view crime not just as a violation of people and relationships, but also as an opportunity for transformative healing for all victims(s), offender(s), family members, friends, witnesses, and members of the community. Conflict creates opportunities for education, socialization, and resocialization of not only the victims and offenders, but of all community members. Conflict is appreciated as an opportunity for moral growth and transformation. The values, and socioeconomic condition of the community are further re-examined in the process. It is generally believed that crime indicates a failure of responsibility. Although the primary responsibility is that of the offender, the culpability of the family and the community is not overlooked. The mutual responsibility of community members for each other in Africa is acknowledged. African people believe crime and nonconformity could be an indication of the social and economic marginalization of the individual.

The victim of a crime or his or her parents or relatives initiate the judicial processes by petitioning either the Chief or an elder who calls on the town crier to announce to the whole community to assemble at the town square. However, there remain offenses that victimize the entire community. The victim is then called upon to present his or her case. The victim is expected to tell the gathering how the action or inaction of the defendant affected him or her. It is believed that victims whose needs are not addressed are potential offenders. The defendant is later called upon to present his or her side of the story. Disputants must actively be involved in the search for facts relevant to the case. In calling witnesses to corroborate their depositions, they must realize that an eyewitness account is superior to testimonies based on hearsay. However, in the absence of primary evidence, secondary evidence will be considered, although subject to rigorous scrutiny. Friends, supporters, or relatives of the disputants may also be called on or may volunteer to speak to help clarify matters where necessary. The credibility and competence of the disputants and their witnesses remain crucial in the ascertainment of evidence. Evidence obtained through threats or by duress is generally disqualified.

Before a judgment is rendered, the facts of the matter must be presented and verified publicly. All efforts are made to establish the truth, which the parties to the conflict must find credible. The composition of a tribunal that looks into a case must also be representative of parties to the dispute. Reasonable people in the community must appraise the tribunal and its processes as fair and just, and so having integrity. The integrity of the system is measured by its consistency and sensitivity based on the normative principles of the community. When a party to a conflict perceives the system as lacking legitimacy, they may refuse to cooperate or conform to the rules of the tribunal. Coercion will also fail as the community's good will is important. Most African judicial processes are negotiative. Disputants are persuaded to accept the tribunal's judgment.

In cases where the truth or falsity of the matter is difficult to prove, oath swearing becomes the only option if the case is to be resolved. Oath swearing and divination is used to identify the wrong doer and to determine guilt. It works both ways. The accused uses oath swearing to demonstrate his or her innocence, whereas the victim uses it to corroborate his or her position. It is believed that the supernatural will acquit the innocent and convict the guilty. If a litigant who swears an oath gets sick and dies within a year, she or he is presumed guilty and that permanently resolves the case. The litigant is absolved of all guilt if she or he does not die after a year of swearing an oath. Either way, the case is finally resolved after the oath swearing. Arbitrators' responsibility over the matter terminates immediately after the oath swearing takes place.

Victims' need for validation, vindication, restitution, and support is a priority in Africa. As Nsereko (1992) rightly observes, the focus of African indigenous justice processes was mainly the victim, rather than the offender. Protecting the victims' rights included recognizing her or his pain or loss, validating and vindicating the victim's situation and concerns, and taking steps to address them. The meting of punishments to offenders is intended to compensate the victims rather than punishing the offender for punishment's sake. Other goals of punishment are the reestablishment of equilibrium and harmony in the community. Compensation to victims is not always in tangible forms. Restitution and atonement for wrongs can be symbolic. Moreover, however serious an offense is in Africa, it can be atoned for with a commensurate sacrifice and reparation.

African indigenous societies had laws and rules that governed the peoples' conduct and social and economic relationships. Conduct norms about what is good, and therefore accepted, and what is bad and prohibited were clearly defined. Behaviors that were harmful and inimical to the well-being of the community attracted formal community sanctions. Thieves, sorcerers, and those involved in other offenses are thought of as embodying moral evil. Their behaviors harm others and undermine good relationships. Nature can also wreak havoc on people. Evil acts such as accidents, terminal illnesses, and other misfortunes are blamed on natural forces. However, it is also believed that bad people can be purveyors of natural evil (Mbiti, 1970).

Nevertheless, African people believe that human beings are inherently good. However, human beings are capable of doing bad things when their conduct fails to conform to the conduct norms of their communities. Offenders' conducts harm the individual victims, their family members, and the community. Offenders can also be harmed by their own actions. Crime also represents the lack of respect, not only for the direct victim, but also for the entire community. Further, violations create fear and distrust and undermine community bonds and harmony.

African societies view themselves as a collective, hence responsible for the well-being of its members, including victims and offenders. In this respect, the conflict resolution process seeks to attend to the wounds and feelings of the victim, and to restore the community to its former position. The road to repair, reconciliation, and reassurance begins when the offender acknowledges that his or her behavior is a violation of people and other relationships, and that violations create obligations to make things right. An offender's expression of remorse and responsibility over the consequences of his or her behavior is a key to peace. Reparation to the victim is further negotiated in an atmosphere devoid of symbols of power and intimidation. The process is educational with the participants involved in the analysis and definition of societal values. Offenders' competence is greatly enhanced in the process. It is noted that when offenders are actively involved in the decision-making process they are more likely to be in accord with the decisions reached.

The offender's empathy and appreciation of the harm his or her actions caused the victim is also greatly enhanced by his or her active participation in the judicial process. In holding the offender accountable, the offender's healing is facilitated to ensure that offensive behavior is not repeated. Strenuous efforts are made to preserve connections between the offender and community members. In condemning the offender's conduct, a parallel message of love, support, understanding, and respect is sent across to the offender. African economies being agribusiness and labor intensive, no individual is expendable, unless the person poses a threat to the survival of the community.

In the event that the offender is not identified, the Almighty will avenge the wrong on behalf of the people. God punishes evildoers. The punishment can even be postponed for another lifetime when the evildoer reincarnates. This explains why peoples' misfortunes are sometimes interpreted as punishment for moral wrongs either committed in the present life or the one before. God is the ultimate defender of the society's moral order. Yet, maintenance of law and order is the responsibility of the "patriarchs, living-dead, elders, priests, or even divinities and spirits who are the daily guardians or police of human morality" (Mbiti, 1970, 213).

In conclusion, African indigenous justice is shaped by restorative, transformative, and communitarian values. There are several forums for doing justice in Africa. Litigants are free to choose which system best addresses their needs. Some of the forums for conflict resolution in Africa include the family matrilineal and patrilineal groups, age groups, village courts, and Chiefs-in-Council. African judicial processes allow for the participation of victims, offenders, their families, and co-villagers. Morality is a corporate affair, crime affects not only the victim, but the whole community. As primary stakeholders in the conflict, the victim, offender, their families, and the entire community are involved in the definition of harm and search for resolution. The judicial process is persuasive and negotiative. Everybody has equal access and participation in the system and decisions are reached through a consensus. No one can arrogate to himself or herself the role of professionals thereby subjugating the voices of the lay people. A major lesson from the system is that social sanctions, even when devoid of punishment, are sufficient to bring people to order.

O. Oko Elechi

References and Further Reading

Amadi, E. (1982). *Ethics in Nigerian Culture*. Ibadan: Heinemann Educational Books (Nigeria) Ltd.

Braithwaite, J. (1989). *Crime, Shame and Reintegration*. New York, NY: Cambridge University Press.

Cayley, D. (1998). *The Expanding Prison: The Crisis in Crime and Punishment and the Search for Alternatives*. Cleveland, OH: The Pilgrim Press.

Christie, N. (1973). *Criminological Data as Mirror for Society.* Oslo: Institute for Criminology and Criminal Law Stenciseries, No. 15.

Christe, N. (1976). *Conflict as Property.* Oslo: Institute for Criminology and Criminal Law Stenciseries, No. 23.

Christie, N. (1981). *Limits to Pain*. Oslo: Universiteteteforlaget.

Dike, C.P. (1986). Igbo traditional social control and sanctions, *in Igbo Jurisprudence: Law and Order in Traditional Igbo Society. Ahiajoku Lecture (Onugaotu) Colloquium*. Owerri, Nigeria: Ministry of Information and Culture.

Elechi, O.O. (1991). *Alternative Conflict Resolution in (Ehugbo) Afikpo*. Oslo: Institute for Criminology and Criminal Law Stenciseries, No. 67.

Elechi, O.O. (1996). Doing justice without the state: The Afikpo (Ehugbo) Nigeria model of conflict resolution. *International Journal of Comparative and Applied Criminal Justice*. Fall, Vol. 20, No. 2.

Elechi, O.O. (1999). Victims under restorative justice systems: The Afikpo (Ehugbo) Nigeria model. *International Review of Victimology*, 6, 359–375.

Elias, T.O. (1956). *The Nature of African Customary Law.* Manchester Press.

Elias, R. (1993). *Victims Still: The Political Manipulation of Crime Victims*. Newbury Park, CA: Sage Publications, Inc.

Fattah, A.E. (1995). *Restorative and retributive justice models: A comparison*, in *Festschrift fur Professor Koichi Miyazawa*, Kuhne, H. (Ed.).

Fattah, A.E. (1998). A critical assessment of two justice paradigms: Contrasting the restorative and retributive justice models, in *Support for Crime Victims in a Comparative Perspective: A Collection of Essays Dedicated to the Memory of Prof. Frederic McClintock*, Fattah, E. and Peters, T. (Eds.). Leuven: University Press.

Gibbs, J.L. Jr. (1973). Two forms of dispute settlement among the Kpelle of West Africa, in *The Social Organization of Law*, Black, D. and Mileski, M. (Eds.). New York: Seminar Press.

Gluckman, M. (1969). The judicial process among the Barotse of Northern Rhodesia, in *Sociology of Law,* Aubert, V. (Ed.). (originally published 1955).

Gyekye, K. (1996). *African Cultural Values: An Introduction*. Accra, Ghana: Sankofa Publishing Co.

Harris, M.K. (1989). Alternative visions in the context of contemporary realities, in *Justice: The Restorative Vision: New Perspectives on Crime and Justice*. Occasional Papers of the MCC Canada Victim Offender Ministries Program and MCC U.S. Office of Criminal Justice, Issue No. 7, February.

Iro, M. (1985). Igbo ethics and discipline, in *The Igbo Socio-Political System*, Papers Presented at the 1985 Ahiajoku Lecture Colloquium. Owerri, Nigeria: Ministry of Information, Culture, Youth and Sports.

Iwuagwu, A.O. (1980). The Ogu corpus and the Igbo concept of the moral law, in *The 1980 Ahiajoku Lectures Colloquium*. Owerri, Nigeria: Ministry of Information and Culture.

Kamalu, C. (1990). *Foundations of African Thought: A World-view Grounded in the African Heritage of Religion, Philosophy, Science and Art*. London, UK: Karnak House.

Morris, R. (1995). *Penal Abolition: The Practical Choice*. Toronto: Canadian Scholars' Press.

Morris, R. (1999). *7 Steps from Misery: Justice to Social Transformation*. Toronto: Rittenhouse, A New Vision.

Njaka, E.N. (1974). *Igbo Political Culture*. Evanston: North Western University Press.

Nsereko, D.D.N. (1991). Extenuating circumstances in capital offenses in Botswana. *Criminal Law Forum*. 2, No. 2, Winter.

Nsereko, N. (1992). Victims of crime and their rights, in *Criminology in Africa*, Mushango, T.M. (Ed.). Rome: United Nations Interregional Crime and Justice Research Institute (UNICRI).

Okere, T. (1986). Law-making in traditional Igbo society, in *Igbo Jurisprudence: Law and Order in Traditional Igbo Society. The 1986 Ahiajoku Lectures Colloquium*. Owerri, Nigeria: Ministry of Information and Culture.

Onwuachi, C.P. (1977). African identity and ideology, in *Festac 77*. London: African Journal Ltd.

Otuu, M.O. (1977). Afikpo (Ehugbo) Age-Grade Organization (A Study in Continuity and Change). Unpublished B.Sc. Thesis, June 1977. University of Nigeria, Nsukka.

Ottenberg, P.V. (1959). The changing economic position of women among the Afikpo Ibo, in *Continuity and Change in African Cultures by* Bascon, W.R. and Herskovits, M.J. (Eds.). Chicago, IL: University of Chicago Press.

Ottenberg, S. (1968). *Double Descent in African Society: The Afikpo Village Group*. Seattle, WA: University of Washington Press.

Ottenberg, S. (1965). Inheritance and succession in Afikpo, in *Studies in the Laws of Succession in Nigeria* by Duncan, J. and Dekkett, M. (Eds.). London, UK: Oxford University Press.

Ottenberg, S. (1971). *Leadership and Authority in an African Society: The Afikpo Village-Group*. Seattle, WA: University of Washington Press.

Parnell, C.P. (1988). *Escalating Disputes: Social Participation and Change in the Oaxacan Highlands*. Tucson: University of Arizona Press.

Pepinsky, H.E. and Quinney, R. (Eds.) (1991). *Criminology as Peace-making*. Bloomington, IL: Indiana University Press.

Rattray, R.S. (1929). *Ashanti Law and Constitution*. Clarendon: Oxford University Press.

Ross, R. (1996). *Returning to the Teachings: Exploring Aboriginal Justice*. Toronto: Penguin Books.

Uchendu, V.C. (1965). *The Igbo of Southeast Nigeria*. New York, NY: Holt, Rinehart and Winston.

Umozurike, U.O. (1981). Adjudication among the Igbo, in *Perspectives on Igbo Culture. The 1981 Ahiajoku Lectures Colloquium*. Owerri, Nigeria: Ministry of Information and Culture.

Van Ness, D. and Strong, H.K. (1997). *Restoring Justice*, 2nd ed. Cincinnati, OH: Anderson Publishing Co.

Van Ness, D. (1989). Pursuing a restorative vision of justice, in *Justice: The Restorative Vision*. Occasional Papers of the MCC Canada Victim Offender Ministries Program and the MCC U.S. Office of Criminal Justice. February 1989 Issue No. 7.

Wilson, A.R. (1986). Customary marriage and divorce in Igbo society, in *Igbo Jurisprudence: Law and Order in Traditional Igbo Society. The 1986 Ahiajoku Lectures Colloquium*. Owerri, Nigeria: Ministry of Information and Culture.

Wiredu, K. (1997). Democracy and consensus in African traditional politics: A plea for a non-party polity, in *Postcolonial African Philosophy: A Critical Reader* by Eze, E.C. (Ed.). Cambridge, Massachusetts: Blackwell Publishers.

Zehr, H. (1989). Stumbling toward a restorative idea, in *Justice: The Restorative Vision: New Perspectives on Crime and Justice*. Occasional Papers of the MCC Canada Victim Offender Ministries Program and the MCC U.S. Office of Criminal Justice. February 1989, Issue No. 7.

Zehr, H. (1990). *Changing Lenses: A New Focus for Crime and Justice*. Waterloo, Ontario: Herald Press.

See also **Criminal Justice System: Models of Operation; South Africa, Crime and Justice in; Sub-Saharan Africa, Crime and Justice in**

Age and the Patterning of Crime

The relationship between aging and criminal activity has been noted since the beginnings of criminology. For example, Adolphe Quetelet, the 19th century geographer and criminologist who in the mid-1800s pioneered the statistical analysis of crime across space, gender, and age, found that the proportion of the population involved in crime tends to peak in adolescence or early adulthood and then decline with age. This age–crime relationship is remarkably similar across historical periods, geographic locations, and crime types. That the impact of age on criminal involvement is one of the strongest factors associated with crime has prompted the controversial claim that the age–crime relationship is invariant (Hirschi and Gottfredson, 1983). However, considerable variation exists among offenses and across historical periods in specific features of the age–crime relationship (for example, peak age, median age, rate of decline from peak age). A claim of "invariance" in the age–crime relationship, therefore, overstates the case (Steffensmeier et al., 1989).

Age–Crime Patterns for the U.S.

The FBI's Uniform Crime Report (UCR) data, particularly the Crime Index (comprising homicide, robbery, rape, aggravated assault, burglary, larceny-theft, and auto theft), document the robustness of the age effect on crime and also reveal a long-term trend toward *younger* age–crime distributions in more modern times. Today, the peak age (the age group with the highest age-specific arrest rate) is younger than 25 for all crimes reported in the FBI's UCR program except gambling, and rates begin to decline in the teenage years for more than half of the UCR crimes. In fact, even the median age (50% of all arrests occurring among younger persons) is younger than 30 for most crimes. The *National Crime Victimization Survey* (NCVS), self-report studies of juvenile and adult criminality, and interview data from convicted felons corroborate the age–crime patterns found in the UCR data (Rowe and Tittle, 1977; Elliott et al., 1983).

Explaining Youthful Offending

In a general sense, physical abilities, such as strength, speed, prowess, stamina, and aggression are useful for successful commission of many crimes, for protection, for enforcing contracts, and for recruiting and managing reliable associates (for a review, see Steffensmeier, 1983). Although some crimes are physically more demanding than others, persistent involvement in crime is likely to entail a lifestyle that is physically demanding and dangerous. Declining physical strength and energy may make crime too dangerous or unsuccessful, especially where there are younger or stronger criminal competitors who will not be intimidated, and thus might help to explain the very low involvement in crime of small children and the elderly.

However, available evidence on biological aging reveals very little correspondence between physical aging and decline of crime in late adolescence. The research literature on biological aging (see especially, Shock, 1984) suggests that peak functioning is typically reached between the ages of 25 and 30 for physical factors plausibly assumed to affect one's ability to commit crimes (strength, stamina, aerobic capacity, motor control, sensory perception, and speed of movement). Although decline sets in shortly after these peak years, it is very gradual until the early 50s, when the decline becomes more pronounced (Shock, 1984). Other commonly mentioned physical variables like testosterone levels peak in early adulthood but then remain at peak level until at least the age of 50. In contrast, the age curves for crimes like robbery and burglary that presuppose the need for physical abilities peak in mid-adolescence and then decline very rapidly. In short, although biological and physiological factors may contribute toward an understanding of the rapid increase in delinquent behavior during adolescence, they cannot by themselves explain the abrupt decline in the age–crime curve following mid-to-late adolescence.

A variety of social and cognitive factors can help explain the rapid rise in age-specific rates of offending around mid-adolescence. Teenagers generally lack strong bonds to conventional adult institutions, such as work and family (Warr, 1998). At the same time, teens are faced with strong potential rewards for offending: money, status, power, autonomy, identity

Table 1. Male and Female Arrest Rates per 100,000 (All Ages), Female Percentage of Arrests, and Male and Female Arrest Profiles (1965–2000 Uniform Crime Reports)

Offense	Male Rates[*]				Female Rates[*]				Female Percentage (of Arrests)[†]				Offender-Profile Percentage[‡] Males		Offender-Profile Percentage[‡] Females	
	1965	1980	1990	2000	1965	1980	1990	2000	1965	1980	1990	2000	1965	2000	1965	2000
Violent																
Homicide	9	16	17	12	2	2	2	1	17	12	10	10	0.1	0.1	0.2	0.1
Weapons	78	140	174	141	5	10	13	12	6	7	7	8	1	2	0.6	0.5
Simple assault	279	369	697	817	32	56	127	221	10	13	15	21	4	9	4	9
Property/Drugs																
Larceny	466	755	894	685	125	298	391	351	21	28	30	34	7	8	14	15
Fraud	62	145	169	160	15	96	128	126	20	40	43	44	1	2	2	5
Drug abuse	66	450	800	1010	10	65	150	182	13	13	16	15	1	11	1	8

[*]Rates are calculated based on 3-year averages and are sex-specific rates (e.g., female rate = no. of female arrests/no. of females in the population × 100,000).

[†]The female percentage of arrests adjusts for the sex composition of the population. It is calculated as follows: [female rate/(female rate + male rate)] × 100.

[‡]The offender profile percentage is the percentage of all arrests within each sex that are arrests for a particular offense; this measure indicates the distribution of arrests by gender.

claims, strong sensate experiences stemming from sex, natural adrenaline highs or highs from illegal substances, and respect from similar peers (Wilson and Herrenstein, 1985; Steffensmeier et al., 1989). Further, their dependent status as juveniles insulates teens from many of the social and legal costs of illegitimate activities, and their stage of cognitive development limits prudence concerning the consequences of their behavior. At the same time, they possess the physical prowess required to commit crimes. Finally, a certain amount of misbehavior is often seen as natural to youth and seen as simply a stage of growing up (Jolin and Gibbons, 1987; Hagan et al., 1998).

For those in late adolescence or early adulthood (roughly age 17–22, the age group showing the sharpest decline in arrest rates for many crimes), important changes occur in at least six spheres of life (Steffensmeier et al., 1989; Sampson and Laub, 1993; Warr, 1998):

1. Greater access to legitimate sources of material goods and excitement: (including jobs, credit, alcohol, and sex)
2. Patterns of illegitimate opportunities: with the assumption of adult roles, opportunities increase for crimes (for example, gambling, fraud, and employee theft) that are less risky, more lucrative, or less likely to be reflected in official statistics.
3. Peer associations and lifestyle: reduced orientation to same-age–same-sex peers and increased orientation toward persons of the opposite sex or persons who are older or more mature.
4. Cognitive and analytical skill development leading to a gradual decline in egocentrism, hedonism, and sense of invincibility; becoming more concerned for others, more accepting of social values, more comfortable in social relations, and more concerned with the meaning of life; and seeing their casual delinquencies of youth as childish or foolish.
5. Increased legal and social costs for deviant behavior.
6. Age-graded norms: externally increased expectation of maturity and responsibility; internal anticipation of assuming adult roles, coupled with reduced subjective acceptance of deviant roles and the threat they pose to entering adult status.

As young people move into adulthood or anticipate entering it, most find their bonds to conventional society strengthening, with expanded access to work or further education and increased interest in "settling down" (Warr, 1998; Hagan et al., 1998). Leaving high school, finding employment, going to college, enlisting in the military, and getting married all tend to increase informal social controls and integration into conventional society. In addition, early adulthood typically involves a change in peer associations and lifestyle routines that diminish the opportunities for committing these offenses (Warr, 1998). Furthermore, at the same time when informal sanctions for law violation are increasing, potential legal sanctions increase substantially.

Variations in the Age Curve

Crime tends to decline with age, although substantial variation can be found in the parameters of the age–crime curve (such as peak age, median age, and rate of decline from peak age). "Flatter" age curves (i.e., those with an older peak age or a slower decline in offending rates among older age groups) are associated with at least three circumstances: (1) cultures and historical periods in which youth have greater access to legitimate opportunities and integration into adult society; (2) population groups for whom legitimate opportunities and integration into adult society do not markedly increase with age (i.e., during young adulthood); and (3) types of crime for which illegitimate opportunities increase rather than diminish with age.

Cross-Cultural and Historical Differences

In simple, nonindustrial societies, the passage to adult status is relatively simple and continuous. Formal "rites of passage" at relatively early ages avoid much of the status ambiguity and role conflict that torment modern adolescents in the developed world. Youths begin to assume responsible and economically productive roles well before they reach full physical maturity. It is not surprising, therefore, to find that such societies and time periods have significantly flatter and less skewed age–crime patterns (for a review, see Steffensmeier et al., 1989). Much the same is true for earlier periods in the history of the U.S. and other industrial nations, when farm youths were crucial for harvesting crops and working-class children were expected to leave school at an early age and do their part in helping to support their families (Horan and Hargis, 1991). By contrast, today teenagers typically work at marginal jobs that provide little self-pride and few opportunities for adult mentorship, and instead segregate them into a separate peer culture. Youth has always been seen as a turbulent time, although social processes associated with the coming of industrialization and the postindustrial age have aggravated the stresses of adolescence, resulting in increased levels of juvenile criminality in recent decades. The structure of modern societies, therefore, encourages crime and delinquency among the young because these societies "lack institutional procedures for moving people smoothly from protected childhood to autonomous adulthood" (Nettler, 1978, 241).

Unfortunately, reliable age statistics on criminal involvement are not available over extended historical periods. Nonetheless, we can compare age–crime distributions over the past 60 years or so in the U.S. and also compare these to early 19th century age–crime distributions reported in Quetelet's pioneering study. The age–crime plots are shown in Table 1 for total offenses and homicide (the most reliable crime statistic). The plots clearly show a trend toward younger age distributions and younger peak ages.

The shift toward a greater concentration of offending among the young may be due partly to changes in law enforcement procedures and data collection. Nevertheless, the likelihood that real changes have in fact occurred is supported by the consistency of the changes from 1830 to 1940–1980, and even from 1980 to roughly 2000. Support for the conclusion that real change has taken place over the past century also is found in the age breakdown of U.S. prisoner statistics covering the years 1890–1980 (Steffensmeier et al., 1989). As with the UCR statistics, the prison statistics show that age curves are more peaked today than a century ago and that changes in the age–crime curve are gradual and can be detected only when a sufficiently large time frame is used. Moreover, research shows that more recent birth cohorts of juveniles are more violent than ones in the past (Tracey et al., 1985; Shannon, 1988).

Together, these findings are consistent with the view that contemporary teenagers in industrialized nations are subject to greater status anxiety than in previous periods of history and that the transition from adolescence to adulthood is more turbulent now than in the past (Friday and Hage, 1976; Greenberg, 1977a; Glaser, 1978). In comparison to earlier eras, youths have had less access to responsible family roles, valued economic activity, and participation in community affairs (Clausen, 1986). This generational isolation has fostered adolescent subcultures oriented toward consumption and hedonistic pursuits (Hagan, 1991; Hagan et al., 1998). The weakened social bonds and reduced access to valued adult roles, along with accentuated subcultural influences, all combine to increase situationally induced pressures to obtain valued goods; display strength, daring, or loyalty to peers; or simply to "get kicks" (Briar and Piliavin, 1965; Gold, 1970; Hagan et al., 1998).

Minority Differences

For black inner-city youths, the problems of youth described above are compounded by persistent racial discrimination and blocked conventional opportunity (Wilson, 1987; 1996). As inner-city blacks move into young adulthood, they continue to experience limited access to high quality adult jobs and are more likely to associate primarily with same-sex peers. As UCR data show, adult offending levels among blacks continue at higher levels than among whites, and the proportion of total black crime that is committed by black adults is greater than the proportion of total white crime that is committed by white adults (Steffensmeier and Allan, 1993). Arrest statistics for homicide or robbery from California further document the flatter age–crime curves among blacks than whites.

Crime Types

The offenses that show the youngest peaks and sharpest declines are crimes that fit the low-yield, criminal mischief, "hell-raising" category: vandalism, petty theft, robbery, arson, auto theft, burglary, and liquor law and drug violations. Personal crimes like aggravated assault and homicide tend to have somewhat "older" age distributions (with median ages in the late twenties), as do some of the public order offenses, public drunkenness, driving under the influence, and certain of the property crimes that juveniles

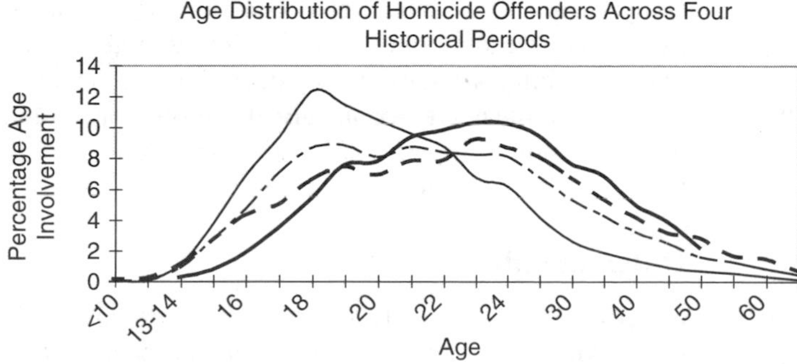

Source: Uniform Crime Reports

FIGURE 1

have less opportunity to commit, like embezzlement, fraud, and gambling (with median ages in late twenties or thirties).

The offenses with flatter age curves are often those for which the structure of illegitimate opportunities increases rather than disappears with age. For example, some opportunities for fraud exist for young people (such as falsification of identification to purchase alcohol or gain entry to "adult" establishments), but as they are too young to obtain credit, they lack the opportunities for common frauds such as passing bad checks, defrauding an innkeeper, or credit card forgery. Similarly, young people have more opportunities for some kinds of violence (for example, street fights or gang violence) but less opportunity for other kinds of violence (for example, spousal violence).

Older people may also shift to less visible crimes such as bookmaking or receiving stolen goods. Or as a spinoff of legitimate roles, they may commit surreptitious crimes or crimes that, if discovered, are unlikely to be reported to the authorities, such as embezzlement, stock fraud, bribery, or price-fixing. Unfortunately, we know relatively little about the age distribution of persons who commit these and related lucrative crimes, but the fragmentary evidence that does exist suggests that they are likely to be middle aged or older (Shapiro, 1984; Pennsylvania Crime Commission, 1991). Evidence also suggests that the age curves for lucrative crimes in the underworld like racketeering or loansharking not only peak much later but tend to decline more slowly with age (Steffensmeier and Allan, 1993; Steffensmeier, 1986).

Still less is known of the age distribution of "respectable" or upperworld offenders who commit lucrative business crimes like fraud, price-fixing, or bribery, as such data are not plentiful. However, data from *New York Times* articles on profitable business crimes (those involving gains of $25,000 or more) during the 1987–1990 period reveals a preponderance of middle-aged or older offenders, with a modal age between 40 and 50 (Steffensmeier and Allan, 1993).

Sex Differences in the Age–Crime Relationship

There appears to be considerable similarity in the age–crime relationship between males and females (Steffensmeier and Streifel, 1991). The UCR arrest statistics from 1940–2000 show that the age curves of male and female offenders are very similar within any given period and across all offenses, with the exception of prostitution. To the extent that age differences between the sexes exist, the tendency is for somewhat lower peak ages of offending among females—apparently because of their earlier physical maturity and the likelihood that young adolescent females might date and associate with older delinquent male peers. But overall, although male levels of offending are always higher than female levels at every age and for virtually all offenses, the female-to-male ratio remains fairly constant across the life span (Steffensmeier and Streifel, 1991). Also, the trend toward younger and more peaked age–crime distributions holds for both sexes.

Variations in Criminal Careers

The youthful peak and rapid drop-off in offending that constitutes the most common societal pattern for conventional crimes is only one of a number of patterns identified when criminal careers are tracked for individual offenders (see Jolin and Gibbons, 1987; D'Unger et al., 1998). Other interesting trends pertain to older offenders.

"Aging Out" of Crime

Research suggests that exiting from a criminal career requires the acquisition of meaningful bonds to conventional adult individuals and institutions (Sampson and Laub, 1993; Warr, 1998). One important tie to the conventional order is a job that seems to have the potential for advancement and that is seen as meaningful and economically rewarding. A good job shifts a criminal's attention from the present to the future and provides a solid basis for the construction of a noncriminal identity. It also alters an individual's daily routine in ways that make crime less likely (Meisenhelder, 1977; Shover, 1983). Other bonds that may lead people away from crime include involvement in religion, sports, hobbies, or other activities (Irwin, 1970).

The development of conventional social bonds may be coupled with burnout or a belated deterrent effect as offenders grow tired of the hassles of repeated involvement with the criminal justice system and the hardships of a life of crime. They may also have experienced a long prison sentence that jolts them into quitting or that entails the loss of street contacts that make the successful continuation of a criminal career difficult. Or offenders may develop a fear of dying alone in prison, especially as repeated convictions yield longer sentences. Still other offenders may quit or "slow down" as they find their abilities and efficiency declining with increasing age, loss of "nerve," or sustained narcotics or alcohol use (Prus and Sharper, 1977; Adler and Adler, 1983; Shover, 1983; Steffensmeier, 1986).

Older Criminals

Older offenders typically fall into two categories: (1) those whose first criminal involvement occurs relatively late in life (particularly in shoplifting, homicide, and alcohol-related offenses) and (2) those who started crime at an early age and continue their involvement into their forties and fifties and beyond. What evidence is available on first-time older offenders suggests that situational stress and lack of alternative opportunities play a primary role. The unanticipated loss of one's job or other disruptions of social ties can push some individuals into their first law violation at any age (Alston, 1986; Jolin and Gibbons, 1987; Agnew 1992).

Older offenders who persist in crime are more likely to belong to the criminal underworld. These are individuals who are relatively successful in their criminal activities or who are extensively integrated into subcultural or family criminal enterprises. They seem to receive relational and psychic rewards (e.g., pride in their expertise) as well as monetary rewards from lawbreaking and, as a result, see no need to withdraw from lawbreaking (Reynolds, 1953; Klockars, 1974; Steffensmeier, 1986). Alternatively, such offenders may "shift and oscillate" back and forth between conventionality and lawbreaking, depending on shifting life circumstances and situational inducements to offend (Adler and Adler, 1983). These older offenders are also unlikely to see many meaningful opportunities for themselves in the conventional or law-abiding world. Consequently, "the straight life" may have little to offer successful criminals, who will be more likely to persist in their criminality for an extended period. But they, too, may slow down eventually as they grow tired of the cumulative aggravations and risks of criminal involvement, or as they encounter the diminishing capacities associated with the aging process.

Effects of Population Age Structure on Crime Rates

The dramatically higher age-specific offending rates for young people suggest that shifts in the age-composition of the population could produce considerable changes in societal crime rates. The so-called "baby-boom" generation born between the end of World War II and the early 1960s brought a large and steady increase in the proportion of the population aged between 12 and 25—the most crime-prone age group—during the 1960s and 1970s, a period when the nation's crime rate was also increasing steadily. Ferdinand (1970) found that about 50% of the increase in the Index crime rate during the 1960s could be attributed to population shifts such as the baby-boom generation's movement into the crime-prone years. Similarly, Steffensmeier and Harer (1989) found that virtually all the reported decreases in the UCR and NCVS Index crime rates during the early 1980s could be attributed to the declining proportion of teenagers in the population, that is, to a "baby-bust" effect.

More recently, Steffensmeier and Harer (1999) report that the large impact of age composition on crime rates during the 1980s has diminished during the 1990s, and that the broad decline in both the UCR and NCVS crime rates since 1992 (the Clinton presidency years) cannot be solely attributed to changes in population age composition. One explanation of the recent downtrend has attributed the decline to dramatic increases in incarceration rates that presumably incapacitate or prevent crimes by locking up high-frequency offenders who commit a disproportionate amount of all crimes. However, the rise in incarceration rates extends backward to at least the late 1970s, and therefore, considerably predates the 1990s drop in crime. Therefore, it appears unlikely that higher imprisonment rates explain much, if any, of the recent drop in crime—just as they do not account for its rise in the late 1980s.

Alternative explanations for recent downward trends in crime rates include the strong economy and low unemployment of the 1990s, an abatement of the crack epidemic of the late 1980s, and the wide variety of community-level criminal justice initiatives undertaken in the past decade, such as Operation Weed and Seed, Pulling America's Communities Together, Safe Futures, and community policing (Kelling, 1998). Also, Steffensmeier and Harer (1999) speculate that offenders may be shifting from risky, low-return offenses like burglary (also robbery) to others that are more lucrative (drug dealing) or less risky (fraud).

Conclusion

Age is a consistent predictor of crime, both in the aggregate and for individuals. The most common finding across countries, groups, and historical periods shows that crime—especially "ordinary" or "street" crime—tends to be a young person's activity. However, the age–crime relationship is not invariant, and in fact varies in its specific features according to crime types, the structural position of groups, and historical and cultural contexts. On the other hand, relatively little is known about older chronic offenders. Clearly, the structure, dynamics, and contexts of offending among older individuals are rich topics for future research.

Darrell Steffensmeier and Jeffery Ulmer

References and Further Reading

Adler, P. and Adler, P. 1983. Shifts and oscillations in deviant careers: The case of upper-level drug dealers and smugglers. *Social Problems* 31:195–207.

Coontz, S. 1997. *The Way We Really Are: Coming to Terms with America's Changing Families*. New York, NY: Basic Books.

Federal Bureau of Investigation. 1935–1997. *Crime in the United States*. Washington, DC: U.S. Government Printing Office.

Ferdinand, T. 1970. Demographic shifts and criminality: An inquiry. *British Journal of Criminology* 10:169–175.
Glaser, D. 1978. *Crime in Our Changing Society.* New York, NY: Holt, Rinehart, and Winston.
Greenberg, D. 1979. Delinquency and the age structure of society. *Contemporary Crisis* 1:66–86.
Greenberg, D. 1982. Age and crime. In *Encyclopedia of Crime and Justice*, Vol. 1, Sanford, K. (Ed.). New York, NY: Macmillan, pp. 30–35.
Hagan, J. 1991. Destiny and drift: Subcultural preferences, status attainments, and the risks and rewards of youth. *American Sociological Review* 56:567–581.
Hagan, J., Heffler, G., Classen, G., Boehnke, K., and Merkens, H. 1998. Subterranean sources of subcultural delinquency beyond the American dream. *Criminology* 36:309–342.
Hirschi, T. and Gottfredson, M. 1983. Age and the explanation of crime. *American Journal of Sociology* 89:522–584.
Irwin, J. 1970. *The Felon*, Englewood Cliffs, NJ: Prentice-Hall.
Jolin, A. and Gibbons, D. 1987. Age patterns in criminal involvement. *International Journal of Offender Therapy and Comparative Criminology* 31:237–260.
Monkkonen, E. 1999. New York city offender ages: How variable over time. *Homicide Studies* 3:256–270.
Nettler, G. 1978. *Explaining Crime.* New York, NY: McGraw-Hill.
Pennsylvania Crime Commission. 1991. *1990 Report-Organized Crime in America: A Decade of Change*. Commonwealth of Pennsylvania.
Quetelet, A. 1833 (1984). *Research on the Propensity for Crime at Different Ages.* (Translated by Sawyer Sylvester.) Cincinnati, OH: Anderson Publishing Co.
Sampson, R. and Laub, J. 1993. *Crime in the Making: Pathways and Turning Points through Life*. Cambridge, MA: Harvard University Press.
Shannon, L. 1988. *Criminal Career Continuity: Its Social Context.* New York, NY: Human Sciences Press.
Shapiro, S. 1984. Wayward Capitalists: Target of the Securities and Exchange Commission. New Haven, CT: Yale University Press.
Shock, N. 1984. *Normal Human Aging: The Baltimore Longitudinal Study of Aging*. Washington, DC: U.S. Government Printing Office.
Shover, N. 1983. The later stages of ordinary property offender careers. *Social Problems* 30:208–218.
Steffensmeier, D. 1986. *The Fence: In the Shadow of Two Worlds*. Totowa, NJ: Rowman & Littlefield.
Steffensmeier, D. and Allan, E. 1995. Criminal behavior: Gender and age. In *Criminology: A Contemporary Handbook,* Joseph, S. (Ed.), pp. 83–114.
Steffensmeier, D., Allan, E., Harer, M., and Streifel, C. 1989. Age and the distribution of crime. *American Journal of Sociology* 94:803–831.
Steffensmeier, D. and Harer, M. 1991. Did crime rise or fall during the Reagan presidency? The effects of an 'aging' U.S. population on the nation's crime rate. *Journal of Research in Crime and Delinquency* 28:330–359.
Steffensmeier, D. 1999. Making sense of recent U.S. crime trends, 1980-98: Age composition effects and other explanations. *Journal of Research in Crime and Delinquency* 36:235–274.
Steffensmeier, D., and Cathy, S. 1991. Age, gender, and crime across three historical periods: 1935, 1960, and 1985. *Social Forces* 69:869–894.
Tracey, P., Marvin, W., and Robert, F. 1990. *Delinquency Careers in Two Birth Cohorts*. New York, NY: Plenum.
Ulmer, J. and William, S.J. The contributions of an interactionist approach to research and theory on criminal careers. *Theoretical Criminology* 3:95–124.
Warr, M. 1998. Life-course transitions and desistance from crime. *Criminology* 36:183–216.
Wilson, J.Q. and Richard, H. 1985. *Crime and Human Nature*. New York, NY: Simon and Schuster.

Aggravating or Mitigating Circumstances

At sentencing, aggravating and mitigating circumstances are used to inform the sentencing decision. A mitigating circumstance is a fact that reduces a convictee's culpability. An aggravating circumstance is a fact that enhances a convictee's culpability. Common aggravating circumstances are prior criminal history, the gravity of the offense, lack of remorse, cruelty and extreme disregard for life, the use of a firearm or other weapon, and flight from prosecution. Common mitigating circumstances include the absence of a criminal history, emotional, physical, or psychological disability, good character, poor family history, a tendered apology to the victim, paid restitution, and remorse.

Generally, in noncapital cases and where there is not a system of sentencing guidelines, sentencing judges exercise considerable discretion over aggravating and mitigating circumstances, including what qualifies as a circumstance and what weight is to be assigned to each circumstance. Aggravating and mitigating circumstances are typically proven by a preponderance of the evidence, although the higher standards, proof by clear and convincing evidence or beyond a reasonable doubt, are sometimes constitutionally or statutorily required. The rules of evidence are relaxed at sentencing. So, evidence that is inadmissible at trial may be received and considered by a sentencing judge, provided it is credible and it is not unduly prejudicial.

A statute may enumerate the circumstances that can be relied upon in increasing or reducing a sentence. A convictee possesses no constitutional right to present mitigating circumstances when a statute mandates a particular sentence. This includes mandatory life imprisonment without the possibility of parole. See, for example, *State v. Farrow*, 118 N.H. 296, 386 A.2d 808 (1978) and *Beard v. State of Indiana*, 262 Ind. 643, 323 N.E.2d 216 (1975)

The law is different in capital cases. Defendants convicted of capital crimes possess an Eighth Amendment freedom from cruel and unusual punishments, as well as a due process right to present mitigating circumstances. (see for example, *Boyde v. California*, 494 U.S. 370 (1990) and *McCleskey v. Kemp*, 481 U.S. 279 (1987)). This right is broadly construed in favor of the convictee. Accordingly, a statute that enumerates the possible mitigating circumstances in capital cases must include an open-ended provision that permits defendants to present evidence not included in the statutory list. Death can not be mandated for any crime, including murder (see *Woodson v. North Carolina,* 428 U.S. 280 (1976) and *Lockett v. Ohio*, 438 U.S. 586 (1978)). Instead, a system of individualized sentencing that narrows the pool of eligible convictees to a smaller number of convictees that possess one or more justifiable aggravating circumstances must exist. If a system of aggravating circumstance is so broad that every eligible convictee possesses a characteristic that supports the imposition of death, the system is violative of both the prohibition of cruel and unusual punishments and of due process.

In an effort to reduce disparity in sentencing, to achieve greater proportionality in punishment, and to facilitate judicial review, the federal government and many states have established systems of sentencing guidelines. The federal government did this through the Sentencing Reform Act of 1984 (P.L. 98-473, Title II, 98 Stat., 1988). This statute established the Sentencing Commission, which was delegated the responsibility of establishing a set of sentencing guidelines that include a narrow range of possible punishments for each offense. The guidelines require sentencing courts to calculate an offense level and a criminal history category for each defendant. Mitigating and aggravating factors are considered when determining both the offense level and criminal history category. The offense level and criminal history category are used to determine the range of punishment from which the court must sentence the convictee. Courts may depart from the prescribed range only when aggravating or mitigating circumstances exist that were not fully taken into consideration by the Sentencing Commission. In addition, the Sentencing Commission has expressly stated that certain factors were considered, but not fully factored into the guidelines. Examples include where the victim provoked the crime, when a defendant was acting under extreme duress, and when a defendant voluntarily disclosed the offense to the government. State sentencing guideline systems are similar in how they operate.

One of the most controversial forms of evidence at sentencing is so-called victim impact evidence. Victim impact evidence typically comes in the form of survivors who testify to the impact the crime has had on their lives. Prior to 1987, victim impact evidence was commonly admitted. This ended with the U.S. Supreme Court decision *Booth v. Maryland*, 482 U.S. 496 (1987) wherein the use of such evidence was held to violate the Cruel and Unusual Punishments Clause of the Eighth Amendment to the Constitution of the U.S. The Court reversed its holding in *Booth* only 4 years later in *Payne v. Tennessee*, 501 U.S. 808 (1991). Although the Court reversed its *per se* bar of victim impact evidence, it also made it clear that sentencing judges are to exclude victim impact evidence that is so unduly prejudicial that it renders sentencing fundamentally unfair.

Proof of an aggravating circumstance sometimes includes evidence of a crime that was committed in conjunction with the offense under sentence. For example, it is common for the use of a firearm to be an aggravating circumstance to violent crimes, such as rape, assault, battery, and murder. Additionally, the use or possession of the firearm may itself be a separate crime. In such cases, a defendant may be both charged and punished for the possession or use and receive a sentence enhancement for the violent crime without violating the Double Jeopardy Clause of the Fifth Amendment to the Constitution of the U.S. Further, the Supreme Court of the U.S. ruled in *United States v. Watts*, 519 U.S. 148 (1997) that the evidence of the second crime may be used to enhance the sentence of the first crime, even if the defendant is acquitted of the second crime. The Court's rationale centered on the differing standards of proof between sentencing and trial, the former commonly being preponderance of the evidence and the latter being beyond a reasonable doubt.

Daniel E. Hall

References and Further Reading

Frase, R. (2000). Is guided discretion sufficient? Overview of state sentencing guidelines, *St. Louis University Law Journal*, 44, 425–446.

Reitz, K. (1998). Sentencing guideline systems and sentence appeals: A comparison of federal and state experiences, *Northwestern University Law Review*, 91, 1441–1506.

See also **Defenses to Criminal Liability: Justifications and Excuses; Sentences and Sentencing: Guidelines**

Aggression and Criminal Behavior

Introduction

Over several centuries, social scientists have attempted to identify the variables that influence the acts of violence and criminal behavior. Although it can be stated with some degree of confidence that no single factor causes criminal behavior, one behavior that has produced much literature as well as controversy is the act of aggression. Aggression is not usually thought of as an emotional state like anger but as an act. Zillmann (1988) defined aggression as a response to any condition that poses a threat to the well-being of another person. Similarly, Rush (2000) defined aggression as any act that inflicts pain or suffering on another individual or where there is the intent to do harm.

When considering the relation of anger and aggression, it is tempting to set up a simple formula: anger is the emotion that gives rise to aggression, the act. Although this simple formula often works in explaining many acts of aggression, it does not account for the situations where individuals become increasingly angry but forego becoming physically aggressive (Robbins, 2000). Most people have inhibitions that prevent them from acting in an aggressive fashion even when they experience situations that might otherwise lead to a violent response (Baumeister, Heatherton, and Tice, 1994). Some aggressive acts do occur, however, without provocation, and therefore, one must keep in mind that while anger does not always lead to aggression, aggression does not always presuppose anger (Robbins, 2000).

Although the majority of our society manages to cope with daily adversity, there are those who fail to control their emotions, which in some cases leads to aggressive and violent behavior. Some of these individuals consciously engage in aggressive and criminal behavior for the payoff or thrill that the moment brings. Still others act out and engage in socially unacceptable behavior because of mental illness or desperation. Like most human behavior, however, the causes of aggression are speculative. Although much research has been produced in an attempt to identify the various factors that can lead to aggressive and criminal behavior, no single factor has been identified. However, some of the factors that seem to work in concert with one another and may assist with understanding aggressive behavior include the individual's biological composition, family interaction and background, peer group association, and social and cultural differences.

Biological Factors, Aggressiveness, and Criminal Behavior

One factor that has contributed to a flurry of interest with regard to genetic abnormalities is the notion of the "born criminal." Mainly in the 1960s researchers became intrigued by a genetic mutation that occurs in about one man in every 1000: the XYY syndrome (Voight et al., 1994). The discovery of this extra Y chromosome subsequently led to extensive research concerning the possible link among aggressive behavior, criminality, and genetic composition. One of America's most famous criminals Richard Speck, who was convicted of murdering eight nurses in Chicago, was originally believed to have an abnormal XYY chromosomal structure. However, it was later learned that neither Speck nor most other violent offenders actually possessed the extra chromosome that was thought to be linked to criminality (Siegel, 1998). As a result of the failure to link the additional chromosome to aggressive and violent behavior the majority of the research related to the XYY chromosome quickly dissipated (Neill, 1996).

Although the causal link between the additional Y chromosome and criminal behavior was not found, other researches emerged that continued to search for a link among genetics, biological composition, and criminality. In 1993, Raine reported that antisocial, aggressive, and violent offenders tended to have low resting heart rates. The main theory underlying this finding was that a low heart rate indicated low autonomic arousal and fearlessness. Therefore, low autonomic arousal was believed to lead to sensation seeking and risk taking in an attempt to increase stimulation, which some believed increased the likelihood of criminality (Raine, 1993). Hawkins et al. (1998) support this theory but believe that there is not enough evidence to establish this condition as a risk factor for future violence, and Van Hulle et al. (2000) question the effects of heart rate on aggressive behavior.

Another research has focused on male and female hormones and their link to aggressiveness. With regard to the male hormone, testosterone, increased levels in both males and females have been found to influence aggressive behavior (Blanchard and Blanchard, 1984), and decreases in estrogen have been associated with female aggression and antisocial behavior (Buchanan, Eccles, and Becker, 1992). In addition to the increase in these hormones, it has been suggested that the onset of the female menstrual cycle and the subsequent release of excessive amounts of sex hormones may also trigger this type of behavior. However, no empirical research has directly linked the menstrual cycle to aggressive, antisocial, or criminal behavior (Siegel, 1998).

Another focus of researchers has been the brain's neurotransmitters, which are chemicals stored in brain cells that carry information. There are many different neurotransmitters, but serotonin has been the chemical that has been linked to aggressive and violent behavior (Reiss and Roth, 1993). Booth and Osgood (1993) support this notion and reported in their study of Vietnam War veterans that a relationship did exist between aggressive and criminal behavior and testosterone levels. Conversely, Cary (1994) suggested that genetics (including neurotransmitters) do not play a strong role in predicting or observing violence.

The biological link between aggressive and criminal behavior continues to be elusive at best. However, research continues to be produced that challenges our thinking about the possibility that there is such a thing as "born criminal." Despite the possibility that one's biological makeup may have the capacity to influence future aggressiveness or criminal behavior, the family structure and its ability to function "normally" has often been the focal point of trying to understand the dynamic nature of human development and socialization.

The Family, Aggressive Behavior, Abuse, and Criminality

Berkowitz (1974) suggests that the early learning and socialization process of children play a key role in the development of aggression and possibly later criminal activity. Supporting this view Torbet et al. (1996) reported that a child who grows up in a dysfunctional family may learn aggressive or antisocial behavior; may not be taught to control unacceptable behavior, delay gratification, or respect the rights of others; or may not be adequately supervised to preclude association with antisocial or delinquent peers.

As a consequence, the child becomes inadequately socialized and unable to constrain his or her behavior within acceptable boundaries.

From a theoretical perspective, family influences on an adolescent's behavior cannot be overstated. Edwin Sutherland's theory of differential association supports the notion that deviant or criminal family members may have the capacity to influence and teach negative behavior to its members (Siegel, 1998). Adding support to Sutherland's theory, Loeber and Dishion (1983) found in their review of 70 studies that family characteristics might influence delinquency and later criminality. They found for example, at age 6, family functioning was a predictor of delinquency, and antisocial behavior and aggressiveness at age 9 indicated delinquent tendencies. In addition, parental criminality at age 10 was a valid predictor of a child's delinquency, and by age 15, academic failure was noted as a significant risk factor for future criminality. Finally, at age 16, if the child was expressing aggressive behavior and involved in delinquency, these behaviors were more likely to continue.

In a similar study, Henggeler (1989) reviewed the relationship between family transactions and child psychosocial functioning in 65 studies conducted over a 30-year period. It was found that delinquent behavior stemmed from three main areas. First, low levels of parental control tended to influence the onset of aggressive behavior. Second, if parental controls were present, but were inadequate or ineffective, youths in these families were at-risk for engaging in delinquent acts. Finally, the antisocial behavior of parents, including the degree to which deviant methods of meeting goals were acceptable, tended to be a strong predictor of delinquent behavior in young family members.

In addition to these findings, child neglect and abuse has been identified as another variable that may cause aggressive and violent behavior. According to Natalucci–Persichetti (1996), childhood abuse and neglect represents a widespread serious social problem that increases the likelihood of delinquency, adult criminality, and general aggressiveness toward others. In addition, poor educational performance, health problems, and low achievement tend to characterize the victims of childhood abuse and neglect. Also important is the fact that neglect alone (not necessarily physical abuse) has been significantly related to violent criminal behavior (Natalucci–Perisichetti, 1996, 55).

With regard to sexual abuse, Moore (1991) found in his study of female offenders at a Kansas youth center that 55–60% of the female offenders had been victims of sexual abuse as children. Moore and his colleagues identified factors that appear to have played a significant role in fostering delinquency among this population including anger and aggression toward others, alienation, distrust of authority and adults, self-blame, substance abuse, and running away. Although sexual abuse does not appear to be a concrete factor that leads *all* sexually abused youths down a road to delinquency, sexually abused juveniles appear to be at greater risk of becoming offenders when compared to nonabused youths (Moore, 1991).

The influence of family members in relation to the cognitive development of children, the interaction between family members, and all types of abuse, appear to significantly increase the probability that a child will engage in aggressive and criminal behavior. Although the family can increase the likelihood that the child will become aggressive and possibly delinquent, it can also serve as a positive model for the child to follow. According to Drowns and Hess (1990) the family is considered the first teacher, role model, classroom, and educator, which influences the value system that the child will develop and use for a lifetime. Although the family appears to greatly influence the development of youth, the adolescent's peer group may also impact the child's conformity with social norms and values, or influence his tendency to engage in aggressive or delinquent behavior.

The Influence of the Peer Group

According to Lingren (1995) peer relations expand to occupy a particularly central role in young people's lives, and new types and levels of peer relationships emerge during adolescence. During this time, peers typically replace the family as the center of socializing and leisure activities. Youths progressing through adolescence tend to have several peer relationships, and confront various "peer" cultures that have very different norms and value systems. Lingren explains that adult perception of peers as being a dangerous influence is inaccurate, and more often than not, the adolescents interacts with individuals who reinforce family values. Supporting this point of view, Reiss and Roth (1993) found that school-age children often rejected physically aggressive children because of their threatening behavior.

The impact on the rejected child, however, may exacerbate behavior problems, making it more difficult for the rejected child to form healthy, positive relationships with nonaggressive youth (Reiss and Roth, 1993). When this type, as well as other types of rejection occur, it is possible that the individual will seek others who behave in a similar fashion or are willing to support or tolerate their negative or aggressive tendencies (Crews and Counts, 1997). Many times these youths and other youths that have been alienated from the larger peer group, find refuge in delinquent subcultures or youth gangs.

According to Gerrard (1964) many gang members show a preference for aggression based on their feeling of inferiority and their fear of being rejected or ignored by others. Consistent with this point of view Spergel (1995) reported that the gang subculture permits youth to identify with a status-providing system that emphasizes violence or the threat of violence as a key means to resolve uncertainty, ambiguity, and the lack of connectedness with the world (p. 168).

It is clear that the peer group or the lack of connection thereof, can be quite strong and have a significant impact on a child's development. Although aggressive and delinquent youths appear to be drawn to other youths with similar backgrounds and behavior, the peer group can reinforce positive and acceptable behavior that is modeled in the home and by significant others. It appears that differences in adolescent preferences for playmates, however, naturally gives rise to some form of rejection, which may be responsible for stimulating aggressive or antisocial behavior and involvement in delinquent subcultures. Although peer relationships may help explain the relationship between aggressive behavior and criminality, social and cultural factors are also important considerations when examining this behavioral phenomenon.

Social and Cultural Explanations of Aggression and Criminal Behavior

When considering the variables that may cause individuals to become aggressive, violent, or even criminal, the person's social and cultural background becomes rather important. For example, Wolfgang and Ferracuti (1982) in their explanation of violence found that the history and circumstances of the society dictates the values, beliefs, and attitudes of its members. Similarly, Baumeister and Heatherton (1996) proposed that subcultures do not promote or encourage aggressive behavior as much as they define the conditions under which such behavior is acceptable.

As a society, America has raised youth to accept violence as a "normal" part of life and that "toughness" is a part of adolescent masculine identity. This mindset has been passed from generation to generation in families from various backgrounds and socioeconomic conditions. In fact, it can be argued that the willingness to resort to violence to resolve interpersonal conflict has been the foundation of male adolescent upbringing for hundreds of years (Crews and Montgomery, 2000).

Today, despite evolving into a more civilized society, the use of guns and other violent means to resolve conflict continues. However, it is possible that the demand for guns and the readiness to resort to their use is in response to perceived dangers within communities in which guns have been purchased. The demand for guns, particularly in major cities, has been fueled by an "ecology of danger," which is often comprised of street gangs, an expanding drug market, and different lifestyles and perceptions about gun possession and violence (Sheley and Wright, 1995). Therefore, aggressive and violent behavior in this context is likely to be a response to what is perceived to be a very real threat of victimization, and the ongoing need to protect oneself, family members, and possessions.

Social groups, communities, and society as a whole determine whether behavior is within acceptable boundaries. Some acts of aggression or violence that occur in one community or society, however, may or may not be acceptable in other parts of the world. Therefore, aggression is not only individual and situation specific, it is also socially defined. In the U.S., as well as in other countries that share similar values, aggressive behavior in some specific situations is actually encouraged. For example, aggressive behavior is valued in the U.S. when it is used as a means of obtaining a competitive edge, particularly in sports and in the corporate business industry. This becomes problematic, however, when the individual fails to harness, control, or shape the aggressive behavior into positive or productive actions, and the individual strays outside the socially prescribed values and norms.

Today the reasons for criminal activity that have resulted from aggression are elusive. What are more perplexing, however, are the compulsive acts of violence that do not progress along a continuum or follow a sequence of steps. These illogical crimes present the most problematic situations for both social scientists and the law enforcement community. Despite the existence of this type of behavior, the links among biological, social, and cultural variables provide possible explanations or clues that may help explain the reasons why one may choose to engage in criminal behavior. Subsequently, the complexity of these variables and their relationship to one another continues to evolve as research produces pieces of a puzzle that may one day provide a definitive explanation as to why aggressive acts sometimes lead individuals to engage in criminal conduct.

JEFFREY A. TIPTON

References and Further Reading

Baumeister, R.F. and Heatherton, T.F. (1996). Self-regulation failure: An overview. *Psychological Inquiry, 7*(1), 1–15.

Baumeister, R.F., Heatherton, T.F., and Tice, D.M. (1994). *Losing Control: How and Why People Fail at Self-Regulation.* San Diego, CA: Academic Press.

Berkowitz, L. (1974). Some determinants of impulsive aggression: The role of mediated associations with reinforcement for aggression. *Psychological Review, 81*(2), 165–176.

Blanchard, D.C. and Blanchard, R.J. (1984). Affect and aggression: An animal model applied to human behavior. In Blanchard, R.J. and Blanchard, D.C. (Eds.), *Advances in the Study of Aggression,* Vol. 1, pp. 1–62. Orlando, FL: Academic Press.

Booth, A. and Osgood, D.W. (1993). The influence of testosterone on deviance in adulthood: Assessing and explaining the relationship. *Criminology, 31*(1), 93–117.

Buchanan, C.M., Eccles, J.S., and Becker, J.B. (1992). Are adolescents the victims of raging hormones: Evidence for activational effects of hormones on moods and behavior at adolescence. *Psychological Bulletin, 111*(1), 62–107.

Bushman, B.J. and Huesmann, L.R. (2000). Effects of televised violence on aggression. In Singer, D.G. and Singer, J.L. (Eds.), *Handbook of Children and the Media,* pp. 223–254. Thousand Oaks, CA: Sage Publications.

Cary, G. (1994). Genetics and violence. In Reiss, A.J. Jr. and Roth, J.A. (Eds.), *Understanding and Preventing Violence. Biobehavioral Influences*, Vol. 2, pp. 21–53. Washington, DC: National Academy Press.

Crews, G.A. and Counts, R.M. (1997). *The Evolution of School Disturbance in America: Colonial Times to Modern Day.* Westport, CT: Praeger Publishers.

Crews, G.A. and Montgomery, R.H. Jr., (2000). *Chasing Shadows: Confronting Juvenile Violence in America.* Upper Saddle River, NJ: Prentice Hall.

Drowns, R. and Hess, K. (1990). *Juvenile Justice.* New York, NY: West Publishing Company.

Elliott, D.S. (2000). Violent offending over the life course: A sociological perspective. In Krasnegor, N.A., Anderson, N.B., and Bynum, D.R. (Eds.), *Health and Behavior,* Vol. 1, pp. 189–204. Rockville, MD: National Institutes of Health, Office of Behavioral and Social Sciences.

Gerrard, N.L. (1964). The core member of the gang. *British Journal of Criminology, 4*, 361–371.

Gershoff, E.T. (2002). Corporal punishment by parents and associated child behaviors and experiences: A meta-analytic and theoretical review. *Psychological Bulletin, 128*(4), 539–579.

Hawkins, J.D., Herrenkohl, T.L., Farrington, D.P., Brewer, D., Catalano, R.F., and Harachi, T.W. (1998). A review of predictors of youth violence. In Loeber, R. and Farrington, D.P. (Eds.), *Serious and Violent Juvenile Offenders: Risk Factors and Successful Interventions*, pp. 106–146. Thousand Oaks, CA: Sage Publications.

Henggeler, S.W. (1989). *Delinquency in Adolescence.* Thousand Oaks, CA: Sage Publications.

Johnson, J.G., Cohen, P., Smailes, E., Kasen, S., Oldham, J.M., et al. (2000). Adolescent personality disorders associated with violence and criminal behavior during adolescence and early adulthood. *American Journal of Psychiatry, 157*(9), 1406–1412.

Lingren, H.G. (1995). *Adolescence and Peer Pressure.* Retrieved on May 22, 2003, from http://www.ianr.unl.edu/pubs/NebFacts/nf211.htm.

Loeber, R. and Dishion, T.J. (1983). Early predictors of male delinquency: A review. *Psychological Bulletin, 94*(1), 68–99.

Moore, J. (1991). Addressing a hidden problem, Kansas Youth Center treats sexually abused female offenders. *Corrections Today, 53*(1), 40–46.

Natalucci-Persichetti, G. (1996). *Juvenile Justice Programs and Trends: Youth Violence a Learned Behavior.* Laham, MD: American Correctional Association.

Neill, P. (1996, June). *Mass Testing for "Delinquency" Gene.* Retrieved on July 12, 1999, from http://www.parascope.com/mx/genel.htm.

Raine, A. (1993). *The Psychopathology of Crime: Criminal Behavior as a Clinical Disorder.* San Diego, CA: Academic Press.

Reiss, A.J. Jr. and Roth, J.A. (1993). *Understanding and Preventing Violence.* Washington, DC: National Academy Press.

Repetti, R.L., Taylor, S.E., and Seeman, T.E. (2002). Risky families: Family social environments and the mental and physical health of offspring. *Psychological Bulletin, 128*(2), 330–366.

Robbins, P.R. (2000). *Anger, Aggression, and Violence: An Interdisciplinary Approach*. Jefferson, NC: McFarland & Company, Inc.

Rush, G.E. (2000). *The Dictionary of Criminal Justice,* 5th ed. New York, NY: Dushkin/McGraw-Hill.

Sheley, J. and Wright, J. (1995). *In the Line of Fire: Youth, Guns, and Violence in Urban America*. New York, NY: Aldine de Gruyter.

Siegel, L.J. (1998). *Criminology: Theories, Patterns, and Typologies*, 6th ed. Belmont, CA: Wadsworth Publishing Company.

Spergel, I.A. (1995). *The Youth Gang Problem: A Community Approach*. New York, NY: Oxford University Press.

Thornton, T.N., Craft, C.A., Dahlberg, L.L., Lynch, B.S., et al. (2000). *Best Practices of Youth Violence Prevention: A Sourcebook for Community Action*. Atlanta, GA: Centers for Disease Control and Prevention, National Center for Injury Prevention and Control.

Torbet, P., Gable, R., Hurst, H., Montgomery, I., Szymanski, L., et al. (1996). *State Responses to Serious and Violent Juvenile Crime*. Office of Juvenile Justice and Delinquency Prevention. Washington, DC: Office of Justice Programs, U.S. Department of Justice.

Van Hulle, C.A., Corley, R., Zahn-Waxler, C., Kagan, J., and Hewitt, J.K. (2000). Early childhood heart rate does not predict externalizing behavior problems at age 7 years. *Journal of the American Academy of Child and Adolescent Psychiatry, 39*(10),1238–1244.

Voight, L., Thornton, W., Barrile, L., and Seaman, J. (1994). *Criminology and Justice*. New York, NY: McGraw-Hill.

Wolf, D.A. (1999). *Child Abuse: Implications for Child Development and Psychopathology.* Thousand Oaks, CA: Sage Publications.

Wolfgang, M.E. and Ferracuti, F. (1982). *The Subculture of Violence: Towards an Integrated Theory in Criminology.* Beverly Hills, CA: Sage Publications.

Zillmann, D. (1988). Cognition-excitation interdependencies in aggressive behavior. *Aggressive Behavior, 14*(1), 51–64.

See also **Biological Theories of Crime: An Overview**

Akers, Ronald L.

Ronald Akers is a sociologist whose research on social learning theory as applied to deviant behavior has been recognized as a key theory in understanding and predicting criminal behavior. Social learning theory is based upon the propositions found in Edwin Sutherland's differential association theory. Akers and an associate, Robert Burgess, modified Sutherland's theory to include the importance of reinforcement in determining the amount and level of deviant behavior. Their new theory, labeled differential association-reinforcement theory, added components of operant (voluntary response) and respondent (involuntary response) conditioning, and also has components of rational choice theory.

According to Akers and Burgess, learning behavior is the result of exposure to both conforming and criminal behavior and definitions of that behavior. A person learns behavior from others (imitation), and then this behavior is reinforced. If the behavior results in positive consequences, or reinforcements, the behavior will continue. On the other hand, negative consequences will help to eliminate the behavior. Thus, positive reinforcements serve to increase and negative reinforcements tend to decrease the strength and amount of criminal behavior. The reinforcers and punishers can be nonsocial, as in the physical effects of drugs or alcohol use, but the principal behavioral effects come from interaction with primary groups of family and friends and secondary groups such as the media. These can be the associations that occur most frequently among peers but may also be within the family. They provide the basic social sources of rewards and punishment that encourage or discourage use or nonuse.

Akers and Burgess explain that learning criminal behavior is no different from learning normative conduct. Both forms of behavior are learnted by social interactions with others, and are a function of consequences. Criminal behavior can be expected when it has been reinforced and defined as desirable. The strength of criminal behavior is a function of the amount, frequency, and probability of reinforcement. As deviant behavior is a form of operant behavior and must be reinforced, it stops if it is no longer reinforced. Reinforcement can come from any social group, including peer groups and gangs.

There are five key points to social learning theory. First is that, the primary learning mechanism is operant conditioning, in which behavior is shaped by the reaction to that behavior or the consequences of that behavior. Second, direct conditioning and imitation of others is important in determining behavior. Third, rewards, or positive reinforcement, as well as avoidance of punishment, strengthen this behavior. Fourth, the determination of whether the behavior is deviant or conforming depends on differential reinforcement. Finally, people learn norms and attitudes from those who are important to them. Generally speaking, our associations with people who are important to us help to shape our behavior (Masters and Roberson, 1990, 209–210).

Since it was originally developed in 1966, Akers has used social learning theory to test deviant behavior in a number of different settings by different populations, including the use of alcohol, drugs, and sexual deviations among students. For example, in 1984, Lanza-Kaduce, Akers, Krohn, and Radosevich applied social learning theory to alcohol and drug use. They found that social learning variables could be used to discriminate between adolescents who ceased using drugs and those who continued to use. The following year, Krohn et al. (1985) used a 3-year panel study of junior and senior high school students to test the concepts of social learning behavior to adolescent cigarette smoking. They found that the concepts of social learning theory could help understand why students continued or ceased smoking. Also in that year, Akers and Cochran (1985) applied social learning theory to adolescent drug use. In this study, the authors find that social learning theory is strongly supported over other theories such as social bonding theory or anomie.

In 1989, Akers, La Greca, Cochran, and Sellers used social learning theory to understand older adults' alcohol behavior. Through a series of face-to-face interviews of 1410 people, 60 years or older, in New Jersey and Florida, they found that drinking among the elderly is related to the norms and behavior of one's primary groups, one's own attitudes toward (definitions of) alcohol, and the balance of reinforcement for drinking. Once again, the researchers found that a person's definitions of drinking are conducive to consumption of alcohol when, on balance, the positive definitions offset negative definitions of drinking. Briefly, the more that association with persons who hold favorable attitudes toward drinking outweighs that with abstainers or persons who hold negative attitudes toward drinking, the more likely one is to drink alcohol. In essence, the choice to drink alcohol is expected to the extent that one has differentially associated with other drinkers, that drinking has been differentially reinforced over abstinence, and that one defines drinking as more desirable than abstinence.

Akers and Lee (1996) used social learning theory to address smoking behavior in adolescents. Using a 5-year longitudinal study of students in grades 7–12, they find that smoking can be expected if it has been differentially reinforced over nonsmoking behavior, and is defined as desirable or justified. Generally, whether students abstained from drugs, chose to use them, and if they continued to use them depended on the past, present, and anticipated future rewards and punishments perceived by the students to be attached to the use or abstinence (the differential reinforcement). By their social interaction with other drug users or abstainers, the students developed attitudes, orientations, and knowledge that were either favorable or unfavorable to using drugs. The more the student defined the behavior as good or justified rather than holding to attitudes counter to drug use, the more likely they were to use it.

In 1998, Akers published a new book to help explain crime rates. In this book, Akers developed the Social Structure–Social Learning Theory of crime. He argues that environments also impact individuals through learning. Crime rates, according to Akers, are a function of social learning theory in a social structure (Akers, 1998).

Nancy Marion

Biography

1960, Indiana University, B.S in secondary education; 1961, Kent State University, M.A. in sociology; 1966, University of Kentucky, Ph.D. in sociology. 1965–1968, assistant professor, University of Washington; 1969–1972, associate professor, University of Washington; 1972–1974, professor, Florida State University; 1974–1980, professor, University of Iowa, and chairman; 1980–1985, professor and chairman, University of Florida; 1994–2001, director of the Center for the Studies in Criminology and Law, The University of Florida; 2001–now, associate dean for faculty affairs, University of Florida; past president of the American Society of Criminology and the Southern Sociological Society.

Selected Writings

Social Learning and Social Structure: A General Theory of Crime and Deviance, 1998. Boston, MA: Northeastern University Press.

Criminological Theories: Introduction and Evaluation. 1994. Los Angeles, CA: Roxbury.

Rational choice, deterrence, and social learning theory: The path not taken, *Journal of Criminal Law and Criminology, 81,* 1990.

Social learning and alcohol behavior among the elderly, *Sociological Quarterly, 30*, 1989.

Deviant Behavior: A Social Learning Approach, 1985, 3rd ed, New York, NY: Wadsworth.

Social learning theory and adolescent cigarette smoking, *Social Problems, 32*, 1985.

Deviant Behavior: A Social Learning Approach, 1973. Belmont, CA: Wadsworth.

Adolescent marijuana use: A test of three theories of deviant behavior, *Deviant Behavior, 6*, 1985 (with Cochran, J.K.).

A longitudinal test of social learning theory: Adolescent smoking, *Journal of Drug Issues, 26*, 1996 (with Lee, G.).

A differential association-reinforcement theory of criminal behavior, *Social Problems, 14*, 1966 (with Robert Burgess).

Cessation of alcohol and drug use among adolescents: A social learning model, *Deviant Behavior, 5*, 1984 (with Lonn Lanza Kaduce, Marvin D. Khrohn, and Marcia Radosevich).

References and Further Reading

Masters, R. and Cliff, R., 1990. *Inside Criminology*. Englewood Cliffs, NJ: Prentice Hall.
Sutherland, E., 1939. *Principles of Criminology*, 3rd ed. Philadelphia, PA: J.B. Lippincott.
Sutherland, E., 1947. *Principles of Criminology*, 4th ed. New York, NY: Harper and Row, Publishers, Inc.

See also **Social Learning Theory**

Alcohol, Tobacco, and Firearms, Bureau of (ATF)

The Bureau of Alcohol, Tobacco, and Firearms (ATF) is a law enforcement agency within the U.S. Department of Treasury. The mission of ATF is to enforce the federal laws and regulations dealing with alcohol and tobacco products, firearms, explosives, and arson by (1) curbing illegal traffic and criminal use of firearms; (2) investigating violations of federal explosives laws; (3) assuring the collection of all tobacco and alcohol tax revenues and suppress illegal manufacture, sale, and deception in the alcoholic beverage industry; and (4) assisting states in eliminating interstate trafficking and distribution of cigarettes to avoid state taxes.

With 24 field divisions located throughout the U.S., ATF annually regulates and licenses approximately 10,000 explosives industry members, over 100,000 Federal Firearms Licensees, and collects approximately 12 billion dollars in tax revenue from alcohol products.

To reduce the illegal use of firearms and enforce federal firearm laws, ATF is responsible for issuing firearms dealers' licenses and monitoring licensee qualification and compliance with federal law. The ATF also works with other federal, state, and local agencies to investigate armed violent offenders and career criminals, narcotics traffickers, and domestic and international arms traffickers (U.S. Department of Treasury web site).

History

The history of ATF is as fascinating as the tasks with which it is charged. Historians trace the agency's origin to the Congressional Act of 1 July 1862, which created the Office of Internal Revenue within the Treasury Department. This act entrusted the Treasury commissioner with collection of taxes on tobacco products and distilled spirits. In 1863, Congress authorized the hiring of three detectives to aid in prevention, detection, and apprehension of tax evaders. In 1875, the office was changed to the Bureau of Internal Revenue, and the number of detectives continued to grow. The 1919 ratification of the Eighteenth Amendment brought fame to these officers, as they were charged with investigating the illicit manufacture of liquors, and in 1920, the officers were given the title of the Prohibition Unit. In 1927, the unit was elevated to Bureau status within the Treasury Department. In 1930, Congress transferred the powers of the Prohibition Bureau to the Department of Justice's new Bureau of Prohibition, with the tax-related and regulatory activities of the Bureau remaining within the Treasury under the jurisdiction of the new Bureau of Industrial Alcohol. When the Twenty First Amendment repealed Prohibition in 1933, the Department of Treasury once again found itself regulating the alcohol industry. In 1934, the Department of Justice prohibition enforcement duties ended, and the Alcohol Tax Unit (ATU) was created within the Bureau of Internal Revenue in the Department of Treasury.

In 1934, in response to organized crime, the National Firearms Act was passed, followed in 1938 by the Federal Firearms Act. In 1942, enforcement of firearms tax regulations was transferred to the ATU. After the Bureau of Internal Revenue became the Internal Revenue Service (IRS) in 1951, laws covering tobacco taxation were added to the division's jurisdiction, and the ATU was renamed the Alcohol and Tobacco Tax Division of the IRS. This title lasted until the passage of the 1968 Gun Control Act, which added regulation of the explosives industry to the division, and shifted its title to Alcohol, Tobacco, and Firearms (ATF) Division. In 1972, Treasury Department Order No. 120-1 transferred the functions, duties, and powers related to alcohol, explosives, and firearms from the IRS to ATF. That same year, ATF was given full bureau status under the Department of Treasury, and has continued in that capacity to date.

Recent Developments and Controversies

Many Americans became aware of ATF because of its involvement in the raid on the Branch Davidian compound near Waco, Texas in early 1993. Led by David Koresh, the Branch Davidians had allegedly amassed a large cache of illegal machine guns and explosives. In an attempt to serve warrants to confiscate illegal weapons and arrest Koresh for violations of the Gun Control Act of 1968, ATF unsuccessfully raided the compound on February 28, 1993. Four ATF agents and three Branch Davidian men were killed, and a number of others were wounded. After the unsuccessful raid, the FBI was called in to take over the operation. After 7 weeks of negotiations, the FBI assaulted the compound with tanks and fire, resulting in a frenzy of executions and suicides by the Davidians.

The controversy surrounding Waco brought about an increase in the Treasury Department's oversight of ATF operations and brought a series of leadership changes at the management and directorship level. John Magaw, the newly appointed director, embarked on a series of changes within the bureau. Magaw supervised the restructuring of the agency to operate more efficiently, including combining special agents and inspectors into one Enforcement Directorate and elevating training to a higher priority. These changes, along with other programs outlined below, have reduced the criticism of ATF brought about by the Waco incident.

The ATF operates the National Tracing Center in Falling Waters, West Virginia, as the sole agency responsible for tracing firearms recovered at crime scenes and used in crimes, tracing approximately 200,000 firearms annually. The ATF also operates Project LEAD, an automated data system that tracks illegal firearms and illegal firearm trafficking, allowing law enforcement agencies to identify the most prolific illegal firearms traffickers in their area.

Additionally, ATF's Gang Resistance Education and Training (GREAT) program is designed to teach third/fourth-grade and fifth/sixth-grade children how to resist negative peer pressure, understand how gangs and youth violence negatively affect their lives, learn how to resolve conflicts without violence, and help children set goals for themselves. Over 1.5 million students have received GREAT training since the program began.

During 2001, ATF initiated approximately 18,500 criminal investigations and recommended 10,206 individuals for prosecution, resulting in over 5000 convictions. They also collected over 14 billion dollars in federal tax revenue from excise taxes imposed on alcohol, tobacco, firearms, and ammunition (ATF Accountability Report for 2001).

ATF continues to be one of the more prominent federal agencies, supporting local, state, and international efforts to control illegal activities in the areas of alcohol, tobacco, and firearms.

David C. May

References and Further Reading

Bureau of Alcohol, Tobacco, and Firearms, *A Report on the Bureau of Alcohol, Tobacco, and Firearms: Its History, Progress, and Programs*, Washington, DC, 1995.

Bureau of Alcohol, Tobacco, and Firearms, *ATF Facts*, Washington, DC.

Moore, J., *Very Special Agents: The Inside Story of America's Most Controversial Law Enforcement Agency—The Bureau of Alcohol, Tobacco, and Firearms*, Champaign, IL: University of Illinois Press, 1997.

U.S. Department of Justice, *Promising Strategies to Reduce Gun Violence*, Washington, DC: Office of Juvenile Justice and Delinquency Prevention, 1999.

U.S. Department of Treasury, ATF Accountability Report, 2001: *Working for a Sound and Safer America through Innovation and Partnership*, Washington, DC: U.S. Department of Treasury, 2002.

See also **Firearms and Criminal Behavior; Firearms and the Law**

Alcohol Use and Criminal Behavior

Ethyl alcohol, ethanol, or alcohol that is drunk, "is soluble in water, has no distinctive taste, does no physical harm (in moderate quantities) and is metabolized at the rate of about 7 grams (or 0.3 ounces) per hour in a normal human body, leaving only carbon dioxide (which is what we breathe out anyway) and water" (Heath, 1995, 1). Yet, this seemingly innocuous substance has been the subject of centuries of impassioned denunciation and bitter condemnation leading to public controversy, debate, and policy aimed at regulating, controlling, and eradicating it. Of course, alcohol has also elicited lavish literary and poetic praise, not to mention being wildly popular in terms of availability and consumption: aspects that Gusfield (1989, 39) refers to as the "carnival point of view," which he argues has generally been neglected by those studying it (for a history of alcohol and its ubiquity, see Austin, 1985; Siegel and Inciardi, 1995).

How to explain this contradiction? Part of the answer to this paradox is the alleged involvement and reported contribution of alcohol to a variety of biological, psychological, social, and legal problems. There has been widespread recognition of several alcohol-related individual health problems (see White, 1991). Alcohol has a strong potential for producing tolerance, habituation, and dependence that may lead to alcoholism. Its connections to cirrhosis of the liver and the neurological disease known as Wernicke-Korsakoff syndrome are well established. The existence of fetal alcohol syndrome among the newborns of alcoholic mothers is a grim reality. Finally, we know that alcohol is related to various cardiovascular and endocrine diseases, and that slight-to-severe cognitive impairment may result among drinkers depending on their consumption patterns (see Dusek and Girdano, 1992). In all of these health-related concerns, alcohol is viewed as a causal factor whose use and abuse result in the deleterious effects identified.

Beyond these health-related concerns lie a variety of issues wherein alcohol has been implicated as a possible precipitating or facilitating (though rarely as a direct causal) factor. These include its part in the commission of a variety of criminal offenses including homicides; aggravated assaults; rape or sexual assaults (see below), and various forms of domestic violence such as spousal and child abuse (see Kurst-Swanger and Petcosky, 2003). And ironically as Nurco et al. (1991) show, those who are dependent on alcohol (despite its legal availability in the U.S.) are more likely to commit serious crimes compared to those who are dependent on cocaine or heroin (despite their illegality). Parker (1995, xiii) makes the following point in explaining why he chose to study alcohol's relationship to the crime of homicide:

> Despite the problem that illegal drug use represents in the U.S., alcohol consumption is dramatically more widespread and much more integrated into everyday life. This makes the study of alcohol and homicide relationship much more pressing and important than that between illegal drug use and homicide.

The focus of this essay will, therefore, be two-fold. First, we will focus on alcohol's relationship to crime and the hypothesized pathways from the former to the latter as uncovered in earlier literature. Second, a longer section will describe recent research trends that has expanded and provided more details on the alcohol–crime nexus. In both sections, the literature cited is illustrative rather than comprehensive.

Alcohol and Crime—Earlier Literature

Marvin Wolfgang (1958) is generally credited with carrying out the seminal work that first reported on the possible linkage of alcohol to crime, specifically violent crime. He found, after examining 588 homicides that occurred in Philadelphia, that alcohol was present in 63.6% of them. Other studies over the decades using varying methods since then have consistently upheld this relationship (e.g., Pittman, 1974; Collins, 1981; Parker, 1995). It has become an accepted part of macro-level aggregate and micro-level situational discussions of crime to note that alcohol is often present where crime is taking place. In general, studies of the alcohol–crime relationship have relied on aggregate statistical measures (e.g., state or city level alcohol consumption rates correlated with crime rates), surveys (e.g., examining individual alcohol consumption along with the criminal activities or asking crime victims regarding the presence of alcohol during criminal events) and testing arrestees or other known offenders for drugs, including alcohol.

Earlier work in the alcohol–crime genre, in general, does not argue that consuming alcohol directly induces or causes anyone to behave criminally. Most often, it is seen as a factor or facilitator that increases the odds of crimes (generally, of violence) taking place. There are three traditional explanations for how the pathway from drinking alcohol to criminal behavior operates (see Conklin, 2003 for details). The first two pay attention to the "effects" of alcohol on individuals, whereas the third considers societal or group definitions of the meaning of alcohol usage. The first suggests that alcohol acts to reduce personal and learned inhibitions against behaving aggressively, physically and verbally.

> To the extent that alcohol lowers social inhibitions and reduces anxiety and guilt, people who have been drinking may act more aggressively than would otherwise have been the case. (Barlow and Kauzlarich, 2002, 64).

The second explanation holds that those who are already motivated to commit crime or are actively involved in criminal activity use alcohol instrumentally. It allows them to calm their own anxieties and to screw up their courage before committing a crime (see Tunnell, 1992). In particular, persistent property offenders are said to sometimes act this way. The third focuses on alcohol's perceived function in American society of being a social lubricant that allows people who consume alcohol to behave differently from their conventional selves, particularly in more aggressive ways. However, this aggression is not a uniform pattern across cultures and social groups. Goode (1989, 117) comments:

> Behavior under the influence, then, does not follow a predetermined biochemically fixed pattern. It, too, has its norms, although they may often be a bit different from those that influence behavior when one is sober. It is not the drug, alcohol, that truly makes anyone do anything.

From this perspective, it is the "permission" that a culture (although this may be untenable as an excuse, legally speaking) gives a drinker, who has assimilated this norm, to behave in nonnormative (e.g., to use verbal insults, to be aggressive or start a fight, to try to engage in forcible sex) ways that results in his or her criminal activity. In this context, the issue of what societies teach their young about "non-pathological" drinking patterns, practices, and behaviors becomes important (Houghton and Roche, 2001).

Alcohol and Crime—Recent Research

It is safe to say that more recent literature has extended and detailed the insights described above. Recent research can be best characterized as introducing new explanatory variables (especially the deleterious effects of alcohol availability), and as shedding more light on alcohol's role as contributory factor in many more offenses. There are three major areas of endeavor.

First, a line of explanatory research continues to provide richer and more detailed information on the nature of the alcohol–crime relationship. Parker (1995), in the most influential work on alcohol and crime published in the past decade, describes what he refers to as the "selective disinhibition" hypothesis. This hypothesis takes the idea of disinhibition discussed earlier and adds the concepts of active and passive constraints to behavioral outcomes in situations where alcohol is present (as determinants of whether or not violence results). Active constraints involve a choice on the part of the drinking individuals as to whether or not to descend into violence. Passive constraints are situation-specific in that because of the setting or environment, the choice of violence is diminished (on a related issue, see Lanza-Kaduce et al., 1997 on predrinking expectations and how they may change situationally as drinking progresses). The hypothesis is tested and supported in two ways. The first using city and state level data, shows that alcohol availability increases homicide rates (see below for more research that focuses on availability). The second suggests that decreases and increases in minimum age for alcohol purchase (fluctuations between 18 and 21) significantly affected youth homicide. Expanding on the approach used in the second study, Parker and Cartmill (1998) have argued persuasively using multivariate time-series analysis, encompassing more than 60 years of data, that fluctuations in homicide rates in the U.S. are affected by alcohol consumption rates.

Other explanatory research into the relationship between alcohol and crime have detailed findings from other countries and introduced new variables into the mix. Chervyakov et al. (2002) report that in Russia, the connections between alcohol and homicide are strong in that 80% of those convicted of homicide were under the influence of alcohol at the time of the offense. Further, where data on both offender and victim are available, "victims were also commonly intoxicated." Masters and Coplan's (1999) intricate model integrates neurobiology and toxicology into an area-based explanation of the alcohol–crime nexus. Finally, Fergusson and Norwood (2000) find that among a birth cohort studied up to the age of 21 in New Zealand, even after taking into account nonobserved and confounding variables, the relationship between alcohol abuse and violence as well as property crime remained intact.

Second, a robust line of research focuses more closely on the role of alcohol in rape or sexual assault. Martin and Bachman (1998) use data from the National Crime Victimization Survey (NCVS) to show that if the perpetrator was drinking, it decreases the likelihood that the rape will be completed, increases the possibility of injury to the victim, and is not correlated with the need for medical assistance for the victim. Ullman et al. (1999) report, based on a national survey of female college students, that the propensity of sexual assault victims to abuse alcohol and the actual use of alcohol by both victim and offender prior to an attack were associated with more severe sexual victimization. They suggest that educational efforts aimed at alcohol use and sexual assault prevention could benefit from incorporating this information. Using data gathered through the NCVS for the years 1992 through 1996, Brecklin and Ullman (2001) further confirm that the use of alcohol by offenders associated with higher risk sexual assaults. This means that if the offender had been drinking, the rape was likely to be a stranger assault, during nighttime, at outdoor locations, and involved greater resistance on the part of the victim. At the same time, alcohol also reduced the likelihood of completion of the rape and was unrelated to whether or not physical injury resulted for the victim. However, culling information from the Uniform Crime Reports, Coker et al. (1998) disagree concluding flatly that avoiding situations where the abuse of drugs and alcohol occurs is likely to lessen the risk of physical injury trauma during sexual assaults. The propensity to report crime (specifically on campus) is also affected by alcohol, according to surveys conducted by Ruback et al. (1999). The college student respondents viewed reporting crime to the police to be more appropriate if victims had not been drinking and even more inappropriate if the victims were underage and had been drinking. The reason underlying this "is the perceived stigma attached to victims who have been drinking" (Ruback et al., 1999, 381). On another note while focusing on the relationship between stalking and domestic violence in Colorado Springs, Colorado Tjaden and Thoennes (2000) note that where stalking is connected to domestic violence, both victims and suspects are less likely to have been using alcohol.

Third, a relatively new line of recent research has considered the impact of alcohol availability (generally, focusing on the number and location of outlets that sell alcohol, such as liquor stores and bars) on crime (see discussion of Parker, 1995 above). These studies begin with the common observation in the United States that decaying urban areas with concentrated poverty, which generally have higher rates of crime, also appear to have thriving businesses centered on alcohol. Speer et al. (1998) investigate the interrelationships between neighborhood characteristics, the density of alcohol outlets and violent crime in Newark, New Jersey. With some qualifications, they do find that alcohol outlet density is a significant predictor of the occurrence of violent crime. Norstrom (2000) reports using time-series data, that in Norway, "a positive and statistically significant relationship was found between density and crimes of violence." The longitudinal method employed here, support the findings of cross-sectional studies that criminal violence grows along with the number of alcohol outlets. Thus, Gorman et al. (2002) conclude in a study of Camden, New Jersey that after controlling for neighborhood social structure, the density of alcohol outlets affected violent crime positively. This was replicated using spatial analysis. There is more. Stevenson et al. (1999) consider the relationship of alcohol to two forms of crime that are rarely studied in connection with it: property damage and public disorder. They find, using data from Sydney and New South Wales, Australia that both of these offenses occur more frequently in areas with higher alcohol sales. They consider this positive relationship causal, but also suggest that higher alcohol sales may also indicate higher levels of opportunity for crime.

We are learning more about the problematic aspects of this popular drug, particularly in terms of its behavioral manifestations, and the troubling consequences of its widespread availability. The correlations and connections between alcohol and various forms of criminal behavior (as well as other problems detailed earlier) have led to various legal measures aimed at curbing, controlling through regulation or completely eliminating production, distribution, and use of the substance. These legal measures represent contemporary forms of sumptuary laws. Anthropologists say such laws reflect larger cultural themes in various societies and social groups and are attempts at regulating or prohibiting the consumption of certain objects and substances. Not unexpectedly, alcohol has often been the subject of such controls (see Heath, 1995 for details from various countries). Historically and contemporaneously, some societies have tabooed the use of alcohol under any and all circumstances (e.g., compulsory abstinence as practiced in Saudi Arabia). Others have restricted its use to ceremonial occasions and ritualistic purposes (e.g., the use of alcohol among Indian tribes in Guatemala). Yet other societies have deemed it as an acceptable recreational substance but subject to certain restrictions (e.g., its status in contemporary United States) that define and closely monitor the circumstances under which it might be produced and used. Alcohol is taxed heavily. Permits are required for selling liquor and it may be done only during particular times on specific days of the week. The locations of establishments that serve alcohol are subject to strict zoning by local government. States define and enforce a legislated minimum age for drinking. Finally, there are laws against driving or boating in an intoxicated state or while under the influence of alcohol, as well as regarding public intoxication. It is clear that the peculiar dilemmas posed by this popular, yet problematic drug, will continue to befuddle humanity.

N. Prabha Unnithan

References and Further Reading

Austin, G.A. (1985) *Alcohol in Western Society from Antiquity to 1800: A Chronological History*, Santa Barbara, CA: ABC-Clio.

Barlow, H.D. and Kauzlarich, D. (2002) *Introduction to Criminology*, 8th ed. Upper Saddle River, NJ: Prentice Hall.

Brecklin, L.R. and E. Ullman, S. (2001) The role of offender alcohol use in rape attacks: An analysis of National Crime Victimization Survey data. *Journal of Interpersonal Violence* 16, 1: 3–21.

Chervyakov, V.V., Shkolnikov; V.M., Pridemore, W. A., and McKee, M. (2002) The changing nature of murder in Russia. *Social Science and Medicine* 55, 10: 1713–1724.

Coker, A.L., Walls, L.G., and Johnson, J.E. (1998) Risk factors for traumatic physical injury during sexual assaults for male and female victims. *Journal of Interpersonal Violence* 13, 5: 605–620.

Collins, J.J., Jr. (1981) *Drinking and Crime: Perspectives on the Relationships between Alcohol Consumption and Criminal Behavior.* New York, NY: Guilford Press.

Conklin, J.E. (2003) *Criminology.* 8th ed. Boston, MA: Pearson Allyn and Bacon.

Dusek, D.E. and Girdano, D.A. (1992) *Drugs: A Factual Account.* 5th ed. New York, NY: McGraw Hill.

Fergusson, D.M. and .Norwood, J. L. (2000) Alcohol abuse and crime: A fixed-effects regression analysis. *Addiction* 95, 10: 1525–1536.

Goode, E. (1989) *Drugs in American Society.* 3rd ed. New York, NY: Alfred A. Knopf.

Gorman, D.M., Speer, P.W., Gruenewald, P.J. and Labouvie, E.W. (2001) "Spatial dynamics of alcohol availability: Neighborhood structure and violent crime." *Journal of Studies on Alcohol* 62, 5: 628–636.

Gusfield, J.R. (1989) Constructing the ownership of social problems: Fun and profit in the welfare state. *Social Problems* 36, 4: 431–441.

Heath, D.B. (1995) *International Handbook on Alcohol and Culture.* Westport, CT: Greenwood Press.

Houghton, E. and Roche, A.M. (2001) *Learning about Drinking.* Philadelphia, PA: Brunner-Routledge.

Kurst-Swanger, Karel and Petcosky, J.L. (2003) *Violence in the Home: Multidisciplinary Perspectives.* New York, NY: Oxford University Press.

Lanza-Kaduce, L., Bishop, D.M. and Winner, L. (1997) Risk/benefit calculations, moral evaluations, and alcohol use: Exploring the alcohol-crime connection. *Crime and Delinquency* 43, 2: 222–229.

Martin, S.E. and Bachman, R. (1998) The contribution of alcohol to the likelihood of completion and severity of injury in rape incidents. *Violence against Women* 4, 6: 694–712.

Masters, R.D. and Coplan, M.J. (1999) A dynamic, multifactorial model of alcohol, drug abuse, and crime: Linking neuroscience and behavior to toxicology. *Social Science Information* 38, 4: 591–624.

Norstrom, T. (2000) Outlet density and criminal violence in Norway, 1960–1995. *Journal of Studies on Alcohol* 61, 6: 907–911.

Nurco, D., Hanlon, T., Balter, M., Kinlock, T.W. and Slaght, E. (1991) A classification of narcotic addicts based on type, amount and severity of crime. *Journal of Drug Issues* 21: 429–448.

Parker, R.N. (1995) *Alcohol and Homicide: A Deadly Combination of Two American Traditions.* Albany, NY: State University of New York Press.

Parker, R.N. and Cartmill, R.S. (1998) Alcohol and homicide in the United States 1934–1995—or one reason why rates of violence may be going down. *Journal of Criminal Law and Criminology* 88, 4: 1369–1398.

Pittman, D.J. (1974) Drugs, Addiction and Crime. In Glasner, D. (Ed.) *Handbook of Criminology,* Chicago, IL: Rand McNally, pp. 209–232.

Rodell, D.E. and Benda, B.B. (1999) Alcohol and crime among religious youth. *Alcoholism Treatment Quarterly* 17, 4: 53–66.

Ruback, R.B., Menard, K.S., Outlaw, M.C., and Shaffer, J.N. (1999) Normative advice to campus crime victims: Effects of gender age, and alcohol. *Violence and Victims* 14, 4: 381–396.

Siegel, H.A. and Inciardi, J.A. (1995) A brief history of alcohol. In Inciardi, J.A. and McElrath, K. (Eds.) *The American Drug Scene: An Anthology.* Los Angeles, CA: Roxbury Publishing Company.

Speer, P.W., Gorman, D.M., Labouvis, E.W., and Ontkush, M.J. (1998) Violent crime and alcohol availability: Relationships in an urban community. *Journal of Public Health Policy* 19, 3: 303–318.

Stevenson, R.J., Lind, B., and Weatherburn, D. (1999) Property damage and public disorder: Their relationship with the sales of alcohol in New South Wales, Australia. *Drug and Alcohol Dependence* 54, 2: 163–170.

Tjaden, P. and Thoennes, N. (2000) The role of stalking in domestic violence reports generated by the Colorado Springs police department. *Violence and Victims* 15, 4: 427–441.

Tunnell, K.D. (1992) *Choosing Crime: The Criminal Calculus of Property Offenders.* Chicago, IL: Nelson-Hall.

Ullman, S.E., Karabatsos, G., and Koss, M.P. (1999) Alcohol and sexual assault in a national sample of college women. *Journal of Interpersonal Violence* 14, 6: 603–625.

White, J.M. (1991) *Drug Dependence.* Englewood Cliffs, NJ: Prentice Hall.

Wolfgang, M.E. (1958) *Patterns in Criminal Homicide.* Philadelphia, PA: University of Pennsylvania Press.

See also **Alcohol Use: Prevention and Treatment; Alcohol Use: The Law; Driving under the Influence (DUI); Public Drunkeness**

Alcohol Use: Prevention and Treatment

Introduction

Patterns of Alcohol Consumption

Alcohol causes over 100,000 deaths each year in the U.S. and contributes to a range of health problems and negative consequences including cancer, liver disease, motor vehicle crashes, violence, crime, and suicides. The majority of alcohol-related problems are experienced by a relatively small percentage of the population. The people that form this segment of the population are considered "heavy drinkers" based on their quantity or frequency of alcohol consumption. Although heavy drinkers comprise only 20% of the adult population, they drink over 80% of the alcohol consumed in the United States. A 2001 survey revealed that nearly half of all Americans aged 12 or older reported alcohol use in the past month, an increase from the previous year. In 1998, the estimated economic cost associated with alcohol abuse was $185 billion for the U.S. Economic costs of alcohol abuse refer primarily to lost productivity, health care expenditures, motor vehicle crashes, and the criminal justice system costs of alcohol-related crime.

Age

Of those who do consume alcohol, rates of heavy drinking are highest among those under the legal drinking age, and it is estimated that underage drinkers account for 20% of all alcohol consumed. Approximately half of all high-school seniors consumed alcohol in the past month and almost one third reported binge drinking (Johnston et al., 2003). Motor vehicle crashes remain the leading cause of death for youth between the ages of 15 and 20, and alcohol is a major contributing factor to such fatalities. The combination of inexperience with driving and alcohol consumption places adolescents and young adults at even greater risk for impaired driving than those 21 and older (Hingson et al., 1994). Among youths, alcohol use is associated with more fatalities than all other illegal drugs combined. Also, underage drinking is associated with an increased chance of alcohol abuse or dependence problems later in life. Thus, early intervention is essential to prevent the development of serious alcohol problems among youths and should be given serious consideration when planning public health programs.

Despite the significant societal costs resulting from alcohol abuse, the alcohol industry spends more than $4.5 billion annually marketing the sale of beverages. Whether intentional or not, the alcohol industry's advertising strategies are appealing to youth and research indicates that exposure to alcohol advertising greatly influences a young person's beliefs about alcohol and their intention to drink. Counter advertising strategies are currently being tested as a means to dissuade alcohol use among youth.

Alcohol Use among College Students

The prevalence of heavy alcohol consumption on U.S. college campuses has been identified as the primary health problem for college students. Alcohol is the number one drug of choice among college students, and college binge drinking rates have increased despite a dramatic rise in alcohol prevention efforts over the past decade. With almost a third of all college students meeting the diagnostic criteria for alcohol abuse, college drinking is beginning to garner attention as a major public health concern, and not just a "rite of passage." The Harvard College Alcohol Study reports a linear relationship between the number of alcoholic drinks consumed and reported alcohol-related problems (Wechsler et al., 2002). Problem drinking in college does more than just result in negative consequences for the individual drinker, it affects other college students as well. Secondhand consequences, those problems experienced by students who had not been drinking, such as disrupted sleep or studies, are now a primary concern for students, parents, and college administrators (NIAAA, 2002).

Alcohol, Crime, and Violence

The association between violent crime and alcohol use is well documented. In addition to the violence induced by heavy alcohol use, short-term effects of alcohol such as disinhibitions and impaired judgment contribute to alcohol-related violent crimes. More than one third of all arrests in the U.S. are associated with alcohol, the majority of which include driving under the influence (DUI), liquor law violations, and drunkenness. Each year, alcohol is a factor in approximately 40% of all violent crimes in the U.S., and over half of incarcerated offenders were under the influence of alcohol or drugs when they committed their crime (BJS, 1998). Alcohol and other drugs have roughly equal roles in crime: 20% of federal inmates reported being under the influence of alcohol at the time of their offense, compared to 22% who report being under the influence of illicit drugs when they committed their crimes (BJS, 1999).

Prevention

A number of policies have proven to be effective in reducing alcohol consumption and alcohol-related problems. Such policies include increased prices of alcohol, restricting alcohol outlets, strengthening and enforcing minimum legal drinking age laws, and controlling alcohol advertising. Alcohol availability is a major contributing factor for underage alcohol consumption, as nearly three quarters of high-school seniors indicated that beer is "fairly easy" or "very easy" to obtain (Johnston et al., 2003). Thus, interventions to prevent underage drinking must include policy changes aimed at reducing youth access to alcohol. Given the widespread use and acceptance of alcohol, especially among youth, environmental prevention strategies are becoming more popular and effective means to create and sustain change.

Minimum Legal Drinking Age (MLDA)

In 1984, the Federal Uniform Drinking Age Act was passed, which encouraged all states to raise the MLDA to 21. The U.S. is one of only a few countries to have the MLDA as high as 21 years. The MLDA of other countries is 18, 16, or none at all. There is debate as to whether or not the MLDA should be lowered from 21 to 18 years. Those who oppose lowering the MLDA point to research that MLDA laws are estimated to have reduced traffic fatalities by more than 10% among those aged 18–20. The MLDA has been credited for reduced alcohol consumption and decreased involvement in alcohol-related fatal crashes for persons under 21 (Hingson et al., 1994).

Excise Taxes on Alcohol

Taxes on alcohol have rarely and only modestly been raised, and existing alcohol tax revenue (approximately $18 billion) does not even begin to cover the costs associated with alcohol abuse, estimated at $185 billion. Increasing excise taxes on alcohol, particularly beer, would not only decrease alcohol-related health problems, but also reduce traffic crash fatalities and crime. Underage drinking would also be reduced from increases in alcohol taxes, as even small increases in beer prices have been shown to reduce the rate of underage drinking (NIAAA, 1996). Proceeds from increased alcohol taxes could fund prevention and education initiatives, treatment services, or the enforcement of alcohol laws, thus making the alcohol industry shoulder more responsibility for the problems caused by alcohol abuse. Although the majority of high-risk drinkers prefer beer, hard liquor is typically taxed at a higher rate than beer and wine. Thus, *equalization*, or taxing all alcohol beverages at equal rates, is currently being explored as a means to reduce impaired driving prevalence through policy change.

Drinking and Driving

The risk of a motor vehicle crash greatly increases as a person's Blood Alcohol Content (BAC) increases. For example, the risk of a single-vehicle fatal crash for drivers with BACs between 0.05 and 0.09% is estimated to be 11 times higher than those who did not consume alcohol; and for those with BACs at or above 0.15%, the risk is 380 times higher (Zador, 1991). Driver's license suspension and license revocation are two of the most effective deterrents to impaired driving among the general population. However, the combination of license suspension with an individualized intervention has been found to be the most effective strategy for reducing recidivism for DUI and alcohol-related crashes.

Under the National Highway Systems Act, all states in the U.S. have enacted a "zero tolerance" law, which reduces the BAC limit to 0.02% or less for drivers under the age of 21. Zero tolerance laws reflect both the MLDA of 21 and that young drivers are at greater risk for motor vehicle crashes, especially for those involving alcohol. After adopting zero tolerance laws, some states have reported as much as a 20% reduction in alcohol-related crashes for those under 21 (Hingson, 1994). Another effective approach to curbing impaired driving among youth is graduated licensing, a process by which drivers are gradually introduced to driving in order to gain experience in both maturity and driving skills through progressive steps before receiving full driving rights.

Treatment

There is a gap between the number of people in need of treatment for alcohol abuse and those who actually receive such services. A variety of factors contribute to this discrepancy in treatment services, such as barriers to accessible treatment, social stigma of alcoholism, and lack of social support. Another potential explanation for the treatment gap is a function of limited insurance coverage, as most workplace insurance plans do not cover a full range of services for the alcohol dependent employee. In addition, insurance policies may restrict the number of sessions, which may not adequately meet an individual's needs. Of the more than 3 million people who received substance abuse treatment in the past year, more than two-thirds consisted of services involving alcohol as the primary or secondary substance of abuse. The following are some examples of the various types of approaches commonly used in the field of alcohol abuse treatment.

Alcoholism Treatment Modalities

Treatment options for those seeking help for alcohol abuse vary from short-term outpatient, to long-term residential treatment. Residential treatment programs may last anywhere from a few weeks to more than a year. Therapeutic community, or TC, is a comprehensive approach developed for substance abuse treatment that is often used in residential treatment programs. The primary goal of TC is to identify all of those areas for change (i.e., negative personal behaviors, lack of social skills, psychological distress) that often lead to drug abuse.

Outpatient treatment offers nonresidential settings where clients can become engaged in a variety of individual, group, or family therapy sessions. Outpatient treatment options vary widely in duration and treatment modalities. Common elements in such treatment programs include group therapy, individual counseling, drug testing, and educational training.

Motivational Enhancement Therapy

Motivational Enhancement Therapy (MET) is based on principles of Motivational Interviewing, a client-centered approach to help individuals build commitment to change. (Miller and Rollnick, 1991). Developed specifically for Project MATCH, MET follows the assumption that the responsibility for change lies within the client (Project MATCH Research Group, 1997). Components of MET include providing individualized feedback concerning the patient's drinking, as well as discussion on the benefits of abstinence, treatment options, and goal setting. MET is a cost-effective approach to treatment, and has been found to overcome the problem of patients' reluctance to begin treatment when compared to traditional treatment methods.

Self-Help Groups

Self-help groups, the most common type of alcohol treatment sought, are based on the premise that sharing with others can be therapeutic for people battling substance abuse and dependence. Those who have experienced similar problems can provide support and serve as motivation for an individual determined to achieve abstinence. One such self-help group is Alcoholics Anonymous, or AA. With more than one million members in 114 countries, AA uses 12 steps of recovery and group participation to assist each other in their recovery.

Future Directions

Alcohol abuse costs more to the society than all illicit drugs combined, especially when one considers such indicators as treatment costs, lost productivity, and alcohol-related motor vehicle crashes. Despite the extensive research on prevention and treatment approaches to reduce alcohol abuse that have yielded numerous effective and promising approaches, there is a need for further investigation to help combat this problem. Individualized prevention approaches such as brief, motivational interventions have shown to be effective in specific segments of the population. Also, environmental strategies, including policy change and enforcement have shown promise in reducing underage alcohol use and its associated problems. It is necessary to continue the growth in alcoholism clinical research to investigate existing treatment methods as well as the emergence of new treatment modalities. Also, further research into the benefits of pharmacotherapy used in conjunction with psychosocial therapy is warranted to explore the potential of medications for alcoholism treatment. Most importantly, it is imperative that those in need of alcohol abuse treatment have access to appropriate services, especially for those committed to abstinence and changing the direction of their lives.

STUART L. USDAN

References and Further Reading

Bureau of Justice Statistics (BJS). *Alcohol and Crime*. U.S. Department of Justice, Office of Justice Programs, 1998.

Bureau of Justice Statistics (BJS). *Substance Abuse and Treatment, State and Federal Prisoners, 1997*. U.S. Department of Justice, Office of Justice Programs, 1999.

Hingson, R., Heeren, T., and Winter, M. Lower legal blood alcohol limits for young drivers. *Public Health Reports* 109(6):738–744, 1994.

Johnston, L.D., O'Malley, P.M., and Bachman, J.G. *Monitoring the Future: National Results on Adolescent Drug Use. Overview of Key Findings, 2002. NIH Pub. No. 03-5374.* Bethesda, MD: National Institute on Drug Abuse (NIDA), 2003.

Miller, W.R. and Rollnick, S. *Motivational Interviewing: Preparing People to Change Addictive Behavior*. New York, NY: Guilford Press, 1991.

National Institute on Alcohol Abuse and Alcoholism (NIAAA). *Preventing Alcohol Abuse and Related Problems. Alcohol Alert* No. 34. Rockville, MD: NIAAA, 1996.

National Institute on Alcohol Abuse and Alcoholism (NIAAA). *Changing the Culture of Campus Drinking. Alcohol Alert* No. 58. Rockville, MD: NIAAA, 2002.

Project MATCH Research Group. Matching alcoholism treatments to client heterogeneity: Project MATCH posttreatment drinking outcomes. *Journal of Studies on Alcohol* 58(1): 7–29, 1997.

Wechsler, H., Lee, J.E., Kuo, M., Seibring, M., Nelson, T.F., and Lee, H. (2002). Trends in college binge drinking during a period of increased prevention efforts. *Journal of American College Health* 50 (5), 203–217.

Zador, P.L. Alcohol-related relative risk of fatal driver injuries in relation to driver age and sex. *Journal of Studies on Alcohol* 52(4):302–310, 1991.

See also **Alcohol Use and Criminal Behavior; Drug Policy: Prevention and Treatment**

Alcohol Use: The Law

Among other countries (see Unnithan, 1985; Millay, 1987) in the 20th century, the U.S. completely outlawed the sale of alcohol between 1919 and 1933. This came about as a result of the long-term efforts of the temperance movement, a significant political force in the 19th and early 20th centuries. National prohibition of alcohol was legislated (through the process of ratifying the Eighteenth Amendment to the U.S. Constitution) and enforced (through the Volstead Act) with the objective of turning the country "dry" and eliminating the problems associated with the use and abuse of the substance. When sale of this popular recreational drug became illegal, organized crime, historians suggest, stepped in and expanded the reach of its networks to make, distribute, and provide alcohol to those who thirsted for it. Private, illegal distillation of alcohol (e.g., "moonshine" whisky and "bathtub gin") was also popular. In the late 1920s, while overall alcohol consumption did decline, it was recognized that drinking continued to be popular among various demographic groups (particularly those who were increasing in population and political significance) in the U.S. It was also recognized that outlawing alcohol completely may not be the best way of dealing with related social and individual problems. National prohibition was repealed by passage of the Twenty-First Amendment. Despite sporadic efforts by what Heath (1989) refers to as the "new temperance movement" the selling and buying of alcohol has continued to be legal since 1933.

However, American society's historical ambivalence ("We like it but wish to restrict it legally.") toward alcohol continues (see Adler and Adler, 1983). Moderate recreational use of alcohol is acceptable and even encouraged (through the mass media, by serving it at gatherings such as parties, etc.). As a result, in most American jurisdictions, there are laws that regulate the sale and consumption of this particular psychoactive (i.e., mood altering) substance. In the U.S., Barlow and Kauzlarich (2002, 190) note that more than two-thirds of drug or alcohol arrests were alcohol-related and that these offenses "constitute this country's number-one law enforcement problem, representing almost a quarter of all police arrests." It is also estimated that there are around a quarter of a million deaths associated with drunk driving in the U.S. annually. The most common alcohol-related offenses that figure in law enforcement activity are the following:

1. Public drunkenness or public intoxication. This is generally defined as appearing in public manifestly under the influence of alcohol or a controlled substance (in Pennsylvania) or profanely cursing, swearing, or being intoxicated in public, whether such intoxication results from alcohol, narcotic drug, or other intoxicant (in Virginia). Sometimes, the issue of the individuals being intoxicated to such a degree that they may endanger themselves or others is also added (e.g., in Texas) into the law. Such behavior often constitutes violations to city or county ordinances, although as seen above, they may be also defined in a state's penal code. Public drunkenness is a classic example of a "public order crime." This means that although the behavior itself (drinking to intoxication) is legal, situational elements (in this case, the context in which the behavior is manifested, i.e., acting drunk in public) are defined as problematic. In addition, both the person who is publicly drunk as well as large sections of the public may not consider the behavior "criminal" in terms of the usual meaning associated with the word or the images evoked by it. Reactions to the behavior are more likely to be connected to its potential for creating a public nuisance and maintenance of order problem (in other words, it affects the predictable flow of business and traffic and may increase the sense of disorderliness in a community). Given its perceived low level of seriousness, it is likely to be treated as a minor offense (e.g., it is a lower level misdemeanor in both Virginia and Texas) that may be dealt with by simply transporting the individual concerned to a detoxification center (often known as the "drunk tank") to sober up and then released without necessarily going through the courts. In spirit (though not in letter) public drunkenness has been decriminalized. However, recent legal developments have included challenges and clarifications to what exactly constitutes the "public" in public intoxication (e.g., does it cover drunken behavior exhibited in a quiet residential area, outside the home of the suspect) and to dealing relatively more severely with repeat offenses of public drunkenness. For example, in 2001 San Francisco adopted a so-called "Three chugs, you're in"

policy that requires the offender to be charged, held over, and brought to court for the fourth instance of public drunkenness.

Research on public drunkenness laws has been relatively sparse. Aaronson et al. (1978) determined using time-series analysis that although formal public intoxication arrests decline following decriminalization; however, the police are likely to develop alternative means for "keeping inebriates off the streets" (e.g., the creation of informal areas that hold such individuals). Snow et al. (1989) found that public intoxication arrest is the leading reason for higher arrest rates associated with members of the homeless (in comparison with the general population of males) in Austin, Texas. However, Novak et al. (1999) have found that aggressive policing of public order offenses such as public intoxication is unrelated to reductions in serious crime (aggravated burglary and robbery) and did not result in spatial displacement of serious crime.

2. Violations of liquor sale and distribution laws. Given the ambivalent position of alcohol in and regional variations within American society (see Mooney et al., 1991), there are many related laws that regulate the general "handling" of the substance. These include (see Janes and Gruenewald, 1991) laws that: specify the alcohol content of various beverages and how these are advertised and marketed; dictate the location of places selling alcohol and the hours of sale; require warning labels on bottles containing alcohol; prevent the sale or serving of alcohol to minors; apply and enforce procedures relating to liquor permits; punish possession by minors and prevent their buying alcohol (perhaps using false identification); and require training of drinking establishment employees on issues and liabilities associated with serving alcohol.

One line of research in this area has focused on the impact of state and local laws on the behavior of those serving as well as consuming alcohol. Holder et al. (1993) report that owners or managers of establishments that serve alcohol were responsive to the legal climate of particular states in that higher liability led to practices that reduced the risk of intoxication among their customers. Berman et al. (2000) note that restrictive levels (dry counties) of local community control over alcohol distribution resulted in significant reductions in homicide and accident rates among Alaska Natives. Related to this matter, Goldsmith and Travers (1988) report that their respondents identified the most common method for obtaining alcohol by minors was through an adult and that the government and law served as the most influential agent in preventing such procurement.

In particular, there has been tremendous interest in evaluating whether increasing the minimum legal age for drinking from 18 to 21 (which all states except Wyoming did under pressure from the federal government in the 1980s and 1990s) has affected behavior. The results are inconclusive. In a comprehensive review of the literature on the issue Wagenar and Toomey (2002) conclude that the "preponderance of evidence indicates that there is an inverse relationship between the minimum legal drinking age and two outcome measures: alcohol consumption and traffic crashes." On the other hand, Evans and Forsyth (1998) found that increasing the drinking age "had little effect on the alcohol consumption of the targeted group" although there was a shift among them from public to private drinking (see Lotterhos et al., 1988; Dodder and Hughes, 1990; Hughes and Dodder, 1992). Somewhat similarly, Mooney and Gramling (1993) find reductions in drinking at "controlled" but not in "uncontrolled" locations as a result of increasing the drinking age to 21 (see also Mooney and Moran, 1994).

Finally, a modest line of research has focused on the impact of warning labels on knowledge about and attitudes toward alcohol and resulting behavior. For example, Hankin et al. (1994) report that warning labels on alcoholic beverages affected knowledge (increased) and drinking during pregnancy (decreased) among inner city African American women. Similar positive reported effects for warning labels were noted earlier by Kaskutas and Greenfield (1992) in a random national telephone sample of adults.

3. Drunk driving. During the 1980s, many states enacted laws against drunk driving generally referred to as either "driving under the influence" (DUI) or "driving with ability impaired (DWAI) and "driving while intoxicated" (DWI) based on blood alcohol levels. Such laws were the result of pressure from groups such as Mothers Against Drunk Driving (MADD) and Students Against Drunk Driving (SADD). More recently in the 1990s, the blood alcohol level required to prove that a driver was drunk has been lowered from 0.1 to 0.08 g alcohol per milliliter of blood. The latter resulted from the insistence of the federal government using the threat of withholding federal highway funds. Drunken driving laws are enforced through a variety of means (see Kinkade and

Leone, 1992; Mastrofski et al., 1994 for related enforcement issues) such as police crackdowns, sobriety checkpoints, intensive patrolling of areas with alcohol-related problems, and increasing associated penalties (e.g., suspending the licenses of drunk drivers, increasing fines, mandatory incarceration, etc.). Breath tests are the common method for determining blood alcohol levels (Ross et al., 1995). Media campaigns against drunk driving continue to be run (Yanovitsky, 2002) periodically. Williams (1994) has emphasized the need for education and public information campaigns particularly for individuals who are not necessarily "at risk" for drunk driving.

Some research has focused on the characteristics of individuals associated with drunk driving. For example, James et al. (1993) found that in Washington State, American Indians were most likely to be arrested for drunk driving. Such arrestees were likely to be unemployed and have histories of substance abuse. Yu et al. (1992) found that between 1978 and 1988 female drunk driving and recidivism increased.

In a landmark, early study of the deterrent effects of drunk driving laws, Ross (1982) concluded the following: initially, following a crackdown, there is a reduction in deaths of intoxicated drivers. This effect decays after some time, although not completely. However, judges may believe newly enacted higher penalties for drunk driving are too harsh and may refuse to impose them, thereby undermining intended outcomes. A decade later, reviewing literature on the effectiveness of DWI sanctions in terms of correctional objectives such as retribution, reform, incapacitation, and general deterrence, Ross (1992) concluded the following. The effectiveness question cannot be answered for retribution; they do not promote reformation; they incapacitate (specifically if driving licenses are revoked); and, they result in general deterrence, "especially to the degree to which sanctions are perceived as swift and certain."

The other research provides a mixed picture with increased penalties affecting the dispositions of some offenders substantially while negligible for others (Kingsnorth and Jungtsen, 1988). Fors and Rojek (1999) report that offenders who were addressed by victim impact panels were less likely to be drunk driving recidivists. A pretrial intervention program of education was found to be more successful than probation in preventing drunk driving recidivism (Lucker and Osti, 1997). Regarding the related issue of specific deterrence, Weinrath and Gartrell (2001) found that sentence length (particularly, those between 3 and 6 months) were crucial in deterring drunk driving recidivism.

N. Prabha Unnithan

References and Further Reading

Aaronson, D.E., Dienes, C.T., and Musheno, M.C. (1978) Changing the public drunkenness laws: The impact of decriminalization. *Law and Society Review* 12, 3: 405–436.

Adler, P.A. and Adler, P. (1983) Dry with a wink: Normative clash and social order. *Urban Life* 12, 2: 123–139.

Barlow, H.D. and Kauzlarich, D. (2002) *Introduction to Criminology*, 8th ed. Upper Saddle River, NJ: Prentice Hall.

Berman, M., Hull, T., and May, P. (2000) Alcohol control and injury death in Alaska native communities: Wet, damp and dry Alaska's local option law. *Journal of Studies on Alcohol* 61, 2: 311–319.

Dodder. R.A. and Hughes, S.P. (1990) Research examining impacts of attempts to change patterns of alcohol consumption and related behaviors. *Mid-American Review of Sociology* 14, 1–2: 145–150.

Evans, R.D. and Forsyth, C.J. (1998) The effects of changing the legal drinking age on the drinking behavior of the underage groups. *International Review of Modern Sociology* 24, 1: 117–128.

Fors, S.W. and Rojek, D.G. (1999) The effect of victim impact panels on DUI/DWI rearrest rates: A twelve month follow-up. *Journal of Studies on Alcohol* 60, 4: 514–520.

Goldsmith, H. and Travers, W.T. (1988) Illicit alcohol procurement by underage persons: Prevention implications and strategies for melioration. *Journal of Offender Counseling, Services and Rehabilitation* 13, 1: 133–162.

Hankin, J.E., F, I.J., Sloan, J.J., Ager, J.W., Sokol, R.J. and Martier, S.S. (1994) Time series analyses reveal differential impact of the alcohol warning label by drinking level. *Applied Behavioral Sciences Review* 2, 1: 47–59.

Heath, D.B. (1989) The new temperance movement: Through the looking glass. *Drugs and Society* 3, 3–4: 143–168.

Holder, H.D., Janes, K., Mosher, J., Saltz, R., Spurr, S., and Alexander, C.W. (1993) Alcohol beverage server liability and the reduction of alcohol-involved problems. *Journal of Studies on Alcohol* 54, 1: 23–36.

Janes, K. and Gruenewald, P.J. (1991) The role of formal law in alcohol control systems: A comparison among states. *American Journal of Drug and Alcohol Abuse* 17, 2: 199–214.

James, W.H., Hutchison, B., Moore, D.D., and Smith, A.J. (1993) Predictors of driving while intoxicated (DWI) among American Indians in the Northwest. *Journal of Drug Education* 23, 4: 317–324.

Kaskutas, L. and Greenfield, T.K. (1992) First effects of warning labels on alcoholic beverage containers. *Drug and Alcohol Dependence* 31, 1: 1–14.

Kingsnorth, R. and Jungsten, M. (1988) Driving under the influence: The impact of legislative reform on court sentencing practices. *Crime and Delinquency* 34, 1: 3–27.

Kinkade, P.T. and Leone, M.C. (1992) The effects of 'tough' drunk driving laws on policing: A case study. *Crime and Delinquency* 38, 2: 239–257.

Lotterhos, J.F., Glover, E.D., Holbert, D., and Barnes, R.C. (1988) Intentionality of college students regarding North Carolina's 21-year drinking age law. *International Journal of the Addictions* 23, 6: 629–647.

Lucker, G.W. and Osti, J.R. (1997) Reduced recidivism among first-time DWI offenders as a correlate of pre-trial intervention. *Journal of Offender Rehabilitation* 24, 3–4: 1–17.

Mastrofoski, S.D., Ritti, R.R., and Snipes, J.B. (1994) Expectancy theory and police productivity in DUI enforcement. *Law and Society Review* 28, 1: 113–148.

Millay, J.B. (1987) Prohibition Pacific style: The emergence of a law banning alcohol in Truk. *Legal Studies Forum* 11, 2: 165–187.

Mooney, L.A. and Gramling, R. (1993) The differential effects of the minimum drinking age law. *Sociological Inquiry* 63, 3: 330–338.

Mooney, L.A and Moran, S. (1994) Libation, location, and legalization: A comparison of 1978 and 1988 alcohol consumption patterns. *Sociological Viewpoints* 10, 1: 45–55.

Mooney, L.A., Gramling, R., and Forsyth, C.J. (1991) Amplification of deterrence: The effects of drinking laws on alcohol consumption patterns. *International Review of Modern Sociology* 21, 2: 73–91.

Novak. K.J., Hartman, J.L., Holsinger, A.M. and Turner, M.G. (1999) The effects of aggressive policing on serious crime. *Policing* 22, 2: 171–190.

Ross, H.L. (1982) *Deterring the Drinking Driver: Legal Policy and Social Control*. Lexington, MA: Heath.

Ross, H.L. (1992) Are DWI sanctions effective? *Alcohol, Drugs and Driving* 6, 1: 61–69.

Ross, H.L., Simon, S., Cleary, J., Lewis, R., and Storkamp, D. (1995) Causes and consequences of implied consent test refusal. *Alcohol, Drugs and Driving* 11, 1: 57–72.

Snow, D.A., Baker, S.G., and Anderson, L. (1989) Criminality and homeless men: An empirical assessment. *Social Problems* 36, 5: 532–549.

Unnithan, N.P. (1985) A cross-national perspective on the evolution of alcohol prohibition. *International Journal of the Addictions* 20, 5: 591–604.

Wagenaar, A.C. and Toomey, T.L. (2002) Effects of minimum drinking age laws: Review and analyses of the literature from 1960 to 2000. *Journal of Studies on Alcohol* 63, 14: 206–225.

Weinrath, M. and Gartrell, J. (2001) Specific deterrence and sentence length: The case of drunk drivers. *Journal of Contemporary Criminal Justice* 17, 2: 105–122.

Williams, A.F. (1994) The contribution of education and public information to reducing alcohol-impaired driving. *Alcohol, Drugs and Driving* 10, 3-4: 197–205.

Yanovotsky, I. (2002) Effects of news coverage on the relevance of drunk driving behavior: Evidence from a longitudinal study. *Journal of Studies on Alcohol* 63, 3: 342–351.

Yu, J., Essex, D.T., and Williford, W.R. (1992) DWI/DWAI offenders and recidivism by gender in the eighties: A changing trend. *International Journal of the Addictions* 27, 6: 637–647.

See also **Alcohol Use and Criminal Behavior; Alcohol Use: Prevention and Treatment; Public Drunkenness**

Ammunitions *See* **Firearms**

Amphetamines

Description and History of Abuse

Amphetamine encompasses a family of synthetic, chemically related nerve stimulants including Benzedrine, Desoxyn, Didrex, Methedrine, Biphetamine, and Dexamyl (Goode, 1999). Amphetamine can be distributed in powder, tablet, liquid, or capsule form. Amphetamine crystals usually appear in white, light pink, or yellow hue and exhibit a pungent odor and bitter taste. Ingestion of amphetamine is accomplished by snorting the powder through the nose, swallowing or dissolving the tablet into a drink, injecting the liquid intravenously, or smoking the drug. Street terms for amphetamine vary by region and social group. Terms commonly associated with amphetamine include speed, crank, crystal, meth, bennies, dexies, and uppers (Miller, 2001).

Benzedrine was first synthesized in 1887 in Germany, nearly 45 years before it was first marketed as an inhalant to treat nasal congestion. Amphetamines have been used medically to treat narcolepsy, attention deficit disorder, depression, obesity, and Parkinson's disease (National Institute on Drug Abuse (NIDA), 1980). Methamphetamine, the most commonly abused of these stimulants today, was first synthesized in Japan in 1919 and closely resembles amphetamine in chemical composition and pharmaceutical effect. Both amphetamine and methamphetamine were used by World War II soldiers to fight fatigue during battle (Goode, 1999). By the late 1950s widespread abuse of amphetamine inhalers and intravenous methamphetamine prompted Congress to pass stringent restrictions on the sale and use of the substances.

Effects of Abuse

A host of short-term and long-term effects are attributed to amphetamine use. Immediate effects of the drugs are similar to a rush of adrenaline. Users will typically experience increased heart rate, increased blood pressure, dilated pupils, and reduced appetite (NIDA, 1980). In addition, amphetamine users may exhibit increased breathing, talkativeness, and aggressiveness, compulsory behavior, and may experience visual and auditory hallucinations. Repeat amphetamine users develop increasing levels of tolerance to the drug and must elevate their dosage to achieve the same effects. Chronic abuse of amphetamine often leads to powerful physical and psychological dependency.

Long-term abuse of amphetamines may result in psychological conditions similar to paranoid schizophrenia. Large, repeat doses of amphetamine often result in extreme panic, hallucinations, paranoia, fever, blurred vision, dizziness, uneven heartbeat, tremors, loss of motor skill, and death (Kalant, 1973). Continued usage may also damage blood vessels, increase the risk of heart failure, and weaken resistance to disease. Individuals discontinuing amphetamine use typically experience a range of withdrawal symptoms: hunger, anxiety, restlessness, and extreme fatigue. Chronic and high dosage users coming off amphetamine binges have been known to collapse for up to 48 hours of disturbed sleep.

Drug Regulation

Prior to 1914, the federal authority over food and drugs was primarily limited to international traffic. States maintained authority over domestically produced and distributed foods and drugs throughout the 19th century. Scientific progress and a shift away from agricultural labor throughout the century altered the context of both food and drug sales (Kurian, 1998). During this time there was no government entity that examined the quality of drugs and food sold on the open market. In response to escalating public concern, all of the states eventually adopted legislation to protect against falsely marketed or dangerous food and drugs; however, considerable differences existed between the state laws. This concern culminated at the end of the 19th century prompting the passage of several laws. The most important of these was the enactment of the Pure Drug and Food Act of 1906, which criminalized the false advertising of patent medicines, and mandated the disclosure of addictive chemicals (Kurian, 1998). This act also charged the Food and Drug Administration, previously the Bureau of Chemistry, with the regulation of these activities. During this time, many states passed additional legislation governing the sale of drugs and food, but no uniform standards were developed.

The passage of the Harrison Act in 1914 placed stringent restrictions on the use, sale, and distribution of opium, coca, and their derivatives (Kurian, 1998). In part, the Harrison Act mandated that the sale of these patent drugs require a prescription from a physician and empowered the FDA to control the traffic of these substances. Despite the awareness of amphetamines' powerful chemical properties, Congress failed to specifically restrict the sale or transport of amphetamine in the Harrison Act's provisions.

It was not until 1951 that the Subcommittee on Narcotics of the House Ways and Means Committee broadened its consideration to include barbiturate and amphetamine abuse as it met to consider necessary restrictions for dangerous drugs (NIDA, 1980). Several bills aimed at reducing the abuse of these substances were introduced between 1954 and 1961. In 1965, Congress enacted the drug abuse control amendments that specified the legal authority of the Food and Drug Administration, extended the record keeping requirements on drug registration and inventories, and increased the restrictions on the sale and manufacture of certain drugs (Musto, 2002). Despite these steps, inadequacies continued to exist in the laws, enabling the legal nonprescription sale of certain amphetamine products as late as 1971.

The Comprehensive Drug Abuse Prevention and Control Act of 1970 served to unify and replace all previous federal legislation governing the use and abuse of restricted drugs (Musto, 2002). This legislation classified all applicable drugs into one of five schedules. These schedules reflect the varying medical utility and abuse potential of each drug. Under the 1970 Act, amphetamine, phenmetrazine, and methylphenidate were classified as Schedule III drugs; while intravenous methamphetamine was further restricted as a level II drug (NIDA, 1980). In 1971, amphetamine, phenmetrazine, and methylphenidate were reclassified as Schedule II drugs, reflecting increased concern for their potential for abuse.

Several bills have been enacted since 1970 in an effort to further stem the abuse of dangerous substances. The Anti-Drug Abuse Act of 1986 heightened the penalties for the possession and trafficking of controlled substances, introduced minimum sentences for proscribed offenses, and imposed sanctions on possession and use (Musto, 2002). Subsequently, the Anti-Drug Abuse Act of 1988 established the Office of National Drug Policy (ONDCP) to formulate the U.S. strategy to combat drug abuse.

Theories on Abuse

Researchers typically approach the subject of amphetamine abuse from one of several theoretical perspectives. Each individual theory uses a unique approach to assessing the nature of drug abuse, however individually these theories may lack the predictive power of a more integrated approach. Some of the most common approaches include biological, sociological, learning-based, and psychological theories (Josi and Roberts, 2003). Biological theories follow a medical model that views drug addiction as a treatable disease influenced by genetics and other biological factors. These theories have also been used to explain alcohol and other substance abuse.

Sociological theories focus on the influence and bonds that develop between an individual and his or her peers, family members, and the community. This theoretical genre contends that the acceptance of or resistance toward drugs by these influential social groups may significantly impact an individual's likelihood for abuse.

Theories based on psychological models typically address the emotional needs of individual users. Psychological theories contend that addicts achieve a form of physiological satisfaction from drug abuse. One widely accepted psychological theory explaining voluntary amphetamine abuse is the reinforcement model (Bozarth, 1994). The reinforcement model theorizes that drugs like amphetamine activate certain chemicals in the brain that serve as positive reinforcers. These reinforcers are activated naturally by factors like food, water, and sex and are thought to increase the release of dopamine producing a pleasurable reaction (Bozarth, 1994). Amphetamine triggers this pleasurable response, especially for first-time users, and individuals abusing the drug become addicted to the dopamine release.

Trends Associated with Abuse

A diverse segment of the population currently uses amphetamines. The 1996 National Household Survey on Drug Abuse estimated that approximately 4.8 million people have used methamphetamine in their lifetime (Goode, 1999). Individuals may turn to amphetamines to help remain awake and alert, enhance initiative, lose weight, or even combat depression. Roughly equal numbers of men and women are estimated to abuse stimulants. Current estimates of abuse vary significantly, ranging from less than 1% to over 5% abusing nationwide.

More recent research reveals a stable amount of amphetamine abuse occurring across the U.S. The Monitoring the Future (O'Malley and Bachman, 2003) survey examined high-school seniors nationwide over a period of years in order to estimate patterns of drug use among youth. Their estimates indicate lifetime prevalence use of amphetamine among high-school seniors decreased from 22.3% in 1975 to 16.8% in 2002 (O'Malley and Bachman, 2003). The National Household Survey on Drug Abuse (NHSDA) estimated lifetime stimulant abuse to be 6.6% during the year 2000 (Substance Abuse and Mental Health Services Administration (SAMHSA), 2002A) and found that stimulant abuse for the past year and past month measured less than 1%.

The Drug Abuse Warning Network (DAWN) collects data from emergency room visits and fatalities related to drug abuse in major metropolitan areas. Their trend data indicate that amphetamine and methamphetamine use is consistently among the top 10 illicit drugs identified in drug-related deaths and is most prevalent in the southwestern region of the U.S. In the 2001 DAWN study, methamphetamine use accounted for over 75% of emergency room visits related to drugs in San Diego (SAMHSA, 2002B). San Francisco reported a fatality rate due to methamphetamine abuse in over 25% of drug-related deaths (SAMHSA, 2002B).

The Drug Use Forecasting (DUF) system measures drug usage among adult and juvenile arrestees during intake into various correctional facilities. In 1995, among those arrested in San Diego 30.6% were methamphetamine users (National Institute of Justice (NIJ), 1996). During the same year, among those arrested in Phoenix 19.5% were methamphetamine users (NIJ, 1996). These data collectively suggest that there has been a slight although steady decline over the past two decades. However, there has been an increase in the amount of not only methamphetamine users but methamphetamine-related deaths as well.

Although no official estimates of clandestine drug manufacturing exist, trends in the number of illegal laboratories may indicate a significant increase in methamphetamine production over the past two decades. Between 1980 and 1994 there was a significant increase in the number of detected clandestine drug labs. Globally and domestically, clandestine methamphetamine manufacturing appears to be most pervasive. During the years 1975 to 2001, the DEA seized 16,504 illegal drug laboratories, 13,931 of which were being used to manufacture methamphetamine (ONDCP, 2003A)

Measurement Difficulties

Due to the illegal nature of amphetamine possession and abuse, accurate measurements of its production, sale, and abuse may prove difficult if not impossible (Miller, 2001). Survey participants, who are by nature volunteers, may be unwilling to admit criminal acts. Such underreporting influences the validity of drug use survey data. Attempts to estimate the prevalence of amphetamine abuse from arrest records is difficult

(NIDA, 1980). It may be impossible to assess what percentage of abuse is reflected using only those individuals apprehended. Also, reporting standards often differ from jurisdiction to jurisdiction, with local precincts potentially overlooking such variables as method of administration. Finally, terminological differences may lead to a lack of comparability in the data collected (Miller, 2001).

Policy and Treatment Implications

The Office of National Drug Control Policy currently designates three national strategy priorities: prevention, treatment, and enforcement (ONDCP, 2003B). Prevention efforts remain the primary federal method for deterring potential amphetamine abuse. Such efforts attempt to draw upon community and family influence to deter abuse, and include the National Youth Anti-Drug Media Campaign, Drug-Free Communities Program, and the Corporation for National and Community Service—Parents Drug Corps Initiative. Treatment programs comprise the second element in the national drug strategy.

The popularity of drug treatment as a crime prevention strategy has led to many different approaches across the country (Josi and Roberts, 2003). Some treatment programs are privately operated, whereas others are part of county courts, state corrections, or mental health departments. Between 1993 and 1999, amphetamine treatment admission rates increased by 250% or more across 14 states and over 100% in another 10 states (SAMHSA, 2001). While many individuals are required to undergo treatment by their probation or diversion agreements, others volunteer or are placed in treatment by their families. Treatment programs vary in the duration, intensity, and format. Such programs include detoxification programs, chemical dependency wards, outpatient clinics, and therapeutic communities. Although addiction is common and difficult to overcome, treatment centers work tirelessly to combat lifetime abuse of amphetamine.

Enforcement, the final strategic component, remains an important focus of governmental policy. The ONDCP pursues several initiatives to achieve enforcement, by providing funding for various DEA initiatives at home and abroad as well as for tracking programs for drugs and drug financing.

Despite efforts to influence the use of amphetamines in the U.S., amphetamine in its various forms continues to be a concern for practitioners in the criminal justice system and in the field of public health. Given the U.S.' ever growing dependency on medication and other controlled substances it is difficult for one to foresee an end to amphetamine and methamphetamine abuse in the near future.

Ashley Blackburn and W. Wesley Johnson

References and Further Reading

Bozarth, M.A. (1994). Pleasure systems in the brain. In Warburton, D.M. (Ed.) *Pleasure: The Politics and the Reality* (pp. 5–16). New York, NY: John Wiley & Sons.

Goode, E. (1999). *Drugs in American Society* (5th ed.). Boston, MA: McGraw Hill.

Johnston, L.D., O'Malley, P.M., and Bachman, J.G. (2003). *Monitoring the Future National Results on Adolescent Drug Use: Overview of Key Findings, 2002* (NIH Publication No. 03-5374). Bethesda, MD: National Institute on Drug Abuse.

Josi, D. and Roberts, L. (2003). Drugs. In *Encyclopedia of Juvenile Justice* (Vol. 1, pp. 140–149). London: Sage Publications.

Kalant, O. (1973). *The Amphetamines: Toxicity and Addiction* (2nd ed.). Toronto: University of Toronto Press.

Kurian, G. (Ed.). (1998). *A Historical Guide to the U.S. Government*. New York, NY: Oxford University Press.

Miller, M. (2001). History and Epidemiology of Amphetamine Abuse in the United States. In Inciardi, J.A. and McElrath, K. (Eds.), *The American Drug Scene* (3rd ed., pp. 216–228). Los Angeles, CA: Roxbury Publishing.

Musto, D.F. (Ed.) (2002). *Drugs in America: A Documented History*. New York, NY: New York University Press.

National Institute on Drug Abuse (NIDA). (1980). *Research Issues 25: Use and Abuse of Amphetamine and Its Substitutes* (DHEW Publication No. ADM 80-941). Washington, DC: U.S. Government Printing Office.

National Institute of Justice (NIJ). (1996). *Research Report: 1995 Drug Use Forecasting Annual Report on Adult and Juvenile Arrestees*. Retrieved on July 16, 2003 from http://www.ncjrs.org/pdffiles/duf1995.pdf.

Office of National Drug Control Policy (ONDCP). (2003a). *Drug Data Summary, January 2003*. Retrieved on July 16, 2003 from http://www.streetdrugs.org/methlabs.htm.

Office of National Drug Control Policy (ONDCP). (2003b). *The President's National Drug Control Strategy 2003*. Retrieved on July 16, 2003 from http://www.whitehousedrugpolicy.gov/publications/policy/ndcs03/index.html.

Substance Abuse and Mental Health Services Administration (SAMHSA), Office of Applied Studies. (2001). *The DASIS Report: Amphetamine Treatment Admissions Increase 1993–1999*. Retrieved on July 16, 2003, from http://www.samhsa.gov/oas/dasis.htm.

Substance Abuse and Mental Health Services Administration (SAMHSA), Office of Applied Studies. (2002a). *Results from the 2001 National Household Survey on Drug Abuse: Volume I. Summary of National Findings* (NHSDA Series H-17 DHHS Publication No. SMA 02-3758). Washington, DC: U.S. Government Printing Office.

Substance Abuse and Mental Health Services Administration (SAMHSA), Office of Applied Studies. (2002b). *Mortality Data from the Drug Abuse Warning Network, 2001* (DAWN Series D-23, DHHS Publication No. SMA 03-3781). Rockville, MD.

See also **Drug Policy: Prevention and Treatment; Drug Use: The Law**

Anti-Semitism *See* **Hate Crime**

Antisocial Personality Disorder and Criminal Behavior

It is unfortunate that the term psychopath is often used as a label for anyone who exhibits persistent tendencies to behave criminally or violently. In fact psychopathic traits are uncommon even among recidivist criminals, and there are certainly examples of people whose freedom from the shackles of conscience has allowed them to be successful in their careers in the business world or in politics without getting into trouble with the criminal law. Blackburn (1993) points out that although—in popular speech and journalism—the term has come to imply a category of *socially damaging* individuals, as it originated in German psychiatry, psychopathic personality meant literally a *psychologically damaged* person.

Early studies of what we would now term psychopathy concentrated upon categorical notions of the condition, or the belief that certain individuals—variously described as morally insane, born criminal, and subject to irresistible atavistic impulses—were qualitatively different from ordinary people (McCord, 1983). Others have adopted a dimensional strategy, regarding psychopathy as the extreme value of a continuum, or as the conjunction of several dimensions (for example, Hans and Sybil Eysenck). McCord argues that the categorical approach is the more fruitful because "a categorical definition provides a decision rule for identifying people similar to those whose peculiarities mark them as *unlike* other criminals." The case of the Burgate House murders, which concludes this essay, appears to support this view. The callous cruelty of the prime mover in this crime appears to be categorically different from the actions and moral values of the overwhelming majority of ordinary criminals, and can be described only by comparison with a small number of very unusual and notorious homicidal offenders.

There have always been differences of opinion about whether one should distinguish between subcategories of psychopathy. Some investigators, such as Robert Hare and his colleagues and students, have followed Hervey Cleckley in excluding from this diagnostic category individuals whose disruptive or asocial behavior cannot be accounted for by the presence of neurotic or psychotic illness—often referred to as primary psychopaths. Others, such as Ronald Blackburn, would recognize a category of secondary psychopaths, whose "antisocial behavior results from dynamic disturbance, and who [are] more properly classified with neuroses or psychoses." McCord and McCord also identify a narrow category, describing the psychopath as "an asocial, aggressive, highly impulsive person who feels little or no guilt, and is unable to form lasting bonds of affection with other human beings" (Blackburn, 1993). Blackburn also identifies himself as one of several researchers who have "adopted the concepts of primary and secondary psychopath to distinguish nonanxious from anxious deviant personalities in antisocial populations."

It will be apparent that descriptions and definitions of psychopathy have been diverse and are often conflicting; this state of affairs made for confusion in clinical diagnosis and retarded research into the origins of the condition and the development of methods of managing and treating psychopaths. In these circumstances, the publication of Cleckley's classic text, *The Mask of Sanity* (1941) was a major development. Cleckley's book provided a detailed list of the most prominent attributes of people usually regarded as psychopathic, supported by a fascinating series of case histories of predatory, manipulative individuals—many of them people with long criminal records, but a few whose talents had led them to considerable success in politics, commerce, and finance. The book also offered a review of distinguishing characteristics of such individuals that might mark them out from ordinary, opportunistic thieves, frauds, and chancers, and identify them as people whose callousness and defects of conscience set them apart from common criminals. Cleckley's book was a masterly work, both because he conveyed, in his case studies, the nature and the diversity of psychopathic behavior, and because he managed to identify the key aspects in which true psychopaths differ from ordinary men and women who had chronic problems with the criminal law. He grasped the connections between the temperamental and interpersonal defects of psychopaths—their inadequacies in relationships with other people—and their characteristically dishonest, callous, and manipulative conduct, and resistance to attempts to treat or retrain them. He lists 16 criteria, each of which is considered and explained in a separate section of the book, and further illustrated by individual case histories. It was originally written for psychiatrists and other medical practitioners, but it has also proved valuable to many relatives and acquaintances of psychopaths and has considerably influenced the work of clinical staff in prisons and secure hospitals.

The first edition of the *Diagnostic and Statistical Manual of Mental Disorders*, published in 1952, did not refer to psychopathy, but it did include a category of "sociopathic personality disturbance, antisocial reaction," which was clearly influenced by Cleckley's book, and by the work of Lee Robins (see Hare and Schalling, 1978). Further editions appeared in 1968 (DSM-II) and in 1987 (DSM-III-R)—the last being extensively described and explained in Blackburn's book.

As Blackburn points out, the term psychopath is a *personality construct*, and is, therefore, not synonymous with criminal, which is a description of the *behavior* of an individual: "Psychopathy is a theoretical construct rather than a palpable entity"—or as Hare (1996) expressed it, "Psychopathy is a socially devastating disorder defined by a constellation of affective, interpersonal, and behavioral characteristics, including egocentricity; impulsivity; irresponsibility; shallow emotions; lack of empathy, guilt, or remorse; pathological lying; manipulativeness; and the persistent violation of social norms and expectations." Although DSM-II described psychopaths (referred to as people exhibiting antisocial personality) as "unsocialized, impulsive, guiltless, selfish, and callous individuals who rationalize their behavior and fail to learn from experience" it did not provide explicit diagnostic criteria for the disorder. It was widely hoped and expected that DSM-III would do so, but as Hare (1996) points out, "the criteria that it *did* present consisted almost entirely of persistent violations of social norms, including lying, stealing, truancy, inconsistent work behavior, and traffic arrests. Among the main reasons given for this dramatic shift away from the use of clinical inferences were that personality traits are difficult to measure reliably and that it is easier to agree on the behaviors that typify a disorder than on the reasons why they occur. The result was a diagnostic category with good reliability but dubious validity, a category that lacked congruence with traditional conceptions of psychopathy."

There was clearly a need, both for clinical purposes and as a secure basis for research, for a standard method of diagnosis and assessment. It was apparent that DSM-III and DSM-IV would not serve in this role. Broad-based personality tests and multitrait inventories, such as the Minnesota Multiphasic Personality Inventory and the California Personality Inventory, had not proved effective in identifying psychopaths. Robert Hare and his colleagues, therefore, set about translating Cleckley's descriptive accounts of psychopathic traits into an assessment procedure, based on a semistructured interview and detailed collateral evidence provided by custodial staff or a study of the individual's record and case notes. The fully developed procedure, named the Psychopathy Checklist, Revised Edition (PCL-R) was published in 1991, and consists of 20 items. The total score provides an estimate of the extent to which a given individual matches the prototypical psychopath. The closer the match, the higher the score, and there is a cut-off point, at and above which the individual is identified, for research and clinical purposes, as the possessor of a psychopathic personality. It is essentially a categorical device, because for most purposes differences in scores above the cut-off point are not regarded as important.

The PCL-R shows a high level of agreement between independent psychologists (inter-rater reliability) and consistency over time. The 20 items are grouped into two classes: one that mainly measures "items having to do with the affective or interpersonal features of psychopathy such as egocentricity, manipulativeness, callousness, and lack of remorse, characteristics that many clinicians consider central to psychopathy" that Hare defines as Factor 1, and "those features of psychopathy associated with an impulsive, antisocial, and unstable lifestyle, or social deviance," defining Factor 2. The items in these two classes, and the factor to which they are related, are listed in the chapter by Hare and Hart in Hodgins, 1993 (p. 105) and the factor loadings for each item are given in Harpur, Hakstian, and Hare (1988). Factor 2 is defined by elements of a disorganized, antisocial, aimless, and parasitic lifestyle that often leads to criminal convictions and to trouble of a kind to which many young men and women, most of whom are not psychopaths, are vulnerable. Factor 1, on the other hand, describes personality traits that are, for the most part, peculiar to the psychopath and are immensely damaging to the society in which he lives. What is being identified is a small number of people (perhaps 1% of the general population, and between 15% and 25% of persistent criminals held in prisons or in secure institutions) who cause damage and distress to others out of all proportion to their numbers. Hare and Hart (1993) remark that it "comes as no surprise that the disorder is implicated in a disproportionate amount of serious repetitive crime and violence ... psychopaths are more criminally active through much of their life span than are other offenders."

In a study of 243 men prisoners in British Columbia, Hare found that convictions for violent offenses appeared in the criminal records of almost all of those diagnosed as psychopaths (97%); the corresponding figure for other prisoners was 74%. Hare and Jutai calculated that although psychopaths committed more offenses than nonpsychopaths during their spells of freedom (about five offenses per year, as contrasted with an average of 3.25 per year of liberty for nonpsychopaths), the mean number of charges per-year-free for *violent* offenses was more than three times higher for the psychopaths than for the nonpsychopaths (Hare and Hart, 1993, 106). These studies employed clinical global ratings rather than the PCL-R, but a later study by Hare and McPherson, using the PCL-R, yielded similar findings.

The greater propensity for violence that is characteristic of psychopaths in the community, indexed by convictions in the courts, is also apparent when they are in prison. They are more frequently involved in assaults and threats than other prisoners, and generally have much worse records of disruptive and unruly behavior. Psychopaths are more likely than nonpsychopathic individuals to recidivate after release from prison, and are much more likely to be convicted of a violent crime. Hare (1996) cites a follow-up study of 299 male offenders released from a federal prison, carried out by Serin and Amos and published in 1995: "Within three years, about 65% of the psychopaths and 25% of the non-psychopaths were convicted of a new crime. The difference was even greater for convictions for violent crimes; about 40% for psychopaths and less than 10% for non-psychopaths."

These studies have established that high scores on the Hare Psychopathy Checklist (PCL-R) are closely associated with a record of frequent, serious offenses, often including violent crimes, while at liberty in the community, and with disruptive conduct, much of it threatening and violent, during periods of imprisonment. They are essentially retrospective studies relating current checklist scores to earlier behaviors. It is not surprising that several investigators have begun to explore the potential of the PCL-R in allocating offenders to particular secure regimes and strategies for control in the community, such as parole and probation supervision, and in predicting the risk that they will behave in a predatory and perhaps dangerous fashion in the future. Hare and Hart (1993) list several studies of this kind. A total of 231 male inmates from prisons and forensic psychiatric hospitals in British Columbia and released on parole or granted discharge from the institution to mandatory supervision in the community were followed up until they had completed the period of parole or supervised release, or were returned to prison or secure hospitals because they had committed further offenses or broken the conditions on which they were released. Psychopaths, identified by high scores on PCL-R, violated the conditions of release faster and more often than did individuals with low scores, and presented more supervisory problems. The high scorers were almost three times more likely to violate the conditions of release, and almost four times more likely to commit a violent crime while on mandatory supervision or parole, than low scorers. To express the results of the study in rather different terms (called survival) the probability of remaining out of prison for at least 1 year was 0.80 for the low-scorers, but 0.34 for the high scorers. Given the nature of the study population, which presumably included a high proportion of men with substantial criminal records, this is an impressive outcome. Hare and Hart also quote a study by Serin, Peters, and Barbaree, published in 1990, in which the PCL-R was administered to 93 men prior to release from a federal prison on unescorted temporary absence. Sixteen had high scores on the checklist, six of whom violated the conditions of temporary absence; none of the 16 low scorers did so. Seventy-seven of the original samples of 93 were subsequently paroled; follow-up data available on 74 of these showed that 27% of the sample failed on parole and were recommitted to prison; the failure rate was 7% for the nonpsychopaths and 33% for the psychopaths. The average time to failure was 8 months for the psychopathic group and 14.6 months for the nonpsychopathic failures. As the authors point out, the PCL-R predicted outcome better than prediction strategies based upon prior criminal history and demographic variables.

These findings suggest that the most effective discrimination between psychopaths and others depends upon a combination of personality traits and an inventory of antisocial behavior, an unstable and parasitic lifestyle, and delinquency and criminal history, represented by the two-factor structure of PCL-R, as distinct from diagnoses prescribed by objective behavior and eschewing assessment of personality characteristics, as embodied in DSM-IV.

There have been many reports indicating that attempts to modify the behavior of individuals committed to forensic hospitals, psychiatric institutions, and prisons have been largely unsuccessful, and these have led to a general belief that psychopaths are not amenable to treatment. This belief is not, as yet, well-substantiated, for several reasons. Committal to custody in forensic institutions and psychiatric prisons, or to ordinary prisons under the special provisions under statutes relating to psychopaths or sexual psychopaths, are based on legal, rather than psychiatric or psychological, considerations, and these often have to do with the complexities of legal defense rather than clinical criteria. In England and Wales, for example, Blackburn found that only a quarter of those sent by courts to special hospitals designed for the care of psychopaths showed characteristics associated with the more specific category of primary psychopath. Harris, Rice, and Cormier (1989) also note that although two-thirds of patients admitted to a Canadian maximum security hospital were diagnosed as antisocial personality, less than a quarter met "DSM-III-R criteria for Antisocial Personality Disorder" (Blackburn, 1993). The reasons for this state of affairs are complex. Some individuals arrive at special hospitals having been diagnosed as psychopathic by medical practitioners who are inexperienced and unskilled in dealing with a rare and unfamiliar condition. Others are, in effect, declared by the courts to be psychopaths, under legislation that allows committal to a secure hospital or prison where appropriate treatment should be available.

The second problem concerns the relation between the treatment technique and the criteria for improvement. It is quite common for the treatment to be based on methods that have been effective with other categories of clinical patients—for example, those whose difficulties are neurotic in origin, who undoubtedly benefit from group therapy, or from membership of a therapeutic community. In the few studies that have been published, the criteria of success are in most instances based upon the subsequent frequency and seriousness of offending, whereas, as Blackburn argues, it would be more appropriate to try to measure personality changes, as the issue is not whether it is possible to restrain psychopaths from further crime, but whether there is any treatment that will make the individuals less psychopathic by making them less predatory, manipulative, deceitful, and cruel. It is generally agreed that as psychopaths grow older their involvement in crime—but not in violent crime—tends to diminish, but there is no reason to believe that they become more decent and humane in their relations with others. Blackburn's (1993) assessment is that "conclusions about the treatability of the classical psychopath rest mainly on studies of poor methodology conducted with vaguely defined samples." This judgment is supported by the meta-analysis by Garrido, Esteban, and Molinero (cited in Cooke, Forth, and Hare, 1996), which found that treatment communities, currently fashionable in the treatment of offenders in correctional programs, are conspicuously ineffective in attempts to change the more dangerous characteristics of psychopaths. Hare (1996) concludes that conventional treatment programs are not only ineffective, but actually promote the destructive behavior of psychopaths by developing their skills in manipulating interpersonal relations.

The connections between psychopathy and violent crime are well illustrated by the murder of five people in England at Burgate House, near Fordingbridge, on the edge of the New Forest in Hampshire, in 1986. The murders were organized by George Stephenson, aged 35. He and his wife worked as handyman and working-housekeeper at Burgate House for about 2 months, but they were dismissed by their employer, Joseph Cleaver, and his son, after repeatedly disturbing the household by engaging in very noisy quarrels. While they were employed at Burgate House they occupied a cottage in the grounds, but had to leave at once, and their marriage came to an end. George Stephenson returned to his home city of Coventry. A few weeks later he recruited two petty criminals with whom he was acquainted, George Daly (24) and his brother John Daly (20) to help him with a burglary. He hired a car, and the three drove south to Hampshire, stopping on the way to buy two cans of gasoline, some cigarette lighters, rubber gloves, twine, stockings (for use as face masks), and three pick-handles. They arrived at Fordingbridge earlier than they had intended, and so went on to the seaside town of Bournemouth, where Stephenson had friends. The couple happened to mention that their television and video recorder were no longer functioning, and Stephenson immediately responded that he knew where to get replacements, and promised to do so.

In the early evening they returned to Burgate House, where Joseph Cleaver (82), who was a wealthy retired publisher, his invalid wife Hilda (also 82), their son Thomas (48) and his wife Wendy (46), and Hilda's nurse–companion, Margaret Murphy (70), were having dinner. The entrance door to the house was unlocked, as George Stephenson knew it would be. The three men burst in, threatened the five residents with violence, and tied them up with the twine. Hilda Cleaver, who was virtually helpless as the result of a stroke, was taken upstairs in her wheelchair. Wendy Cleaver was taken off to a bedroom by Stephenson, and raped in an extraordinarily brutal fashion by each of the three men. Then John Daly was ordered by Stephenson to strangle Wendy, and, by now very frightened, did so. Stephenson and George Daly soaked the carpets with the gasoline and used the firelighters to start the fire, which burned immediately and with intense heat. The other four members of the household (Wendy was already dead) perished in the blaze. The criminals seized a rifle and three shotguns, various items of modest value, including video equipment, and all the money they could find—the equivalent of US$130—and returned to Coventry, making a detour to deliver the television receiver and video recorder to Stephenson's friends in Bournemouth. This was a serious mistake, and played an important part in the police investigation that was to follow.

Stephenson's second error was a curious one. He had explored Burgate House with some thoroughness while he was employed there; he had a good grasp of the layout of the house and its outbuildings, and of the routine followed by the five residents. They entered, as has been said, through the unlocked entrance door, but, as he knew he would be suspected of the crime, Stephenson was careful to make it appear that the burglars had broken in, smashing windows and breaking furniture. He had tried to convince the Daly brothers that they were to carry out a straightforward burglary in which no-one would be hurt, but—given the nature of the purchases that he made during the journey from Coventry—it is clear that he had already decided that none of the victims would survive the crime (which must have gradually dawned on his two companions). The large supply of gasoline was intended to burn down the house and destroy all evidence of the murders and rapes. What Stephenson failed to notice was that the house was constructed of reinforced concrete, which is highly resistant to fire, and so the blaze was confined to a small part of an upper floor. The five bodies were very badly burned, but there was enough forensic material to identify them, and other evidence of what had happened on the ground floor, which was untouched by the fire.

The murders were widely reported in the local and national press, as homicides are comparatively rare in Britain, and multiple murder of such ferocity was almost without precedent. One morning Stephenson, watching television news at his lodgings in Coventry, realized that he was looking at a photograph of himself. After giving the matter some thought, he decided to travel down to Fordingbridge by rail, give himself up to the police, and blame the Daly brothers for planning and carrying out the brutal murders. He arrived in Fordingbridge in the afternoon, and visited four public houses (taverns) in the town, where he was bound to be recognized. In one of them he encountered a couple of tourists playing pool, and demanded the right to play the winner; he stayed for a long session, which was so successful that they agreed to play again the following evening. He stayed with them for a little more than 2 hours, and before he left he took a newspaper from his pocket and showed them the headlines and pointed to the photograph, saying proudly, "That's me!" In the early hours of the morning he went to call the police from a public telephone. He waited, by now seriously drunk, until they arrived and arrested him.

At the trial, George Daly was stoical and impassive, his younger brother John was bewildered and tearful, but George Stephenson was confident, even cocky, often smiling at the judge and staring menacingly at the jury during the 4 weeks of court proceedings. He was visibly surprised and indignant when he was convicted and sentenced, with his companions, to life imprisonment. He subsequently appealed against his convictions without success.

Stephenson had a long and undistinguished history of crime, much of it petty and opportunistic, including burglary, housebreaking, fraud, deception, handling stolen property, and illegal possession of a handgun, but he also had a reputation and record of serious violence. He was on bad terms with his brother, having been caught burgling his house. He had an erratic and intermittent work history. On the other hand, people found him good company. "He had the gift of the gab, pleasant to talk with—he charmed his way into a lot of pairs of panties. He was good at his job, a good conman—into swindling you out of your money, not beating it out of you" were comments volunteered by his brother in the course of a television interview. His behavior was calculating and manipulative, persuading George Daly to become involved in the burglary, and exploiting the vulnerability of John Daly to implicate him in rape, murder, and arson. He also sought to escape the blame for the burglary and murders by claiming that he was "only the driver," and had remained in the car throughout; he insisted that George Daly had planned the whole venture. The five victims met cruel, humiliating deaths, but Stephenson showed no concern or remorse, clearly believing that he was justified in exacting revenge for which he saw as unfair dismissal from his job. The damage and misery that he inflicted on the five murdered victims, their relatives, and their friends in the town of Fordingbridge were immense, and his wife was driven to attempt suicide. It was a striking example of the destructiveness that flows from psychopathic traits.

GORDON B. TRASLER

References and Further Reading

American Psychiatric Association. (1994) *Diagnostic and Statistical Manual of Mental Disorders* (4th ed.). Washington, DC.

Blackburn, R. (1993) *The Psychology of Criminal Conduct.* New York, NY: Wiley.

Cleckley, H. (1976) *The Mask of Sanity* (5th ed.). St. Louis, MO: Mosby.

Cooke, D., Forth, A.E., and Hare, R.D. (Eds.) (1996) *Psychopathy: Theory, Research, and Implications for Society.* Dordrecht, The Netherlands: Kluwer.

Hare, R.D. Psychopathy: A clinical construct whose time has come, *Criminal Justice and Behavior* 23 (1996).

Hare, R.D. and Schalling, D. (Eds.) (1978) *Psychopathic Behavior: Approaches to Research,* New York, NY, and Chichester, UK: Wiley.

Hare, R.D. and Hart, S.D. (1993) Psychopathy, Mental Disorder and Crime, in *Mental Disorder, and Crime,* Sheilagh, H., Ed., Newbury Park, CA, Sage Publications.

Harpur, T.J., Hakstian, R., and Hare, R.D. (1988) Factor structure of the psychopathy checklist, *Journal of Consulting and Clinical Psychology,* 56.

Hollin, C.R. (1989) *Psychology and Crime: An Introduction to Criminological Psychology,* London, UK and New York, NY: Routledge.

McCord, J. (1983) The psychopath and moral development, in William, S.L. and James, M.D. (Eds.) *Personality Theory, Moral Development, and Criminal Behavior.* Lexington, MA: DC Heath.

Siddle, D.A.T. and Trasler, G.B. (1981) The psychophysiology of psychopathic behavior, in Margaret, J.C. and Peter, G.M. (Eds.) *Foundations of Psychosomatics.* Chichester, UK: Wiley.

Trasler, G.B. Relations between psychopathy and persistent criminality: Methodological and theoretical issues, in Robert, D.H. and Daisy, S. (Eds.) (1978) *Psychopathic Behavior: Approaches to Research,* Chichester, UK: Wiley.

See also **Psychological Theories of Criminal Behavior; Psychopathy and Criminal Behavior**

Appeals and Posttrial Motions

The importance of, and procedures related to, posttrial motions and appeals, like so many other aspects of criminal justice, vary greatly among countries. It is not possible in this essay to thoroughly address the variations that exist or to discuss all the similarities and differences. Rather, the primary focus will be on the posttrial and appellate process in the U.S. Additionally, there will be some discussion on the appellate process in other nations.

U.S.

Perhaps one of the least understood aspects of the criminal adjudication process in the U.S. is that of posttrial motions and appeals. Both are mechanisms for correcting errors that occur during the trial process and for ensuring the integrity of the criminal trial. Such error correction does not, however, occur in a vacuum. Rather, there is a great deal of deference given to the trial process that limits the efficacy of the posttrial and appeals, procedures in changing the outcome of a trial. What occurs at trial is rarely ever altered by a posttrial proceeding or appeal. Yet, both avenues are necessary to insure the ultimate reliability of the trial process by providing a safety valve in the event something goes drastically wrong at trial.

There is also a unique relationship between posttrial motions and appeals. In most jurisdictions, it is necessary to first raise an issue in a posttrial motion before presenting it in an appeal. This procedure is referred to as "preserving an issue for appeal." If an issue is not presented first to the trial court via a posttrial motion, it will often be considered waived and unreviewable on appeal. The reasoning behind this approach is to allow the trial judge an opportunity to rectify any trial errors or other defects before conviction. This prevents a party from "laying in the weeds" and raising an issue for the first time on appeal. It is always more desirable to let the trial judge who presided over the trial to remedy any defects contemporaneous to the conclusion of the trial.

Before discussing posttrial motions and appeals in more depth, it is first necessary to understand the nature of the errors or defects that can be raised in such processes. There are two broad categories of errors that can be used to challenge a trial outcome: legal and factual. Legal errors are those matters involving legal rulings by the judge such as admission of evidence or jury instructions. Factual defects deal with such things as sufficiency of the evidence, credibility of witnesses and the weight to be given to the evidence. There is generally much greater deference given to the factual findings and determinations than that given to legal issues. The facts of the case are seldom considered in appeals. This is so because factual matters are best decided at the time when the evidence is the freshest, the witnesses are observable directly and their credibility subject to firsthand assessment. Legal issues, on the other hand, can theoretically be decided at any time, even months or years after the trial. Factual matters also receive tremendous deference because they are often determined by the jury, which receives special respect under the American justice system.

There are essentially four types of posttrial motions that can be made following a criminal trial. They are a motion for directed verdict, a motion to reconsider, a motion for a judgment of acquittal, and a motion for a new trial. Each of these serves a unique function in the posttrial process.

A motion for a directed verdict is not actually made at the end of the trial. Instead, it is presented at the end of the case but before the judge submits the matter to the jury for deliberation. The motion for directed verdict asks the judge to take the case from the jury and decide it as a matter of law. In other words, with this type of motion, the judge is asked to rule that because of the evidence, or lack thereof, a reasonable jury could only rule one way. Therefore, the court will avoid submitting the matter to the jury and will instead enter judgment consistent with the evidence. If there is any reasonable dispute about the evidence, then the motion must be denied. As one can imagine, in light of the tremendous deference given to juries under the American legal system, judges are reluctant to grant such a motion. In fact, the standard that is applied, that no reasonable jury could find a certain way, insures that the motion for directed verdict will only be granted in the very rare case where there is virtually no evidence to support an opposite judgment.

The motion to reconsider will be usually be made after the completion of the trial and is designed to give the trial judge the first opportunity to change any rulings made during the trial. Such a motion can also be used to ask a judge to alter a sentence imposed following conviction. Although judges are generally reluctant to change their own prior rulings, the motion to reconsider gives them one last opportunity to do so before an appeal.

The motion for judgment of acquittal, which is sometimes referred to as a motion for judgment notwithstanding the verdict, asks the trial judge to change the verdict of guilty to that of not guilty. The standard to be applied to this motion is similar to that used for a motion for directed verdict. The judge can only set aside a guilty verdict if, when viewing the evidence in a light most favorable to the prosecution, no reasonable jury could have found the defendant guilty. If any reasonable jury could have found the defendant guilty, then the judge must let the verdict stand. The standard applied to this motion is extremely deferential to the jury.

The motion for a new trial is commonly made by defendants after a guilty verdict. The essence of such a motion is to convince the judge of the need to retry the case. There are generally three bases for a motion for a new trial: newly discovered evidence, trial error, and sufficiency of the evidence. The standard applied to a motion for a new trial is usually one of discretion. That is, a motion for a new trial will not be granted if the trial judge, in her discretion, decides there are no defects in the trial process sufficient to affect the reliability of the outcome. As with all the posttrial motions, a trial judge is generally reluctant to find fault with the proceeding that they have presided over.

The appellate process is very much different from the criminal trial. There is no live testimony, no introduction of evidence, and no fact finding. Rather, a criminal appeal is primarily an after-the-fact paper process. All matters are submitted to the appellate court in a written form. The appeals court reviews the written materials in the light of certain standards and assesses the reliability of the outcome and the fairness of the procedures in the criminal trial. The appellate court then has several options. It can affirm the trial outcome, reverse the decision and order a new trial, or reverse the outcome and enter judgment on behalf of the defendant. Whether a new trial is ordered or judgment is entered for the defendant depends on the basis for the reversal and issues of double jeopardy.

Typically, only the defendant can appeal in a criminal case. This is because the Fifth Amendment to the U.S. Constitution generally prohibits subjecting a defendant to more than one criminal trial for the same offense. There are a few instances where the government can appeal, such as where the trial court granted a defendant's pretrial motion to suppress evidence. Otherwise, the defendant is the appealing party in most criminal cases.

There is a time limit in which an appeal must be filed, usually 30 days from the entry of judgment in the trial court or disposal of any posttrial motions if any were filed. The appealing party is responsible for submitting a written brief to the appellate court as well as the trial record, consisting of all materials filed in the case and the transcripts of all court proceedings. The responding party, in turn, files a responsive brief. In most jurisdictions, the defendant is allowed to file a final reply brief. There are numerous rules in most jurisdictions concerning such things as the timing of the briefs, the color of the brief covers, the length of the briefs, the citation format, and so forth.

Once the briefs and trial record are filed with the appellate court, the case is assigned to a panel of judges. Although the number of judges that decide each case varies in different jurisdictions, the number is typically three. The judges are usually rotated so that the same judges are not always on the same panel. The panels always consist of an odd number of judges to avoid tie votes, and a simple majority is needed to decide a given appeal.

The appeals panel will consider the written briefs and the trial record in deciding the case. In some instances, the appellate court will request or allow the appellate attorneys to present oral argument in support of their respective positions. There are numerous rules that apply to the oral argument process such as the order of presentment, length of time, and decorum. The recent trend in some appellate courts is to minimize or eliminate oral arguments, especially in what are perceived to be simple or straightforward appeals. This movement to do away with oral argument is generally not popular among attorneys who prefer any opportunity to further their case.

Once the appeals court has considered the briefs, the trial record, and any oral arguments, it will decide the case. The judges do not ordinarily decide a case immediately following oral argument, except in matters of special urgency. Rather, they take the matter under advisement, and, depending on the caseload of the court, decide the case some time thereafter. They usually hold a conference in which the judges discuss the case and vote. In the vast majority of cases, the judges will be unanimous in their decision. In some cases, however, there may be a majority and minority position on how the case should be decided. Typically, one of the judges in the majority will be assigned to write an opinion in the case.

Most appellate courts issue written opinions deciding the cases before them. Some of those opinions are, in turn, published in books called reporters as well as in online databases. There is a recent trend with some appellate courts to issue unpublished opinions in cases the court believes add little or nothing to an existing body of law. This is being done primarily in an effort to be more efficient and to save on publication costs. The decision to not publish certain opinions remains controversial.

A critical issue to understanding the appellate process is awareness of the standards of review that are applied by the appellate court. These standards of review are designed to preserve the integrity of the trial process and to promote some degree of efficiency in the criminal adjudication process. There are typically three standards of review applicable in most criminal appeals. They are *de novo*, abuse of discretion, and sufficiency of the evidence.

Each standard of review serves a different purpose. *De novo*, or anew, is applied to purely legal questions that were decided by the trial judge, such as evidentiary rulings or jury instructions. The abuse-of-discretion standard is used to assess discretionary rulings by the trial judge. For example, discretionary matters governed by this standard might include the decision to let a particular witness testify or the denial of a motion for a new trial. There are various formulations of the standard used to measure the sufficiency of the evidence. The most common is to ask whether any rational trier of fact, when viewing the evidence in a light most favorable to the prosecution, could have returned a guilty verdict.

These three standards of review vary in their degree of deference with *de novo* being the least and sufficiency of the evidence being the most deferential. Again, there is a compelling desire in the American system of criminal jurisprudence to preserve the sanctity of the jury or the judge in their fact-finding function.

Statistically, most verdicts in criminal cases are upheld on appeal. The appeals process is not designed to retry the case or to consider such matters as the credibility of the witnesses or the weight of the evidence. The primary purpose of any appeal is to oversee the trial process in an effort to guarantee fair procedures and a reliable outcome. At the point all appellate options are exhausted, a criminal case becomes final, subject only to *habeas corpus* review in the appropriate situation.

Other Nations

France has a multilevel appellate process. It has several courts of appeal that consider decisions of the lower correctional court or the police court. It also has a supreme court called the Court of Cassation that has a criminal chamber that reviews criminal cases. As a general rule, the Court of Cassation only reviews questions of law and leaves all factual questions for determination by the lower courts. If it decides the law was incorrectly interpreted, it will send the dispute back to a new court for a new decision.

In the former Soviet Union, there was only one appeal allowed from the court of original jurisdiction to an immediately superior court. To file an appeal, only a general complaint against the judgment was allowed. The specific grounds for a successful appeal were one-sidedness or incompleteness of the judicial investigation, substantial violation of criminal procedural law, incorrect application of criminal law, lack of correlation between the court findings and the evidence, or the lack of correlation between the punishment and the seriousness of the crime or the nature of the defendant.

Great Britain has a criminal division of its court of appeal. Most of the appeals that come before it are challenges to sentences and are thus dissimilar to the appeals brought in the U.S. The Criminal Appeal Act gives the criminal division the authority to quash a conviction if the judge thinks it is unsatisfactory without any showing of any particular error. The entire appellate process up to the actual hearing is almost totally within the control of the Registrar of Criminal Appeals. The principal document filed by the appellant is called the perfected grounds for appeal that states the basis for appeal plus supporting arguments.

Although many nations provide an appeals process in criminal cases, the actual procedures are quite varied. There are differences, for example, in what can be challenged and the standards of review that apply. The commonality, however, is that the appeal provides the criminal defendant an opportunity to challenge his or her conviction or sentence in a higher court.

MILO MILLER

References and Further Reading

American Bar Association, *A Contrast between the Legal Systems in the United States and in the Soviet Union*, 1968.

Childress, S. and Martha D., *Federal Standards of Review*, Lexis Publishing, 1999, 3rd ed.

Cooley, J.W., *Callaghan's Appellate Advocacy Manual*, Clark Boardman Callaghan, 1995.

Koeltl, J.G. and Kiernan, J. Eds., *The Litigation Manual—Special Problems and Appeals,* The American Bar Association, 1999, 3rd ed.

Knibb, D.G., *Federal Court of Appeals Manual,* West Publishing, 1998.

Martineau, R.J., *Appellate Justice in England and the United States*, William S. Heine & Co, Inc., 1990.

McLean, I., *Criminal Appeals: A Practical Guide to Appeals to and from the Crown Court*, Sweet & Maxwell, London, UK, 1980.

Small, D.L., *Going to Trial,* The American Bar Association, 1999, 2nd ed.

Stern, R.L., *Appellate Practice in the United States,* The Bureau of National Affairs, 1989, 2nd ed.

Tigar, M.E. and Tigar J.B., *Federal Appeals—Jurisdiction and Practice,* West Publishing, 2000.

See also **Courts in the U.S.: Structure and Functions**

Arraignment

The arraignment session is where a defendant accused of a crime enters a formal plea before a judge or magistrate to the charge(s) for which he or she has been arrested or summoned. Generally, a defendant enters one of three pleas: "not guilty," "guilty," or "no contest," formally *nolo contendre.* (This latter plea has the same practical effect as a guilty plea, but entering it shields the conviction from being used against the offender in a subsequent civil action.) When a defendant is incapable of entering a plea (usually due to issues of mental competence), or refuses to enter a plea, a judge will generally enter a "not guilty" plea on the defendant's behalf.

Arraignments may take place whether a defendant is "in custody" or "out-of-custody." Most felony defendants remain in custody prior to their first court date, or *initial appearance*, at which time if the charge is not dismissed—bail is set. Whether or not a felony defendant is released on a monetary bail or a recognizance bond (nonmonetary release based on one's promise to appear in court), he or she is expected to appear, with her or his lawyer, at one's arraignment.

The time frame for arraignment sessions differs on the felony and misdemeanor levels. On the misdemeanor level, the arraignment is often a defendant's *initial appearance*, whereas on the felony level, the *initial appearance* and the *arraignment* are separate court proceedings. Misdemeanor arraignments usually take place within 24 hours of arrest, but on weekends may be delayed for up to 72 hours. Although felony *initial appearances* fall within the same general time restrictions, felony arraignments do not take place until after an *indictment* or *information* determines that there is enough evidence to bind a defendant to trial. In the absence of such evidence, a *dismissal* occurs. Therefore, as a rule of thumb, felony arraignments in the U.S. take place anywhere from 10–14 days following a defendant's *initial appearance.*

Arraignment sessions differ substantively on the misdemeanor and felony levels. On the misdemeanor level, the arraignment session tends to be collapsed with the defendant's Initial Appearance, where bail is routinely set for defendants who plead "not guilty." Misdemeanor defendants may also appear at an "out of custody" arraignment session after being released one of four ways: (1) Defendants may have received citations and been released in the field by the police (*field* or *citation releases*); (2) Following transportation by the police to a police station, defendants may be released on their promise to appear in court once they are fingerprinted and information about them is obtained (*station house release*); (3) Misdemeanor defendants and some felony defendants (depending on the jurisdiction) may be released from custody in a prearraignment status through *prebooking release.* (In these instances, pretrial release agencies screen defendants for possible release while on the grounds of the county jail, but in a facility outside the jail itself. Prebooking release programs emerged in the 1980s as strategies designed to relieve jail overcrowding, particularly in jurisdictions that were facing federal court-ordered mandates to reduce and maintain jail populations to a certain number of prisoners.) Qualified defendants then may be released, at times with specified conditions and supervision, on their promise to appear at their next scheduled court date; and (4) After being fingerprinted and "booked" into the jail, a defendant posts a cash bond, a predetermined amount of money that is required to facilitate a defendant's pretrial release from custody.

Guilty pleas are more often entered than not at misdemeanor arraignment sessions, a fact that did not go unnoticed in the report of President Johnson's Commission on Law Enforcement and Administration of Justice, *The Challenge of Crime in a Free Society* (1968). The President's Commission graphically depicted how "assembly line justice" operates in misdemeanor courts, or courts of limited jurisdiction, which are not part of the state court system. Often referred to by statute as "police courts," these judicial entities are also known as Municipal Courts, City Courts, County Courts, Justice of the Peace Courts, and, in a word, lower courts:

> The Commission has been shocked by what it has seen in some lower courts. It has seen cramped and noisy courtrooms, undignified and perfunctory procedures, and badly trained personnel. It has seen dedicated people who are frustrated by huge caseloads, by the lack of opportunity to examine cases carefully, and by the impossibility of devising constructive solutions to the problems of offenders. It has seen assembly line justice.

"Assembly line justice," or the rapid processing of cases within a courtroom environment, is the norm at both felony and misdemeanor arraignment sessions. A City Court magistrate, observed repeatedly over a duration of years, would playfully explain to defendants that they had the right to plead one of three ways: "chocolate," "vanilla," or "strawberry." Yet, despite this attempt at introducing levity into the courtroom, due to the fact that pleas of guilty and no contest must be made knowingly and voluntarily, this particular magistrate consistently made sure that defendants were aware of their rights. ("Rights are like a leg in cast," he was known to pontificate. "Both must be exercised to gain strength.") However, U.S. courts, in particular the lower courts, are more concerned about speed, and what Samuel Walker (2001) refers to as the functioning of the "courtroom work group," than they are about justice. In the lower courts, on the conveyer belt of assembly line justice, "cash register justice," in which fines are routinely in accordance with the offense, prevails. Over the years, despite technological advances, this phenomenon has not dramatically changed.

What has changed significantly concerning arraignments in U.S. courtrooms since *The Challenge of Crime in a Free Society* was published is the use of *video arraignments.*

Introduced in the 1980s, video arraignments are viewed as cost effective measures that eliminate the need to transport prisoners from the jail facility to the courthouse. Viewed by some as Orwellian in nature, judge, and defendant face each other via separate television monitors that are located in both the court where the judge is located—and the jail, where the incarcerated defendant enters her or his plea to the charge(s) for which he or she has been accused. The defendant's attorney and the prosecutor are physically present, either on one side or the other of the television, video, or computer screen. By 1994, when over 800 jurisdictions were known to employ video court technology, the National Center for State Courts (2003) stopped maintaining its registry of such proceedings (MacMillan, 2003). Today, according to the NCSC, video court technology has become commonplace and widely implemented. Video arraignment procedures, however, are employed on a less frequent basis than are video initial appearance proceedings.

Michael C. Elsner

References and Further Reading

Packer, H.L., Two models of the criminal process, *University of Pennsylvania Law Review* 113 (1964).

President's Commission on Law Enforcement and Administration of Justice, *The Challenge of Crime in a Free Society*, New York, NY: Avon Books, 1968.

Reinkensmeyer, M.W. and Doktor, J.M., The promise of court technology: Reality or fiction? pp. 93–102 in *The Improvement of the Administration of Justice*, 7th ed., Griller, G.M., and Stott, E.K., Jr., Eds., Washington, DC: American Bar Association, 2002.

Shelden, R.G. and Brown, W.B., *Criminal Justice in America: A Critical View*, Boston, MA: Allyn and Bacon, 2003.

Walker, S., *Sense and Nonsense about Crime and Drugs*, 5th ed., Belmont, CA: Wadsworth, 2001.

Wright, B., *Black Robes, White Justice*, New York, NY: Lyle Stuart, 1993.

Personal Communication with Jim MacMillan, National Center for State Courts, July, 2003.

See also **Arrest; Due Process**

Arrest

An arrest, through legal authority, deprives a person of individual liberty. It is the means by which a defendant enters the criminal justice system. If the system may be seen as a motor vehicle, then arrests may be likened to the vehicle's gasoline tank. Using this analogy, arrestees provide the fuel that enables the engine of criminal justice to run. Arrests, effectuated by police officers, generally take place in one of two ways: (1) through physical arrests, in which suspects accused of committing crimes are taken into custody, and usually handcuffed, transported to a pretrial holding facility, fingerprinted, and booked into jail; and (2) through field, or citation, releases, in which defendants are not physically arrested but instead are released on their written promise to appear in court at a specified date and time. A third type of arrest, station house releases, used in such cases as driving while intoxicated (DWI) and driving while under the influence (DUI), involve transporting an in-custody suspect to a police station, fingerprinting the arrestee, obtaining other information as necessary, and releasing him or her, often into the custody of a responsible third party, pending his or her arraignment in court. As a rule, only misdemeanor, and not felony, suspects are released either in the field or from the station house.

Arrests take place on a similar basis for juveniles, most of whom enter the juvenile justice system. Juveniles may be arrested for either delinquent offenses, acts for which adults may be arrested, or status offenses, which are directly linked to the age of the juvenile. Examples of status offenses include underage drinking, truancy, and curfew violations. Across the U.S., in increasing numbers, juveniles who are arrested for serious delinquent offenses, such as robbery and murder, are being remanded to the criminal justice system where they are treated as adults.

Although the public perception of crime is largely shaped by images of violent and dangerous criminals, available arrest statistics do not bear this out. Conservatively, on the adult level, roughly two out of three arrests in the U.S. involve misdemeanors, less serious criminal offenses that are routinely punishable by up to a year in jail, as opposed to felony offenses, for which convicted offenders may be sentenced to prison terms greater than 1 year. Depending on the city, county, or jurisdiction, physical arrests of suspects accused of committing misdemeanor offenses may double, triple or quadruple the number of physical arrests for felony defendants. When one includes the number of out-of-custody misdemeanor arrests in a given time frame, then the misdemeanor to felony arrest ratio may be as high as ten to one. Unfortunately, the Uniform Crime Report (UCR) statistics of the U.S. Federal Bureau of Investigation (FBI) was not designed to classify offenses as either misdemeanor or felony. Similarly, the definitive *Sourcebook of Criminal Justice Statistics* (2002) does not publish data that specifically address misdemeanor offenses because classification of offenses varies from state to state.

On both the felony and misdemeanor levels, arrests take place through one of two ways: on the basis of probable cause or through the issuance of a warrant. Most arrests do not involve the execution of a warrant, but three types do exist: (1) a lower court judge may issue a felony arrest warrant when presented with a sworn affidavit by a police officer. Usually, these are requested if the police are seeking entrance to a private residence or establishment for the purpose of effectuating an arrest. (2) A Grand Jury, guided by a prosecutor, determines that sufficient evidence exists for charges to be brought against a criminal suspect, and issues an arrest order through a Grand Jury warrant. Grand Jury investigations, conducted in secret, involve compelled testimony and the examination of criminal law violations prior to an arrest. The execution of the Grand Jury warrant marks the beginning of the criminal justice process, or at least the portion of the process that is visible to the public eye. (3) If a defendant fails to appear in court, fails to pay a fine, or otherwise fails to comply with a judicial or other order while on pretrial or postconviction release, then a judge may issue a *bench warrant* for the defendant's or the offender's arrest.

It has been estimated that roughly 25% of all felony arrests are dismissed at a defendant's initial court appearance, although no national database tracks cases from arrest to conviction or dismissal. Due to the fact that the UCRs of the FBI only reflect arrests for selected "index" crimes, and not the case outcomes (or dispositions), what is commonly called "the crime rate" should more accurately be referred to as "the arrest rate."

In his classic work, "Two Models of the Criminal Process," Herbert Packer (1964) outlined the competing Crime Control and Due Process models that operate within the U.S. criminal justice system. Both are ideal types, or constructed schemes that serve, in the words of sociologist Max Weber, "the purpose of offering an ideal typical means of orientation" (Gerth and Mills, 1946). In other words, ideal types are abstract formations, or definitions, that focus on a given phenomenon's typical characteristics. In this sense, Packer's Crime Control and Due Process models are not reflected in the real world in an absolute way, but they do enable us to view two extremes of how the U.S. justice system may function. In reality, the criminal justice system that operates in the U.S. incorporates aspects of both models outlined by Packer.

The Crime Control model posits that the crime repression is the most important element of the criminal justice system. Its focus is administrative efficiency, and it seeks to quickly identify, arrest, and process criminal offenders. Its key component is discretion, which is administered at the police and pretrial stages of the criminal justice process. Ideally, under this model, arrestees quickly plead guilty, are sentenced to prison terms, and through their incapacitation, pose no threat to society. From the vantage point of those who champion the Crime Control model, it breaks down because of procedural due process rights that are granted to criminal suspects.

Packer's Due Process model posits that the preservation of individual liberties is the most important element of the criminal justice system. This model's focus is judicial reliability, and it is anchored in the notions of adversarial justice and the presumption of innocence. The law, not discretion, guides the decision-making process, which is rendered in the courtroom. "It is better to let 99 guilty persons go free than to convict one innocent person," is its motto. Although viewed as an obstacle course, and not as an assembly-line, the Due Process model's wheels of justice nonetheless rotate in a mechanical nature. Justice, however, is carried out not on an individual basis, but systematically. Justice is said to be blind, as evidenced by its symbol, a blindfolded woman (perhaps based on either the Roman goddess Justitia or the Greek goddess Themis) who holds the scales of justice from one of her hands, while brandishing a sword in the other.

Police typically are reactive, and respond to reports of crime. On occasion, they are proactive, but this is an exception to the rule. Perhaps the best known criminological study that has addressed this issue is the "Kansas City Preventive Patrol Experiment," which demonstrated that routine, random police patrols have no effect on and do not reduce both reported and unreported crime. Moreover, patrolling in marked police cars was found to make no difference in terms of how safe citizens felt, and in their actually becoming crime victims. A subsequent study of note, the "Newark Foot Patrol Experiment," similarly concluded that increased foot patrols by police officers had no effect on the crime rate, although said patrols were said to positively impact the "fear of crime" experienced by citizens.

Usually on the basis of reactive, rather than proactive, investigations, most arrests take place when police apprehend an individual who is believed to have committed an offense. Discretion enables police to arrest or not arrest suspects whom they apprehend. A common law enforcement technique involves the use of informants ("snitches"), or persons who—in lieu of being arrested or prosecuted—supply law enforcement officials with information regarding the commission of other crimes. Typically, informants are used in cases of both low-level drug users or dealers and high-level organized crime and racketeering investigations. Such cases may also involve the use of undercover police officers and detectives, whose responsibilities differ from those of uniformed police officers. Over time, detectives and undercover police, often with the aid of informants, use techniques of investigation and surveillance to arrest larger numbers of people who may be charged in a conspiracy.

While now conspiracy laws are a standard operating procedure of police and prosecutors, Clarence Darrow (1932), perhaps the most renowned defense attorney in U.S. history, had this to say at a time when their use was not so prevalent:

> If there are still any citizens interested in protecting human liberty, let them study the conspiracy laws of the United States. ... The conspiracy laws magnify misdemeanors into serious felonies. If a boy should steal a dime a small fine would cover the offense; he could not be sent to the penitentiary. But if two boys by agreement steal a dime then both of them could be sent to the penitentiary as conspirators. ... If A is indicted and a conspiracy is charged, or even if it is not charged, the state's attorney is allowed to prove what A said to B and what B said to C while the defendant was not present. Then he can prove what C said to D and what D said to E, and so on, to the end of the alphabet ... These conspiracy laws. ... have gone so far that they can never be changed except through a general protest by liberty-loving men and women, if any such there be, against the spirit of tyranny that has battered down the ordinary safeguards that laws and institutions have made to protect individual rights.

Arrests may also take place with no intent, on part of the police, for a prosecution to ensue. These "bad" arrests may occur for a variety of reasons: (1) some are made for altruistic purposes, such as when mentally ill persons are deemed in need of treatment or public drunks may appear to need shelter and protection; (2) some attempt to "sweep the streets clean" of public nuisances, such as disorderly persons, visible panhandlers, and prostitutes; (3) some involve the use of informants, such as low-level drug users and dealers; and (4) others involve the administration of "street justice," in which the act of arrest is meant to send a message to a criminal suspect, despite the lack of evidence that would warrant further prosecution.

In terms of the discretion used by police, the distinction has been made between selective law enforcement and discriminatory enforcement. "Driving while black" and "racial profiling," terms that surfaced in the late 20th century, are reflective of discriminatory law enforcement practices that are widely used in the U.S. However, the phenomenon of law enforcement operations targeting low-income, urban communities that are primarily inhabited by Latinos and African Americans is hardly new. In 1970, Ramsey Clark, who was then the attorney general of the U.S., wrote the following:

> Perhaps the most difficult and troublesome procedural issue in police-community relations is arrest. Arrest standards must be clearly understood by the police and uniformly applied. The public must also understand the rules and believe they are equally enforced. Citizens must respect arrest procedures as being firm but fair; too often the authority for arrest is vague, capriciously applied, and inadequately reviewed. Arrest has been used as a technique of intimidation to maintain ghetto order. "Law and order" sounds ominous to the ghetto dweller, because it implies force and he has known order without law.

Police stop and frisk suspicious persons in some parts of some cities as a regular enforcement technique. A careful search of persons arrested on probable cause will be necessary sometimes for the safety of the officer. But if the technique is used without probable cause to believe a violent crime has been committed and if it is used excessively, if it is abused it will undermine the very purpose of the police department. It will negate their opportunity to communicate, to relate, to serve the public, because there will be a loss of respect, there will be fear and no confidence. In parts of some cities most males over 10 years have been frisked by police, often without cause.

More than 25 years later, the National Criminal Justice Commission, a group convened by the National Center on Institutions and Alternatives (NCIA) and comprised of public officials, scholars, and criminal justice officials, echoed similar sentiments (Donziger, 1996):

> The first place where racial disparities are usually measured is at the point of arrest. Most studies reveal what most police officers will casually admit: that race is used as a factor when the police decide to follow, detain, search, or arrest. Some police officers believe that race provides a legitimate and significant basis to suspect a person of criminal behavior. To justify the use of race in forming this suspicion, these officers might point to racial disparities in arrest patterns: if minorities get arrested more often, they argue, then the minorities must be committing more crime. This is a self-fulfilling statistical prophecy: racial stereotypes influence police to arrest minorities, thereby creating the arrest statistics needed to justify the racial stereotype.

"It seems that no matter what Black men do in their cars, they are targets for criminal suspicion," writes criminologist Katheryn Russell in *The Color of Crime* (1998). Black men are subjected to vehicle stops for a variety of reasons, she notes, including the following:

- Driving a luxury automobile.
- Driving an old car.
- Driving in a car with other Black men.
- Driving in a car with a White woman.
- Driving early in the morning.
- Driving late at night.
- Driving a rented automobile.
- Driving too fast.
- Driving too slowly.
- Driving in a low-income neighborhood, known for its drug traffic.
- Driving in a White neighborhood.
- Driving in a neighborhood where there have been recent burglaries.
- Fitting a drug courier profile.

In a compilation by Russell of famous African American men "who report that they have been unfairly stopped and harassed by law enforcement officers," attorneys on both sides of the aisle in the O.J. Simpson trial, defense attorney Johnnie Cochran and prosecutor Chris Darden, are represented. Other professionals on the list include: actors, athletes, authors, businessmen, journalists, musicians, and pastors, as well as three esteemed professors: Cornel West, Roger Wilkins, and William Julius Wilson. "To avoid being stopped and questioned by police," Miles Davis, the renowned jazz artist, "would call and notify the Beverly Hills police department *before* leaving home."

Today, with respect to police–community relations, the so-called "war on drugs," which has been in operation for more than two decades, has greatly exacerbated the racial, ethnic, and social-class tensions that exist throughout the U.S. Arrest statistics have soared since the current U.S. drug war was officially launched by President Reagan in 1982. The "war on drugs," in actuality, is not being waged against illicit substances, but instead aims its weapons and uses its resources against people, primarily people of color who have limited economic resources. Statistics clearly bear this out.

Marc Mauer, author of *Race to Incarcerate* (1999), points out the impact of the drug war on the African American community in the U.S. "can be mapped out by looking at two overlapping trends. First, there has been an enormous increase in the number of drug arrests overall; second, African Americans have constituted an increasing proportion of those arrests." Whereas, there were 581,000 arrests for drug offenses in 1980, that number nearly doubled, to about 1.1 million, by 1990, and nearly tripled, approaching 1.5 million, in 1995. While African Americans comprised 13% of the U.S. population in 1980, they accounted for 21% of drug possession arrests that year. By 1992, 36% of all adults arrested for drug possession were Black, dropping slightly thereafter. Figures for juveniles are even more striking: whereas African Americans represented only 13% of all juvenile drug possession arrests in 1980, this figure climbed to 40% by 1991, before falling to 30% in 1995. Meanwhile, drug use statistics consistently reveal that Blacks use illicit drugs at roughly the same rate as they are represented in the general population, at about 15%. Arrest figures for the sale of illicit drugs are even more revealing: whereas African Americans accounted for 35% of such arrests in 1980, the figure rose to 49% by 1995.

Although the law of arrest is rooted in common law and Constitutional safeguards, the tremendous increase of drug-related arrests over the past 20 years challenges the limits of the Fourth Amendment, which prohibits unreasonable searches and seizures. Common police practices, instituted since the current "war on drugs" has been declared, include: pretextual stops of motor vehicles; "jump out squads," in which police officers frisk and detain citizens without warning of any kind; consent searches; "no knock warrants," and "drug sweeps."

MICHAEL C. ELSNER

References and Further Reading

Clark, R., *Crime in America*, New York, NY: Simon and Schuster, 1970.

Darrow, C., *The Story of My Life*, New York, NY: Charles Scribner's Sons, 1932.

Donziger, S.R., Ed., *The Real War On Crime: The Report of the National Criminal Justice Commission*, New York, NY: HarperCollins, 1996.

Gerth, H.H. and Wright, M.C., *From Max Weber: Essays in Sociology*, New York, NY: Oxford University Press, 1946.

Harris, D.A., *Profiles in Injustice: Why Racial Profiling Cannot Work*, New York, NY: New Press, 2003.

Kelling, G.L., Pate, T., Diekman, D., and Brown, C.E., *The Kansas City Preventive Patrol Experiment: A Summary Report*, Washington, DC: The Police Foundation, 1974.

Mauer, M., *Race to Incarcerate*, New York, NY: New Press, 1999.

Milller, J., *Search and Destroy*, Cambridge, UK: Cambridge University Press, 1996.

Packer, H.L., Two models of the criminal process, *University of Pennsylvania Law Review* 113 (1964).

Pastore, A.L. and Maguire, K., Eds., *Sourcebook of Criminal Justice Statistics 2001*, Washington, DC: U.S. Department of Justice, Bureau of Justice Statistics, 2002.

The Police Foundation, *The Newark Foot Patrol Experiment*, Washington, DC: The Police Foundation, 1981.

President's Commission on Law Enforcement and Administration of Justice, *The Challenge of Crime in a Free Society*, New York, NY: Avon Books, 1968.

Russell, K.K., *The Color of Crime*, New York, NY: New York University Press, 1998.

See also **Arraignment; Police: Patrol**

Arson: Extent and Correlates

Arson is defined by the Uniform Crime Report system as any "willful or malicious burning or attempt to burn, with or without intent to defraud, a dwelling, house, public building, motor vehicle or aircraft, personal property of another, etc." According to the U.S. Fire Administration, an estimated 45,000 intentionally set fires occurred in the U.S. in 2001. For the same year, the FBI reported nearly 70,000 arsons. Accordingly, accuracy may be compromised as arson fires are not always investigated by law enforcement officials. In some communities (75% of all fire companies in the U.S. are comprised of volunteers) arson is investigated by the local fire marshal or fire department volunteers. Arson fires account for an estimated 25–40% of all reported incidents. Estimates on yearly deaths, resulting from arson, range from 350 to 700, with over 4000 people losing their lives between 1992 and 2001 in the U.S.

According to the 2001 U.C.R., most reported arson fires occurred in structures (over 42%) with 60% of those arsons occurring in single occupancy homes. About 30% of the arsons were committed in or on motor vehicles followed by 25% of other types of properties, like crops, timber, and the like. The U.S. law enforcement agencies cleared 16% of the arsons and they arrested nearly 19,000 people. Forty-nine percent, nearly half of those arrested, were juveniles. Males comprised 84% of those arrested. Seventy-seven percent were white.

There has been a paucity of empirical research on arson, with virtually no examination of the phenomenon outside the urban context (Stahura and Hollinger, 1988). Nevertheless, the scarce literature available provides three emerging explanations. First, the experts, supported by official statistics, agree that arson is attributed to juvenile delinquency. Over 50% of those arrested in the U.S. for arson are under the age of 18. Second, a smaller, but better researched category of firesetting behavior is attributed to the pyromaniac or psychologically deranged person. Finally, it is estimated that between 10% and 20% of all intentionally set fires can be attributed to arson-for-profit schemes. The following discussion briefly expands upon the aforementioned fire-setting explanations.

Firesetting by children and adolescents is a dangerous act that often has grave consequences, including destruction of property, personal injury, and death (Sakheim and Osborne, 1999). Lewis and Yarnell (1951) conducted one of the first scientific investigations into the psychological dynamics of the juvenile fire setter, where the firesetters' family, social, and psychiatric backgrounds were studied. They found among firesetting juveniles a high incidence of family dysfunction, including alcoholism, psychosis, criminality, and illegitimacy. Later, research by Kaufman (1961) found a high incidence of emotional disturbance, including hyperactivity, psychosis, rage reactions, and enuresis in firesetting cases by juveniles. The motives for juvenile firesetters were found to be intense pleasure, a cry for help, retaliation, or a desire to reunite the family. Further, more useful motive categories, accidental, purposeful, psychotic, neurotic, and revengeful, have been developed. Interestingly, juvenile firesetters tend to set fires along with other juveniles and these acts take place close to home (Santilla et al., 2003).

Pyromaniacs, the second group of researched arsonists, are intensely fascinated with setting fires and are thrilled by watching things burn. When Moore, Thompson-Pope, and Whited (1996) compared groups of psychiatric patients, one being firesetters and other not, they found the firesetting group to score significantly higher on psychasthenia, schizophrenia, and mania scales. The firesetting group also scored higher on a variety of emotional- and behavioral-problem scales. These scales include depression, alienation, bizarre mentation, anger, conduct problems, school problems, and negative treatment indicators. This group was found to be fearful, worried, and withdrawn. Moreover, they were found to have low self-esteem and somatic problems along with a wide range of psychological problems including excesses in behavior such as impulsiveness and acting out. Obsessive compulsive firesetters (e.g., pyromaniacs) may have an early interest in fire and most likely they cannot solve problems very well. They are exposed to stressors in life such as parental psychopathology, abuse, and parental absence. Firesetting, for them, is seen as a manifestation of both anxiety and anger and is a complex level of antisocial behavior.

The final category of firesetting research focuses on the for-profit firesetter. Accordingly, Brady (1983) postulated that arson outstrips all other index crimes in terms of injuries, deaths, and property losses. He argues that arson is a consequence of economic decisions by profit-making bodies such as banks, real estate developers, and insurance industries that desire to control neighborhood destabilization in order to make money. Arson for profit has become a crime venue for organized crime members, professional fire setters, corrupt governmental officials, and small property owners desperate to escape losing investments due to urban decay. Brady bases his thesis on the finding that the most common fire sites are located in the older cities of the Northeast and Midwest. City fires in New York City, for example, have been highly concentrated in black and Hispanic neighborhoods. This was also found to be the case in cities like Hoboken, Paterson, and Denver. Arson, in these cities, is a problem associated with the disinvestment of urban slums, exacerbated by the high presence of abandoned buildings, absentee landlords, and banking or governmental policies that support urban decay as a natural process of social change. Arson, then, most likely occurs in those neighborhoods that have been drained of their capital and mortgage power.

In sum, the dominant popular image of the arsonist has been the crazed pyromaniac who sexually enjoys observing the flames of his own doing. Indeed, Inciardi (1970) concluded that most of the 138 imprisoned arsonists he studied were primarily motivated by sexual excitement or the desire to gain revenge. However, the sociology of arson challenges that assumption and takes us directly into the hearts of our inner cities where profit and greed take an opportunistic advantage of urban blight. Forensic scientists, psychologists, sociologists, and others interested in the correlates of arson also cannot forget the role juvenile delinquency plays in this most devastating of criminal events.

John T. Krimmel

References and Further Reading

Brady, J. (1983) Arson, urban economy, and organized crime: The case of Boston. *Social Problems* 31(1): 1–27.

Inciardi, J. (1970) The adult firesetter. *Criminology* 8(2): 132–149.

Kaufman, I. (1961) Crimes of violence and delinquency in schizophrenic children. *Journal of the Academy of Child Psychiatry* 1: 269–283.

Lewis, N. and Yarnell, H. (1951) Pathological firesetting. In *Nervous and Mental Disease Monographs* 82. Nicholasville, KY: Coolidge Foundation.

Moore, J., Thompson-Pope, S., and Whited, R. (1996) MMPI-A profiles of adolescent boys with a history of firesetting, *Journal of Personality Assessment* 67(1): 116–126.

Sakheim, G. and Osborne, E.(1999) Severe vs. nonsevere firesetters revisited, *Child Welfare* 78 (4): 1–12.

Santilla, P., Hakkanen, H., Alison, L., and Whyte, C. (2003) Juvenile firesetters: Crime scene actions and offender characteristics, *Legal and Criminological Psychology* 8: 1–20.

Stahura, J. and Hollinger, R. (1988) A routine activities approach to suburban arson rates, *Sociological Spectrum* 8; 349–369.

See also **Arson: The Law**

Arson: The Law

Arson is a catastrophic and devastating crime in terms of life and property loss. Statistics indicate that acts of purposeful firesetting for profit, for revenge, political motives, or to hide the evidence at a crime scene are on the rise. It is estimated that between 500 and 1000 people every year are killed because of arson. Moreover, upward of 2 billion dollars in property damage is the result of this crime, not to mention mounting insurance costs and related government liabilities associated with fighting fires (Uniform Crime Report, 2001).

Arguably, arson is the easiest of the major crimes to commit, the most difficult to detect or solve, and the hardest to prosecute in court. The act of arson, that is the malicious burning of the dwelling of another, was a felony at common law. The earliest common law felonies were homicide, rape, arson, larceny, and robbery; and a felony at common law was punishable by the possibility of death to the convicted. Although in early English times the death penalty was possible upon conviction many escaped the fate through pardons, voluntary forfeiture of personal property or the benefit of clergy.

The common law elements of arson include malicious burning and dwelling of another. The term dwelling was defined as a place usually used for sleep. At common law a person could not be convicted of arson if he set fire to his own dwelling or a building not used for sleeping. Further, there never was a specific requirement of the level of damage caused. A mere charring was significant for an arson case. Modern statutes eliminate the common law technicalities of a dwelling and the requirement that the structure be that of another. By the 19th century most crimes had been identified and given full definition. In America, the colonists almost always followed common law but adopted statutes to fit their circumstances. The new laws were a mix of common law and statutory regulations. Present-day law is also a mixture of common laws and statutes but the goal of the model penal code seeks to clearly define all crimes. Thus, arson in modern law has been defined in such as fashion as to address the previously stated unclear crime elements and intent (*mens rea*).

The federal law on arson (18 USCS 81) states, "Whoever within the special maritime and territorial jurisdiction of the U.S., willfully and maliciously sets fire to or burns a building or structure or vessel, and machinery or building materials or supplies, military of naval stores, munitions of war, or any structural aids or appliances for navigation or shipping, or attempts or conspires to do such an act shall be imprisoned for not more than 25 years." This federal statute (unlike some state statutes) sets the punishment and does not grade the offense for sentencing purposes other than to provide a maximum exposure to punishment.

In order for the government to prove the crime of arson, it must show beyond a reasonable doubt that, first, there was a fire and witnesses must testify as to the date and time of the fire, how authorities received notice of the fire, and the nature of the alarm. Secondly, the government must demonstrate what part of the building was actually burned. Blackening or discoloration of paint is not viewed as a crime of arson, but more appropriately prosecuted as criminal mischief. Finally, the government must show that the fire was of incendiary origin and that it was willfully and intentionally set.

Some states have expanded their definitions of arson. New Jersey, for example in their crime code lists arson as NJSA 2C:17-1 (2003) and includes in its definition that a person is guilty of arson if he starts a fire or sets off an explosion where he knowingly placed another person in danger of death or serious bodily injury. The crime of arson is committed if a person sets fire with the intention of collecting insurance money or to exempt the property from any state provision. Also, if a forest is set ablaze the person starting the fire is guilty of arson. The New Jersey statute also makes it a crime with an enhanced penalty to set fire to a church, synagogue, or other places of worship.

It is clear that the definitions of common law arson were not adequate to stem the current-day tide of felonious arsons in the U.S. The common law definition of arson contained the basic elements of malicious burning of another person's dwelling. These statutes were not enough. Federal and state statutes were developed to address felonious arsons set on a persons' own property and those arsons set for insurance purposes or on religious properties. Moreover, the state and federal statutes adequately address arson where fire has been set and a person is placed in danger of harm or death.

The emerging modern-day definitions of arson have a marked connectedness between the nature of the crime and the law. As the crime of arson intensifies in depth and breath the changes in the law have adapted. We have seen the statutes redefine felonious arson as the targets and the perpetrators change.

JOHN T. KRIMMEL

References and Further Reading

New Jersey Criminal Law (2003) 2C:17-1 Arson and related offenses. *United States Code* (2003) Title 18 USCS 81.

United States Department of Justice (2003). *Crime in the United States*, Uniform Crime Reports, Washington, DC.

See also **Arson: Extent and Correlates**

Art Crime

Art is one of the most profound expressions of our creativity and one of our most lasting legacies. Throughout history, art has been a reflection of the cultural, social, and political aspects of all societies. The art market consists of a wide range of different kinds of art, which includes photographs, sculptures, works in glass, ceramics, antiquities, and works on paper (that is, prints, drawings, and watercolors). Art crime encompasses a variety of illegal activities such as art theft, fraud, forgeries, fakes, and vandalism. Although the first four of these categories are associated with the illicit trade and smuggling of art, and transnational criminal organizations, vandalism is conducted by individuals with personal or political reasons and does not usually involve organizations. The illegal excavation or looting or archaeological sites of cultural property is also a form of art crime (Bernick, 1999).

Art crime is not a new phenomenon. Stories of fakes, forgeries, and stolen cultural treasures have been a part of the history of the world for centuries (Greenfield, 1995). However, the improved accessibility of art and the acceptance of contemporary art as an investment have contributed to the upward trend in art crime, particularly art theft, over the last few decades when private ownership has become more prevalent. Reports of stolen art received by the International Foundation for Art Research more than tripled in the late 1970s and recent estimated values of international art theft have been in the vicinity of US$2 billion and US$6 billion per year (International Foundation for Art Research, 1995). Around US$200 million worth of antiquities are smuggled out of Turkey yearly, primarily taken from burial sites and ancient cities (Doxey, 1996). The government of the People's Republic of China claims that 40,000 tombs were robbed in 1989 and 1990, and gangs managed to smuggle out huge statues 1000 years old or more (WuDunn, 1992). Italy recorded 230,000 art thefts from 1970 to 1990, British losses were estimated at US$1.5 billion a year and the Czech Republic said it was losing about 10% of its national patrimony per year to theft and smuggling (Blumenthal, 1996). The 1990 theft of 12 paintings from the Isabella Stewart Gardner Museum in Boston has been estimated to be valued at US$300 million. They were stolen by thieves posing as police officers who gained entry to the museum (Boston Police, 2000). The paintings, which included the only known seascape by Rembrandt as well as one of the few extant paintings by Jan Vermeer, have still not been recovered.

To combat art theft, the art community and the insurance industry established the Art Loss Register in 1991. The Art Loss Register currently has offices in New York, London, and Cologne in Germany. This is a permanent computerized database of stolen and missing works of art, antiques, and valuables and operates on an international basis to assist law enforcement agencies. The public as well as law enforcement can register stolen art. On average the Art Loss Register records approximately 1200 items per month and since its inception it has helped recover over US$100 million in stolen art (Kisluk, 1999).

However, as is the case with all crime, there is a low reporting rate for art theft. A great deal of the stolen art is unreported to such central bodies as Interpol and perhaps not even to the local law enforcement authorities, particularly in developing countries (James, 2000). The recovery rate for stolen art reported to the International Foundation for Art Research, Interpol and the FBI has been estimated to be as low as 10% and conviction of criminals for crimes involving art is even lower (Aarons, 1998).

Younger and less well-known artists over the centuries have found that there was money to be made by reproducing the works of better known artists. One notable forger during the 1930s and 1940s was van Meegren, who specialized in the paintings of the 17th century Dutch master, Vermeer. Van Meegren did not copy Vermeer originals, but created paintings in the artist's style, such as "Supper at Emmaus." This painting was declared to be one of Vermeer's finest works until years later when it was discovered to be a fake. Van Meegren was eventually convicted of forgery in 1947 after selling the supposed Vermeers to the Germans during the occupation of Holland (Conklin, 1994). Another well-known forger was John Drewe who was convicted in a London court in 1999 of two charges of forgery and one of conspiracy to defraud for the sale of 15 forged paintings of 9 modern masters. These masters included Giacornett, Braque, Chagall, Matisse, and Klee. All of these had been sold through Sotheby's, Christie's, and Phillips. Although Drewe did not actually produce the forged paintings (this was done by artist John Myatt, whom Drewe had specifically approached), he was the master of authenticating Myatt's works by creating fraudulent provenances (James, 2000).

Art also lends itself to money laundering. Money laundering occurs when luxury goods are purchased for the purpose of converting illicit cash into "clean assets," together with concealing the source or use of the funds (National Crime Authority, 1991). As with other luxury items, art can be attractive to the money launderer because of the absence of controls in the industry, the high value of quality art, and difficulties associated with determining the true value of art unless an experienced valuer is used. There is also an active market for quality art and no cash reporting requirements (National Crime Authority, 1991). It is also known that crime related to art and cultural property is significant, as is its inextricable relationship to major and organized crime. Groups as diverse as the American, Italian, and Russian Mafias, the IRA and Colombian cocaine cartels have been identified as being involved. They can be conclusively linked to drugs and arms dealing, and those involved are dangerous and capable of violence (Hill, 1995).

Although art theft and art forgery are of real concern to some individual countries, it is the international environment that potentially provides many opportunities for art crime. The high prices that can now be demanded for paintings and antiquities often means that the supply through legal means is not sufficient. Economic and political instability in some parts of the world, together with less stringent border controls make trafficking in illegal art easier. Organized crime and its ability to evade law enforcement agencies can also have a large impact on the illegal art market. To effectively counter these symptoms, a dedicated approach to art crime is needed both within internal law enforcement agencies of the countries involved and also between international law enforcement agencies.

MARIANNE JAMES

References and Further Reading

Bernick, L., 1999, Art and antiques theft, in Einstein E. and Amir, M., Eds., *Organized Crime: Uncertainties and Dilemmas*, Office of International Criminal Justice, the University of Illinois, Chicago.

Blumenthal, R., 1996, Museums getting together to track stolen art, *New York Times*, 14 July 1996, p. C13.

Boston Police, 2000, Robbery of priceless works of art from the Isabella Stewart Gardner Museum. Available at http://www.fbi.gov/majcases/arttheft/art.htm.

Conklin, J.E., 1994, *Art Crime*, Praeger, Westport, CO.

James, M., 2000, Art Crime, *Trends and Issues in Crime and Criminal Justice* No. 170, Australian Institute of Criminology, Canberra, ACT, Australia.

Kisluk, A., 1999, Stolen art and the art loss register, paper presented at the *Art Crime: Protecting Art, Protecting Artists and Protecting Consumers Conference Convened by the Australian Institute of Criminology*, 2–3 December, Sydney.

National Crime Authority, 1991, Luxury goods industry, Chap. 22, *Money Laundering in Australia—Taken to the Cleaners* (NCA protected, cited with permission), National Crime Authority, Sydney.

WuDunn, S., 1992, China is fighting for its soul: Its looted antiques, *New York Times*, 8 December, p. 18.

Doxey, J., 1996, Stemming the flow: Turkey's fight against the illegal importation of its antiquities, *The Middle East,* July–August, no. 258, p. 35.
Greenfield, J., 1995, Art theft and the art market, *The Return of Cultural Treasures,* 2nd ed., Cambridge University Press, Cambridge.
Hill, C. 1995, Art crime linked to drugs and arms, *Law and Order*, May.
International Foundation for Art Research, 1995, *DEA Operations Nets 3 Pictures*, International Foundation for Art Research, New York.

See also **Forgery; Money Laundering**

Assault and Battery: Extent and Correlates

The terms "assault" and "battery" were developed at common law as separate criminal acts, and only recently have states begun to view them as interchangeable terms (Md. Code. Ann., Criminal Law, § 3-201 [2002]; R.I. Gen. Laws § 11-5-3 [2003]). At common law, assault occurred when one person acted in a manner that indicated force would be used to injure another person. Actually touching or injuring the other person was battery at common law. The two terms have been commonly used in combination because a battery by definition usually included an assault.

At common law, assault was a crime resulting in a mental or emotional harm, but no physical harm. Two different acts arose out of the common law definition to be recognized as assault by state and local jurisdictions. The first type of assault is called tort type (Kan. Stat. Ann. § 21-3408 [2002]). The elements of tort type assault are similar to the elements of the civil wrong (tort) of assault. Tort type assault requires intentionally putting another person in reasonable apprehension of imminent bodily harm. Tort type assault addresses those situations in which an aggressor threatens to physically harm another person even though the aggressor may have no intention of actually carrying on with his threat. (See, for example, Fla. Stat. ch. 784.011 [2003]; 2003 Nev. Stat. § 200.471.) A few states are reclassifying this criminal act as the crime of "threat" or "menace" (Conn. Gen. Stat. § 53a-62 [2003]; Colo. Rev. Stat. § 18-3-206 [2003]).

The second type of assault is called attempted battery type assault. The elements of the attempted battery type assault require an actor to attempt to commit a battery but fail to actually touch his intended victim (W. Va. Code § 61-2-9 [2003]). Attempted battery type assault can be differentiated from tort type assault by analyzing the intent of the aggressor. When the aggressor actually intends to cause physical harm but fails he has committed an attempted battery type assault. When the aggressor has no actual intent to cause a physical harm, he merely wishes to threaten, he has committed a tort type assault. (See, for example, § 720 Ill. Comp. Stat. 5/12-1 [2003].)

Most jurisdictions recognize some form of the crime of aggravated assault, but the elements of that crime depend upon the underlying version of assault adopted by the jurisdiction. In some states, the crime of assault becomes aggravated when the aggressor's act involves the use of a deadly or dangerous weapon. (See, for example, Or. Rev. Stat. § 163.165 [2001]; Mich. Comp. Laws § 750.82 [2003].) Other states elevate the crime of assault to aggravated assault depending upon the level of harm inflicted. (See, for example, Tex. Penal Code Ann. § 22.02 [LexisNexis, 2004]; Me. Rev. Stat. Ann. tit. 17-A, § 208 [2003].) It is also not unusual for state laws to follow the Model Penal Code and combine both the concept of method of threat and the concept of amount of harm into a single aggravated assault statute (Model Penal Code, § 211.1 (2) [1962]). For example, South Dakota's aggravated assault law criminalizes both "[a]ttempts to cause serious bodily injury to another" and an actual injury to another person (S.D. Codified Laws § 22-18.1.1 [LexisNexis, 2003]). Illinois has created a more unusual definition of aggravated assault. Although that state's aggravated assault law has an element related to the use of a weapon during the commission of a simple assault, the primary focus of that law is on the characteristics of the victim known to the offender at the time of the act (§ 720 Ill. Comp. Stat. 5/12-2 [2003]).

At common law the crime of battery required physically touching another person, but did not require a physical harm. Today, most states recognize two different acts as the crime of battery. The first type of battery, bodily harm, typically requires that the actor intentionally or recklessly cause bodily harm to another person (W. Va. Code § 61-2-9 [2003]; Cal. Penal Code § 242 [2003]). This type of battery can be elevated to aggravated battery when the actor uses a deadly or dangerous weapon to complete the crime.

The second type of battery recognized today is the offensive touching type of battery. This type of battery requires that the actor intentionally cause physical contact with another person in a rude, insulting, or angry manner, but does not require that the victim suffer bodily harm (Kan. Stat. Ann. 21-3412 [2002]; Ga. Code Ann. § 16-5-23 [2002]). The premise of this type of battery is that the victim suffered a nonconsensual touching. Offensive touching includes acts such as spitting, poking, or prodding a victim with one's finger, or intentionally bumping into another person. Although offensive acts do not usually result in serious bodily harm in and of themselves, poking or prodding a victim with a deadly or dangerous weapon increases the severity of this crime to aggravated battery in some jurisdictions.

A few states further categorize battery as simple battery or aggravated battery. Simple battery usually refers to crimes of battery resulting in a low level of harm. Criminal battery resulting in a great degree of harm may be charged as aggravated battery even when no weapon is used to commit the crime (Ga. Code Ann. § 16-5-24 [2002]).

Many states are moving away from the common law concepts of assault and battery. These jurisdictions include acts of physical harm, classified as battery at common law, within the statutory definition of assault. (See, for example, S.D. Codified Laws § 22-18.1.1 [LexisNexis, 2003]; N.H. Rev. Stat. Ann. § 631:2 [2003]; Ariz. Rev. Stat. § 13-1203 [2003].) This group of states has eliminated battery as a separate classification of crime within their criminal codes (Neb. Rev. Stat. § 28-308 [2002]; Ala. Code §13A-6-22 [2003]; Haw. Rev. Stat. § 707-711 [2003]). The New York Statutory Code explains why that state eliminated the common law crime of battery. In that state the level of physical injury that the criminal justice system seeks to prevent and prosecute has evolved into "considerably more than the common law concept of a battery, which may amount to no more than a technical touching" (N.Y. Penal Law § 120.00 [Consol. 2003]). Therefore, in New York, offensive sexual acts that cause no actual physical harm are dealt with as sex offenses, whereas "petty slaps, shoves, kicks and the like delivered out of hostility, meanness and similar motives" are covered by the more minor offense of harassment (N.Y. Penal Law § 120.00 [Consol. 2003]). Other types of touchings resulting in no actual physical harm are no longer included within the criminal code.

At common law very serious harm to a victim was neither assault nor battery, but was categorized as the separate crime of "mayhem." Usually, mayhem was defined to include the malicious disabling of a victim or the permanent disfigurement of a victim. Because the intent of those criminal acts was to limit a victim's ability to earn a living, or interact with society, the penalty for mayhem was necessarily greater than the punishment imposed for the crime of battery. A few states continue to criminalize the common law version of mayhem (Miss. Code Ann. § 97-3-59 [2004]; Cal. Penal Code § 203 [2003]; Mass Gen. Laws ch. 265, § 14 [2003]). Most states, however, include the common law acts of mayhem as elements of either aggravated assault or aggravated battery (Va. Code Ann § 18.2-51 [2003]).

Technical battery makes the infliction of unnecessary physical harm an illegal act. Technical battery may be charged when an individual is legally permitted to cause some level of harm, but exceeds the scope of permission granted by the victim. A tattoo artist might be charged with technical battery if he inserts a tattooing needle deeper into the client's body than is necessary to make the tattoo if his intent is not related to tattooing.

Consent may constitute a defense to a charge of battery when the person inflicting the physical harm is acting with permission and in the interests of the injured party. For example, a surgeon may begin an operation by cutting a patient with a knife, but this act is not battery because the patient has consented to the harm and the doctor's intent is to benefit the patient.

When developing the Uniform Crime Reporting System in 1960, the Federal Bureau of Investigation (FBI) avoided the difficulties inherent in attempting to categorize the wide variety of definitions of assault and battery used by state and local jurisdictions. Instead, that agency followed the *Model Penal Code* (*Model Penal Code*, § 211.1(2) [1962]). Pursuant to that definition neither type of simple assault as understood at common law was deemed serious enough to justify the effort and expense of inclusion in the Uniform Crime Reports. Offensive touching type battery is also excluded from the Uniform Crime Reports. Only crimes resulting in serious physical harm were included in a category generically termed "aggravated assault" (Federal Bureau of Investigation, *Crime in the 2002, United States*, Section II at 3 [hereinafter, Uniform Crime Reports]). In this way, the Uniform Crime Reports limits its data collection to those aggravated assaults that are "an unlawful attack by one person upon another for the purpose of inflicting severe or aggravated bodily injury" (Uniform Crime Reports, §VII, 454). The FBI further limits reportable aggravated assaults to those assaults involving the use of a weapon or some other means likely to produce death or great bodily harm (Uniform Crime Reports, § VII, 454). It should be noted that this definition does not restrict aggravated assaults to crimes with a high level of harm actually caused, but rather focuses upon the potential harm that could occur based upon the weapon or means involved.

Aggravated assaults accounted for 7.5% of the total crimes reported in the Uniform Crime Reports in 2002 (Uniform Crime Reports, § II, 11). This figure represented a slight drop in both the number of aggravated assaults included in the 2001 Uniform Crime Report, and also the percentage of aggravated assaults to total crime, continuing a 9-year decline for that offense (Uniform Crime Reports, § II, 66; § IV, 242). However, aggravated assault still accounted for the largest percentage of all violent crimes reported in 2002: 62.7% (Uniform Crime Reports, § II, 37).

Aggravated assaults as reported by the Uniform Crime Reports have been further broken down into categories based upon the weapon used in the assault. Almost 28% of all aggravated assaults occurred by means of the attacker using his or her own body (personal weapons) to inflict harm upon the victim. Firearms were used in 19% of aggravated assaults and knives or cutting instruments were the weapon used in 17.8% of these crimes. More than 35% of all weapons, however, were clubs or other blunt instruments that could be used to inflict harm upon a victim (Uniform Crime Reports, § II, 216).

Almost 80% of all persons arrested for aggravated assault were male (Uniform Crime Reports, § IV, 251). Eighty-seven percent of all persons arrested for this crime were 18 years of age or older (Uniform Crime Reports, § IV, 250). For males, the age groups with the highest number of reported aggravated assaults were those 16–30 years of age (Uniform Crime Reports, § IV, 246). While females accounted for an overall smaller percentage of criminal acts, the age groups ranging from 13 to 44, all showed more than 1500 crimes per year with a spike to 2500 crimes per year in the 20–22 year age group.

Racially, those categorized as white equaled 63.4% of the total group arrested for aggravated assault in 2002 (Uniform Crime Reports, § IV, 252). Blacks constituted 34.2% of those arrested for aggravated assault in 2002, and other races accounted for the remainder of the total.

ALISON MCKENNEY BROWN

References and Further Reading

Black, H.C., et al. (1979). *Black's Law Dictionary,* 105 (5th ed.). St. Paul, MN: West Publishing.

Federal Bureau of Investigation (2003) *Crime in the United States, 2002.* Federal Crime Reports, Washington, DC: Government Printing Office.

Hails K.J. (1997). *Criminal Law.* Incline Village, NV: Copperhouse Publishing.

See also **Assault and Battery: The Law**

Assault and Battery: The Law

The crime of assault generally requires the intent of one person to inflict injury or offensive contact on another person. A threat of inflicting injury or offensive contact can constitute assault, as long as that threat is immediate; thus, an assault need not involve an actual touching. Specific intent is not required for an assault to take place; in other words, the actor need not have intended that the specific result occur, only that some injury or offensive contact take place. Thus, if a person intends to strike another on the shoulder and ends up striking the person's skull instead, an assault has still taken place regardless of the fact that the actor's original intent was not the action carried out. Mere words will not constitute a criminal assault; there must also be a present ability to carry out the intended act. Hence, a threat to carry out some action at a future time will not be considered an assault. Because assault involves a person's intent, authorities differ on whether a person can be prosecuted for an attempt to commit assault, or if the prosecution of an assault assumes attempt. Assault charges often form the basis for other crimes such as domestic violence, child abuse, and abuse of the elderly. Federal statutes make it a crime to assault certain types of government officials and establish sentence enhancements for hate crimes, which include assaults against persons of certain minority and other legally protected groups. In developing the common law of assault, the English courts also developed an aggravated assault category. English law also recognizes certain types of behavior that do not constitute criminal assault, such as boxing and contact sports.

Assault charges are often accompanied by battery charges. Battery is generally defined as a wrongful physical contact with another, without that person's consent. In many states, the two charges are combined into one, as "assault and battery," because instances of assault and battery are often carried out at the same time or within very close proximity of each other. A completely accidental touching does not arise to the level of a battery, but a touching brought about by the negligence of the actor may constitute battery. A touching is offensive for purposes of establishing a battery if that touching would offend a reasonable person's sense of dignity. In some jurisdictions, one must show that some bodily injury or physical harm was inflicted to prove that a battery took place. However, an assault can exist on its own, and it is often said that battery is the lethal culmination of an assault. Both assault and battery can constitute the basis for a civil lawsuit as well as supporting criminal charges.

Other countries have assault laws similar to those in the U.S. In Australia, a differentiation is made between "assaults", which are criminal in nature and "assault and/or battery", which is considered a tort or civil action. Most intentional acts that result in the interference of a person's bodily integrity will be considered both a crime and a civil wrong. Interestingly, in Australia, female genital mutilation is also considered an "assault" for which both criminal and civil actions may be undertaken.

English law also differentiates between assault and battery. In England, "common assault" is considered a summary offense, although the definitions of assault and battery are similar to those used in the U.S., with assault constituting an act that places someone in fear of an act and battery existing when a person actually applied unlawful force to another person. In England, a person could also be charged with "assault occasioning actual bodily harm." This offense requires proof of assault or battery, as well as some sort of physical harm or significant psychiatric harm.

English case law requires that recklessness constitutes sufficient *mens rea* for the offense of assault. In fact, in one case, the English courts declared that silence can constitute assault; in that case intimidating, although silent, phone calls, were considered an assault. However, any threat must be immediate; the threat of some future action will generally not rise to the level of assault.

Tina M. Fryling

References and Further Reading

Dietz, L.H., *Assault and Battery, American Jurisprudence 2d. 6*, Matthew J.C., Ed., Danvers, MA: West Group, 1999.

Doerner, W.G. and Steven, P.L., *Victimology*, 2nd ed., Cincinnati, OH: Anderson Publishing Co., 1998.

Fletcher, G.P., *Crime of Self-Defense*, Birmingham, Ala: Notable Trials Library, 1991.

Hagan, F.E. *Criminology,* 4th ed., Chicago, IL: Nelson-Hall, 1998.

Hindelang, M.J. *Sourcebook of Criminal Justice Statistics*, Washington, DC: U.S. Department of Justice, Bureau of Justice Statistics, 1999.

Odem, M.E. and Clay-Warner, J., *Confronting Rape and Sexual Assault,* Wilmington, DE: Scholarly Resources, Inc., 1988.

See also **Assault and Battery: Extent and Correlates; Domestic Assault: Extent and Correlates; Domestic Assault: The Law**

Assembly Line Justice

See **Due Process**

Asset Forfeiture

Societal standards concerning the legitimacy of various forms of wealth accumulation are reflected in law. The criminal law is the standard by which guilt is determined and appropriate and proportionate sanctions specified, one of which is asset forfeiture. Asset forfeiture occurs when a property owner, whose property is said to be directly involved in an applicable criminal action, has property (i.e., assets) seized by law enforcement. Seizure of assets is the first of several steps taken by law enforcement and the legal system in a multifaceted process also involving the criminal and civil courts.

After personal assets are seized, either through surrender or force, judicial action to forfeit ownership of such property to the government occurs. Property subject to seizure includes contraband (e.g., drugs, stolen merchandise, illegal weapons), resources used to help facilitate the crime (e.g., car, house, boat, money), and objects that constitute the proceeds of the crime (e.g., money, cars, jewelry). Applicable criminal action can be anything from terrorist activity to organized crime activities, such as gambling, depending on current statutes. Most often in situations involving forfeiture, however, the pertinent criminal action will be a drug offense. This is most certainly the result of the recent history of drug enforcement law and policy reform, in particular the expansion of law enforcement powers provided by the "War on Drugs."

There is a very distinct boundary that separates two fundamentally different types of asset forfeiture. Criminal asset forfeiture occurs when a person, charged and convicted of a crime, is then forced to surrender ownership of the assets implicated in alleged criminal events. The other type of asset forfeiture is civil asset forfeiture. The major difference is that criminal asset forfeiture is dependent on the conviction of the accused, whereby this accused property owner is afforded all the due process rights and protections against unwarranted punishment (Hyde, 1995). Civil asset forfeiture happens completely independent of any criminal trial, and the property owner's proven guilt or innocence is theoretically inconsequential to the forfeiture. In civil forfeiture cases, the property is, in essence, being charged with criminal involvement, virtually ignoring the property owner's interest in the asset(s). These *in rem* proceedings allow law enforcement to seize a suspected criminal's assets without requiring the agency to mount a criminal prosecution. If a property owner feels that his or her assets were seized unduly then he or she must then become the claimant in a civil case whereby he or she must endure relaxed due process protections (including standard of proof, indigent owner, and self incrimination) to retain ownership of his or her property.

The history and origins of asset forfeiture can be traced back thousands of years. In the time of the Hebrew Exodus from Egypt God instructed Moses that an ox that gores a man should be put to death (Exodus, 21, 28). The verse establishes the long-lived notion that property, in this case an ox, can be held responsible for reprehensible actions even though it is unable to morally comprehend any such events (Hyde, 1995). The notion is pressed further in Medieval England by the custom of deodands (Sutton, 1997). Deodand, meaning "god-gifts" (Cawthon, 1989) or "to be given to God" (*Calero-Toledo v. Pearson Yacht Leasing Co.* 94 S. Ct. 2080, 1974) is a word used to describe property (be it an animal or an inanimate object) that was seized by the Crown as a result of the property causing the death of a human (EOAF, 2002). The actual practice of asset forfeiture would soon be realized in England and eventually the U.S. from amidst the Admiralty laws that governed maritime trade and traffic in both countries. Forfeiture of a vessel or the cargo was often a punishment assigned by admiralty courts for vessels caught smuggling or avoiding customs duty fees or taxes (Williams, 2002). British admiralty standards were adopted in U.S. statutes from the outset of early America. In 1789, for example, the first U.S. Congress established the legal use of civil forfeitures in certain circumstances. That Congress also provided jurisdiction of admiralty cases to the federal court (Pratt and Petersen, 1991; Williams, 2002).

In 1827, the Supreme Court posited a ruling that established the legal basis for civil asset forfeiture in America. It was determined that property, in fact, could be civilly charged and seized for an offense independent of the guilt of the involved owner or possessor (*In Re the Palmyra 1827*, Williams, 2002). Later, during the War between the States, the Confiscation Act of 1862 was passed, legalizing the seizure of confederate property (Hyde, 1995; Pratt and Petersen, 1991; Williams, 2002). The issue faced several Constitutional problems that were later justified by the Supreme Court as acceptable because of the extraordinary circumstances of war.

Twentieth century America has seen a relative explosion in forfeiture statutes and practices. The prohibition era of the 1920s gave law enforcement officials the power to seize assets used in the "production, importation, and consumption of alcoholic beverages" (Hyde, 1995, 23). Then, in response to the bourgeoning problems of organized crime, the U.S. Congress passed three important acts. The "Racketeer Influenced and Corrupt Organization Act" (RICO) includes provisions to the *Organized Crime Control Act of 1970*, along with the *Comprehensive Drug Abuse Prevention and Control Act of 1970* and the *Continuing Criminal Enterprise Act* (CCE), all of which strengthen law enforcement initiatives to thwart organized crime. The main advancement was that now not only could law enforcement seize contraband, but also the property used to facilitate the crime and property that represented the proceeds of the crime were subject to forfeiture (Williams, 2002). The idea was to impede the organizations' ability to financially maintain or expand itself by hurting them where it counts—in the pocketbook (Warchol and Johnson, 1996).

The American "war on drugs" began during the 1980s set forfeiture into the commonly used context that we know today. The war on drugs produced significant legislation, such as *the Comprehensive Crime Control Act of 1984* and the *Anti-Drug Abuse Act of 1986*. Scholars posit that these acts expanded the government's forfeiture powers with three major developments: (1) the introduction of the Asset Forfeiture Fund to house those assets and proceeds seized by the Department of Justice, (2) the establishment of the Equitable Sharing Program made it possible for the federal government to get assistance from, and share proceeds with, state and local agencies, and (3) the newfound ability to offer percentages of the proceeds to informants that assist in the detection of certain illegal activities that eventually leads to forfeiture (Warchol and Johnson, 1996; Miller and Selva, 1994).

Although research on asset forfeiture is relatively limited, there are several studies that provide good insight on some of the characteristics and conditions that surround current asset forfeiture policies and practices. In a very broad exploratory study, Warchol and Johnson (1996) examined several procedural aspects of forfeitures from one federal judicial district, finding that "monetary instruments" are most often pursued on the legal grounds that they were the proceeds of a drug transaction, that "real property" was more likely to be pursued on the charge that it was used to facilitate a drug transaction, and that the average time for an entire civil forfeiture action, from initiation to final disposition was less than 1 year. They also noted certain trends in forfeiture practice, for example, asset seizures worth more than $100,000 were more likely to involve a proactive, or preplanned, investigation and, even though real property was the most frequently seized asset, conveyances (vehicles, vessels, or aircraft) were the most likely assets to result in forfeiture. Also, reactive investigations tended to result in a higher percentage of forfeiture dispositions, and much lower dismissal dispositions than those investigations that were preplanned.

Although this study is limited to one geographic space, its significance lies in its exposure of common procedural characteristics of civil asset forfeiture cases. It also provides an empirical basis for the common mistrust of law enforcement motivations by relating characteristics such as property value to other variables such as proactive or reactive investigation types. If law enforcement does in fact have an impure motive, then they would probably give proactive investigative attention to assets that are worth more money, which was found to be the case in the Warchol and Johnson (1996) study.

Miller and Selva (1994) pioneered the academic criticism of law enforcement motives in a study where one of the authors infiltrated the world of drug enforcement exposing unintended consequences that naturally accompany the practice of forfeiture. Their most significant finding was that the priorities of drug enforcement had shifted to asset seizure, instead of drug control. Consequently, investigations and seizures were selected based on the assets of the suspect and not necessarily on the threat to society, such as the quantity of drugs they possess (i.e., the prioritization of profitability over culpability).

Worrall (2001) examined the issue of law enforcement dependency on forfeiture proceeds, directly asking the executives of a large sample of police agencies around the United States if civil asset forfeiture was necessary as a budgetary supplement. A substantial number of agencies responded that they strongly agreed that there is agency reliance on civil forfeiture proceeds, this dependency much less evident in smaller and rural agencies. Warchol, Payne, and Johnson (1996) compared the use of civil and administrative forfeitures with criminal forfeiture and found that administrative forfeitures are simply forfeitures where the property owner makes no challenge to the seizure. Civil and administrative forfeitures were also found to account for approximately 99% of all forfeitures studied across four major federal judicial districts in 1991 and 1992. The authors argue that such procedures significantly disadvantage citizens, claimants, or the accused although conveniently expediting the work of the government. Vecchi and Sigler (2001) studied law enforcement officers in southeastern Florida to identify officer perception of asset forfeiture goals and whether officer attitudes were consistent with policy. Agents or officers belonging to federal agencies were much less concerned with "funding the agency" as a goal of forfeiture, while members of local agencies focused more on income generation.

Civil asset forfeiture is surrounded by controversy. Major points of contention include the constitutionality of the practice, especially as it pertains to the Fourth, Fifth, and Eighth Amendments to the Constitution (Pratt and Petersen, 1991; Tonry, 1996), the facilitation of corrupt law enforcement motives and practices, and civil rights concerns (Hyde, 1995).

Due process procedures are often overlooked in civil asset forfeiture cases because the property is being charged independent of the person involved, and property has no due process protections (Jensen and Gerber, 1996). This harsh reality significantly disadvantages indigent owners that cannot afford an attorney to represent their property in civil court. The standard of proof that the state must meet to realize forfeiture is only a "preponderance of the evidence," instead of "beyond a reasonable doubt." The Civil Asset Forfeiture Reform Act of 2000 has attempted to improve some of these conditions, including shifting the burden of proof to the state. The additional concessions in the Act are not strong enough, however, to really allay other due process and constitutional problems.

One lingering concern regarding current forfeiture practices involves the Fourth Amendment protection against unreasonable searches and seizures as well as the exclusionary rule (Pratt and Petersen, 1991). The Second Circuit has stated, "an illegal seizure of property does not immunize that property from forfeiture" (*U.S. v. $37,780 in U.S. currency* 920 F.2d 159, *1990*). Nelson (1992) argues that because police officers in civil forfeiture cases are in pursuit of forfeiture, instead of conviction, that the exclusionary rule offers little deterrence in guiding their search and seizure practices.

The next controversy pertains to the Fifth Amendment's provision against self-incrimination. The Fifth Amendment affirms that a person not be compelled to be a witness against himself in a criminal case. It does not, however, disallow adverse consequences to those unwilling to testify in a civil forfeiture case to avoid loss of assets (Pratt and Petersen, 1991; U.S. Constitution). Tonry (1996) points out that pitting an individual against a civil case and criminal case for the same charge or action may also violate the Fifth Amendment's protection against double jeopardy. To date, *United States v. Ursery* (116 S. Ct. 2135, 1996) sets the standard that double jeopardy claims in this context are not valid because civil forfeiture is remedial in nature rather than punitive, although other courts have been inclined to disagree.

A final point of contention within asset forfeiture law comes from the Eighth Amendment's protection against the imposition of "excessive fines." Cases in the past have seen largely valuable seizures result from relatively minor crimes (*United States v. One 1986 Mercedes Benz* 846 F.2d 2, 1988), calling into question the constitutional principle of proportionality. While drug-related forfeiture cases are, in fact, subject to Eighth Amendment protection against excessive fines (*Austin v. United States* 113 S. Ct. 2801, 1993), legal standards offer minimal protection in real-world instances where cases seldom reach the juncture of judicial scrutiny.

Several researchers have shown their disagreement with law enforcement initiatives and motivations concerning asset forfeiture practices, generally contending a conflict of interest between budget supplementation and crime control (Hyde, 1995; Miller and Selva, 1994; Blumenson and Nilsen, 1998). Hyde (1995) points out that another problem with asset forfeiture is that there is no legislative oversight for much of the revenue generated through asset forfeiture. With no legislative oversight, the agencies become more self-sustaining and less accountable and responsive to their governing body and citizenry. Zalman (1996) sternly rejects parts of asset forfeiture on the grounds that it undermines the fundamental "Lockean principles" upon which our entire republican society is grounded.

Finally, innocent owners present another problem for asset forfeiture. Past cases, such as *Bennis v. Michigan* (116 S. Ct. 994, 1996), have not made being an innocent owner a legitimate defense in retaining one's property. The Civil Asset Forfeiture Reform Act of 2000 has alleviated much of this concern by establishing a uniform innocent owner defense standard.

Despite the existence of a federal office overseeing asset forfeiture, the practice, rather conspicuously, has not been examined on par with the vast level of resources involved. None of the major federal funding agencies (e.g., the National Institute of Justice and the Bureau of Justice Statistics) have funded empirical investigation, thus many dimensions of the forfeiture phenomenon remain unknown. Foremost among the unanswered research questions specific to forfeiture is the role of legal culture on the practice of forfeiture. Presumably, the extent of forfeiture-oriented policing corresponds to actual level of illicit drug activity within an area, but the true level of forfeiture practice may be more a result of prosecutor training concerning forfeiture law.

J. MITCHELL MILLER AND ROBERT A. FOSTER, JR.

References and Further Reading

Blumenson, E. and Nilsen, E. (1998). Policing for profit: The drug war's hidden economic agenda. *University of Chicago Law Review*, 65, 35–114.

Cawthon, E. (1989). New life for the deodand: Coroners' inquests and occupational deaths in England, 1830–46. *American Journal of Legal History*, 33 (2), 137–147.

The Civil Asset Forfeiture Reform Act of 2000. Public Law 106–185, 106th Congress.

The Executive Office for Asset Forfeiture (EOAF). (2002). Available at http://www.eoaf.treas.gov/. United States Department of the Treasury.

Exodus, 21: 28. The New King James Version.

Hyde, H. (1995). Forfeiting Our Property Rights: Is your property safe from seizure? Washington, DC: Cato Institute.

Jensen, E. L. and Gerber J. (1996). The civil forfeiture of assets and the war on drugs: Expanding criminal sanctions while reducing due process protections. *Crime and Delinquency*, 42 (3), 421–434.

Miller, J.M. and Selva, L.H. (1994). Drug enforcement's double edged sword: An assessment of asset forfeiture programs. *Justice Quarterly*, 11 (2), 313–335.

Nelson, W.P. (1992). Should the Ranch Go Free Because the Constable Blundered? Gaining Compliance with Search and Seizure Standards in the Age of Asset Forfeiture. *California Law Review*, 80, 1309–1359.

Pratt, G.C. and Petersen, W.B. (1991). Civil forfeiture in the second circuit. *St. John's Law Review*, 65, 653–672.

Sutton, T. (1997). The deodand and responsibility for death. *Journal of Legal History* [Great Britain], 18 (3), 44–55.

Tonry, M. (1996). *Forfeiture laws, Practice, and Controversies in the U.S.*: A report to the Max-Planck institute, Freiburg. Unpublished Report.

Vecchi, G.M. and Sigler, R.T. (2001). *Assets Forfeiture: A study of policy and its practice*. Durham, NC: Carolina Academic Press.

Warchol, G.L. and Johnson, B.R. (1996). Guilty property: A quantitative analysis of civil asset forfeiture. *American Journal of Criminal Justice*, 21 (1), 61–81.

Warchol, G.L., Payne, D.M., and Johnson, B.R. (1996). Criminal forfeiture: An effective alternative to civil and administrative proceedings. *Police Studies*, 19 (3), 51–66.

Williams, H.E. (2002). *Asset Forfeiture: A Law Enforcement Prospective*. Springfield, IL: Charles C. Thomas Publisher.

Worrall, J.L. (2001). Addicted to the drug war: The role of civil asset forfeiture as a budgetary necessity in contemporary law enforcement. *Journal of Criminal Justice*, 29,171–187.

Zalman, M. (1996). Judges in their own case: A Lockean critique of law enforcement asset sharing in drug forfeiture law and practice. *Criminal Justice Review*, 21 (2), 1996.

See also **Drug Control Policy: Enforcement, Interdiction, and the War on Drugs; Police: Brutality and Corruption; Organized Crime: Enforcement Strategies**

Attachment Theory

See **Psychological Theories of Criminal Behavior; Social Control Theory**

Attempted and Incomplete Offenses

Criminal attempt is one of three traditional inchoate or incomplete offenses. The doctrine of attempted crime has a long history that predates treatment by English common law. Common law held that criminal attempt must involve both specific intent and some action toward the completion of a crime. By the 19th century, Anglo-American law had settled on a criminal attempt doctrine that considered it a separate, albeit incomplete crime (Fletcher, 1998).

As with other offenses, prosecution of criminal attempt requires proof of both the criminal mental state and act. Two theories of criminal attempt have emerged—one focusing on the act as a manifestation of "dangerous conduct" and the other emphasizing the mental state as indicative of an underlying "dangerous person" (Samaha, 1999). These theories consider the criminal scheme and the proximity to the completion of the attempted crime. An offense of criminal attempt has three essential elements. First, the mental state of specific intent whereby the perpetrator purposely intends that the object offense be completed. Second, that the offender engaged in actions that went "beyond mere preparation" toward the completion of the crime. Third, that the crime was not consummated or completed. Modern statutes typically view criminal attempt as a separate and distinct incomplete crime, regardless of the crime being attempted (Kaci, 1997).

Numerous legal and physical factors contribute to the determination of whether a person engaged in criminal attempt. Dimensions of the *actus reus* or criminal act component of criminal attempt can present legal difficulties in prosecuting the offense. Though the establishment of criminal attempt requires the showing that an act constitutes more than preparation, those acts fall somewhere between criminal thought and the completed crime. Courts have developed several standards to analyze at what point a person moves past preparation but falls short of the consummated crime. They seek to reconcile how many steps or levels a person must progress through to constitute criminal attempt. Determination of steps that go beyond preparation is usually based on four standards. The "physical proximity" standard ascertains how close the perpetrator came to completing the offense. It is an analysis of the progression of criminal conduct toward consummation of the crime.

"Probable desistance" is a standard that examines the actor's progress past a point where a reasonable person would have discontinued their steps toward completion of the crime. Using the "equivocality" approach, courts consider whether the postpreparation actions have any other logical purpose than the intended crime (Samaha, 1999). Many courts use the *Model Penal Code* "substantial steps" approach. It assesses whether the person's actions were sufficient to corroborate their criminal intent to commit the object offense (*Model Penal Code* § 5.01 1980). Courts continue to struggle with the issue of how many steps past preparation are required to establish criminal attempt.

Other factors can influence the sufficiency of the requisite elements of criminal attempt. Some statutes or courts require that the perpetrator engage in an "overt act" toward the commission of the crime, in conjunction with passing beyond mere preparation (Klotter, 1994). Extraneous circumstances can interfere with the completion of a crime as in the case of "legal impossibility" or "factual impossibility." Legal impossibility refers to the circumstance where the actor intends to commit an offense and engages in what he or she believes is prohibited conduct. However, criminal prosecution is not possible because the conduct is not illegal. In the case of factual impossibility, a person may be prosecutable for criminal attempt even if events beyond the perpetrator's control prevent him from completing the intended crime. An example is if a person attacked another with intent to kill but the victim, unbeknownst to the perpetrator, was already deceased. Thus, the offender may be prosecuted for an attempted crime even though extraneous factors had prevented the consummation of the offense. Under these conditions, the individual developed the necessary criminal intent and engaged in actions beyond preparation necessary to complete the intended act. Most courts have rejected impossibility as a defense to prosecution for criminal attempt and have concluded that the person may be criminally liable based on his mental state and act in furtherance of criminal attempt (Gardner and Anderson, 2003).

Though courts may conclude that various acts of preparation such as procuring items for use in crime, enticement, or planning activities may not satisfy the required steps of criminal attempt, these conducts may nonetheless be prohibited by law. Voluntary abandonment or renunciation is another issue that arises in the analysis of criminal attempt. Logically, if a person voluntarily halts their actions before moving beyond preparation, that may negate the criminal intent required to prosecute criminal attempt. Some courts have held that once the individual demonstrates the necessary criminal intent, coupled with sufficient steps beyond preparation, they have committed criminal attempt. Hence, renouncing his progression of actions past preparation may not offer an adequate defense to prosecution if the person has moved far enough toward consummation with intent to commit a crime. Other courts, however, have viewed such renunciation as a means of negating the requisite mental state for criminal attempt.

Criminal attempt is established as a separate crime that is frequently punishable at one degree lower that the object offense. In many state statutes, this is a consistent approach used for all of the inchoate offenses (i.e., attempt, conspiracy, solicitation); however, some punish criminal attempt in thc samc way as the object offense (Kaci, 1997). Criminal attempt is a difficult offense to prosecute because of the complexity of determining the progression of events beyond preparation. Hence, many courts use a variety of standards to arrive at a conclusion about the necessary steps one must move beyond to establish criminal attempt. Though the variance of factors influencing the *act* can be confounding (i.e., impossibility, nonconsummation, renunciation or abandonment, and required steps), the requisite mental state is usually specific intent. Impossibility defenses are rarely accepted in the prosecution of criminal attempt. The most pivotal determinant in deciding whether a person has committed criminal attempt is their movement "beyond preparation." Thus, the demarcation between legal thoughts and illegal attempted crime often hinges on that point.

William P. Bloss

References and Further Reading

Fletcher, G., *Basic Concepts of Criminal Law*, New York, NY: Oxford University Press, 1998.

Gardner, T. and Anderson, T., *Criminal Law,* 8th ed., Belmont, CA: West/Wadsworth, 2003.

Kaci, J., *Criminal Law*, Incline Village, NV: Copperhouse Publishing, 1997.

Klotter, J., *Criminal Law,* 4th ed., Cincinnati, OH: Anderson Publishing, 1994.

Model Penal Code, American Law Institute, 1980.

Samaha, J., *Criminal Law,* 6th ed., Belmont, CA: West/Wadsworth, 1999.

See also ***Actus Reus*****; Conspiracy to Commit a Crime**

At-Risk Youth

See **Juvenile Delinquency**

Attica

See **Prison History: U.S.**

Australia, Crime and Justice in

Introduction

Australia covers an area of around 3 million square miles (8 million square kilometers) and has an ethnically diverse population of 19 million drawn largely from Europe, South and East Asia, and the Middle East. Prior to colonization by Britain after 1788, Australia was populated for more than 40,000 years by around 1 million indigenous people. Since then the indigenous population has dropped to 380,000, constituting just 2% of the current overall population.

The administration of criminal law differs around the nation, a federation of six states and two territories. For example, in Western Australia, Queensland, Tasmania, the Northern Territory, and the Australian Capital Territory, criminal offenses are codified, while in South Australia, New South Wales, and Victoria, criminal law derives from common law and statute. Definitions of crime as well as patterns of policing, adjudication, and punishment vary between states and territories. Some criminal laws are administered by the Commonwealth and apply to the whole of the population.

Crime

Since 1900, official rates of criminal offending have displayed few fluctuations. A downward trend coincided with the First and Second World Wars, none too surprising given that thousands of those considered "most at risk" of offending—poorly educated or unemployed young men—were enlisted and stationed abroad. Since 1945, rates of homicide, rape, robbery, assault, and theft have climbed slowly, partly the result of widening differences in income levels.

Information about crime in Australia can be discerned from official police statistics and victim surveys. Police statistics track the rate of reported crime per 100,000 people and provide some details about the nature of offenders, victims, and crimes. In 1998, police statistics revealed 284 victims of murder and 49 victims of manslaughter—a combined rate of 1.8 victims per 100,000, less than one homicide per day. For more than 20 years, around 87% of homicide offenders have been male. Chances of becoming a victim of homicide increased for the unemployed and for unmarried men aged between 25 and 44, females aged between 15 and 24, and indigenous people. This last group faced the greatest risk of becoming homicide victims, with a rate seven times greater than the wider population. "Stranger" homicides were rare, with 80% of victims sharing some relationship with offenders. In all but 5% of cases, homicides resulted in a single fatality. Mass murders involving four or more victims occur, on average, at one per year. One involved the shooting by a lone offender of 35 men, women, and children at Port Arthur in Tasmania in April 1996. In the last four decades, nine serial killers have been brought to justice. In 2000, in the Snowtown killings, four defendants were charged with ten murders in South Australia.

In 1998, there were 709 recorded victims of assault and 77 victims of sexual assault per 100,000 persons. Two out of every five assaults occurred in homes, and just over one in five in public places. Women were more vulnerable to being assaulted in the home, whereas men were more likely to be assaulted in public. With the important exception of sexual assault, men experienced assault at a greater rate than women.

Property-related crime accounted for 70% of recorded crime. Just under half a million unlawful entries of property with intent to commit an offense (including burglary, breaking and entering, and some stealing) were recorded in 1998. In addition, there were 131,000 motor vehicle thefts and just over half a million other thefts (including pickpocketing, bag snatching, and shoplifting).

The 1998 national victimization survey indicates varying levels of discrepancies between reported and unreported crime. About 2% of motor vehicle thefts and 22% of household break-ins go unreported. Figures for robbery and sexual assault are much higher, with 50% and 67% of incidents, respectively, eluding official criminal statistics. Victimization rates differed between jurisdictions, with Western Australia reporting highest rates for motor vehicle theft and actual and attempted break-ins, and the Australian Capital Territory the highest levels of sexual and nonsexual assaults.

A 1998-99 national survey asked persons over the age of 18 to identify the criminal activity that concerned them the most. Ninety-one percent cited illegal drugs, 83% family violence, 83% sexual assault, and 86% other physical assaults. When asked about their own neighborhood, 65% listed housebreaking, 53% motor vehicle theft, and 46% graffiti and vandalism. Respondents were also asked how safe they felt. Ninety-three percent felt safe or very safe if they were home alone during the day, with slightly less saying they felt safe after dark. These perceptions of crime differed vastly from officially recorded crime rates.

Crime prevention programs exist in all jurisdictions, usually administered by local councils. Some of the better known initiatives have included education and publicity campaigns aimed, for example, at drunk driving, domestic violence, and homophobic violence; broad community development approaches such as those facilitating a dialogue between young and elderly about fear of crime; targeted programs including those teaching automotive and teamwork skills to at-risk youth; situational prevention initiatives such as security cameras, high-tech alarms, and scratch-resistant surfaces; and police informant campaigns such as Crime Stoppers. Nevertheless, these activities have not been able to displace the rhetoric of law and order as the primary means of preventing crime.

Justice

In 1998-99 governments allocated A$5.5 billion (A$286 per person) to the criminal justice system—71% to policing, 7% to criminal courts administration, and 21% to correctional services—an annual average increase in public spending of 4% since 1994-95.

Each state and territory has its own police force with the Australian Federal Police functioning both as local police for the Australian Capital Territory and as investigators of crimes (such as drug offenses and money laundering) that cross state and national borders. The National Crime Authority is responsible for dealing with organized crime. As of 1998-99 about 52,000 police were employed around Australia, with just under a third being female. However, women occupied less than 1% of the 2000 most senior positions. Generally speaking, reaction to, rather than primary prevention of, crime dominates policing. Despite critical findings of police violence and corruption by the 1989 Fitzgerald Royal Commission in Queensland, the Human Rights and Equal Opportunity Commission in 1991, and the 1997 Wood Royal Commission in New South Wales, a national survey conducted in 1998 and 1999 had, respectively, half and two-thirds of respondents agreeing that police treat people "fairly and equally" and provide satisfactory levels of service.

The number of cases appearing before courts increased by 20% in the late 1990s. Although court structures differ between states and territories, each jurisdiction adopts the adversarial model of justice, meaning the prosecution (the Crown) decides the charges the defendant will face and seeks to prove guilt beyond all reasonable doubt. In higher courts, which hear approximately 7% of all criminal cases, the prosecution is usually led by staff representing the Director of Public Prosecutions. In lower courts, where a high proportion of cases involve minor traffic infringements, prosecutors are typically police officers. The accused has a right to be represented by a lawyer where the offense is serious, and, if necessary, the cost will be borne by the state. Convicted offenders may appeal against their conviction or sentences to the relevant appeal court. In some circumstances, the prosecution may appeal against the leniency of a sentence. The highest court of appeal is the High Court of Australia.

Although there have been numerous calls to reign in judicial discretion in matters of sentencing, the power of the bench remains largely intact. Nevertheless, there have been moves to impose minimum periods of imprisonment on courts. Mandatory sentencing laws have been introduced in Western Australia ("three strikes" and the offender goes to prison), New South Wales, and the Northern Territory ("one strike") for particular kinds of property offenders. Such laws have led to an increase in the prison population and have been criticized as being inflexible, ineffective, discriminatory against indigenous offenders, and in violation of international human rights obligations under the International Covenant on Civil and Political Rights. However, more liberal sentencing options do exist. For example, the New South Wales Drug Court in western Sydney diverts heroin-addicted nonviolent offenders from prison by handing offenders a suspended sentence during which they are required to participate in an intensively supervised 12-month drug program.

With the abolition of capital punishment in New South Wales in 1985, imprisonment stands as the most severe sanction across Australia. In 1998-99 there were approximately 18,000 persons serving custodial sentences in public prisons (82 facilities) and about 2000 persons serving such in private prisons (15 facilities)—an imprisonment rate of 145 and a punishment rate of 362.5 persons per 100,000 adults. Men constituted 94% of custodial prisoners, and their average sentence was 4.7 years. Nearly half of all sentenced prisoners were convicted for crimes involving actual or threatened violence, 9% for drug-related offenses and only one-quarter for property offenses. For women, the average custodial sentence was 3.1 years, and the most common offenses that led to imprisonment were fraud, breaking and entering, dealing and trafficking in drugs, and robbery. Women continue to experience all kinds of problems relating to child rearing, health services, and the masculine culture perpetuated by correctional staff. On average, nearly two thirds of all prisoners had served previous time in jail. Between 1983 and 1998 the rate of imprisonment increased by over 50%, placing considerable strain on correctional services—throughout 1998-99 the number of people imprisoned in Queensland, Western Australia, South Australia, and the Australian Capital Territory exceeded prison capacity.

Community-based sanctions are used three times more often than imprisonment. Eighty percent of offenders placed on these programs are male. Such programs are used with offenders who would not be sent to prison, to divert offenders from prison, or as a postcustodial early-release program. Community-based sanctions include financial penalties (fines), supervised community-based penalties (such as community service orders, intensive supervision orders, and home detention), unsupervised community-based penalties (bonds), and conditional release (parole).

Recently, advocates of a "get tough" approach to juvenile crime have authorized increased police powers and harsher sentences for youth. On the other hand, most jurisdictions have also adopted a restorative approach, involving formal or informal police cautioning for minor offenses and family conferencing for more serious issues where offenders have acknowledged their guilt.

Aboriginal juveniles were 10 times more likely to appear in court, and aboriginal adults were 29 times more likely to be arrested and 17 times more likely to be imprisoned than other Australians. The 1994 National Aboriginal and Torres Strait Islander Survey found that approximately 20% of indigenous people aged over 13 had been arrested or detained over the previous 5 years. On an average between 25% and 33% of aboriginal males experience imprisonment during their lives. Indigenous women made up almost half of women arrested and held in custody and were over 13 times more likely to go to prison than their nonindigenous counterparts. As a result of their overrepresentation in prisons, aboriginal people died in custody at a rate 23 times greater than nonindigenous Australians. In 1993, Amnesty International concluded that the Australian criminal justice system left indigenous Australians vulnerable to highly disproportionate levels of incarceration and to cruel, inhuman, or degrading treatment.

Conclusion

The Australian criminal justice system is finding it increasingly difficult to respond to political, economic, and social demands. Governments use the criminal justice system as a device for transforming the structural issues that traditionally lead to offending into individual issues that speak of the offender's lack of responsibility or self-restraint. Although a large proportion of Australians feel safe and secure in the operation of the criminal justice system, the failure of official police statistics to include information on government, corporate, or environmental crimes reflects the continuing targeting of the powerless rather than the powerful. Not surprisingly, many groups feel Australian criminal justice consistently serves all manner of interests but their own.

MARK HALSEY AND MARK ISRAEL

References and Further Reading

Australian Illicit Drug Report, 1998–99 (2000).

Australian Institute of Criminology, *Australian Crime: Facts and Figures, 1999,* Canberra: Australian Institute of Criminology, 1999.

Chappell, D. and Wilson, P.R., Eds., *The Australian Criminal Justice System: The Mid 1980s*, Sydney: Butterworths, 1986; updated edition, as *Crime and the Criminal Justice System in Australia: 2000 and Beyond*, 2000.

Findlay, M., Odgers, S., and Yeo, S.M.H., *Australian Criminal Justice*, South Melbourne, Victoria: Oxford University Press, 1994; 2nd ed., 1999.

Harding, R.W., *Private Prisons and Public Accountability*, New Brunswick, NJ: Transaction, and Buckingham, Buckinghamshire: Open University Press, 1997.

Johnston, E., *National Report,* 5 Vols., Canberra: AGPS, 1991.

McLennan, W., *Women's Safety, Australia, 1996*, Canberra: Australian Bureau of Statistics, 1996.

Mouzos, J., *Homicidal Encounters: A Study of Homicide in Australia, 1989–1999*, Canberra: Australian Institute of Criminology, 2000.

O'Malley, P. and Sutton, A., Eds., *Crime Prevention in Australia: Issues in Policy and Research*, Annandale, New South Wales: Federation Press, 1997.

Productivity Commission, *Report on Government Services, 2000,* Canberra: AustInfo, 2000.

See also **Penal Colonies; United Kingdom, Crime and Justice in**

B

Babylonian Legal Traditions

Rise of Babylon

The Babylonians were one of four invaders in the ancient Near East to unify the diverse city-states of Mesopotamia, a region situated between the Tigris and Euphrates rivers in modern day Iraq. Dating back to the formation in Mesopotamia of the world's first cities (ca. 3500–3000 BCE), scorching deserts and vast swamplands had inhibited unification of the region, ensuring that early Mesopotamian cities would develop into independent states by 3000 BCE. The Semitic chieftain Sargon of Akkad succeeded in briefly uniting Mesopotamia under his rule around 2300 BCE. When Sargon's Akkadian Empire declined around 2000 BCE, a period of chaos and civil war raged for nearly 400 years. Eventually, the power void left by the Akkadian empire was filled by a Semitic people from the city of Babylon, whose most notable ruler, King Hammurabi, conquered Mesopotamia between 1800 and 1750 BCE, thereby founding an empire that reached from southwest Iran to eastern Syria.

Hammurabi and the Origins of the Code

Like all unifiers of culturally and politically diverse areas, Hammurabi faced the problem of how to administer justice when the legal norms of formerly autonomous city-states conflicted with each other. The problem was especially acute in cases in which the parties hailed from different city-states. Each litigant would turn to the laws of his city-state to resolve it, and the potential for fractious dispute over the choice of law would always be at hand. In order to address this issue, Hammurabi reserved to himself the power to decide these cases. What would eventually emerge as a written "code" of legal principles binding throughout the Babylonian Empire may have been Hammurabi's decisions in particular cases reduced to writing. The Code may have, in other words, a basis in the "common law" determinations of the King and his agents. In 1901-02, archaeological excavations at Susa in southwest Iran uncovered a diorite stele from the second millennium BCE inscribed with the Code of Hammurabi. At the time of its discovery, it was the oldest set of written laws in world history. Although later excavations have unearthed at least three legal codices in Mesopotamia yet older than Hammurabi's, none of them can rival the latter for the range and intensity of its influence on subsequent Western civilization.

The Laws

The laws that make up the Code of Hammurabi are grouped in at least 260 sections, and pertain to the following areas of law:

Administration of Justice
Offense against Property
Real Estate and Domiciles
Merchants and Agents
Women, Marriage, & Inheritance
Crimes against the Person

Professional Fees & Responsibilities
Agriculture
Rates of Hire
Slave Ownership

These substantive areas of law are preceded by a prologue that vouches for Hammurabi's credentials as a lawgiver (he was appointed by the gods "to cause justice to prevail in the land"), and by an epilogue that adjures his successor to "pay attention to the words I have inscribed on my stele,... that he may pluck out the evil and the wicked from his land, and make the flesh of his people glad." Concerning the laws themselves, four characteristics are particularly striking for the modern reader. First, there was little formal equality within the Code, which incorporated the four-fold social divisions of Mesopotamian society (nobility, free clients of the nobility, commoners, and slaves). Babylonian law stipulated that the different social classes enjoyed different legal protections. The nobility were punished less severely for harming commoners than for harming other aristocrats, whereas the persons of slaves were devalued below the members of all other classes. Law #200, for example, holds that "if a man knock out a tooth of a man *of his own rank*, they shall knock out his tooth." Sometimes the laws expressed the double badge of inferiority that victims who were both women and slaves wore in Babylonian society. We read in Law #170 that "if a man strikes the daughter of a free man and causes her to cast that which is within her womb, he shall pay ten shekels of silver for that which is within her womb. If that woman dies as a result, they shall put his daughter to death." If, on the other hand, the woman who died was a slave, the penalty was another fine.

Second, the Code of Hammurabi required that the punishment meted out roughly fit the crime. Clearly, this principle did not extend to crimes committed by a perpetrator on a victim from a lower class but if both the perpetrator and victim belonged to the same class, proportionalism was obligatory. The following provisions reflect this "eye for an eye" principle of equivalence:

#1. If a man accuse another man of murder but is unable to prove it, the accuser shall be put to death.
#3. If a man perjure himself or cannot establish testimony offered in a case involving life, that man shall be put to death.
#53. If a man neglects to maintain his dike and does not reinforce it, and a break is made in his dike and the water carries away the farmland, the man in whose dike the break has been made shall replace the grain that has been damaged.
#196. If a man destroy the eye of another man, they shall destroy his eye.
#197. If he break another man's bone, they shall break his bone.

An aspect of the Code reminiscent of modern legal systems, captured in #53 above, is the importance it ascribes to damages as a means of making whole an aggrieved victim. Losses sustained through the willful or negligent conduct of others were fully compensable—either through an equal harm being inflicted on the accused, or the transfer of property from the offender to the victim. Restitution is one of the Code's dominant themes.

Third, the Code may represent the first effort in human history to promote consumer protection. If a builder faultily constructed a house that later collapsed, killing the occupants, the builder was put to death. If a merchant sought to increase the interest rate on a loan, he forfeited the full amount of the loan. These and similar provisions evidence a desire by Hammurabi to ensure fairness in commercial transactions.

Finally, Hammurabi's Code reflects the universal legal subordination of women in the ancient world. Like its cultural milieu, the Code assigned to the husband almost absolute power over his *ménage*. So capacious was the range of this power that a man could legally sell his wife and children into slavery in order to repay his debts (Law #117). On the other hand, the Code at times strove to protect the lives and well-being of women, as it did in requiring a man who sought to divorce a barren wife to pay her the amount of her "marriage price" and return her dowry (Law #138).

Administration of Justice

As the divinely appointed representative of the gods, Hammurabi and his Babylonian successors were responsible for dispensing justice to their people. An older Mesopotamian tradition, however, allowed private disputes to be resolved by a citizens' assembly, a practice that persisted into the age of the Babylonian empire. All free male citizens were eligible to serve on the citizens' assembly. Sometimes, a case might first be lodged with the king, who would then refer it to the citizens' assembly for adjudication. Officials referred to as "judges" existed in the region as early as the 24th century BCE. Whether they functioned as judges in the modern sense of the term, however, is debatable. Some scholars of ancient law contend that Babylonian judges were probably more akin to assessors who provided assistance to the citizens' assembly in its deliberations. On the other hand, Babylonian documents suggest that the role of judges—particularly in the earliest phases of the Empire—may have been quite active, and the role of the assembly comparatively passive. The need for energetic judges may have been enhanced by a lack of interest among the Babylonians in serving on the assembly. Despite their power in judicial proceedings, Babylonian judges confronted stringent demands imposed by the Code that required them to preserve their judgments, once established, without later alteration. If a judge violated this injunction, he faced a hefty financial penalty and permanent expulsion from the assembly.

The Babylonians of Hammurabi's era brought their cases to the assembly for determination, where a distinctive procedure then unfolded. Evidence was presented by both sides in the dispute. When the evidence clashed or proved inconclusive, the citizens' assembly or the judges could order the litigants to swear an oath before the gods at a temple. The severity of punishment for perjuring oneself before the gods was so intimidating that it sometimes induced one of the parties to quail, resulting in a verdict in favor of the party who took the oath. In an actual case of robbery recorded in Babylonian documents, for example, the judges demanded that the defendant take an oath, which he refused to do. The plaintiff won the case and damages were assessed against the defendant. When the evidence was inconclusive and both parties took an oath before the gods, the assembly or judges determined the verdict through ordeal, a common means of decision-making in premodern legal cultures. The litigants were thrown into the river: whoever sank was deemed guilty. (Note that the Medieval English trial by ordeal reversed the procedure, declaring innocent the party who sank.) The Code of Hammurabi decreed that allegations of witchcraft, if unproven in the assembly, were to be decided by ordeal. If the accused "witch" drowned, then the accused was found guilty, and the accuser received the drowned party's property. If the accused floated, then the accuser was executed and his property given to the accused.

Earlier Mesopotamian Laws and Influence of the Code of Hammurabi

The importance of the Code of Hammurabi in the history of Western legal systems does not reside in its systematization or its novelty. The Code made no pretensions to be an exhaustive codification of Babylonian law; neither Hammurabi's prologue nor his epilogue stakes such a claim, nor do the provisions of the Code cover every legal issue that must have arisen in the daily round of life in the Empire. Moreover, since its discovery in the early 20th century, archaeologists have located three other written sources of Mesopotamian law that predate Hammurabi's Code, i.e., the Laws of Ur-nammu, Lipit-ishtar, and Eshnunna. Scholars speculate that, long before the founding of the Babylonian Empire, every city-state in the region may have possessed its own set of law adapted to local conditions. The most ancient of extant laws, those of Ur-nammu, are written in Sumerian and date back to the Ur III Dynasty (circa 2200 BCE). A comparative reading of these earlier legal texts and the Code of Hammurabi reveals that the notion of proportionalism (*lex talionis*) preexisted the Code by several centuries. The significance of the Code thus lies neither in its codification of Babylonian law nor in its originality, but in transmitting Mesopotamian legal norms to subsequent Western civilization. The vehicle of transmission was the Kassites, a people of unknown origin who temporarily conquered and ruled Babylonia (circa 1595–1200 BCE). The period of Kassite rule was noteworthy for its peace and prosperity as the Kassites advanced northward and southward in quest of access to the profitable trade of the Mediterranean coast. They extended their realm to modern Bahrain in the South while cultivating amicable relations with Egypt and possibly Mycenaean Greece (as suggested by the Kassites' knowledge of Linear B, the language of the Mycenaeans). During the three hundred year "Kassite Interlude," the Kassites preserved the literary, scientific, religious, and legal heritage of Mesopotamian culture, which gradually spread throughout the Near East. Their preservation and diffusion of Babylonian legal thought, with its emphases on restitution, proportionality, and equity, would later influence three of the primary wellsprings of Western civilization: Israel, Greece, and Rome.

Michael Bryant

References and Further Reading

Driver, G.R. and Miles, J.C., *The Babylonian Laws*, Vols. 1 and 2, Oxford University Press, Oxford, U.K., 1952, 1955.

Kraus, F.R., Ein zentrales Problem des altmesopotamischen Rechtes: Was ist der Codex Hammurabi, *Geneva*, new series VIII, 283–296 (1960).

Kuhrt, A., *The Ancient Near East*, Vols. 1 and 2, Routledge, New York, 1995.

Potts, D.T., *Mesopotamian Civilization*, Cornell University Press, Ithaca, NY, 1997.

Saggs, H.W.F., *The Babylonians: A Survey of the Ancient Civilisation of the Tigris-Euphrates Valley*, The Folio Society, London, 1999.

Snell, C., *Life in the Ancient Near East, 3100-332 BCE*, Yale University Press, New Haven, CT, 1997.

See also **Judeo-Christian Legal Traditions; Retribution**

Bail: Reform

Usually when we hear the word bail, we think of money paid for the release of a defendant confined to some form of detention. According to *Black's Law Dictionary*, bail is money as a provision for release from custody usually set by the judge at a defendant's initial appearance. Bail is thought of as being fundamental to the idea of releasing a defendant because they are innocent until proven guilty. Essentially, bail is the defendant's personal promise that he or she will appear in court. However, this paints a fairly restrictive representation of bail. Those working under and studying the criminal justice system would tell you it represents one of the most important decisions in our system of justice. Traditionally, under the Magna Carta and English common law, bail was a provision that those accused of a crime would appear for their court proceedings. Throughout various stages of history this provision took many forms, from the defendant giving an oath, to leaving one's property in the short-term custody of officials to ensure the presence of that person at trial.

Eventually, the U.S. grew in both population and industry and therefore one's oath or property was not sufficient to guarantee their appearance for trial. These practices were ultimately replaced with cash bail, or money for the pretrial release of a defendant. It was at this point that bail bondsmen, and the act of bonding someone out of jail were established and became a popular way to make bail. It was also at this nexus that bail became problematic because it was seen as a form of economic discrimination. Those who could afford bail were released and those who could not were detained. This practice was criticized as being punishment of the innocent before they were proven guilty.

Legal Right to Bail

Contrary to popular belief, the Eighth Amendment does not guarantee the right to bail, it only protects against excessive bail. Although judges generally have no limits on the amount of bail they can impose, bail is not supposed to be a form of punishment. The Supreme Court ruled on bail and the Eighth Amendment in the case of *Stack v. Boyle* (342 U.S. 1, 1951), ruling bail to be a traditional freedom before trial. Bail becomes excessive when it is above a reasonable amount necessary to guarantee a defendant's appearance for trial. The court also ruled that bail should be similar in similar cases, and that bail may be higher if there is sufficient evidence to support the increase. Although this case did not authorize a right to bail, it did provide guidance to the courts in that if bail is set, its amount should not be frivolous, unusual, or beyond a person's ability to pay.

Problems with Bail and Pretrial Detention

Those being detained pretrial make up a greater proportion of inmates than those serving time after conviction. This has led to the worsening of jail conditions all over the U.S. The nation's jails are not only overcrowded, but are dangerous, have very poor living conditions, and a place where rehabilitation is nonexistent. Many jails have now been ordered by the court to reduce their populations as well as improve their living conditions. There is also evidence that those who are detained pretrial are more likely to receive prison sentences upon conviction, and for longer periods. Despite these problems, the U.S. Supreme Court has upheld the use of preventative detention as constitutional.

Preventative Detention and Due Process

In the case of *United States v. Salerno* (481 U.S. 739, 1987), the Supreme Court ruled that preventative detention does not violate the due process clause. They stated "Congress formulated the detention provisions not as punishment for dangerous individuals, but as a potential solution to the pressing societal problem of crimes committed by persons on release," adding that "preventing danger to the community is a legitimate regulatory goal." Finally, "The government's regulatory interest in community safety can, in appropriate circumstances, outweigh an individual's liberty interest" (481 U.S. 739, 1987, p. 746–748). This case justifies using preventative detention as a crime control method, and shows a concern for the protection of the community. Essentially, the Supreme Court ruled preventative detention does not violate the due process.

In a related case, *Schall v. Martin* (467 U.S. 253, 1984), the Supreme Court upheld the constitutionality of a New York preventative detention law for juveniles. The Court stated that the law "served the legitimate state objective of protecting the child and society from the potential consequences of his criminal acts." The

Court also limited juvenile detention to 17 days, provided that juveniles be aware of the charges against them, gave them a hearing to be informed of their rights, and afforded representation by counsel.

The Preventative Detention Controversy

Those who advocate bail reform cite the Eighth Amendment as proof that all those accused of a crime should be afforded bail. They believe this to be fundamental to the principle of innocent until proven guilty. However, this view is contested by those that believe public and community safety is more important, and that by releasing offenders we open ourselves and our property up to increased victimization. People holding this latter view have seen some support with the implementation of many preventative detention statutes that dictate certain defendants—those who are dangerous or pose some sort of risk—be imprisoned before trial. For instance, the Bail Reform Act of 1984 allows preventative detention if a judge believes that no single condition or combination of conditions will convincingly assure the defendant's appearance in court, and the safety of the community. Many states have also included some type of preventative detention components in their bail systems. These generally serve to restrict bail eligibility by limiting the right to bail for defendants who have priors and defendants charged with certain crimes.

Bail Reform in the 1960s

Numerous attempts have been made at reforming bail and eliminating the use of bail bonding agents. Until the 1960s, monetary bonds were the principal form of bail. Essentially, those who had sufficient financial resources were able to make bail and be released whereas those who were indigent would be detained. Today many defendants are released on their own recognizance (ROR) without having to post bail. ROR was established by the Vera Institute of Justice in 1961 with their Manhattan Bail Project. The Manhattan Bail Project was a collaborative research project between New York City criminal courts and law students. The project sought to provide New York City's criminal courts with more information about a defendant's background and community ties better enabling judges to make informed decisions about bail. The findings suggested that this background information helped the judges to assess whether or not the defendant would return for trial. The research team used a quantitative scale that relied on adding and subtracting points to make a decision about release. A minimum of five points was needed to qualify for a recommendation to the judge that the defendant be released. Ultimately, the judge had the final say in whether or not a defendant would be released ROR. Additionally, law students working with the Vera Institute followed up with each defendant to remind them of their obligation to appear in court. By linking ROR decisions to community ties and the nature of the offense using the 5-point scale, and using follow-up procedures like telephone calls and mail reminders, the project was correct about defendants returning over 99% of the time.

The Manhattan Bail Project was the impetus for the passage of the Bail Reform Act of 1966 and the implementation of ROR programs in courts all over the country. The 1966 Act established that ROR be considered before cash bail is set and also allowed deposit bail, mandating that the 10% fee, being paid to bondsmen, be paid to the court instead. This 10% fee would make it easier for more defendants to make bail than if the full bail amount was required for release. The 10% fee would then be refunded to the defendant at the end of the trial.

Bail Reform in the 1970s and 1980s

Despite its success, the Bail Reform movement was slowed by public outcry in response to some defendants committing new crimes while on pretrial release. As such, the Bail Reform Act of 1984 made several changes to federal pretrial release and detention practices. For instance, under the Bail Reform Act of 1966, a judge was required to impose only those provisions necessary to ensure the defendant's appearance in court. Also, a defendant could only be held without bail in capital cases. The Bail Reform Act of 1984 also stipulated that when judges make release decisions, they consider not only the assurance of the defendant's appearance in court, but also the safe protection of individuals and their communities. Judges generally have four options under this act; release on non-financial conditions, release on the condition that the defendant meet financial conditions of bail, detention for failure to meet conditions of bail, or detention without bail. The last option allows detention for certain categories of offenders and offenses. More specifically, the 1984 Act authorizes "pretrial detention for defendants charged with crimes of violence, offenses with possible life (or death) penalties, major drug offenses, and felonies, where the defendant has a specified serious criminal record" (USDOJ, Bureau of Justice Statistics, p. 2).

Bail Reform Today

The bail system in the U.S. has come a long way since cattle were placed in the property of local officials to ensure a defendant's appearance in court. A number of bail systems have been used since then, including: release on recognizance (ROR), which requires that the defendant only promise to appear and no money is required; private bail, in which an individual other than the defendant posts bail; surety bail, where the defendant pays a bonding agent to bail them out; and deposit bail, where the defendant pays a percentage (usually 10%) of the bail amount to the court.

Bail reforms have encouraged the greater use of non-financial forms of release as well as establishing procedures to ensure protection of the community. Although it appears that bail in the U.S. has progressed substantially, there remains more to accomplish. Bail practices still vary greatly from state to state, and most states are yet to adopt the due process based framework for decisions about detention that has been incorporated into the federal system. Another problem needing immediate attention is overcrowding in the nation's jails. In the U.S., jails are filled primarily with poor and minority defendants who cannot afford to raise bail, leading critics to contend that race and other extra legal factors occupy an important role in release decisions. Recently however, John Goldkamp and colleagues have experimented with using a presumptive set of bail guidelines to help judges responsible in making release decisions. This experiment was conducted based on the assumption that judicial discretion was a primary cause for the disproportionate number of poor and minority persons being detained pretrial. Results of this study have been positive in some cities, better enabling judges to make informed decisions about release. This study could serve as an important guide for future reforms, and could prove to be an effective means for alleviating jail overcrowding.

Those who advocate bail reform cite the Eighth Amendment and the principle of innocence until proven guilty as a foundation for the pretrial release of all defendants accused of a crime. Those contesting this position believe that the safety and protection of the community are more important than the freedom of individuals charged with committing a crime, especially when the crimes are violent or the criminals are dangerous. Until the Supreme Court decides to hand down another ruling on the issue of bail and pre-trial detention, persons supporting these views are likely to stand firm in their beliefs. Therefore, it is likely that debate about the preventative detention controversy as well as bail reform issues will continue.

RICHARD D. HARTLEY

References and Further Reading

Black, H.C., *Black's Law Dictionary*, 6th ed., West Publishing Co., St. Paul, MN, 1990.

Goldkamp, J. *Two Classes of Accused*, Ballinger, Cambridge, MA, 1979.

Goldkamp, J., Gottfredson, M., Jones, P., and Weiland, D. *Personal Liberty and Community Safety: Pretrial Release in the Criminal Courts*, Plenum, New York, 1995.

Thomas, W.H., *Bail Reform in America*, University of California Press, Berkeley, CA, 1976.

Vera Institute of Justice, *Programs in Criminal Justice*, Vera Institute of Justice, New York, 1972.

United States Department of Justice, Bureau of Justice Statistics, *Pretrial Release and Detention: The Bail Reform Act of 1984*, Washington, DC.

See also **Bail: Right to; Criminal Law: Reform**

Bail: Right to

Bail is the device used by courts to allow persons charged with a crime to be released by posting financial security or agreeing to certain terms of release. Bail holds its roots in Anglo-Saxon law, developed by kings in 673–687 A.D. At that time, it was required that persons accused of a crime pay "bohr" to the family of the victim. This "bohr" would be returned to the accused if he was subsequently found innocent. Further, English law provided that certain offenses, such as murder and treason, were "non-bailable" offenses. The Habeas Corpus Act of 1679 established an offender's right to bail and outlined the procedure to be used to determine the amount of bail set for an individual.

The Eighth Amendment to the Constitution of the U.S. provides that "excessive bail shall not be required." However, the Constitution does not specifically grant persons charged with criminal offenses the right to bail. Generally, the right of a defendant to be released on bail is within the discretion of the courts and legislature, although state constitutions may also grant a right to bail. Congress has historically provided the right to bail for defendants in the federal system beginning with the Judiciary Act of 1789 and continuing with the Federal Rules of Criminal Procedure, which provided bail to all persons arrested for a noncapital offense. The Federal Bail Reform Act, originally enacted in 1966 and substantially revised in 1984, provides defendants with the right to bail.

When granting bail, a court must balance the state's interest in both protecting society and prosecuting crimes with the presumption of innocence of the accused. Bail allows defendants an opportunity to prepare a defense to criminal charges and prevents punishment prior to a person's conviction. Some states require that a person be released on bail if the state is not ready to bring that person to trial within a specified number of days. Bail also furthers the court's interest in keeping a defendant in the jurisdiction of the court, thereby insuring that person's appearance at further judicial proceedings.

The right to bail is available at several different points in the criminal process, including prior to trial, prior to sentencing, and upon appeal. A Supreme Court Justice can allow release on bail when a person has appealed a state court criminal proceeding to the Supreme Court, subject to that state's bail requirements. In such cases, bail is generally granted unless the appeal is frivolous or taken to delay proceedings. All judicial officers, including appellate and trial court judges, possess the right to grant bail. Magistrates also have the authority to grant bail when conducting preliminary hearings.

The Bail Reform Act of 1984, 18 U.S.C.S. § 3144, was enacted following concerns of the criminal justice system in the 1970s and 1980s that society was being harmed when dangerous criminals were released on bail. That Act recognizes that there are some persons who should not be released on bail in order to protect society. However, the Act also recognizes that setting only monetary bail orders may be a violation of a person's constitutional rights, in accordance with the excessive bail provision of the Eighth Amendment. The Act presumes that defendants should be released on personal recognizance, unless it can be determined that such a release would not ensure either the return of the person for court proceedings or the safety of the community. Release on personal recognizance provides that rather than posting monetary collateral, a person can be released from custody after signing a release form agreeing that he or she will attend all required proceedings. Factors that a judicial officer or magistrate must consider in order to determine whether to release a person on his or her own recognizance include information regarding the person's past and present employment, family ties and relationships, past and present residence, reputation, character, mental condition, criminal record, previous appearances in court, current charge, the existence of others who would support the character of that person, and other relevant factors.

The Supreme Court has stated that requiring excessive amounts or conditions of bail may violate the due process. The 1984 Federal Bail Reform Act provides that bail cannot be set at an amount so high that it, in effect, results in the pretrial detention of a person. In other words, if a judge decides that the community will not be harmed by the release of a defendant, he must set bail at an amount that is only high enough to further the interest of the protection of the community, but not so high as to prohibit that person from being able to obtain release.

The Bail Reform Act eliminates any assumption that all defendants are entitled to bail, by eliminating the right to bail for persons charged with particular serious felonies. Section 3142(f) of the Bail Reform Act provides that if a defendant is charged with certain felonies or was involved in a crime of violence, a crime for which the maximum sentence is life imprisonment or death, or certain drug offenses, that person will not receive bail as long as the government can demonstrate that no release conditions would safeguard the community. Additionally, section 3142(e) disallows bail if the judicial officer making the decision to grant or deny bail has probable cause to believe that the accused possessed a firearm during the commission of the felony. The Bail Reform Act assumes that no bail amount would safeguard the community for such felons. Additionally, the judicial officer determining whether to grant bail should consider the specifics of the crime allegedly committed, the weight of evidence existing against the person, the person's character, whether the person was already involved in the court system for another offense, and the potential of danger to any person in the community, including witnesses to the case, if the person is released from custody on bail.

A person's right to receive bail and what conditions can be imposed upon such decisions continue to be controversial points of law. Since the passage of the 1984 Act, courts have considered whether provisions of the Bail Reform Act are unconstitutional, especially whether certain conditions under which a person will not receive bail are considered punitive in nature, go against the presumption of innocence implied in the constitution, or violate equal protection.

Other countries that have followed the western system of criminal justice also provide a right to bail as part of those systems. For example, the Ukraine in August 1991 began to form a new justice system and provided that bail could be available to every defendant. However, various limitations were placed on the amount of bail set. For example, the amount of bail required could not be less than the amount of damages claimed by a victim in a civil suit, and no upper limit was set. Additionally, in the Ukraine, bail can be kept by the tribunal to satisfy a judgment or other penalties owed to the victim. Some countries, such as New Zealand, have no formal bail statutes, and any bail provisions in existence come from common law. New Zealand courts generally follow Canadian court rulings in their determination of bail factors. South Africa, in the postapartheid era, has made great strides in the area of bail. Its 1993 Constitution gives detainees the right to be released "with or without bail," depending on the circumstances. The legislature of that country has been given the power to regulate bail, and future standards are most likely to be developed. The bail systems in other countries following the western system of criminal justice are similar to, but not exactly the same as, the system of bail in the U.S.

Tina M. Fryling

Further Reading

Goldkamp, J.S., Criminal Law: Danger and Detention: A Second Generation of Bail Reform, *Northwestern School of Law Journal of Criminal Law & Criminology*, 76, 1985.

Goldkamp, J.S. and Gottfredson, M.R., *Judical Guidelines for Bail: The Philadelphia Experiment*, U.S. Dept. of Justice, National Institute of Justice, Washington, DC, 1984.

Goldkamp, J.S. and Gottfredson, M.R., *Policy Guidelines for Bail: An Experiment in Court Reform*, Temple University Press, Philadelphia, PA, 1985.

Ryan, M.K. and Olson, B.K., Preliminary Proceedings: Bail. *Georgetown Law Journal*, 88, 2000.

Thomas, W.H., *Bail Reform in America*, University of California Press, Berkeley, CA, 1976.

Waldman, M., Bail and Recognizance, in Matthew J. Canavan, Ed., *American Jurisprudence*, 2nd ed. 8A, Danvers, MA, West Group, 1997.

See also **Bail: Reform**

Ballistics

See **Police: Forensic Evidence**

Bank Robbery

From Jesse James and John Dillinger to today's less colorful desperados, the bank robber is the quintessential American outlaw. Bank robbery has been an indigenous American crime with enduring mystique and populist appeal. The theme of banks as passive, even deserving victims—"moneylenders" in the service of economic elites—may resonate with the public, particularly during periods of economic decline (Kirchner, 1999).

Most bank robberies that occurred during the years prior to World War II were committed by a limited number of criminals or criminal gangs. Dillinger, Bonnie and Clyde, "Pretty Boy" Floyd, "Baby Face" Nelson, "Machine Gun" Kelly and the Barker gang were elevated to public-enemy status by J. Edgar Hoover and helped him transform the FBI into the major federal law enforcement agency. Armed with fast cars and automatic weapons, these gangs engaged in daring raids, police shootouts, hostage-taking and high-speed chases. They provided visible targets and massive manhunts resulted in lethal ambush or their capture. The era of the professional bank robber was seemingly over.

After the enactment of the Federal Banking Act of 1934 (18 U.S.C. Section 2113), bank robbers were pursued across state lines, targeted by the FBI, prosecuted under federal law, and subjected to long prison terms. After attaining a peak in 1932 with 609 robberies at the height of the Great Depression, the number of bank robberies plummeted to 411 in 1934 to 129 in 1937. This trend continued until 1943 when only 24 bank robberies were reported.

Following the war, bank robbery rates climbed steadily, fueled by the entry of a large number of amateurs with a declining number of full-time criminals. The number of reported robberies steadily rose from several hundred in the 1950s to 2500 in the early 1970s. Increasing numbers of drug offenders drove the number higher to around 6000 during the 1980s, attaining a peak in 1991 with 9388 robberies, falling to 6599 in 1999, then increasing to 7127 in 2000 and 8500 in 2001, ending a decade-long decline.

The principal reasons for this overall increase were the growth in the money supply and the proliferation of branch banking (Gould, 1969). Banks have entered new markets, spread out into the suburbs and extended their hours to better serve the public, increasing the number and availability of potential targets. In 2001, 93% of bank robberies involved branches (Erickson and Balzer, 2003). Branch banks with lower police presence are more vulnerable than the more fortified central banks.

The inherent conflicts between commercial and security interests are usually resolved in favor of the bottom line. In the effort to improve accessibility to customers, banks have cultivated an open appearance, there is an abundance of lighting and glass to enhance visibility, physical barriers separating tellers and customers have been removed, and there are no armed guards on duty. Banks that are conveniently located near freeways to be more customer-friendly also facilitate rapid escape. Banks have few incentives to hire armed guards or install expensive security systems. Because of the limited amount of cash kept in tellers' tills, time locks on bank vaults and federal deposit insurance, losses from bank robbery that usually range from a few hundred to a few thousand dollars are often considered a cost of doing business.

Whereas banks are enticingly easy to rob, successful escape is problematic. Target-hardening and limiting access to cash have made lucrative scores rare. Silent alarms, cameras mounted in multiple locations, recorded serialized currency ("bait money"), explosive dye packs, tracking devices, and high public visibility deter most professional robbers because they know they are likely to get caught. Because of monitoring devices, witnesses, lack of planning, repetitive modus operandi, enforcement efforts, and human error, serial bank robbers are much more likely to be caught than other chronic offenders. The serial bank robber continues to be a small but persistent presence.

Bank Robbers

Most information about bank robbers comes from interviews with incarcerated offenders or those released on parole. Captives and former captives would seem to represent the population of offenders well since the vast majority gets caught. Arrest and conviction rates range from 70 to 80% and 80% of those convicted on federal charges receive prison sentences of 10 years or more (Haran and Martin, 1977). The statutory maximum penalty for bank robbery is 20 years but most first convictions result in three to four year sentences. Subsequent federal convictions carry long prison terms and no chance for early release, bringing an extended hiatus if not an abrupt end to a serial robber's career.

Although most of Camp's (1968) sample was involved in other crime, few were recidivists. Only 3 of the 132 convicted bank robbers he interviewed had served a prior sentence for bank robbery. Serial bank robbery and recidivism may be increasing. Twenty-eight percent of recent Canadian bank robbers had prior bank robbery convictions (Desroches, 2002). Recidivism among bank robbers convicted on state charges is likely to be higher because of shorter prison terms. Very few states provide special penalties for bank robbery.

Haran and Martin (1977) examined the pre-sentence investigations of 500 robbers and found the profile of the federal bank robber changed radically during a single decade in eastern New York. In the mid-1960s, a typical bank robber was a white male in his late twenties or early thirties, who carefully planned his robberies for maximum payoff and was captured only after an intensive investigation. A decade later, bank robbers were generally black, younger, unsophisticated, and many were apprehended shortly after the holdup. FBI statistics indicate that in 2001, 49% of arrestees were black and 42% white (Erickson and Balzer, 2003). The average offender is a male in his late twenties, making him older and more likely to be white than other armed robbers.

The most representative study of bank robbery (Camp, 1968) concluded that most bank robbers are amateurs who have "nothing to lose" and commit the crime out of financial desperation, unemployment, debt or threat of bankruptcy. Today, drug addiction and short run hedonism are major causes of bank robbery (Haran and Martin, 1977; Desroches, 2002). Most robbers enjoy the taste of affluence and the creature comforts that the relatively large amount of cash provides. Robbers are often generous with their family and friends and sponsor an ongoing party filled with entertainment, clothes, cars, sex, gambling, and drugs.

Even those who regard bank robbery as a short-term solution to a financial problem do not have the legitimate resources to meet their basic needs—let alone sustain a life of consumptive leisure. Eighty percent of Canadian bank robbers were unemployed prior to committing the crime and very few were even looking for work (Desroches, 2002). Except for cars, few purchase material goods or invest their money but many squander the money. This may account for the low recovery rate of less than 20% (Erickson and Balzer, 2003). Some of the missing money may be hidden away but most was probably spent living the high life. Most robbers have no alternative source of income and when the money is gone there are strong incentives to repeat the crime.

Types of Bank Robbery

There are basically three types of bank robbers. They are the note-pusher or "beggar bandit," the solo gunman, and the robbery gang (Desroches, 2002). Note jobs account for over half of all incidents (Erickson and Balzer, 2003). This robber waits in line posing as a customer and passes a note or makes a quiet verbal threat. The bandit instructs a single teller to empty the cash drawer. His success depends upon anonymity. No weapon is openly displayed. The robber blends in with the bank customers and then blends in with public pedestrians if all goes well. He is aware that banks instruct their employees to comply with the robber's request as quickly as possible to minimize the risk of violence. The criminal is usually allowed to exit the bank with several hundred to several thousand dollars before an alarm is sounded. The FBI has turned the investigation of most of these incidents over to local authorities and most are prosecuted as state rather than federal crimes (Kirchner, 1999).

The lone gunman is a robber demanding money from several different tellers by displaying a real or simulated weapon. Solo gunmen do not usually jump the counter but instead order a teller to collect the money while he watches the behavior of customers and other employees. The conditions are rather delicate for one person to handle and the stability of the encounter is uncertain if not precarious. The robber cannot turn his back on the door nor his victims and he does not exercise the degree of complete control over the situation that is characteristic of takeovers by armed gangs.

Under these circumstances, some lone gunman may use politeness and reassurance instead of shock and intimidation to exert control. Willie Sutton was the legendary "gentleman bandit" who robbed scores of banks over a 25-year career. Sutton disguised himself as a police officer, telegraph messenger, maintenance man, and mailman. He carried a Thompson submachine gun that was never fired and he was noted for his polite demeanor. More recently, Edwin Dodson, an owner of a Hollywood antique shop, began robbing banks to support a cocaine and heroin habit. Dodson mostly robbed banks in affluent areas—64 during one crime spree in 1983–1984. He used an unloaded starter pistol and soft-spoken personal charm to manage his victims (Rehder, 2003).

Robbery Gangs

Armed gangs typically engage in violent "takeovers." Menacing gunmen frighten and terrorize employees and customers with exaggerated gestures, verbal threats, obscenities and occasional violence. The tactic is to shock everyone into submission under imminent threat of death. About 80% of Haran and Martin's (1977) federal inmates and 43% of Canadian offenders (Desroches, 2002) had associates. Whereas most gangs operate with two or three members, some include as many as six. Some gangs are loose transient relationships whereas others are relatively permanent and rooted in friendship. Some groups spend the night together before the robbery. Others meet for breakfast before the job.

Partners choose roles based on personal preferences, skills and background. There is no particular leader. Decisions are reached collectively. Deference may be shown to the person who originated the plan and laid the groundwork or those with the most experience (Letkemann, 1973). Gang leadership can also be exercised through intellect and charisma (Weyermann, 1992). Generally the basic roles include the "money grabber" or "bagman" who leaps over the counter to empty the tellers' tills. The "doorman" or "floorman" enters the bank and establishes control and monitors employees and customers, "lookouts" maintain surveillance over internal and external points of entry and the "wheelman" drives the getaway car (Desroches, 2002). Most gangs combine these roles into two or three positions.

The first positions are the most pivotal (Letkemann, 1973; Desroches, 2002). The doorman is the only member who is always armed. He instigates the takeover by entering first, brandishing his weapon and shouting commands. The robber would like to separate tellers from the counter and officers from their desks before they can sound the alarm. He may herd employees into a corner or demand that they lie on the floor. He is generally the last to exit the bank. The doorman is likely to be the most experienced and the person who can be trusted with weapons. Weapons are used as props and if they are fired it is usually a sign that something has gone wrong. Just as it takes emotional stability for this role, the person who jumps the counter must have some physical agility and may therefore be younger.

The more successful offenders plan their crimes. They at least have to procure weapons, disguises and vehicles. Most use handguns because they are concealable, some prefer assault rifles for their intimidating effect and others favor sawed-off shotguns as their weapon of choice. Caps and sunglasses, ski masks, wigs, nylon stockings and Halloween masks are all common disguises.

Getaway cars tend to be nondescript vehicles stolen for the occasion and given different license plates. The vehicle is usually parked on a street or lot adjacent to the bank in an unobtrusive location. The stolen car is usually used to escape to the site of another vehicle where the robbers switch cars. Disguises may be left behind in the stolen car. The second car may be concealed in a rented private or public parking garage where the exchange is less visible. The bandits may double-back or drive in a different direction in their own car or cars. Their main concern is to get off the streets as quickly as possible (Letkemann, 1973).

More meticulous robbers may observe at what times there are fewer employees and customers, "case" alternative targets, observe armored car deliveries or analyze escape routes and police patrols. Some gangs locate central cash tills, vault and safety deposit box locations or identify head tellers and managers (Weyermann, 1992). Sophisticated gangs may make prior arrangement to launder stolen cash or plan for medical and legal contingencies if they are injured or captured (Letkemann, 1973).

"The Boys" were a successful robbery gang composed of three to six friends who grew up together in an impoverished industrial area in Des Moines. During their 20-year career of robbing banks, armored cars, and jewelry stores, "The Boys" stole $10 to $12 million, most of which was never recovered. Their biggest score was $3.3 million stolen from the First National Bank depository in Tucson in 1981. They were later prosecuted for the crime but were acquitted by an apparently sympathetic jury. The gang was known for its meticulous planning including learning the names of bank employees, wiping down cars and bank counters and using "crazy glue" on their hands to avoid leaving fingerprints (Weyermann, 1992).

"The Trenchcoat Robbers" were two middle-aged men, a locksmith and a salesman, who robbed 27 banks over a 15-year period, including a $4.5 million Tacoma, Washington bank robbery, the largest in U.S. history. They would spend several weeks in remote cities casing each bank. The locksmith would open the bank door after closing time or during the night so they would surprise employees when the vault was likely to be open and no customers present. They dressed alike to confuse the witnesses. Once they were forced to take hostage and exchange gunfire with police before the police lost them in a well-planned escape maneuver. The identity of the robbers was discovered as a result of a tip to the IRS that the locksmith was paying for a new house in cash. After being stopped for speeding, he was arrested on weapons charges and his girlfriend tried to bail him out with bait money from the Tacoma heist (Kotlowitz, 2002). He and she both cooperated with the FBI in return for reduced sentences.

Bank robbers tend to rob several banks over a short period of time and most are caught within a few weeks or months (Desroches, 2002). If they initially elude capture, the experience is likely be easy, exciting and, for the amount of time invested, profitable. Few robbers express concern about cameras, alarms or other security measures. They do not anticipate nor do many encounter resistance. Robbers feel safe when they are not initially apprehended. As their self-confidence grows, they become better at their task. With each success, their modus operandi crystallizes into predictable patterns. These repetitive routines and disguises give serial bank robbers a distinctive identity that investigators often tag with a unique nickname. If the robber's profile and predictable behavior does not lead to his arrest, it does provide investigators with enough evidence to link him to past crimes. Once the police or FBI knows who the robbers are, it is most likely that every one of the robbers will eventually make a mistake or be identified by a witness or informant if they do not fall into a police dragnet.

Violent Robberies

Even when bank robberies were declining during the 1990s, the proportion of violent "takeover" robberies increased and may account for as many as one-third of the cases in some cities (Rehder, 2003). In armed takeovers, a substantial amount of cash is usually taken from several tellers and sometimes from the vault. Incidents of violence are also more likely to occur. The weapon is designed to frighten and immobilize the victims. There is the danger that employees may be so shaken that they may not respond quickly to the robbers' demands. A weapon may rarely be discharged for intimidation purposes or for destroying barriers, but if people are hurt, something has gone wrong.

Any delay poses a threat to a successful holdup. Robbers expect the crime to be easy and victims to be cooperative. When problems are encountered, they may become frustrated because of time constraints. Robbers must assume that the silent alarm system has been activated when they make a dramatic entry and the encounter must be over within seconds or minutes. Technology has elevated the level of stress and danger in armed bank robbery and after two minutes the robbers could face armed police intervention (Rehder, 2003).

A robber is hesitant to use his gun on a civilian, especially since women are the likely victims. However, many seem prepared to use violence against and express contempt for the "hero-type" whose actions are considered irrational and dangerous. Deadly robberies do occur in which employees and customers have been murdered by summary execution but these incidents are less frequent in bank robbery than in other forms of commercial robbery.

Most people who are injured are struck with weapons rather than shot. In about 3% of robberies, victims are injured or hostages taken. From 100 to 150 employees and customers are injured each year and about 100 are taken hostage. Most deaths result from confrontations and shoot-outs with police and the robber is the person usually killed. Of the 23 deaths in 2001, 19 were perpetrators; of the 14 killed in 2002, nine were robbers (Erickson and Balzer, 2003).

One of the most violent episodes involved a short succession of commando-style robberies inspired by the movie *Heat*. In May 1996, Larry Phillips, Jr. and Emil Matasareanu, a real estate con artist and a failed computer consultant, stormed into a Bank of America wearing ski masks, body armor and firing automatic weapons. They had carved up Kevlar bullet-proof vests to cover nearly their entire bodies and strapped on extra magazines of ammunition for their AK-47s. After blasting open the Plexiglas bandit barrier with armor-piercing bullets, 30 employees and customers were ordered inside the vault while the robbers stuffed $750,000 in duffle bags and fled. A month later they successfully repeated this scenario at another Bank of America branch.

The following February, they were spotted by a patrol car as they entered yet another Bank of America office. This time, the bank had taken the precaution of reducing the amount of cash in the vault and lacing the money with dye packs. The robbers wasted valuable time searching for additional money while patrol cars gathered outside. As they attempted to flee, they turned their automatic weapons on the police while news helicopters hovered overhead. Because of their body armor they were initially impervious to police fire. Phillips pulled several different weapons from the trunk of the getaway car, walking alongside, using the vehicle as a shield and firing at officers. After his ammunition was spent, Phillips killed himself with a handgun and Matasareanu was fatally wounded by fire from police SWAT units. The hour-long firefight left 15 people injured, including ten police officers, but no one except the robbers were killed.

Prevention

Although federal law requires camera and alarm systems, surveillance cameras that reuse videotape produce grainy black-and-white images of robbers that lack sufficient detail to help law enforcement identify the suspects. However, replacing the fuzzy pictures produced by old equipment with digital or closed-circuit camera systems is expensive. Armed guards are also expensive. Bankers concerned with liability may not want armed employees on the premises. Some risk can be reduced by hiring uniformed off-duty police officers as guards.

"Bandit barriers" are bullet-resistant Plexiglas and steel partitions that extend from the top of the counter to the ceiling of the bank, separating tellers and the vault area from the customers in the lobby. "Man traps" are enclosed entrances where metal detectors activate locks if a gun is detected, sealing the suspect inside the vestibule. "Man traps" are rare. Only 10% of the banks employ armed guards or bullet-resistant enclosures. Less than one-third use dye-packs (Erickson and Balzer, 2003).

Note jobs can be reduced by requiring customers to remove hats, hoods and sunglasses when entering the bank so their features are visible to surveillance cameras. Placing an employee in the lobby to greet customers can also enhance vigilance. Hiring more male tellers may discourage some robbers. Banks are advised to vary times of armored car deliveries and quickly separate bulk cash into separate locked containers.

Perhaps the most cost-efficient deterrent is employee training. Training should be ongoing because of high employee turnover in teller positions. Discrete placement of dye packs and bait money should be practiced. Employees should be instructed to observe the height, weight, race and clothing of the robber as well as any identifiable physical features, scars, tattoos or other marks. Employees should quickly comply with all the robber's demands and sound the alarm only after he turns to exit. Doors should immediately be locked to avoid the robber's reentry and a hostage situation as well as to preserve the crime scene. Areas the robbers may have touched should be sealed off and customers should be asked to remain until the police arrive. Counseling should be available to reduce post event trauma.

Target-hardening has been effective in reducing the number of bank burglaries. Vaults have become almost impenetrable and are governed by time locks. Alarm and surveillance systems limit the amount of time one can spend committing the crime. Banks have however spent relatively little on security measures to deter bank robbery. The rising number of bank robberies may require banks to consider more rigorous security devices and procedures.

Donald Scott

References and Further Reading

Camp, G.C., *Nothing to Lose: A Study of Bank Robbery in America*, Ph.D. dissertation, Yale University, 1967.

Desroches, F., *Force And Fear: Robbery in Canada*, Canadian Scholars' Press, Inc., Toronto, Ontario, Canada, 2002.

Erickson, R.J. and Balzer, K.M., *Summary and Interpretation of Bank Crime Statistics, 2001*, Athena Research Corp., San Diego, CA, 2003.

Gould, L.C., The Changing Structure of Property Crime in an Affluent Society, *Social Forces*, 48 (1969).

Haran, J.F. and Martin, J.M., The Imprisonment of Bank Robbers: The Issue of Deterrence, *Federal Probation*, 41 (1977).

Kirchner, L.R., *Robbing Banks: An American History 1831–1999*, Da Capo Press, Cambridge, MA, 1999.

Kotlowitz, A., The Trenchcoat Robbers, *New Yorker*, 78 (2002).

Letkemann, P., *Crime as Work*, Prentice-Hall, Englewood Cliffs, NJ, 1973.

Rehder, W.J., *Where the Money Is: True Tales from the Bank Robbery Capital of the World*, WW Norton & Co., New York, 2003.

Weyermann, D., *The Gang They Couldn't Catch: The Story of America's Greatest Modern-Day Bank Robbers—And How They Got Away With It*, Poseidon Press, Crofton, MD, 1993.

See also **Robbery as an Occupation; Robbery: Extent and Correlates; Robbery: The Law**

Battered Woman Defense to Criminal Liability

The battered woman defense to criminal liability is not exclusively available to women and generally is not separated from claims of self-defense or duress. It can be raised by any person who has been brutalized repeatedly, particularly by an intimate partner, but this entry will sometimes use gendered language both for convenience and in recognition that most cases in the justice system in fact involve battered women and battering men. In the modern view, evidence of a "battering relationship" and the psychological impact of that relationship is admissible to help the finder of fact address issues raised in traditional defenses, usually self-defense, but sometimes defense of a third person or duress.

Battered person syndrome evidence is usually offered through expert testimony of a mental health professional or sometimes a social work professional. In addition to bearing on possible defenses, the evidence helps the finder of fact understand what is otherwise a puzzling aspect of the narrative: "Why did she stay?" If there is a conviction, the evidence also has relevance to the issue of punishment.

Evidence of battering is offered most often in homicide or aggravated assault cases. When homicide or aggravated assault occurs during a battering incident, the courts are presented with a classic case of self-defense. The battering evidence is easily admitted as part of the story that makes sense of the particular fight that is the subject of the trial.

The harder case is where the victim in a battering relationship assaults the batterer in a manner that appears particularly offensive, such as when he is asleep or otherwise caught unawares, or by poison, or by a homicide-for-hire transaction. In this kind of case, the prosecutor may take the position that self-defense does not apply because the defendant was in no *imminent* danger. Her use of force was not reasonable. The law of self-defense does not apply to revenge killings.

This position began to be challenged in the seventies as the legal system responded to a civil rights movement on behalf of battered women. Criminal defense lawyers began offering expert testimony on the psychological impact of battering and the difficulty of leaving battering relationships, particularly Lenore Walker's "cycle of violence" theory.

Walker, who often found herself in the role of defense expert, argued that domestic violence is not constant but rather follows a repetitive cycle and the "tension building" phase of that cycle may in fact be distant in time from the last battering incident but nonetheless is a time when a battered woman reasonably perceives "imminent danger." Her perception is colored by the number of times she has been through the cycle of violence, and the time just before an eruption is, in her experience, much more dangerous than the time just after when the batterer may in fact be apologetic rather than aggressive.

Before self-defense will apply, the defendant's belief that she must use force to protect herself from imminent danger must be reasonable. Most jurisdictions require that her belief be objectively reasonable—that is, a belief that would be held by a reasonable person in the same or similar circumstances. In those jurisdictions, the battering evidence is offered to show part of the circumstances that shaped the belief. A minority of jurisdictions apply a subjective test of reasonableness, which allows the battering evidence in direct support of the battered woman's testimony that she feared for her life.

Because these developments in evidence law are fairly recent, many battered persons are currently serving substantial prison sentences for homicide received under rules that did not allow evidence of battering to come before the judge or jury. Several states have initiated review of these cases with the objective of identifying appropriate candidates for executive clemency.

In addition to proving the state of mind of the defendant for the purpose of showing self-defense, battering evidence may also be offered to show why the defendant needed to use force in defense of a third person, most often a child. The task of persuasion in defense of a third person may be difficult when no prior acts of violence have been directed against the child, but battered women's syndrome testimony might help explain why the woman did not defend herself yet would defend her child. In jurisdictions that admit the battered woman syndrome evidence, this use of it is not particularly controversial.

On the other hand, battered woman syndrome evidence has been offered with mixed results in cases where the woman is charged as a party to the homicide of her child for failure to protect the child from the batterer. The result of living in fear is said to be paralysis in a situation where the parent has a duty to protect the child. Feminists argue that the battered woman in this situation is likely to get prosecuted whether or not she attempts to protect the child.

Another controversial extension of battered woman syndrome evidence is in support of a duress defense when the claim is that the defendant committed a crime because he or she feared the batterer, typically a property offense alleged to have been ordered by the batterer. The issue is similar to self-defense in that the duress defense normally requires proof of an *imminent* threat of death or serious bodily injury. Although fewer jurisdictions allow this use of battering evidence, the trend is to expand it to duress cases, on the theory that the issue in both duress and self-defense is what the chronically abused person would reasonably believe to be an imminent threat.

If American courts were more receptive to a "diminished capacity" (mental health oriented) defense, then the admissibility of battered woman syndrome evidence might have followed a slightly different path, as it has in Great Britain. British courts first admitted the evidence to show what they call "diminished responsibility," treating battered woman syndrome as a mental defect, but having the evidence available at all began to bring it to bear on self-defense or "provocation."

Canada does not recognize what the British call "diminished responsibility" and some American jurisdictions call "diminished capacity," and therefore Canadian courts have treated battered woman syndrome evidence in a manner similar to the American trend, as relevant to self-defense or provocation.

In Australia, battered woman syndrome evidence has been admissible since 1991 as relevant to self-defense, provocation, and duress. Of course, it has long been accepted in most Anglophone jurisdictions after conviction to support an argument in mitigation of sentence, and Australia is no exception.

STEVE RUSSELL

References and Further Reading

Boland, B.I.Z., Battered Women Who Act Under Duress, *New England Law Review*, 28 (1994).

Callahan, A.R., Will the 'Real' Battered Woman Please Stand Up? In Search of a Realistic Definition of Battered Woman Syndrome, *American University Journal of Gender and the Law*, 3 (1994).

Daniels, C.R., Ed., *Feminists Negotiate the State: The Politics of Domestic Violence*, University Press of America, Lanham, MD, 1997.

Downs, D.A., *More Than Victims: Battered Women, the Syndrome, Society, and the Law*, University of Chicago Press, Chicago, IL, 1996.

Gagne, P., *Battered Women's Justice: The Movement for Clemency and the Politics of Self-Defense*, Twayne Publishers, New York and Prentice Hall International, London, 1998.

Murdoch, J.B., Is Imminence Really Necessity? Reconciling Traditional Self-Defense Doctrine With The Battered Woman Syndrome, *Northern Illinois University Law Review*, 20 (2000).

Stubbs, J. and Tolmie, J., Falling Short of the Challenge? A Comparative Assessment of the Australian Use of Expert Evidence on the Battered Woman Syndrome, *Melbourne University Law Review*, 23 (1999).

Walker, L.E., *The Battered Woman Syndrome*, 2nd ed., Springer-Verlag, New York, 2000.

Walker, L.E., *Terrifying Love: Why Battered Women Kill and How Society Responds*, Harper and Row, New York, 1989.

Wannop, A.L., Battered Woman Syndrome and the Defense of Battered Women in Canada and England, *Suffolk Transnational Law Review*, 19 (1995).

See also **Domestic Assault: Law; Duress as a Defense to Criminal Liability; Self-Defense as a Defense to Criminal Liability**

Beccaria, Cesare

Nearly two and a half centuries after proposing his ideas for reforming the legal and penal systems of Europe, Cesare Beccaria's philosophy remains an important topic of discussion in criminology today. To be sure, he has long been considered a founder of the classical school of criminology and his proposals have shaped the legal systems of several countries, including that of the U.S.

Despite his various accomplishments, Beccaria is today best remembered for one singular achievement. In 1764, at the age of 26, he produced the highly renowned essay, *On Crimes and Punishments*. This slim volume, first published anonymously, was a scathing indictment against the brutal abuses of the legal and penal practices of eighteenth century continental Europe. In short, the treatise was a clarion call to radically transform the penal system and criminal procedure of the time.

Generally, the legal and penal systems of eighteenth-century Europe were extremely abusive and brutal. Owing to the fact that much of it was unwritten, the law was frequently applied in an uncertain, haphazard, and biased manner. It was common for people to be accused of crimes without their knowledge. The corruption of prosecutors and judges was also a widespread problem. In addition, because there was little or no due process of law, the accused lacked legal protections such as the right to a speedy and public trial by an impartial jury. Finally, many punishments involved a variety of agonizing torments and hundreds of offenses were punishable by death, usually in an aggravated fashion.

In light of the abusive conditions on the Continent, Beccaria advanced several general recommendations for legal reform. First, he declared that the legislature alone, and not the judiciary, should have the power to enact and interpret the law. This clear demarcation between the legislature and judiciary we now refer to as "the separation of powers." Second, Beccaria argued that because society's contractual nature does not discriminate between individuals on the basis of their social status, so too should the laws be applied equally, regardless of a person's station in life. In other words, all citizens are to be guaranteed the equal protection of the laws. Third, Beccaria urged that the laws be written clearly and simply so that everyone is sure to understand them. Fourth, he reasoned that since people are rational it is only logical that the laws also be rational. A rational legal code requires that the laws be stated generally and systematically so that they can be applied uniformly to similar types of conduct. Fifth, Beccaria recommended that the burden of proof be shifted from the accused to the court. Sixth, during Beccaria's time there was no difference in treatment between the accused and the convicted. Attempting to rectify this injustice, he wrote that a defendant found innocent of a criminal charge must not be stigmatized with a negative label. Finally, Beccaria vehemently denounced the secret accusations so prevalent in his day. Secret accusations not only encourage informers to lie, he stated, they also create an atmosphere of suspicion in which everyone is regarded as a potential enemy. Beccaria's objective in proposing these and other reforms was to devise a legal system that administered justice in a fair, equitable, and logical manner.

As regards penology, Beccaria saw aggravated and violent punishments as possessing an element of overkill. Accordingly, he argued that punishment must be proportional to the crime and must not exceed its reasonable limits. In his view, punishment should not be simply a means of exacting vengeance and tormenting the offender. Instead its primary purpose should be to deter, or prevent future acts of criminality. Beccaria further maintained that for punishment to be an effective deterrent it must meet three criteria: severity, swiftness, and certainty.

Considering people's hedonistic nature, the severity of punishment should just slightly outweigh the pleasure derived from the crime. Anything over that calculation, Beccaria contended, is superfluous and tyrannical. Moreover, Beccaria stated that subjecting the offender to intense forms of castigation is counterproductive to the goal of deterrence. To his way of thinking such severe punishment served to incite individuals to commit the very crimes it is intended to prevent.

Based on the principles of what would later be known as behavioral psychology, Beccaria argued that swiftness of punishment is necessary so that the connection between the pleasure of the crime and the pain of the penalty is resolutely impressed in people's minds. Accordingly, he suggested that the accused be tried as speedily as possible in order to minimize the time that elapses between the commission of the crime and its punishment.

According to Beccaria, the third condition, the certainty of punishment, is the most important for successful deterrence. If people believe that there exists a high probability of getting caught and punished for their criminal actions, they will refrain from engaging in that behavior. In sum, Beccaria's three criteria of severity, swiftness, and certainty decrease the likelihood that punishments will be motivated by the irrational desire for revenge and applied arbitrarily. Conversely, the three criteria increase the likelihood that punishments will be motivated by the goal of deterrence and applied systematically.

As a result of Beccaria's *On Crimes and Punishments*, legal and penal reforms took place in various countries throughout Europe. The book's popularity and impact also extended to North America. Its "spirit" can be found in documents central to the political development of the U.S. such as the Declarations of Causes and Independence, the Constitution, and the Bill of Rights. For example, Beccaria's concern with the excesses of punishments is found in the doctrine of proportionality as stipulated in the Eighth Amendment to the U.S. Constitution: "Excessive bail shall not be required, nor excessive fines imposed, nor cruel and unusual punishments inflicted." Thomas Jefferson and John Adams were influenced by and quoted from Beccaria's book. Benjamin Rush, a noted physician and signer of the Declaration of Independence, also made reference to Beccaria in an essay that Rush wrote on the injustices of capital punishment.

A. Javier Treviño

Biography

Born in Milan, Italy, March 15, 1738; son of aristocrats. Educated at the Jesuit College in Parma; Law degree from the University of Pavia, 1758; Professor of Political Economy at the, Public Economy and Commerce, Palatine School in Milan, 1768; Appointed to the Supreme Economic Council of Milan, 1771; Died on November 28, 1794.

Selected Works

Del disordine e de' rimedi delle monete nello stato di Milano nell' anno 1762, 1762.

Dei Delitti e delle Pene, 1764; translated as *On Crimes and Punishments*, translated by Henry Paolucci, 1963; Macmillan Publishing Co. edition., 1777.

References and Further Reading

Beirne, P., Inventing Criminology: The 'Science of Man' in Cesare Beccaria's *Dei Delitti e Delle Pene*, *Criminology*, 29 (1991).

Caso, A., *America's Italian Founding Fathers*, Branden Press, Boston, MA, 1975.

Devine, F.E., Cesare Beccaria and the Theoretical Foundations of Modern Penal Jurisprudence, *New England Journal of Prison Law*, 7 (1982).

Jenkins, P., Varieties of Enlightenment Criminology: Beccaria, Godwin, de Sade, *British Journal of Criminology*, 24 (1984).

Maestro, M.T., *Voltaire and Beccaria as Reformers of Criminal Law*, Octagon Books, New York, 1972.

Maestro, M.T., *Cesare Beccaria and the Origins of Penal Reform*, Temple University Press, Philadelphia, PA, 1973.

Monachesi, E., Cesare Beccaria, in Mannheim, H., Ed., *Pioneers in Criminology*, 2nd ed., Patterson Smith, Montclair, NJ, 1972.

Newman, G., and Marongiu, P., Penological Reform and the Myth of Beccaria, *Criminology*, 28 (1990).

Phillipson, C., *Three Criminal Law Reformers: Beccaria, Bentham, Romilly*, Dent, London, 1923; reprint, Smith, Montclair, NJ, 1970.

Young, D.B., Cesare Beccaria: Utilitarian or Retributivist? *Journal of Criminal Justice*, 11 (1983).

See also **Capital Punishment, History of International; Deterrence, General; Deterrence, Specific (Special)**

Becker, Howard S.

Before he entered academia, Howard Becker spent many years as a piano player entertaining in taverns. Sociology, he claims, was a sideline. Starting his academic career in this way—he now feels—allowed him to miss many of the pitfalls of conventional approaches to standard problems in criminology. He claims to never have thought of himself as a criminologist, but just a sociologist. Yet Howard Becker is one of the premiere theorists of the discipline. This honor, he asserts, has been thrust upon him.

Becker favored the interactionist perspective, which briefly asserts that human behavior is a process of action and interaction between individuals. His work on the identification of deviance, what has come to be known as labeling theory, has been marked as an integral theoretical perspective in the study of criminology.

Outsiders: Studies in the Sociology of Deviance (1963), served to crystalize previous attempts made by Tannenbaum (1938), Lemert (1951), Kitsuse (1962), and Erikson (1962) at drawing attention to the importance of societal reaction as a mechanism in the formation of the deviant identity. Becker contributes two central concepts to the theorizing on the acquisition of the deviant identity. The importance of the reaction to nonconformist behavior and the dynamics and selectivity of rule enforcement are conceptualized as paramount in the identification of deviant offenders.

In essence, Becker asserts that rule-makers create deviance in that they outline guidelines of proper conduct. Rule-breakers, those who violate conventional norms and values, become labeled as outsiders. Therefore deviance is not inherent to the individual, or the act, but in the reaction to the behavior and the application of labels to nonconformists. The deviant is, therefore, someone who has been successfully labeled as a rule-breaker by another, or group of others. The labeling process is a product of the interaction between one who is carrying out a behavior, or set of behaviors, and the moral entrepreneur(s) who witness and interpret these actions as either deviant or nondeviant. Howard Becker also notes that deviant behavior does not develop in a social vacuum. Rather, is the product of a series of sequential events leading up to the point of the behavior being carried out, culminating in the labeling of the offender.

In *Outsiders*, Becker outlines four basic types of deviant behavior. First, "conformists" are those who are not rule-breakers, nor are their actions perceived as rule violations. Those who violate a rule, and are perceived as a deviant, are considered "pure deviants." However, this is not the only social situation in which labeling of behavior occurs. One can be labeled deviant, yet commit no behavioral rule violation. Becker identifies these individuals as being "falsely accused." They are interesting in that they suffer all the stigma of the rule-breaker, without carrying out the deviant act. Even more interesting are those "secret deviants" who commit deviant acts that go undetected.

The actual application process of the label to the offender, Becker notes, is a selective one. The physical, social, and cultural context in which the behavior takes place has to be considered when estimating whether or not deviant behavior will be identified. For example, smoking marijuana is currently prohibited by law in the U.S. However, where and when it is smoked and with whom are mitigating factors in whether a crime is reported to police. If the drug is consumed alone, or with other drug users, it is less likely that this behavior will be identified as deviant by a moral entrepreneur, or rule-maker. If, on the other hand, it is consumed in a public park while small children are playing, parents may find this behavior offensive and request officer assistance to curtail the offending action.

Becker argues that a final step in the successful acceptance of the deviant identity by one who violates conventional norms lies in the movement of that individual into an organized group, or the realization that they are already part of a deviant organization. This can have a powerful effect on how the rule-breaker perceives his or her own identity in relation to the world around them. Subcultures form when individuals who share or participate in similar deviant activities develop, and abide by, a set of alternative norms and values inclusive of the specific form of deviance.

Indeed, Becker's use of the interactionist perspective in explaining the process of labeling of rule-breaking behavior was one of the first explanations of deviant behavior to acknowledge the dynamics of power in the identification of norm violation. Some critical theorists, who theorize about the nature of power in rule formation and the offender identification process, have adopted various ideas put forth by Becker and others. Labeling theory conceptualizes the process of power in differential identification and variable social control of rule violators through both informal (e.g., by shaming or gossip) and formal (e.g., by police or courts) systems of crime control.

One central criticism of this theory surrounds the concept of the "secret deviant." If, as Becker asserts, societal reaction is important in the deviant labeling process, is an act that is not brought to the attention of the public, in fact, deviant? In other words, is deviance inherent to the individual committing the act, or is it solely the product of societal reaction? This has been countered with the argument that the individual may engage in self-labeling of their own behavior. The offender knows it is wrong, and anticipates that other members of his or her society will disapprove. The secret deviant therefore carries out the socially disapproved act(s) while taking precautions to avoid detection.

Finally, the resulting label, if applied successfully to and accepted by the offender, can become a controlling identity, or master status. Becker warns that treating those who are identified as having committed a rule violation as generally deviant, rather than committing a specific act of deviance, may lead to a self-fulfilling prophecy. John Braithwaite (1989) extends the interactionist perspective in his book, *Crime, Shame, and Reintegration*, not only acknowledging the damaging effects of the labeling process, but also suggesting that there may be positive alternatives to punishment that reintegrates offenders back into society.

HANNAH SCOTT

Biography

Born in Chicago, Illinois, April 18, 1928; Educated at the University of Chicago, A.B., 1946; M.A., 1949, Ph.D., 1951. Research associate, Chicago Area Project, 1951–1953; Instructor, University of Chicago, 1952–1953; Project Director, Community Studies, Inc., Kansas City, Missouri, 1955–1962; research sociologist, Institute for the Study of Human Problems, Stanford University, 1962–1965; associate to professor of sociology, Northwestern University 1965–1991; Editor, *Social Problems*, 1961–1964; professor of sociology, University of Washington, 1991–1998; adjunct professor, School of Music, University of Washington, 1995–1998; Adjunct professor, University of California, Santa Barbara, 1998–present. Currently retired and living in San Francisco.

Selected Works

The Professional Dance Musician and His Audience, *American Journal of Sociology*, 57 (1951).
Becoming a Marijuana User, *American Journal of Sociology*, 59 (1953).
Marijuana Use and Social Control, *Social Problems*, 3 (1955).
Outsiders: Studies in the Sociology of Deviance, 1963; revised edition 1973.
The Other Side: Perspectives on Deviance, 1964.
Conventional Crime, *Orthopsychiatry and the Law*, 1968.
Sociological Work: Method and Substance, 1970.
Practitioners of Vice and Crime, in *Pathways to Data*, Habenstein R., Ed. (1970).
Art Worlds, 1980.
Exploring Society Photographically, edited, 1982.
Doing Things Together: Selected Papers, 1986.

References and Further Reading

Braithwaite, J. *Crime, Shame, and Reintegration*, Cambridge University Press, Cambridge, U.K., 1989.
Cullen, F. and Cullen, J. *Toward a Paradigm of Labeling Theory*, University of Nebraska, Lincoln, NE, 1978.
Erikson, K., Notes on the Sociology of Deviance, *Social Problems*, 9 (1962).
Kitsuse, J., Societal Reaction to Deviant Behavior: Problems of Theory and Method, *Social Problems*, 9 (1962).
Lamert, E., *Social Pathology*, McGraw-Hill, New York, 1951.
Pfohl, S., *Images of Deviance and Social Control: A Sociological History*, McGraw-Hill, New York, 1994.
Schur, E.M., *Labeling Deviant Behavior: Its Sociological Implications*, Harper and Row, New York, 1971.
Schur, E.M., *Labeling Women Deviant: Gender, Stigma, and Social Control*, Temple University Press, Philadelphia, PA, 1983.
Tannenbaum, F., *Crime and the Community*, Ginn, New York, 1938.
Wright, C., *Constructions of Deviance in Sociological Theory: The Problem of Commensurability*, University Press of America, Lanham, MD, 1984.

See also **Braithwaite, John; Labeling and Symbolic Interaction Theories of Criminal Behavior**

Bentham, Jeremy

English social philosopher Jeremy Bentham devoted his life to writing about a variety of subjects including legal reform. Accordingly, he produced a series of books on such related issues as moral philosophy, criminal jurisprudence, and penology. However, Bentham's most important work, in which he formulated a set of tenets that provide a guide for legal reform, was *An Introduction to the Principles of Morals and Legislation* (1789). In this volume he described and developed much of his moral philosophy, which reflects his most famous doctrine, "the principle of utility."

The legal and penal systems of Europe during the late 18th century, the time when Bentham proposed his reforms, were highly irrational. The law was applied by judges in an arbitrary, inconsistent, and contradictory manner so that, from one jurisdiction to another, practices varied to an extraordinary degree. Moreover, the infliction of punishment on the accused was characterized by vindictiveness and a high degree of cruelty. In addition, innocent persons were frequently the victims of this capricious application of law and punishment. Against this background of gross injustices Bentham called for the rational revision of the legal and penal systems of Europe.

Bentham's campaign for reforming the criminal law has its theoretical basis in the principle of utility. His philosophy begins with one simple assertion about the nature of human conduct: after rationally considering their options, people inevitably pursue pleasure and avoid pain. Thus, according to Bentham, an action possesses utility if it tends to produce pleasure or happiness, or tends to prevent pain or unhappiness. Bentham believed that "the greatest happiness of the greatest number," was the foundation of morals and legislation. It is this notion—that what is morally obligatory is that which produces the greatest amount of happiness for the greatest number of people—which Bentham argued should guide all legislation. Any action that does not maximize the greatest happiness is, therefore, morally—and legally—wrong.

Bentham developed a felicific ("happiness-making") calculus to measure the amount of pleasure and pain that a particular act possesses for the individual whose interest is being considered. According to him, lawmakers, in order to effectively deter crime through punishment, must calculate the sum total of pleasure and pain resulting from a criminal act. Bentham proposed that the value of a pleasure, or pain, can be measured according to its: (1) *intensity*; (2) *duration*; (3) *certainty* or *uncertainty*; (4) *propinquity* or *remoteness*; (5) *fecundity*, or the chance that a pleasure is followed by other pleasures, a pain by further pains; (6) *purity*, or the chance that a pleasure is followed by pains and vice versa; (7) *extent*, that is, the number of persons affected by the pleasure or pain. To measure the value of pleasure and pain of any act we are to take the balance, which, if on the side of pleasure, will give the act's good tendency and if on the side of pain, will give bad tendency.

Bentham maintained that since potential criminals rationally calculate the pleasures and pains that arise from committing a crime, the felicific calculus would serve to set the amount of punishment necessary to deter crime. However, given that punishment is itself an evil, if it is to be imposed at all, it must to be imposed only insofar as it helps to prevent some greater evil. Punishment, Bentham argues, should not be inflicted where it is (1) *groundless*, where there is no mischief for it to prevent; (2) *inefficacious*, where it cannot prevent the mischief; (3) *unprofitable*, or too expensive, where the cost of punishment outweighs the cost of the harm it seeks to prevent; (4) *needless*, where the mischief may be prevented, or cease of itself, without punishment.

Bentham then states that when punishment is necessary to deter crime, there are four goals in calculating the proportion between crime and punishment that must be considered in legislation. First, the ultimate goal should be the prevention of all crime. To achieve this goal, the pain of the punishment must not be less than the pleasure derived from the crime. Second, if a person is intent on committing a crime, the next goal is to induce that person to commit a less serious crime. This means that the punishment for a serious offense must be sufficiently painful to induce the person to prefer committing a less serious offense. Third, when a person has actually decided to commit a crime, that person should be persuaded by the threat of punishment to do no more mischief than necessary. Consequently, the pain of punishment should be adjusted to fit the seriousness of the offense, so that for every increase in the seriousness of the offense the punishment may serve as a deterrent. Finally, the last goal of legislation should be to prevent crime as cheaply as possible. Punishment, therefore, should not be more painful than what is necessary to deter crime. Bentham believed that these four goals, if appropriately incorporated into law, would serve to bring a person's pursuit of their own happiness in line with the best interests of the community as a whole.

Bentham's belief that the ultimate goal of punishment is deterrence led him to agitate for penal reform because prior to the late 18th century severe and cruel punishments were routinely inflicted on offenders. Additionally, hundreds of crimes were punishable by death, usually in an aggravated fashion, and prisons were places where offenders were systematically subjected to all sorts of torments. Furthermore, incarceration was not a function of the prison during this period.

Given these non-utilitarian practices, Bentham, in 1791, designed the Panopticon (Greek, meaning "all seeing")—a model prison where all prisoners would be visually isolated from each other, while being continually observed by a small number of guards. Bentham believed that the Panopticon's architectural design—which consisted of a three-storied circular or polygonal building with individual cells around its perimeter and an inspection tower for the guards at its center—would do no less than reform prisoners and eliminate crime. Most Panopticon-style prisons, including two constructed in the U.S.—the Western State Penitentiary in Pittsburgh, Pennsylvania and part of Stateville prison in Joliet, Illinois—have been abandoned as impractical. A prison design that allowed guards to watch inmates at all times proved to have the disadvantage of enabling inmates to observe the actions of guards.

A. Javier Treviño

Biography

Born in London, England, February 15, 1748; son of a lawyer. Educated at Westminster School; Entered Queen's College, Oxford, 1760; Studied law at Lincoln's Inn, 1763; Called to the bar, 1772; Died in London, England on June 6, 1832.

Selected Works

A Fragment on Government, 1776.
An Introduction to the Principles of Morals and Legislation, 1789.
Panopticon; or The Inspection-House, 1791.
Théorie des peines et des récompenses, 1811.
Constitutional Code, 1830.

References and Further Reading

Foucault, M., *Discipline and Punish: The Birth of the Prison*, Vintage Books, New York, 1979.
Geis, G., Jeremy Bentham, in Mannheim, H., Ed., *Pioneers in Criminology*, Patterson Smith, Montclair, NJ, 1972.
Harrison, R., *Bentham*, Routledge & Kegan Paul, London, 1983.
Hart, H.L.A., *Essays on Bentham: Studies in Jurisprudence and Political Theory*, Clarendon Press, Oxford, U.K., 1982.
Lyons, D., *In the Interest of the Governed: A Study in Bentham's Philosophy of Utility and Law*, Clarendon Press, Oxford, U.K., 1973.
Parekh, B., Ed., *Jeremy Bentham: Ten Critical Essays*, Frank Cass, London, 1974.
Phillipson, C., *Three Criminal Law Reformers: Beccaria, Bentham, Romilly*, J.M. Dent and Sons, London, 1923.

See also **Beccaria, Cesare; Deterrence, General; Deterrence, Specific (Special)**

Biochemical Theories of Criminal Behavior

Throughout history theorists have attempted to explain the causes of criminal and delinquent behavior. One area of theory and research has focused on the biological components that influence involvement in criminal activity. One area that biologists have investigated is the role that neurochemicals play in behavior. Whereas this area has examined numerous explanatory models, two specific theories that have garnered recent attention surround the effects of hormones and attention deficit hyperactivity disorder (ADHD) on crime and delinquency.

Historical Development

Similar to psychological theories of crime, biological theories focus on the individual differences in persons that affect behavior. Unlike sociological explanations, however, biological theories reject the supposition that free will determines behavior. Instead, these theories center on the interaction between biological predisposition and sociological or environmental influences. As such, in response to the emphasis placed on scientific methodology and research, biologists sought to identify, through scientific analysis, these biological predispositions.

Initially, biological theories were employed to explain criminal behavior by the presence of physical traits. For example, body type and other physical characteristics were thought to be indicative of criminality. Whereas these theories were subsequently refuted, they did lay the framework for further research. Based on the observations that many criminals display aggressive and deviant tendencies early in life, biologists first set out to determine if behaviors in general and criminality specifically could in fact be inherited. The quest to examine this key question led to genetic studies of twins and adoptees. These studies, although finding different strengths of the relationship, in general show that identical twins are more likely to both engage in crime than fraternal twins. In addition, adoptees are more similar to their biological parents than their adoptive parents in terms of criminality. The findings of these studies suggest that hereditary factors may influence or predispose deviant behavior. Once this potential genetic basis of crime was uncovered, researchers began to seek out other biological causal factors.

Food Allergies and Dietary Influences

Although the link between diet and criminal behavior has not been firmly established, researchers have investigated its possible association. In doing so, food allergies and additives have been implicated as potential sources of violence, hyperactivity, and irritability. Foods that have substances in them that may cause allergic reactions and subsequent behavior problems include chocolate, cheese, milk, citrus fruit, wheat, and eggs. When such foods are consumed by an individual who is allergic, it is believed that swelling occurs in the brain. This swelling is thought to limit higher-order cognitive functioning, thus increasing the amount of impulsive and antisocial behavior.

Other studies have investigated the diets of persons who have engaged in crime or deviance. These studies have implicated additives in foods, such as monosodium glutamate, aspartame, xanthines, dyes, and artificial flavorings, as potentially producing aggressive behaviors. Perhaps most widely publicized has been the link between sugar consumption and levels of blood sugar and crime. It is thought that diets that are high in refined sugars may lead to hyperactive or aggressive behavior. In light of this assertion, some prisons have reduced the amount of refined sugar in the meals served to inmates. Not only have prisons recognized the possible link between sugar and violence, the criminal law has also recognized the role that diet may play in behavior. The "Twinkie defense" was used by Dan White in his murder trial to explain the erratic behavior that led up to his murdering a fellow supervisor. He blamed this murder on his consumption of Twinkies and Coca-Cola along with other high-sugar foods. Luckily, for White, the jury apparently believed his defense and convicted him of manslaughter rather than murder.

An individual's blood sugar level is another potential source of aggressive behavior. Persons who are hypoglycemic have low levels of blood sugar. This condition can be particularly harmful to brain functioning and can result in headache, anxiety, confusion and also aggression. Studies of blood sugar levels have revealed that violent male offenders are in fact more likely to have hypoglycemia than nonoffenders.

Hormonal Influences on Crime

With the advent of more sophisticated research methodologies and the development in knowledge regarding the human brain, scientists have concluded that biochemical differences may exist between criminals and noncriminals. Dating back to the mid-1800s, scientists recognized that hormones produced by the endocrine system have effects on behavior. In the 1920s, Schlapp and colleagues proposed that biochemical deficiencies and dysfunctions are responsible for all criminal behavior. Specifically, Schlapp believed that one third of all prison inmates had experienced a toxic infection or problems with gland functioning. Building upon these early works, more recent attention has been given to the relationship between levels of estrogen and testosterone and aggression and crime.

Research suggests that high levels of testosterone, the male gonadal hormone, is associated with increased levels of aggression in both women and men. This conclusion has been supported in studies of teenagers, adults, and prisoners. Recent studies show that testosterone may not directly influence aggressive behavior; rather, its effects may be mediated by social interaction. Specifically, persons with increased levels of testosterone tend to express more irritability and frustration, which causes them to be less capable of healthy social interactions. That is, situational factors may interact with high testosterone levels to elicit aggressive responses.

Testosterone may also interact with levels of neurotransmitters to produce aggression. One such neurotransmitter that has been implicated in aggressive behavior is serotonin. Serotonin is produced by the brain and when released, calms an individual down. Persons who possess high levels of testosterone may be at an increased risk for aggressive or violent behavior if they do not produce serotonin in the amount sufficient enough to calm their naturally aggressive responses.

Although females are generally less aggressive than males and produce smaller amounts of testosterone, some women may possess higher than normal levels of testosterone, possibly leading to higher levels of aggressive behavior. Other women may react to the fluctuations in hormones associated with the onset of menstruation. This relationship was first articulated after researchers determined that many crimes perpetrated by females were done so during the premenstrual and early menstruation periods. After ovulation, the ratio of the "female" hormones, estrogen and progesterone, becomes imbalanced. This imbalance is thought to contribute to the alterations in physical symptoms and mood that may subsequently cause some women to become aggressive or violent.

Although research has shown mixed support for the relationship between the menstrual cycle and aggression, it has been found that at least some women respond to hormonal changes with irritability and aggression. Notably, research of incarcerated women has shown that many women report being the most aggressive during the premenstrual phase. In addition, other researchers have found that many women who physically abuse their children do so during this same phase, reportedly feeling severe irritability during this time. Similarly, evidence exists that testosterone levels in women may also affect aggression. That is, for both women and adolescent females, high levels of testosterone are associated with violent behavior.

It should be noted, however, that research in this area is limited and oftentimes potentially flawed. It is possible that there are mediating variables not taken into account in the current available research. In other words, it is possible that changes in hormone levels alone do not account for aggressive behavior. Instead, these hormonal changes may affect a third, unspecified variable (such as self-control or social bonds) that leads to aggressive responses. Rather than directly affecting behavior, hormones may instead interact with social factors to produce criminal behavior. Secondly, it is possible that the heavy reliance on self-reports of aggressive behavior and the timing of menstruation may be problematic. Solely relying on recall of when menstruation occurs can potentially lead to inaccurate results if women can not accurately remember the specific dates of their past menstrual cycles. Because researchers have attempted to link aggression to particular points during the cycle, error about cycle times can lead to faulty conclusions.

In addition to these methodological issues, linking hormones to crime and aggression also leads to ethical and ideological concerns. First, it is possible that if persons are found to have high levels of testosterone, they may be encouraged to undergo chemotherapy as a mechanism of prevention, even in the absence of criminal behavior. Whereas it may be useful to identify those *criminals* who may have elevated levels, there are potential ethical problems with manipulating a person's hormones against their will. A second concern is that the findings of researchers have led defense attorneys to use premenstrual syndrome as a defense for crimes committed by some women. Whereas it may be possible that the menstrual cycle is linked to crime, blaming behavior hormonal fluctuations on could potentially be detrimental to women as a whole. As such, it is possible that using menstruation as an explanation for crime may lead society to revert to questioning the ability of women to perform duties and control their emotions.

Attention Deficit/Hyperactivity Disorder

In addition to hormonal influences on crime, other biochemical deficiencies may be responsible for criminality in both adults and juveniles. Deficiencies in specific neurotransmitters, substances secreted by neurons in the brain, may be linked to antisocial behaviors such as substance abuse and crime. In investigating this relationship, it has been found that a lack of certain neurotransmitters like serotonin and dopamine is evident in many persons diagnosed with the behavioral disorder Attention Deficit Hyperactivity Disorder (ADHD).

Persons with ADHD typically exhibit a range of symptoms that are due to impulsive behavior that is seemingly erratic. Often, persons suffering from ADHD evince behaviors that are not appropriate in a specific setting. Additionally, because persons with ADHD are easily distractible, they are unable to give sufficient levels of attention or concentration to age-appropriate tasks. Children in particular often show impairments in functioning in the home, in school, and in their friendships. Notably, not only is ADHD associated with short-term problems, persons with ADHD are likely to have persistent, long-term problems academically, vocationally, and personally.

Originally termed minimal brain dysfunction or minimal brain damage, ADHD is the most widely diagnosed behavioral disorder of childhood. Estimates of prevalence for American youths under the age of 18 range from 3% to 10%. Whereas official diagnosis is made by a physician, parents and teachers often refer children to doctors and psychiatrists based on their own observations at home or in the classroom. Thus, children may be misperceived as having ADHD when in fact they do not. Because of the reliance on referrals for what may be "normal" child behaviors, it has been suggested that ADHD is overdiagnosed in the U.S. An additional problem with diagnosis lies in the high co-occurrence of other disorders. In particular, conduct disorder and ADHD are often both present in individuals. Because the two disorders share many common symptoms, it is difficult to distinguish between them, thus possibly leading to further misdiagnosis.

Another potential problem with diagnosis of ADHD is that no consensus exists regarding its cause. While it is generally thought that the cause of ADHD is biological in nature, no specific test has been developed to test this assertion. Some research has shown that ADHD could have a genetic basis. Studies have revealed that the frequency of ADHD and other disorders is higher in the relatives of persons with ADHD than in those who do not suffer from ADHD. This genetic link suggests a biological cause. In investigating this relationship, researchers have proposed that the development of ADHD is a result of deficiencies in certain neurochemicals. Specifically, defects in the central nervous system limit the brain's ability to properly metabolize the neurotransmitters serotonin, dopamine, and norepinephrine. Imbalances of these neurotransmitters have been associated with behavioral abnormalities such as impulsivity and aggression.

Other research suggests that ADHD may be a result of low cortical arousal. The brains of persons suffering from ADHD show a lack of activity in areas responsible for arousal and alertness. Importantly, low levels of arousal, as indicated by tests of the autonomic nervous system, are often found among offenders. Farrington (1987) found a significant relationship between low heart rate and convictions for violent offenses. Although the exact causal linkages are unknown, it is thought that a lack of arousal may in fact cause persons with ADHD to seek out stimuli in their environments. These stimuli oftentimes involve engaging in illegal or deviant activities. Together, imbalances in neurochemicals and the lack of arousal may lead to persons engaging in stimulation-seeking behaviors (e.g. crime).

Importantly, although ADHD is most commonly diagnosed in children, prospective studies have shown that ADHD often persists into adolescence. Because many criminals begin offending during adolescence, this finding is particularly salient to the criminal justice researcher. A review of the research reveals that adolescents with ADHD are more likely to be suspended from school and admitted into juvenile justice facilities. Other researchers have found that juveniles with ADHD are more likely to report engaging in violence and are also more likely to have come into contact with the criminal justice system for their violent acts. Juveniles who suffer from ADHD are also more likely to engage in other antisocial behaviors. Specifically, research shows that juveniles with ADHD often have problems with drugs and/or alcohol. Although it is not clear if ADHD actually causes substance abuse, they co-occur in a substantial portion of juveniles. In summary, persons with ADHD often engage in a constellation of problem behaviors that may increase their risk of coming into contact with the criminal justice system.

Not only does ADHD persist into adolescence, research suggests that its symptoms and effects are also present into adulthood. Specifically, follow-up studies of children with ADHD show that up to two-thirds possess ADHD symptoms as adults. Whereas research shows that having ADHD in adulthood is not solely responsible for engaging in crime, adults with ADHD are more likely to have been arrested, convicted, and incarcerated than persons without such a diagnosis. Moreover, like juveniles, adults with prior diagnoses of ADHD are significantly more likely to develop problems with alcohol and drugs and to engage in other antisocial behaviors.

Similar to persons who have problems with hormonal imbalances, persons with ADHD often respond to medications. Administration of central nervous system stimulants is one of the most common modes of treatment for both children and adolescents. In fact, such chemotherapy has been shown to be effective in reducing restlessness and impulsivity and has been found to aid in concentration and frustration management. Although treatment with medication appears to be an effective option, it can also lead to problems for the criminal justice system. Not all persons with ADHD will respond favorably to stimulants. These persons may subsequently be singled out for other less rehabilitative punishments based on their apparent inability to be "cured." In addition to treatment issues, the criminal justice system will also have to deal with a range of other issues associated with ADHD. Persons may attempt to use their suffering from a behavioral disorder as a defense or excuse for their criminal activity. Although such defenses have not been received favorably in courts, it is possible that ADHD may be viewed as a mitigating factor in both trials and in sentencing. Also, because many persons with ADHD do often come into contact with the criminal justice system, it is imperative that facilities be equipped with proper diagnostic tools, medications, and trained counselors.

It is apparent that whereas biochemical factors may not alone cause criminality, they likely play a role in the etiology of deviance. Because of this relationship, researchers in criminal justice and in the scientific community have recently begun to investigate the relationship between both hormonal imbalances and ADHD and participation in crime. This attention given to biochemical theories by scientists in a range of fields will enable further collaboration among disciplines. These pursuits have led to the formation of more integrated criminological theories which recognize biosocial influences. In addition, they have aided researchers in their quest to articulate developmental theories that incorporate prenatal, genetic and psychosocial elements. Research in these areas has revealed that factors within an individual and in society influence behaviors. Further investigation into these influences will surely arise in response to, in part, the research that has been conducted on biochemical theories of crime.

LEAH E. DAIGLE

References and Further Reading

Diagnosis and Treatment of Attention Deficit Hyperactivity Disorder, *NIH Consens Statement Online*, 16, 1–37 (Nov. 16–18, 1998).

Farrington, D.P., Implications of Biological Findings for Criminological Research, in Mednick, S.A., Moffitt, T.E., and Stack, S.A. Eds., *The Causes of Crime: New Biological Approaches*, Cambridge University Press, Cambridge, U.K., 1987, pp. 42–64.

Fishbein, D.H., *The Science, Treatment, and Prevention of Antisocial Behaviors: Application to the Criminal Justice System,* Civic Research Institute, Inc., Kingston, NJ, 2000.

Fishbein, D., The Psychobiology of Female Aggression, *Criminal Justice and Behavior*, 19, 99–126 (1992).

Goldstein, S., Attention-Deficit/Hyperactivity Disorder: Implications for the Criminal Justice System, *FBI Law Enforcement Bulletin*, 66, 11–16 (1997).

Maes, M. and Coccaro, E.F. Eds., *Neurobiology and Clinical Views on Aggression and Impulsivity*, John Wiley & Sons, New York, 1998.

Niehoff, D., *The Biology of Violence: How Understanding the Brain, Behavior, and Environment Can Break the Vicious Circle of Aggression*, The Free Press, New York, 1999.

Schlapp, M. and Smith, E., *The New Criminology*, Boni & Liveright, New York, 1928.

See also **Biological Theories of Criminal Behavior; Neurophysiological Theories of Criminal Behavior; Psychological Theories of Criminal Behavior**

Biocriminology *See* **Biological Theories of Criminal Behavior; Genealogical Studies of Crime**

Biological Theories of Criminal Behavior

There are three broad "biological" approaches to the study of criminal behavior: evolutionary, behavior genetics, and neurophysiological. These theories are more aptly called biosocial theories, since they stress that the environment mediates, and often initiates, all biological phenomena relevant to behavior. Evolutionary psychologists stress the universality of a human nature developed in response to challenges faced in ancestral environments, and that this evolved nature is always expressed contingently. Behavior geneticists accent the point that genes influence, but do not determine, how we respond to the environment. Genes facilitate the activation of behaviors we have decided to perform, and are thus really at our beck and call rather than the other way around. For their part, neuroscientists inform us that apart from some vital "hard wired" functions, the brain wires itself by the selective retention of neural pathways in response to environmental inputs.

Biosocial theories are theories of criminality, not crime. The confusion of these terms often leads to faulty arguments about why biology is irrelevant to criminological understanding. Crime is a legal label placed on socially disapproved behavior, and the definition, spread, concentration, and prevalence of crime is rightfully the domain of traditional sociological criminology. Criminality, on the other hand, is a property of individuals, a continuous trait that is itself an amalgam of other continuous traits, and thus belongs to a more inclusive kind of criminology. Criminality involves the willingness to violate social norms and individual rights regardless of whether these violations have been criminalized, a willingness that indexes a relative lack of empathy, conscience, self-control, and fear, as well as self-centeredness, and a penchant for risky behavior.

Biosocial theories have never been popular with American criminologists. This may change in the near future as biosocial arguments become increasingly difficult to ignore. Two recent addresses to the *American Society of Criminology* by presidents Charles Wellford (1997) and Margaret Zahn (1999) called for more biologically informed criminological theory. We have seen increasingly more journal space being devoted to biosocial criminology over the last decade, and significantly more space being devoted to it in criminology textbooks. Except for textbooks authored by Marxist/radical theorists, who still tend to link biosocial theories to racism, sexism, and other pejorative "isms," biosocial theories are given fairly balanced treatment in most of them (Wright & Miller, 1998).

Evolutionary Theories

Evolutionary theorists look for ultimate causes, and ask about how what we now call criminal behavior might have been adaptive in ancestral environments. *Homo sapiens* is a cooperative species with reciprocal altruism being the primary mode of relationship maintenance. Cooperative species provide niches for "cheats," i.e., those who signal cooperation and then default. Cheats gain resources at no cost to themselves, and cheating may thus have promoted biological fitness. *Fitness* refers to reproductive success (the maintenance of an organism's genes in future generations), therefore the specific theories addressed here focus on reproductive strategies (mating effort versus parenting effort) and the tactics that flow from them. Evolved traits (deception, egoism, aggression, sensation-seeking) were selected to foster reproductive success, not criminality, but they also serve that purpose.

Cheater theory focuses on the different reproductive strategies of males and females. The major factor in female reproductive success has been to secure and hold on to the assistance of a mate to raise her offspring, and thus females have evolved a strategy inclining them to be choosier than males about with whom they will mate. Male reproductive success potentially increases with the number of females a male can have sex with, and thus males have evolved a desire for multiple partners. Males can respond to the more reticent female strategy by complying with female preferences and assist a single female raise their offspring, or they can either trick or force a female to have sex and then move on to the next female. These two strategies have been called *Dad vs. Cad*. Just as almost all males have committed some form of delinquent act during adolescence, they have probably used cheater tactics (falsely proclaiming love and fidelity and the use of some form of coercion) to obtain sex in their youth.

The "dad" strategy is facilitated by the social emotions, particularly love and empathy, and the "cad" strategy is likely to be followed well after adolescence by males deficient in these emotions. Criminal behavior is facilitated by the same traits that make for the successful pursuit of a cheater sexual strategy. Cheater theory does not postulate that criminal behavior reflects a defective genome. Rather it reflects a normal, albeit morally regrettable, alternative followed by a large percentage of males during adolescence and by a small subset of males over the life-course. Linda Mealey (1995), the major proponent of cheater theory, avers that this small subset (psychopaths) are genetically "programmed" to adopt a cheater reproductive strategy, and that this "programming" spills over into all other areas of social interaction.

Conditional adaptation theory (CAT) proposes that people adopt different reproductive strategies depending on their early experiences. A uniform reproductive strategy would not be evolutionarily viable for all individuals since circumstances often vary drastically. According to CAT, the early home environment represents a prototype for children, providing them with a set of expectations regarding interpersonal relationships that set them on two distinct reproductive pathways. Individuals will tend to adopt an unrestricted (promiscuous) sexual strategy if they learned during their childhood that interpersonal relationships are ephemeral and unreliable (as indexed by such things as parental divorce, witnessing others engaging in short-term relationships, and lack of attachment to parents or caregivers). Individuals who experienced the opposite (stable pair bonding and secure parental attachment) will tend to adopt a more restricted strategy. Needless to say, neither strategy is consciously chosen, but rather flows from subconscious expectations based on early experiences of the stability or instability and quality of interpersonal relationships.

As with cheater theory, Jay Belsky (1997), the leading proponent of CAT, avers that the same suite of traits that facilitate an unrestricted sexual strategy also facilitate criminality, and that traits useful for focusing resources on parenting effort, such as conscientiousness, empathy, and altruism, are also conducive to prosocial activity.

Alternative adaptation theory (AAT) differs from CAT in that it proposes that humans are arrayed along a continuum regarding where they tend to focus their reproductive efforts largely for genetic rather than environmental reasons. At one end is mating effort (effort devoted to seeking multiple sex partners) and at the other is parenting effort (effort devoted to rearing young). The best demographic predictors of where reproductive effort is focused are also the best demographic predictors of criminal behavior: age and gender. Mid-adolescence to early adulthood is a period of intense male reproductive effort replete with competitiveness, risk-taking and violence aimed ultimately at securing more mating opportunities than the next male. In general, males and the young emphasize mating effort and females and older persons emphasize parenting effort.

David Rowe (1996), the main proponent of AAT, agrees with cheater theory and CAT that the traits useful for focusing on mating effort are readily coopted for other deceptive practices. Rowe adds intelligence to his theory, maintaining that low IQ people will tend to gravitate toward mating effort because they typically do not have the ability to gain the resources needed for parenting effort, and have a reduced ability to learn the moral norms of society.

r/K theory posits that all animal species can be arranged on a continuum in terms of resources they expend on parenting effort. The continuum ranges from zero for rapidly developing and prodigious reproducers, to extensive for species that produce few slowly developing offspring. Oysters are extremely r-selected (quantity reproducers), and humans are extremely K selected (quality reproducers).

This continuum is also posited to exist within species, with some individuals possessing more r-selected traits than others, and some possessing more K-selected traits. According to the major proponents of r/K theory, Lee Ellis (1987) and J. Philippe Rushton (1995), criminal behavior is the result of the expression of r-selected behavioral traits. Because males are relatively more r-selected than females, this theory partially accounts for the overrepresentation of males in criminal populations. According to this theory, criminals have been found to be more r-selected than people in general. Studies have shown that, *on an average*, criminals have shorter gestation periods, lower birth weight, earlier puberty, come from larger families, have early onset of sexual behavior, have more sexual partners, and form less stable bonds with others.

Neurological Theories

Neuroscientists seek to discover brain structures and functions among identified criminals that may serve to explain their antisocial behavior. The three most prevalent neurological theories of criminal behavior are suboptimal arousal, reward dominance, and prefrontal cortex dysfunction theories. Just as all evolutionary theories converge on the issue of mating versus parenting effort, these three theories converge on sensation-seeking and impulsiveness, although each theory focuses on different brain systems. The mechanisms explored by these theories may constitute the proximal mechanisms that facilitate the evolved reproductive strategies that evolutionary theories explore at a more ultimate level.

Suboptimal arousal theory maintains that people prefer a level of environmental stimulation that is neither too low nor too high. Arousal levels are primarily a function of the sensitivity of the reticular formation, the network of neurons originating at the spinal cord and projecting into many areas of the brain. Individuals who are unusually sensitive to incoming stimuli will learn to avoid behaviors that elevate arousal to unpleasant levels, and those who are unusually insensitive (suboptimally aroused) will engage in behavior that will increase cortical arousal to an acceptable level. Individuals with attention deficit hyperactivity disorder (ADHD) are in this category. Suboptimal arousal theory alleges that criminals are chronically underaroused relative to people in general, often engaging in provocative acts (substance abuse, fighting, impulsive and risky behavior) in an attempt to alleviate low arousal, which is subjectively experienced as boredom. The major proponents of suboptimal arousal theory are Hans Eysenck (1977) and David Lykken (1995).

Reward dominance theory focuses on two opposing neurological control systems: the behavioral activation system (BAS) and the behavioral inhibiting system (BIS). The BAS is a reward motivator moving us to seek food, sex, and other pleasurable features of the environment, and the BIS alerts us to desist when we have had enough. The BAS is dopamine facilitated and the BIS is serotonin facilitated, and the two systems are balanced in most people. Other people are reward dominant, meaning that they are unusually sensitive to reward cues and unusually insensitive to punishment cues (a lead foot and faulty brakes). Criminals, and especially psychopaths, tend to be overly sensitive to the short-term rewards accompanying antisocial behavior and relatively insensitive to the negative long-term effects of it. Herbert Quay (1988) and Jeffrey Gray (1987) are the major proponents of this theory.

Prefrontal dysfunction (PFD) theory begins by noting that the prefrontal cortex (PFC) is responsible for a number of uniquely human attributes, such as making moral judgment, planning for the future, analyzing, synthesizing, and modulating emotions, all of which are collectively referred to as *executive functions.* These executive functions are quite clearly involved in prosocial behavior. Damage to the PFC often results in impulsive antisocial behavior, a reduced ability to control emotions, and an inability to empathize with others. The damage does not have to be physical, as in a blow to the head; it is often more likely to be the result the maternal ingestion of alcohol or drugs during critical periods of the fetus's brain development.

Adrian Raine (1993), the major figure in PFD theory, claims that the theory can account for some of the physiological arousal factors observed in antisocial individuals by relating physiological functioning to psychological processes. EEG and brain imaging studies show a moderate to strong positive correlation between measures of physiological arousal and arousal of the prefrontal cortex. ADHD individuals manifest low PFC arousal, although this may be more a problem of reticular formation arousal rather than PFC arousal.

Behavior Genetics

Behavior genetics does not have a distinct theory of criminal behavior. Rather, it is interested in identifying genetic contributions (e.g., impulsivity/hyperactivity, aggression, and low IQ) to traits associated with it, and may be viewed as aiding the endeavors of traditional theory rather than seeking to develop its own theory. For instance, strain theory argues that criminal behavior is a function of a perceived inability to achieve a middle-class lifestyle legitimately, but fails to explore the determinants of socioeconomic status (SES) beyond claims of societal discrimination. Extending strain theory to the realm of behavior genetics might involve exploring the genetic underpinning of the major determinants of SES, such as intelligence and conscientiousness. Similarly, self-control theory could benefit from an understanding of the behavior genetic concept of gene to environment correlation, and of the genetics of serotonin, the neurotransmitter underlying levels of self-control.

Determining genetic effects is accomplished through family, twin, and adoption studies that allow for the calculation of heritability coefficients (h^2), which are estimates (ranging between 0.0 and 1.0) of the genetic contribution to a trait in a given population. Heritability coefficients thus allow us to calculate the contribution of the environment to that trait ($1 - h^2$) also. Heritability estimates fluctuate in different populations and in different environmental conditions, which has the benefit of allowing researchers to assess the relative importance of the mix of environmental and genetic factors over time and place.

Because of high base rates of juvenile delinquency we find that genes only account for about 7% of the variances in delinquency, but about 43% of the variance in adult offending (Lyons, et al., 1995). The famous Danish adoption study (Mednick, Gabrielli, and Hutchings, 1984) found modest genetic affects across the entire sample, but strong affects for 37 male adoptees whose biological fathers had three or more criminal convictions. This mere 1% of the cohort accounted for 30% of the cohort's convictions. These studies suggest that genetic influences on antisocial behavior may be weak to nonexistent beneath some unknown threshold, but quite strong above it. Pooling subjects at minimal genetic risk for antisocial behavior with a small minority at great genetic risk, has the effect of elevating estimates of genetic vulnerability overall while simultaneously minimizing them for those most involved in offending.

ANTHONY WALSH

References and Further Reading

Belsky, J., Attachment, Mating, and Parenting. *Human Nature*, 8, 361–381 (1997).

Ellis, L., Criminal Behavior and r/K Selection: An Extension of Gene-Based Evolutionary Theory. *Deviant Behavior*, 8, 149–176 (1987).

Ellis, L. and Hoffman, H., Eds., *Crime in Biological, Social, and Moral Contexts*, Praeger, New York, 1990.

Ellis, L. and Walsh, A., Gene-based Evolutionary Theories in Criminology, *Criminology*, 35, 229–276 (1997).

Ellis, L., and Walsh, A., *Criminology: A Global Perspective*. Allyn & Bacon, Boston, 2000.

Fishbein, D., *Biobehavioral Perspectives in Criminology*. Belmont, CA: Wadsworth, 2000.

Gray, J., *The Psychology of Fear and Stress*, McGraw-Hill, New York, 1987.

Lykken, D., *The Antisocial Personalities*, Lawrence Erlbaum, Hillsdale, NJ, 1995.

Lyons, M., True, W., Eusen, S., Goldberg, J., Meyer, J., Faraone, S., Eaves, L., and Tsuang, M. Differential Heritability of Adult and Juvenile Antisocial Traits, *Archives of General Psychiatry*, 53, 906–915 (1995).

Mealey, L., The Sociobiology of Sociopathy: An Integrated Evolutionary Model. *Behavioral and Brain Sciences*, 18, 523–559 (1995).

Mednick, S., Gabrielli, W., and Hutchings, B., Genetic Influences in Criminal Convictions: Evidence from an Adoption Cohort. *Science*, 224, 891–894 (1984).

Quay, H., The Behavioral Reward and Inhibition System in Childhood Behavior Disorders, in Bloomingdale, L.M., Ed., *Attention Deficit Disorder*, Vol. 3, Pergamon Press, Oxford, U.K., pp. 176–186.

Raine, A. *The Psychopathology of Crime: Criminal Behavior as a Clinical Disorder*. San Diego: Academic Press. (1993).

Rowe, D. An Adaptive Strategy Theory of Crime and Delinquency, in Hawkins, J., Ed., *Delinquency and Crime: Current Theories*, Cambridge University Press, Cambridge, U.K., 1996, pp. 268–314.

Rushton, J.P., Race and Crime: International Data for 1989–1990. *Psychological Reports*, 76, 307–312, 1995.

Walsh, A., *Biosociology: An Emerging Paradigm*, Praeger, New York, 1995.

Walsh, A., Behavior Genetics and Anomie/Strain theory, *Criminology*.

Wellford, C. Controlling Crime and Achieving Justice: The American Society of Criminology 1996 Presidential Address, *Criminology*, 35, 1–11 (1997).

Wright, R. and Miller, J., Taboo Until Today? The Coverage of Biological Arguments in Criminology Textbooks, 1961 to 1970 and 1987 to 1996. *Journal of Criminal Justice*, 26, 1–19 (1998).

Zahn, M., Thoughts on the Future of Criminology. The American Society of Criminology Presidential Address, *Criminology*, 37, 1–15 (1999).

See also **Body-Type Theories of Criminal Behavior; Evolutionary Theories of Criminal Behavior; Genetic Theories of Criminal Behavior; Neurophysiological Theories of Criminal Behavior**

Blackmail

See **Extortion and Blackmail**

Blood Alcohol Content

See **Alcohol Use: The Law; Driving Under the Influence (DUI)**

Blumstein, Alfred

Alfred Blumstein's involvement in criminological research began with his involvement as Director of Science and Technology for the President's Commission on Law Enforcement and Administration of Justice from 1966 to 1967. In this position, he was instrumental in the establishment of a single telephone number (911) made available nationwide that Americans could call for police assistance. His research over the past twenty years has covered many aspects of criminal justice, including demographic trends, youth violence, incarceration patterns, criminal careers, and drug enforcement policy.

The U.S. has seen a steady, dramatic decline in the violent crime rate (which includes rapes, robberies, homicides and assaults) starting slightly in the 1970s through the mid 1990s. The reasons for these declines are not entirely clear and several explanations have been promoted. Alfred Blumstein has been at the forefront of the discussions about the implications of this decline and the nexus between crime rates and specific social, demographic, economic and political trends. Some experts have credited tougher incarceration policies, such as mandatory minimum sentences, abolition of parole, and catchy political public policy lingo like "Three Strikes and You're Out" that is reactionary to the public's fear of crime. Blumstein and other criminologists have observed that demographic trends in the U.S. population may be the better explanation. His research indicates that the age of individuals is a significant demographic factor contributing to their level of involvement in criminal activities. He notes that younger persons are more likely to commit most violent crimes, particularly those between the ages of 18 and 24. He refers to this age category as the crime prone years and notes that as individuals get older their likelihood of the involvement in criminal activity significantly declines. For instance, the increase in violence in the U.S. during the late 1980s and early 1990s was due primarily to an increase in violent crime committed by individuals under age 20. In addition, Blumstein's research indicates that the increase in youth homicide is directly related to greater accessibility to handguns, which converted ordinary fist fights into intensified violence, often resulting in homicide. It was once believed that juvenile gun violence was primarily concentrated in lower-class urban communities, chiefly among African American males. The Columbine high school shooting and similar incidents across the country at suburban, middle and upper class neighborhoods supports his research that the availability of handguns is a contributing factor to youth violence. Dr. Blumstein's research has highlighted several other interrelated factors that have also contributed to the surge in youth violence. Among these are the increasing illegal drug trade of crack cocaine and lack of desirable employment for youth.

The U.S. has always had a violent crime problem, particularly compared to other industrialized countries. The best way to address crime, like many other social problems, is often at the center of debate and varies along political party lines. Congressional committees often seek the expertise of Dr. Blumstein in developing policy in this area. For instance, he often testifies before the congressional committees focusing on gun violence, drug offenses, and sentencing. Many criminologists, including Dr. Blumstein, argue that the billions of dollars being spent on incarcerating offenders for longer and longer terms has had only a marginal impact on crime rates and crime prevention. Data used by Dr. Blumstein shows that the number of people in prison continues to climb to staggering levels, yet the U.S. has not seen a significant decline in crime rates. Nevertheless, policy makers often sway towards public opinion in which voters find a sense of safety in policies that promulgate stiffer sanctions and longer prison sentences. In fact, as America grapples with the infiltration of drugs, particularly crack cocaine, Blumstein's research has shown that the current incarceration rate for drug offenders alone is higher than the incarceration rate for all crimes combined during the half-century from the 1920s into the 1970s. Consequently, Blumstein and other criminologist have tried to encourage a more rational dialogue supported by empirical data that points out that most Americans are relatively safe. And yet a misconception about the gravity of violent crime continues and effectiveness of strategies for combating crime continues to fuel public policy. Consequently, many state prisons are bulging at the seams and paying astronomical costs to feed and house prisoners.

In the policy arena, Blumstein argues that there is a plethora of information and research on crime, yet policy makers often design policies that are inconsistent with the research. According to Blumstein, this is also evident in the lack of priority that has often been given by funding agencies to adequately support research on violence, particularly its causes and the impact of crime prevention strategies.

Dr, Blumstein has also studied parole violations by offenders convicted of murder, robbery, assault, burglary, drugs, and sexual assault. He concluded that parole violators represent an increasing number of prison admissions. For instance, parole violators comprised 18% of all admissions, by 1996 that percentage had grown to 35%. This is a policy area where he has brought attention to the need to provide postrelease programs to help offenders transition back into their communities upon the completion of their sentences, an area that is often under-funded by government agencies.

Crime is a very complex phenomenon and the scholarly research of Dr. Blumstein has significantly advanced knowledge in many aspects of crime, including incapacitation, prison populations, career criminals, and drug enforcement policy. His many scholarly works include *The Crime Drop in America*, which synthesizes a significant portion of the research on crime trends. A pending book co-authored with Brian Forst, entitled *Errors of Justice*, focuses on the errors commonly made from policing to prosecution that often places the perception of fairness in the criminal justice system in a negative light.

JACQUELINE SMITH-MASON

Biography

Born in New York City, June 3, 1930; Education: Cornell University, B.S. engineering physics, 1951, Ph.D. operations research, 1960; University of Buffalo, M.S. statistics; John Jay College of Criminal Justice of the City University of New York, honorary degree of Doctor of Laws. Chairman, Pennsylvania Commission on Crime and Delinquency, 1979–1990; Pennsylvania Commission on Sentencing from 1986–1996. Director, Office of Urban Research and member of the Research Council, 1968–1969. Chair, National Academy of Science Committee on Research on Law Enforcement and Administration of Justice, 1979–1984. President, American Society of Criminology (ASC), 1991–1992, ASC's Sutherland Award, 1997. Currently professor, H. John Heinz School of Public Policy and Management at Carnegie Mellon University; Director, National Consortium on Violence Research.

Selected Writings

Violence by Young People: Why the Deadly Nexus? *National Institute of Justice Journal*, 229 (1995):3–9.

Youth Violence, Guns and the Illicit Drug Industry. *Journal of Criminal Law and Criminology*, 88, no. 4 (1995).

Interaction of Criminological Research and Public Policy, *Journal of Quantitative Criminology*, 12 no. 4 (1996): 349–362.

Exploring Recent Trends in U.S. Homicide Rates (with Richard Rosenfeld). *Journal of Criminal Law and Criminology*, 88, no. 4 (1998).

The Crime Drop in America (with Joel Wallman). Cambridge University Press, 2000.

Judicial Policy Making and the Modern State: How the Courts Reformed America's Prisons (with Malcom M. Feeley, Edward L. Rubin, and David Farrington). Cambridge University Press, 2000.

Errors of Justice: Nature, Sources and Remedies (with Brian Forst and David Farrington), Cambridge University Press, 2004.

U.S. Criminal Justice Conundrum: Rising Prison Populations and Stable Crime Rates. *Crime and Delinquency*, 44 (January): 129.

See also **Criminal Careers/Chronic Offenders**

Body-Type Theories of Criminal Behavior

Body-type theorists suggest that criminality is predicted by an offender's physique or external observable physical characteristics (Schmalleger, 1999) and that an individual's propensity for criminal behavior can be assessed by examination of their physical appearance and characteristics. Body-type theories emerged from the larger biological and positivistic schools of criminology, which argue that the basic determinants of human behavior are physiologically based or inherited. The body-type perspective emerged at the turn of the twentieth century and is most commonly associated with the works of Caesare Lombroso, Charles Goring, E.A. Hooton, and William Sheldon. Each theorist and the tenets of his theory are discussed in this article.

Caesare Lombroso (Lombroso-Ferrero, 1972) began the exploration of the relationship between body types and criminality based on the Darwinian theory of evolution. Lombroso's study of prisoners convinced him that convicts often had distinctive physical types at birth, and that these features matched those of the primitive man discussed by Darwin. Lombroso thus argued that criminal behavior was associated with "physical atavism," and described a number of physical characteristics that atavists shared (e.g., sloping foreheads, long arms, and sloping shoulders). Lombroso's work met numerous criticisms that have since led most criminologists to dismiss his theory as archaic and invalid, but his work served as important forerunner for the body-type theorists who followed him.

Charles Goring (1913), an English prison physician, compared the physiological characteristics of nearly 3000 prisoners with physical characteristics of British soldiers, university students, and noncriminal hospital patients. He determined that "atavists" were no more likely to be found among criminals than noncriminals and argued vehemently that the results from his study discredited Lombroso's notions that "atavistic born criminals" were responsible for most criminality. Nevertheless, he did not conclude that criminals had no distinguishing characteristics that set them apart from noncriminals and closed his work by suggesting that "…evidence conclusively shows that, on the average, the criminal of English prisons is markedly differentiated by defective physique as measured by stature and body weight…"(Article 370).

Hooton was an American physical anthropologist who attempted to correct many of the criticisms of Lombroso's and Goring's earlier work by comparing a control group of 3203 nonincarcerated individuals with 13,873 inmates from ten states along 107 physiological dimensions (Hooton 1939). Hooton determined that there were physiological differences between criminals and noncriminals and between criminals convicted of different offenses. In general, he found criminals to be smaller than noncriminals. Additionally, the more serious criminals were found to be larger than the less serious criminals. He further identified distinct physical characteristics that were associated with the type of crime an individual committed (e.g., first degree murderers were more likely to be balding, with broad noses, pointed chins, and square-shouldered than their criminal counterparts). From his data, he suggested that crime was not an exclusively sociological phenomenon, but had biological linkages as well.

Whereas each of the aforementioned works met numerous criticisms from a wide variety of scholars, their efforts to associate body types with criminality spurred the more accepted research of the American physician William Sheldon. Sheldon developed a system he called "somatotyping," in which he argued that each individual could be characterized in terms of three physical and temperamental components. He called these three components endomorphy, mesomorphy, and ectomorphy.

Individuals with endomorphic builds tended to be soft and round, outgoing, and relaxed; those with mesomorphic builds were athletic, muscular, large-boned, and aggressive; and those with ectomorphic builds were tall, thin, fragile, introverted, and delicate. Sheldon argued that each individual could be scored on all three components with their score expressed on a seven-point scale. For example, an individual who scored 2-1-7 would exhibit few endomorphic or mesomorphic characteristics, but strong ectomorphic characteristics.

Sheldon then used his index to rate 200 delinquent, runaway, and "unmanageable" boys between the ages of 15 and 21 in Boston (Sheldon, 1949). He determined that the boys scored high in mesomorphy and low in ectomorphy, and that chronic delinquents scored higher in mesomorphy than their less delinquent counterparts. Thus, Sheldon argued that mesomorphic individuals were more prone to criminality. This finding has been replicated with a wide variety of samples by a number of other researchers (see Glueck and Glueck, 1950; Cortes and Gatti, 1972).

Thus, body-type theorists argue that criminals (on an average) have different physiques than noncriminals. Whereas early body-type theorists suggested that criminals were smaller on an average than noncriminals, later research has suggested that criminals tend to be more mesomorphic and less ectomorphic than noncriminals. As Wilson and Herrnstein (1985) suggest, the aforementioned evidence "...leaves no doubt that constitutional traits correlate with criminal behavior" (Article 91). Nevertheless, even the most resolute body-type theorists do not argue that all mesomorphs will be criminals or all criminals will be mesomorphs. Mesomorphs are found among noncriminals while both endomorphs and ectomorphs are found among criminals. Even Sheldon noted that mesomorphs are not only the predominant physical type among criminals, but among other occupations as well.

Whereas Lombroso, Hooton, and Sheldon believed that criminals could be identified by physical characteristics such as mesomorphic body types, few current criminological researchers would assert that a mesomorphic body type *causes* one to become criminal. As such, although body-type theorists may be correct in stating that one's physique is associated with criminality, it would be misleading to suggest that body-type theorists can identify criminals at birth. In sum, then, although body-type theorists assert that mesomorphs are more prone to criminality, most theorists recognize that crime is caused by a combination of mesomorphic body type in conjunction with other social and environmental factors.

Furthermore, if one were to accept that individuals with a specific body type were more likely to be criminal than others, the policy implications would be potentially immense. Whereas few current researchers or policymakers would suggest crime reduction measures as drastic as segregated isolation (placing mesomorphs on reservations), sterilization (to prevent mesomorphs from reproducing) or eugenics (reducing the likelihood of mesomorphic body types through selective breeding), each of the above has been discussed by some as an option for preventing crime relating to other biological predictors (e.g., intelligence, and mental disorders). In fact, in *Buck v. Bell* (1927), the U.S. Supreme Court blessed state-enforced sterilization statutes, with Justice Holmes declaring in the majority opinion: "It is better for all the world, if instead of waiting to execute degenerate offspring for crime, or to let them starve for their imbecility, society can prevent those who are manifestly unfit from continuing their kind" (Buck v. Bell, 1927).

In an effort to avoid policies such as those just mentioned and that would be discriminatory and ineffective, many current criminologists dismiss the association between body type and criminality as circular. Is it mesomorphy that causes criminal behavior, or rather, the harsh, difficult life of criminals on the streets and in prisons that causes mesomorphy? These criminologists argue that it is impossible to separate one's body type from other social, economic, and environmental factors that contribute to criminality. In other words, whereas the presence of a mesomorphic body type may increase the likelihood that one will become criminal, criminality is not absolutely determined by body type. Thus, whereas one's body type may provide a precursor and a context for criminal behavior, this context is often eclipsed by socialization, acculturation, and environment.

DAVID C. MAY

References and Further Reading

Cortes, J.B. and Gatti, F.M., *Delinquency and Crime: A Biopsychological Approach*, Seminar Press, New York, 1972.

Glueck, S. and Glueck, E.T., *Physique and Delinquency*, Harper, New York,1956.

Goring, C., *The English Convict: A Statistical Study*, Darling and Son, London, 1913.

Hooton, E.A., *Crime and the Man*, Harvard University Press, Cambridge, MA, 1939.

Lombroso-Ferrero, G., *Criminal Man*, Patterson Smith, Montclair, NJ, 1972 (originally published in 1911).

Sheldon, W.H., *Varieties of Delinquent Youth*, Harper & Brothers, New York, 1949.

Wilson, J.Q. and Herrnstein, R.J., *Crime and Human Nature*, Simon and Schuster, New York, 1985.

See also **Biological Theories of Criminal Behavior; Genetic Theories of Criminal Behavior**

Bond

See **Bail: Right to**

Bonger, Willem A.

Willem Adriaan Bonger (1876–1940), the Dutch criminologist who wrote one of the first Marxist or socialist studies of criminality, is widely recognized as one of the pioneers in the development of modern criminology (Mannheim, 1955). Bonger's reputation largely was made on the basis of his magnum opus—and dissertation—*Criminalite et Conditions Economiques* (1905) (Van Heerikhuizen, 1987). *Criminality and Economic Conditions* was selected in 1916 by the prestigious American Institute of Criminal Law and Criminology to be translated and published as a volume in its distinguished Modern Criminal Science Series. This made the work accessible to the English-language world and provided Bonger with an international reputation in the world of criminology.

Bonger was a very prolific writer in areas other than criminology, only three of his criminological works have been translated into English: *Criminality and Economic Conditions* (1916), *Introduction to Criminology* (1936), and *Race and Crime* (1943). His general sociological writings on suicide, morality, religion, surplus labor, war, and historical change have never been made accessible to non-Dutch scholars. Likewise, his political writings on extremism, dictatorship, democracy, labor unions, intellectuals and socialism, and international politics have never been translated into English. This has resulted in an unfortunate separation of Bonger's criminological thinking from his general sociological and political theories (Bianchi, 1976).

Bonger was a socialist Marxist. His involvement in active socialism began when he still was a student. Interest in socialism and Marxism was quite common among young Dutch intellectuals in Bonger's time. The German socialist Karl Kautsky wrote that, perhaps with the exception of Russia, he had found nowhere a greater theoretical interest in socialism than in the Netherlands (H. Bonger, 1950:xi). He was the editor-in-chief of the *Socialistische Gids* (1916–1939), the main publication of the Dutch socialist party. As a socialist intellectual, he gave a large number of public lectures and speeches, wrote newspaper articles and political pamphlets, and authored several scholarly works related to socialism.

Although Bonger never developed a full-fledged theory of crime (van Heerikhuizen, 1987), he did formulate a set of fairly clear-cut ideas about the relationship between capitalism and crime.

Bonger reasoned that a capitalist economic system promotes egoism. All crimes—economic, sexual, political and pathological—committed by both the economically powerless and the powerful, Bonger argued, were the result of egoism engendered by a capitalist economic system (Beirne and Messerschmidt, 2000).

Crime should be approached primarily as a social fact. Although psychological and biological factors may be important in explaining individual criminality, environmental factors are of crucial importance in explaining crime. This sociological reasoning is also reflected in *Race and Crime* (1936), which states that racial differences in crime must be explained primarily by differences in socioeconomic conditions.

Bonger's ideas initially failed to receive recognition among American criminologists whose mode of thinking was hard to reconcile with his socialist analysis. Howcvcr, with the resurgence of interest in Marxist social theory in the late 1960s and early 1970s in the U.K. and the U.S., Bonger's works began to be routinely cited in American and British criminology texts. Typically, these texts portrayed Bonger as a theorist "ahead of his time," a "forerunner to modern conflict criminology," as someone whose thinking was antithetic to the dominant modes of thinking of early twentieth century criminology. (However, for a different view see Ineke Haen Marshall and Dennis E. Hoffman, The Life and Times of Willem A. Bonger, a paper presented at the annual meeting of the Academy of Criminal Justice Sciences, 1984.) The image of Bonger as "the odd man out" (of mainstream early twentieth century thinking, that is) is further strengthened by the considerable time gap between Bonger's treatise on the relationship between crime and economic conditions (i.e. capitalism) (1916) and the first appearances of radical or Marxist criminology in the U.S. and Great Britain more than half a century later.

In the late 1960s and early 1970s, when conflict criminology emerged as an alternative to mainstream criminology, Bonger's work as "the first Marxian criminologist" came under close scrutiny. Ironically, Bonger was severely criticized as not being truly Marxist (Turk, 1969; Taylor, Walton and Young, 1973). These criticisms are not fair, since Bonger himself never claimed to have developed a Marxist theory of crime. Bonger greatly admired Karl Marx as sociologist and economist; however, he despised "dogmatic" Marxism (H. Bonger, 1950). Although most of his contemporaries viewed him as a Marxist, Bonger himself preferred to label his work "economic-sociological" rather than to apply the Marxist label of "historical-materialistic" (Valkhoff, 1950). This is consistent with the historical reality of the early Dutch socialist movement that was characterized by a distaste for radicalism, extremism, revolution. Bonger's Marxism was a "clear reformist, progressive, evolutionary socialism" (Valkhoff, 1950).

Bonger was also a criminal justice reformer. He was involved in attempts to make the Dutch criminal justice system more humane and more effective. He was a strong supporter of parole and suspended sentences. He strongly opposed the use of incarceration except for short sentences, for observation, for "recalcitrant elements," and "incorrigibles" (Valkhoff, 1950: xxxiii). He rejected retribution as a rationale for punishment and saw capital punishment as a "barbaric" remnant of earlier times (Valkhoff, 1950: xxxix). Bonger was also instrumental in preparing the groundwork for the Dutch Psychopath Laws.

Finally, Willem Bonger was a humanist. In his own words (when explaining his reasons for becoming a socialist):

> My deepest motivation was social compassion and a democratic consciousness. It always has been, for me, an unbearable thought that there is so much misery in such a rich world; feelings of human solidarity...run in my blood (H. Bonger, 1950:xi and xii; in Dutch).

Willem Bonger committed suicide after the Dutch capitulation to the Germans in May 1940.

INEKE HAEN MARSHALL

Biography

Born in Amsterdam, the Netherlands, September 16, 1876. Educated at the University of Amsterdam, Faculty of Law, Ph.D., 1905. Managing clerk in the insurance firm Brak and Moes, Amsterdam, 1905–1914; partner in the insurance firm Brak en Moes, Amsterdam, 1914–1922; professor in sociology and criminology, University of Amsterdam, 1922–1940. Founder of the *Nederlandse Sociologische Vereniging* (Dutch Society of Sociology), 1936; editor-in-chief of *De Socialistische Gids* (scientific monthly of the Dutch socialist party), 1916–1939. Died in Amsterdam, the Netherlands, May 15 1940.

Selected Works

"*Criminalite et Conditions Economiques*," Ph.D. dissertation, University of Amsterdam, 1905; as *Criminality and Economic Conditions*, translated by Henry P. Norton, Boston: Little, Brown and Company, 1916.

Criminality and Economic Conditions. Abridged and with an Introduction by Austin T. Turk, Bloomington and London: Indiana University Press, 1969.

Inleiding tot de Criminologie, Haarlem: Bohn, 1932; as *An Introduction to Criminology*, London: Methuen, 1936.

Ras en Misdaad, Haarlem: Tjeenk Willink, 1939; as *Race and Crime*, translated by Margaret Matthews Hordyk, New York: Columbia University Press, 1943; Montclair, N.J.: Patterson Smith, 1969, 1972.

Verspreide Geschriften, Amsterdam: De Arbeiderspers, 1950. Compiled and edited by Bonger, H., J. Valkhoff & B. van der Waerden.

References and Further Reading

van Bemmelen, J., Willem Adriaan Bonger, in Mannheim, H., Ed., *Pioneers in Criminology*, Stevens & Sons, London, 1960.

Beirne, P. and Messerschmidt, J., *Criminology*, 3rd ed., Westview Press, Boulder, CO, 2000.

Bianchi, H., De Radicale Criminologen en Bonger, *Tijdschrift voor Criminologie*, 18, 202–208 (1976).

Bonger, H., Korte Levensschets van Prof. Mr. W.R. Bonger, in Bonger, W.A., Ed., *Verspreide Geschriften*, De Arbeiderspers, Amsterdam. (Compiled and edited by Bonger, H., J. Valkhoff & B. van der Waerden, 1950.)

van Heerikhuizen, B., *W.A. Bonger, Socioloog en Socialist* [*W.A. Bonger, Sociologist and Socialist*], Wolters-Noordhof/Forsten, Groningen, 1987.

Mannheim, H., *Pioneers in Criminology*, Patterson Smith, Montclair, NJ, 1955.

Marshall, I.H. and Hoffman, D.E., The Life and Times of Willem A. Bonger, paper presented at the Annual Meeting of the Academy of Criminal Justice Sciences, 1984.

Peters, T. and van Weringh, J., Eds., De Actualiteit van Bonger, Special volume, *Nederlands Tijdschrift voor Criminologie*, 18, 145–216 (1976).

Taylor, L., Walton, P., Walton and Young, J., *The New Criminology. For a Social Theory of Deviance*, New York, 1973.

Turk, A.T., Introduction, in Bonger, W.A., *Criminality and Economic Conditions*, abridged edition, Indiana University Press, Bloomington, IL, 1968.

Valkhoff, J. Bonger's Werken, in Bonger, W.A. *Verspreide Geschriften*, N.V. De Arbeiderspers, Amsterdam, (Compiled and edited by Bonger, H., J. Valkhoff & B. van der Waerden, 1950.)

See also **Critical Criminology: An Overview; Marxist Theories of Criminal Behavior**

Boot Camps and Shock Incarceration

In recent years, shock incarceration programs—also known as correctional boot camps—have become a popular intermediate sanction for nonviolent offenders. These programs vary in content and structure but, generally speaking, they are modeled after military boot camps and emphasize "strict discipline, physical training, drill and ceremony, military bearing and courtesy, physical labor, and summary punishment for minor misconduct" (Morash and Rucker, 1990). They are designed to provide a short but harsh sentence (typically 3 to 6 months) within the context of a controlled and disciplined environment.

After making their first appearance in Georgia and Oklahoma in 1983, shock incarceration programs spread rapidly across the U.S. and now appear in most states. These programs (or, at least, various elements of these programs) have also appeared, on a smaller scale, in other parts of the globe, including the United Kingdom. And over the years, several provincial governments in Canada have considered the use of shock incarceration programs to deal with young offenders.

Yet, despite unprecedented growth in such programs during the past decade—particularly in the U.S.—shock incarceration should not be viewed as an innovative approach to corrections. Similar, military-style tactics of crime control were also popular in the nineteenth century (Morash and Rucker, 1990; McCorkle, 1995). Rather, the recent growth of shock incarceration programs can be interpreted as a revival of the military model of corrections, which emphasizes the importance of traditional values such as discipline, hard work, and respect for authority. As McCorkle (1995: 366) observes, "in the current era of turmoil," such an approach is embraced by the public because it locates the problem of crime in the breakdown of traditional values, suggests a remedy, and promises a return to social order and stability.

Several other factors have also contributed to the newfound popularity of the military model. Shock incarceration programs are popular among politicians and criminal justice officials because they are viewed as a cost-efficient remedy for prison overcrowding (Byrne, Lurigio, and Petersilia, 1992). Moreover, they are consistent with a "get tough" approach to crime and are seen as a possible solution to the high rates of recidivism associated with traditional incarceration (Lutze and Brody, 1999; Van Vleet, 1999). In comparison to traditional prison life, the strict regimen of the boot camp is said to reduce conflict between inmates, build confidence and self-respect, and offer an environment that is more conducive to rehabilitation. Moreover, some programs place a strong emphasis on offender rehabilitation by supplementing the boot camp experience with opportunities for counseling, drug and alcohol treatment, education (GED), and vocational training.

Although shock incarceration has widespread appeal, it has nonetheless been a target for critics who view it as a shortsighted and possibly counterproductive response to crime. In particular, shock incarceration programs have been criticized for their apparent emphasis on masculine stereotypes and aggressive confrontation—characteristics that are believed to foster, rather than deter, antisocial attitudes and behaviors (Lutze and Murphy, 1999). For example, such programs are frequently associated with the image of tough and domineering staff members, who ridicule feminine traits and yell and shout at inmates. As Morash and Rucker (1990) are forced to ask: "Why would a method that has been developed to prepare people to go to war, and as a tool to manage legal violence, be considered as having such potential in deterring or rehabilitating offenders?"

Shock incarceration programs have also been criticized for exposing inmates to humiliating and abusive forms of treatment, including demeaning verbal reprimands (e.g., "scumbag," "sissy," "fool") and physical challenges that have the potential for serious injury (e.g., excessive exercise in foul weather, carrying logs or other heavy objects). These forms of treatment appear to be inconsistent with those that characterize effective rehabilitation programs, such as treatment that is perceived to be caring and just. Moreover, given reports of actual injury sustained by boot camp participants, some researchers believe that future lawsuits are likely on the grounds of "cruel and unusual" punishment (Lutze and Brody, 1999).

Research on the actual nature and impact of shock incarceration has produced mixed results, whether the findings of interest concern inmates' perceptions of the boot camp environment, attitude change, recidivism, or system-level impact (such as a reduction in correctional costs or prison overcrowding). Before reviewing the results, it is important to note that such research does not often lend itself to general statements about the impact of shock incarceration programs, due to considerable variation in program structure and content (MacKenzie and Brame, 1995; Zhang, 1998). For example, some boot camp programs rely almost exclusively on military drill and physical training, while others combine military and physical components with counseling, education, and substance abuse treatment.

Substantial variation also exists in the age of boot camp inmates and the manner in which they are selected for participation. While most correctional boot camps have been designed for young adult offenders, a growing number of camps have been developed for juveniles. In some states, participation in a boot camp program is decided by the sentencing judge, whereas in other states correctional officials have the discretion to refer inmates. Consequently, the results of evaluation studies frequently vary from state to state.

Given the concerns about the possibly abusive atmosphere of correctional boot camps, several studies have focused on inmates' perceptions of the boot camp environment. Based on a national study, Styve et al. (2000) found that, in comparison to youths in traditional correctional facilities, boot camp juveniles tend to view their correctional environment as more positive and more conducive to rehabilitation. Even after adjusting for important individual differences, boot camp juveniles—in the majority of comparisons—were more likely to perceive their environment as safer and as having "more therapeutic programming, activity, structure, and control, and a more thorough preparation process for release from the facility" (Styve et al., 2000).

Although these findings challenge arguments regarding the potentially "harmful" effects of the boot camp environment, they do not eliminate concern. In comparison to inmates in a traditional prison setting, Lutze and Murphy (1999) find that adult inmates in a Pennsylvania boot camp program are more likely to perceive the correctional environment as supporting male sex-role stereotypes (e.g., as one stressing aggressive behavior and endorsing ridicule of feminine traits). Moreover, inmates who perceive the environment as possessing more masculine stereotypes tend to report relatively high levels of stress, isolation, and conflict with staff and other inmates.

Nevertheless, some studies report positive attitude change during program participation, with the attitudes of boot camp inmates becoming more positive toward themselves, their future, and those around them (MacKenzie and Shaw, 1990; McCorkle, 1995). It may not be appropriate, however, to attribute such change to the unique paramilitary environment of the correctional boot camp. For instance, McCorkle (1995) also observed positive attitude change among regular prison inmates, who were assigned to a treatment-oriented, non-paramilitary program.

Research has failed to produce any consistent or conclusive evidence that exposure to shock incarceration, in general, decreases the likelihood of future offending (Zhang, 1998). In the most comprehensive evaluation to date, Mackenzie et al. (1995) examined data in eight states, comparing the recidivism rates of boot camp graduates to prison parolees, probationers, and boot camp dropouts (taking into account age, race, and possession of a prior criminal record). The results of the evaluation were mixed. In a few states, boot camp graduates fared better than their comparison groups, and were less likely to experience subsequent arrest or revocation of parole. In one state, they actually fared worse and tended to exhibit relatively high rates of recidivism. On an average, however, no significant difference in recidivism was observed between boot camp graduates and those exposed to traditional sanctions—a finding that is consistent with the bulk of research in this area.

The general failure of shock incarceration programs to reduce recidivism is not surprising. By and large, the design of such programs is not guided by research on the characteristics of effective rehabilitation programs. Nor is the design of such programs inspired by an explicit criminological theory (Zhang, 1998). Rather, shock incarceration programs are built on the assumption that young offenders need to be "straightened out," given a kick in the pants, and effectively disciplined. While this assumption fits well with a "get tough" approach to crime and has widespread appeal, by itself it is not viewed by criminologists as providing an adequate basis for effective recidivism-reduction efforts (see Finckenauer and Gavin, 1999).

Few studies have examined the system-level impact of shock incarceration programs, even though this is an important area of research. Even if correctional boot camps do not produce significant reductions in recidivism, they may still prove to be relatively cost-efficient and help to reduce prison overcrowding. Research on system-level effects is limited, however, because in most states correctional boot camps are too small in size to have much influence.

Nonetheless, certain data suggest that, in some states, shock incarceration programs have helped to alleviate prison overcrowding (MacKenzie and Parent, 1991; MacKenzie and Piquero, 1994; U.S. General Accounting Office, 1993). In a handful of states, shock incarceration programs have also been less expensive to operate than traditional prisons. On an average, however, these programs do not generate substantial cost savings (U.S. General Accounting Office, 1993).

An important issue raised by existing system-level studies is that of "net widening"—the filling of boot camps with offenders who, in the past, might have otherwise received probation or some other lesser sanction. If such offenders are funneled to boot camps in great numbers, these programs cannot be expected to produce cost savings or alleviate prison overcrowding. In fact, if the availability of boot camp programs contributes to substantial net widening, then these programs may generate unanticipated costs. The possibility of net widening may help to explain why the observed system-level impact of shock incarceration programs is not consistently positive, but varies considerably from state to state. Ultimately, careful planning and administration are required to ensure that shock incarceration programs lead to intended system-level outcomes (MacKenzie and Piquero, 1994).

Although shock incarceration in general has not yet been shown to represent a particularly promising alternative to traditional sanctions, a final verdict must await future research (Zhang, 1998). For instance, most recidivism studies have relied on official sources of data and have examined a limited range of outcome variables (Zhang, 1998). Future studies would benefit from an examination of self-report data, a variety of recidivism and outcome measures (including employment, community and familial reintegration, and long-term adjustment), and greater use of experimental design.

Future studies would also benefit from a more detailed examination of offender and program characteristics. It is possible that shock incarceration may have positive effects on some offenders but not others, depending on age, race, education, criminal history, and other factors. It is also possible that certain program characteristics may increase the likelihood of positive outcomes, such as the availability of educational opportunities, vocational training, treatment for drugs and alcohol, and the presence of trained and motivated staff. Future research that is designed to examine these possibilities may help to explain why some programs have shown promising results, while others have not (Zhang, 1998). Such research may also suggest guidelines concerning the use, modification, or future development of shock incarceration programs.

TIMOTHY BREZINA AND JAMES D. WRIGHT

References and Further Reading

Byrne, J.M., Lurigio, A.J., and Petersilia, J., Eds., *Smart Sentencing: The Emergence of Intermediate Sanctions*, Sage, Newbury Park, CA, 1992.

Finckenauer, J.O. and Gavin, P.W., *Scared Straight: The Panacea Phenomenon Revisited*, Prospect Heights, Illinois: Waveland, 1999.

Lutze, F.E. and Brody, D.C., Mental Abuse as Cruel and Unusual Punishment: Do Boot Camp Prisons Violate the Eighth Amendment?, *Crime and Delinquency*, 45:2 (1999).

Lutze, F.E. and Murphy, D.W., Ultramasculine Prison Environments and Inmates' Adjustment: It's Time to Move Beyond the 'Boys will be Boys' Paradigm, *Justice Quarterly*, 16:4, (1999).

MacKenzie, D.L. et al., Boot Camp Prisons and Recidivism in Eight States, *Criminology*, 33:3 (1995).

MacKenzie, D.L. and Brame, R., Shock Incarceration and Positive Adjustment During Community Supervision, *Journal of Quantitative Criminology*, 11:2 (1995).

MacKenzie, D.L. and Parent, D., Shock Incarceration and Prison Overcrowding in Louisiana, *Journal of Criminal Justice*, 19 (1991).

MacKenzie, D.L., and Piquero, A., The Impact of Shock Incarceration Programs on Prison Overcrowding, *Crime and Delinquency*, 40:2 (1994).

MacKenzie, D.L. and Shaw, J.W., Inmate Adjustment and Change During Shock Incarceration: The Impact of Correctional Boot Camp Programs, *Justice Quarterly*, 7:1 (1990).

McCorkle, R.C. Correctional Boot Camps and Change in Attitude: Is All this Shouting Necessary, *Justice Quarterly*, 12:2 (1995).

Morash, M. and Rucker, L.A., Critical Look at the Idea of Boot Camp as a Correctional Reform, *Crime and Delinquency*, 36:2 (1990).

Styve, G.J., et al., Perceived Conditions of Confinement: A National Evaluation of Juvenile Boot Camps and Traditional Facilities, *Law and Human Behavior*, 24:3 (2000).

U.S. General Accounting Office, Prison Boot Camps: Short-Term Prison Costs Reduced, But Long-Term Impact Uncertain, Government Printing Office, Washington, DC, 1993.

Vleet, V. and Russell, K., The Attack on Juvenile Justice, *Annals of the American Academy of Political and Social Science*, 564 (1999).

Zhang, S.X., In Search of Hopeful Glimpses: A Critique of Research Strategies in Current Boot Camp Evaluations, *Crime and Delinquency*, 44:2 (1998).

See also **Corporal Punishment**

Braithwaite, John

John Braithwaite was born in Queensland, Australia in 1951. He completed both his undergraduate and graduate studies at the University of Queensland in Brisbane, receiving a Ph.D. in sociology in 1977. He served for a year as a lecturer in the University of Queensland's Department of Anthropology and Sociology, and then joined the staff of the Australian Institute of Criminology in Canberra for four years (1978–1982). He left the institute to take up a position as the executive director of the Australian Federation of Consumer Organizations. Following this stint in a policy and advocacy position he was appointed to the faculty of the Research School of Social Sciences at the Australian National University (ANU) in 1984, rising to professorial status in 1988. In 2001 he was awarded a Federation Fellowship by the Australian government.

Few criminologists have distinguished themselves in as many different areas of the discipline. Braithwaite's work on white-collar crime, begun at the Australian Institute of Criminology in the late 1970s, contributed to the renaissance of that subfield. His ambitious book, *Corporate Crime in the Pharmaceutical Industry* (1984), was an unusually systematic case study of fraud, bribery, antitrust, occupational health and safety, environmental and product safety breaches in one industry. The chilling effect of libel laws delayed its publication by four years. His work on corporate offending evolved into the analysis of business regulation more generally, and his book with Ian Ayres, *Responsive Regulation* (1992) established an analytical paradigm that provided the framework for regulatory discourse in the 1990s. This was followed by *Global Business Regulation* with Peter Drahos (2000) that addressed the role and influence of international regulatory authorities, nongovernment organizations, and markets.

Braithwaite's work on regulatory theory has informed his thinking on criminological theory, and vice versa (Braithwaite, 2000; Braithwaite, 2002). His keen sense of social justice, visible in the book *Inequality, Crime and Public Policy* (1979) emanating from his Ph.D. thesis, is reflected in the landmark *Not Just Deserts: A Republican Theory of Criminal Justice* (with Phillip Pettit). The work for which he is perhaps best known is on restorative justice, and it too draws on his philosophical commitment to social justice. His book *Crime, Shame and Reintegration* (1989) received an enthusiastic response not only from scholars, but also from activists and practitioners who were seeking an alternative to the instinctive retributivism that had grown to dominate western criminal justice systems, at substantial cost but without achieving much in the way of crime reduction. His idea of reintegrative shaming, inspired in part by Asian culture, attracted tremendous interest around the world, and has influenced the implementation of numerous restorative justice programs. His work on restorative justice has also meant significant benefits to victims of crime, who have traditionally felt neglected and marginalized by the criminal justice system (Strang, 2002).

One of the great strengths of Braithwaite's work has been his commitment to applied criminology. As a result, Braithwaite has been a strong supporter of empirically testing criminological theory, including his own. In the early 1990s, Braithwaite and colleagues undertook a major study of Australian nursing home regulation that sought both to improve the quality of care in nursing homes and also to understand empirically how regulatory agencies performed at the coal face (Makkai and Braithwaite, 1994). This was followed by the establishment of the Re-Integrative Shaming Experiments (RISE) in the mid 1990s at the ANU in collaboration with the Australian Federal Police. The largest controlled experiment ever undertaken in Australian criminology, the RISE Project was designed to test whether restorative justice conferences are a more effective and just means of dealing with offenders and victims.

The restorative justice conferences evaluated in the RISE study were underpinned by Braithwaite's theory of reintegrative shaming. They were found to produce no significant difference in later reoffending rates compared to court for property and drink driving offenders, but a significant drop in reoffending by violent offenders (about 40% less than those who went to court). Of arguably greater significance was the fact that victims of crime were more satisfied with conferences than with conventional court proceedings (Australian Institute of Criminology 2003). His most recent work, with Eliza Ahmed, Nathan Harris and Valerie Braithwaite focuses on shame management and pride management. This work is showing empirically that shame displacement (into angry blaming of others) and narcissistic pride is associated with higher levels of workplace and school bullying. In contrast, shame acknowledgment and humble pride is associated with lower levels of bullying. Restorative justice in this work is conceived as a strength-based strategy that nurtures humble pride in offenders and their families and that nurtures shame acknowledgment, remorse, apology and forgiveness. As a result restorative justice is conceived as a useful vehicle for delivering commitment to crime prevention implementation that works.

Braithwaite is author or coauthor of 16 books and scores of articles, chapters, and review essays. In 1991, he received the Michael J. Hindelang Award of the American Society of Criminology for the most outstanding contribution to criminology in the previous three years (for *Crime, Shame and Reintegration*). The following year, he received the ASC's Sellin-Glueck Award for lifetime scholarly contributions to the discipline of criminology by a non-North American criminologist. In the year 2000, he received the Hart Socio-Legal Book Prize (for *Global Business Regulation*). He is a fellow of the American Society of Criminology.

In addition to his academic achievements, Braithwaite has distinguished himself in the world of public policy. His leadership of the Australian consumer movement, his ten years of service (1985–1995) as part-time commissioner of the Australian Trade Practices Commission, and his four years as a member of the Australian Prime Minister's Economic Planning Advisory Council, complemented his international policy activities, including consultancies for the Organization for Economic Cooperation and Development, the United Nations Office for Drug Control and Crime Prevention, and the Singapore Juvenile Court.

Braithwaite has been instrumental in promoting the careers of many young criminologists in Australia as well as promoting the ideas of Australian scholars to the wider international audience. He has encouraged young scholars to see the study of crime and deviancy as a viable and socially useful enterprise. He has sought to do this through graduate and postdoctoral supervision, collaboration with other scholars, and commitment to both the discipline of criminology and multidisciplinary work. There is no doubt that John Braithwaite is Australia's most distinguished criminologist.

Peter Grabosky and Toni Makkai

Biography

Born in Ipswich, Queensland, Australia, July 31, 1951; son of Richard and Joyce Braithwaite. Educated at the University of Queensland, B.A. (Hons), 1972; Ph.D. in sociology, 1977; Federation Fellow, professor, and Convenor of the Regulatory Institutions Network, Australian National University, 2001–; professor, Australian National University 1992–2001; professorial fellow in Law, Research School of Social Sciences, Australian National University, 1988–1992; senior research fellow, Australian National University 1984–1988; director, Australian Federation of Consumer Organizations 1982–1984; criminologist, Australian Institute of Criminology 1978–1982; lecturer, Department of Anthropology and Sociology, University of Queensland, 1977–1978; senior teaching fellow, School of Humanities, Griffith University, 1977.

Selected Writings

The Impact of Publicity on Corporate Offenders (with B. Fisse). SUNY Press, 1983.

Corporate Crime in the Pharmaceutical Industry, London and Boston, Routledge & Kegan Paul, 1984. (Japanese edition, Sanichi Shobo, 1992.)

Of Manners Gentle: Enforcement Strategies of Australian Business Regulatory Agencies (with Peter Grabosky). Oxford University Press, 1986.

Crime, Shame and Reintegration. Cambridge University Press, 1989.

Not Just Deserts: A Republican Theory of Criminal Justice (with P. Pettit). Oxford University Press, 1990.

Responsive Regulation: Transcending the Deregulation Debate (with I. Ayres). Oxford University Press, 1992.

Corporations, Crime and Accountability (with B. Fisse). Cambridge University Press, 1993.

Global Business Regulation (with P. Drahos). Cambridge University Press, 2000.

Shame Management Through Reintegration (with E. Ahmed, N. Harris, and V. Braithwaite). Cambridge University Press, 2001.

Restorative Justice and Responsive Regulation. Oxford University Press, 2002.

References and Further Reading

Braithwaite, J., Restorative Justice: Assessing Optimistic and Pessimistic Accounts, in Torny, M., ed., *Crime and Justice: A Review of Research*, Vol. 25, 1–127, 1999.

Braithwaite, J., *Regulation, Crime and Freedom*, Ashgate Publishing Limited, 2000.

Braithwaite, J., *Restorative Justice and Responsive Regulation*, Oxford University Press, 2002.

Hagan, J. and Peterson, R., Introduction, in Hagan, J. and Peterson, R., Eds., *Crime and Inequality*, Stanford University Press, Stanford, CA, 1995.

Makkai, T. and Braithwaite, J., Reintegrative Shaming and Compliance with Regulatory Standards, *Criminology*, 32:3, 361–385, 1994.

Scheff, T., Review Essay: A New Durkheim, *American Journal of Sociology*, 96:3, 741–746.

Strand, H., Repair or Revenge: Victims and Restorative Justice, Clarendon Press, Oxford, U.K., 2002.

Australian Institute of Criminology, *Restorative Justice in Australia*. http://www.aic.gov.au/rjustice/rise/index.html (visited 8 October 2003)

Bribery and Graft

A bribe is something, such as money or a favor, offered or given to a person in a position of trust to influence that person's views or conduct. Bribery is an important form of political corruption. Political corruption is defined as "any illegal or unethical use of governmental authority for personal or political gain" (Benson, 1978). Corruption occurs to accomplish one of two broad goals, material gain or power. Material gain can involve personal enrichment, or illicit contributions to election campaigns (Simon & Hagan, 1999).

One term closely associated with bribery is graft. Political graft is the illegal act of taking advantage of one's political position to gain money or property (Amick, 1976). Graft can take several forms. First is the outright bribe, where an individual, group, or corporation offers money to a public official for a favor. Or the government official may demand money in return for a favor, which is political extortion.

A third type occurs when a public figure is offered the opportunity to buy securities at a low price; then, when the price goes up, the briber purchases the securities back, at a great profit to the bribee. Finally, a fourth variant is the kickback, where contractors, engineering and architectural firms, and others pay back the official responsible for granting a lucrative government contract with a percentage of that contract.

This article will focus on various fields of graft, areas in which corruption is most likely to occur (Simon, 2002).

Goods and Services

The federal government spends billions of dollars on an array of goods and services from U.S. businesses including military hardware, space systems, research projects, and numerous other goods and services. Suppliers and repair contractors have been guilty of billing the government for undelivered materials and work never performed. Also, store managers have accepted money and other gifts from firms that sell to the government. In return, the companies are allowed to charge in excess for their merchandise (Simon, 2002). Bidding for contracts is a process especially susceptible to bribery, especially when the bidding is not competitive.

Public Funds and Property

The use of public moneys is a ready source of corruption by those in political power. Bribery occurs in deposits of government funds in banks and loans to and joint investment with businesses (Miller, 1992). Another potential area for corruption is the misuse of public property. Government officials have discretionary powers over public lands. They decide, for example, which ranchers will have grazing rights, which lumber companies will have rights to timber lands, and what policies will control the extraction of minerals and petroleum from lands owned by the government. Fortunes can be made or lost depending on favorable access to these lands. Of course, such a situation is susceptible to bribery and extortion (Simon, 2002).

Tax Assessment, Collection, and Government Regulation

The taxation function of government is one that has enormous potential for graft. Tax assessors have great latitude because many of their decisions are subjective. They are obvious targets for bribes to reduce assessments. Officials at the federal level are also susceptible to bribes involving taxation. Internal Revenue Service (IRS) personnel investigating income tax evasion can be bribed to look the other way. So, too, can Customs officials.

Government officials are required by law to inspect foods (such as grain and meat) to ensure that they are not contaminated and to grade them according to quality. Agents have received bribes to allow questionable items to pass inspection. Abuses also abound in government efforts to control certain business activities, such as gambling and the sale of alcohol where the granting of licenses is involved.

The areas of zoning, planning, and building codes are highly subject to graft, since the decisions can provide or eliminate great financial advantage. Decisions in these areas can establish which individuals or organizations will have a monopoly. Overnight, such decisions can make cheap land valuable or priceless land ordinary. And the decisions can force all construction to be done by certified employees. Again, government officials and businesspeople can abuse the government's discretionary powers for individual gains (Gross, 1992).

The relationship between giving money to and receiving favorable decisions from legislators is not always a subtle one, however. Numerous scandals in American history have involved bribing legislators to vote either in favor of or against various pieces of legislation.

Law Enforcement

The police have great decisional latitude. Unlike other aspects of the criminal justice process, the police often deal with their clients in isolation and their decisions are not subject to review by higher authorities. The police have the power to continue or terminate the criminal-processing procedure. Accordingly, the position of the police personnel exposes them to extraordinary pressures and temptations. Police corruption is most likely with the enforcement of so-called victimless crimes, especially narcotics and other drugs. Over 80% of the police work in the U.S. has to do with the regulation of private morals. Laws prohibiting gambling, sex between consenting adults, pornography, liquor, and drug use are examples of such victimless crimes.

Elections

The hallmark of representative democracy is that all people have the fundamental right to vote for those who will administer and make the laws. Those in power have often defied this principle of democracy, however, as they have minimized, neutralized, or even negated the voting privileges of the lower classes, minorities, third parties, and the opposition. Throughout U.S. history, it has been a common practice for the majority in legislatures (at all levels) to revise political boundaries for their advantage. This tactic, known as gerrymandering, occurs when the party in power designs the political boundaries to negate the power of the opposition.

Certainly many elections have been won through illegal activities. The supporters of certain candidates to control the vote use violence and intimidation. In this century, violence has been aimed at southern African Americans to keep them from registering, thus ensuring white supremacy. Most election frauds involving illegal voting, false registration, and bribery have occurred in areas of one-party dominance, especially in cities controlled by a political machine. This has kept the machine in power at the local level and has delivered votes in state and federal elections to one party, thus increasing the scope of the machine's power (Benson, 1978).

Political campaigns often involve illegal or at least immoral behavior by the candidates and their supporters to achieve the advantage over one another. Behavior such as espionage, bribery, sabotage, crowd agitation, lying, and innuendo occur quite regularly. The primary goal of these tactics is to negate the strength of opponents by spreading rumors about their character, especially regarding his or her sex life and association with unsavory individuals.

Whatever forms bribery or graft take, it is clear that the deviance involved can be achieved by corrupt individuals or by a corrupt system and that power, violence, and money are often employed to achieve certain goals in all sectors of life.

David R. Simon

References and Further Reading

Amick, G. (1976) *The American Way of Graft* (Princeton, NJ: The Center for the Analysis of Public Issues).

Benson, G.C.S. (1978) *Political Corruption in America* (Lexington, MA: D.C. Heath & Company).

Gross, M. (1992) *The Government Racket: Government Waste from A to Z* (New York: Bantam Books).

Miller, N. (1992) *Stealing from America* (New York: Paragon House).

Simon, D.R. (2002) *Elite Deviance*, Seventh Edition (Boston: Allyn & Bacon).

Simon, D.R. and Hagan, F. (1999) *White-Collar Deviance* (Boston: Allyn & Bacon).

See also **White-Collar Crime: Definitions; White-Collar Crime: The Law**

Bullying *See* **Schools and Delinquent Behavior**

Burglary as an Occupation

Definition of Burglary

The manner in which burglary is defined has undergone tremendous changes. The common law definition of burglary was the "breaking and entering of a dwelling house of another in the nighttime with the intent to commit a felony therein" (*Black's Law Dictionary,* 1990, p. 197). Several components of the common law definition raised serious issues with the legal classification of the act of burglary, as well as the prosecution of such an act. First, the common law definition required that the offense be committed during the night. Therefore, offenses committed at any time when "natural light" was present did not fit the definitional constraints of burglary. Second, the definition required the intent of the person to commit a felony. Without proof of intent, the act did not constitute burglary. Third, the person had to actually enter the dwelling for the crime of burglary to have occurred. If actual entry was not attained or was caught before entering the dwelling, then the burglary charges were not applicable. Fourth, the "dwelling of another" requirement caused issues. The "dwelling" requirement carried the implication that the victim actually resided in the structure, leaving storage or temporary structures uncovered. These strict components of the common law definition made the indictment and prosecution of burglary extremely difficult. Ultimately, these difficulties led to the revision of the statutory definition of burglary (Reid, 2003).

Partially in response to the difficulties encountered with the common law classifications of burglary, the current definition has been expanded to provide for more comprehensive coverage. According to the Uniform Crime Report (FBI, 2001), burglary is defined as "the unlawful entry into a structure to commit a felony or theft." Modern statutory definitions are much less restrictive than the common law definition, as they don't usually require that an individual actually break into the structure. This definition also removes the dwelling requirement for the burglary, in place allowing for burglary of structures. Current statutes provide for three basic classes of burglary: (1) forcible entry (2) unlawful entry without force and (3) attempted forcible entry (Brown, 2001).

Data and Research

Statistical information regarding burglary is captured and reported in the Uniform Crime Report (UCR) compiled annually by the Federal Bureau of Investigation. Burglary is considered a Part I or index crime. According to the UCR there were approximately 2 million incidents of burglary during 2000. This number has been declining with a 36% decrease since 1996. Preliminary estimates for 2002 indicate that burglary has increased by 1.5%. These statistics include both residential and commercial burglaries. This number is not considered to be completely accurate, as many burglaries are not reported to police and thus not included in the UCR measures (FBI, 2001). The National Crime Victimization Study (NCVS) reported a total of 3.4 million burglaries during 2000. This study has also noted a decrease in burglaries with 2001 having one third fewer burglaries than in 1973 (USDOJ, 2001). The estimated cost of burglary during 2000 was approximately $3 billion (FBI, 2001).

Research into burglary has provided us not only with the likely targets of burglars, but also a typology of professional burglars. Data from the NCVS and the UCR provide us with information regarding the likely targets of burglars. According to 2000 data, residential structures were the most likely target of burglars with rental units being victimized more frequently than owner-based units. Most of these burglaries occurred during the day with the rate of nighttime burglaries declining in recent years. These, most often, occur during the week. The most likely targets of residential burglaries were individuals of Hispanic or African American descent. Finally, the majority of burglaries occurred in the South (FBI, 2001; USDOJ, 2001; Wiesel, 2002). Wright and Decker (1994) also found that the primary areas which residential burglars search are the master bedroom and the living room.

One out of every three burglaries that occurred during 2000 targeted commercial structures (FBI, 2001; USDOJ, 2001). Wright and Decker (1994) found commercial burglars prefer to target retail stores rather than warehouses. For those individuals who do target warehouses, they target locations that are removed from any pedestrian or automobile traffic and that are located in wealthier areas.

Types of Burglars

Research has provided the general profile of the typical burglar: male, young, and underprivileged (Shover, 1991). These offenders select their targets based on a number of factors. Offenders usually target houses that are located in areas familiar to them. They also assess the specific location of the house prior to selecting their target. For instance, houses on dead end streets and those with access to busy roadways are more likely to be the target of a burglar. The visibility of the house from the roads or other houses is also a factor. Houses located in areas where others cannot see them or that are obstructed by trees and foliage are often targeted because of the low likelihood that the burglar will be caught. Finally, burglars tend to weigh the potential rewards for their actions in their decisions to commit this crime (Wiesel, 2002).

Extensive research into the area of career burglars has also lead to the promulgation of several typologies. One of the more well-known typologies was offered by Shover (1972). Through his research he was able to distinguish a successful type of burglar, which he termed the "good burglar." The characteristics of a "good burglar" were identified as follows:

1. the individual is competent in the technical areas required to carry out the act of burglary,
2. the individual maintains a level of personal integrity that involves a high level of dedication to the career,
3. the individual specializes in burglaries,
4. the individual succeeds financially, and
5. the individual possesses the ability to avoid punishment in terms of prison time.

The status of "good burglar" is one that is bestowed upon a burglar by other professional burglars. In order to achieve this status, Shover (1972) noted that four key requirements were essential. First, the burglar must learn the skills from other seasoned burglars. Second, the individual must be able to form professional collaborations (or gangs). Third, "good burglars" have the ability to obtain inside information to enable them to successfully complete their "job." Fourth, the individual must develop sufficient contacts to sell the stolen goods.

Wright and Decker (1994) also identified several types of burglars. One of the primary types of burglars they found were "active burglars." These individuals steal for the benefit of getting money to maintain their party lifestyle. Simply put, these individuals wish to party, but do not want the responsibilities associated with traditional employment opportunities. Thus, they turn to the profession of burglary. While these individuals may seek a party lifestyle, they still maintain a high degree of professionalism. These individuals are very job oriented and possess a sense of ethics about their work. Yet, while they put effort into their jobs, they seek to focus that effort on activities that will provide substantial financial rewards (Wright and Decker, 1994).

Researchers have also identified a career ladder for professional burglars. Cromwell, Olson, and Avary (1991) found that these individuals actually advance through stages as their skill and professionalism increase. They specified three stages through which career burglars pass. The first, which they titled the novice stage, involves the learning of a skill from older professionals in the field. During the second stage, the journeyman stage, individuals begin to branch out on their own. These burglars actually start selecting their own targets and preparing their own strategies for accessing such targets. The final stage is the professional stage. The status of a professional burglar denotes that the individual has attained a specialized level of skills and abilities that is recognized by peers (Cromwell, Olson, and Avary, 1991).

Theories

Perhaps the most widely used explanation for professional burglars is the rational choice theory. This theory is predicated upon the belief that offenders conduct a potential cost/benefit analysis of their actions. Thus, the offender makes a cognizant decision to commit a crime. The assumption is that the more profitable the outcome of the action under scrutiny, the more inclined an individual might be to commit the act. The role of consequences or punishment for such actions cannot be ignored. Although such consequences often exist, the individual calculates the potential benefits to be more appealing than the possibility of the consequences, thus making a rational decision to commit the act. This approach to the explanation of burglary, however, is not without its critics. Wright and Decker (1994) argue that rational choice theories do not give enough credence to the role that emotions may play in the crime of burglary, a view which Shover (1972) shares. They also argue that rational choice theories don't take into account the "cultural context" in which the crime was committed. As they note, such crime does not occur in a vacuum, thus it is important to take into account all of the factors that may influence an individual's behaviors (Wright and Decker, 1994).

Routine activities theory, a specific theory under the auspices of rational choice, has also been used to explain burglary. Specifically, this theory posits that three things must be in place for crime to occur. First, you must have a motivated offender. Second, you must have the availability of suitable targets. Finally, there must be an absence of capable guardians. When these three things are present, then crime can occur. This theory is applicable to burglary on many levels. First, most burglars are motivated by the desire to obtain money. Second, burglars tend to target properties that are lucrative in nature. Property unlikely to yield goods that would bring a substantial amount of money is unlikely to be targeted. Third, as Wright and Decker (1994) point out, most burglars select their targets according to absence of some type of security measures, for example, the capable guardian. Many burglars will not target properties where dogs, alarms, or numerous people, that is, factors that make targets unsuitable, are present (Shover, 1991).

Theorists have also been quick to use social disorganization to explain burglary. According to this theory, the characteristics of a community are the likely causes of crime. In areas where there is high poverty, transient populations, and a mixture of commercial and residential properties, there is likely to be decay in the social norms. This decay leads to areas of increased criminal activity. The increase in crime allows for the transmission of the skills and knowledge regarding criminal behavior from older persons to younger ones. As far as burglary is concerned, evidence exists that areas affected by social disorganization are more likely to have increased levels of burglary. However, as Wright and Decker (1994) note, the social disorganization explanation is most applicable to areas where only small pockets of poverty exist. In such areas where a large amount of poverty exists, there is a lack of suitable targets for burglars.

Along the lines of the social disorganization theory, the criminal opportunity theory offered by Hannon (2002) has also received some empirical support with regards to burglary. A primary tenet of the theory involves the opportunity saturation hypothesis. This hypothesis states that economic deprivation and property crimes have a "curvilinear" relationship. This relationship is evident in areas of economic deprivation. When such deprivation is limited, there is a positive effect on crime. In areas where economic deprivation is severe, there is a negative effect on crimes. The criminal opportunity theory is relevant to burglary in that economic deprivation plays a role in the motivation for burglary. Yet, when economic deprivation is severe, then burglary is less frequent. However, when there is only a limited amount of economic deprivation within an area, then burglaries are more likely to occur (Shover, 1991).

Burglary is also frequently explained by Sutherland's differential association (1959). Differential association theory identifies several important steps that precede the commission of crime. First, criminal behavior is learned. Second, learning occurs through interaction with others. Third, learning occurs most frequently in small, intimate groups. Fourth, the techniques and attitudes involved in criminal behaviors are learned. Fifth, crime occurs when individuals develop attitudes that favor criminal behavior over those that favor abiding by the laws. In his research Shover (1972) found support for the explanatory abilities of this theory regarding burglary. Professional burglars repeatedly revealed that they had learned the "tricks of the trade" from other, professional burglars. The role of learning theory in burglary has also been supported by Cromwell, Olson and Avary (1991) through their findings that indicated burglars progress through various stages in their careers. In order to proceed to the next stage, individuals must learn the precise skills and techniques needed to be successful burglars. "Novices" in the field learn these skills from older, experienced burglars. Hoheimer (1975) also found that burglars learned their trade from others.

Prevention

Efforts to reduce burglaries have been ongoing for numerous years. One of the most common efforts, based on the tenets of rational choice theory, is the use of deterrent strategies. A central assumption underlying this theory is that an increase in the risk of punishment will result in a decrease in the commission of crime. Therefore, strategies designed to increase the likelihood of being caught and punished have been implemented. In keeping with the specific routine activities theory, many of these strategies involve approaches like a hardening of the target, or the removal of a suitable target. Such approaches would involve the placing of locks on windows and doors, installation of additional dead bolts, or even bars on doors and windows. The use of security alarms, closed circuit television cameras, and dogs (or at least the appearance of dogs via a sign) have also been a frequent prevention approach. Even the simple marking of property through the recording of serial numbers or the affixing of a particular mark have been deemed to be essential components of deterrent strategies. Research has supported the deterrent effect of such strategies. Cromwell, Olson, and Avary (1991) found that the primary reasons for non-offending was the fear of punishment. Wright and Decker (1994) also found that deterrent strategies were effective in the prevention of burglary.

At the community level, strategies such as the formation of Neighborhood Watch groups have also been undertaken. Although found to be effective in increasing residents' use of target hardening strategies, Neighborhood Watch programs have generally been found to be unsuccessful (Wiesel, 2002). Communities have also come together and formulated specific strategies for prevention in their area. For instance, many neighborhoods use gated communities or increased security patrols as a deterrent effect. There is also evidence suggests that strategies that relying solely on the use of increased security devices are often less effective than those that use such approaches in combinations with other strategies (Wright and Decker, 1994).

Law enforcement agencies have joined in the prevention effort with regards to property crimes such as burglaries. Many agencies offer support to Neighborhood Watch programs, as well as provide educational materials to residents detailing ways to secure their property. In areas where a significant number of burglaries occur, many agencies have begun identifying the hot spots for such activity through the use of GIS. Increasing the levels of patrol in the identified hot spots in an effort to increase the likelihood of catching and punishing burglars, has been a common strategy for the prevention of burglaries (Wiesel, 2002).

Conclusion

Just what constitutes an effective and appropriate response to the crime of burglary is debatable. In a recent article, Matt Robinson (2000) argues that for crime prevention strategies to be effective, they must occur at all levels of society—from individual to groups to communities and even society. An effective prevention effort for burglaries would consist of participation at all levels. For the individual, it is important that specific strategies to minimize the suitability of the target should occur. Such strategies may be as simple as the installation of additional locks or as complex as the revamping of the house for measures such as close circuit monitoring or security alarms. At the group level, the simple reorganization of the family schedule to allow for at least one individual to be in the home during the day might be appropriate. At the community level, actions could consist of coordination with neighbors to insure the presence of someone in the neighborhood at all times or the formation of a Neighborhood Watch group. At the societal level, the use of crime prevention education programs would be applicable.

The response to professional or career burglars is comprehensive and complex. These individuals pose an even greater challenge for law enforcement and victims, as they possess a different set of motivations and skill levels than ordinary or petty perpetrators of burglary. Many theorists argue that the elimination of the persistent property offenders, especially the burglars, will not occur until the societal conditions that contribute to their offending are removed.

Lisa Hutchinson Wallace

References and Further Reading

Black, H.C., Eds., *Black's Law Dictionary*, West Publishing, St. Paul, MN, 1990.

Brown, S., Esbensen, F. and Geis, G., *Criminology: Explaining Crime and Its Content*, Anderson Publishing, Cincinnati, OH, 2001.

Cromwell, P., Olson, J. and Avary, D. *Breaking and Entering: An Ethnographic Analysis of Burglary*, Sage, Newbury Park, CA, 1991.

Decker, S. and Wright, R., Perceptual Deterrence among Active Residential Burglars: A Research Note, *Criminology*, 31 (1993).

Federal Bureau of Investigation, *Crime in the United States*, Uniform Crime Reports 2000, Washington, DC, U.S. Department of Justice, 2001.

Gleason, J.M. and Barnum, D.T., Crime Does Pay: An Analysis of the Burglary Profession, *Interfaces*, 7 (1977).

Hannon, L., Criminal Opportunity Theory and the Relationship between Poverty and Property Crime, *Sociological Spectrum*, 22 (2002).

Hoheimer, F., The Home Invaders: Confessions of a Cat Burglar. *Chicago Review*, 1975.

LaFave, W.R. and Scott, A.W. Jr., *Criminal Law*, West Publishing, St. Paul, MN, 1986.

Reid, S.T., *Crime and Criminology*, Boston, McGraw Hill, MA, 2003.

Robinson, M., From Research to Policy: Preventing Residential Burglary Through a System Approach, *American Journal of Criminal Justice*, 24 (2000).

Shover, N., Structures and Careers in Burglary, *Journal of Criminal Law, Criminology, and Police Science*, 63 (1972).

Shover, N., *Great Pretenders: Pursuits and Careers of Persistent Thieves*, Westview Press, Boulder, CO, 1996.

Shover, N., Burglary, in Tonry, M.J., Ed., *Crime and Justice*, University of Chicago Press, Chicago, IL, 1991.

Siegel, L.J., *Criminology*, 8th ed. Wadsworth Thomson Publishing, Belmont, CA, 2003.

Stevenson, R., Forsythe, L. and Weatherburn, D., The Stolen Goods Market in New South Wales, Australia: An Analysis of Disposal Avenues and Tactics, *British Journal of Criminology*, 41 (2001).

United States Department of Justice, *Criminal Victimization in the United States, 2001*, U.S. Government Printing Office, Washington, DC, 2001.

Wiesel, D.L., *Burglary in Single Family Homes*, U.S. Government Printing Office, Washington, DC, 2002.

Wright, R.T. and Decker, S.H., *Burglars on the Job: Street Life and Residential Break-Ins*, Northeastern University Press, Boston, MA, 1994.

See also **Burglary: Extent and Correlates; Burglary: The Law**

Burglary: Extent and Correlates

What Is Burglary?

Burglary is defined by the Federal Bureau of Investigation (FBI) as the unlawful entry into a structure to commit a theft or any other felony. Burglary does not necessarily require the use of force to gain entry. In fact, most completed burglaries are not achieved through the use of force. Burglary is a crime defined as an act not against persons but against households. Household burglary includes completed burglaries achieved through forcible entry, completed burglaries achieved without force, and attempted forcible entry.

Extent of Burglary in the U.S.

Criminologists gain information about the nature and extent of burglary from two main sources produced by the U.S. government, the FBI's Uniform Crime Reports (UCR) and the *National Crime Victimization Survey* (NCVS), produced by the Bureau of Justice Statistics (BJS). Criminologists also have studied both active and incarcerated burglars in self-report studies. According to the 1999 NCVS, there were almost 29 million violent and property crimes experienced by the more than 200 million Americans aged 12 years or older. This includes 3,652,000 completed or attempted burglaries, of which 3,065,000 were actually completed. The rate of household burglary in 1999 was 34.1 per 1000 households, meaning that about 3.4% of all households in the U.S. experienced either a completed or attempted burglary. The largest share of household burglaries (1,890,000) were achieved without force.

The UCR only showed 2,099,739 household burglaries in 1999. This means only about 58% of completed and attempted household burglary victimizations were reported to the police in 1999. Statistics from the BJS suggest that victims only report about one out of every three property crimes and that victims are most likely to report their victimizations to the police when they are violent in nature, when an injury results, when lost items are valued at $250 or more, or when forcible entry has occurred. Statistics from the police show that burglaries make up about one in five of all crimes known to the police and one in five of all property crimes. Police statistics also show that most residential burglaries occur during the day (60%) when people are at work or away from the household for other reasons.

Extent of Burglary Internationally

Despite the common assertions that crime rates are so much higher in the U.S. than in other countries, results from the International Crime Victims Survey (ICVS) suggest otherwise. This victimization survey of residents in Australia, Belgium, Canada, Denmark, England and Wales, Finland, France, Japan, the Netherlands, Northern Ireland, Poland, Portugal, Scotland, Spain, Sweden, Switzerland, and the U.S., show that many crimes actually occur more frequently in other countries.

Results from the 2000 ICVS show that the proportion of households with a completed or attempted burglary was highest in Australia (7%), England and Wales (5%), and Canada, Denmark, and Belgium (all 4%). Burglary rates in the U.S. are less than 2% and are generally exceeded by other countries, including New Zealand and Czechoslovakia. Burglary rates are high in these countries in part because they contain a significant proportion of semidetached or detached homes, which provide better opportunities for offenders.

Effects of Burglary Victimization

Many people consider burglary to be the "rape" of property crimes, because of the drastic personal consequences it can have on its victims. Burglary has many effects on individual victims, as well as society in general. Perhaps the most prevalent effect is the fear it causes because virtually everyone has at some time worried about his or her home being burgled. Among the impacts of residential burglary on victims include loss of property and money. According to the 1999 UCR, burglaries known to the police produced more than $3 billion in losses to victims. The average loss associated with residential burglaries was $1,441 per offense. Other results of burglary victimization include the potential for physical injury, posttraumatic stress disorder, immobility, and costs to the state (including the investigation, apprehension, prosecution, conviction, and sentencing of the offender). Victims tend to have a lack of access to postvictimization services. It has been demonstrated that victims go through stages or phases of grief, anger, shock, disbelief, fear, and sadness as a result of burglary victimization, much like victims of rape. Burglary affects neighbors, friends, and family (e.g., emotional trauma).

Correlates of Burglary Victimization

Most burglaries occur in the hotter months (e.g., July and August), while the fewest occur in February. Certain types of households are more likely to be victimized by burglary than others. The BJS provides information on how demographic characteristics relate to victimization risk.

Race of Household Head. African Americans generally experience property crimes, regardless of the type, at higher rates than whites. For example, in 1999, 250 black and 190 white households per 1000 were victims of property crime overall. Fifty-three black and 32 white households per 1000 were burglarized in 1999. Persons of other races experienced overall property crime and burglaries at rates lower than African Americans.

Ethnicity of Household Head. Generally, Hispanic households are characterized by higher rates of overall property crime, motor vehicle theft, and theft than non-Hispanic households. However, Hispanic and non-Hispanic households are burglarized at roughly similar rates (37 and 34 burglaries per 1000 households, respectively, in 1999).

Household Income. The NCVS demonstrates that the relationship between annual household income and property crimes depends upon the type of crime being considered. For example, in 1999, higher income households were less susceptible to burglary, but more susceptible to theft.

Region. In 1999, Western households had the highest rate of overall property crime. Western, Southern, and Midwestern households experienced similar burglary rates, and Northeastern households had the lowest burglary rate in the nation.

Place of Residence. As usually shown by the NCVS, urban households were the most vulnerable to overall property crime in 1999, including burglary. Suburban households were more likely to experience all forms of property crime except burglary than were rural households. Rural households were burglarized at rates greater than suburban households during 1999 (33 versus 27 burglaries per 1000 households, respectively).

Home Ownership. Property crime is significantly more likely to occur in rented properties. In 1999, for example, rented properties experienced 48% higher rates of overall property crime, including 85% higher rates of burglary than owned households.

Burglary Trends

The NCVS is a better measure of crime trends since the factors that affect victim recall and reporting to researchers are more constant than those that affect the UCR crime trends. According to the NCVS, crime rates are at their lowest rates since the inception of the survey. They have generally declined since 1973 and have continued a downward trend since the redesign of the survey in 1993. Victimization rates in 1999 were the lowest recorded since the survey's creation in 1973. Aside from an increase between 1973 and 1974, the overall property crime rate has declined since the inception of the NCVS. After a period of slow decline that was interrupted by an increase from 1980 to 1981, the burglary rate fell each year through the rest of the period. The 1999 household burglary rate was about a third that of the adjusted rate of 1973 (34 burglaries per 1000 households).

UCR data do show that only 14% of burglary offenses led to arrests in 1999. This means that 86% of burglaries did not produce arrests. The majority of arrests in 1999 (81%) were of adults, while 19% were juveniles. The highest percentage of juvenile arrests for burglaries occurred in cities with less than 10,000 population (25%).

Who Is the Burglar?

In general, a burglar is a property offender who does not engage in dangerous or confrontational behavior. Burglary is a passive crime in which offenders try to avoid any form of contact with their victims. Most burglars are males (87% of arrests in 1999), most burglars are under the age of 25 years (63% of arrests in 1999), and most burglars are Caucasian (69% of all arrests in 1999).

Criminologists claim that there are at least two types of burglars, including the less skilled, who probably is satisfied with tackling available targets regardless of the potential for yield, and the more skilled burglar, who would insist on tackling a profitable target. The notion that there is more than one "type" of offender is common in the literature. Others suggest there are three types of burglars, including *planners* who plan target selection far in advance of their offenses, *searchers* who actively explore an area for suitable targets immediately prior to their offenses, and *opportunists* who simply locate suitable targets by happenstance. Most criminologists place burglars along some form of continuum, with the *novice* burglar at one extreme and the *professional* burglar at the other. The novice may be just beginning his or her career as a burglar or may only commit the crime occasionally, while the professional burglar is viewed, within the burglary world, as an elite. The novice can be considered a part-time offender while the professional is more a career criminal. The most important point is that all burglars are not necessarily brilliant and daring. As noted above, most residential burglars enter unoccupied residences during the daytime when houses are deserted, not when people are at home, which would require greater skills and is much riskier.

Why Does Burglary Occur?

Criminological theory has clearly and consistently demonstrated a relationship between spatial characteristics of the physical environment and crime. From the *Chicago School of Criminology* and its predecessors, to the most recent environmental and ecological theories of criminal behavior, it has been shown that criminal incidents occur in predictable patterns. Criminal behavior does not occur randomly so observable patterns are not a function of chance. Residences within any given neighborhood do not have an equal potential for becoming the target site for a burglary. Their risks are dependent on factors in the physical environment.

Four primary environmental characteristics related to the offense of residential burglary have been identified, including *surveillability*, *accessibility*, *non-occupancy* of residents, and *routine activities* of surrounding areas. *Surveillability* is the degree to which a residence is observable by others. Generally, residences that are less visible to neighbors and passersby are more vulnerable to burglary. *Accessibility* is the degree to which a residence can be entered and exited with relative ease. Generally, residences that are more accessible to offenders are more likely to be burglarized. Many burglary studies also show that residences are at highest risk for burglary when they are left unoccupied. Burglar interview studies and analysis of times of burglary demonstrate the importance of *non-occupancy* in the occurrence of burglary. Burglars simply prefer to enter residences when residents are not home. In fact, burglars use some very clever methods to determine whether people are home, and also track the daily activities of household members and neighbors to determine the best times to enter unoccupied residences. Burglars may even approach potential targets when residents are home and attempt entry prior to their actual offense, by ringing the doorbell or knocking on the door of a residence. They may claim to need to use the telephone, that their car is broken down on the side of the road, or that they need to borrow some item from the kitchen of a neighbor, in order to stake out the property and its contents.

Routine activities include the amount of movement around a residence. Some studies show that higher levels of automotive traffic around a residence increase the risk of burglary victimization, while others suggest that higher levels of pedestrian traffic are related to lower burglary victimization rates. Engaging in legal activities away from the home (e.g., work and leisure) increases the possibility of burglary victimization. Living in a neighborhood where most residents have similar schedules has also been found to increase the risk of burglary victimization, since it is easier to predict when residences will be left unoccupied.

Several theoretical positions about criminal behavior generally have been examined in burglary research to explain these findings. In order of development, the most prominent of these are referred to as *rational choice theory*, *opportunity theory*, *routine activities theory*, and *crime pattern theory*. Each of these approaches is intimately related.

"Rational" refers to the fact that criminals process information and evaluate alternatives and "choice" suggests that they make decisions. A characteristic of rational behavior is risk avoidance. Risk plays a role in target selection among burglars. The level of risk is one of the factors that make a target "good" or "bad." Offenders plan to reduce the level of risk associated with committing criminal offenses through selection of the most suitable targets. As a result, differential levels of risk associated with different targets lead to differential risks of victimization for potential victims. Burglary offenders often behave in a rational fashion, since they prefer to commit crimes that provide the highest benefits and pose the lowest risks. When motivated by drugs or a desire to commit acts of violence, burglary can be far less rational and dangerous for residents.

Opportunity theory holds that criminal behavior most often reflects offenders' exploitation of perceived opportunities. It is a situational theory since it places emphasis on the specific elements of the crime and not on the characteristics of the offender. Burglars see residences as suitable opportunities when they are attractive because of high payoffs and little risk. Rational offenders are most likely to take advantage of available opportunities.

Routine activity theory suggests that crime results from the convergence of three elements in time and space: a presence of potential or motivated offenders; a presence of suitable targets; and an absence of capable guardians to prevent the criminal act. The greater the degree to which daily life pulls people away from their residences (for work and leisure) and allows potential offenders the freedom to travel, the more likely that burglary will occur, particularly when potential victims possess greater amounts of property suitable for stealing. Offenders discern suitable targets through the course of routine, normal, or patterned recreational or work activities of victims, thus increasing the likelihood of the commission of offenses.

Crime pattern theory posits that criminal behavior is the end point in a decision process or sequence of decision steps that begins with a rational offender and is only possible with suitable opportunities for crime. The suitability of a target is a function of the characteristics of the target and the characteristics of the target's surroundings. In the case of burglary, offenders determine which targets are good and which are not so good by developing images or "mental templates" through previous experiences. According to this theory, a burglary offense starts with the desire or willingness to engage in crime, which is "triggered" by the presence of a criminal opportunity (such as an unoccupied house with windows left open, which also is hidden from the view of neighbors because of overgrown bushes). Whether the offense actually occurs depends on the offender's readiness to commit the crime, the suitability of the target for offending, and the presence or absence of capable guardians to protect the property.

MATTHEW B. ROBINSON

References and Further Reading

Bennett, T. and Wright, R., *Burglars on Burglary: Prevention and the Offender*, Gower Publishing, Brookfield, VT, 1984.

Brown, B. and Altman, I., Territoriality and Residential Crime: A Conceptual Framework. In Brantingham, P. and Brantingham, P., Eds., *Environmental Criminology*, Sage, CA, Beverly Hills, 1981.

Cohen, L. and Cantor, D., Residential Burglary in the United States: Lifestyle and Demographic Factors Associated with the Probability of Victimization, *Journal of Research in Crime and Delinquency*, 18 (1981).

Cohen, L. and Felson., M., Social Change and Crime Rate Trends: A Routine Activity Approach, *American Sociological Review*, 44 (1979).

Cromwell, P., Olson, J., and Avary, D., *Breaking and Entering: An Ethnographic Analysis of Burglary*, Sage, Newbury Park, CA, 1991.

Felson, M., Routine Activities and Crime Prevention in the Developing Metropolis, *Criminology*, 25 (1987).

Felson, M., *Crime and Everyday Life: Insights and Implications for Society*. Pine Forge Press, Thousand Oaks, CA, 1994.

Garofalo, J., Reassessing the Lifestyle Model of Criminal Victimization, in Gottfredson, M. and Hirschi, T., Eds., *Positive Criminology*, Sage, Newbury Park, CA, 1987.

Maguire, M. and Bennett, T., *Burglary in a Dwelling*, Heinemann, London, 1982.

Rengert, G. and Wasilchick, J., *Suburban Burglary: A Time and Place for Everything*, Charles C. Thomas, Springfield, IL, 1985.

Reppetto, T., *Residential Crime*. Ballinger, Cambridge, MA, 1974.

Robinson, M., Environmental Characteristics Associated with Residential Burglaries of Student Apartment Complexes, *Environment and Behavior*, 29 (1997).

Robinson, M., Accessible Targets but not Advisable Ones: The Role of Accessibility in Student Apartment Burglary, *Journal of Security Administration*, 21 (1998).

Robinson, M., Lifestyles, Routine Activities, and Residential Burglary Victimization, *Journal of Crime and Justice*, 22 (1999).

Robinson, M., From Research to Policy: Preventing Residential Burglary Through a Systems Approach, *American Journal of Criminal Justice*, 24 (2000).

Rountree, P. and Land, K., Burglary Victimization, Perceptions of Crime Risk, and Routine Activities: A Multilevel Analysis Across Seattle Neighborhoods and Census Tracts, *Journal of Research in Crime and Delinquency*, 33 (1996).

Van Kesteren, J., Mayhew, P., and Nieuwbeerta, P., *Criminal Victimization in Seventeen Industrialised Countries: Key Findings from the 2000 International Crime Victims Survey*, Netherlands Ministry of Justice Research and Documentation Centre, The Hague.

Winchester, S. and Jackson, H., *Residential Burglary: The Limits of Prevention*. Home Office Research Study No. 74, Her Majesty's Stationary Office, London, 1982.

Wright, R. and Decker, S., *Burglars on the Job: Streetlife and Residential Break-Ins*. Northeastern University Press, Boston, 1994.

Wright, R. and Logie, R., How Young House Burglars Choose Targets, *The Howard Journal*, 27 (1988).

See also **Burglary as an Occupation; Burglary: The Law**

Burglary: The Law

Introduction

There is a growing concern on how to combat the frequency of burglaries in the U.S. This is not simply because of the staggering rate of burglaries, but also because burglaries can lead to more complicated crime scenes. For instance, if the dwellers of the home discover a burglary in progress, there is the potential for further forms of criminality, such as assault. While burglary, by definition, does not involve a person-on-person offense, the Common Law still describes burglary as a heinous offense. This is due to the fact that terror or fear is inflicted upon the victim.

Every individual is entitled to the right of habitation. Habitation implies the right to feel secure in one's own home. Thus, burglary and more precisely the fear that the victims experience from this crime, infringe upon the right to habitation. The following entry will give a broad, legal history of burglary, some straightforward facts about the crime, and a brief explanation of the role of burglary in the criminal justice system today.

History

Burglary is an act that has been with man through many civilizations. Thus, burglary has also existed under many different legal structures and systems throughout history. In fact, even the first known written law, known as the Code of Hammurabi, contains codes about burglary.

The Code of Hammurabi contains 282 codes, or laws. Three of these codes, codes 21 through 23, explicitly deal with stealing and the home. Burglary or "breaking and entering" is described as an offense where the punishment is death. Code 21 states, "If anyone breaks a hole into a house, he shall be put to death before that hole and burned." The language that the code is written in differs little from that of today's, but the message is the same. Defacing or vandalizing someone's home was done at one's own peril. What should be realized here, however, is not necessarily the harshness of the punishment. Instead, the punishment illustrates the amount of respect and value associated with a home. This great amount of respect and value for the home yielded a law insistent on protecting it.

Code 22 further added, "If anyone is committing a robbery and is caught, then he shall be put to death." Of course, the punishment for violating the two codes discussed thus far can only be exercised if the offender is caught. Therefore Code 23 maintained, "If the robber is not caught, then shall he who was robbed claim under oath the amount of his loss, then shall the community on whose ground and territory and in whose domain it was completed compensate him for the goods stolen." In other words, code 23 states that if the criminal is not caught, the victim will swear truth to the amount of stolen property. The community in which he lives will then repay him for the stolen goods.

As stated above, Hammurabi's Code viewed burglary as a death penalty offense. In later years the Common Law continued this principle. Common Law did not consider burglary as a crime against the property, but rather as an offense against the habitation of individuals. Common Law specifically viewed burglary as breaking and entering a house, at night with the intent to commit a felony. Given this rather specific definition of burglary, four components must then be met in order to have a burglary.

The first component addressed in the definition is that one must break and enter. Again, this definition is very strict so there must be physical evidence showing breaking into the dwelling. Also, these two acts (breaking and entering) had to be committed on the same occasion. For instance, if an individual broke into a house one night, but waited until the next night to enter, a burglary was not committed.

The second element addresses what locations can be burglarized. The location had to be a house, apartment, or inn rooms. Barns and warehouses were included as locations that could be burglarized but certain guidelines had to be met. For instance, the structures must be located on the same parcel of land as the home of a resident. Also, it was not enough to simply own the house or dwelling. The house must be inhabited in order to have its surrounding buildings protected by the burglary law. The basis for this rested on the idea of curtilage, or the presence of other buildings and structures on a property.

The third component was the time of day. The fact that the act occurred at night was central and required for the concept of burglary under the Common Law. If the offense occurred during the day, a burglary was not committed.

The fourth component of the definition of burglary is intent. Aside from the above three elements being required and met, an offender must also have the intent to commit some felony. It can be any felony such as but not limited to murder, robbery, or rape.

Keep in mind that this is simply an exploration of a strictly written Common Law definition of burglary. The offense and definition of burglary has undergone some modifications since its Common Law inception. Today, burglary, as a crime, is more inclusive of other elements. For instance, *Black's Law Dictionary* still includes the Common Law definition but simply by way of background. Later, though, the dictionary gives a broader definition and defines burglary as, "the common law offense of breaking and entering another's dwelling at night with intent to commit a felony." The second part of the definition goes on to broaden the scope of the crime. In fact it says, "The modern statutory offense of breaking and entering any building—not just a dwelling, and not only at night—with the intent to commit a felony."

Dealing with definitions of crimes can be rather difficult. Burglary is no different. The definitions of burglary are all similar. Realize, however, that the laws do vary from state to state. Some states simply have burglary charges whereas others have first, second, and even third degree burglary charges.

Generally, whether the burglary is completed is irrelevant. In other words, even an attempt is classified as a burglary. As long as the person has no legal right to be present in the structure, a burglary has occurred. If breaking and entering occurs in a hotel or vacation residence, for instance, a burglary would still have occurred. In this situation, the act would be a burglary for the household whose member or members were staying there at the time the entry occurred.

Facts

About half of all burglaries involve residences. The official data, however, do not distinguish inhabited parts of houses from garages or similar structures on the property. Given the data, burglars break into a house, apartment or condominium every 11 seconds. This is not saying that there is a regular occurrence of offenses; instead, stating that burglaries occur every 11 seconds simply illustrates how often a burglary might occur, on an average. Most reports estimate that between 50 and 60% of all residential burglaries are committed in the daylight. One can now see why the legal definition of burglary has evolved to disregard time of day.

Uniform Crime Reports (UCR), which are compiled and published by the Federal Bureau of Investigation (FBI), can aid individuals who wish to examine burglary. A recent UCR survey indicated that 32% of the entries into residences are made through unlocked doors and windows. Again, the older definition of burglary would not have classified these instances as burglaries.

The annual losses experienced by burglary victims are estimated at $3.1 billion. The average loss per residential burglary is $1350. Each victim's loss, of course, can vary greatly from this average loss value; however, only reported cases are used to estimate losses and rates of occurrences. There may be many more burglary occurrences that simply go unreported.

Differences in the nature of burglary offenses occur across time and space. For some reason, July has the greatest number of reported burglaries while February has the least. As well, the South has the highest volume of burglaries. In fact, 42% of all burglaries committed and reported occur in the southern U.S. In contrast, the Northeast has the lowest amount of reported burglaries. Reported burglaries in the Northeast account for only 14% of all burglaries in the U.S.

Sixty-five percent of all burglaries are by forcible entry. In other words, these burglaries did in fact include breaking and entering into a structure. Twenty-eight percent of burglaries were committed by unlawful entry. This is not necessarily breaking into the dwelling. The remaining 7% were reported as attempted forcible entry. When employing today's legal definition of burglary, even an attempted burglary is considered burglary.

Unfortunately official data sources contain weaknesses. Not only are the data limited to reported burglaries, but also when an unlawful entry results in a violent confrontation with the occupant, the offense is counted as a robbery rather than a burglary. Nationally, these types of confrontations occur in only one fortieth of all residential burglaries. Although this issue may seem negligible when discussing burglary rates, it should still be addressed and acknowledged.

In summary, these figures suggest that, on an average, the likelihood of a serious personal attack on any American in a given year is about 1 in 550. The actual risk for slum dwellers or residents of ghettos is considerably higher. For most Americans, however, the risk of being burglarized is actually less than 1 in 550. In other words, a person's given risk of being burglarized can vary greatly. This variation is dependent on the type of neighborhood or area in which one lives.

Burglary and the Criminal Justice System

Burglary is expensive and frightening. Having one's home broken into and ransacked is an experience that unnerves almost anyone. Additionally, research indicates that burglars are seldom caught. Being a victim of burglary can be stressful but knowing that the perpetrator is still on the loose can be traumatic for some victims. Since burglary is frequent, costly, upsetting, and difficult to control, it makes great demands on the criminal justice system. The nature of this crime causes society to look for and demand results from the criminal justice system.

Preventing and solving burglaries pertains to the front line of the criminal justice system, law enforcement agencies. Burglary prevention calls for and assumes imaginative methods of police patrol. Solving burglaries demands great investigative patience and resourcefulness. Recent changes in law enforcement tactics, such as community policing, will ideally yield better control over burglary and overall crime. Community policing, for instance, involves a combination of efforts between highly trained police personnel and the residents of the area the police patrol. Residents are crucial to the success of controlling burglary. Such community involvement includes Neighborhood Watch programs. Instead of simply leaving the burglary reduction task to law enforcement agencies, residents actively assist in the process.

When police apprehend burglars, the courts enter the picture. Appropriately dealing with individual burglars is a difficult and delicate problem for prosecutors and judges. Burglary is indeed a serious crime and thus can carry heavy and harsh penalties. Additionally, many burglary offenders are habitual or professional criminals. Many more offenders are youthful or marginal offenders. Criminal sanctions in their most drastic form might do more harm than good to these individuals. To address this potential, some statutes make petit larceny an alternative to a felony for purposes of proving burglarious intent.

The final component that burglars travel through in the criminal justice system is corrections. Burglars are probably the most numerous of serious offenders in the correctional system. Still, given the number of incarcerated burglary offenders, it is a plausible assumption that this crime may be a reason for Americans' high perceptual fear of crime. Moreover, the prevalence of the two major crimes of burglary and robbery may be a significant, if not the major, reason for America's alarm about crime. Finding effective ways of protecting the community from these two crimes would undoubtedly do much to make "crime," as a whole, significantly less frightening.

A study in London has found that a history of burglary is a strong predictor of recidivism. In other words, when comparing an offender with a history of burglary to an offender with no history of burglary, the offender with the history of burglary is significantly more likely to re-offend. Even after controlling for all other factors, a history of burglary still predicted recidivism.

There are two possible explanations for this phenomenon. First, offenders who specialize in burglary commit a high number of burglary offenses. Thus, the offenders who specialize in burglary have a high probability of being caught and, of course, a history of burglary. This is not to say that many burglars are apprehended. In fact, of all UCR Index Crimes, burglary has the lowest clearance rate (12.7%). Instead, what should be understood is that although the police clearance rate for burglaries is low, burglars who commit many burglaries have a high probability of being caught and re-caught. Clearly, this could be a viable reason why burglars with a history are more likely to re-offend.

The second theory or explanation that supports the data indicating that a history of burglary is a strong predictor of recidivism is current police tactics. Evidence suggests that police agencies target known offenders. Police know of the burglars and know of the habitual offenders' modes of operation. This in turn helps the police target and seize career burglars. Operations such as "Bumblebee" for example, targeted known burglars.

Burglary and the Courts

The courts have aided in further extrapolating the legal definition of burglary. For instance, in *Taylor v. United States* (495 U.S. 575, 1990) the Court held that burglary, regardless of its exact definition or label, is burglary so long as the basic elements remain. These elements include an unlawful or unprivileged entry into, or remaining in, a building or other structure. Additionally, the entry must accompany the intent to commit a crime. Given this definition, some jury instructions actually require the jury to find all the elements of generic burglary in order to find the defendant guilty.

Taylor is important because statutes vary within and between states in reference to burglary. It is difficult to understand burglary law or any law if the definition continuously varies by state. For example, in Massachusetts the definition of burglary is the breaking and entering of a dwelling house in the nighttime with the intent to commit a felony. Not all jurisdictions require the nighttime elements. Thus, *Taylor v. United States* (1990) added a more standardized definition of burglary. Although states still have both varying definitions of burglary and punishment, the *Taylor* case is a step toward making the definition of burglary more universal.

In *Eduardo v. State* (70 Cal. App. 4th 591, 1999), a juvenile court case, the juvenile committed first-degree residential burglary. The child broke into a garage attached to a duplex house from which he stole a bicycle. The juvenile's defense was a claim that the garage was not an inhabited dwelling within the meaning of the penal Code. Therefore, the act he committed was not first-degree residential burglary.

The Court of Appeals, however, found that the garage was indeed an inhabited dwelling. This verdict was in spite of the fact that the only entrance to the garage was an exterior door. The court built its argument on the fact that the garage was attached to a multiunit dwelling. The appellate court held that not only are individual units of a multiunit building dwelling houses but also that the multiunit building itself is a dwelling house. The court went on to protect any basement room or garage attached to a dwelling house under burglary statutes. In fact, any attachment that is "under the same roof with the living quarters, functionally connected to the living quarters, and an integral part of the living quarters is part of the inhabited dwelling house."

The appellate court also held that the tenants should have expected to encounter a resident or a guest of the other unit in the garage. The juvenile in this matter, however, was neither a guest nor a resident. Thus, it was reasonable for the tenants to expect protection from unauthorized intrusions of the garage. With regard to entrances considered for burglary, the Court of Appeals further expanded the scope of burglary law. The defense argued that since the only entrance to the garage was an exterior door, a burglary could not have been committed. The court ruled that the nature of the entrance was irrelevant. The proper focus was then on the proximity of the structure to the dwelling. The rationale is that the closer the structure is to the dwelling, the more potential there is for confrontation. Confrontation, of course, opens the door for additional and possibly more serious crimes.

Conclusion

Burglary has been defined as breaking and entering any dwelling house by night with intent to commit a felony therein. The object of punishing such a breaking and entering is not to simply prevent trespass. Today, the punishment is instead based on our society's recognition that burglary is among the first steps toward wrongs of a greater magnitude; examples potentially include robbery or murder. In crimes such as robbery and murder the function of intent, when proven, appears more clearly than in theft. The intent, however, is still precisely similar.

Burglary can be seen as an index to the probability of committing more serious crimes in the future. Criminal law seeks to prevent these future forms of criminality. Here the law gives evidence that this is the true explanation. For example, an indictment for burglary that charges that the defendant broke into a dwelling house and stole certain property, is just as good as one which alleges that he broke in with intent to steal—the law assumes future criminal acts stem from burglary.

In short, burglary has been with man throughout history. Though the definition has evolved and will in all likelihood continue to evolve, the seriousness of this crime has not changed. The right to property and feeling secure in one's home are long standing desires. Today the right to feeling secure in one's home is still well respected and, quite frankly, demanded in the U.S. Therefore, burglary will always be viewed as a serious crime and will thus always have the attention of the American criminal justice system.

Sean Maddan

References and Further Reading

Blackstone, W., *Commentaries on the Laws of England*, Vol. 4, University of Chicago Press, Chicago, IL, 1979.

The Burglary Prevention Council, www.burglaryprevention.org, 2003.

Crime in the United States, 2001, Federal Bureau of Investigation, Washington, DC, 2002.

Garner, B.A., *Blacks Law Dictionary*, 7th ed., West Group, St. Paul, MN, 2000.

Hammurabi, in Johns, C.H., Johns (Translator), *The Oldest Codes of Law in the World*, The Law Book Exchange, Ltd., New York, 2000.

Holmes, O.W., Jr., *The Common Law*, Dover Publications, Inc., New York, 1991.

Presidents Commission on Law Enforcement and Administration of Justice, *The Challenge of Crime in a Free Society*, Avon, New York, 1968.

See also **Burglary as an Occupation; Burglary: Extent and Correlates**

C

Campus Crime

Crime on college and university campuses is by no means a new phenomenon. What is new is that in the mid to late 1980s, crime on campuses was catapulted to the agendas of federal and state policy makers, campus administrators, and the courts. The concern over campus crime has not waned. In 1998, the 4064 institutions of higher education in the U.S. had an enrollment of just over 14.5 million students and nearly 3 million faculty and staff. The sheer number of potential victims (and offenders) suggests that campus crime will remain an agenda item.

The concern over campus crime occurred in part because of national and local media coverage highlighting violence against students, faculty, staff, and visitors that happened on or near campuses. The media, including the *Chronicle of Higher Education's* annual campus crime report and routine coverage of campus crime issues, continue to paint a picture of increasing violence on campus. This portrayal has shattered the "ivory tower" image of the college campus and replaced it with another image—the campus as a "hot spot" of heinous criminal activity where guns, binge drinking, and illegal drugs create many opportunities for violence among students. The "hot spots" image, however, is contrary to Lizotte and Fernandez's estimate that between 1974 and 1991, the rate of violent crime on campus steadily decreased by 27%—from 88 incidents per 100,000 students to 64 incidents per 100,000 students. Volkwein, Szelest, and Lizotte, as well, reported a decreasing trend in on-campus property crimes from 1980 to 1992.

Court Cases and Anticrime Legislation

Toward the latter quarter of the 20th century, state courts also became involved with campus crime. In several states, liability lawsuits were successfully filed against colleges or universities either by students who had been victimized on campus or by the student victim's parents. The courts have generally ruled that colleges and universities have (1) a duty to warn students about known risks and (2) a duty to protect them with adequate security protection. They have awarded both compensatory and punitive damages to student plaintiffs when the victimization is "foreseeable."

Other lawsuits have raised additional legal issues concerning the secrecy and handling of campus crime. The highest state-level courts and the U.S. Supreme Court agreed to hear these cases; their attention demonstrates the importance of legal issues associated with campus crime. These cases include: (1) a lawsuit demanding access to the records of student disciplinary proceedings, (2) a lawsuit invoking the civil rights provision of the federal Violence against Women Act of 1994 and Title IX gender discrimination law to seek damages for an alleged on-campus "gang" rape, and (3) a student suing a university for mishandling the internal judicial process that led to his suspension based on a rape charge.

No lawsuit alleging failure to provide adequate campus security has received more notoriety and achieved more long-term results than the one brought by the Clery family against Lehigh University in

Pennsylvania. Following the brutal rape and murder of their daughter, Jeanne, in her dormitory room on campus in 1986. The Clerys sued the university and won an out-of-court settlement against the institution. The loss of their daughter ignited their grassroots activism and led them to create a nonprofit organization, Security on Campus, Inc., in 1987.

The Clery's activism provided the vehicle that enabled other campus crime victims and their parents to organize and gain a hearing for their safety concerns. Together they lobbied state and federal governments to pass legislation forcing colleges and universities to publicize their campus crime statistics. One point among their arguments was that little was known about the extent and nature of campus crime. It is noteworthy that during the 1980s, less than 15% of the nation's colleges and universities voluntarily reported their campus crime statistics to the Federal Bureau of Investigation's annual Uniform Crime Report (UCR), which began collecting these institutions' crime statistics in 1972.

In 1988, Pennsylvania was the first state to enact legislation requiring colleges and universities to report campus crime statistics publicly; 18 states have since passed similar or stricter reporting legislation (e.g., Tennessee). In 1990, Congress passed the Student Right-to-Know and Campus Security Act (hereafter referred to as the Security Act), which required colleges and universities that participate in federal financial aid programs to publish statistics for specific on-campus FBI Index offenses (e.g., murder, rape, robbery, aggravated assault, burglary, and motor vehicle theft), hate crimes, and arrests for liquor law and drug abuse violations and weapons possession. The law also mandated that institutions make available their respective crime prevention and security policies and procedures.

Congress has maintained a steady interest in campus crime issues. In 1992, Congress amended the Security Act to include the Campus Sexual Assault Victim's Bill of Rights, which, among other requirements, mandated schools to provide the basic rights for victims of sexual assault and to develop written policies dealing with sexual assault on campus. The 1992 amendments also changed the reporting of rape statistics to the reporting of forcible sexual offenses and nonforcible sexual offenses beginning in 1993. The Security Act was amended again in 1998 to require reporting of statistics for additional crimes (e.g., murder and nonnegligent manslaughter and arson) and for the geographic locations of crimes (e.g., residential facilities for students on campus, public areas immediately adjacent to or running through the campus, and certain noncampus facilities); the act also requires extensive campus security-related provisions, keeping a daily public crime log, and clarified and expanded hate crimes reporting (e.g., disability was added to the list of possible prejudged motivations). There is also a requirement that the Department of Education collect, analyze, and report to Congress on the incidences of campus crime. The 1998 amendments also formally changed the name of the Security Act to the Jeanne Clery Disclosure of Campus Security Police and Campus Crime Statistics Act (hereafter referred to as the Clery Act).

During the 1990s, Congress authorized three federal agencies—the Department of Justice, the General Accounting Office (GAO), and the Department of Education—to examine several different aspects of campus crime. First, in 1996 the Bureau of Justice Statistics issued a report describing the functions (e.g., patrol and response and criminal investigation and enforcement), expenditures, pay, and number of reported crimes for campus law enforcement agencies serving U.S. 4-year colleges and universities with 2500 or more students. The report also described the types of crime-related policies and programs operating within these agencies (e.g., general crime prevention, date rape prevention, and victim assistance). Second, in 1997 Congress directed the GAO to examine compliance with the Security Act. This report concluded that schools were having difficulty in consistently interpreting and applying some of the law's reporting requirements. Third, in 1997 the Department of Education issued a study done by the National Center for Educational Statistics that examined the extent of campus crime and security at 5317 institutions in the 50 states, the District of Columbia, and Puerto Rico. Fourth, in January 2001 the Department of Education released its report to Congress on the 3-year incidence of crime on campuses and facilities of these colleges and universities (i.e., 1997, 1998, and 1999), as required by the Clery Act.

Congress, as part of the Violence against Women Act, appropriated monies for basic research to examine the sexual victimization of college women and for schools to address the prevention of violence against women on campus. During 1999 and 2000, the Department of Justice awarded close to $15 million to 39 colleges and universities to develop and implement or improve campus-based programs and services for victims of sexual assault, domestic violence, and stalking.

Variables Affecting Campus Crime

Only recently have social scientists turned their attention to crime and related issues on college campuses. Some of the studies have used official estimates of campus crime to answer questions about the extent and the nature of crime on campus and to examine the correlates of campus crime rates. For example, in 1978, McPheters published one of the first studies of campus crime using official data from 38 colleges and universities in California. He found that the proportion of students living in dormitories and the proximity of the campus to urban areas with high rates of unemployment were strong predictors of official rates of campus crime (i.e., all FBI Index crimes in 1975). Fox and Hellman examined the 1979 UCR-based crime rates for 222 colleges and universities. They reported that property offenses, and in particular, larceny-theft, had the highest incidence. Their analysis revealed that campus size (in acres) and low academic quality (SAT or ACT scores of incoming freshmen) were strongly associated with campus crime rates; the location of the campus (urban, suburban, or rural), although not related to overall campus crime rates, was related to rates of campus violence. Sloan analyzed crimes known to campus police at 500 colleges and universities during the 1989–1990 academic year. Similar to Fox and Hellman's findings, his analysis revealed that most offenses known to the police were property related (64% burglary and theft related and 18% vandalism). His research strongly suggests that the characteristics of the institution (e.g., the setting, population per acre, and academic quality), the characteristics of students attending the institution (e.g., percentage of part-time students, percentage of students living on campus, and percentage of students under the age of 25), and security measures used by the campus (e.g., the number of campus police or security officers per 1000 students and crime prevention programs or services) were significantly related to rates of crime.

Using UCR and survey data from campus police agencies at 530 2-year and 4-year schools during the 1991–92 academic year, Fernandez and Lizotte examined the relationship between campus crime rates and crime rates in the community surrounding the campus. Although their results indicated little general support for a reciprocal relationship between campus crime rates and community crime rates, they uncovered a reciprocal relationship between rates of campus motor vehicle theft and rates of motor vehicle theft in the surrounding community. They reported that community characteristics and community crime rates affected rates of motor vehicle theft and robbery on campus. They concluded that, with some exceptions (motor vehicle theft, burglary, and robbery), campus crime rates were influenced by campus characteristics, and community crime rates were influenced by community characteristics.

Bromley (1992), also using UCR data on campus crime, compared campus crime rates at public state universities in Florida with crime rates in the surrounding cities and counties. He found that regardless of the size of the university or surrounding community population and regardless of the location of the school (e.g., urban, rural, or suburban), campuses had significantly lower crime rates (per 1000 population) than did the surrounding cities and counties. Bromley's research suggests that college campuses have lower rates of reported crime than do the cities and counties in which they are located. The research of Volkwein and his colleagues comparing on-campus violent crime rates to the national violent rates supports Bromley's results. Their research showed that between 1974 and 1992 campuses were over 10 times safer than the nation in general.

Researchers have criticized the measurement biases inherent in "official" crime rates and the narrow range of offenses (e.g., rape, courtship violence, and sexual harassment) examined by a large number of sexual victimization researchers. Later researchers have begun to administer general victimization surveys to students and faculty to collect information about different types of personal and property offenses.

Patterns in Crime Victims and Types of Victimization

Neither college students nor faculty are sheltered from experiencing victimization, with some types of crime experienced at a higher rate than other types and some types of students and faculty being at higher risk than others. The only national-level study of 3472 college students at 4-year schools reported that 24% of the sample had experienced at least one type of on-campus victimization during the 1993–94 academic year (e.g., violence, theft, living quarters crimes, threats, and harassment). Similar to the results from studies using the official crime statistics, Fisher et al. (1998) reported that the on-campus theft rate per 1000 students outnumbered the on-campus violent victimization rate almost four to one. Students were particularly at risk for having their property stolen (114.6 victimization rate per 1000 students) as compared to being the victim of a violent crime (31.7 per 1000 students). A closer look at these results reveals that sexual assaults and simple assaults were the two most common types of violent victimization on campus (12.7 per 1000 students and 12.1 per 1000 students, respectively). Personal larceny without contact had the highest on-campus theft victimization rate (109.5 per 1000 students); it was the most frequent on-campus victimization across all the offenses. Burglary was the most widespread form of on-campus living quarters victimization (37.2 per 1000 students). Rates of vandalism on campus were comparatively high (54.4 per 1000 students). Verbal and telephone harassment was fairly widespread on campus (66.0 per 1000 students); threats were less common (10.7 per 1000 students).

Few studies of faculty victimization have been published. Similar to the student pattern of on-campus victimization, a case study of faculty at the University of Cincinnati reported that 27% of the respondents had been victimized on campus during the last year. Even fewer faculty, 5%, experienced violent crime on campus.

Campus crime research is in its infancy stages. Thus, the question concerning why students and faculty become victims has not been fully answered. Little research has been done that examines on-campus the determinants of student and faculty victimizations within a theoretical framework. Fisher et al. (1998), using the lifestyle or routine activities framework, reported that students who lived in all-male or coed dormitories, spent long periods of time on campus (e.g., residents who spent most nights on campus), spent more money on nonessential items, were members of athletic groups, male, and young, were more at risk of experiencing a theft on campus. Group membership in a fraternity or sorority reduced the likelihood of experiencing an on-campus theft. Contextual variables were also significant predictors of on-campus theft: victimization was higher among those who attended schools with a "climate" of theft (i.e., high overall theft rates) and lower for those at schools where a larger percentage of students lived on campus. In contrast to property victimization, few of the measures assessing routine activities concepts were related to the risk of being a victim of on-campus violent crime. Students who led "risky" lifestyles—that is, who partied on campus several nights per week and were more likely to take recreational drugs—were more likely to be victims of on-campus violent crime, and those who attended a nonmandatory crime prevention program had a lower risk compared to those who did not attend.

Wooldredge et al. (1992), testing routine activities theory, found similar results for faculty as Fisher et al. (1998) found for students, further supporting this theory. Those faculty who were on campus after hours increased their risk of property victimization, whereas those who had offices within shouting distance of colleagues, taught in the building where their office was located, and had an office in the most secure building on campus were at decreased risk. Faculty who were on campus after hours, walked alone on campus, and socialized with students increased their risk of experiencing an on-campus personal crime.

The large body of sexual victimization research consistently has found that a substantial percentage of college women are the victims of aggression, including physical violence (e.g., hitting, slapping, and kicking), date rape, acquaintance rape, and sexual harassment. For example, Fisher, Cullen, and Turner's (2000) national-level study of 4446 college women found that 1.1% of them had experienced a completed or attempted rape on campus since school had begun in the fall of 1996 (approximately a 7-month reference period).

A small body of research has appeared that provides data on the incidence of stalking against college women. Using a 6-month reference period with a sample of female students from nine colleges and universities, Mustaine and Tewksbury (1999) reported that 10.5% of the females in their sample said that they had been a victim of behavior that they defined as stalking. In the only national-level study of stalking among college women, Fisher et al. (2000) reported that 13% of the sample indicated that they met the legal definition of having experienced stalking since school had begun in the fall of 1996. Close to half (45.6%) of the pursuit behaviors that constituted stalking happened on campus, and 23% happened both on campus and off campus.

Campus Security

In response to the changing image of the extent and nature of campus crime, the role and functions of campus police have evolved from night watchmen-security guards to law enforcers-service providers. Contrary to the image of the campus security guard locking the doors of buildings, almost all campus law enforcement agencies serving public schools now use sworn officers with general arrest powers granted by state or local governments. Furthermore, almost all public campuses have armed officers. Many campuses have begun to use community-oriented policing strategies as part of their law enforcement philosophy.

Campus law enforcement agencies now sponsor crime prevention programs (including crime and fear reduction educational programs, campus watch programs, campus escort services, and programs that use student officers to assist in patrolling campus); they also have begun to assess the security risks of new building construction. To illustrate, the Bureau of Justice Statistics reported that 85% of the campus law enforcement agencies located in 4-year schools with 2500 or more students operated a general crime prevention unit or program designed to educate students and employees on how to reduce their risks of victimization. Approximately, 66% of the agencies had programs designed specifically for date rape prevention and 60% had programs designed specifically for stranger rape prevention. About half had alcohol education programs or drug abuse programs on campus. About a third of the agencies had victim assistance programs.

Official statistics, student and faculty victimization surveys reveal a common theme: college and university campuses are not immune to criminal activity. The vast majority of campus crimes involve theft-related victimization. Nonetheless, college women are at a high risk for sexual victimization and violence, often by acquaintances. The developing body of research suggests that campus crime is a multifaceted issue that continues to be the focus of much concern. The legal and political issues surrounding campus crime and the determinants of campus crime and victimization are complex and deserve further scholarly investigation.

BONNIE S. FISHER

References and Further Reading

Bromley, M.L., Campus and community crime rate comparisons: A statewide study, *Journal of Security Administration* 15 (1992).

Fernandez, A. and Alan, J.L., What's happening to rates of campus crime? *The Public Perspective* (November/December, 1993).

Fernandez, A. and Alan, J.L., An analysis of the relationship between campus crime and community crime: Reciprocal effects? In *Campus Crime: Legal, Social, and Policy Perspectives,* edited by Bonnie, S.F. and John, J.S., Springfield, IL: Thomas, 1995.

Fisher, B.S., Crime and fear on campus, *American Academy of Political and Social Science* (May, 1995).

Fisher, B.S. and Francis, T.C., Measuring the sexual victimization of women: Evolution, current controversies, and future research, in *Criminal Justice 2000*, Vol. 4, *Measurement and Analysis of Crime and Justice*, Washington, DC: U.S. Department of Justice, 2000.

Fisher, B.S. and Sloan, J.J. Compilers, *Campus Crime: Legal, Social, and Policy Perspectives*, Springfield, IL: Thomas, 1995

Fisher, B.S., et al., Crime in the ivory tower: The level and sources of student victimization, *Criminology* 36 (1998).

Fisher, B.S., Cullen, F.T., and Turner, M.G., *The Sexual Victimization of College Women,* Washington, DC: U.S. Department of Justice, 2000.

Fox, J.A. and Hellman, D.A., Location and other correlates of campus crime, *Journal of Criminal Justice* 13 (1985).

Lewis, L. and Ferris, E. *Campus Crime and Security at Postsecondary Institutions*, Washington, DC: U.S. Department of Education, 1997.

McPheters, L.R., Econometric analysis of factors influencing crime on the campus, *Journal of Criminal Justice* 6 (1978).

Mustaine, E.E. and Tewksbury, R.A., Routine activity theory explanation for women's stalking victimizations, *Violence against Women* 5 (1999). National Center for Education Statistics: Digest of Education Statistics, 2000. Available at www.nces.ed.gov/pubs2001/digest/.

Reaves, B.A. and Goldberg, A.L., *Campus Law Enforcement Agencies, 1995*, Washington, DC: United States Department of Justice, 1996.

Sloan, J.J., The correlates of campus crime: An analysis of reported crimes on college and university campuses, *Journal of Criminal Justice* 22 (1994).

Sloan, J.J., Fisher, B.S., and Cullen, F.T., Assessing the Student Right-to-Know and Campus Security Act of 1990: An analysis of the victim reporting practices of college and university students, *Crime and Delinquency* 43 (1997).

Security on Campus, Inc. Available at www.campussafety.org.

Smith, M.C. and Fossey, R., *Crime on Campus: Legal Issues and Campus Administration,* Phoenix, AZ: Oryx Press, 1995.

Student Right-to-Know and Campus Security Act, Public Law No. 101-542 (1990) amended by Public Law No. 102–26, 10(e) (1991) [name changed to Jeanne Clery Disclosure of Campus Security Policy and Campus Crime Statistics Act, 20 USC 1092(f) (1998)].

United States General Accounting Office, *Campus Crime: Difficulties Meeting Federal Reporting Requirements*, Washington, DC: General Accounting Office, 1997.

Volkwein, J.F., Bruce, P.S., and Alan, J.L., The relationship of campus crime to campus and student characteristics, *Research in Higher Education* 30 (1995).

Wooldredge, J.D., Francis, T.C., and Edward, J.L., Victimization in the workplace: A test of routine activities theory, *Justice Quarterly* 9 (1992).

See also **Alcohol and Criminal Behavior; Rape, Acquaintance and Date; Sexual Harassment; Vandalism**

Canada, Crime and Justice in

Canada is a democratic federation of ten provinces and three territories occupying the northern half of North America. Canada's overall quality of life, as measured by the United Nations, has consistently ranked at or near the top of the world, despite pockets of severe deprivation. Most of Canada's 30 million people reside in urban areas, and most live within 200 miles of the U.S. border. Above this band of settlement, geographic conditions tend to be harsh, and the population is thinly spread. Both as a trading nation and as one of the world's four largest immigrant reception countries, Canada is open and vulnerable to international economic and political conditions. With respect to crime and crime policies, Canada shares a great deal with other common law nations such as the U.S., England and Australia.

Crime Problems

Victimization surveys (such as the *General Social Survey*) show that the most commonly reported crimes in Canada are relatively minor offenses against persons or property. Roughly one in four Canadians reports being a victim of at least one crime in the previous year. Less than half of these incidents are reported to the police. The main reason cited for nonreporting is that the incident was not important, although there may be many other reasons why, for example, only one third of assaults are reported. The *International Crime Victims Survey* (1995) places Canada just about in the middle of the western nations with respect to crime victimization, both minor and serious. This rank is lower than the U.S., but higher than Austria, France, or Sweden.

Police-reported crime figures show that Canada has low rates of violent crime and high rates of property crime. The most frequent property offense is "theft under $5000." At over 2000 incidents per 100,000 population, "theft under" amounted to more than half of all reported property crimes in 1999. The most frequent violent crime was simple (level 1) assault. At just under 600 incidents per 100,000 population, simple assault accounted for 8 out of 10 reported violent offenses.

Since 1921, Canada's homicide rate, just slightly above 2 per 100,000 population (it peaked at 3.1 in 1973), has consistently been less than one third that of the U.S., but nearly twice as high as the homicide rate of most European countries. Unlike the U.S., the murder rate in Canada is higher in the relatively unsettled north and northwest, not in the core of large cities. Canada's robbery rates are as much as 50% lower than those of the U.S. When gun-related offenses are taken out of the equation, however, crime rates in the two countries are quite similar, and similar to crime rates in Australia, England, and Wales.

Property and violent crime rates rise from east to west, and are generally highest in the northern territories. Government spending for justice services is less than $200 per capita in each of the Maritime provinces of the southeast, but over $600 per capita in the far North. These figures reflect higher availability of guns and alcohol, as well as higher levels of poverty and social disorganization that characterize aboriginal communities and the frontiers of settlement.

As in other nations, crime in the suites attracts less attention than crime in the streets, and, despite reasonably strong legislation, these offenses are underreported and underprosecuted. The Transparency International (TI) 1999 survey shows that both political and business corruption is perceived to be among the lowest in the world. Canada is, however, second highest on TI's list of international bribe payers, perhaps as a reflection of the country's dependence on foreign trade. Although incidents of patronage, dubious party financing, and improper distribution of government funds have been exposed, they are not on a scale or frequency seen in many other countries. The lack of large-scale corruption of government and business activities in Canada has been attributed to features such as a strong democratic system with effective opposition parties, independent legislative and judicial branches, police who are largely independent of political masters, and an alert and vocal media presence.

Organized crime in Canada includes the traditional Italian and Sicilian "mobs," Asian Triads and newer groups unleashed by disorder in the former Soviet Union. It also includes "home grown" organizations such as ethnic gangs and aboriginal gangs. Biker gangs such as the Hell's Angels have a strong presence in Canada. Biker violence has been particularly pronounced in Quebec, where an attempted takeover of the local Rock Machine, a rival biker gang, by the Hell's Angels in 1994 precipitated a long running series of bombings, brutal executions, and bystander injuries. Most Canadians are touched by the financial effects of organized crime, even though they are largely unaware of it.

Canada has always experienced substantial levels of smuggling of both goods and migrants. With an undefended land border that is roughly three thousand miles long, the longest coastline in the world, (thinly populated and characterized by many places suitable for secret landings), several border-straddling semi-independent native reserves, smuggling has a long and almost honored history in Canada.

Terrorist and insurgent crime has rarely been aimed at Canada. Terrorist activities aimed at changing conditions in Ireland, Armenia, India, and elsewhere have occasionally been financed and launched from Canadian soil. An example of this is the bombing of Air India flight 182 in 1985.

Crime Policies: The Criminal Law

According to the HEUNI *Crime Guide* (1988) Canadians and Americans were about equally likely to have taken personal protective measures against crime. Less than 20% report having installed a burglar alarm, but most people have locks to secure their significant possessions, and there is increasing interest in "defensible space" planning. For most Canadians, the manifest primary line of defense against crime is the criminal law and the criminal justice system.

The *Criminal Code of Canada* is the law for all who are 18 years of age or older in Canada. It is based on the common law of England as enacted by Parliament and adapted over the years to fit a federal and multicultural society. There is a separate law for "young offenders." The Youth Criminal Justice Act (in force as of April 1, 2003) generally parallels the adult system, but with additional protections for youths and lower maximum sentences. Although there has been substantial American influence on Canadian law and on Canadian court practices, there are also areas where the two countries diverge. This is partly because Canada has evolved in different ways, and partly because Canada is more strongly influenced by European models than by the U.S. Some of these diverging policies are outlined as follows:

Death Penalty. The last executions in Canada took place in 1962, and the death penalty was officially abolished in 1976. The maximum sentence for first degree murder is "Life-25"—life imprisonment with the first chance of parole set at 25 years. In the most common cases, there is provision for reassessment of the parole date after 15 years have been served. This "faint-hope" clause has rarely been successful. An Ekos poll (June 2000) reported that only 49% of Canadians favor reinstatement of the death penalty, and, except in the immediate aftermath of particularly heinous crimes, the trend has been toward less support rather than more. This may partly be because of a number of highly publicized cases of individuals who served decades in prison because of wrongful convictions, and may be related to findings that the abolition of the death penalty had no discernable effect on homicide rates. The Supreme Court of Canada (2001) has severely restricted the possibility that Canada will extradite an accused person who will face the death penalty in the extraditing country.

Guns. Canada lacks a revolutionary background and has no historic right for each citizen to "bear arms." Carrying of handguns by ordinary citizens has been banned since 1930. On December 6, 1989, the worst single-day mass murder on Canadian soil took place when an "antifeminist" gunman used a semiautomatic rifle to murder 14 women at a college in Montreal. This, and publicity from similar incidents in the U.S., helped to put pressure on Parliament to legislate even tighter restrictions. Since 1995, all firearms must be registered, handguns are "restricted" to purposes such as target shooting, gun collecting, and occupational use, and combat weapons are prohibited. Gun owners are required to take the Canadian Firearms Safety Course or its equivalent. Police have been given enhanced powers to search for and confiscate firearms. The legislation, which targets law-abiding as well as criminal users of guns, has been highly unpopular among hunters and farmers, among others, but enjoys wide support, particularly in the cities. The Criminal Code of Canada prohibits possession of a firearm for dangerous purposes, and possession of a concealed weapon. Using a firearm in the commission of certain indictable (felony) offenses is itself an offense that attracts mandatory minimum sentences.

Drugs. Canada's legislation reflects an early reliance on the punishment-oriented model of the U.S., which is supported by international agreements. Although the laws themselves have undergone little change, the actual practice of the Canadian criminal justice system has gradually become less punitive. The "harm reduction model" (which includes compassionate community policing, needle exchanges, and other supports) has been gaining favor. Polls repeatedly show that more than half of Canadians favor decriminalization of marijuana, and more than 80% favor legalization of medical marijuana. (The US-based Lindesmith Center has helped to fund efforts to translate these attitudes into actual court practices.) Drug use, even hard drug use, is increasingly viewed as a health problem rather than a crime problem. It is also increasingly recognized that keeping drugs illegal exacerbates the violence and organized crime associated with drug use.

Abortion. Canadian Criminal Code provisions that restricted women's access to abortion were struck down by the Supreme Court of Canada in 1988 as an unconstitutional infringement of a woman's right to the security of her person. Unless or until Parliament produces new law, Canada has no criminal legislation on the subject of abortion.

Rape. In 1982, new legislation replaced the offense of rape with the new offense of "sexual assault." Sexual assault can take the form of unwanted touching, and need not involve penetration. There are three levels of sexual assault, graded by the amount of violence involved. Level 3, aggravated sexual assault, can be charged when the victim is wounded. The maximum penalty for Level 1 is 10 years, for Level 2 is 14 years and for Level 3 is life. Sexual assault laws apply equally to men and women. Spouses are no longer immune to prosecution. "Rape shield laws" limit access to the complainants' records (such as counseling records). Such rules have increased the probability of successful prosecution of these offenses. Still, victimization data shows that only one tenth of sexual assault events are reported to police, and victims still feel that the courts victimize them again.

Organized Crime

Canada has been concerned about its reputation for weak legislation that attracts organized crime. Changes introduced in the mid-1990s mean that the Criminal Code now has provisions that parallel the U.S. Racketeer Influenced Corruption Organizations Act (RICO). Members of criminal gangs who are convicted of offenses may serve stiffer sentences, prosecutors can get at ill-gotten assets by way of the Proceeds of Crime Act (1997) and banks and lawyers are under stringent reporting rules with respect to suspicious monetary transactions. Canada is involved in many cross-border and international efforts to find resolutions to problems of transborder crimes such as telemarketing fraud, money laundering, missing children, and high-tech crime.

Crime Policies: The Criminal Justice System

Approximately 3% of all government spending goes to the six sectors of the justice system (policing, courts, legal aid, criminal prosecutions, adult corrections, and youth corrections.) Public police are the first line of enforcement against crime. The largest public police force in Canada is the Royal Canadian Mounted Police (RCMP), which serves as a federal force throughout the nation, but acts as provincial and municipal police under a contract arrangement in all provinces and territories except Ontario and Quebec. Some provinces and larger municipalities have their own police forces. On the whole, Canadian police forces have a good reputation for integrity, despite cases of corruption of individual officers, particularly those working in areas such as drug enforcement. Canada's *General Social Survey* (*GSS*), consistently shows that a majority of Canadians feel that their local police are approachable (66%), ensure the safety of citizens (62%) and do a good job of enforcing the laws (54%). Only half (49%) felt that police responded rapidly to calls. Private security forces are the fastest growing segment of policing and have a large impact with respect to social control in shopping malls and other privately owned places where the public gathers.

Canada's criminal courts are adversarial common law courts. Although terminology differs (summary conviction and indictable offenses correspond to the categories of misdemeanor and felony, the prosecutor is often called "the Crown"), most Americans would find little to surprise them in a Canadian court. Lower courts handle the vast bulk of criminal prosecutions, whereas higher courts deal with more serious offenses and with appeals. The Supreme Court of Canada, established at the Federal level, has more power than the highest courts of most other countries. It hears appeals from decisions of the appeal courts in all the provinces and territories. Its judgments are final. The only recourse for parliament, if it is dissatisfied with the outcome, is to create new legislation. Canadian criminal courts tend to exercise much more control over press coverage than is tolerated in the U.S. Despite the Supreme Court of Canada ruling (*Dagenais v. CBC*, 1994) that the right to a fair trial does not always take precedence over the right to a free press, Canadian courts still make use of sweeping publication bans that are allowed when there is a substantial risk to fairness of the trial and no other measure will prevent this. This factor was shown quite dramatically with respect to the highly publicized trial of O.J. Simpson in the U.S. and the contemporaneous prosecutions of Paul Bernardo (Teale) and his wife Karla Homolka, an attractive young couple who were convicted in the random kidnap and murder of teenaged girls. As a result of an almost total ban on publication, Canadians learned far more about the American case than they did about their own.

Most Canadians regard the courts as fair, but those most involved with the courts are less positive. Although most research has failed to document overall discrimination with respect to sentencing, there have been some high-profile inquiries in Nova Scotia, Ontario, and Manitoba that suggest the presence of pervasive systemic injustice in policing, adjudication, and correctional practices. A Royal Commission investigation (1990) into the unjust homicide conviction of a native youth (Donald Marshall) condemned the entire system of criminal justice in the province of Nova Scotia, as well as the behavior of selected individuals who abused their power. Similarly, the Manitoba Aboriginal Justice Inquiry (1999) severely criticized that province's unequal treatment of aboriginals, both as complainants (crime victims) and as persons in conflict with the law.

In Canada, inmates serving sentences of 2 years or more are incarcerated in federal institutions and those serving less than this are assigned to provincial jurisdiction. At roughly 130 inmates per hundred thousand population, Canada has always had very high incarceration rates compared with all other western nations, except the U.S., which incarcerates at a rate almost five times as high. Prisons are much smaller than the American norm, and have, in comparison with most other nations, a relatively high rate of success in the control and rehabilitation of offenders. Most Canadians, however, are unaware of this success, and very critical of the corrections system. Tufts (2000) reported that barely a quarter of Canadians think the prisons are doing a good job in supervising offenders. The lack of faith in the rehabilitative potential of the corrections system makes reintegration difficult. As in other nations, the costs of incarceration are rising to levels that are encouraging the use of restoration and other alternatives that are perceived to be less expensive.

Among the provinces, there are differences in the extent to which social problems are met with criminal justice responses. Quebec, a mainly French-speaking province with extensive ties with Europe, tends to emphasize preventative and rehabilitative goals and its own approach to justice issues even more than is true of other provinces. British Columbians tend to be the most fearful of crime and the most critical of the justice system.

Other Factors in Crime and Crime Control Responses

In addition to the factors discussed above, Canada's crime and crime policies are influenced by patterns of inequality and opportunity.

Inequality and Multiculturalism. Although inequality is not as great as in the U.S., there are nonetheless great differences between citizens who are well-positioned to achieve affluence legitimately and those who are not, as well as differences in respect for, and commitment to the dominant values and rules enshrined in the Criminal Code of Canada. These differences vary by social class, ethnicity, "race," gender, and region. This results in the overrepresentation of the poor, some ethnic groups, aboriginals and blacks, and males in the criminal justice system. Although most members of immigrant groups and ethnic subcultures are law abiding, some cultural practices (such as genital mutilation) are illegal in Canada.

Statistics on race and crime are not normally released in Canada, because of the perception that such data are subject to misuse. It is clear that groups that are poor and socially marginalized are more likely to contribute to the statistics on crime. Data from the Solicitor General (1999) show that aboriginals are seriously overrepresented in Canada's courts and correctional institutions as both perpetrators and victims of crime. Overall in Canada, the nonaboriginal incarceratison rate is less than 60 per 100,000, whereas the aboriginal rate is over 400. In some provinces the aboriginal rate is over 1200. Although aboriginals constitute 2% of the general adult population, they comprise 17% of individuals in provincial or territorial or federal custody. This reality has led to an increasing commitment to develop alternative systems that will respect and strengthen indigenous forms of social control without eroding the fairness of a uniform justice system.

Opportunity. The lifestyles of Canadians provide criminal opportunities. Families tend to live in single-family homes that contain many portable possessions. These homes are often unguarded while the adults engage in work or recreation, and the children participate in day-care, school, and after-school activities. Young Canadians who like to party at night are particularly likely to be targets of robbery or assault, and there are youth subcultures that promote criminal activities. Although alcohol is regulated by provincial liquor control boards, illegal drugs are not difficult to obtain. On the other hand, Canadian society is relatively peaceful and stable, providing little incentive or opportunity for vigilantism and "disorderly" crime. The decline in crime rates in the 1990s through to the early 2000s has been attributed to factors such as the aging population, decline in the relative size of the crime prone age group, a healthy economy, and more effective forms of surveillance, detection, and prevention.

Linda B. Deutschmann

References and Further Reading

Archer, D. and Gartner, R., *Violence and Crime in Cross-National Perspective*. Yale University Press, 1987.

Bell, S.J., *Young Offenders and Juvenile Justice*: *A Century after the Fact*. Scarborough, Ontario: ITP Nelson, 1999.

Beare, M., *Criminal Conspiracies: Organized Crime in Canada*. Scarborough, Ontario: ITP Nelson, 1996.

Beirne, P. and Hill, J., *Comparative Criminology: An Annotated Bibliography.* Criminal Justice, Research and Bibliographical Guides No 3. Westport, CT: Greenwood Press, 1991.

Brantingham, P. and Easton, S., *Crime Costs in Canada*. Burnaby: Simon Fraser University, Crime Prevention Analysis Laboratory, 1998.

Canadian Center for Justice Statistics, Statistics Canada, *Canadian Crime Statistics 1999*. Ottawa: Ministry of Industry Catalogue No. 85-205-XPE, 2000.

Dagenais v. CBC [1994] 3 S.C.R. 835.

HEUNI *Crime Guide*. Helsinki: HEUNI, 1998.

Kangaspunta, K., Joutsen, M., and Ollus, N., Eds., *Crime and Criminal Justice Systems in Europe and North America: 1990–1994*. Helsinki: HEUNI, 1998.

Mayhew, P. and Van Dijk, J.J.M., *Criminal Victimizaton in Eleven Industrialised Countries*: *Key Findings from the 1996 International Crime Victims Survey.* Den Haag: Ministerie van Justitie, WODC, 1997.

Transparency International, *The Corruption Perceptions Index*, available at http://www.transparency.de/documents/cpi/index.html, 1999.

UNIDCP *World Drug report, 1997*. Published for the United Nations Development Programme. Oxford, UK: Oxford University Press, 1997.

Schmalleger, F., MacAlister, D., McKenna, P.F., and Winterdyk, J., *Canadian Criminal Justice Today: An Introductory Text for the 21st Century*, Toronto: Prentice Hall, Allyn and Bacon Canada.

Silverman, R.A., Teevan, J.J., and Sacco, V.F., Eds., *Crime in Canadian Society*, 6th ed. Toronto: Harcourt Brace, 2000.

Tufts, J., Public Attitudes toward the Criminal Justice System, *Juristat.* Canadian Center for Justice Statistics, Statistics Canada Catalogue No. 85-002-XPE. 20 (12) 2000.

See also **France, Crime and Justice in**

Capital Punishment: U.S. History

America's experience with capital punishment began in 1608, when Captain George Kendall, a councilor for the Virginia colony, was executed for being a spy for Spain. Capital punishment, or the death penalty, was one of the punishments brought to the New World by the early European settlers.

Colonies varied in the crimes for which the death penalty could be legally imposed. For example, the Massachusetts Bay Colony had 12 death-eligible crimes. South (New) Jersey, on the other hand, originally did not allow capital punishment, but the prohibition only lasted 45 years. In Pennsylvania, capital punishment was allowed only for treason and murder. Most of the British colonies, however, had statutes similar to those of the Massachusetts Bay Colony.

Since Kendall's execution in 1608, more than 19,000 executions have been performed in the U.S. under civil (as opposed to military) authority. It has been estimated that a total of between 20,000 to 22,500 people have been executed by legal authority in the U.S. since 1608. That total does not include the approximately 10,000 people lynched in the 19th century. Compared to more recent times, colonial Americans used the death penalty sparingly. For example, more executions were conducted in the 1930s (1676) than in the 1600s and 1700s combined (1553).

Nearly all of the people executed during the past four centuries in America have been adult men. Of the approximately 19,000 documented executions, only about 2% have been women. Ninety percent of the women were executed under local, as opposed to state, authority, and the majority (87%) was executed prior to 1866. The first woman executed in America was Jane Champion in the Virginia colony in 1632. She was hanged for killing and concealing the death of her child who was fathered by a man who was not her husband.

About 2% of the approximately 19,000 people executed have been juveniles who committed their capital crimes prior to their 18th birthday. Most of them (69%) were black, and nearly 90% of their victims were white. The first juvenile executed in America was Thomas Graunger in Plymouth colony in 1642 for the crime of bestiality. He was 16 at the time of his crime and execution. The youngest nonslave executed in the U.S. was Ocuish Hannah. She was hanged for a murder she committed when she was 12 years old. Hannah was executed in New London County, Connecticut on December 20, 1786.

Among the first people in the U.S. to organize others against the death penalty was Dr. Benjamin Rush (1747–1813), a Philadelphia physician and signer of the Declaration of Independence. Rush questioned the Biblical support for capital punishment and the belief that it was a general deterrent to crime. He did not believe that the example of executions dissuades people from committing crimes they have contemplated committing. To the contrary, he thought that capital punishment might increase crime. Reflecting Enlightenment philosophy, Rush maintained that the social contract was violated whenever the state executed one of its citizens. In the late 18th century, Dr. Rush attracted the support of Benjamin Franklin and William Bradford, Pennsylvania's and later U.S. Attorney General, among others. It was at Franklin's home in Philadelphia that Rush became one of the first Americans to propose confinement in a "House of Reform" as an alternative to capital punishment. As envisioned by Rush, houses of reform would be places where criminals could learn to be law-abiding citizens through moral education. At least in part because of the efforts of Rush and his colleagues, in 1790 the Walnut Street Jail in Philadelphia was converted into the world's first penitentiary—an institution devoted primarily to reform.

Largely as a result of Bradford's efforts, Pennsylvania became the first state in legal proceedings to consider degrees of murder based on culpability. Before this change, the death penalty was mandated for anyone convicted of murder, regardless of circumstance. Like Rush, Bradford did not believe that capital punishment deterred crime, citing the example of horse stealing, which at the time was a capital offense in Virginia and the most frequently committed crime in the state. Because of the severity of the penalty, convictions for the crime were hard to obtain. Pressure from abolitionists also caused Pennsylvania to repeal the death penalty for all crimes, except first-degree murder. Many people were drawn to Rush's ideas, and petitions to abolish the death penalty were introduced in several state legislatures, although half a century would pass before the first state abandoned capital punishment.

Between 1800 and 1865, use of the death penalty increased significantly. The number of executions rose almost 60% over the number of executions during the entire 17th and 18th centuries. From the Civil War until

1880, the number of executions dropped by two thirds, however, from 1880 to the turn of the century, the number of executions increased to about a thousand each decade.

The period between, approximately, 1825 and 1850 was a time of reform in America. During this era, death penalty abolitionists received a boost from antisaloon and antislavery sentiment. Several death penalty abolitionist societies were organized, especially along the eastern seaboard and, in 1845, the American Society for the Abolition of Capital Punishment was founded. By 1850, death penalty abolitionist societies were also working in Tennessee, Ohio, Alabama, Louisiana, Indiana, and Iowa. The chief reasons for this antideath penalty activity likely were the increase in the number of executions and liberal sympathies generated within the abolitionist movement.

In 1834, Pennsylvania became the first state to hide executions from the public by requiring them to be conducted in jails or prisons. Only a few authorized officials and the relatives of the condemned were allowed to attend. New York, New Jersey, and Massachusetts enacted similar policies the following year. Apparently, legislators were willing to sacrifice any general deterrent effect of witnessing executions to escape the "public disorder, rioting, and even murder" that sometimes accompanied the public spectacles, especially the botched executions and last-minute reprieves. The last public execution was held in Galena, Missouri in 1937.

In 1838, Tennessee became the first state to enact a discretionary death penalty statute for murder. Before then, all states employed mandatory death penalty statutes that required anyone convicted of a designated capital crime to be sentenced to death. Between the Civil War and the end of the 19th century, at least 20 additional jurisdictions changed their death penalty laws from mandatory to discretionary ones. Except for a few rarely committed crimes in a handful of jurisdictions, mandatory capital punishment laws were removed from all penal codes by 1963.

This change from mandatory to discretionary death-penalty statutes, which introduced unfettered sentencing discretion into the capital-sentencing process, was considered, at the time, a great reform in the administration of capital punishment. Ironically, it was unfettered sentencing discretion that the Supreme Court declared unconstitutional in its landmark *Furman v. Georgia* decision in 1972.

In 1846, the state of Michigan abolished the death penalty for all crimes, except treason, and replaced the penalty with life imprisonment. The law took effect the next year making Michigan, for all intents and purposes, the first English-speaking jurisdiction in the world to abolish capital punishment. The first state to outlaw the death penalty for all crimes, including treason, was Rhode Island, in 1852; Wisconsin was the second state to do so a year later. Although no other states abolished the death penalty during this period, most states outside South began reducing the number of death-eligible crimes, generally to only murder and treason. Opponents of the death penalty, who initially benefited from general abolitionist sentiment, saw concern with capital punishment wane as the Civil War approached. Attention shifted to the growing antislavery movement.

Not until well after the Civil War did Iowa, in 1872, and Maine, in 1876, become the next states to abolish the death penalty. However, legislatures in both states reversed themselves, and reinstated the death penalty in 1878 (Iowa) and in 1883 (Maine). In 1887, Maine reversed itself again and abolished capital punishment and, to date, has not reinstated it. Colorado abandoned capital punishment in 1897, but restored it in 1901.

During the Civil War, a major change took place in the legal jurisdiction of executions. Before the war, all executions were conducted locally—generally in the jurisdiction in which the crime was committed. However, on January 20, 1864, Sandy Kavanagh was executed at the Vermont State Prison. He was the first person executed under state, as opposed to local, authority.

This shift in jurisdiction was not immediately adopted by other states. After Kavanagh, there were only about two state or federally authorized executions per year well into the 1890s; the rest were locally authorized. That pattern changed dramatically during the next 30 years. In the 1890s, about 90% of executions were imposed under local authority, but by the 1920s, about 90% were imposed under state authority. These changes reflected a general trend toward the strengthening of state power over local jurisdictions. Today, all executions are imposed under state authority, except those conducted in Delaware, Montana, the federal government, and the military.

As the U.S. entered the 20th century, a new age of reform called the "Progressive Movement" began. Death penalty abolitionists benefited from the critical examination of American society that characterized the era and achieved a series of successes, albeit in most cases temporary ones. Between 1907 and 1917, six states outlawed capital punishment entirely (Kansas 1907; Minnesota 1911; Washington 1913; Oregon 1914; South Dakota 1915; Missouri 1917) and three states (Tennessee 1915; North Dakota 1915; Arizona 1916) limited the death penalty to only a few rarely committed crimes, such as treason or the first-degree murder of a law enforcement official or prison employee. Tennessee also retained capital punishment for rape. The momentum, however, failed to last. By 1920, five states had reinstated the death penalty

(Arizona 1918; Missouri 1919; Tennessee 1919; Washington 1919; Oregon 1920). It has been argued that the reinstatement of capital punishment in the five states was at least partly the result of a media-inspired panic about the threat of insurrections inspired by criminals.

The death penalty abolitionist movement fell on hard times during Prohibition and the Great Depression (roughly from 1920 to 1940). Only the determined efforts of members of the American League to Abolish Capital Punishment, founded in 1925, and a few high-profile abolitionists, such as attorney Clarence Darrow and Lewis E. Lawes, the abolitionist warden of New York State's Sing-Sing Prison, kept the movement alive. Despite their efforts, more capital offenders were executed during the 1930s than in any other decade in American history; the average was 167 executions per year. The most executions in any single year were in 1935 when 199 offenders were put to death. Furthermore, of the ten states that abolished capital punishment for all crimes after 1850, only three—Minnesota, Maine, and Wisconsin—had not restored the death penalty by the 1950s. No state abolished the death penalty between 1918 and 1957. In contrast, after World War II, most of the advanced western European countries abolished the death penalty or severely restricted its use. Great Britain did not join them until 1969.

Beginning in the 1950s, partly as a result of the lingering horrors of World War II and the movement by many allied nations to either abolish the death penalty or restrict its use, the number of executions in the U.S. began to drop precipitously—from 1289 in the 1940s to 715 during the 1950s. From 1960 through 1972 (actually, 1976), there were only 191 executions in the U.S. For the same reasons, along with the decline in executions, the abolitionist movement in the U.S. was able to claim some modest achievements in the late 1950s. Besides resurrecting debate in some state legislatures, the (then) territories of Alaska and Hawaii abolished the death penalty in 1957. Delaware did the same in 1958, only to reinstate it 3 years later in 1961.

The civil rights movements of the 1960s also galvanized abolitionist sentiment. Four states abolished the death penalty (Michigan in 1963 for treason; Oregon 1964; Iowa 1965; and West Virginia 1965), and two states (New York 1965 and Vermont 1965) sharply reduced the number of death-eligible crimes.

Although specific methods of execution had been legally challenged as early as 1890, the fundamental legality of capital punishment itself was not subject to legal challenge until the 1960s. It had long been argued that the Constitution or, more specifically, the Fifth Amendment, authorized capital punishment and that the framers of the Constitution, at least a majority of them, did not object to it. Given such evidence, it made little sense to argue that capital punishment violated the Constitution.

That conventional wisdom was challenged in a 1961 *University of Southern California Law Review* article written by law Professor Gerald Gottlieb. Gottlieb argued that "the death penalty was unconstitutional under the Eighth Amendment because it violated contemporary moral standards, what the U.S. Supreme Court in *Trop v. Dulles* (356 U.S. 86, 1958) referred to as "the evolving standards of decency that mark the progress of a maturing society" (p. 101). In *Trop* and *Weems v. United States* (217 U.S. 349), both nondeath penalty cases, the latter decided in 1910, the Court departed from the fixed or historical meaning it had always used in deciding whether a particular punishment was cruel and unusual in violation of the Eighth Amendment. In *Weems*, the Court opined that the cruel and unusual punishment provision "would only offer paper, illusory protection if it was restricted solely to the intent of the Framers." Consequently, the Court declared that the meaning of the Eighth Amendment is not limited by the Framers' intent, but that it changes with evolving social conditions; specifically, "the evolving standards of decency that mark the progress of a maturing society."

Professor Gottlieb took an extreme position toward the death penalty, calling for its complete abolition. Most of the other attacks on the penalty during this period were more moderate, seeking its reform. In 1959, for example, drafters of the American Law Institute's Model Penal Code suggested two legal reforms in the way capital punishment was administered. The first was a bifurcated trial consisting of a guilt phase, where guilt or innocence was the principal issue to be determined, and a penalty phase, where the imposition of either a life or death sentence was the sole issue. The second reform was the use of enumerated aggravating and mitigating circumstances to guide and restrict the sentencing authority's (judge or jury) discretion during the penalty phase of the bifurcated trial. Both of those procedural reforms would later be incorporated into the new, post-*Furman* (1972) death penalty statutes.

Problems with the administration of capital punishment had long been a focus of attack by death penalty opponents, but they were also a source of consternation to proponents of the penalty who wanted it "done right." By the 1960s, some reform in the process of putting capital offenders to death seemed necessary. Most importantly, at least three members of the Supreme Court agreed. Justices Goldberg, Brennan, and Douglas believed the Court should decide whether the death penalty for a rapist who had not taken a life violated the Constitution's Eighth Amendment. It seemed the appropriate time for a test case on the matter.

The defendant selected for the test case was William L. Maxwell, a 22-year-old black man who in 1961 was charged in Arkansas with the rape of a white woman. Maxwell was convicted of the crime and sentenced to death the following year. His initial appeal to the Arkansas Supreme Court claimed that there was a pattern of racial discrimination in the way that Arkansas juries handled rape cases. The appeal was denied. Maxwell's attorney, with the help of lawyers from the NAACP Legal Defense Fund, then drafted a writ of habeas corpus for review by the federal courts. In each of the courts—first the U.S. District Court, then the Court of Appeals for the Eighth Circuit, and, finally, the U.S. Supreme Court—the writ was rejected. This all occurred during 1964 and 1965.

Maxwell's fate was finally determined by the U.S. Supreme Court on June 1, 1970 (*Maxwell v. Bishop*). The Court, however, did not directly address Maxwell's principal claim that racial discrimination on the part of jurors, who had total discretion in the sentencing decision, affected death cases for rape in at least some Arkansas counties. Instead, the Court vacated (disallowed) Maxwell's death sentence on the narrower grounds that several prospective jurors in Maxwell's case were improperly removed during *voir dire* because of their general opposition to the death penalty. As for the problem of juror discretion and, presumably, the racial discrimination that it sometimes allowed, the Court, in footnote four of the *Maxwell* decision, announced that it would address that issue early in the 1970 term. What the Court could not know at this time was that it was embarking on a road that would eventually lead to the complete abolition of capital punishment in the U.S.

Another consequence of the *Maxwell* case, as well as two other death penalty cases decided by the Supreme Court in 1968 (*Witherspoon v. Illinois* and *United States v. Jackson*), was the unofficial suspension of all executions until some of the more problematic issues with the death penalty could be resolved. The last execution in the U.S., before a brief moratorium on executions, was held in June of 1967, when Luis Jose Monge was executed in Colorado's gas chamber. The moratorium on executions would last 10 years until 1977 when Gary Gilmore requested to be executed by the state of Utah.

In 1972, William Henry Furman's lawyers argued with the Supreme Court that unfettered jury discretion in imposing death for murder resulted in arbitrary or capricious sentencing in violation of the Fourteenth Amendment right to due process and the Eighth Amendment protection against cruel and unusual punishment. Furman's challenge proved successful and, as a result, on June 29, 1972, the U.S. Supreme Court set aside death sentences for the first time in its history.

A practical effect of *Furman* was the Supreme Court's voiding 40 death penalty statutes and the sentences of 629 death row inmates. However, 36 states immediately proceeded to adopt new death penalty statutes designed to meet the Court's objections. The constitutionality of the new death penalty statutes was quickly challenged, and on July 2, 1976, the Supreme Court announced its rulings in five test cases. In *Woodson v. North Carolina* and *Roberts v. Louisiana*, the Court rejected "mandatory" statutes that automatically imposed death sentences for defined capital crimes. However, in *Gregg v. Georgia*, *Jurek v. Texas*, and *Proffitt v. Florida*, the Court approved "guided discretion" statutes that set standards for juries and judges to use when deciding whether to impose the death penalty. The first person to be executed under the new guided discretion statutes was Gary Gilmore in Utah in 1977. Gilmore's execution marks the beginning of the modern death penalty period.

Currently, 40 jurisdictions in the U.S. have death penalty statutes (38 states, the U.S. government, and the U.S. Military), and 13 jurisdictions do not (12 states and the District of Columbia). Since Gilmore's execution in 1977 (through January 1, 2001), 683 people have been put to death under legal authority in 31 states. More than 80% of those executions have occurred in southern states, and three states—Texas, Virginia, and Florida—account for more than half of all executions conducted during the modern death penalty period. Texas alone has executed more than a third of the total and nearly three times as many people as Virginia—the state that has executed the second largest number. As of January 1, 2001, 3726 inmates were awaiting their executions on death rows throughout the U.S.

Robert M. Bohm

References and Further Reading

Acker, J.R., Bohm, R.M., and Lanier, C.S., Eds., *America's Experiment with Capital Punishment: Reflections on the Past, Present and Future of the Ultimate Penal Sanction*. Durham, NC: Carolina Academic Press, 1998.

Bedau, H.A., Ed., *The Death Penalty in America: Current Controversies*. New York, NY: Oxford University Press, 1997.

Bedau, H.A., Ed., *The Death Penalty in America*, 3rd ed. New York, NY: Oxford University Press, 1982.

Bohm, R.M., *Deathquest: An Introduction to the Theory and Practice of Capital Punishment in the United States*. Cincinnati, OH: Anderson, 1999.

Bowers, W.J., Pierce, G.L., and McDevitt, J.F., *Legal Homicide: Death as Punishment in America, 1864–1982*. Boston, MA: Northeastern University Press, 1984.

Coyne, R. and Entzeroth, L., *Capital Punishment and the Judicial Process*. Durham, NC: Carolina Academic Press, 1994.

Haas, K.C. and Inciardi, J.A., Eds., *Challenging Capital Punishment: Legal and Social Science Approaches*. Newbury Park, CA: Sage, 1988.

Johnson, R., *Death Work: A Study of the Modern Execution Process*, 2nd ed. Belmont, CA: West/Wadsworth, 1998.

Paternoster, R., *Capital Punishment in America*. New York, NY: Lexington, 1991.

Van den Haag, E. and Conrad, J.P., *The Death Penalty: A Debate*. New York, NY: Plenum, 1983.

Vila, B. and Morris, C., Eds., *Capital Punishment in the United States: A Documentary History*. Westport, CT: Greenwood, 1997.

Zimring, F.E. and Hawkins, G., *Capital Punishment and the American Agenda*. Cambridge, UK: Cambridge University Press, 1986.

See also **Homicide: Law**

Capital Punishment: World History

Capital punishment, or the death penalty, refers to execution as a punishment for crime. Because crime is a violation of a political jurisdiction's criminal law, capital punishment as such did not exist prior to the advent of the nation–state, though, before then, many people lost their lives for their transgressions through private, informal justice. The earliest reference to capital punishment is found in the Code of Urukagina. Urukagina was a king of the Sumerian city–state of Lagash. Written in about 2350 BCE, the Code provided, among other things, that thieves and adulteresses be stoned to death with stones inscribed with the name of their crime.

The first known death sentence in a legal proceeding was imposed in about 1850 BCE (place not provided). Three men and a woman were charged with the murder of a temple employee. The woman, the victim's wife, knew about the murder plan but remained silent. Nine witnesses testified against the four defendants and asked for the death penalty in each case. Two other witnesses testified that the victim's wife had been abused by her husband, was not present at the murder, and was materially worse off since her husband's death. The wife's life was spared but the three men were executed in front of the victim's house.

The Code of Hammurabi (approximately 1780 BCE) also provided for capital punishment. Hammurabi (r. 1795–1750 BCE) was Babylonia's best-known king. The Code of Hammurabi is considered the first great, comprehensive code of laws. The Code combined very enlightened aims, such as "to prevent the strong from oppressing the weak [and] to enlighten the land and to further the welfare of the people," with barbaric punishments. The phrase "an eye for an eye and a tooth for a tooth" captures the guiding principle for punishments in Hammurabi's Code. Under the Code the death penalty could be imposed for 25 crimes. As an example, a house builder could be put to death if a house he built collapsed because it was not built strong enough and killed the owner. If the house owner's son died because of the collapse, then the builder's son could be executed.

One of the earliest death sentences (according to the source, the first death sentence historically recorded) was imposed on a member of the Egyptian nobility in the 16th century BCE. He was accused of practicing magic and ordered to take his own life. During this period non-nobility was usually killed with an ax.

Moses, the leader of the ancient Hebrews, is believed to have received The Ten Commandments from God in around 1300 BCE. The book of the Bible that contains The Ten Commandments, Exodus, also contains an extended list of legal rules as well as appropriate punishments for their violation. The punishments are based on the "eye for an eye" principle of Hammurabi's Code. In Exodus and other books of the Old Testament the death penalty is prescribed for many offenses: murder; manslaughter; bearing false witness on a capital charge; kidnapping or stealing a man; cursing God; idolatry; disobedience of religious authority; laboring on the Sabbath; false prophecy in the name of God; child sacrifice; striking, cursing or rebelling against a parent; adultery and unnatural vice; prostitution or harlotry under certain circumstances; sorcery; incest; sodomy and bestiality; and keeping an ox known to be dangerous, if it kills a person. Offenders were executed by stoning—the standard method of judicial execution in Biblical times—and, in some cases, burning, beheading, strangling, and shooting with arrows. Occasionally, corpses of executed lawbreakers were hung in public as an example to others, and sometimes, the corpse of the executed person was mutilated. However, the ancient Hebrews were not as vengeful and barbaric as it may appear. In practice, Hebrew law made it very difficult to execute a capital offender.

In 621 BCE, Draco, an Athenian citizen, created the first written laws of Greece. The Draconian Code made capital punishment the penalty for many crimes and provided that the state had the exclusive right to punish persons accused of crime. The Code thus replaced customary law and private justice, at least formally. The Code also distinguished, perhaps for the first time, between intentional and unintentional murder, making the former subject to the death penalty and the latter to less severe punishments. In making the distinction, the importance of moral responsibility in law was recognized, again probably for the first time. The Draconian Code is known for the harshness of its punishments and, indeed, by today's standards they were harsh. However, they were probably more humane than punishments in customary law.

Solon, an Athenian statesman, produced a new legal code that repealed all of Draco's Code except for the laws governing homicide in 594–593 BCE, primarily because of the harshness of Draconian punishments. During the next two centuries, the severity of the laws and punishments decreased even further. Capital punishment became mandatory for only the most serious crimes such as temple robbery, high treason, and intentional homicide. It was no longer imposed for idleness, common theft, or destruction of sacred olive trees, as it was under Draco's Code. Methods of execution also became more humane. For example, poisoning by drinking hemlock increasingly replaced hurling the offender alive into a pit. Perhaps the most famous person executed BCE was the Greek philosopher Socrates who, in about 399 BCE, was required to drink poison for heresy and corruption of youth.

The Roman Law of the Twelve Tables was produced in 450 BCE and it, too, provided for capital punishment. Methods of execution were different for nobles, freemen, and slaves. Execution methods included crucifixion, drowning at sea, burial alive, beating to death, crushing to death (with animals or stones), burning alive, and impalement. For parricide (murder of a parent) the condemned was put in a sack that contained a dog, a rooster, a viper, and an ape and thrown into a body of water. Capital crimes included willful murder of a freeman or a parent, theft by a slave, the burning of a house or a stack of corn near a house, the cutting or grazing of crops planted by a farmer, cheating by a patron of his client, perjury, making disturbances at night in the city, or publication of libels and insulting songs. By the fourth century BCE, however, the harshness of the laws and the severity of the punishments had already begun to decline. From the 2nd century BCE to near the end of the Republic (about 27 BCE), the death penalty was rarely imposed on Roman citizens, who instead were allowed to go into exile. However, after that, during the Empire and until the fall (476 CE), laws and punishments returned to their pre-republic harshness and severity. Arguably, the most infamous execution of all time occurred about 29 CE, when the Romans crucified Jesus Christ.

In the 7th century CE, 400 years after seven feuding kingdoms were united to form an Empire that is now China, a new legal code was developed. The T'sang Code revised earlier Chinese legal codes and standardized legal procedures throughout the Empire. The Code listed crimes and punishments, including capital punishment. Under the Code, only two methods of execution were allowed: beheading or hanging.

During the 12th and 13th centuries (the Middle Ages) when the Catholic Church dominated social life in Western Europe, capital punishment began to be used widely for religious crimes, despite New Testament references seemingly against it. Before then, pre-Christian legal codes generally listed fewer crimes and milder punishments than those imposed later under religious auspices. Religious authorities created some of the more barbaric methods of execution. They included the rack, the wheel, the iron maiden, burning at the stake, and impaling in the grave. A primary purpose of those execution methods was to cause prolonged suffering before death so that in the interim, heretics had the opportunity to confess, repent, and receive salvation.

Also during the Middle Ages, the criminal code of the Holy Roman Empire, which informed the later codes of Austria, Prussia, and Germany, prescribed capital punishment for many crimes and many of the methods of execution favored by the Catholic Church, as well as some new ones. For example, burning at the stake was the punishment for sorcery, arson, sodomy, and counterfeiting. Murderers, depending on the heinousness of the crime, were beheaded, dragged behind horses, torn apart by claws, or broken on the wheel. Dismemberment was the punishment for treason; beheading for robbery, rape, abortion, and major brawls. Burglars and robbers could be hanged. The penalty for blasphemy was either execution or mutilation. Women who committed capital crimes were executed by drowning; however, for the crime of infanticide, a woman could be impaled and buried alive. France's criminal code at the time, although based on different traditions, was similar to the codes of Austria, Prussia, and Germany at least with respect to capital punishment.

By the 10th century CE in Britain, hanging from the gallows had become the most frequently used method of execution. Popular earlier methods included throwing the condemned into a quagmire. In the next century, William the Conqueror, who opposed killing except in war, prohibited peacetime executions for any offense. He preferred mutilating criminals instead.

During the early Middle Ages in Britain, following the lead of the Catholic Church, capital punishment was frequently accompanied by torture. Both major and minor crimes were typically punished by either hanging or drowning, although women convicted of high treason were burned to death and men accused of the same crime were hanged and drawn and quartered. Upper-class criminals could be beheaded. A person could be burned to death for marrying a Jew. For those suspects who would not confess their crimes, pressing was used. Pressing involved placing increasingly heavier weights on the offender's chest until he or she suffocated. In the 16th century, under King Henry VIII, an estimated 72,000 people were executed for their crimes, which included offenses such as marrying a Jew, not confessing to a crime, and treason. In 1531, boiling was approved as a method of capital punishment. Records show that some people boiled for up to 2 hours before they finally died.

In Britain over the next two centuries, the number of capital crimes continually increased to more than 200 in the 1700s. People could be executed for stealing things worth more than 40 shillings from a house, stealing things worth more than 2 shillings from a store, cutting down a tree, robbing a rabbit warren, counterfeiting tax stamps, and pocketpicking. However, because the punishment so often outweighed the crime, juries in Britain frequently failed to convict in such cases. Partly as a result of this problem of "jury nullification," in the 1820s and 1830s more than 100 of the more than 200 capital offenses were eliminated. In 1840, an attempt was made to abolish capital punishment in Britain altogether, but the attempt failed. However, other attempts to abolish capital punishment throughout Europe in the 19th and 20th centuries were more successful.

An important influence on the practice of capital punishment from the latter part of the 18th century on was the Italian Cesare Beccaria's treatise *On Crimes and Punishments*, published in 1764. In that work, Beccaria provided a reasoned argument against the death penalty. He claimed, among other things, that capital punishment is counterproductive because of the example of barbarity it provides; that, as a general deterrent, it is less effective than life imprisonment; and that, in any event, capital punishment violated the social contract (or the tacit agreement that citizens forfeit certain freedoms in exchange for protection from the state). Beccaria believed that the only circumstance in which capital punishment might be necessary is when it was the only way to prevent a revolutionary from destroying a country. A direct effect of Beccaria's argument was the abolition of capital punishment, albeit temporarily, in Russia, Austria, and Tuscany in the late 18th century. However, the real importance of the work was that it planted death penalty abolitionist seeds that would sprout more fully in the next century.

Beccaria's influence was weak in France, however. In 1791, the French Assembly approved the use of the guillotine for people condemned to death, and it was used quite extensively during the French Revolution. The French did not abandon the guillotine until 1977—the year of the last execution—and did not abolish capital punishment altogether until 1981.

From the end of the 18th century through the end of the 19th century, 10 countries either abolished capital punishment in law or abandoned it in practice and have never reinstated it. Those countries and the year of abolition or abandonment are Liechtenstein (1785), Iceland (1830), Cape Verde (1835), Monaco (1847), San Marino (1848), Portugal (1849), Brazil (1855), Venezuela (1863), Netherlands (1870), and Costa Rico (1877). Additionally, in 1848, France abolished capital punishment for all political crimes, and, in 1863, England limited capital punishment to murder, treason, and piracy. Italy also abolished capital punishment in the 19th century but restored it for a brief period under fascism in the 20th century.

In the 20th century, prior to World War II, another 10 countries either abolished or abandoned capital punishment. Some of them, however, still permit the death penalty in time of war or under military law, and some of them executed Nazi collaborators after World War II. The 10 countries are Panama (1903), Norway (1905,), Ecuador (1906), Uruguay (1907), Columbia (1909), Sweden (1910), Paraguay (1928), Nicaragua (1930), Denmark (1933), and Mexico (1937). During World War II and shortly there after another eight countries either abolished or abandoned capital punishment (although some of them still permit it in time of war or under military law): Honduras (1940), Switzerland (1942), Andorra (1943), Malta (1943), Finland (1944), Italy (1947), West Germany (1949), and Luxembourg (1949). During the 1950s and 1960s, 14 more countries joined the ranks of the abolitionists: Austria (1950), Greenland (1954), Ireland (1954), Israel (1954, except for the execution of Adolph Eichmann in 1962 for "crimes against humanity"), New Zealand (1957), Canada (1962), Cyprus (1962), the U.K. (1964), Fiji (1964), the Dominican Republic (1966), Hong Kong (1966), the Solomon Islands (1966), Australia (1967), and the Vatican City State (1969). Besides the countries that abolished or abandoned capital punishment during these periods, many of the countries that retained the death penalty have used it infrequently. Between 1958 and 1962, four countries accounted for about half the world's executions (reliable information was not available for the communist bloc nations). They were, in order from most to least, South Africa, Korea, Nigeria, and the U.S.

In the 1970s and 1980s another 15 countries abolished or abandoned the death penalty: Greece (1972), Haiti (1972), El Salvador (1973), Spain (1975), Poland (1976), France (1977), Nepal (1979), Peru (1979), Mozambique (1986), Hungary (1988), Namibia (1988), Cambodia (1989), Romania (1989), Slovakia (1989), and Slovenia (1989). The worldwide trend continued in the 1990s with at least 13 more countries joining the abolitionist ranks: Croatia (1990), Czech Republic (1990), Angola (1992), Guinea-Bissau (1993), Mauritius (1995), Micronesia (1995), South Africa (1995), Belgium (1996), Georgia (1997), Azerbaijan (1998), Bulgaria (1998), Estonia (1998), and Lithuania (1998). A number of factors are contributing to the worldwide death penalty abolitionist trend. One factor is the view widely held in Europe and elsewhere that capital punishment is a violation of human rights. A second more practical factor is the requirement of both the European Union and the 40-nation Council of Europe that member nations renounce the death penalty.

As of April 2000, 108 nations of the world had either abolished capital punishment in law or practice, and 87 nations had retained it. According to Amnesty International, there were about 1600 legally authorized executions throughout the world in 1998 and at least one in 37 different countries. Nations with the most executions in 1998 were China (with 1067), the Democratic Republic of the Congo (with 100), the U.S. (with 68), Iran (with 66), and Egypt (48). More than 80% of all executions conducted worldwide in 1998 were in those five nations. In 1999, the five countries of China, the Democratic Republic of the Congo, Iran, Saudi Arabia, and the U.S. accounted for 85% of the more than 1800 legally authorized executions in the world.

Robert M. Bohm

References and Further Reading

Beccaria, C., *On Crimes and Punishments*, translated, with an introduction by Harry Paolucci. Indianapolis, IN: Bobbs-Merrill, 1975.

Bedau, H.A., Ed., *The Death Penalty in America: Current Controversies*, New York, NY: Oxford University Press, 1997.

Bowers, W.J., Pierce, G.L., and McDevitt, J.F., *Legal Homicide: Death as Punishment in America, 1864–1982*. Boston, MA: Northeastern University Press, 1984.

The Death Penalty Information Center, available at www.deathpenaltyinfo.org/dpicintl.html.

Durant, W., Our oriental heritage, Part 1 of *The Story of Civilization*, New York, NY: Simon & Schuster, 1954.

Erez, E., Thou shalt not execute: Hebrew law perspective on capital punishment, *Criminology* 19, 1981.

From the Middle Ages to ..., available at www.metaphor.dk/guillotine/Pages/History.html.

Gorecki, J., *Capital Punishment: Criminal Law and Social Evolution*. New York, NY: Columbia University Press, 1983.

Hood, R., *The Death Penalty: A World-Wide Perspective*, Oxford, UK: Clarendon Press, 1996.

Reggio, M.H., History of the Death Penalty, available at www.pbs.org/wgbh/pages/frontline/shows/execution/readings/history.html.

Schabas, W.A., *The Abolition of the Death Penalty in International Law*, Cambridge, UK: Cambridge University Press, 1997.

The World Wide Legal Association, The Timetable of World Legal History, available at www.wwlia.org/hist.htm.

See also **Beccaria; Cesare**

Carjacking

See **Motor Vehicle Theft**

Central America, Crime and Justice in

It is virtually impossible to think of Central America without being reminded of the political controversy that has surrounded the region during the past century. One cannot discuss the concepts of crime and justice in Central America without examining the political climate that has affected the systems of justice in most of the countries in this region of the world. The following discussion will attempt to explain the political factors that have affected the social construction of crime while examining how the concept of justice has changed in meaning and practice.

Central America forms a long isthmus that serves as a bridge between North and South America. It is made up of an area of about 201,903 square miles and includes the countries of Guatemala, Belize, El Salvador, Honduras, Nicaragua, Costa Rica, and Panama (Center for the Administration of Justice). Although all these countries share cultural similarities (ethnicity, language, religion, customs), each one of them enjoys the benefit of being unique in the administration of justice. Therefore, the concepts of crime and justice in Central America must be studied both generally (that is, as they apply to all Central American countries) and individually, with respect to each country. Further, it is important to recognize that both the meaning of crime and the interpretation of justice have dramatically changed in the Central American region as a result of the shift in the late 20th century from dictatorship and totalitarianism to democratic governance.

Origins

It seems that ever since Christopher Columbus discovered the Central American region in 1502, political struggle has not ceased. In the 20th century, political instability brought on by dictatorships, socialism, and civil war has contributed to a state of anomie in which law is seldom respected and crime is politically defined.

Spanish colonial criminal procedure was notorious for being based on inequalities between subjects and rulers and for emphasizing protection of the crown's property. Its procedure focused on the role of the judge as investigating magistrate. It also divided the process into the stages of investigation and trial. The first stage was known for the absence of counsel, defendants who were uninformed of the charges against them, and the use of torture to obtain confessions. The second stage consisted of a judicial review of the materials presented in the investigation (Rico and Salas, 1991).

Political reformers in the Central American colonies were greatly affected by the revolutions that took place in France and the U.S. in the late 18th century. In fact, the reforms made as a result of these two revolutions were looked upon by Central American reformers with admiration and respect. Thus, it is not surprising that the Napoleonic codes and the U.S. Constitution influenced the language and principles used in the crafting of constitutional law in the Central American region. Of these, the European influence (i.e., the Napoleonic codes) was stronger. This is largely because of the fact that when Central American scholars traveled to European countries it was a common practice to bring back the latest criminal justice-related trends. This habit of copying European criminal justice practices still continues today and has led some to conclude that "Latin American codification could be characterized as legislation by tourism" (Rico, 1985). As will be apparent in the following discussion, today's Central American judicial procedures largely reflect their European inheritance.

Criminal Justice Procedures

The court-related procedure to be followed in a particular case is largely determined by the nature and classification of the offense. Central American countries classify crimes as *delitos* and petty crimes as *delitos menores.* Although there is some agreement among most Central American nations on how a particular offense should be classified, there is much variance in the manner in which procedures are followed. For instance, Panama does not have any written procedures for the trial of minor cases (*delitos menores*) despite the fact that a judge has the authority to sentence the offender to up to 2 years in prison (Center for the Administration of Justice).

Aside from the common processes, Central America follows several extraordinary procedures, which include a jury trial, trial for minor offenses, special trials for crimes committed by public officials, juvenile trials, and special tribunals. Of all these, the most controversial have been special tribunals, which have become popular during military periods.

Nicaragua

In 1979, Nicaragua ended its two-year civil war with the triumph of the Sandinista regime. This Marxist–Leninist group forced dictator Anastasio Somoza into exile after a 40-year rule. During the first few months of the Sandinista regime, Nicaragua adopted the Sandinista Criminal Decree 1233, which established the "Tribunales Populares anti-Somocistas" (TPAs) (Taboada, 1987). The TPAs were special tribunals whose goal was to convict and render sentences upon the large number of Somoza followers in captivity. At the time, Nicaragua's rural areas had the highest concentration of political prisoners, because most Somoza followers had fled to the countryside (Corte Suprema de Justicia, 1981). Therefore, the rural courts were in desperate need of assistance in the handling of criminal cases. Not being close to urban settings, and therefore, not subject to anyone's oversight, the TPAs suspended the rule of law and seemed to emphasize conviction rate rather than due process. The common verdict was either a long prison sentence or immediate death, the latter without the benefit of appeals or due process. In the past 10 years, the practice of these courts has been abolished in all Central American countries, including Nicaragua. Many attribute this to the birth of democracy in the region.

Nicaragua has the oldest code of criminal procedure of all the Central American countries. It dates back to 1879, whereas the other Central American countries enacted their codes of criminal procedures in the 1970s and 1980s. It is noteworthy that this is the case: despite the fact that Nicaragua experienced the most violent civil war of all Central American countries, its code of criminal procedure survived.

Individual Rights Issues

Although it is clear that crime in Central America is deeply rooted in its political atmosphere, politics has also influenced questionable practices of those sworn to uphold and administer the law. Despite the fact that the constitution of most Central American nations includes language guaranteeing the rights of all citizens while ensuring due process, many of these guarantees have not been enforced, as demonstrated by the numerous cases filed before organizations such as Amnesty International that report human rights violations. This abuse of legal rights is particularly true of countries that have experienced civil wars (Guatemala and Nicaragua) or military coups (Honduras, El Salvador, and Guatemala).

The concept of crime is socially defined in Central American countries. That is, the citizenry agrees on the behavior that should be considered unacceptable or undesirable. The criteria used to determine this behavior are deeply rooted in the mores and powerful religious convictions of the citizenry. Although it would not be accurate to state that crime is also viewed as sin, one could argue that Central American countries hold the belief that crime is evil and therefore should be abolished. The emphasis here is on the fact that crime should be abolished, and not necessarily on the manner in which this behavior is to be prohibited. One could argue that most of these countries hold crime control as a priority and dismiss due process as a nuisance (Packer, 1964).

Profound political differences have also influenced the social construct of crime. Some of the Central American nations have added language to their criminal codes that prohibits certain behaviors against a particular political group. Unfortunately, many of these laws have been interpreted in distorted ways; thus, individuals are punished who have merely exercised freedom of expression against powerful political figures.

Costa Rica

Of all the Central American countries, Costa Rica has been the most politically stable. Many regard it as a safe haven, because it has taken steps to remain on neutral political ground. Costa Rica's peaceful mentality has prevailed to the extent that its government does not have an army. It is the only Central American government without a military unit. It enjoys a peaceful environment in which crime is regarded as an extraordinary phenomenon. This is in contrast to other Central American countries, where the occurrence of crime is regarded as the norm. In addition, Costa Ricans have added momentum to their economic growth by promoting the beauty of their country to the international community (particularly to the U.S.). This ongoing advertising campaign has helped make Costa Rica into the tourism Mecca of Central America.

Crime Statistics

None of the Central American countries has a formal crime reporting system. Statistics on crime rates are mere guesses or projections based on inaccurate reporting mechanisms. This is largely because of the fact that until recently, most Central American countries had a police force that was largely part of the military component. That is, the military served the function of a civilian police force. Thus, the reporting of crime data was done through the military leadership, which was primarily interested in maintaining control and perceived crime-related information as unimportant. Recently, countries such as El Salvador and Nicaragua have founded a civilian police force in charge of public affairs. This phenomenon will have a significant impact on the collection of crime data. It is hoped that Central America will initiate an educational campaign aimed at informing the public and private sectors of the importance of collecting and analyzing crime statistics.

Central American countries have had a long history of certain crimes (i.e., murder, kidnapping, drug possession, and distribution), but since democratization, the civilian and militarized police forces have faced additional challenges. With the return of former exiles to countries such as El Salvador and Nicaragua, the local police in these countries have had to adjust to a different criminal element. For example, gang activity in El Salvador is becoming a challenge to local law enforcement. Not only do police confront ritualistic gang behavior similar to that of gangs in the U.S. (i.e., painting graffiti, claiming territory as their own, and declaring war against other gangs), but it has also become common for police to respond to a gang-related incident and to become confused when gang members speak English to one another in an attempt to elude police. In Nicaragua, similar circumstances have prompted the local police to become educated on gang activities in the U.S. in an effort to be better equipped to address the Nicaraguan gang problem.

The future of crime and justice in Central America is uncertain. Every time countries such as Honduras, Nicaragua, or El Salvador hold a democratic election, the consequent peaceful transfer of power reinforces the notion that democracy may have a place in the Central American community. Further, democratization has a positive impact on the notion that crime should be controlled but never at the expense of sacrificing the due process rights of the citizenry. Perhaps in the near future the rights provided by the constitutions of Central American countries will be upheld and guaranteed to all citizens.

Alejandro del Carmen

References and Further Reading

Center for the Administration of Justice. Florida International University. *Los Codigos de Justicia*.

Rico, J.M. and Salas, L. (1991). *Codigos Latinos de Procedimiento Penal*. Mars Editores. San Jose, Costa Rica.

Rico, J.M. (1985). *Crimen y Justicia en America Latina,* 3rd ed. Mexico. Siglo xxi.

Taboada, T.A. (1987). *Aspects of the Evolution of Law in Sandinista Nicaragua*. Allen and Unwin, Inc. Winchester, MA.

Corte Suprema de Justicia. (1981). *Boletin Nacional (de Nicaragua)*. Managua, Nicaragua. America Central. Edicion Oficial.

Packer, H. (1964). *Two Models of the Criminal Process*. University of Pennsylvania Law Review. (November 1964).

See also **Cuba, Crime, and Justice in; Organized Crime: Mexican Mafia**

Chambliss, William J.

In the late 1950s, William Chambliss was an average student at the University of California, Los Angeles, who struggled with his classes while he worked 40 hours a week to pay tuition. His interactions with Donald R. Cressey, who became an early mentor during his undergraduate studies, changed the course of his life and career. It was Cressey who encouraged Chambliss to study sociology and, in 1955, he received a B.A. in psychology with minors in sociology and English. Cressey, a student of Edwin H. Sutherland, believed that criminologists should "work in pursuit of the truth, not in pursuit of criminals"—a notion that would influence a great deal of Chambliss' work.

Over the years, Chambliss has become perhaps the most famous critical criminologist in the world. His work on organized state crime has an international scope that developed from an interest in 16th and 17th century piracy—actions that exemplified the state's complicity in criminal behavior. He has studied and taught in Zambia, Austria, Wales, Sweden, Norway, England, Hong Kong, and Nigeria. He attributes the direction of his research to John Dewey who, as quoted by Chambliss, said that a good researcher will "scratch where it itches." According to his former student and sociologist of law scholar Kitty Calivita, he possesses a unique sense to ask the right questions.

Chambliss' studies on organized crime developed almost serendipitously as he undertook a field research project to determine how police make the decision to arrest. In 1962, he began a participant observation study in a Seattle slum area. At the time, he was told that Seattle's low crime rate and lack of organized crime would limit his findings. But for the next 5 years, Chambliss became closely connected to the city's seedier side where he developed unusual friendships and lasting contacts as he unearthed a prosperous underground criminal network. His entry into this world of crime was facilitated by Millie, an exprostitute and drug addict, who worked as a waitress at a cafe frequented by Chambliss and who arranged access to a back room poker game. In 1969, his exposure of organized crime in Seattle resulted in threats to his family, including his three small children. An offer to work in Wisconsin presented the perfect opportunity to leave behind a corrupt world that had supplied excellent research data, but also had put his personal safety at risk.

During his research in Seattle, Chambliss became close friends with a thief named Harry King, who had specialized in safecracking from 1910 to 1960. The original 1972 publication of *Boxman: A Professional Thief's Journey*, a collaboration between Chambliss and King, presented an inside view of a world of deviance. The book recounts King's experiences and reflections on his victims, the professional criminal rackets, and prison life.

Chambliss' interest in the sociology of law became the impetus for his classic 1964 study of vagrancy laws and the evolution of criminal law. Inspired by Jerome Hall, Chambliss traced the history of vagrancy law that developed as lawmakers responded to socially perceived needs and passed laws accordingly. Jeffrey Adler's (1989) critique of the work declared that criminologists should not continue to cite the article as an authoritative source on the historical development of criminal law. Adler accused Chambliss of exaggerating the anticrime orientation of early vagrancy codes and the narrow class interest that those laws served. In response, Chambliss ("On Trashing Marxist

Criminology") noted that Adler's appraisal represented an outgrowth of the structured bias against Marxist theory in the publication process of mainstream journals.

Chambliss views the first edition of *Law, Order and Power* that was published in 1971 with Robert Seidman as his most important work. The book is a Marxian analysis of the American justice system that characterizes the legal order as a "self-serving system to maintain power and privilege" (p. 4). Chambliss and Seidman argue that legal norms reflect interest-group activity (e.g., large corporations), not the "public interest."

Chambliss also is celebrated for "The Saints and the Roughnecks"—an article that has been reprinted innumerable times. The work is based on observations of the activities and behaviors of two small-town male gangs at Hanibal High School. The two groups engaged in similar levels of delinquency, both in frequency and seriousness. The behavior of the white, lower-class Roughnecks, however, was perceived by the police and community as more deviant than the Saints, who were from upper-middle-class families. The Saints participated in school activities and were seen as good kids with bright futures. The labeling of the Roughnecks ultimately reinforced their pattern of deviancy as their self-conceptions diminished and sense of alienation increased.

Disillusioned by the Vietnam War and what he viewed as governmental efforts to suppress free speech, Chambliss traveled to Scandinavia in the mid-1970s. His ground-breaking work, *On the Take: From Petty Crooks to Presidents* (first published in 1978) was written in a rustic cabin by kerosene lantern outside Oslo, Norway. Chambliss' expose of crime, business, and politics was based on interviews with hundreds of people, including drug dealers, CIA agents, drug enforcement officials, politicians, addicts, gamblers, and international smugglers. The work describes how and why organized crime flourished while those in authority remained indifferent to the phenomenon. The analysis focuses on politicians, law enforcement agents, and business people who were intimately involved in corruption. The research includes organized crime activities in Seattle, Miami, New York, and the opium fields of Thailand and Turkey.

Chambliss' *Power, Politics and Crime* (1999) is a sweeping indictment of crime policy, that reveals the disparities between the ideal and the reality of law. Examining issues ranging from the failed war on drugs to the corruption of the criminal justice system, Chambliss argues that crime has overtaken the U.S., despite a decline in crime rates, because of misinformation from the media, politicians, and criminal justice agencies. He argues that the law enforcement industrial complex profits from the building of prisons and that crime control technologies perpetuate myths about the threat of street crime. Law, in some cases, is seen as a mechanism of oppression, as officials emphasize policing in minority ghettos, but ignore corporate, organizational, political, and white-collar crime. Inherent biases and problems in the criminal justice system are related to minority group social alienation, middle class cynicism, and the diversion of resources from other government needs such as education.

Chambliss' primary theoretical influence developed from the work of German economist and philosopher Karl Marx. Although the works of Marx present no specific analysis of crime and criminal law, his framework on capitalist societies laid a foundation for the development of a conflict perspective in criminology. According to Chambliss, the needs, characteristics, ideologies, and institutions are a reflection of that society's historical condition—especially the material conditions (the mode of production) at that particular historical moment. A Marxist analysis shows how the social needs of the society contribute to the oppression of the lower classes and the need to develop workable recipes for change (praxis). Chambliss argues that criminal behavior is explained by the forces of class interests and class struggle, and by contradictions inherent in the social relations created by the society's particular mode of production. He notes that the most important force behind criminal law creation is the economic interest and political power of those social classes that either own or control the resources or occupy positions of authority in the state bureaucracies.

Mainstream criminologists sometimes dismiss his work as being too radical, although Chambliss has withstood this criticism. As evidence supporting the strength and tenacity of his ideas, Chambliss was elected president of the American Society of Criminology, serving in 1988 and received the Edwin H. Sutherland award in 2003.

Mary Dodge

Biography

Born in Buffalo, New York, December 12, 1933. Educated at University of California, Los Angeles, B.A., 1955; Indiana University, Bloomington, Indiana, M.A. in Sociology, 1960, Ph.D. in Sociology with a minor in Law, 1962. Assistant professor, University of Washington, Seattle, 1962–1966; associate professor and chair of the department of sociology, University of California, Santa Barbara, 1967–1973; professor, University of Delaware, Newark, 1976–1986; professor, George Washington University 1986–present. President of the American Society of Criminology, 1988; 1992–1993; president of the Society for the Study of Social Problems, 1993.

Selected Works

A Sociological Analysis of the Law of Vagrancy, *Social Problems* 12 (1964).

Law, Order, and Power (with Robert B. Seidman), 1971.

Boxman: A Professional Thief's Journey, New York, NY: Harper & Row, 1972, reissued as *Harry King: A Professional Thief's Journey*, New York, NY: John Wiley, 1984.
The saints and the roughnecks, *Society* 11 (1973).
On the Take: From Petty Crooks to Presidents, 1978; revised edition, 1988.
State-Organized Crime, *Criminology* 27 (1989).
Policing the Ghetto Underclass: The Politics of Law and Law Enforcement, *Social Problems* 41 (1994).
Power, Politics and Crime, 1999.

References and Further Reading

Adler, J., A historical analysis of the Law of Vagrancy. *Criminology*, 1989.
Klockars, C., The contemporary crises of Marxist criminology. *Criminology*, 1979.
McCord, J. and Laub, J., *Contemporary Masters in Criminology*. New York, NY: Plenum Press, 1995.
Passas, N., *Organized Crime*. London, UK: Darmouth Publishers, 1994.
Quinney, R., *Crime and Justice in Society*. Boston, MA: Little Brown, 1968.
Taylor, I., Walton, P., and Young, J., Eds. *Critical Criminology*, London, UK: Routledge and Kegan Paul Ltd., 1975.

See also **Cressey, Donald R.; Critical Criminology**

Chesney-Lind, Meda

Criminology is, for the most part, a social scientific discipline dominated by White men. Most of the empirical and pedagogical work done on crime and its control ignores the experiences of girls and women, especially those who are not of European decent. Still, a review of the contemporary literature on topics of central concern to criminologists reveals that feminist research, theories, and policy proposals are gradually moving from the margins to the forefront of the criminological enterprise. This much-needed transition is due, in large part, to the scholarly, pedagogical, and political efforts of Meda Chesney-Lind, who is currently Professor of Women's Studies at the University of Hawaii at Manoa.

Chesney-Lind has devoted considerable intellectual, emotional, and physical energy to influence criminologists around the world to always remember girls and women and to treat gender as more than a variable to be included in multivariate statistical analyses. However, like other leading feminist scholars who study crime and social control, Chesney-Lind does not concentrate only on writing and orally presenting critiques of androcentric or "gender-blind" scholarship and policies. For example, she has generated a substantial amount of rigorous empirical and theoretical work on the United States criminal justice system's harsh treatment of women and girls who come into conflict with the law, female youth gangs, juvenile robbery, child sexual abuse, sexual harassment, and the ways in which child abuse and poverty propel females into crime.

That she received the following prestigious awards for her contributions to a sociological understanding of these and other topics is an important statement on the impact she has had on criminology, feminism, and criminal justice studies: the Western Society of Criminology's 1992 Paul Tappan Award for Outstanding Contributions to Criminology; the American Society of Criminology's 1992 Michael J. Hindelang Award for the most Outstanding Contribution to Criminology; the 1994 Distinguished Scholar Award from the American Society of Criminology's Division on Women and Crime; the American Society of Criminology's 1996 Herbert Block Award for Outstanding Services to the Society and the Profession; the Western Society of Criminology's 1997 Morrison-Gitchoff Award; the National Council on Crime and Delinquency's 1997 Cressey Award; and the 2000 Major Achievement Award from the American Society of Criminology's Division of Critical Criminology. She was also named as a Fellow to the American Society of Criminology in 1996 and received several awards from the University of Hawaii for her scholarship and service to her university and to the nonacademic community.

Among her most recent path-breaking contributions to criminology is her widely read and cited book *The Female Offender: Girls, Women, and Crime* (1997). This work motivated many researchers around the world to carefully and systematically examine the relationship between sexual, physical, and psychological abuse in family or household settings and females' involvement in crime. Unfortunately, as pointed out by

Chesney-Lind, the only choice many girls and women have is to either stay in brutal homes or to escape from parents, spouses, and other relatives who cause them much pain and suffering. Leaving, however, as documented by Chesney-Lind, creates new problems, such as poverty, unemployment, homelessness, and other highly injurious outcomes of patriarchal capitalism. Lacking adequate social support and legitimate means of employment, crime, then, is the only perceived means of survival. *The Female Offender* also sensitizes us to the fact that even if runaway girls do not commit serious crimes, they are often officially designated as criminal anyway because they resisted their parents' patriarchal control and rejected traditional gender roles.

What sets Chesney-Lind apart from other feminists who study criminological issues is her ongoing in-depth focus on girls and how ethnic, class, and gender inequality contribute to them coming into conflict with the law. This is not to say that she is not concerned with adult female offenders, their life histories, and the extremely punitive societal reactions to their offenses. Indeed, she has done extensive research on women and is heavily involved in grass roots efforts to reduce women's imprisonment through progressive community-based strategies. Still, Chesney-Lind is one of the few feminist criminologists who consistently talks to girls, publicly advocates for them, and who is passionately committed to developing a rich understanding of what life is like from their perspective. Her latest book, an edited collection titled *Girls and Gangs in America* (1999), is another example of how dedicated Chesney-Lind is to enhancing a sociological understanding of girls' lives and to helping them achieve gender, class, and racial or ethnic equality.

In addition to experiencing family violence, poverty, unemployment, racism, and a host of other serious social problems, many socially and economically excluded girls and women are further victimized by a vicious antifeminist backlash heavily fueled by conservative journalists, politicians, and academics. For example, it is now common to read newspaper articles stating that women are just as violent as men and that advanced industrial societies are currently experiencing an unprecedented feminist-driven epidemic of violent crimes committed by "bad" or "unruly" females. A large body of international research shows that nothing could be further from the truth, and Chesney-Lind is currently challenging media accounts of females. Much of her work in this area involves presentations to local organizations and the writing of newspaper articles. *The Female Offender* constitutes another significant challenge to backlash journalism and strongly suggests that academics publicly confront media personnel and others who paint hurtful images of the feminist struggle for gender equality.

For Chesney-Lind, teaching and mentoring are just as important as scholarship and activism. Consider that she has, for over two decades, inspired many students and junior faculty to achieve the highest disciplinary standards and to overcome their fear of being attacked by journalists, academics, and others intent on protecting the patriarchal status quo. Chesney-Lind has also made many major contributions to professional, regional, and national organizations (e.g., the American Society of Criminology) that have resulted in numerous changes, such as an increase in the number of feminist papers presented at academic conferences and much more female involvement in committees.

In sum, Chesney-Lind has clearly helped transform criminology. She has also played an integral role in the ongoing and constantly evolving struggle to enhance females' physical, psychological, and economic well-being, and influenced many students and established academics to make gender analysis a core component of their scholarly work on crime and its control.

WALTER S. DEKESEREDY

Biography

Born in Woodward, Oklahoma, 22 January. Educated at Whitman College in Walla Walla, Washington, B.A. in Sociology, 1969; University of Hawaii at Honolulu, M.A. in Sociology, 1971; University of Hawaii at Honolulu, Ph.D. in Sociology, 1977. Sociology Instructor, Honolulu Community College, 1973–1985; associate professor, Women's Studies Program, University of Hawaii at Manoa, 1990–1993; director, Women's Studies Program, University of Hawaii at Manoa, 1994–present; professor, Women's Studies Program, University of Hawaii at Manoa, 1998–present. Fellow, Western Society of Criminology, 1988; Michael J. Hindelang Award for the Most Outstanding Contribution to Sociology, American Society of Criminology, 1992; Distinguished Scholar Award, Division on Women and Crime, American Society of Criminology, 1994; Fellow, American Society of Criminology, 1996; Herbert Bloch Award for Outstanding Services to the Society and the Profession, American Society of Criminology, 1996; Major Achievement Award, Division on Critical Criminology, American Society of Criminology, 2000.

Selected Works

Judicial paternalism and the female status offender, *Crime & Delinquency* 23 (1977).

Women and crime: The female offender, *Signs: Journal of Women in Culture and Society* 12 (1986).

Feminism and criminology (with Kathleen Daly), *Justice Quarterly* 5 (1988).

A reformulation and partial test of the power control theory of delinquency (with Mary Morash), *Justice Quarterly* 8 (1991).

Girls, Delinquency, and Juvenile Justice (with Randall G. Shelden), 1992; 2nd ed., 1998.

Representations of gangs and delinquency: Wild in the streets? (with Paul A. Perrone), *Social Justice* 24 (1997).

The Female Offender: Girls, Women, and Crime, 1997.
Female Gangs in America: Essays on Girls, Gangs, and Gender (edited with John M. Hagedorn), 1999.

References and Further Reading

Belknap, J., *The Invisible Woman: Gender, Crime, and Justice*, Belmont, CA: Wadsworth, 1996.
Boritch, H., *Fallen Women: Female Crime and Criminal Justice in Canada*, Toronto: Nelson, 1997.
DeKeseredy, W.S., Review of Meda Chesney-Lind's *the female Offender: Girls, Women, and Crime*, *Justice Quarterly* 16 (1999).
DeKeseredy, W.S., *Women, Crime and the Canadian Criminal Justice System*, Cincinnati, OH: Anderson, 2000.
Faith, K., *Unruly Women: The Politics of Confinement and Resistance*, Vancouver, WA: Press Gang, 1993.
Miller, S.L., Ed., *Crime Control and Women: Feminist Implications of Criminal Justice Policy*, Thousand Oaks, CA: Sage, 1998
Raffel P., Barbara, and Sokoloff, N.J., Ed., *The Criminal Justice System and Women: Offenders, Victims, and Workers*, 2nd ed., New York, NY: McGraw-Hill, 1995.
Renzetti, C.M. and Goodstein, L., Eds, *Women, Crime, and Criminal Justice*, Los Angeles, CA: Roxbury, 2000.

See also **Feminist Theories of Criminal Behavior; Gangs, Girl**

Chicago School

See **Sociological Theories of Criminal Behavior**

Child Abuse: Extent and Correlates

Child abuse is not a new phenomenon; parents and other adults have mistreated children throughout history. Until the latter part of the 19th century little public information was available on the subject and little was done to protect child victims, however, because of the prevailing belief in the privacy of the family and the notion that children were essentially the "property" of their parents, especially their fathers. In the U.S., public authority to intervene was initially granted in 1874 in New York City, with the case of Mary Ellen Wilson, an illegitimate 8-year-old child who was repeatedly beaten and otherwise abused by her guardian. As there were no agencies charged with protecting children from abuse, a concerned church worker asked Henry Bergh, President of the Society for the Prevention of Cruelty to Animals, to intervene. Mr. Bergh obtained an attorney to act on Mary Ellen's behalf, and the case was successfully prosecuted. Mary Ellen was removed from her guardian and placed in a home for children, and her guardian was sentenced to a year of labor in prison (Crosson-Tower, 1999). In 1875, Elbridge Gerry, the attorney who had defended Mary Ellen, founded the Society for the Prevention of Cruelty to Children (SPCC), and an organized effort to address the problem of child maltreatment began.

Other cities established chapters of the SPCC, which expanded its activities beyond intervention in cases of child abuse and neglect to also include advocacy for children in poverty and situations of family violence. Officials in Cook County, Illinois, established a separate juvenile court in 1899, which assumed jurisdiction over child deprivation cases as well as cases of delinquency, and other counties followed suit. These agencies helped bring national attention to the plight of children, culminating in a White House Conference on Dependent Children in 1909. A federal Children's Bureau was established in 1912, and The Child Welfare League of America was established in 1915. The American Humane Association added children to its agenda soon afterward, and the Social Security Act of 1930 mandated "child welfare services for neglected dependent children and children in danger of becoming delinquent" (Williams, 1983). It was not until the late 1940s, however, when physicians began to speak openly about the problem of child abuse, that the issue was defined as a social problem and a concerted effort across disciplines was begun to find out more about the extent and correlates of child maltreatment.

John Caffrey, a radiologist, began to notice in the 1940s that X-ray findings of some child patients did not correspond to parents' versions of the child's injuries. Caffrey suspected that in some cases of child injuries, parents were the ones responsible. When his suspicions were made known to other physicians, they felt he might be correct. In 1962, Dr. C. Henry Kempe, chairman of the Department of Pediatrics at the University of Colorado's School of Medicine, and his colleagues published what is now known as a landmark article, entitled "The Battered-Child Syndrome," in the *Journal of the American Medical Association.* Kempe defined the syndrome as "a clinical condition in young children who have received severe physical abuse, generally from a parent or foster parent," and advised health care providers to look for a "marked discrepancy between clinical findings and historical data supplied by the parents" as an indicator (Kempe, 1962). Kempe and his associates began studies of the problem and an attempt to document cases. In 1962, the American Humane Association found 662 cases of child abuse that had been reported to the press (Parton, 1985).

The University of Colorado Medical Center provided funding to establish the National Center for the Prevention of Child Abuse and Neglect in 1972 to engage in research and provide training to professionals. In 1974, exactly 100 years after the case of Mary Ellen, the U.S. Congress passed the Child Abuse Prevention and Treatment Act, which, among other things, established a National Center on Child Abuse and Neglect within the Department of Health, Education and Welfare. The Center's functions were to engage in research, establish a clearinghouse, distribute training material, fund demonstration projects, and study the effectiveness of child abuse and neglect reporting laws and the proper role of the federal government in assisting state and local child abuse intervention efforts. In addition, the Act required states to adopt procedures to identify, treat, and prevent child abuse and to maintain data and report to the Department of Housing, Education and Welfare (HEW) on how well those procedures were working. State health and welfare agencies also were required to cooperate with one another to coordinate the treatment of child abuse and neglect cases. Failure to comply with these requirements would jeopardize states' eligibility for certain funds under the Social Security Act (Crosson-Tower, 1999).

Since the passage of the Child Abuse Prevention and Treatment Act, all states have developed statutes addressing mandatory reporting requirements, public agency responsibilities, civil and criminal interventions, and record-keeping standards, although these may vary somewhat from state to state. The National Center on Child Abuse and Neglect includes four main types of maltreatment in the definition of child abuse and neglect:

1. Physical Abuse: the infliction of physical injury as a result of punching, beating, kicking, biting, burning, shaking or otherwise harming a child;
2. Child Neglect: failure to provide for the child's basic needs, which can be physical, educational, or emotional;
3. Sexual Abuse: fondling a child's genitals, intercourse, incest, rape, sodomy, exhibitionism, and commercial exploitation through prostitution or the production of pornographic materials; and
4. Emotional Abuse: acts or omissions by the parents or other caretakers that have caused or could cause serious behavioral, cognitive, emotional, or mental disorders.

Although these types can occur separately, they more commonly occur in combination. In particular, emotional abuse is likely to be present when any of the other forms of maltreatment occur. In each state known or suspected cases of child abuse and neglect are reported to the local child protective services (CPS) agency. Workers investigate reports that meet designated criteria and screen out cases that cannot be substantiated. If a case of child abuse or neglect is confirmed, then the agency will actively intervene, offering a range of treatment options depending on the family's particular situation. If the case is serious enough, the perpetrator(s) may be prosecuted in criminal court.

The most recent data on child abuse and neglect at the national level are from 2001. These data are from states' reports to the National Child Abuse and Neglect Reporting System (NCANDS) (U.S. Department of Health and Human Services 2003). It is important to remember that all official data only represent those cases brought to the attention of public agencies. There is no way to know the true extent of child abuse among the population. It is also important to know that each state may have different criteria for screening cases "in" or "out," which may, to some extent, depend on internal agency policy and available resources. Thus, national data can only serve as indicators of the extent of the problem and cannot provide an accurate account. In 2001, approximately three million referrals of child abuse and neglect were received by local CPS agencies, involving approximately five million. A referral may include more than one child. Of these referrals, 33% were screened out, and 67% were opened for further investigation. Of those cases investigated, child abuse or neglect was confirmed in 28%. Thus, there were approximately 560,000 cases of confirmed child abuse and neglect in 2001, involving an estimated 903,000 victims, for a rate of 12.4 per 1000 children in the United States. The rate has continued to decrease each year since reaching a peak of 15.3 per 1000 in 1993. The largest category of maltreatment was neglect, accounting for 57% of victims. Another 19% of victims suffered physical abuse, whereas 10% were sexually abused, and 9% or fewer were victims of psychological abuse or medical neglect. Approximately 9% of children experienced a recurrence of abuse or neglect within 6 months after the initial substantiated incident, indicating that child maltreatment is a chronic problem in a significant number of families. Younger children, children who had experienced neglect or multiple forms of maltreatment, children who were maltreated by their mothers, and those who had been prior victims were most vulnerable to continued abuse or neglect.

Very young children (age 0–3) were most likely to be victims of abuse or neglect, with 28% of victims in that age group. Victimization rates decreased as the child's age increased. Male and female children were about equally likely to be victims of all types of maltreatment (48% males, 52% females) except sexual abuse, where females are generally about three times as likely to be victims as males. Victimization rates varied by race or ethnicity of the child: 50% of victims were white, 25% were African American, 15% were Hispanic, 2% were American Indian or Native Alaskan, and 1% were Asian or Pacific Islanders. The vast majority of children who were victims of child abuse and neglect were mistreated by one or both of their parents (more than 80%), with the majority of perpetrators being female (59%). However, female parents are generally more likely to be responsible for neglect, whereas males are more likely to inflict sexual abuse. The median ages for perpetrators were 31 for females and 34 for males.

In 2001 an estimated 1300 children died as a result of abuse or neglect. Again, very young children were most at risk, with children less than 1-year old accounting for 41% of deaths, and children less than 6 comprising 85%. Perpetrators of child fatalities are primarily parents, and they tended to be younger than perpetrators of child abuse or neglect in general. Consistent characteristics of perpetrators from a variety of studies indicate that in addition to being young they tend to be high school dropouts, poor, depressed, have difficulty coping with stress, and often victims of violence themselves. Some experts believe the number of child fatalities as a result of child abuse or neglect is much higher than what is reported through official channels. In 1995, the U.S. Advisory Board on Child Abuse and Neglect estimated child deaths as a result of abuse and neglect to be about 2000 per year, and the National Center for Prosecution of Child Abuse puts the estimated number closer to 5000. The underreporting is believed to result in part from the fact that some child deaths are labeled as accidents, child homicides, and Sudden Infant Death Syndrome (SIDS). Another problem is the lack of a standard definition of child fatality from abuse or neglect used by social services agencies, medical professionals, researchers, and law enforcement officials. Some states are attempting to address these problems through the establishment of multi-disciplinary, multi-agency Child Fatality Review Teams that establish protocols to provide a coordinated approach to the investigation of child deaths. The teams may also try to obtain services for surviving family members, provide information to assist in the prosecution of perpetrators, develop recommendations to improve community response to child abuse and neglect, identify promising prevention efforts, and suggest improvements in training for front-line workers.

Since Kempe and his associates began to study the dynamics of child abuse and neglect in the 1960s, researchers and professionals from several disciplines have sought to understand why parents and other adults mistreat the children entrusted to their care. Numerous theories have been proposed, with the focus ranging from individual pathology to the parent–child relationship to the family environment to larger social or cultural conditions. Most often, however, some combination of psycho-social risk factors is present that places a given family in jeopardy. As might be expected, the larger the number and more severe the risk factors, the higher the risk for child maltreatment.

As mentioned earlier, neglect is consistently the largest category of child maltreatment, comprising over half of all confirmed cases. In spite of that fact, the dynamics involved in neglectful families have been the least studied. Because the vast majority of neglect cases come from families in the lower socioeconomic strata of society, neglect has traditionally been associated primarily with poverty. However, asserting that improvement in the standard of living of many families who neglect their children does not improve the neglect situation, Crittendon (1999) proposes that there may be a third variable responsible for both the neglect and the other frequent correlates of poverty (e.g., unemployment, unmarried, social isolation). She suggests that poor interpersonal social skills, particularly the inability to establish and maintain long-term, productive relationships with others, may be at the core of neglectful parenting. Interpersonal skills deficits may be because of faulty cognitive processing, lack of emotional attachment, or some combination of the two.

Perhaps the most frequently studied type of child maltreatment is physical abuse. Early studies of physical abuse focused primarily on the characteristics of the abuser, identifying such characteristics as inability to control anger, depression, low frustration tolerance, low self-esteem, rigidity, inability to empathize, use or abuse of alcohol and drugs, and health problems. As more families were studied, some researchers began to suggest that certain child characteristics also seemed to be correlated with abuse, such as exhibiting difficult behaviors, possessing physical or mental disabilities, and being very young. Characteristics of the parenting styles of abusive parents were identified as problematic as well, such as having unrealistic expectations of children, viewing the parenting role as stressful, holding negative perceptions of the child, and lacking adequate basic parenting skills. From a more sociological perspective, researchers have identified factors in the family as a whole that are important contributors to the likelihood that physical abuse will occur. These factors include other violence in the home (i.e., spouse abuse), the intergenerational practice of physical child abuse, marital problems, and few positive family interactions. Other sociological factors that affect the likelihood of physical child abuse occurring are poverty, especially dependence on public assistance; living with a single parent; unemployment, underemployment, or blue-collar employment of the adults in the household; situational stress; and social isolation. In addition, cultural approval of violence in general and corporal punishment in particular, and power differentials in the family and the larger society may be contributors as well (review of the literature in Barnett, Miller-Perrin, and Perrin, 1997; Crosson-Tower, 1999).

Similar to the research on physical abuse, the focus of early studies on child sexual abuse was on the characteristics of the perpetrator. Whereas recent data from the National Child Abuse and Neglect Reporting System show that approximately 75% of perpetrators of child sexual abuse are males, other researchers (Walters, 1975; Groth, 1979; Rush, 1980) have found males to be 95–98% of perpetrators. The difference may be as a result of an increase in the proportion of female perpetrators in recent years, to different study populations, and to different definitions of abuse employed by the researchers. Typically, though, there have been few women perpetrators of child sexual abuse, and those tend to be accomplices to males, isolated single parents, adolescent female babysitters, or women who have become romantically involved with adolescent males.

A review of the literature (see Barnett, Miller-Perrin, and Perrin, 1997; Crosson-Tower, 1999) identifies numerous risk factors associated with child sexual abuse. Children who are most vulnerable tend to be females who have not gone through puberty; children who are socially isolated, quiet, and passive; children who are emotionally needy and trusting; and children who generally appear unhappy and depressed. Perpetrators are likely to be male and to have been victims of physical or sexual abuse themselves as children. They tend to lack empathy and have poor impulse control, be somewhat passive, and use or abuse alcohol and other drugs. They generally lack appropriate hetero-social relationship skills and are sensitive about their sexual performance with adult women; thus, like the children they victimize, they often feel dependent, lonely, needy, and inadequate. In addition, perpetrators tend to be sexually attracted to children, they often fantasize about sexual relations with children, and they use various cognitive distortions to rationalize their behavior. Certain family dynamics may also increase the likelihood of child sexual abuse, particularly if both the victim and the perpetrator are living in the home. These factors include other violence in the family (i.e., spouse abuse) or parental conflict, generally unhappy family life, absence of biological father and presence of a nonrelated adult male, and a poor parent–child relationship. In addition, a mother who has less than a high-school education, who works outside the home, who is disabled or otherwise ill, and who has a history of sexual abuse herself may also place a child at higher risk for sexual abuse. A sociological perspective adds sociocultural factors that may play a part as well, such as patriarchal households; a lack of development of empathy in males; socializing males to be stoic; socializing men to be attracted to women who are younger, smaller, and more vulnerable than they are; social sanctioning of sexual relations between adults and children; the objectification of sex partners; and the proliferation of child pornography. In addition, there is a lack of attention to children's sexual development and the tendency to sexualize emotional needs.

As emotional or psychological abuse is very difficult to define and identify, there is little research on that type of child maltreatment apart from other types of abuse or neglect. A few studies have found, though, that parents who psychologically abuse their children tend to have more psycho-social problems themselves, difficulty with interpersonal relationships, poor coping skills, a lack of social support networks, and inadequate child management skills (Perberton and Benady, 1973; Hickox and Furnell, 1989).

The information presented thus far, is based on research conducted primarily in the U.S. It is important, however, to recognize that there are differences in the extent and dynamics of child maltreatment among racial, ethnic, or cultural groups within the United States as well as between the United States and other countries and cultures. Nevertheless, attempts to clearly define these differences are limited by a lack of research in some cases, and a lack of comparability of research in others. For example, several industrialized countries (e.g., the U.K., Australia, Canada, Sweden, Finland) have conducted research on child maltreatment, but these studies often use different samples, data-collection methods, operational definitions of abuse and neglect, and reporting categories. On the other hand, many less developed countries or cultures have done little or no research on child maltreatment, and what we know about their child-rearing practices often comes more from anthropological studies (e.g., Korbin, 1981) and anecdotal reports. Unlike other industrialized countries that share some general concepts about what constitutes child maltreatment, less developed countries or cultures may not identify what we would consider child maltreatment as such (e.g., female genital mutilation, footbinding, female infanticide), or what is identified as abuse in those settings may be behaviors that we consider normal and even preferable for rearing healthy children (e.g., toilet training, having young children sleep alone). Even within the same country or culture, definitions of child maltreatment may vary over time, and they may reflect child-rearing practices that were once deemed functional for survival in that cultural context but have outlived their usefulness.

In examining what research has been done in other countries or cultures, one common theme that emerges is the difficulty in separating the effects of ethnicity and poverty on parent–child relations, as abuse or neglect seems to be more prevalent among lower socioeconomic groups, which are often disproportionately comprised of the minority group(s) in a country or culture. Another common factor is the negative effect of stress, whether the source is personal, social, or imbedded in the larger community (e.g., economic, rapid social change, traumatic event) (Garbarino and Ebata, 1983). Nevertheless, there do appear to be some cultural or ethnic differences in the extent and dynamics of child abuse or neglect. Based on a cross-cultural study, Korbin (1981) identified four main factors that seem to affect the incidence of child maltreatment: the cultural value of children, beliefs about special categories of children (handicapped, illegitimate, etc.), beliefs about age-appropriate abilities and developmental levels, and the extent of social support for child rearing among family and community.

Given the difficulty in reaching common definitions and measures of child abuse and neglect across countries and cultures, in an effort to establish some means of comparison UNICEF (2003) recently conducted a study of only child deaths attributable to physical child abuse and neglect, as reported to the World Health Organization, among the 30 industrialized countries who are members of the Organisation for Economic Co-operation and Development. The researchers found that approximately 3500 children under the age of 15 die each year from physical abuse and neglect in the industrialized world. According to their calculations, the three countries with the highest rates of child deaths as a result of maltreatment are Portugal, Mexico, and the U.S., in that order, and they have rates 10–15 times higher than the average, with 3.7, 3.0, and 2.4 deaths per 100,000 children. Belgium, the Czech Republic, New Zealand, Hungary, and France have rates from four to six times higher than the average, at 1.1–1.3 per 100,000, whereas Spain, Greece, Italy, Ireland, and Norway have very low rates, at fewer than 0.2 per 100,000. As with child deaths as a result of maltreatment in the United States, the risk of death from maltreatment worldwide is three times greater for children from birth to one than for those from one to four, and the group from one to four has twice the risk of the group from five to fourteen.

The UNICEF study emphasizes the complexity of trying to obtain comparable data for child abuse or neglect beyond the narrow category of death and the fact that no one really knows the true extent of child maltreatment in the world. For example, officials in Australia say that substantiated cases of physical abuse are 150 times the level of abuse-related deaths and estimate that the ratio would rise to about 600:1 if neglect, sexual abuse, and emotional abuse were included. French officials say that there are approximately 300 substantiated cases of child abuse and neglect for every abuse-related death, whereas Canadian officials estimate the ratio in their country to be more than 1000:1. A survey of 3000 18–24 year olds conducted by the National Society for the Prevention of Cruelty to Children in the U.K. found that 7% reported that they had suffered serious physical abuse, and about 25% reported that they had suffered severe physical abuse at the hands of their parents, but the definitions of abuse were purposefully subjective. A self-report study in Egypt found that 37% of children reported being beaten or tied up by their parents, with 26% claiming injuries, such as fractures, loss of consciousness, or permanent disability. An Ethiopian study found that 21% of urban schoolchildren and 64% of rural schoolchildren reported that they had received bruises and swelling as a result of parental punishment.

Despite the variation in definitions and measures, there do appear to be commonalities in factors associated with child maltreatment reported by all countries. The most commonly occurring factors are these: lower socioeconomic class and minority race or ethnicity, single parenthood, unemployment, domestic violence, family breakdown, child not living with biological parents, social isolation, child ill-health or disability, parental or caregiver mental ill-health, alcohol or drug abuse, teen parenthood, low educational level of parent or caregiver, and parents who were abused themselves as children. Across countries poverty and stress, along with alcohol or drug abuse, appeared to be the factors most closely and most consistently associated with high levels of child abuse and neglect. The UNICEF study points out that there tends to be an association between high levels of child abuse and cultures with a high level of acceptance and use of physical punishment, and that seven countries so far—Austria, Denmark, Finland, Germany, Iceland, Norway, and Sweden—have passed laws explicitly prohibiting the physical punishment of children.

In summary, child abuse and neglect is a complex phenomenon. The causes and correlates of child maltreatment cross many domains, including individual, interpersonal, familial, social, and cultural factors. Further, the negative consequences affect not only the individuals involved, but also societies and the global community as a whole. Additional research needs to be conducted to determine effective interventions so that future generations of children around the world may be spared from physical, sexual, and psychological trauma.

SANDRA S. STONE

References and Further Reading

Barnett, O.W., Miller-Perrin, C.L., and Perrin, R.D., *Family Violence across the Lifespan: An Introduction*, Thousand Oaks, CA: Sage Publications, 1997.

Briere, J., Berliner, L., Bulkley, J.A., Jenny, C., and Reid, T., Eds., *The APSAC Handbook on Child Maltreatment*, Chicago, IL: American Professional Society on the Abuse of Children, 1996.

Crittendon, P.M., Child neglect: Causes and contributors, in *Neglected Children: Research, Practice, and Policy*, Dubowitz, H., Ed., Thousand Oaks, CA: Sage Publications, 1999.

Crosson-Tower, C., *Understanding Child Abuse and Neglect*, 4th ed., Boston, MA: Allyn and Bacon, 1999.

Garbarino, J. and Ebata, A., The significance of ethnic and cultural differences in child maltreatment, *Journal of Marriage and the Family* November (1983): 773–783.

Groth, A.N., *Men Who Rape*, New York, NY: Plenum Press, 1979.

Hickox, A. and Furnell, J.R.G., Psychosocial and background factors in emotional abuse of children, *Child: Care, Health and Development* 15 (1989): 227–240.

Kantor, G.K. and Jasinskie, J., Eds., *Out of the Darkness: Contemporary Perspectives on Family Violence*, Thousand Oaks, CA: Sage Publications, 1997.

Kempe, H., Silverman, F., Steele, B., Droegemueller, W., and Silver, H., The battered-child syndrome, *Journal of the American Medical Association* 181 (1962): 17–24.

Korbin, J.E., Ed., *Child Abuse and Neglect: Cross-Cultural Perspectives*, Berkeley, CA: University of California Press, 1981.

Parton, N., *The Politics of Child Abuse*, London, UK: Macmillan, 1985.

Pemberton, D.A. and Benady, D.R., Consciously rejected children, *British Journal of Psychiatry* 123 (1973): 575–578.

Rush, F., *The Best Kept Secret*, New York, NY: McGraw-Hill, 1980.

UNICEF, A League Table of Child Maltreatment Deaths in Rich Nations, *Innocenti Report Card* no. 5, Florence, Italy: UNICEF Innocenti Research Center, September 2003.

U.S. Department of Health and Human Services, *Child Maltreatment 2001: Reports from the States to the National Child Abuse and Neglect Data System*, Washington, DC: U.S. Government Printing Office, 2001. Available at http://nccanch.acf.hhs.gov.

U.S. Advisory Board on Child Abuse and Neglect, *A Nation's Shame: Fatal Child Abuse and Neglect in the United States*, Washington, DC: Department of Health and Human Services, 1995.

Walters, D., *Physical and Sexual Abuse of Children*, Bloomington, IL: Indiana Unversity Press, 1975.

Williams, G., Child protection: A journey into history, *Journal of Clinical Child Psychology* 12 (1983): 236–243.

See also **Child Abuse: Prevention and Treatment; Child Molestation**

Child Abuse: Prevention and Treatment

Definitions and Types of Abuse

Child abuse is a malady found in all sectors of society. Males and females of all ages, races, family incomes, and from all different areas are possible victims of child abuse. Child abuse and neglect have been present in society throughout history. Infanticide, ritual killings, maiming, and cruel punishments have all been documented from the past. Historically in American society, children were viewed differently from how they are today and as a result they were often victims of abuse. Parents did not become as involved emotionally with their children and children were not given exclusive protection under American law. Another factor that influenced child abuse was religion. Punishments, such as beatings, were seen as an appropriate technique of discipline, even though today this would be considered child abuse. The first efforts to oppose child abuse took place as early as 1655. By the early 1800s, public officials were legally sanctioned to take children from homes where parents were abusive or negligent.

Today, every state has put forth laws to ensure reports of child abuse. There are many definitions of child abuse, and state laws vary on what is considered in this crime. The following is a general definition taken from the Model Child Protective Services Act:

> An "abused or neglected child" is one whose physical or mental health or welfare is harmed or threatened with harm by acts of omission or commission on the part of his or her parent or other persons responsible for the child's welfare.

Types and forms of child abuse include sexual abuse, physical abuse, psychological abuse, emotional neglect, and other forms of abuse. Thousands of children annually are victims of child abuse and neglect, and several studies present data on the extent of this problem. According to the National Center for Child Abuse and Neglect, four in 1000 children are physically assaulted in the U.S. every year, and an estimated 652,000 children were confirmed to have been abused and neglected each year. Eighty-four percent of these were moderately or severely wounded or impaired.

The impact of child abuse comes in a variety of ways. Physical abuse may influence the child's feelings about him or herself, view of other people, and behavior toward others. There may also be physical effects of the abuse, such as injury to the brain, limbs, eyes, ears, and vital organs. Damage resulting from abuse could lead to mental retardation, blindness, deafness, or delayed development. Children that have been abused may have low self-concept and slow thinking. They are often more aggressive, anxious, and antisocial and language and motor skills could possibly be delayed.

Just as the effects of child abuse vary, so do causes of child abuse. Rigorous emotional strain, psychopathology, or family stress could be a cause of child abuse. Also, the family's history of violence may lead to child abuse. Problems as a result of poverty, unemployment, marital stress, and having little social communication could also be causes. Parents' attitudes and views of children could also be factors. Parents who do not favor children may take their frustration of having unwanted offspring out on the child.

One of the most common topics in child abuse is sexual abuse. Sexually abused children have become the focus of public concern. According to the American Humane Association, the actual scope of the problem is not known because thousands of cases never get reported. An estimated 10–25% of all preadolescent females had some sexual contact with adults, and 19% of females were sexually abused before the age of 12 by someone at least 5 years older. Sexual abuse does not occur to females only. It is estimated that 9% of males were sexually abused before the age of 12 by a person at least five years older.

Sexual abuse may have some of the most traumatic effects on children and extend on into adulthood. A sexually abused child may show many physical symptoms and become socially isolated. As an adult, the person may abandon sexual activity or experience sexual problems.

Prevention and Treatment

Prevention of child abuse requires action on the part of many groups. Community and family members are responsible for aiding in the prevention of child abuse. Educating the community to stop child abuse before it occurs lays the groundwork for prevention of child abuse. Community education and other classes increase awareness of abuse and its prevention, improve parenting skills, and teach personal safety skills to children. Making the community aware of the signs of child abuse and individuals watching for those signs could prevent it from occurring again. Family support services usually offer prevention programs for families with significant needs to improve situations linked with child abuse. It is also important to strengthen family relationships and parenting skills. Parent support groups, educational programs, and activities for children and parents that encourage positive communication and problem solving within the family are important in child abuse prevention. Teaching youth how to protect themselves from abuse and what to do if an incident occurs is vital in preventing abuse. In general, youth are afraid to report abuse. By educating youth, it is possible that the fear will be taken away and youth will be more apt to report any act.

Treatment of children who have been abused is a lengthy and complex process. Treatment usually involves several professionals from different agencies; typically including a physician who is trained to assess and treat the abused child, a mental health specialist, a child-protective services worker, the police, and the prosecuting attorney. All of these individuals working together is vital to the success of the treatment process. A physical examination is important when there is evidence of physical or sexual abuse. The examination may contain important information and cause the court to become involved. Psychological considerations are also important. It is traumatic to a child when he or she is removed from parents, siblings, friends, and school. The child should be kept at home if possible to safeguard the psychological connections and continue relationships. It is crucial to evaluate the psychological impact on the child. This is done by determining the depth of the abuse and assessing the impact on the child.

Therapy is a common treatment for child abuse. Individual therapy, group therapy, and family therapy are all used in child abuse treatments. Therapy should help the child put feelings and needs into words, control impulsive actions by channeling the aggression into another activity, improve interpersonal relationships with family and peer groups, and treat children who show low self-esteem, depression, aggressiveness, and severe management or behavior problems. Having the child respond to stories with certain themes, having the child wish for anything he or she wants, and having the child draw freely are all ways to both assess and treat an abused child. A frequent technique used by therapists includes anatomical dolls in sexual abuse cases. The dolls are used to extract information about the abuse from the child. The child does not realize what he or she is telling, so the child is not afraid and information about the abuse is received.

In cases of both physical and emotional abuse, the child may be taken out of the home. This alleviates the abuse, but treatment may take years. The degree of abuse, degree of emotional distress, parents' mental state, family situation, and parents' willingness to cooperate are all considerations when deciding whether to remove a child from the home. Taking the child from the home may be beneficial to the child. The child no longer lives in fear, can be himself or herself, and can focus on school and friends. Usually, when children are removed from the home and placed in foster care or an institution, the child receives therapy.

It is common to see one who has been abused as a child to carry on the effects into adulthood. Many adults who were abused as children never spoke of it and they have carried it with them since childhood. Therapists who work with adults who were abused as children have one goal and that is to repair the client's self-image. Many adults who were abused as children are reluctant to go for therapy, and therapy may be one of the first intimate relationships that they have. Personal questions are asked and a trust must be built between the client and therapist for therapy to be successful. When the bond is formed, the goal is to challenge the client's perceptions and beliefs he or she already has and to find out how they affect present performance in daily life. The client may have emotionally not matured because the circumstances needed for development were not given at the appropriate developmental stages. Blame taken by clients is a big issue. Clients need to realize that they are not at fault for the abuse and that they should not judge themselves when they attain adulthood. When the adult client has a positive self-concept, increased self-esteem, does not see dependency as a weakness, tolerates pain, has gone through grief, expresses feelings, and manages or ceases depression the client is making great progress in therapy.

Group therapy can be significant in treating adults who have been abused as children. Group therapy gives an opportunity to interact with others, to get positive feedback, to experiment with issues of safety and trust, and to meet and socialize with others who have gone through similar experiences. Individual therapy should be completed before group therapy so the individual will be able to discuss past abuse without being devastated. In group therapy, goals are usually set by the group itself. It is important that all group members get equal time to speak and that no one feels uncomfortable. One technique often used in group therapy is having the members draw themselves. Group members give feedback on the drawings and this gives the member an idea of how others view him or her. Listing strengths and weaknesses also help group members to acknowledge their strengths and see the value of themselves as being abused as a child usually damages self-concept. Along with bringing childhood pictures and keeping a journal, group therapy seeks to have the clients build self-esteem and connect with others like them.

Not only do the abused children need treatment, but the abusing adults do too. In family abuse cases, primarily, a family evaluation must take place to determine if the family is treatable. If the case involves intense physical or sexual abuse, it is often beneficial to have the perpetrator hospitalized or leave home for 3 or 4 weeks so that an evaluation and treatment process can be completed. Parents that abuse their children need to understand that anger is a feeling and emotion, whereas abuse is a behavior. They need to realize that angry feelings are normal and everyone gets mad and upset, but abuse is not the way to express anger. Parents must recognize their feelings so that they can handle and control it instead of exploding. Taking a time-out to gather thoughts and control, communicating feelings to the child, stopping the use of alcohol, and reducing stress are all ways to prevent and treat abuse by a parent.

There are many national programs that aim to combat child abuse. Though not all cases of child abuse are reported, it is up to adults in the community to be aware and report any suspicions of abuse. The treatment of not only abused children and adults who were abused as a child is fundamental, but also treatment of the abusive adult is critical in stopping child abuse.

JACQUELINE DAVIS

References and Further Reading

Briere, J.N. 1992. *Child Abuse Trauma.* Newbury Park, CA: Sage Publications, Inc.

Gil, E. 1988. *Treatment of Adult Survivors.* Walnut Creek, CA: Launch Press.

Giovannoni, J.M. 1989. Definitional issues in child maltreatment. Cicchetti, D. and Carlson, V. *Child Maltreatment: Theory and Research on the Causes and Consequences of Child Abuse and Neglect.* New York, NY: Cambridge University Press.

MacKinnon, L.K. 1998. *Trust and Betrayal in the Treatment of Child Abuse.* New York, NY: The Guilford Press.

Veltkamp, L.J. and Miller. T.W. 1994. *Clinical Handbook of Child Abuse and Neglect.* Madison, CT: International Universities Press, Inc.

Webb, L.P. and Leehan. J. 1996. *Group Treatment for Adult Survivors of Abuse.* Thousand Oaks, CA: Sage Publications, Inc.

Wiehe, V.R. 1996. *Working with Child Abuse and Neglect.* Thousand Oaks, CA: Sage Publications, Inc.

See also **Child Abuse: Extent and Correlates; Child Abuse: The Law; Child Molestation**

Child Abuse: Law

Child abuse is not a recent phenomenon. Children have been the victims of abuse by their parents, caretakers, or others since the beginning of recorded history. Child abuse knows no absolute boundaries of race, socioeconomic status, or culture. Historically, children had no legal rights. Infants were particularly vulnerable to abuse. Early records document the legal and moral acceptance of infanticide. In Egypt, the Pharaoh ordered the death of all male children when Moses was born. Similarly, King Herod called for infanticide when Jesus was born. Children who were born illegitimate, of the female gender, with birth defects, or came from poor families were often killed by their parent or by someone in the village. Greeks believed that handicapped children could pass on their deficits to their offspring and should not be allowed to live. Indeed, the most celebrated philosophers of that time, Plato and Aristotle, strongly supported and recommended enacting laws prohibiting defective children to live.

Infanticide was not the only method of abuse practiced by early civilizations. During the middle ages, families often mutilated or severed limbs from children to make them more effective beggars. Children were also brutalized during the Industrial Revolution. They were forced to work in mills, orphanages, or workhouses under an apprenticeship system that legally indentured children to their masters for 7 years. In England, many scholars noted the particularly vile situation the chimney sweeps faced. William Blake, a well-known physician and humanitarian, wrote "these waifs were purposefully kept small and thin so that they could clamber up narrow, soot-clogged flutes." Yet, societies around the world continued to embrace harsh child labor policies. In fact, as late as 1866, a Massachusetts legislative report noted that child labor was an economic boom to society.

Eight years later in 1874, an infamous case in New York City involving 8-year-old Mary Ellen Wilson made headline news. Mary Ellen was being abused and neglected (starved) by her adoptive parents. Her case was reported by a concerned humanitarian to the local magistrate. However, there were no laws prohibiting parents from abusing their children, only laws that made it illegal for people to abuse their animals. The abuse of animals statute was used to address Mary Ellen's tenuous situation. Her adoptive mother was sent to jail and the Society for the Prevention of Cruelty to Children was formed in 1875.

Despite the outcry that Mary Ellen's case brought, it would be decades before the U.S. and other countries acknowledged the brutality of these practices and afforded legal protections to children, let alone bestowing legal rights to children. Children generally were considered property and valued (or devalued) depending on the parent's property rights and society's perception of their worth.

The creation of the idea of child abuse is largely credited to C. Henry Kempe, a physician who studied child abuse and described the concept *battered child syndrome.* Kempe and his associates (1962) provided clinical case histories to point out that many children were injured or even died as a result of physical abuse. They also pointed out that neglect was often present in abuse cases. Thus, the battered child syndrome defined the specific features of abuse cases that physicians could apply when conducting physical and radiological examinations of children. Interestingly, Kempe noted that physicians were reluctant to assume the role of investigator and prosecutor despite overwhelming evidence of abuse. Kempe's work was pivotal in establishing the first mandatory reporting laws.

Today all states in the U.S. have mandatory reporting laws and reporting agencies, usually called Child Protective Services. There are four common domains of these reporting laws: (1) the definition of what constitutes abuse, (2) the level of certainty the reporter must have, (3) legal sanctions for those who fail to report, and (4) the type of legal immunity from civil and criminal liability for those who act in "good faith." Beyond this, states vary dramatically in terms of legal definitions of abuse and imposing legal sanctions.

States have also expanded the legal duty of reporting abuse cases to include other professionals who come into regular contact with children. Some states even require the average citizen to report abuse (there are about 40 different professionals specifically named in mandatory reporting laws across the U.S.). States vary in who they define must report child abuse.

The term "abuse" generally can be divided into four legal categories: First, physical abuse denotes that a child has suffered injury that did not result from accidental means. Second, sexual abuse involves exploitation of the child through some form of sexual activity. Both physical abuse and sexual abuse laws provide for narrow definitions and physical symptoms coupled with specific circumstances and physical and sexual intent.

Third, neglect, the most common form and most frequently reported type of abuse, is the failure to provide the child with supervision, and physical, medical, and educational needs along with supervision.

Fourth, emotional neglect is now recognized by some states as an act that inflicts psychological harm to the child. Neglect and emotional abuse are ambiguous, providing broad and vague definitions as well as circumstances.

Mandatory reporting laws have been used as an explanation for the rising number of child abuse victims. Many legal and research scholars suggest that other variables can explain this causal connection: public awareness and accountability and society's change in attitude and perception regarding child protection. Currently, the U.S. Department of Health and Human Services (1998) estimates that just over 900,000 children are victims of abuse and neglect. About one half are cases of neglect, one quarter include physical abuse, and about one in seven involve sexual abuse. It is also estimated that 2.8 million children are currently at-risk for becoming victims of some form of abuse. Tremendous strides have been made in addressing child abuse, yet it is clear that it continues to be a serious social problem.

LANETTE P. DALLEY

References and Further Reading

Brenner, R.H., *Children and Youth in America*, Vols. 1–3. Cambridge, MA: Harvard University Press.

Child Abuse Prevention and Treatment Act of 1974, 42 U.S.C.S sec. 5101–5115 (1979, Cum. Supp. 1988).

Helfer, R.E. and Kemp, R.S., *The Battered Child*, 4th ed. Chicago, IL: The University of Chicago Press, 1987.

Kempe, C.H., Silverman, F.N., Steele, B.F., Droegemueller, W., and Silver, H.K., The battered child syndrome, *Journal of the American Medical Association*, 181 (1962) 105–112.

Levine, A. and Levine, M., *Helping Children: A Social History*, New York, NY: Oxford University Press.

Meriwether, M.H., Child Abuse Reporting Laws: Time for a Change. *Family Law Quarterly*, 20, (1986) 141–171.

National Center on Child Abuse and Neglect, *Child Abuse and Neglect: State Reporting Laws*, Washington, DC: Clearinghouse on Child Abuse and Neglect Information, 1979–1999.

U.S. Department of Health and Human Services, *Administration for Children and Families Report*, 2000.

Wallace, H., *Family Violence*, 2nd ed. Boston, MA: Allyn and Bacon, 1999

Kalichman, S.C., *Mandated Reporting of Suspected Child Abuse Ethics, Law and Policy*, Washington, DC: American Psychological Association 1993.

See also **Child Abuse: Extent and Correlates; Child Abuse: Prevention and Treatment; Child Molestation**

Child Molestation

Child molestation covers a wide range of acts that cause considerable psychological harm to children. Throughout the world, child molestation generally refers to conduct where adolescents or adults seek sexual arousal and obtain sexual arousal from interactions with children or adolescents interact with prepubescent children. This conduct covers fondling, anal, oral, or vaginal penetration, exposing one's private parts to children, having children touch or kiss one's private parts, or touching children's other body parts (e.g., feet) for sexual arousal. Laws against child molestation require the proof that the touching was for sexual gratification.

It is very difficult to obtain any accurate estimate of the prevalence of child molestation. First, many cases are never reported or are reported long after the incident. More than half of the victims in a national U.S. sample waited 5 years before disclosing that they had been victims of child molestation and typically confiding only in friends. One quarter had never told anyone about the victimization. A comparison of information from social services with official arrest records indicated that there were 2.4 reoffenses based on social service records for each arrest noted (Marshall and Barbaree, 1988). Studies of sex offenders who are guaranteed anonymity reveal that many sex offenders report engaging in multiple undetected acts of fondling, penetration, and exhibitionism toward children. In a 1987 study (Abel et al.), 651 sex offenders, who were guaranteed anonymity, admitted to 291,737 sex acts against 195,407 victims under the age of 18; on the average, each offender committed 75 crimes that were not detected. In Matabeleland, Zimbabwe, half of the sexual abuse of children is detected through sexually transmitted diseases, including HIV. Researchers agree that multiple sources are needed to provide the most accurate measure of child sex abuse and recidivism among child molesters.

Children and teenagers are more at risk of sexual assaults and abuse than are adults. In the U.S., two thirds of all prisoners who were convicted of rape or sexual assault had offended against a child victim, and more than two thirds of sexual assaults reported to the police involved minors under the age of 18. Based on survey data, children compared to adults have experienced (but not disclosed to authorities) a much higher rate of sexual abuse. Similar distributions are found in other countries. In the Netherlands, 40% of the female children under age 16 reported sexual abuse in a survey. In Belgium, 50% of all females and 80% of all males that are sexually assaulted are minors. In Matabeleland, Zimbabwe, child sexual abuse accounts for 40–60% of the rape cases brought to the attention of the court.

Very young children also are frequently victims. In the U.S., 14% of all victims are under age 6, and 34% were between 6 and 11 years old. Children are about half of the victims of forcible sexual assaults and the majority of victims of forcible fondling, sodomy, and sexual assault with an object. Girls also are at more risk of child sexual abuse, though a significant percentage of boys also experience such abuse. Child sexual abuse occurs in every socioeconomic level and ethnic group.

In the U.S., most sexual assaults known to the police occur in residences with only 30% occurring in other places. Teenagers are more likely to be sexually assaulted outside of a residence. Weapons are rarely used in sexual assaults against children, only 2% involved a gun and 6% involved a knife or club. Children are most likely to be victimized around mealtimes or in the mid-afternoon when schools are dismissing students.

The characteristics of child molesters are confined to those who have been reported to the authorities, and the studies primarily are conducted in the U.S., England, Canada, Australia, and European countries. Child molesters represent a very diverse group of individuals. Adolescents commit about one quarter of all child molestation cases, and in the U.S. accounted for 47% of molestation victims under the age of 6. Of the child molestation cases known to the police, acquaintances are responsible for 60% of the offenses, family members offended in 27% of the cases, and strangers in 13% of the cases in the U.S. Strangers are responsible for only 3% of the assaults against children younger than 6 and are most likely to victimize children between the ages of 12 to 17. Most (96%) child molesters are male, with women offenders more likely to assault children under the age of 6. Other countries such as Africa, Canada, the Netherlands, Germany, and England report that the majority of offenders victimized acquaintances and family members, and only a small percent victimized strangers.

Overall child molesters compared to nonoffenders are lonelier, are less assertive, and have lower self-esteem and report an inability to cope with negative feelings. Most child molesters deny the harm that they cause their victims and have an inability to take the perspective of their victims. Child molesters also often attribute some of the blame for the offense on their victim (i.e., they claim the child initiated or wanted the contact). Nonincestuous child molesters have more sexual arousal toward children than toward adults. Only a small proportion of child molesters, however, meet the criteria of being diagnosed as pedophiles. Pedophiles clinically are persons who are only sexually attracted to prepubescent children and have had sexual urges, fantasies, and behaviors toward children for at least 6 months. Some studies have attempted to isolate different groups within this offender population, specifically comparing incest offenders and molesters of children outside of the family.

Studies have found that child molesters can be classified into three categories based on psychological profiles, including those who are (1) underdeveloped sexually and emotionally, (2) psychiatrically disturbed, and (3) characterologically disturbed. Those who are underdeveloped sexually and emotionally have low self-esteem, are over-controlled, and have anxiety about their sexual adeptness and sexual identity. Members of the psychiatrically disturbed group have at least one psychiatric disorder, and those in the characterologically disturbed group have significant personality problems. Personality problems include psychopathic deviants (who are self-centered, manipulative, remorseless, and insensitive toward others) and those with passive aggressive personalities (who are immature, hostile, and resentful about dependence upon other people). Other schemes exist for classifying child molesters, but no one classification system accounts for all the diversity within the child molester population.

Based on data from the FBI National Incident-Based Reporting System in the U.S. from 1991 to 1996, the perpetrator was arrested in 27% of all sexual assault victimizations reported to the police. Many sexual assaults and abuses against children are not criminally prosecuted; it is estimated that prosecutors do not pursue criminal charges in one quarter to one half of the cases reported to the police in the U.S. In Germany, less than 15% of the sexual abuse/assault cases reach a conviction. Weak evidence is often the reason that the case is not prosecuted. Children may change their stories, there may be no corroborating evidence, and it can be difficult to convince juries that very young children are being truthful. Sexual assaults of young children are the least likely to result in arrest. In one sample of prepubescent children, doctors found forensic evidence in only 25% of the cases of sexually abused children examined within 44 hours of the assault. Most of the evidence was found on the child's clothing. Furthermore, swabbing the body for forensic evidence is fruitless after 24 hours past the assault. In addition to the strength of the evidence, prosecutors may consider the prior criminal history of the offender, the duration of the abuse, the use of force, and the child's relationship to the perpetrator in the decision to file charges.

Prosecutorial decisions are important because offenders who are charged are typically found guilty. Most defendants charged with child molestation (about 84%) plead guilty; if the case goes to trial, there is about a 64% chance of a guilty verdict. Some studies have looked at how the criminal justice system handles accused child molesters compared to those accused of nonsexual crimes. These two groups receive very similar outcomes. Both groups have similar levels of plea bargaining, with more than half of the accused perpetrators given a reduced charge in exchange for a guilty plea. The chance of acquittal for cases that go to trial also is similar to the chance of acquittal in other felony cases.

A recent study compared crime, conviction, and incarceration rates of sex offenders in England and the U.S. (Langan and Farrington, 1998). The U.S. has a three-time higher rate of reporting sexual assaults to the police compared to England. Sex offenders are more likely to be incarcerated and receive longer prison sentences in the U.S. than in England. About three quarters of convicted child sex offenders receive some incarceration time, with about 38% incarcerated for over 1 year. The offender's prior criminal history and number of victims are the best predictors of the amount of time served. Victim characteristics, including relationship to the offender, are not related to the severity of the sentence. Between 25% and 64% of child molesters receive a probation sentence with conditions jurisdictions in the U.S., Canada, and England. Many jurisdictions in the U.S. and Canada now have intensive sex offender probation programs to provide closer supervision of sex offenders in the community. This includes visits and searches of their home and mandates for sex offenders to attend group therapy while they serve their probation sentence. Some jurisdictions, such as the state of Arizona, have implemented lifetime probation sentences for convicted sex offenders.

Public pressure to increase confinement for sex offenders directly influenced the creation of punitive policies toward sex offenders in New Zealand, Australia, England, the U.S., and Canada. Lawmakers in these countries have taken radical measures to protect the public from child molesters. The U.S. and England have implemented sex offender registration laws that require sex offenders convicted of felonies to register their home address with their local police station. Laws also provide for the arrest of sex offenders found on or near school grounds. Several countries have passed laws requiring sex offenders released on parole to take sex-drive-reducing medication as a condition of parole. The U.S., England, Canada, and Australia have extremely long prison-terms for offenders convicted as "sexual predators," and some states in the U.S. also allow for the civil confinement of dangerous and mentally ill sexual predators after the completion of their prison term. All of these laws reflect the view that child molesters are an extremely dangerous group who must be managed in order to protect the children of society.

Criminal justice professionals and the public are concerned about the possibility that child molesters will commit additional offenses while they live in the community. The rate of committing new offenses (recidivism) varies depending on the measure used (e.g., self-reported crimes, new arrests, or new convictions), the amount of time that has expired since the offender's last arrest, and the sample of offenders (e.g., child molesters on probation, those released from prison, or those released from mental institutions). Based on a review of studies conducted primarily in Australia, the U.S., Canada, and England, recidivism among child molesters was 12.2% for sexual offenses, 9.9% for violent nonsexual offenses, and 36.9% for other crimes. However, studies that use long follow-up periods (25 years or more) show that recidivism rates exceed 50% for child molesters, suggesting that these offenders are at risk of offending throughout their lives.

Which child molesters are at a higher risk of committing another sex crime? The most stable predictor of recidivism is the degree to molesters are sexually aroused only by children (to the exclusion of adults), based on research conducted primarily in Australia, the U.S., Canada, and England. Pedophiles, as the media and public suspect, are the most dangerous offenders. Other risk factors for committing a new sex crime are the number of different types of sexual perversions (paraphilias) possesses by the offender and the number of the offender's prior arrests for sex crimes. Child molesters who are psychopathic deviants are at a high risk of committing a new sex crime. Unfortunately, most probation and parole departments do not have information on child molesters' personality profiles or objective sexual preferences. There have been several crude risk assessment scales developed in Canada, England, and the U.S. to provide rough indicators of the likelihood of reoffending. These scales predict recidivism through characteristics related to the offense and the offender's known prior criminal history. Offense characteristics that indicate a higher risk for reoffending include the victimization of males and strangers, noncontact sex offenses (i.e., exhibitionism or voyeurism), and the use of violence. Criminal history characteristics that indicate a higher risk for offending include prior convictions for sexual offenses and nonsexual violence crimes. In addition, these scales assign a higher risk to offenders who never married and those between the ages of 18 and 25.

One problem with risk assessment scales is that they typically measure only variables that cannot change. What are some characteristics that probation officers and therapists can target to lower the risk of reoffense? The few studies that have addressed this question suggest that recidivists (compared to nonrecidivists) have less ability to manage their anger, have attitudes tolerant of sexual offending, have ready access to victims, and have antisocial lifestyles. In addition, they are uninterested in treatment and attempt to deceive probation officers, and often miss scheduled appointments. Research shows a small but significant reduction in the risk of committing a new sex crime if offenders sentenced to serve community-based sentences successfully complete cognitive-behavioral sex offender group therapy (this therapy attempts to stop risky behaviors and cognitive distortions before the cycle of sexual assault leads to a new offense). It is unclear whether prison-based treatment programs for child molesters reduce recidivism.

A description of sex offender treatment is available in many countries including Belgium, Czech Republic, England, Germany, the Netherlands, and North America, and all of these countries use a form of cognitive-behavioral group therapy with supplemental behavioral or biochemical treatment as needed. Which child molesters are more likely to benefit from and complete treatment? Child molesters have very high dropout rates in treatment programs, especially when they are not required to attend treatment as a condition of probation or parole. Furthermore, studies indicate that child molesters with psychopathic deviant personality styles may be very good at fooling therapists; it appears that they learn new ways to approach child victims and to manipulate and deceive people in group therapy programs. Psychopathic deviants are less likely to complete treatment than are other sex offenders; even if they complete treatment, they are more likely to commit a subsequent offense. Child molesters who victimized both their own children and children outside their family and both boys and girls are less likely to complete treatment. Sex offenders with a substance abuse disorder and a history of non-violent criminal offending are more likely to graduate from treatment programs. One study also indicates that married offenders with high reading abilities are likely to complete treatment successfully. Cognitive-behavioral therapy requires an ability to read and to communicate clearly as well as an ability to understand criminal motivations and risky behaviors. Other treatments include behavioral therapies to reduce inappropriate sexual arousal to children and hormonal and drug treatments to reduce sex drive. The three most common drugs used for the reduction of deviant sexual behavior are cyproterone acetate (which is used in Canada, England, and European countries, but not approved in the U.S.), Provera (used in 70 countries, but not approved in the U.S.) and medroxyprogesterone acetate (which is used in the U.S., Canada, England, and European countries). In recent years, serotonin reuptake inhibitor antidepressants have been used to lower sex offenders' deviant sexual urges and fantasies, and have fewer side effects than the hormonal or antiandrogens drugs. Child molesters generally are reluctant to remain on hormonal drug therapy, which may explain why some therapists try antidepressants as a way to lower deviant sexual urges.

Do victims of child molestation suffer from psychological and interpersonal adjustment problems in later life? Several studies show that child sexual abuse victims have higher rates of depression, lower self-esteem, and other psychological adjustment problems than nonvictims. On the other hand, child sexual abuse accounts for only a small amount of the variation in levels of depression, self-esteem problems, and other psychological symptoms. The relationship between child sexual abuse and various psychological problems persists even after controlling for such factors as family stability, alcohol and drug abuse by parents, and the quality of the relationship with peers and teachers.

What conditions or characteristics determine the effects of child sexual abuse on psychological adjustment in adult life? Gender appears to be unrelated to this adjustment; men and women appear to have similar reactions to having been molested as children as they grow older. The quality of attachment with significant others is related to how much child sexual abuse will affect the later psychological adjustment of victims. Those who have a less secure and more fearful attachment style are more affected by child molestation and have worse psychological problems in later life. Victims of childhood sexual abuse also tend to be more distant and controlling in interpersonal relationships that contributes to problems in marriages and friendships. Strong interpersonal relationships and social supports provide a safety net that may reduce the harmful consequences of child sexual abuse. Importantly, most victims of child molestation do not become child molesters in their adult life.

Given the harmful consequences that may occur from child molestation, it is important to prevent these abuses. There have been several programs created to prevent child molestation in several countries.

Approximately, 66% of grade school children have participated in child sexual abuse prevention programs in the U.S. These prevention programs attempt to teach children the difference between appropriate and inappropriate touching, that they should protest touching that feels bad, and when not to keep secrets. Children who participate in these prevention programs have a better understanding of these concepts than other children. Programs that show greatest success have a greater number of sessions, teach concrete rules about appropriate and inappropriate touch, include behavioral skills training, and allow children to role play and physically rehearse correct responses in the sessions. One study has found that children who participated in prevention programs had a lower rate of sexual abuse than children who did not participate. More research is needed to determine the actual impact of prevention programs on reducing the rate of sexual abuse. There have been suggestions on how to improve prevention programs. Davis and Gidycz suggest that children of all ages participate in these programs for longer periods of time. Children also have difficulty applying the concepts they learn in these programs to adults they know, such as parents, other family members, and regular caretakers. In these programs, instructors should clearly and repeatedly emphasize that most child molesters will be adults the children know, and not strangers.

LORETTA J. STALANS

References and Further Reading

Christian, C.W., Lavelle, J.M., De Jong, A.R., Loiselle, J., Brenner, L., and Joffe, M., Forensic evidence findings in prepubertal victims of sexual assault, *Pediatrics*, 106(1), 1612–1627, 2000.

Abel, G.G., Becker, J.V., Mittlelman, M.S., Cunningham-Rathner, J., Rouleau, J.L., and Murphy, W.D., Self-reported sex crimes of nonincarcerated paraphilics, *Journal of Interpersonal Violence*, 2, 3–25, 1987.

Cullen, B.J., Hull, S.P., Funk, J.B., and Haaf, R.A., A matched cohort comparison of criminal justice system's response to child sexual abuse: A profile of perpetrators, *Child Abuse and Neglect*, 24(4), 569–577, 2000.

Davis, K.M. and Gidycz, C.A., Child sexual abuse prevention programs: A meta-analysis, *Journal of Clinical Child Psychology*, 29(2), 257–265, 2000.

Falkenhain, M.A., Duckro, P.N., Hughes, H.M., Rossetti, S.J., and Gfeller, J.D., Cluster analysis of child sexual offenders: A validation with Roman Catholic priests and brothers, *Sexual Addiction and Compulsivity*, 6, 317–336, 1999.

Fisher, D., Beech, A., and Browne, K., Comparison of sex offenders to nonoffenders on selected psychological measures, *International Journal of Offender Therapy and Comparative Criminology*, 43(4), 473–491, 1999.

Gibson, L.E. and Leitenberg, H., Child sexual abuse prevention programs: Do they decrease the occurrence of child sexual abuse? *Child Abuse and Neglect*, 24(9), 1115–1125, 2000.

Hanson, K.R. and Thornton, D., Improving risk assessments for sex offenders: A comparison of three Actuarial Scales, *Law and Human Behavior*, 24(1), 119–136.

Jumper, S.A., A meta-analysis of the relationship of child sexual abuse to adult psychological adjustment, *Child Abuse and Neglect*, 19(6), 715–728, 1995.

Langan, P.A. and Farrington, D.P. (1998). *Crime and Justice in the United States and in England and Wales* (1981–1996). Washington, DC: Bureau of Justice Statistics U.S. Department of Justice.

Levesque, R.J.R., Sentencing sex crimes against children: An empirical and policy analysis, *Behavioral Sciences and the Law*, 18, 331–341, 2000.

Meursing, K., Vos, T., and Coutinho, O., Child sexual abuse in Matabeleland, Zimbabew, *Social Science and Medicine*, 41(12), 1693–1704.

Polizzi, D.M., MacKenzie, D.M., and Hickman, L.J., What works in adult sex offender treatment? A review of prison- and non-prison-based treatment programs, *International Journal of Offender Therapy and Comparative Criminology*, 43(3), 357–374, 1999.

Prentky, R.A., Knight, R.A., and Lee, A.F.S., *Child Sexual Molestation: Research Issues,* U.S. Department of Justice: NCJ 163390, 1997.

Roche, D.N., Runtz, M.G., Hunter, M.A., Adult attachment: A mediator between child sexual abuse and later psychological adjustment, *Journal of Interpersonal Violence*, 14(2), 184–207, 1999.

Special Issue on Sex Offender Treatment: *Journal of Interpersonal Violence*, 14(3–4), 1999.

Snyder, H.N., *Sexual Assault of Young Children as Reported to Law Enforcement: Victim, Incident, and Offender Characteristics.* Bureau of Justice Statistics: NCJ 182990, July 2000. Available at http://www.ojp.usdoj.gov/bjs/abstract/saycrle.htm.

Whiffen, V.E., Thompson, J.M., and Aube, J.A., Mediators of the link between childhood sexual abuse and adult depressive symptoms. *Journal of Interpersonal Violence*, 15(10), 1100–1120, 2000.

Winick, B.J. and Fond, J.Q.L., (Eds), Special theme: Sex offenders: Scientific, legal and policy perspectives, *Psychology, Public Policy, and Law*, 4(1/2), 1998.

See also **Child Abuse: Extent and Correlates; Child Abuse: Prevention and Treatment; Child Abuse: Law**

Child Neglect *See* **Child Abuse**

China, Crime and Justice in

China is one of the oldest civilizations in the world, with a written history of more than 4000 years. Like other long-standing civilizations, China has a long legal tradition. An ancient classic book "Shang Shu," which is a compilation of very ancient documents by Confucius and other Confucian scholars, records that the ancient Chinese used the words "crime" and "penalty" as far back as 2200 BCE. "Shang Shu" also records that five penalties—tattooing, disfigurement, castration, mutilation, and death—were included in "Yu Xing," the law of Xia Dynasty (2100–1600 BCE). Archaeological evidence shows that the Chinese developed and administered codified law and justice as far back as 300 BCE.

The central concepts of imperial law and justice were the Confucian concept of "Li" (moral code) and the legalist school's concept of "Fa" (law). Originally, "Li" referred to the rules set by the early king, Zhougong, in the Western Zhou Dynasty (1100–771 BCE) as a basis for upper-class behavioral norms. "Li" includes rituals and functions as a system of customary laws. The basic spirit of the "Li" is to outline the rules that govern the ordered status system of relationships among people and set behavioral expectations for each social position. The central principles are the domination and submission relations between the emperor and his ministers, fathers and sons, and husbands and wives. To Confucius, the Western Zhou (1100–771 BCE) was an ideal and exemplary society. If all people observed the expectations of their social positions, society would be free of social conflict, orderly, organized, and harmonic. Governing through moral example and persuasion was far superior to rule through rigid legal codes and severe punishment.

To realize the ideal of "Li," the emperor and government must exercise "Ren Zhen," that is, the treatment of his people in a humanitarian manner, rather than in a cruel and punitive way. A central tenet of the Confucian school of thought is that human beings are born with good natures and have the fundamental capacity to pursue a virtuous life. People can and should persistently cultivate themselves to pursue the four virtues: humanity (Ren), righteousness (Yi), propriety (Li), and wisdom (Zhi). Virtues are to be achieved through the education of the mind. Evil, deviance, and crime are because of bad external influences; therefore, offenders are fundamentally rehabilitable and can be reintegrated back into society through education and moral persuasion. The internalization of the "Li" is the fundamental route to achieving social order.

In contrast to Confucianism, legalists believe that human beings are born with the desire for gratification. Innate selfishness and greed distract human beings from following morals and laws. Therefore, all human beings have the potential to do wrong. Social order can only be achieved by punishment and enforcement of the law. Legalism was the dominant political philosophy of the Qin Dynasty (221–206 BCE), the first dynasty that united China. It was infamous for cruelly punishing dissidents and minor offenders. The dynasty was very short lived and overthrown by peasant revolutions. The fall of the dynasty was historically attributed to its reliance on the law and cruel punishment for social control, and was often cited as a support for Confucius' idea of rule by "Li."

One of the first things that founding emperor Liu Bang of the Western Han dynasty (206 BCE–24 CE) did was to eliminate all the cruel laws of the Qin Dynasty. Later emperors of Han dynasty after Wudi (140–88 BCE) established Confucius' teachings as the official ideology of the state while implementing the law as a secondary measure for social control. Later, most emperors adopted this basic model. Throughout imperial China, dynasties promulgated many legal codes. These codes all strongly reflect the ethical norms of Confucianism, including strengthening the ultimate authority of the state, the preservation of dominance-submissive social relations between emperor and his ministers, fathers and sons, and husbands and wives, while being less concerned with the defense of individual interests. To a large degree, imperial law and justice were moralistic in nature. The penal code was designed to strengthen the Confucian moral code. A remarkable characteristic of the Chinese law and justice system was its effort to control not only undesirable behavior, but also to control the deviant mind.

Dynasties developed a complex judicial hierarchy. They were both penal and administrative in nature. The magistrates at the local level exercised the powers of judge, prosecutor, and police chief in addition to filling the role of head of the local government. Traditional legal principles included the emperor's power to determine guilt and punishment of high-ranking officials, the presumption of guilt, the nonexistence of defense attorneys, reduced punishment for the aged and young, reduced or exempted punishment for shielding offenders who are family members, and reduced punishment if the offender confessed before prosecution. The justice traditions also included the handling of disputes by local extrajudicial organizations. Going through the formal criminal justice system for a dispute was considered "losing face." The clan and village typically settled conflicts through mediation and by imposing sanctions according to local customs to maintain peace and order, and to achieve social harmony. Contemporary Chinese criminal justice is still influenced in many ways by these historical and cultural traditions.

Crime rates are unknown for imperial (before 1911 CE) China. There are no available systematic records on the level of crime during the period of the Republic of China (1912–1949). After the communists took power in China in 1949, crime statistics were not published until 1987, when the first Chinese law *Yearbook* was published. It is generally accepted by researchers that crime rates in China were very low during the prereform years. Based on official sources, the average number of crimes annually was 290,000 from 1950 to 1965, while the population was around 0.6 billion. During the period of the "cultural revolution" (1966–1976), there are no statistical records on crime.

Crimes have increased significantly since economic reform was launched in 1978. As China's economy evolves from a state socialist command economy to a market economy, Chinese society has experienced profound social changes. The total crime rate tripled from 55.91 per 100,000 people in 1978 to 163.19 per 100,000 in 1998. The rate started to increase in 1978, reached a first peak in 1981 but then decreased over the next few years. The rate remained relatively low until 1987, at which point a sharp increase began. The total crime rate reached a second peak in 1991. A pronounced decrease followed 1991. Levels were fairly steady from 1992 to 1995. The rate once again moved upward between 1997 and 1998. Similar to what is found in other nations, violent crime rates are generally much lower than property crime rates. Homicide rates increased very little, rape rates actually fell a little. Property crimes increased the most. Theft constitutes about 60% to 80% of total crime. As economic reform proceeds, economically motivated crimes have increased faster than other crimes.

The extent of the crime problem can also be reflected by the rate of recidivists, who commit crime at least twice, and chronic offenders, who have been arrested five or more times. No systematic information is available to the extent of recidivism and chronic offense in China, but a few examples provide insight into the general picture. For example, in 1995, the Chinese government reported that the recidivism rate for 1994 was between 6% and 8%. In comparison, it is widely accepted that the rate of adult recidivism in the U.S. is approximately 60%. A study led by Wolfgang in Wuhan, China, in 1995 did not find a chronic offender group, whereas he and his colleagues in Philadelphia found that 6.3% of the juveniles of their sample were chronic offenders, who were responsible for more than half of the juvenile delinquency. A study by Liu, Messner, and Liska in 1997 found that when administrative violations were included, in 1992, only 0.26% of the inmates in Tianjin, China were chronic offenders. However, as profound social changes occur in China, new studies are needed to discover change and new patterns.

Contemporary Chinese law and criminal justice are different in many aspects from western models, especially Anglo-American adversarial systems. However, as China moves to modernize its legal system along with the economic reforms, it has begun to adopt much from Western systems. The current system is an amalgam of influences from communist political ideology and China's cultural and historical tradition.

When the communist party established the People's Republic of China (PRC) in 1949, China formally followed the Soviet Union's legal model as it set up its law and criminal justice system. The system stresses the revolutionary nature of the state and functioned to consolidate the socialist system. However, the late communist leader Mao Zedong, much influenced by the Chinese traditions, preferred to downplay the role of laws and formal systems. For 30 years following 1949, China practiced a largely informal system of criminal justice. China had no codified criminal law and criminal procedural law until economic reform began. In 1979, the National People's Congress enacted the PRC's first criminal law and criminal procedural law. This was a landmark development in China's criminal justice system. The organic law of the people's courts and organic law of the people's procuratorates enacted in 1980 laid out a hierarchy of courts and prosecution system, consisting of the Supreme, higher, intermediate, and basic court and procuracy, corresponding to government at national, provincial, prefectures, and municipalities directly under the provinces, and counties. In 1982, the People's Congress passed a newly revised constitution. In 1996, China revised the 1979 criminal procedural law and then revised the criminal law in 1997. These new laws systematically built the formal Chinese criminal justice system of today.

The Chinese approach to certain basic principles of criminal justice is best reflected in its criminal justice process. Chinese criminal procedural law stipulates that the police are in charge of investigation, detention, and preliminary review of criminal cases. The people's procuratorate approves the arrest, conducts procuratorial proceedings and investigation, and initiates public prosecution. The people's court is responsible for adjudication. The procedural law emphasizes that throughout the entire criminal process, the police, procurators, and courts must base their decisions on facts and strictly follow the law.

Generally, the police have strong discretionary powers to detain a suspect. In China, not all lawbreaking is defined as crime. For an act to be criminal, it must be serious enough to be prohibited by the criminal law. Minor crimes are treated as violations and punished primarily by the police according to the "Regulations of the PRC for Security Administrative Punishment," and "Rules for Reeducation through Labor." Administrative punishment carries fines of up to 200 Chinese yuan, administrative detention for up to 15 days, and confinement to reeducation through labor camps for up to 3 years. The courts do not determine administrative punishment; the police decision is central in rendering administrative punishment. In the arrest proceedings for criminal charges, the police must have a warrant. The arrestee or detainee and their families are entitled to a notice of reasons for the arrest or detention, and of the place of confinement within 24 hours, unless the investigation would be hampered or notification is impossible.

Interrogation must begin within 24 hours of the detention or arrest. The detainee or arrestee should be released immediately if no legitimate grounds are found. When the police consider it necessary to formally arrest a detainee, they must submit the request for arrest to the procuratorate for approval within 3 days or, in difficult circumstances, 7 days. The procuracy must either approve the arrest or order the release of the detainee within 7 days. During the investigation, procedural law strictly forbids extorting confessions through means of torture or use of threat, enticement, deceit, or any other illegal means. Except in emergency situations, searches must be conducted with a search warrant. The detention of the accused person, pending investigation, should not exceed 2 months. If necessary, a 1-month extension may be granted by the procuratorate at the next higher level.

Procurators are responsible for decisions regarding prosecution. A procurator is required to make a decision on prosecution within one month to one and half months. When they find further investigation is needed, procurators can carry out the investigation, or order the police to conduct further investigation. If evidence is found to be sufficient, the procurators initiate a public prosecution by filing an indictment presenting the facts of the crime charged and evidence. When the procurator's decision is to not prosecute, the accused must be released immediately.

The trial includes four stages: investigation, debate, discussion by the collegiate bench, and judgment by the court. The collegiate bench typically includes three judges or a judge and two assessors. When adjudicating minor cases, the local court is allowed to use only one judge. The court reaches conclusions based upon the evidence presented in the trial and the arguments made by the prosecution and the defense. The trial judges decide the verdict and sentence by majority rule, except for the most difficult or important cases, which are decided by the Adjudication Committee of the court. The newly revised procedural law stipulates that for cases where there is insufficient evidence to prove the guilt of the defendant, a not guilty verdict should be given. All trials are supposed to be public except when the cases involve minors, state secrets, or personal intimacies.

Legal representation is an essential element of due process in the Western criminal justice system. The Chinese constitution states that the accused has the right of defense. The criminal procedural law stipulates that the accused has the right to defend him or herself and also to choose to be defended by a lawyer, a relative, a friend, or a citizen recommended by a social organization. In the case involving a minor, possible death penalty, or persons with deficiency, who do not have a defender, a public defender will be designated by the court. However, the emphasis in the Chinese process is not on protection of the rights of the defendant, but to ensure the state and public's security, maintain social order, and to protect the interests of the public. Procedural law specifies that the duty of the defense lawyer is, on the basis of the facts and the law, to present materials and opinions proving that the defendant is innocent, that this crime is minor, or that he should receive a mitigated punishment or be exempted from criminal responsibility, to safeguard the lawful rights and interests of the defendant. The purpose of the defense counsel is to help the court render a just verdict and protect the legitimate rights and interests of the defendant. He must under no circumstances fabricate evidence, distort facts, or use deceptions to help his client; these actions are crimes, punishable by law.

It is expected that a defense lawyer should persuade the defendant to reveal to the court concealed facts to seek its leniency, and not to manipulate the facts and bend the law to win a case and help an accused escape criminal responsibility. The official stance has been that the defense counsel is not bound by the will of the accused. Lawyers should be loyal to the interest of the socialist cause and the people. Only recently have these expectations been emphasized less and the rights of the defendant emphasized more.

Assumption of innocence is an essential element of the Western system. The prevailing Chinese tradition was assumption of guilt with an emphasis on confessions. Recent development in Chinese procedural law places emphasis on facts and hard evidence. The law neither specifies an assumption of innocence nor an assumption of guilt as principles; Instead, the emphasis is on basing decisions on facts and taking the law as the criterion. The law stipulates that evidence can be used as the basis of judgment only after it is verified. Confession alone cannot be used as evidence to convict.

Judicial independence is a major principle of Western laws. Chinese law stipulates that the people's courts administer justice independently and are subject only to the law. However, it has been a practice that communist party committees review major case decisions. The 1997 revised criminal procedural law made changes to limit the practice and stated that proper party leadership over judicial organs should be only on principles and policy lines and not on concrete and routine matters.

Equality before the law was stipulated in the 1954 constitution, the first constitution of PRC. However, it was often repudiated as a bourgeois concept in various political campaigns. In 1979, the criminal procedural law once again stipulated that all citizens are equal before the law, irrespective of their nationality, race, sex, occupation, social origins, religious belief, education, property status, or duration of residence. It was declared that former landlords, rich peasants, and their descendants would no longer be discriminated against as long as they supported socialism. In practice, when the offender is a high-ranking official and a communist party member, it is conventional that the party will take over the case to determine the party disciplinary punishment first. It is usually the case that only after the offender is dismissed from the party that criminal prosecution and court proceedings start.

The criminal procedure allows one appeal to the court of the next higher level. It used to be that appealing might entail heavier punishment. The 1979 criminal procedural law specified that the court of second instance might not increase the penalty; although this does not apply to a case appealed by the procuracy. All death penalties must be submitted to the Supreme Peoples' Court for examination and approval.

The Chinese corrections system is built on the principle of rehabilitation. It emphasizes justice system's restorative function. In dealing with punishment, the Chinese are heavily influenced by cultural tradition. They believe crime must be punished, and that deterrence works, but criminal punishment is only a last resort when education and prevention, which primarily rely on extrajudicial processes and social organizations, fail. The Chinese firmly believe that most criminal offenders can be reformed through physical labor, political and moral education, and assistance in changing their environment. Offenders can eventually be reintegrated back into society and become productive citizens. The goal of correction is to bring about a change of heart and mind of offenders, through a process that begins with compulsion through forced labor and moral education, to repentance, and to the forming of a work ethic. The Chinese put heavy emphasis on forced labor as an essential means to rehabilitation, as diligent and honest work is highly valued by Chinese cultural tradition. Work ethic and skills are considered vital to resisting bad environmental influences. Whereas the Western legal tradition and systems is more concerned with inmates' rights and their fair treatment, the Chinese system focuses on the goal of society and collectives, and conformity and changes in the minds of offenders.

The contemporary Chinese criminal justice system has many unique features and weak points, notably its insufficiency in protecting the rights of the accused. These are partially attributable to its traditional emphasis on the importance of states and collectives over individual citizens. As China rapidly modernizes its economic and social institutions, changes are continuing to occur. Given China's increasing importance in this increasingly globalized world, understanding its changing crime and criminal justice system is a great challenge but an important task.

Jianhong Liu

References and Further Reading

China Law Yearbook Press. *Law Yearbook of China*. Beijing: China Law Yearbook Press, 1987–1998.

Leng, S. and Chiu, H., *Criminal Justice in Post-Mao China: Analysis and Documents*, Albany, NY: State University of New York Press, 1985.

Liu, J., Zhang, L., and Messner, S.F., Eds., *Social Control in a Changing China*, Westport, CT: Greenwood Publishing Group, 2001.

Liu, J., Messner, S.F., and Liska, A.E., Chronic offenders in China, *International Criminal Justice Review* 7 (1997).

National People's Congress of People's Republic of China. *Constitution of the People's Republic of China*, Beijing: Foreign Languages Press, 1994.

National People's Congress of People's Republic of China. *The Criminal Law of the People's Republic of China*, Beijing: Legal Press, 1997.

National People's Congress of People's Republic of China. *The Criminal Procedure Law of the People's Republic of China*, Beijing: Legal Press, 1996.

Troyer, R.J., Clark, J.P., and Rojek, D.G., Eds., *Social Control in the People's Republic of China*, New York City, NY: Praeger Publishers, 1989.

Ren, X., *Tradition of the Law and Law of the Tradition: Law, State, and Social Control in China*, Westport, CT: Greenwood Press, 1997.

Yang, H., Ed. *Chinese Legal History*, Beijing, Press of Chinese University of Politics and Law, 1994.

See also **Organized Crime: Chinese Tongs and Triads**

Citation Research in Criminology and Criminal Justice

Citation Analysis

The technique of citation analysis is widely used in the evaluation of the prestige and impact of scholars, university departments, academic journals, and individual scholarly works not only in criminal justice but in such disparate fields as physics, medicine, biochemistry, economics, psychology, and sociology. It provides an objective quantitative method for determining the impact of a scholar, journal, or department on the field. Citation analysis assumes first that the most highly cited works are those that were considered most useful or important by other scholars, and second that citations indicate the influence of the work on the field (although there is some question as to whether citation counts accurately measure the quality of a given work). Similarly, those journals that are highly cited are considered to be the most prestigious or influential within the field.

There is a significant body of research in various academic fields that demonstrates the strong relationship between citation counts and other measures of scholarly influence, professional prestige, and intellectual reputation. Citation counts have been found to be highly correlated with peer ratings of professional eminence, scholarly recognition, scholarly productivity, and the receipt of scholarly prizes (such as the Nobel Prize in physics). Researchers have also found correlations between citation counts and ratings of the prestige of university departments and doctoral programs. Unlike other measures of influence and prestige (e.g., peer rankings, professional awards), citation analysis is truly objective and not subject to personal bias or special interest. Counting journal publications by individuals or departmental faculty is a more quantitative method than peer rankings but is a measure of productivity rather than influence on the field. Publication of an article does not automatically mean that it will be read, cited, or considered by others to be of significance. Overall, it appears that citation analysis is the most reliable and objective method of measuring influence and prestige in a field of study.

As a method of measuring influence, citation analysis is not perfect; there are several concerns and problems related to it. One issue is the possibility of bias against scholars working in less populated topic areas; they may have fewer colleagues to cite their work. Another concern is that citation counts do not distinguish between positive, negative, and neutral citations but count them all equally. However, citation analysts have found that the vast majority of citations are positive or neutral, and also argue that research that stimulates criticism may still be considered influential. Citation counts may also be affected by the productivity of the researcher; researchers have found that the most-cited criminology scholars tend to be those with longer publication records. Finally, it is also possible that citation selection may be influenced by social factors, such as personal likes and dislikes, attempts to please journal editors, or by a desire to inflate individual or departmental citation counts. However, despite these difficulties, citation analysis is generally accepted as a valid technique.

Citation Indexes

The most common way of gathering criminology citation data is through the use of indexes produced by the Institute for Scientific Information, such as the *Social Sciences Citation Index* (SSCI). These list all bibliographic references made in a large number of social science journals. However, this method has several drawbacks. First, indexes such as SSCI do not include references in all published works; several important criminology journals (e.g., *Justice Quarterly)* are not included. In addition, works cited in books or book chapters are not indexed. Second, listings in SSCI provide only initials and surnames of cited authors. This could cause confusion when several scholars share the same surname and first initial (e.g., Patricia and Paul Brantingham, Jacqueline and Joseph Cohen, Douglas and David Smith). Citations of married women may appear under more than one surname (e.g., Ilene Nagel, Ilene Bernstein, Ilene Nagel-Bernstein). Another problem with citation indexes such as SSCI is that any clerical or other errors in the original reference lists or bibliographies, such as misspelled names, incorrect author initials, or incorrect publication dates, are repeated in SSCI. Finally, SSCI includes self-citations. Although it is perfectly justifiable for scholars to cite themselves, especially when building on their prior research, self-citations do not indicate the influence of the cited work on other scholars. Because only the first author of a cited work is included in SSCI (thus penalizing junior authors in collaborative works), it is difficult to exclude self-citations when using SSCI.

Other Citation Resources

A second method, which is more time consuming but arguably more accurate than employing citation indexes such as SSCI, is to examine reference lists of journals, textbooks, scholarly books, and other sources within a field and count the number of citations to a given scholar, work, or journal. Although this method can be tedious, it does avoid many of the problems inherent in the use of SSCI. We have successfully used this method to produce a substantial body of citation research in criminology and criminal justice. The goal of our research is not only to identify the most cited (and arguably most influential) scholars during a particular time period, but also to identify the most influential topics during that period and thus document the historical development of the field of criminology and criminal justice.

Conclusion

The use of citation analysis in criminology was pioneered by Wolfgang, Figlio, and Thornberry (1978) in a book entitled *Evaluating Criminology.* Twenty years later, this in-depth study inspired a new work by Cohn, Farrington, and Wright (1998), *Evaluating Criminology and Criminal Justice*. Both contain objective bodies of research and both have generated a significant amount of controversy regarding the use of this technique. Some criminologists find citation analysis threatening whereas others actively oppose research involving citation analysis and may even attempt to prevent the publication of articles using this approach. At the same time, many scholars find the results of citation analysis research fascinating and consider them a contribution to the field. Recent citation analyses that we conducted have been cited as a partial justification for scholars receiving major awards from the American Society of Criminology and used in dossiers prepared for promotion applications. Overall, although the approach is controversial, it does appear to be both valid and reliable, and is clearly one of the best methods for measuring prestige and influence within the field of criminology and criminal justice.

ELLEN G. COHN AND DAVID P. FARRINGTON

References and Further Reading

Cohn, E.G. and Farrington, D.P. (1996). Crime and Justice and the criminology and criminal justice literature. In Morris. N. and Tonry, M. (Eds.), *Crime and Justice: A Review of Research* 20: 265–300. Chicago, IL: University of Chicago Press.

Cohn, E.G. and Farrington, D.P. (1998). Assessing the quality of American doctoral program faculty in criminology and criminal justice, 1991–1995. *Journal of Criminal Justice Education*, 9(2): 187–210.

Cohn, E.G. and Farrington, D.P. (1998) Changes in the most-cited scholars in major American criminology and criminal justice journals between 1986–1990 and 1991–1995. *Journal of Criminal Justice*, 26(2): 99–116.

Cohn, E.G., Farrington, D.P., and Wright, R.A. (1998). *Evaluating Criminology and Criminal Justice*. Westport, CT: Greenwood Press.

Gordon, R.A. and Vicari, P.J. (1992). Eminence in social psychology: A comparison of textbook citation, Social Sciences Citation Index, and research productivity rankings. *Personality and Social Psychology Bulletin* 18: 26–38.

Regoli, R.M., Poole, E.D., and Miracle, A.W. Jr. (1982). Assessing the prestige of journals in criminal justice: a research note. *Journal of Criminal Justice* 10: 57–67.

Shichor, D. (1982). An analysis of citations in introductory criminology textbooks: A research note. *Journal of Criminal Justice* 10: 231–237.

Thomas, C.W. (1987). The utility of citation-based quality assessments. *Journal of Criminal Justice* 15: 165–171.

Wolfgang, M.A., Figlio, R.M., and Thornberry, T.P. (1978). *Evaluating Criminology.* New York, NY: Elsevier.

Wright, R.A. (1995). The most-cited scholars in criminology: A comparison of textbooks and journals. *Journal of Criminal Justice* 23: 303–311.

Wright, R.A. (1996). Do introductory criminology textbooks cite the most influential criminologists? *American Journal of Criminal Justice* 20: 225–236.

Classical Criminology

Many criminologists regard the classical school as the advent of criminology per se. It at least served as the vehicle for first viewing crime as a product of natural forces, supplanting supernatural explanations of behavior, including crime. The shift to classicism cannot be understood absent the social context of the Middle Ages, for it represented above all a reform movement, a challenge to the status quo. Classical thinking about crime truly qualifies as a paradigm shift and continues to provide the foundation for a free will based or rational choice school of criminology.

Preclassical Middle Age understanding of crime is most clearly reflected in the Holy Inquisition, extending roughly over a 600-year period between the 12th and 18th centuries A.D. The Roman Catholic Church and the governmental authorities of most European countries formed an alliance to combat the perceived evils of witches and heretics. The ranks of those that the church and state wished to control included not only thieves, murderers, and the like, but also eccentrics, political dissidents, social critics, the mentally ill, and a wide range of other deviants. All manner of torture and execution were employed to rid society of these unwanted elements. The church provided the philosophical reasoning for the inquisitorial era, whereas the state provided the means of enforcing the religious mandates. Those who violated the norms, which tightly reigned the bounds of acceptable behaviors, were deemed possessed by evil spirits. Moreover, those who dared question the truth of inquisitorial reasoning were declared heretics, an offense itself calling for death.

By the 18th century the Holy Inquisition reached its pinnacle, spreading torture and killing across Europe. The most common methods of execution were burning at the stake, hanging, drowning, beheading, stoning, and quartering (tying the subject's limbs to four horses and driving them in different directions to rip the body apart). Even these horrible deaths were sometimes preceded by long agonizing tortures such as breaking multiple bones in the feet through the sequential tightening of metal "boots," a gradual stretching of the entire body on specially designed racks, disemboweling and a plethora of mutilations. In short, unthinkable cruelty was the order of the day for contending with "crime." Moreover, these tortures and executions were meted out at the arbitrary will of officials of the church and state with no means of defense available to the condemned. Finally, they were only inconsistently applied; so many behaviors were deemed offensive that discretion was necessitated less the population shrink to unacceptable levels.

It was in this context of cruel, arbitrary, and inconsistent administration of justice that the classical school of criminology emerged. In fact, it can best be seen as a reaction to this state of affairs. First and foremost, classical criminology then evolved as a reform movement sympathetic to humanitarian concerns wrought by the Inquisition. It was part and parcel of the Enlightenment, a broad social movement of the 18th century juxtaposed to the premises of the inquisitorial era.

It is the Italian philosopher Cesare Beccaria (1738–1794) who is most frequently credited with the development of classical criminology. In fact, he is typically praised in criminology texts as the "Father of Classical Criminology." This view is rooted in his authorship of *Dei deliti e delle pene (On Crimes and Punishments)*, published in 1764. It was a small treatise, just over 100 pages in length, that was originally published anonymously to avoid the wrath of the inquisitors. Beccaria's fears were well-founded for the work was severely attacked, resulting in calls for his execution and condemnation of the book by the Catholic Church. The tide, however, quickly turned and Beccaria became a celebrated figure.

Whatever credit Beccaria merited for the ideas expressed in *On Crimes and Punishments* and however critical the work was in influencing the shift to the classical paradigm for understanding crime, it is clear that he stood on the shoulders of the Enlightenment philosophers of the era. Beccaria was really a novice in the scholarly conceptualization of crime, having written the treatise to fulfill an assignment as a member of a small literary club. The influence of social contract philosophers such as Rousseau, Locke, Hobbes, and Hume were particularly evident, as were the works of such contemporary Enlightenment philosophers as Montesquieu, Diderot, and Voltaire.

Classical criminology was deeply rooted in utilitarianism, often defined as the greatest happiness principle. It viewed all human suffering as bad, and saw the driving force in society as a need to reduce overall suffering. It was believed that some pain, however, may be necessary to reduce the sum total of human suffering. Inherent in the notion of a social contract, in fact, is that all persons give up some benefits in order to secure others. Thus the function of the organized state is to require that all citizens relinquish certain rights such as access to the property of another, striking another out of anger, and sexual access to persons deemed unacceptable. In return, those same protections are extended to all members of the state. Violations of the social contract are designated crimes and it is to the benefit of all citizens that crimes be punished. Thus although punishment was viewed as bad within the classical philosophical tradition, it was necessary to enforce the law undergirded by the social contract. Punishment to the classicist becomes a necessary evil, exemplified when the punishment that parents mete out to children is softened by the adage, "this hurts me more than it hurts you."

The concept most important to the classical conception of crime is that of deterrence, which cannot be understood without reference to punishment or the imposition of suffering. Stated concisely, deterrence is the prevention of crime through the use or threat of sanctions to dissuade persons from violating the social contract. Punishment of law violators, though evil in itself, serves the utilitarian goal of preventing crime. Beccaria opened his important essay by noting that the object of the classical school was to prevent crime. In short, the utilitarian goal of crime prevention paved the way for punishments, administered in accordance with the principles of deterrence theory. This school of thought then is characterized by its rationality and emphasis on humanitarian reform, but also by utilitarianism, which incorporates punishment for the good of the whole. Only by understanding the social and historical contexts in which this theory emerged can the seeming conflict between punishment and humanitarianism be understood. Moreover, it is necessary to understand the assumptions that were incorporated into classicism.

The classical paradigm is premised upon a particular conception of human nature. It is assumed that all persons are rational, that they have free will, and that they are hedonistic. Within original or pure classical thought, all persons were regarded as equal along each of these dimensions. The rationality assumption, for example, envisions each human being as equally capable of engaging in a thought process and arriving at the best decision regarding how to behave under a given set of circumstances. Free will assumes that persons have the same array of choices available and that there are no impediments to selecting the most rational choice. Hedonism depicts each human as driven by a desire to pursue whatever is pleasurable to them and to avoid whatever is painful. Thus rational free-willed actions are driven by a desire to experience pleasure and to avoid pain. To the extent that these assumptions about human nature are valid, deterrence seems obtainable. At the same time, however, to the extent that they are incorrect, the deterrence called for by the classical school is attenuated.

Given a fixed human nature whereby people are rational, have free will, and are hedonistic, behavior can be controlled through threats of appropriate punishments. As detailed by the founders of the classical school, if the appropriate sanction is relatively certain, severe, and swift, it follows that crime will be deterred. If the prospect of punishment is not certain enough, not severe enough, or is delivered too slowly, crime will not be deterred. If, on the other hand, the punishment is too severe, it is more than is necessary to deter and, therefore, all beyond the effective deterrent threshold is unjust punishment. Classical criminology was, after all, developed in response to the atrocities of the Inquisition and was intended to bring about fair and effective punishments. Any punishment beyond what was necessary to deter crime was deemed non-utilitarian, and therefore, unjustifiable. Fair punishment was the necessary evil to the utilitarian end of reducing suffering through the prevention of crime. As Beccaria cautioned, it was necessary to control the private passions of us all for the common good of humankind.

Because of its focus on developing a system for the delivery of fair and effective punishments, classical criminology has sometimes been dubbed administrative criminology. Particularly after the demise of classical thinking with the shift to positivism in the late 19th century, and continuing for nearly a century, this was about the only value recognized from the classical era. In any case, given the logic outlined above, it made sense for classical criminology to concentrate on the administrative details of a system of justice. It was that search for fair and effective principles for the administration of justice that provided classical criminology with the historical legacy of an important reform movement.

Several ideas lay at the basis of the classical reforms. Perhaps foremost, and in contrast to later criminological thinking, attention was directed almost exclusively to the law and not to the individual criminal. This was rooted in the assumption that all people, as rational and hedonistic beings, are both capable of any type of criminal behavior and fortunately, at the same time, are malleable under the influence of law. With these assumptions in place it was not necessary to address criminal motivation because all persons held the potential to offend should they see prospects for gaining advantage over others. In the context of the social contract, we all want the protection that it provides without giving up the rights that this entails. It is only the system of justice, by threatening delivery of sanctions to would-be violators of the conditions of the contract, that insures conformity. Consequently, classical criminology needed only to examine the administration of law to ensure that proper sanctioning mechanisms were in place to influence the rational decision making of the citizenry at large.

The focus on fair and effective punishment under law, coupled with the assumption that there were no individual differences underlying crime, obviated any need for discretion in the application of law. To the contrary, this logical framework condemned differences in treatment between offenders. Beccaria was adamant, at least in the first edition of *On Crimes and Punishments*, in arguing that judges should not be accorded discretionary authority. Given the social context that Beccaria and the Enlightenment philosophers were reacting to, it is understandable why there was such a strong indictment of individualized justice, for abuse of power was inherent in the cruel and arbitrary justice system that was being critiqued. If they overreacted to the use of discretion in the administration of law, as history has indicated to be the case, this might be forgiven in light of the abuses they were protesting.

Rather than individualized determinations, Beccaria and the classicists called for punishing the crime (that is all violators of the same statute) proportionate to the objective harm caused. Criminal intent as well as any differences between offenders were irrelevant to them. Thus past record was not deemed relevant, nor was the age of the offender or other circumstances surrounding their crime. This gave rise to one of the stumbling blocks in translating classical ideas into policy. In England, Jeremy Bentham (1748–1832), much influenced by Beccaria's essay, most notably struggled to translate the idea of proportional punishment into pragmatic guidelines for the administration of justice. In examining what he called felicity calculus, the balancing of pleasure and pain, Bentham painstakingly detailed what he deemed to be appropriate punishments for a full range of criminal transgressions. His efforts and the thoughts of other representatives of the classical school were inhibited by bold assumptions regarding human calculus. For example, they envisioned a linear relationship between the seriousness of offenses and the punishment necessary to deter them, overlooking potential temptations that many people might experience regarding minor offenses versus the rare motivation to engage in the most heinous offenses. In contemporary society, for example, temptations to drive too fast or cheat on taxes are widespread, whereas relatively few people would struggle with decisions regarding cannibalism, incestuous relations with their children or bestiality, even if the punishments for such behaviors were substantially less severe than their rank order in a seriousness scale might call for.

The centerpiece of classical reform lay in its call for shifting the control of the justice process. The reformers stridently called for wresting this power from the church and monarchies. Thus Beccaria delineated a separation of powers, wherein the legislative branch of government would be charged with the responsibility of determining the will of the people and identifying those behaviors that should be specified as criminal transgressions. He emphasized that criminal prohibitions and their consequences should be widely disseminated in order to gain the desired deterrent effect. The law was to be applied by the judicial branch of government, only in the sense of determining guilt or innocence, and not in interpreting the intent or following the spirit of the legislators' intent. No role was left for the church, obviating that social institution to a status independent of government powers and effecting the separation of church and state.

As the classical school was reacting largely to contemporary abuses, it is not surprising that Beccaria condemned torture, though interestingly, not corporal punishment. His opposition to torture was based on the rationale that it should err in either direction, eliciting false confessions from the weak or failing to acquire confessions from the stalwart, but guilty, individual. Absent any utilitarian value to offset the evil inherent in torture, he found it unjustifiable. It could not help to determine guilt, and one could not be punished until found guilty. Once found guilty, there was justification only for the specified punishment and not for any more. Beccaria also opposed capital punishment on two grounds. First, he argued that it was illogical that any individual would agree to a contract whereby violation was punishable by death. Thus he felt that the death penalty was inconsistent with the social contract basis of the proposed system of justice. Secondly, he argued that life imprisonment would be more dreadful because the suffering would be drawn out over such a longer period than an execution. Consequently, he projected a greater deterrent effect for a sentence of life in prison than for the death penalty.

The classical school had a profound impact on all segments of systems for the administration of justice throughout Europe and ultimately the Western world. First, criminal procedure was revamped in pursuit of a rational and humane framework for the deterrence of crime. Though the procedural reforms emanating from classicism might seem passe to 21st century Americans, they were revolutionary at the time. The procedural protections extended to criminal suspects provided the foundation for criminal procedure in Western democracies. They included the right to a trial by jury, the right of the accused to confront witnesses, the right to present evidence on one's own behalf, the right to have legal counsel and protection against *ex post facto* laws.

These changes were possible because many legislators and other government figures took the classical proposals to heart. In England, for example, Sir Samuel Romilly devoted some dozen years in the English Parliament to introducing and seeking the passage of such reforms.

Beccaria's *On Crimes and Punishments* also provided the impetus for police reform. The process was slow, but received a jumpstart from the careful political maneuvering of Sir Robert Peel. Peel served as the Home Secretary of England early in his political career, securing passage of the London Metropolitan Police Act of 1829. The legislation relied upon Beccaria's book as its theoretical guide and was designed to prevent crime by way of deterrence. As Peel applied the deterrence concept to police operations, the random patrol of officers in clearly discernable uniforms would convey a sense of police omnipresence. Owing to the risk that a police officer could round the corner at any time and effect an arrest, crime was expected to be deterred. Although there was originally staunch public resistance to centrally organized policing, the "Bobbies" or "Peelers" were eventually accepted in England and this force became the model for Americans and other Western nations to emulate.

Classical criminology also had implications for penology. As a humanitarian reform movement, the new way of thinking called for dramatic reductions in the cruelty that had characterized preclassical treatment of assorted miscreants, criminals, and debtors. Several widespread forms of notably inhumane treatment were abolished as a result of the reform movement. All manner of tortures as well as retribution-based infliction of pain to elicit confessions were disallowed. Corporal punishment, however, continued to be practiced based on the pleasure or pain principles of deterrence. Segregation of the incarcerated by age, gender, and types of offense was implemented. No longer were males confined with females, adults with children, or debtors with felons. In short, although jail and prison conditions remained harsh by today's standards, they improved dramatically. The use of convict galley ships (called hulks) for confinement ceased, as did the practice of transporting offenders to foreign jurisdictions.

Classical criminology generally called for an increase in the use of incarceration to serve as the punishment proper, rather than merely a holding facility until the real punishment (e.g. torture, transportation, or service on a hulk) was initiated. This raised a question of prison design that Bentham became particularly interested in. He devoted extensive time and financial resources to the development of a prison model he called the Panopticon. The design consisted of a circular guardhouse at the center of the facility with straight corridors aligning the entrances to individual cells and protruding straight from it. From this central location, a limited staff of guards could monitor the entire facility. The plan never took hold in Bentham's native England, and was used only in a few American prisons (e.g., Western Penitentiary in Pittsburgh and Stateville Prison in Illinois). Although the plan seemed practical, it overlooked the psychological effect of the overwhelming isolation that it entailed.

The time for these reforms was ripe when Beccaria's work circulated. It was quickly translated from Beccaria's native Italian to several languages, including English, French, Spanish, German, Dutch, Polish, Russian, and Greek. His sudden fame brought invitations to meet with the renowned French philosophers of the day, such as Voltaire, Diderot, Helvetius, and D'Alembert. Moreover, his work so impressed reform-minded political leaders around the world that it yielded changes at lightening speed. Among the political leaders he strongly influenced were not only some aristocrats of his homeland but figures throughout the Western world such as Sir Samuel Romilly and Sir Robert Peel in England, the Empress Maria Theresa of Austria, King Gustavus III of Sweden, and Catherine II of Russia. Revolutionaries in France and America were notably impacted by Beccaria's work, as reflected in the French Declaration of the Rights of Man and the Bill of Rights contained in the Constitution of the U.S. Most of the latter's extension of procedural protections to criminal suspects can be traced to Beccaria's work. Reading the American Bill of Rights is much like reading Beccaria's 1764 essay.

Many of the reforms of the classical school were perhaps overreactions to the injustices plaguing European societies in the 1700s. As such, experience in administering these reforms revealed some practical problems and led some to retreat from classical principles after only a few years. Beccaria's recommendations were, for example, strictly embodied in the French Code of 1791 that was drafted in the aftermath of the French Revolution. Experiences with the new code led to revisions in 1810 and 1819 that softened the strict adherence to classical premises. First, classicists assumed the presence of rationality among all persons, but experience quickly dictated that the mentally ill and children should logically be exempted from this assumption, so they were. Similarly, practical experience in administering the new laws soon suggested that intent may sometimes seem more pertinent than the actual harm caused by someone, so this focus has remained a cornerstone of Western criminal law. Third, although discretionary decision making served as a focal point for the resentment of unjust decision making and was thus eliminated in early classical revisions of law, some measure of discretion became allowable in later legal codes. Laws, in other words, began to allow judges to select sentences within certain parameters depending upon the specific circumstances of crimes and offenders. Although some criminologists depict these changes as representing a so-called "neo-classical" school of thought, others see them as part of the evolution of the classical school and point out that even Beccaria's own writings provide the basis for some of these changes.

The classical school of criminology has had a lasting impact. It provided the dominant intellectual explanation of crime for over 100 years, until it was largely supplanted by positivist thinking under the influence of Auguste Comte and criminologists such as Ceasare Lombroso. Moreover, its practical impact on the administration of justice within the Western world has never entirely subsided. To the contrary, neoclassical thought has continued to serve as the cornerstone of law, criminal procedure, policing, and broad criminal justice philosophy to the present. Although the effectiveness of the key concept of deterrence was dismissed by criminologists for most of the 20th century, it was reinvigorated beginning in the late 1960s. Over the last one third of the 20th century, the concept of deterrence was subjected to vigorous scientific testing and careful theoretical elaboration. Although classical thinking has broadened, giving rise to a more complex rational choice school of thought, much of early classicism remains intact within this contemporary school of thought. This modern version of classical criminology captures a substantial portion of criminological attention and has substantially impacted the direction of theory and policy.

Stephen E. Brown

References and Further Reading

Beccaria, C., *Dei deliti e delle pene,* 1764; as *On Crimes and Punishment,* translated by Paolucci, H., Indianapolis, IN: Bobbs-Merrill, 1963.

Beirne, P., Inventing criminology: The 'Science of Man' in Cesare Beccaria's dei delitti e delle pene (1764), *Criminology* 29 (1991).

Brown, S.E. and Esbensen, F., Thoughts on deterrence: Evolution of a theoretical perspective, *International Journal of Offender Therapy and Comparative Criminology* 32 (1988).

Brown, S.E., Esbnensen, F., and Geis, G., *Criminology: Explaining Crime and Its Context*, 4th edition, Cincinnati, OH: Anderson, 2001.

Johnson, H.A., *History of Criminal Justice*, Cincinnati, OH: Anderson, 1988.

Maestro, M.T., *Cesare Beccaria and the Origins of Penal Reform*, Philadelphia, PA: Temple University Press, 1973.

Martin, R., Mutchnick, R.J., and Austin, W.T., *Criminological Thought: Pioneers Past and Present*, New York, NY: Macmillan, 1990.

Phillipson, C., *Three criminal Law Reformers*, Montclair, NJ: Patterson Smith, 1970.

Roshier, B., Controlling Crime: *The Classical Perspective in Criminology*, Chicago, IL: Lyceum, 1989.

Wright, R.A., *In Defense of Prisons*, Westport, CT: Greenwood Press, 1994.

See also **Beccaria, Ceasare; Bentham, Jeremy; Deterrence, General; Deterrence, Specific**

Classification of Offenders

In a very broad sense, the classification of offenders involves the gathering and use of information in order to make decisions about the sentencing, placement, or treatment of those found in violation of the law. The types of methods and practices of offender classification by correctional professionals have a long history in the U.S. and are still evolving.

Offender classification in general guides decision making in the criminal justice system. Correctional professionals who are new to the field often find the use of standardized classification methods (incorporating interviews or survey instruments) to be useful as a guide during the early part of their careers. Veterans in the profession of corrections use standardized methods of classification in order to better manage what often may seem like an ever-increasing caseload. There are a variety of classification methods or tools available today (some are better than others). Some of the best tools in use for the purpose of offender classification offer all the benefits of assessment in general. These benefits include the ability to make a decision about an offender's level of risk to the community, the appropriate treatment placement, the construction of a viable and relevant case-management plan, and the measurement of individual change in the offender's personality and life circumstances over time.

Methods of offender classification, when properly implemented, can help to reduce bias in criminal justice decision making by restricting major decisions to factors or variables that are not "extra-legal" (or outside the law, such as gender, race/ethnicity, or marital status). By subtracting extra-legal factors from the decision making process, protection and legitimization are offered to the various choices made by correctional professionals. In addition, if an agency or a large correctional treatment program implements a classification method system-wide, large populations can be managed more effectively. In sum, correctional agencies that use a classification method are in a much better position to incorporate what is known as the "risk principle."

The risk principle in corrections specifies that high intensity (and often expensive) sanctions and treatment options should be reserved for the highest-risk offenders and low-intensity sanctions and treatment options should be reserved for low-risk offenders. Some research has shown that an offender's likelihood of recidivism can actually be increased if they receive a sanction or treatment option that is too intense for them. The incorporation of a standardized offender classification tool early in an offender's journey through the system is one way to estimate the level of risk before punishments or treatment programs begin.

There are four common principles underlying offender classification: risk, need, responsivity, and professional discretion. In general the principle of risk means assessing the likelihood or probability that the offender will commit additional criminal activity. The assessment of risk may involve making the determination that an offender is better suited for placement in an institutional or residential setting, as opposed to a correctional option in the community (e.g., probation).

The principle of need involves assessing the "criminogenic" or crime-producing needs the offender may possess in his or her person or environment. For example, drug addiction or a hostile nonsupportive family environment is often regarded as a "criminogenic" need. Quantitative research in criminal justice and criminology has uncovered a host of predictive criminogenic needs. It stands to reason that an individual who possesses many criminogenic needs is much more likely to commit additional criminal behavior than an individual who possesses few criminogenic needs. The proper assessment of criminogenic needs also translates very well into "treatment targets"—those factors or variables that need to be changed (most often through treatment) in order to help the offender cultivate and maintain a crime-free lifestyle.

The principle of responsivity involves the assessment of various factors about the offender that may impact their readiness for treatment or their ability to comply with correctional sanctions. Responsivity factors include (but are not limited to) the convictee's level of psychological development, intellectual ability, motivation, and personality characteristics. The assessment of responsivity often may involve the use of various psychological assessment tools, aptitude tests, or consultation with a psychologist or psychiatrist. One way to consider these first three principles of classification could be that risk and need indicate what an offender needs, whereas responsivity indicates how the offender needs it.

The principle of professional discretion generally involves the "override" of whatever classification method or tool may be in place at a correctional agency or program. Regardless of the method, there will be times that the correctional professional does not believe that the level of risk or need indicated by the tool is the true level of risk or need. In such cases, the professional may make the decision to override the classification method and base decisions on unstructured "clinical" observations or some outstanding offender characteristic (such as a history of sex offending).

Throughout history, offender classification has undergone a distinct evolution. In fact, offender classification may be thought of as having experienced three phases. Early classification tools, or first-phase methods, relied heavily (if not solely) on static factors—those factors that cannot change. These static factors most often included criminal history or historical, personal, or social factors (e.g., abusive parents) that would always exist in the offender's past. Second-phase methods relied on these factors as well, but gave particularly heavy consideration to substance use and abuse factors. Third-phase methods of offender classification rely primarily on dynamic factors—variables that can change through appropriate correctional intervention (e.g., educational levels and work skills). It is the incorporation of dynamic criminogenic factors that allows third-phase methods of offender classification to out-perform first- and second-phase methods. It is the dynamic criminogenic factors that allow for the identification of treatment targets and, perhaps most importantly, the measurement of offender change as participation in correctional treatment occurs.

Not all methods of offender classification are of equal value. In fact, even with the best third-phase methods of classification, there are many potential pitfalls that can neutralize benefits (relating to the eccentricities of human behavior). Nonetheless, criminal justice research supports the fact that agencies and programs that incorporate a standardized, objective method of offender classification perform better than agencies that do not. Offender classification is undoubtedly the engine that can drive individual case planning as well as agency (or even state-wide) correctional agendas (relating to punishment and rehabilitation).

Alexander M. Holsinger

References and Further Reading

Andrews, D.A. and Bonta, J., *Psychology of Criminal Conduct*, Cincinnati, OH: Anderson Publishing Co., 1998.

Andrews, D.A., Robinson, D., and Balla, D., The risk principle of case classification and the prevention of residential placements: An outcome evaluation of share the parenting, *Journal of Consulting and Clinical Psychology*, 54, 1 (1986).

Andrews, D.A., Kiessling, J.J., Mickus, S., and Robinson, D., The construct validity of interview-based risk assessment in corrections, *Canadian Journal of Behavioral Science*, 18, 3 (1986).

Bonta, J. and Motiuk, L.L., Utilization of an interview-based classification instrument: A study of correctional halfway houses, *Criminal Justice and Behavior*, 12, 3 (1985).

Clements, C.B., Offender classification: Two decades of progress, *Criminal Justice and Behavior*, 23, 1 (1996).

Latessa, E.J. and Allen, H.E., *Corrections in the Community*, Cincinnati, OH: Anderson Publishing Co., 1999.

Latessa, E.J. and Holsinger, A., Importance of evaluating correctional programs: Assessing outcome and quality, *Corrections Management Quarterly*, 2, 4 (1998).

Van Voorhis, P., Overview of offender classification systems, in *Correctional Counseling and Rehabilitation*, Van Voorhis, P. and Braswell, M. (Eds.), Cincinnati, OH: Anderson Publishing Co., 2000.

See also **Corrections: Federal Bureau of Prisons; Institutional Corrections**

Clemency and Pardons

Historically, the rulers of nations have exercised the power both to punish those who offend against their laws and to exercise leniency or clemency toward them. Most modern nation states have incorporated this power of clemency into their governmental structures. However, unlike many premodern regimes where the power was personally held by the ruler and exercised free of external constraint, most contemporary states provide for the exercise of clemency within the formal regulatory frameworks of their legal systems. As a creature of the law, the precise nature of the power and the conditions under which it may be validly exercised vary from jurisdiction to jurisdiction. Nevertheless, we may generally define clemency in law as an act exercised by a state's legally designated representative (most commonly the chief executive officer of the state) that suspends, reduces, or removes entirely the punitive consequences of criminal behavior. The power is not exercisable in relation to private or civil wrongs.

Clemency in law takes a variety of forms, each of which may be subject to a different regulatory regime. For example, the execution of a criminal sentence upon a convicted offender may be temporarily postponed by way of an executive order known as a reprieve. Alternatively, a court-ordered sentence may be permanently commuted to—that is, substituted by—a lesser sentence. Both of these forms of clemency are often exercised in relation to capital offenses, with the result that the death penalty is either postponed or commuted to life imprisonment. During the 18th and 19th centuries in England, many of those sentenced to death for certain criminal offenses (such as stealing, for example) had their penalty subsequently commuted to transportation to the American or Australian colonies in order to meet a growing demand for labor in those places.

A pardon is a form of clemency by which an individual offender may be either absolutely or conditionally absolved from the legal consequences of his or her offense. Depending on the legal regime in place, pardons may be granted at any time after the commission of the offense. Though they are usually granted following conviction, they are occasionally offered prior to the offender even being charged or convicted. The pardon of former U.S. President Richard Nixon (for crimes committed during the Watergate scandal) by his successor Gerald Ford is a notable example here. As a result of a pardon an offender may avoid trial, conviction or a sentence and receive absolution from any legal disabilities that might attach to conviction (such as a statutory disability from holding public office).

Finally, an amnesty is a form of clemency that differs from a pardon largely in that it is granted to a class of persons rather than to a specific individual. Further, it is usually granted to those liable to be charged and tried rather than to those already convicted. Because the purpose of an amnesty is most often political, it is generally offered to groups of people who have committed crimes against the state—rather than against specific persons. Historically, amnesties have been offered in response to widespread rebellion or civil disobedience. A well-known example was that granted by Abraham Lincoln at the conclusion of the American Civil War to Confederate soldiers who by their rebellion were in breach of Union laws. It was justified on the grounds that the interests of the nation as a whole would not have been served by prosecuting such a large number of the population. More recently, many countries such as the U.K. have issued general amnesties for the possession of illegal firearms in order to reduce the number of such weapons in circulation throughout the society. Such amnesties are generally offered only for a limited period of time and often precede a toughening up of sanctions for such offenses.

The political and practical merits of an executive power of clemency have provided an important rationale for its continued maintenance. The power has also been justified on the grounds that human institutions are inevitably imperfect; the criminal justice system is no exception. Therefore, it has been argued that there is some utility in maintaining an extrajudicial mechanism by which errors committed by that system in the course of prosecuting and punishing offenders may be corrected. Similarly, the power has been justified as offering a mechanism by which justice may be achieved in those cases where a strict application of the criminal law—and, particularly, its sentencing provisions—would produce an unjust outcome (Hoffstadt, 2001). Defenders of the clemency power have maintained that it offers an important extrajudicial safeguard should the judicial system fail or otherwise operate in a manner not consistent with the public interest or public standards of justice.

On the other hand, skeptics have questioned whether such a power is the best means of achieving these ends. Some have argued for the correction of defects in the criminal justice system by overt legislative means. Others have accepted the limited role a clemency power might play but have called for greater legislative and judicial input into the issuing of politically-motivated amnesties and pardons by the executive (Moore, 1985; Walker, 1999). These concerns have been particularly acute within those jurisdictions where the executive officer in question has a broad discretion and is subject to minimal regulation in the exercise of the power. For example, in the U.S., the presidential power of clemency is only voluntarily regulated, by means of a purely advisory Office of the Pardon Attorney. Further, the exercise of the president's power has been held by the Supreme Court to be largely immune from judicial investigation into and review of its merits (*Conn. Bd. of Pardons v. Dumshcat*, 452 US 458 (1981)).

In such jurisdictions, important questions arise in relation to ensuring the propriety of clemency decisions. With so little regulation of the process, the risk of arbitrariness and abuse is heightened. In societies subject to the rule of law, such unconstrained power appears to stand in potential breach of the fundamental requirements of due process, procedural regularity, equal treatment, and public accountability. Critics have argued that the risks of abuse and injustice cannot be addressed by mere faith in the holder of the office but only by an increased legal regulation of the decision-making process.

On the other hand, defenders of a relatively unregulated power have argued that its flexibility and responsiveness to unpredictable political and legal contingencies would be impeded by undue regulation. Further, they have pointed out that in nations such as the U.S., any serious abuse of the power by a democratically accountable executive officer would inevitably come to the attention of the legislature and public and would render that officer liable for impeachment by the legislature or, at the very least, to informal sanctions in the court of public opinion.

Questions as to the degree of regulation required to enable the clemency power to be exercised both effectively and justly—and, indeed, as to whether such a power is the best means of achieving its ends at all—arouse much debate. Though not easily resolved, they are important questions that intersect with some of the most fundamental issues of contemporary law and politics.

Anthony J. Connolly

References and Further Reading

Bentham, J., *An Introduction to the Principles of Morals and Legislation*. London, UK: Methuen, 1970.

Capital University Law Review 28, 3 (2000) (Special issue on clemency and capital punishment).

Hanauer, P., *Pardon and Parole, American Jurisprudence* (2nd ed.) 59 (1987).

Hoffstadt, B.M., Normalising the federal clemency power, *Texas Law Review* 79 (2001).

Kant, I., *The Metaphysical Elements of Justice*. New York, NY: Bobbs-Merrill, 1965.

Kobil, D.T., The quality of mercy strained: Wresting the pardoning power from the king, *Texas Law Review* 69 (1991).

Moore, K.D., *Pardons: Justice, Mercy and the Public Interest*, New York, NY: Oxford University Press, 1989.

Sebba, L., The pardoning power—A world survey, *Journal of Criminal Law and Criminology* 68, 1 (1977).

Smart, A., Mercy, *Philosophy* 43 (1968).

University of Richmond Law Review, *Clemency and Pardons Symposium* 27 (1993).

Walker, N., Aggravation, mitigation and mercy in *English Criminal Justice*, London, UK: Blackstone Press, 1999.

See also **Administrative Law**

Climate and Criminal Behavior

Introduction

The notion that climate and weather can affect criminal behavior has persisted throughout history and is evident in language, legends, and literature. Tempers "reach the boiling point" and people get "hot under the collar" when angry. Cicero observed that "The minds of men do in the weather share/Dark or serene as the day's foul or fair." In Shakespeare's *King Lear*, the king's mad and manic episodes are accompanied by violent winds and storms.

One of the most surprising results to emerge from recent research is that many of these old beliefs have turned out to be wrong. For example, research into the relationship between lunar phases and behavior (e.g., Rotton and Kelly, 1985) indicates that there is little, if any, truth to the notion that people act strangely when the moon is full. Similarly, the idea that "rain is a policeman's best friend" also appears to be false. A recent review of both published and unpublished research (Rotton and Cohn, 2003) found that weak and inconsistent results have been obtained for most weather variables (e.g., humidity, wind speed, sunlight or cloud cover, and barometric pressure). This review indicated that temperature is the only weather variable consistently and reliably related to criminal behavior, and even the relationship between temperature and crime has turned out to be much more complex than anyone (scholars or the public) originally thought.

This essay looks at the possible influences of weather and climate on criminal behavior. "Weather" describes temporal variations in meteorological conditions (usually monthly, daily, or hourly averages), whereas "climate" refers to spatial or geographical variations (usually data averaged over at least 35–75 years).

Climate and Crime

It is difficult to separate out effects attributed to climate from those attributed to history, culture, and social class. In the U.S., southern states have both higher temperatures and higher rates of homicide than northern states. However, it has been found (Rotton, 1993) that when factors such as southern culture, literacy, and variations in socioeconomic conditions are controlled for, correlations between temperature and violent crimes are no longer significant. This suggests that regional and socioeconomic factors, rather than temperature, may be responsible for the higher rate of violence in southern states.

However, although climate does not appear to affect criminal behavior directly, Rotton and Cohn (2002) postulate that it may act as a moderator that determines the size of relationships between weather variables and crime. They suggest that high temperatures have stronger effects on criminal behavior in cold than in temperate regions whereas low temperatures exert stronger effects in warm regions.

Weather and Crime

Research has consistently found significant relationships between temperature and various types of criminal behavior. In general, field research has demonstrated that there is a definite positive correlation between temperature and violent crime, with more violent crime reported to the police on warm than cool or cold days. Cohn and Rotton (2001) recently uncovered a similar relationship between temperature and property crime. However, it appears that the size and even the shape of these relationships depend upon other factors such as the time of day. For example, research conducted in both Minneapolis and Dallas found that the relationship between temperature and assault was strongest during the evening hours, which is the coolest part of the day (Cohn and Rotton, 1997; Rotton and Cohn, 2000a). However, temperature's correlation with assaults was not significant during the early afternoon, which includes the warmest hours of the day.

A number of other weather variables have been examined for their relationship with criminal behavior. Although people often say, "it's not the heat—it's the humidity," most studies have failed to uncover a reliable relationship between humidity and violent crime. Similarly, most studies that consider wind speed have failed to uncover relationships between air velocity and crime, and investigators have yet to uncover any relationship between barometric pressure or change in air pressure and crime. Mixed results have been obtained in studies that included sunlight, although this may be because of the lack of consistency in how this variable is operationalized. Finally, of the studies that examined rainfall, only two have found any relationship with criminal behavior and their results were contradictory.

Theory: Explaining the Relationships

Attempts to explain the relationship between temperature and crime tend to focus either on emotional states (the psychological perspective) or on behavior patterns (the criminological perspective). Rotton and Cohn (2000b) attempted to integrate these two perspectives by combining elements of Cohen and Felson's (1979) routine activities theory with Baron's (1978) negative affect escape model. This integration suggests that uncomfortably hot and cold temperatures cause a negative effect that discourages social interaction and keeps people apart; that is, individuals either try to escape uncomfortably hot and cold temperatures or else avoid such conditions. Escape and avoidance result in fewer opportunities for victims and motivated offenders to come into contact with each other on cold and very warm days than on more temperate ones. Temporal variables, such as time of day and day of week, moderate the relationship between temperature and crime by also affecting opportunity; for example, offenders and victims are more likely to come into contact with each other during evening and weekend hours than during the day, when many people are busy at work or school or engaged in other routine activities.

This integration received strong support from a cross-sectional time-series analysis (Rotton and Cohn, 2001) that examined whether assaults were committed outdoors or inside climate-controlled structures. On the one hand, assaults were a linear function of temperature inside buildings: The warmer it is, the more likely individuals are to spend time indoors, to come into contact with family and friends, and to have violent encounters. On the other hand, more assaults occurred outdoors during comfortably warm than either uncomfortably cool or hot periods: During temperate periods, both victims and offenders are more likely to be outdoors. This pattern is consistent with the idea that extreme temperatures lead to less violence by reducing the probability that victims come into contact with motivated offenders.

Ellen G. Cohn and James Rotton

Further Reading

Baron, R.A. Aggression and heat: The 'long hot summer' revisited, in *Advances in Environmental Psychology: The Urban Environment,* Vol. 1, Baum, A., Singer, J.E., and Valins, S. (Eds.), Hillsdale, NJ: Erlbaum, 1978.

Bell, P.A., Greene, T.C., Fisher, J.D., and Baum, A., *Environmental Psychology*, 5th ed., Fort Worth, TX: Harcourt Brace, 2001.

Cohen, L.E. and Felson, M., Social change and crime rate trends: A routine activity approach, *American Sociological Review* 44, 1979.

Cohn, E.G. and Rotton, J., Assault as a function of time and temperature: A moderator-variable time-series analysis, *Journal of Personality and Social Psychology* 72, 1997.

Cohn, E.G. and Rotton, J., Weather, seasonal trends, and property crimes in Minneapolis, 1987–1988: A moderator-variable time-series analysis of routine activities, *Journal of Environmental Psychology* 20, 2001.

Rotton, J., Geophysical variables and behavior: LXXIII. Ubiquitous errors: A reanalysis of Anderson's (1987) 'temperature and aggression,' *Psychological Reports* 73, 1993.

Rotton, J. and Cohn, E.G., Climate, weather, and crime, in *The New Environmental Psychology Handbook*. John Wiley and Sons, 2003.

Rotton, J. and Cohn, E.G., The Ins and Outs of Temperature and Assault, paper presented at the annual convention of the American Psychological Association, San Francisco, August, 2001.

Rotton, J. and Cohn, E.G., Violence is a curvilinear function of temperature in Dallas: A replication, *Journal of Personality and Social Psychology* 78, 2000a.

Rotton, J. and Cohn, E.G., Weather, disorderly conduct, and assaults: From social contact to social avoidance. *Environment and Behavior* 32, 2000b.

Rotton, J. and Kelly, I.W., Much ado about the full moon: A meta-analysis of lunar-lunacy research, *Psychological Bulletin* 97, 1985.

See also **Routine Activities Theories of Criminal Behavior**

Cloward, Richard A.

The contributions of Richard Cloward to criminological theory may be traced to the work of the classical sociological theorist Emile Durkheim and the contemporary work of theorist Robert Merton. In his work *Suicide* (1897) Durkheim argued that anomie is one of the conditions that lead to high rates of suicide. Anomie is described as a state of normlessness in which structural social controls break down. Merton expanded on the concept of anomie in 1938 by applying the term to modern industrial societies, specifically the U.S. According to Merton, anomie takes place when there is a discrepancy between the cultural goals that are valued by a society and the legitimate means for achieving these goals. Merton noted that in American culture great emphasis is placed on material success that is to be achieved by legitimate opportunities such as high levels of education and occupational endeavors. But for Merton, this drive for wealth was not in keeping with the reality of disadvantaged minority groups who did not have equal access to legitimate opportunities. This situation produces strain that pressurizes such groups to achieve success by any means possible, even delinquency. Merton's theory led the way for later works that have been variously named "strain theory," "subcultural theory," and "class-oriented theory." For example, Albert Cohen expanded on Merton's work by emphasizing the structural sources of strain that lead to deviance in the lower class.

Cloward and his associate, Lloyd Ohlin, sought to integrate the work of Durkheim and Merton with social structural theories such as Cohen's and Sutherland's differential association that stresses that delinquency is learned in association with criminal behaviors or noncriminal behaviors. Out of this merger the "differential opportunity" theory was developed. Cloward and Ohlin were critical of Merton's assumption that lower-class individuals who are denied access to legitimate means of success will naturally have access to illegitimate opportunities. In a 1959 publication, Cloward purposed that the means for both illegitimate and legitimate success are unequally distributed. According to Cloward and Ohlin, individuals become deviant or conformists depending on their learned environments. Differential opportunity theory was in keeping with Merton's idea that deprivation of legitimate means for achieving success produced strain that leads to delinquency, but the kind of delinquency that will be learned depends on the illegitimate opportunities that are made available within particular neighborhoods. Therefore, deviance would likely not occur if an individual has little or no access to illegitimate opportunities. When a delinquent subculture develops, its form depends on the kind of illegitimate opportunities that are available in a particular area.

Cloward and Ohlin identified three delinquent subcultures: the criminal, the conflict, and the retreatist. A criminal subculture is mostly found in lower-class ethnic neighborhoods where professional criminals are highly visible and conventional role models are largely absent. In such an environment youth associate with adult offenders and are often encouraged to mimic their criminal behaviors. The kinds of crimes committed are usually those that involve acquisition of income, including theft, extortion, and fraud. The conflict subculture is characterized by an absence of either conventional or criminal adult role models and youth are unable to gain either legitimate or illegitimate opportunities for success. In such a culture, weak social controls lead to violence as a way to gain status. The retreatist subculture comprises so-called "double failures" who cannot make it in either the criminal or conflict subculture. Access to both legitimate and illegitimate opportunities is limited and youth retreat into drug abuse. Differential opportunity theory has been criticized for its lack of empirical evidence. Contemporary researchers note that gangs continue to be concentrated in lower-income ethnic neighborhoods but gang subcultures do not neatly fit into Cloward and Ohlin's categorizations. Other critics have noted the problems associated with the operational definitions of such terms as "double failures" and "differential opportunity." Further, some researchers note that neighborhoods with high delinquency rates are made up of not one but several subcultures. Despite these charges, differential opportunity theory is highly regarded as an important extension of the work of anomie theory, strain theories, and social structural theories.

Cloward has been praised for his achievements as a theorist, an educator, and a social worker. In 1957, Cloward and Ohlin embarked on a 3-year study of juvenile offenders at the research center of Columbia University. Out of this study the "Mobilization for Youth" program was established. The goal of the program was to help lower-class Manhattan youth to gain the necessary skills to overcome the structural obstacles to success. A major emphasis of the organization was to make training programs and employment opportunities more accessible. In his later works, Cloward became more involved in studies of public welfare and is well-known for his collaborative works with Frances Fox Piven: *Regulating the Poor: Functions of Public Welfare* (1971) and *Poor People's Movements: Why They Succeed, How They Fail* (1977).

LAUREL HOLLAND

Biography

Born in Rochester, New York, 25 December, 1926. Educated at University of Rochester, B.A., 1948; Columbia University, M.S.W., 1959; Ph.D., 1958; Adelphi University, D.H.L. 1985; Hunter College, D.H.L., 1999. Professor, Columbia University, 1954—. Dennis Carroll Award, 1965; C. Wright Mills Award, 1972; Founders Award, Society for the Study of Social Problems, 1991; Herman D. Stein Award, 1992; Lifetime Achievement Award in Political Sociology, 1995; Lifetime Achievement Award for Social Administration and Policy Practice, 1995; Lifetime Achievement Award of the National Association of Social Workers, 1999; Distinguished Career Award for the Practice of Sociology, American Sociological Association, 2000; Significant Lifetime Achievement in Social Work Education Award, 2001.

Selected Writings

Illegitimate means, anomie, and deviant behavior, *American Sociological Review* 24, 2 (1959).
Delinquency and Opportunity: A Theory of Delinquent Gangs, 1960, with Ohlin, L.E.
Regulating the Poor, 1971, with Piven, F.F.
The Politics of Turmoil, 1974, with Piven, F.F.
Poor People's Movements: Why They Succeed, How They Fail, 1977, with Piven, F.F.
The New Class War, 1982, with Piven, F.F.
The Mean Season, 1987, with Fred B., et al.
Why Americans Don't Vote, 1988, with Piven, F.F.
The Breaking of the American Social Contract, 1997, with Piven, F.F.

References and Further Reading

Cohen, A.K., *Delinquent Boys: The Culture of the Gang*, New York, NY: The Free Press, 1955.
Cohen, A.K. and James, F.S., Jr., Research in delinquent subcultures, *Journal of Social Issues* 14 (1958).
Cullen, F.T., Were Cloward and Ohlin strain theorists? *Journal of Research in Crime and Delinquency* 25, 3 (1988).
Durkheim, E., *Suicide*, 1897; translated by John A. Spaulding and George Simpson, New York, NY: Free Press, 1951.
Helfgot, J., *Professional Reforming: Mobilization for Youth and the Failure of Social Science*, Lexington, MO: Heath (1981).
Maris, P. and Rein, M., *Dilemmas of Social Reform*, 2nd ed., Chicago, IL: Aldine, 1973.
Merton, R., Social structure and anomie, *American Sociological Review* 3 (1938).
Merton, R., *Social Theory and Social Structure*, Glencoe, IL: Free Press, 1957.
Merton, R., Social conformity, deviation and opportunity structures: A comment on the contributions of Dubin and Cloward, *American Sociological Review* 24 (1959).
Schrag, C., Delinquency and opportunity : Analysis of a theory, *Sociology and Social Research* 46 (1962).
Sutherland, E., *Principles of Criminology*, 3rd ed., Philadelphia, PA: J.B. Lippincott, 1939.

See also **Strain Theories: Recent Developments**

Club Drugs

The origins of contemporary American club culture can be traced to the European island of Ibizia, located off the cost of Spain. It was the summer of 1987, and this summer getaway village became the birthplace of a music revolution—the "rave" movement. In the 1 years since, this youth movement has transfixed nightlife for many eager participants into venues where they can abandon their anonymity and, if only temporarily, themselves. Unfortunately, the means to such pursuits have been through the use of club drugs.

Although these substances do not share similar pharmacological properties, they are the most commonly used drugs in club venues across Europe and the U.S. In descending order, the "club drugs" taxonomy consists of the following:

- 3,4-methylendioxymethamphetamine—MDMA or Ecstasy
- Gamma-hydroxybutyrate—GHB or its precursor, gamma-butyrolatone, GBL
- Cocaine
- Methamphetamine
- Amyl nitrites—Poppers
- D-Lysergic acid diethylamide—LSD
- Ketamine—Special K
- Phencyclidine—PCP
- Flunitrazapam—Rohypnol

This essay will focus on providing a summary descriptive profile of the two most popular club drugs; MDMA (Ecstasy) and GHB.

3,4-methylenedioxymethamphetamine, MDMA, is referred to by some as a psychedelic amphetamine. It was first synthesized by Merck pharmaceuticals in 1912 and later patented in 1914. Although many believe its original use was as an appetite suppressant, there remains much contention about this point of view. However, what is known is that prior to its prohibition in 1986, MDMA was used in therapeutic sessions with individuals suffering from posttraumatic stress disorder (PTSD). Its cachet as a "party" drug did not evolve until the 1980s. MDMA's allure as a club drug stems from what users commonly describe as "the most physiologically and psychologically intense orgasm in a pill" which is actually a referent to how MDMA functions: (a) blockage of serotonin reuptake, (b) induction of serotonin release, and (c) induction of dopamine release (Malberg and Bonson, 2001).

MDMA is usually sold in tablet form (as such, they are commonly known in the streets as wafers, rolls, beans, X, and E) with monikers such as Mitsubishi,

Mercedes, Rolls Royce, Smiley Faces, Pink Hearts, Smurfs, and Harry Potters. Ecstasy is also available in white powder form which, in the street market, is commonly referred to as either pure caps or mollies. A standard dose of Ecstasy is between 80 and 150 mg per tablet. The street price of Ecstasy varies according to geography and amount of pills purchased. The base price can range from $20.00 to $40.00 per pill. If purchased in white powder form, the price can range anywhere from $35.00 to $50.00, although it should be noted a major factor in the pricing of Ecstasy is the amount of adulterants contained therein. The biggest threat to Ecstasy users lies in the fact that no one can guarantee the purity of, or presence of, pharmaceutical grade MDMA in each pill. Some of the most common adulterants found include caffeine, ephedrine, and a host of amphetamine-related substances. This represents a substantial risk to the unsuspecting user.

As with most drugs, the overall effects of MDMA are mediated by one's physiology, overall drug-using history, health status, and food intake prior to consuming "E." Generally, onset is between 20 and 90 minutes after taking the drug (which can be consumed orally, intranasally, or intravenously, and for some, by introduction into the bloodstream via the anal cavity). The user will generally feel the reported serotonin "rush" between 5 and 20 minutes after onset—this is what users typically describe as the "rolling" experience. Within 2 to 3 hours the user will experience the plateau phase, and the "come down" usually settles in during the last 1 to 2 hours of an E-trip. The aftereffects of the drug can last anywhere from 2 to 32 hours, depending on how much was consumed. Some positive effects, as reported by users, include extreme mood lift, willingness to communicate, increased energy, increased sensitivity to stimuli, and sense of community among the group of users.

Reported negative effects include short-term memory loss, headaches, vertigo, mild-to-severe depressive episodes, mild-to-extreme jaw clenching and teeth grinding. Illegal manufacturing of MDMA occurs mostly in European countries. MDMA is a Schedule I substance under the Controlled Substance Act (CSA).

Gamma-hydroxybutyrate, or GHB, is by far the second most popular of the club drugs. In the past, its legitimate use included the treatment of narcolepsy and alcoholism, and as an anesthetic, but its use has been discontinued because of unwanted side effects. In the 1980s, use of GHB as a bodybuilding supplement gained in popularity and in the 1990s, recreational or illicit use of GHB as a "party" drug came into vogue. In the late 1990s, GHB gained infamy as a "date" rape drug because of its powerful sedative effects whereby potential victims were rendered completely unconscious and vulnerable to sexual predators.

In the streets, GHB is commonly referred to as G, Liquid Ecstasy, Grievous Bodily Harm, and Goop. Its price varies according to geography but it is usually sold for a couple of dollars per dose or per capful. As such, it generally comes in liquid form but powder GHB is available. Because of the fact that it is primarily distributed as a mixed solvent, users have a difficult time determining its strength, thereby making it nearly impossible to ascertain the appropriate dosage. As a result, mild-to-severe overdose episodes are much more common, especially when mixed with alcohol. The overall attraction of GHB as a club drug is because of the fact that mild doses often mirror the effects found with MDMA. Moreover, as a cost-saving mechanism, some users employ GHB as a substitute for alcohol. The manufacturing of GHB is purely domestic and with most of the precursor chemicals readily available, its control is much more of a challenge for law enforcement. According to the CSA criteria, GHB is a Schedule I drug.

WILSON R. PALACIOS

References and Further Reading

Beck, J. and Rosenbaum, M., *Pursuit of Ecstasy: The MDMA Experience*. Albany, NY: State University of New York Press, 1994.

Boys, A., Lenton, S., and Norcross, K., Polydrug use at raves by a Western Australian sample. *Drug and Alcohol Review* 16 (1997).

Hammersley, R., Khan, F., and Ditton, J., *Ecstasy and the Rise of the Chemical Generation*. New York, NY: Routledge, 2000.

Holland, J., Ed., *Ecstasy: The Complete Guide: A Comprehensive Look at the Risks and Benefits of MDMA*. Rockester, VT: Park Street Press, 2001.

Lowinson, J.H., Ruiz, P., Millman, R.B., and Langrod, J.G., *Substance Abuse: A Comprehensive Textbook,* 3rd ed. Baltimore, MD: Williams and Wilkins, 1997.

Malberg, J. and Bonson, K.R., How MDMA works in the brain, in *Ecstasy: The Complete Guide: A Comprehensive Look at The Risk and Benefits of MDMA*, Julie H., Ed., Rockester, VT: Park Street Press, 2001.

Nicholson, K.L. and Balster, R.L., GHB: A new and novel drug of abuse. *Drug and Alcohol Dependence* 63 (2001).

Reynolds, S., *Generation Ecstasy: Into the World of Techno and Rave Culture*. New York, NY: Little, Brown and Company, 1998.

See also **Designer Drugs**

Cocaine

Cocaine is the active alkaloid that is extracted from the leaves of the *Erythroxylon coca* plant that contains between 0.5% and 1% cocaine. *Erythroxylon coca* grows in the high Andes region of South America. Chewing the leaves of the plant as a remedy for fatigue, nausea, and altitude sickness has been a custom in the region for as long as written records of human practice exist (Van Dyke and Byck, 1986).

The actual word "coca" comes to us from the Aymara Indians, a local tribe living in the area now known as Bolivia, and translates as "plant." The Aymara were conquered by the Inca in the 10th century. Coca received elevated religious status in the Incan Empire, being used prominently in religious ceremonies, marriages, rites of prophecy, and initiation rituals for "haruaca," young Incan noblemen. The production and use of coca were tightly regulated in Incan society. Incan rulers restricted production to state-owned plantations and restricted its use to rituals and as a special gift bestowed on the favored only by Incan royalty. Use among the general population was heavily regulated and restricted (Grinspoon and Bakalar, 1985).

The use of coca was introduced to the general populace only after the Spanish conquest of the Incan Empire. Under an edict issued by King Philip II coca was made available as a labor-enhancing substance, a food substitute, and an ameliorative for hunger. Social norms that regulated its use among the Inca disappeared with the passage of time under Spanish rule (Grinspoon and Bakalar, 1985).

Coca use and production remained restricted because the plant does not grow in Europe and the harvested leaves lost their efficacy during the long voyage from South America. It was not until 1750 that botanist Joseph de Tussie was able to successfully transfer the first plants to Europe. Nonetheless coca was highly praised in writings by visitors to South America for its stimulant attributes and is usefulness in easing breathing difficulties at high altitudes (Grinspoon and Bakalar, 1985).

Cocaine as a drug was not isolated from the plant until the mid-19th century. Dr. Aschenbrant, a Bavarian army physician, initiated the first recorded use of cocaine as a medicine, treating asthenia and diarrhea with the drug. In 1859, the Italian physician Dr. Mantegazza published what is probably the earliest tract on cocaine, praising its widespread potential for medical use (Van Dyke and Byck, 1986).

It was at about the same time that cocaine began appearing in nonmedicinal substances as well. Angelo Mariani patented the formula for and produced "Vin Mariani," a wine containing 6 mg of cocaine. Vin Mariani was used medicinally by some people, but was also popular at social events, and was the preferred drink served at social gatherings hosted by Pope Leo VXIII and King William III. Another contemporary example of nonmedical use was the inclusion of cocaine in the original formula for Coca-Cola patented in 1886 (Grinspoon and Bakalar, 1985).

Use of cocaine among the literati was common. Sir Arthur Conan Doyle used the drug and made his fictional hero Sherlock Holmes a user who found cocaine useful in sharpening his powers of deduction. Robert Louis Stevenson, it is believed, wrote his novel about Dr. Jekyll and Mr. Hyde under the influence of the drug. In addition, Alexander Dumas, Jules Verne, and Thomas Edison were acknowledged cocaine users who praised the drug's qualities (Grinspoon and Bakalar, 1985).

Dr. W.H. Bentley brought cocaine to the U.S. as a drug to cure opium, morphine, and alcohol addiction in 1878. Sigmund Freud was both a user and an advocate of cocaine, arguing it was effective in treating depression and morphine addiction. One of Freud's students, Dr. Koller, introduced the use of cocaine as a local anesthetic in 1884. The major pharmaceutical firm Parke-Davis was selling cocaine as an additive in cigarettes, as an ingredient in an alcohol-based drink called "Coca Cordial," as a nose spray, as a tablet, and as an injectable fluid by 1890 (Van Dyke and Byck, 1986).

The first signs of medical reticence about cocaine use appeared between 1885 and 1890. Reports on the negative psychological and physical reactions associated with using cocaine as an antidote to morphine addiction surfaced in the medical literature. Because common medical practice at the time was to treat morphine addiction by combining cocaine and morphine, it is unclear whether these reports actually reflected problems with cocaine, the results of reducing morphine doses to addicts or of combining two drugs with such antagonistic pharmacological properties. An unfortunate side effect of this confusion was the linking of cocaine and morphine in international attempts to control addictive or dangerous drugs despite their almost opposite qualities and effects. This confusion is one of the reasons why early efforts to regulate cocaine were undertaken (Van Dyke and Byck, 1986).

Snorting cocaine was quite fashionable among the wealthy, artists and writers in America by 1890. Several policies and practices implemented over the next several decades impacted use rates. For instance, in 1903, cocaine was removed as an active ingredient in Coca Cola and Novocain was developed and used as a local anesthetic that led to a reduction in the medicinal use of cocaine. The passage of the Pure Food and Drug Act of 1904 and the Harrison Narcotics Act in 1914 instituted controls on over-the-counter medicines that limited availability. Around the same time, personal use of cocaine was criminalized in Europe, but medical use continued until the introduction of amphetamines in the 1930s (Grinspoon and Bakalar, 1985).

It was not until the 1970s that cocaine, as a recreational drug, resurfaced in the U.S., Canada and Europe. Although very popular, increases in cocaine's use were slowed by its prohibitive price, selling in the U.S. for between $100 and $150 per gram, and an acceleration in the growth of cocaine use began in the mid-1970s and extended into the early 1980s. The legal suppression of amphetamine use, failed U.S. drug control policies in South America, and the activities of CIA-backed paramilitary groups in Central and South America combined to increase availability and reduce the consumer price. By the end of the 1980s, the supply of cocaine in the U.S. had increased by more than 400%, the purity of imported cocaine had more than doubled, and the wholesale price at a port of entry had declined by about 500%. Use, although relatively stable in terms of numbers, spread to all social strata of American society (Lyman and Potter, 1998).

In the 1980s, U.S. intelligence agents working with the Nicaraguan contras in an attempt to overthrow the government of Nicaragua (1) solicited funds for the operation from the Medellin Cartel; (2) provided logistical air support for cocaine flights to the U.S. and allowed the cartels use of contra-landing strips in Costa Rica; (3) arranged State department payments to companies owned by drug traffickers, ostensibly as part of a humanitarian relief operation; and (4) allowed the contras to deal in large quantities of cocaine themselves. Recent investigations have revealed that a sizeable portion of the cocaine being sold to Los Angeles-based street gangs for the production of crack came from the contras (Scott and Marshall, 1991).

Although snorting cocaine continued to be the most common modality of use (about 90% of users), increased availability led to new modalities, particularly smoking the drug, either freebasing it or smoking crack. In South America, cocaine is smoked in the form of "basuko," a coca paste created by the first step in the extraction process, with a cocaine content as high as 90% (Van Dyke and Byck, 1986).

Cocaine works by extending and strengthening the activity of the neurotransmitters noradrenaline and dopamine, resembling the effects of amphetamines in a much milder fashion. Cocaine does not create tolerance, and its effects last for a maximum of 1 hour when snorted (less when smoked). Cocaine is not physically addictive. It is, however, a powerfully reinforcing drug that can lead to patterns of increased frequency of use (Fagan and Chin, 1991).

In the 1980s and 1990s, media and state portrayals of cocaine described it as a highly addicting drug. These accounts usually depicted cocaine addicts suffering the anguish of their cocaine "addiction" with horrifying consequences for their personal lives. This socially created view of cocaine addiction went uncontested for three basic reasons. First, there was very little data from which to evaluate the claims. Second, this view of cocaine as an addicting drug was promoted as part of the drug war and, therefore, was unlikely to be contested by the state itself. And finally, the only early data that were available came from alleged cocaine addicts in treatment or seeking treatment (Lyman and Potter, 1998).

Over the years, additional research has produced data that contradict this view. For example, the preponderance of the evidence shows that cocaine, no matter what the mode of administration, is not especially addictive for human beings (Fagan and Chin, 1991). For example, the 1990 NIDA household survey of drug use found that 11% of Americans reported they had used cocaine. But, only 3% had used it in the past year and only 0.8% had used cocaine in the past month. This means that roughly 2.7% of cocaine users had patterns of use that might fall into a category of addictive behavior. A similar Canadian study found that only 5% of current cocaine users used the drug monthly or more frequently. Other studies demonstrate that only a very small proportion of cocaine users are persistent abusers, much less addicts (Lyman and Potter, 1998).

Among a small minority of long-term, persistent cocaine users, characteristics of dependence do develop. For example, of 50 regular, persistent cocaine users studied over a 10-year period, only five demonstrated the characteristics of compulsive users at any point in the 10 years. These persistent users, even during periods of heavily increased use, did not progress to habitual patterns of cocaine use. Similar studies of regular cocaine users in Canada, Scotland, Australia, and Holland all found controlled use to be the common pattern. These studies showed the level of use and problems associated with use came and went during the study period. The most frequent response to problems incurred in using cocaine was to quit or greatly cut back use, once again, hardly the characteristics of addiction (Kappeler, Blumberg, and Potter, 2000).

Crack is a chemical form of cocaine sold on the streets. It is composed of water, cocaine, ammonia, and bicarbonate of soda. It has a melting point of 96 degrees centigrade that allows it to be smoked. Because cocaine's effects are increased when the concentration of the drug in the body rises quickly, smoking cocaine produces a more intense, but shorter "high" than snorting the drug.

Studies have shown that in the U.S., where street-level cocaine is highly adulterated with other substances, greater preference is shown for crack. In the Netherlands, where cocaine is less adulterated and less costly, consumer preference is strongly oriented toward sniffable forms of the drug. It is important to note that 92% of cocaine-related deaths result from smoking the drug, and only about 10% of all cocaine users smoke cocaine rather than snort cocaine (Kappeler, Blumberg, and Potter, 2000).

In the mid-1980s the media and the states' drug war bureaucracy worked in concert to create a "drug scare," a historical period in which all manner of social difficulties, such as crime, health problems, the failure of the education system, were blamed on a chemical substance—crack. The crack scare linked the use of crack-cocaine to inner-city Blacks, Hispanics, and youth. In the 1970s, when the use of expensive cocaine hydrochloride was concentrated among affluent Whites, both the media and state focused their attention on heroin, seen as a drug of the inner-city poor. Only when cocaine became available in the form of inexpensive crack, and after its use spread to minority groups and the poor, was it widely portrayed as a social problem (Beckett, 1994).

Media coverage of crack, beginning in 1986, was intense. *Time* and *Newsweek* ran five cover stories each on crack during 1986. NBC ran 400 evening news stories on crack between June and December 1986; and all three networks ran 74 drug stories on their nightly news in July 1986. These stories repeated highly inflated and inaccurate estimates of crack use and warnings about the dangers of crack that were out of all proportion to the available evidence (Reinarmann and Levine, 1989).

The fact is that by 1986 crack use was no longer growing. Research from the National Institute of Drug Abuse showed that the use of all forms of cocaine had reached its peak 4 years earlier and had been declining ever since. At the height of the drug scare, crack use was relatively rare. Surveys of high school seniors showed that experimentation with cocaine products had been decreasingly steadily since 1980. The government's own drug use statistics showed that 96% of young people in the U.S. had never even tried crack. The media portrayal of crack use was out of all proportion to reality. The intense coverage of crack may have created new markets for the drug and slowed the decline in use that had already been under way for almost a decade (Beckett, 1994; Orcutt and Turner, 1993; Reinarmann and Levine, 1989).

As a result of the crack scare, new state and federal laws were passed increasing mandatory sentences for crack use and sales. Ironically, these laws resulted in a situation where someone arrested for crack faced the prospect of a prison sentence three to eight times longer than a sentence for cocaine hydrochloride, the substance needed to produce crack. In addition, the crack scare resulted in the racialization of the drug war. Starting with the crack scare of the 1980s, both the state and the media have gone to extraordinary lengths to tie illicit drug use to African Americans while ignoring heavy drug use among affluent Whites. Half of all television news stories about drugs feature Blacks as users or sellers, whereas only 32% of the stories feature Whites. This is out of all proportion to the known patterns of drug use. About 70% of all cocaine and crack users are white and about 14% are black. The media's overemphasis on African American drug use is matched perfectly by the police enforcement activity. Blacks represent 48% of all individuals arrested on drug charges, roughly three and a half times their actual rate of use (Beckett, 1994; Kappeler, Blumberg, and Potter, 2000).

In the mid-1980s reports also began to surface about the negative effects of cocaine use by mothers on their developing fetuses. Although the use of any drug is inadvisable during pregnancy, the panic that resulted from early research claims about cocaine's damage to fetuses and the laws passed by the state and federal governments in response to that research clearly exaggerated the harm and created policies that did far more damage to the mother and fetus than the drug itself (Phillip Coffin, 1996).

The early research, particularly a 1985 case study, suggested that prenatal cocaine use could result in several health problems related to fetal development, the health of the newborn, and future child development. Quickly thereafter, several other studies linked prenatal cocaine use to maternal weight loss and nutritional deficits; premature detachment of the placenta; premature birth; low-birth weight; reductions in infant body length and head circumference; rare birth defects, bone defects, and neural tube abnormalities (Coffin, 1996).

The media widely repeated these research findings, creating the impression that an epidemic of "crack babies" was plaguing the medical community. The intense publicity and a proclivity for dealing with drug issues with harsh measures led to new laws in response to the "crack baby crisis." Laws were passed that required doctors and nurses to report pregnant drug users to child welfare authorities. Other laws required child welfare agencies to take children away from mothers who had used drugs while pregnant. Many states criminalized drug use during pregnancy; in July 1996, the South Carolina Supreme Court upheld a law which allowed women to be imprisoned for up to 10 years for prenatal drug use (Coffin, 1996).

In this flurry of activity, few took note of continuing research on the issue of prenatal cocaine use that seemed to call the whole "crack baby scare" into question. Subsequent reviews of the early studies on prenatal cocaine use found serious methodological difficulties, including the absence of any control groups; not distinguishing cocaine from other substances in the studies; and lack of follow-up studies noting the health and development of the newborn (Coffin, 1996).

One of the most serious problems with the early studies suggesting a "fetal cocaine withdrawal syndrome" was that they were "non-blind," meaning that the individuals making the observations were told in advance which infants had mothers who had used cocaine during pregnancy. This biased the research and contradicted other observations from doctors and nurses who reported cocaine-exposed children to be indistinguishable from other children. In subsequent blind studies, therefore, it came as no surprise that observers were unable to detect the presence of "fetal cocaine withdrawal syndrome." (Coffin, 1996).

In addition, research using control groups found no increased risk of sudden infant death syndrome (SIDS) among cocaine-exposed infants. Earlier studies suggesting a possible relationship between SIDS and maternal cocaine use had failed to control for one of the most important variables in SIDS deaths, the socioeconomic status of the mother (Coffin, 1996).

In reviewing all the studies on both animals and humans it is now clear that no study has been able to establish a causal link between maternal cocaine and poor fetal development, and epidemiological studies have not detected any increase in birth defects that could be associated with cocaine use during pregnancy, although it is likely that cocaine, like any other psychoactive substance that enters the bloodstream, has the potential to impact on fetal and newborn development (Coffin, 1996).

Rather than maternal cocaine use, most of the scientific evidence points to the lack of quality prenatal care, the use of alcohol and tobacco, environmental agents, and heredity as primary factors in poor fetal development and birth defects. Inadequate prenatal medical services have been positively associated with prematurity and low birth weight. The provision of quality prenatal care to cocaine using mothers and non-cocaine using mothers significantly improves fetal development. Without question it is the use of alcohol, resulting in fetal alcohol syndrome, which is responsible for the most severe birth defects. Tobacco use has also been strongly associated with low birth weight, prematurity, growth retardation, SIDS, low cognitive achievement, behavioral problems, and mental retardation. Other factors far surpassing cocaine use in their impact on fetal and newborn development are poverty and lead exposure (Coffin, 1996).

The legal responses to the "crack baby scare" did much more harm than good to both the mothers and the children. Making substance abuse during pregnancy a crime kept mothers from prenatal medical care, thereby endangering the fetus far more than would be the case with drug use, and discouraged them from seeking drug treatment. When babies were removed from maternal care as a result of alleged drug use, social service agencies found it very difficult to find homes for infants labeled as "crack babies" because of the alleged behavioral problems that might occur during infancy and early childhood. In addition, enforcement of maternal drug abuse laws was also clearly and blatantly racist. Over 80% of the women subjected to prosecution under those laws were African Americans or Latina women (Coffin, 1996).

By the 1990s both cocaine use and the illegal cocaine markets had stabilized in the U.S. and Europe. As of 2001, 27.7 million adults in the U.S. had used cocaine, with at least 1.6 million using it on a monthly basis. Additionally, 6.2 million American adults had used crack, with 400,000 using it on a monthly basis (SAMHS, 2002: 109, 110, 129 and 130). Although European use levels are not calculated for every country, the Netherlands, which measures use in a manner consistent with that used in the U.S., reports much lower use levels, despite a much more lenient drug policy toward cocaine users. The Netherlands reports only 2.1% of their adult population has ever used cocaine, compared with 12.3% in the U.S., and only 0.2% has used it in the last month, compared with 0.7% in the U.S. So, in the Netherlands, with a no-arrest drug policy for possession and use, cocaine use is between 350% and 586% lower than in the U.S. (University of Amsterdam, 1999).

In addition, the economics of cocaine have demonstrated a clear stabilization in the cocaine market. In fact, cocaine is available at a lower price, in greater quantity and at a higher grade than ever before. In the U.S. the cost of cocaine at the retail level has declined from $423.09 per gram in 1981 to $211.70 per gram in 2000. In addition, the purity level of that retail gram has increased from 36% in 1982 to 61% in 2000. At the wholesale level, the cost of cocaine has declined even more markedly from $125.43 a gram in 1981 to $26.03 a gram in 2000 (Abt Associates, 2001, 43).

Similarly, in Europe, during the 1990s the price of cocaine fell by 45% (UNODCCP, 1999, 86).

GARY W. POTTER

References and Further Reading

Abt Associates. *The Price of Illicit Drug: 1981 through the Second Quarter of 2000*. Washington, DC: United Nations Office for Drug Control and Crime Prevention, 2001.

Beckett, K., Setting the public agenda: 'Street crime' and drug use in American politics, *Social Problems* 41 (1994).

Coffin, P., *Cocaine and Pregnancy: The Truth about Crack Babies*, New York, NY: The Lindesmith Center, 1996.

Fagan, J. and Chin, K., Social processes of initiation into crack, *Journal of Drug Issues*, 21 (1991).

Grinspoon, L. and Bakalar, J., *Cocaine: A Drug and Its Social Evolution*, New York, NY: Basic Books, 1985.

Kappeler, V., Blunberg, M., and Potter, G., *The Mythology of Crime and Criminal Justice*, Prospect Heights, IL: Waveland Press, 2000.

Lyman, M. and Potter, G., *Drugs in Society*, 3rd ed. Cincinnati, OH: Anderson, 1998.

Orcutt, J. and Turner, J.B., Shocking numbers and graphic accounts: Quantified images of drug problems in the print media, *Social Problems* 40 (1993).

Reinarmann, C. and Levine, H., Crack in context: Politics and media in the making of a drug scare, *Contemporary Drug Problems* 16 (1989).

SAMSHA (Substance Abuse and Mental Health Services Administration), U.S. Department of Health and Human Services. *Results from the 2001 National Household Survey on Drug Abuse: Volume I. Summary of National Findings*. Rockville, MD: Office of Applied Studies, 2002.

Scott, P.D. and Marshall, J., *Cocaine Politics*, Berkeley, CA: University of California Press 1991.

United Nations Office for Drug Control and Crime Prevention (UNODCCP). *Global Illicit Drug Trends, 1999*. New York, NY: UNODCCP, 1999.

University of Amsterdam, Centre for Drug Research. *Licit and Illicit Drug Use in the Netherlands*. Amsterdam: University of Amsterdam, 1999.

Van D., Byck, C., and Byck, R., *Cocaine*, *Scientific America* 246 (March 1986).

See also **Drug Use and Criminal Behavior; Drug Use: Extent and Correlates**

Cohen, Albert

Albert Kircidel Cohen (1918–), a sociologist whose work holds a prominent place in the advancement of theoretical criminological thought, is widely credited as a pioneer in the development of subcultural theory. He is Professor Emeritus at the University of Connecticut, an American Society of Criminology Fellow, a past editor of the *American Sociological Review* (1967), and was the president of the Society for the Study of Social Problems from 1970 to 1971. He also received a Senior Fulbright award to the Philippines in 1987. His major works include *Delinquent Boys: The Culture of the Gang* (1955) and *Deviance and Control* (1966).

The majority of criminology and criminal justice texts begin the discussion of subculture theory with the work of Al Cohen (Shoemaker, 1984; Reid, 1990; Lilly, Cullen, and Ball, 1989; Martin, Mutchnick, and Austin, 1990). Others, however, have chosen to minimize Cohen's contribution (Bartol, 1980; Vold and Bernard, 1986). This lack of consensus raises the question of whether Cohen's theory stands alone as a cultural accounting of crime, or if it is more an extension and synthesis of previously established theories. The answer lies in examination of not just Cohen's writings, but also his background and academic training.

Perhaps no student of sociology has ever enjoyed exposure to the level of instruction as much as Al Cohen. He enrolled in courses taught by prominent sociologists, most notably Talcott Parsons and Robert K. Merton, while an undergraduate during the 1930s at Harvard. While pursuing a master's degree at Indiana University, Cohen studied under criminology's founding father, Edwin Sutherland. After service in the Army during World War II, he returned to Harvard as a doctoral student, where he was associated with George Homans (Martin et al., 1990). Of these scholars, Merton and Sutherland substantially molded Cohen's interest with their strain and differential association theories, respectively. It is because of these influences that his works have been occasionally omitted from reviews of the subculture literature. Specifically, it has been alleged that Cohen focuses on the internal social conditions of subcultures, culminating in a strain theory dependent on social structural forces, instead of a more appropriate focus on the essence of a subculture (Vold and Bernard, 1986).

Cohen's repute as the founder of a distinct subcultural theory is based on his most famed work, *Delinquent Boys: The Culture of the Gang* (1955). In this revised version of his doctoral dissertation, Cohen develops a general theory of subcultures through a detailed commentary on delinquent gangs. Gang-based delinquency is dissected into five major categories: prevalence, origins, process, purpose, and problem. Prevalence refers to the uneven distribution of delinquency across class sectors in society. From a strain theory orientation, Cohen concluded that some groups were more anomic and moved toward deviance as a result of social constraints.

The delinquent prone groups were predominantly from working-class backgrounds. From an interactionist perspective, Cohen postulated that individuals from the bottom end of the socioeconomic scale shared difficulty in conforming to the dominant society that largely rejected them. The emergence of subcultures, then, is an alternative by various persons to their mutual rejection, a collective response to a shared problem. The process by which subcultures form and evolve is one of trial and error, a redefining of accepted norms likened to crowd behavior. Cohen notes that although "collective outbursts" as a way of solving problems are usually temporary and soon wane, they often succeed in establishing subcultures that, once created, can assume a life of their own (1955).

The purpose of the subculture is an accepting and supportive belief system that benefits individuals and is perpetuated through interaction with the subgroup. The benefit may be material, but also psychological in terms of positive reinforcement, a necessary ingredient for continued out-group existence. Group members may profit by increased self-esteem and social status, and these micro-level advantages foster greater group cohesion, although pronouncing the differences in value systems of the subculture and the larger society. Repudiation of social standards and norms is a defining characteristic of a subculture that necessarily results in cultural conflict (Vetter and Silverman, 1980).

In his focus on delinquent gangs, Cohen noticed class-differentiated degrees of drive and ambition that manifested in individual responsibility. Because of social-structural constraints largely beyond their control, lower-class youths experience a socialization process that devalues success in the classroom, deferred gratification, long-range planning, and the cultivation of etiquette mandatory for survival in the business and social arenas (Cohen, 1955). Cohen also observed that working-class juveniles generally did not participate in wholesome leisure activity, opting instead for activities typified by physical aggression, consequently stunting the development of the intellectual and social skills valued in the mainstream culture. The overall learning experience of lower-class males leaves them ill prepared, says Cohen (1955, 129), to compete in a world gauged by a "middle-class measuring rod." Their deficiencies are most noticeable in the classroom, where working-class youth are frequently overshadowed and belittled by their middle-class counterparts. Turning to membership in a delinquent gang is but a normal adaptation to status frustration resulting from clashing cultures.

Reviews of Cohen's gang theory of delinquency have been comparatively favorable, one early exception being an *American Sociological Review* article (Kitususe and Dietrick, 1959) that took issue with methodological considerations. It was contended that Cohen failed to present adequate support for what was basically an untestable theory. In response to this criticism, others (Martin et al., 1990) have considered the matter to be an issue of perspective. The criticism of verification has merit from a positivistic viewpoint, but Cohen's book is pure theoretical narrative; its objective is to recognize conceptual distinctions between juvenile and adult crime and the uneven distribution of delinquency throughout society that prompts the creation of gangs (Shoemaker, 1984).

Cohen has remained active during his retirement, continuing to attend the annual meetings of the American Society of Criminology. He gave an invited presentation to the Academy of Criminal Justice Sciences in Chicago in 1997 and has occasionally written with junior theorists building upon his work (Miller, Cohen, and Bryant, 1997; Miller and Cohen, 1996).

J. Mitchell Miller

References and Further Reading

Bartol, C.R. (1980). *Criminal Behavior: A Psychosocial Approach*. Englewood Cliffs, NJ: Prentice-Hall.

Cohen, A.K. (1966). *Deviance and Control*. Englewood Cliffs, NJ: Prentice-Hall.

Cohen, A. (1955). *Delinquent Boys: The Culture of the Gang*. Glencoe, IL: The Free Press.

Kitsuse, J. and Dietrick, D.C. (1959). Delinquent boys: A critique. *American Sociological Review*, 24: 208–215.

Lilly, J.R., Cullen, F.T., and Ball, R.A. (1989). *Criminological Theory: Context and Consequences*. Newbury Park, CA: Sage Publishers.

Martin, R., Mutchnick, R.J., and Austin, W.T. (1990). *Criminological Thought: Pioneers Past and Present*. New York, NY: Macmillan.

Miller, J.M., Cohen, A.K., and Bryant, K.M. (1997). On the demise and morrow of subculture theories of crime and delinquency. *Journal of Crime and Justice*, 2, 167–178.

Miller, J.M. and Cohen, A. (1996). Gang theories and their policy implications, in *Gangs: A Criminal Justice Approach*. Cincinnati, OH: Anderson Publishing.

Reid, S.T. (1990). *Crime and Criminology*. Fort Worth, TX: Holt, Rinehart, and Winston, Inc.

Shoemaker, D.J. (1984). *Theories of Delinquency: An Examination of Explanations of Delinquent Behavior.* New York, NY: Oxford University Press.

Vetter, H.J. and Silverman, I.J. (1978). *The Nature of Crime.* Philadelphia, PA: W.B. Saunders Company.

Vold, G.B. and Bernard, T.J. (1986). *Theoretical Criminology,* 3rd ed. New York, NY: Oxford University Press.

See also **Gangs: Theories; Subculture Theory; Sociological Theories of Crime**

Cohort Research

Cohort research involves the use of a research design in which a group of subjects sharing some common characteristic or event is studied over time. Historically, according to the *Oxford English Dictionary* (OED), the word "cohort" referred to a body of infantry in the Roman army, of which there were 10 in a legion. More recently, in the social science field of demography, we see the term being used to refer to a group of persons possessing a common statistical characteristic (OED Online, 2001).

When scientists conduct research, they must develop a plan for study. As part of this process, they consider who or what they are going to study, when they are going to study, and for how long they are going to study. Designs that involve the study of subjects at one point in time are called cross-sectional designs, whereas those that study a group repeatedly over time are called longitudinal designs. One type of longitudinal design is the cohort design. This is considered an "event-based design," as "data are collected at two or more points in time from individuals in a population defined by a common starting point or event" (Schutt, 1999, 173). Such efforts may be prospective, in which data are collected as subjects move into the future, or retrospective, whereby the researcher collects information on the prior history of the subjects.

The field of demography (the statistical study of human populations) makes frequent use of this approach. The best-known and most widely used defining event is the year of birth of the subject (referred to as a birth cohort). In 1965, N. B. Ryder, a sociologist (and demographer), wrote a piece on the value of the cohort perspective for the behavioral and social sciences generally (Ryder, 1965). He argued for the utility of this technique for the study of many different substantive issues, and his work has been described as "a seminal contribution to the subject" (Mason and Fienberg, 1985, 1). Ryder noted that each (birth) cohort has a "unique location in the stream of history" (Ryder, 1985, 11), and that by using this technique, researchers could study temporal changes within a cohort or examine differences between cohorts. This design is thus well suited to the study of process and change.

Cohort research is conducted throughout the world, although the use of birth cohorts in the study of delinquency is relatively recent. Criminological studies that have used the cohort design have been conducted in the U.S., England, New Zealand, Denmark, Finland, China, and Puerto Rico. In criminology, other cohorts have been defined and constructed based on a group of offenders sharing some common characteristic, such as the type of offense committed (for example, sex abuse defendants, adolescent murderers, or seriously mentally ill arrestees). Studies have been conducted on groups of arrestees, handgun purchasers, prison inmates treated for HIV/AIDS, juvenile detainees, and parolees, all in a given place and time. The cohort design has been used to study a variety of behaviors, attitudes, and opinions in the field of criminology.

For example, Guttridge and colleagues, interested in the criminal activity of violent offenders, studied the criminal careers of all males born in Copenhagen, Denmark from 1944–1947 (Guttridge et al., 1983). A cohort of college students was studied to examine the effect of victimization on fear of crime and attitudes toward the justice system (Dull and Wint, 1997). Widom (1998), using a prospective cohort design, has explored the relationship between early child abuse and neglect and later delinquent or criminal behavior. A number of studies have tested the "Easterlin hypothesis," investigating whether larger birth cohorts have higher crime rates (e.g., Steffensmeier, Streifel, and Shihadeh, 1992; Savolainen, 2000). Researchers from California retrospectively studied a cohort of handgun purchasers in that state to examine whether those with prior misdemeanor convictions were more likely to be charged with new crimes than those without priors (Wintemute et al, 1998).

One of the most important and influential cohort studies in criminology was spearheaded by Thorsten Sellin and Marvin E. Wolfgang. It was the first U.S. birth cohort study in criminology. Wolfgang, Figlio, and Sellin studied a cohort of 9945 males born in 1945 who resided in Philadelphia from their 10th to their 18th birthdays (Wolfgang et al., 1972). Data were gathered on a number of sociodemographic variables, including educational factors, residential mobility, and socioeconomic status. This study demonstrated the value of the cohort design for studying processes over time. It investigated the prevalence and incidence of the official delinquency of these youth, looking for patterns and trends in their criminal careers. The researchers studied issues such as offense specialization, offense escalation, recidivism, and age at onset. Comparisons were made between the offending and nonoffending cohort subjects, as well as among the offending subjects. This project produced the now well-known finding that a small minority of chronic offenders, about 6% of the cohort, was responsible for the majority (52%) of the crimes. This analysis was extended to the study of a 10% sample of the cohort, investigating the criminality of this group in their young adult years, to age 30 (Wolfgang, Thornberry, and Figlio, 1987). The follow-up study included interview data on the subjects to age 26 in addition to official arrest data. Wolfgang et al. determined that subjects with long and serious juvenile careers were likely to have long and serious adult careers. In addition, the tendency to specialize in a particular type of offense in a criminal career was relatively rare.

The 1945 Philadelphia birth cohort study, as it became known, was replicated and extended to the study of males and females born in Philadelphia in 1958, of which there were 27,160 (Tracy, Wolfgang, and Figlio, 1985, 1990). As was the case in the first study, delinquency was correlated with lower socioeconomic status, poor school achievement, school dropout, and residential instability. On the other hand, the members of the second cohort committed more crimes and more serious crimes than the cohort born earlier. There were also notable gender differences; males were more likely to be delinquent than females, and more likely to be frequent and serious offenders. Wolfgang's most recent involvement in cohort research involves his supervision of a birth cohort study in the People's Republic of China (Wolfgang, 1996). More than 5000 persons born in 1973 in the Wuchang district of the city of Wuhan were studied, with the ultimate goal being to investigate the delinquency of all those in the entire city of Wuhan who met this criterion.

Other influential studies using this design have been conducted in Racine, Wisconsin, and Dunedin, New Zealand. Lyle Shannon, using the Philadelphia cohort project as a model, studied three birth cohorts born in 1942, 1949, and 1955 over a period of 28 years (Shannon et al., 1988). He was interested in the relationship of crime and delinquency to the ecological structure of the city of Racine. Shannon et al. confirmed the finding that a small number of cohort members were responsible for a disproportionate share of the offenses. In New Zealand, more than 900 children were followed from birth until age 18. This extensive effort explored issues such as the link between personality and criminal behavior, childhood onset versus adolescent onset antisocial conduct problems in males, the association between mental disorders and violence, and variations in offending trajectories (see Krueger et al., 1994; Moffitt et al., 1996; Arseneault et al., 2000).

As a longitudinal approach, the cohort design has the benefits of greater ease in sorting out trends and causal relationships. Cohort research allows the scientist to better study changes over time. Farrington (1979) noted the utility of longitudinal research for the examination of continuities and discontinuities between earlier and later ages and the effects of particular events of life experiences on the course of development.

Conversely, there are a number of practical and methodological problems with the design. It can be a time-consuming and costly design to use. Given that a cohort is a unique group in time and space, there is a potential difficulty in terms of the generalizability of results. Further, researchers may have trouble disentangling cohort effects (those as a result of membership in the cohort) from the effects of age (as a result of maturation) or period (as a result of social, historical, or environmental changes that affect all members of society; Mason and Fienberg, 1985; Lab, 1988).

Pamela Tontodonato

References and Further Reading

Arseneault, L., Moffitt, T.E., Caspi, A., Taylor, P.J., and Silva, P.A., Mental disorders and violence in a total birth cohort: Results from the Dunedin Study, *Archives of General Psychiatry* 57, 10 (2000).

Bursick, R.J., Jr., Erickson could never have imagined: Recent extensions of birth cohort studies, *Journal of Quantitative Criminology* 5 (1989).

Dull, R.T. and Wint, A.V.N., Criminal victimization and its effect on fear of crime and justice attitudes, *Journal of Interpersonal Violence* 12, 5 (1997).

Farrington, D.P., Longitudinal research on crime and delinquency, in *Crime and Justice: An Annual Review of Research*, Vol. 1, Morris, N. and Tonry, M. (Eds.) Chicago, IL: University of Chicago Press, 1979.

Guttridge, P., Gabrielli, W.F., Jr., Mednick, S.A., and Van Dusen, K.T., Criminal violence in a birth cohort, Ch. 11 in *Prospective Studies in Crime and Delinquency*, Van Dusen, K.T. and Mednick, S.A. (Eds.), Boston, MA: Kluwer Nijhoff Publishing, 1983.

Krueger, R.F., Schmutte, P.S., Caspi, A., Moffitt, T.E., Campbell, K., and Silva, P.A., Personality traits are linked to crime among men and women—Evidence from a birth cohort, *Journal of Abnormal Psychology* 103 (1994).

Lab, S.P., Analyzing change in crime and delinquency rates: The case for cohort analysis, *Criminal Justice Research Bulletin*, Sam Houston State University, 3, 10 (1988).

Mason, W.M. and Fienberg, S.E. (Eds.), *Cohort Analysis in Social Research: Beyond the Identification Problem*, New York, NY: Springer-Verlag, 1985.

Menard, S., Demographic and theoretical variables in the Age-Period-Cohort analysis of illegal behavior, *Journal of Research in Crime and Delinquency* 29, 2 (1992).

Moffitt, T.E., Caspi, A., Dickson, N., Silva, P., and Stanton, W., Childhood-onset versus adolescent-onset antisocial conduct problems in males: Natural history from ages 3 to 18 years, *Development and Psychopathology* 8 (1996).

Ryder, N.B., The cohort as a concept in the study of social change, in *Studying Aging and Social Change: Conceptual and Methodological Issues*, Hardy, M.A. (Ed.), Thousand Oaks, CA: Sage Publications, 1997 (reprinted from *American Sociological Review,* 30 (1965).

Savolainen, J., Relative cohort size and age-specific arrest rates: A conditional interpretation of the Easterlin effect, *Criminology* 38 (2000).

Schutt, R.K., *Investigating the Social World*, Thousand Oaks, CA: Pine Forge Press, 1999.

Shannon, L.W., McKim, J.L., Curry, J.P., and Haffner, L.J., *Criminal Career Continuity: Its Social Context*, New York, NY: Human Sciences Press, 1988.

Steffensmeier, D., Streifel, C. and Shihadeh, E.S., Cohort size and arrest rates over the life course: The Easterlin hypothesis reconsidered, *American Sociological Review* 57, 3 (1992).

Tracy, P.E., Wolfgang, M.E., and Figlio, R.M., *Delinquency in Two Birth Cohorts: Executive Summary*, Washington, DC: U.S. Department of Justice, 1985.

Tracy, P.E., Wolfgang, M.E., and Figlio, R.M., *Delinquency Careers in Two Birth Cohorts*, New York, NY: Plenum Press, 1990.

Widom, C.S., Child victims: Searching for opportunities to break the cycle of violence, *Applied and Preventive Psychology* 7 (1998).

Wintemute, G.J., Drake, C.M., Beaumont, J.J., Wright, M.A., and Parham, C.A., Prior misdemeanor convictions as a risk factor for later violent and firearm-related criminal activity among authorized purchasers of handguns, *JAMA* 280, 24 (1998).

Wolfgang, M.E., *Delinquency in China: Study of a Birth Cohort*, Washington, DC: U.S. Department of Justice, National Institute of Justice, 1996

Wolfgang, M.E., Figlio, R.M., and Sellin, T., *Delinquency in a Birth Cohort*, Chicago, IL: University of Chicago Press, 1972.

Wolfgang, M.E., Thornberry, T., and Figlio, R., *From Boy to Man, From Delinquency to Crime*, Chicago, IL: University of Chicago Press, 1987.

See also **Cross-Sectional and Longitudinal Research; Sellin, Thorsten; Wolfgang, Marvin E.**

Colonial America, Crime and Justice in

The colonial period in our nation began in 1607, when the first permanent English settlement was established in Jamestown, Virginia. This period lasted until the new nation declared itself independent of Great Britain on July 4, 1776.

From the start, the colonists needed a method of justice that would punish offenders and deter future criminals. Originally, the Virginia Company, which sponsored the Jamestown settlement, decided that, to ensure order, it was best to allow the resident governor (who was appointed by the king) to institute a system of military law. This meant that the governor had maximum authority. In most cases, the governor established harsh sanctions for those who broke the norms of the society. This included death for the crimes of treason, murder, burglary, rape, robbery, and forgery.

As the colonies developed and became more independent, they began to create their own systems of justice. As most of the new settlers were of British descent, they held English values, norms, and social institutions, and they looked to the English ways of dealing with crime and disorder as models for their own systems. The colonists established a system based upon the English criminal codes, including the English system of law enforcement, courts, and punishment.

In these early communities, an offense against God was an offense against society, and vice versa. The boundary between violation of human law and violation of God's law was unclear: crime and sin were the same thing. The colonists had a high degree of consensus over what was appropriate behavior, and they used the criminal law to suppress any behavior they thought would threaten the values and moral standards of the community. If a colonist dissented from religious orthodoxy or expressed beliefs other than that which was popular, they could be whipped and fined.

However, serious crime was not a problem in colonial communities. There were few instances of predatory crime. Offenses such as murder, robbery, rape, and burglary were not common. Most crimes that occurred were misdemeanors, such as cursing, blasphemy, fornication, adultery, and drunkenness. However, offenses such as sexual promiscuity, drunkenness, idleness, heretical religious views, or failure to attend church were more common.

Because there was not much serious crime, the colonists created a system of justice that relied on informal methods rather than on formal agencies to punish wrongdoers. Offenders were more likely to be judged by their church congregation members than to be prosecuted in a court of law (because many times, courts and sheriff were hundreds of miles away). Church members acted as judge and jury, and could impose punishments ranging from admonition or rebuke to banishment from the congregation. The most common colonial punishment was a demand for public acknowledgment of wrongdoing in the presence of fellow church members. This punishment served to shame the offender, and reinforce the sense of obligation to other members of the community.

In addition to the church, the townspeople and family were principal agencies of social control. This often happened in the New England colonies, where offenders had to face a town meeting where the dispute was aired in public. In most cases, people were expected to monitor the behavior of their neighbors and report offenses. Because there was such intense neighborhood surveillance, patrol by a public police was unnecessary.

Fines and imprisonment were used to discourage blasphemy and failure to attend church. As the residents of the early colonies were familiar with each other, there was little anonymity. Most colonists were related by blood or marriage. Thus, the identification of criminals was easy. Any potential flight to avoid prosecution meant living on your own in the wilderness or with native tribes. Communities would often expel those who would not conform, or anyone who was undesirable.

Over time, the colonies developed different systems of justice based on the natural conditions in which they were located. There was a great difference in climate and access to trade between the colonies, as well as the social and religious structure. Massachusetts, which was founded by Puritans, had a more religious citizenry. Thus there was more of an influence of the Old Testament reflected in its laws. Each crime and punishment were supported by an appropriate Bible verse. The laws of Massachusetts, called the Massachusetts Body of Liberties, imposed corporal punishment for idolatry, blasphemy, witchcraft, murder, sodomy, adultery, kidnapping, bearing false witness, conspiracy, and insurrection. In one part of Massachusetts, Salem, the citizens carried out trials to determine if the, accused were witches, because it was thought that the devil was present in the community. In the end, nineteen witches were executed and seven more were sentenced to die.

The systems of justice that evolved in the colonies of Pennsylvania and New York were much different from that in Massachusetts. Pennsylvania was founded by Quakers, who established a far more humane justice system than in Massachusetts, with fewer offenses punishable with corporal punishment. The colony of New York, unlike the other colonies, had more immigrant populations that influenced the justice systems that developed. Dutch, German, French, Jewish, Scots-Irish, Irish, and English settlers each came to New York to establish lives. As there was great diversity, it was harder to rely on community norms and values to maintain public order.

The Southern colonies had other issues that northern colonies did not have, so yet another system of justice was established. Controlling slaves was one of the major tasks of the law in the South; the criminal law was used as a means of racial control. The fear of slaves and slave revolts was a major factor in the Southern criminal justice systems. These colonies developed daytime slave patrol systems in the 1740s, which preceded northern city police departments. Slaves did have access to the courts, but only rarely did the courts side with slaves. People of color (both slaves and free citizens) in the Southern colonies had few, if any, legal rights. The court proceedings were designed to reinforce the idea that slave masters had full authority over slaves and servants. At the same time, the Southern justice system also allowed more freedom in the private behavior of citizens, tolerating sexual promiscuity and private dispute settlement through duels.

During the colonial period, there was no juvenile justice system. In most colonies, the family had the primary responsibility for controlling the behavior of children. Children were often whipped for unsocial behavior, especially in the South.

As the colonies developed and became more complex, the community standards changed as well. The colonies could no longer rely on shared religious values and mores to define and reinforce acceptable behavior. The English system of justice the colonists had been using was no longer acceptable to settlers, who had fled England and the harsh government that limited people's religious beliefs. Thus, the colonies created a more advanced system of justice that included law enforcement, courts, and punishments to mete out justice.

Law Enforcement in the Colonies

Before the revolution, colonists held to the belief that community members had a basic responsibility to help maintain order. Thus, there was little formal law enforcement in the colonies. But as the colonies grew, the need developed for some system of policing. Originally, the colonists followed the English models of law enforcement. These agencies were loosely organized and not too effective. As they were still relying on citizen initiative in stopping crime, the police simply reacted to reported criminal events, which were few. They only responded to complaints brought to them and did not engage in preventive patrol. Many agencies did not have sufficient personnel to investigate those crimes that were reported. Over time, more methods of policing were established in the colonies, each one specific to the needs of the individual community. Three types of policing agencies that were instituted were the county sheriff, town constables, and night watchmen.

The county sheriff was appointed by the governor to oversee the formal aspects of law enforcement, such as making arrests, serving subpoenas, selecting juries, and supervising the jails and prisons. He was also an administrator who performed general governmental duties such as collecting taxes, supervising elections, and maintaining the roads. The sheriffs were paid through a system of fees for performing different tasks. The county paid him for services rendered, such as serving subpoenas or collecting taxes.

Corruption was prevalent in most sheriffs' offices. The sheriff was considered one of considerable prestige and power. The position was generally given to a member of the local elite, so they were untrained in the law. As the sheriff got paid more fees for collecting taxes than administering justice, they focused more on nonjustice functions. The sheriff billed the county for housing prisoners, and in some colonies, the jailer sold meals to the prisoners. It was common for the sheriff to take bribes from prisoners and their families for better accommodations, or to sell whiskey to the prisoners. In some cases, they would take bribes to release prisoners or fix the juries. Sheriffs would often embezzle public funds. In fact, it became such a problem that in 1730, the Pennsylvania colony felt the need to pass laws that would prohibit sheriffs from extorting money from prisoners or selling "strong liquors" to any person under arrest.

Town constables (who enforced local laws) did much of the day-to-day work of law enforcement, enforcing local laws. This included serving warrants, making arrests, inspecting taverns for drunks, arresting drunk persons, or questioning suspected vagrants on the streets. The job was not a full-time position, so most constables were ordinary citizens and were often elderly individuals. They were untrained, unskilled, and did not know the law. They earned fees by serving civil papers and arresting criminal suspects. They often ignored many violations, and enforced the law arbitrarily.

Night watchmen, like constables, were not trained in law. Their responsibilities revolved around protecting the city from crime and fires during nighttime hours. The men patrolled the city to watch for drunks, suspicious individuals, fires, or possible riots. Unfortunately, the night watch system was not effective. The watchmen were comprised of a rotating duty of all men in the community, and were usually paid no more than 50 cents a night. In many instances, the more affluent men paid others to take their turn. Often, these substitutes turned out to be drunks and petty criminals. Other members of the night watch were lazy, incompetent, and corrupt. There were often too few watchmen on duty to be effective, especially if there were a major problem, and in most cities the watchmen were not adequately equipped to maintain order. The ineffectiveness of the night watch became a serious problem as disorder (including public drunkenness and rioting) was a serious and constant problem in many colonial cities.

Under these systems of law enforcement, citizens could not report offenses. A victim of crime had to initiate action against an offender by going to court to swear out a warrant and by requesting the assistance of the constable in serving the warrant and making an arrest. Police officials could not respond effectively. Often, ordinary citizens responded themselves. Political entities sometimes offered rewards to the public for the apprehension of felons, and citizens could be called on to form posses to pursue criminals.

Courts in the Colonies

The courts that developed in the colonies began very small, but each of the colonies eventually developed their own individual court structures. For example, Virginia had a system of county courts manned by local planters who were assisted by sheriffs and constables. The county courts heard civil cases, minor criminal cases, and all criminal cases involving black slaves. Legal proceedings involving serious criminal charges were heard by the general court at the colonial capital in Jamestown. In New England, minor offenses were tried in local and county courts, with justices of the peace serving as magistrates. Serious criminal offenses were prosecuted in the highest court of the colony or in special courts of "oyer and terminer" ("hear and conclude"). These were temporary bodies that combined a judicial function with an investigatory one, and were convened by the governor for unusual circumstances only.

As the colonies grew, their courts became more formal, complex, and specialized. Formal courts first appeared in Virginia; Plymouth, Massachusetts; Maryland; and Connecticut. In these early colonial courts, the personnel administered English Common law, drawing from examples and cases set forth by the English. The Massachusetts Bay Colony established a powerful body known as the General Court that acted as both a legislature and the highest court of the colony.

The colonies developed superior courts to hear criminal and civil cases. The courts had different names in different colonies: Provincial Court in Maryland, Court of Assistants in the Massachusetts Bay Colony, the Court of Magistrates in New Haven, the General Court in Virginia, and the Court of Trials in Rhode Island. These courts heard a wide variety of both civil and criminal cases, such as persons accused of witchcraft or even murder. Eventually, some colonies established trial courts headed by a chief justice and several associate justices. Appeals from the trial courts were heard by the governor and his council and became known as courts of appeals. At this time, the courts also carried out administrative duties, including setting and collecting taxes, supervising the building of roads, and licensing taverns. At the county level, justices of the peace handled most minor cases. The more serious cases were handled by a collective group of justices of the peace.

There were no prosecutors in the colonial courts. Instead, cases were privately initiated. Criminal defendants had few legal rights, there were only a few trained lawyers, and only a few defendants who could afford their services. Sentencing of offenders was highly individualized. Court officials had much discretion in disposing of cases in a manner that would be appropriate according to that community's norms. The justices in these early courts were often members of the community's social elite. The court positions were often passed down from father to son, rather than to the most qualified individual. Most justices had no formal legal education and were not trained lawyers. They used the courts to reinforce their authority and maintain law, order, and the dignity of their class. Court day became a time for the elite to discuss business, politics, or just socialize.

Punishments in the Colonies

To punish criminal behavior, the colonists relied most often upon corporal punishments that inflicted physical pain on the offender. People found guilty were whipped, put in stocks or pillory, flogged or maimed as the primary means to control deviant behavior. Sometimes, people in the pillory had their ears nailed to the wood and were forced to pull them free upon release. Women who were found guilty of gossiping were immersed in the ducking stool. In Pennsylvania, women were publicly whipped for bearing children out of wedlock. Serious or repeat offenders were branded on the face with hot irons. An adulterer would be branded with an A, a burglar with a letter B on his forehead. Sentences were often carried out in a public arena. A common punishment was to whip offenders in the town square, or to publicly humiliate an offender for an hour in the stocks or the pillory.

The gallows were used frequently for more serious crimes. Criminals were sentenced to death not only for murder, rape, adultery, or kidnapping, but also for minor crimes such as picking pockets, burglary, robbery, blasphemy, and horse stealing. An offender could be burned at the stake or hanged in the public square, where hundreds or even thousands of colonists could watch. In some cases, offenders could be sentenced to the gibbet, which was an iron cage that held for days the body of a criminal already executed by hanging.

Other punishments existed in the colonies, but they were rarely used. There was little or no imprisonment. Jails existed, but they were used primarily as a holding facility to hold defendants awaiting trial, or to punish those who were unable to pay their debts. When people were in jail, there were no distinctions made among the prisoners. For the most part, jails were overcrowded with inadequate sanitation and widespread disease. Colonists were sometimes sentenced to pay fines or pay restitution for property crimes and other minor offenses against public decency. For very serious offenses against the community, offenders were banished from the colony. If the offender returned, they could be hanged.

There was no probation but "peace bonds" did exist. In this case, criminal offenders were ordered to post a cash bond and to report to the court in lieu of punishments. These were often used for people who had not been convicted of an offense.

The American Revolution: The End of the Colonial Period

The American Revolution brought new ideas about society, government, and criminal justice. The writers of the Declaration of Independence and the Constitution had optimistic views of human nature, and gave specific rights to people accused of crimes, and to those otherwise involved in the justice system. Values were changing throughout the nation and in criminal justice as well. William Penn and the Quakers supported a more humane treatment of offenders, and regarded corporal and capital punishments as barbaric. John Howard wrote about the conditions of prisons in England and Wales, shocking many with his stories of mistreatment. Jeremy Bentham's ideas of utilitarianism (that people can logically choose how to act by calculating the relative amounts of pleasure and pain derived from various actions) became very popular. Benjamin Rush (a physician and signer of the Declaration of Independence) maintained that excessive punishments only serve to harden criminals. He was opposed to capital punishment and advocated the penitentiary as a replacement for capital and corporal punishment. And Cesare Beccaria fought to bring order and rationality to criminal laws and procedures. He argued that society needed a system that would guarantee all people equal treatment before the law, and proposed that punishment should fit the crime. All of these people helped those working for justice move out of the colonial period, and into one that was considered to be a more humane system of justice.

Nancy Marion

References and Further Reading

Johnson, H.A. 1988. *History of Criminal Justice*, Anderson Publishing Company.

Walker, S. 1998. *Popular Justice: A History of American Criminal Justice*, New York, NY: Oxford University Press.

Walker, S. 1999. *The Police in America*, Boston, MA: McGraw-Hill.

See also **Customary Law; Witchcraft and Heresy**

Commercial Sex *See* **Prostitution**

Common Law *See* **English Legal Traditions**

Community Corrections

The definition of community corrections (also often referred to as intermediate sanctions) is controversial for a number of reasons. First and foremost, the field of community corrections is dynamic, with new programs and practices appearing regularly. Secondly, some argue that probation should be considered a form of community corrections, whereas others argue that probation is a unique sentence and should not be discussed as equivalent to other forms of community corrections. Nevertheless, most practitioners and researchers agree that community corrections include those correctional programs delivered in the community that are more stringent than probation and less severe than imprisonment. These sanctions are designed to supervise convicted offenders in lieu of incarceration (either by local, state, or federal authority) and: (1) provide a variety of services to clients or offenders (e.g., employment and substance abuse counseling); (2) heighten client or offender responsibility regarding payment of fines, victim compensation, and restitution orders; and (3) provide for a continuation of punishment through more controlled supervision and greater personal accountability (Champion, 1996). Community corrections is the part of the criminal justice system that provides services and sanctions to offenders in the community with the idea that it is important to maintain positive ties between the offender and the community in which they live.

Most community corrections programs originated in the late 1960s and 1970s. There were a number of factors that combined to bring about the growth of community corrections during that time period. First, the Federal Prisoners Rehabilitation Act of 1965 was passed, requiring that furloughs, work release, and community treatment facilities be made available for federal offenders. Secondly, the President's Crime Commission report of 1967 argued that corrections systems should not just incapacitate, but should reintegrate the offender into the community, restore family ties, and, overall, rebuild the bond between the offender and the community. Finally, amid rising crime rates during that period, the criminal justice system received tremendous criticism, culminating in an article by Robert Martinson and his colleagues that appeared in 1974 and concluded that neither probation, parole, nor incarceration had a significant impact on reducing crime among offenders sentenced to those programs. As a result, a number of innovative correctional programs administered in the community were developed as alternatives to probation, parole, and imprisonment. These programs have continued until present and even the harshest critics admit that, at worst, these programs are no less effective than either prison or probation in reducing the recidivism of clients.

The rationale for community corrections involves five related ideas. First, imprisonment is too severe a punishment for many offenders, particularly offenders convicted of less serious crimes. Few would argue that a person convicted of writing bad checks or shoplifting should be imprisoned. Nevertheless, regular probation may not be an effective deterrent to keep them from engaging in future crime, so alternative punishments are needed. Secondly, traditional probation does not work for many offenders. Most researchers agree that regular probation is not an effective supervision tool for offenders who do not want to be rehabilitated. Thus, community corrections give criminal justice decision makers alternatives other than incarceration to deal with these offenders. Thirdly, justice can be served by having options in between probation and imprisonment. Though some would argue that regular probation is not a stringent enough penalty for many crimes, community corrections programs can punish the offender more severely without the use of imprisonment or incarceration. Further, most community corrections programs are less expensive than imprisonment; state and local jurisdictions can thus save money and effectively deter crime when using sentences in the community. Finally, community corrections allow criminal justice officials to alleviate prison and jail overcrowding. With the development of community corrections programs, criminal justice decision makers can now save prison for those offenders who pose the greatest threat to society and who commit the most serious offenses.

Although most admit that community corrections present vital alternatives to probation and imprisonment, corrections experts have nevertheless identified a number of problems faced by community corrections programs. The most significant problem faced by community corrections is net widening. Net widening is the idea that instead of reducing control exerted over offenders' lives, the introduction of community corrections has extended control. As asserted above, one of the purposes of community corrections is to alleviate jail and prison overcrowding by offering additional sentencing alternatives to criminal justice decision makers. Critics of community corrections argue that by allowing criminal justice decision makers a choice of more options than prison or probation, instead of assigning into community corrections offenders who otherwise would have been incarcerated, decision makers are diverting people from probation. According to these critics, then, community corrections programs often supervise offenders who would have been sentenced to regular probation had the community program not existed.

A similar problem also exists in selecting offenders. Some argue that the seriousness of the offender's crime should be used as the criteria for placement in prison or community corrections; others argue that the offender's response to rehabilitation services should be used as the criteria for selection. Despite the debate, the reality is that officials who administer community corrections programs often are unwilling to accept offenders convicted of serious crimes, even though the chances of an offender being rehabilitated are very good.

A final problem faced by community corrections programs involves selecting which agencies should administer the program. In many jurisdictions, traditional corrections agents argue that they should administer the community corrections programs to maintain program coherence throughout the jurisdiction. Critics of this model argue that because traditional correctional organizations must give highest priority to institutional program administration, they cannot provide adequate supervision of offenders in community corrections programs. These critics favor the creation of separate community corrections departments to administer these programs. Little research has investigated which of the administrative models is more effective; future research will have to determine that answer.

An important legal development in the area of community corrections came about with the implementation of community corrections acts in the early 1970s in the states of Minnesota, Iowa, and Colorado. A community corrections act is a statewide mechanism through which funds are granted to local units of government to plan, develop, and deliver correctional services at the local level. Community corrections acts establish local community corrections agencies, facilities, and programs and provide local sentencing options that can be used in lieu of imprisonment in state institutions. These acts allow local governments to take offenders who pose little or no risk to the public and release them into the community under close supervision. Local jurisdictions are given financial rewards from the state for sentencing offenders to locally administered community corrections programs, again saving limited prison space. Soon after this legislation originated in the aforementioned states, community corrections acts spread throughout the country.

Despite the fact that community corrections acts vary from state to state, they also share a number of similarities. First, community corrections acts are enacted by state legislatures and are authorized statewide. Thus, each locality within the state can take advantage of the funds granted by the act. Second, community corrections acts define the relationships between agencies, specifying the roles to be performed and distributing the power between state and local governments. Finally, community corrections acts endorse locally determined sanctions and services, and provide state funding and authority for new sanctions and services to be used to place offenders in the community (Harris, 1996). Many authors argue that without these provisions, community corrections programs would never have gained the level of popularity they have presently achieved.

In the U.S. and throughout the world, there are a wide variety of community corrections programs. These programs range from fines to shock incarceration and boot camp programs. As many of the programs are discussed in greater detail in this encyclopedia (e.g., boot camps, diversion, electronic monitoring, home confinement, and shock incarceration), each will be only briefly discussed here.

Fines are the most used form of community corrections and are often combined with other sentences such as probation or diversion. In fact, over $1 billion in fines is collected annually in the U.S. Nevertheless, compared with other Western democracies, the U.S. makes little use of fines as the sole punishment for crimes. A number of reasons exist, but judges cite the difficulty of collecting and enforcing fines, as well as the fact that fines punish affluent offenders to a lesser degree than poor offenders. To counter these criticisms, day fines are commonly used in Europe and South Africa. A day fine is a criminal penalty based on the amount of income an offender earns in a day's work. In other words, the sentencing official sentences the convicted offender to a number of days instead of a financial penalty. This monetary amount of the fine is calculated as the cost of a day of freedom, or the amount of income an offender would have to forfeit if they were incarcerated. Thus, the day fine is said to punish each offender equitably, regardless of their income.

Another community corrections program that has become popular is shock incarceration. Shock incarceration is a short period of incarceration followed by a sentence reduction. The offender is sentenced to a jail or prison term; after the offender has served 30–90 days, the judge adjusts the punishment by placing the offender on regular probation or home confinement. The assumption is that the offender will find the incarceration experience so distasteful, they will not want to commit another crime. Boot camp experiences (where offenders are placed in highly structured programs emphasizing rigorous physical exercise, drills, and ceremony, akin to basic training in the military) have been added as a part of shock incarceration.

Originating in England, day-reporting centers are facilities where probation violators attend day-long intervention and treatment sessions. The actual administration of these facilities varies widely, but most day-reporting centers incorporate a mix of common correctional methods, including close supervision, individual and group therapy, and drug and alcohol counseling. Relatively few evaluations have been performed of these programs, so it will be interesting to see how successful they are in reducing recidivism.

Other community corrections programs include community service (where offenders are required to provide a specified number of hours of free labor in some public service), forfeiture (seizure by the government of property or other assets used in or gained from criminal activity), diversion (where the defendant agrees to abide by certain conditions set by the prosecutor to avoid incarceration), intensive supervision probation (where the officer more closely supervises the offender than under regular probation), and home confinement (offenders serve their sentences under strict curfews in their home).

A number of evaluations of community corrections programs have been performed with a wide variety of positive and negative results. Gendreau (1995) argues that for community corrections programs to succeed they must have the following characteristics: (1) intensive cognitive, social learning, and behavioral or psychological services are provided to the offender the last 3–9 months; (2) target antisocial attitudes and values; (3) tailor programs that match the offender's needs, personality, and learning style; (4) positive reinforcement is used much more frequently than punishment to modify behavior; (5) train therapists to relate to offenders in positive and sensitive ways; and (6) place offenders in pro-social activities and make it difficult for them to maintain previous antisocial ties.

For community corrections to function effectively, Clear and Cole (2000) argue that three continuing problems need to be addressed. First, some method must be devised to ensure that criminal justice decision makers resist the urge to place offenders otherwise headed to probation in more restrictive correctional contexts (net widening) so that community corrections programs are delivered to the appropriate offenders. Secondly, community support for community corrections programs must increase. Active efforts should be undertaken to ensure that citizens' fears of offenders in the community can be reduced. Finally, the goals of community corrections must be clarified. No program can operate with goals that are not clearly defined, and community corrections programs today have a number of competing goals (e.g., reducing prison and costs, community protection, and rehabilitation).

Others, however, argue that the present system of community corrections needs to be modified so that interventions at the community level have a more "restorative" goal. These critics argue that community corrections programs should be designed so that victims have access to court and correctional processes that allow them to structure offender obligations that will encourage the offender to take responsibility to ensure that the victim is "made whole again." Additionally, these critics argue that the community should be involved in holding the offenders accountable, supporting victims, and providing opportunities for offenders to be reintegrated into the community. These critics argue that community corrections acts should be amended to focus on the protection of the fundamental rights of the victims.

Despite the rhetoric and controversy surrounding the goals and future of community corrections, one fact is clear: community corrections programs are dynamic and will continue to improve as they take on a much larger role in the correctional practices of the future.

David C. May

References and Further Reading

Anderson, D., *Sensible Justice: Alternatives to Prison*, New York, NY: The New Press, 1998.

Austin, J. and Irwin, J., *It's about Time: America's Imprisonment Binge*, 3rd ed., Belmont, CA: Wadsworth, 2000.

Byrne, J.M., Lurigio, A.J., and Petersilia, J., *Smart Sentencing: The Emergence of Intermediate Sanctions*, Newbury Park, CA: Sage, 1992.

Lerman, P., *Community Treatment and Social Control*, Chicago, IL: University of Chicago Press, 1975.

Morris, N.J. and Tonry, M., *Between Prison and Probation: Intermediate Punishments in a Rational Sentencing System*, New York, NY: Oxford University Press, 1990.

Reiman, J., *The Rich Get Richer and the Poor Get Prison*, 5th ed., Boston, MA: Allyn and Bacon, 1998.

See also **Community Service and Restitution Programs; Juvenile Justice: Corrections; Sentences and Sentencing: Guidelines**

Community Justice Programs

See **Community Service and Restitution Programs; Restorative Justice**

Community Service and Restitution Programs

Community service is a requirement by the court that convicted offenders should undertake unpaid work for the benefit of the community. Numerous examples of criminal sanctioning with an emphasis on the performance of work with a socially useful purpose can be identified historically. However, the first modern community service program was developed in Alameda County, California in 1966 when certain road traffic offenders were required by the municipal court to perform unpaid work for the community.

The development of community service in the U.S. received a particular impetus when, in 1976, the Law Enforcement Assistance Administration made available funding for the development of community service programs for adult offenders. Two years later the Office of Juvenile Justice and Delinquency Prevention provided resources to enable the development of community service programs for juvenile offenders in 85 counties and states. As McDonald (1986) observed, many programs ceased when the initial funding expired, but others obtained alternative sources of finance, including local and state support.

Community service orders were first introduced on a *legislated* basis in England and Wales in 1973, with the new orders administered and supervised by the probation service. The Criminal Justice Act of 1972 enabled offenders aged 17 years and over who had been convicted of an offense that was punishable by imprisonment to be ordered to undertake between 40 and 240 hours of unpaid work. Community service orders proved to be a popular measure with the courts: the availability of this sentencing option was extended throughout England and Wales in 1974 and introduced in Scotland in 1979.

The formal incorporation of community service into the criminal justice system was watched with interest by other countries and the British experience served as a model for schemes that were subsequently developed elsewhere. During the 1970s community service was introduced in differing formats in several other non-European countries, including Australia, Canada, and New Zealand and in most of Western Europe (Albrecht and Schädler, 1986). Community service was most often introduced, as in Britain, as a direct alternative to short periods of incarceration. In some countries (such as Luxembourg and Norway) community service could be substituted for prison as a condition of pardon whereas in others (such as Germany, Italy, and Switzerland) community service orders could be imposed instead of imprisonment for fine default (van Kalmthout and Tak, 1988). A few countries resisted the addition of community service to their repertoire of criminal sanctions. Sweden, for example, rejected it on the basis that it had a limited impact on the use of imprisonment and was incompatible with a social structure that regarded work as a privilege.

In the U.K., community service orders were intended to serve as alternatives to short prison sentences, though it appeared that they were often used by the courts as alternatives to other noncustodial sentences such as fines. They have also been used disproportionately as a sanction for young men and women who have tended to be underrepresented on these orders. Morris and Tonry (1990) concluded that community service was most commonly used in the U.S. for white-collar offenders, juveniles, and for minor offenses but suggested that these sanctions should be used for a wider range of offenses and offenders. Increasingly community service has been used in the U.S. as an element of intensive probation programs where it represents one component of a package of measures (which can include house arrest, counseling, financial compensation to victims, and drug testing) imposed upon the probationer. In England and Wales, the 1991 Criminal Justice Act enabled courts to combine community service with a period of probation supervision, in what is referred to as a combination order.

Despite the apparent popularity of community service as a sentencing option in various jurisdictions, fundamental concerns have been expressed about its underlying philosophy and apparent ability to fulfill simultaneously a number of sentencing aims (Pease, 1985). This is reflected to some extent in the nature and range of activities that community service may involve. Offenders are given community service work in a variety of settings and are engaged in many different types of unpaid work. They may, for example, work alongside other offenders in supervised teams or they may carry out their community service working for a public or not-for-profit agency. Sometimes, the work the offender is required to perform is related in some way to the type of offense committed (e.g., persons convicted for cruelty to animals who are required to work in animal shelters), though more usually it is not.

Community service has been said to contain elements of punishment, restitution, and rehabilitation. In the U.S., community service is sometimes considered a form of restitution. These programs have been particularly popular with juvenile offenders. Restitution involves holding the offender accountable for his or her actions while compensating victims for the harm caused. It most commonly involves the offender providing monetary compensation to the victim in proportion to the loss or damage incurred but it also may involve the offender carrying out unpaid work for the victim.

Community service is often defined as symbolic restitution because it is the community that benefits rather than the individual victims of crime. Frequently used as an intermediate sanction which is perceived as less punitive and restrictive than prison but more so than probation, it has been widely referred to as representing a fine on the offender's free time (McDonald, 1992). Construed in this way, community service would not be considered to be an explicitly rehabilitative sanction. However, it has also been suggested that the experience of performing unpaid work for the community may bring about positive changes in offenders' attitudes and behavior. Some studies have found that restitution in general and community service in particular are associated with lower recidivism rates than alternative sanctions such as prison and probation, though other studies have produced contradictory results (Schiff, 1998). There is, however, some evidence that completion rates are higher and recidivism rates are lower when the work carried out is capable of providing some intrinsic satisfaction and reward and the offender can readily recognize its worth.

Gill McIvor

Further Reading

Albrecht, H. and Wolfram, S., Eds., *Community Service: A New Option in Punishing Offenders in Europe*, Freiburg: Max Plank Institute for Foreign and International Penal law, 1986.

Ervin, L. and Schneider, A., Explaining the effects of restitution on offenders; Results from a national experiment in juvenile courts, in *Criminal Justice, Restitution and Reconciliation*, Galaway, B. and Hudson, J. (Eds.), Monsey, NY: Criminal Justice Press, 1990.

McDonald, D.C., *Punishment without Walls: Community Service Sentences in New York City*, New Brunswick and London: Harvard University Press, 1986.

McDonald, D.C., Unpaid community service as a criminal sanction, in *Smart Sentencing: The Emergence of Intermediate Sanctions*, Byrne, J.M., Lurigio, A.J., and Petersilia, J. (Eds.), Newbury Park, CA: Sage, 1992.

McIvor, G., *Sentenced to Serve: The Operation and Impact of Community Service by Offenders*, Aldershot and Brookfield: Ashgate, 1992.

Morris, N. and Tonry, M., *Between Prison and Probation: Intermediate Punishments in a Rational Sentencing System*, New York, NY: Oxford University Press, 1990.

Pease, K., Community service orders, in *Crime and Justice: An Annual Review of Research*, Vol. 6, Tonry, M. and Morris, N. (Eds.), 1985.

Schiff, M., Restorative justice interventions for juvenile offenders: A research agenda for the next decade, *Western Criminology Review*, 1, 1, 1988, available online.

van Kalmthout, A.M. and Tak, P.J.P., *Sanctions-Systems in the Member-States of the Council of Europe: Part 1*, Deventer: Kluwer, 1988.

See also **Community Corrections; Juvenile Justice: Corrections; Sentences and Sentencing: Guidelines**

Comparative Crime and Justice

Origins

Shortly after systematic data collection initiatives began during the first decades of the 19th century, scholars started to compare conviction and other criminal justice data. Between 1750 and 1805 systematic data collection began in Sweden (von Hofer, 1991) and England and Wales (Elmsley, 1996). Later, data on trials and then data on convictions began to be collected in France, the Kingdom of the United Netherlands (including the actual Netherlands, Belgium and Luxembourg), the major German principalities (e.g., Baden) and the Protestant Swiss cantons (Zurich, Geneva) after the Napolean wars (Killias, 2001). The Belgian Adolphe Quételet (1796–1874) was among the first scholars to look at these data comparatively. His main work was first published in 1831. Later, data were collected on suicide and illegitimate births. These so called *morality statistics* were used as "indicators" of the morality of different European nations. From there, it was only a short step to the "discovery" of *anomia* by Durkheim (1897) who, in his writings, widely referred to these as "morality indicators" as opposed to mere measures of crime and criminal justice decisions.

The problematic validity of data on trials or convictions as indicators of crime has been well recognized from the beginning of comparative research in this area. For example, the Genevan botanicist Alphonse de Candolle (1830/1987) described in an article first published in 1830 what later became a standard critique of such indicators. Quételet's anticipation of such criticisms led to him defending his use of conviction statistics. Quételet argued (or perhaps hoped) that the proportion of crime that appears in statistics would remain stable over time and space (Quételet, 1831/1984).

From Trivial Use to the Dismissal of Comparative Data

Since the beginnings of comparative analyses dating back to the first half of the 19th century, criminology has oscillated between continued naive data collection on one hand, and, on the other hand, dismissing all efforts to use comparative data to test criminological theories. Both positions were ill-designed to advance knowledge. The rejection of such data, as of criminal justice data in general, which is predominant in some continental European countries, has slowed the process of testing theories in a comparative perspective, as attempted by scholars with a multilingual background like Hermann Mannheim (1965). Criminal justice policies vary widely across the world. Therefore, this attitude deprives criminology of the chance to evaluate comparatively their merits and pitfalls, and also to provide policy-makers with relevant feedback in order to help them to improve or change their current policies. Thus, it seems that the lack of comparative research may have prevented policy-makers and the public from learning from the significant experiences accumulated in other countries. For example, crime control has, overall, not been less successful in countries with low or moderate incarceration rates than in those with very large prison populations, such as the U.S. and Russia.

From Two-Country Studies to Multinational Research

Some studies have compared two countries with presumably different levels of crime. For example, studies have been conducted in Switzerland, Japan, and some Latin American countries, e.g., the study on homicide by Neapolitan (1994). Recent examples include studies comparing England and Wales with the U.S. (Langan and Farrington, 1998), England and Wales with Sweden (Farrington and Wikström, 1993), Scotland and Sweden (McClintock and Wikström, 1990), the former Soviet Union and Western countries (Shelley, 1981), and the Nordic countries (von Hofer, 1997). Such studies allowed a very accurate assessment of the validity of several indicators in the countries studied, because of the particular familiarity of the scholars with the contexts at stake. However insightful and suggestive they may be, studies limited to comparing only two or three countries do not allow theories to be tested (as two cases do not make a sample). Archer and Gartner (1984) conducted what is perhaps the only multinational study that used crime statistics over roughly one century for as many as 40 countries.

Multinational data collection initiatives are considered to be more useful than traditional cross-country studies, because they provide relevant data on many countries. However, it is accepted that such studies will never represent an ideal random sample of all existing nations, because of the fact that there is no clearly defined universe out of which a random sample could be drawn. Over the last decades, a number of multination research projects have been developed. One of the first such projects was developed by Interpol (*Interpol crime statistics*), which regularly published data on police-recorded crime for a significant number of countries. However, it should be noted that the data were collected by the relevant national authorities, and Interpol published the data as it received them. Given the many problems involved in the measurement of crime, this type of data collection did not help reduce the widespread skepticism toward comparative data among criminologists. The *United Nations (UN) Crime Surveys* that were conducted every 5 years from 1973 collected data on police-recorded offences, and also criminal justice data on selected topics, such as sentencing and prison populations. As these surveys relied on official national sources, the data shared many of the shortcomings of the Interpol crime statistics. In more recent years, however, several United Nations Institutes (HEUNI at Helsinki, UNICRI at Torino, Italy) have devoted considerable energy and expertise in scrutinizing beyond the surface the validity of the data provided (Kangaspunta, Joutsen, and Ollus, 1998). Thus, the UN surveys have become a major data source, particularly when interpreted using other sources of international data, such as the international crime victimization surveys (Marshall, 1998). In addition, they have provided valuable data on several criminal justice indicators whose validity is less problematic, such as those on prison populations (Kuhn, 2000, 1998).

A related initiative came from the Council of Europe, shortly after many nations in Eastern and Central Europe had joined that organization. This initiative drew on the former experience of the UN crime and criminal justice surveys, but was inspired mainly by the *American Sourcebook of Criminal Justice Statistics*, which has been published annually since 1973 by the U.S. Department of Justice. The working group in charge of the new initiative organized a network of national correspondents in each country to act as experts, and not as official government representatives. Thus, the focus was on the "expertise" and not on the official position of those in charge of providing the data. In addition, each member of the working group was responsible for a number of countries he or she was somewhat familiar with. Data were not merely accepted but were scrutinized in order to assess face validity (Killias and Rau, 2000). Although not yet satisfactory, the figures collected using this process were considered much more plausible than anything collected previously. Of particular value was combining data from the international crime surveys with data on police-recorded offences and offenders, convictions (including sentences imposed) and corrections (time served, number of prisoners or serving other sanctions, as collected since the 1980s by the Council of Europe, under the responsibility of Pierre Tournier). These kinds of data also provide information on the "costs" of offending in the different countries, and, thus, on the "outcomes" of more or less punitive policies. The *European Sourcebook of Criminal Justice Statistics* was first published in 1999 using data collected during 1990–1996 for 36 nations. The second edition will be extended to include more countries; it was scheduled for publication in 2002.

The year 1988 saw the beginning of the development of the International Crime Victimization Survey (ICVS). The emergence of computer-assisted telephone interviews (CATI) made it possible to conduct standardized surveys with large national samples in many countries at affordable costs. The ICVS drew mainly on two methodologies. Firstly, it drew largely on the methodology successfully tested in two national Swiss crime surveys that were conducted in 1984 and 1987 (possibly the first such surveys ever conducted using CATI). Secondly, it also drew on a questionnaire that was mainly inspired by the British Crime Surveys (whose main researcher was Pat Mayhew). The first ICVS was conducted in 11 Western European countries, and in the U.S., Canada, and Australia in 1989 (van Dijk, Mayhew, Killias, 1990). The idea for this survey originated from the Research and Documentation Center of the Ministry of Justice of the Netherlands (whose director at that time was Jan van Dijk); the center has continued to play a decisive role in this project over the years. Later sweeps of the survey followed in 1992, 1996, and 2000 (Mayhew and van Dijk, 1997; van Kesteren, Mayhew, and Nieuwbeerta, 2000), with the inclusion of an increasing number of countries from outside the Western hemisphere (Alvazzi del Frate, 1998). Despite criticisms, the ICVS data have been found to be more suitable for cross-country comparisons than police data. For example, for the nations covered by the *European Soucebook of Crime and Criminal Justice Statistics*, the rate of burglary was found to vary from 1 to 7 when using ICVS data, and from 1 to 262 when using police data. This latter difference is of course, beyond any plausibility. Therefore, survey data are much more valid for cross-country comparisons, whatever the merits of police data for longitudinal research may be (von Hofer, 2000).

Another multinational project started in 1992 built on the success of the ICVS. Josine Junger-Tas (at that time director of the Research and Documentation Center of the Netherlands) initiated the first international self-reported delinquency study (ISRD), covering 12 countries, including the U.S. (Nebraska) and 11 European nations (Junger-Tas, Terlouw, and Klein, 1994). Despite its less rigorously standardized methodology, the ISRD is likely to promote further the understanding of the role of certain factors currently assumed to be associated with delinquency, such as family disruption and school failure.

In summary, the 1990s saw the emergence of a large number of multinational data collection initiatives that are likely to promote further the understanding of different levels of crime, and to assess the comparative merits of particular national policies.

Potentials of Multinational Research

Whereas research comparing two or three countries may generate feasible hypotheses at best, multinational research allows hypotheses to be tested and thus can be used to answer controversial issues. Compared with research based on sub-units of one nation (e.g., counties, provinces or states) multinational studies have the advantage of offering generally much larger variations in both dependant and independent variables. Crime rates, as well as criminal justice responses, typically vary much more between nations than within nations, which means that multinational tests are, generally speaking, much more powerful than comparisons of states and counties, as are common in American research. The following examples illustrate this point.

Firstly, the ICVS data have also given way to a number of innovative analyses on factors associated with different levels of crime rates, such as situational circumstances, "anomia" (measured as a feeling of having no chance of economic improvement) and structural variables, such as urbanization (van Dijk, 1998). Using the same line of reasoning, it may well be that the very low crime rates in Japan and, more generally, in Asia are as a result of the high costs associated with offending, in particular stigmatization not only of offenders themselves, but even of their relatively remote relatives, rather than "integrative shaming" (Braithwaite, 1989) or other "tolerant" policies (Miyazawa, 1997; Killias, and Sahetapy, 1999).

Secondly, for many years, scholars in the U.S. have debated whether prison populations are driven mostly by crime trends or by policy shifts (e.g., Zimring and Hawkins, 1991, 1997). Research based on the *European Sourcebook of Crime and Criminal Justice Statistics*, and particularly on the detailed data on convictions, sentencing, and prison populations, provided from as many as 36 European nations has shown that the answer is a complex one (Aebi and Kuhn, 2000). It was found that the prevalence of convictions for very serious offences, such as homicide, and the severity of sentences for less serious offences, such as drug trafficking and burglary, contributed about equally to the—widely varying—imprisonment rates within Europe, explaining together about half of the variance in the dependant variable. This finding is, intrinsically, quite plausible. Homicide and other very serious crimes are, in almost all countries, punished with very long sentences; thus, countries with huge homicide rates, such as Russia and other Eastern European nations (about 10 times those of Western Europe), will "naturally" end up having large prison populations. On the other hand, the length of sentences meted out for much more frequent medium offences, such as burglary and drug trafficking, will influence the size of the prison population, particularly in nations with low or medium homicide rates.

A third example is offered by the international self-reported juvenile delinquency (ISRD) project. Family disruption and school failure have generally been known to be strongly associated with juvenile delinquency. This conclusion has been largely based on research conducted in the U.S., which, as a result of its quantitative preeminence, has largely shaped international knowledge on these issues. Recently published findings from the ISRD project suggest, however, that these conclusions may be much less valid in Western Europe than in the Anglo-Saxon world (Junger-Tas et al., 2003). The reason may be that, because of differences in the educational systems, school failure is, in the long term, less damaging to careers in Europe than in America, or that "broken homes" may have quite different social implications on the two sides of the Atlantic. Multinational research may also be helpful to assess the "real" weight of certain explanatory variables, such as the availability of guns in homicides and other violent events (Killias, van Kesteren, and Rindlisbacher, 2001), or of the lack of efficiency and reliability of government services and corruption, as has been assessed by the ICVS (Alvazzi and Pasqua, 2000).

Finally, the comparative crime data file of Archer and Gartner (1984) allowed the identification of the detrimental effects of wars on violent behavior, because of the long-term perspective and the large number of countries included. Archer and Gartner have also been able to reject the idea that crime in major cities developed along (and as a result of) population growth. Instead, they argue that it was the central position of a city which, at all times, seems to have shaped the concentration of crime (and other human activities) on its territory.

Deficits of International Cooperation

So far, criminal justice policies have widely remained a national domain, despite increasing international cooperation. The wide variety of approaches and policies may be seen not only as a source of concern, but also as a chance for mutual learning from successes and failures. However, this advantage will come into play only if different policies are carefully evaluated, and the results of these evaluations disseminated to policymakers in other countries and to the scientific community at large. This has not been common so far; however, and scientific communication across national and language borders has remained the exception rather than the rule. Part of the problem is the lack of international platforms where researchers can exchange their experience without being drawn back by hierarchical structures and national prejudice.

International criminological organizations may have to play a significant role in promoting multinational research initiatives, and in stimulating exchange across national borders in general. Whereas the American Society of Criminology has achieved this role for many years, making it extremely easy for researchers to locate specialists in any relevant field within the U.S., no such organization has existed so far in other continents, and in particular in Europe. The newly established European Society of Criminology may, eventually, grow to a size where it will be able to stimulate exchange across the continent and with the U.S. as much as the American Society of Criminology has succeeded over many years. There is no doubt that comparative research will be greatly stimulated by international platforms of this kind.

Martin Killias

References and Further Reading

Aebi, M.F. and Kuhn, A., Influences on the prisoner rate: Number of entries into prison, length of sentences and crime rates, *European Journal on Criminal Policy and Research*, 8, 1 (2000), 65–75.

Alvazzi del F.A., *Victims of Crime in the Developing World*, Rome: UNICRI 1998.

Alvazzi del F.A. and Pasqua, G. (Eds.), *Responding to the Challenges of Corruption*, Rome: UNICRI 2000.

Archer, D. and Gartner, R., *Violence and Crime in Cross-National Perspective*, New Haven, CT/London: Yale University Press, 1984.

Barclay, G., The comparability of data on convictions and sanctions: Are international comparisons possible? *European Journal on Criminal Policy and Research*, 8, 1 (2000), 13–26.

Braithwaite, J., *Shame, Crime and Reintegration,* Cambridge, UK: Cambridge University Press, 1989.

De Candolle, A., Considération sur la statistique des délits, *Déviance et société* 11, 4 (1987), 352–355 (first published in 1830).

Durkheim, E., *Le Suicide*, Paris: Presses universitaires de France 1960 (first published in 1897).

Elmsley, C., *Crime and Society in England*, 1750–1900, 2nd ed., London, UK: Longman, 1996.

Farrington, D.P. and Wikström, P.H., Changes in crime and punishment in England and Sweden in the 1980's, *Studies in Crime and Crime Prevention* 2 (1993), 142–170.

Junger-Tas, J., Terlouw, G., and Klein, M., (Eds.), *Delinquent Behavior among Young People in the Western World*, Amsterdam: Kugler, 1994.

Junger-Tas, J., Ribeaud, D., and Marshall, I.H., Delinquency in an International Perspective. *The International Self-Reported Delinquency Study* (2003).

Kangaspunta, K., Joutsen, M., and Ollus, N., (Eds.), *Crime and Criminal Justice Systems in Europe and North America* 1990–1994, Helsinki: HEUNI, 1998.

Killias, M., *Précis de criminologie*, 2nd ed., Berne (Switzerland): StŠmpfli, 2001.

Killias, M. and Rau, W., The European sourcebook of crime and criminal justice statistics: A new tool in assessing crime and policy issues in comparative and empirical perspective, *European Journal on Criminal Policy and Research,* 8, 1 (2000), 3–12.

Killias, M. and Sahetapy, J.E., Communities and crime: The unexpected outcomes of an Asian dinner, *European Journal on Criminal Policy and Research*, 7, 4 (1999), 532–532.

Killias, M., van Kesteren, J., and Rindlisbacher, M., Guns, violent crime, and suicide in 21 countries, *Canadian Journal of Criminology*, 43, 4 (2001), 429–448.

Kuhn, A., Sanctions and their severity, in Kristina, K., Matti, J., and Natalia, O. (Eds.), *Crime and Criminal Justice Systems in Europe and North America* 1990–1994, Helsinki: HEUNI 1998, 115–137.

Kuhn, A., *Détenus: Combien?, Pourquoi?, Que faire?*, Berne (Switzerland): Haupt, 2000.

Langan, P.A., and Farrington, D.P., *Crime and Justice in the United States and in England and Wales 1981–1996*, Washington, DC: U.S. Department of Justice, 1998.

Mannheim, H., *Comparative Criminology*, 2 Vol., London: Routledge & Kegan, 1965.

Marshall, I.H., Operation of the criminal justice system, in Kangaspunta, K., Joutsen, M., and Ollus, N. (Eds.), *Crime and Criminal Justice Systems in Europe and North America 1990–1994*, Helsinki: HEUNI 1998, 54–114.

Mayhew, P. and van Dijk, J.J.M., Criminal Victimization in Eleven Industrialized Countries: Key Findings from the 1996 International Crime Victims Survey, The Hague (NL): WODC, 1997.

McClintock, F.H. and Wikström, P.H., Violent crime in Scotland and Sweden: Rate, structure, and trends, *British Journal of Criminology*, 32, 4 (1990), 207–228.

Miyazawa, S., The enigma of Japan as a testing ground for cross-cultural criminological studies, in Nelken, D. (Ed.), *Comparing Legal Cultures*, Aldershot (UK): Dartmouth, 1997, 195–214.

Neapolitan, J. L., Cross-national variation in homicides: The case of Latin America, *International Criminal Justice Review*, 4 (1994), 4–22.

Quételet, A., *Research on the Propensity for Crime at Different Ages* (translated by Sylvester, S.F.), Cincinnati (OH): Anderson 1984 (first published in 1831).

Shelley, L.I., *Crime and Modernization. The Impact of Industrialization and Urbanization on Crime*, Carbondale, IL: Southern Illinois University Press, 1981

van Dijk, J.J.M., Mayhew, P., and Killias, M., *Experiences with Crime accross the World*, Deventer (NL)/Boston, MA: Kluwer, 1990.

van Kesteren, J., Mayhew, P., and Nieuwbeerta, P., *Criminal Victimisation in Seventeen Industrialised Countries*, The Hague: WODC, 2000.

von Hofer, H., *Criminal Statistics over three Centuries*, Stockholm: Statistics Sweden, 1991.

von Hofer, H., *Nordic Crime Statistics 1950–1995*, Stockholm: Department of Criminology, University of Stockholm, 1997.

von Hofer, H., Crime statistics as constructs: The case of Swedish rape statistics, *European Journal on Criminal Policy and Research*, 8, 1 (2000), 77–89.

Zimring, F.E. and Hawkins, G., *The Scale of Imprisonment*, Chicago, IL: The University of Chicago Press, 1991.

Zimring, F.E. and Hawkins, G., *Crime is not the Problem: Lethal Violence in America*, New York, NY: Oxford University Press, 1997.

See also **International Crime Statistics; International Crime Trends; International Policing**

Competency to Stand Trial

See **Insanity and Diminished Responsibility as a Defense to Criminal Liability**

Computer Offenses

Many social scientists, economic experts, and political leaders now believe that we are living in an "information society." The diffusion and deepening of the information technology revolution has seen the proliferation of networks connecting economies, social and political structures, scientific communities, and disorganized and diffuse populations. These processes have created what Manuel Castells (1996) calls a network society. Although information communication technologies (ICTs) allow legitimate global economies and knowledge networks to exist, they also allow for a darker side that sees the illegitimate use of information networks. Castells (1998) identified what he called the global criminal economy as a defining feature of network society. Organized criminal groups that were once national in scope can now employ global networks to further their illicit dealings. Information technology has enabled criminal groups to interact with other criminals on a global scale, to traffic illegal goods more effectively and anonymously, and to identify potential victims at a click of a button.

Whereas Castells (1998) was more concerned with organized mafia criminal structures, his thesis allows us to understand how and why criminals have incorporated information technologies (IT) into their deviant behaviors. From large-scale money laundering to petty instances of computer hacking, the criminal has turned to IT to further facilitate "traditional" criminal activity, and to create new ways of committing crimes. Essentially with new opportunity follows crime. The digital networked age provides not only established criminals with new ways of committing crime, but also empowers previously nondeviant individuals, drawing them into new criminal behaviors. At one end of the spectrum we see organized criminals taking advantage of new technologies and networks to facilitate their illegalities, whereas at the other extreme the "empowered small agent" is able to commit crimes that were previously beyond their means (Pease, 2001).

Untangling the Web: Defining Cybercrime

Before categorizing types of cybercrime it is important to distinguish what is criminal behavior and what is not in relation to computer use or misuse. As advances in technology escalate at a rate unparalleled by everyday institutional mechanisms, it is no surprise that the law is slow to respond to high-tech criminal activity. The McConnell Report (2000) identifies 42 countries that are yet to update their legal systems to cope with the threats of cybercrime. Where advances have been made, it is questionable whether the scope of new and adapted bodies of jurisprudence can remain ahead of deviant enterprise. Certain forms of hacking, obscene electronic materials, and online stalking have been met with legal rationalization, although many other forms of computer related activities escape regulation because of their esoteric nature. For example, certain activities, such as bomb talk (discussions surrounding the manufacturing of explosives), some forms of online textual violence (see Mackinnon, 1997), and until recently racist and xenophobic online behavior (see Mann, Sutton, and Tuffin, 2002) escape regulation but are still arguably harmful. As a result it has become acceptable, and more analytically fruitful, to consider harms instead of crimes in relation to computer use or misuse. Examining how one's behavior on a computer network can negatively effect an individual, be it financially or psychologically, allows for a greater scope in understanding both criminal and noncriminal computer related activities.

In attempting to define crimes and harms that take place on computer networks, it is important to consider the spatial and temporal dimensions of crime and deviance. "Traditional" crimes exhibit certain general characteristics. Often they are static in terms of time and space. Perpetrators very often have to be present at a certain time and in a certain place to carry out a crime. To a lesser extent the same might be said for a victim of a crime; in order for them to become a victim they or their property must come into contact with a perpetrator in a certain space and at a certain time (especially the case for violent crimes). For a crime to be committed it must be recognized as a crime within these spatial-temporal constraints. Therefore, the law and conventional social understanding at the time and place must recognize a behavior as illicit for it to be labeled as criminal. Finally, Wall (1999) notes that criminology has traditionally focused on the offender rather than the victim or the offence, and that in the majority of cases, the offender has a disadvantaged socioeconomic background.

The characteristics of cybercrimes and harms can vary from those of traditional crimes. There is little adherence to the spatial-temporal restrictions characteristic of conventional crimes. This is primarily as a result of the burgeoning growth of new electronic information and communications technologies (Woolgar, 2002). Networked societies allow for time and space to be distanciated, meaning that an action in one spatial-temporal boundary may have an effect outside of that restriction (Giddens, 1990). In relation to criminal activity, this means that individuals are able to attack their victims at a distance. The temporal dimension of crime is also affected; new ICTs allow criminals to make deals or harass a victim in compressed periods of time, given the distance covered. A fraudulent transaction can take place over thousands of miles in milliseconds and a harasser can subject their victim to derisory discourse at great distance in real time. Further, unlike traditional crimes the perpetrators of cybercrimes and harms are more likely to have more affluent socioeconomic backgrounds.

Given these inconsistencies, there is contentious debate over what constitutes a cybercrime (Wall, 1999). This uncertainty is further reflected in legal discourse, where issues over jurisdiction inflate the debate. As cybercrimes can span national boundaries and legal jurisdictions, questions over what body of law should apply complicate issues of retribution. In contradiction, Wall (2001) identifies that the trans-jurisdictionality of some cybercrimes can prove beneficial in attaining a conviction. The notion of "forum-shopping" has allowed prosecutors to identify in which region an investigation and conviction would be most successful. The two case examples Wall (1999) gives come from both sides of the Atlantic. In the case of *R v. Arnold* and *R v. Fellows* (1996) jurisdiction was handed over from U.S. to U.K. law enforcement as it was thought a conviction would be more likely. Similarly in *United States of America v. Robert A. Thomas* (94-6648) and *Carleen Thomas* (94-6649) (1996) the prosecution was moved from California to Tennessee given that the differing body of law in the latter state would be more effective at securing a conviction.

The contention surrounding legal discourse in relation to cybercrime is mirrored in other political and social arenas. Three multilateral organizations are currently involved in shaping high-tech crime policy: the European Union (EU), the Council of Europe (COE), and the G8. Other organizations, such as the Organisation for Economic Cooperation (OECD), the United Nations, Interpol, and Europol, have been involved to a lesser extent. None of the organizations has offered a definitive definition of cybercrime. The United Nations highlighted the problem of definition in its *Manual on the Prevention and Control of Computer-Related Crime* (United Nations, 1995) stating that although there is consensus among experts, these definitions have been functional and hence too specific. A similar position was held by the Council of Europe. The Committee on Crime Problems decided to leave out any definition of high-tech crime in its Convention on Cybercrime (2001), allowing individual jurisdictions to apply their own definitions based on their specific body of law. The Council of Europe does, however, provide a working definition for Europol, the European law enforcement organization responsible for fostering effective co-operation of member states in order to tackle organized crime. However, this definition is narrow, in that it only relates to attacks on automated data-processing systems. This is in part because of Europol's existing mandate that already covers certain crimes that can be committed over computer networks (drug and arms trafficking, counterfeiting, trafficking in human beings, child pornography, illegal immigration networks, etc.) nullifying the need for a more comprehensive definition of cybercrime.

Recognizing the complex nature of cybercrimes, others have had more success with defining them. Wall (1998) has recognized that computer-related crimes can be categorized in three main ways. First, it has provided a vehicle for the further facilitation of existing harmful activities. Wall (1998) identifies that computer networks have become a communications vehicle that facilitates the commission of "traditional" criminal activities. Everyday crimes have then migrated or have been reengineered to function online. A typical example might be the use of the Internet by pedophiles who have used the anonymity that is granted to every Internet user to "groom" children in unregulated chat rooms, and to maintain and build networks where illegal images and even victims are exchanged. Further, Mann and Sutton (1998) show how a group of burglars posed as trainee locksmiths on a locksmiths' newsgroup in order to obtain new methods of lock picking.

The second category of computer related crime identified by Wall (1998) involves the creation of new opportunities for harmful activity that are currently recognized by existing criminal or civil law. Examples would be the creation of new kinds of obscenity through computer-generated images (pseudo-photographs) and computer fraud. Third, entirely new forms of harmful activities that are of dubious legal status have emerged with the increased use of the Internet. Essentially the Internet has allowed for the creation of a new environment within which novel forms of misbehavior are engineered. At one level, these include the unlawful appropriation of intellectual property such as images, software, music, and video products. At the extreme, cases of virtual violence have been reported on many occasions, where online community members have been verbally attacked and harassed by other Internet users. In the most extreme scenario, cases of virtual rape have been reported (Mackinnon, 1997). It is these kinds of computer-related crimes that are posing the greatest challenge to legal systems and are undergoing constant evaluation in terms of understanding and interpreting the kinds of potential harm they can cause.

Wall (2001) further identifies four main typologies that prove useful in trying to understand these types of deviant cyber activity: *cyber*trespass, *cyber*obscenity, *cyber*theft, and *cyber*violence.

Cyber Trespass

Cyber trespass is the invasion of private space on the Internet by a hacker. Young (1995) identifies several types of hackers, including utopians, who believe they are helping society by demonstrating its vulnerabilities, and militant activists, who are aggressively anti-establishment and use their technical knowledge to cause harm to their targets, be they individuals or institutions. Wall (2001) identifies four categories of illicit activity conducted by these individuals. First is the deliberate planting of viruses. These could be designed to disable a particular function or they could be sleeping viruses designed to be neutralized only after a ransom has been paid. On a less organized level viruses are sometimes distributed via the Internet and email to cause general chaos—the so-called "Love-Bug" realized in 2000 being an example.

The second type of activity is the deliberate manipulation of data, such as web pages, so that they misrepresent the organization or person they are supposed to represent. Several political party websites have been targeted by hackers on the run-up to general elections in the U.K. Manifestos have been rewritten in sarcastic and satiric fashion. In more serious circumstances, following the introduction of Megan's law (Sex Offender Registration Act, 1996) the misrepresentation of pedophiles' names and addresses on the Internet in some American states could prove detrimental, both physically and psychologically, to innocent individuals. The anonymity granted to every Internet user often means the process of identifying the perpetrator of such acts is very difficult if not futile.

The remaining two kinds of activities are associated with Wall's (2001) further categorization of hackers, the *cyber* spy and the *cyber* terrorist. *Cyber* spies break access codes and passwords to enter classified areas on computer networks. The primary aim of the *cyber* spy is to appropriate classified knowledge. In comparison, *cyber* terrorism can take many forms, including denial of service attacks (DoS), where entire servers are brought to a standstill, halting business and sometimes even whole economies. Military strategists are also preparing to counter "information warfare," so defined when intruders enter major computer systems and cause damage to their contents, thus causing considerable damage to the target. It is known that such intruders can infiltrate and tamper with national insurance numbers and tax codes, bringing economies to a standstill (Wall, 2001). Such evidence suggests a gap seems to be opening between society's increasing dependence upon ICTs and its ability to maintain and control them (Taylor, 2001).

Taylor (2001), having conducted extensive research into hackers, provides alternative characterizations based on function. Firstly, he outlines Levy's (1984) hacker "generations," detailing the "true" hackers of the 1950s and 1960s, who were seen as the pioneers in their field, hardware hackers who were responsible for opening access to hardware during the 1970s and game hackers of the 1980s who generated games for the hardware. Taylor (2001) adds three more types of hackers, bringing the typologies up to date. He describes the hacker or cracker as an individual who illicitly breaks into other computer systems, much the same as Wall's cyber spy. Microserfs are those individuals who once belonged to, or are still associated with, hacker groups but work within corporate structures, such as Microsoft. Finally, Taylor (2001) talks of hactivists, those hackers who are motivated by political drive.

Cyber Obscenity or Pornography

It is important to distinguish what is meant by pornography and how it manifests on the Internet. A distinction can be drawn between child pornography, which is illegal, and mainstream pornography, which is legal. Child pornography is a special case and is generally considered illegal in many countries. For this reason it provides a challenge for regulation on the Internet (Grace, 1996). It is also recognized that there is no settled definition of "conventional" pornography in a multinational space such as the Internet. Further, cultural, moral, and legal variations make it difficult to define "pornographic content" in a global society (Akdeniz, 1997). The debate over obscene material on the Internet is contentious because the laws that govern this material differ so drastically between countries. In Britain, for example, individuals regularly consume images that might be classed as obscene in many Middle-Eastern countries. In seeking to clarify this issue the European Commission's Green Paper on the Protection of Minors and Human Dignity in Audio-Visual and Information Services (1998) highlighted the need to distinguish between illegal acts, such as child pornography, which are subject to penal sanctions, and children gaining access to sites with pornographic content, which is not illegal but may be deemed as harmful for children's development. Nonetheless, differences in classification between countries create problems when information of a seemingly pornographic content is internationally transmitted via the Internet.

Several studies have been conducted focusing on the availability of pornographic material on the Internet. Although the Carnegie Mellon Study was methodologically flawed, its finding that at least half of Internet content was related to pornography drew mass attention from the media, which saw the genesis of the first Internet moral panic (Rimm, 1995). Another project, employing content analysis, examined Internet pornographic graphic images (Mehta and Plaza, 1994). Other studies have conducted similar content analyses of written pornography found on newsgroups (Harmon and Boeringer, 1997). Each study voiced how simple it was to access various incarnations of pornography via the Internet. Content analyses of written pornography also showed a tendency to use violence within the narrative, more so than magazine pornography (Harmon and Boeringer, 1997).

Pornography on the Internet is available in many different formats, ranging from pictures and short animated movies to sound files and textual stories (Akdeniz, 1997). These sites and newsgroups are accessible through the Internet by any online user. Whereas some discussion groups are free to access, most of the websites with pornographic content require proof of age and payment by credit card to access their materials (Akdeniz, 1997). The legal requirement of proof of age verification and the cost that customers are obliged to pay meant that the online pornographic industry was one of the first to venture into e-commerce. The online sex industry is one of the more successful e-commerce ventures, and paved the way for other online businesses. The desire to legitimize the industry resulted in the establishment of Adult Sites against Child Pornography (ASACP). This organization, and others like it, go to form part of a wider network of Internet governance (Wall, 2001).

Prosecutions for the production of online pornography are rare. In the majority of situations, the producers of this material go to great lengths to secure their websites from underage access. Age verification systems are in operation on many sites, whereas others require the use of a major credit card. However, regulation is complex given trans-jurisdictionality. When addressing the issue of pornography the limited police resources are directed toward more serious infringements of the law—such as online pedophile networks. However, current U.K. legislation does stipulate that it is an offence to send "by means of a public telecommunications system, a message or other matter that is grossly offensive or of an indecent, obscene or menacing character" (Akdeniz, 1997). Although arrests have been made in the U.S. for sending similar obscene messages (see *United States of America v. Jake Baker and Arthur Gonda,* 890 F. Supp. 1375; 1995 U.S. Dist.), similar trends have not been mirrored to such an extent in the U.K.

Policing of the Internet and newsgroups is beginning to emerge as part of the Home Office's drive toward further proactive policing methods. Operation Starburst in July 1995 was one of the first international investigations into pedophile rings and the Internet. As a result of the investigation nine British men were arrested (Akdeniz, 2000). Operation Starburst was the first investigation to uncover a direct link between child abuse and the use of the Internet (Akdeniz, 1997). The recognition that the Internet is an avenue for the trafficking of illegal pornographic images was also embodied in criminal law. The UK Criminal Justice and Public Order Act of 1994 widened the definition of a publication to include a computer transmission, which led to the prosecution of Fellows and Arnold in *R v. Fellows* and *R v. Arnold* 1996. Governance of Internet content is, at present, a contentious debate. The reasons for regulation may seem obvious at first, however, currently it might be thought inappropriate to regulate mainstream pornography on the Internet as it is readily available in the streets.

Cyber Theft

Wall (2001) identifies two types of *cyber* theft. The first is the appropriation of intellectual property where, for example, music or video has been recorded and digitally reproduced and distributed over computer networks. The most notorious successful prosecution for this type of *cyber* theft was in the case of *A&M Records, Inc. v. Napster, Inc.* (239 F.3d 1004, 9th Cir. 2001) where the defendant was accused of distributing and selling copyrighted musical material. The Digital Millennium Copyright Act (DMCA), 1998 was introduced to update U.S. law for the digital age. Certain aspects of the act made Internet service providers (ISPs) liable for copyright violations. Although the DMCA was comprehensive enough to satisfy the World Intellectual Property Organization's (WIPO) treaties, there were still concerns over its inadequate protections for copyright owners. The proposed Berman Bill (2002) in the U.S. allows copyright owners to effectively violate the law in protection of their products. The bill allows for the hacking of any computer that is downloading copyright material from a peer-to-peer network. It becomes clear that the bill allows for action tantamount to vigilante justice with copyright owners acting as prosecutor, judge, and jury. Because of such opposition from digital civil libertarians it is questionable whether the bill will actually be implemented.

The second type of *cyber* theft is the appropriation of virtual money, or more accurately the appropriation of credit card numbers. The important issue here is that the offender does not actually need to have the physical credit card. All of the relevant details are available from discarded credit card receipts or can be obtained through unsecured (unencrypted) online credit card transactions.

Cyber Violence

Cyber violence is the term used to describe online activities that have the potential to harm others via text and other "digital performances." These activities manifest in visual and audio forms, meaning the violence is not actually physically experienced. *Cyber* violence can be delineated by its perceived seriousness. Least serious are heated debates on message boards, often referred to as flaming (Joinson, 2003). At worst, a defamatory remark may be made about someone's inferior intellect or flawed argument. These exchanges are considered minor in terms of violence because of the fact that their consequences never amount to anything more than a bruised ego.

More serious are "digital performances" that are hate-motivated. To take two examples, racial and homophobic hate-related online violence is in abundance in the form of extremist web pages (Mann, Sutton, and Tuffin, 2003). While protected under freedom of speech laws in the U.S., these sites employ shocking tactics to drum up support for their extremist view points. In particular, some sites go as far as to display images of hate-related homicide victims in distasteful ways to heighten their very often misguided outlook on society's monitories (Schafer, 2002). The use of derogatory homophobic and racist text in these sites, combined with the use of inappropriate imagery and sound, results in a digital performance that is violent and potentially psychologically harmful, not only to the victim's family but also to the wider community.

Of potentially more harm are the violent activities of online stalkers. Cyber stalking involves the use of electronic mediums, such as the Internet, to pursue, harass or contact another in an unsolicited fashion (Petherick, 2000). Most often, given the vast distances that the Internet spans, this behavior may never manifest itself in the physical sense, but this does not mean that the pursuit is any less distressing. Petherick (2000) states that "there are a wide variety of means by which individuals may seek out and harass individuals even though they may not share the same geographic borders, and this may present a range of physical, emotional, and psychological consequences to the victim." Yet there still remains some concern that cyber stalking might be a prelude to its physical manifestation (Reno, 1997).

The Internet allows communication with another person unconstrained by social reality, thus creating a certain psychodynamic appeal for the perpetrator who chooses to become a cyber stalker (Meloy, 1998). Only written words are used, and other avenues of sensory perception are eliminated; one cannot see, hear, touch, smell, or emotionally sense the other person. There is also, if one wants, a suspension of real time. Messages can be sent and electronically stored, and their reception is no longer primarily dictated by the transport time of the medium, but instead by the behavior of the receiver. Meloy (1998) explains "some individuals may always return their phone calls the day they receive them, while reviewing their e-mail at leisure."

Meloy (1998) contends that these unusual circumstances provide opportunities for the stalker and presents a series of suppositions concerned with the medium itself. First, Meloy (1998) notes how the lack of social constraints inherent in online communication means that potential stalkers become disinhibited. Therefore, certain emotions and desires endemic to stalkers can be directly expressed toward the target more readily online than offline. Second, while online the absence of sensory-perceptual stimuli from a potential victim means that fantasy can play an even more expansive role as the genesis of behavior in the stalker.

A more contentious debate in cyber violence literature exists around the phenomenon that has become known as "virtual rape" (MacKinnon, 1997). These cases of virtual violence have completely escaped any legal rationalization. In the most famous case a hacker was able to enter an online community and take control over community members' actions (Dibble, 1993). Because movement and action within virtual communities is expressed through text, the "virtual rapist" was able to manipulate people's actions against their will. What essentially followed was a salacious depiction of violent rape upon several individuals in real time. Although no one was physically harmed, community members reported being traumatized by the event. This case was taken so seriously that the whole community (over 1000 members) voted on what action should be taken against the perpetrator. The imperative point to be made here is that the physical self of the perpetrator, the individual who exists in the offline world, could not be harmed, only his online persona could be punished. The effectiveness of such punishment is then questionable.

Levels of Computer Related Crime

Any attempt to quantify computer related offenses is flawed because of a lack of reporting and recording. In most cases, individuals may not realize an offence has occurred, and indeed it may have not, given the dubious legal status of these acts. Others may feel the acts are not serious enough, that the police would not be interested, or that an alternative method of meditation is required. The statistics that are available are published by voluntary and public organizations set up to support victims of online harassment and to map the extent of business related cybercrime.

In particular, attempting to accurately quantify the prevalence of *cyber* violence is complex. The infrastructures required to identify and record such instances are yet to be put in place. Definitional issues still complicate the matter. However, the statistics that are made available by some voluntary organizations may shed partial light on the pattern of *cyber* violent victimization. In 2002, the organization Working to Halt Online Abuse (WHOA) received an average of 100 communications a week concerning online harassment, 95% of which were legitimate. The majority of cases (81.5%) were resolved by the Internet service provider, leaving 18.5% of cases which called upon the police and legal system. The majority of victims were white females aged between 18 and 25, and in most cases the harassment occurred either through email or an online chat. Many organizations like WHOA collect similar data. Unfortunately collection is far from systematic, and little collaboration exists among organizations. The victimization patterns that have been identified from these data are not an accurate picture of online crime, and a substantial dark figure exists.

Similar, to WHOA, but on a far more systematic level, the Computer Security Institute (CSI) and the FBI in the U.S. conduct an annual computer crime and security survey, gathering information from over 500 corporations, government agencies, financial institutions, medical facilities, and universities (a similar survey is conducted in Australia). Each year the survey provides data on the prevalence of high-tech illegal activities covering hacking, fraud, and denial of service attacks, among many others. In 2003, the survey uncovered that 56% of the respondents detected computer security breaches within the last 12 months. The 44% of the respondents who were willing or able to quantify their financial losses reported losing over 200 million dollars in the financial year through various forms of high-tech crime (Richardson, 2003). Up until 2003 (where financial losses dropped by almost 60% from the previous year) these figures have increased on an annual basis, providing some evidence that the high-tech crime problem is far from under control. Although these statistics may be more accurate than those collected by voluntary Internet organizations, the CSI and FBI can be criticized for overemphasizing the problem. Calculations of financial loss and the actual harm corporations suffer from high-tech crimes are difficult to accurately calculate. The figures provided are more than likely an overestimation that only proves to add to public hysteria over the prevalence and harmfulness of cybercrime.

Regulating Computer-Related Crime

Government's desire to take advantage of networked information technologies has also resulted in calls for regulation and control of certain forms of electronic information. The Internet in particular has proven a challenge to regulators in terms of intellectual property rights, access to obscene or harmful content and the protection of minors. This can be seen in the drafting of the Berman Bill (2002) and the Communications Decency Act (CDA) (1996) in the U.S. and the various attempts by the EU to control Internet content and behaviors (such as the EU Action Plan on Promoting the Safe Use of the Internet, 1997, and the Convention on Cybercrime, 2001). These attempts to regulate and govern Internet content and behaviors have often been met with staunch opposition from cyber civil liberties campaigners. Such opposition saw the successful challenge of the CDA (1996), a decision more than likely to be mirrored in the challenge to the Berman Bill (2002). Technically the Internet is difficult to regulate. Its capacity to span the globe, ignorant of national boundaries, means that no one body of law has precedence over what can and cannot be distributed.

However, it is a misnomer to state that the Internet and other forms of computer-mediated communication are not subject to any form of regulation. In fact, it may be more appropriate to talk of the governance of the Internet instead of regulation, as the discourse of governance lends itself to the very nature of the Internet. Governance refers to the "regulation of relationships in complex systems" (Rhodes, 1994) which "can be performed by a wide variety of public and private, state and non-state, national and international, institutions and practices" (Hirst and Thompson, 1995). The Internet is a complex system of interconnections between technologies, organizations and individuals. Any attempt to govern such a complex system of interconnectivities requires a diverse and dynamic approach. Walker and Akdeniz (1998) provide an overview of a governing framework that is both diverse in its constituent components and dynamic in its approach:

- Global international regulatory solutions by the likes of OECD and the United Nations.
- Regional supranational legislation such as by the European Union.
- Regulations by individual governments at a national or local level, such as through police squads and customs control units.
- Self-imposed regulation by the ISPs with industry-wide codes of conduct, which would transcend national boundaries.
- Trans-national and national pressure groups made up of end-users.
- Rating systems such as Platform for Internet Content Selection (PICS).
- Self-imposed regulation, such as through software filters, to be used by end-users.
- Hotlines and pressure organizations to report illegal content such as child pornography. The Internet Watch Foundation (IWF) is one such incarnation in the U.K. The EU Action Plan set up in January 1999 is also an initiative that incorporates the use of hotlines.

Evidence already exists in support of this hierarchy of governance. The blurring of private and public regulation is recognizable in the increased sales of security software for end-users and the continued establishment of local and regional policy development. The European Commission's Action Plan: Promoting the Safe Use of the Internet (1997) was one of the earliest pieces of legislation to recognize the necessity for a multilayered and multijuridical approach to the regulation of Internet content. The action plan, therefore, aimed to set up a European network of hotlines to report illegal content such as child pornography. It also sought to establish a clear set of criteria for the identification and filtration of what it termed "harmful" or "illegal" content. However, little discussion was given to what was actually meant by either of these terms in relation to child pornography. Nonetheless, the plan sought to increase the awareness among children and parents of the dangers of using the Internet, and to encourage vigilant self-regulation where possible.

More recently, the Convention on Cybercrime (2001) might be considered one of the most systematic and international attempts at regulating "harmful" and criminal activities that employ the use of computers. The aim of the European Commission was to approximate substantive law in the area of high-tech crime. It was considered that with common definitions, incriminations, and sanctions, high-tech crime could be successfully regulated. Four areas were focused upon: offenses against the confidentiality and integrity of computer data and systems; computer-related offenses; content-related offenses; and offenses related to infringements of copyright and related rights. Further, additions to the convention concerning content that is xenophobic in nature have also been added. However, the convention is not yet in force. Although 36 countries (including four non-COE member states) signed the treaty in November 2001, only

Albania and Croatia have so far ratified the convention. In order for the convention to take effect at least three member states have to ratify the treaty. There are also major concerns that the convention jeopardizes certain civil liberties and places an unreasonable burden on Internet service providers. Further, it is questionable whether the content constraints espoused by the convention would be adopted in the U.S. given First Amendment rights.

MATTHEW WILLIAMS

References and Further Reading

Akdeniz, Y. (1997) Governance of pornography and child pornography on the global internet: A multi-layered approach, in Edwards, L. and Waelde, C. (Eds.), *Law and the Internet: Regulating Cyberspace*, London, UK: Hart Publishing.

Akdeniz, Y.W.C. and Wall, D. (2000) *The Internet, Law and Society*, London, UK: Longman.

Castells, M. (1996) The rise of the network society, *The Information Age: Economy, Society and Culture*, Vol. I. Oxford, UK: Blackwell.

Castells, M. (1998) The end of the millennium, *The Information Age: Economy, Society and Culture*, Vol. III. Oxford, UK: Blackwell.

Dibble, J. (1993) A rape in cyberspace; or, how an evil clown, a Haitian trickster spirit, two wizards, and a cast of dozens turned a database into a society, *The Village Voice.* Available at http://www.levity.com/julian/bungle.html, accessed on 01/08/00.

Giddens, A. (1990) *The Consequences of Modernity*, Oxford, UK: Polity Press.

Grace, S. (1996) Testing Obscenity: An International Comparison of Laws and Controls Relating to Obscene Material, Home Office Research Study 157.

Harmon, D. and Boeringer, S (1997) A content analysis of internet-accessible written pornographic depictions, *Electronic Journal of Sociology*, 3, 1. Available at http://www.sociology.org/content/vol003.001/boeringer.html.

Hirst, P. and Thompson, G. (1995) Globalisation and the Future of the Nation State, *Economy and Society*, 24, 408–422.

Joinson, A.N. (2003) *Understanding the Psychology of the Internet*, New York, NY: Palgrave Macmillan.

Levy, S. (1984) *Hackers: Heroes of the Computer Revolution*, New York, NY: Bantam Doubleday Dell.

Mackinnon, R.C. (1997), Virtual rape, *Journal of Computer Mediated Communication*, 2, 4. Available at http://www.ascusc.org/jcmc/vol2/issue4/mackinnon.html, accessed on August 16, 2000.

Mann, D. and Sutton, M. (1998), Netcrime: More change in the organisation of thieving, *British Journal of Criminology*, 38, 2.

Mann, D.S.M. and Tuffin, R. (2003) The evolution of hate: Social dynamics in white racist newsgroups, *Internet Journal of Criminology*, Available at www.flashmousepublishing.com, accessed on April 12, 2003.

McConnell International (2000) Cybercrime and Punishment: Archaic Laws Threaten Global Information, McConnell International.

Meloy, J.R. (1998) The psychology of stalking in Meloy, J.R. (Ed.) *The Psychology of Stalking: Clinical and Forensic Perspectives*, London, UK: Academic Press Ltd.

Mehta, M.D. and Dwaine, E.P. (1997) Content analysis of pornographic images available on the Internet. *The Information Society*, 13, 2: 153–162, original study presented in October 1994.

Pease, K. (2001) Crime futures and foresight: Challenging criminal behaviour in the information age, in David, S.W. (Ed.) *Crime and the Internet*. London, UK: Oxford University Press.

Petherick, W. (2000) *Cyber-Stalking: Obsessional Pursuit and the Digital Criminal*. Available at http://crimelibrary.com/criminology/cyberstalking, accessed on May 2, 2001.

Reno, Rt.H.J. (1997), *Keynote Address to the Meeting of the G8 Senior Experts Group on Transnational Organised Crime*, Chantilly, VA. Available at http://www.usdoj.gov/criminal/cybercrime/agfranc.htm, accessed on March 20, 2002.

Rhodes, R.A.W. (1994) The hollowing out of the state: The changing nature of the public services in Britain, *Policing Quarterly*, 65, 138–151.

Richardson, R. (2003) *CSI/FBI Computer Crime and Security Survey*, CA: Computer Security Institute.

Rimm, M. (1995) Marketing pornography on the information superhighway: A survey of 917,410 images, descriptions, short stories, and animations downloaded 8.5 million times by consumers in over 2000 cities in forty countries, provences and territories, *The Georgetown Law Journal*, 83, 1849.

Schafer, J.A. (2002) Spinning the web of hate: Web-based hate propagation by extremist organisations, *Journal of Criminal Justice and Popular Culture*, 9, 2, 69–88.

Taylor, P. (2001), Hacktivism: In search of lost ethics?, in David, S.W. (Ed.) *Crime and the Internet*, London, UK: Routledge.

Thomas, D. and Loader, B.L. (2000) Cybercrime: Law enforcement, security & surveillance in the information age, London, UK: Routledge.

Wall, D. (2001) Cybercrimes and the Internet, in David, S.W. (Ed.) *Crime and the Internet*, London, UK: Routledge.

Wall, D.S. (1998) Policing and the regulation of cyberspace, *The Criminal Law Review*, Special Edition on Crime, Criminal Justice and the Internet, 79–91.

Wall, D.S. (1999) Cybercrimes: New wine, old bottles? in Davies, P., Francis, P., and Jupp, V. (Eds.) *Invisible Crimes: Their Victims and their Regulation*, London, U.K.: MacMillan, 105–139.

Woolgar, S. (2002) *Virtual Society?—Technology, Cyberbole, Reality*, Oxford, UK: Oxford University Press.

Young, L.F. (1995) United States computer crime laws, criminals and deterrence, *International Yearbook of Laws, Computers and Technology*, 9, 6, 1–16.

See also **Consumers, Crimes against; Hackers: History, Motivations, and Activities**

Confessions *See* **Interrogation and Confessions**

Conflict and Consensus Theories of Law

At first blush, the explanation of why certain acts and certain people in this society are labeled "criminal" seems straightforward. We call acts "crimes" when they pose a threat to society, and we label people "criminal" when we catch them committing those acts. However, such an explanation is not as simple and instructive as it might appear, for it leaves unanswered a number of questions. For example, can we speak of society as if all members are affected similarly by crime? Who decides specifically what types of acts should be considered illegal? Can we easily say what constitutes a threat to society or to groups within it? Is breaking the law the only criterion for gaining criminal status, and will it ensure such status? Having raised such questions, we examine two theoretical approaches to understanding what shapes definitions of crime: consensus and conflict models.

Consensus Theory

Throughout most of the 20th century, social theorists assumed that definitions of acts and persons as deviant or criminal reflected a value consensus within society. Within the consensus model, law was viewed as a reflection of custom and a codification of societal values, as an institution functioning to settle disputes that arise when values and norms occasionally become cloudy, and as an expression of social control when an individual deviates too far from the normatively acceptable. Indeed, deviance itself and the ensuing reaction to it were seen by some as necessary to the proper functioning of a society in that various forms of deviance were thought potentially to remind members of a community about the interests and values they share, to strengthen social bonds, and to reassure community members of their own moral normality and righteousness. Importantly, some also pointed out that punitive reactions to deviance may lead to repressive societal conditions that stifle creativity and critical societal self-examination. As well, if social solidarity is weak in the first place, deviance and reactions to it may further divide a community into factions (Durkheim, 1958; Mead, 1918; Coser, 1956).

These themes have informed considerable research. Based upon his study of deviance rates in the early Puritan colonies, for example, Erikson (1966) noted that "crime waves" were matters of shifts of public attention from one form of trouble to another. In fact, despite "crime waves," crime rates remained relatively stable over the six decades he examined. This suggested to Erikson a "deviance quota," that is, the encouragement or allowance by the social system of a sufficiently functional amount of deviance. Deviance and reactions to it set the boundaries of acceptable behavior and provided a sense of stability and direction for the fledgling Puritan society. As time passed, deviance would cause the society to refocus on its character and mission, to reemphasize the common beliefs and interests of its members (Lauderdale, 1976).

Inverarity (1976) attempted to extend Erikson's work through a study of lynchings in Louisiana between 1889 and 1896. Prior to the late 1800s, the South was a white-dominated, relatively closed, united society. Two general white classes existed, a wealthy planter, merchant, and industrialist class and a larger, poorer class of farmers and laborers. Their relationship was fairly harmonious, even if economically inequitable. Although blacks at this time were considered inferior by both white classes, they were able to vote. In the late 1800s, the black vote was controlled by the wealthy class, which used it to solidify its power position.

White solidarity collapsed briefly in the early 1890s, however, with the advent of the Populist revolt, an abortive attempt to capture economic and political power by some members of the lower classes. Inverarity pointed out that this disunity coincided with an increase in lynchings, primarily of blacks but also of whites, in Louisiana parishes. He posited that the lynchings were a societal mechanism to counter the lack of social unity by rallying people against their "common enemies." After the Populist movement collapsed in the 1890s, the white South reunited and lynchings declined in Louisiana. In Inverarity's opinion, the decline reflected the lessened need for a unifying mechanism. As Erikson had suggested in his study of the early Massachusetts colonies, the societal response to deviance in the South had functioned to strengthen a social system whose unity was threatened.

Erikson's and Inverarity's research drew criticism. The Puritan colonies and, to some extent, southern communities in the late 1800s represented small, apparently highly homogenous societies. Overall, the "functions of crime" thesis seems to apply far better to smaller societies than to larger, heterogeneous ones. As a society expands and becomes more differentiated, it tends to form clusters, smaller subcultures, and economic groups that differ from one another in worldview, social status, and economic interests. Generally, these groups compete for various scarce economic and status rewards in society. Crime and deviance *within* these smaller segments of a society may serve the same unification and boundary maintenance functions as crime may serve in smaller societies such as the Puritan colonies. More importantly, however, definitions of and reactions to crime and deviance in the larger society are tied integrally to competition and conflict *among* the smaller segments or interest groups.

Many critics of the consensus approach will not accept the notions of value consensus and functions of deviance even for the smaller society. They argue that were consensus in the small society really present, deviance would be rarer and the use of legal threats to deter deviance rarer still. They note that "societal needs" and the functioning of social phenomena like deviance to meet those "needs" are impossible to document. They note too that the argument that laws are created in the interests of a few and then shape public values is as plausible as the belief that public values shape law. Thus, whereas the consensus position assumes that the state (specifically, legal mechanisms and processes) represents the interests of the majority, many historical studies trace a given law to the interests of a powerful minority. By contrast, no studies have tied a law directly to the expressed will of a majority independent of the influence of some interested minority (Beck and Tolnay, 1990; Chambliss and Seidman, 1982; Michalowski, 1985).

Finally, most empirical grounding of the notion of "functions of deviance" to date relies on historical or field observation studies. The major exception is the work of Liska and Warner (1991) who employ data concerning crime, victimization, and social interaction among respondents in a 26-city survey. They find that, in our urban society, the reaction to high crime rates increases the social isolation of citizens rather than bringing them closer together in common indignation. Ironically, in many cases the effect of the decrease in social interaction is to *lower* the crime rate. Crimes like robbery intensify fears and, therefore, constrain social activity; this in turn reduces the number of targets for robbers.

Conflict Theories

If power struggles characterize smaller societies and shape law and its enforcement to the extent that critics of the consensus model claim, it seems unlikely that the consensus model can describe accurately the sources of criminal definitions in larger societies. For this reason, an alternative approach became increasingly popular among criminologists in the last three decades of the century: the *conflict* model. The U.S. version of this approach for the most part focused upon shapers and processes of legislation, law enforcement, and correction. The British version, especially as it was rendered in the 1970s (Taylor, Walton, and Young, 1973), exhibited a far more critical, theoretical bent, seeking to locate not only the issue of crime and punishment but even the manner of their study (the questions and methods of modern criminology) in the larger context of the changing Western capitalist society (Garland and Sparks, 2000).

Although not all conflict models are alike, three themes cut across all models: the relativity of criminal definitions, the role of control of major social institutions in maintaining interests, and the definition of law (legislation and enforcement) as an instrument of power.

Regarding relativity, the conflict perspective posits that no act or individual is intrinsically moral or immoral, criminal or noncriminal. If a criminal label is attached to an act or a person, there is an underlying reason: such definitions serve some interests within society. If these labels are tied to interests, then they are subject to change as interests change. Thus, every definition of an act as immoral, deviant, or criminal (or the converse) must be viewed as tentative, always subject to redefinition. Prime examples of the process of shifting definitions are seen in our perpetually changing attitudes, laws, and law enforcement patterns concerning "vices." The conflict theorist argues as well that even apparently universal acceptance of a criminal definition, over a long period, will have its origins in the protection or furtherance of some group's interests.

Regarding control of social institutions, conflict theorists argue that, in maintaining and enhancing interests within a society, such control is more effective than force or compromise. Force calls attention directly to interest preservation and basically dares others to summon enough counterforce to alter the power structure. Compromise is preferred to force because all parties involved somehow benefit; yet, compromise still carries liabilities. The granting of concessions indicates the absence of absolute power in the hands of any one interest group. It highlights the weaknesses of certain parties and encourages others to organize further to exploit those weaknesses.

Control of such institutions as the law, religion, education, government, economics, and science means control of the world views of members of society, especially regarding questions of interests and power. With respect to the problem of crime and criminals, control of legal institutions means that more powerful groups gain legal support for their interests by outlawing behavior and attitudes that threaten them or by focusing attention away from their own wrongdoings. Control of other institutions, such as religion and education, is used to promote the interests of the more powerful by shaping the opinions of the less powerful concerning the legitimacy of the economic, political, and legal status quo. It should be noted that control of such institutions often exceeds mere instrumental use of them. Instead, the powerful also have their own world views shaped by the institutions they control. Their efforts to shape law reflect not only perceptions of interests but also a whole value set that labels such interests inherently right and necessary to the health of the collectivity.

Finally, whereas consensus theorists view law as an institution expressing common societal values and controlled by the majority in society, conflict theorists view law as "a weapon in social conflict" (Turk, 1976). Those who own the law fight to keep it; those who want it fight to get it. Indeed, rather than simply reducing conflict, law also produces it by virtue of its status as a resource to be won by some combatants and lost by others. Most obviously, control of the legal order represents the ability to use specified agents of force to protect one's interests. Beyond this, decisions concerning economic power are made and enforced through law. Further, control of the legal process means control of the organization of governmental decisions in general, and decisions concerning the structure of institutions such as public education. Even the attention commanded by the workings of law (police, trials, and so forth) may serve to divert attention from more deeply rooted problems of power distribution and interest maintenance. In sum, if law is an instrument sought after and employed by interest groups to enhance their position in society, and if criminal law forbids certain acts, we can reasonably define crime as acts perceived by those in power as direct or indirect threats to their interests (Quinney, 1970).

Most contemporary conflict theories derive from Marxian analyses of competing class interests and argue, therefore, that law in this society is rooted in class conflict (Michalowski, 1985; Jacobs and Helms, 1996; Hochstetler and Shover, 1997). Theorists differ, however, concerning who is behind legislation and law enforcement: essentially a single dominant class or a number of relatively powerful, competing interest groups (Domhoff, 1991). Those who favor dominant class theories conceptualize conflict as perpetual, dynamic tension between those who own or control the means of production (factories, machinery, investment capital) and those who work for these owners turning raw materials into saleable goods. Within this framework, some theorists view the state as the mere pawn of the dominant owner class, and thus portray legislation and state action as mechanisms by which to control workers. Others see a more complicated relationship, one that finds the owner class seeking self-restraint in order to avoid drawing the line between its interests and those of the workers too sharply. For these theorists, the state is viewed as at least somewhat autonomous and acting at times against the short-term interests of the dominant class (Allen, 1991; Campbell and Linberg, 1990; Prechel, 1990). The state, then, becomes yet another party to conflict, pursuing its own self-interests and capable of error in assessing the need for and the effects of policy and legislation (Quadagno, 1994; Skocpol and Amenta, 1986).

Yet another cadre of conflict theorists offers a broader explanation of the legal process. *Pluralist theorists* argue that the legal process is not controlled by one or two specific interest group but emerges from or is shaped by the conflicting interests of a multiplicity of groups. The object of conflict is not always economic interest; it may also reflect status concerns and moral and ideological commitments (DiMaggio, 1997). Hence, much of what occurs in legal conflicts is symbolic rather than purely instrumental (Galliher and Cross, 1983). Pluralists consider conflict highly dynamic as new groups vie for power and as groups in power (including the state) seek to maintain their position and often err through oversight, misdefinition of situations, and miscalculation of policy effects. Thus, the passage of a given law may reflect the rising or falling sociopolitical fortunes of these various groups. The movement toward increased criminalization of "hate crimes" (offenses committed against persons because of their race or sexual orientation), for example, demonstrates the growing political clout of groups that have traditionally lacked such influence (Grattet, Jennesss, and Curry, 1998).

Although they appear to capture the crucial elements and dynamism of the creation and maintenance of law in the larger, modern society, conflict theories are not immune to criticism. Those that focus almost wholly upon a dominant elite class often fail to consider noneconomic influences on legal processes and generally underestimate the role of the state in shaping law. In turn, theorists who focus on the development of the short-term neutrality or impartiality of the state have yet to link short-term autonomy with the hypothesized long-term bias of the state toward capitalism. They seem as well to underemphasize historic, state-sanctioned, legal discrimination against segments of the worker population (for example, African Americans and women).

The strength of the pluralist approach is essentially the weakness of the more Marxian theories. Pluralists argue that much of the use of legal process involves the competing interests of many parties, not simply the maneuverings of an economic elite or of the state looking out for the long-term interests of that elite. Countering the pluralists, more class-oriented theorists argue that intergroup competition for both instrumental and symbolic legal support is a mirage, that ruling elites "allow" such competition (as long as it does not threaten specific ruling elite interests) in order to promote the impression that a society is diversified and democratic. This claim is, for all intents and purposes, untestable. Yet, pluralists may be open to the more modest criticism that they do not listen closely enough to the Marxian theorists' message. Thus, although they pay lip service to power differentials, to the economic clout of corporations, and to a semiautonomous state, they exclude these elements from most of their analyses of legislation.

In part, the absence of attention focused by pluralists on elites is because of the types of law creation studied by pluralists. Pornography laws, for example, reflect the activity of groups of roughly equal power and organization, and such laws tend not to threaten any specific corporate interests. Yet, how might pluralists explain tax law structure or weak legal control of corporations responsible for oil spills despite very organized and strong efforts to assert such control (Molotch, 1970)? The answer lies in the pluralist penchant for defining elite involvement in the legal process as defensive, that is, as reacting only to direct economic threat. Surely, the dominant class is sufficiently aware of its interests and sufficiently organized to pursue them that much of its activity is anticipatory and aimed at enhancement as well as at protection of interests.

Finally, Coleman (1985) argues that the pluralist model pays insufficient attention to the outcomes of conflicts as opposed to the process by which conflicts occur. He focuses his claim on the effects of the Sherman Antitrust Act on the petroleum industry. Antitrust legislation would seem to epitomize the tenets of the pluralist model: an amalgam of populist forces able to constrain major corporate interests. Yet, the resources of the petroleum companies have permitted them to dodge the effects of the legislation aimed at them. Companies were able to delay legal proceedings until the political climate changed; they contributed substantially to the campaigns of politicians who could influence their situations; they concealed their holdings and their activities from public and government view; and they threatened state and local economies with plant closings. In short, Coleman argues, antitrust laws have been enforced against petroleum interests rarely and poorly. The pluralist roots of antitrust law, in this instance, would seem a mirage, though, in other instances, such a conclusion would seem unwarranted (Dobbin and Dowd, 2000).

In sum, the conflict perspective seems to address more aggressively and more convincingly the issue of the workings of the legal process than does the consensus model. Despite criticisms of elements of its many brands, the conflict perspective's basic argument cannot be ignored: Laws do not simply appear miraculously on our law books, and they do not epitomize "society's" values. Instead, the acts and people we call criminal and our concern with crime at any given time reflect the activity of groups in this society seeking legal support for economic, ideological, and status interests. Sometimes, only a few groups are involved in the struggle for legal support; other times, many groups compete. The issue contested in a legal struggle may be explicit and instrumental, or it may be symbolic of some greater conflict. The ebb and flow of law reflects the ebb and flow of interest groups, and laws emerging from this process must be viewed as tentative and negotiable.

In the coming years, we can expect to see a broader theoretical and more global approach to understanding law and crime as a function of conflict among social and economic interest groups. The impetus for this expansion of our explanatory framework comes from British and Australian criminologists, as it did in the 1970s (Braithwaite, 2000; Garland, 1996; Taylor, 1999). Their approach is based upon changes in the world economy, technology, and national and international redistribution of skilled and unskilled labor during the past 30 years. An increasingly global economy has transformed our notions of both production and consumption. As corporate investment in research, development, production, and trade has blurred traditional borders, so has the perceived need for stability and management of risk moved beyond those borders. Social control, historically framed in local and national terms by U.S. criminologists, is becoming more transnational in scope. The welfare state is, in the eyes of the critical theorists in question, being jettisoned in favor of softer regulatory devices affirming of free-market economics. The political climate that reflects this transformation and shapes societal conceptions of social problems is now characterized by antiwelfare policy and cultural conservatism. It is difficult to imagine, British and Australian critical criminologists argue, understanding law and crime control apart from their increasingly postmodern context.

JOSEPH F. SHELEY

References and Further Reading

Allen, M.P., Capitalist response to state intervention: Political finance in the new deal, *American Sociological Review*, 56, 5 (1991).

Beck, E.M. and Stewart, E.T., The killing fields of the deep south: The market for cotton and the lynching of Blacks, 1882–1930, *American Sociological Review*, 55, 4 (1990).

Braithwaite, J., The new regulatory state and the transformation of criminology, *British Journal of Criminology*, 40, 2 (2000).

Campbell, J. and Lindberg, L., Property rights and the organization of economic activity by the state, *American Sociological Review*, 55, 5 (1990).

Chambliss, W.J. and Seidman, R., *Law, Order, and Power*, 2nd ed., Reading, MA: Addison-Wesley, 1982.

Coleman, J.W., Law and power: The Sherman Antitrust Act and its enforcement in the petroleum industry, *Social Problems*, 32, 3 (1985).

Coser, L., *The Functions of Social Control*, Glencoe, IL: Free Press, 1956.

DiMaggio, P., Culture and cognition, *Annual Review of Sociology*, 23 (1997).

Dobbin, F. and Dowd, T.J., The market that antitrust built: public policy, private coercion, and railroad acquisitions, 1825 to 1922, *American Sociological Review*, 65, 5 (2000).

Domhoff, G.W., *The Power Elite and the State: How Policy is Made in America*, Hawthorne, NY: Aldine de Gruyter, 1991.

Durkheim, E., *The Rules of Sociological Method*, translated by Solloway, S.A. and Mueller, J.H., Glencoe, IL, 1958.

Erikson, K., *The Wayward Puritans*, New York, NY: Wiley, 1966.

Galliher, J.F. and Cross, J.R., *Moral Legislation without Morality*, New Brunswick, NJ: Rutgers University Press, 1983.

Garland, D., The limits of a sovereign state: Strategies of crime control in contemporary society, *British Journal of Criminology*, 36, 4 (1996).

Garland, D. and Sparks, R., Criminology, social theory, and the challenge of our times, *British Journal of Criminology*, 40, 2 (2000).

Grattet, R., Jenness, V., and Curry, T., The homogenization and differentiation of hate crime law in the United States, 1978–1995: Innovation and diffusion in the criminalization of bigotry, *American Sociological Review*, 63, 2 (1998).

Hochstetler, A. and Shover, N., Street crime, labor surplus, and criminal punishment, 1980–1990, *Social Problems*, 44, 3 (1997).

Inverarity, J., Populism and lynching in Louisiana: A test of Erikson's theory of the relationship between boundary crises and repressive justice, *American Sociological Review*, 41, 2 (1976).

Jacobs, D. and Helms, R.E., Toward a political model of incarceration, *American Journal of Sociology*, 102, 2 (1996).

Lauderdale, P., Deviance and moral boundaries, *American Sociological Review*, 41, 4 (1976).

Liska, A. and Warner, B., Functions of crime: A paradoxical process, *American Journal of Sociology*, 96, 6 (1991).

Mead, G.H., The psychology of punitive justice, *American Journal of Sociology*, 23, 5 (1918).

Michalowski, R., *Order, Law, and Crime*, New York, NY: Random House, 1985.

Molotch, H., Oil in Santa Barbara and power in America, *Sociological Inquiry*, 40 (1970).

Prechel, H., Steel and the state: Industry politics and business policy formation, *American Sociological Review*, 55, 5 (1990).

Quadagno, J., *The Color of Welfare: How Racism Undermined the War on Poverty*, New York, NY: Oxford University Press, 1994.

Quinney, R., *The Social Reality of Crime*, Boston, MA: Little Brown, 1970

Skocpol, T. and Amenta, E., States and social policies, *Annual Review of Sociology*, 12 (1986).

Taylor, I., Walton, P., and Young, J., *The new criminology: For a social theory of deviance*, London, UK: Routledge and Kegan Paul, 1973.

Turk, A., Law as a weapon in social conflict, *Social Problems*, 23, 3 (1976).

See also **Marxist Theories of Criminal Behavior; Race and Ethnicity and Criminal Behavior; Sociological Theories of Criminal Behavior**

Consent as a Defense to Criminal Liability

The idea of consent as a defense to criminal liability must be placed in the context of the sovereign as the ultimate victim in every criminal case. In English common law, criminal activity was "against the peace of our Lord the King." In modern parlance, a crime is "against the peace and dignity of the state." In this context, there is no such thing as a "victimless crime." The sovereign is always the victim and the question is whether the sovereign has the power to prevent particular conduct, a more serious question for a modern republic than it ever was for an absolute monarchy.

When the sovereign, the government, defines a crime, it often includes lack of consent as an element of the offense because unless the conduct is without consent there is no governmental interest at stake. Therefore, theft is often a taking of property without the consent of the owner. Rape is sexual intercourse when one party has not consented.

When consent is raised as a defensive issue in a rape case, it is often for the purpose of exploring whether the government can prove absence of consent and, until recently, exploring the complaining witness's sexual history. This tactic is claimed by those who practice it to be a method of testing the government's case and by those who deplore it to be a method of embarrassing the complainant to the degree that she becomes a reluctant witness.

Modern rape statutes often contain shield laws that require the defendant to put on some evidence tending to show consent before exploring the complainant's sexual history. In addition, there is a trend away from the common law idea that consent is presumed in sexual relations within marriage. Spousal rape is becoming common in the statute books, but it remains rare in court because prosecutors are reluctant to address the consent issue without fairly strong evidence of coercion.

Sometimes, the government claims an interest that precludes recognizing consent as a defense. In the case of statutory rape, an individual under the "age of consent" cannot agree to sexual intercourse because of the government's interest in protecting children and the government's power to define who is a child.

In most jurisdictions, euthanasia and aiding suicide are crimes to which even the most carefully documented consent will not function as a defense. The interest of the government in protecting the life of its citizens is considered to trump the interest of a citizen in ending his or her own life. There is movement away from this position in some jurisdictions toward laws allowing physician-assisted suicide in cases where an illness is terminal and particularly painful.

Assault and battery cases raise a number of questions that are answered in particular jurisdictions by weighing the government interests and the private interests at stake. Sometimes that weighing takes place in the legislature and sometimes in the courts, but the general trends are the same across jurisdictions.

Consent to medical treatment is consent to conduct what would otherwise be battery, and medical professionals often get consent in writing for this reason in addition to the purpose of documenting warnings given to the patient about potential risks of treatment.

Playing contact sports normally implies consent to the assaults and batteries that are within the rules of the game. Injuries from contact sports can be quite serious, including death and permanent paralysis, but if the injuries result from blows inflicted within the rules of hockey or boxing or football, there is normally no basis for criminal prosecution. However, criminal prosecution is possible when injuries result from violations of the rules of a game, such as a high stick in hockey, a low blow in boxing, or tackling with the facemask in football.

Some jurisdictions recognize a "mutual combat" defense to battery that is essentially a consent theory. When evenly matched people decide to fight, the law could impose criminal sanctions on the winner, on both combatants, or on neither combatant. Sometimes, this choice is dictated by law, but more often by the charging decisions of police officers or prosecuting attorneys.

Consensual sadistic or masochistic sexual activity is sometimes legal and sometimes not, and the result is almost always determined by case law. The government's interest in not recognizing a consent defense is the same as in the case of prostitution transactions or sodomy, where the consent of the parties is irrelevant. The government is considered to have a legal interest in controlling the private sexual expression of its citizens, and interest stated in terms of preventing disease, protecting the family, or upholding morality.

In Great Britain, sadistic and masochistic sexual activity is illegal without regard to consent: *Regina v. Brown*, 1 A.C. 212 (House of Lords 1994). This position was upheld by the European Court of Human Rights: *Case of Laskey, Jaggard and Brown v. The United Kingdom*, 109/1995/615/703-705 (1997). In the U.S., the majority view is that consent will be a defense unless the activity results in injury. This may be a tacit recognition that American privacy law makes regulation of private consensual conduct very difficult, or it may be a drawing of the line where the government's interest outweighs individual interests. The government's interest is a remnant of the common law crime of maiming, which offended the sovereign because it left a subject unable to fight for his king.

When consent is a defense, the consent must normally be given before the otherwise criminal conduct. Consent given afterward is sometimes called "condonation," and is more akin to forgiveness than to what is normally understood as consent. Although the law does not consider after-the-fact consent to be a defense, prosecuting attorneys will often drop charges when the nominal victim chooses not to proceed. As representative of the actual victim, the government, the prosecutor has the authority to subpoena the nominal victim and require testimony, but few prosecutors care to invest limited resources in cases with reluctant witnesses.

STEVE RUSSELL

References and Further Reading

Biebel, J.H., I thought she said yes: Sexual assault in England and America, *Suffolk Transnational Law Review*, 19 (1995).

Chad, H., *Principles of the Law of Consent with Special Reference to Criminal Law, Including the Doctrines of Mistake, Duress, and Waiver*, Bombay: Bombay Education Society Press, 1897.

Dripps, D.A., Beyond rape: An essay on the difference between the presence of force and the absence of consent, *Columbia Law Review*, 92 (1992).

Schultz, L.G., Ed., *Rape Victimology*, Springfield, IL: Thomas, 1974.

White, D.V., Sports violence as criminal assault: Development of the doctrine by Canadian courts, *Duke Law Journal*, 1986 (1986).

See also **Rape, Acquaintance and Date; Rape, Marital; Rape, Forcible: Extent and Correlates; Rape, Forcible: Law**

Conspiracy to Commit a Crime

Conspiracy is a very complex concept in modern criminal law. It is both an attempt to explain the level of criminal intent (*mens rea*) and a crime in and of itself. Conspiracy also is complicated in that it has been applied to the *process* of planning a crime, and to *groups* who participate in the process of planning a crime. The focus here will be on the process rather than the nature of the conspiratorial entity.

Conspiracy: A Definition

At its most basic level, a conspiracy is an implicit or explicit agreement by two or more people to commit a crime. The parties may or may not all know one another. Conspiracy—like attempt and solicitation—is considered an *inchoate offense*. This means that the substantive crime has not been completed, or perhaps it cannot be completed.

In some jurisdictions the planning process itself is sufficient for a conspiracy to exist, and no overt act in furtherance of the crime is necessary. The difficulty associated with conspiracy to commit a crime is that the prosecutor is placed in the position of having to establish the mental state of those people who have entered into a conspiratorial agreement. Against this requirement is the notion in Anglo-American law that individuals cannot be punished for their thoughts. Thus, to counter the objection that people are being punished for what they are thinking, some jurisdictions have required that some act, although not necessarily a "substantial" one, must have taken place to demonstrate the conspirators' criminal intent. Beyond being considered an inchoate offense, conspiracy to commit a crime may be charged along with the completed substantive offense. The following sections distinguish the two approaches to charging on conspiracies.

Conspiracy as an Inchoate Offense

As previously noted, conspiracy exists when two or more persons enter into an agreement to commit a crime, and conspirators are considered complicitous in the acts committed by others in carrying out the contemplated offense. The primary purpose for treating conspiracy as a crime is to allow law enforcement authorities to intervene and make arrests prior to any attempt to commit the target offense. In other words, the police do not have to allow the conspirators to set the crime in motion before they can act. Such an approach should prevent further crimes from occurring.

Conspiracy as a Crime

In addition to viewing conspiracy as an inchoate offense, conspiracy can be charged as a crime, in addition to a completed substantive offense. For instance, if two college students agree to rob a convenience store and only one actually carries out the robbery, one could be charged with robbery but both could be charged with conspiracy to commit robbery. Furthermore, the student who helped plan the robbery, but who did not participate directly in the crime could be charged as an accessory to robbery, and in some jurisdictions if both students were present during the robbery the prosecuting attorney might charge both with robbery as well as with conspiracy to commit robbery.

Under common law, conspiracies are not like the related inchoate offenses of attempt and solicitation in that when the target offense is completed attempts and solicitations cease to exist. Legally, this is characterized as those offenses being merged into the substantive offense. By contrast, for conspiracies, charging on both the substantive offense and conspiracy is possible, and this has become a frequent tactic employed by U.S. attorneys in federal cases, particularly those involving the Racketeering Influenced Corrupt Organizations (RICO) Act. The fact that conspiracies do not merge into the planned offense is one criticism of the common law concerning conspiracies. To address this criticism, the Model Penal Code provides that in most instances an individual cannot be charged with both conspiracy and the target offense.

Punishments for Conspiracies

Under common law, conspiracies were treated as misdemeanors regardless of the target offense. Today, some states still follow the common law tradition, but in other states this is no longer true. States that have "reformed" criminal codes, particularly the 37 states that have based their criminal law revisions on the Model Penal Code, tend to grade conspiracies based on the nature of the planned offense. Thus, a conspiracy to commit a misdemeanor would be a misdemeanor and conspiracy to commit a felony would be a felony. The only exception under the Model Penal Code involves conspiracies to commit a first degree felony; these offenses typically call for the most serious punishments—such as life in prison or the death penalty—and conspiracies in those instances are graded as less serious felonies.

Defenses against Conspiracy Charges

There are a number of possible defenses that can be raised to conspiracy charges, but the two most commonly encountered are "impossibility" and "abandonment." First, although there is no complete agreement in case law, most agree that neither factual nor legal impossibility is a defense to the charge of conspiracy. In essence, the view has been that people who conspire to commit what they believe to be a crime—even if the behavior actually does not constitute a crime, or they are precluded from consummating the act—are considered threats to society anyway. Thus, impossibility typically cannot be asserted as a defense to conspiracy, and if it is offered it will not be successful.

Second, like impossibility, in many states withdrawal or abandonment is not recognized as a defense against conspiracy. The reason for this is related to the definition of conspiracy itself. Unlike substantive crimes, where a person may decide completely against committing the offense and renounce all efforts to that end, with conspiracy the "crime" has occurred once two or more people have agreed to perform an illegal act. Thus, the thought (the mental process or *mens rea*) has been formed and the crime of conspiracy already has been committed once the agreement is reached, and once the crime is committed the effort cannot be renounced or the effort abandoned. Nevertheless, a few states provide by statute for the defense of renunciation and they recognize that a person who has entered into a conspiratorial agreement may withdraw from that agreement and notify law enforcement authorities in order to avoid criminal liability for the subsequent acts of co-conspirators.

G. Larry Mays

References and Further Reading

Dressler, J., *Understanding Criminal Law*, 3rd ed., New York, NY: Matthew Bender & Co., 2001.

Fletcher, G.P., *Basic Concepts of Criminal Law*, New York, NY: Oxford University Press, 1998.

Scheb, J.M. and Scheb, J.M., II, *Criminal Law*, 3rd ed., Belmont, CA: Wadsworth Publishing Co., 2003.

See also **Accomplices, Aiding and Abetting; Solicitation to Commit Crime**

Consumers, Crimes against

The types of crimes referred to as "crimes against consumers" fall within the broad category of white-collar crimes. A variety of behaviors can be considered crimes against consumers. Consumers fall victim to crimes such as false advertising, faulty and unsafe products, unfair business practices, and fraud on a daily basis. These types of crimes are so prolific in our society it is nearly impossible to accurately estimate the number of victims and the total cost of crimes against consumers. Included in this article is a discussion of some of the early researchers who addressed this problem, examples of behaviors that typify crimes against consumers, possible theoretical explanations for such crimes, and some of the legal remedies that have been put in place to protect consumers from victimization.

Behaviors and Types of Criminals

At a time when biological explanations for criminal behavior were widely popular and accepted, Edwin Ross wrote *Sin and Society* (1907). In his text, Ross addressed the criminal behaviors of seemingly upstanding citizens and businessmen. Contrary to the atavistic born criminal described by Lombroso, Ross's criminal did not suffer from inherited criminal traits or lack sufficient evolution. Rather, Ross's "criminaloid" was a respected member of the community who used his position in society and in the business world to prey upon others. The criminaloid was an opportunist who capitalized on weaknesses in the legal system and used others to do his "dirty work" in order to maintain a clean reputation. Ross argued that the criminaloid would continue to victimize the public until public morality or laws forced him to stop.

Ross's criminaloid is very much alive and well in today's society. Respected public figures and corporate leaders continue to use their powerful positions and influence to victimize the trusting public. In 1949, Edwin Sutherland published *White Collar Crime* in which he addressed the relationship between the social status of an individual and the misuse of one's occupation to commit crimes. In the text, he discusses the advantages money and power afford the white-collar criminal in avoiding arrest and conviction, as well as the differential or preferential treatment they are often shown within the criminal justice system.

Ultimately, the white-collar criminal and the street criminal are more similar than different. Both victimize the public and result in financial and emotional costs to society as a whole. The two differ, however, in how they victimize the public, the level of fear the public feels toward them, and their treatment within the criminal justice system. A robber might steel a purse or wallet while threatening the victim with a gun in a dark ally at night, but a white-collar criminal picks your pockets, dwindles your savings account, and threatens your health and safety using a fountain pen in a well-lit office during broad daylight.

The American capitalistic economy is founded on the principle "let the buyer beware." It is this very foundation that lends itself to crimes against consumers. By accepting this principle, responsibility for victimization is shifted from the seller or producer of a good or service to the consumer. It is the responsibility of the consumer to be careful, cautious, and leery of the businessperson and their wares. Failure to do so is too often seen as illustrating an irresponsible consumer rather than an unscrupulous businessperson or industry.

Techniques and Types of Crimes

Consumer fraud and false advertising are two common crimes against consumers. Enticing consumers to purchase goods or services through the use of deceitful means or misrepresentation are characteristics of consumer fraud and false advertising. Sellers shamelessly misrepresent the quality or ability of their product or service to the consumer. Sometimes disclaimers can be found in the fine print of a product or service, leaving little recourse for the jilted consumer. Similarly, sellers might misrepresent who they are either by lying or subtly implying something about themselves. For example, dressing an actress in a white lab coat in a commercial or advertisement for an herbal supplement might give the impression that the spokesperson is a doctor. After making this assumption, some consumers might be more inclined to believe the spokesperson's claims because a "doctor" made them. Celebrity endorsements are another popular way to lend legitimacy and notoriety to a product. The public often trusts the opinions of celebrities and may wish to emulate them. For years, celebrity endorsers were not required to be familiar with the products they peddled. Only recently did the Federal Trade Commission (FTC) require celebrity endorsers to base their comments on honest beliefs based on personal findings or experience (ABA, 2000). Additionally, consumers often trust the expert opinions of mechanics, contractors, and other service persons who are willing to sell them services and products they do not need or overcharge consumers for products and services they do need. It has been estimated that 30% of the billions of dollars American consumers spend annually to fix their automobiles is spent on unnecessary work (Glickman, 1981).

Two tactics used by retailers to swindle money from consumers are the bait and switch and chiseling techniques. A bait and switch scam is accomplished when an advertiser makes a tempting offer to sell a product or service but does not intend or want to sell the advertised product or service (Rosoff, Pontell, and Tillman, 2003). The advertised item is simply a lure used by merchants fishing for consumers. The consumer is strongly encouraged to purchase a more expensive item after learning more about the advertised item.

Consumers are also bilked out of their money by a sales technique known as chiseling. This is a systematic means of taking consumers' money, most often undetected by the consumer. For example, by calibrating the scales at a deli to overweigh products priced by weight, the consumer pays for goods they did not receive. Though the weight might be off by only a few ounces and the cost only a few cents to the consumer, the practice can result in significant profits for merchants over the course of a few days, weeks, or even years. Chiseling can occur in a variety of settings the consumer frequents such as at the gas pump and supermarket, but even utility companies and telephone services "round up" to the nearest whole unit, which results in consumers paying for services they did not use and greater profits for the company.

Competition is one of the cornerstones of capitalism. When companies agree to fix prices or rig the bidding process for a contract, competition is eliminated and consumers suffer. Price fixing typically results in inflated prices for goods and services. Therefore, consumers pay more for goods and services than if companies were competing for their patronage. Similarly, when competitors agree to rig a contract bidding process competition is eliminated not by the consumer or contract seeker but by the competitors themselves. In this scenario, even the lowest bid might be inflated and result in overcharging the consumer.

Within the practice of price fixing is another sinister crime against consumers—price gouging. Price gouging occurs when companies take advantage of perceived or real shortages of a good or monopolize a market (Rosoff, Pontell, and Tillman, 2002). For example, in the face of a pending hurricane or aftermath of a natural disaster, homeowners may find themselves paying inflated prices for building materials, as well as increased labor costs for repairs. Numerous examples of price fixing can be found in a variety of industries. Often, companies who take part in price gouging are preying on consumers' fears and their own industry projections. Regardless of whether the shortage or projection comes to fruition, fears and reports of oil shortages result in higher gas prices, crop projection reports result in higher grocery bills, and even weather forecasts can change the price of some items consumers need. Price gouging is an opportunistic crime. Take for example the pharmaceutical industry. Outrageous profits have been gained by monopolizing on the medical needs of individuals whereas soaring prescription costs are blamed on increasing research and development costs (Rosoff, Pontell, and Tillman, 2003).

Described above are some examples of crimes against consumers. An exhaustive discussion of all crimes against consumers is beyond the scope of this article. Consumers can be victims of telephone and telemarketing scams such as 900 phone numbers, unsafe products from defective automobiles to children's toys, outrageous interest rates charged by rent-to-own centers and credit card companies that target poor consumers, and the list goes on. Measuring the true amount of crimes against consumers is virtually impossible. Reporting is problematic at best. Often consumers are unaware they have been victims of crimes such as price fixing or chiseling. Frequently, consumers are embarrassed that they have been duped out of their money by a conman or advertiser and are reluctant to report the incident. Still others are unaware of who to report the crime to and what the authorities can do about the situation.

Theories of Crimes against Consumers

Several theoretical explanations can be used to explain why crimes against consumers occur. According to Coleman (1994) the American culture that breeds greed is a good philosophy. America is a culture of excess. If some is good, then more is better. Our unquenchable desire for more wealth and power creates a breeding ground for unscrupulous acts. In a similar vain, some researchers have asserted that there are corporate cultures that allow and even reward behaviors of this type. Cultural expectations may stem from the leader of the company or be considered part of the industry in general (Rosoff, Pentall, and Tillman, 2002). One need only think of the stereotypical used car industry, auto repair industry, and advertising industry to understand corporate culture theory.

Although there are societal and institutional explanations for crimes against consumers there are also countless individual explanations. One can apply Merton's (1938) modes of adaptation to crimes against consumers, arguing such behaviors are a form of innovation. Equally applicable is Gottfredson and Hirschi's (1990) general theory of crime in which the authors explain that all criminal behavior is the product of lack of self-control.

Consumer Protection

Early examples of federal legislation that was passed to address the problem of crimes against consumers included the Sherman Antitrust Act (1890) and the Clayton Act (1914) that prohibited monopolistic competition, price fixing, and price discrimination. The Pure Food and Drug Act (1906) required over-the-counter medicine manufacturers to correctly label the inclusion of certain drugs to better inform the consumer.

More recently, the Nutritional Labeling and Education Act (1990) requires food manufacturers to include the nutritional content of foods on the product's label. In addition, claims about the health benefits of a product must be based on "significant scientific agreement." However, the Food and Drug Administration, the first agency created to enact and enforce standards in the food processing industry, recently decided to relax the restrictions on health claims and allow manufacturers to print claims even if they are not based on conclusive scientific evidence (Martin, 2003). The new guidelines call for a grading system by which beneficial health claims will be analyzed. The scale is based on an A–D rating system. All claims which receive a B–D rating, ranging from good but inconclusive scientific evidence (B) to little scientific evidence (D) will require a disclaimer. Time will tell if this system of rating claims will prove beneficial to consumers or if it will simply open the door for more confusion and exploitation of consumers.

AMIE R. SCHEIDEGGER

References and Further Reading

American Bar Association (1990). Endorser liability. *ABA Journal*. May 1990: 24, 29.

Coleman, J.W. (1994). *The Criminal Elite* (3rd ed). New York, NY: St. Martin's.

Glickman, A.P. (1981). *Mr. Badwrench: How You Can Survive the $20 Billion-a-Year Auto Repair Rip off.* New York, NY: Wideview Books.

Gottfredson, M.R. and Hirschi, T. (1990). *A General Theory of Crime.* Stanford, CA: Stanford University Press.

Martin, A. (2003). FDA relaxes rules for food health claims. *Chicago Tribune*, July 30, 2003.

Merton, R. (1938). Social structure and anomie. *American Sociological Review*, 3, 672–682.

Rosoff, S.M., Pontell, H.N., and Tillman, R.H. (2002). *Profit without Honor: White-Collar Crime and the Looting of America* (2nd ed). Upper Saddle River, NJ: Prentice Hall.

Rosoff, S.M., Pontell, H.N., and Tillman, R.H. (2003). *Looting America: Greed, Corruption, Villains, and Victims*. Upper Saddle River, NJ: Prentice Hall.

Ross, E.A. (1965). *Sin and Society: An Analysis of Latter-Day Inequity.* New York, NY: Houghton, Mifflin.

Sutherland, E.H. (1983). *White-Collar Crime: The Uncut Version.* New Haven, CT: Yale University Press.

See also **Corporate Crime; White-Collar Crime**

Containment Theory

In the early 1940s, Walter Reckless suggested that a variation existed in the respective crime rates among different social groups in the U.S. To a large extent, this variation resulted from their ability to contain or accept norm-violating behavior during the process of social change and cultural conflicts.

In the late 1950s and early 1960s, a group of scholars, namely, Walter Reckless, Simon Dinitz, Ellen Murry, and Frank Scarpitti, began to argue that there is a relationship between personal and social controls. The discussion continued until the emergence of control and self-esteem theories in the early 1970s.

It was Reckless who specifically outlined his theoretical framework of the containment theory in "A New Theory of Delinquence and Crime," published in *Federal Probation* in 1961. The publication was based on his research on delinquent boys and girls in Columbus, Ohio. Reckless's containment theory argues that both internal forces and external forces operate on individuals as they make decisions to either commit or avoid committing crime in diverse situations. Further, Reckless contends that both criminal and noncriminal behaviors can result from the interaction of inner and outer forces within an individual or forces outside the individual.

In Reckless's theory there are four main components operating in two different directions: (1) "inner pushes and pulls" toward committing criminal behavior (motivating forces), (2) "outer pressure and pulls" toward committing criminal behavior (motivating forces), (3) "inner containments" (restraining forces), and (4) "outer containments" (restraining forces).

Inner pushes and pulls are a person's basic human needs and wants, similar to Freud's id-like desires. Outer pressure and pulls refer to an individual's immediate surrounding or environment, such as one's living conditions, (un)employment, and deviant or nondeviant associates. Specifically, whereas pulls are usually defined as the rewards from criminality (financial gains or criminal status), the pressures are those social forces that draw the individual away from law-abiding behavior, e.g., criminal labeling. On the other hand, inner containments are similar to Freud's superego, an individual's tendency to follow the conventional norms and rules. This tendency would prevent the individual from committing criminal behavior. Finally, outer containments are social laws, rules, and policies that sanction criminal actions.

Imagine Reckless's containment theory as a hierarchical structure that describes an individual's ability to contain social and psychological conflicts. At the top level, there are outer (social) pressure and pulls. When an individual is facing social pressures, such as poverty, family problem(s), lack of opportunity, or class or social inequality, a negative life experience starts. Further, if associated with bad peers or influential deviants within a criminal subculture (social pulls), one is more likely to commit criminal behavior. At the bottom level, there are psychological factors called inner pushes and pulls. These factors are usually an individual's personality, characteristics, and perceptions of the social environment. They may include aggressiveness, materialism, pleasure seeking, rebellion, guilt reaction, and perceived social inadequacy and inferiority. According to Reckless, the degree of these motivating inner factors varies within an individual, depending upon how strongly the other two restraining components can balance.

At the middle level are the other two factors acting as barriers with canceling effects: inner containment and outer containment. Inner containment is a type of self-image associated with the level of an individual's internalization of a moral consciousness. This internalization of a moral consciousness often results from family supervision, discipline, and education. It also comes from a person's social norms and expectations. An individual usually uses this internalized self to judge his or her actions when his actions are in conflict with either society or another individual. Outer containment, on the other hand, represents societal sanctions, for instance, laws, rules, regulations, and policies that inhibit criminal behavior.

Although these four forces have combined effects on an individual's behavior and simultaneously push or pull him in criminal or noncriminal directions, Reckless believed that a strong inner containment, such as a strong self-image from a positive internalization, will deter a youth from the pressures of criminogenic influences in the environment. In other words, the type of self-image one has is a major predictor of which of these forces will dominate one's behavior. According to Reckless, nondelinquents are able to maintain law-abiding behavior simply because they are able to maintain a strong self-image in the face of environmental pressures toward criminality. On the other hand, delinquents often come from broken homes and have not been properly socialized or supervised by their families, peer groups, schools, and adult friends. The containment theory is often categorized under social control process theories with sociological perspective.

The containment theory, like every major theory, has been criticized in several aspects. First, certain concepts in the theory are not clearly defined and thus seem to be vague, for example, what is a poor self-concept? Second, the theory sounds conceptually reasonable but is very difficult to test empirically, for instance, how bad must company be for it to constitute bad company? Are the concepts of "inner pushes and pulls," "outer pressure and pulls," "inner containments," and "outer containments" testable in reality? Next, the containment theory fails to answer why some poorly contained youths commit violent crimes whereas others do property crimes. Finally, the theory needs to be tested in cross-cultural settings for its validity and reliability.

JOHN Z. WANG

Principal Writings

Criminal Behavior, New York, NY: McGraw-Hill, 1940.

The Crime Problem, New York, NY: Appleton-Century-Crofts, 1961.

Self-concept as an insulator against delinquency, with Dinitz, S. and Murray, E., *American Sociological Review*, 21 (1956).

A new theory of delinquency and crime, *Federal Probation*, 25 (1961).

Pioneering with self-concept as a vulnerability factors in delinquency, with Dinits, S. *Journal of Criminal Law, Criminology, and Police Science*, 58 (1967).

References and Further Reading

Hirschi, T., *Cause of Delinquency*, Berkeley, CA: University of California Press, 1969.

Kaplan, H., Self-attitudes and deviant response, *Social Forces*, 54 (1978).

Murray, E., Dinitz, S., and Reckless, W.C., The good boy in high delinquency area: four years later, *American Sociological Review*, 25 (1969).

Nye, F.I., *Family Relationships and Delinquent Behavior*, New York, NY: John Wiley, 1951.

Redl, F. and Winerman, D., *Children Who Hate*, Chicago, IL: Free Press of Glencoe, 1951.

Reiss, A.J. Jr., Delinquency as the failure of personal and social controls, *American Sociological Review*, 16 (1951).

Schrag, C., Delinquency and opportunity: Analysis of a theory, *Sociology and Social Research*, 46 (1962).

See also **Psychological Theories of Criminal Behavior; Reckless, Walter; Sociological Theories of Criminal Behavior**

Control Theory *See* **Self-Control Theory; Social Control Theories of Criminal Behavior**

Convict Criminology

There are a significant number of former prisoners studying criminology and becoming professors. As a result of their experiences of arrest, trial, and years of incarceration, they have insight that promises to update and inform what we know about crime and correction. Since 1997, exconvict criminology and criminal justice professors have organized sessions at annual meetings of the American Society of Criminology, the Academy of Criminal Justice Sciences, and the American Correctional Association. These professors discuss and analyze a number of themes related to jails and prisons.

The New School of Convict Criminology

The conference presentations were used to build a working group of exconvict and nonconvict critical criminologists to invent the New School of Convict Criminology. This is a "new criminology" led by exconvicts who are now academic faculty. These men and women, who have worn both prison uniforms and academic regalia, served years behind prison walls, and now as academics, are the primary architects of the movement. As exconvicts currently employed at universities, the convict criminologists openly discuss their personal history and distrust of "mainstream" criminology.

Regardless of criminal history, all the group members share a desire to go beyond "managerial" and "armchair" criminology by conducting research that includes ethnography and an "inside perspective." In contrast to normative academic practice, the "convict criminologists" hold no pretense for value-free criminology and are partisan and proactive in their discourse. This includes merging convict, exconvict, and critical voices in their writing. As Rideau and Wikberg (1992) wrote, "That's the reality, and to hell with what the class-room bred, degree toting, grant-hustling 'experts' say from their well-funded, air-conditioned offices far removed from the grubby realities of the prisoners' lives."

Convict Criminologists

The exconvicts can be described, in terms of academic experience, as three distinct cohorts. The first are the more senior members, full and associate professors, some with distinguished research records. A second group of assistant professors is just beginning to contribute to the field. The third, only some of whom have been identified, are graduate student exconvicts.

Although all these individuals provide convict criminology with unique and original experiential resources, some of the most important contributors may yet prove to be scholars who have never served prison time. A number of these authors have worked inside prisons or have conducted extensive research on the subject. The inclusion of these "non-cons" in the new school's original cohort provides the means to extend the influence of the convict criminology while also supporting existing critical criminology perspectives.

Convict criminologists recognize that they are not the first to criticize the prison and correctional practices. They pay their respects to those who have raised critical questions about prisons and suggested realistic humane reforms. The problem they are most concerned with is that identified by Todd Clear in the foreword to Richard McCleary's *Dangerous Men* (1978/1992), "Why does it seem that all good efforts to build reform systems seem inevitably to disadvantage the offender?" The answer is that, despite the best intentions, reform systems were never intended to help convicts. Reformers rarely even bothered to ask the convicts what reforms they desired. The new school "consultants" correct this problem by entering prisons and directly asking the prisoners what they want and need.

Ethnographic Methodologies: Insider Perspectives

Convict criminologists specialize in "on site" ethnographic research where their prior experience with imprisonment informs their work. They interview in penitentiary cellblocks, in community penal facilities, or on street corners. Their method is to enter jails and prisons and converse with prisoners. This may include a combination of survey instruments, structured interviews and informal observations and conversations. As former prisoners they know the "walk" and "talk" of the prison, as well as how to gain the confidence of the men and women who live inside. Consequently, they have earned a reputation for collecting quality and controversial data.

Exconvict academics have carried out a number of significant ethnographic studies. John Irwin, for example, who served a prison sentence in California, drew upon his experience to write the *The Felon*, *Prisons in Turmoil*, *The Jail* and *It's about Time* (with James Austin). Richard McCleary, who did both state and federal time, wrote his classic *Dangerous Men* based on his participant observation of parole officers. Charles M. Terry, a former California and Oregon state convict, wrote about how prisoners used humor to mitigate the managerial domination of penitentiary authorities. His recent book, *The Fellas*, discusses how convicts overcome prison and chemical addiction. Three exconvict professors, Stephen C. Richards, Charles M. Terry, and Daniel S. Murphy, co-authored an essay on lady hacks and gentlemen convicts. Greg Newbold, having served prison time in New Zealand, wrote *The Big Huey*, *Punishment and Politics*, and *Crime in New Zealand* to analyze crime and corrections in his country. Stephen C. Richards and Richard S. Jones, both former prisoners, used "inside experience" to inform their studies of prisoners returning home. Alan Mobley gave his perspective on private prison corporations (with Gilbert Geis). Richard S. Jones wrote *Doing Time*, about the prison experiences of first-time prisoners (with Thomas J. Schmid). Finally, Jeffrey Ian Ross and Stephen C. Richards coauthored *Behind Bars* and coedited *Convict Criminology*, which includes nine chapters by exconvict academic scholars.

Language and Point of View

The convict criminologists all share an aversion to the language used in most academic research writing on crime and corrections. Typically, researchers use words like "offender" and "inmate." In comparison, convict criminology prefers to use convicts, prisoners, or simply men or women. The distinction is important because it illustrates the different point of view of researchers and authors who have never been incarcerated with those that have. "Offender" and "inmate" are managerial words used by police, court officials, and criminal justice administrators to deny the humanity of defendants and prisoners. To the ear of a former prisoner, being referred to as an offender or inmate is analogous to a man being called a boy, or a women being called a girl. Clearly, the feminists' struggle to redefine how women were addressed and discussed taught an important lesson to the convict criminologists: words are important.

Respect for Convict Authors Still in Prison

A number of convict criminologists continue friendships and working relationships with writers in prison, some of which are well published in criminology. This includes Victor Hassine, a prisoner in Pennsylvania who wrote *Life without Parole*; Wilbert Rideau, a convict in Louisiana who wrote *Life Sentences* (with Ron Wikberg); and Jon Marc Taylor, serving time in Missouri and the author of numerous newspaper and journal articles. The exconvict academics use correspondence, phone calls, and prison visits to communicate with these prisoners, in order to stay current with prison conditions.

The convict authors write serious commentaries on prison life. Unfortunately, much of their research and writing, although critically informed, based on their experiences inside prisons, may only be partially grounded in the academic literature. After all, many of these authors lack or have difficulties obtaining the typical amenities that most scholars take for granted. For example, they may not have access to a computer for writing, to a university library, or to colleagues educated in criminology. They struggle to write by hand, or with broken or worn out machines, and may have difficulty obtaining basic supplies like paper, envelopes, and stamps. In addition, their phone calls are monitored and recorded, and all their mail is opened, searched, and read by prison authorities. In many cases they suffer the retribution of prison authorities, including denial of parole, loss of good time credit, physical threats from staff or inmates, frequent cell searches, confiscation of manuscripts, trips to the hole, and disciplinary transfers to other prisons.

In comparison, convict criminologists have academic resources and credibility to conduct a wide range of research and writing. This allows them to use developments in theory, methodology, and public policy to develop their discourse. As academics they know the scholarly literature on prison, including how issues have been debated over the years in various venues. This knowledge provides them with the opportunity to generalize from research findings, and to understand better how prison conditions compare over time, from state to state, or country to country.

Recent Policy Recommendations

Convict criminologists have come up with several policy recommendations. Many of these build upon the ideas of prison reform activists, progressive policy makers, and critical criminologists. First, the group advocates dramatic reductions in the federal and state prison population through diversion to community corrections programs. Today, many men and women are sentenced to prison for nonviolent crimes. These people should be evaluated as candidates for early release, with the remainder of their sentence to be served under community supervision. The only good reason for locking up a person in a cage is if he or she is a danger to the community. A prisoner should have an opportunity to reduce his or her sentence by earning "good time credit" for good behavior and program participation. Unfortunately, many state correctional systems, following the federal model, have moved toward determinate sentencing. This so called "truth in sentencing" has limited provisions for "good time" reductions in sentences, and no parole.

One problem with reducing the prison population is predicting who might commit new crimes. Despite numerous attempts, there is still no reliable instruments to predict the potential risk of either first-time or subsequent criminal behavior by either free or incarcerated individuals. The problems are many, including "false positives," which predict a person to be a risk who is not. Conversely, "false negatives" are persons predicted not to be dangerous who turn out to be so. Even so, the fact is that our science is less than successful at devising classification schemes, and prediction scales are not adequate rationale for failing to support reductions in prison admissions and population.

Second, convict criminologists support the closing of large-scale penitentiaries and reformatories, where prisoners are warehoused in massive cellblocks. Over many decades, the design and operation of these "big house" prisons has resulted in murder, assault, and sexual predation. A reduced prison population housed in smaller institutions would be accomplished by constructing or redesigning prison housing units with single cells or rooms. Smaller prisons, for example, with a maximum of 500 prisoners, with single cells or rooms, should become the correctional standard when we begin to seriously consider the legal requirement for safe and secure institutions. As a model, we should turn to European countries that have much lower rates of incarceration, shorter sentences, and smaller prisons.

Third, there is a need to listen carefully to prisoner complaints about long sentences, overcrowding, double celling, bad food, old uniforms, lack of heat in winter and air-conditioning in summer, inadequate vocational and education programs, and institutional violence. The list grows longer when a careful look is taken into how these conditions contribute to prisoners being poorly prepared for reentry to the community and the large number that return to prison.

Fourth, strong evidence exists that prison programs are underfunded because administrators and legislators continue to emphasize custody at the expense of treatment. Prisoners should be provided with opportunities for better paid institutional employment, advanced vocational training, higher education, and family skills programs. It is true that most institutions have "token" programs that serve a small number of prisoners. For example, a prison may have paid jobs for 20% of its prisoners, low-tech training, a GED program, and occasional classes in life skills or group therapy sessions. The problem is that these services are dramatically limited in scope and availability.

Convicts need to be asked what services and programs they want and need to improve their ability to live law-abiding lives rather than assume and then implement what we believe is good for them. One recommendation is that prisoners be provided with paid employment, either inside or outside of the prison, where they will earn enough to pay for their own college credit tuition. At the very least, all prisons should have a program that supports prisoners to complete college credit courses by correspondence.

At the present time, most U.S. prison systems budget very little for prisoner programs. Instead they spend most of the money on staff salaries and security. This is because prison administrators are evaluated on preventing escapes and maintaining order in their institutions. So, the prisons are operated like zoos where human beings live in cages, with few options to develop skills and a new future.

Convict criminologists advocate prison administrators being evaluated on their delivery of programs and the reduction of parole violation, recidivism, and the "return rate" of prisoners to their prison system. It is no longer acceptable for prisons to neglect prisoner needs for vocational, educational, and life skills programs and services.

Fifth, convict criminology advocates voting rights for all prisoners and felons. The U.S. is one of the few advanced industrial countries that continue to deny prisoners and felons voting rights. They suggest that if convicts could vote, many of the recommendations advocated would become policy because the politicians would be forced to campaign for convict votes. State and federal government will only begin to address the deplorable conditions in prisons in the U.S. when prisoners and felons become voters. Prisoners are no less interested than free persons in exercising the right to vote. To the contrary, if voting booths were installed in jails and prisons, convict criminologists predict the voter turnout would be higher than in most outside communities.

Sixth, they advocate that prisoners released from prison have enough "gate money" that would allow them to pay for 3 months worth of rent and food. The excons could earn some of this money working in prison industries, with the balance provided by the institution. All prisoners exiting correctional institutions should have clothing suitable for applying for employment, eye glasses (if needed), and identification, including a social security card, state ID or drivers' license, and a copy of their institutional medical records. They should be given credit for time served on parole supervision. Also, the use of drug and alcohol testing as the primary cause of parole violations needs to be addressed.

Seventh, the most controversial policy recommendation is eliminating the snitch system in prison. The snitch system is used by "guards" in old-style institutions to supplement their surveillance of convicts. It is used to control prisoners by turning them against each other and is therefore responsible for ongoing institutional violence. Convict criminologists argue that if the recommendations for a smaller population, housed in single cells or rooms, with better food and clothing, voting rights, and well-funded institutional programming were implemented, the snitch system would be unnecessary. Furthermore, in a small prison, with these progressive reforms, prison staff would no longer be forced to behave as guards, but instead would have the opportunity to actively "do corrections" as correctional workers. The staff would be their own eyes and ears, because they would be actively involved in the care and treatment of prisoners.

Finally, they support the termination of the drug war. Military metaphors continue to confuse thinking and complicate the approach to crime and drug addiction. For example, the theory of judicial deterrence, discussed as a rationale for sentencing in nearly every criminal justice textbook, is derived from the "Cold War" idea of nuclear deterrence. This idea evolved into mutually assured destruction (MAD), which was the American rationale for building thousands of nuclear bombs to deter a possible Soviet nuclear attack. The use of deterrence and war has now bled over from the military strategic thinking to colonize criminal justice. The result is another cold war for the U.S., this one against its own people. Convict criminologists advocate an end to the drug war, amnesty for drug offenders, and a reexamination of how the criminal justice priorities are set.

Pros and Cons of Convict Criminology

The first strength of convict criminology is that it is based on a bottom-up, inside-out perspective that gives voice to the millions of men and women convicts and felons. The second is that the group is composed of men and women who have served prison time in many different environments, including the Federal Bureau of Prisons, various state systems, different countries, and at different levels of security. Altogether, the founding members of the group have served over 50 years in prison. Finally, it should be remembered that it would have been much easier for the exconvict professors to conceal their past and quietly enjoy their academic careers. Instead, they decided to "come out" of the closet, develop their own field of study, and take up the fight against the liberal-conservative consensus that continues to ignore the harm done by mass incarceration in the U.S.

There are two weaknesses of this new field. First, most of the exconvict professors are white males. This is the result of two facts: over 90% of prisoners are male, and very few minorities leave prison prepared to enter graduate school. To some extent, this problem is being addressed through active recruitment of minorities and women into the group. For example, the group does include feminist noncon criminologists who conduct prison research.

Second, because the group is partisan and activist it is clearly biased in its approach to research and publication. On the other hand, the convict criminologists would argue that given the prejudice most people, academics included, have against criminals, convicts and felons, the idea of value-free prison research is at best a polite fantasy. The only solution to this dilemma is for all researchers who contribute to the literature to discuss their biases openly, including former criminal justice personnel.

Conclusion

Convict criminology is a new way of thinking about crime and corrections. The alumni of the penitentiary now study in classrooms and serve as university faculty. The old textbooks in criminology, criminal justice, and corrections will have to be revised. A new field of study has been created, a paradigm shift occurred, and the prison is no longer so distant.

STEPHEN C. RICHARDS AND JEFFREY IAN ROSS

References and Further Reading

Austin, J., Bruce, M.A., Carroll, L., Mc Call, P.L., and Richards, S.C. 2001. The use of incarceration in the United States. American Society of Criminology National Policy Committee. *Critical Criminology: An International Journal*, 10, 1: 17–41.

Austin, J. and Irwin, J. 2001. *It's about Time*. Belmont, CA: Wadsworth.

Austin, J., Richards, S.C., and Jones, R.C. 2003a. Prison release in Kentucky: Convict perspective on policy recommendations. *Offender Programs Report*, 7, 1: 1, 13–16.

Austin, J., Richards, S.C., and Jones, R.C. 2003b. New ideas for reforming parole in Kentucky. *Offender Programs Report*, 7, 2: 19–20, 22, 24.

Irwin, J. 1970. *The Felon*. Englewood Cliffs, NJ: Prentice-Hall.

Irwin, J. 1980. *Prisons in Turmoil*. Boston, MA: Little, Brown and Company.

Irwin, J. 1985. *The Jail*. Berkeley, CA: University of California Press.

Jones, R.S. and Schmid, T.J. 2000. *Doing Time*. Stamford, CN: JAI Press.

McCleary, R. 1978, 1992. *Dangerous Men: The Sociology of Parole*. New York, NY: Harrow and Heston.
Mobley, A. and Geis, G. 2000. The corrections corporation of America AKA the prison realty trust. In Gilbert, M. and Shichor, D. (Eds.), *Privatization in Criminal Justice: Past, Present and Future*. Cincinnati, OH: Anderson, pp. 202–226.
Newbold, G. 1982, 1985. *The Big Huey*. Auckland, NZ: Collins.
Newbold, G. 1989. Punishment and Politics: The Maximum Security Prison in New Zealand. Auckland, NZ: Oxford University Press.
Newbold, G. 2000. *Crime in New Zealand*. Palmerston North, NZ: Dunmore.
Richards, S.C. and Jones, R.S. 1997. Perpetual incarceration machine: Structural impediments to post-prison success. *Journal of Contemporary Criminal Justice*, 13, 1: 4–22.
Richards, S.C. and Ross, J.I. 2001. The new school of convict criminology. *Social Justice*, 28, 1: 177–190.
Richards, S.C. and Ross, J.I. 2003. Convict perspective on the classification of prisoners. *Criminology & Public Policy*, Vol. 2, No. 2: 243–252.
Richards, S.C., Terry, C.M., and Murphy, D.S. 2002. Lady hacks and gentlemen convicts. In Alarid, L.F. and Cromwell, P. (Eds.), *Contemporary Correctional Perspectives: Academic, Practitioner, and Prisoner*. Los Angeles, CA: Roxbury, pp. 207–216.
Richards, S.C., Austin, J., and Jones, R.S. 2004a. Thinking about prison release and budget crisis in the blue grass state. *Critical Criminology* (at press).
Richards, S.C., Austin, J., and Jones, R.S. 2004b. Kentucky's perpetual prisoner machine: It's all about money. *Review of Policy Research*, Vol. 24, No. 1 (at press).
Rideau, W. and Wikberg, R. (Eds.). 1992. *Life Sentences: Rage and Survival Behind Bars*: Times Books.
Ross, J.I. and Richards, S.C. 2002. *Behind Bars: Surviving Prison*. New York, NY: Alpha.
Ross, J.I. and Richards, S.C. 2003. *Convict Criminology* (Eds.). Belmont, CA: Wadsworth.
St. John, W. 2003. Professors with a past: Ex-convict criminologists say time they spent as prison inmates adds special insight to their research and their teaching, in *The New York Times*, August, 9: A13–A14.
Terry, C.M. 1997. The function of humor for prison inmates. *Journal of Contemporary Criminal Justice*, 13, 1: 23–40.
Terry, C.M. 2003. *The Fellas: Overcoming Prison and Addiction*. Belmont, CA: Wadsworth.

See also **Critical Criminology: An Overview; Radical Theories of Criminal Behavior**

Corporal Punishment

Introduction

Corporal punishment has been used as a means of controlling different forms of misbehavior. It has been used as a way of disciplining children who are acting in a bad manner. This ability to mete out corporal punishment on children has not been the sole domain of parents and family members. School authorities and administrators have also used corporal punishment as a tool to curb problem students. But corporal punishment has not been confined to children or adolescent misbehavior. Historically, it was used as a means of disciplining adult offenders with unruly behavior who had been sent to correctional institutions. Although predominantly meted out by correctional officers in the past, it was not unheard of for inmates to impose corporal punishment on other inmates.

There is no way of knowing when or where the use of corporal punishment first originated; it is older than civilization, and probably, all primitive races used it. Before the development of organized education, physical force was the primary means of socializing children. Before the birth of prisons in Europe and America, the whip had been a key instrument of penal practice. Together with other physical punishment and tortures, corporal punishment gave formal expression to the punitive obsessions of medieval criminal justice. Historical works have illustrated how corporal punishment was used in ancient Greece, Rome, and Russia.

Corporal punishment primarily affects the criminal justice system in two contexts: (1) Correctional institutions and (2) Court involvement with schools. This encyclopedia entry examines the incidence and nature of corporal punishment within both of these arenas. Although the courts have served as an important intermediary in the use of corporal punishments in prisons and jails, both of these will be discussed under the banner of correctional institutions. What follows is, first, a discussion of corporal punishment in correctional institutions and how court involvement helped in the abandonment of corporal punishment as a legitimate penalogical interest. Following this is a discussion of how the courts have viewed and acted toward corporal punishment in public schools.

Corporal Punishment in Correctional Institutions

Correctional institutions and the use of corporal punishment have an intertwined history dating back to the first prisons in America. For the majority of correctional history, correctional officers have had wide discretion when punishing troublesome prisoners. These officials controlled all facets of prisoner life; and, in doing so, the officers had many options of punishment for unruly prisoners. Prisoners who misbehaved could be subjected to the hole, restriction of food, or lose other privileges. Correctional officers could also subject prisoners to corporal punishment—beatings with whips, boards, fists, or other means of inflicting physical pain.

Different definitions of corporal punishment are fairly universal in nature. Corporal punishment has been defined as the infliction of physical pain upon an inmate as a punishment for the violation of a prison rule or regulation. These forms of conduct can include whippings, the use of cold showers, electrical shocking devices, and suspension from cell bars by handcuffs; this list is by no means all encompassing. Legal dictionaries define corporal punishment as physical punishments that are distinguished from pecuniary punishment or fines; this implies any kind of punishment inflicted on the body. Corporal punishment, then, is nothing more than the "infliction of pain" as part of a sanction.

Corporal punishment was used as a tool of punishment until the 1960s, when the courts took a stance against it. By the time the federal courts examined corporal punishment and moved toward abolishing the practice, most states had already abandoned or were in the process of abolishing this practice as a viable punishment option. The major effect of different court actions was to bring the remaining states into compliance with the rest of the states that had abolished the practice. The end of corporal punishment has its origins in the Arkansas correctional system in the 1960s.

Talley v. Stephens (247 F. Supp. 683, 1965) marked the beginning of the end for the whipping style of corporal punishment in the U.S. In *Talley*, prisoners in the Arkansas correctional system brought suit against the state. Talley and the other prisoners argued that they had been unconstitutionally subjected to cruel and unusual punishments, and that they had been denied access to the Courts. The court described the corporal punishment process as it was administered in Arkansas prisons. Corporal punishment consisted of blows with a leather strap 5 feet in length, 4 inches wide, and about one-fourth inch thick, attached to a wooden handle or shaft about 6 inches long. This punishment was inflicted by the assistant warden of the prison. A prisoner who was to be whipped was required to lie down on the ground fully clothed, and the blows were inflicted upon his buttocks.

In this case, the court held that although persons convicted of crimes lose many of the rights and privileges of law-abiding citizens, it is established that they do not lose all of their civil rights. On the other hand, convicts must be disciplined, and prison authorities must be given wide latitude and discretion in the management and operation of their institutions, including the disciplining of inmates. The court recognized, however, that the courts, at this time, could not take over the management of correctional facilities. The problem the court had with the Arkansas correctional system was that there were no written rules or regulations prescribing what conduct or misconduct would bring on a whipping or prescribing how many blows would be inflicted for a given act of misconduct. In this particular case, Talley had been whipped a number of times by the warden and by a "line rider" assigned to Talley's long line. This line rider, Pike, was a convicted murderer serving a sentence for beating to death a warden in Mississippi.

The court held that: "The Court's unwillingness to say that the Constitution forbids the imposition of any and all corporal punishment on convicts presupposes that its infliction is surrounded by appropriate safeguards" (247 F. Supp. at 687, 1965). Corporal punishment must not be excessive. Corporal punishment must be inflicted as dispassionately as possible and by responsible people. Corporal punishment must be applied in reference to recognizable standards whereby a convict may know what conduct on his part would cause him to be whipped and how much punishment given conduct may produce. Without these safeguards, a prison system could not continue to use corporal punishment. In the case of the Arkansas experience, the court ruled that those safeguards did not exist. Until these conditions were established, the further use of corporal punishment on prisoners was halted. The *Talley* case did not ban corporal punishment; however, it did pressurize Arkansas to develop procedures for meting out these types of punishments—standards and procedures that were supposed to prevent arbitrary, discriminatory, and excessively brutal beatings.

Three years after the courts handed down the *Talley* decision, the courts were again faced with the issue of corporal punishment. Again the stage for the case was set in the Arkansas correctional system. In *Jackson v. Bishop*, 404 F.2d 571 (1968), it was claimed that the District Court erred in refusing to hold that corporal punishment of prisoners is cruel and unusual punishment within the meaning of the Eighth Amendment to the U.S. Constitution, and in holding that the whipping of prisoners was not unconstitutional per se. *Jackson* further outlined how whipping was the primary disciplinary measure in the Arkansas system. The strap was used to hurt inmates' pride, to preserve discipline, and to improve the work level of the inmates.

Blackmun, in his decision, noted that neither side in *Talley v. Stephens* had appealed the decision. Blackmun then concluded that Jackson was correct in the position that Arkansas' use of the strap, irrespective of safeguards, was unconstitutional. As a result of the *Talley* decision, Arkansas had changed its practices on corporal punishment. By 1966, new rules and procedures had been implemented that were used until the district court again halted the use of corporal punishments. The new rules had stated certain major offenses that would warrant corporal punishment in Arkansas. Several rules were listed that would garner the use of physical force; a few examples of violations included: homosexuality, agitation, insubordination, making or concealing weapons, refusal to work when medically certified able to work, and participating in or inciting a riot.

Under the new policy, no inmate was authorized to inflict corporal punishment under color of prison authority on another inmate. Punishment was not to exceed 10 lashes with the strap and this punishment was to be determined by a Board of Inquiry. No punishment was ever to be administered in the field as the severity of the punishment could be increased as a result of the heat of the moment. However, these new policies and procedures concerning corporal punishment had been created in a very quick manner, and, hence, an adequate corporal punishment policy in the State of Arkansas still did not exist. The post-*Talley* rules and regulations were still not found to provide adequate safeguards.

The *Jackson* case ended on a more fatal note for the whipping form of corporal punishment than the *Talley* case had. The court had no difficulty in reaching the conclusion that the use of the strap in the penitentiaries of Arkansas was punishment that ran afoul of the Eighth Amendment's prohibition on cruel and unusual punishment. The strap's use, irrespective of any precautionary conditions that may be imposed, ran counter to contemporary concepts of decency and human dignity and precepts of civilization. The use of corporal punishment also violated those standards of good conscience and fundamental fairness enunciated by this court in the several preceding cases. In this, corporal punishment was not declared unconstitutional *per se*, but because no proper procedures were ever instituted that would ensure the inmates rights against the arbitrary use of the strap, and thus, protect the inmates' rights against cruel and unusual punishment, corporal punishment in prisons was abandoned.

The *Jackson* opinion indicated that standards and procedures could not keep abuses from occurring. Just because new standards were in place, it was not ensured that officials would always follow the written procedures. In Arkansas, excessively brutal whippings still took place. It was presumed by the court that this would be the case in any correctional issue that still used corporal punishment as a means of controlling inmates. The beatings generated hatred among the prisoners; this hatred served to hinder any progress toward the rehabilitation of inmates or preparing them for their return to society. Even though the court found at this time that corporal punishment was unconstitutional in correctional institutions, less than a decade later the courts would examine the issue of corporal punishment in a different setting, with a much different outcome.

Corporal Punishment and Schools

In March 1994, an American teenager, Michael Fay, was convicted of vandalism in Singapore. Part of his sentence included six blows from a cane, though that number was eventually reduced to four. While this was occurring and after Fay had received the blows, the idea of corporal punishment as a correctional and disciplinary measure came again to the attention of American society. Shortly after Michael Fay's caning, numerous public opinion surveys were conducted, by the news media, producing mixed results. The general consensus regarding the mood of Americans toward corporal punishment, as reported by the surveys, was that most Americans surveyed approved of the government of Singapore imposing caning—a duly authorized and historically employed form of sanction under their system of law. A few states, California and Louisiana, even tried to enact legislation extending corporal punishment from the classroom and making it a sentencing option for juvenile offenders. None of this legislation was ever passed, but corporal punishment has remained a viable disciplinary option for school children.

Just as with correctional issues, corporal punishment has been a tool used by school teachers and administrators when disciplining wayward students since the inception of organized primary education. In schools, though, there is less of a consensus as to both the effectiveness and legality of the physical disciplining of students. The courts have historically denoted a difference between the use of corporal punishment in schools and in prisons. As corporal punishment in schools has been viewed under a different lense, the way in which the courts have handled the issue of corporal punishment in the school setting has met different ends. Although research has indicated differential findings on the efficacy of using corporal punishment as a means of keeping order, the courts have continuously found that schools are warranted in using physical punishments if necessary.

Until 1977, the courts were somewhat disjointed in their views of corporal punishment in the school setting. For instance, two cases were heard in 1974 that pertained to the use of force on students with different outcomes. In *Nelson v. Heyne* (491 F.2d 352, 1974), the Seventh Circuit Court of Appeals determined that corporal punishment in schools was cruel and unusual punishment. However, in *Bramlett v. Wilson* (496 F.2d 714, 1974), the Eighth Circuit Court of Appeals found that only in certain circumstances did corporal punishment violate the Constitution's ban on cruel and unusual punishment. A certain resolution to the issue of physically disciplining students came in 1977.

In *Ingraham v. Wright* (430 U.S. 651, 1977), corporal punishment in public schools was definitively examined by the Supreme Court. In 1970, two students, Ingraham and Andrews, who were enrolled in a Florida junior high school, were paddled numerous times for misbehaving. In this case, the Court contended that the use of corporal punishment in America as a means of disciplining school children dated back to the colonial period. Corporal punishment has survived the transformation of primary and secondary education from the colonials' reliance on optional private arrangements to the present system of compulsory education and dependence on public schools. Despite the general abandonment of corporal punishment as a means of punishing criminal offenders, the practice continues to play a role in the public education of schoolchildren in most parts of the country. Professional and public opinion is sharply divided on the practice, and has been for more than a century. The Court could discern no trend toward its elimination. The Court argued that teachers and school administrators were not bound by the Eighth Amendment because the common law gave them the ability to use force for the "proper education and discipline" of the child. If a school teacher or administrator went too far in the use of physical force, then that person would be subject to criminal or civil sanctions. It is interesting that the Court came to this conclusion as, just under a decade earlier in *Jackson v. Bishop*, the court had declared the use of corporal punishment in prisons unconstitutional. As illustrated above, corporal punishment had a long history in prisons as well, but it was declared unconstitutional in the correctional setting.

Prior to the decision in *Ingraham*, the National Educational Association appointed a task force to examine corporal punishment in schools. This committee argued for the dissolution of such policies in public schools. This task force also suggested that students should play more of a role in the disciplinary process in schools; if students and staff worked together, students would have more of a stake in the process. However, teachers are very limited in their resources when dealing with problem children in generally overcrowded classrooms. There have been some suggestions for different means of handling students. Most of this comes from management research that argues for management training for teachers that focuses on personality conflicts and the ability to identify ineffective management strategies. These different disciplinary strategies aside, corporal punishment continues to be a punishment option for teachers and school administrators.

Conclusion

This encyclopedia entry has examined the use of corporal punishment in correctional institutions and in schools and how the judicial branch has reacted to this form of discipline. The courts have taken a split view on the use of corporal punishment in both of these types of environments. Although the courts have adamantly ruled against physical disciplinary forms in prisons and jails, the judiciary has viewed that the use of corporal punishment in public schools is not a violation of the Constitution's ban on cruel and unusual punishment. Although the majority of research on this issue has been and continues to be from the perspective that discipline does not require reinforcement by physical means, especially in the case of schools, the future of corporal punishment in the criminological enterprise is mostly an artifact of an earlier time in the evolution of the criminal justice system.

Within correctional institutions, the use of corporal punishment as a means of punishing inmates for bad behavior was being disused by most prisons long before a court in the Eighth Circuit Court of Appeals declared that no policy could ever be created that would halt the abuses inherent in any strategy of corporal punishment. Situational factors associated with corporal punishment in prisons still arise in the courts. In 2002, the Supreme Court heard *Hope v. Pelzer* (No. 01-309, 2002), a case that dealt with the qualified immunity of correctional officers who engage in the practice of physically disciplining correctional inmates. The future of corporal punishment in correctional institutions will likely revolve around isolated cases like this one that occur sporadically throughout time.

If there is any future to the study of corporal punishment in criminology, it will be in regard to different courts' stances on the use of physical beatings in public schools. For now, courts at all levels seem reluctant to overturn the decision handed down in *Ingraham v. Wright*, which allows school teachers and administrators to mete out corporal punishment to students with bad behavior. Many schools across the nation have begun to abolish the use of force on students. This is similar to the way in which corporal punishment met its end in the correctional institution. The beginning disuse of force in the school setting could suggest an end to corporal punishment in schools in the not-too-distant future.

SEAN MADDAN

References and Further Reading

Black, H.C., *Black's Law Dictionary*, 6th ed, St. Paul, MN: West Group, 1998.

Edwards, T.D., Can (or should) we return to corporal punishment?—Yes, in Fields, C.B. (Ed.), *Controversial Issues in Corrections*. Boston, MA: Allyn and Bacon, 1999, pp. 219–230.

Harrison, M. and Gilbert, S., *Schoolhouse Decisions of the United States Supreme Court*, San Diego, CA: Excellent Books, 1997.

Hyman, I.A. and James, H.W., Corporal Punishment in American Education: Readings in History, Practice, and Alternatives, Philadelphia, PA: Temple University Press, 1979.

Maddan, S. and Hallahan, W., Corporal punishment in the 21st century: An examination of supreme court decisions in the 1990s to predict the reemergence of flaggelance," *Journal of Crime and Justice* 25(2): 97–120, 2002.

Midgley, J.O., Corporal punishment and penal policy: Notes on the continued use of corporal punishment with references to South Africa," *The Journal of Criminal Law and Criminology* 73(1):388–403, 1982.

Palmer, J.W. and Stephen, E.P., *Constitutional Rights of Prisoners*, 6th ed., Cincinnati, OH: Anderson Publishing Co., 1999.

Paquet, R.A., Judicial Rulings, State Statutes, and State Administrative Regulations Dealing with the Use of Corporal Punishment in Public Schools, Palo Alto: R & E Research Associates, 1982.

Scott, G.R., The History of Corporal Punishment: A Survey of Flagellation in its Historical, Anthropological, and Sociological Aspects, London: T. Werner Laurie Ltd., 1886.

Smith, C.E., *Law and Contemporary Corrections*, Belmont, MA: West/Wadsworth Publishing Company, 2000.

See also **Child Abuse: The Law; Punishment Justifications; Schools and Delinquent Behavior**

Corporate Crime

Though attention to the phenomenon of corporate crime remains marginal to the discipline of criminology, a focus on illegal abuses of power by economic entities and their key agents in fact has a long history. For example, within the social sciences, many of the so-called "classical" sociologists—including Marx, Weber, Durkheim, Simmel, Pareto—each paid some attention to such phenomena, though of course their central concerns were not with corporate crime *per se*, but with business illegalities as indices of certain social structures, changes, or norms. Within criminology, a concern with the illegal activities associated with economic activity is traceable back to the work of Willem Bonger in The Netherlands and E. A. Ross in the U.S.

Beyond academia, the American traditions of muckraking and populism focused critical scrutiny upon the activities of both robber barons and "big business" in general in the latter years of the 19th and early years of the 20th centuries. By this time, however, corporations had been granted by the state the legal privileges of incorporation and limited liability, these developments easing the way for similar legal innovations in Britain in the 1860s, closely followed by France. In the face of popular opposition, corporations had won telling legal protection from exposure to accountability for their socially harmful activities.

The first major piece of criminal law designed to control corporate activity was the Sherman Anti-Trust Act, passed in the U.S. in 1889, prohibiting conspiracies in the restraint of trade—though, as Edwin Sutherland noted, this proved more likely to be used against trade unions than business organizations. This was followed during the Progressive Era in the U.S. by other forms of legislation regulating the economic activities of business. It was not until the 1960s and 1970s that there emerged a wave of social regulation in the U.S.—laws designed to prohibit corporate damage to the environment, consumers, and workers—which quickly spread throughout many advanced western economies. The latter part of the 20th century witnessed some rather contradictory developments regarding the regulation of corporate activity, although combinations of deregulation, decriminalization, and the "downsizing" of regulatory agencies appeared to be the norm, at least in the context of social regulation (Snider, 2000).

It is the path-breaking work of Sutherland that is usually credited with spurring more recent academic concern with corporate crime, though in this origin lies the source of much of the ongoing confusion as to what constitutes corporate crime. In a famous presidential address to the American Sociological Association in 1939, and in a series of papers, articles, and a book published between 1940 and 1949, Edwin Sutherland developed the concept of "white-collar crime"—"a crime committed by a person of respectability and high social status in the course of his occupation" (Sutherland, 1983, 7). He thus challenged the stereotypical view of the criminal as typically lower class, because "powerful business and professional men" also routinely commit crimes. The principal distinction between the crimes of the upper and lower classes was the implementation of the criminal laws that apply to them: "upper class" criminals often operate undetected, if detected they may not be prosecuted, and if prosecuted they tend to receive relatively lenient (and overwhelmingly financial) penalties.

Given these insights, Sutherland sought to produce a more encompassing and abstract definition of crime, requiring the "legal description of an act as socially injurious and legal provision of a penalty for the act" (Sutherland, 1983, 46). Thus, although his definition of "crime" retained a reference to law, he sought to encompass within it illegalities other than those proscribed by *criminal* law. Sutherland's rationale here was that the content of laws and such legal distinctions are themselves social products, and that "crimes" are illegalities that are contingently differentiated from other illegalities by virtue of the specific administrative procedures to which they are subject.

Important as Sutherland's naming of this concept of "white-collar" crime was, it generated significant theoretical and conceptual confusion, not least because having defined white-collar crime in terms of persons, Sutherland proceeded to study corporations (Cressey, 1989). What he actually did was highlight the phenomenon of corporate crime.

Notwithstanding notable exceptions—for example, some of the work of Geis through the 1960s—very little academic attention focused upon *corporate* crime in the immediate aftermath of Sutherland's clarion call to criminology. It was not until the end of the 1960s and the beginning of the 1970s that there occurred a reemergence of attention to corporate crime as one aspect of a more general proliferation of both an academic concern with "white-collar" crime and a popular and political concern with the socially harmful effects of corporate activity. Clearly the emergence of these two areas of concern is closely related (Geis et al., 1995). Post-Watergate America saw the country enter something of a crisis of legitimacy, a context that tainted all powerful organizations with more than a whiff of both corruption and criminality. This was a ripe context for the emergence of a social movement against corporate crime (Kramer, 1989). And so in the early to mid-1970s, over three decades after Sutherland had famously attempted to turn the attention of American criminology to white-collar crime, there appeared to be something of an upsurge in academic and indeed popular interest in the criminal and socially irresponsible activities associated with corporations.

One element of increased attention to both corporate and white-collar crime was a series of attempts to achieve definitional and conceptual clarity regarding the different phenomena to which these terms referred. One recent, and significant, stage in the delineating of corporate crime was the development of the distinction between occupational and organizational crimes. Although occupational crimes occur when individuals or groups of individuals make illegal use of their occupational position for personal advantage and victimize consumers or their own organization, organizational illegalities, a subset of which are corporate crimes, are individual or collective illegalities that are perceived as helping to achieve, or are congruent with, organizational goals set by the dominant coalition within an organization (Sherman, 1982). This being said, it is important that the distinction between organizational and occupational crimes is not overdrawn, as what appear to be occupational crimes are often encouraged, required, or tolerated for a variety of reasons within corporations, furthering their ends. To focus in an overly restrictive manner on occupational crimes may obscure the origins of certain acts in criminogenic corporations, industries or markets that can produce *both* occupational and organizational crime.

Ultimately, there remains no universally accepted definition of corporate crime. Corporate crime has been treated—albeit differently and with greater or lesser adequacy—by criminologists and social scientists whose concerns have been with business crime, commercial crime, crimes of capital, crimes of the powerful, crimes at the top, crimes of the suites, economic crime, elite deviance, occupational crime, organizational deviance, and white-collar crime. More recently, Ruggiero has added to definitional disputes through seeking to document empirically and grasp theoretically the seemingly increasingly complex relationships between legitimate organizations and organized crime factions (Ruggiero, 1996).

However, one definition that has entered more general usage views corporate crime as illegal acts or omissions, punishable by the state under administrative, civil, or criminal law, which are the result of deliberate decision making or culpable negligence within a legitimate formal organization. These acts or omissions are based in legitimate, formal, business organizations, made in accordance with the normative goals, standard operating procedures, or cultural norms of the organization, and are intended to benefit the corporation itself (Pearce and Tombs, 1998, 107–110, 1983; Schrager and Short, 1977).

This definition distinguishes occupational from organizational crime and corporate crime from organized crime. It also incorporates Sutherland's insight that the distinctions between different forms of illegalities—criminal, civil, or administrative—are largely contingent. This is particularly important given the power of corporate representatives to influence the passage, implementation, enforcement, and interpretation of laws—a power that some have argued has been augmented with the reemergence of conservative political views on an international scale (as evidenced by the repeal or nonenforcement of laws regulating corporations) (Snider, 2000).

Why so much attention to the problem of definition here? Largely because the failure to achieve definitional and conceptual clarity is particularly significant in the sphere of corporate crime research. These problems are exacerbated by the type of corporate crime research that has been done, the state of theoretical development within this area of inquiry, and the relationship between corporate crime research and criminology.

Thus much corporate crime research has been devoted to establishing the extent, or even the very fact, of corporate crime. One important context for this endeavor is that most nation-states fail to collate data on corporate crime—a fact that both follows from, and reinforces, the marginalization of corporate crime from political and popular discourse on crime. If official quantification matters in such discourses, then the lack of corporate crime data is related to its lack of political representation as a law and order problem. Given this absence of usable official corporate statistics in almost all jurisdictions, one strand of corporate crime research has sought to document the quantitative scale of such offending. Typically, this has involved the use of large datasets, focusing most notably upon the largest corporations of any one nation-state, most notably the Fortune 500 in the U.S. This very exercise was first engaged in by Sutherland (1983); some years later, one of the landmark texts of corporate crime research presented results from a similar exercise (Clinard and Yeager, 1980). Efforts have also been made to use such datasets to isolate empirical correlates of offending, such as industry, size, profitability, and so on. Given the relative paucity of data available with which to work, however, findings from such empirical efforts remain highly contentious, save for the overwhelming conclusion that corporate offending is widespread and pervasive.

Various forms of qualitative work also have been undertaken around corporate crime. Within this case-study tradition, two strands of work should be noted. On the one hand, there now exist numerous posthoc studies of corporate crimes that attempt to reconstruct the causes, modus operandi, and consequences of the event or set of events in question—a classic work in this context is Geis's documentation of the antitrust conspiracy in the heavy electrical equipment industry in the U.S. (Geis, 1967). A second strand within the case study genre has entailed examinations of a particular incident or set of events—such as the infamous case of the deaths associated with the design fault in the Ford Pinto (Cullen et al., 1987)—largely with a view to determining via social science that an incident constituted illegality even in the absence of any successful legal action.

A further broad tradition of academic work is also devoted to specific types or categories of corporate crimes, raising issues of extent, consequences, modus operandi, and appropriate modes of regulation and sanction. Notable here are the categories of: financial crimes, including illegal share dealings, illegal mergers and takeovers, bribery, tax evasion, transfer pricing, and other forms of illegal accounting; offenses committed directly against consumers, such as illegal marketing and sales practices, the sale of unfit goods, cartel pricing, illegal labeling, and fraudulent safety testing; crimes arising directly out of the employment relationship, such as offenses against laws regarding equal treatment, violations of wage laws, health and safety offenses; and crimes against the environment, including illegal emissions to air, water, and land, waste dumping, and the provision of false information to regulatory authorities.

Finally, there now stands a body of work devoted to industry-specific case studies, notably in the car, chemicals, financial services, oil, and pharmaceuticals sectors. The classic study herein must surely be Braithwaite's (1984) account of corporate crime in the pharmaceutical industry. As with the strictly quantitative work, such efforts have demonstrated the scale and pervasiveness of corporate crimes across societies.

Taken together, these bodies of work also demonstrate that the economic (not to mention physical and social) costs of corporate offending far outweigh those associated with "conventional" or "street" offending—a conclusion that is difficult to contest even while recognizing that attempts to calculate estimates of the "costs" of any form of crime are fraught with difficulty. Even studies of single examples of corporate crime—such as the illegal activities of corporations in the Savings and Loans debacle—are enough to support this general conclusion.

A second general issue associated with the lack of definitional and conceptual clarity associated with corporate crime research is the commonplace observation that this area of research remains under-developed in its ability to produce real theoretical insight (Cressey, 1989)—even if we should be wary of seeing this as a problem too peculiar to corporate crime research, given that much the same criticism could be made of over 100 years of conventional crime research. However, to the extent that this charge is plausible, then there are some plausible elements of an explanation for it.

For one thing, understanding corporate crime requires modes of explanation and analysis that extend far beyond criminology—indeed, the key focus may need to be the *corporation*, rather than *crime*, a focus that entails an analysis of the nature and operation of the corporate entity through both organizational analysis and political economy. Relatedly, explanatory concepts developed within criminology over the past century have largely failed to make any effort to encompass corporate crime within their explanatory ambit, even if there is no necessary reason why concepts such as anomie, relative deprivation, rational choice theory and so on should not have explanatory value in the sphere of economic activity and organization. Second, corporate crime research has historically been led by U.S. researchers, and it is clear that such work has raised issues about the peculiarity—or generalizability—of findings beyond that national context. Third, issues of generalizability are also raised by the use of industry or event case studies, as well as by the related, and almost universal focus on larger corporate actors to the neglect of small and medium sized enterprises.

This does not deny that there have not been important contributions to theory-building in corporate crime research. It is established that among the factors to be taken into account in explaining the nature and incidence of corporate crime are: the cultures and subcultures of organizations; the opportunity structures—physical, moral, and psychological—which are differentially created by varying organizational forms, and in particular internal lines of decision making and accountability; the industries and markets within which corporations operate, as some market and industrial contexts have been identified as particularly criminogenic; the opportunity structures presented by regulation in the widest senses; and macro economic, political and social contexts, within which are to be found both material and ideological factors more or less conducive to the incidence of corporate crime.

A third general phenomenon associated with the lack of conceptual clarity in the field of corporate crime research is the fact that much of this work has proceeded either at the margins of, or indeed beyond, criminology. Corporate crime researchers have frequently attempted to squeeze their concerns into a discipline that remains wedded to state-defined crime and criminal law, each of which is largely understood in individualistic and interpersonal terms. Indeed, it is little surprise much of the work around corporate crime has been conducted by critical criminologies, which are based upon a commitment to a critique of dominant definitions of crime and criminal law, while at the same time examining the processes of criminalization (and, thus, at times, noncriminalization).

The continued marginalization of corporate crime within the discipline of criminology requires corporate crime research to begin by asserting its legitimacy, a constant problem because of its extension of the term "crime," first, to those acts or omissions punishable beyond the criminal law and, second, because of the desire to include as crimes acts or omissions that have never been defined as such through any criminal justice process. These shifts beyond both the criminal law and formal legal processes have opened up corporate crime researchers to charges of acting as moral entrepreneurs or crusaders, engaged in politicking, bad science, and so on (see, for example, Shapiro, 1983). Further, corporate crime research—as research on the relatively powerful—also faces enormous methodological difficulties, may be relatively unattractive to the funders of research, and is unlikely to produce immediately usable policy proposals, all of which may further explain its relative omission from dominant criminological agendas.

Corporate crime is a problematic and contested area of inquiry. Notwithstanding these definitional, conceptual, methodological, and theoretical disagreement and problems, it speaks to phenomena which on almost any criterion one chooses—the nature and extent of economic, physical, and social harms—is a significant crime and social problem. Indeed, there are some reasons for thinking that corporate crime research should proliferate. These include: the spread of the corporate form, as privatization has been championed across nation-states; diversification in the nature of corporate structures and organization; the seemingly increasing international nature of much corporate activity; associated claims regarding the growing power of corporations vis-à-vis national governments and populations and resistance associated with these trends; and the dogged persistence of so-called "quality of life" issues such as environmental protection, which emerged to prominence in the Western capitalist states in the 1960s onward. Against these trends, and militating against corporate crime research, should be noted both the ongoing glorification of business activities in capitalist economies, alongside the power of corporations to seek, via their political allies, the decriminalization of their activities through the introduction of various forms of self-regulation or through simple deregulation, each of which appear to be significant trends in contemporary capitalist nation-states (Snider, 2000).

Lastly, and to take us right back to the discipline of criminology, corporate crime research remains worthwhile because it can revitalize the discipline itself. Corporate crime research should encourage criminological reflexivity and debates; a focus upon corporate crime entails continual scrutiny of the coverage and omissions of legal categories, the presences and absences within legal discourses, the social constructions of these categories and discourses, their underpinning of treatment within and development through criminal justice systems, the ways in which particular laws are enforced (or not enforced), interpreted, challenged, and, of no little significance, the contours of the discipline of criminology itself.

STEPHEN TOMBS

References and Further Reading

Box, S., *Power, Crime and Mystification*, London, UK: Tavistock, 1983.

Braithwaite, J., *Corporate Crime in the Pharmaceutical Industry*, London, UK: Routledge and Kegan Paul, 1984.

Clinard, M.B. and Yeager, P.C., *Corporate Crime*, New York, NY: Free Press, 1980.

Cressey, D., The poverty of theory in corporate crime research, in *Advances in Criminological Theory*, Adler, F. and Laufer, W.S. (Eds.), New Brunswick, NJ: Translation, 1989.

Cullen, F.T., William, J.M., and Gray, C., *Corporate Crime Under Attack*, Cincinnati, OH: Anderson, 1987.

Geis, G., White-collar crime: The heavy electrical equipment anti-trust cases, in *Criminal Behavior Systems*, Clinard, M.M., and Quinney, R., New York, NY: Holt, Rinehart and Winston, 1967.

Geis, G., Robert, F.M., and Laurence, M.S., Introduction, in *White-Collar Crime. Classic and Contemporary Views*, Geis, G., Meier, R.F., and Salinger, L.M., New York, NY: Free Press, 1995.

Kramer, R.C., Criminologists and the social movement against corporate crime, *Social Justice* 16 (1989).

Pearce, F., *Crimes of the Powerful*, London, UK: Pluto, 1976.

Pearce, F. and Steve, T, *Toxic Capitalism: Corporate Crime and the Chemical Industry*, Aldershot, UK: Ashgate, 1998.

Ruggiero, V., *Organised and Corporate Crime in Europe. Offers that can't be refused*, Aldershot, UK: Dartmouth, 1996.

Schrager, L.S. and James, F.S., Towards a Sociology of Organisational Crime, *Social Problems*, 25 (1977).

Shapiro, S.P., The new moral entrepreneurs: corporate crime crusaders, *Contemporary Sociology* 12 (1983).

Sherman, L., Deviant organisations, in *Corporate and Governmental Deviance*, David, E. and Lundman, R. (Eds.) New York, NY: Oxford University Press, 1982.

Snider, L., The sociology of corporate crime: An obituary (Or: Whose Knowledge Claims Have Legs?), *Theoretical Criminology* 4 (2000).

Sutherland, E.H., White-collar criminality, *American Sociological Review* 5 (1940), reprinted in *White-Collar Criminal: The Offender in Business and the Professions,* Geis, G., New York, NY: Atherton Press, 1968.

Sutherland, E.H., *White Collar Crime: The Uncut Version*, New Haven, CT: Yale University Press, 1983.

See also **Bonger, Willem; Sutherland, Edwin H.; White-Collar Crime, Definitions of; White-Collar Crime: Enforcement Strategies; White-Collar Crime: Law; White-Collar Crime: Theories**

Corpus Delicti

The phrase *corpus delicti* does not mean dead body, but "the body of the crime," and every offense has its *corpus delicti*. For example in *Bussey v. State,* a Texas court held "To establish the *corpus delicti* in arson cases, it is necessary to show (a) that the house was designedly set on fire, and (b) that the accused did it or was criminally connected therewith"; 474 S.W.2d 708 (Tex. Crim. App. 1972). The *corpus delicti* has two components: (1) an unlawful injury, and (2) an individual's unlawful conduct as a source of that injury. To establish a *corpus delicti* there must be proof that a specific injury, harm, or loss resulted, and that someone is responsible for the injury (i.e., the injury was not accidental) (Perkins and Boyce, 1982). Establishing a *corpus delicti* requires that the government only prove that a crime has been committed. The identity of the perpetrator is not required and proof of the *corpus delicti* may be based on circumstantial evidence (*Government of Virgin Islands* 938 F2d 401).

Most *corpus delicti* cases have involved homicides where, typically, the prosecution must show first that a human being is dead (rather than simply disappeared, in those circumstances where no body has been produced, to ensure that the victim will not reappear alive and well at a later time); and second, the death can be attributed to another's unlawful conduct (rather than by accident, suicide, or natural causes) (LaFave and Scott, 1986).

Under the common law, the production of the body of a missing person was generally not required in order to establish the *corpus delicti* for homicide (Perkins and Boyce, 1982). Although this "no-body-required" rule applies today in both federal and most state law cases, under the old Texas Penal Code, one of the elements of the *corpus delicti* of murder in Texas was that the body of the deceased "must be found and identified." (Texas Penal Code Ann. Article 1204 (Vernon, 1925) provided: "No person shall be convicted of any grade of homicide unless the body of the deceased, or portions of it, are found and sufficiently identified to establish the fact of the death of the person charged to have been killed.") In 1974, Texas repealed the requirement that a victim's body be found in order to prove the *corpus delicti* of homicide (e.g. *Williams v. State* 629 S.W.2d 791 (noting the omission of the body-must-be-found requirement under the new Texas Penal Code)). Nevertheless, the Texas Court of Criminal Appeals still requires that the body of the deceased be found and identified (e.g. *Harris v. State* 738 S.W.2d 207 (holding that homicide victim's body must be found and identified)).

One rationale provided for the "no-body-required" rule is that a murderer should not be entitled to acquittal simply because he successfully disposes of a victim's body. Similarly, the "successful concealment or destruction of the victim's body should not preclude prosecution of his or her killer where proof of guilt can be established beyond a reasonable doubt" (*State v. Zarinsky* 143 N.J. Super. 35).

The *corpus delicti* is of significance today primarily in cases where part of the evidence is an extrajudicial (i.e., out of court) confession of the defendant. Historically, the *corpus delicti* doctrine incorporated the almost-universal American rule that in order to convict a defendant of a crime based upon an extrajudicial confession or admission, the defendant's statement must be corroborated by some evidence of the *corpus delicti* (LaFave and Scott, 1986).

It is important to note that the *corpus delicti* rule no longer exists in the federal system. Federal courts and a number of state courts have adopted the "trustworthiness" doctrine that emphasizes the reliability of the defendant's confession over the independent evidence of the *corpus delicti* (Id.). Under the "trustworthiness" doctrine, direct proof of the *corpus delicti* is not required.

The U.S. Supreme Court adopted the trustworthiness doctrine as the "best rule" in *Opper v. United States,* 348 U.S. 84 (1954). In *Opper,* the Court rejected the original *corpus delicti* doctrine, holding instead that confessions, admissions, and exculpatory statements must be corroborated by "substantial independent evidence that would tend to establish the trustworthiness of the statement" (348 U.S. at 93). The Court considered it to be "sufficient if the corroboration supports the essential facts admitted sufficiently to justify a jury inference of their truth" (Id.). Rather, the prosecution must introduce substantial independent evidence that would tend to establish the trustworthiness of the statement, the independent evidence serving a dual function, namely, tending to make the admission reliable, thus corroborating it, while also establishing independently the other necessary elements of the offense (Id.).

Despite the doctrine's nonapplicabilty in the federal system and a few state courts, most jurisdictions continue to follow the original *corpus delicti* doctrine requiring proof from another source that a crime has occurred. The requirement that the *corpus delicti* be sufficiently corroborated by independent evidence is rooted in the premise that the examination of this additional evidence will avert the danger that a crime was confessed to, when in fact no such crime was committed by anyone. Thus, the rule exists to prevent the conviction of an innocent person.

LAVERNE MCQUILLER WILLIAMS

Refererences and Further Reading

Perkins, R.M. and Boyce, R.N. *Criminal Law*, 3rd ed., Mineola, NY: The foundation Press, 1982.

See also **Elements of Crime**

Corrections: Careers

Careers in the corrections field are abundant and diverse. Many of the career paths available in the corrections field are often overlooked by outsiders, and many of the jobs that are available are frequently misunderstood. In actuality, there are hundreds of thousands of jobs available in the field of corrections. There are also many jobs opening up all the time, as new prisons and jails open, existing ones grow larger and more offenders are sentenced to community corrections. The types of jobs that are most commonly thought of in corrections are that of a correctional officer or a probation officer. However, even if these are the most common jobs, they are nowhere all that are available.

The correctional industry covers all types of correctional services, from supermax prisons to minimum security community correctional facilities, to probation officers to persons who provide programming or treatment for offenders, and many "regular" jobs such as food service, plumbers, secretaries, and business-office staff. Especially when talking about institutional corrections it is important to remember that in at least some states prisons are quite large places, holding several thousand inmates. This means that some prisons are larger than many small towns, and yet also need to provide many of the same types of services (i.e., jobs) that are found in free communities.

In addition to the "regular" types of work that are available in corrections there are also a number of specialized populations with whom you can work. There are juvenile corrections services, prisons for female offenders, growing numbers of elderly offenders, mentally ill offenders and myriad other "special" types of offenders. However, many of the jobs available in corrections also do not require much, if any, contact and interaction with offenders. Many of the administrative and support positions have minimal direct contact with criminal offenders.

What follows is a look at some of the major categories of types of careers that are available in the corrections field. This is by no means an exhaustive listing. Anyone interested in finding out about the full range of career opportunities in corrections should contact a local, state, or the federal corrections agency to review the job classifications that are available.

Administrative Positions

The top positions that many correctional staff strive for are those at or near the top of the agency or organization that oversees corrections for a particular geographic or political area. At the top is the Commissioner or Director of Corrections, usually at the state, city, or county government level. The commissioner or director, along with an executive management team (other top administrators who report directly to the commissioner or director), are the individuals who develop policies, oversee finances, and have the final say in decisions. These are the people who make the "big" decisions about how a system or agency will be organized and what it will actually do. The goals, direction, structure, budgeting, and major changes in actions for the organization are determined at this level. The actual jobs available at these levels, and the names for the positions, will vary widely across states and local communities; therefore, it pays to spend some time studying the organizational charts of agencies and reviewing some of the publications these organizations produce to get a better sense of what the various job titles are, and which individuals have what sets of responsibilities.

Policy or Legal Staff

In every organization, there are positions that are focused on keeping the organization and its staff members out of legal trouble, and responding to legal questions and challenges. In corrections, there are many legal questions, and for reasons that are too numerous to discuss here, many lawsuits that need to be defended. Typical issues about which lawsuits are filed include allegations of mistreatment, property damage or loss, and claims of inmates that they are being denied access to basic services such as legal advice, medical services, religious services, and education. Lawsuits sometimes come from inside the organization as well, as employees may file lawsuits about working conditions, allegations of discrimination, or other labor issues.

In addition, policy or legal staff members deal with all aspects of the operations of correctional facilities and programs. Literally every aspect of how a correctional institution or program functions is guided by at least one (and often more) law. By carefully developing and continually reviewing operating policies many of the "bigger" legal challenges can be avoided. Legal or policy staff members also are often involved in negotiations regarding contractual agreements or inconsistencies in policies between the organization and other units of government. There is no shortage of work for staff working in legal or policy administrative positions.

Information Staff

The use and management of many types of information in corrections continue to become both increasingly important and more carefully monitored and controlled. As a growth industry, the amount of information that is used and must be stored, organized, and to which access must be provided grows and changes every year. There is an obvious need for highly skilled staff to design and maintain ways to coordinate all of this information in an easy-to-use manner. Especially in the areas of computer and other technologies there is an increasing need for highly educated and highly skilled management information specialists, media specialists, and researchers.

One frequently overlooked type of information staff is that of the researcher. Many government officials and policy makers want and need to know which programs are effective, what the recidivism rates for offenders are, and other issues. With resources scarce and efficiency demanded, there is a significant need for persons trained and skilled in research to conduct evaluations and outcome studies to determine which activities work and for which offenders. Correctional researchers not only try to determine which programs work or do not work, but they also look at what makes a program more or less successful and what trends can be predicted for the future. Many correctional departments work with colleges, universities, or research organizations to complete such studies, but most agencies also have some type of in-house research capabilities as well.

Human Resources Staff

Like any large organization, correctional agencies need staff that recruit, hire, train, and retain staff members, as well as handle personnel matters. These core tasks will be with a human resources office. In addition, these staff members (in most jurisdictions) need to deal with union contracts and grievances, employee or supervisor conflicts, and reviews of job posts to determine the staffing needs of the organization.

Having a good human resources staff is especially important for a growing industry, where there is an almost constant need for new employees. Additionally, as our population ages and more persons move to retirement, many job openings are created. As a result, recruiting, selecting, and training new staff members are significant sized tasks, and often require innovative and creative approaches. Opportunities for creative, progressive thinking and highly motivated persons are abundant in the human resources career areas of corrections.

Careers in Correctional Institutions

To discuss the types of careers that are available in prisons and jails, it must be remembered that correctional facilities come in all sizes and will range from needing just about any type of job that is found in society (doctors, lawyers, plumbers, landscape technicians, accountants, cooks, recreation leaders, teachers, counselors, secretaries, and even chaplains) to small facilities that have only a handful of staff members (and then usually only security staff). The types of career options outlined here are only some of the more numerous types of opportunities. However, there are many, many different types of jobs available in correctional institutions.

Security Staff

When most people think about a career in corrections, they usually think about positions in security, or what is most commonly referred to as a correctional officer. These are the most numerous positions in corrections. It is important, however, to keep in mind that maintaining security is not just the responsibility of security staff: every person who works in a correctional institution is responsible for security.

The staff persons with primary responsibilities for maintaining security, however, are security staff. Correctional officers, as entry level career positions, carry out the majority of the tasks centered on keeping inmates in, outsiders out, and order on the inside. The actual tasks of correctional officers range from working in housing units to transporting offenders to monitoring inmate activities in open areas, programming offices, work shops, and recreational areas for checking staff and visitors in and out of the institution and processing newly arriving and leaving inmates. Ultimately, it is the correctional officers who ensure control within the facility.

Although the majority of a correctional officer's time, energy, and attention is directed at keeping a facility secure, there are many different aspects of the job of a correctional officer. For example, a correctional officer in a women's prison may have different issues or problems with which to contend than an officer in a maximum security prison for men. Both of these types of officers will have different experiences than a correctional officer in a major city jail, which will also differ from what a correctional officer experiences in a small, rural jail. And, for security staff in a juvenile correctional institution, things are likely to be different yet.

One common question about correctional officers is what type of weapons they carry. The answer is simple, the only weapons usually carried by a correctional officer are his or her hands and brain. Correctional officers do not carry firearms (contrary to the beliefs of many). To have guns anywhere inside a jail or prison is considered too dangerous (in case inmates were able to get hold of them). Rather, correctional officers carry out their tasks using only their brains, mouths and bodies; in some jurisdictions correctional officers may carry pepper spray or a baton, but this is not in all jurisdictions or among all security staff members.

The actual responsibilities of a correctional officer may include a wide variety of tasks, such as controlling and directing the movement of inmates, visitors, and other staff members; patrolling the perimeter of the institutional grounds; overseeing intake or release of offenders; or being a member of a crisis response team.

Moving up the ranks—security staff members are almost always organized in a quasi-military fashion with ranks designated with military labels (sergeant, lieutenant, captain, etc.)—correctional officers may move into supervisory and eventually administrative positions. As one's rank increases one has less contact with inmates and more contact with both staff in general and other supervisors. Because of the large growth of corrections, and the ever-present need for additional staff members, a corrections career provides promotional opportunities fairly quickly.

Facility Executive Staff

Facility executive staff are similar to administrative positions in the larger organization, but they hold primary responsibilities for what happens within their individual institution (or, their area or program within the institution). At the top of the facility executive staff hierarchy is the position of warden (or superintendent). Just like the commissioner or director of the larger corrections department, the warden or superintendent has the final say on all activities in an institution. The warden or superintendent is the individual who is responsible for overseeing all of the personnel in the institution, is responsible for making and implementing policies and procedures, and is the person with whom ultimate responsibility stops. They are the person in charge, completely, of a particular institution.

In addition to the warden or superintendent, the executive management team of a correctional institution is also comprised of one or more deputy wardens (overseeing entire areas of operations, such as security or programs), security captains (usually the highest ranking security staff person(s) who direct the deployment of correctional officers), housing unit directors, and directors of individual program areas (the academic school, recreation, psychological services, medical department, etc.). At this level, these managerial staff persons have most of their interactions with their peers or the executive management staff one level above them; these individuals will also usually be involved in at least some provision of actual services to inmates.

Program Staff

In addition to providing a safe and secure place for inmates to be housed, correctional institutions are also expected (and in some jurisdictions legally required) to provide some types of programming designed to treat inmates' problems and (hopefully) rehabilitate offenders. Academic education, ranging from basic literacy and adult basic education all the way through college courses, needs to be arranged and provided by qualified (usually certified) teachers. Treatment programs for substance abuse, sex offenders, mental illness, and poor social skills are often provided, and require both professional treatment providers and support staff to facilitate the program's operations. Other common (and popular with inmates) types of programs include recreational programs (including arts and crafts, organized sports, and other diverse types of leisure activities) and religious programming. Trained (and again usually certified) professionals are needed to organize and implement these types of programs. Providing inmates with skills through either institutional jobs or vocational training may come in almost any type or form. Inmate industry and work training programs include such diverse things as computer programming and repair, data entry, auto mechanics, electrical work, masonry and carpentry, textile production, printing and graphic design, culinary arts, agriculture, furniture construction and repair, and even cosmetology. All of these types of industry or training programs need qualified professionals to oversee the work of inmates and to provide them instruction.

Almost all incarcerated offenders are also assigned a person responsible for developing an individualized case plan that outlines the offender's needs and a recommended or required course of programming. From conducting and reviewing all of the assessments provided to inmates to developing a case plan and ultimately preparing a release plan, the case manager provides guidance, monitoring, and accountability for offenders. The case manager, in essence, is the individual who watches over the inmate, not to monitor their day-to-day or minute-to-minute activities, but rather in terms of how the correctional institution can best meet both their needs and the needs of society in terms of preparing the inmate for release back to the community.

Support Staff Positions

Like any organization, correctional facilities need administrative support staff. These include everything from data entry clerks to payroll administrators, mailroom staff, executive secretaries, and individuals to organize and maintain inmates' records. Support staff positions include both those that do have a large amount of inmate contact and many that have essentially no contact with inmates.

Careers in Community Corrections

In addition to offering opportunities for working in a jail or prison, corrections also has many career opportunities working with the much larger population of offenders under community corrections supervision. In some ways, these career paths are similar to those in correctional institutions (working with criminal offenders, focusing on administration or supervision, or programming) and in other ways community corrections work is very different (work is in many locations, a smaller number of offenders are assigned to individuals, offenders are often (but not always) convicted of lesser offenses). Community corrections, although serving a much larger number of offenders actually has fewer jobs and fewer specific types of jobs than are available in prisons and jails. Because many of the services that must be provided when offenders are housed, fed, and cared for are not provided to offenders on probation or parole, the jobs associated with doing these tasks are not present.

Supervision Staff

Jobs that are centered on supervising and monitoring the activities of offenders—probation and parole officers—are the centerpiece of community corrections work. The responsibilities and actual job tasks associated with these career paths have changed dramatically over the last couple of decades. The goals for probation and parole officers, however, have not changed. The expectation is that these officers monitor and process offenders for the purpose of public safety. In some jurisdictions probation and parole officers are sworn law enforcement officers with the authority to arrest and detain offenders who do not comply with the conditions of their supervision; however, this is not a universal power.

The basic function associated with probation and parole officers is the supervision and monitoring of offenders who live in the free community. This is accomplished via offenders making scheduled visits to the officer's office; following up with offenders at their homes, jobs, or schools; ensuring that offenders attend mandated programs; sometimes monitoring offenders' whereabouts through electronic means; administering drug and alcohol tests; and monitoring police records to detect any contact (including arrests) that offenders have had with the police. One aspect of the probation or parole officer position that has changed is that whereas at one time the job was considered fairly evenly divided between the supervision role and a treatment-oriented role, the idea of probation or parole officers working with offenders in a treatment-oriented, social work style has been significantly diminished. These staff still recommend and refer offenders to treatment programs and services, but these tasks today are a smaller component of the job than they were in the past.

Probation officers begin their work with offenders shortly after conviction, when they complete assessments of offenders for the court to use in determining sentencing. Parole officers encounter offenders as they are released from prison and must report to the officer to learn the expectations imposed on them for their time in the community. Regardless of the type of supervision, the supervision officer is responsible for monitoring whether the offender abides by the conditions imposed by the court and if the offender is not in compliance, the supervision officer may initiate processing to send or return the offender to incarceration.

Other Community Corrections Careers

In addition to the position of probation or parole officer, all of the standard organization-supporting positions—administrative, support staff, and programming—that are found in either a typical governmental bureaucracy or a correctional facility will be in a community corrections agency. The primary difference between doing these jobs in community corrections versus in a prison or jail is the setting. The clientele is largely the same, the legal mandates and the restrictions are very similar, and the nature of the work and the work environment are largely the same.

There are a multitude of career options available for someone interested in corrections. These opportunities include those that focus directly on interactions with offenders and those that have little or no interaction with offenders. Many "regular" types of jobs are also involved in corrections. This is a growing industry offering many challenging opportunities.

RICHARD TEWKSBURY

References and Further Reading

American Correctional Association. 2004. *Careers in Criminal Justice*. Lanham, MD: American Correctional Association.

Justice Research Association. 2000. *Your Criminal Justice Career: A Guidebook*. Upper Saddle River, NJ: Prentice-Hall.

Wadsworth Publishing. 2003. *Wadsworth's Guide to Careers in Criminal Justice*, 2nd ed. New York, NY: Wadsworth Publishing.

See also **Careers in Law and Legal Services; Criminology and Criminal Justice Careers; Probation and Parole: Careers**

Counsel, The Right to

In the U.S. the right to be represented by counsel (an attorney) is embodied in the Sixth Amendment to the Constitution, which provides that, "In all criminal prosecutions, the accused shall enjoy the right … to have the assistance of counsel for his defense." As with many aspects of criminal law in the U.S., the right to the assistance of counsel did not spring forth spontaneously from the imagination of the Framers. Instead, its basis is found in the legal tradition of England that permeates much of American criminal law.

The Right to Counsel in Historical Perspective

Prior to the late 17th century, there was only a limited use of counsel to argue occasional points of law. Use of counsel in these instances was more a function of assisting the court, rather than any concern for the defendant. Counsel was also available in misdemeanor cases, but not for felonies or treason (Heller, 1951). According to Langbein (1994), the belief was that the court served as counsel for the defendant. The right to assistance of counsel was not formally recognized until 1695. The passage of the Treason Act of 1695 allowed for assistance of counsel in cases of treason or misdemeanors. The Act resulted from a perceived need for a balance against the consistent use of prosecutors in treason trials, and a questioning of the impartiality of the court (Langbein, 1994). Once this door was opened, the use of counsel began to expand to ordinary felons, starting in the 1730s (Langbein, 1994). Still, it was not until 1836 that Parliament officially granted a full right to the assistance of counsel in all felonies.

English law, not surprisingly, followed the colonists to the New World. However, as Francis Heller (1951) notes in his 1951 history of the Sixth Amendment, it was not a wholesale transfer. The colonists were not above making a few adjustments. By the early 1700s, prosecution in the colonies had become the purview of public prosecutors—full time government officials whose presence increased the imbalance between the states and the uncounseled defendant. By the time of the Constitutional Convention, 12 of the 13 original states had responded to this imbalance by including a right to counsel in their constitutions (Heller, 1951). Its inclusion in the Sixth Amendment to the new national constitution was almost natural. Indeed, the right to jury trial was considered the more important protection, with the right to counsel a safeguard of that right (Heller, 1951). Yet, although the right to jury trial is rarely debated today, "the right to counsel, a privilege of limited practical value for nearly 150 years, … [attained] a significance plainly not contemplated by the Framers" (Heller, 1951, 139).

Today we refer to the "right" to counsel. However, originally it was seen as a privilege more than a right. The Sixth Amendment only ensured that counsel would not be kept out of the proceedings if the defendant desired representation and could afford it. It did nothing to guarantee access to counsel if the defendant could not afford one, or could not find someone willing to take his or her case. That did not change until 1932, through the case of *Powell v. Alabama,* 287 U.S. 45 (1932). *Powell* was the first case to recognize the right to assistance of counsel as an entitlement that should be provided to the defendant. Justice Sutherland's powerful language set the foundation or basis for the right to appointed counsel that is followed in a long line of subsequent cases. As such, it bears repeating here:

> What, then, does a hearing include? Historically and in practice, in our own country at least, it has always included the right to the aid of counsel when desired and provided by the party asserting the right. The right to be heard would be, in many cases, of little avail if it did not comprehend the right to be heard by counsel. Even the intelligent and educated layman has small and sometimes no skill in the science of law. If charged with crime, he is incapable, generally, of determining for himself whether the indictment is good or bad. He is unfamiliar with the rules of evidence. Left without the aid of counsel he may be put on trial without a proper charge, and convicted upon incompetent evidence, or evidence irrelevant to the issue or otherwise inadmissible. He lacks both the skill and knowledge adequately to prepare his defense, even though he had a perfect one. He requires the guiding hand of counsel at every step in the proceedings against him. Without it, though he is not guilty, he faces the danger of conviction because he does not know how to establish his innocence. If that be true of men of intelligence, how much more true is it of the ignorant and illiterate, or those of feeble intellect. If in any case, civil or criminal, a state or federal court were arbitrarily to refuse to hear a party by counsel, employed by and appearing for him, it reasonably may not be doubted that such a refusal would be a denial of a hearing, and, therefore, of due process in the constitutional sense.

For all its powerful language, *Powell* had an important limitation. It dealt only with capital cases. There was still no right to appointed counsel for other felonies—many of which involved harsh prison sentences. In addition, *Powell* was based on the due process clause of the Fifth Amendment, rather than on the specific guarantee of counsel granted in the Sixth Amendment. Six years later the U.S. Supreme Court expanded the *Powell* reasoning to justify a Sixth Amendment right to appointed counsel in all *federal* felony cases where the government sought to deprive a defendant of life or liberty. In writing the opinion for *Johnson v. Zerbst*, Justice Black noted that:

> The Sixth Amendment stands as a constant admonition that if the constitutional safeguards it provides be lost, justice will not "still be done." It embodies a realistic recognition of the obvious truth that the average defendant does not have the professional legal skill to protect himself when brought before a tribunal with power to take his life or liberty, wherein the prosecution is presented by experienced and learned counsel (*Johnson v. Zerbst*, 304 U.S. (1938)).

It was not until the famous case of *Gideon v. Wainright*, 372 U.S. 335 (1963), dramatized in the movie *Gideon's Trumpe*, that the right to have appointed counsel was extended to state felony prosecutions. The right was later expanded to misdemeanor charges that involved incarceration in *Argersinger v. Hamlin*, 407 U.S. 25 (1972).

The Sixth Amendment Right to Counsel

The historical foundations of the right to counsel still left open a number of questions that have been addressed by case law over the years. When does the right attach? What is a criminal prosecution? How is indigence defined for purposes of appointing counsel? Does the right guarantee effective counsel?

In addressing the first question, the Court for a number of years followed what has been termed the "critical-stage analysis." This analysis asked whether the confrontation between the defendant and the prosecuting authority at a particular stage created a chance of substantial prejudice against the defendant, and whether counsel could help avoid that prejudice. Following this analysis, the Court held that the right to counsel applied to postindictment line-ups (*United States v. Wade*, 388 U.S. 218 (1967)), sentencing hearings (*Memph v. Rhay*), and preliminary hearings on the merits of the case (*Coleman v. Alabama*, 399 U.S. 1 (1970)).

Concerned that the critical-stage analysis was too broad, the Burger Court sought to narrow the definition of "criminal proceeding" and limit the point at which the Sixth Amendment right attached. The Court in 1973 set forth the "trial-like confrontation" test that holds that "counsel is … to be provided to prevent the defendant himself from falling into traps devised by a lawyer on the other side and to see to it that all available defenses are proffered" (*United States v. Ash*, 413 U.S. 300, 317 (1973)). Under this test, the right to counsel does *not* attach to such things as photo identifications (*United States v. Ash*), probable-cause hearings (*Gerstein v. Pugh*), and court-ordered psychiatric evaluations (*Estelle v. Smith*, 451 U.S. 454 (1981)).

Although defendants now have a firm and established right to assistance of counsel, they also have a right to represent themselves if they wish. The Sixth Amendment's right to counsel can be waived. The waiver must be knowing, intelligent, and voluntary—it cannot be assumed. As Justice Black wrote in *Johnson*:

> This protecting duty imposes the serious and weighty responsibility upon the trial judge of determining whether there is an intelligent and competent waiver by the accused. Although an accused may waive the right to counsel, whether there is a proper waiver should be clearly determined by the

> trial court, and it would be fitting and appropriate for that determination to appear upon the record.

The Fifth Amendment Right to Counsel

The holdings in such cases as *Johnson* and *Gideon* dealt with the Sixth Amendment's right to assistance of counsel in criminal proceedings. What happens in situations prior to the initiation of criminal proceedings? The Fifth Amendment has been held to provide a right to counsel during custodial interrogations.

This right was made clear in the famous case of *Miranda v. Arizona*, which required certain warnings be given to suspects in custody before they can be questioned. Under *Miranda*, the Court held that:

> without proper safeguards the process of in-custody interrogation of persons suspected or accused of crime contains inherently compelling pressures which work to undermine the individual's will to resist and to compel him to speak where he would not otherwise do so freely. In order to combat these pressures and to permit a full opportunity to exercise the privilege against self-incrimination, the accused must be adequately and effectively apprised of his rights and the exercise of those rights must be fully honored.

These warnings included the right to have an attorney present when being questioned, and to have an attorney provided if the suspect could not afford one.

In point of fact, *Miranda* was not the first case to apply the right to counsel to interrogation proceedings. In *Massiah v. United States*, 377 U.S. 201 (1964) the Court applied a Sixth Amendment right to counsel to an interrogation *after* the defendant had been formally indicted. In *Escobedo v. Illinois*, 378 U.S. 478 (1964), the Court dealt with an unindicted defendant and excluded his confession when his requests for counsel had been denied and his attorney had been turned away by the police. Unlike *Miranda*, however, the Court in insisting on the right to counsel at that stage argued, under the Sixth Amendment "critical-stage" test, that once the police have focused on an individual as a suspect, such a stage had been reached, prosecution has begun, and the right attaches.

The key difference in the *Miranda* approach was to create what is now often referred to as a Fifth Amendment right to counsel. In this sense, the right to counsel is part and parcel of needed precautions to ensure that the defendant is not coerced into confessing—thus violating the privilege against self-incrimination. Indeed, the *Miranda* opinion often refers to the circumstances in *Escobedo* as implicating that privilege.

The denial of the defendant's [Escobedo's] request for his attorney thus undermined his ability to exercise the privilege—to remain silent if he chose or to speak without any intimidation, blatant or subtle. The presence of counsel, in all the cases before us today, would be the adequate protective device necessary to make the process of police interrogation conform to the dictates of the privilege. His presence would ensure that statements made in the government-established atmosphere are not the product of compulsion.

The presence of an attorney, and the warnings delivered to the individual, enable the defendant under otherwise compelling circumstances to tell his story without fear, effectively, and in a way that eliminates the evils in the interrogation process. Without the protections flowing from adequate warnings and the rights of counsel, all the careful safeguards erected around the giving of testimony, whether by an accused or any other witness, would become empty formalities in a procedure where the most compelling possible evidence of guilt, a confession, would have already been obtained at the unsupervised pleasure of the police.

Today, the Sixth Amendment right to counsel is applied to numerous circumstances encountered *after* the government has initiated formal proceedings of some type. The Fifth Amendment version, by contrast, applies to situations arising *prior* to formal proceedings, such as police interrogations after arrest but before charging.

In enforcing the Fifth Amendment right, the Court has held that once a suspect in custody requests an attorney, all questioning must cease unless reinitiated by the defendant or his attorney (*Edwards v. Arizona,* 451 U.S. 477 (1981)). This does not, however, apply to questioning about a different crime from the one for which an attorney was requested (*Maine v. Moulton,* 474 U.S. 459 (1985)).

Assessing the Right to Counsel via Miranda

Because police questioning takes place behind closed doors, it has been extremely difficult to judge empirically the effect of the right to counsel during police interrogations—particularly with regard to the need for and role of confessions. Much of the literature in this area has been written from the perspective of the privilege against self-incrimination. However, as discussed above, the right to counsel and the privilege against self-incrimination under *Miranda* are intertwined; indeed, the right to counsel was promoted under *Miranda* as a safeguard ensuring the privilege against self-incrimination. For that reason—and because there has been much debate on whether the presence of counsel at interrogations has encouraged or discouraged statements—the empirical literature assessing the effect of *Miranda* is worth reviewing.

Normative research on *Miranda* asks whether we as a society want to insist on a right to silence and if so, what costs are we willing to accept. Empirical debates focus on trying to establish the actual costs and benefits of *Miranda*; how many confessions or convictions have we lost since the advent of the *Miranda* requirements (*see* Leo and Thomas, 1998).

With regard to the normative debate about *Miranda*, a number of questions have been raised, including whether the rights overprotect suspects who should be encouraged to tell the truth, whether the coercive nature of interrogation causes even innocent people to incriminate themselves, what the constitutional relationship is between the *Miranda* requirements and the Fifth and Sixth Amendments, and issues regarding the actual origins and intent of the right to silence. For example, in 1986 a Department of Justice Report argued that *Miranda* should be viewed as a prophylactic rule of procedure, rather than a constitutional requirement (Justice, 1996, 1997). On the other hand, Schulhofer (1987) defends *Miranda* based on constitutional doctrine and policy, whereas Caplan (1985) attacks *Miranda* on those same policy grounds. Taking a different perspective, Herman (1987) is one of many authors who have supported *Miranda* on practical grounds, arguing that the rules provide better control of police and prosecutors and is easier for courts to apply than the old voluntariness doctrine (Herman, 1987).

A number of scholars feel that only through empirical assessments of the costs and benefits of the *Miranda* rules can we decide what we are willing to accept and what we are willing to give up with regard to the rights of criminal suspects. Studies done in the mid-1960s (just after *Miranda*) attempted to study its use and effect and compare it with pre-Miranda results. These studies are widely acknowledged to have numerous methodological problems (Leo and Thomas, 1998, 171). Nonetheless, despite these problems, Paul Cassell—an ardent critic of the *Miranda* decision—sought to conduct an empirical study of the costs of *Miranda* by looking at the early *Miranda* studies. Cassell, in his analysis of the studies, attempted to assess the costs of *Miranda* by considering the number of confessions lost because of the warnings, and the number of those lost confessions that were required for conviction. Averaging together the assessments of the "more reliable" *before and after* studies, Cassell came up with a "tentative estimate that *Miranda* has led to lost cases against almost 4 percent of all criminal suspects in this country who are questioned" (Cassell, 1996, 438). Multiplying this by numbers drawn from the 1994 Uniform Crime Reports, Cassell translates this to 28, 000 suspects lost in violent crimes and 79,000 for property crimes per year. Later, Cassell conducted his own study with Bret S. Hayman (Cassell and Hayman, 1996). They gathered their data by attending all of the screening sessions at the Salt Lake City District Attorney's office for a 6-week period (Cassell and Hayman, 1996). They found that only 33.3% of interrogations were successful, and argued that "our 33.3 percent overall success rate … is well below the 55–60 percent estimated pre-Miranda rate and, therefore, is consistent with the hypothesis that Miranda has harmed the confession rate" (Cassell and Hayman, 1996, 228).

Not surprisingly, Cassell's claims caused a stir and numerous responses. Leo and Thomas sum up these responses by noting that:

> [T]here has been a great deal of criticism and debate among many of the authors of this section: Paul Cassell has critiqued the earlier impact studies and readjusted estimates of Miranda's effect upward; Stephen Sculhofer has critiqued Paul Cassell's work and readjusted his estimates downward; Cassell and Hayman have readjusted Richard Leo's estimates upward; and George Thomas has readjusted Cassell and Hayman's estimates downward. Despite these disagreements, the empirical study of law in action is once again informing the larger debate about Miranda's ongoing legitimacy and vitality (Leo and Thomas, 1998, 171).

The vitality and legitimacy of the *Miranda* decision was affirmed in the Court's 1999–2000 term, when they put to rest any question of whether *Miranda* was a constitutional requirement. In *United States v. Dickerson*, 530 U.S. 428, 120 S. Ct. 2326 (2000), the Court held that:

> *Miranda*, being a constitutional decision of this Court, may not be in effect overruled by an Act of Congress, and we decline to overrule *Miranda* ourselves. We therefore hold that *Miranda* and its progeny in this Court govern the admissibility of statements made during custodial interrogation in both state and federal courts.

Given this reaffirmation, it is unlikely that—despite the numerous debates—the *Miranda* requirements will cease to be an integral part of the rights accorded to defendants, including the right to assistance of counsel.

Due Process Right to Counsel

In areas not covered by either the Sixth Amendment's "criminal proceedings" or the Fifth Amendment's privilege against self-incrimination, the due process clause of the Fifth and (by incorporation) Fourteenth Amendments has been used to provide a right to counsel. The question centers on whether fundamental fairness requires the assistance of counsel in a particular proceeding. Thus, a right has been found for a first appeal as of right (*Evitts v. Lucey*, 469 U.S. (1985)) and some parole and probation violation hearings (*Gagnon v. Scarpelli*, 411 U.S. 778 (1973)), but not on discretionary appeals (*Ross v. Moffitt*, 417 U.S. 600 (1974)), or for collateral attacks (*Pennsylvania v. Finley* 481 U.S. 551 (1987)).

The Right to Counsel in Comparative Perspective

To the extent that a right to the assistance of counsel is granted during police interrogations, it is a much more limited right in Europe and, to some extent, even in England (Van Kessel, 1998). In France, for example, the right attaches only 20–36 hours after initial questioning. In the U.K., the right to counsel during interrogations dates back only to the Police and Criminal Evidence Act of 1984. Even when it is offered, the presence of counsel may not discourage incriminating statements, as is the case in the U.S. Van Kessel (1998) poses two reasons for this. First, on both the Continent and in the U.K., the role of the attorney is not as adversarial as in the U.S. The role of the defense attorney is merely to make sure that the defendant is treated properly, not to obstruct the system's search for the truth. Second, there is a perception that it is the duty of all citizens to cooperate in the search for the truth, and that there are considerable benefits to those who cooperate early. In comparison, the role of the defense attorney in the U.S. is more adversarial, challenging, and serves as a protective barrier between the defendant and the state.

The evolution from a privilege to a right to counsel, coupled with the expansion of other defendants' rights, has also had profound effects on the structure and organizational culture of the American legal system. Hermann et al. (1977) point out that more attorneys were required for more defendants, and required earlier in the process. This has led to the development and prevalence of institutions such as public defender offices, and local defense bar available for court appointment. In addition, Feeley argues that the rise of the use of defense counsel is a key factor in the rise of plea bargaining. In the heyday of the adversarial system, trials were perfunctory affairs where a defendant was rarely represented, was unable to challenge the evidence in any meaningful way, and where prosecutors (often police officers) rarely talked to witnesses beforehand. Today, we have dedicated criminal justice professionals making full use of pretrial activities and case reviews—resulting in sufficient information for both sides to come to an agreement about the strengths or weaknesses of a case long before trial.

For these reasons, short of a massive change in the legal culture of the U.S., the right to counsel—like the privilege against self-incrimination—is likely to remain a fundamental aspect of the criminal justice system in the U.S.

STEPHANIE MIZRAHI

References and Further Reading

Boyce, R.N. and Perkins, R.M. *Criminal Law and Procedure*, 8th ed., New York, NY: Foundation Press, 1999.

Caplan, G.M. Questioning Miranda, in *The Miranda Debate: Law, Justice, and Policing*, Leo, R.A. and Thomas, G.C. (Eds.), Boston, MA: Northeastern University Press, 1998.

Cassell, P.G. Miranda's social costs: An empirical reassessment, *Northwestern Law Review* 90 (1996).

Cassell, P.G and Hayman, B.S. 1996, Police interrogation in the 1990's: An empirical study of the effects of Miranda, in *The Miranda Debate: Law, Justice and Policing*, Leo, R.A. and Thomas, G.C. (Eds.), Boston, MA: Northeastern University Press, 1998.

Feeley, M.M. 1982, Plea bargaining and the structure of the criminal process, in *The Criminal Justice System: Politics and Policies*, 5th ed., Cole, G.F. (Ed.), Pacific Grove, CA: Brooks/Cole.

Heller, F.H. 1951, The Sixth Amendment to the Constitution of the United States: A Study in Constitutional Development, Lawrence, Kansas: University of Kansas Press.

Herman, L. 1987, The supreme court, the attorney general, and the good old days of police interrogation, in *The Miranda Debate: Law, Justice, and Policing*, Leo, R.A. and Thomas, G.C. (Eds.), Boston, MA: Northeastern University Press, 1998.

Langbein, J.H. 1994, The historical origins of the privilege against self-incrimination at common law, 92 *Michigan Law Review* 1047 (1994).

Leo, R.A. and Thomas, G.C. (Eds.), *The Miranda Debate: Law, Justice, and Policing*, Boston, MA: Northeastern University Press, 1998.

Samaha, J., *Criminal Procedure*, 4th ed., Belmont, CA: West/Wadsworth, 1999.

Schulhofer, S.J. 1987, Reconsidering Miranda, in *The Miranda Debate: Law, Justice, and Policing*, Leo, R.A. and Thomas, G.C. (Eds.), Boston, MA: Northeastern University Press, 1998.

United States Department of Justice, Office of Legal Policy (1996, 1997). Report to the attorney general on the law of pretrial interrogation, in *The Miranda Debate: Law, Justice, and Policing*, Leo, R.A. and Thomas, G.C. (Eds.), Boston, MA: Northeastern University Press, 1998.

Van Kessel, G., European perspectives on the accused as a source of testimonial evidence, *West Virginia Law Review* 100 (1998).

Whitebread, C.H. and Slobogin, C. 2000, *Criminal Procedure: An Analysis of Cases and Concepts*, 4th ed., New York, NY: Foundation Press, 2000.

See also **Courts in the U.S.: Structure and Functions; Criminal Courts: Personnel; Trials, Criminal**

Counterfeiting

Counterfeiting is the intentional process of falsifying a document or other item with the intentions of deceiving. The counterfeiting of a national currency, obviously, is one of the most important and, for government, worrisome forms of document falsification. In order to carry out everyday business transactions, it is essential for people to trust and have faith in their national currency. Thus, great efforts are placed on bolstering anticounterfeiting enforcement mechanisms in the U.S. and elsewhere.

Although an exact figure for the amount of counterfeit dollars or "funny-money" cannot be given, it is estimated that each year nearly one-half billion counterfeit U.S. dollars circulate in this country and abroad. Counterfeiting, to be sure, is not a new phenomenon. In this country, as early as the American Revolution, the British were such prodigious counterfeiters that the people lost faith in most money, prompting the saying "not worth a Continental." Counterfeiters during the Civil War were so successful that nearly one-half of all bank notes in the U.S. were fake.

During the late 18th through the mid-19th centuries, the U.S. was not alone in combating such ubiquitous currency counterfeiting. The French and English, to name the most well-known, were constantly searching for ways to limit the harmful effects of counterfeiting and end the widespread problem of circulating fake money. The French and English used the death penalty to deter counterfeiters. In England, between 1797 and 1817, more than 300 people were executed and many more exiled to Australia for counterfeiting; the French, during this period, guillotined nearly 1300 people for passing forged notes. Differing from contemporary counterfeiters, the early French and English culprits were often unwitting, often illiterate, poor women unable to tell the difference between real and fake bills.

One contributing factor to such large-scale counterfeiting was the lack of a standardized money production system. In the U.S., local areas were responsible for manufacturing their own money, with approximately 1600 state banks designing and printing their own bills, making it virtually impossible for the public or government agencies to detect counterfeits among the 7000 varieties of authentic notes. This currency diversity was changed by the adoption of a homogeneous national currency in 1863. Counterfeiting, however, was not the sole reason for adopting a single currency. Rather, it was extremely difficult for interstate commerce to function without a national currency; exchange rates between states were often more costly to merchants than international exchange rates.

Regardless of all the motives for adopting a uniform national bank note, creative individuals possessing the necessary technology quickly became adept at falsifying the new bills. Counterfeiting, therefore, was still a major problem plaguing the American law enforcement community. The Treasury Department, facing this challenge, on July 5, 1865, created the U.S. Secret Service agency with the sole responsibility of fighting counterfeiting. It is no doubt that the Secret Service was, relatively speaking, successful at combating counterfeiting. The U.S. government, following the French and English, nonetheless persistently sought alternative technological measures to reduce the circulating of fake bills.

It was reasoned that with increased technological savvy, nations could mass produce a standardized currency that was difficult to counterfeit. A Philadelphia inventor named Jacob Perkins, making use of a steam-powered engine and steel instead of copper plates, created a technique known as siderography, ensuring that all paper notes were identical. The U.S. Bureau of Printing and Engraving made use of Perkins' technique, and, in 1877, with a meager six-person crew became responsible for printing all U.S. currency.

At the close of the 19th century, the combined effect of standardization, industrial equipment, and increased law enforcement vigilance spurred a decrease in counterfeiting. This only lasted for a short time before law enforcement agencies detected another area of counterfeiting needing attention. It was during the 1920s that international or cross-border counterfeiting became a national and international problem. As international trade gained prominence, the need to establish a stable, trusted currency became a central concern for the League of Nations. In 1923, therefore, the international police organization Interpol was created to monitor counterfeiting and other international crimes. Then, in 1929, the League required all members yet to possess one to create a law enforcement arm focused on combating national and international counterfeiting, with Interpol serving as the international anticounterfeiting office.

From the first quarter of the 20th century until the present, Interpol has fought international counterfeiting. Interpol was responsible for apprehending nearly

114,000 offenders for counterfeiting U.S. currency in 2001 alone. Actually, it was the pervasiveness of international counterfeiting, most notably the superbill, a high-quality 100 dollar bill that circulated throughout much of the 1990s, that brought about currency design changes in 1996. The superbill is believed to have been the work of counterfeiters in Syria and Iran and used to purchase arms on the global black market.

This major style change—the first of its kind since 1928—was a consequence of the infiltration of the superbill and an 800% increase in home counterfeiting between 1996 and 1998, thanks, in large part, to the increased quality of ink jet copiers and printers. Once again, diffuse technological improvements and technical know-how spurred an upsurge in counterfeiting, requiring government officials to invent new anti-counterfeiting measures. The design changes in the mid-1990s included a security thread imbedded in the paper fibers and a watermark that becomes visible when held under ultraviolet light.

Anyone caught possessing, manufacturing, or altering U.S. currency larger than a 5-cent piece is subject to federal prosecution. This prosecution can result in between a $2000 and $15,000 fine and 5–15 years in prison. Counterfeiting, with its potential to destabilize national currency and provide unscrupulous nations fake money to purchase weapons, is a major national security issue for the U.S. and other nations. It is essential to maintaining trust in a unified currency to minimize counterfeiting; in order to do this, law enforcement agencies must stay abreast of technological movements easing the counterfeiting process.

RICHARD TEWKSBURY AND MATTHEW DEMICHELE

References and Further Reading

Glaser, L. *Counterfeiting in America: The History of an American Way to Wealth.* New York, NY: Crown Publishers, 1967.

Kenneth, S. *Counterfeiting in Colonial America.* New York, NY: Oxford University Press, 1957.

United States Secret Service: *Secret Service History Timeline.* Available at http://www.secretservice.gov/history.shtml

United States Secret Service: *Interim Strategic Plan,* FY 2003-FY 2008. Available at http://www.secretservice.gov/sp_index.shtml.

United States Secret Service: *Know Your Money.* Available at http://www.secretservice.gov/know_your_money.shtml.

United States Treasury Department. 2000. *The Use and Counterfeiting of United States Currency Abroad [Electronic Resource]: A Report to the Congress.* Washington, DC. Available at http://purl.access.gpo.gov/GPO/LPS20133.

Counterterrorism

See **Terrorism; Terrorism: The Law**

Courts in the U.S.: Structure and Functions

Trying to describe the structure of all court systems in the U.S. is a daunting task. The nation has one of the most intricate and complex court structures of any country in the world, and this structure is a clear reflection of its culture and historical development. The judicial branch of government in the U.S. is decentralized and fragmented. Elements can be found at all three levels of government. In fact, there is not a single court structure, but really 52 different sets of courts: one for the federal government (including courts for U.S. territories and possessions), one for the District of Columbia, and 50 distinctive state court systems. There are courts entirely of a local nature as well. Most of the court systems in the U.S. trace their character back to the English legal heritage, but courts have developed at different times (for example, as different states entered the Union), and they have evolved in response to changing legal and social pressures. In order to understand the complexity of structures and functions among courts, it is necessary to examine the constitutional and statutory bases for the creation of courts; the notions of federalism, comity, and judicial review; the similarities and differences between federal and state courts; the hierarchical structure of these courts; and the concept of unified versus nonunified courts. As each level of courts is described, a general discussion will be included of the attorneys and judges who serve in those courts.

Bases for the Creation of Courts

In most states, the provision for the creation of courts exists in the state constitution. Occasionally, states also will have statutory provisions dealing with the creation, elimination, or jurisdictional definition of courts. State courts are responsible for applying and interpreting state laws, but state judges also are obligated to adhere to the Constitution and statutes of the U.S.

In the federal system the fundamental basis for court structure is Article III of the U.S. Constitution, which provides, in part, that "The judicial Power of the United States, shall be vested in one supreme Court, and in such inferior Courts as the Congress may from time to time ordain and establish." Thus, the Constitution provides only the broadest parameters for the federal court system and leaves to Congress the authority to establish the number, types, and jurisdictions of federal courts, as well as the number of federal judges and their qualifications. With the Judiciary Act of 1794, the First Congress provided the structure for the federal judicial system that still exists today. This legislation set the number of Supreme Court justices for the Court's first term and established the nature of the federal trial and appellate courts. In the two centuries since this legislation was passed, Congress has from time to time expanded the federal court system by adding judges, courts, and jurisdictional authority over additional types of cases. Seldom have members of Congress restricted the powers of the courts, although they have the authority to do so. What the Congress cannot do is remove a federal court judge from the bench, short of impeachment, or reduce the salaries of federal judges while they are serving in office.

In addition to the so-called Article III or constitutional courts, Congress also has power under Article I (the legislative article) "To constitute Tribunals inferior to the supreme Court." From time to time Congress has established so-called legislative courts. Legislative courts differ from Article III (constitutional) courts in that they exercise administrative responsibilities. These courts also exist to help administer certain pieces of legislation. Examples of legislative courts include the U.S. Tax Court and the Court of Veterans Appeals. The judges serving in these courts are appointed for specific terms and do not enjoy the life tenure provided for Article III court judges.

Federalism, Comity, and Judicial Review

It is impossible to understand the way courts are organized and operate in the U.S. without understanding the legal and political concepts of federalism and comity. When the U.S. became a nation, the states already had court systems in place. The framers of the Constitution debated at length whether state courts routinely should handle cases of first instance, leaving appeals of a more significant nature to the national courts. In the end a compromise was struck. There would be state courts and federal courts, each with unique, but interrelated, responsibilities. The notion of federalism expressed the idea that both the state and federal levels of government—in this case the judicial branch—have responsibilities that each of them must discharge. Thus, we have court systems for each of the states, and these courts primarily are concerned with application and interpretation of state laws and constitutions. We also have a single court system for the national government, and although the federal courts primarily deal with interpreting the U.S. Constitution and the statutes enacted by the U.S. Congress, at times the federal courts are called on to review state court actions or to rule on the constitutionality of state laws. Federalism, as it applies to courts in this country, is a reflection of a political compromise between the framers of the Constitution who held opposing viewpoints on what the new republic should look like. On the one hand, there was a group of the founding fathers who pressed for a strong national government (these were the so-called federalists). On the other hand, there were those who placed greater confidence in the ability of the states to govern and to protect the rights of their citizens. For this reason, the U.S. does not have a unitary national court system the way many nations around the world, particularly the countries in Europe, do.

In addition to federalism, comity also plays a significant role in federal–state court relations. The principle of federalism would assert that although state and federal courts have their own unique legal domains, in cases involving conflicts in interpretation, federal law ultimately must prevail. By contrast, the ideology of comity would acknowledge that federal courts should give deference to state courts in every situation possible. Comity assumes that federal courts would intervene in state matters or overrule state courts only in the most extreme circumstances. Thus, these two politico-legal principles often create a dynamic tension in federal–state court relations.

The concept of judicial review developed early in our nation's history, and it distinguishes the courts in the U.S. from those in other nations. The U.S. Supreme Court first asserted its right to rule an act of Congress unconstitutional in the case of *Marbury v. Madison,* 1 Cranch 137 (1803). From this basis the notion of judicial review evolved to mean that courts formally and informally have the authority to review and rule on the legality (or constitutionality) of acts of the federal and state executive and legislative branches, and even decisions of other courts. This authority can be counterbalanced by the actions of the executive and legislative branches of government in enacting new laws. Nevertheless, judicial review provides a symbolically powerful tool that often (but not always) is exercised cautiously by both state and federal courts.

Comparing Federal and State Courts

Certain features are similar when we compare federal courts with state courts. The concept of jurisdiction provides the clearest understanding of the similarities, and some of the differences. Jurisdiction, when applied to courts, means the legal authority to hear and decide cases, and it can be divided into three parts: geographic, subject matter, and hierarchy. Geography and subject matter will be treated here, and the notion of hierarchical differentiation will be examined at greater length in a following section.

Courts are limited by political geography to hearing cases that occur within certain areas. This is embodied in the legal principle of venue. That is, state legislatures and the U.S. Congress can define judicial boundaries within which cases can be heard. The normal rule of thumb is that cases will be heard where a crime was committed or where the civil breach or violation was said to have occurred. The exception, of course, is that there can be a change of venue in cases that have generated enough pretrial publicity so as to affect the potential for a fair trial. The federal courts have much greater latitude in this regard than the state courts have. For example, although federal cases typically are heard in the federal court district in which the act occurred, technically speaking a federal case can be moved to any federal district in the U.S., if there is a compelling reason to do so. An illustration of this involves the trial of Timothy McVeigh, who was charged with bombing the Murrah Federal Building in Oklahoma City, Oklahoma. As a result of the extensive pretrial publicity in that case and fear over potential juror bias, the trial was moved to the federal court in Denver, Colorado. In state proceedings, a trial might be moved from one judicial district to another within the state, but states do not have the luxury of moving a case into another state to be tried.

Subject matter jurisdiction is another area on which we can compare and contrast state and federal courts. Some courts are specialized by subject matter, and some have broadly defined jurisdictions. At the most basic level we can categorize courts as having civil jurisdiction, criminal jurisdiction, or both (as we will see in a following section, these are called unified courts). Courts that have criminal jurisdiction alone are responsible for processing violations of their jurisdictions' criminal codes. Some states—for example, New York (New York City only), Tennessee, and Texas—have courts that exclusively possess criminal case jurisdiction. Many states also have local courts (that may not be part of the state court apparatus), and some of these courts exercise criminal jurisdiction over specific local infractions such as traffic violations.

Beyond the simple civil–criminal distinction, the specialized subject matter jurisdiction courts found in a number of states include probate courts (handling wills and inheritances, as well as mental health and related cases; in Maryland these are known as orphan's courts; in New York State they are surrogate's courts), juvenile courts (some states have separate juvenile courts statewide, and some have separate juvenile courts in selected counties), tax courts (to hear a variety of tax-related issues), police courts, water courts (found mostly in western states where water rights are critical), family courts, municipal courts (limited to violations of city ordinances), justice of the peace courts, mayor's courts (in Louisiana and Ohio; similar courts are known as alderman's courts in Delaware), courts of claims, worker's compensation courts, and environmental court (in Vermont). Three states—Arkansas, Mississippi, and Tennessee—have specialized civil courts known as chancery courts. Chancery courts are a holdover from the English legal tradition, and they exercise what is known as equity jurisdiction. Equity issues arise when the statutory law may not offer adequate remedies or when applying the law strictly would cause an injustice. All other states have merged equity and law in the jurisdictions of their courts.

Unlike the 35 states that have at least some courts of specialized subject matter jurisdiction, the federal courts handle both civil and criminal cases, and they have merged law and equity jurisdiction. Several states have adopted this model, and the notion of unified courts will be addressed in a later section.

Hierarchical Structure

Federal and state courts are organized around hierarchical jurisdictions as well as around subject matter jurisdiction. However, it is important to emphasize that federal courts and state courts exist side by side, not one set of courts above the other. The various court systems differ in the number of levels or tiers they contain. For example, the federal court system is composed of three tiers. State courts vary from the simplest (South Dakota) with two tiers, to the most complex (New York and Texas are prime examples) with four tiers. Each type of court system has a hierarchical structure to it. The most basic hierarchical distinction is between trial courts (also called courts of first instance, or courts of original jurisdiction) and appellate courts. These can be subdivided further into trial courts of limited or inferior jurisdiction and those of general trial jurisdiction. Appellate courts can be classified as intermediate appellate courts and courts of last resort. Each of these levels will be considered in terms of where they exist and the distinctive functions they perform.

There are a variety of courts of limited or inferior jurisdiction in the U.S. Most of these courts operate at the local level, and they are known by such names as municipal courts, justice (or justice of the peace) courts, police courts, mayor's or alderman's courts, and magistrate's courts. Some of these courts hear only misdemeanor criminal cases such as traffic offenses and violations of local ordinances. Typically, a conviction in one of these courts can result in a fine or local jail time up to 1 year (although sentences above 6 months are unusual). In some states, courts of limited jurisdiction also may be responsible for limited civil jurisdiction, and they become, by design or by default, the small claims courts. There is no court of limited jurisdiction in the federal system. The U.S. magistrate judges, who issue warrants, conduct bond hearings, and handle minor civil and criminal offenses, actually operate under the umbrella of the district court judges.

Several features characterize the operation of limited jurisdiction courts in the U.S. First, many of these tribunals are courts of nonrecord. In simplest terms this means that as a routine matter these courts do not produce transcripts of proceedings. The parties to a case may privately hire a court reporter to produce a transcript, but in most instances there will not be a court reporter present for hearings and trials. Therefore, if a case is appealed it will go to a court of general trial jurisdiction on the basis of a trial *de novo*, or an entirely new trial. Second, many of the cases are minor enough that attorneys may not be present for either side. For example, in small claims cases and in many traffic offenses, the attorneys' fees may be greater than the possible award or fine. Therefore, it makes little sense to hire an attorney for most of these cases. If no jail time is possible—and this is the situation in many traffic cases—the court is not obligated to appoint an attorney for a defendant who cannot afford one. In serious misdemeanor cases where incarceration up to 1 year could result, the court will appoint attorneys for indigents. Third, many of these courts are characterized by the speed and informality with which they process cases. Observers are sometimes astounded at the number of cases these courts can dispose of in a given session, and a substantial number of the cases result in guilty pleas. The consequence of this is that limited jurisdiction courts are accused of dispensing "rough justice" or "assembly line justice." It has been said of some of these courts that defendants (particularly in traffic cases) can either plead guilty or be found guilty. Fourth, in some localities limited jurisdiction courts have provisions only for bench trials. That is, they do not conduct jury trials. Occasionally these courts may conduct six-person jury trials for certain types of cases. Fifth, as a reflection of our nation's judicial history, harking back to the presidency of Andrew Jackson, limited jurisdiction courts may not require judges to be licensed attorneys. In fact, in some states there is no educational requirement (beyond the general education that may be required for all office-holders) for judges in these courts. A few of these judges are appointed, but most are elected in either partisan or nonpartisan elections. Finally, the limited jurisdiction courts often lack the dignity and decorum present in most general jurisdiction trial courts. The limited jurisdiction courts may meet in police stations or be held in government buildings other than the county courthouse. Large numbers of litigants or defendants come and go at a rapid pace, and the general atmosphere does not resemble the television or movie image of what a trial looks like.

Unlike the courts of limited jurisdiction, the general trial courts are courts of record. In the federal system the general trial courts are known as the district courts. States may have from one to four federal court districts, but by legal custom no district crosses a state line. State courts of general trial jurisdiction are known by a variety of names including superior courts, district courts, county courts, and circuit courts.

The general jurisdiction courts keep transcripts of all proceedings, and these transcripts form the basis for appeals. Virtually every case appearing in general trial jurisdiction courts will have attorneys representing the parties on both sides. Formality and procedural regularity will characterize the general trial courts. The notions of substantive and procedural due process—although not mentioned specifically—will be very much a part of case processing. Perhaps as many as 80–90% of the cases processed by general trial jurisdiction courts will result in guilty pleas—with or without an explicit plea bargain. However, these courts do have the capacity to conduct jury trials, and these trials typically embody the image that most people associate with courts in the U.S.

Criminal cases in state general jurisdiction courts are presented by a prosecuting attorney. State and local prosecutors may be known as district attorneys (the most common designation), state's attorneys, commonwealth attorneys, or county attorneys. The vast majority of these officials are elected in partisan elections within a given jurisdiction, and they typically serve 4-year terms. Local prosecutors' offices normally employ a number of assistant prosecutors who handle the day-to-day responsibilities of grand jury presentations, arraignments, pretrial hearings, and trials. Prosecutors often use their very visible positions to seek other state or local political offices, and many assistant prosecutors find the district attorney's office a good place to gain experience after graduating from law school. In the federal district courts criminal cases are presented by the U.S. Attorneys. There are 94 U.S.

Attorneys, one for each of the federal court districts, and these individuals are nominated by the president and confirmed by the U.S. Senate. U.S. Attorneys serve at the pleasure of the president and under the very broad (and sometimes remote) direction of the attorney general of the U.S. When a new president is elected all U.S. attorneys submit their resignations and typically all are accepted. In the offices of the U.S. attorneys are assistant U.S. attorneys chosen by the U.S. attorney for a particular district. Some of these individuals are career prosecutors, and some serve a few years in this office to gain legal experience and visibility.

Judges in general trial courts are required by law or custom in most jurisdictions to be licensed attorneys. Several states even require that these judges have practiced law for a certain number of years before being qualified to serve as a judge. Some states appoint trial judges, but most elect them in partisan or nonpartisan elections. Increasingly, states are turning to the merit selection system (the Missouri Plan) to choose their judges. These judges may be removed from office through impeachment or through "failure to retain" votes. Judges in the federal trial courts (the district courts) all are appointed by the president of the U.S. and confirmed by the U.S. Senate. All federal judges serve life terms, during good behavior, and only may be removed from office through the process of impeachment. Finally, in contrast to the limited jurisdiction courts, the courts of general trial jurisdiction frequently are housed in courtrooms with wood-paneled walls and dark carpeting. Lawyers and litigants speak in hushed tones, and there is an atmosphere of reverence that almost resembles a house of worship.

The first-level appellate courts are known as intermediate appellate courts. Thirty-nine states have one or more intermediate appellate courts. The names may vary from state to state, but in most states they are known as the court(s) of appeals. In the federal system, the U.S. Courts of Appeals are the intermediate appellate courts. These courts sometimes are referred to by their traditional name of circuit courts, since they are organized into 11 numbered circuits (or clusters of geographically contiguous states), plus a Court of Appeals for the District of Columbia and a Court of Appeals for the Federal Circuit, both of which meet in Washington, DC. Each state is completely within the boundaries of a federal appellate circuit, and no circuit divides a state.

The intermediate appellate courts are distinguished by three features. First, they are collegial courts. This means that they decide cases in panels of judges (sometimes in small groups of three to five judges, or sometimes by all members of a court). The decisions are rendered by majority votes, and most of these courts produce written and published opinions that serve as guides to the trial courts under them. Second, relatively few cases ever are appealed and most of them that are appealed never get beyond the intermediate appellate courts. Third, the basis for an appeal must be an error of law, not an error of fact. In most instances this means that an appealable error was made by the trial judge, and the appeal is not based simply on an adverse verdict. Judges in the intermediate appellate courts may be appointed or elected in state courts. An increasing number of states are turning to merit selection systems to choose and retain these judges. In the U.S. Courts of Appeals the judges are chosen by the president and confirmed by the U.S. Senate.

The highest level appellate courts in the state and federal systems are known generically as the courts of last resort. The most common name applied to these courts is "supreme court," but that name is not used in all states. For instance, the courts of last resort in Maryland and New York are known as the Court of Appeals. Oklahoma and Texas have divided courts of last resort with the State Supreme Court hearing only civil cases and the Court of Criminal Appeals hearing criminal cases. Quite often in state courts of last resort the state attorney general will represent the state in various legal matters. When the federal government is a party to a case before the U.S. Supreme Court, the solicitor general, an official appointed by the president and who serves in the U.S. Department of Justice, represents the U.S.

Like the intermediate appellate courts, courts of last resort are collegial courts. However, unlike some intermediate appellate courts, most courts of last resort hear cases *en banc*. That is, all of the judges (or justices, as they frequently are called) sit together as a group to hear and decide cases. In virtually all instances opinions by courts of last resort are written and published to serve as precedents for lower-level courts in the court system. Obviously, the opinions of the U.S. Supreme Court get the most attention because of the small number of cases decided by that court each year, the magnitude of the issues raised in many of the cases, and the fact that in many instances these decisions apply to all federal and state courts. Again, judges and justices of the courts of last resort may be appointed, elected, or chosen by merit in the state court systems. Justices of the U.S. Supreme Court, like all federal court judges, are nominated by the president and confirmed by the U.S. Senate.

Unified versus Nonunified Courts

The general notion of unified courts already has been presented, but not in an explicit way. Three elements typically are present in a unified court system, and the federal courts provide a model for most unified state court systems. The most fundamental component of a unified court system is lack of specialized courts. Unified systems may have specialized judges—hearing juvenile, domestic relations, or probate cases, for example—but they do not have specialized courts. One of the chief aims is to eliminate courts that can hear only limited types of cases, or courts that have overlapping jurisdictions. Second, unified court systems have centralized budgeting and financing. At the state level this means that the state government assumes the responsibility for preparing (or assisting in the preparation of) the budget for the judicial branch and that funding comes from state sources rather than relying on local funding for operations. A principal assumption is that statewide financing produces a broader and more stable basis for funding the courts. This area provides something of a dynamic tension. On the one hand, the judicial branch is a coequal branch of government along with the executive and legislative branches. On the other hand, the judicial branch may be dependent on the executive branch for developing a budget and the legislative branch for funding state court operations. Third, unified courts normally have centralized administration and rule-making authority. All state courts and the federal system now have an administrative body, typically known as the Administrative Office of the Courts (AOC) or a similar title. Rule-making authority allows the court of last resort, acting through the AOC, to provide broad policy guidance to local courts and to prescribe day-to-day operational procedures as well. The clear trend in court systems in the U.S. has been toward more unified courts, with greater state financing and centralized administration.

The assumption most frequently cited in regard to court reform and especially court unification is that unified courts are more efficient. Interestingly enough, efficiency is not necessarily a concept that is associated with courts, and many of the actors working in U.S. courts fear that justice will be sacrificed to efficiency. Nevertheless, around the country there are strong movements to professionalize court administration, to make courts more open to public scrutiny (for example, through televised trials), to make them more responsive to social problems (the development of specialized drug, drunk driving, and domestic violence courts), and to remove the influences of partisan politics and money in the choice of judges. One measure of the degree to which court reforms have taken hold is the development of judicial standards or conduct commissions in most states. Beginning with California in the early 1960s, states increasingly are establishing judicial conduct commissions as mechanisms to hear complaints of misconduct against judges. These commissions allow for judicial discipline short of the cumbersome and protracted process of impeachment. They also may respond to situations that partisan elections or recall elections might not deal with adequately. A number of reform efforts are under way in both state and federal courts. The most basic conclusion that can be drawn from most of these efforts is that, fundamentally, the American public is pleased with the way courts operate but that they believe there is always room for improvement.

G. Larry Mays

References and Further Reading

Abadinsky, H., *Law and Justice*, Chicago, IL: Nelson-Hall, 1988; 4th ed., 1998.

Barnum, D.G., *The Supreme Court and American Democracy*, New York, NY: St. Martin's Press, 1993.

Carp, R.A. and Stidham, R., *Federal Courts*, Washington, DC: CQ Press, 1985; 3rd ed., 1998.

Carp, R.A. and Stidham, R., *Judicial Process in America*, Washington, DC: CQ Press, 1990; 3rd ed., 1996.

Eisenstein, J. and Jacob, H., *Felony Justice: An Organizational Analysis of Criminal Courts*, Boston, MA: Little, Brown, 1977.

Holten, N.G. and Lamar, L.L., *The Criminal Courts: Structures, Personnel, and Processes*, New York, NY: McGraw-Hill, 1991.

Mays, G.L. and Gregware, P.R., Ed., *Courts and Justice*, Prospect Heights, IL: Waveland Press, 1995; 2nd ed., 2000.

Neubauer, D.W., *America's Courts and the Criminal Justice System*, North Scituate, MA: Duxbury Press, 1979; 6th ed., Belmont, CA: West/Wadsworth, 1999.

Robertson, J.A., compiler, *Rough Justice: Perspectives on Lower Criminal Courts*, Boston, MA: Little, Brown, 1974.

Rottman, D.B., et al., *State Court Organization 1998*, Washington, DC: U.S. Department of Justice, Office of Justice Programs, Bureau of Justice Statistics, 2000.

Stolzenberg, L. and D'Alessio, S.J., compilers, *Criminal Courts for the 21st Century*, Upper Saddle River, NJ: Prentice Hall, 1999.

Vago, S., *Law and Society*, Upper Saddle River, NJ: Prentice Hall, 1981; 6th ed., 2000.

See also **Criminal Courts: Administration and Organization; Criminal Courts: Lower; Criminal Courts: Personnel; Grand Juries; Judges; Juries and Juror Selection; Supreme Court, U.S.**

Courts in the U.S.: Supreme Court

The U.S. government comprises three branches: the judicial, the executive, and the legislative. The U.S. Constitution defines each branch of government and gives them specific powers and duties. The scope and nature of the judicial branch, for instance, is defined in Article III of the Constitution. Article III, Section 1 specifically gives rise to the Supreme Court of the U.S. (which has also become referred to as the "Court of Last Resort" or "The High Court"). Article III, Section 1 states that "the judicial power of the United States, shall be vested in one Supreme Court, and in such inferior Courts as the Congress may from time to time ordain and establish."

Article III, Section 2 continues to define the scope and nature of the Supreme Court. The Supreme Court has jurisdiction over many types of cases, which include the following: all cases concerning the U.S. Constitution, all cases concerning laws of the U.S., treaties made with other countries, and legal controversies between states. Additionally, the Supreme Court acts as the ultimate oversight of all other state and federal judiciaries. Finally, the Chief Justice of the Supreme Court presides over impeachment trials. The Supreme Court is the pinnacle of the U.S. judiciary, and clearly has the potential to play a significant role in its legal system.

There are nine justices on the Supreme Court, one of which is given the title of Chief Justice. The current members of the court, as of January 2001, include the following in order of most recent appointment: Stephen Breyer, Ruth Bader Ginsburg, David Souter, Clarence Thomas, Anthony Kennedy, Antonin Scalia, Sandra Day O'Connor, John Paul Stevens and Chief Justice William Rehnquist. The Chief Justice is typically the justice who has been on the court the longest, is appointed by the president, and will normally write the majority decision if it concurs with his or her opinion. Finally, the decisions of the Supreme Court during any era are characteristically referred to in terms of the Chief Justice (e.g., during the 1960s, when Earl Warren was Chief Justice, the court was known as the "Warren Court").

The president nominates justices, and the Senate has the power to either confirm or deny the nomination. The U.S. Constitution does not specify particular rules or factors that may be used in either the nomination or confirmation process. Often, the president will nominate a qualified appointee who holds views that are consistent with his political party. This can create problems in the confirmation process, particularly when the political party to which the president does not belong dominates the Senate. Also, if many senators (regardless of party affiliation) have ideological disagreements with the nominee on controversial issues (e.g., in recent years abortion), confirmation may be difficult. Throughout the history of the U.S. the Senate has defeated several nominees, many because of ideological or political beliefs. In these cases, the Senate has rejected the nominee for largely political and ideological reasons as opposed to whether the nominee was qualified. The first nominee defeated for ideological reasons by the Senate was John Rutledge, who was nominated to be the Chief Justice by George Washington in 1795. Opposed to the ratification of Jay's Treaty (which was crafted to avert a commercial war with England), Rutledge was defeated by senators who favored it. In recent times, Democrats defeated Robert H. Bork, who was Ronald Reagan's nominee in 1987, largely because of his conservative political and legal leanings. In other instances, the nominee never made it before the Senate because of political pressures. For example, when former President Ronald Reagan nominated Douglas Ginsburg, the nomination was quickly withdrawn after it was discovered that Ginsburg had smoked marijuana. In other cases, however, the Senate has approved very controversial nominees, as was the case in 1937 when former Klu Klux Klan member Hugo Black was confirmed. Clearly, the successful appointment of any justice to the Supreme Court is not only a matter of qualifications and merit, but also political and ideological considerations.

Part of the reason why Supreme Court appointments are so controversial is that after being confirmed by the Senate, justices serve a lifetime appointment. As such, justices may stay on the bench for many years, as was the case with William Douglas, who served 36 years between 1939 and 1975. Unless a justice resigns, he or she cannot be removed from the bench unless they are impeached. The impeachment criteria for justices is defined by the Constitution, and is the same as it is for all federal judges and the president, who can be impeached if found guilty of: "treason, bribery, or other high crimes and misdemeanors." Only one justice has been subject to impeachment hearings. In 1805, Republicans subjected Justice Samuel Chase to the impeachment process for political reasons (namely, his public attacks on then President Jefferson). Chase was eventually acquitted. Some have argued that his impeachment trial served as an important legal landmark establishing that political differences alone are not impeachable crimes. Nevertheless, groups will occasionally call for the impeachment of a justice who does not rule in their favor on important issues, as was the case with the John Birch Society, who called for the impeachment of Chief Justice Earl Warren in the 1960s.

Since the Supreme Court's inception, its members have struggled with not only how to interpret the Constitution, but also how active they should be in influencing policy and legal matters. Historically, conservative interpretivists have argued that the role of the Supreme Court in influencing policy and law should be very limited, and that its decisions must be based upon a strict interpretation of the Constitution. Liberal noninterpretivists, on the other hand, have argued that it is necessary for the Supreme Court to articulate what the Constitution should mean given the current historical context. As such, liberal noninterpretivists have generally argued that the Supreme Court can and should take an active role by exerting its power in the legal arena. Meanwhile, conservative interpretivists have argued that the Supreme Court should severely limit its role in such matters. Like most issues, the question of Constitutional interpretation has polar extremes. Most justices fall somewhere between the extremes of the strict interpretivists on one side and the strict noninterpretivists on the other. As will become more evident later, the degree to which the members of the Supreme Court decide to exert their collective power depends largely on how its members interpret the Constitution, and whether they choose to take an active role in shaping criminal justice policy.

Each year, the Supreme Court is asked to consider thousands of cases, most of which are filed as *writs of certiorari*. *Writs of certiorari* are requests to review the proceedings of lower courts. When considering a *writ of certiorari*, the justices have complete discretion over whether they will hear the case. Rather than having every justice read each and every of the approximately 5000 cases that are filed each year, the "cert pool" decides whether to hear a case. The "cert pool" consists of eight justices. Each justice has several clerks who read through the cases that are filed. The clerks prepare memoranda for each case and then submit them to the other members of the "cert pool." If four justices agree the case has merit and should be heard by the court, the *writ of certiorari* is granted and arguments are presented to the court. In recent years, the Supreme Court has granted *certiorari* to less than 100 cases annually. When the Supreme Court decides not to hear a case, the last decision made by the lower court from which it was appealed stands.

Since the Constitution gives the Supreme Court the ultimate authority to declare state and federal laws constitutional, decisions by the Supreme Court have had significant influences on the legal system in the U.S. Importantly, it has had major influences on both the criminal justice system and the juvenile justice system. Many of these decisions came during what has been termed by several as the "due process revolution" of the 1960s under the Warren Court.

Throughout the 1960s, there was a great deal of social and political unrest in the U.S. During this period the civil rights movement gained momentum, college students protested the war in Vietnam, the women's rights movement exerted itself, and violent protests occurred in many urban areas, notably the race riots in Watts and Detroit. Against this backdrop, several cases came before the Supreme Court that concerned individual rights in the criminal justice system. These rights, also sometimes referred to as "due process rights," include the procedural safeguards afforded every citizen accused of a crime. Intended to protect citizens from the arbitrary actions of government officials, due process rights ensure that citizens are not denied their liberty without due process of law (as granted by the 14th Amendment). The Supreme Court has, under the Incorporation Doctrine, ruled that the 14th Amendment extends due process rights to every citizen of the U.S., regardless of how any particular state may choose to define them. In reference to criminal procedure, these rights are defined in the Bill of Rights in the Fourth, Fifth, Sixth, and Eighth Amendments, which respectively concern search and seizure, self-incrimination, a speedy and fair trial with counsel, and cruel and unusual punishment.

Mapp v. Ohio (367 U.S. 643, 1961) was the culmination of the Incorporation Doctrine in reference to the Fourth Amendment, and significantly shaped modern law enforcement practices with reference to search and seizure, as well as the use of illegally seized evidence. The issues at stake in *Mapp v. Ohio* were twofold. The first concerned whether state police officers had to comply with federal standards in making searches. The second issue was whether evidence seized without a proper warrant was admissible in court. Earlier, the Supreme Court had ruled in *Wolf v. Colorado* (338 U.S. 25, 1949) that state law enforcement officers could not arbitrarily search a suspect's home. However, the *Wolf* decision did not apply the exclusionary rule (i.e., that illegally seized evidence is not admissible in court) to states. Thus, the Supreme Court was asked to consider whether both federal standards applied to state law enforcement officers in *Mapp v. Ohio*. In a vote of 5-3 they ruled that both standards did apply to states. Criminal justice scholars and practitioners have debated the effect of *Mapp v. Ohio*, but the end result has been that law enforcement officers must adhere to strict standards before searching structures. Failure to do so may result in crucial evidence being ruled inadmissible in court.

A few years after *Mapp v. Ohio*, the Supreme Court was once again asked to consider the Incorporation Doctrine, this time with reference to the Sixth Amendment and the right to counsel. Earl Gideon, a resident of Florida, was charged with breaking into a pool hall. Gideon did not have the means to hire counsel and asked the Florida court to appoint one. The court refused Gideon's request, forcing him to represent himself as best he could with his limited knowledge of the law. Gideon was convicted, but later filed a *habeas corpus* petition with the Supreme Court. (A *habeas corpus* petition—questioning the lawfulness of detention—is sometimes used as a method of requesting the Supreme Court to hear a case.) In *Gideon v. Wainwright* (372 U.S. 335, 1963) the Supreme Court ruled 9-0 that all defendants accused of serious crimes must be provided counsel by the state if they cannot afford it. The implications of *Gideon v. Wainwright* on the criminal justice system were far-reaching. Currently, every state has some mechanism to provide counsel to indigent clients, the most prominent of which is the public defender system.

Three years later another important due process case came before the Supreme Court: *Miranda v. Arizona* (384 U.S. 436, 1966). Of all the due process cases of this period, *Miranda* was arguably the most widely debated and contentious. At stake in *Miranda v. Arizona* was whether criminal defendants were unknowingly forfeiting their Fifth Amendment right against self-incrimination during police interrogations. Subsequently, the court was also asked to consider whether such confessions could be used in court.

The Supreme Court ruled that once the police detain a suspect, due process rights are applicable. Therefore, suspects do not have to answer questions after being arrested unless they knowingly and willfully give up their constitutional right against self-incrimination. Additionally, *Miranda* specified four other rights that must be read to criminal defendants once they are arrested. The substance of these rights have become popularized in police television shows and movies: (1) you have the right to remain silent; (2) anything you say can and will be used against you; (3) you have the right to an attorney and to have him or her present during questioning; (4) if you cannot afford a lawyer, one will be provided to you. Collectively, these rights embody the essence of the Fifth Amendment and serve as a reminder to criminal defendants that their right against self-incrimination applies to all stages of the criminal justice system from the point of arrest forward.

Critics have charged the Warren Court with hampering the ability of law enforcement personnel to gain confessions from suspects. Some have argued that "Mirandizing" suspects allows thousands of criminals to go free each year. The conservative Rehnquist Court ruled 7-2 in *Dickerson v. United States* ((99-5525) 166F.3d 667, 2000) that the *Miranda* requirements are constitutionally protected.

In 1972 the Supreme Court handed down another controversial ruling in *Furman v. Georgia* (408 U.S.238, 1972). In the *Furman* decision the Court ruled that the application of the death penalty constituted cruel and unusual punishment because of its random application. In other words, many people who were technically eligible for the death sentence were not charged with a capital offense. At that time, there were over 600 death row defendants awaiting execution in 39 states; all were halted by the *Furman* decision. However, 4 years later the death penalty was reinstated after the Court's ruling in *Gregg v. Georgia* (428 U.S. 153, 1976). In the *Gregg* decision, the Court ruled that the death penalty did not constitute cruel and unusual punishment if mechanisms were implemented by states to ensure that aggravating and mitigating factors were weighed during sentencing.

In respect to the juvenile justice system, the Supreme Court handed down several rulings in the 1960s that would forever change the scope and nature of the juvenile courts. Since its inception, the juvenile court system had focused on rehabilitation. As such, juvenile courts did not extend due process rights to clients. Historically, due process rights were not afforded to juveniles because the juvenile courts were viewed as nonadversarial social welfare systems intended to act in the best interests of the children. In other words, the juvenile court was not viewed as punitive, coercive, or adversarial like the adult courts, and thus there was no reason to extend the rights afforded to adult criminal defendants to juveniles. In the 1960s, however, the rehabilitative ideal of the juvenile court was attacked. Progressives, who viewed the court as a coercive agent of social control, believed that juveniles should have rights if they can be denied liberties and freedoms by the court. Conservatives, on the other hand, attacked the juvenile courts for being "soft" on juvenile offenders and for emphasizing what they believed to be an ineffective and outdated ideal: rehabilitation. In a series of decisions in the 1960s the Supreme Court began to extend due process rights to juveniles.

In *Kent v. United States* (383 U.S. 541, 1966), the Supreme Court clarified the procedural safeguards extended to juveniles facing waiver to adult court. At issue in *Kent v. United States* was whether a juvenile offender could be waived to the adult court without a hearing. The Supreme Court ruled the following in *Kent*: (1) juveniles do have the right to a hearing before the juvenile court waives jurisdiction; (2) juveniles have a right to counsel during these hearings; (3) the juvenile court's social record of the juvenile must be given to counsel if it is requested; and (4) the juvenile must be given a statement of the reasons for the waiver. In addition, the Supreme Court included an appendix to *Kent* that contained seven criteria that should be considered by juvenile courts before waiving jurisdiction to the adult system.

One year later, another important juvenile case came before the Supreme Court, *In re Gault* (387 U.S. 1, 1967). Gault was a 15-year-old boy who was arrested for making lewd telephone phone calls to his neighbor. Gault was taken into custody with no effort made to notify his parents. Throughout the proceedings in the *Gault* case, no sworn testimony was made by anyone (including the woman who accused him), and no particular facts were stated. Additionally, there was no counsel present and the probation officer's report was not made available to Gault or his parents. Gault did, in fact, confess to this crime, but was never told he could remain silent. Eventually, Gault was sentenced to a state industrial school until he reached the age of 21. If Gault had been an adult, the maximum sentence he would have received would have been a small fine and 2 months in jail.

The Supreme Court overturned the *Gault* conviction, ruling that the due process clause of the Fourteenth Amendment applied to juvenile proceedings. These due process rights include the right of notice, the right against self-incrimination, the right to counsel, and the right to confront witnesses. As such, the *Gault* decision by the Supreme Court extended many due process rights to the juvenile courts.

While *In re Gault* extended due process rights to the juveniles, questions remained concerning other rights and standards applied in the adult system. For example, *In re Winship* (397 U.S. 358, 1970) concerned the question of the degree of proof needed in juvenile proceedings. The Supreme Court ruled in *Winship* that proof beyond a reasonable doubt was the standard that the juvenile courts must use to find juveniles guilty. One year later the Supreme Court was asked to determine whether juveniles had a constitutional right to a jury trial in juvenile courts. The Supreme Court ruled in *McKeiver v. Pennsylvania* (403 U.S. 528, 1971) that some due process rights, like the right to a jury trial by one's peers, were not required as part of due process. (The *McKeiver* decision gave states the option of using jury trials if they wished.) Observers of the Supreme Court have noted that the *McKeiver* decision prevented the juvenile courts from becoming completely adversarial like the adult courts.

Many have argued that throughout the 1970s and 1980s the Supreme Court became increasingly conservative, both in its composition and rulings. For example, between 1980 and 1992 former Presidents Reagan and Bush appointed a total of five justices. Current Chief Justice Rehnquist had been appointed by former President Nixon, and is also conservative. Thus, six of the current justices are at least moderately conservative. In addition, two of the Reagan or Bush appointees are widely viewed as being the most conservative on the Supreme Court: Antonin Scalia and Clarence Thomas. Conservative justices have played a significant role in deciding many important cases in recent years, and have been charged by some with eroding due process rights extended in the 1960s. For example, in *Illinois v. Wardlow* ((98-1036) 183 Ill. 2d 306, 701 N.E. 2d 484, 2000), the Supreme Court ruled that unprovoked flight in a "high crime neighborhood" constituted reasonable suspicion whereupon a police officer could legally conduct a stop and frisk. Others, however, have applauded such decisions as empowering the police to reduce crime.

Given the election of President George W. Bush in 2000, most scholars of the Supreme Court are of the opinion that it is likely that conservative justices would be appointed if additional vacancies should arise during his term. Political struggles between liberals and conservatives may make very conservative appointments difficult, particularly if the nominee has controversial beliefs about divisive issues like abortion. In the end, what is certain is that the Supreme Court will continue to play a significant role in the workings of the criminal justice system, and that the ideological beliefs of its members will likely continue to influence its decisions.

RICK A. MATTHEWS

References and Further Reading

Abraham, H., Justices, *Presidents, and Senators : A History of the U.S. Supreme Court Appointments from Washington to Clinton*, New York, NY: Rowman and Littlefield, 1999.

Feld, B., *Bad Kids: Race and the Transformation of the Juvenile Courts*, New York, NY: Oxford University Press, 1999.

Hall, K., Ely, J., Grossman, J., and Wiececk, W., Ed., *The Oxford Companion to the Supreme Court of the United States*, New York, NY: Oxford University Press, 1992.

Hall, K., Ed., *The Oxford Guide to United States Supreme Court Decisions*, New York, NY: Oxford University Press, 2001.

Irons, P., *A People's History of the Supreme Court*, New York, NY: Penguin, 2000.

Lazarus, E., *Closed Chambers: The Rise, Fall, and Future of the Modern Supreme Court*, New York, NY: Penguin, 1999.

Levy, L.W., *Origins of the Bill of Rights* (Contemporary Law Series), New Haven, CT: Yale University Press, 1999.

Levy, L.W., *Original Intent and the Framers' Constitution*, Chicago, IL: Ivan R. Dee, 2000.
Smith, C., *Critical Judicial Nominations and Political Change*, Westport, CT: Praeger, 1993.
Urofsky, M., Editor, *The Supreme Court Justices: A Biographical Dictionary*, New York, NY: Garland, 1994.
Yalof, D.A., *Pursuit of Justices: Presidential Politics and the Selection of Supreme Court Nominees*, Chicago: IL, University of Chicago Press, 1999.
Yarbrough, T.E., *The Rehnquist Court and the Constitution*, New York, NY: Oxford University Press, 2000.

See also **Courts in the U.S.: Structure and Functions**

Crack *See* **Cocaine**

Cressey, Donald R.

In a prolific career spanning nearly 40 years, Donald R. Cressey published on virtually every subarea in criminology, including theories of crime, corrections and punishment, law and justice, white collar crime, and organized crime. His wide-ranging influence continues today not only through his writings, but also through his influence on former colleagues and students. In 1950, Cressey received his Ph.D. from Indiana as Edwin Sutherland's last Ph.D. student. Following Sutherland's death, he became co-author of the highly-influential textbook, *Principles of Criminology* (Sutherland and Cressey, 1955), which went through eleven editions. The book dominated the discipline for decades because it essentially defined the field and moreover was the source of the complete statement of Sutherland's theory of differential association.

Through his work on *Principles*, and through his own research and writings, Cressey became the leading spokesperson for differential association theory. In 1960, he published "Epidemiology and Individual Conduct," which argued that differential association theory was not just an individual-level theory of criminal behavior, in which a person becomes delinquent after learning an excess of definitions favorable to crime. Rather, the theory also accounted for aggregate rates of crime with the structural and organizational concepts of normative conflict and differential social organization. According to the latter, a crime rate of a group or society is determined by the extent to which the group or society is organized in favor of crime versus against crime. Cressey also evaluated criticisms, corrected misunderstandings, and assessed empirical evidence relevant to the theory. He wrote many articles on differential association, most notably showing how the theory could explain compulsive crimes, such as kleptomania and pyromania—which at first glance appeared to be exceptions to the theory (1954), and later showing how the theory could be applied to rehabilitate criminals (1965). Here, he argued for using criminals (confederates) to present anticriminal definitions to other criminals (targets), which would help tip the ratio of criminal and anticriminal definitions for both the target *and* confederate.

Cressey's work on differential association actually began much earlier with his Ph.D. dissertation on embezzlement, which he later published as *Other People's Money* (1953). In an exemplary piece of theory construction, Cressey used the method of analytic induction—a rigorous search for negative cases in developing a generalization—to arrive at a situational explanation of embezzlement. Using interview data with imprisoned embezzlers, he concluded that trust will be criminally violated when one has an unshareable financial problem, perceives the problem can be solved secretly by violating trust, and applies verbalizations that allow one to abscond with the funds while maintaining a favorable self-image. His concept of verbalizations became the basis of Sykes and Matza's techniques of neutralization. Cressey published numerous articles on white collar crime, drawing parallels between variations in rates of restraint of trade by industry and variations in rates of delinquency by neighborhood, analyzing the causes and controls of management fraud, and critiquing the concepts of organizational and corporate crime (e.g., 1980). In the latter, he argued that the concepts of organizational crime and corporate crime are legal fictions, as organizations cannot engage in intentional behavior, and should be redefined as acts of individuals, using concepts such as managerial fraud.

Early in his career, Cressey (1960) participated in a Social Science Research Council group (including luminaries Lloyd Ohlin, Richard Cloward, Gresham Sykes, among others) to study prisons. The group popularized the study of prisons and developed a functionalist approach to the study of prisons. Beginning here, Cressey wrote a series of articles arguing that, although treatment goals in correctional systems did not effectively change criminals, they nevertheless served as an ideological justification for fair and humane conditions of custody. Cressey was especially astute in understanding how conflicting goals of the prison led to contradictory directives to custodial staff, how social order depends on the consent of the governed even in a coercive organization like the prison, and how the inmate social system functions to produce order in the prison. Cressey later came to rethink the functionalist approach to the inmate system, and with John Irwin (1962) sparked an exciting theoretical and empirical controversy over the functionalist versus important theory of inmate culture and organization. Their new perspective argued that inmate cultures did not result entirely from prison conditions shaping inmates stripped of their previous cultural baggage. Rather, inmate cultures were in part imported from criminal subcultures outside the prison (forming the "thief" culture) and from inmates' previous prison experience (forming the "convict" culture).

Throughout his career, Cressey was concerned with discretionary decision making in the criminal justice system, not only in prisons but also among police and in the courts. He saw discretion as an outgrowth of the need for law and justice not merely to punish and control offenders mechanically, but also to maintain the "consent of the governed." When properly exercised, discretion can help fit the *abstract* categories of the law to *concrete* cases of (law violating) behavior in ways that increase justice and soften penalties, relative to a mechanical imposition of law. Viewed in this light, proposals for reforming criminal justice by abolishing discretion or eliminating plea bargaining is unlikely to produce a more fair or humane system (Rosett and Cressey, 1976). Late in his career, Cressey (1978) wrote about disturbing trends that saw academic criminology move from basic research to applied research and justice policy move from rehabilitation and prevention to deterrence.

In the 1960s, Cressey agreed to serve as an advisor to the President's Crime Commission, Task Force on Organized Crime. His report on the structure and functions of organized crime in America, which served as the basis of his best-selling monograph *Theft of the Nation* (1969), became the official position of the commission. Drawing on police reports and confidential government documents, Cressey analyzed the structure of the cartel, described it as a loosely federated alliance of families, each of which employed a rigid vertical authority structure. He showed how this structure made crime more rational and thereby thwarted police methods of eradicating crime. In particular, a buffer insulates a boss from prosecution, a corruptor and corruptee nullify the justice system, and an enforcer and executioner function as an internal judicial system enforcing the Mafia code. Furthermore, Cressey argued that a national crime commission existed, consisting of a dozen or so bosses of the most powerful Cosa Nostra families, and operated principally to settle disputes among families. Cressey maintained that an effective policy to combat organized crime must recognize its organizational nature—attacking the positions, rather than merely its incumbents. He recommended defining organizational crime as a new form of crime and then providing special legislation to deal with it. His ideas influenced the passage of the Racketeer Influenced Criminal Organizations Act, which allowed federal prosecutors to charge suspects with individual offenses, plus the additional charge of doing so as part of a criminal organization. Cressey's research was important not only because it was one of the best analyses of organized crime, but also because it legitimized the study of organized crime as respectable for sociologists and criminologists.

Cressey's contributions extend beyond his voluminous writings. He was an adroit administrator, serving as department chair at UCLA, dean of his college at UC Santa Barbara, and as a member of many commissions and advisory panels, including several presidential commissions. He was elected president of two national associations. But perhaps his most important role was in mentoring students, both graduates and undergraduates. His legacy lives on in former Ph.D. students, such as Kenneth Polk, Sheldon Messinger, David Luckenbill, Ross Matsueda, and Dario Melossi, as well as undergraduates he enticed into the discipline, such as Aaron Cicourel, Egon Bittner, William Chambliss, and John Irwin.

Ross L. Matsueda and Ronald L. Akers

Biography

Born in Fergus Falls, Minnesota, 27 April 1919; son of a switchboard operator at a hydro station. Educated at Iowa State, B.S. in Sociology; Indiana University, Ph.D. in Sociology. Lecturer, UCLA,1949–1951; Assistant Professor, UCLA, 1951–1956; Research Associate, University of Chicago 1955–1956; Associate Professor 1956–1958, UCLA; Professor and Chair of Sociology, UCLA 1958–1961; Dean of College of Letters and Science, UC Santa Barbara, 1962–1967; Professor of Sociology UC Santa Barbara 1962–1986; Professor Emeritus, UC Santa Barbara 1986–1987. President of the Pacific Sociological Association 1959–1960; President of International Symposium on Victimology, 1976. Died Santa Barbara, California, 21 July 1987.

Selected Writings

Principles of Criminology, 1955, 5th–10th eds. (with Sutherland, E.H.), 11th ed. (with Sutherland, E.H. and Luckenbill, D.F.), 1992.
Other People's Money, 1953.
The differential association theory and compulsive crimes. *Journal of Criminal Law, Criminology and Police Science* 45 (1954).
Epidemiology and individual conduct: A case from criminology. *Pacific Sociological Review* 3 (1960).
Theoretical Studies of the Prison (with Cloward and others), 1960.
Thieves, convicts, and the inmate culture, (with John Irwin) *Social Problems* 10 (1962).
Social psychological foundations for using criminals in the rehabilitation of criminals. *Journal of Research in Crime and Delinquency* 2 (1965).
Theft of the Nation, 1969.
Justice by Consent (with Rosett, A.I.), 1976.
Criminological theory, social science, and the repression of crime. *Criminology* 16 (1978).
Management fraud, accounting controls, and criminological theory, in *Management Fraud* (1980).

References and Further Reading

Akers, R.L. and Matsueda, R.L., Donald R. Cressey, An intellectual profile of a criminologist. *Sociological Inquiry* 59 (1989).
Colomy, P. and Donald R. Cressey, A personal and intellectual remembrance. *Crime and Delinquency* 34 (1988).
Cressey, D.R. 1988. Learning and living, in *Sociology and Autobiography*, Berger, B., Ed., Berkeley, CA: University of California.
Laub, J.H. and Donald R. Cressey, *Criminology in the Making: An Oral History*. Boston, MA: Northeastern University Press. Chapter 7.
Ohlin, L., In memoriam: Donald R. Cressey (1919–1987). *Crime and Delinquency* 34 (1988).
Polk, K. and Gibbons, D.C. The uses of criminology, the rehabilitative ideal, and justice. *Crime and Delinquency* 34 (1988).
Irwin, J. Donald Cressey and the sociology of the prison. *Crime and Delinquency* 34 (1988).
Albini, J.L. Donald Cressey's contributions to the study of organized crime: An evaluation. *Crime and Delinquency* 34 (1988).

See also **Differential Association Theory; Neutralization or Drift Theory**

Crime Commission Reports

Crime became the focus of numerous commissions in the 20th century, beginning in Chicago after World War I when businessmen called for get tough enforcement and prosecution following a wave of bank and payroll robberies (Chicago Crime Commission: see Douthit, 1975; Peterson, 1945; Chamberlin, 1920; Sims, 1920). The 21st century started with a warning by two commissions on national security and terrorism that attacks on American soil could soon inflict heavy casualties, just months before thousands died in New York City and Washington, DC in September 2001 (National Commission on Terrorism, 2000; U.S. Commission on National Security, 21st century 2001).

Whereas many recommendations of the commissions were either rejected or ignored (e.g., abolish plea bargaining by the National Advisory Commission on Criminal Justice Standards and Goals; require college degrees of police by several study groups beginning with the President's Commission on Law Enforcement and the Administration of Justice), others were adopted and became law, policy, or procedure in the criminal justice system. Each commission tried to assess problems and needs and suggest remedies for crime and justice dilemmas plaguing American society. Below is a capsule of the work, findings, and recommendations of the major commissions, presented in chronological order.

Chicago Crime Commission

In 1917, a number of banks were robbed and payrolls of several businesses were stolen, leading to a committee of prominent citizens being appointed by the Chicago Association of Commerce to a Committee on Prevalence and Prevention of Crime. This committee's major recommendation was the creation of a permanent Chicago Crime Commission, which was formed and began work in January 1919. More than 100 businessmen—primarily bankers, storeowners, and lawyers—were appointed, and a staff of investigators, statisticians, and office workers were hired to support the work (Douthit, 1975; Peterson, 1945; Chamberlin, 1920; Sims, 1920).

The commission sought to reduce burglary and larceny, which it held were costing Chicago businesses $12 million or more each year and had made their burglary insurance rates the highest in the nation (Chamberlin, 1920). A major early recommendation was to create a State Bureau of Criminal Records to "keep tabs" on police activity, and when this was rejected by the state, the commission set up its own records system (with other states and the federal government to follow their lead later). In general, the commission recommended stepped-up enforcement and prosecution to provide "swift and sure punishment" as a deterrent to crime (Sims, 1920). The commission was a precursor to two dozen similar operations established in cities and states across the nation during the 1920s in response to "crime waves" (Douthit, 1975; Crimes, 'Crime Waves,' 1919; Fosdick, 1921).

U.S. National Crime Commission

Appointed by President Calvin Coolidge in 1925, Commission Chairman Mark O. Prentiss described the objective as "a war on crime"—the first known acknowledgement of crime as a federal government problem and the first use of the term "war on crime" at the national level. The commission worked for 4 years, with the highlight being the National Crime Conference in 1927 that brought together state and municipal authorities from across the country, as well as representatives of 26 crime commissions and 50 other organizations directly involved in coping with crime (Douthit, 1975). The conference proceedings (US National Crime Commission, 1927) reflect the mood of the nation in this "crime wave," and recommendations were to move away from the 1900–1917 era of rehabilitation and to return to "good old-fashioned hard justice" with longer sentences, tighter criminal court procedure, and abolition of probation, parole, and indeterminate sentencing (Douthit).

National Commission on Law Observance and Enforcement (Wickersham Commission)

The National Crime Commission had barely finished its report when incoming President Herbert Hoover in 1929 created a commission chaired by George W., Wickersham to investigate law enforcement and courts use of "illegal means" to bring offenders to justice (National Commission on Law Observance and Enforcement, 1931)—a counter to the Coolidge-appointed Crime Commission. The new commission was heavily populated by defense attorneys and influenced—both in its creation and its recommendations—by Northwestern University Law School Dean John H. Wigmore. Staff assistance was provided by the Board of the *Harvard Law Review* and the New York Voluntary Defenders Association. A questionable murder conviction in California of J. Mooney and Warren K. Billings played a role in precipitating the appointment of the commission, but was not considered in the work of the group.

In the preface of its report, the commission (1931, 1) decried "abuses of power" by "inefficient and delinquent officials" in their "misguided zeal." "Respect for law, which is the fundamental prerequisite of law observance, hardly can be expected of people in general if the officers charged with enforcement do not set the example of obedience to its precepts" (p. 1).

The commission spent considerable effort to ferret out the problem of "the third degree," which it defined as "the employment of methods that inflict suffering, physical or mental, upon a person in order to obtain information about a crime" (p. 19). Prosecutorial unfairness also received major attention and led to a recommendation to create a Federal Code of Criminal Procedure (eventually legislated). The commission concluded that law enforcement needed a complete overhaul, whereas unfair prosecution was a problem of individuals rather than systemic. "Some kinds of lawless enforcement of law like the 'third degree' or searches and seizure without warrants required by law appear to result from a definite official policy in certain regions favoring habitual disregard of particular legal rules. The remedy for an abuse of this sort involves the serious difficulty of altering rooted official habits" (National Commission on Law Observance, 1931, 340).

Major recommendations included: (1) establish minimum time that must be provided to prepare a defense in criminal cases; (2) require judges to be disqualified for bias; (3) require the state to provide its list of witnesses to the defense; (4) require representation by counsel for the accused; (5) place persons on the juror list "regardless of color"; (6) simplify and clarify laws regarding what previous or other offenses of the defendant can be admitted into the record; (7) allow comment on the failure of the accused to testify; (8) abolish the "fee system" under which judges, prosecutors, and other court officials are paid from fines and court costs assessed against the defendant ("The income of persons concerned with the administration of justice should not depend on the fact of conviction," p. 342); (9) allow the trial judge to comment on the "weight of the evidence" (i.e., instruct jurors on law and advise on facts, to counter unfairness in the prosecution); (10) give appellate courts power to reduce sentences without a new trial; and (11) give appellate courts power to grant new trials "if required by justice" (p. 343).

In its final comment, the commission warned changes in the machinery of justice could not alone prevent unfairness. "The most important safeguards of a fair trial are that these officials want it to be fair and are active in making it so" (p. 347).

President's Commission on Law Enforcement and Administration of Justice

More than three decades after the Wickersham Commission, the next major crime commission was created by Executive Order 11236 on July 23, 1965, by President Lyndon B. Johnson in "recognizing the urgency of the Nation's crime problem and the depth of ignorance about it" (President's Commission on Law Enforcement and Administration of Justice, 1967, v). Nicholas deB. Katzenbach chaired the commission while James Vorenberg of Harvard Law School served as executive director. The 19 commissioners, 63 staff members, 175 consultants, and hundreds of advisers sponsored three national conferences, conducted five national surveys, held hundreds of meetings and interviews with "tens of thousands" of persons on their way to documenting the crime and justice problem in America and making some 200 recommendations to "lead to a safer and more just society" (p. v). The commission called for "a revolution in the way America thinks about crime," citing an independent random survey of 1700 persons in which it was found 91% admitted to committing acts for which they could have gone to jail or prison—exploding the myth that crime results from the activities of a small number of hardcore offenders.

The commission also cited the "enormous variety" of acts that constitute crime, the need for citizen involvement to control crime, the evidence that most crime is never reported to authorities, and the high fear of crime that had "eroded the basic quality of life of many Americans" (p. v.) The commission held "a significant reduction of crime" was possible if seven objectives were vigorously pursued: (1) prevent crime by seeing all Americans have a stake in the "benefits and responsibilities" of American life, law enforcement is strengthened, and criminal opportunities are reduced; (2) add options and techniques to deal with the wide variety and types of offenders; (3) eliminate injustices in the criminal justice system and seek to achieve respect and cooperation of citizens; (4) attract "more and better" people to employment in the criminal justice system; (5) increase basic and operational research about the criminal justice system; (6) fund at substantially higher levels police, courts, and correctional agencies; and (7) unite citizens plus business, civic, religious, and government organizations at all levels to plan and implement the necessary changes (p. v).

In its report, *The Challenge of Crime in a Free Society*, the commission documented the elements and complexity of the "criminal justice system" and presented a flow chart (pp. 8–9). Chief among the systemic recommendations were the creation of uniform crime reporting nationwide and separation of the Crime Index of the Uniform Crime Reports into two parts—crimes of violence and crimes against property—and strengthening of communities by providing resources for neighborhood anticrime programs such as the creation of Youth Service Bureaus to help children before they turn to crime in frustration or for lack of alternatives.

The 200 recommendations were generally broad in scope even when focused narrowly. For example, among the some 40 recommendations under "Juvenile Delinquency and Youth Crime" were recommendations to "expand counseling and therapy," "reduce racial and economic segregation," "develop better means for dealing with behavior problems," and "create new job opportunities" (p. 294). Taken together, however, they called for a more tolerant, caring, and attentive society to the needs of youth, particularly those living under severe conditions of poverty, family disorganization, and racism. Emphasis was on the prevention of youth crime through assistance such as that from Youth Service Bureaus, and for separation of adolescents from adult offenders, with a focus on saving children from the harshness of the system and keeping as many juveniles as possible out of the system altogether.

For police, the commission recommended a college degree as an employment prerequisite as well as better training and the recruitment of more minorities. It also called fors establishment of community relations programs with a focus on improving interactions with "the poor, minority groups, and juveniles." Also recommended were increased salaries, in-service training, lateral entry, guidelines for use of discretion, legal advisers, firearms use policies, and pooling of resources (p. 295).

For courts, adding "dignity and effectiveness" to the lower courts was stressed, along with implementing bail reform so more poor defendants could remain in the community prior to trial, "fair and visible" plea bargains, increasing the scope of pretrial discovery, considering "whether" to retain capital punishment, establishing presentence investigations for all convicted offenders, abolishing jury sentencing in noncapital cases, establishing procedures for "just and uniform sentencing," providing for better selection, training, and monitoring of court personnel, creating "single, unified State courts systems," and improving facilities and compensation for witnesses and jurors (pp. 296–297).

For corrections, the focus was on providing more alternatives to incarceration—especially strengthening probation and parole and adding intensive treatment and other community-based programs. For institutions, the emphasis was on improving selection and training personnel along with better diagnostic and screening of inmates in order to provide better programs for them (pp. 297–298).

In a section on organized crime, the commission recommended more investigative grand juries and more focus on laws and procedures to seek out organized crime, such as immunity grants, wiretapping and eavesdropping, and witness protection (p. 298). In a brief list concerning narcotics and drugs, the commission recommendations were broad—conduct research and develop educational materials while increasing staffs of the Bureau of Customs and Narcotics. On drunkenness, the recommendations were more specific—eliminate public drunkenness as a crime when not accompanied by disorderly conduct, establish more detoxification programs, and expand aftercare and research (p. 298).

On weapons, the commission recommended stricter firearms control laws, such as a ban on the transportation and possession of "military-type weapons" and denial of firearms to dangerous persons, plus registration of all guns. It also called for required permits to possess or carry handguns, and a prohibition on interstate sales (p. 299).

A Task Force on Science and Technology led to several commission recommendations ranging from providing universal access to police call boxes to the creation of a single, uniform police telephone number (e.g., "911"), increasing coordination and sophistication of police communications systems, seeking a new fingerprint recognition system (which was later computerized), and establishing a National Criminal Justice Statistics Center (now the Bureau of Justice Statistics) (p. 300). The Task Force on Research led to commission recommendations for a coordinated public and private effort to provide needed research, including organizing research units in criminal justice agencies, expanding university research, and establishing a National Foundation for Criminal Research (now the National Institute of Justice) (p. 300).

Finally, in a chapter entitled "A National Strategy," the commission commented on the need for national commitment and implementation of its recommendations and called for the establishment of agencies or officials in every state and city "responsible for planning and encouraging implementation in criminal justice" as well as the initiation of an eight-point federal support program.

Many of the President's Commission's recommendations were implemented in part through the creation of the Law Enforcement Assistance Administration (LEAA) to assist state and local governments in crime control and justice arenas, and through the LEAA-created National Advisory Commission on Criminal Justice Standards and Goals (see discussion below) to refine the process and develop an implementation strategy. Many scholars see the President's Commission as the most comprehensive examination of crime ever conducted in America.

National Advisory Commission on Civil Disorders

Executive Order 11365 issued by President Lyndon Johnson on July 29, 1967, established this bipartisan commission to study a "divided nation" in the wake of bloody and destructive riots in the nation's cities (National Advisory Commission on Civil Disorders, 1968). Chaired by Otto Kerner, Governor of Illinois, with New York City Mayor John Lindsay as cochair, the commission was composed of two U.S. senators, two U.S. representatives, representatives of labor, industry, civil rights, and police groups, with numerous advisors. The major conclusion was: "Our nation is moving toward two societies, one black, one white—separate and unequal" (p. 1).

In an introduction, *New York Times* reporter Tom Wicker wrote: "Reading it [the Commission report] is an ugly experience but one that brings, finally, something like the relief of beginning. What had to be said has been said at last, and by representatives of that white, moderate responsible America that, alone, needed to say it" (p. xi).

The disorders were found to be led by "middle class" Blacks, mostly in northern cities, because they "were mistrustful of white politics, they hated the police, and they were proud of their race, and acutely conscious of the discrimination they suffered. They were and they are a time-bomb ticking in the heart of the richest nation in the history of the world," Wicker wrote (pp. vii, x–xi). Citing the need for jobs, housing, schools, and fair police and media practices, the commission recommended three guiding principles for reform: (1) mount programs on a scale equal to the dimension of the problems; (2) aim programs for high impact in the immediate future in order to quickly close the gap between promise and performance; and (3) undertake new initiatives and experiments that can change the system of failure and frustration that dominates the "ghetto" and weakens U.S. society (p. 1). Finally, the commission said, "The alternative is not blind repression or capitulation to lawlessness. It is the realization of common opportunities for all within a single society" (p. 1).

National Commission on Causes and Prevention of Violence

Less than a year after creating the Civil Disorders Commission, but in the wake of the assassinations of both civil rights leader Dr. Martin Luther King Jr.

and Sen. Robert Kennedy, President Johnson on June 6, 1968 issued Executive Order 11412 to create what became known as the Riots Commission (National Commission on Causes and Prevention of Violence, 1969). Chaired by Dr. Milton S. Eisenhower, with Lloyd N. Cutler as executive director, the 15 commissioners represented a cross section of America—black and white, male and female, young and old, Republican and Democrat—and its professions (e.g., education, law, religion, politics, psychology, history, labor, and philosophy) from all sections of the country. Its task was to seek out causes and prevention of violence of all types—murder, assassination, and assault especially—as well as causes and prevention of disrespect for "law and order." The commission's report was made to incoming President Richard Nixon.

In the report, *To Establish Justice, to Insure Domestic Tranquility*, the commission issued 81 recommendations in 10 areas, chief among them: (1) provide more resources "to establish justice and insure domestic tranquility" as promised in the U.S. Constitution; (2) increase welfare benefits after the Vietnam War was concluded; (3) double the investment in the criminal justice process; (4) increase foot patrol and police–community relations; (5) provide low-cost drugs, such as methadone, to hardcore drug users; (6) identify and provide special treatment for violence-prone persons; (7) provide jobs and homes for all Americans; (8) expand Secret Service efforts to protect federal officeholders and candidates; (9) have the National Rifle Association educate the people on the dangers of firearms; (10) abandon violent television programming for children; (11) lower the voting age to 18 and reform the military draft system; and (12) expand paid public service opportunities for youth (pp. 271–282).

President's Commission on Campus Unrest

President Richard Nixon, on June 13, 1970, established this commission in response to violent demonstrations and riots on campuses—including deadly encounters between students and police or national guard at Jackson State (MS) College and Kent State (OH) University (President's Commission on Campus Unrest, 1970).

Chaired by former Pennsylvania Governor William W. Scranton, the commission held 13 days of hearings and conducted investigations (e.g., interviews of students, faculty, and staff) in Jackson and Kent as well as Lawrence, KA, issuing its report Sept. 26, 1970. The commission told the president, "nothing is more important than an end to the war in Indochina" to curtail campus unrest (p. 9). Secondly, the commission recommended the president renew a national commitment to full social justice and work to restore trust and responsibilities of minorities and students in general. To government agencies, the commission called for increased integration of schools, more financial aid for Black students and for predominantly Black colleges, and for strict control over the sale and possession of explosive materials. For law enforcement, more training and equipment to handle civil disorders on campuses was recommended, whereas for students, the basic message was to lower the level of protest without giving up their rights to free speech and dissent, noting there was no right of students to "dictate policy."

Still, overall the commission found: "Most protests, even today, are entirely peaceful and orderly manifestations of dissent ... protected by the First Amendment" (President's Commission on Campus Unrest, p. x).

National Advisory Commission on Criminal Justice Standards and Goals

The Law Enforcement Assistance Administration (LEAA), created as a response to the call by the President's Commission on Law Enforcement and Administration of Justice for a federal response to crime, appointed this commission on October 20, 1971 to formulate for the first time national criminal justice standards and goals for crime reduction and prevention at state and local levels (National Advisory Commission on Criminal Justice Standards and Goals, 1973). Governor Russell W. Peterson of Delaware chaired the commission and LEAA General Counsel Thomas J. Madden was executive director. The LEAA provided $1.75 million in discretionary grants to support the work of the independent commission, whose membership represented a broad spectrum of state and local government.

The commission released and discussed its standards at a National Conference on Criminal Justice held Jan. 23–26, 1973, in Washington, DC. The nearly 400 standards and goals in five areas—criminal justice system, police, courts, corrections, and community crime prevention—were included in six volumes, including the summary document, *A National Strategy to Reduce Crime.* Priorities and goals included a two-level attack on five crimes—homicide, forcible rape, aggravated assault, robbery, and burglary. By 1983—a decade after the report—"high-fear (stranger-related) offenses in the five crime categories were to be cut in half" and specific goals for reduction of all crimes in the categories were set between 25 and 50% (p. 7).

Among the recommendations: SYSTEM—institute crime specific planning, develop and make maximum use of data collected through criminal justice information systems, establish criminal justice education and training standards and curriculum, and revise criminal codes and procedures; COMMUNITY CRIME PREVENTION—dispense government services through neighborhood centers, coordinate youth services through Youth Service Bureaus independent of the juvenile justice system, create drug intervention and treatment programs at the community level, expand education and employment opportunities for disadvantaged youths, and implement designs for buildings and neighborhoods to reduce criminal opportunity; POLICE—formulate and publicize policies governing police functions, objectives, and priorities, including the use of discretion, establish geographic team policing and involve the public in neighborhood crime prevention efforts, establish crime laboratory certification standards, and upgrade entry-level educational and training requirements while offering incentives for police to seek higher education; COURTS—prohibit all plea bargaining in all courts by 1978, assure the period from arrest to trial does not exceed 60 days for felonies or 30 days for misdemeanors, formulate alternatives to the Exclusionary Rule, and select judges on merit only with mandatory retirement at age 65; CORRECTIONS—guarantee offenders' access to courts, legal assistance, and legal materials, establish rules of inmate conduct and grievance procedures, implement formal diversion programs, develop a comprehensive correctional classification system for institutions and community-based programs, develop a range of community-based alternatives to incarceration, and authorize police to divert juveniles from the criminal justice process.

R. Eugene Stephens

References and Further Reading

Chamberlin, H.B., The Chicago crime commission—How the businessmen of Chicago are fighting crime, *Journal of Criminal Law and Criminology* 11 (1920).

Crime, 'Crime Waves,' Criminals and the Police, *Literary Digest* 60 (1919)

Douthit, N., Police professionalism and the war against crime in the United States, 1920s–1930s, in *Police Forces in History*, Mosse, G.L., London and Beverly Hills: Sage, 1975.

Fosdick, R., The crime wave in America, *New Republic* 26 (1921).

National Advisory Commission on Civil Disorders, *Report of the National Advisory Commission on Civil Disorders*, New York, NY: E. P. Dutton, 1968.

National Advisory Commission on Criminal Justice Standards and Goals, *A National Strategy to Reduce Crime*, Washington, DC: US Government Printing Office, 1973.

National Commission on the Causes and Prevention of Violence, *To Establish Justice, To Insure Domestic Tranquility*, Washington, DC: US Government Printing Office, 1969.

National Commission on Law Observance and Enforcement, *Report of Lawlessness in Law Enforcement*, Washington, DC: US Government Printing Office, 1931.

Peterson, V.W., *Crime Commissions in the United States*, Chicago, IL: (No Publisher Cited), 1945.

Pfiffner, J., The activities and results of crime surveys, *American Political Science Review* 23 (1929).

Prentiss, M.O., War on the growing menace of crime, *Current Opinion* 23 (1925).

President's Commission on Campus Unrest, *Report of the President's Commission on Campus Unrest*, Washington, DC: US Government Printing Office, 1970.

President's Commission on Law Enforcement and Administration of Justice, *The Challenge of Crime in a Free Society*, Washington, DC: US Government Printing Office, 1967.

Sims, E.W., Fighting crime in Chicago, *Journal of Criminal Law and Criminology* 11 (1920).

US National Crime Commission, a Full Report of the Proceedings of the National Conference on the Reduction of Crime Called by the National Crime Commission, Washington, DC: US Government Printing Office, 1927.

Wigmore, J.H., The National Crime Commission: What will it achieve, *Journal of Criminal Law and Criminology* 16 (1925).

See also **Criminal Law Reform**

Crime, Definitions of

"Crime" is a widely invoked and broadly familiar term. An aspiration to define crime in a single, formal manner—repudiating all other definitions as incorrect, or wrong—is futile. Rather, we have to accept that the term "crime" refers to different things, and then be clear about which meaning is being invoked in a particular context.

There are perhaps a dozen ways to define crime, but within criminology, the five most popular are the legalistic, humanistic, constructionist, political, and moralistic definitions.

The *legalistic definition of crime* has been dominant, and such a conception of crime is most readily embraced by a literate public. The simplest legalistic definition of crime defines it as a violation of the criminal law, or conduct leading to criminal prosecution (Michael and Adler, 1933; Tappan, 1947). In legal terms, a crime involves both conduct (or action) and intent (*mens rea*). The action may be inchoate, or not fully realized (e.g., it is a crime to attempt to hire someone to kill a spouse, even if no further action occurs). Intent should not be confused with premeditation, or the specific intent to cause a grievous harm (e.g., a person who spontaneously punches another person, causing a fatal injury, can be charged with a degree of homicide, even though the fatal injury was neither planned nor anticipated). The proscribed action must be shown to have some causal relationship to the injurious outcome. An individual may be deemed incapable of forming criminal intent (e.g., because of being underage or mentally ill), and overall circumstances may be taken into account in determining whether or not a crime occurred.

The legalistic definition of crime differentiates forms of crime. An ancient distinction exists between crimes that are *mala in se*—or evil in themselves—and *mala prohibita*—or crimes because they are prohibited (Blackstone, 1979). More familiarly, the most serious crimes are designated as felonies; less serious crimes are designated as misdemeanors. The terms infractions or citation offenses are used for minor violations, such as jaywalking, prohibited by local ordinances.

If crime through most of history was thought of principally in terms of conventional, predatory offenses such as murder, rape, robbery, and burglary, Edwin H. Sutherland (1945) challenged this way of defining crime when he introduced the concept of white-collar crime. Such crime is committed by respectable members of society (often of high social status) in the context of a legitimate occupation. But Sutherland incorporated into this conception activities that are not defined as crime by the criminal law; rather, much of this activity evokes a response from regulatory or civil law.

Legalistic definitions of crime have been challenged as ideologically biased in some way, with calls for adopting criteria other than criminal, civil, or regulatory law to define crime (Friedrichs, 1992). Conflict theorists, radical criminologists, and critical criminologists emphasize that crime is an ideological construct, and the conventional adoption of legalistic definitions of crime as inherently biased. A *humanistic definition of crime* has been advanced by Herman and Julia Schwendinger (1970), who called for a definition that would focus on objectively identifiable harm to human beings and violations of human rights as the criteria for labeling an activity a crime. By such criteria imperialism, racism, sexism, and other such oppressive conditions should be viewed as crimes. The Schwendingers argued that criminologists should not defer to the vested interests in society the exclusive right to define crime. In a similar vein, Larry Tifft and Dennis Sullivan (1980) have argued that we should define crime in terms of needs-based social harms inflicted by the powerful on less powerful people, independent of formal legal institutions; accordingly, actions that contribute to the denial of food, clothing, and shelter—and the realization of human potential—should be recognized as crime. Further, Ronald C. Kramer (1985) has specifically called for a humanistic definition of crime as willful social harm. Raymond Michalowski and Ronald Kramer (1987) have called for recognition that in an increasingly globalized world transnational corporations engage in demonstrably harmful activities that fall in "the space between the laws," but that ought to be recognized as crime. And David Kauzlarich, Ronald Kramer, and Brian Smith (1992) are among those who have called for extending the definition of crime more broadly to the harmful activities engaged in by states, especially those governmental actions that violate international human rights.

Another way to define crime is via the *constructionist* or labeling perspective, which holds that crimes are distinguished from other acts precisely because they have been defined as crimes by people whose reactions matter. Pursuing this reasoning, what makes behavior distinctive are the kinds of reactions it calls forth. The labeling perspective views crime as status rather than as behavior, and would define crime as a label that is attached to behavior and events by those who exercise power (Barlow and Kauzlarich, 2001).

The fourth major way to define crime is *moralistically*. Pro-life activists, for example, embrace a definition of crime that emphasizes moralistic criteria. Accordingly, abortion is characterized as a crime and, indeed, a crime of the first magnitude: willful murder of fetuses. Its criminal status is rooted in the view that abortion is fundamentally at odds with the law of God and is accordingly both immoral and criminal.

Finally, if legalistic definitions of crime emanate out of a political system, some definitions of crime may be regarded as purely political, formulated and applied quite independently of the legal system. In this sense, a *political definition of crime* encompasses the brute exercise of political power. In totalitarian political systems in particular, those whose actions (or attributes) are fundamentally offensive or threatening to the political elite are defined and treated as guilty of serious crimes, and are dealt with accordingly. As a classic illustrative case, the Jews in Nazi Germany (and in countries occupied by Nazi Germany) were ultimately defined as guilty of the crime of being Jewish, and millions of Jews were accordingly systematically exterminated. Although a series of laws in Nazi Germany stripped Jews of their rights as citizens, no law was ever passed declaring it a crime to simply be of Jewish extraction, and legal proceedings were not the means used to identify, seize, transport, and ultimately to exterminate Jews. Here, then, is a case where brute political power was used to impose the label criminal on a whole people.

In conclusion, the term "crime" means different things in different contexts. Rather than imagining that crime can be defined in one way we should be sensitive to the fact that crime is a construct, defined differently for different purposes.

DAVID KAUZLARICH AND DAVID O. FRIEDRICHS

References and Further Reading

Barlow, H.D. and Kauzlarich, D. *Introduction to Criminology.* 8th ed. Upper Saddle River, NJ: Prentice-Hall, 2001.

Blackstone, W. *Commentaries on the Laws of England (1765–1769)*, Chicago, IL: University of Chicago Press, 1979.

Friedrichs, D.O. White collar crime and the definitional quagmire: A provisional solution. *Journal of Human Justice* 3 (1992).

Henry, S. and Lanier, M., Eds. *The Nature of Crime: Controversies over the Content and Definition of Crime*, Boulder, CO: Rowman & Littlefield, 2001.

Kauzlarich, D., Kramer, R.C., and Smith, B. Toward the study of governmental crime: Nuclear weapons, foreign intervention, and international law. *Humanity and Society* 16, 4 (1992).

Kramer, R.C. Defining the concept of crime: A humanistic perspective. *Journal of Sociology and Social Welfare* 12: 469–487 (1985).

Michael, J. and Adler, M. *Crime, Law and Social Science*, New York, NY: Harcourt, Brace and Company, 1933.

Michalowski, R.J. and Kramer, R.C. The space between the laws: The problem of corporate crime in a transnational context. *Social Problems* 34: 34–53 (1987).

Quinney, R. *The Social Reality of Crime*, Boston, MA: Little, Brown.

Schwendinger, H. and Julia. Defenders of order or guardians of human rights? *Issues in Criminology* 5, 2 (1970).

Sutherland, E.H. Is 'white-collar crime' crime? *American Sociological Review* 10 (1945).

Tappan, P. Who is the criminal? *American Sociological Review* 12 (1947).

Tifft, L.L. and Sullivan, D.C. *The Struggle to Be Human: Crime, Criminology, and Anarchism*, Sanday, UK: Cienfuegos Press, 1980.

See also **Elements of Crime; Sutherland, Edwin E.; Typologies of Crime and Criminal Behavior; White-Collar Crimes, Definitions of**

Crime Laboratories

See **Police: Forensic Evidence**

Crime Mapping

A geographic information system (GIS) is a set of computer-based tools that allow a person to modify, visualize, query, and analyze geographic and tabular data. Crime analysis in the law enforcement setting is the systematic study of criminal activity along with sociodemographic, temporal, and spatial factors in order to inform crime prevention and decision making. Consequently, computerized crime mapping is the process of using a geographic information system in combination with crime analysis techniques to focus on the spatial context of criminal and other law enforcement activity. Examples of analysis range from examining the number of crimes per patrol area for resource allocation, to determining travel patterns of a serial offender for apprehension purposes.

Although computerized crime mapping has become a standard practice among many law enforcement agencies, the mapping of crime has not always been conducted with the aid of computers. The placement of hand drawn dots on a map to indicate the locations of crime incidents or shading areas to indicate crime characteristics of an area has been practiced since the early 1800s. In fact, one of the first maps analyzing crime was created in France in the 1820s. The map depicted areas of France shaded to show a comparison of national data on education to national data on crimes committed against property and persons.

The use of crime mapping in the U.S. began some time later, primarily because the country itself was relatively new which meant that reliable maps, especially of newly acquired territories, were not readily available, and census data were not regularly collected. Thus, the first substantive crime mapping in the U.S. was conducted in the 1920s and 1930s by urban sociologists such as Park, Thrasher, Shaw, and Myers. Their crime research and related crime maps linked crime and delinquency to factors such as social disorganization and poverty. In fact, Shaw and McKay's spatial analysis of juvenile delinquency and social conditions in Chicago is considered to be one of the foremost examples of crime mapping in the first half of the 20th century.

In the 1960s and 1970s, the first computerized crime maps were made although their creation was greatly restricted by both the cost and availability of advanced technology. These maps were not of high quality by today's standards as they were printed on dot-matrix printers that used letters and symbols to draw the map, but they were an improvement over manual crime mapping methods. For a more complete history of crime mapping, see the books by Weisburd and McEwen (1988) and Harries (1999).

In addition to being used historically in criminological research, crime mapping has been used in law enforcement for some time. As base maps depicting geographic features such as streets and city boundaries have been available, police departments have used them to determine patrol areas, emergency routes, as well as to find specific addresses during patrols. Police departments have also mapped crime, though this process has historically been manual, in that dots were drawn on paper maps by hand and push pins were placed on larger maps posted to the wall to represent crime locations. Pins with different colored heads or flags with dates or types of crimes written on them were used for more detailed depictions of crime locations. In fact, these manual maps may still be used today by law enforcement agencies that lack the funding or the personnel necessary to implement computerized crime mapping.

Even though these manual methods may still be used today, they are limited in their analytical value. That is, the chronology of the incidents is difficult to determine, and the pins or dots do not have readily accessible associated attributes, e.g., crime type, address, or date, of that particular crime, i.e., looking at one of these maps, one only sees the pins and in some cases various colors, but no additional data about the incident or its location. In fact, using this type of mapping to depict crimes at one particular location is problematic because it is difficult to place more than one pin, much less numerous pins, on a single address. In fact, once the maps are cluttered with a day, week, or month's worth of incidents, the maps must be completely redone, and prior crime data are lost. In the case of wall maps, the base map has to be replaced periodically because there are so many holes that the streets and names become unreadable.

With the significant improvements in computer technology since the early to mid-1990s, such as memory size, processing speed, and printing quality, geographic information systems and law enforcement data have become available on desktop computers, thus making high quality electronic crime mapping a reality. Even though some law enforcement agencies and researchers have been conducting crime mapping for some time, awareness of computerized crime mapping and its importance to crime prevention and policing increased significantly in the mid-1990s.

From 1995 to 2000, several books on crime mapping concepts, research, and case studies were published; the U.S. government formulated the Crime Mapping Research Center within the National Institute of Justice to promote research, evaluation, development, and dissemination of GIS technology and the spatial analysis of crime; and the U.S. government, through the Office of Community Oriented Policing Services and the National Institute of Justice, granted funding to establish crime mapping technology in law enforcement agencies as well as to provide training and technical assistance to agencies conducting crime mapping.

In addition to advances in crime mapping technology, improvements in general technology have made police and geographic data more readily available. Law enforcement data such as crime, arrests, accidents, and calls for service have become available electronically through computer aided dispatch (CAD) systems as well as through electronic records management systems (RMS). In addition, geographic information such as street and census information are now widely available in electronic format and are provided free or at minimal cost from a variety of government and commercial resources. All these improvements have helped to advance the field of crime mapping beyond manual methods or the use of large, costly mainframe mapping systems and bring it to the desktop computer.

The introduction of GIS technology to the field of crime analysis has dramatically improved law enforcement efforts to both understand and respond to criminal activity. Law enforcement agencies apply crime mapping principles and technology in many different ways. In short-term application, crime mapping is being used to identify immediate patterns for crimes such as residential and commercial burglary, auto theft, or theft from vehicle. For example, mapping is useful for examining the relationship between auto theft and recovery. Spatial analyses of auto theft incidents may reveal clusters of activity at specific locations, and it may also highlight factors that increase the likelihood of auto theft, such as the proximity of a location to the freeway or another escape route. In addition, analysis of recovery locations, along with recovery conditions, may lead to the identification of a vehicle "chop shop" in a particular neighborhood. Another example of a short-term application of crime mapping is the use of aerial photography to conduct environmental analyses of crime locations. For example, an aerial photograph of a mall and its parking lot mapped in combination with incidents of theft from vehicles might reveal the characteristics of a high crime incident area of the parking lot, such as access from a wooded area.

Crime mapping is used in long-term applications to analyze the relationship between criminal activity and indicators of disorder, such as a high volume of vacant property or disorder calls for service; to assist in geographic and temporal allocation of resources, i.e., patrol officer scheduling and determining patrol areas; to examine patterns of crime at or around specific locations, such as schools, bars, or drug treatment centers; to calculate crime rate information, such as numbers of residential burglaries per household; and to incorporate crime with qualitative geographic information such as teen-age hangouts, student pathways to school, or drug and prostitution markets.

Crime mapping is also a valuable tool for law enforcement agencies, researchers, and media organizations to convey criminal activity information to the public. Since the mid to late 1990s, the Internet has become the primary method for disseminating information. Images depicting maps of crime along with corresponding tables and definitions are regularly posted to police department as well as news organization Web sites. For example, one method for reducing public requests for neighborhood crime information is to place monthly or weekly crime maps on a Web page that the public can access on their home computer or at the local library.

Some law enforcement agencies have taken Web-based mapping one step further by developing applications that allow users to create their own crime maps by choosing a time period, crime type, and geographic area. Finally, mapping is being used to assist in the sex offender notification process by allowing individuals to input an address, typically at home or school, and identify convicted sex offenders within a certain radius of that address.

A great deal of research and application of crime mapping focuses on "hotspots." Hotspots are defined in many different ways in crime mapping literature, but in the most general sense, they are clusters of activity in a particular area. There are many different methodologies for determining hotspots just as there are many different types of hotspots. For example, a cluster can be defined as a few incidents or many incidents, depending on the time frame of the analysis, the area of interest, and the type(s) of crime considered. For example, an analysis of frequency of crime in the entire U.S. will show hotspots of activity around Los Angeles, Chicago, and New York City. However, an analysis of the city of Los Angeles itself would yield hotspots in specific neighborhoods. These more concentrated hotspots could not be distinguished in an analysis of the entire U.S. because the area under examination is too large.

Additionally, for an analysis of crimes occurring over the last year versus the last week, a hotspot might consist of 50 cases or three cases, respectively. Finally, by combining incidents with demographic characteristics such as population to determine hotspots of crime by population density, areas of New York and Los Angeles may no longer be considered hotspots because their populations are so large and would offset their relative frequency of crime. In sum, "hotspot" is a general term by which data are analyzed in many different ways.

In addition to the type of data, the time period of the data, and the area covered, there are various statistical methods used to determine hotspots. These range from the noncomputerized "eyeball" technique (simply looking at the map and determining clusters) to advanced methods such as hotspot area ellipses, kernel density, and K-means statistics.

Finally, a combination of advanced GIS technology and spatial statistics, theories such as environmental criminology, and the widespread acceptance of innovative law enforcement practices such as crime prevention through environmental design (CPTED) have led the way for highly advanced applications of spatial analyses of criminal activity. Some examples of these advanced applications include determining hotspots in three dimensions, e.g., in high-rise buildings; geographic profiling, which is determining the probable residence of serial criminals from the locations related to the crime such as the crime site, the body dumping site, or the victim's residence; mapping cellular telephone calls placed during the commission of a crime to assist prosecutorial efforts; or using nighttime aerial photography to determine whether more crimes occur in less lighted areas.

Although the practice of mapping criminal incidents can be traced back to the 19th century, the advent of GIS technology and the relatively recent development of computerized crime mapping have dramatically enhanced the ability to both understand and respond to criminal activity. In combination with other crime analysis tools, spatial analysis and depictions of crime and other law enforcement data are an effective method for highlighting geographic and other types of patterns that may not otherwise be evident.

RACHEL BOBA

References and Further Reading

Block, C., Dabdoub, M., and Fregly, S., Eds. *Crime Analysis through Computer Mapping*, Washington DC: Police Executive Research Forum, 1995.

Brantingham, P. and Brantingham, P., *Patterns in Crime*, New York, NY: MacMillan, 1984.

Chou, Y., *Exploring Spatial Analysis in Geographic Information Systems*, Santa Fe, New Mexico: OnWord Press, 1996.

Clarke, K., *Getting Started with Geographic Information Systems*, 2nd ed., Englewood Cliffs, NJ: Prentice Hall, 1998.

Eck, J. and Weisburd, D., Eds., *Crime and Place (Crime Prevention Studies,* Vol. 4*)*, Monsey, NY: Willow Tree Press, 1995.

Harries, K., *Mapping Crime: Principle and Practice*, Washington DC: US Department of Justice, Office of Justice Programs, 1999.

Hirschfield, A. and Bowers, K., Eds., *Mapping and Analysing Crime Data: Lessons from Research and Practice.* New York, NY: Taylor & Francis, 2001.

LaVigne, N. and Wartell, J., Eds., *Crime Mapping Case Studies: Successes in the Field*, Vol. 1. Washington DC: Police Executive Research Forum, 1998.

LaVigne, N. and Wartell, J., Eds., *Crime Mapping Case Studies: Successes in the Field*, Vol. 2. Washington DC: Police Executive Research Forum, 2000.

Rossmo, D.K., *Geographic Profiling*. Boca Raton, FL: CRC Press, 2000.

Turnbull, L., Hendrix, E., and Dent, B., Eds., *Atlas of Crime: Mapping the Criminal Landscape*, Phoenix, Arizona: Oryx Press, 2000.

Weisburd, D. and McEwen, T., Eds., *Crime Mapping and Crime Prevention*. Monsey, NY: Willow Tree Press, 1998.

See also **Crime Prevention**

Crime Prevention

Preventing crime and building safer societies comprise the goals and aspirations of policy makers, criminal justice practitioners, civil servants, community activists, teachers, and parents across the world. No one disputes the need to make our cities, states, and neighborhoods safer to live and works in. People universally desire their environments to be free from crime problems.

Crime prevention is an amorphous term used variously to describe the environments, settings, perspectives, and programmatic approaches that aim to build safer societies. In general terms, crime prevention involves any effort that either stops a crime from ever occurring or reduces the likelihood that further crimes will occur in the future. This essay identifies key crime prevention concepts, provides an overview of some selected perspectives on crime prevention and briefly summarizes the literature of what works in preventing crime.

Crime Prevention Concepts

During 1996, Lawrence W. Sherman and his colleagues from the University of Maryland prepared a report titled *Preventing crime: What works, what doesn't and what's promising* for the U.S. Congress that synthesized much of the extant crime prevention literature (see Sherman et. al, 1997). According to Lawrence Sherman, crime prevention *practices* are defined as ongoing routine activities that are intended to prevent crime. Most of these practices are unfunded and merely comprise the day-to-day efforts of people in everyday life. Examples of crime prevention practices include parents making sure their children come home at a particular time at night, schools specifying start and end times to the school day, and shop owners observing customers and making sure they do not steal their merchandise.

Crime prevention *programs*, as defined by Sherman, include focused efforts that seek to change, restrict, or create a routine practice in a crime prevention setting. Crime prevention programs are diverse in nature and can include church programs that discourage parents from spanking their children; family-based programs that discourage children from watching violent television programs, shows or movies; and police crackdown programs that enforce truancy laws.

Crime prevention *settings* are defined by Sherman as being a social stage for playing out various roles such as parent, child, neighbor, employer, teacher, and church leader. Sherman and his colleagues identify seven major institutional settings including communities, families, schools, labor markets, places, police agencies, and other criminal justice agencies.

Crime prevention *strategies* are defined as broad and distinctive categories of crime prevention approaches that offer important guidance on how governments may approach the task of building safer societies. Michael Tonry and David P. Farrington, in their edited volume titled *Building a Safer Society: Strategic Approaches to Crime Prevention* (1995), identify four strategic approaches to crime prevention including law enforcement, community, situational, and developmental prevention.

John Last (1980) distinguishes three kinds of prevention in the public health arena that are often adapted to describe preventive approaches in criminal justice settings (see Moore, 1995). *Primary crime prevention* seeks to prevent crime from ever occurring by implementing programs that manipulate environments that make crime possible or likely to occur. Environments such as families, communities, and schools feature prominently in this category of crime prevention. *Secondary crime prevention* seeks to identify cases, people or situations early in some developmental process that will lead to more serious crime problems if these cases, people, or situations are not altered. Again, families, schools, and communities are typically the locust of intervention programs in this category of crime prevention. The difference between primary prevention and secondary prevention is that people, places, or situations that exhibit *risk factors* that are known to correlate with crime problems are singled out and targeted within this secondary category of crime prevention. Finally, *tertiary crime prevention* intervenes after a crime problem is well established and seeks to minimize the long-term consequences of the crime problem. Rehabilitative programs in prisons, schools, and families feature in this category of crime prevention.

Criminological scholars talk much about risk factors, protective factors, and resilience to crime. These concepts have major links to the crime prevention literature and are thus important concepts to define. *Risk factors* are those characteristics that, through careful research, have been identified as being correlated with criminal behavior or a crime event. Some well-known risk factors include childhood disruptive behaviors (such as aggression and hyperactivity), cognitive deficits (such as low IQ, inattentiveness, poor school performance), parental deviance, parental discord, ineffective discipline, poor supervision, socially disorganized neighborhoods, and association with deviant peers. *Protective factors* are defined as the inverse of risk factors and are generally referred to as those characteristics that insulate people or places from crime. *Resilience* is defined as the process of being insulated from previous exposure to criminogenic risk.

Four Crime Prevention Approaches

Michael Tonry and David P. Farrington (1995) in their edited volume titled *Building a Safer Society: Strategic Approaches to Crime Prevention*, identify four major strategic approaches to crime prevention: community-based prevention, situational crime prevention, developmental prevention, and law enforcement. These four approaches provide a useful framework to describe the theory and practice of crime prevention. Importantly, these four strategic approaches variously occur in what Sherman and his colleagues (1997) describe as institutional settings: communities, families, schools, labor markets, places, police agencies, and other criminal justice agencies.

Community crime prevention refers to the actions intended to change the social conditions that are believed to sustain crime in residential communities. "Community-based" crime prevention efforts are organized around local institutions such as families, friendship networks, clubs, associations, and organizations and are aimed at changing the social structure of particular communities (see Hope, 1995).

Lawrence Sherman (1997) categorizes community-based crime prevention around five risk factors: community composition, social structure, oppositional culture, legitimate opportunities, and social and physical disorder. *Community composition* refers to the kinds of people who live in a community. Intervention efforts that seek to alter the composition of communities include, for example, programs that open up opportunities for poor people living in inner-city ghettos to relocate to the suburbs.

Social structure refers to the interaction of people in communities and how they either increase or decrease capacities of local communities to control crime. Intervention efforts that aim to improve the social structures in communities include community mobilization programs (e.g., increasing voluntary association participation and membership) and efforts to help and reduce the number of single-headed households.

Oppositional culture refers to the rejection of mainstream economic and social life and the adoption of an oppositional identity with its own values and aspirations. The social institutions that are targeted to address the criminogenic conditions underpinning these oppositional cultures include labor markets, places, and communities. Crime prevention programs, such as efforts to increase the participation of "at-risk" young adults in mainstream jobs, figure prominently in this category.

Criminogenic commodities refer to those factors that facilitate crime conditions. Factors such as drug use, alcohol abuse, and gun ownership are typically identified as neighborhood "commodities" (or characteristics) that correlate highly with high rates of violence. Prevention programs such as drug and alcohol treatment and gun control programs comprise the types of interventions that seek to reduce criminogenic commodities.

Finally, Sherman (1997) refers to *social and physical disorder* as a key risk indicator that needs to be targeted within the auspices of community crime prevention. The "Broken Windows" thesis, as proposed by James Q. Wilson and George Kelling, provides the theoretical foundation for this aspect of community crime prevention. Wilson and Kelling suggest that neighborhoods exhibiting signs of social and physical decay send visual and social cues that nobody cares. These "signs of decline" may lead to an invasion of more serious crime problems (Wilson and Kelling, 1982). Public drunkenness, decayed buildings, and disorderly public behavior (such as playing loud radios in public places) are all examples of social and physical disorder. Prevention programs such as neighborhood clean-ups and enforcement of building code violations (see Mazerolle and Roehl, 1998) seek to reduce the signs of social and physical decay.

Situational crime prevention seeks to reduce opportunities for specific categories of crime by increasing the associated risks and difficulties and reducing the rewards (Clarke, 1995). Situational prevention comprises "measures directed at highly specific forms of crime that involve the management, design, or manipulation of the immediate environment in as systematic and permanent a way as possible so as to reduce the opportunities for crime and increase its risks as perceived by a wide range of offenders" (Clarke, 1983, 225).

This definition of situational crime prevention encompasses a wide range of techniques that aim to reduce the situational correlates that increase opportunities for crime problems.

Ronald Clarke (1992), as the principal author of the situational approach to crime prevention, identifies 12 main techniques for crime prevention. Four of these techniques are designed to reduce the rewards of crime and include target removal (e.g., removing car radios), identifying property (e.g., vehicle licensing), removing inducements (e.g., graffiti cleaning), and rule setting (e.g., hotel registration). Four techniques are designed to increase the efforts that potential offenders have to go through in order to commit a crime and include target hardening (e.g., steering column locks), access control (e.g., fenced yards), deflecting offenders (e.g., street closures), and controlling facilitators (e.g., gun control). Finally, four techniques are designed to increase the risks associated with committing a crime and include entry or exit screening (e.g., baggage screening), formal surveillance (e.g., burglar alarms), surveillance by employees (e.g., closed circuit television systems), and natural surveillance (e.g., neighborhood watch).

Ronald Clarke and Ross Homel (1997) have since suggested that the number of techniques of situational prevention can be expanded by including a set of situational approaches that remove excuses and thus reduce opportunities for crime. Examples of removing excuses include stimulating conscience (e.g., T.V. advertisements sending the message that drunk driving kills) and facilitating compliance (e.g., providing public transportation at bar closing hours).

Richard Tremblay and Wendy Craig (1995) define *Developmental crime prevention* as being based on the idea that criminal activity is determined by behavioral and attitudinal patterns that have been learned during an individual's development. Ross Homel and his Australian colleagues advocate a developmental approach to crime prevention and suggest that the approach "… involves intervention early in developmental pathways that lead to crime and substance abuse. It emphasises investment in 'child friendly' institutions and communities, and the manipulation of multiple risk and protective factors at crucial transition points, such as around birth, the preschool years, the transition from primary to high school, and the transition from high school to higher education or the workforce" (Homel et al, 1999, 10).

Early intervention programs that are theoretically linked to the developmental notion of crime prevention include programs that begin in infancy such as family support and early education. Preschool programs such as parent training, child skills training, and cognitive enrichment also fall under the umbrella of early intervention programs. Similarly, early primary years training such as programs that improve a child's problem-solving skills as well as programs that train parents and teachers to improve their behavior management skills are part of the array of early intervention programs that are theoretically linked to the field of developmental criminology.

Law enforcement is broadly defined by Michael Tonry and David Farrington (1995) as a crime prevention approach that operates directly through deterrence, incapacitation, and rehabilitation and indirectly through effects on socialization. Tonry and Farrington suggest that criminal laws can operate in an indirect manner when people refrain from illegal behavior simply because they have been socialized to respect and adhere to the law. They also suggest that the enforcement of criminal laws can have a direct preventive effect.

Much skepticism exists as to the direct preventive value of the criminal law and law enforcement. For example, preadjudication programs, such as mandatory arrest policies (in the Minneapolis Domestic Violence Experiment) that systematically remove and arrest domestic violence perpetrators at the scene of a domestic dispute have been found, under certain conditions, to directly prevent future domestic incidents. But replication studies of the original Minneapolis experiment were far less convincing of even the short-term benefits of mandatory arrest policies for domestic violence.

Social scientists are equally skeptical of the preventive effects of incapacitation programs such as three-strike laws (automatic imprisonment for repeat violent offenders), selective incapacitation policies (automatic prison sentences for offenders identified as being statistical risks for future offending), and rehabilitative efforts that are, for example, mandated through prison or community correction programs.

Social scientists often claim that law enforcement (in the broadest sense of deterrence, incapacitation, and rehabilitation) can make only minimal contributions to crime prevention. Indeed, two famous criminologists, Michael Gottfredson and Travis Hirschi, commentating on the role of the police in crime prevention, conclude that "… no evidence exists that augmentation of police forces or equipment, differential police strategies, or differential intensities of surveillance have an effect on crime rates" (Gottfredson and Hirschi, 1990, 270). However, there is a growing literature that suggests that there are, in fact, some direct preventive benefits of law enforcement.

The following section explores what works in preventing crime. What we know works in preventing crime is categorized around the four strategic approaches: law enforcement, community, situational, and developmental.

What Works in Preventing Crime

The breadth of crime prevention interventions and the vast literature (some good, some not-so-good) surrounding evaluations of various local, state, and federal crime prevention programs make the synthesis of what works in preventing crime a daunting task. Two government mandated reports, one in the U.S. and one in Australia, attempted to synthesize the extant literature on what works in crime prevention. In the U.S., the report is titled *Preventing crime: What works, what doesn't and what's promising* and written by Lawrence Sherman and his University of Maryland colleagues (Sherman et al. 1997). In Australia, the report is titled *Pathways to prevention* by Ross Homel of Griffith University and his colleagues (Homel et al., 1999) from various government and university departments across the country. These two reports summarize what we know works in preventing crime and they provide recommendations for the future. Below is a synopsis of some of the most important, successful and scientifically evaluated crime prevention programs.

Law Enforcement

Skeptics traditionally doubt the crime prevention outcomes of programs that revolve around law enforcement. In recent years, however, there has been a growing body of scientific evidence that suggests that some law enforcement programs can, indeed, prevent crime.

Growing scientific evidence documents the success of some policing programs and their ability to prevent and reduce crime problems. In particular, increased directed patrols and problem-oriented policing in street corner hotspots of crime, proactive arrests of serious repeat offenders, proactive drunk-driving arrests, and arrests of employed suspects for domestic assaults are identified as law enforcement programs that work.

Despite a long history lamenting that "nothing works" in terms of rehabilitation, we now have substantial evidence that shows that rehabilitation programs, under certain circumstances, do indeed work in preventing crime. Rehabilitation programs that seek to change offender propensities to commit crimes in the future and rehabilitation programs with specified, particular and highly focused characteristics can prevent future involvement in crime. We also know that prison-based, therapeutic, and community treatment of drug-involved offenders prevents future offending and that incapacitating offenders who continue to commit crimes at high rates has been found, under certain conditions, to be an effective crime prevention strategy.

Substantial research has demonstrated the value of rehabilitation programs as a crime prevention strategy. Doris Layton MacKenzie, in her chapter in *Preventing crime: What works, what doesn't and what's promising* (Sherman et al., 1997) reveals that effective rehabilitation programs tend to be structured and focused, using multiple treatment components that focus on developing skills and use behavioral modification methods. Moreover, MacKenzie concludes that effective rehabilitation programs provide for substantial, meaningful contact between the treatment personnel and the participant.

Community Crime Prevention

Community crime prevention is an amorphous concept covering decades of research and a vast array of programs that one could categorize as "community-based." Programs such as neighborhood watches, gun buy-back programs, recreation programs, and community mobilization programs feature in this crime prevention category.

The most effective community-oriented prevention programs tend to be school-based intervention programs. Denise Gottfredson, in her chapter in *Preventing crime: What works, what doesn't and what's promising* (Sherman et al., 1997) concludes that the following programs have scientific evidence to support their success as crime prevention initiatives: programs aimed at building school capacity to initiate and sustain innovation; programs aimed at clarifying and communicating norms about behaviors by establishing school rules, improving consistency of their enforcement, and communicating norms through school-wide campaigns or ceremonies; and comprehensive instructional programs that focus on a range of social competency skills and that are delivered over a long period of time to continually reinforce skills.

From a labor market perspective, Shawn Bushway and Peter Reuter in their chapter in Preventing crime: *What works, what doesn't and what's promising* (Sherman et al., 1997) conclude that short-term vocational training programs for older male exoffenders no longer involved in the criminal justice system is an effective community-based crime prevention initiative.

Finally, traditionally-oriented community-based crime prevention programs that have some promise include gang violence prevention programs as well as volunteer mentoring programs that focus on reducing substance abuse. Big Brothers and Big Sisters Programs have been identified by Lawrence Sherman (Sherman et al., 1997) as being a volunteer mentoring program with the most promise.

Situational Crime Prevention

Situational crime prevention and the police management approach that uses much of the techniques of situational prevention, namely problem-oriented policing, are relatively new approaches to crime prevention. Perhaps for this reason, the scientific evidence about what works in this area of crime prevention is especially weak. Nonetheless, John Eck, in his chapter in *Preventing crime: What works, what doesn't and what's promising* (Sherman et al., 1997) identifies several situational and problem-oriented policing approaches to crime prevention that work. Nuisance abatement to control drug dealing and related crime at private rental places is the intervention program that has the most scientific evidence to conclude that it is a worthwhile crime prevention strategy (see also Mazerolle and Roehl, 1998).

Although John Eck laments the lack of scientific rigor within the situational crime prevention literature, he concludes that there are generally positive indications that blocking opportunities at places has much promise. He also suggests that metal detectors for entry or exit screening and street closures are two situational measures that are promising types of intervention tactics.

Developmental Crime Prevention

Ross Homel, Lawrence Sherman and their colleagues (Homel et al., 1999) identify a number of prevention programs within the developmental category of crime prevention that have scientific evidence to document their success. Of most note are long-term frequent home visitation programs that are combined with preschool programs, infant weekly home visitation programs, and family therapy by clinical staff for delinquent and predelinquent youth.

LORRAINE GREEN MAZEROLLE

References and Further Reading

Clarke, R.V. Situational crime prevention: Its theoretical basis and practical scope. Tonry, M. and Morris, N. (Eds.) *Crime and Justice: A Review of Research.* Vol. 4. Chicago and London, University of Chicago Press, pp. 225–256. 1983.

Clarke, R.V.(Ed.) *Situational Crime Prevention: Successful Case Studies.* Harrow and Heston, New York, 1992.

Clarke, R.V. Situational crime prevention. Tonry, M. and Farrington, D. (Eds.) *Building a Safer Society: Strategic Approaches to Crime Prevention*, Vol. 19. Crime and Justice: A Review of Research. Chicago and London, University of Chicago Press, pp. 91–150. 1995.

Clarke, R. and Homel, R. A revised classification of situational crime prevention techniques. In *Crime Prevention at a Crossroads.* Edited by Steve Lab, Cincinnati, OH: Anderson Publishing Co. and Academy of Criminal Justice Sciences, pp. 17–30, 1997.

Gottfredson, M. and Hirschi, T. *A General Theory of Crime.* Stanford, CA: Stanford University Press, 1990.

Homel, R. and others, *Pathways to Prevention: Developmental and Early Intervention Approaches to Crime in Australia*, National Crime Prevention, Canberra, Australia, 1999.

Hope, T., Community crime prevention. Tonry, M. and Farrington, D. (Eds.) *Building a Safer Society: Strategic Approaches to Crime Prevention*, Vol. 19. Crime and Justice: A Review of Research. Chicago and London, University of Chicago Press, pp. 21–90. 1995.

Last, J., Scope and methods of prevention. In *Public Health and Preventive Medicine*, 11th ed., Last, J.M. (Ed.) New York, NY: Appelton-Century-Crofts.

Mazerolle, L.G. and Roehl, J. (Eds.) *Civil Remedies and Crime Prevention.* Crime Prevention Studies, Vol. 9. Criminal Justice Press, Monsey, NY. 1998.

Moore, M.H. Public health and criminal justice approaches to prevention. Tonry, M. and Farrington, D. *Building a Safer Society: Strategic Approaches to Crime Prevention*, Vol. 19. Crime and Justice: A Review of Research. Chicago and London, University of Chicago Press, pp. 237–262. 1995.

Sherman, L., Gottfredson, D., MacKenzie, D., Eck, J., Reuter, P. and Bushway, S. *Preventing Crime: What Works, What Doesn't and What's Promising*, University of Maryland, College Park, MD, 1997.

Tonry, M. and Farrington, D. *Building a Safer Society: Strategic Approaches to Crime Prevention*, Vol. 19. Crime and Justice: A Review of Research. Chicago and London, University of Chicago Press. 1995.

Tremblay, R. and Craig, W.M. Developmental crime prevention. Tonry, M. and Farrington, D. (Eds.) *Building a Safer Society: Strategic Approaches to Crime Prevention*, Vol. 19. Crime and Justice: A Review of Research. Chicago and London, University of Chicago Press, pp. 151–236. 1995.

Wilson, J.Q. and Kelling, G. Broken windows: The police and neighborhood safety. *The Atlantic* 249, 29–38, 1982 (March).

See also **Crime Mapping; Farrington, David P.; Gangs: Enforcement, Intervention, and Prevention Strategies; Law Enforcement; Police: Patrol; Police: Private Security Forces**

Criminal Anthropology

For centuries, man has studied man. The science of anthropology has shaped understanding of human beings. Anthropological research has resulted in great strides in such fields of study as history, biology, medicine, and culture. With the vast amount of knowledge attainable from anthropological studies, it is not unexpected that the science has also been used to understand human behavior. Social scientists, psychologists, researchers, and society in general have offered theories to explain deviant behavior. Prior to and through the first half of the 19th century, explanations of criminal or deviant human behavior were based on spiritual and biological rationales; however, Italian professor and physician Cesare Lombroso introduced an anthropological perspective on the matter in 1876 with his manuscript *L'Uomo Delinquente* ("The Criminal Man"). Lombroso's theory became known as *criminal anthropology.*

Lombroso is considered the father of criminology, particularly in relation to positivistic theories. He expanded the theories of physiognomy (determining individual character from physical appearance) and phrenology (determining individual character from distinctiveness of skull features) that were given credence in early 19th century social science. In his early studies, Lombroso added psychology and Darwinism to explain the phenomenon of a "born criminal."

While performing an autopsy on a known thief, Lombroso identified what he termed a *median occipital fossa*, a depression on the portion of the skull where the spine adjoins. Lombroso recognized this distinctive characteristic as being similar to that found in rodents and other inferior animals. Realizing that animalistic nature steals, injures, and kills for protection and survival, Lombroso theorized that those individuals who are deviant have specific characteristics transferred genetically through human evolution. In essence, criminal or deviant behavior is a throw-back or atavistic to more primitive ancestors.

Upon his initial discovery, Lombroso performed numerous autopsies on known criminals and identified a significant amount of shared characteristics with primitive man. Characteristics such as skull size, ear size and position on the head, chin shape, wrinkles, amount of hair, length of extremities, brain symmetry, and even tattoos were studied and compared to the same characteristics of primates. Lombroso furthered his studies by analyzing characteristics of known living criminals and noncriminals as well as the mentally disabled, termed "lunatics." Lombroso found that among his study subjects, the known criminals exhibited more distinctive physical and behavioral ape-like characteristics. Lombroso conducted extensive work in the European penal system and relying on his atavistic theory persuaded penitentiary officials to alter sentencing rules so that punishments would fit the criminal, rather than the crime. Lombroso asserted that born criminals could not be rehabilitated under any conditions and were best served by lifelong incarceration. He supported this argument with recidivism rates of those determined to be born criminals.

Lombroso planned to employ impartial researchers to test his theory using 300 study subjects divided into three categories, "born criminals," individuals with criminal tendencies, and noncriminals with no criminal tendencies, stressing that criminals would exhibit some irregularity, or "stigmata," when compared to noncriminals. Although this initiative was not carried out, Lombroso stood by his ideals and further suggested that in any society there exists a small group whose heredity is more closely related to human primitive ancestors than the majority. Subsequently, such a group's members will exhibit more primitive, or apish, behaviors (i.e., criminal or deviant behaviors).

Throughout his career, Lombroso continued to study the links binding psychology and anthropology to criminal behavior. He did begin accepting environmental factors as causation later in his career, but asserted the existence of only three types of criminals expressed as *born criminals*, *insane criminals*, and *criminaloids*. The born criminals were those who reflected Lombroso's earlier studies. They were born with a predisposition to commit crime and were, as Lombroso described, atavistic. Insane criminals exhibited deviant behavior as a result of mental illness, which at the time included alcoholism, epilepsy, schizophrenia, and the like. Lombroso described the majority of criminals as criminaloids. He explained that these are born with the predispositional tendency to commit criminal or deviant acts, but the tendencies are repressed until an environmental factor, such as climate, finances, or relationships, gives rise to manifestation of the tendency.

The theory that criminality and deviance is a direct result of anthropological features and that criminals are born immediately became a target of critics, researchers, and scientists in the late 1800s. Although criminal anthropology is still not widely accepted as a plausible explanation of criminal or deviant behavior, Cesare Lombroso's work began a renaissance of social science and psychological research geared toward criminology. The introduction of criminal anthropology began the positivist criminology movement that continues to vie with classical criminology today. Despite the lack of acceptance of criminal anthropology, the idea of incorporating the discipline of anthropology in the criminal justice arena has continued, particularly with regard to forensic investigations.

Forensic anthropology is the analysis of skeletal and human remains to determine identity and assisting pathologists with concluding causes of death. The science of forensic anthropology is a growing field of study made popular and enhanced by the research of Dr. William Bass, Professor Emeritus of the University of Tennessee, via his establishment and caretaking of the controversial "Body Farm." As a result of Dr. Bass' extensive research of human and skeletal remains, forensic anthropology has become an invaluable tool for criminal justice professionals.

M. Patrick Long

References and Further Reading

Bass, B. and Jefferson, J. (2003). *Death's Acre: Inside the Legendary Forensic Lab; the Body Farm; Where the Dead Do Tell Tales*. G.P. Putnam's Sons: New York, NY.

Broeckmann, A. (revised, 1996, 1995). Criminal anthropology: A semiology of indexicality in *A Visual Economy of Individuals: The Use of Portrait Photography in the Nineteenth-Century Human Sciences*. Chapter 4, PhD thesis for University of East Anglia: Norwich, England. Available at http://www.v2.nl/abroeck/phd.

Gould, S.J. (March, 1976). Criminal man revived. *Natural History*, 85 (3), 16.

Hibbert, C. (2003, 1963). *The Roots of Evil: A Social History of Crime and Punishment*. Sutton Publishing: Phoenix Mill, United Kingdom.

Johnson, H.A. (1990). *History of Criminal Justice*. Anderson Publishing Co.: New York, NY.

Vold, G.B., Bernard, T.J., and Snipes, J.B. (1998). *Theoretical Criminology*, 4th ed. Oxford University Press: New York, NY.

See also **Body-Type Theories of Criminal Behavior; Lombroso, Cesare**

Criminal Careers and Chronic Offenders

Brief History of Criminal Careers

A criminal career is defined as the characterization of the longitudinal sequence of crimes committed by an individual offender (Blumstein et al., 1986, 12). Among offenders, criminal careers can vary substantially. For example, at one extreme some offenders' careers may consist of only one offense, whereas at another extreme some offenders' careers may consist of numerous crimes such that these offenders are considered career or chronic offenders. It is this latter group of individuals who tend to commit serious offenses with high frequency over extended periods of time (Blumstein et al., 1986, 14). Given the frequency of crime among these chronic offenders, it is little surprise that early identification of these offenders in their criminal career has spurred policies of selective incapacitation.

The study of criminal careers and career criminals has been the focus of social science research for over a century. For example, early research on criminal careers started with classic case studies and life histories of individual offenders. One prominent example is Shaw's (1930) *The Jack Roller*. This autobiographical account of a delinquent's experiences, influences, attitudes, and values spearheaded a research agenda that influenced an entire generation of research into criminal careers and career criminals.

One prominent example of early, quantitative research on criminal careers was undertaken by Sheldon and Eleanor Glueck. These authors studied criminal career patterns in the state of Massachusetts. Their major studies focused on the causes of juvenile delinquency and adult crime, as well as assessing the effectiveness of correctional treatment in controlling the future course of criminal behavior. Their most prominent contribution to criminal career literature came with the publication of *Unraveling Juvenile Delinquency* (1950).

This project compared 500 persistent delinquents from two correctional schools in Massachusetts to 500 nondelinquents chosen from the Boston public schools. The two groups were matched case by case on age, race or ethnicity (birthplace of both parents), neighborhood, and measured intelligence. Criminal activity comparisons across the groups were conducted by the Gluecks at ages 25 and 32, and follow-up criminal activity information has been collected and analyzed by Robert Sampson and John Laub (1993) and subsequently published in *Crime in the Making*.

In what has been described as one of the key "turning points in criminological research in the United States" (Morris, 1972, vii), Marvin Wolfgang, Robert Figlio, and Thorsten Sellin (1972) studied the arrest histories of a birth cohort of 9945 Philadelphia males from birth through age 17. Their findings, published as *Delinquency in a Birth Cohort*, yielded several important findings. First, they uncovered that a substantial fraction of the cohort had been arrested at least once; however, most were not arrested again. Second, a small subset of the cohort was arrested numerous times. These "chronic offenders," representing about 6% of the cohort, were responsible for over 50% of the criminal arrests of the cohort by age 17.

The findings of this study led to a number of replication efforts both in the U.S. and abroad, including a second Philadelphia birth cohort study that included females (Tracy et al., 1990). For example, longitudinal studies of criminal careers have been carried out in London, Stockholm, New Zealand, Finland, Denmark, and Puerto Rico, as well as several U.S. cities including Pittsburgh, Rochester, Denver, and Providence. Researchers have documented findings from these studies in great detail, and much quantitative information has been learned regarding criminal careers.

The Criminal Careers Report

The single most influential summary report on criminal careers and career criminals was published by the National Academy of Sciences as *Criminal Careers and "Career Criminals"* in 1986 (Blumstein et al.). This two-volume publication presented a thorough review of the knowledge based on criminal career patterns and also shaped the ensuing research agenda for the remainder of the 20th century. The authors of this report reviewed the literature on several criminal career topics including participation in criminal careers, dimensions of active criminal careers, methodological issues in criminal career research, crime control strategies using criminal career knowledge, and the use of criminal career information in criminal justice decision making.

In this report Blumstein and his colleagues (1986, 1) partitioned aggregate rates of criminal activity into two components: the percentage of the population that commits crime and the nature and extent of activity of those people who are actively engaging in crime (i.e., active offenders). This distinction is important because the first component, participation, is associated with efforts to prevent individuals from ever becoming involved in criminal behavior in the first place, whereas the second component, encompassing frequency, seriousness, and career length, is central to the decisions of the criminal justice system. Frequency is defined as the rate of criminal activity among those offenders who are active. Seriousness refers to the gravity of the offenses committed. And career length refers to the length of time an offender is active, fully recognizing that there could be intermittence throughout one's offending career. That is, there could be several starts and stops over the course of one's criminal career.

Research on Criminal Careers

The criminal career volume established a research agenda that held several key assumptions. One critical assumption made by the authors concerned their argument that frequency, seriousness, and the length of the criminal career varied across offenders. The implication of this argument is such that the offending patterns of different individuals varied from one another. Therefore, different theoretical explanations and policy responses would have to be developed to fully account for the wide variation of criminal careers evidenced among the offending population.

Several scholars have deemed this and other predictions made by Blumstein et al. worth pursuing. Researchers have asked (1) if all criminal careers traverse a similar trajectory, or if there are different types of criminal careers, (2) if criminals specialize in the kinds of crimes they engage in over their careers, (3) if an early age of arrest distinguishes chronic offenders, (4) if desistance is abrupt or resembles a glide path, (5) if the correlates of one criminal career dimension are similar to the other criminal career dimensions, and so on.

Evidence on these and other fronts is slowly emerging, and several tentative conclusions can be reached. For example, researchers have discovered that the factors that predict initiation into criminal behavior are not necessarily the same as the factors that predict persistence in—and desistance from—criminal behavior. Other researchers have found that the factors predicting an early onset of offending vary from the factors that predict late onset of offending. Finally, researchers have uncovered that criminal careers are not marked by specialization in offending; that is, the criminal career of active offenders evidences a wide array of different types of offenses. At the same time, some scholars have even argued that the commission of a violent offense throughout the course of one's criminal career is random and that violence is primarily a function of increasing frequency. That is, frequent offenders tend to incur violent offenses more so than less-frequent offenders.

Amid this evidence, perhaps one finding that all scholars recognize, albeit for different reasons, is the observation that offenders are likely to be heterogeneous in their propensity to violate the law. Researchers have discovered that the arrest rates (lambdas) of offenders vary both within offenders over time and across offenders at the same and other times. Thus, scholars have recognized the need to account for the wide-ranging arrest rates of offenders. Daniel Nagin and Kenneth Land (1993) have developed a sophisticated statistical model that takes into account the heterogeneity of offense rates and models this criminal propensity in a discrete form. Their statistical model has led to major insights into criminal careers and career criminals.

Challenges to the Criminal Careers Concept

The criminal careers report, and all that emanates from it, has been controversial. At its core, the criminal careers paradigm is built around certain concepts, specifying a particular research agenda and establishing criteria for assessing the value and validity of empirical research (Greenberg, 1996). Sociologists Travis Hirschi and Michael Gottfredson have rejected the criminal careers concept, going so far as to suggest that employing longitudinal data to study criminal careers would be a waste of precious financial resources and that the findings from longitudinal data would not be an improvement over the findings from cross-sectional data. Their point is embodied in an article they published in 1986: "The true value of lambda would appear to be zero."

At the core of this debate is the relationship between age and crime, one that is fundamental to the criminal careers paradigm. Hirschi and Gottfredson contend that the (aggregate) age-crime relationship is roughly the same for all offenders at all times and places. Moreover, they argue that the relationship is largely unaffected by life events. Finally, although they believe that some offenders offend at higher rates than other offenders, they claim that attempts to identify chronic offenders have failed, therefore implying that differences among offenders are more distinctions in degree than kind; that is, there are not different types of offenders, just different degrees of offenders with some offenders having a higher offense rate than other offenders. As can be seen, Hirschi and Gottfredson claim that neither the criminal careers agenda nor longitudinal research has much to offer criminological theory or public policy.

Another key point of contention between criminal careers supporters and opponents concerns the idea of selective incapacitation. The essence of selective incapacitation is the correct identification and isolation of the small group of high-rate offenders early in their criminal careers in order to prevent their future criminal acts. According to Blumstein, Cohen, and Farrington (1988), there is an obvious benefit in focusing imprisonment on offenders with the highest offending rates at any time: it would lead to a large crime reduction per prisoner. Gottfredson and Hirschi (1986, 217) claim that the identification of such chronic offenders does not occur until that offender is "on the verge of retirement." Therefore, at the point in time when a criminal career is peaking (late teens), Gottfredson and Hirschi claim that the (aggregate) offense rates of such individuals begin a precipitous decline toward zero.

Blumstein and colleagues agree with Gottfredson and Hirschi that if lambda were to decrease with age, then it would pose important problems for a policy of selective incapacitation. On the one hand, Gottfredson and Hirschi claim that lambda declines after the peak age; yet on the other hand, Blumstein et al. claim that the decline in the aggregate offense rate after a teenage peak does not require that individual lambdas follow a similar pattern, and this is precisely the issue under the selective incapacitation argument.

The answer to this question is decidedly important for matters of both theory and policy. To date, the evidence is mounting that although aggregate offense rates rise during adolescence and peak in the late teenage years, individual lambdas do not necessarily follow this progression. In fact, there is a substantial amount of lambda heterogeneity among offender populations such that aggregate age or crime depictions hide the wide variation of offense rates among offenders (Nagin and Land, 1993). And although most offenders trend toward desistance as adulthood ensues, small subgroups of criminal offenders continue to offend at exceedingly high rates of criminal activity (Piquero et al., 2001). These findings have led to major insight into criminal careers that would likely not have materialized had it not been for the methodological advances put forth in the 1990s.

Policy Implications of the Criminal Careers Concept

The dimensions outlined by the criminal careers paradigm necessitate dimension-specific policy responses. For example, one of the key dimensions refers to participation. Knowledge of the factors that influence an individual's decision to participate in criminal behavior could aid the development of prevention techniques in early childhood. Similarly, knowledge on the correlates of persistence could assist scholars and policy officials to better develop intervention approaches, which could be used to alter the course of a criminal career. Finally, further study into the reasons why offenders temper their offending rates over their careers as well as study into the factors that correlate with an exit out of criminal careers is important for policy officials in their effort to thwart lengthy criminal careers.

Although not anticipated by criminal careers supporters, one recent policy response to chronic offenders is the development of "three-strikes" crime control policies. At their core, these policies recommend a lengthy prison term (upward of 25 years) for an offender's third felony. Aimed at incapacitating chronic offenders, these policies have been subject to lengthy debate, and research on the effectiveness of such policies will take time to materialize. At present, two studies have questioned the usefulness of three-strike policies. Schmertmann and his colleagues (1998) conducted a simulation study where they examined the long-term financial and bed-space implications of a three-strike policy. Their analysis indicated that the financial costs of such policies would be extremely large because of the "graying" of the prison population, and the resultant health care costs, and these significant costs would come at the price of not-so-significant decreases in criminal activity. Toward that end, Piquero et al.'s (2001) study of high-risk parolees from the California Youth Authority indicated that by age 30, most offenders had exhibited very small arrest rates, although there was a group of offenders who continued to offend at high rates; but even their arrest rates were on a downward trajectory.

Future Direction for Research on Criminal Careers

Knowledge on criminal careers continues to push forward. Future studies will likely focus on six key areas for which little information is currently available. The first concerns subgroup differences on criminal career dimensions. For example, little research has been conducted in an effort to compare the extent to which whites and nonwhites resemble (or differ from) one another on the various criminal career dimensions of participation, frequency, specialization, persistence, and career length. Moreover, we continue to have very little quantitative information about the criminal career patterns of female offenders. This avenue of research has much to offer matters of theory as well as policy.

A second area of future research concerns the criminal career dimension of desistance. Research on career length has been slow to materialize because it virtually requires scholars to follow offenders until their death to ensure that their criminal career is really over. A recent methodological development by Bushway et al. (2001) may help researchers overcome this limitation. These scholars advance a statistical approach that can help scholars study desistance without following offenders until death. Knowledge on career length also has direct implications for the age or crime debate as well as policy proscriptions of selective incapacitation and three strikes. Information on the length of criminal careers could seriously undermine these policies, which are based on the assumption that criminal careers are lengthy.

A third and related future research direction lies in the study of intermittence. Perilously little is known about the various stops and starts criminal offenders evidence throughout their criminal careers, and extant theory has been slow to develop accounts as to why offenders stop for certain periods of time and then why these same offenders resume their criminal activity.

A fourth important area for future research efforts is the comparison of self-report and official records as measurements of criminal career dimensions. Much of the early research on criminal careers was carried out with official records. Given the limitations with this measurement strategy, researchers have recently incorporated self-report protocols into their analytic strategies, and some interesting insights have been uncovered. For example, Nagin and his colleagues (1995) found that although offenders appeared to have refrained from criminal activity, at least as measured by conviction records, self-report surveys indicated continued criminal involvement in less detectable offenses. Future studies will likely employ both measures simultaneously to determine similarities and differences in criminal career dimensions.

A fifth research direction concerns the extent to which contextual characteristics influence various criminal career dimensions. Much like the early life history criminal career research, several recent theoretical expositions anticipate contextual influences on criminal career dimensions, especially those related to onset and persistence. Primarily as a function of increased cost, research efforts have been slow to collect the sorts of contextual information necessary for an application to criminal career dimensions. Future studies will likely collect this information to examine how contextual and individual risk factors influence the various criminal career dimensions. Two recent efforts by Lynam and his colleagues (2001) and Piquero and Lawton (2001) suggest that this contextual or individual approach will provide important information.

The final research direction concerns the integration of quantitative information on criminal careers with qualitative information from offenders throughout the course of their lives. Although extremely costly, the integration of qualitative data has helped researchers unpack the meaning of life events. As such, researchers have been better able to understand exactly why certain life events matter more than others in their relation to desistance from criminal offending. Research by Laub and Sampson (1999) has led this quantitative or qualitative integration, and continued efforts in this area appear likely.

The nature of the criminal careers paradigm is such that it invites the application of dynamic, or life-course, theories to account for the developmental aspects of key criminal career dimensions. These theories anticipate different types of criminal offenders, each of whom has a separate etiology and evidences distinct patterns of criminal offending. Future research efforts will likely test these theoretical accounts with sophisticated methodological tools to better understand patterns of criminal careers.

Alex R. Piquero

References and Further Reading

Blumstein, A., et al., Eds., *Criminal Careers and "Career Criminals,"* 2 Vols., Washington, DC: National Academy Press, 1986.

Blumstein, A., Cohen, J., and Farrington, D.P., Criminal career research: Its value for criminology, *Criminology* 26 (1998).

Bushway, S., et al., A developmental framework for empirical research on desistance, *Criminology* 39 (2001).

Gottfredson, M.R. and Hirschi, T., The true value of lambda would appear to be zero: An essay on career criminals, criminal careers, selective incapacitation, cohort studies, and related topics, *Criminology* 24 (1986).

Greenberg, D.F., *Introduction in Criminal Careers,* Vol. 1, Greenberg, D.F., Ed., Aldershot, Hampshire, and Brookfield, Vermont: Dartmouth, 1996.

Laub, J.H. and Sampson, R.J., Integrating quantitative and qualitative data, in *Methods of Life Course Research: Qualitative and Quantitative Approaches,* Giele, J.Z. and Elder, G.H., Jr., Eds., Thousand Oaks, CA: Sage, 1998.

Lynam, D., et al., The interaction between impulsivity and neighborhood context on offending: The effects of impulsivity are stronger in poorer neighborhoods, *Journal of Abnormal Psychology* 109 (2001).

Nagin, D.S. and Land, K., Age, criminal careers, and population heterogeneity: Specification and estimation of a nonparametric, mixed Poisson Model, *Criminology* 31(1993).

Nagin, D.S., Farrington, D.P., and Moffitt, T.E., Life-course trajectories of different types of offenders, *Criminology* 33 (1995).

Piquero, A.R. and Lawton, B., Person-environment interactions explain criminal offending in adulthood, in *Advances in Life-Course Research: New Frontiers in Socialization*, Settersten, R. (Ed.) New York, NY: JAI Press, 2001.

Piquero, A.R., et al., Assessing the impact of exposure time and incapacitation on longitudinal trajectories of criminal offending, *Journal of Adolescent Research* 16 (2001).

Sampson, R.J. and Laub, J.H., *Crime in the Making: Pathways and Turning Points through Life*, Cambridge, MA: Harvard University Press, 1993.

Schmertmann, C.P., Amankwaa, A.A., and Long, R.D., Three strikes and you're out: Demographic analysis of mandatory prison sentencing, *Demography* 35, 4 (November 1998).

Shaw, C.R., *The Jack-Roller: A Delinquent Boy's Own Story*, Chicago, IL: University of Chicago Press, 1930; reprint, with a new introduction, 1966.

Tracy, P.E., Wolfgang, M.E., and Figlio, R.M. *Delinquency Careers in Two Birth Cohorts*, New York, NY: Plenum Press, 1990.

Wolfgang, M.E., Figlio, R.M., and Sellin, T., *Delinquency in a Birth Cohort*, Chicago, IL: University of Chicago Press, 1972.

See also **Burglary as an Occupation; Drug Trafficking as an Occupation; Prostitution as an Occupation; Recidivism; Robbery as an Occupation; Theft, Professional**

Criminal Courts: Administration and Organization

The criminal courts have steadily evolved over America's history, from a general system with poorly trained lawyers in the prerevolution era, to the highly complex and specialized system that exists today. Indeed, today's system involves a number of key actors and it makes an effort to combine ideas of due process with crime control, as well as deterrence with rehabilitation. Attempts to satisfy both of these initiatives present great challenges for the court system in America today, challenges that will continue to shape the very nature of the courts.

The origins of America's court system are found in the American colonies of the 17th and 18th centuries, and as expected, they were strongly influenced by

England's court system. Today, America's criminal court system has developed into its own unique system and is broken down into two main subsystems: state and federal courts (Schmalleger, 1991). This dual court system developed in congruence with the ideas of limited federal intervention into state governmental affairs. Thus, each state developed with a number of state and federal courts, each serving a separate function.

State courts today are typically broken down within local county or district courts that have jurisdiction over specific areas of the state (Gaines, Kaune, and Miller, 2000). Appeals courts and the State Supreme Courts have further authority over the proceedings within the district or county courts, only superseded by the U.S. Supreme Court. State courts can be additionally categorized into courts of limited jurisdiction and courts of general jurisdiction. Although courts of limited jurisdiction typically hear less serious misdemeanor and traffic and small claims cases, courts of general jurisdiction can hear any state criminal case and are much more likely to involve jury trials and appeals (Schmalleger, 1991).

The federal court system has also developed substantially since its initial setup during America's independence. As with the state system, the federal system comprises district, appeals, and a Supreme Court (Weston and Wells, 1987). District courts try all cases in the federal system and have jurisdiction over all federal criminal cases. Although federal appeals courts are generally first in line to review appeals of decisions from lower courts, the U.S. Supreme Court has the ultimate ruling authority on such appeals. The Supreme Court may also review decisions of State Supreme Courts (Weston and Wells, 1987).

In both the local state courts and federal district courts, there are similar members of the courtroom work group. The main staff members in the courts are judges, prosecutors, and defense attorneys (Weston and Wells, 1987). Although police are at the center of the criminal justice system in the U.S., they have played a diminished role in the court process in comparison to many other countries (Fairchild and Dammer, 2001). For instance, it was not until 1985 that England transferred responsibility of prosecuting cases away from the police to independent prosecutors (Fairchild and Dammer, 2001). Although this separation between police and prosecution of cases has been established for the sake of greater impartiality in the court system, the drawback is the lack of coordination between the two agencies (police and prosecution).

Although most U.S. federal district courts share the same stages in processing criminals, there are differences among the steps found across the state courts. The differences are somewhat minimal, however, and all courts include pretrial functions, trial stages, and the sentencing phase. The initial role of the court comes through either a magistrate's review, whereby a judge reviews the validity of the arrest, or at the first appearance. According to *McNabb v. U.S.* (318 U.S. 332, 1943), all defendants in the U.S. must be brought before a magistrate within 48 hours of arrest and apprised of the charges on which they are being held.

One important element of a first appearance in most states is the bail hearing. Depending on the severity of the offense, the likelihood of appearance at trial, and other characteristics, the judge sets a bail amount on the defendant. Defendants can either post the full amount of bail set by the court or seek bail through a professional bail bondsman who will charge them a percentage (usually 10% or 15%) of the bail. Perhaps the most troubling aspect of bail comes in the potential hardship on indigent offenders who cannot afford to free themselves before trial (Weston and Wells, 1987). The ultimate fear would be an increased likelihood of a guilty plea by defendants facing the dilemma of time spent in jail awaiting trial, versus going ahead and pleading to an offense that will only result in probation or an intermediate sanction.

During the entire court process and up to the verdict, the defense and prosecution have the opportunity to agree on a guilty plea. Although a great deal of attention in popular culture, documentaries, and criminal justice textbooks is placed on the trial process, the plea bargain is the reality for most criminal justice cases (Acevedo, 1999). In fact, a plea results in about 90% of all criminal prosecutions in the U.S. today (Gaines et. al., 2000).

The plea can have mutual benefits to each side, as a defendant who is afraid of the trial outcome can plead to a lesser charge and escape the harsher punishment associated with a trial conviction, and the prosecution can secure punishment for the defendant without risking a trial verdict (Weston and Wells, 1987). The main criticism of plea-bargaining is that it may encourage innocent defendants to plead guilty to a crime they did not commit (Acevedo, 1999). Moreover, even guilty defendants are not ultimately convicted of the crime that they committed, removing this version of justice from the vision contemplated by the founding fathers (Acevedo, 1999).

Plea-bargaining is considered by many to be a necessary evil within the court process, as it allows the large volume of cases to be processed within a realistic timeframe. Indeed, several states and jurisdictions have attempted bans or limitations on plea-bargaining, including Alaska, El Paso County in Texas, and Bronx County in New York (Acevedo, 1999; Carns and Kruse, 1992; Weninger, 1987). These experiments ultimately ended in prosecutors with overly large caseloads, overwhelmed public defenders, and lenient sentences and increased dismissals by judges as a response (Acevedo, 1999: Carns and Kruse, 1992; Weninger, 1987). These findings, as well as court rulings stating that plea-bargaining is constitutional (*U.S. v. Goodwin* 457 U.S. 268, 278, 1982) and essential (*Santobello v. New York*, 404 U.S. 257, 260, 1971), suggest that plea-bargaining will be a reality of the court system in the U.S. for years to come.

If a plea-agreement is not made early within the court process, and if the case is serious enough, the defendant may either be provided a preliminary hearing or a grand jury hearing. Which one of these hearings the defendant receives depends upon the state in which the defendant is tried, and whether it is a federal charge or state charge. In the U.S., the federal government and about half of the states use grand jury hearings, which are more secretive and provide the defendant fewer rights than preliminary hearings (Weston and Wells, 1987). A judge makes the decision in the preliminary hearing, whereas a group of citizens (usually 23) decides the indictment hearing. Both hearings are used to determine whether there is enough evidence to proceed with the prosecution of the defendant (Weston and Wells, 1987).

Once the defendant has been arraigned on charges, the possibility of a trial becomes more likely. Although a plea-bargain can be made up until the trial verdict is given, the more time and resources that prosecutors place into a case, the more likely that the plea offer will not be as desirable for the defense. Of course, this may depend somewhat on the strength of the case and whether there is any public pressure placed upon the prosecution for a trial.

If the defendant decides to plead guilty, it is typically a guilty or *nolo contendere* plea. The *nolo contendere* plea requires the permission of the court and prosecution, and it has the same legal effect as the guilty plea (Weston and Wells, 1987). However, this plea cannot be used against the defendant in any future civil proceedings (Weston and Wells, 1987).

If the defendant pleads not guilty to the charges and the case progresses to the trial date, then a jury is selected through a process called *voir dire*. The process of *voir dire* is used to select juries in the U.S., which typically includes 12 members, but can consist of fewer members for nonserious offenses, depending on the state (Westong and Wells, 1987). These jury members are given the responsibility of deciphering the facts presented to them and coming up with a verdict of not guilty or guilty.

The process of *voir dire* and the duties of jurors in the U.S. differ somewhat from other countries in the world. Countries such as Germany do not have jury trials and allow judges or a panel of judges to handle all adjudications, whereas England and France have juries that have slight differences from the American system (Fairchild and Dammer, 2001). For instance, America's system of *voir dire* allows the prosecution and defense great leeway in altering the shape of the final jury, even through the use of psychological assessment of the conviction or acquittal potential of jurors in the selection pool (Barber, 1999). The English system, though allowing jurors to have more impact on the course of the trial process through their own questions to defendants, does not allow the defense or prosecution to recreate the jury once it has been selected. In other words, the jury that is originally selected randomly is in most cases the same jury that will end up at trial (Hirschel and Wakefield, 1995).

As the U.S. is an adversarial system, defendants do not have to take the stand in their own defense during trial. This differs from countries with inquisitorial systems, where the emphasis is placed more on the defendants' ability to explain the charges against them (Fairchild and Dammer, 2001). Whereas the inquisitorial process stresses judicial overview of the investigation of the criminal offense, the adversarial system focuses on competition of the prosecution and defense in order to balance both sides of the justice system and bring out the truth (Fairchild and Dammer, 2001).

Once the jury has decided the guilt or innocence of the defendant through the standard of reasonable doubt, the sentencing phase ensues. In less serious cases in the U.S., judges are solely responsible for the sentence handed out, whereas juries make a recommendation in the more serious cases, which judges tend to highly regard.

Finally, some controversial policies today are found in the sentencing phase. Two such policies include determinate sentencing and victim impact statements. Determinate sentences are used in some states within the U.S. and provide the judge with the power to set a flat-line term that must be served by the defendant (Weston and Wells, 1987). This lack of wiggle room provided by these sentences has ultimately lead to questions about the efficiency and ethics surrounding this practice. Victim impact statements are also becoming popular today, and allow victims or their families to assert the impact that the crime of the defendant has had on their lives. A potential problem is that these statements may lead to disparate treatment of defendants who committed the same offense (Newman, 1995). It will be interesting to note the extent to which these policies are used as the court system continues to develop.

BRION SEVER

References and Further Reading

Acevedo, R. (1999) Is a ban on plea bargaining an ethical abuse of discretion? A Bronx County, New York case study, Stolzenberg, L. and D'Alessio, S. (Eds.) *Criminal Courts for the 21st Century*, Upper Saddle River, NJ: Prentice Hall.

Barber, J. (1999). The jury is still out: The role of jury science in the modern American courtroom, Stolzenberg, L. and D'Alessio, S. (Eds.) *Criminal Courts for the 21st Century*, Upper Saddle River, NJ: Prentice Hall.

Carns, T. and Kruse, J. (1992). Alaska's ban on plea bargaining reevaluated, *Judicature*, 75: 310–311.

Fairchild, E. and Dammer, H. (2001). *Comparative Criminal Justice Systems*, 2nd ed. Belmont, CA: Wadsworth.

Gaines, L., Kaune, M., and Miller, R. (2000). *Criminal Justice in Action*. Belmont, CA: Wadsworth.

Hirschel, D. and Wakefield, W. (1995) *Criminal Justice in England and the United States*. Westport, CT: Praeger.

Newman, W. (1995). Jury decision making and the effect of victim impact statements in the penalty phase, *Criminal Justice Policy Review*, 7: 291–300.

Schmalleger, F. (1991). *Criminal Justice Today*. Englewood Cliffs, NJ: Prentice Hall.

Weninger, R. (1987). The abolition of plea bargaining: A case study of El Paso County Texas, *UCLA Law Review*, 35: 265–278.

Weston, P. and Wells, K. (1987). *The Administration of Justice* (5th ed.). Englewood Cliffs, NJ: Prentice Hall.

See also **Criminal Courts: Lower; Criminal Courts: Problems in**

Criminal Courts: Felony

State courts handling felonies are generally courts of general jurisdiction, meaning that they are able to hear virtually any type of case at trial, regardless of the subject matter, parties involved, or level of importance. There are over 3500 of these courts in the 50 states. The state trial courts have different titles in different states. Alabama, Arkansas, Florida, Hawaii, Illinois, Kentucky, Maryland, Michigan, Mississippi, Missouri, Oregon, South Carolina, South Dakota, Tennessee, Virginia, West Virginia, and Wisconsin refer to their felony courts as *circuit courts*.

Alabama, Arizona, California, Connecticut, Delaware, District of Columbia, Georgia, Indiana, Maine Massachusetts, New Hampshire, New Jersey, North Carolina, Rhode Island, Vermont, and Washington call their felony courts *superior courts*. *District court* is the title used in Colorado, Idaho, Iowa, Kansas, Louisiana, Minnesota, Montana, Nebraska, New Mexico, North Dakota, Oklahoma, Texas, Utah, and Wyoming. Ohio and Pennsylvania are the only two states to refer to their trial courts as *courts of common pleas* and the state of New York alone calls its trial level courts *supreme courts*.

Judges are selected for these courts by four main methods. Partisan elections select judges in 13 states. These judges are nominated by a political party and run in the general election against the other party's nominee. Sixteen states use nonpartisan elections. Eight states use a merit selection process. In this process, the governor selects a candidate from a list of qualified candidates prescreened by a committee of community leaders, attorneys, etc. After being selected, judges are placed on the ballot unopposed in the next election, with voters indicating whether or not to retain the individual. Eight other states rely on gubernatorial appointments, where judges are usually appointed to judgeships as rewards for prior political contributions. The remaining states use various methods of selection.

Felonies are the most serious category of criminally offenses, as distinguished from misdemeanors. Most present day felony crimes have their origins in common law. Common law was law that developed from the customs of the English people and incorporated into early English court decisions. These court decisions then became precedents for future court decisions. In common law a felony was a heinous act that passed your land rights to the king and the punishment was death. The common law felonies were murder, arson, mayhem (which is the disabling of an eye or a limb), rape, robbery, larceny, burglary, escape from prison, and sodomy.

Presently, 36 states have abolished common law offenses and have adopted substantive criminal law codes. They are Alabama, Alaska, Arizona, Colorado, Connecticut, Delaware, Florida, Georgia, Maine, Minnesota, Missouri, Montana, Nebraska, New Hampshire, New Jersey, New Mexico, New York, North Dakota, Ohio, Oregon, Pennsylvania, South Dakota, Tennessee, Texas, Utah, Virginia, Washington, and Wyoming. In the remainder of the country, the common law survives either expressly or by implication. In substantive criminal law codes, a felony is usually defined as a crime carrying a sentence in excess of 1 year in a state penal institution. A misdemeanor by contrast is a less serious category of crime, typically carrying a sentence of less than 1 year in a local jail facility. Some states however, do have felony offenses that carry less than 1 year. For example, in Ohio a fifth-degree felony carries possible sentences of 6–12 months.

In order to treat some crimes as more serious than others, state legislatures have divided felonies into categories or degrees. As indicated above, the state of Ohio has five categories, with a first-degree felony being the most serious level and fifth degree being the least serious category of crime.

Within each level or degree are a range of possible sentences. Again, as stated above a fifth-degree felony can carry 6–12 months whereas a first-degree felony results in a sentence of 3–10 years. The statutory scheme for each state sets out possible criteria as to which sentence within the range should be given to any individual defendant based on the specific characteristics of the crime committed as well as the prior record of the defendant.

All persons who are charged with crimes recognized as felonies are entitled to representation by a qualified attorney based on the Sixth Amendment to the U.S. Constitution. In the case of *Gideon v. Wainwright* the U.S. Supreme Court stated, "The right of one charged with crime to counsel may not be deemed fundamental in some countries. But it is in ours." Prior to this 1963 case only individuals charged with capital murder were entitled to counsel if unable to afford one.

Criminal cases generally speaking reach felony courts by one of two paths. Most cases reach felony court after having had initial court proceedings in a court of limited jurisdiction, commonly called municipal court. Persons who are arrested and charged with felonies appear in municipal courts following their arrest. Bail is set at the initial hearing, counsel is appointed for an indigent defendant and a hearing is often set called a preliminary hearing. At that hearing the municipal court judge will determine if probable cause exists to bind the matter over to the grand jury, or to allow the case to proceed. If the matter is bound over to the grand jury a secret grand jury proceeding is held, outside the hearing of the defendant, to determine if probable cause exists to issue an indictment. An indictment is the formal charging instrument in a felony criminal case.

In other circumstances, the entire municipal court portion of the proceeding is skipped and the felony charge is brought by taking the case directly to the grand jury. This process is called direct indictment or secret indictment.

Regardless of which method is used to seek an indictment, the initial proceeding in felony court is the arraignment. Here the accused enters a plea of guilty or not guilty. Regardless of the guilt of the accused, a not-guilty plea is typically entered at this point in the proceedings. The not-guilty plea for an admittedly guilty person is seen merely as way to begin the process of having the case move through the court system. For individuals who wish to contest the charges against them the not-guilty plea sets the process toward trial in motion. Defendants also have the opportunity to enter a plea of guilty at arraignment. However, although the majority of defendants do in fact plead guilty it is rare for the pleas to be made at the time of arraignment. An important, but rarely seen plea that can be entered is the Alford guilty plea. This plea permits a defendant to enter a plea of guilty while protesting his or her innocence. Based on a U.S. Supreme Court case, *North Carolina v. Alford*, this plea allows a defendant to voluntarily, knowingly, and understandingly consent to the imposition of a prison term even if he is unwilling or unable to admit his participation in the acts constituting the crime. An additional plea, no contest or *nolo contendere* plea, is also occasionally permitted. This plea permits the defendant not to contest the criminal charge against him or her although recognizing that the court will make a finding of guilty. In most circumstances, the plea can only be made with the court's permission.

At arraignment, other issues can also be raised. A plea of not guilty by reason of insanity can be raised at this time if counsel for the defendant feels that the defendant was legally insane at the time of the commission of the offense. The defendant is then referred for a psychiatric or psychological evaluation and a report is made to the court as to whether or not the defendant was able to appreciate the wrongfulness of his actions at the time of his criminal activity. Questions regarding a defendant's mental fitness or competency to proceed to trial can also be raised at the time of arraignment and are usually raised before the original entering of a plea. Again, the defendant is referred for a psychiatric or psychological evaluation and a determination is made as to whether or not the defendant is mentally fit to participate in the legal system and to understand the nature of the criminal charges against him or her. The issues as to a defendant's competence can be raised at any time in a criminal proceeding and can be raised by the defense counsel, the prosecution or even the judge can raise the issue based on their own observations of the defendant.

Counsel for the defendant also frequently argues bond at the time of arraignment regardless or whether or not bail had previously been set in the earlier court appearances. In setting bond, the court considers the nature of the charges against the defendant, any prior criminal record and the likelihood that the defendant will return for future court appearances if released on bond.

The major work in a felony criminal case begins after the arraignment. Motions are typically filed by both sides, the prosecution and the defense. For example, a defense attorney might file a motion alleging that her client was wrongfully searched or that a confession was coerced. Following a reply by the prosecution, the trial judge will set an oral hearing where testimony is presented to determine if the motion has merit. Defense counsel might also assert that a search warrant was obtained without probable cause or that his client should have a trial separate from other potential codefendants. On each of these matters, the trial judge must make a ruling. The rulings can be made with or without a hearing. Often the hearings are seen as a minitrial, an opportunity for each side to get a look at the evidence the other side has to offer.

It is also during this time period that the two sides begin to exchange information in a process known as discovery. The judge presiding over the case typically supervises the process. If either side fails to cooperate with the other in the exchange of information the trial judge may issue sanctions against the attorney for failing to cooperate.

At times, defense counsel may feel he or she is entitled to information regarding the case that the prosecution does not wish to disclose. The defense will then file a motion asking the court to compel or require the prosecution to disclose the information.

Following the discovery process, the prosecutor and the defense counsel attempt to resolve the case by way of a plea, making the need for a trial moot. The parties attempt to receive a plea bargain or negotiated plea. In a plea bargain, often some counts or charges are dropped or dismissed in exchange for a plea to other counts. The negotiated plea may include counts, charges, or the two sides may actually agree on a sentence for the defendant. This proposed resolution of the case must be presented to the trial judge. The judge will then determine if he or she feels the plea bargain is a fair and equitable resolution of the case. A judge is not required to accept a plea bargain simply because it is presented by the parties. The final responsibility resides with the judge who is responsible for the sentencing of the defendant regardless of whether or not a plea bargain was entered into by the parties.

Most cases are resolved by way of plea bargains resulting in guilty pleas by the defendant. In 1998 guilty pleas accounted for 94% of all felony convictions. If a case cannot be resolved by way of a negotiated plea or plea bargain and the defendant is not willing to plead as charged the matter must be set for a trial.

Prior to accepting a plea of guilty the judge must determine that the decision is being knowingly, voluntarily, and intelligently made. All states have a litany of rights that the judge must read to the defendant prior to accepting the plea. The purpose of the litany is to ensure that the defendant is aware that he or she has certain constitutional rights that will be waived by the entering of a plea of guilty. These rights include: the right to trial, the right to cross-examine the witnesses against one, the right to compulsory process (the right to subpoena witnesses on your own behalf), the Fifth Amendment right against self-incrimination, and in most instances the right to an appeal.

Persons charged with a felony are guaranteed a trial by jury. A defendant may chose to waive a jury and try his case to the trial judge, however, this is done infrequently. Defendants also are guaranteed a speedy trial by law. The time for speedy trials differs from state to state but normally an incarcerated defendant must be brought to trial within three or four months. This time requirement can be extended however by agreement of the parties, by defense motions and tactics, or the court. In 1998, the average time from arrest to sentencing was just over 7 months.

Most states require a 12-person jury for felony cases. Florida, Louisiana, South Carolina, Texas, and Utah use fewer than 12 people for noncapital felony cases, arguing that the Sixth Amendment to the U.S. Constitution does not require that a jury be comprised of any specific number of people. Louisiana and Oregon allow nonunanimous felony verdicts, which the U.S. Supreme Court has ruled is permissible. Most other states require unanimous verdicts.

In each step of a criminal trial, the prosecution has the opportunity to go first. This is because the prosecution has the burden of proving the defendant guilty by proof beyond a reasonable doubt. The steps in the criminal trial are jury selection, called *voir dire*; opening statements; and the presentation of witnesses and evidence by the prosecution. The defense has the opportunity to cross-examine each witness presented by the prosecution.

After the prosecution has presented its witnesses and evidence, the trial court must determine if enough evidence has been presented to permit the trial to continue. If the court finds that the state has not presented sufficient evidence the charges against the defendant are dismissed and the defendant is discharged or free to go. If the judge decides that sufficient evidence has been presented, the defendant may either present witnesses of his or her own or simply rest without presenting any evidence. If the defendant chooses to present witnesses, those witnesses are subject to cross-examination by the prosecution just as the defense had had the opportunity to cross-examine the prosecution's witnesses. In some instances the state has the opportunity to present rebuttal witnesses. This means that if they can rebut or refute any evidence presented by the defendant they may call witnesses to the stand to do so.

After all the evidence has been presented, each side has the opportunity to present closing arguments. Again, because the prosecution has the burden of proof they are permitted to go first and last in their effort to convince the jury or court to convict the defendant.

Before the jury begins its deliberations, the judge reads to the jury the law that relates to the case and the charges the defendant is facing. This is called the jury charge or jury instructions. After hearing the instructions the jury retires to begin its deliberations. Upon reaching a verdict, the jury notifies the judge and the verdict is announced in the courtroom. If the jury is unable to reach a verdict, or is hung, the defendant may be retried or the case may be dismissed. This decision rests solely with the prosecution.

Following conviction at trial, a defendant is sentenced to an appropriate prison term. He or she is then advised of his or her right to an appeal. Criminal defendants are entitled to an attorney at their first appeal as of right.

Ninety-five percent of felony convictions in 1998 occurred in state felony courts. The rest were convicted in federal court.

The responsibility of the trial felony court does not necessarily end with the conviction of a criminal defendant. If the trial court determines that an offender is capable of remaining in the community following conviction, the offender is typically placed on a period of probation supervised by the trial court. The court sets certain rules and regulations that the convicted felon must follow, and if the person fails to follow the rules, a prison sentence may subsequently be imposed by the judge who originally placed the person on probation.

The felony trial judge's responsibilities may also involve supervising individuals who were found to be not guilty by reason of insanity. State statutes provide that the trial court judge who presided over the determination of insanity be responsible for supervising the individual. Periodic hearings are held to determine if an insanity acquittee is still in need of court ordered hospitalization and frequently even after the individual has left a psychiatric hospital and has returned to live in the community the felony court is responsible for his supervision.

In recent years the felony court's supervision has been extended to include sexual offenders. Following conviction for a sexually related offense, sexual offenders are required to register with local law enforcement and to notify the authorities when they change their address pursuant to a state notification statute. These notification statutes are typically called "Megan's Law" after the 1994 murder, kidnapping and rape of 7-year-old Megan Kanka. The court has the responsibility for making a determination as to the risk of future sexual offenses, and the higher the risk that the sex offender has of reoffending, the more stringent the notification requirements will be. Failure to follow the notification and registration requirements set forth by the court typically results in a new charge of failure to register.

State felony courts are also responsible for oversight of state postconviction proceedings. In these proceedings a convicted criminal defendant is permitted to return to the court where his or her conviction occurred and argue why the conviction is void or voidable. However, only evidence that was not presented in the original proceeding may be presented to the court.

PATRICIA MILLHOF

References and Further Reading

Bureau of Justice Statistics Bulletin, October 2001, NCH 190103, *Felony Sentences in States Courts*, 1998.

Del Carmen, R.V., Criminal procedure, law and practice, in Garland, N. M. (Ed.), *Criminal Law for the Criminal Justice Professional*, Glencoe McGraw-Hill, 2003.

Holten, N.G., *The Criminal Courts: Structures, Personnel and Processes*, McGraw-Hill, 1991.

Reid, S.T., *Criminal Law*, Mc-Graw-Hill, 2004.

Territo, L., *Crime and Justice in America: A Human Perspective*, 6th ed., Pearson Prentice Hall, 2004.

See also **Courts in the U.S.: Structure and Functions; Criminal Courts: Administration and Organization**

Criminal Courts: Lower

In the U.S., state trial courts are generally divided into two categories: courts of limited jurisdiction and courts of general jurisdiction. Courts of limited jurisdiction are often referred to as lower courts. In 1998, such courts existed in all but four states, the District of Columbia and Puerto Rico (U.S. Department of Justice, 1998).

Historical Overview

Although the first lower courts date back to the Old Testament (Exodus 18:13–26), lower courts in America originate from the justice of the peace and magistrate courts of 14th century England. During the 19th century a majority of the U.S. continued the tradition of lower courts through either the local election or appointment of justices of the peace, police magistrates, mayors who also had judicial responsibilities, or other officers. Though the geographical area over which such courts could hear cases varied from state to state, it was, and remains to this day, generally limited to the confines of a precinct, town, city, parish, or county. Despite a history in which many states have looked to the lower courts as sources of revenue through fines and court costs, few local courts receive funding from their state. Rather, the municipality or county funds most locally.

The justice of the peace is the judicial figure generally associated with local justice in rural territories. Whereas rural America has historically been viewed as a safe haven from the serious crimes occurring in metropolitan areas, rural areas have always endured their fair share of disorderliness, minor assaults, petty thefts, and the like. Such criminal activity necessitated the need for local lower courts. The education and experience of justices of the peace varied greatly. Many were not lawyers or law-trained. Nevertheless, many justices of the peace in rural areas not only managed their own trial dockets but also handled the preliminary stages of felony cases until arrangements could be made for a court of general jurisdiction to take over the matter. Although in the 1920s all states incorporated justices of the peace as an important component of their judicial system, by the middle of the 20th century changing circumstances and reformist pressures resulted in a decline in these courts (Steury and Frank, 1996). As of 1998, justice of the peace courts existed in only 12 states: Arizona, Arkansas, Delaware, Louisiana, Mississippi, Montana, Nevada, New York, Oregon, Texas, Utah, and Wyoming (U.S. Department of Justice, 1998).

In metropolitan areas, police magistrate courts served as the urban counterpart of the justice of the peace courts. Such courts were presided over by either the mayor or a designated police official. A combination of law enforcement official and judicial officer, the police magistrate not only adjudicated common lesser offenses, but also provided legal advice to the police, set bond on arrestees, and conducted preliminary hearings in felony cases. Over a period of time the inherent conflicting duties of the police magistrate led to its abolition and the creation of two distinct positions: the police legal advisor and the municipal court judge. In 1998, municipal courts existed in 29 states (U.S. Department of Justice, 1998).

During the 20th century, lower courts experienced considerable criticism and change. Historically, the impartiality of many lower courts was called into question by the existence of the fee system (that paid the judicial officer directly from fees assessed against defendants found guilty). The demise of the notorious fee system began when the U.S. Supreme Court ruled that a judge in a misdemeanor case is disqualified from adjudicating the case if the judge's fee depends on the conviction of the defendant (*Tumey v. Ohio*, 273 U.S. 510, 1927). Within 50 years, the high court once again addressed another controversial issue pertaining to lower court judges: Should lower court judges be attorneys? In *North v. Russell*, 427 U.S. 395 (1976), the court held that nonlawyers do not deny defendants equal protection, nor do they violate the due process clause of the Fourteenth Amendment. Although some states, such as California and Iowa, now require that lower court judges be attorneys, only 57% of lower court judges in the U.S. were attorneys in 1988 (Neubauer, 1999).

By the 1980s criticisms of the quality of justice dispensed in the lower courts led many states to initiate various reforms, such as increased emphasis on judicial education. By the end of the 20th century at least 31 states mandated judges of limited jurisdiction to have a requisite number of judicial education hours before taking the bench. Additionally, 44 other states require continuing judicial education (U.S. Department of Justice, 1998). Although such efforts to reform the lower courts have resulted in beneficial changes in some jurisdictions, the problems facing local trial courts remain as varied as the courts themselves. In general, however, the most pressing problems of lower courts continue to involve inadequate financing, inadequate facilities, lax court procedures, and unbalanced caseloads (Neubauer, 1999).

Contemporary Function of Lower Courts

In terms of contemporary operations, many lower courts perform both magistrate and trial court functions.

Magistrate Functions

Although a majority of lower courts do not adjudicate felonies, many are nevertheless involved in the preliminary stages of felony cases and serve an important gate-keeping function for the trial courts of general jurisdiction. As magistrates, many lower court judges issue arrest and search warrants. Additionally, though their responsibilities vary by jurisdiction, lower court judges frequently perform the following magistrate duties: (1) holding an initial appearance; (2) setting bail and conditions for pretrial release; and (3) conducting preliminary hearings.

An initial appearance is required promptly after the arrest of the suspect (generally within 24 hours of arrest; *County of Riverside v. McLaughlin*, 111 S.Ct. 1661, 1991). At the initial appearance, the judge informs the defendant of his or her rights and explains the formal charge or charges pending against the defendant. If the arrest was made without a warrant, probable cause may be determined. In some jurisdictions, it is at this stage that indigency and the appointment of counsel may be determined. If the judge has jurisdiction over the offense, he may accept a plea. In such cases, roughly one third to two thirds of all criminal defendants plead guilty during the first appearance (Alfini, 1981). It is important to note, however, that many law violations observed by a peace officer do not result in arrest. Increasingly, peace officers issue citations to the accused. The peace officer retains a copy of the citation that contains the suspect's signed promise to appear before the court at a designated time and date. Failure to appear can result in a warrant being issued for both the failure to appear and for the original underlying offense.

If the accused has not been released by law enforcement prior to being brought before the court, the judge, acting as a magistrate, will set bail and in some cases order special conditions for pretrial release. The accused can generally secure release in one of the following four ways: (1) post the full amount of bail in money (i.e., a cash bond); (2) use property as collateral for release (i.e., a property bond); (3) post bail through a third person (i.e., a surety bond); or (4) release on one's own recognizance in lieu of a monetary bond (i.e., personal bond). The law generally requires that bail be set at an amount to assure the appearance of the accused, weighing his or her financial resources and ties to the community. The Eighth Amendment to the U.S. Constitution forbids the requirement of excessive bail.

Following arrest, suspects in the U.S. are entitled to a timely preliminary hearing before a neutral magistrate to determine if probable cause exists that justifies detaining the defendant prior to trial (*Gerstein v. Pugh*, 420 U.S. 103, 1975). The right to a preliminary hearing is limited to alleged felonies. The general underlying function of a preliminary hearing is to protect citizens and society from the consequences and financial costs of unwarranted prosecutions. Although preliminary hearings are sometimes sought by the defense counsel as a tactic to discover evidence, they are usually brief, if held at all. The preliminary hearing screens few cases out of the criminal process because of the minimal amount of evidence necessary to detain a defendant based on probable cause.

Trial Court Function

Although the trial court function of lower courts varies from state to state, lower courts generally have jurisdiction over nonfelony criminal cases. Such offenses include local ordinances and state misdemeanors punishable by fines or incarceration in a local jail for a term not to exceed 1 year (many lower courts also have jurisdiction over small claims in civil lawsuits). In 1992, 71% of all filings in lower courts pertained to traffic cases (Ostrom, 1994). Although the volume and types of cases being heard in the lower courts has continued to increase, by the mid-1990s the number of traffic offenses declined by 20%. This decrease can be attributed to the decriminalization or transfer of less serious traffic offenses from the lower criminal courts to administrative proceedings in the executive branch of government (Ostrom and Kauder, 1996). Most states have even further jurisdictional subdivisions among courts of limited jurisdiction. Whereas some lower courts only have jurisdiction of fine-only offenses, others hear misdemeanor cases punishable by a fine and time in jail. Lower courts in Delaware, Georgia, Mississippi, Ohio, Rhode Island, and Texas have incidental appellate jurisdiction, hearing appeals from other lower courts of limited jurisdiction (e.g., traffic courts: U.S. Department of Justice, 1988). Appellate procedures also vary among states. Some lower courts use a court reporter or mechanical means to record trial proceedings. In such courts of record, appeals are based on the merits of the appellate record and transcript. In courts of nonrecord, appeals result in a trial *de novo* (i.e., the case is tried once again as if the first trial never occurred). Only a small percentage of defendants in lower courts exercise their right to a trial. Most of these are bench trials (before a judge without the option of a jury). The constitutional right to a trial by jury only applies to defendants charged with offenses punishable by imprisonment for more than 6 months (*Baldwin v. New York*, 399 U.S. 66, 1970). Although at least 19 states allow for jury trials in lower courts, they are often limited to offenses punishable by incarceration in jail. Some state constitutions, such as that of Texas, allow for jury trials in all criminal matters, including fine-only offenses.

Conclusion

Although popular culture fixates on felony trials and the events transpiring in courts of general jurisdiction, the reality is that relatively few citizens ever come into contact with such courts. In contrast, whereas lower courts are not the frequent focus of media attention, they collectively have a tremendous impact on the public's perception of the American judicial system. Lower criminal courts constitute 84% of all the American courts. Lower court judges constitute 66% of the American judiciary. Over 61 million cases, 72% of all state cases, were filed in lower courts in 1995 (Ostrom and Kauder, 1996). Yet, despite the fact that more Americans come in contact with these courts than all other levels of the judiciary combined, the lower courts are the least studied segment of the judicial system (Steury and Frank, 1996).

RYAN KELLUS TURNER

References and Further Reading

Alfini, J.J., Ed., Symposium on misdemeanor courts, *Justice System Journal* 6 (1981).

Neubauer, D.W., *America's Courts and the Criminal Justice System*, 6th ed., Belmont, CA: West/Wadsworth, 1999.

Ostrom, B.J., *State Court Caseload Statistics: Annual Report*, Williamsburg, VA: National Center for State Courts, 1994.

Ostrom, B.J. and Neal, K., *Examining the Work of State Courts*, Williamsburg, VA: National Center for State Courts, 1996.

Steury, E.H. and Nancy, F., *Criminal Court Process*, St. Paul, MN: West Publishing, 1996.

United States Department of Justice, Office of Justice Programs, Bureau of Justice Statistics, *State Court Organization*, (1998).

See also **Courts in the U.S.: Structure and Functions; Criminal Courts: Personnel, Trials, Criminal**

Criminal Courts: Personnel

As most U.S. criminal law is state law, the structure of the courtroom work group can vary among 50 jurisdictions, without even considering other U.S. territories and the federal system. The functions that must be performed by the courtroom work group are similar across jurisdictions, and it is that similarity of function that makes general description possible.

Courtroom function, like courtroom architecture, centers on the judge. The judge's primary function is to apply the law, either directly or by explaining the law to the jury. Federal judges are appointed by the president (normally upon the recommendation of the local senator) and serve for life. State court judges, which is to say most judges, are selected by a bewildering array of methods ranging from partisan election to gubernatorial appointment. Terms vary widely, but most state court judges must stand for reelection or reappointment periodically. Many jurisdictions limit the question to whether the incumbent judge should be retained rather than considering all interested candidates.

Judicial elections are thought to inject some democracy into the least democratic branch of government. Other methods are thought to better assure that judges remain independent in the face of community sentiment. These two goals are diametrically opposed and the opposition is nowhere as important as in criminal courts. It is easy for judicial candidates to run against crime, but somewhat more difficult to run in favor of fair trials.

The basic qualifications for judges are generally stated in the statutes creating the judgeships. In spite of the primary function of the judge to interpret the law, many judges on the lower levels (justice of the peace courts, and city courts) do not hold law degrees and are not licensed attorneys. As the responsibilities of the court for more complex cases rise, so do the qualifications required of the judge and the number of support personnel assigned to the court. The following personnel are often found in general jurisdiction trial courts.

Prosecutor. It is the function of the prosecuting attorney to represent the government's position in criminal cases. The government's position in a criminal case may seem self-evident, but in fact prosecutors are subject to serious ethical constraints within the adversary system. Most jurisdictions require the prosecutor not merely to convict, but to see that justice is done. Taken to its logical conclusion, this stricture places as much duty upon the prosecutor to assure a fair trial as upon the judge. The duty of a prosecutor to seek justice conflicts with the pressure of working within the adversary system to win at any cost.

Defense attorney. A criminal defendant is entitled to the assistance of a lawyer in every case where imprisonment is to be imposed upon conviction. The defense attorney is spared the prosecutor's conflicting roles within the adversary system because, within the system, the defense attorney is obligated to get the best result possible for his or her client within the facts and the law. Unlike the prosecutor, for example, the defense attorney seldom has the duty to disclose facts that would hurt the defense case. However, the defense attorney's role in providing a fair trial for all accused and advocating for anyone who needs an advocate (often on a court-appointed basis) can cause emotional turmoil for the attorney as well as unwarranted damage to the reputation of a defense attorney who must advocate for an extremely unpopular accused.

Defense attorneys are employed directly by criminal defendants who can afford them. Indigent defendants may be represented by public defender offices or by private attorneys appointed by the court. Some jurisdictions require all practicing attorneys to share in the duty to represent indigent persons, either by personal service or by paying a "buy out" fee into a fund to compensate court-appointed lawyers.

Court reporter. Most jurisdictions still record the proceedings of trial courts by a certified shorthand reporter (CSR) using a stenograph machine, although handwritten shorthand notes are not completely unknown. Modern stenographs are often equipped for computer-assisted transcription (CAT), which makes the production of a trial record much faster. Some jurisdictions have switched from shorthand reporting to audio or video recording, with or without a CSR. If the recorded trial record is not reduced to writing, the time saved is often paid back when the appellate court must play all the parts of the recording that relate to issues being appealed. If the recorded trial record is reduced to writing, this is done either by a CSR or someone with similar responsibilities.

Bailiff. The bailiff is sometimes a peace officer and sometimes not, sometimes armed and sometimes not, but always charged with keeping order in the courtroom and communicating with the jury. The bailiff is sometimes employed by a law enforcement agency within the jurisdiction of the court (e.g., the sheriff's office within a county) and sometimes employed by the judge, but always acts under the immediate direction of the judge.

Court clerk. Sometimes the judge is responsible for the keeping of the court's records and sometimes a separate agency is responsible, but in either case some person must keep track of the case files as they are used by the judge. Case files typically contain a docket sheet on which the judge notes any actions taken pending the entry of a written order. Many courts, especially in urban areas, are beginning to use electronic docket sheets. The judge makes his notes with a keyboard on the bench, and a hard copy docket sheet is printed out if needed.

Together, these personnel represent the courthouse work group in the U.S. Because they work together every day, their familiar interactions can be intimidating to a stranger in the courtroom. The strangers in courtrooms are typically the people whose lives are being changed by the lawsuits on trial: crime victims and criminal defendants. This estrangement is likely even greater for court participants in Britain, where a criminal defendant does not even directly hire his own barrister (trial lawyer).

The American courtroom evolved from England, so an American walking into a courtroom in Great Britain or Wales would recognize the general layout. Juries are relatively scarcer in British courts than in American courts, but even in the U.S. jury trials are the exception rather than the rule. The British Bar maintains a traditional distinction between barristers (trial lawyers) and solicitors (office lawyers), although the modern trend is "fusion," with solicitors being granted rights of audience in lower courts and barristers engaging in some office practice. When a barrister is engaged to argue a case, that is still typically done through a solicitor and a barrister has a professional duty not to "refuse a brief" without good cause, a custom that insulates British barristers from the damage to reputation that American lawyers may suffer for representing unpopular persons. Indigent criminal defendants in Great Britain are issued vouchers with which to retain a solicitor, who then engages a barrister as in any other case.

Solicitors are the "lower" branch of the British Bar, and the "higher" branch of barristers is further stratified among "pupils" (apprentices who are allowed to plead cases during their training), "juniors," and barristers who have "taken the silk" and become "Queen's Counsel." Many dispute resolutions that would be considered judicial functions in the U.S. are handled in Great Britain by barristers, but the professional judges of the High Court are appointed by the Queen upon the advice of the Lord Chancellor, who bases his advice upon a much more intensive review of professional experience and reputation than was conducted when the candidate was first offered the silk. It is unusual for a barrister to be appointed to the Court of Appeal or the House of Lords without first serving on the High Court, and as all evaluations for the silk or for the bench take place within the profession, the process is less overtly political than judicial selection in the U.S.

STEVE RUSSELL

References and Further Reading

Abraham, H.J., *The Judicial Process*, New York, NY, Oxford University Press, 1998.

Cohen, H., The English legal profession revisited—again, *The Journal of the Legal Profession* 19 (1995).

Gershman, B.L., *Prosecutorial Misconduct*, New York, NY, Clark Boardman, 1990.

Kunen, J.S., *How Can You Defend Those People?* New York, NY, Random House, 1983.

Maute, J.L., Looking backward: Alice's adventures in wonderland: Preliminary reflections on the history of the split English legal profession and the fusion debate (1000–1900 A.D.), *Fordham Law Review* (2003).

Megarry, R.E., Barristers and judges in England today, *Fordham Law Review* 51 (1982).

Neubauer, D.W., *America's Courts and the Criminal Justice System*, Belmont, CA, Wadsworth, 1999.

Tague, P.W., Ensuring able representation for publicly-funded criminal defendants: Lessons from England, *University of Cincinnati Law Review* 69 (2000).

See also **Criminal Courts: Administration and Organization**

Criminal Courts: Problems in

Early in the 21st century, the criminal court system faces a daunting series of operational and perceptional problems as its paradigm has shifted from a deterrence-based model to an increasingly incapacitative model. This new court system is characterized by burgeoning caseloads, increased punitiveness, and a sustained legacy of unfavorable public perceptions. As a framework for addressing criminal court problems, this article will cluster concerns in three primary areas: (1) efficiency, which involves the actual day-to-day workings of the criminal court system; (2) effectiveness, which concerns whether the court system's strategies actually manage the problems that they purport to address; and (3) legitimacy, which concerns the court system's fairness, as well as the public's perception of the system.

Efficiency

The concern here is whether the criminal court system's productivity is maximized. In other words, are the courts efficiently using their available resources? The efficiency concern is critical because the criminal court system is massive and massively funded. There are over 15,000 criminal courts in the U.S., handling approximately 14 million arrests each year, which result in 24 million cases. Court dockets continue to grow, even as overall crime rates decrease. Between 1973 and 2002, victimization decreased from 44 million to 23 million persons, even though the population increased during the same time period. Between 1993 and 2002, FBI Index crimes decreased almost every year; however, between 1992 and 2000, felony convictions in combined state and federal courts actually increased 3% (Bureau of Justice Statistics, 2003). Between 1984 and 1998, state court felony filings increased 65% (Ostrom and Kauder, 1999), although crime rates were generally falling. As Neubauer (2002, 250) writes, "Most state trial court systems were unable to keep pace with the increasing volume of criminal cases. The number of cases disposed of each year is less than the number filed." Consequently, despite the decline in overall crime rates, many state courts do not try a defendant until the case is over 1 year old, and often over 2 years old.

Although the cost of case delays is difficult to quantify, the consequences are nevertheless serious. For defendants in jail, there are costs associated with jail-space and loss of liberty and productivity. Prosecution priorities are frequently focused on defendants in jail; once defendants leave jail, defense attorneys frequently have a perverse incentive to maximize a case's age: Prosecutors may leave the office, and witnesses and evidence may disappear. Older cases are more likely to be dismissed or receive a favorable disposition. Consequently, older cases lead to more dismissals or more lenient sentences.

The decentralization of state court systems prevents the optimally efficient allocation of court resources. It is perhaps a misnomer to term the state court system a "system" as the structure of the system is typically disunified. The thousands of state courts are organized into a multitude of frequently overlapping jurisdictions. The bulk of cases are handled in magistrate courts, which typically do not share caseloads with other courts. Court reformers have called for increased centralization, as decentralization prevents overburdened courts from shifting caseloads to other courts (Neubauer, 2002).

Particularly in state courts, incomplete and dilatory information-exchange systems delay case resolution and foster a trial-by-ambush approach. There is typically a considerable lag between a defendant's arrest and the defense attorney receiving discovery materials and a prosecution settlement offer. Rules governing discovery do not require either the prosecution or defense to exchange all their information. For example, the prosecution is not required to turn over witness lists, work product, or interview notes. Consequently, both sides often go to trial without knowing the full quality of the other's evidence.

Effectiveness

The effectiveness of the criminal court system is a paramount concern considering the financial and human costs involved in its processes. The modern criminal court system has largely been predicated on deterrence, along the lines proposed by Italian thinker Cesare Beccaria (1764–1992). The Beccarian model presumes that potential offenders are rational actors, who will maximize the utility of their actions by properly weighing the benefits and detriments of their actions' anticipated consequences. By increasing the severity of crimes and the likelihood of apprehension, the deterrent effect is increased, and rational offenders will choose to avoid crime.

Over the last three decades, increasingly punitive and incapacitative laws have increasingly shifted the criminal court focus away from the Beccarian model (see, e.g., Garland, 2001, 199). Beginning in the 1970s, as crime rates were rising, criminal justice policy makers began questioning whether rehabilitation worked (see, e.g., Martinson, 1974). Lawmakers such as Edward Kennedy blamed the court system's leniency for rising crime rates. Ronald Reagan's presidency brought a "war on drugs," which resulted in tremendous incarceration increases. During the 1980s and 1990s, numerous mandatory minimum laws were passed. During that same time period, legislatures frequently created violent and no-parole offenses, which adjusted parole eligibility. At the same time, new laws have allowed for juveniles to be prosecuted in adult courts in limited cases. Unsurprisingly, prison populations ballooned. Between 1980 and 2001, the number of people in prison, on probation, or on parole increased by a factor of three, to 6 million. By 2002, the number had reached 6.7 million, or 1 in 32 of all adults (Bureau of Justice Statistics, 2003). Between 1980 and 2002, incarceration increased fourfold to over 2,000,000 (Ibid). As of 2003, 1 in 37 Americans has been incarcerated at some point (Justice Policy Institute, 2003). The new punitiveness is an extremely expensive, generalized approach to crime control, emphasizing both deterrence and incapacitation. Deterrence itself may be misplaced in light of recent criminological research suggesting that offenders consistently fail to make rational decisions (see, e.g., Gottfredson and Hirschi, 1990) and that criminal propensities tend to remain relatively stable over time (see, e.g., Bushway, Brame, and Paternoster, 1999). Incapacitation is an extraordinarily costly social control mechanism. In 1998, costs per inmate per year at state prisons, federal prisons, and jails were $20,261, $21,837.95, and $19,903, respectively (Camp and Camp, 1999). Those incarcerated are publicly stigmatized by a lifelong criminal record and an associated decline in earning power. The costs of incarceration are not simply borne by the criminal justice system and prisoners but by their families. Children of incarcerated parents, for example, are at high risk for delinquency. Garland (2001, 204) sees high social costs in the increased use of penal institutions: The new crime-control arrangements do, however, involve certain social costs that are, over the long term, less easily accommodated: the hardening of social and racial divisions, the reinforcement of criminogenic processes; the alienation of large social groups; the discrediting of legal authority; a reduction of civic tolerance; a tendency toward authoritarianism—these are the kinds of outcomes that are likely to flow from a reliance upon penal mechanisms to maintain social order.

Respected criminologists such as Lawrence Sherman (2003) have decried the failure of criminal courts to develop justice models that take into account an offender's nonrational, emotional character. The generalized nature of the criminal court system is particularly problematic in that alternative justice models found in specialized courts have provided established benefits (see, e.g., in criminal domestic violence contexts, Gover, MacDonald, and Alpert, 2003; in drug court contexts, Belenko, 1998.)

Legitimacy or Fairness

Criminal courts are instruments of social control. As such, courts not only maintain order but frequently a particular kind of order: a certain power structure and the interests and values of those within the power structure (Crystal, 2001). Parsons (1962, 71) predicts that the influence of law will be strong when there are "strong informal forces reinforcing conformity" with the legally institutionalized tradition, but weak in situations when the fundamental social values are in acute conflict (Parsons, 1962, 71). Courts help to maintain legitimacy by operating according to the law and with the appearance of fairness. Court decisions that are perceived as unfair run the risk of destabilizing entire communities, as in the aftermath of the Rodney King verdicts.

There is considerable evidence that the public does not believe in the fairness of the criminal court system. Such attitudes have been consistent over the last three decades. In the late 1960s, for example, more than 90% of surveyed Americans felt that the court system was unfair (Funkhouser and Popoff, 1969). In a University of Connecticut survey of 1000 respondents (Veilleux, 2000):

> Eighty percent say prosecutors will bend rules at least sometimes in order to obtain a confession. ... Twenty-four percent say judges make decisions based on their personal beliefs, not law. Ninety percent think defense attorneys will hide facts often (56 percent) or sometimes (34 percent) to protect their client.

Low public perceptions of the court system appear related to underlying fairness problems. This article will consider the public's perception of unfairness in criminal courts in three primary areas: discrimination, modern advocacy, and economics.

Racial perceptions about the criminal court system appear linked to underlying realities. In the previously mentioned University of Connecticut survey (Veilleux, 2000), nearly half of all respondents felt that judges treat White defendants better than their African American counterparts, 12% felt that race was always a factor in criminal trials, 68% felt that race was sometimes a factor in criminal trials, 80% felt that race is at least sometimes a factor in criminal trials, and 67% felt African Americans are more likely to be stopped by police than whites. Nearly half (46%) of the respondents believed that African Americans or Hispanics are less likely to receive as fair a trial as Whites. In step with public perceptions regarding the influence of race, there is a growing body of evidence that criminal courts discriminate against minorities. For example, independent studies have found that African Americans receive disproportionately harsher punishments for juvenile crime (Bishop and Frazier, 1996; Abeyratne and Sizemore, 1999; Building Blocks for Youth, 2000). Studies have found that victim race affected prosecutorial decisions to seek the death penalty (Smith, 1987; Paternoster and Kazyaka, 1991). In 2000, there were more African American males in prison or jail than in college (791,600–603,032), though, in 1980, the opposite was true (463,700–143,000) (Butterfield, 2002).

The public perception of American lawyers remains abysmally low. According to a 2002 Columbia Law School survey (Citizens for Judicial Accountability, 2003), two-third of Americans think that lawyers are overpaid, about half think attorneys do more harm than good, and four in ten think lawyers are dishonest. On the question of honesty only politicians were ranked below lawyers.

In the same study, 41% of respondents felt that lawyers do more harm than good. Part of the public perception problem is as a result of the increasing litigiousness of American society, which has made lawyers feared. Modern movies and television shows have repeatedly depicted lawyers as devious, deceitful, and frequently wealthy. Lawyers have contributed to their low public perception through advertisements, which are increasingly unregulated. Perhaps, related to the public's poor perception of lawyers is the ethical mandate of zealous advocacy. The zealous advocacy ethic actually encourages extremes of advocacy (Pizzi, 1999), which may threaten the legal system's integrity (Shutt, 2002).

"Zealous advocacy" is the lawyer's duty to "represent a client zealously within the bounds of the law" (Code of Professional Responsibility, Canon 7, 1969). Such a standard was eventually adopted by all states (Morgan and Rotunda, 1999). Other than suborning perjury, the boundaries of zealous advocacy lack clear definition: A criminal defense attorney is charged with zealously pursuing all avenues of defense for his client. It is difficult to overstate the importance of the zealous advocacy principle, which serves as a corrective procedure, protecting individuals from procedural abuses. But unrestrained zealous advocacy can damage the legal profession's reputation and undermine the public's trust in the justice system (Elkins, 2002). The client's legal benefit is the highest good, often at the expense of the tribunal's truth-finding function. Motivated by zealous advocacy, ambush tactics are acceptable, even mandated. The ethic itself creates selective pressures for attorneys because prospective clients will want attorneys who will be as zealous as possible. As a central ethic, zealous advocacy creates its own doublespeak culture. A defense attorney will warn a client at the initial meeting that, should the client admit committing the offense, the attorney cannot later have him or her testify otherwise, and, therefore, the client should just tell the attorney what the client wants the attorney to know. Under this ethic, the defense attorney is not concerned with the actual truth; rather, the defense attorney is solely interested in securing an advantageous result for the client.

There is a public perception that money creates favorable results in the criminal justice system. In the same University of Connecticut survey, 65% of respondents felt that public defenders will not perform as well as paid lawyers, and 68% believed judges treat wealthy people better than less well-off people. Again, public perception appears linked to an underlying problem. Sociologists such as Donald Black (1994) have argued that socioeconomic status is an important factor in justice experiences, citing widespread evidence linking economic resources to favorable court results. For example, the socioeconomics of jailing continue to disfavor the poor, despite a series of bail reform measures in the 1960s and 1970s. Bail amounts are typically set based on community risk and regardless of an individual's ability to pay; consequently, the very poor often remain in jail until their court date. The appointed counsel system underscores the different justice experiences of the poor and the wealthy. Public defenders are typically overworked, underpaid, and inexperienced. Although there is no empirical evidence linking public defenders with less favorable trial outcomes, appointed counsel typically have less time to devote to particular cases. Public defenders often have fewer investigative resources; it is common, for example, for public defenders to do their own investigations. As evidenced by the O.J. Simpson case, wealthy people can afford to hire the most experienced and successful trial attorneys, investigators, and experts. In essence, the public perception that money creates favorable results reflects the empirical reality of a court system that unintentionally favors the wealthy.

J. Eagle Shutt

References and Further Reading

Abeyratne, S. and Benita, S. *Juveniles Waived to Criminal Courts in Ohio (1995–1997) (Adjudication and Disposition)*. Columbus, OH: Office of Research, Ohio Department of Youth Services.

Beccaria, C. 1992. *An Essay on Crimes and Punishment*. Boston, MA: Branden Publishing Co.

Belenko, S. (1998). Research on drug courts: A critical review. *National Drug Court Institute Review*, I(1), 1–42.

Bishop, D.M. and Frazier, C.E. Race effects in juvenile justice decision-making: Findings of a statewide analysis. *Journal of Criminal Law and Criminology* 86(2):392–414.

Black, D. (1994). *The Social Structure of Right and Wrong*. San Diego, CA: Academic Press.

Building Blocks for Youth. (2000). *Youth Crime/Adult Time: Is Justice Served?* Washington, D.C.

Bureau of Justice Statistics. (2003). *Court Organization Statistics*. Retrieved on January 1, 2004 at http://www.ojp.usdoj.gov/bjs/courts.htm.

Bureau of Justice Statistics. (2003). Corrections Statistics. Retrieved on January 1, 2004 at http://www.ojp.usdoj.gov/bjs/correct.htm.

Bushway, B.R. and Raymond, P. Assessing stability and change in criminal offending: A comparison of random effects, semiparametric, and fixed effects modeling strategies. *Journal of Quantitative Criminology* 15(1):23–61.

Butterfield, F. (2002). Study finds big increase in black men as inmates since 1980. New York Times, August 28, 2002.

Camp, G.M. and Graham, C.C. (1999). *The Corrections Yearbook*. Middletown, CT: Criminal Justice Institute.

Citizens for Judicial Accountability. (2003). Lawyers seek to improve image. Retrieved on January 1, 2004 at http://www.judicialaccountability.org/lawyersseekto.htm.

Code of Professional Responsibility. (1969). American Bar Association.

Crystal, J. 2001. Criminal justice in the Middle East. *Journal of Criminal Justice* 29(6):469–482.

Elkins, J.R. (1992). The moral labyrinth of zealous advocacy. *Capital Law Review* 20:735–796.

Garland, D. The Culture of Control: Crime and Social Order in Contemporary Society. Chicago, IL: University of Chicago Press.

Gottfredson, M. and Travis, H. (1990). *A General Theory of Crime*. Stanford, CA: Stanford University Press.

Gover, A., John, M., and Geoffrey, A. Combating domestic violence: Findings from an evaluation of a local domestic violence court. *Criminology and Public Policy* 3(1): 109–132.

Justice Policy Institute. (2003). Retrieved on January 1, 2004 at www.justicepolicy.org.

Martinson, R. (1974). What works? Questions and answers about prison reform. *The Public Interest* 22.

Morgan, T.D. and Rotunda, R. (1999). *Professional Responsibility*, 7th ed. New York, NY: Foundation Press.

Neubauer, D.W. (2002). *America's Courts and the Criminal Justice System*, 7th ed. Belmont, CA: Wadsworth.

Ostrom, B. and Neal, K. (1999). *Examining the Work of State Courts, 1998*. Williamsburg, VA: National Center for State Courts.

Parsons, T. (1962). The law and social control, *Law and Sociology*, Evan, W.M. (Ed.). The Free Press, pp. 56–72.

Paternoster, R. and Marie, K.A. (1991). An examination of comparatively excessive death sentences in South Carolina 1979–1987. *New York University Review of Law and Social Change* 17:101–159.

Pizzi, W.T. (1999). *Trials without Truth*. New York, NY: New York University Press.

Sherman, L.W. (2003). Reason for emotion: Reinventing justice with theories, innovations, and research—The American Society of Criminology 2002 Presidential Address. *Criminology* 41(1):1–38.

Shutt, J.E. (2002). From the field: On criminal defense, zealous advocacy, and expanded ethics dialogue. *Journal of Crime and Justice* 25(2).

Smith, M.D. (1987). Patterns of discrimination in assessments of the death penalty: The case of Louisiana. *Journal of Criminal Justice* 15(4):279–286.

Veilleux, R. 2000. *Criminal justice poll shows distrust of America's legal system*. Retrieved on January 1, 2004 at http://www.news.uconn.edu/REL00069.htm.

See also **Criminal Courts: Administration and Organization; Criminal Courts: Felony; Criminal Courts: Lower; Criminal Courts: Personnel**

Criminal Justice Funding, The State Role in

The state plays several different roles in receiving and administering criminal justice grant funds. Part of this variance is caused by federal regulation and part is caused by differences in the way that states choose to allocate and administer funds. States often serve as a pass through agency for federal funds and subgrant them to state agencies, local jurisdictions, and private nonprofit organizations according to federal criteria, program areas, and state priorities. The governor in each state designates a particular entity to administer each grant funding stream. In some states, this entity may be the governor's office itself. The amount of federal funds received on an annual basis usually is determined on the basis of a formula such as population, or in the case of juvenile justice funding, the population under age 18. Exceptions are often made for small states and U.S. territories, which receive a specific allocation regardless of population. In many funding streams, federal regulations require states to subgrant, or pass through, a certain percentage of their allocations to agencies and organizations at the local level. Exceptions to this requirement may be made in the cases of states that are centralized, in which many or all services are provided by the state.

Some grant programs include entitlements, in which a portion or all of the funds must be subgranted to local jurisdictions according to a specific formula that calculates data such as law enforcement expenditures, crime statistics, and population. In a competitive process, a request for proposals or concept papers is issued and applications may be reviewed by peer review committees, professional grant administrators, an advisory board, or a combination of these. Examples of federal funding passed through state agencies are the Byrne Formula funds from the Bureau of Justice Assistance (BJA), the Victims of Crime Act (VOCA) from the Office for Victims of Crime, and the Juvenile Accountability Incentive Block Grant (JAIBG) from the Office of Juvenile Justice and Delinquency Prevention (OJJDP).

States may also allocate their own funds to support criminal justice programs. In these cases, the funds are usually allocated to the state agency that implements programs most relevant to the goals of the funds, not to a purely administrative agency. The funds are often distributed and expended according to the established needs and priorities of that agency and any constituent or satellite offices it may operate at the local level. These agencies coordinate services and may subcontract to local authorities or private organizations for direct services. In other cases, they may be distributed on the basis of a competitive subgrant process. An example is the State Victims Assistance Program (SVAP) in South Carolina. Funds are generated through the South Carolina Department of Corrections Inmate Work Release Program. Ten percent of inmate wages is transferred to the grants administrative arm of the South Carolina Department of Public Safety, which then subgrants the funds on a competitive basis to complement and coordinate with the federal VOCA program. In other cases, certain fees collected statewide are distributed directly to county authorities, such as fees from alcohol consumption that go to local alcohol and drug abuse agencies to develop treatment, intervention, and prevention programs to help divert offenders or potential offenders from entering the criminal justice system.

In cases where the state subgrants funds to other state and local agencies, an important role of the state is to monitor the progress of subgrants both programmatically and financially. Programmatic monitoring helps ensure that the program is being implemented as described in the application, data are being collected to measure the objectives, and the goals or outcomes are being met. If this is not occurring, the state can assist program staff in overcoming barriers and improving both the process and outcomes. Such programmatic assistance can result in more solid data to demonstrate the effectiveness of a project, thereby increasing the chances that additional funding can be secured to continue the project, whether from the current funding source or a new one. Financial monitoring helps to ensure that expenditures are reasonable and appropriate and that state and federal financial guidelines are followed. State grant administrators can assist subgrantees in navigating what are often labyrinthine regulations regarding issues such as bidding procedures, state contract requirements, and supplantation. The degree of programmatic and financial monitoring varies considerably among states and among individual state agencies that administer grant funds and oversee program implementation.

A valuable but often overlooked role of the state in criminal justice funding is that of technical assistance provider to agencies and organizations at both the state and local levels. State agencies that receive and administer federal allocations are often very knowledgeable about other funding opportunities as they become available, such as federal discretionary funds. Because discretionary funds are not passed through a state administrative agency, organizations at the local level may apply directly to the federal government for funding. State grant administrative agencies may be very helpful in disseminating these funding notices as well as assisting local or state agencies as they apply for federal, state, or private funding. They may be willing to answer questions, provide contact information, and review applications to provide recommendations for improvement. This capacity to provide technical assistance varies greatly, not only from state to state but within each state as well.

In sum, the state's role in criminal justice funding can take many forms, and these forms are largely dependent on the original funding source and its concomitant regulations. Importantly, the state role is not necessarily limited to merely disbursing grant funds from state or federal sources. It can serve as a disseminator of information about funding opportunities of many types, provide information about best practices and model programs, facilitate more effective program operation and improve outcomes through programmatic and financial monitoring, and assist agencies and organizations in improving grant applications. A state may also involve its citizens by soliciting and coordinating public input into the determination of funding priorities to the extent that it has the flexibility to do so. Citizen involvement may extend to serving on advisory boards or peer review committees for state agencies.

LAURA D. WHITLOCK

References and Further Reading

The South Carolina Department of Public Safety, Office of Justice Programs website, www.scdps.org/cjgp.

The Office of Juvenile Justice and Delinquency Prevention website, www.ojjdp.ncjrs.org.

The Bureau of Justice Assistance website, www.ojp.usdoj.gov/bja.

The Office for Victims of Crime website, www.ojp.usdoj.gov/ovc.

The South Carolina Department of Alcohol and Other Drug Abuse Services website, www.daodas.state.sc.us.

The Catalog of Federal Domestic Assistance website, www.cfda.gov.

Justice Information Center website, www.ncjrs.org.

See also **Evaluation and Policy Research; National Institute of Justice**

Criminal Justice System: Definition and Components

The criminal justice system is defined as the aggregate of agencies that are mandated to respond to alleged violations of the public order, to test the validity of accusations, and to ensure that appropriate sanctions are applied where warranted. Fulfillment of this mandate requires legislation, policing, adjudication, sentencing, and sanctions. These five activities are carried out by four interrelated components of the system: the legislature (insofar as it makes criminal laws or confirms the validity of court-made criminal laws within its jurisdiction), police (who identify violations and violators), courts (that ascertain guilt and sentencing), and corrections (that carries out court-mandated sentences). Each of these components consists of a set of designated actors, working within designated agencies. Each agency impacts on the others, and the result is not necessarily, or even usually, a smoothly running system.

The first component of the criminal justice system is criminal law. Substantive criminal law defines which actions can be treated as "criminal." Generally, these are actions seen as violations of the state's right to maintain social order. They are offenses against the state, rather than "civil" or "tort" offenses, which are citizen-to-citizen disputes (suits). Federal states may provide for each federated state (province or canton) to have its own criminal code (the U.S., Switzerland), or may limit criminal jurisdiction to the central government (Canada).

Substantive criminal laws usually specify an action or omission that is prohibited (*actus reus*), the degree of subjective awareness that must be established with respect to it, such as negligence, recklessness, or conscious intention (the required *mens rea*), the appropriate defenses (such as necessity or duress), and the range of penalties that can be invoked upon conviction. Procedural criminal law establishes which agents of the justice system, under what circumstances, can initiate, conduct, terminate, appeal, or review the conduct of a criminal prosecution. Procedural law covers, for example, when and how police, courts, and corrections may conduct surveillance, interrogate, seize evidence, lay a charge, or release those who have been detained. Criminal law is bounded by constitutional rules, international agreements, and human rights legislation.

The second component in criminal justice is "policing." Policing may be done by people working in quasi-military agencies called police, but is sometimes also done, or assisted, by private security agents, the military, or any other persons delegated this power by the state. Unauthorized (vigilante) policing is outside the system, because it usurps the role of the state. Policing involves identifying certain events as crimes, identifying the person or persons who may be held responsible for them, and using procedures such as arrests or summons to bring such persons to the attention of the prosecutors' office and the intake level of the court system. Policing can be reactive (a response to a specific call for help), proactive (involving active investigation, often undercover), or preventative (maintaining police presence, assisting in crime prevention efforts).

The third component in the system is adjudication (official weighing of the evidence), usually most visible in the trial court, but also includes pretrial investigation, plea bargaining, and appeal (review). The court, as a component in the criminal justice system, brings together many actors representing differing and potentially conflicting interests. The predominant roles are prosecution, defense, witnesses, judge, and (sometimes) jury. Victims who are not called witnesses have no official presence in criminal adjudication. The prosecutor (in some systems known as the procurator) has the task of reviewing the pretrial evidence and, if prosecution is warranted, presenting the case for the state. As an officer of the court, the prosecutor should ensure that the accused's rights are not violated, and should allow all legally admissible evidence to be available to the defense. This is often violated in practice. The defense counsel is also considered to be an officer of the court, even when retained by the defendant. As such, the defense is restricted by court rules. The defense attempts to show that there is insufficient evidence to support the charge as laid, and is likely to attack any procedural errors (especially rights violations) that have occurred. Not every modern system includes a jury, and most limit its use to serious felony cases heard in higher courts. In jury trials, the jury is expected to rule on the "facts" (what actually happened), whereas decisions about the application of the law are supposed to be the province of the presiding judge. In practice, this distinction is difficult to maintain, and "jury nullification" (refusal to convict in the face of the evidence) is a potential outcome. Court systems vary immensely with respect to the qualifications required for prosecutors and judges, the processes leading to their appointment or election, the quality and availability of defense counsel, and the selection of juries.

Also considered part of adjudication is sentencing. Although a sentencing decision is nominally made by the judge, juries may have an impact through their decision to convict on a higher or lower level of charge, and their recommendations, if requested. Also, the law is often written in a way that establishes not only maximum and minimum sentences (in terms of fines or length of incarceration, for example), but mandatory sentences under certain circumstances.

A final aspect of adjudication is appeal. Appeals by either the prosecution or the defense are hedged by many rules. They may result in a new trial or direct substitution of a new verdict or sentence. A jury verdict of acquittal cannot be overturned, but a new trial can be ordered. Appeals are usually allowed only if a significant violation of procedural rules can be demonstrated, or significant new evidence has emerged. The highest court of the land normally considers only appeals that it consents to hear on the basis of important issues in law.

The fourth component in the system is corrections, which comes into play if the convicted individual is deemed to require supervision. If the sentence has been a fine, or time already served in pretrial detention (remand), or, as in some Islamic systems, an amputation or flogging, the individual does not fall under the corrections component of the system. If, however, the individual is sentenced to probation or some form of detention (prison, penitentiary, or electronic monitoring) the corrections subsystem is responsible for providing this. Corrections has incompatible goals (revenge, punishment, control, and rehabilitation). Corrections also prepares the offender for release, sometimes providing or subcontracting postrelease supervision, for example, through parole officers, halfway houses, or day-reporting centers.

Overall, criminal justice systems do not run smoothly. For example, if mandatory penalties are increased beyond what the police or the courts regard as reasonable, police may refuse to charge or judges may refuse to convict. If the courts send too many offenders into the corrections system, it may respond by increasing early release or by keeping offenders under substandard, potentially dangerous, and criminogenic conditions.

Criminal justice systems vary a great deal with respect to their role in the balance of crime control and protection of individual rights, and to the extent to which justice translates into fairness. Inequality may be fostered by laws that criminalize possession of one drug rather than another, and by courts that view white collar and dominant group offenders as less criminal than others. Societies vary a great deal in the extent to which they resort to the criminal justice system as a solution to problems of public order, and most are actively working to develop alternative approaches, such as restorative justice.

LINDA B. DEUTSCHMANN

Further Reading

Cole, G.F., compiler, *Criminal Justice: Law and Policies*, North Scituate, MA: Duxbury Press, 1972; Cole, G.F. and Gertz, M.G. (Eds.), *The Criminal Justice System: Politics and Policies,* 7th ed. Belmont, CA: West/Wadsworth, 1998.

Cook, J.R., *Asphalt Justice: A Critique of the Criminal Justice System in America*, Westport, CT: Praeger, 2001.

Courtless, T.F., *Corrections and the Criminal Justice System: Law, Policies, and Practices*, Belmont, CA: West/Wadsworth, 1997.

Dwyer, J., Neufeld, P.J., and Scheck, B., *Actual Innocence: Five Days to Execution, and Other Dispatches from the Wrongly Convicted*, New York, NY: Doubleday, 2000.

Fairchild, E.S., *Comparative Criminal Justice Systems*, Belmont, CA: Wadsworth, 1993; 2nd ed., Fairchild, E. and Dammer, H.R. (Eds.), Belmont, CA: Wadsworth/Thomson Learning, and London, UK: Thomas Learning, 2001.

Hirsch, J.S., *Hurricane: The Miraculous Journey of Rubin Carter*, Boston, MA: Houghton Mifflin, and London, UK: Fourth Estate, 2000.

Reichel, P.L., *Comparative Criminal Justice Systems: A Topical Approach*, Upper Saddle River, NJ: Prentice-Hall, 1994; 2nd ed., 1999.

Schmalleger, F., *Criminal Justice Today: An Introductory Text for the 21st Century*, Englewood Cliffs, NJ: Prentice-Hall, 1991; 6th ed., Upper Saddle River, NJ: Prentice-Hall, 2001.

Stojkovic, S., Klofas, J., and Kalinich, D.B., (Eds.), *The Administration and Management of Criminal Justice Organizations: A Book of Readings*, Prospect Heights, IL: Waveland Press, 1990; 3rd ed., 1999.

Washington, L., *Black Judges on Justice: Perspectives from the Bench*, New York, NY: New Press, 1994.

See also **Criminal Justice Funding: The State Role; Criminal Justice System: Models of Operation; Discretion and the Criminal Justice System; Mass Media and the Criminal Justice System; Public Opinion and the Criminal Justice System**

Criminal Justice System: Models of Operation

Systems

A system, as defined by *Webster's Collegiate Dictionary*, is a "regularly interacting or interdependent group of items forming a unified whole." However, the conventional notion of a criminal justice system is actually a somewhat misleading characterization of a rather complex maze of criminal justice organizations in the U.S. A better way of thinking about it is to consider it as two distinct parts—national (federal) and local (states, counties, cities, etc.). Thus, the American criminal justice system is highly decentralized, with local community norms contributing significantly in shaping the various subunits of criminal justice organizations.

The Criminal Justice System Is Distinctive

Most organizations would like to believe that they are engaged in systematic-rational decision making. Criminal justice organizations are similar, but because of the unique nature of their work there are some differences. In particular, criminal justice organizations are distinguished by their broad use of discretion, operational resources, chronology of operations, and filtering or gate-keeping activities. Hence, system output may be affected by internal and external environmental factors as noted in systems theory analyses.

Discretion

Discretionary decision making by criminal justice professionals is pervasive and necessary for effective and efficient operations. Discretionary power is typically justified along two dimensions: justice and resources. Clearly, every violation of law cannot possibly be prosecuted because of costs—both human resources and institutional capacity. For example, in large urban environments experiencing significant violent crime and where calls for service drive much of what police officers do, it would not be uncommon for officers not to make arrests for minor violations to ensure the availability of officers for more serious offenses. Similar reasoning may apply for a judge who is confronted with sentencing a first-time youthful offender for a nonserious crime. He or she may make the decision to impose probation rather than incarceration—thus providing the offender with the chance for reform while also being mindful of the limited prison space within the correctional system. These types of actions fall within the discretion of criminal justice professionals and demonstrate how the activities of one subsystem may affect another.

Operational Resources

The criminal justice system is analogous to other public sector organizations in that it *generally* does not produce its own resources. Rather, it relies on public funds typically in the form of taxes to support operations. Salaries, retirement, equipment, and support staff must be paid for out of the treasuries of local, state, and federal budgets. This reliance on public funds requires efficient utilization—requiring periodic accountings. Furthermore, justice professionals are accountable to legislators, city managers, mayors, city councils, and "we the people" taxpayers. The level of funding will be a function of the political process at both the national and local levels. Thus, political leaders, representing their constituents, will ultimately impact the levels of funding a community will find for its criminal justice organizations. In most communities, the police and public safety initiatives comprise the largest part of their respective budgets.

Chronology of Organizational Operations

The criminal justice system has discrete tasks that are performed largely in a rational manner. Yet because of the nature of the system's interdependence on other parts, the actions of one part may affect the actions of another. For example, the prosecutor can only prosecute individuals who are arrested by the police. If officers make discretionary decisions not to arrest, the prosecutor will have no knowledge of the offense—likewise with the prosecutor. If he or she makes a discretionary decision not to prosecute and takes the case under advisement, then the case never goes to trial or before a judge and jury. So, correctional professionals will never become involved in the case.

Filtering and Gate-keeping

The criminal justice system performs a filtering process wherein cases are screened. Depending upon the facts and circumstances of each case and the discretionary activities of criminal justice professionals, the decisions made at various points in the system could result in a person or persons not being arrested; cases taken under advisement or dropped by the prosecutor; cases forwarded for trial; cases dismissed or probation ordered at trial; cases tried; or persons incarnated after passing through the system. Some cases will be plea bargained; some will have individuals admit guilt, and finally some will involve the entire sequence ending in conviction and sentencing. Most cases are not tried, and in fact, although many cases enter the system, very few result in conviction and punishment.

Principal Subsystems and Operational Models

The primary criminal justice subsystems are (1) police, (2) prosecutors, (3) courts and judges, and (4) corrections. These entities deal directly with people charged with violations of criminal laws. Collectively, they include over 60,000 agencies, both public and private, with annual budgets of over $74 billion and roughly 1.7 million employees.

Police

With approximately 17,000 public organizations in the U.S. it is easy to understand how fragmented and complex the criminal justice system is. Policing is dominated by local government activity, with agencies disbursed through counties, towns, and cities and over 1,019,496 full-time employees. Of this amount, 708,022 are full-time sworn personnel (69%) and 311,474 nonsworn (civilian) personnel (31%). Additionally, these agencies have roughly 99,000 part-time sworn personnel. Overall, U.S. policing is comprised of small police departments that operate within their own independent jurisdictional authority. The police function focuses generally on four primary areas: (1) peace keeping, (2) apprehending law violators and crime fighting, (3) crime prevention, and (4) social services. Variations in policing models have changed over the years and are now undergoing significant innovations.

Peace keeping is a rather broad area, but is arguably one of the most important aspects of any police operation. It involves a host of activities that focus on protecting the rights of people in a range of situations, from domestic disturbances to bar room brawls.

The apprehension of law violators and crime fighting is often touted by the public as the most essential police function. Yet this area of policing accounts for only a small percentage of the officer's time. Officers are typically not engaged in the types of activities seen on television shows or the movies.

Crime prevention activities deal largely with educating the public about crime in the community and community awareness. It focuses on reducing the number of potential situations in which crimes may occur, thereby reducing the incidence of crime.

Social service activities constitute a rather large range of activities, from recovering stolen property, traffic control, providing directions to visitors, assisting the mentally ill and the elderly, to helping find lost pets. These types of mundane activities are not only expected by communities, but also are typically very visible and necessary to any community.

Of course, because American cities differ in governmental structure and demographics, one could expect to find variations in policing. As noted in James Q. Wilson's classic study, citizens expect their local police practices and behaviors to reflect community norms. Hence, local political cultures will, in part, determine the style of policing. Wilson identified three styles of policing: the watchman style, the legalist style, and service style.

The *watchman* style focuses on order maintenance wherein police officers are afforded considerable discretion and concentrate largely on maintaining the peace. Minor violations may be ignored—particularly juvenile activities and traffic.

The *legalistic* style is characterized by professionalism and focuses on law enforcement activities such as aggressive enforcement geared toward visible street crimes that pose threats to personal safety and property. This style may also be attentive to juvenile offenders, drug arrests, prostitution, and other nuisance types of crimes. Police agencies that employ this type of legalist enforcement practice use strict application of the law as the guiding force that ultimately directs their activities, thereby suggesting one community standard. This type of policing tends to ignore variations in standards for different groups of people such as juveniles, minority populations, gay populations, and others.

The *service* style is most likely to be found in middle class communities. These communities want their police to focus not only on serious crimes such as burglaries or crimes against persons, but also to pay limited attention to minor infractions. The expectations of these community members are a quasi-individualized style of policing.

However, the activities of most patrol officers have been described as being similar to medical doctors specializing in general practice. As such, officers must be knowledgeable in a variety of areas and be able to quickly diagnose symptoms and, where appropriate, provide a cure or refer to a specialist such as detectives or other specialized units. But in most communities the patrol division is the largest and most visible part of the department and is typically characterized as the backbone of police operations. They respond to calls for service 24 hours a day and must be prepared to address any type of situation ranging from armed robberies to international terrorism. However, in small departments the patrol division *is* the entire police department. Nevertheless, patrol functions revolve largely around answering calls for assistance or service and maintaining a visible presence for deterrence purposes, and investigation of suspicious people or activities.

Patrol Officer Functions

There are nearly 800,000 full-time sworn law enforcement officers in the U.S. and their responsibilities encompass a large range of activities. They are focused along three dimensions: responding to calls for assistance, observance of suspicious activities, and maintaining a visible police presence in the communities served. Of course, depending on the size and complexity of the communities served, their duties will be quite varied. Yet, when most officers are not engaged in responding to calls for service they may be attempting to practice preventive patrol techniques with the idea of creating a visible presence for the purpose of deterring potential criminal activity. Nevertheless, as noted by one chief in a major metropolitan city, "when the people call we must respond and we must respond quickly." In some communities, foot patrol is a key policing technique that attempts to bring officers closer to the community. Although this is a laudable technique, in an age of highly mobile criminal offenders officers must be able to respond quickly. In fact, the public they serve demands it.

Community Oriented Policing

Community oriented policing attempts to build partnerships with citizens for the purpose of having community members help in deciding approaches to make communities safe. It focuses on extensive collaboration between the police and the community. Community policing has been well received because of the alleged deficiencies in traditional—quasi-military police models. One problem with this form of policing is that it means different things to different police departments and communities. In fact, it is defined differently across many jurisdictions. For example, in many large urban cities it could mean more aggressive patrol and a zero tolerance approach to crime and disorder. Or, in a smaller middle class or affluent community with relatively limited serious crime it may mean simply talking more to local residents and business personnel. Essentially, no definitive encompassing definition is available that may be generalized to and applicable for "all" police departments.

Problem Oriented Policing

Problem oriented policing is somewhat comparable to the community approach, but it focuses on resolving root causes of community instability and crime rather than treating symptoms of it. Quality of life issues are of paramount importance under this model wherein officers are encouraged and required to look beyond police department resources for problem resolution. So, an eclectic approach is used that could include the use of other city, state, or federal services; the business community, social service, and nonprofit organizations, the media, the military, the fire department, and other agencies as needed. The problem oriented approach, therefore, attacks community problems using multiple lines of sight and resources.

A New Model and Synthesis

According to the U.S. Department of Justice Office of Community Oriented Policing, a new postacademy field-training program for law enforcement agencies is being implemented in select communities. It is the first new innovation in over 30 years. The Police Training Officer (PTO) program merges both community policing and problem-solving policing philosophies and techniques and comprises eight components: (1) citizen complaint intake and investigation issues, (2) community policing to reduce domestic violence, (3) early identification and intervention strategies, (4) effective management of overtime, (5) ethics for the individual officer, (6) racial profiling: issues and dilemmas, (7) use of force issues in a community policing environment, and (8) school-safety conference. The program, originally tested in Reno, Nevada, was then pilot-tested by the Savannah, GA, Lowell, MA, Colorado Springs, CO, Richmond, CA, and Charlotte-Mecklenburg, NC police departments. Early results of this training have been promising in that it has produced well-trained officers who are prepared to serve their individual communities.

Federal Law Enforcement

According to the Bureau of Justice Statistics, as of June 2002, 93,000 full-time personnel authorized to carry firearms worked for federal agencies in all 50 states and the District of Columbia. The duties of federal officers vary considerably. Criminal investigations accounted for 40% of their activities, 22% police response and patrol, corrections 18%, noncriminal investigation and inspection 14%, court operations 4%, and security protection about 1%. The number of federal law enforcement officers increased 19% at the Bureau of Alcohol, Tobacco and Firearms, 11% at Customs, and 8% at the Department of Immigration and Naturalization Service, which is now under the umbrella of the Department of Justice. Federal agencies enforce specific federal laws and are part of the executive branch of government. The Federal Bureau of Investigation (FBI) has the widest range of operations. It typically investigates numerous federal violations along with any other areas not encompassed by other federal law enforcement agencies.

A New Model: Convergence of Local and Federal Law Enforcement

Substantial federal collaboration has occurred since the mid-1980s—but most notably since the events of September 11, 2001. In the mid-1980s there began a significant trend toward more federal jurisdiction and local cooperation with police and prosecutors. This has been most remarkable in larger urban U.S. cities plagued by pervasive drug and gang activities. This type of collaboration has been extremely helpful in numerous large-scale drug and gang investigations where local authorities lacked sufficient resources to conduct their operations effectively. The result has been improved law-enforcement coordination, significant intelligence sharing, and innovative problem-solving techniques. The reasons collaboration began to proliferate was based on the dual needs of federal agencies and local authorities. For example, federal law enforcement needed additional personnel and more extensive geographic coverage to investigate specific federal crimes. But local police needed greater access to national criminal information; more undercover agents unfamiliar to local criminals and criminal organizations; access to cross-jurisdictional law enforcement powers and to more sophisticated investigative methods; and tougher federal penalties for certain crimes. Just as important is the need for federal and local authorities to pool scarce resources and to coordinate investigative activities to avoid duplicitous activities, thus decreasing danger to officers. Although some tend to believe that the federal role in local law enforcement is too great, the general feeling is that this sharing of expertise, resources, and in some cases training has been a positive step toward addressing the problem of crime in an ever-changing complex society. Yet the most significant example of federal and local police cooperation is most evident following the events of September 11th with the institution of the Office of Homeland Security. Local and federal law enforcement must now be able to address issues involving: intelligence and warning; border and transportation security; domestic counterterrorism; protecting critical infrastructure and key assets; defending against catastrophic threats; and emergency preparedness and response. Because local police will typically be the first responders in the event of an attack, the need for extensive federal and local convergence is necessary. Consequently, conventional models of police and criminal justice activities are undergoing rapid and significant change.

The Prosecutorial System

Just like the policing subsystem, the prosecutorial subsystem is largely a function of local and state governments, with federal crimes prosecuted by the U.S. attorney. U.S. attorneys are appointed by the president and are housed in the U.S. Department of Justice. However, because most offenses involve state law violations, local criminal justice systems are pervasive. Every state elects an attorney general who has the legal power and authority to initiate prosecutions under the right conditions.

The Prosecuting Attorney—Federal

Within the American criminal justice system, prosecution of offenders rests largely with state and local jurisdictions. However, when federal law is involved, U.S. attorneys, who are all members of the Department of Justice, have jurisdiction. There are 94 U.S. attorneys and 2000 assistant U.S. attorneys. U.S. Attorney offices are maintained in each of the 94 federal district courts. Each U.S. attorney is appointed by the president of the U.S. and must be approved by Congress and then confirmed by the Senate. U.S. attorneys serve a 4-year term in office. Federal prosecutors have a significant role in the criminal justice system. They represent the federal government in court and their activities must be conducted in a fair and balanced manner in an effort to afford justice to the accused while also vigorously representing the government.

The Prosecuting Attorney—State and Local

On the state level where most offenders are prosecuted, each state has an attorney general, who is elected to office. He or she is responsible for both civil and criminal activities. To assist the attorney general, he or she may have numerous assistant state attorneys, very similar to the federal government. There may be wide variations in terms of scope and level of prosecution. For example, according to the Bureau of Justice Statistics, in 2001:

- Half the prosecutors' offices nationwide employed nine or fewer people and had a budget of $318,000 or less;
- The 2314 state court prosecutors' offices employed over 79,000 attorneys, investigators, and support staff, a 39% increase from 1992 and 13% from 1996;
- Over three-quarters of the nation's chief prosecutors occupied full-time positions compared to about half in 1990. Sixty-five percent of all offices had at least one full-time assistant attorney;
- Forty-one percent of the prosecutors' offices had a staff person who had been threatened or assaulted compared to 49% in 1996;
- Approximately 69% of all offices indicated having proceeded against an estimated 32,000 juveniles in criminal court; four out of ten offices prosecuted computer-related crimes (felony or misdemeanor) against their state's computer statutes;
- About 23% of prosecutors' offices assigned prosecutors to handle community-related activities.

Clearly, as noted throughout this essay, variations in demographics, economic resources, law and politics, along with vast prosecutorial discretion could impact both the role of the prosecutor and the effect and output of the criminal justice system.

The Defense Attorney

Defense attorneys play a central role in the criminal justice system. These lawyers represent the accused and the convicted offender in their dealings with criminal justice officials—including prosecutors, police, and courts. Within this system, the defense counsel could appear with his or her client at the police station after initial arrest to provide advice concerning interrogation and to make sure that rights are not violated. Defense attorneys may typically appear at the initial appearance with the accused before a judge to seek pretrial release or seek bail or challenge the basis of the arrest. Furthermore, defense counsel may be with the accused during preliminary hearings, arraignment, pretrial, trial, sentencing, and appeal. One primary function of defense counsel is to ensure that the accused is afforded a fair trial and to be diligent advocates for them. They are obligated to challenge legal points of law asserted by prosecutors and to advise clients of their rights.

Dual Criminal Justice Court System

The court system in the U.S. is a dual system consisting of federal and state courts. The U.S. Supreme Court provides oversight of sorts for both systems. Federal courts focus largely on issues involving "federal questions" or those problems wherein the accused has allegedly violated laws involving the national or federal government. Overwhelmingly, however, most criminal actions are brought in state courts—most notably at the trial court level of city and various county governments. These systems are highly decentralized with the idea that the citizenry should be close to its court system.

Federal Court System

The federal court system consists of the Supreme Court of the U.S., Circuit Court of Appeals, and District Courts. Initially, the federal court system was to be the least powerful among the three branches of government. However, because of the complexity of a dynamic American society the federal court system, particularly the Supreme Court, has significantly impacted the criminal justice system.

The judges who serve on the federal judiciary are nominated by the president and ultimately confirmed by the Senate for lifetime appointments. No formal qualifications to be a judge exists in the Constitution and federal judges are removed involuntarily only through impeachment and conviction by Congress. The Constitution is also silent on the size of courts. It only stipulates that there shall be one Supreme Court and such inferior courts as deemed necessary by Congress to create. Furthermore, although the Constitution does not discuss the notion of overturning the actions of Congress or the president, it has been doing so under the guise and power of judicial review made famous in a case called *Marbury v. Madison* (5 U.S. (1 Cranch) 137, 2 L.Ed. 60, 1803).

The federal court system is a dual state and federal system. We have one federal system and 50 corresponding state systems. Each one has layers: trial courts typically referred to as district courts, courts of appeal, and supreme courts. These court systems have their own particular sets of activities. For example, if an individual is accused of breaking a criminal law of the state of Illinois, he or she will be tried in an Illinois state court. However, if the controversy involves a federal law in the state of Illinois, the case will be tried in a federal district court. A common issue involving cases concerns jurisdiction. There are two types of jurisdiction: original and appellate. Original jurisdiction is focused on fact finding and the actual judging of the case. Essentially, a court with original jurisdiction over a case is where the trial will take place that will include lawyers, witnesses, and judge and jury. Federal district courts are trial courts and are considered courts of original jurisdiction and have power over almost all federal cases.

Appellate jurisdiction occurs when a court reviews the procedures and actions of a lower court. Trials are not conducted at the appellate level and evidence is not heard. The appellate judge merely judges the lower court judge's procedures in adjudicating the case—not whether the individual or parties are guilty.

The Supreme Court is distinctive in the federal system in that it has both original and appellate jurisdiction. In most instances, the Supreme Court is sitting in appellate jurisdiction and thus hearing appeals. Yet under some circumstances the Supreme Court is responsible for hearing evidence and judging the facts of a case compatible with a typical trial setting.

Corrections

Corrections administration in the U.S. is fragmented and diverse largely because of the various levels of government. Every level of government, to some extent, has some responsibility for corrections and thus—among the federal, state, and local governments—one can observe significant variation. Adult corrections, juvenile corrections, and federal corrections may involve significantly different levels of government and agency responsibility. Within the adult system, the correctional function includes pretrial detention, probation and parole, halfway houses, houses of corrections, county prisons, state prisons, county parole, and state parole. The juvenile system may include detention, probation supervision, dependent/neglect, training schools, private placements, and juvenile aftercare.

Federal Corrections

Congress created the U.S. Bureau of Prisons in 1930 in an attempt to provide humane professional care to inmates. Central to its mission was to "ensure consistent and centralized administration of the eleven federal prisons in operation at that time." As of 2003, the bureau has 104 institutions, six regional offices, a central office, two staff training centers, and 28 community corrections offices. The bureau's area of responsibility encompasses the control, custody and care of approximately 171, 000 federal offenders. A little over 144,500 inmates are confined in bureau-operated correctional institutions and detention centers. The remaining inmates are confined in privately operated prisons, detention centers, community correctional centers, juvenile facilities, and some facilities operated by state and local governments.

State Corrections Systems

All states have a department that deals exclusively with corrections. However, the responsibility for these programs varies. For example, in some states the corrections department operates probation and parole but in other states probation is under the control of the judiciary with parole handled separately. There is considerable variation among the several states on how correctional policy is administered. Much of it has to do with variations in state law, tradition, and structure of government. Although there is considerable variance, most state correctional systems are generally quite large and old. The institutions are typically characterized by the types of inmates incarcerated and could range from maximum to minimum security facilities. Maximum security facilities focus on tight custody and discipline. They typically may resemble a fortress of sorts with guard towers, barbed wire, and a quasi-military approach to administration of services. Prisoners must adhere to a strict routine with the institution focusing on preventing escape. Medium security facilities, although they resemble the maximum institutions in appearance, attempt to create a somewhat different atmosphere. It is less structured, rigid, and generally less stressful. Prisoners in these institutions normally have more privileges and more contact with outside visitors, frequent mail, and more exposure to amenities such as radio, television, and computers. These medium security institutions account for about 49% of state inmates, thus incarcerating the bulk of offenders. A major issue confronting the correctional community is overcrowding resulting from increasing incarceration rates derived from the "war on drugs" and mandatory minimum sentences. In fact, according to the Bureau of Justice Statistics:

- In 2000, 6.7 million people and at year end 2002, 3.1% of all U.S. adult residents or 1 in every 32 adults were on probation, in jail or prison, or on parole.
- State and federal prison authorities had 1,440,655 inmates at mid-year 2002, 1,277,127 under state jurisdiction, and 163,528 under federal jurisdiction.
- Local jails held or supervised 737,912 persons awaiting trial or serving a sentence at mid-year 2002. About 72,400 of these were persons serving their sentence in the community.

As one can see, the criminal justice system is large, complex, and is capable of adjusting to a dynamic American and global society where change, chaos, and complexity are the norm. Yet, for all of its complexity, the system in general and its numerous subsystems in particular, provides for the most equitable administration of justice of any society in the history of human kind.

Morris A. Taylor

References and Further Reading

Bureau of Justice Statistics. (2002). *Census of State and Local Law Enforcement Agencies*, 2000.

Bureau of Justice Statistics. (2003). *Federal Law Enforcement* Officers, 2002.

Easton, D. (1979). *A Framework for Political Analysis*. Chicago, IL: University of Chicago Press.

Eck, J. and Spelman, W. (January 1987). *Problem Oriented Policing*. National Institute of Justice, Research in Brief.

Gilsinan, J. (1989). They is Clowning Tough: 911 and the Social Construction of Reality. *Criminology*, 27 (2), 329–343.

Goldstein, H. 1990. *Problem-Oriented Policing*. New York, NY: McGraw-Hill.

Herbert, S. (1997). *Policing Space: Territoriality and the Los Angeles Police Department*. Minneapolis, MN. University of Minnesota Press.

Office of Community Oriented Policing Services: U.S. Department of Justice. (2003). *First New Post-academy Police Officer Field Training Program in 30 Years Emphasizes Community Problem Solving Skills Over Traditional Response Methods*. Available at http://www.cops.usdoj.gov/default.asp.

Russell-Einhorn, M. (2003). *Fighting Urban Crime: The Evolution of Federal-local Collaboration*. National Institute of Justice, Research in Brief. December

Swanson, C., Territo, L., and Taylor, R. (2001). *Police Administration: Structures, Process, and Behavior*, 5th ed., Prentice Hall.

The National Strategy for Homeland Security: Office of Homeland Security, Executive Summary (2003). Available at http://www.whitehouse.gov/homeland/book/sect1.pdf.

Understanding the Federal Courts (2004). Available at http://www.uscourts.gov/understand02/.

Webster's New College Dictionary. (1995). Houghton Mifflin Company.

Wilson, J.Q. (1967). *Varieties of Police Behavior: The Management of Law and Order in Eight Communities*, Cambridge, MA: Harvard University Press.

See also **Corrections: Federal Bureau of Prisons; Courts in the US.; Criminal Justice System: Definitions and Components; Police: Administration and Organization.**

Criminal Justice Theorizing

Introduction: Crime Theory Substituting for Criminal Justice Theory

What is criminal justice theory? What does it mean to theorize criminal justice phenomena? Amazingly, despite the large number of academic programs and scholarly works dedicated to studying criminal justice, our field has hardly asked, let alone answered, these fundamental questions (exceptions include Bernard and Engel, 2001; Marenin and Worrall, 1998; Hagan, 1989). A strong theoretical infrastructure is the heart and soul of any area of study. The time is past due to begin recognizing and developing a theoretical foundation explicitly intended to make theoretical sense of criminal justice.

It is not that criminology and criminal justice studies are not experienced with theory and the activity of theorizing. Our field has amassed an impressive body of theoretical work. Its focus, however, has concentrated mostly on answering the why of crime and explaining crime rates. When we use the term "theory" in our field, we are generally referring to crime theory. Our "theory courses" and "theory textbooks" concentrate almost exclusively on explaining crime. Theoretical research in our field, as evidenced by the articles published in *Criminology* and *Justice Quarterly*, mostly test preexisting explanations for crime. Our field's theoretical infrastructure is built on explanations of crime, not criminal justice.

An underlying assumption in our field is that the discipline of criminology is more interested in explaining the why of crime and thus by nature more theoretically oriented. It follows, then, that studying criminal justice is necessarily a policy-based pursuit more interested in effecting practical crime-control initiatives, as derived from theories of crime (Gibbons, 1994). Studying criminal justice is tacitly relegated to the limited role of discerning "how to" and "what works"—laudable objectives, but incomplete insofar as understanding the nature of our formal reaction to crime. Dantzker's (1998, 107) delineation between criminology and criminal justice is typical of this view.

Criminology is the scientific study of crime as a social phenomenon—that is, the theoretical application involving the study of the nature and extent of criminal behavior. Criminal justice is the applied and scientific study of the practical applications of criminal behavior—that is, the actions, policies, and functions of the agencies within the criminal justice system charged with addressing this behavior.

Are not both criminology and criminal justice studies diminishing their theoretical integrity with this conception? Surely the study of criminal justice, by both criminological and criminal justice scholars, has involved far more than merely describing its functioning and devising means of crime control. There is no reason that the study of criminal justice cannot be approached in the same way Dantzker views the study of crime. By slightly modifying his quote, criminal justice studies could similarly be viewed as *the scholarly examination of criminal justice as a social phenomenon—that is, the theoretical application involving the study of the nature and extent of criminal justice behavior.*

Some traditional criminological theorists might take exception to this view. After all, they would argue, crime theory has already been used as the foundational material for developing *models* of criminal justice functioning (see Einstadter and Henry, 1995). This approach to understanding criminal justice takes traditional crime theories and infers a model of criminal justice functioning based on that particular conception of crime causation. Although modeling criminal justice functioning does shed important theoretical light on the system, even those involved in the activity admit that these models do not constitute the development of theory (Einstadter and Henry, 1995). This exercise also reinforces the notion that there can be no other theoretical foundation for understanding criminal justice behavior, besides those preexisting theories designed to make theoretical sense of crime.

Some *critical* criminological theorists might also take exception. Critical criminology has a rich body of work theorizing the behavior of the state, the legal apparatus, trends in social control, and oppressive crime control policies. In fact, compared to their analysis of criminal justice behavior, explaining law breaking has been a secondary pursuit. This is one reason critical scholarship often seems out of place in most criminological theory textbooks: their object of study—an oppressive crime control apparatus—does not coincide well with theories focused only on crime causation. Even when critical criminologists explore the causes of crime, they most often focus on the oppressive features of how the state differentially defines acts as crime among marginalized groups (again, focusing on state behavior). Seen this way, critical criminology is more engaged in theorizing criminal justice than crime.

Criminal Justice Theory: Varieties and Possibilities

Theorizing crime has proved to be a complex endeavor. The object of study is difficult to identify and agree upon, a plethora of theories compete for prominence, and determining the strength and worth of these theories is wrought with controversy and conflicting evidence. This description is not meant as an indictment; rather, criminological theory's complexity and conflicts render it dynamic and intellectually stimulating.

Theorizing criminal justice possibly harbors even more potential for this type of complexity and stimulation. The central reason is the multifaceted nature of our object of study. The entity we call "criminal justice" actually comprises numerous objects of study—including the criminal justice system, each of the major components within that system (police, courts, corrections, juvenile justice), crime control agencies and practices that fall outside the formal criminal justice system (private sector controls, social services), and other participants in criminal justice including, but not limited to, academic researchers, the media, the legislative body, and the public.

The following questions are just a sample of the types of inquiry we're interested in when theorizing criminal justice.

- How do we best make theoretical sense of the criminal justice apparatus's (CJA) long-term historical development?
- What accounts for the steep growth in power and size of the CJA over the last 30 years?
- How do we best make theoretical sense of current and possible future trends associated with the CJA?
- On what theoretical basis can we best understand various controversial issues facing the CJA (e.g., racial profiling, death penalty, erosion of constitutional safeguards, privatization, etc.)?
- On what theoretical basis can we best make sense of past and current criminal justice reform efforts, including what drives them and why they succeed or do not?
- How does the CJA affect the larger society in which it operates? Conversely, what societal forces shape the CJA?
- How do we best make theoretical sense of the behaviors of criminal justice practitioners?
- What best explains the internal functioning and practices of criminal justice agencies?

These questions demonstrate that our field's crime theories, because they have been constructed specifically to explain crime, are insufficient for providing adequate answers. Attempting to explain the behavior of the state, public agencies, the criminal law apparatus, trends in crime-control thinking and practice, private crime-control organizations, and trends in social control necessitate a theoretical infrastructure unique to these unique objects of study.

Numerous approaches to developing criminal justice theory are possible. One was already mentioned: constructing models of criminal justice functioning based on differing theories of crime. David Duffee (1990) has taken the more traditional approach by attempting to articulate a general theory of criminal justice, grounded in the context of local communities. Of course the development of a grand theory that accounts for all social, political, economic, and cultural influences would likely be an impractical undertaking. Another avenue has been to answer specific theoretical questions about a specific object of study. David Garland (2001), for example, limits his theoretical analysis to the question of what accounts for the rapid growth of the criminal justice system over the last 30 years (focusing primarily on the correctional subsystem). Other researchers concentrate on explaining individual practitioner behavior—such as why some police officers engage in corruption. Finally, some academics have worked on developing normative theories of criminal justice, concentrating on philosophical principles intended to guide criminal justice practices (Braithewaite and Pettit, 1990; Ellis and Ellis, 1989).

Theoretical Orientations—Infrastructure Beginnings

Despite these various avenues for developing criminal justice theory, our field still does not have a well-recognized theoretical infrastructure about criminal justice. To begin the process of rectifying this situation, Kraska (2004), in his book, *Theorizing Criminal Justice: Eight Essential Orientations*, has taken the unique approach of identifying and articulating the contours of eight different "theoretical orientations" found in traditional and contemporary scholarship about the criminal justice system and trends in crime control. Theoretical orientations are not specific theories ready made for testing; rather, they are broad-based interpretive constructs. Each orientation frames how we think about criminal justice phenomena, guiding the questions we might ask, influencing the research and specific theory testing we might conduct, orienting our interpretations of criminal justice phenomena, and affecting policy and practice. These orientations are organized around the notion of metaphor—an approach that helps us make theoretical sense of criminal justice by relating it to something else. Figure 1 illustrates the major features, concepts, and ideas associated with the eight metaphors employed.

Perusing these eight orientations should demonstrate that our field actually has a rich set of theoretical lenses through which to make sense of criminal justice phenomena, aside from theories about crime. The multitheoretical approach found in Figure 1 not only catalogs the diversity of thinking in our field of study, it also avoids the ethnocentric tendency in academics to view phenomena through a single theoretical filter. Even though the system's metaphor has predominated, influential work has also been done using the interpretive orientation (social constructionism or cultural studies), the political framework, the oppression orientation, and most recently, studying criminal justice through the lens of "late modernity."

Major Features/ Elements	***Rational/ Legal***	***System***	***Packer's C.C. vs. D.P.***	***Politics***	***Social Constructionist***	***Growth Complex***	***Oppression***	***Late-Modernity***
Intellectual tradition	Neo-classical; legal formalism	Structural-functionalism; biological sciences; organizational studies	Liberal legal jurisprudence; legal realism; socio-legal studies	Political science; public administration	Interpretive school; symbolic interactionism; social constructionism	Weber; Frankfurt School; critical public administration	Marx; feminism; critical sociology; race studies	Foucault; governmentality literature; postmodernism
Key concepts employed	Rational-legalistic, rule-bound; taken for granted	Functional; equilibrium; efficiency; technology; external forces; open system; closed system	Value-cluster; efficiency, crime control values; due process values; needs-based values	Ideology; conflict; symbolic politics; policy making/ implementing; state, community	Myth; reality; culture; symbols; legitimacy; moral panic; impression-management institutional theory	Bureaucracy building; privatization profit; complex; technical rationality; merging complexes	Dangerous classes; gender; patriarchy; racism; class bias; conflict model; structural thinking; dialectics; praxis	Actuarial justice; neo-liberal politics; exclusive society; safety norm; incoherence in CJ policy
Central objects of study	CJ system; rational decisions; law enforcement	CJ system; what works; technology; subsystem focus	CJ system; criminal law process; police and courts	CJ system; legislators; policy-making and implementing	Entire CJ apparatus; myth; media; organization culture; legitimacy; use of language	Entire CJ apparatus, dynasty building, privatization	Entire CJ apparatus; inequality; patriarchy; racism	Entire CJ apparatus and beyond; impact of late modern changes
Purpose of the CJ system and apparatus	Control crime; punish offenders; maintain peace and security	Control crime primary focus; various sub-purposes; efficient processing of accused; maintain safety in society	Control crime overall; purpose is ambiguous and tension-filled between crime control, due process, and need-based values	Purpose contingent on political climate; CJ is tool for political capital; rational administration of policy	Purpose is relative; socially constructed; management of appearances; maintain legitimacy	Growth in size and power; financial gain; political gain; build bureaucracy	Oppress marginalized in society; controlling those perceived as threatening status quo	Purpose is confused; technical management of excluded; fetish for safety, complex of controls
Why the rapid CJ expansion in the last 30 years?	Legal reaction to increased law-breaking (forced reaction theory)	CJ system reacting to increases in crime (forced reaction theory)	Pendulum swing toward crime control values; choosing punitiveness	Politicians exploiting problem; politicized drug war; shift in ideology	Moral panics; media exploitation; run-away cultural process; crime as scapegoat	Dynasty building; growth complex; merging private with public; CJ with military	Control of threatening groups; marginalized used as scapegoats; crisis in state legitimacy	Crisis in state sovereignty; risk aversive society; growth complex; moral indifference

FIGURE 1 Criminal Justice Theoretical Orientations.

Major Features/ Elements	*Rational/ Legal*	*System*	*Packer's C.C. vs. D.P.*	*Politics*	*Social Construc-tionist*	*Growth Complex*	*Oppression*	*Late-Modernity*
Underlying conception of crime	Definition of crime is not questioned; crime is a rational choice	Definition of crime is not questioned; crime is a rational choice	Definition of most crimes is not questioned; status offenses are over-reach of criminal law; crime is a rational choice	Image/definition of crime community-driven; partisan ideology also drives image of crime; crime is a political construct	Definition of crime relative; myths about crime rampant; overcriminalzation; moral entrepreneurs guiding definition	Definition of crime driven by desire to expand; image manipulated for purposes of CJ growth; crime is raw material for industry	Definition of crime driven by those with economic, cultural and political power; definition of crime is a product of race/gender/ class inequality	Negligence and safety threats defined as criminal; late modern controls do not require acts to be defined as criminal
Assump-tions about agency and practitioner motives	Well-intended; protecting; serving; rule following; law abiding; professionalism	Rational decision makers; efficient; adapting to external forces	Role/goal conflict; mixed messages; mimic the value-messages provided from public	Responsive to politics; interest-based; ideological pulls; power-players	Constructing problems for existing solutions; reacting to moral panics; culturally bound; managing appearances	Self-serving; power-building; quest for immortality; means over ends; bureaucratic survival; technical over moral thinking	Institutional racism, sexism, classism; often unaware of oppressive end-result of their own activities	Navigating through massive transformations, late modern forces; good intentions, disturbing results
Level of emphasis on reform	Strong; emphasis on rules, policies	Strong; efficiency, technology, rational decision making, control discretion	Minimal as applied in the discipline; but could be a strong emphasis based on the tone of Packer's book	Varies; strong emphasis on policy reform for most; some use mostly as a way to understand	Low to moderate; most use only as a way to understand; some emphasis on reforming culture and myth-busting	Low to moderate; primarily used to understand; some emphasis on methods of limiting growth	Strong; promoting economic/ social justice; eliminating racial and gender oppression	Low to moderate; primarily a needed intellectual exercise; better theory leads to understanding, leading to better practice
Solutions to problems facing CJA	More resources; greater efficiency; reduce discretion; professionalism	Seamless harmony; what works research; reduce discretion; new technology; efficiency	Healthy balance of values; ensure system of checks and balances; decriminalization	De-politicize; research; local democratic control; control interest groups	Myth-busting; deconstruct moral panics; media accountability	Beware of growing complex; limit growth; resist privatization watchdogs needed	Reduce size and power of CJA; emphasis on social/ economic measures, social justice	Few recommendations; latent concern for freedom; mostly analytical orientation
Issues and controver-sies of concern	Deterrence; defending the virtues and honor of the CJS	Abuse of discretion; cutting-edge technology; streamline/ centralize operations	Erosion of Constitutional rights; governmental intrusiveness	Federalization; symbolic politics; ideological intensification	Media/ bureaucrat/ political exploitation; mythology; symbolic policies; war rhetoric; images of race/gender	Exponential growth; private/ public; military/ police blur	Violence against women; drug wars impact on marginalized; racial profiling	Growth of system; changes in social control; rise of surveillance society

FIGURE 1 *Continued.*

Major Features/ Elements	*Rational/ Legal*	*System*	*Packer's C.C. vs. D.P.*	*Politics*	*Social Construc-tionist*	*Growth Complex*	*Oppression*	*Late-Modernity*
Methodo-logical tendency	Legal research; advocacy research	Quantitative policy and evaluative research; macro-quantitative studies	Legal research; socio-legal studies	Historical research; quantitative; interpretive	Interpretive methodolo-gies; cultural studies	Descriptive; quantitative; investigative; historical	Qualitative and quantitative; historical; critical ethnography	Recent historical analysis; some quantitative being done on new penology
What the future might hold	Crime control efforts intensify; increased professiona-lism; forced reaction to terrorism threat	Greater system integration; enhanced technology; greater efficiency; well-coordinated response to terrorism threat	Pendulum swings between crime control and due process; crime controls continued emphasis likely with war on terrorism	Interest group influence intensifies; irrational policies due to partisan ideology; further federalization of CJS due to war on terrorism	Moral panics intensify; irrational policies; media and governmental influence grows in construction of myths; especially in light of war on terrorism	Merging growth industries; runaway growth in power and size due to war on terrorism	CJ apparatus becomes more oppressive to poor, women, and minorities; war on terrorism used to further control and oppression	Uncertainty and fears of risk intensifies; enhanced soft control measures; blurring of traditional distinctions; terrorism threat intensifies; security conscious society

FIGURE 1 *Continued*

Conclusion: Nothing as Practical as a Good Theory

In 1998, Marenin and Worrall (1998, 465) asserted that "criminal justice is an academic discipline in practice but not yet in theory." Our field has not placed high value on this endeavor for two primary reasons. The first has already been discussed—crime theory suffices. The second is more difficult to overcome: although exploring the why of crime has *prima facie* importance, our field has not articulated nor acknowledged what value theorizing criminal justice provides us. Some assume, in fact, that studying criminal justice is inherently and necessarily atheoretical because it concentrates on practice. The notion that practice can somehow be severed from theory has been thoroughly debunked in most other major fields of study (Bernsetin, 1976; Fay, 1977; Habermas, 1972; Carr and Stephens, 1986). Theory and practice are implied in one another; no policy analysis, implementation, strategic plan, or practitioner action is devoid of theory. To deny the integral role theory plays in all these instances is to remain ignorant of its influence.

Theorizing criminal justice phenomena should also not be viewed as an endeavor intended exclusively for practical change. Numerous scholars in our field, including myself, find studying our society's reaction to crime intellectually stimulating in and of itself. Throughout my career, I have been fascinated by criminal justice phenomena—much like a biologist studies the animal kingdom or an astronomer studies the solar system (see Kraska, 2001). Studying humans and organizations attempting to control wrongdoing (and sometimes engaging in wrongdoing while trying to control it) yields intriguing insights about the nature of society, our political landscape, and cutting-edge cultural trends. In short, how we react to crime tells us a lot about ourselves and where our society might be headed.

Theories are repositories for substantive thought, impossible to avoid filters for thinking through our history and major contemporary issues and trends, the foundational material through which we develop innovative solutions to our problems, and the backdrop for all research in our field—whether it be policy based, descriptive, or theoretical. Numerous contemporary scholars are beginning to study criminal justice using more modern conceptions of system theory, social constructionism, Foucauldian theory, feminist theory, and late modernism. The time appears right for our field to begin placing a higher value on developing a theoretical infrastructure about criminal justice.

PETER KRASKA

References and Further Reading

Bernard, T. and Engel, R. (2001) Conceptualizing criminal justice theory. *Justice Quarterly* 18(1): 1–30.

Bernstein, R.J. (1976) *The Restructuring of Social and Political Theory*. London, UK: Methuen University Press.

Braithewaite, J. and Pettit, P. (1990) *Not Just Deserts: A Republican Theory of Criminal Justice*. Oxford, UK: Clarendon Press.

Carr. W. and Stephens, K. (1986) *Becoming Critical: Education, Knowledge and Action Research*. London, UK: The Falmer Press.

Dantzker, M.L. (1998) *Criminology and Criminal Justice: Comparing, Contrasting, and Intertwining Disciplines*. Boston, MA: Butterworth-Heinemann.

Duffee, D.E. (1980, 1990) *Explaining Criminal Justice: Community Theory and Criminal Justice Reform*. Prospect Heights, IL: Waveland Press.

Einstadter, W. and Henry, S. (1995) *Criminological Theory: An Analysis of its Underlying Assumptions*. New York, NY: Harcourt Brace Publishers.

Ellis, R.D. and Ellis, C.S. (1989) *Theories of Criminal Justice: A Critical Reappraisal*. Wolfeborro, NH: Longwood Academic.

Fay, B. (1977) *Social Theory and Political Practice*. London, UK: George Allen and Unwin.

Gibbons, D.C. (1994) *Talking About Crime and Criminals: Problem and Issues in Theory Development in Criminology*. Englewood Cliffs, NJ: Prentice-Hall.

Hagan, J. (1989) Why is there so little criminal justice theory? Neglected macro- and micro-level links between organizations and power. *Journal of Research in Crime and Delinquency* 26(2): 116–135.

Habermas, J. (1972) *Knowledge and Human Interests*. Translated by J.J. Shapiro, London, UK: Heinemann.

Kraska, P.B.(2001) *Militarizing the American Criminal Justice System: The Changing Roles of the Armed Forces and Police*. Boston, MA: Northeastern University Press.

Kraska, P.B. (2004) *Theorizing Criminal Justice: Eight Essential Orientations*. Prospect Heights, IL: Waveland Press.

Marenin, O. and Worrall, J. (1998) Criminal justice: Portrait of a discipline in progress. *Journal of Criminal Justice* 26(6): 465–480.

See also **Criminology and Criminal Justice: A Comparison; Criminology as a Social Science; Criminology: Definitions**

Criminal Law: Definition, Sources, and Types

The term “crime” has been defined as any social harm made definite and punishable by law (Schmalleger, 2002). Law has been defined as “that which is laid down, ordained, or established. A rule or method according to which phenomena or actions co-exist or follow each other. That which must be obeyed and followed by citizens, subject to sanctions or legal consequences” (Black, 1951, 1028). The term “criminal law” then refers to the body of governing rules regulating acts that result in harm to society and provide for the sanctions against those who violate such rules. When someone violates a facet of the criminal law, it is said that this person has committed a crime. It is generally accepted that there are two types of crimes, felonies and misdemeanors. However, there are some who further distinguish between types of crime and consider small offenses routinely punishable through a ticket to be a separate type of crime known as an infraction or violation (Samaha, 1996; Schmalleger, 2002).

Criminal law is one of the most important aspects of the criminal justice system because it provides for several things. First, criminal law protects members of society through the regulation of activities that are deemed unsafe, and therefore, maintains a certain semblance of social order. Second, criminal law regulates what activities are considered to be improper in the eyes of society. Finally, the criminal law deters individuals from committing criminal acts by providing for the form and severity of punishment for those who commit criminal acts. The level of punishment levied upon a violator is dependent upon the type of crime for which they are convicted. Individuals found guilty of a felony are routinely sentenced to death in extreme cases or incarceration for 1 year or more in less extreme cases. If a misdemeanor has been committed then the individual convicted will receive a fine, a sentence of less than 1 year, or a combination of the two punishments (Scheb and Scheb, 1999).

History of Criminal Law

The American system of criminal law has been impacted by an extensive number of scholars, philosophers, and events dating back centuries. Understanding of the criminal law requires an introduction to the development of codified law. One of the earliest forms of codified law was the Code of Hammurabi, a stone pillar located near the city of Susa that is believed to have been created around 1750 B.C. The Code of

Hammurabi is best known for its somewhat brutal treatment of those who violated the established laws. The Code strictly followed the doctrine of *lex talionis*, or the belief of an eye for an eye. Many of the crimes enumerated in the code were punishable by death or dismemberment. For example, consider the following punishments discussed in the Code: any man who sleeps with another's wife shall be put to death, a son who strikes his father shall have his hands cut off, and if a nobleman puts out the eye of another nobleman, his eye shall be put out.

The Code of Hammurabi, although an important piece of history involving criminal law, is believed to have had limited direct impact on the development of American criminal law. According to Schmalleger (2002), the value of the Code of Hammurabi lies in its being the first instrument to formalize both the punishment and the criminal acts. Prior to the Code's existence, individuals could be punished severely for engaging in activities that were deemed inappropriate; however, the punishments may have been unknown by those who committed the act. The Code of Hammurabi corrected this by specifying which punishments would be inflicted for which crimes. The Code of Hammurabi was the beginning of codification for law and punishment and many other nations would follow this precedent.

One such nation that followed Hammurabi's example in codifying the law was that of the Roman nation. The Justinian Code was written by Roman emperor Justinian I and, unlike Hammurabi's Code, is considered to have had a substantial impact on the development of American law. The Justinian Code was the first formalized set of rules to provide for two categories of law: public laws and private laws. Public laws dealt with regulation of the government and private laws dealt with contracts between citizens and injuries to citizens. When the Emperor Claudius conquered England, the issue of codified law was imparted upon the English people through the use of Roman might (Schmalleger, 2002). From the Justinian Code developed the concept of codifying legal rights into what we would today call statutes, or guidelines defined by those who govern our society and are enforced with all of the powers the state maintains.

Codification is of course an important development regarding how our laws are represented to the people, but understanding of how the criminal law has developed requires an explanation of where the laws to be codified originated. American criminal law was strongly influenced by the English concept of common law. The term "common law" refers to law that was inherent in the customs of the communities, and therefore, common among those in society. The beginning of understanding of common law can be traced back to the Norman Conquest of 1066. Prior to the Norman Conquest, English law was considered to have been a clutter of local laws and customs applied by the various courts that were already in operation (Scheb and Scheb, 1999). However, upon conquering England, William the Conqueror declared himself the protector of English law and began dispatching judges to travel in circuits around the country settling disputes. Lacking some form of established guidelines, these judges relied upon the common customs of the people within the communities where they were led to hold court. Judges would empirically examine customs related to the issue in question and would provide a ruling on the basis of this examination.

Over time, these decisions were recorded as a means of providing guidance to other judges who might encounter similar situations and not have prior experience with the issue. The process of relying on the opinions of previous judges came to be known as *stare decisis*, which literally translates into "let the decision stand." The process of *stare decisis* is still employed extensively in our justice system today, although now, it is more often referred to as deference to case law (Scheb and Scheb, 1999). Current opinions are catalogued in book format and made available to attorneys and interested parties. With recent advances in technology, it is now even possible to obtain these decisions from the comfort of one's home or office, without the need to search through the court reporters.

Understanding of the common law also requires a brief introduction to the concept of natural law, which refers to law that originates from a source higher than a society's rulers and is understood to be binding on people regardless of whether there is a lack of guidance from the state or whether the state contradicts the natural law (Reid, 2003). Many people often assume that the term "natural law" means law that comes from God. Although the term refers to law from a higher order, this does not necessarily mean that it is law from God. Aristotle spoke often of the natural law in his writings; however, Aristotle was not necessarily a believer of one god. The natural law is more appropriately labeled as law that can be empirically assessed when one considers the overall values and beliefs of humans. Proof of this belief can be found by considering that there are some wrongs regarded as wrong that do not depend upon the understanding of written statutes. One example of this concept is that of the crime of murder. The vast majority of humans, regardless of religious and geographic locations, consider murder an inappropriate act. In considering this, it becomes clear that the natural law was a forerunner of the common law, as the judges who wrote on common law were similarly searching for natural law answers to their questions even if they were not aware of the presence of such a concept.

Numerous philosophers and jurisprudential theorists have discussed the natural law. However, two of these individuals are perhaps better representatives of the concept. These individuals are Saint Thomas Aquinas and Sir William Blackstone. Thomas Aquinas was a Dominican monk who was educated in the philosophy of Aristotle and other great philosophers, a situation that surely impacted his beliefs on the issue of law and order. Sir William Blackstone was a professor of common law at Oxford, who converted his lectures into a series of definitive works on the common law known as *Commentaries on the Laws of England.*

Thomas Aquinas was a strong supporter of Aristotle's philosophy of man and natural law, but he could not support all of Aristotle's beliefs because they perhaps came into contact with his own deeply ingrained religious beliefs. Aquinas, therefore, modified Aristotle's discussion on the natural law and stated that law was divided into four categories: (1) eternal law, (2) natural law, (3) human law, and (4) divine law. Aquinas believed that eternal law was law that governed the nature of a universe that was eternal in existence (Himma, 2001). Natural law was then the portions of eternal law that governed the behavior of human beings as humans were the only beings possessing free will. Further, it was Aquinas' belief that human law could not circumvent the natural law. In his great work, *Summa Theologica*, Aquinas stated, "every human law has just so much of the nature of law as is derived from the law of nature. But if in any point it deflects from the law of nature, it is no longer a law but a pervasion of law" (Himma, 2001, citing Aquinas). Here, Aquinas was stating that human law is a form of natural law implemented through man's understanding of nature. However, Aquinas further believed that any law passed by humans but in contradiction to that of nature is in fact not a true law but is instead the result of a human's perversion or corruption.

Sir William Blackstone, in his *Commentaries on the Laws of England*, provided additional support for Aquinas' views when he stated that all law receives its force and authenticity from the natural law and that there can be no valid law that conflicts with the natural law. The debate over whether natural law can truly supercede human law is still one that is debated today. It is generally accepted that human law must reign supreme, as failure to do so could result in complete anarchy as citizens could argue against the authority of any law by calling its conflict with the natural law into question (Himma, 2001). Such a scenario would lead to a situation of complete and total anarchy if left unchecked.

Blackstone's importance to the development of American criminal law goes beyond his belief and support of the natural law. Blackstone is considered to have been one of the most influential individuals in the development of American law because he began the formalization of English common law that would become the model for America's legal system. Following the American Revolution, portions of the English law were rejected in the American colonies on grounds they were monarchial. At this time, it was believed that crime was becoming viewed more as a sin than as an assault on an individual. Some scholars suggest that evidence of this belief can still be found in legislation that regulates liquor, gambling, sexual behavior, and any other activity historically considered to be a matter or morals and not safety (Nelson, 1967).

In their quest to develop a separate legal system, the founding fathers of America relied heavily on Blackstone's *Commentaries*. After all, here was a work that had created great controversy upon its publication because many of Blackstone's contemporaries were dissatisfied with his codification, and as some would argue his simplification, of the English common law. The *Commentaries* provided American scholars with an in-depth examination of the common law that had never before been possible. The American colonies individually began subscribing to the common law beliefs to the extent that they did not contradict the newly established Constitution. Today, many states still employ the common law system, with the exception of the State of Louisiana, which subscribes to the Napoleonic Code (Scheb and Scheb, 1999).

The common law maintains a minimal impact on the criminal law system of the U.S. today, as there are three primary recognized sources of criminal law in America: (1) the U.S. Constitution, (2) case law, and (3) criminal law statutes. The U.S. Constitution is the country's most important document and has been termed a "living document" because of its ability to avoid becoming outdated despite the fact the work was completed over 200 years ago. It should be noted that few acts are criminalized in the Constitution, with the only clearly defined criminal act being that of treason, or betraying one's country. Instead, it is through the Constitution that criminal procedure is clearly defined and protected through the first ten amendments to the Constitution, the Bill of Rights. The Constitution is believed to impact the development of criminal law by establishing limitations on which acts can be criminalized. Under the protection of the Constitution, an act may only be criminalized when the need to regulate such activity is believed to be so great that the need to protect the larger society will outweigh the potential harm that could come to a few citizens (Schmalleger, 2002).

Case law today is much like the Constitution in that there are few criminal activities declared through case law. The Constitution provides for regulation of which activities can be criminalized, and although the document has withstood the test of time, there are still some situations that the founding fathers could not have foreseen when they drafted the Constitution. When the Constitution is unclear or appears to be inapplicable to the criminalization of an activity or behavior, then it is through case law that society is provided with an interpretation. Through the evaluation of prior cases the courts provide what is many times a clearer definition of what constitutes a violation of the criminal law.

Criminal law statutes are legislative acts passed by Congress that regulate and occasionally criminalize the activities of citizens. It is statutes that form the greatest source of criminal law today. The Congressional branch is provided for by the Constitution and operates on the belief that its members are enacting laws designed to protect the citizens who have placed the elected official in office. Many of the crimes considered to be of great threat to the safety of society are already criminalized, leaving those in Congress to invoke a majority of criminal sanctions that seek to protect property and livelihood. One example of legislation designed to protect livelihood is that of statutes criminalizing violations of copyright permissions of materials and information.

Elements of Criminal Law

To prove a criminal act under the criminal law it is required that the prosecution prove two very important issues: the *actus rea* and the *mens rea*. *Actus rea* refers to the actual act being committed. The courts have long held that a man cannot be punished for his thoughts alone. Punishment may only be brought about in situations where the thoughts themselves are acted upon and the resulting act is considered illegal by the society in which the act takes place. Additionally, an individual may be found to have committed the *actus rea* for a crime even if they did not in fact commit an act. This is possible through acts of omission or acts where the individual committed a criminal act through their failure to act in a given circumstance. Along with the *actus rea*, criminal law requires an examination of the *mens rea*. *Mens rea* refers to the state of mind or intent of the individual committing the criminal act. The *mens rea* is not a physical thing, and therefore, can be hard to prove in some cases. Many times the only method of proving the *mens rea* is through examination of the *actus rea*. It is through the argument that there was no *mens rea* that many defense attorneys today argue that their client cannot be guilty of a crime because they may not have understood what it was they were doing (Samaha, 1996).

There are also two divisions of criminal law: crimes that are *mala in se* and crimes that are *mala prohibita*. *Mala in se* refers to crimes that are wrong in and of themselves. Under the common law there were nine primary crimes that fell under this heading: murder, manslaughter, rape, sodomy, robbery, larceny, arson, burglary, and mayhem. *Mala in se* crimes were routinely viewed as acts that threatened not only the victim but the entire society. For this reason, many of these crimes were punished by death of the offender. *Mala prohibita* refers to acts that are wrong because the state has labeled them as wrong. With the exception of the previously discussed nine crimes and treason, all other crimes were considered to have fallen under this category and were punished in a far less severe manner. Examples of crimes that are *mala prohibita* include: speeding, consumption of alcohol, prostitution, and all acts that are wrong because society has deemed them wrong and passed statutes criminalizing the behavior (Sigler, 1981).

Offenses that are *mala prohibita* are routinely referred to as strict liability offenses. When proving a strict liability claim, the prosecution is not required to show intention, which means the individual's *mens rea* becomes a moot issue. The example used by Scheb and Scheb (1999) is that of the crime of statutory rape. Despite the fact that the young girl may have looked like she was over the age of consent, the man was ultimately responsible for insuring that his partner was of legal age. In this case, despite the fact that the man had no idea he was engaging in an illegal sexual encounter, he may still be found guilty and punished as if he had intentionally engaged in sexual acts with a known minor. It has been stated that as punishments continue to grow in length and severity it is only a matter of time before judges restrict the crimes for which individuals can be held strictly liable (Scheb and Scheb, 1999).

Finally, there are two types of criminal law briefly introduced earlier: misdemeanors and felonies. Historically, misdemeanors were considered to be the result of legislative activity by those in charge of protecting society's interest, whereas felonies were considered acts that were fundamentally wrong. The issue of whether an act is fundamentally wrong returns to the issue of acts that are *mala in se* versus acts that are *mala prohibita*. A misdemeanor would closely parallel an act that is *mala prohibita* and a felony would parallel an act that was *mala in se*.

When an individual is convicted of a misdemeanor, he or she is normally confined to a correctional facility for a period of time less than 1 year. Felonies result in the individual convicted being sentenced to a correctional facility for a period of time greater than 1 year. Misdemeanants or individuals convicted of misdemeanors, are generally housed with the local sheriff whereas those convicted of felonies are normally housed in state or federal prisons. However, the decision as to where a felony offender is housed can be based upon a myriad of factors. Individuals convicted of a crime violating federal law will normally be housed within one of the federal prisons administered by the Federal Bureau of Prisons, whereas those convicted of crimes violating state law are housed within the correctional facility ran by the state in which the crime occurred. Local jails may agree to house felony offenders in situations where the state prison is overcrowded, where the housing arrangements are stipulated in a plea bargain, or where the sheriff requests that the individual be housed within his facility in place of the state prison.

Current and Future Developments in Criminal Law

As society moves into the 21st century, it is generally believed that all crimes *mala in se* are criminalized in current statutes. The same cannot be said, however, in regard to crimes that are *mala prohibita*. Two of the greatest legal debates of the past decade have been arguments concerning whether there is a need to decriminalize or modify the criminal law statutes relating to drug usage and prostitution. These crimes are commonly referred to as victimless crimes, and therefore, have led some to argue that the regulation of the activities is outside the realm of the state's authority. Crimes such as these are believed to be upheld out of nothing more than a reliance on past beliefs that the law must be influenced by the morals of society. The war on drugs has resulted in the reduction of numerous other federal programs, and the results of the war are such that few believe the efforts are reaping a satisfactory return on investment. The decriminalization of drugs is an open area for debate and is the subject of the research projects of many criminologists and experts in the criminal justice field today.

Another difficulty facing the current legal system is the globalization of the world and the increase in reliance on the Internet. In the early 1990s, the Internet and the World Wide Web were released for public use. Although many were slow to accept the benefits of the new technology, by the late 1990s one survey conducted by the Computer Emergency Response Team Coordination Center (CERT/CC) stated that 96% of businesses were maintaining some form of presence on the Internet and the World Wide Web. As a result of the Internet and the Web's increased popularity, more people have begun "signing on" to the Internet and maintaining some form of presence. Society's reliance on the computer and the Internet has developed an entirely new wave of potential victims for individuals who would rely on technology to commit their criminal activities.

It should be noted that computers were already being used in the commission of criminal acts before the release of the Internet. During the late 1980s, the legislature took notice of the problems caused by individuals who employed computers in the commission of criminal activities and established the *Computer Fraud and Abuse Act*, which criminalized activities that involved the use of computers in the destruction of data stored on federal computers. The problem has been that the legislation only criminalized activities against federal interest computers. By early 2002, however, the combination of Internet connectivity and the prevalence of computers combined to make computer-related crime even more serious and diverse. A few of the crimes involved attacks against federal computer systems; however, a majority of the crimes were merely reincarnations of traditional crimes that targeted individuals. For example, the crime of distributing or purchasing child pornography is not a new crime, but the activity has more than doubled since the release of the Internet and the advancement of computer technology (Casanova, 2000). Today, pedophiles and others who traffic in the abuse of children are capable of mass production and distribution of their materials. Other crimes, such as stalking, barely had time to develop before the use of computers modified the elements of the criminal offense. Stalking was only recognized in the early 1990s as a criminal activity, and now the trend appears to be an increase in cyberstalking, or stalking that occurs in the virtual world. Both forms of harassment are dangerous to victims, as each inflicts a level of emotional distress and a feeling of being unsafe. However, the criminal law has only recently begun to reflect the activity as being a criminal act (McGraw, 1995; Brenner, 2001).

The rapid level of development in technology has led to the question of whether it is possible to keep up if the law remains reactive and not proactive. Those who commit these newer versions of crime through the use of technology have not been able to escape punishment in most cases. However, the individuals assigned to bring these criminals to justice have been forced to modify their approach to investigating and presenting evidence in order to find someone guilty under criminal law statutes that had not previously considered the issue of technology. The debates over the revocation of criminal laws concerning drugs and sexual activity are sure to continue, but it appears that the addition of laws regulating the Internet and the quickly shrinking world are certain to maintain a powerful presence in the discussion of criminal law in the coming years.

Robert Moore

References and Further Reading

Aquinas, T. (1947). *Summa Theologica.* New York, NY: Benziger Brothers.

Black, H. (1951). *Black's Law Dictionary.* St. Paul, MN: West Publishing Co.

Blackstone, W. (1979). *Commentaries on the Laws of England.* Chicago, IL: University of Chicago Press.

Brenner, S.W. (2001). Defining cybercrime: A review of state and federal law, *Cybercrime: The Investigation, Prosecution and Defense of a Computer-Related Crime*, Clifford, R.D., (Ed.), pp. 11–69, Durham, NC: Carolina Academic Press.

Casanova, M. (2000). The history of child pornography on the internet. *Journal of Sex Education and Therapy*, 25, 245–252.

Computer Fraud and Abuse Act. 18 United States Code 1030 (1989); Amended 1996, 2001.

Himma, K. (2001). Natural law. *The Internet Encyclopedia of Philosophy.* Retrieved on August 24, 2003, from http://www.utm.edu/research/iep/n/natlaw.htm.

McGraw, D. (1995). Sexual harassment in cyberspace: The problem of unwelcome e-mail. *Rutgers Computer and Technology Law Journal*, 21, 491–518.

Nelson, W. (1967). Emerging notions of modern criminal law in the revolutionary era. *New York University Law Review* 42, 461.

Pethia, R. (1999). Testimony to the Commerce and Economic Development Subcommittee on Electronic Commerce—Commonwealth of Pennsylvania. Retrieved on August 21, 2003 from http://www.cert.org/congressional_testimony/PA_ecommerce_hearing_sep99.html.

Reid, S. (2003). *Crime and criminology.* Boston, MA: McGraw-Hill.

Samaha, J. (1996). *Criminal law.* New York. NY: Wadsworth.

Scheb, J. and Scheb, J. (1999). *Criminal law and procedure.* New York, NY: Wadsworth.

Schmalleger, F. (2002). *Criminal law today.* Upper Saddle River, NJ: Prentice Hall.

Sigler, J. (1981). *Understanding Criminal Law.* Boston, MA: Little Brown and Company.

See also **Criminal Law: Reform; Crime, Definitions of**

Criminal Law: Reform

Lessons Learned in the Last Fifty Years

Many students often get confused between "substantive law" and "procedural law." For the purposes of this essay, it is important to clear up similar confusions. Administration of justice requires the components of justice—i.e., substantive law—and the process of justice—i.ė., procedural law. The "components of justice" include the definitions of criminal activity, culpability, and defenses whereas the "process of justice" includes pretrial, trial, and posttrial procedures. The current essay will not address how the process of the criminal justice system has evolved such as bail reform, exclusionary rule modifications, the imposition of Amber alerts, and new federal procedural legislation such as the USA Patriot Act I and II. Contrarily, the current essay focuses on reforms to the components of justice.

In summary, the current essay will address the major thrusts of criminal law reform within the last 50 years. First, we will address criminal law reform in general—especially with regard to statutory construction. Second, two reform movements that have had a major impact on criminal law reform will be discussed. These movements include reforms to sex crimes and family violence crimes. The current essay will then discuss the defenses that have experienced the most prominent reform in the last 50 years. Finally, this essay will address what we have learned—and, what we have not learned—from the reforms that have already taken place as a guide to reforms in the future.

Criminal Law Reform: An Introductory Lesson

The purpose of criminal law is to define actions that violate community norms of right and wrong. Criminal law is instituted for the purpose of running an effective, civilized society (Gainer, 1998). A civilized society is thrown into chaos without a set of rules to govern the behavior of its citizens. More specifically, criminal law is formalized and codified to define outer boundaries of acceptable human behavior beyond which citizens should not freely act (Gainer, 1998). Criminal law acts as an educative tool to shape shared norms. However, as Robinson (2002) argued, the law—by itself—cannot shape norms. Prohibition serves as a good example of this phenomenon. Criminal law is only as powerful as its citizen's compliance to that law.

In order to accomplish these purposes, a community must not only provide complete coverage of all defined criminal activity, but it should also ensure that there are no overlapping laws that might cause confusion (Gainer, 1998). Criminal law formation also must be understandable with fair notice of what is prohibited on the one hand and what is permitted on the other (Gainer, 1998). Without a clear line to what is prohibited, citizens may feel frozen to act at all. Criminal law is to set outer boundaries without restricting the rights of citizens within a particular community.

It is important to understand that criminal law reform may *follow* a particular charge of a community rather than *leading* that particular charge and shaping the norms of any particular group of people (Robinson, 2002). Arguably, the one reform that has had the largest impact on criminal law formation in the last 50 years has been American Law Institute's Model Penal Code—MPC, hereafter—created in 1962 (Gainer, 1998; Kadish, 1999). The MPC attempted to provide a model criminal code as a method of updating and revising outdated legislative attempts to codify common law.

Although the MPC has had a strong effect on state criminal codes (and glimpses of influence on the federal criminal code), other reforms to criminal laws have been created as a judicial response rather than a legislative response. Although the purpose of the judiciary is to interpret the law, they often create law through judicial review of the U.S. Constitution. As will be evident in the section entitled "Reforms to Sex Crimes," the judiciary can change the course of legal understanding of what is prohibitive and what is permissive.

The ultimate purpose of this essay is to articulate the debate about whether we have learned any lessons about criminal law reform in the last 50 years. Although the MPC has provided a model criminal code, there remain lessons to be learned. Understanding the following reform movements can better instruct us on how to proceed in future reforms.

Reforms to Sex Crimes

Legal scholars can learn a few lessons by examining reforms to particular sex crimes. Two areas of the criminal law are especially educative in this movement: pornography or obscenity and sexual assault. It is important, first, to acknowledge the importance of feminism to this movement of reformation. Feminism fleshed out important issues about women's liberty and the sexual revolution. Feminism taught us lessons about the right of free expression and the need to protect women—and men, alike—from physical, emotional, and sexual attacks by all individuals—not merely complete strangers. Feminism fought—and still fights—for equality among men and women with all of the protections that equality demands.

Issues regarding obscenity have been a major debate of reform in the U.S. ever since the Supreme Court made their decision in *Roth v. United States* (354 U.S. 476, 1957). In *Roth*, the Court decided that obscenity is not a protected expression under the First Amendment of the U.S. Constitution. The real question, though, is what material is obscene and what material is "acceptable" free expression? Several judicial decisions are instructive to answer this question more accurately.

First, the decision in *Regina v. Hicklin* (England, L.R. 3, 1868) stated that if isolated passages of a literary piece were considered obscene, then the whole passage was deemed obscene. This test, known as the "Hicklin Test," was adopted by the Supreme Court until the decision in *Roth*. Therefore, the restriction of the particular expression within which an isolated, obscene passage was located did not violate the First Amendment of the U.S. Constitution. In other words, the decision in *Regina v. Hicklin* ruled that obscenity was judged by the impact of a particular isolated passage rather than the impact of the whole work.

Although the judicial decision in *Hicklin* guided legal scholars to understand how to mete out what was obscene and what was not, other scholars were eager to produce a more modern test of obscenity. Two different sources offered a "dominant theme" approach to define obscenity. The Supreme Court in 1957 made a dominant theme argument in *Roth v. United States* and *Alberts v. California* (354 U.S. 476, 1957) (see Hixson, 1996). The MPC offered a dominant theme approach in their statutory definition of obscenity. Material was no longer found obscene if merely an isolated passage was deemed obscene. On the contrary, the new dominant theme test only found the material obscene—and not protected by the First Amendment—if the dominant theme of the material was obscene.

A final trend in the obscenity debate was to tap into the community standards of changing morals in today's society. The Court in *Roth v. United States* also espoused this type of analysis by requiring the state to apply contemporary community standards. Therefore, not only must the impact of the material as a whole be deemed as obscene but also the definition of "obscene" must be based on what the community deems as obscene.

The reforms with the most impact within the sexual crime reform movement, though, are reforms of sexual assault within the last 50 years. The rape reform has affected the expansion of the definition of rape in three different ways: definitions of victims or offenders, definitions of "sexual conduct," and definitions of misappropriations of sexual advances.

The crime of rape has generally met up with several changes that have been common to most jurisdictions.

Some states supported all of the proposed changes whereas other states made small steps toward reform (Spohn and Horney, 1992). First, the definition of rape has changed immensely over the years. The common law definition of rape only required penile sexual intercourse by a man with a woman—not his wife—with the use of force against her will. The modern definition of rape—or, sexual assault—does not require penile penetration, does not require a male offender, does not require a female victim, and allows for an individual to be prosecuted for the rape of his or her spouse (see, Spohn and Horney, 1992).

Second, common law required a showing of nonconsent that often required evidence of the victim's resistance. The current rape laws have eliminated this requirement. In other words, victims of sexual assault no longer have to offer evidence about their resistance. Scholars suggested that requiring victims to show resistance to the attack would further jeopardize the victim's personal safety (Spohn and Horney, 1992).

A final major reform to rape law was the creation of rape shield laws. Prior to reform, defendants were allowed to offer the victim's past sexual behavior into evidence to prove consent, thereby eliminating one of the requisite elements of rape. However, rape shield laws limit admissibility of such evidence and protect victims from humiliation during a trial (Spohn and Horney, 1992). However, these rape shield laws do not completely eliminate the use of the victim's past sexual behavior. A defendant can admit evidence of past sexual behavior between the victim and defendant, current sexual conduct with a third party to prove semen, pregnancy, or diseases contracted from the third party rather than the defendant, and past sexual behavior to impeach the prosecutor's assertion of the victim's character in his or her sexual practices (Spohn and Horney, 1992).

The real question, though, is whether these reforms affected attitudes and behaviors within the administration of justice. Spohn and Horney (1992) found that rape law reforms in Michigan—the most significant rape reform state—had very little impact on officials' evaluations of which factors were important in guiding their decisions in a rape case. For the most part, they found that officials in the field—namely, prosecutors, defense attorneys, and judges—determined the relevant, statutory factors to be the most influential in their decisions in a rape case.

Although it is important to understand the impact of reforms on attitudes and beliefs about how justice operates under new rape laws, it is equally important to understand the impact on the actual administration of justice under the reforms. Spohn and Horney (1996) found that reforms had very little impact in most jurisdictions. Even disaggregating the data into jurisdictions with mild reforms and jurisdictions with severe reforms, Spohn and Horney (1996) did not find consistent increases in the number of complaints, indictments, or convictions even though the reforms should have widened the net of potential cases.

Where do we go from here? Although much broader lessons will be addressed in the last section, the one immediate lesson we can learn is that law has changed and, for the most part, has changed for the better. That is, feminism has encouraged reforms to criminal law that have not only given women a voice in their own right to express themselves, but they have also given them certain protections. We can learn more lessons about criminal law reform by examining the most prominent reforms in family violence.

Reforms to Family Violence Crimes

Family violence is another area of the criminal law that has experienced major reforms. The term "family violence" is used to explain interrelationships including immediate family members—that is, spouses and children. Although domestic violence issues have traversed interrelationships extended beyond the family, this essay focuses on "family" violence with regard to criminal law reform. This essay is intended to paint a broad stroke over the topic of criminal law reform. The first area of family violence addressed in this essay is child abuse or neglect and the second is spousal abuse.

The government's interests of children were a result of the "child-saving movement" (see Feld, 1999). Out of this movement, the doctrine of *parens patriae* was created and adopted by every state. This doctrine gives the justice system the power to act in the best interests of the child. With regard to child abuse or neglect laws, over the last 50 years states have stepped into family situations more often where abuse or neglect are evident. The state protects individuals—especially children—who cannot protect themselves (Myers, 1998).

Several laws have been created with the intention to protect children. Because some of these recent laws are more procedural in nature, they will only bear mentioning. One of these is sex offender registration (see Brooks, 1996). In most jurisdictions, a sex offender must register with the state or local community. Another law—Megan's law—is inextricably linked to sex offender registration and requires states to notify the public that convicted sex offenders are living in the local community (see Brooks, 1996).

Another stance within child abuse or neglect law reforms is the creation of criminal liability for not reporting suspected child abuse. The first child abuse reporting law was enacted in California in 1963 (Myers, 1998). Initial child abuse reporting laws required physicians to report suspected physical abuse of their child patients. However, these child abuse reporting laws have expanded in several ways. Now, other professionals must report child abuse. These professionals range from educators to social workers to childcare providers. In essence, any professional who works with children similarly has a duty to report suspected child abuse (Myers, 1998).

Some states have mandatory reporting procedures whereas other states have permissive reporting procedures (Myers, 1998). In these later jurisdictions, discretion is allowed that might introduce disparate treatment based on many different factors including—but not limited to—sex, age, race, or socioeconomic status. The ramifications of not reporting can range anywhere from minor civil action to criminal action (Myers, 1998). Also, other forms of abuse are falling under the umbrella of child abuse or neglect, such as sexual abuse, mental abuse, and emotional abuse. However, professionals are finding it difficult to differentiate between "normal" discipline practices and abuse.

Criminal law reform with regard to family violence has not only occurred within child abuse or neglect laws, but it has also been important within spousal abuse. We have already discussed the reforms in rape law. One important issue regarding the reforms of rape law that addresses spousal abuse is the marital exception rule. One of the requisite elements of common law rape was that the victim could not be the offender's wife. Therefore, in common law, it was not a crime for a husband to force sexual intercourse on his wife. The rape law has been modified to eliminate this marital exception rule.

Often, women are without adequate resources to relocate or escape the debilitating abuse they receive from their spouses (Coker, 2001). Although mandatory arrest procedures are beyond the purview of this essay because they deal with procedural law, it has been argued that mandatory arrest policies can extend the state's control over its citizens (Coker, 2001). Therefore, even though feminism attempted to protect women from abusive situations, advocates of feminism find themselves in a struggle with state control over women's actions.

A final issue that will be discussed in further detail later is the advent of the battered spouse syndrome that has become more accepted as an excused defense. The defense is allowable when the spouse experiences extensive or persistent physical or emotional abuse that induces a mental incapacity to know right from wrong (see Kadish, 1999). This mental incapacity is a learned helplessness where the spouse believes there is no way out other than to kill or seriously harm his or her spouse in order to avoid future abuse.

Although similar lessons can be learned from reforms to criminal laws with regard to family violence as they were learned from reforms to sex crime laws, different wrinkles appear. Although laws have changed for the better by protecting children and—for the most part—women, these reforms provide a much more expansive state power than was originally intended. Whether this is acceptable or not will be addressed in the last section.

Reforms to Definitions of Defenses

We can learn lessons about reforms to criminal defenses just as we have learned about reforms to criminal liability. The most profound reforms with regard to criminal defenses in the last 50 years are the insanity defense and the battered spouse syndrome defense. These defenses have had a significant impact on the administration of justice.

Since John Hinckley's trial case for the assassination attempt on President Ronald Reagan in 1981, the defense of insanity has experienced several important changes. There are two ways insanity can be used as a defense in a trial case. First, a defendant can plead "not guilty by reason of insanity," which allows for the defendant to be sent to a mental health facility until they are rehabilitated, at which point they can be released into the community. Another way to institute an insanity defense—which is actually a recent retributive reform—is "guilty but mentally ill," which requires the defendant to serve the rest of his or her sentence after being released from the mental health facility.

The purpose of redefining the insanity defense is not only to provide a more retributive action by increasing perceived public safety but also to reduce the number of insanity acquittals and to prevent early release from mental hospitals (Steadman, McGreevy, Morrissey, Callahan, Roberts, and Cirincione, 1993). Steadman et al. (1993) addressed these objectives by examining how reforms changed the administration of justice—if at all. They found that states that abolished the insanity defense did not eliminate its use. Cases that would have been eligible for the insanity defense claim were merely displaced to findings of incompetency to stand trial (Steadman et al., 1993). Although virtually no one was acquitted after the abolition reform, the administration of justice for these defendants remained fairly consistent before and after the reform took place.

Another major change to the insanity defense during the post-Hinckley era was the change in the tests of insanity. The tests, themselves, have changed over time. For example, a test of insanity that has probably gained the most notoriety is the *M'Naughten* Rule, which states that the individual is legally insane if he had a mental defect at the time of the crime that caused him not to know right from wrong (see *M'Naughten's Case,* 1843). The Court in *Durham v. United States*

(214 F.2d 862, D.C.Cir., 1954) rejected the right–wrong test and adopted the product test that states that if the defendant suffered a mental defect during the time of the crime *and* that the mental illness was the actual cause of the crime, then the defendant can claim insanity (see, *Durham v. United States*, 1954). However, this rule was also later stuck down fairly quickly. The *M'Naughten* Rule was popularly used until the 1960s when the "substantial capacity" test was proposed. Most jurisdictions today have accepted this test. The defendant must have a mental defect and, as a result of that defect, must lack the substantial capacity to appreciate the wrongfulness of their act or to conform their conduct to the requirements of the law (see Steadman et al., 1993).

With the changes in the tests of insanity, there came the reforms to the burden of proof of insanity defenses. Because of the latest need to keep dangerous defendants off the streets, reformers have required the defendant to wield more of the burden to prove their case for an insanity defense (Steadman et al., 1993). These reforms, though, have produced little—if any—changes in the processing of such cases. Steadman et al. (1993) found depreciable differences in the number of insanity pleas made, the success rates of such defenses, and the length of confinement for those found legally insane by the court.

However, one reform that has produced some significant results in changing how the system operates is the introduction of the "guilty but mentally ill" defense. The number of insanity pleas in jurisdictions with this type of defense increased—albeit gradually. This defense was also used most often for violent offenders and these defendants received longer sentences or commitments compared to similar "sane" defendants (Steadman et al., 1993).

Another defense that has recently come to the forefront is the use of the battered spouse syndrome defense. Although several other syndromes were attempted—such as premenstrual syndrome, Vietnam Vet, and addiction—only the battered-spouse-syndrome-defense has been accepted consistently (Kadish, 1999). The first case to accept the battered-spouse-syndrome-defense was *State v. Kelly* (478 A.2d 364, N.J. 1984).

As previously discussed, battered spouse syndrome is permitted as a defense where one spouse has been physically—and emotionally in limited circumstances—abused on a persistent basis to create a situation for which the only way to escape the situation is to commit a violent act against the abusing spouse. Using this defense excuses the battered spouse from criminal liability. Although nonconfrontational killings—that is, situations where the battered spouse attacks her abusing spouse while the spouse is sleeping or is in an inactive, nonthreatening state—provides special problems, it is not entirely impossible to be successful under the defense (Kadish, 1999). In other words, the defense requires the battered spouse to feel an immediate threat of violence. If the abusing spouse is sleeping, then the battered spouse is no longer under immediate threat. Depending on the circumstances, though, the battered spouse can win her case under a battered-spouse-syndrome-defense strategy.

Have We Learned Our Lesson?

Criminal laws have been modified over the last 50 years to where they are today. We have noticed an array of influences from broad movements such as feminism to specific incidents such as John Hinckley's assassination attempt on President Ronald Reagan. These influences have changed the course of criminal law in America. However, have they improved our criminal law agenda for the better? Just as a mother asks her child, we must ask ourselves, "have we learned our lesson?"

Since the MPC was founded in the early 1960s, legislators have become keenly aware of statutory construction of the criminal law. Some problems, though, still exists, especially in the federal criminal code. Criminal codes still remain long, complex, and duplicative—in other words, similar criminal acts are defined in multiple sections of the criminal code. It is important to keep criminal law simple and brief so that citizens have reasonable notice of what is prohibited and what is permissive.

As with most cultures and societies, differences between right and wrong change over time. The same is true with regards to sex crimes—especially with obscenity or pornography. The question, though, is whether morals should change or not. Some would argue that morals should not change over time; they should remain constant. What was wrong 50 years ago is now right? Again, criminal law must be simple. Changing the debate about whether material is obscene or not can create confusion within citizens' minds. Complexity can occur when confusion about what is right and what is wrong is introduced.

However, some would argue that change in how we view the world is a natural progression. Societies and nations consistently change in their natural environments. Therefore, it is neither good nor bad that criminal law merely fashions itself around these natural changes. As previously stated, criminal law is often a reflection of its community rather than a driving force. Societies progress and criminal law merely progresses with them.

Scholars may disagree whether morals should change or not with regard to obscenity or pornography, but all scholars agree that the archaic common law of rape needed to be reformed. When it comes to violence, no one tolerates outdated laws. Today, we cannot imagine that forcing sex upon one's spouse is not a crime or that other types of penetration are not crimes.

Reforms to family violence crimes have experienced interesting challenges. First, when it comes to child abuse, qualified professionals find it difficult to report child abuse or neglect for marginal cases. Second, more professionals are required to report abuse or neglect; however, some of these professionals are not qualified for such tasks and could be liable for missing a diagnosis. Third, protections of children and women through recent criminal law reforms have expanded state authority over them as well as their assailants, which is contrary to feminist's beliefs that citizens—especially women—should be free from state control.

Finally, defenses to criminal liability have also been reformed. It is evident that some laws and legal rationales are molded and reformed as a result of particular "moral panic" events. These events are clearly catalysts for particular issues with regard to reforms. The biggest threat to good criminal law reform, though, is the lack of preparation and impatience of lawmaking. Without careful consideration and thoughtful reasoning, law reforms can become muddled by present day events that truly do not change the administration of justice on a daily basis. Such is the argument of the changes to the insanity defense post-Hinckley. However, other defenses—such as the battered-spouse-syndrome-defense—can be well researched in multiple disciplines.

There have been many lessons learned about criminal law reform—especially in the last 50 years. We still have much to learn about reforming the criminal law. Statutory formations remain quite complex by using difficult language, lengthy code formation, and overlapping sections within the criminal code. Legislators must remember brevity and simplicity should be primary goals in statutory construction in order for citizens to understand what is prohibited.

The struggle between lawmaking and law interpretation is evident within current judicial rulings. The creation of the law should be a legislative decision and not a judicial one, even though particular rulings previously addressed have done the exact opposite. Too many hands involved in changing the criminal law exacerbate the initial problem of complexity.

Finally, although it is inevitable that particular events will drive legislation, criminal code formation must remain carefully considered with a reasonable amount of debate. Legislation should not be made in the matter of days but also should avoid years of delay. If laws are not carefully considered, a community's citizens may not feel compelled to comply with such laws.

Some recent reforms that could learn from previous successes and failures of past reforms are gun law reform, drug law reform, and reforms on terrorism. These most recent reforms must learn from the lessons provided by reforms in the last 50 years: avoid complexity, consider the progressive state, carefully consider legislative reform, and leave the lawmaking to the legislators.

Jeremy D. Ball

References and Further Reading

Brooks, A.D., Megan's law: Constitutionality and policy, *Criminal Justice Ethics, 15* (1996).

Coker, D., Crime control and feminist law reform in domestic violence law: A critical review, *Buffalo Criminal Law Review, 4* (2001).

Feld, B.C., *Readings in Juvenile Justice Administration*, New York, NY: Oxford University Press, 1999.

Gainer, R.L., Federal criminal code reform: Past and future, *Buffalo Criminal Law Review, 2* (1998).

Hixson, R.F., *Pornography and the Justices: The Supreme Court and the Intractable Obscenity Problem*, Carbondale, IL: Southern Illinois University Press, 1996.

Kadish, S.H., Fifty years of criminal law: An opinionated review, *California Law Review, 87* (1999).

Myers, J.E.B., *Legal Issues in Child Abuse and Neglect Practice,* 2nd ed., Thousand Oaks, CA: Sage, 1998.

Robinson, P.H., Should the victims' rights movement have influence over criminal law formulation and adjudication? *McGeorge Law Review, 33* (2002).

Spohn, C.C. and Horney, J., The impact of rape law reform on the processing of simple and aggravated rape cases, *The Journal of Criminal Law and Criminology, 86* (1996).

Spohn, C. and Horney, J., *Rape Law Reform: A Grassroots Revolution and Its Impact*, New York, NY: Plenum Press, 1992.

Steadman, H.J., McGreevy, M.A., Morrissey, J.P., Callahan, L.A., Robbins, P.C., and Cirincione, C., *Before and After Hinckley: Evaluating Insanity Defense Reform*, New York, NY: The Guilford Press, 1993.

See also **Criminal Law: Definition, Sources, and Types**

Criminalistics *See* **Police: Forensic Evidence**

Criminal Profiling *See* **Investigate (Psychological) Profiling**

Criminalization and Decriminalization

Criminalization and decriminalization appear at first blush to be mirror images of one another as concepts. However, defining, refining, and amplifying shows that there is more to this pair of criminological constructs than meets the eye.

Criminalization is the process of creating a crime and making conduct previously lawful illegal, frequently for the protection of society, though the goal might also be one such as economic regulation. In contrast, decriminalization refers to a process (be it legislative, judicial, or otherwise) whereby conduct that has been unlawful is, if not officially legalized, then at least no longer deemed and punished as a crime; such a process oftentimes provides further liberty to members of society. The processes, as will be discussed, may emanate from different sources, but both relate to the question of what is a crime.

By definition, a crime is generally composed of two essential pieces, the *actus reus* (the conduct) and the *mens rea* (the intent or the guilty mind). As a general matter (and leaving aside jurisdictional issues), where the conduct takes place and the requisite level of intent for the particular crime are both provable, there is liability for criminal culpability (or blame). In the ordinary course, and with the exception of strict liability crimes, which are *per se* violations requiring no intent, the burden of proof is upon the prosecution to prove the elements of a crime beyond a reasonable doubt. Assuming that there is sufficient evidence to prove the elements of the crime beyond a reasonable doubt, and absent a viable defense placing either the intent or the conduct in issue, there may be a conviction for a crime.

This seemingly simple formula inevitably becomes complicated when one factors in that law is a reflection of social norms. This may take the form of codification and legislation, or of common law and case development. These are, in no small measure, professional formulations of moral value systems, which may change or evolve over time. For example, stalking behavior was not legally codified as criminal conduct until the 1990s, starting with the first antistalking legislation in California in 1990. By the end of the decade, every state in the U.S. had some form of particularized antistalking law, as did the U.K. and other countries. Some of these laws had been expanded (for example, to include additional forms of conduct or provide additional protections for certain classes of targeted victims, such as minors) or refined after judicial challenges (most often with regard to the requisite intent necessary to support a conviction). If there were no antistalking laws prior to the antistalking movement and legislation criminalizing stalking during the 1990s, does this mean that the conduct did not exist previously? Does it mean that the level of intent of the actors, who could now be prosecuted as criminals, necessarily changed? The answer to both of these rhetorical questions would be in the negative. Rather, the social norms of what was acceptable changed, and the process of criminalizing stalking took place in multiple jurisdictions in a very short time frame.

In contrast, the process of decriminalization and legalization has been taking place for the past 50 years with regard to loving and marrying. During the early part of the 20th century, it was illegal as a matter of law in some states to marry someone of another race. It was not until 1967 that the U.S. Supreme Court, in the case of *Loving v. Virginia* (388 U.S. 1, 87 S.Ct. 1817, 18 L.Ed. 2d 1010, 1967), held that the felony of miscegenation, marriage between a white person and a person of another race, should be struck down because there should be no restriction placed upon the freedom solely based upon racial classification or composition. In 1999 came the first of a series of cases holding that same-sex couples should be entitled to the same benefits and protections afforded by the law to married opposite-sex couples. Ironically, in the subsequent 2003 Massachusetts case, *Goodridge v. Department of Health* (2003 Mass. LEXIS 814, 2003), the court notes that it has the obligation of defining liberty and related entitlements, and specifically eschews the role of mandating its own moral code, citing a recent U.S. Supreme Court case. That case, *Lawrence v. Texas* (123 S.Ct. 2472, 2003), in fact, was an opportunity whereby the Supreme Court had the opportunity to reconsider its deeply divided 1986 decision in *Bowers v. Hardwick*, holding that there was no fundamental right to engage in homosexual sodomy in view of traditional moral and legal prohibitions against sodomy. Hence, what was criminal conduct proceeds to be decriminalized, and in fact, appears to be along the path to legalized protections.

A more complicated case presents itself for the study of criminalization and decriminalization in the question of physician-assisted suicide. Euthanasia has been, and currently remains, technically illegal as a matter of Anglo-American law. However, the law on the books and the law in practice diverge in the medical hastening of death. For example, one physician, Dr. Timothy Quill, wrote an article about how he gave a cancer patient drugs so that she could self-medicate to overdose; when Quill was brought before a grand jury, the grand jury declined to issue an indictment. Could one not call this *de facto* decriminalization, as one could call cases where the prosecution declines to prosecute as a matter of discrimination? Could one not call early acquittals of the self-styled "Dr. Death," Dr. Jack Kevorkian (see *People v. Kevorkian*, 2001WL 1474986 (Mich.App.), No. 221758 (Ct. App. Mi. 2001))—wherein both the conduct of assisting in suicides and the intent to do so were repeatedly and well documented—jury nullification, and again *de facto* decriminalization of the newly enacted assisted suicide bans of the 1990s? Conversely, is it not reasonable to consider the murder conviction of Kevorkian, notwithstanding a viable defense as to causation or the *actus reas*, to be a criminalization of increasingly aggressive conduct moving toward euthanasia? Yet, during the same period of time that the Michigan legislature codified the criminalization of physician-assisted suicide, the people of Oregon passed a measure, which was codified into law, decriminalizing and *permitting* physician-assisted suicide under controlled circumstances, a law that has survived repeated challenges (see *State of Oregon v. Ashcroft*, 192 F. Supp. 2d 1077, 2002 U.S. Dist. LEXIS 6695 (D. Ct. Oregon 2002)).

It is imperative to recognize that criminalization and decriminalization themselves reflect neither absolute rights nor absolute wrongs. Rather, these processes tend to show an evolution and a symbiosis of the legislatures, the courts, prosecutors, and defense attorneys, sometimes the defendants themselves, sometimes juries. Equally, patterns of enforcement, such as prosecution and sentencing proceedings, emerge as inextricably intertwined when studying impact of criminalization and decriminalization of conduct upon members of different races, genders, socioeconomic groups, geographic locales, and those subject to other factors. The social sciences of psychology, sociology, criminology, and anthropology come to the fore in considerations and explorations of what is being criminalized or decriminalized, or as in the intriguing case of physician-assisted suicide, both simultaneously. The politics of criminalization and decriminalization, juxtaposed with the role of social sciences in legal decision making, and considered concomitantly with the evolution of social norms and economic effects of changing the law or its implementation, offer as many questions as answers in an underexplored area of research.

DEMETRA M. PAPPAS

References and Further Reading

Lacey, N., Criminology, criminal law and criminalization, in Maguire, M., Morgan, R., and Reiner, R. Eds., *The Oxford Handbook of Criminology*, 2nd ed., Clarendon Press, Oxford, 1997, pp. 437–450.

Maguire, M., Morgan, R., and Reiner, R., Eds., *The Oxford Handbook of Criminology*, 2nd ed., Clarendon Press, Oxford, 1997.

Fletcher, G., *Rethinking Criminal Law*, Little Brown and Co., Boston and Toronto, 1978.

Pappas, D.M., Stopping New Yorkers' stalkers: An anti-stalking law for the millennium, *Fordham Urban Law Journal*, 27, 945–952 (2000).

See also **Drug Control Policy: Criminalization and Decriminalization**

Criminology and Criminal Justice: A Comparison

Academic disciplines are distinguished by the nature of their theoretical project, by the domain questions, concepts, and preferred methodological approaches that structure scholarly attention, define what is worth investigating, and suggest legitimate interpretations of observations and data.

In that sense, criminology is best defined as concerned with the question of criminality, the reasons why particular individuals and groups engage in the deviance defined as criminal by a society. Criminologists seek to understand the causes of criminal actions. Different schools of thought and theoretical approaches within the discipline are identified by the major causal connections they see between specified antecedent conditions and criminal behavior; such conditions may be the biological or genetic make-ups of individuals, the personality patterns, values, norms, and social connections they acquire through early and adult socialization processes, their life course and significant events that they experience, or the general societal conditions in which they are raised, live, and work. Though the unit of analysis is the individual, theories explaining criminal acts range across all levels of analysis. Criminology tends to be oriented toward pure research and theorizing, though the policy implications of knowledge gained may be implied or analyzed.

Criminal justice, in contrast, seeks its theoretical *raison d'etre* in the dual concepts of crime control and social order, that is, in the processes and institutions developed by a society to deal with, control, and mitigate criminal acts and their individual and social consequences (harm, fear, disorder, instability). Criminal justice scholars study the ways in which law develops, the processes by which deviance and crime become defined and placed on social and political agendas, and the institutions and policies devised by publics, policy makers, and practitioners to control and manage the threats to social order and well-being posed by criminal activities. Criminal justice scholars are content to use existing theories, or develop new approaches, as long as these help in understanding the development, use, and effectiveness of control policies or processes of reproducing order. Criminal justice has a strong policy orientation (how can information be used to improve policy) yet analysis can remain at a purely theoretical level, be content with understanding the processes and decision-making patterns characteristic of criminals and crime control practitioners (i.e., police, prosecutors, judges, correctional personnel).

A simple way of characterizing the essential difference is that criminologists deal with the beginning of the social problem of crime and disorder (why it happens) whereas criminal justice scholars deal with the way in which societies organize themselves to respond to the crime problem in an effective and just manner.

Yet academic disciplines do not exist in an institutional vacuum nor are they immune to practical considerations. Disciplines become located in organizational units of universities (departments, research centers) and in professional associations that promote and protect the views and interests of their members. Hence, one finds departments of criminology and of criminal justice in many universities, sometimes by themselves and sometimes located within other departments (e.g., criminology in sociology and criminal justice in political science departments).

The distinction between disciplines defined by their theoretical projects versus their status as organizations has consequences for the development of each discipline and its recognition by others as a legitimate field of scholarly inquiry and teaching specialization. Defined by their substantive questions and foci, the two disciplines are engaged in mutually supportive research and as a teaching, with each discipline approaching a common question from its dominant perspective. The goal is the same—to understand the incidence and prevalence of criminal activities and to control them through public and private policies. Criminologists and criminal justice scholars work together to understand why crime happens in order to devise policies that will make a difference for the safety and well-being of a society. The specific focus of research, however, reflects discretion and preference of individual scholars. Some wish to study, develop, and test particular theories why crime occurs; others are more interested in why control institutions (e.g., police or the courts) engage in the policies they do; others, still, are interested in how social order is defined and normalized within different societies. The fact that different scholars look at the problem of crime and control at different levels of analysis and from different perspectives, and derive personal satisfactions from their work in distinct ways (some are enthralled by the theoretical elegance of an explanation or the pyrotechnics of statistical techniques, others by their capacity to enhance safety or promote a version of justice that achieves salience in public thinking) is no great matter. In the end, the understandings developed by each will achieve a reenforcing mutuality that makes it possible for societies to understand more completely and respond more effectively and justly to the problem of crime.

Viewed, though, as organizational units, criminology and criminal justice are competitors for resources, students, prestige, and academic and policy influence. The process of becoming a discipline that is sufficiently well defined to achieve legitimacy in the eyes of fellow scholars is complex, takes time, and may lead to competition and even the stereotyping of goals and aspirations (e.g., Jeffery et al, 1991). This has undermined the natural convergence of criminology and criminal justice toward the common enterprise of understanding and dealing with crime.

Criminology and criminal justice developed separately over time as theoretical and organizational enterprises. Criminology arose from traditional sociological concerns—the underpinnings of social order, explanations of deviance and criminality, the influence of individual, group, and contextual factors on individual behavior—and still embodies within its theoretical and methodological approaches mainly conventional sociological concepts and themes. As the subject matter of criminology gained interested researchers and teachers, these scholars began to define themselves as somewhat distinct from scholars dealing with other sociological areas of inquiry and ultimately founded their own professional association, the American Society of Criminology (ASC) in 1957. The goal of the ASC is to promote its theoretical project as well as to protect the identity of criminology as a separate discipline, entitled to organizational autonomy and attendant benefits within universities (budgets, students, and professors).

Criminal justice is a more recent discipline than criminology (the professional association of criminal justicians—the Academy of Criminal Justice Sciences—was founded in 1963) and grew mainly from and through the efforts of a group of practitioners and academics whose interests lay in applied social policies, specifically police science. During the 1970s, when federal money became available for training a vast multitude of workers in criminal justice institutions, many police science departments converted themselves into criminal justice departments, espousing a complex and multidisciplinary, almost eclectic, approach to problems of crime control. Two concerns drove this change. One was the hope for academic respectability, the need to shed its (inaccurate but widely held) image as an applied, technical, vocational training program and become accepted by other scholars as a serious, theoretically inclined, and methodologically sophisticated area of research and teaching. The second reason reflected a need to convince important audiences beyond the university—politicians, publics, interest groups, and policy makers—that this new discipline could make a contribution to public well-being.

Criminal justice succeeded easily with the social audience but less well with its academic peers, many of whom continued to see criminal justice as ill-defined, lacking focus or domain concepts, unable to move beyond applied thinking to theoretical complexity, and ill-fitting within the organizational arrangements of universities. Criminal justicians (an awkward term that well captures the newness of the discipline and its combination of theoretical and applied focus) sometimes see criminologists as unable to develop theoretical progress and agreement on what causes crime, hence irrelevant to effective or just crime control policy. At the polar end of misperceptions (overstated here to make the point), criminal justice scholars see criminology as but a small part of the understanding of crime and control, although criminologists think of criminal justice as merely the practical application of knowledge about crime gained by true scholars.

But currently, the similarities outweigh the differences. Both criminology and criminal justice have specific theoretical interests, domain concepts, professional status, and organizational identity. They differ in the vocabulary used to stress disciplinary status. Criminologists tend to do pure whereas criminal justice scholars tend to do policy relevant research; criminology is still the child of sociology whereas criminal justice trumpets its multidisciplinary inclinations and freedom; and criminologists deal largely with individual units of analysis whereas criminal justice scholars tend to focus on the personal, institutional, and societal levels of theory and explanation. One can suspect that in the future, criminology and criminal justice will converge even further. Three solid indications of the trend toward convergence are dual members (who belong to both the ASC and the ACJS); the overlapping of citations used in scholarly work (criminologists citing criminal justice scholars, and vice versa—see, Cohn and Farrington, 1998); and—a less direct indicator—the listing of jobs in the professional newsletters (criminology positions that are advertised in ACJS newsletters, and criminal justice positions that are listed in ASC newsletters). All three show an upward trend. In short, academic disciplines do not stand still but respond to professional, academic, economic, and societal pressures. These pressures currently tend to favor convergence.

Otwin Marenin

References and Further Reading

Cohn, E.G. and Farrington, D.P., Changes in the most-cited scholars in major American criminology and criminal justice journals between 1986–1990 and 1991–1995, *Journal of Criminal Justice*, 26, 2, 1998.

Cullen, F., Fighting back: Criminal justice as a discipline, *ACJS Today*, 13, 1995.

Jeffery, C.R., Myers, L.B., and Wollan, L.A., Crime, justice and their systems: Resolving the tension, *The Criminologist*, 16, 1991.

Marenin, O. and Worrall, J. Criminal justice: Portrait of a discipline in progress, *Journal of Criminal Justice*, 36, 1998.

Morn, F., *Academic Politics and the History of Criminal Justice Education*, Westport, CT: Greenwood Press, 1995.

Sorensen, J., Widmayer, A.G., and Scarpitti, F.R., Examining the criminal justice and criminological paradigms: An analysis of ACJS and ASC members, *Journal of Criminal Justice Education*, 4, 1994.

See also **Citation Research in Criminology and Criminal Justice; Internet Resources in Criminology and Criminal Justice**

Criminology and Criminal Justice: Careers

The criminal justice major and the study of criminology is intended for students interested in pursuing careers of graduate study in law enforcement, corrections, the courts, law, education, social services, government, criminology, forensic science or criminalistics, private security, and public administration. There are many skills needed in order to achieve success in the field of criminal justice. Often criminal justice professionals are required to have written and oral resentation skills. Further, understanding societies' reactions to crimes is a skill that is most effective in the area of criminal justice. Included in societies' understanding of crime is an understanding of the impact of gender and race within the context of criminal justice. These skills address the ethical and moral values associated within the context of understanding the impact, and nature of the field of criminology and criminal justice.

Next, an understanding of quantitative skills is key to working well within the field of criminal justice. These research strategy skills include research and scientific methods that allow the criminal justice professional to think critically. Further, as the field is subject to trends and changes that are affected by societal changes, and moreover, the globalization of crime, research strategies are needed in order to combat and confront challenges associated with the social control aspect of crime and justice. Therefore, the criminal justice professional needs to have an understanding of the nature of crimes.

Decision-making techniques, patience, and a strong background in humanities, social science, and natural science will contribute to a keen understanding and career success in the field of criminal justice. Further, a criminal justice professional needs to have a broad understanding of criminal law and the criminal justice system. This includes knowledge of legal structures such as courts.

Finally, those who seek jobs in the administrative section of the criminal justice field need to have supervision and management skills. Again, decision making, problem-solving techniques along with patience contribute greatly to this career choice. For instance, as an administrator the use of interviewing skills would serve as an asset as you build your criminal justice organization. Therefore, the ability to not only analyze social problems and develop solutions but to recognize and identify those who would be an asset in that process in the criminal justice organization with which you are affiliated contributes positively to the field.

Careers in Corrections

As prison populations continue to soar in the U.S., the field of corrections has broadened. This is another choice area for careers in the field of criminology and criminal justice. There are several areas within which one could find employment in corrections. Further, for those interested in the counseling aspects of corrections, there are a myriad of occupations. For instance, a correctional treatment specialist provides guidance or support to inmate populations while working solely with inmates. Similarly, a corrections counselor guides and counsels inmates during their incarceration. Further, this counselor conducts individual and group counseling sessions. A juvenile justice counselor is assigned to state youth divisions to work with juveniless, from persons in need of supervision to hard-core adolescents delinquents. A prerelease program correctional counselor helps clients in their transition from custody to society. This person must be able to interact well with inmates. A prerelease program employment counselor provides vocational guidance for those soon to be released from incarceration. Vocational counselors provide educational programs in vocational specialties to determine learning needs, abilities, and other facts about inmates and provide other career training through work programs. Further, recreation counselors conduct and supervise the social activities of inmates. Education counselors ensure that the inmate's choice of program is in relation to his or her goals.

For persons interested in entering the field of corrections as an officer there are several capacities within which a person could fashion his or her career. For instance, a corrections officer works in the capacity of a guard who observes and supervises inmates in a correctional facility. A parole officer, however, is employed in a correctional facility or private agency to investigate and take action for parole violations. Parole officers are usually trained in the use of firearms. A probation officer conducts presentence reports and evaluations concerning release conditions along with working toward the rehabilitation of the offender while supervising the offender once he or she is released. A juvenile probation officer provides intake, investigation, and supervising service to family court for juveniles. This officer is also required to work with youths and their families while balancing a heavy caseload.

Other positions with corrections include prerelease program halfway house managers whose responsibilities are similar to a corrections officer or prison administrator in that this position requires strong administrative skills. A most important career choice within this field is the prison warden position that includes overall supervision and administration of correctional facility and the ability to plan, direct, and coordinate programs along with expert knowledge of all phases of corrections operation. Clinical psychologists work closely with inmates as members of the prison's interdisciplinary health care team. A person desiring to be in this position must have a doctorate degree. Similarly, academic teachers and professors employed at all levels within the correctional facility instruct in basic remedial courses designed to increase rudimentary English, reading, or math abilities. Classification and treatment directors apply the principles of management to the overall planning of correctional programs along with assigning inmates to particular programs, and review inmate case reports.

Finally, there are specialists employed within corrections. For instance, caseworkers or HIV specialists help HIV-infected inmates cope with their emotional and health related concerns. Similarly, substance abuse specialists provide individual and group counseling and can be found in correctional institutions, prerelease, and other alternative detention programs. Certain correction programs require specific training in substance abuse along with a degree in counseling.

Homeland Security Act and Jobs in the Department of Homeland Security

On November 25, 2002, President Bush signed the Homeland Security Act of 2002 into law. The purpose of the Act is to restructure and strengthen the executive branch of the federal government in an attempt to deal with the threat of terrorism. Having established the Act, the government officially established the Department of Homeland Security, whose primary mission it is to prevent and protect us from acts of terrorism on our own soil.

The Department of Homeland Security (DHS) requires the cooperation of several federal, state, and local government agencies. USA Jobs, the government's official central job bank, created the following list of federal agencies that are likely to hire for homeland security jobs, to fulfill their new roles under the Act. Eventually, the different employment systems will be rolled into one under the DHS. Some also offer entry-level, work-study and internship programs, to prepare high-school and college students and grads for homeland security jobs. These agencies include the following:

- U.S. Capitol Police
- Centers for Disease Control and Prevention
- U.S. Coast Guard Civilian Jobs
- U.S. Customs Service
- Federal Bureau of Investigation
- Federal Emergency Management Agency
- Federal Law Enforcement Training Center
- Food and Drug Administration
- Federal Protective Service
- Immigration and Naturalization Service
- U.S. Border Patrol
- Immigration Inspectors
- National Infrastructure Protection Center
- Homeland security jobs are through the FBI
- National Institutes of Health
- U.S. Secret Service
- Bureau of Diplomatic Security
- Transportation Security Administration
- U.S. Park Police

Many agencies have already established the homeland security jobs, from which the Department of Homeland Security will draw its expertise. In fact, under the Act, most, if not all, functions of several federal agencies have been or will be transferred to the Department of Homeland Security.

What Is the Key to a Successful Career in Criminology and Criminal Justice?

Today a person choosing a career in any field is required to have a college education along with the ability to write and speak well. Problem-solving techniques, the ability to learn new information quickly, and work well with others in a team are a must if one desires to continue in his or her career successfully. Criminal justice graduates seeking a career must use their education in a wide variety of fields. Further, the criminal justice graduate may seek future career avenues that may relate more to personal career interests, work values, and transferable skills than any specific academic major. Experiences within a particular field are extremely important in preparing criminal justice students for life after college. These experiences can be in the form of internships, part-time jobs, or volunteer positions. These experiences allow students to develop specific knowledge and skills that help to solidify their career choice, and improve their chances of employment after graduation. The following is a representative sample of job titles of former graduates with a criminal justice major. Students who obtain employment immediately upon graduation not only have the best college records, but they also are willing to relocate. Some of the following jobs also require education beyond a bachelors degree. There are opportunities for men and women in all these fields, some examples of which include:

Federal Law Enforcement and Investigative Agencies

Department of Agriculture—Office of Inspector General; Department of Defense—Army Criminal Investigation Division, Army Military Police, Defense Security Service, DOD Security, Naval Criminal Investigative Service, Navy Shore Patrol, USAF Air Police; Department of Health and Human Services—Food and Drug Administration; Department of the Interior—Bureau of Indian Affairs, Fish and Wildlife Service, National Park Service, U.S. Park Police; Department of Justice—Border Patrol, Drug Enforcement Administration, Federal Bureau of Investigation, Immigration and Naturalization Service, U.S. Marshals Service; Department of Labor; Labor Management Service; Department of State—Office of Security; Department of Transportation—Motor Carrier Safety, U.S. Coast Guard; Department of The Treasury—Bureau of Alcohol, Tobacco and Firearms, Customs Port Investigators, Internal Revenue Service, U.S. Customs, U.S. Secret Service; Other Federal Agencies—Central Intelligence Agency, Civil Aeronautics Board, Environmental Protection Agency, Federal Aviation Agency, Federal Communications Commission, Federal Deposit Insurance Corporation, Federal Trade Commission, National Security Agency, Securities and Exchange Commission, Supreme Court Police, U.S. Capitol Police, U.S. Postal Inspection Service, Veterans Administration.

State Law Enforcement and Investigative Agencies

Alcoholic Beverage Commission; Attorney General's Office; Auditor General's Office; Casino Control Commission; Conservation Department; Crime Commission; Environmental Protection; Fish and Boat Commission; Game Commission; Highway Patrol; Identification Division; Investigative Bureau; Liquor Control Board; Marine Police; Narcotics Bureau; Natural Resources Division; Public Safety Department; State Police.

Local Law Enforcement and Investigative Agencies

County—county detectives, county police, district attorney's office, park police, sheriff's department; Municipal—city, borough, township, or village police department, school district police, fire district marshal.

Private Security

Armored car; campus safety; courier; industrial security; insurance adjuster; insurance fraud investigator; private investigator; retail loss prevention; transportation safety specialist.

The Courts

Bailiff; clerk of court; constable; court administrator; crier; federal court staff; paralegal; probation officer; prothonotary; state court staff; support services counselor; victim service specialist.

Corrections

Board of Probation and Parole; community treatment facilities; county adult probation; county juvenile probation; county jails; detention facilities; federal bureau of prisons; federal probation; juvenile institutions; prisoner aid agencies; state department of corrections.

Criminalistics
Federal, state, and local crime laboratories.

Traffic Control and Safety
Police traffic divisions; safety associations; safety council; traffic commission; transportation departments.

Drug Abuse Control and Rehabilitation
Addiction prevention programs; drug law enforcement agencies; rehabilitation centers.

Youth Agencies
Children and youth services; community organizations (e.g., Boys and Girls Club); juvenile aid bureau; state youth boards.

Postbaccalaureate Education

A criminal justice education is a very good preparation for law school, as well as for the pursuit of master's level studies in criminal justice, criminology, police science, and in public administration.

Generally, students who want to make a larger impact in the field of criminal justice continue their education, receiving their master's, juris doctor or doctor of philosophy degrees. Seeking such degrees may take 2–10 years. Jobs requiring additional educational skills, such as a graduate degree in criminal justice or a law degree, include the following:

Attorney	Contracts Administrator
Coroner	Substance Abuse Counselor
FBI Agent	Law Librarian
Criminal Investigator	Police Detective
Warden	Penologist
Criminologist	Private Investigator
Corrections Facilities Manager	

Federal Job Sites

USA Jobs—Federal Job Listings (http://www. usajobs.opm.gov/)
Jobs with the Transportation Security Administration (http://www.tsa.gov/public/display?theme=2&content=589)
U.S. Secret Service (http://www.treas.gov/usss/index.shtml)
IRS Criminal Investigation jobs (http://www.treas.gov/irs/ci/recruit/)
Naval Criminal Investigative Service jobs(http://www.ncis.navy.mil/careers/HowToApply.html)
National Security Agency careers (http://www.nsa.gov/programs/employ/index.html)
INS Border Patrol Jobs (http://jsearch.usajobs.opm.gov/getjob.asp?jobid=18686709)
US Park Police job info (http://www.nps.gov/uspp/findex.htm)
Opportunities with the UN & other international organizations (http://www.state.gov/p/io/empl/11076.htm) (http://www.state.gov/p/io/empl/)
Pentagon Force Protection Agency- officer positions (http://www.pfpa.mil/employment.html)
US Postal Inspector jobs (http://www.usps.com/postalinspectors/employmt.htm)
Federal Bureau of Prisons jobs (http://www.bop.gov/hrmpg/hrmcorrectionalofficer.html)
FBI jobs (http://fbijobs.com/)
CIA careers (http://www.cia.gov/employment/index.html)
Dept of Treasury, Bureau of Engraving & Printing—officer jobs(http://www.moneyfactory.com/hr/document.cfm/95/248/1742)
PoliceEmployment.com (http://www.policeemployment.com/)
Lawenforcementjob.com (http://www.lawenforcementjob.com/)
MonsterTRAK (http://www.monstertrak.com)
Criminal Justice jobs (http://criminaljusticejobs.com/)
Lawyers (http://www.bls.gov/oco/ocos053.htm)
Paralegals (http://www.bls.gov/oco/ocos114.htm)
Police and Detectives (http://www.bls.gov/oco/ocos160.htm)
Judges, Magistrates and Other Judicial Workers (http://www.bls.gov/oco/ocos272.htm)
Private Detectives and Investigators (http://www.bls.gov/oco/ocos157.htm)
State and Local government workers (http://www.bls.gov/oco/ocos157.htm)
Careers in Law and Order (http://www.saludos.com/cguide/lguide.html#top)
Federal Law Enforcement Career Resources (http://www.concentric.net/~extraord/law.htm)
Criminal Justice Resources (http://www.icpsr.umich.edu/NACJD/links.html)
Pre-Law Handbook (http://oncampus.richmond.edu/academics/as/polisci/prelaw/)

Organizations and Associations

North Carolina Department of Correction (includes divisions of Prisons, Adult Probation and Parole, Alcohol and Chemical Dependency Programs, etc.) (http://www.doc.state.nc.us/)

US Department of Justice (http://www.usdoj.gov/)
Federal Bureau of Investigation (http://www.fbi.gov)
National Federation of Paralegal Associations (http://www.paralegals.org/)
National Association of Legal Assistants (http://www.nala.org/)
Central Intelligence Agency (http://www.cia.gov)
American Bar Association (http://www.abanet.org/)
National Organization of Black Law Enforcement Executives (http://www.noblenatl.org/)
National Drug Enforcement Officers Association (http://www.ndeoa.org)
National Sheriff's Association (http://www.sheriffs.org/)
National Security Agency (http://www.nsa.gov/)

UNCW Resources

UNCW Graduate Follow-up Survey Data (http://www.uncw.edu/stuaff/stulife/assessment_services;/pg_survey_pages/intro.htm)
Data for Criminal Justice grads (http://www.uncw.edu/stuaff/stulife/assessment_services/) (pg_survey_pages/Criminal%20Justice%20survey%20page.htm)
UNCW Sociology, Anthropology and Criminal Justice Department (http://www.uncw.edu/soccrj/)

RAMONA BROCKETT

References and Further Reading

Lambert, S.E. and Regan, D., *Great Jobs for Criminal Justice Majors*. McGraw Hill, 2001.
Morgan, M. *Careers in Criminology*, McGraw-Hill, 2000.
Stephens, R.W., *Careers in Criminal Justice*, 2nd ed., Allyn & Bacon, 2001.
Stinchcomb, J.D. *Opportunities in Law Endorsement and Criminal Justice Careers*, Revised ed., McGraw-Hill, 2002.

See also **Corrections: Careers; Law and Legal Services: Careers; Law Enforcement: Careers; Probation and Parole: Careers**

Criminology as Social Science

Criminology consists of the study of the social problem of crime, including the processes of making and breaking laws as well as society's reaction to the phenomenon (Sutherland, 1939). As an academic field of study, criminology meets the standards of a social science, defined as:

> The entirety of those disciplines, or any particular discipline, concerned with the systematic study of social phenomena. No single conception of science is implied by this usage, although there are sociologists who reject the notion that social studies should be seen as scientific is in any sense based on the physical sciences (Jary and Jary, 2001).

The social sciences (e.g., sociology, political science, anthropology, economics) differ from the natural or hard sciences (e.g., chemistry, physics, biology) in more ways than just addressing dissimilar subject matter. The natural sciences enjoy a much longer history, dating back to the European Enlightenment era, whereas most of the social sciences did not appear on the university setting prior to the 20th century. The utilization of society as laboratory yields implications for inquiry surrounding the inability of social scientists to adequately eliminate mitigating factors in hypothetic, deductive, and experimental research designs. As an alternative methodological approach, social science largely relies on quasi-experimental research design, which emulates hard science, generally.

The social sciences are heavily rooted in and subscribe to the major philosophies of science, most notably positivism and subjectivism. Positivism has been the dominant paradigm influencing research theory symmetry throughout the social sciences for several decades. According to the *Dictionary of the Social Sciences* (Gould and Kolb, 1964, 530), positivism is "a philosophical approach, theory or system based on the view that in the social as well as in the natural sciences sense experiences and their logical and mathematical treatment are the exclusive source of all worthwhile information." Derived from the social thought of Comte, Newton, and the Vienna Circle, the logic of positivism sets the standard for contemporary social science theory testing and both pure and applied research, primarily through the logic and use of variable analysis. Variable analysis emphasizes reductionism, categorization, and measurement toward the goals of establishing correlation and causality. This style of inquiry, called positivistic criminology, is rooted in empiricism, which is often erroneously thought to characterize quantitative research featuring statistical analyses.

Subjectivism, or interpretivism, differs from positivism in its fundamental assumptions concerning the nature of inquiry. A dynamic and developmental perspective that fosters a qualitative naturalistic research style, subjectivism, also known as interpretivism, has become established as the foremost inquiry alternative to positivism in the social sciences, generally, and in criminology, specifically. Subjectivism is a methodological approach to inquiry positing that social phenomena cannot be objectively observed *per se*, rather each concept is constructed and understood by shared meanings. Whereas positivism seeks to eliminate any subjectivity or bias from both the researcher and the subject, interpretivism encourages consideration of participant perception of human actions. Qualitative research methods, both observational and interactional, facilitate this approach, which, despite the widespread equaling of empiricism and statistical analysis, is inherently sense oriented and thus empirical.

Another standard by which to define a field of study as a science is theory, that is, a set of explanations specific to the field in question. The various social sciences are shaped by specific theories, typically derived from larger social perspectives, namely functionalism, power conflict, and symbolic interactionism. Criminology certainly draws on each of these larger perspectives in its leading theories. Functionalism and its emphasis on normative consensus clearly influences classical criminology and its more modern extensions of deterrence and rational choice theories. Virtually all of critical criminology is either directly or indirectly derived from social conflict perspectives on society and symbolic interactionism affects a variety of crime causation and response theories, such as routine activities theory, reintegrative shaming theory, and labeling theory.

Whether attempting to validate a theory, exploring new phenomena, or evaluating the operational effectiveness of a juvenile or criminal program, criminologists employ a broad range of research methods, both quantitative and qualitative, but strive to do so from a theoretical orientation. Accordingly, a strong case can be made for criminology as a social science.

The issue of criminology as a social science stems from both its embeddedness in sociology and the erroneous assumption that criminology and the complimentary field of criminal justice are synonymous. Although it is clear that criminology is a social science, the boundaries between and hierarchal order of the other crime-focused academic fields relative to criminology are muddled. Criminology, historically, has been considered a major area of specialization within its mother discipline, sociology, the refinement and evolutionary outcome of the sociology of deviance. Criminology today remains both a primary research focus and formal track of undergraduate and graduate studies within sociology departments, but has also splintered from sociology at many colleges and universities to become an independent discipline (a trend in the social sciences since the 1970s responsible for several relatively "young" fields such as child and family studies, women's studies, and African American studies).

Criminology is often confused and contrasted with criminal justice, which emerged on the college setting during the 1970s—about the time criminology was becoming somewhat independent from sociology. Criminal justice was largely shaped by and reflected the spirit of the times, which included the civil rights movement, the Vietnam War, and a general liberalization of the popular culture.

These social movements, along with unprecedented levels of juvenile delinquency, presented widespread challenges for law enforcement management and social order maintenance. The nation's response was the Law Enforcement Administrative Act (LEAA) that sought to resource criminal justice and enhance the professionalism of police administrators. Accordingly, criminal justice (originally known as "police studies" or "police science") programs of study were established in institutions of higher education throughout the country. The LEAA served to define criminal justice as an applied and practitioner-oriented field of study, contrasting it with the more theoretical orientation of criminology.

Today, the paradigmatic conflict between criminal justice as applied science and criminology as social science lingers, but has been largely resolved. The two are naturally complementary and have become so intertwined in coverage and research focus that differences are often a matter of semantics.

J. Mitchell Miller

References and Further Reading

Gould, J. and Kolb, W.L., Eds. (1964). *A Dictionary of the Social Sciences*. New York, NY: The Free Press of Glencoe.

Jary, D. and Jary, J. (2000). *Sociology: The HarperCollins Dictionary*. New York, NY: HarperCollins.

Schuetz, A. (1943). The problem of rationality in the social world, *Economica*, 10, 130–149.

Schuetz, A. (1953). Common-sense and the scientific interpretation of human action, *Philosophy and Phenomenological Research*, 14, 1–38.

Schuetz, A. (1973). *Collected Papers*, Natanson, M. The Hague: Martinus Nijhoff.
Sutherland, E.H. (1939). *Principles of Criminology*, 3rd ed. Philadelphia, PA: J.B. Lippincott.

See also **Criminology and Criminal Justice: A Comparison; Criminology: Definition; Criminology: Historical Development**

Criminology: Definition

Defining the parameters of the field called criminology is quite deceptive. On the one hand, it seems a simple task. Deconstructing the term, we have "ology" or "the study of," combined with "crim," representing crime or criminals. Thus, the typical dictionary definition will tell us that criminology is the study of crime and criminals. Often it will be added that a scientific method of study is used, consistent with the views of mainstream contemporary scholars. The "study of crime" is also congruous with the historical origin of the term. Although the earliest "criminologists," sometimes dubbed the "fathers of criminology," actually preceded the label, appearance of the term soon followed. The Italian Raffaele Garofalo, one of Cesare Lombroso's followers, is often credited with coining the term in 1885, but French anthropologist Paul Topinard is identified by others as the first to call the subject "criminology," as he did in an 1887 publication. It is at least clear that the study of crime is older than the terms "criminology" and "criminologist"; Cesare Beccaria (considered by many to be the founder of classical criminology) was a philosopher, whereas Cesare Lombroso (considered by many to be the founder of scientific criminology) was a physician who considered himself a criminal anthropologist.

The brief definition above is more limited than controversial. The challenge in defining criminology becomes evident, however, with efforts to expand the definition to make it more informative. As noted, just injecting the term "scientific" into the simplest definition generates some controversy. Just as Beccaria was a philosopher and Lombroso a physician, the sources or methods of study for acquiring knowledge in criminology still are not completely agreed upon. Critical criminologists, especially postmodernists and some feminists, reject the scientific method as the sole or primary approach for seeking explanations of crime. In short, there is little more that can be said to define criminology without generating some controversy. What can be done is to identify a number of issues that seem to separate criminological perspectives and to specify those that are more often subscribed to or are more "mainstream."

Many criminology textbooks launch into their subject matter without even defining criminology. Some offer extremely brief definitions that fail to depict the lack of consensus within the field. Those criminological works focused on presenting theoretical developments or research findings simply do so within the framework of their concerns and do not typically digress to debate the appropriate content of the larger discipline. Yet, perhaps, some of the best syntheses of the issues raised in attempting to define criminology can be found in a minority of textbooks. The classic text development of a definition of criminology comes from Edwin H. Sutherland's work, and this is probably the most widely employed definition that is comprehensive enough to offer some clarity regarding the scope and complexity of criminology. Sutherland generally subdivided the discipline into three areas considering the making of laws, the breaking of laws, and the social reactions to behavior that violates the law. In the words of the ninth edition of his classic text, coauthored with Donald R. Cressey, criminology comprises: "(a) the sociology of law, which is an attempt at systematic analysis of the conditions under which criminal laws develop …; (b) criminal etiology, which is an attempt at scientific analysis of the causes of crime; and (c) penology, which is concerned with the control of crime …" (Sutherland and Cressey, 1974, 3) While representing mainstream criminological thought, each of the three subdivisions identified by Sutherland and Cressey raise objections in various corners.

First, Sutherland implied here, and made quite explicit elsewhere, that he regarded criminology as a sociological domain. In fact, largely owing to his influence criminology became overwhelmingly a sociological enterprise during the 20th century in the U.S. Yet other disciplines have and do lay claim to criminology. In recent years one of the most robust developments in the field has been interdisciplinary study, often integrating components drawn from diverse "parent disciplines" (biology, economics, geography, and psychology) into complex theoretical models. Second, Sutherland advocated a scientific approach that, although still dominant, is not the exclusive method of criminological study. Sutherland's view of the criminologists' role in studying criminal behavior also has a particular focus: explaining the causes of the behavior. Sutherland was a staunch advocate of theory and although this view also continues to represent mainstream thinking, many criminologists focus on the gathering and presentation of facts, neglecting theory. Another development since Sutherland's time is the emergence of criminal justice, a field that studies various institutional responses to criminal behavior (e.g., law enforcement, the courts, and corrections). Some scholars see this field as distinct from criminology, whereas Sutherland viewed the study of the reactions to crime as part of criminology *per se*.

A number of other debates about the very nature of criminology keep the field lively. One of the most dramatic of these is the question of how crime itself should be defined. Should criminologists only study socially harmful conduct that violates criminal legal statutes and comes to the attention of law enforcement officials, or should they expand their research to include criminal behavior that goes undetected by the police and conceivably to other socially harmful behaviors that are not violations of criminal law? Sutherland broached this debate when he urged criminologists to study white-collar offenses (e.g., price fixing and unfair labor practices by large corporations) that seldom result in arrests and sometimes violate the administrative regulations established by government agencies, but not criminal laws. Social reaction theories, such as labeling, view the criminal label as relative and focus on behaviors independent of legal status.

One of the old debates that plagues the field is whether criminology is, or can be, value-free. Some argue that ideology dramatically effects criminological work and that affiliation with particular theoretical orientations inevitably color one's thought. This in turn leads to concern about the role of criminology and crime policy. Elliott Currie, for example, is well-known for offering policy commentary that is rooted in liberal criminological theory. In contrast, James Q. Wilson's recommendations come from a conservative theoretical vantage. Other criminologists believe that the discipline should seek a pure truth, undiluted by policy considerations. The dominant perspective nowadays seems to be that criminology should play some role in informing policy.

In sum, there is considerable disagreement regarding exactly what criminology is or should be. The stumbling blocks relate to the methods of study, the role of theory, the larger disciplinary identity or identities that should exist, disagreement over what qualifies as the "crime" to be studied, the relationship of the discipline to the realm that some call criminal justice studies, theoretical preferences, the appropriate ties between criminology and policy, and the influence of ideology. This vast arena of debate may give the impression that there is little agreement. Among all those who view themselves as criminologists, this is probably a fair assessment, for it is a highly diverse field. However, if we identify the mainstream or dominant perspective, realizing that even these perceptions are rather fluid, we can see the outline of a generally accepted definition of criminology. It is one that sees the study of crime as a scientific enterprise with roughly equal emphasis on the roles of theory development and testing. It is a view that tolerates, and sometimes encourages, interdisciplinary exchanges and development of integrated theories. It incorporates an appreciation of the relativity of crime, facilitating cross-cultural comparisons and historical analyses. Finally, mainstream criminology strives to inform policy in practical and meaningful ways.

Stephen E. Brown

References and Further Reading

Brown, S.E., Esbensen, F., and Geis, G., *Criminology: Explaining Crime and its Context*, 5th ed., Cincinnati, OH: Anderson Publishing Co., 2004.

Currie, E., *Crime and Punishment in America*, New York, NY: Henry Holt and Co., 1998.

Sutherland, E.H. and Cressey, D.R., *Criminology,* 9th ed., New York, NY: J.B. Lippencott Co., 1974.

Vold, G.B., Bernard, T.J., and Snipes, J.B., *Theoretical Criminology,* 4th ed., New York, NY: Oxford University Press, 1998.

See also **Beccaria, Cesare; Cressey, Donald R., Lombroso, Cesare; Sutherland, Edwin H.**

Criminology: Historical Development

Although contemporary definitions vary in the exact words used, there is considerable consensus that criminology involves the application of the "scientific method" to the study of variation in criminal law, the causes of crime, and reactions to crime (Akers, 2000). This combination of method and substance evolved over time with the expectation for a scientific methodology in place by the late 19th century, and acceptance of the broad, tripartite, substantive focus established by the middle of the 20th century.

Criminology is an interdisciplinary field of study, involving scholars and practitioners representing a wide range of behavioral and social sciences as well as numerous natural sciences. Sociologists played a major role in defining and developing the field of study and criminology emerged as an academic discipline housed in sociology programs. However, with the establishment of schools of criminology and the proliferation of academic departments and programs concentrating specifically on crime and justice in the last half of the 20th century, criminology emerged as a distinct professional field with a broad, interdisciplinary focus and a shared commitment to generating knowledge through systematic research.

One ultimate goal of criminology has been the development of theories expressed with sufficient precision that they can be tested, using data collected in a manner that allows verification and replication. The theoretical dimension of criminology has a long history and ideas about the causes of crime can be found in philosophical thought over 2000 years ago. For example, in *Politics*, Plato's student Aristotle (384–322 B.C.) stated that, "poverty engenders rebellion and crime (Quinney, 1970)." Religious scholars focused on causes as diverse as natural human need, deadly sins, and the corrupting influence of Satan and other demons. The validity of such theories was founded in religious authority and they were not viewed as theories, subject to verification through any form of systematic observation, measurement, and analysis.

Rational, naturalistic philosophies about people and society grew in prominence during the 18th century. Enlightenment philosophers such as Montesquieu, Voltaire, Cesare Beccaria, and Jeremy Bentham criticized political and legal institutions and advocated social reforms based on the assumption that people were rational, deliberative beings. Such ideas constituted the first major school of organized, "naturalistic" thought about criminal law, criminality, and appropriate responses to crime—the Classical School. Such perspectives were called "naturalistic" because they constructed theories locating the causes of crime in natural characteristics of human beings as opposed to "supernatural" theories emphasizing demonic causes. Classical theorists assumed that most people were capable of rational calculation of gains and costs and that criminality was a choice. Laws were to be designed and enforced based on that principle. Contemporary "deterrence theory," "rational choice theory," and "social learning theory" in criminology incorporate these same assumptions.

The philosophical emphasis on rationality, coupled with the growing acceptance of scientific observation in the study of the natural world, first converged in the work of "European cartographers" in the mid-19th century. The cartographers "charted" crime and other social problems using statistics compiled by government officials, an approach that would dominate criminology for much of its history. The cartographers compiled and analyzed statistics on crime in Belgium (Adolphe Quetelet), France (A. M. Guerry), Germany (Alexander von Oettingen), and England (Henry Mayhew, Joseph Fletcher, Charles Booth). They were the first to recognize the distinction between crime as a property of societies, regions, or social settings and criminality or criminal behavior as a characteristic of individuals. Wealthy areas of their societies could have higher property crime rates than poor areas because of access to property (availability or opportunity in 20th century criminology) regardless of the characteristics of the individuals committing crimes. This "ecological" or "geographic" approach became a central feature in the work of one of the founders of a sociological approach to deviance, the French scholar, Emile Durkheim. In his classic work, *Suicide* (1897), he depicted both suicide rates and crime rates as normal features of society that could be studied empirically and linked to variations in religious, familial, and political characteristics.

In England, Henry Mayhew (1851, 1862) documented patterns of crime and delinquency in the nation and in London. He was particularly interested in "rookeries" of crime in London—areas that had had traditions of crime for several centuries. He complemented his documentation of the distribution of crime with delineation of the experiences of people in specific areas based on interviews of the people in those areas and narratives provided by professional criminals. The use of such "ethnographic" material was a major contribution to the development of criminology as a social science. Moreover, Mayhew believed that habitual, repetitive offenders were the crux of the crime problem—a belief shared by many contemporary criminologists who view "career" offenders as responsible for an inordinate amount of crime and delinquency.

Voss and Petersen (1971) note that the work of the European cartographers was eclipsed by the influence that Charles Darwin had on a variety of disciplines in the late 19th century. In *Descent of Man* (1871) Darwin argued that, although more highly evolved in terms of certain skills, humans were merely one species in the animal world. Darwin's ideas influenced two "schools" of criminology, the Italian "positivists" and the "Chicago school" in America. Although the cartographers were the first to apply scientific methods to the study of crime, the Italian physician Cesare Lombroso is credited as the "father" of criminology as a "scientific" discipline. Lombroso's approach was "positivistic" in that generalizations about crime and criminality were to be derived from observations and measurements of people and societies (i.e., application of the "positive" methods of science). He reported on climatic, social, and economic correlates of crime, but his most consequential work on individual criminality emphasized biological traits. Criminality was correlated with primitive characteristics indicative of earlier stages of primate human evolution called atavism. His *Crime, Its Causes and Remedies* (1911) was one of the first major research monographs on crime.

A revolutionary development in theories of problem behavior (including crime) at the beginning of the 20th century was psychoanalytic theory, formulated by Sigmund Freud. The psychoanalytic school emphasized instinctive urges shared by all humans (id) that could result in criminality without adequate awareness of reality and probable consequences (ego) or a social conscience (superego). The healthy human personality allowed satisfaction of urges within the limits set by the external social and physical world. Mental and behavioral problems result from abnormal personality development. Inadequate superego or ego development is particularly relevant to understanding criminality. In later years August Aichhorn (1936) and Kate Friedlander (1947) applied psychoanalytic perspectives to delinquent youth (delinquency refers to the criminal offenses of nonadults and for much of history included noncriminal behaviors called "status offenses").

Another challenge to the emphasis on biological traits in the explanation of criminality was Willem Bonger's Marxist theory elaborated in 1916 in *Criminality and Economic Conditions*. Bonger argued that economic organization is fundamental to the explanation of crime and criminality. Patterns of crime over time and social space could be explained in terms of the distribution of poverty, inequality, and fluctuations in the economy. Individual criminality could be attributed to the money-driven "egoism" engendered in Western capitalist society. Self-centered egoism facilitated criminality, although inhibiting forces such as adult supervision could overcome such pressures.

The American foundation for a sociological criminology was developed by scholars and researchers associated with the University of Chicago in the first quarter of the 20th century. Charles Darwin had prompted interest in the study of the relation between living organisms and their environment (ecology) and two sociologists, Robert Park and Ernest Burgess (1921), extended that concept to encompass human groups (human ecology). Concepts used in the description of plant and animal ecology were applied to the development of human relationships (e.g., competition, dominance, succession, and symbiosis). In the process of seeking shelter and work people formed "natural areas" with the resources at their disposal, determining their proximity to the central business area and surrounding industry. Although debates emerged about the factors determining who got sorted into what area (e.g., resources, discrimination or cultural preferences), the "zones" that emerged as Chicago grew were found to have distinct rates of crime, delinquency, and other problems. In short, patterns of human misbehavior were not random but were organized in a systematic fashion.

The most consequential research for the development of criminology was Clifford Shaw and Henry McKay's study of Chicago (1929) that described and sought to explain the distribution of a variety of social problems in the city of Chicago. The observation that certain areas tended to keep high rates despite successive changes in the ethnic groups residing in them suggested that those problems were (a) generated by the social conditions experienced by these groups rather than by any genetic or biological predisposition and (b) by "traditions of crime and delinquency" that develop and are perpetuated through interaction among new and established members of social areas.

In addition to analyzing the distribution of problems among social areas, the scholars and researchers constituting the Chicago school systematically documented the activities, culture, and organization of distinct groups of people in the city of Chicago, ranging from *The Polish Peasant* (William Thomas and Florian Znanieki, (1927) and *The Ghetto* (Louis Wirth, 1928) to *The Hobo* (Nels Andersen, 1923), the *Taxi-Dance*

Hall (Paul Cressey, 1932) and *The Gang* (Frederick Thrasher, 1927). In his research on gangs, Thrasher identified regularities in the emergence of gangs that still hold true today.

Based on his training at the University of Chicago, Edwin Sutherland expanded and systematized a sociological explanation of crime and criminality in editions of his *Principles of Criminology*, first published in 1924. By the 1939 version, he had developed a clear set of propositions. He proposed an explanation that emphasized (1) conflicting definitions of appropriate and inappropriate conduct as key to the distribution of crime among social settings and (2) differential association with people communicating conflicting definitions to explain individual criminality. Sutherland's systematic elaboration of a theory of both crime and criminality in a set of nine fundamental propositions earned him honors as the most influential theoretical criminologist of the 20th century. Applied to delinquency, the central proposition of differential association was simply that "A person becomes delinquent because of an excess of definitions favorable to violation of law over definitions unfavorable to violation of law." Definitions were the symbolic messages communicated in everyday interactions with significant others such as parents, peers, and teachers. Sutherland's perspective was defended and applied to a variety of types of crime by his student, Donald Cressey.

By the 1940s, the notion that certain areas of cities were criminogenic because they were disorganized had been replaced by a notion that such areas were differentially organized. High rate areas had different traditions or competing and conflicting subcultural traditions. With his work on *Culture, Conflict and Crime* in 1938, the University of Pennsylvania criminologist Thorsten Sellin played a major role in reinforcing the shift away from social disorganization and toward conflicting subcultural norms in the explanation of crime. Solomon Kobrin, who did some of his graduate work at Chicago and worked at Shaw and McKay's Institute for Juvenile Research, added to this shift by stressing the duality of conduct norms in the urban child's neighborhood. Similar ideas about the subcultural origins of gang delinquency were elaborated in later years by Walter Miller, a cultural anthropologist. In the 1960s, Marvin Wolfgang and Franco Ferracuti proposed an explanation of regional, racial, and demographic variations in violence in terms of subcultural norms and traditions as well.

A distinct theoretical tradition emphasizing a specific type of disorganization as a source of criminality was elaborated by the Columbia sociologist Robert K. Merton in 1938. Merton expanded on the notion of anomie that had been introduced by Emile Durkheim in the explanation of suicide. Durkheim had argued that economic crises and fluctuations could drive people to suicide because rules regulating behavior become unstable and ambitions get out of step with reality. Applying a similar logic, Merton argued that high rates of deviance are generated in anomic social systems where there is a strong emphasis on economic success coupled with inequality in opportunity to realize success legitimately. The pursuit of success by illegal "innovative" means is viewed as one adaptation to strain. Illegal innovation in pursuit of commonly shared success goals is viewed as a common lower-class response to frustrated ambitions but there are other ways to adapt as well. Some people might adapt to strain by giving up pursuit of success goals and retreating through the use of drugs, suicide, or mental illness. Still others might rebel and attempt to change the system.

The logic of Merton's theory with its emphasis on widely shared goals coupled with unequal opportunity is the basis for designating it as a "strain" theory. Other theorists have followed the same logic when introducing other forms of discrepancy between goals and means as a source of frustrated ambitions. In 1955, Albert Cohen took issue with Merton's rather instrumental view of lower class crime and delinquency and introduced emotion and anger into strain theory. He sought to explain male gang delinquency and what he believed to be the hostile, negativistic content of a gang contraculture. The source of anger and hostility was status frustration. Such frustration was generated by the widely shared desire for the good opinion of teachers coupled with limited possession of the social and cultural attributes necessary to achieve such respect. Just as Merton's innovators could overcome limited opportunity through criminal and delinquent activity, Cohen's youth could solve status problems collectively by reversing conventional standards of evaluation. A delinquent contraculture was a collective solution to lower-class status frustration.

Another elaboration of strain theory logic was proposed by Richard Cloward and Lloyd Ohlin in *Delinquency and Opportunity* (1960). They proposed that the outcome of strain varied depending on the nature of illegitimate opportunities available to youth. If adult criminal enterprises were available, the outcome would be a criminal subculture of delinquent youth. In settings where organized illegitimate opportunities were not available, delinquent gangs would exhibit the characteristics of a violence-prone, conflict subculture. Youth who were unable to join or succeed in conflict or criminal subcultures were double failures and candidates for retreatist subcultures. Their theory was a theoretical integration of elements of Merton's strain theory and Sutherland's theory emphasizing illegal associations and opportunities.

Two popular types of theories addressing the crime problem in the 1960s and 1970s were (1) critical, radical, and Marxist theories and (2) labeling theories. Both British (e.g., Paul Hirst, Geoff Pearson, Ian Taylor, Paul Walton, and Jock Young) and American (William Chambliss, Anthony Platt, Austin Turk, Richard Quinney, Herman, and Julia Schwendinger) criminologists mounted radical challenges to traditional criminological theories and methods and located the source of societal problems in the capitalist political and economic systems. Criminality among the disadvantaged was a natural outcome of their economic marginality. With little or nothing to lose, few promising alternatives and continual pressures to prove one's worth through material possessions, criminality becomes a relatively attractive choice. Radical critics also believed that the focus of criminology on street crimes and the crimes of the powerless detracted from attending to more fundamental criminogenic problems in society such as inequality and racism.

A labeling theory of juvenile delinquency had been advocated quite early in criminology by Frank Tannenbaum in *Crime and the Community* (1938). Tannenbaum applied the notion of self-fulfilling prophecies to juvenile delinquency. He argued that problems of delinquency were compounded by dramatizing them and that the innocent play of urban youth was often transformed into something evil through law enforcement. Howard Becker, Kai Erickson, Erich Goode, John Kitsuse, Edwin Lemert, Edwin Schur, and others developed the perspective in the study of drug problems, delinquency, and other forms of deviance. Such arguments grew in popularity during the protests of the 1960s and 1970s when all government institutions were under attack. Too many activities were being criminalized by the government and various interest groups were viewed as transforming minor problems, believed to be matters of choice (abortion, marijuana use, etc.), into major crime problems. Labeling theories shared much in common with radical theories, attributing the persistence of crime problems to ill-conceived societal reactions to them. Like radical criminologists, labeling theorists were critical of traditional causal perspectives. Rather than focus on the causes of criminality, they highlighted the role of interest groups in shaping the law and law enforcement to their own advantage. The critiques of criminology by radical and labeling theorists helped solidify the threefold scope of criminology as the study of law making and reactions to law breaking as well as the study of law breaking.

A major methodological development in criminology played a role in the development of some of the arguments of radical and labeling theorists. In the 1940s, sociologists began experimenting with the use of questionnaires and surveys, asking people to report on their own involvement in crime and delinquency and the technique gained popularity in the late 1950s with the work of F. Ivan Nye and James F. Short, Jr. (1957). Not only did Nye and Short show the feasibility of the self-report method in the study of delinquency, but their findings immediately challenged conventional assumptions about social class in relation to crime and delinquency. The fact that some of the patterns that had dominated criminological discourse appeared to be products of law enforcement rather than variations in behavior, provided a foundation for radical and labeling critiques of the system.

The self-report technique became the dominant method of studying delinquency in the 1960s and 1970s, and UCR data or police statistics were nearly totally avoided. Indeed, two major theories dominating theoretical discourse in the 1970s and 1980s were linked intimately to the development of survey methods—Travis Hirschi's social control theory (1969) and Ronald Akers's social learning theory (1977). In contrast to earlier American theories, neither social control theory nor social learning theory focused specifically on variations among classes or demographic categories of people. Both proposed more immediate variables that affect criminality, regardless of their distribution in the social system. Hirschi's social control theory shared many of the characteristics of earlier social disorganization theories and similar theories proposed by Scott Briar and Irving Piliavin, F. Ivan Nye, Walter Reckless, Albert Reiss, Gresham Sykes and David Matza, and Jackson Toby. When applied to delinquency the theory posited that the odds of delinquent behavior were low when youth were emotionally bonded to others (attachment), committed to conventional goals (commitment), accepted laws as morally binding (belief), and were occupied in conventional activities (involvement). Although most of these variables had been proposed in earlier theories, Hirschi's elaboration drew considerable attention because he identified crucial differences between this perspective and both strain and cultural deviance theory. Moreover, he presented empirical tests relevant to his view of those distinctions using self-report survey data.

As a theory of criminality, social learning theory emerged from a combination of principles derived from behaviorist operant learning theory (most closely identified with the psychologist B.F. Skinner) and other psychological theories stressing vicarious learning and imitation (Albert Bandura and Richard Walters). Robert Burgess and Ronald Akers reformulated differential association theory in terms of operant learning theory in 1966, and Akers elaborated a more general social learning theory in later works. According to social learning theory, the balance of criminal or delinquent conduct versus conforming behavior is a function of (a) differential reinforcement of those behaviors, (b) differential learning of norms or rules that govern behavior at other times and (c) the observed behavior and its consequences for primary sources of reinforcement such as parents and friends. In contrast to the exclusive emphasis of social control theory on barriers, social learning theory added learned motivational forces. Moreover, although it was originally proposed as a reformulation of Sutherland's theory, the inclusion of nondefinitional and nonsocial learning processes distinguishes it from that perspective. Aker's theory focused on learning experiences that could be measured using survey data and most research on that perspective has relied on that methodology.

An earlier line of theoretical development involving learning theories stressed principles of classical learning and was applied specifically to crime by Gordon Trasler (1962). Trasler argued that criminal and delinquent behaviors are most probable for people who are resistant to escape-avoidance conditioning. Such conditioning requires that cues in learning situations have been coupled with unpleasant involuntary nervous and glandular system reactions that prompt avoidance of those situations in the future. If such coupling has not occurred or the individual's autonomic nervous system (ANS) is slow to react or recover, then such conditioned reactions will not inhibit criminal or delinquent behavior.

The most recent lines of theoretical development in criminology have been feminist critiques of patriarchal biases in criminological theory and research; attempts at theoretical integration; elaboration of a "routine-activities" (opportunity) theory of crime and victimization; new, modified versions of disorganization, control, strain, and anomie theories; and development of a "life-course" perspective on crime.

The feminist critique is similar to the radical and Marxist critiques of criminology in the 1960s. Whereas radical critics chastised criminologists for ignoring "upperworld" crime and the differential enforcement of laws by social class, feminist critics argue that female crime has been ignored, and that many observed patterns are products of differential law enforcement by gender. They also argue that theories developed to explain male crime and delinquency ignore dimensions of the female world and female experiences that are relevant to the explanation of low rates for violence and serious property crime as well as survival strategies such as prostitution and runaway. Among the pioneer female criminologists attempting to overcome these problems are Freda Adler (1975), Rita Simon (1975), and Meda Chesney-Lind (1974). They helped to transform the study of gender and crime into one of the central research topics bridging the 20th and 21st centuries.

Theoretical integration has taken several forms. One form is the attempt to combine elements of strain, cultural deviance, and control theory into an integrated theory. Delbert Elliott, David Huisinga, and Suzanne Ageton (1985) have proposed an integrated theory of delinquency in which high levels of status frustration (a strain theory variable) and weak conventional bonds (a control theory variable) lead youth to seek out and imitate delinquent peers (a differential association-social learning variable) with delinquent peers as the major intervening mechanism leading to delinquency. This form of integration focuses on proximate causal mechanisms in each theory and ignores conflicting assumptions at the macro-level concerning such issues as delinquent subcultures, contracultures, and the structural origins of motivational forces.

Another form of integration combines biological, psychological, and sociological variables. James Q. Wilson and Richard J. Hernstein (1985) propose an integrated theory emphasizing criminality as a choice that is affected by variables at the biopsychological level such as conditionability and psychopathology as well as proximate mechanisms stressed by control, strain, and cultural deviance theorists. Although proposed as a theory, there is no clear specification of the range of variables to be included. All the theory demands is the inclusion of some variables from each category.

Modified versions of disorganization, control, and strain theory have been proposed recently as well. Tenets of the social disorganization approach have been revitalized by Rodney Stark (1980) in the form of a social integration theory and Robert Bursik and Harold Grasmick (1993) in their specification of the different ways in which neighborhoods or areas can be organized or disorganized. John Hagan, A.R. Gillis, and John Simpson (1985) combine the neo-Marxist emphasis on power relationships as the most crucial dimension of stratification with some elements of social control theory to predict a positive relation between class and delinquency. Michael Gottfredson and Travis Hirschi (1989) have proposed a modified version of control theory emphasizing "self-control" as the key mechanism for understanding criminality and other forms of reckless, fraudulent, or dangerous behavior. Opportunity to commit offenses is included as a variable as well, a notion borrowed from another recent theory called "routine activities theory." Lawrence Cohen and Marcus Felson (1979) propose to explain crime and victimization rates in terms of the availability and vulnerability of people and property, variables that affect the opportunity for crime. Although not proposed as a theory of individual criminality, opportunity to commit crimes can affect the degree to which other causal factors actually result in criminal or delinquent behavior. Finally, Charles Tittle (1995) has combined ideas from a variety of these theories and proposed a "control-balance" theory of deviance and crime in which various forms of deviance can be attributed to deficits or surpluses of power or control.

Modified versions of strain theory have been developed as well. Robert Agnew (1992) has proposed a version of strain theory called a "general strain" theory, arguing that criminality is affected by (a) actual or anticipated failure to achieve virtually any positive goal, (b) the actual or anticipated removal of positively valued stimuli, and (c) actual or anticipated presentation of negatively valued stimuli. On a more ecological or global level, Steven Messner and Richard Rosenfeld (1994) have elaborated an "institutional anomie" theory in which high crime rates are a product of a breakdown in social institutions caused by dominance of pecuniary, economic values, or goals. Both generalized strain and institutional anomie theories draw on ideas from a variety of theories, but maintain the anomie-strain tradition.

Another recent development in criminological theory and research is advocacy of a "life course perspective." This approach can be contrasted with perspectives such as "self-control" theory in which the causes of criminal behavior and the experiences associated with it are products of traits established quite early in childhood. The life course perspective draws on other theories such as social control and social learning to explain different paths taken at various crucial points in the course of peoples' lives. Robert Sampson and John Laub (1993), Rolf Loeber (1996), Mark Warr (1998), and others.

The basic methods used to build criminology as a scientific discipline—analysis of official data, ethnographies, and self-report surveys—were developed between the mid-19th and mid-20th centuries. The major methodological developments in the late 20th century include the compilation and analysis of victimization survey data, longitudinal panel surveys, and improvements in both national and international data on officially recognized crime. The collection of data on victimization and the experiences of victims have provided an alternative measure of crime over time and crime on an ecological scale as well as facilitating the study of reactions to crime (e.g., decisions to call the police and fear of crime). Research designs that follow panels or cohorts of subjects over long periods of time have allowed criminologists to address issues of causal order and to examine variations over the life course. Finally, the compilation of more detailed data on officially recognized crimes on a national (e.g, the F.B.I. Supplementary Homicide Reports) and international (United Nations and World Health Organization) scale have stimulated new lines of research on types of homicide and global variations.

Although it is common to define criminology in terms of the convergence of a subject matter with a methodology, criminology has also been defined broadly as "the cluster of fields that bear some relation to crime" (Quinney, 1970). This cluster consists of justice personnel, faculty of schools of criminal justice, policy analysts, academics with specific disciplinary allegiances (e.g., sociologists, psychologists, anthropologists) and a growing number of people with degrees in criminology and forensic science. Such diversity is reflected in the proliferation of professional associations with more than 30 national or international associations or organizations of professionals with interests in criminology, ranging from the World Society of Victimology to the Correctional Education Association.

Two major associations in the U.S. are the American Society of Criminology and the Academy of Criminal Justice Sciences. The American Society of Criminology was established in 1958 but grew out of efforts to organize education for law enforcement that began in the 1940s. Soon after its establishment, the dominant orientation within the society shifted toward criminological theory and research with less emphasis on issues central to justice education and law enforcement (Morris, 1974). Partly in response to this shift, the Academy of Criminal Justice Sciences was established in 1963 with a focus on criminal justice research, criminal justice education, and policy analysis. Although there is an overlap both in membership and subject matter, the Academy encompasses more practitioners and law enforcement personnel than the American Society of Criminology.

Several decades ago, Richard Quinney (1970) argued that "a unified field of criminology will probably never be achieved because of the fact that several; distinct intellectual and occupational enterprises are engaged in the study and control of crime." Criminologists do share in common a belief that they are creating and applying knowledge or theories founded in some form of scientific research. However, there will continue to be lively debates about the merits of different theories, different methods, and different ways of contributing to knowledge about crime.

GARY JENSEN

References and Further Reading

Adler, F. *Sisters in Crime*. New York, NY: McGraw-Hill, 1975.

Akers, R.L. *Criminological Theories: Introduction, Evaluation, and Application*. 3rd ed. Los Angeles, CA: Roxbury Press, 2000.

Bonger, W. *Criminality and Economic Conditions*. Boston, MA: Little Brown, 1916.

Gottfredson, M. and Hirschi, T. *A General Theory of Crime*. CA: Stanford University Press, 1990.
Hirschi, T. *Causes of Delinquency*. Berkeley, CA: University of California Press, 1969.
Lombroso, C. *Crime, Its Causes and Remedies*. Boston, MA: Little Brown, 1911
Quinney, R. *The Problem of Crime*. New York, NY: Dodd, Mead and Company, 1970.
Sampson, R J. and Laub, J.H. *Crime in the Making: Pathways and Turning Points Through Life*. Cambridge, MA: Harvard University Press, 1993.
Sellin, T. *Culture, Conflict and Crime*. New York, NY: Research Council, 1938.
Shaw, C., Zorbaugh, F., McKay, H.D., and Contrell, L.S. *Delinquency Areas*. Chicago, IL: University of Chicago Press, 1929.
Sutherland, E.H. *Principles of Criminology*. Philadelphia, PA: J.B. Lippincott, 1939.
Tannenbaum, F. *Crime and the Community*. New York, NY: Columbia University Press, 1938.
Thrasher, F.M. *The Gang*. Chicago, IL: University of Chicago, 1927.
Voss, H.L. and Petersen, D.M., Eds. *Ecology, Crime and Delinquency*. New York, NY: Appleton-Century-Crofts, 1971.
Wilson, J.Q. and Herrnstein, R.J. *Crime and Human Nature*. New York, NY: Simon and Schuster, 1985.
Wolfgang, M. and Ferracuti, F. *The Subculture of Violence*. London, UK: Tavistock, 1967.

See also **Criminology and Criminal Justice: A Comparison; Criminology as Social Justice; Criminology: Definition**

Critical Criminology

Critical Criminology as Structural Theory

Criminological theory can be divided into three broad kinds based on where their advocates believe or assume the source of crime is located: individual, social process, and structural. Critical criminology refers to a group of theories of the structural type. Individual-based theories assume that the causes of crime lie either in individual choice (classical and neoclassical) that may be limited by opportunity or circumstance (rational and situational choice), or in bio-psychological differences (biological, trait-based personality, or psychological), or in some combination of these choices and internal forces. Social process-based theories such as social learning, social control, and labeling theory believe that the ongoing social relations between members of groups influence the meaning of individuals' choices and actions, including whether they violate rules and laws, and what consequences follow from such violation. In contrast, social structure-based theories, such as anomie, strain, social ecology, conflict, and those grouped under the term critical criminology, assume that external forces, resulting from the configuration and organization of society as a whole, shape the nature of social institutions, and within these, channel the behavior of humans and their interaction.

Critical criminology, although a structural theory, differs in significant ways from the more reformist-oriented structural theories of strain and social ecology, although having some similarities with conflict. Moreover, although critical criminology emphasizes the crucial importance of social structure it also considers human agency to be significant, and sees society as a distinctly human product that can be changed through human actions. Thus, social structure only has the appearance of an external force; critical criminology's role is to demystify that appearance to facilitate social change.

Critical criminology (not to be confused with critical social theory of the Frankfurt School) is not one distinct theory but an umbrella term for a range of different critical structurally-oriented theories. In its most inclusive interpretation, critical criminology includes the following theories: conflict, radical, left realist, anarchist or abolitionist, peacemaking, critical feminist, critical race, queer, postmodernist, constitutive, chaos, and topology. A more restrictive interpretation would exclude the first three of these, reserving the term "critical" for theoretical developments that are post-1970s, and those primarily influenced by non-Marxist social theory.

Types of Crime

The range of theories associated with critical criminology has changed and expanded over time, although there are underlying unifying themes that cut across these differences. In its broadest interpretation, critical criminology includes all theoretical positions that see the source of crime stemming from societally generated conflict, fueled by a system of domination, based on inequality, alienation, and injustice. Critical theories are similar in their claim that crime is the direct or indirect outcome of conflict between different segments of society. They see members of society divided by their differences, and they challenge the way difference is exploited as a basis of power and interest. They typically advocate a change from criminal justice to the broader concept of social justice. Looking at the similarities among these critical criminologies, they all assume that segments of society, based on whatever difference, exist in relations of inequality to each other, meaning that some segments have more power than others, existing in a hierarchical relationship to each other. Individual humans are seen as products of these hierarchical power structures. Although theorists variously recognize a degree of individual human agency, ultimately they see humans as repressed, co-opted, and manipulated for the benefit of dominant powerful interests.

Crime, from the critical criminological perspective, is harm that comes from difference in power, and it can be manifest in several ways. One manifestation occurs when dominant groups or segments define the behavior of subordinate segments as threatening their interests. Dominant groups use law as a weapon to criminalize others' behavior, and use the criminal justice system to enforce their group's definitions of reality about what is unacceptable (this use of law can be considered as one kind of "state crime"). Groups or segments do this for the purpose of preserving their own dominant positions in the social order.

A second manifestation of crime to the critical criminologist is the direct abuse and disrespect of subordinate segments by dominant segments, such as when corporations pollute the environment, or violate health and safety regulations designed to protect employees (corporate and organizational crime, also called "suite crime"). This harm is compounded by the legal loopholes or purchased legal protection that limit the consequences to which the powerful are liable. Another version of this kind of disrespect occurs when whites, males, or heterosexuals marginalize and discriminate against blacks, women, gays, and lesbians.

Third, critical criminologists see crime as a form of resistance by subordinate segments to their domination and to perceived economic and social injustices. Resistance is manifest through such means as riots, looting, workplace theft, sabotage, and civil disobedience (also called political crime or collective crime). Crime as resistance is also seen in political action campaigns and protests.

Fourth, to the critical criminologist, crime is the harm created by a society being competitively divided such that personal, individual, and egotistic interests are pursued at the expense of social, collective, altruistic, or humanistic interests. Critical criminologists believe that many of the crimes that the structurally powerless commit on each other, such as interpersonal violence, theft, hate, and domestic abuse (called "street crimes"), are the result of this competitive individualization.

Defining Critical Criminology

Critical criminology is designated "critical" for several reasons. It is "critical" because theorists neither accept nor limit themselves to state definitions of crime. They prefer to define crime as social harm or as violations of human rights. Nor does critical criminology accept that the individual offender causes crime independently of the wider social context, without also considering how offenders have themselves been "victimized." Such victimization occurs, first, by society through its inequities, dehumanization, and alienation and subsequently, by the criminal justice system, through its selective processing of the powerless for punishment. Critical criminologists are critical too, because they oppose the existing social order of inequality, facilitated through the capitalist, patriarchal, or race-divided organization of society. They question the purpose and methods of the criminal justice system, which they see as a reflection of the dominant power structure, rather than an instrument to correct injustice or achieve social justice. Finally, they are critical because the policy changes they advocate usually demand a radical transformation, not just of criminal justice, but the total social and political organization of society. Thus, instead of seeing some people as inherently "bad apples" (individual theories) or as causing other apples to go bad (social process theories), critical criminologists see the society as a "bad barrel" that will turn most of the apples bad that are put into it; the only solution is a new barrel. In seeking to understand this cluster of critical criminologies it is helpful not only to identify what they have in common, but also to outline how their analyses diverge from each other.

Theories of Critical Criminology

Critical criminological theories differ over what they take to be the nature and relative importance of the differences that are the basis of social inequality. These differences include class, race, gender, ethics or morality, ideology, religion or belief, social status, and for some, an infinite variety of yet to be constructed differences. Conflict theory, for example, challenges group power, especially elite group power. Radical criminology (both its instrumental and structural

Marxist versions) challenges class power, especially dominant class power; left realism challenges the rights of the powerful to control state institutions, especially the police; feminism (radical, Marxist, socialist, and postmodernist) challenges male power and the patriarchal social structure based on it; queer theory challenges heterosexual power and the homophobia that results from it; critical race theory challenges white power, especially white supremacy; anarchist and peacemaking criminology challenges governmental power and the power of "professionalism"; and postmodernist and constitutive theory (including varieties of chaos theory) challenge all bases of power and inequality based on known and yet to be constructed differences.

Differences between Critical Criminologists

In 1958, George Vold developed a conflict theory that was rooted in the classic late 19th century sociology of George Simmel and the 1950s reformist sociology of Ralf Darendorf, Louis Coser and Thorsten Sellin. Here society was seen as divided on several dimensions, made up of numerous groups, each defining their own interests and struggling for the power to define and control public issues. Conflict theorists recognize that crime may stem from differences in economic wealth, a clash of cultures, or from the outcome of symbolic and instrumental struggles over status, from differences in ideology, morality, religion, race, and ethnicity. Thus, Austin Turk argued that some groups, claiming an allegiance to mainstream culture, become dominant by gaining control of key resources. Dominant groups are able to criminalize the behavior of those deviating from their own cultural standards and behavioral norms. Conflict criminologists, saw crime as having both instrumental and symbolic roots in a multidimensional fragmented society, with struggles for control occurring at multiple sites of difference.

Other critical criminologists in the early 1970s, however, such as the British "new criminologists" Ian Taylor, Paul Walton, and Jock Young and American radicals such as Richard Quinney, William Chambliss, Tony Platt, and Steven Spitzer, drew on the classic works of Karl Marx and Friedrich Engels and Marxist theory's application to crime at the beginning of the 20th century by Dutch criminologist Willem Bonger. They believed that the social and symbolic dimensions of inequality were mere epiphenomenona, consequences of a deeper *economic* conflict. They saw this conflict rooted in economic power and in the appropriation and concentration of wealth by minority class interests in class-divided societies. They point to the structure of capitalism, based on the private ownership of property, which renders a society "crimogenic" by generating vast inequalities of wealth that provide the conditions for crime. But Marxist criminologists differed over the issue of whether the state is manipulated by dominant economic ruling class interests who also mystify the system that sustains their domination (instrumental Marxism), or whether the impersonal constituent forces of capitalism are responsible for its maintenance and reproduction (structural Marxism). Instrumentalists see the economic base of society as shaping the need to define behavior as crime and the intensity of enforcement strategies. Structural Marxist criminology conceptualizes a dual or many-headed power structure in which the state serves a semiautonomous role in relation to specific powerful economic interests whose position is supported by the monetary mechanism and corresponding influences from a variety of social institutions, including religion and education. Through its mediating influence, the worst excesses of economic exploitation, and the crises these create, are controlled and mitigated in the interests of legitimating the long-term maintenance of the whole capitalist system. As a result, the state and other elements of this superstructure appear as neutral elements in the power structure, allowing capitalist inequality to prevail without obvious challenge.

In contrast to conflict and Marxist theorists, critical feminist criminologists, such as Carol Smart, Meda Chesney-Lind, Kathleen Daly, and Sally Simpson, see the major division around which conflict emerges as patriarchy. This is the "law of the father" in which male activities and accomplishments are more valued than those of females, and in which societal institutions, from the family to the factory, are structured to privilege men. These critical feminist criminologists challenged the gender-structured world but have different emphases.

A similar transcendent position has also been adopted by critical race and by queer theorists. They began by observing the different ways minority groups were treated, and how the legal system obscures racial identity, resulting in white and heterosexual standards being imposed on everyone. They moved to oppose systemic discrimination, prejudice, bigotry, economic marginalization, harassment, and oppression. The ultimate challenge is to help bring social change that reduces the harms caused by these social and institutional structures of difference. Indeed, many, such as critical race theorist Katheryn Russell, now see a value in exploring the intersections of these structures of inequality and difference based on class, race, gender, and sexual preference.

Instead of class, gender, race, or sexual preference, anarchist criminologists such as Larry Tifft and Dennis Sullivan writing initially in the late 1970s and Jeff

Ferrell in the 1990s, see all hierarchical systems of power and authority, whatever their configuration, as flawed. They believe that hierarchical systems of authority and domination should be opposed and that existing systems of justice should be replaced by a decentralized system of negotiated justice in which all members of society participate and share their decisions. According to Ferrell, recent anarchist criminology is an "integration" of critical approaches that seeks to relate crime as a meaningful activity of resistance to both its construction in social interaction and its larger construction through processes of political and economic authority. Anarchists call for total replacement of the existing system of state-run criminal justice with a mutual aid system of warm, living, decentralized, face-to-face justice. This should be a system of "restorative justice" that incorporates the 1980s "peacemaking" and "abolitionist" ideas of Harold Pepinsky and Richard Quinney, rather than war making and fear mongering, typical of state control and punishment.

In a polar opposition to the idealism of anarchist criminology, "left realism" was a position founded in the 1980s by Jock Young, Roger Matthews, John Lea, and Brian MacLean. Instead of what they saw as romantic celebrations of the offender as a primitive revolutionary, argued by some "idealist" Marxist theorists and anarchists, left realists focus on the reality and seriousness of harm to the powerless created by the similarly structurally powerless "street" offenders. Unlike critical perspectives, which focus on crimes of the powerful, definitions of crime, and "victimization" of powerless offenders by the state, left realism emphasizes the relationship between offenders, victims, and the criminal justice system. Left realists want to both strengthen and democratically control the criminal justice system of capitalist society, believing that the law can provide the structurally powerless with real gains, if not ideal victories.

Finally, and most recently, through the work of Stuart Henry, Dragan Milovanovic, Peter Manning, Bruce Arrigo, Gregg Barak, and T.R. Young, the 1990s saw the arrival in critical criminology of postmodernist influenced constitutive theory, which also incorporated ideas of social constructionist theory, chaos theory, semiotics, and topology theory, into an integrated critical theory. At its simplest, constitutive theory recognizes that the social structures of inequality are not only the source of the harm that is crime, but that the inequalities themselves are crimes. Moreover, these inequalities are generated by human agents through their use of discourse (talk). Once created, these socially constructed complex systems of inequality are self-perpetuating in their own expansion, and are sustained through the continued investment of energy into a discourse that constantly elaborates the inequality.

Evaluation

Critical criminology has fared better at providing new ways to see the world than it has at being proven through empirical research findings, or at delivering social justice. Early formulations of critical criminology lend themselves readily to the criticism that they either tend toward romanticism, as in anarchism and left idealism or to the dogmatic and doctrinal, as in instrumental Marxism or radical feminism. In either case, they embodied an unrealistic and untestable air of "conspiracy theory." Some critics have pointed out that critical criminology's class-based revelations are rather unremarkable, merely a restatement of the old Robin Hood adage that the poor steal from the rich to survive but also, like the rich, they steal for greed.

In the late 1970s, Carl Klockars attacked the weak empirical base of much Marxist criminology and argued that radicals misrepresent capitalist societies as destructively class divided, when in reality, class divisions can be beneficial, and that many divisions involve interest groups that unite people across class boundaries. The instrumental Marxist view has been criticized by outsiders and insiders alike for obscuring the diversity and conflict within both the state and corporate elites. Critics point out that not all law is designed to protect ruling capitalist class interests but is intended to protect the overall system of capitalism. Like left realists such as Jock Young, Klockars later asserted that the state actually empowers of oppressed people's rights as genuine, not as a sham or a mystification. Klockars accused early critical theorists of ignoring the contradictory facts, such as crime in socialist societies and the apparent low crime rate in some very capitalistic societies like Switzerland and Japan. Moreover, by implicitly, if not explicitly, romanticizing socialism, early critical theorists failed to take into account the known dehumanizing conditions that socialism, as practiced in large portions of the world, produced. Furthermore, the implicit deterministic character of early versions of critical criminology minimized the self-generated uncooperative behavior of humans. Thus, these criminologists were unprepared for the wholesale rejection of socialist practice and their adoption of the crudest and more exploitative principles and practices of capitalism.

Most recently, critical and radical criminologists have been forced to acknowledge that other dimensions of social inequality such as race, gender, and sexuality are also important. Yet these other versions of critical criminology have also been subject to criticism. Stanley Cohen sees left realism's reformist turn as a reflection of both the aging of radical criminologists and the tempering of their ideas in response to broader social developments such as stable conservative governments, growing awareness of the relevance of feminism and ecology movements, and the collapse of state socialism. Left realism has been challenged for its central contradictions between the call for increased powers of the state to control crime, and their preferences for a minimalist state, subject to public scrutiny and accountability. It has been questioned for taking the spotlight off crimes of the economically powerful outside the state, especially those of corporations. The most damning criticism comes from feminist scholars who, like Phil Scraton, have argued that the construction of the realism or idealism debate has been diversionary, regressive, and purposefully misrepresentative of the advances within critical feminist criminology since the mid-1970s. Feminists claim that left realism, like radical criminology generally, has remained gender blind and as such remains part of the "male stream" ignoring activism, research, and theory drawn from women's experiences.

However, feminist criminologist positions have their own inherent weaknesses. Not the least of these stems from the very notion that gender is the central organizing theme, which some have accused of essentialism, exclusionism, and implicit racism. In spite of recognizing the socially constructed nature of "femininity" and "sexuality," there is a failure to reference the different cultural experience, socialization patterns, and experiences in the labor market and criminal justice system of black women. This does not deny a gender analysis but requires that gender include sensitivity to racial and ethnic differences. Such a sensitivity would also need to overcome the simplistic black and white distinction within a gender analysis. Different cultural experiences, such as those of Latino women, Asian women, American Indian women, and women with disabilities, would also benefit from such a broadened feminist analysis.

Though it is early to evaluate the impact of postmodernism on criminology, especially its more recent adventures into chaos theory, topology theory, and catastrophe theory, its influence is being felt in the increased questioning of traditional criminological concepts, and especially through the constitutive criminological challenge. Postmodern contributions have been criticized for their obscure language, difficult prose, and for claiming that there are no absolute standards by which to judge outcomes and effects. Critical criminology has faced considerable criticism over the years from more traditional rivals, but more recently, it is the criticism from within that has been the most devastating. The most important challenge facing critical theorists is how to develop a transcendent position that applies its critique to any criteria of difference that is used by one group to privilege themselves over others, while simultaneously recognizing the unique historical and local features of any specific differences. Moreover, how do critical criminologists problematize difference, while using difference to distinguish themselves from the mainstream? Finally, perhaps the ultimate challenge is the implementation in practical terms of their theoretical challenge. How does one realistically bring about the necessary broader changes that critical theories of crime imply in a society where by far the majority is substantially invested in reproducing the very system that these theorists are criticizing? The hope is that humans locked in their local struggles will become aware that their specific issues are merely a facet of the underlying problem and that unless this is addressed the problems will emerge in another form. Of course, the paradox is that such a revelation requires the very identification with others' humanity that is undermined by a system based on difference and division.

Stuart Henry

References and Further Reading

Arrigo, B.A., *Social Justice/Criminal Justice: The Maturation of Critical Theory in Law, Crime and Deviance*. Belmont, CA: West/Wadsworth, 1999.

Barak, G., *Integrating Criminologies*, Boston, MA: Allyn and Bacon, 1998.

Kathleen, D. and Maher, L., *Criminology at the Crossroads: Feminist Readings in Crime and Justice*. New York, NY: Oxford, 1998.

Henry, S. and Milovanovic, D., *Constitutive Criminology: Beyond Postmodernism.* London, UK: Sage, 1996.

Lynch, M.J., Michalowski, R.J., and Groves, W.B., *The New Primer in Radical Criminology: Critical Perspectives on Crime, Power and Identity.* Willow Tree Press, 2000.

MacLean, B.D. and Milovanovic, D. (Eds.) *Thinking Critically about Crime*. Vancouver: Collective Press, 1997.

Messerschmidt, J., *Masculinities and Crime.* Lanham, MD: Rowman and Littlefield, 1993.

Martin, D.S. and Milovanovic, D. (Eds.) *Race, Gender and Class in Criminology.* New York, NY: Garland, 1996.

Milovanovic, D. (Ed.) *Chaos, Criminology and Social Justice*. New York, NY: Greenwood, 1997.

Reiman, J., *The Rich Get Richer and the Poor Get Prison: Ideology, Crime and Criminal Justice*. Boston, MA: Allyn and Bacon, 1998.

Russell, K.K., *The Color of Crime*. New York, NY: New York University Press, 1998.

Young, J. and Matthews, R., *Rethinking Criminology. The Realist Debate.* London, UK: Sage.

See also **Consensus and Conflict Theories of the Law; Feminist Theories of Criminal Behavior; Left Realism; Marxist Theories of Criminal Behavior; Peacemaking Criminology; Radical Theories of Criminal Behavior; Postmodern and Constitutive Criminology**

Cross-Sectional and Longitudinal Research

Cross-sectional research refers to research in which data are collected for a set of cases (individuals, or aggregates such as cities or countries) on a set of variables (for example, frequency of illegal behavior, attitudes toward illegal behavior), and in which data collection occurs specifically (1) *at* a single time, and (2) *for* a single time point or a single interval of time (hereafter, both will be referred to as time periods). Analysis of purely cross-sectional data can examine *differences between cases* but not *changes within cases*. Different disciplines define longitudinal research differently (Menard, 1990, 4–5), but a broad definition would include research in which (1) data are collected *for* more than one time period, (2) possibly but not necessarily involving collection of data *at* different time periods, and (3) permitting analysis that, at a minimum, involves the measurement and analysis of change over time within the same cases (or in comparable cases, for change at the aggregate level).

Although some researchers would consider the collection of data *at* different time periods as a defining characteristic of longitudinal research, it is also possible in principle to collect *retrospective* data, in which the data are collected *at* a single period but *for* more than one period. For example, a respondent may be asked to report on all of the times he or she has been a victim of crime, or has committed a crime, over a span of years up to and including her or his lifetime. In contrast to retrospective studies, *prospective* longitudinal data collection involves the repeated collection of data with usually short recall periods: crimes committed or victimizations experienced in the last week, month, 6 months, or 1 year, or data on attitudes, beliefs, and sociodemographic characteristics at the time the data are collected.

Longitudinal research serves two primary purposes: to describe patterns of change, and to establish the direction (positive or negative, from Y to X or from X to Y) and magnitude (a relationship of magnitude zero indicating the absence of a relationship) of causal relationships (Menard, 1990, 5–20). Change is typically measured with respect to one of two continua, chronological time (for historical change) or age (for developmental change). Sometimes it is difficult to disentangle the two. If older individuals are less criminal than younger individuals, is this because crime declines with age, or is it possible that older individuals were always less criminal (even when they were younger) and younger individuals will remain more criminal (even as they get older), or some combination of the two? With cross-sectional data, it is not possible to disentangle the effects of history and development. Even with longitudinal data, it may be difficult, but with data on the same individuals both at different ages and different time periods, it at least becomes possible.

There are several different types of longitudinal designs (Menard, 1990, 22–31), and all of them have been used in major studies in crime and delinquency. The different longitudinal designs are illustrated in Figure 1. In a *total population design*, we attempt to collect data on the entire population at different time periods. An example of a total population design would be the Federal Bureau of Investigation's (annual) Uniform Crime Report (UCR) data on arrests (for most crimes), or data on crimes known to the police (for the FBI Index offenses of murder, rape, robbery, aggravated assault, larceny, burglary, motor vehicle theft, and arson). Although coverage is not, in fact, 100% complete (the same is true for the decennial census), the intent is to include data on the entire U.S. population. From year to year, individuals enter the population (by birth) and exit the population (by death), so the individuals to whom the data refer overlap substantially, but differ somewhat, from one period to the next, and may differ substantially over a long time span (for example, from 1950 to the present). UCR data are used to measure aggregate rates of change or trends in arrests and crimes known to the police.

Repeated cross-sectional designs collect data on different samples in different periods. A good example of a repeated cross-sectional design is the annual sample of high-school seniors on which data are collected in the Monitoring the Future (MTF) study (Johnston et al., annual). Each year, MTF samples over 100 public and private high schools and collects data on up to several hundred respondents in each school. Because a new sample is drawn each year, there is in principle no overlap (it is possible that someone repeats the senior year and moves from a school sampled in one year to a school sampled in the next, but this is likely to be exceedingly rare) from one year to the next. Data from the MTF study are used, for example, to examine aggregate trends for American high school seniors in illegal behavior, particularly alcohol and illicit drug use.

Revolving panel designs are designs in which a set of respondents is selected, interviewed for more than

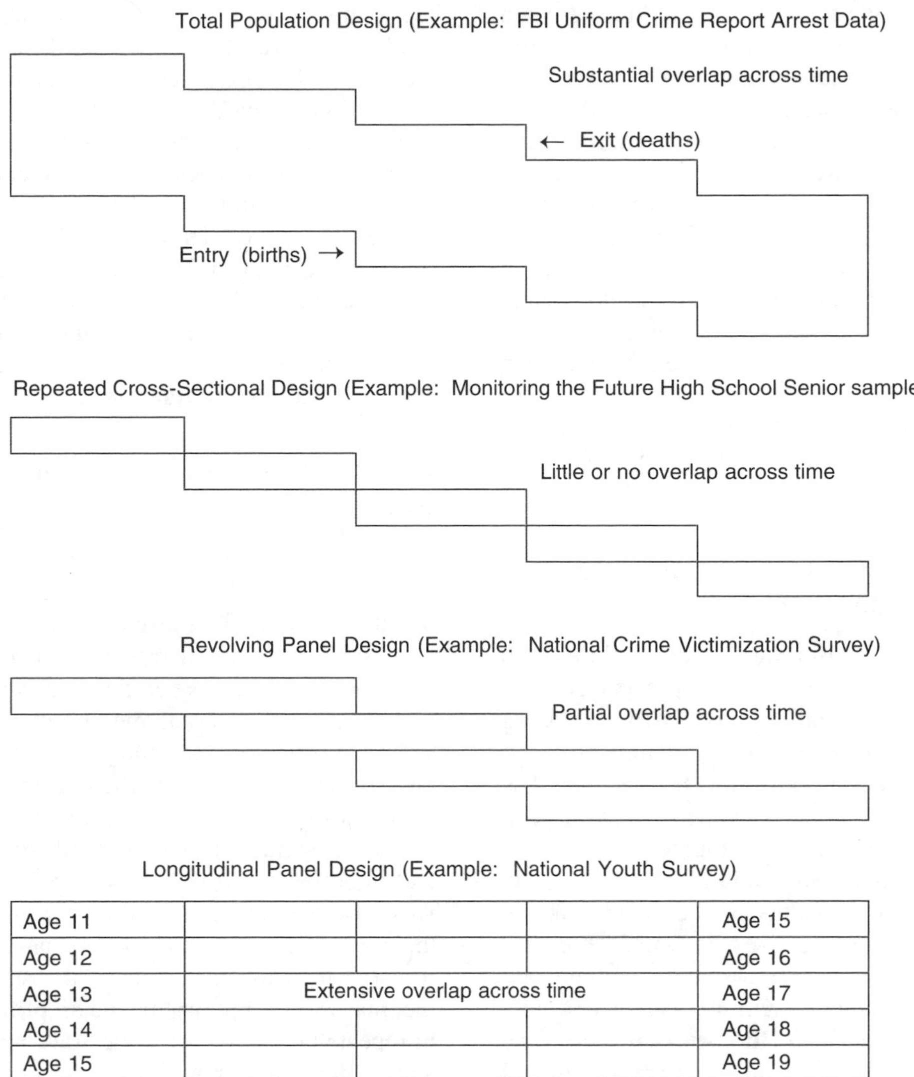

FIGURE 1 Types of Longitudinal Designs (adopted from Menard, 1990).

one time period, then replaced by a new set of respondents. The revolving panel design is used in the National Crime Victimization Survey (NCVS; Bureau of Justice Statistics annual). Households are selected and interviewed seven times over a 3-year period, once at the beginning, once at the end, and at 6-month intervals between entry and exit. At the end of the 3-year period, a new household is selected to replace the old household. Replacement is staggered, so every 6 months approximately one sixth of the households in the NCVS are replaced. It is important to note that the NCVS has historically been a sample of households, not individuals; whenever an individual or a family moved from a household, interviews were conducted not with the original respondents, but with the (new) occupants of the original household. Because each household is replaced after 3 years, only short-term longitudinal data are available for individuals. At the national level, however, the NCVS is one of the most widely used sources of data on aggregate changes over time in rates of crime victimization and, by implication, the rate at which those offenses included in the NCVS (limited to offenses with identifiable victims) are committed.

The *longitudinal panel design* is the design most generally recognized in different disciplines as a true longitudinal design. An example of the longitudinal panel design is the National Youth Survey (NYS; see, for example, Menard and Elliott, 1990). The NYS first collected data on self- reported illegal behavior including substance use *in* 1977 but *for* the preceding year, 1976. (In the first year only, it also collected data on parents of the adolescent respondents.) It then collected data at 1-year intervals, for 1977–1980, and thereafter at 3-year intervals, for 1983–1992, and (as this is being written) plans are underway to collect data on the original respondents once again in 2001 and

2002. Unlike all of the types of longitudinal research discussed so far, there is no entry into the sample after the first year. The respondents interviewed in the most recent year were a subset of the respondents interviewed in the first year: some of the original respondents were not interviewed because of death, refusal to participate, or failure to locate the respondent. In contrast to the UCR, MTF, and NCVS, the NYS is used less to examine aggregate historical trends in crime than to examine intra-individual developmental trends, and to examine causal relationships to test theories of crime. In this latter context, the NYS has been used to study the time ordering of the onset of different offenses and predictors of offending, and to construct cross-time causal models that can only be tested using longitudinal data (Menard and Elliott, 1990).

The Debate about Cross-Sectional versus Longitudinal Models in Criminology

In most social science disciplines, there is little or no question regarding the superiority of prospective longitudinal data and longitudinal models for analyzing within-individual change or causal relationships, but criminology has been an exception to this rule. The argument began in the context of the age–crime relationship and the evolution of developmental and criminal career perspectives in criminology (Vold et al., 1998, chapter 17). Proponents of the developmental and criminal career perspectives had made the case that longitudinal research was essential for the study of developmental change or criminal career research, in particular to examine the relationship between crime and age. Michael Gottfredson and Travis Hirschi argued that cross-sectional research was adequate to study the age–crime relationship, which they asserted was invariant both historically and cross-nationally (Gottfredson and Hirschi, 1987). In addition to subsequent research on the invariance of the age–crime relationship, which has produced mixed results (Vold et al., 1998), Menard and Elliott (1990) responded to Gottfredson and Hirschi with a defense of longitudinal research, and in particular, *prospective* longitudinal research involving short-recall periods.

First, Menard and Elliott demonstrated that there was strong evidence of respondents' forgetting their past behavior when long-recall periods were used. They compared 1-year and 10-year recall periods, asking respondents in 1987 to indicate whether they had "ever" committed any of nine serious offenses (assaults, thefts, illicit drug sales), about which they had been asked in previous waves of the NYS. Of the offenses *that had been previously admitted by respondents*, fewer than half were reported in the 10-year retrospective recall data. Given prior admission of these same offenses, deliberate concealment seemed unlikely, but recall failure would be consistent with studies in other social sciences (Menard, 1990, 39–42). In addition, Menard and Elliott addressed the issue of causal order with a test comparing predictions from control theory and social learning theory regarding the onset of association with delinquent friends and onset of illegal behavior. They found that respondents were much more likely to have delinquent friends before they became involved in illegal behavior (as predicted by social learning theory). They also demonstrated how results of causal analyses differed for cross-sectional and longitudinal data.

Potential Problems in Longitudinal Research

This is not to say that longitudinal research is without its problems. On the contrary, there are more potential threats to longitudinal research than to cross-sectional research. Longitudinal research potentially has all of the problems of cross-sectional research with respect to internal and external measurement validity, measurement reliability, sampling error, refusal to participate, or nonresponse to particular items, the appropriateness of questions to the population being studied, effects of interactions between subjects or respondents and interviewers or experimenters or observers, relevance of the research, and research costs. Some of these issues are even more problematic for longitudinal research than for cross-sectional research. For example, biases in sampling may be amplified by repetition in repeated cross-sectional designs, and costs are typically higher for a multiple-year longitudinal study than for a single-year cross-sectional study.

There are also additional dangers (Menard, 1990, 32–44). As already noted above, respondent recall failure may result in underreporting of illegal behavior if long-recall periods are used. Respondents who are repeatedly interviewed may learn that giving certain answers results in follow-up questions, and may deliberately or unconsciously avoid the burden imposed by those questions, a problem known as panel conditioning. Relatedly, the potential problem of interaction between the respondent or subject and an experimenter or interviewer or observer producing invalid responses may be exacerbated when there is repeated contact between the experimenter or interviewer or observer and the respondent or subject in a prospective longitudinal design. In later waves of a prospective panel study, respondents may have died or become incapable of participating because of age or illness, or may refuse to continue their participation, or researchers may have difficulty locating respondents, resulting in panel attrition. (In retrospective research, the corresponding problem is that individuals who should have been included to insure a more representative sample may have died or otherwise become unavailable before the study begins.) Particularly in prospective longitudinal sample survey research, an important question is whether attrition is so systematic or so great that the results of the study can no longer be generalized to the original population on which the sample was based.

Measurement used at the beginning of a longitudinal study may come to be regarded as obsolete later in the study, but changing the measurement instrument means that the data are no longer comparable from one time to the next. An example of this is the change in the way questions were asked in the NCVS in 1992. The new format produced a substantial increase in reported victimizations. A comparison was made between the rates of victimization reported using the old and the new method, but only in a single year. Thus, it remains uncertain whether attempts to "adjust" the victimization rates to produce a closer correspondence between the old and the new methods are really successful, especially for examining long-term trends in victimization. In developmental research, a parallel problem is the inclusion of age-appropriate measures for the same concept (for example, bonding) across the life course. For example, in adolescence, bonding may occur primarily in the contexts of family of orientation (parents and siblings) and school, whereas in adulthood it may occur more in the contexts of family of procreation (spouse and children) and work. One is then faced with the dilemma of asking age-inappropriate questions, or of using different measures, whose comparability cannot be guaranteed, for different stages of the life course.

In cross-sectional research, we may have missing data because an individual refuses to participate in the research (missing subjects), or because the individual chooses not to provide all of the data requested (missing values). In longitudinal research, we have the additional possibility that an individual may agree to participate in the research and to provide the requested data at one or more periods, but may refuse or may not be found at one or more other periods (missing occasions). Some techniques for analyzing longitudinal data are highly sensitive to patterns of missing data, and cannot handle series of unequal lengths, thus requiring dropping all cases with missing data on even a single variable on just one occasion. Problems of missing data may be addressed in longitudinal research either by imputation of missing data (replacing the missing data by an educated guess, based on other data and the relationships among different variables in the study, sometimes including imputation of missing occasions), or by using techniques that allow the use of partially missing data in the analysis (Bijleveld et al., 1998, 43–44).

Longitudinal Data Analysis

Longitudinal research permits us to use dynamic models, models in which a change in one variable is explained as a result of change in one or more other variables. Although we often phrase statements about causal relationships as though we were analyzing change, with cross-sectional data we are really examining how *differences* among individuals in one variable can be explained in terms of *differences* among those same individuals in one or more predictors. It has been relatively commonplace to draw conclusions about *intraindividual change*, or change within an individual respondent, from findings about *interindividual differences*, or differences between different respondents. To return to an earlier example, Gottfredson and Hirschi (1987) asserted that cross-sectional data on age differences in illegal behavior were adequate to study changes in illegal behavior over the life course. There are certain conditions under which it is possible to estimate dynamic models using cross-sectional data, but those conditions are restrictive and relatively rare in social science research (Menard, 1990, 64–69). It is generally more appropriate to use longitudinal data, and to analyze the data using statistical techniques that take advantage of the longitudinal nature of the data. Longitudinal data analysis techniques (for a general introduction, see Bijleveld et al., 1998) include time-series analysis for describing and analyzing change when there a large number of time periods (for example, changes in imprisonment rates as a function of changes in economic conditions); latent growth curve models and hierarchical linear models for describing and analyzing both short- and long-term change within individual subjects or cases, and relationships among changes in different variables (for example, changes in violent criminal offending as a function of changes in illicit drug use); and event history analysis, to analyze influences on the timing of qualitative changes (for example, timing of the onset of illicit drug use as a function of academic performance).

Cross-sectional research cannot disentangle developmental and historical trends, and the description and analysis of historical change requires the use of longitudinal data. The description and analysis of developmental trends can be attempted using cross-sectional data, but the results will not necessarily be consistent with results based on longitudinal data. Testing for the time ordering or sequencing of purported causes and effects in developmental data can only be done with longitudinal data. Although there are cross-sectional methods for modeling patterns of mutual causation, more powerful models that allow the researcher to examine such relationships in more detail, including the explicit incorporation of the time ordering of cause and effect, require longitudinal data. Briefly, there are analyses one can perform with longitudinal data that cannot be performed with cross-sectional data (analyses of time ordering of cause and effect, of the impact of long recall periods, of the differences between cross-sectional and longitudinal models), but one can do anything in longitudinal analysis that can be done in cross-sectional analysis (by taking a single cross section in the longitudinal data, for example, by analyzing one year of the NYS data). Cross-sectional data remain useful for describing conditions at a particular time period, but increasingly in criminology, as in other social science disciplines, longitudinal data are recognized as best for research on causal relationships and patterns of historical and developmental change.

SCOTT MENARD

References and Further Reading

Bijleveld, C.C.J.H. and van der Kamp, L.J.T., with Mooijaart, A., van der Kloot, W.A., van der Leeden, R., and van der Burg, E., *Longitudinal Data Analysis: Designs, Models, and Methods*, London, UK and Thousand Oaks, CA: Sage, 1998.

Bureau of Justice Statistics, *Criminal Victimization in the United States*, Washington, DC: U.S. Department of Justice (annual).

Federal Bureau of Investigation, *Crime in the United States*, Washington, DC: U.S. Department of Justice (annual).

Gottfredson, M. and Hirschi, T., The methodological adequacy of longitudinal research on crime and delinquency, *Criminology* 25 (1986).

Johnston, L.D., Bachman, J.G., and O'Malley, P.M., *Monitoring the Future: Questionnaire Responses from the Nation's High School Seniors*, Ann Arbor, MI: Institute for Social Research (annual; order of authorship varies).

Menard, S., *Longitudinal Research*, Thousand Oaks, CA: Sage, 1990.

Menard, S. and Elliott, D.S., Longitudinal and cross-sectional data collection and analysis in the study of crime and delinquency, *Justice Quarterly* 7 (1990).

Vold, G.B., Bernard, T.J., and Snipes, J.B., *Theoretical Criminology*, 4th ed., New York, NY: Oxford University Press, 1998.

See also **National Crime Victimization Survey (NCVS); Uniform Crime Reports (UCR)**

Cuba, Crime and Justice in

General Characteristics

In 1492, Christopher Columbus claimed the island of Cuba for the Spanish crown, and for the next 400 years Cuba remained under nearly-continuous Spanish jurisdiction. In the mid-1800s Cuban nationalists began a series of armed struggles for Cuban independence. Just as Cuban nationalists were about to win independence in 1899, the U.S. declared war against Spain. The subsequent peace treaty ending the wider Spanish-American war effectively transferred sovereignty over Cuba from Spain to the U.S. For the next 60 years U.S. business and financial interests dominated the Cuban economy and government until 1959, when a revolutionary movement led by Fidel Castro seized power from the U.S. supported government of Fulengcio Batista.

Cuba's recent history can be divided into four periods, each with its own implications for law, crime, and justice on the island. The first period, from 1959 to the early 1970s, was characterized by revolutionary experimentation in all areas of social organization. The most notable experiment within the justice system during this time was the creation of popular tribunals (*tribunales de base*) that emphasized informal proceedings and using ordinary citizens as lay prosecutors, advocates, and judges rather than filling these positions with formally trained jurists.

In the early 1970s, Cuba began institutionalizing the socialist, economic, and political arrangements that had emerged during the preceding decade. During this second revolutionary phase, Cuba promulgated a new constitution, reorganized most of the administrative offices of government, and replaced the prerevolutionary legal system with one that reflected the beliefs and practices of its emerging socialist political economy. In 1973, the Cuban government implemented a new Law of Judicial Organization that replaced the *tribunales de base* with a more formalized court system, ended the private practice of law in favor of government-regulated group practices known as *bufetes colectivos*, and strengthened the emphasis on "socialist legality." This era also brought increasingly close relations with the Soviet Union, and increased economic dependence on the trading bloc of socialist nations.

The mid-1980s began a period focused on the "rectification" of earlier errors, particularly those that were deemed to have resulted from following too closely a Soviet model of development. During this period Cuba instituted a new penal code that decriminalized some offenses, reduced penalties for crimes overall, and began experimenting with a broader range of alternatives to incarceration including probation and correctional labor without incarceration.

The collapse of the Soviet Union and the disappearance of European socialism in the early 1990s ushered in an era termed the "special period," which was characterized by significant economic contraction and then a slow return to growth by the late 1990s. In an effort to craft new development strategies that would enable Cuba to expand trade relations with the now predominantly capitalist world, while still retaining key elements of its socialist agenda, the Cuban government modified its economic system in a number of important ways. These changes included legalizing the use of foreign currency by Cubans, the passage of laws to attract more foreign investment, expanding the sphere of legal self-employment and small-business activity, and some cut-backs in government subsidies.

Legal System

The Cuban legal system is a composite of the three major stages of Cuban history. Reflecting its past as a Spanish colony, Cuba is a civil law state that emphasizes written codes rather than precedent, and that uses an inquisitorial system of criminal procedure similar to that of Spain and France, rather than the adversarial system of criminal procedure found in the U.S. and Britain. Intermingled with this civil law system are elements of Anglo-American practice such as *habeas corpus* and a greater separation of courts and prosecutors than was normally characteristic of socialist states during the Soviet era. Finally, over 40 years of legal development guided by Marxist legal theory have imparted a strong socialist character to Cuba's legal system. Key elements of Cuba's socialist legality are (1) an emphasis on substantive rather than juridical measures of justice, (2) the use of law as a proactive tool for socialist development, (3) limited use of formal legal mechanisms for the resolution of private disputes, (4) the use of informal "social courts" to resolve conflicts such as housing and labor disputes, (5) direct citizen involvement in the judicial and crime control procedures, and (6) a system of state-organized law collectives to provide low-cost legal services nationwide. One change that has resulted from Cuba's increasing integration into the world market economy, however, has been an increased use of formal, legal suits to resolve economic disputes.

Crime Patterns: 1960–2000

During the first three periods of Cuba's socialist experiment, the island was known for remarkably low rates of ordinary crime and a widespread sense of public safety. These low crime rates resulted from a variety of factors. One of these was Cuba's socialist system of production and distribution that focused on providing all Cubans with the basic necessities of food, clothing, shelter, education, health care, and recreation. Although this strategy produced an average living standard that was lower than was typical in developed North American and European nations, it eliminated the desperate poverty that typically engulfs the majority of those living in less developed nations. Reductions in levels of absolute poverty, in turn, reduced the kinds of thefts and violence that typically reach high levels among the poor in the urban centers of most less developed countries.

For its first three decades, Cuba's socialist distribution system not only reduced levels of absolute poverty, but it also narrowed the range of economic inequality. This contributed to low levels of routine crimes against persons and property in several ways. First, relatively few Cubans had access to luxury items such as new cars, top-of-the-line electronics, or high-style clothing. This meant that the average Cuban was not surrounded by others who seemed to have more than they did. Although differences in levels of income and consumption were not eliminated under Cuba's socialist economy, their range was substantially narrowed. As a consequence, the material resentments that typically motivate much property crime in market societies was reduced. Second, the limited availability of discretionary material goods significantly reduced the available targets for crime in Cuba. Because there were relatively few discretionary goods to steal or to buy with stolen money, the temptations toward property crime were reduced. The relatively equal distribution of goods further reduced the likelihood of property crime because increasing one's consumption through illegal means was readily obvious to others, making the offender liable for investigation.

Cuba's socialist project reduced crime, not only by changing patterns of material distribution, but by giving many Cubans a sense of commitment to the society. In its first two decades in power, Cuba's socialist government involved masses of young citizens in campaigns to improve literacy, build housing, and improve public health facilities. By the early 1970s, Cuba also had instituted a number of overseas programs to provide assistance to other less developed nations. As part of these "internationalist" projects, thousands of young Cubans worked in Latin America and Africa as teachers, doctors, and public health workers. Taken together these domestic and international projects gave many young people—typically a society's most crime-prone group—a sense of participation and belonging, thus reducing the proportion of youth drawn toward deviant or illegal pursuits as a way of finding community, identity, or material satisfaction.

Since the disappearance of Cuba's socialist trading partners in the early 1990s, the Cuban government has pursued a number of market-oriented strategies to maintain its economic development. These have led to an increase in certain kinds of street crimes. The Cuban government reports an increase in property crimes such as theft (particularly against tourists), and public prostitution has reappeared in Havana. In 1999, the Cuban government instituted new, more stringent crime control measures, to address the growth in these crimes. These measures included the creation of special police detachments to prevent crime in areas heavily frequented by tourists, and an increased emphasis on strict observance of the law.

RAYMOND J. MICHALOWSKI

References and Further Reading

Baloyra, E.A. and Morris, J.A. (Eds.) *Conflict and Change in Cuba*. Albuquerque, NM: University of New Mexico Press, 1993.

Behar, R. *Bridges to Cuba/Puentes a Cuba*. Ann Arbor, MI: University of Michigan Press.

Castro, F. *Neoliberal Globalization and the Global Economic Crisis*. Havana: Office of the Council of State, 1999.

Eckstein, S. *Back from the Future: Cuba under Castro*. Princeton, NJ: Princeton University Press, 1994.

Evenson, D. *Revolution in the Balance: Law and Society in Contemporary Cuba*. Boulder, CO: Westview, 1994.

Kaplowitz, D.R. *Anatomy of a Failed Embargo: U.S. Sanctions against Cuba*. New York, NY: Lynne Rienner, 1998.

Michalowski, R.J. Between citizens and the socialist state: The negotiation of legal practice in socialist cuba. *Law and Society Review,* 29 (1995).

Platt, T. Cuba and the politics of human rights. *Social-Justice*. 15 (2): 38–54 (1988).

Roy, J. The Helms-Burton law: Development, consequences, and legacy for inter-American and European-US relations. *Journal of Interamerican Studies and World Affairs* (Fall 1997) 39 (3): 77.

Salas, L. *Social Control and Deviance in Cuba*. New York, NY: Praeger Publishers, 1979.

Zatz, M.S. *Producing Legality: Law and Socialism in Cuba*. New York, NY: Routledge, 1994.

See also **Central America, Crime and Justice in; Organized Crime: Cuban Gangs**

Cultural Criminology

Cultural criminology investigates the many ways in which the activities and beliefs of criminals, the political and organizational ideologies of criminal justice, and the dynamics of media and popular culture converge in everyday life. Highlighting the importance of image, style, and representation in the construction of crime and crime control, cultural criminology explores the complex process through which illicit subcultures, the mass media, political authorities, criminal justice professionals, and others contest the meaning of crime and criminality.

As conceptualized by Ferrell (1999), Ferrell and Sanders (1995), Presdee (2000) and others, cultural criminology constitutes a critical perspective on crime and crime control designed to resonate with the distinctive dynamics of contemporary society. Building on the groundbreaking work of Cohen (1971, 1980), Hebdige (1979) and other British cultural theorists—work that investigated the situated symbolic meanings of illicit subcultures, the mediated (or negotiated) dynamics of social control, and the contested collisions of the two—cultural criminology similarly attempts to account for the symbolic politics of crime and crime control. As such, cultural criminology functions to develop the analytic tradition of British cultural and media studies; to expand the scope of contemporary sociological analysis by exploring the "symbolic" component of symbolic interaction across both small groups and larger media institutions; and to sharpen the analytic edge of critical criminology by attuning critical criminological analysis to the essential role of image and representation in the exercise of power and the construction of crime.

Cultural criminologists contend that this attention to image and representation is essential if we are to make sense of crime and crime control within a social order now largely defined by mediated dynamics. Drawing on Manning's (1998) notion of "media loops," and on postmodernist notions of referentiality and intertextuality, cultural criminologists argue that vital public debates increasingly hinge on contested images of crime and crime control, and on the subsequent images of these images that emerge in an endless, media-driven spiral. As key issues concerning criminality, policing, incarceration, and justice are negotiated within this mediated spiral, so too are power and ideology, as those with greater access to the machinery of media production set public agendas and define the boundaries of public debate around crime and crime control.

Cultural criminologists emphasize, though, that the dynamics of symbolism and style define not just broad public debates over crime, but the specific workings of criminal subcultures themselves. Cultural criminologists understand illicit subcultures to be more than residues of shared social space or illegal activity. Instead, they conceptualize them as subterranean communities of alternative meaning, organized around elaborate conventions of appearance, vocabularies of motive, and stylized presentations of self (Leblanc, 1999). In this sense, illicit subcultures are understood to be communities that produce situated meaning—that is, values and perceptions specific to the shared lives and activities of their members. And in many illicit subcultures, situated media of communication are also produced—from the graffiti of hip hop artists and hobos to the underground videos and websites of gang members.

Because of this, cultural criminologists employ a range of research methodologies designed to explore both general media dynamics and situated meanings. Using content and structural analysis, textual deconstruction, and imaginative counter-reading, many cultural criminologists work to unravel complex, mass media constructions of crime and crime control. Other cultural criminologists rely on ethnographic methodologies to investigate the subtle, situated images and representations constructed by criminals and criminal subcultures, and to achieve a degree of *verstehen* (interpretive understanding) in regard to subcultural meanings and emotions. Still others attempt to integrate these two sets of methods as they explore the contested interplay of mass culture and subcultural meanings (Kane, 1998). In this way, cultural criminology has come to constitute as much a methodological manifesto as a theoretical orientation, rejecting older positivist notions of science and scientific objectivity in favor of a criminology grounded in critical interpretation and attentive understanding (Ferrell, 2001).

Cultural criminologists bring these methodological and theoretical perspectives to bear on an astounding range of contemporary controversies, many of which ride the blurry boundaries between media and crime. The 1970s punk band The Clash sang of "turning rebellion into money," and cultural criminologists today note a number of parallel transformations. They investigate the many ways in which contemporary society turns crime into media, and thus into entertainment and money, through patrol car and courtroom cameras, "reality" television programs, crime films, television dramas, and the proliferation of crime news coverage (Surette, 1998). They explore the manifold ways in which mediated representations turn crime into politics, as moral entrepreneurs launch mediated campaigns of moral panic over crime and criminals, political figures build political capital by marketing imaginary solutions to media-driven crime problems, and criminals (and those criminalized) promote images of themselves as romantic outlaws or political outsiders. In all of this, cultural criminologists emphasize that crime and crime control are increasingly becoming a public carnival, a media circus, and a hall of mirrors where images mostly reflect each other.

These insights suggest that criminal justice policy must recognize and address the complex symbolic universe in which crime and crime control now unfold. This recognition in turn implies, for example, that the policing of a postmodern world increasingly will incorporate everyday mediated practices, will intertwine with mass media operations, and will focus not only on people and practical situations, but on illicit images, cybercrime, and the situated media of criminality. At the same time, cultural criminology cautions against the distorted images and stereotypes that regularly underwrite mediated anticrime campaigns, and offers both the analytic tools for exposing and correcting these distortions (via "newsmaking criminology") (Barak, 1994). Some argue that these orientations reveal cultural criminology's all-too-ready acceptance of a world overrun by media and governed by image; cultural criminologists counter, though, that as new mediated arrangements of power emerge, criminologists must acknowledge them and critically confront their implications if they are to work effectively toward a more just society.

An emergent orientation, cultural criminology continues to reshape the theory and practice of contemporary criminology, as more and more criminologists overtly incorporate an analysis of mediated dynamics and a sensitivity to alternative images and situated styles into their work. More broadly, cultural criminology seems to have instigated a quiet revolution in criminology, such that its traditional domains of inquiry—juvenile delinquency, drug use, and policing—have in many ways now reemerged as domains of inquiry into the mediated representations and contested meanings of these phenomena.

Jeff Ferrell

References and Further Reading

Barak, G., Ed., *Media, Process, and the Social Construction of Crime: Studies in Newsmaking Criminology*, New York, NY: Garland, 1994.

Cohen, S., Ed., *Images of Deviance*, Harmondsworth, UK: Penguin, 1971.

Cohen, S., *Folk Devils and Moral Panics*, London, UK: Macgibbon and Kee, 1980.

Ferrell, J., Cultural criminology, *Annual Review of Sociology* 25 (1999).

Ferrell, J., *Tearing Down the Streets*, New York, NY: St. Martin's/Palgrave, 2001.

Ferrell, J. and Sanders, C.R., Ed., *Cultural Criminology*, Boston, MA: Northeastern University Press, 1995.

Hebdige, D., *Subculture: The Meaning of Style*, London, UK: Methuen, 1979.

Kane, S., *AIDS Alibis: Sex, Drugs, and Crime in the Americas*, Philadelphia, PA: Temple University Press, 1998.

Leblanc, L., *Pretty in Punk: Girls' Gender Resistance in a Boys' Subculture*, New Brunswick, NJ: Rutgers University Press, 1999.

Manning, P.K., Media loops, in *Popular Culture, Crime, and Justice*, Bailey, F. and Hale, D., Eds., Belmont, CA: West/Wadsworth, 1998.

Presdee, M., *Cultural Criminology and the Carnival of Crime*, London, UK: Routledge, 2000.

Surette, R., *Media, Crime, and Criminal Justice: Images and Realities*, 2nd ed., Belmont, CA: West/Wadsworth, 1998.

See also **Subcultural Theories of Criminal Behavior**

Curfews

A curfew prohibits people from public spaces during specified time periods. The origins of curfews are unclear but historical sources suggest they first entered the Anglo-American legal tradition as a public safety measure imposed by Alfred the Great (849–899) that required the residents of Oxford, England to cover their fires every evening when the market square bell was rung. After 1066, the Norman conquerors of England added a more explicit social control dimension to this practice when they imposed strict curfews to prevent nighttime assembly and agitation by the subjugated Saxons. In fact, many etymologists believe the word curfew entered the English language from the Old French phrase "cuevrefeu" that derived from the words "couvirir," to cover, and "feu," fire.

In the U.S. there is a long tradition of *ad hoc* emergency curfews as a temporary response to civil unrest, natural disasters, or threats to national security. Permanent curfews were used in the pre-Civil War south to keep slaves and free blacks off city streets, and during World War II curfews were imposed upon people of Japanese descent. Though the courts validated such racially-based curfews at the time they were enacted, they would not withstand judicial scrutiny today. However, in modern times permanent nonemergency curfews commonly prohibit nighttime access by all adults and juveniles to public parks, and as with *ad hoc* temporary emergency curfews, courts have consistently rejected the argument that such limited curfews are unjustified infringements of civil liberties.

The most common, and controversial, contemporary curfews are those that restrict the public presence of juveniles during certain parts of the day throughout an entire community. Less common and more provocative are ordinances that prohibit juveniles from limited areas within a community—usually high-crime neighborhoods or commercially important districts. Juvenile curfews first gained widespread acceptance in the U.S. in the 1890s and since then their popularity has waxed and waned with changes in public concern over delinquency and youth victimization. The "curfew movement" that swept the U.S. in the 1890s was driven by a concern for the welfare of children but it was also part of a broader effort to control and socialize the urban masses of immigrants, whose children were seen as the source of an epidemic of "child crime." It is estimated that by 1900 at least 3,000 municipalities had enacted juvenile curfew ordinances in the belief that requiring youths to be at their homes after nightfall would reduce delinquency, protect children from the dangers and vices of city streets, and encourage parental responsibility. Increased levels of youth crime during and after the Second World War, during the mid-1960s and early 1970s and then again during the late 1980s and early 1990s, led many citizens and public officials to again accept the logic of the original juvenile curfew movement and resulted in the widespread enactment of new curfews, revisions of longstanding—but largely forgotten—curfews and increased levels of enforcement. By 2000, curfews were present in nearly 80% of major American cities and untold numbers of smaller municipalities.

The resurgence of juvenile curfew laws in the 1990s produced a legal and policy debate framed by the same pro- and anti-curfew arguments of the past, intensified by crucial factors and issues unique to contemporary urban America, and highlighted by a limited but growing body of empirical research focused on the impact and effectiveness of juvenile curfews. As in the past, curfews of the 1990s were subjected to legal challenges. The American Civil Liberties Union, the usual sponsor of these challenges, sometimes alleged vagueness and overbreadth but more argued against curfews on constitutional grounds. The most common constitutional objection is that curfews establish a suspect classification based on age, result in selective enforcement based on race, and thus violate the Equal Protection Clause. Opponents also argue that curfews unjustifiably infringe upon fundamental rights of free movement, assembly, and family privacy. Further, it is argued that curfew enforcement transgresses the due process rights of juveniles through unreasonable search and seizure and forced self-incrimination.

Numerous state and federal courts have issued conflicting rulings on juvenile curfews but most decisions overturning a curfew have been based on vagueness and overbreadth (faults easily remedied through legislative revision) and not on issues of fundamental fairness. Moreover, curfew ordinances in several cities (e.g., Dallas, TX; Charlottesville, VA; and Washington, DC) have survived strict scrutiny by federal district and appellate courts. Two factors were particularly crucial in those procurfew decisions. First was the presentation of delinquency and youth victimization statistics evidencing a nexus between the age classifications created by the curfew, the timeframe of the curfew, and the compelling interest of the city in protecting youths. Second was the inclusion of numerous exceptions, or defenses, that permit youths to remain in public places during curfew hours. Examples of such defenses include returning home from a religious, school or civic function, interstate travel, or exercising First Amendment rights. Short of a definitive Supreme Court ruling that they violate fundamental rights, well-crafted, narrowly tailored juvenile curfews, supported by reasonable and appropriate crime statistics, have a good chance of withstanding legal challenge.

All available findings from opinion surveys and focus groups evidence majority support for curfews and a widespread belief that such ordinances can effectively reduce delinquency and protect youth. Surveys conducted at the national level and at the city level have shown broad support for curfews. Respondents living in jurisdictions with a curfew have favored them, as have respondents in areas without a curfew. Every group of respondents polled—adults, parents of teenagers, policy makers, and teenagers themselves—have favored juvenile curfews. Even groups of teenagers living an inner city high-crime neighborhoods subject to an exceptionally strict curfew have professed overwhelming support for the curfew although simultaneously expressing concern over unfair curfew enforcement and admitting to frequent curfew violations. Such consistent and broad-based support clearly shows that the public understands and accepts at face value the underlying commonsense arguments in support of curfews. Such support also means that even if curfews do not work they still have significant political and symbolic value. At some basic level, they reassure the public and allow policy makers to claim credit for taking a visible and popular action in response to a serious problem.

The underlying arguments for curfews are simple and straightforward. First, limiting the times when youths may be out in public will reduce their opportunities to both engage in crime and to be victimized. As youths do not have the same rights as adults' curfews are possible. As youths account for a disproportionate amount of both crime and victimization, juvenile curfews are reasonable. Further, groups of unsupervised youths pose elevated risks of crime and delinquency and thus are even more justifiably subject to formal social control mechanisms such as curfews. The significant increases in youth violence and homicide in the late 1980s only strengthened those arguments. Additionally, it is argued that by both bolstering the efforts of responsible parents and motivating less responsible parents toward increased involvement and supervision curfews can actually strengthen families.

Supporters of curfews also argue that police enforcement will identify those youths at greatest risk of delinquency and victimization, will identify those parents who are unwilling or unable to exert sufficient control over their children, and thus can bring social service programs into a family situation in dire need of intervention. From this perspective, curfew violations are not primarily seen as punishable offenses. More exactly, they are seen as warning signs and opportunities for evaluation and, if necessary, the initiation of a wide array of youth and family services. A curfew ordinance may also serve as a legitimate means for patrol officers to engage in basic questioning and investigation and thus lead to the discovery and prevention of delinquency. Alternatively, curfews can serve as the basis for periodic sweeps aimed at hotspots of juvenile misbehavior or as the basis for intense crackdowns as a response to a string of serious high profile, late-night crimes involving youths.

However, many individuals are less willing to simply accept the commonsense assumptions and arguments described above. Curfew opponents ask for evidence to verify pro-curfew assumptions, present alternative possibilities, and raise entirely new issues and objections. Contemporary curfew opponents raise many of the same issues and questions that framed previous debates. Among the reoccurring objections are questions such as these. Is it not likely that a curfew will only succeed in shifting delinquency and youth victimization to different times of the day and different locations not subject to the curfew? Why is it that most curfews do not apply to the time of day—middle and late afternoon—-when the most delinquency and youth victimization takes place? Do the police not have better things to do than process curfew violators? Who will pay for taking care of curfew violators whose parents are not to be found? Is the cost of curfew enforcement justified? How many juveniles will curfews unnecessarily drag into the justice system? We know that most police "crackdowns" only produce short-lived gains or they become cost prohibitive, why would curfew enforcement be any different? How realistic is it that over the long run, adequate social services will be provided to the families of persistent curfew violators or that they will make a meaningful difference? What will be the impact of a curfew on youths who are at greater risk at home than away from home?

Some questions about curfews, particularly those that involve issues of violent youthful offenders and the impact of race, are more relevant to the 1990s. Why would youths bold enough to be involved with guns, drugs, and violence heed a curfew ordinance or worry about the consequences of an infraction? Even if curfew enforcement efforts are able to identify serious violent juvenile offenders, how realistic is it to expect family support services to have a meaningful impact on either such offenders or their families? Given the tension, mistrust, and hostility between law enforcement and minority youths in most cities, how can curfew enforcement be fair and unbiased? Why will curfews not simply increase the existing overrepresentation of minority juvenile offenders in the criminal justice system? Are curfews not simply one more get tough overreaction by a biased majority community operating more on fear and bias and less on reason and an understanding of the root causes of urban crime.

Fortunately, there is a growing body of reasonably rigorous, objective, and systematic social science research that addresses key questions about curfews. Specifically for the first time in the history of juvenile curfews, there are multiple empirical studies that measure the impact of curfews on crime prevention, on crime displacement, and on the detection of criminal activity. Other empirical studies studied the characteristics of curfew violators, in part to probe the questions of racial discrimination and bias in enforcement. Unfortunately, in a recent exhaustive review of this research Adams (2003) only found 10 studies that first included offending and victimization as outcome measures and then made before and after statistical comparisons of outcome measures. More unfortunately, none of the 10 studies employed strong research designs. Working within the limitations of various research designs, it was found that the research conclusions did not support the argument that curfews reduce crime and victimization. Some studies showed no impact of curfews on crime, and in the remaining studies, the curfews were nearly as likely to increase crime as decrease it. Also, curfew enforcement rarely led to the discovery of serious crime. Most curfew violators were only arrested for curfew related violations. More rigorous empirical evaluation research on curfews is needed and until such research is completed the debate that started with the first curfew movement in 1890s continues into the 2000s.

William J. Ruefle

References and Further Reading

Adams, K. 2003. The effectiveness of juvenile curfews at crime prevention. *Annals of the American Academy of Political and Social Science* 587: 136–159.

Crowell, A. 1996. Minor restrictions: The challenge of juvenile curfews. *Public Management* 78: 4–9.

Fritch, E.J., Caeti, T.J., and Taylor. R.W. 1999. Gang suppression through saturation patrol, aggressive curfew enforcement and truancy enforcement: A quasi-experimental test of the Dallas anti-gang initiative. *Crime and Delinquency* 45: 122–139.

Hemmes, C. and Bennet, K. 1998. Out in the street: Juvenile crime, juvenile curfews and the Constitution. *Gonzaga Law Review* 34: 267–327.

Hemmes, C. and Bennett, K. 1999. Juvenile curfews and the courts: Judicial response to a not-so-new crime control strategy. *Crime and Delinquency* 45: 99–121.

Hirschel, D.J., Dean, C.W., and Dumond, D. 2001 Juvenile curfews and race: A cautionary note. *Criminal Justice Policy* Review 12: 197–214.

Hunt, A.L. and Weiner, K. 1977. The impact of a juvenile curfew: Suppression and displacement in patterns of juvenile offending. *Journal of Police Science and Administration* 5: 407–412.

Lersch, K.M. and Sellers, C. 2000. A comparison of curfew and noncurfew violators using a self-report delinquency survey. *American Journal of Criminal Justice* 24: 259–269.

Levy, D.L. 1997. The Dade County juvenile curfew ordinance: A retrospective examination of the ordinance and the law that supports its constitutionality. *St. Thomas Law Review* 9: 517–545.

Levy, D.T. 1988. The effect of driving age, driver education, and curfew laws on traffic fatalities of 15–17 year olds. *Risk Analysis* 8: 569–74.

Males, M.A. 2000. Vernon, Connecticut's juvenile curfew: The circumstances of youths cited and effects on crime. *Criminal Justice Policy Review* 11: 254–67.

McDowell, D., Loftin, C., and Wiersema, B. 2000. The impact of youth curfew laws on juvenile crime rates. *Crime and Delinquency* 46: 76–91.

Note. 1984. Assessing the scope of minors' fundamental rights: Juvenile curfews and the constitution. *Harvard Law Review* 97: 1163–1181.

Note. 1994. Juvenile curfews and gang violence: Exiled on main street. *Harvard Law Review* 107: 1693–1710.

Office of Juvenile Justice and Delinquency Prevention. 1996. *Curfew: An Answer to Juvenile Delinquency and Victimization?* Washington, DC: Office of Juvenile Justice and Delinquency Prevention.

Presuser, D.F., Williams, A.F., Zador, P.L., and Blomberg, R.D. 1984. The effect of curfew laws on motor vehicle crashes. *Law and Policy* 6: 115–128.

Public Agenda. 1997. *Kids These Days: What Americans Really Think about the Next Generation*. New York, NY: Farkas and Johnson.

Reynolds, K.M., Ruefle, W., Jenkins, P., and Seydlitz, R. 1999. Contradictions and consensus: Youths speak out about juvenile curfews. *Journal of Crime and Justice* 22: 171–192.

Reynolds, K.M., Seydlitz, R., and Jenkins, P. 2000. Do juvenile curfew laws work? A time-series analysis of the New Orleans Law. *Justice Quarterly* 17: 205–230.

Reynolds, K.M., Thayer, R.E., and Ruefle, W. 1996. *Preliminary Findings—The New Orleans Juvenile Curfew: Impact on Teens, Parents, Delinquency and Victimization.* Paper presented at the 1996 Annual Conference on Criminal Justice Research and Evaluation.

Ruefle, W. and Reynolds, K.U. 1995. Curfews and delinquency in major American cities. *Crime and Delinquency* 41: 347–363.

Ruefle, W. and Reynolds, K.M. 1996. Keeping them at home: Curfew ordinances in 200 American cities. *American Journal of Police* 15: 63–84.

Ruefle, W. and Reynolds, K.M. 1998. Juvenile curfews in the 1990s: Policy, practice and impact. *Children's Legal Rights Journal* 18: 73–77.

Rhyne, C. 1943. Municipal curfew for minors—model ordinance annotated. Washington, DC: National Institute of Municipal Law Officers.

Sherman, L. 1995. The police, in James, Q.W. and Jane, P. (Eds.), *Crime*. San Francisco, CA: Institute for Contemporary Studies.

Sherr, P. 1992. The juvenile curfew ordinance: In search of a new standard of review. *Washington University Journal of Urban and Contemporary Law* 41: 163–193.

Sutphen, R.D. and Ford, J. 2001 The effectiveness and enforcement of a teen curfew law. *Journal of Sociology and Social Welfare* 28: 55–78.

Townsend, J. 1896. Curfew ordinances for city children. *North American Review* 163: 725–730.

U.S. Conference of Mayors. 1997. *A Status Report on Youth Curfews in America's Cities: A 347-City Survey.* Washington, DC: U.S. Conference of Mayors.

See also **Gangs: Enforcement, Intervention, and Prevention Strategies; Juvenile Delinquency: Definitions and the Law; Juvenile Delinquency: Extent, Correlates, and Trends**

Customary Law

Definition

The greatest problem in defining customary law is that the concept itself is a legal fiction over which much ink has been spilt during the past 150 years. Beginning with Sir Henry Maine's (1861, 1863) works on so-called "ancient law," western legal scholars have attempted to distinguish custom from law in terms that supported their ethnocentric views of laws and societies other than their own. Essentially, the argument has been over the form of the law rather than its functions. In juridical terms, customary law may be defined as the unwritten, uncodified laws of pre- or proto-urban societies. In anthropological terms, however, as all laws are simply "rules for living together" (Ryan, 1995), customary law may be regarded as those behavioral norms that have been legitimized over time through their internal acceptance by individual members of a given society or group. Customary law and legal systems typically focus on the resolution of interpersonal conflict and restoration of order through (1) a strong focus on individual rights, (2) collective decision making, (3) the use of corrective rather than punitive sanctions, and (4) the acceptance of sanctions as prerequisite for continued group membership (Allott and Woodman, 1985; Hoebel, 1954; Keon-Cohen, 1982; Pospisil, 1978; Rasing, 1984; Rouland, 1979, 1994; Tyler, 1985; van den Steenhoven, 1955, 1959; Yabsley, 1984). Customary law is typically practiced in small scale, heterogeneous societies (e.g., tribal groups), and within subcultures (e.g., outlaw biker gangs). Interestingly, customary law does not refer to a single entity, but rather it may be likened to an umbrella under which criminal law (violations of the social order), matrimonial law (marriages, divorces, adoption, inheritance, and family relations), game law (hunting and fishing), and business law (trading practices) are all covered. It is possible, therefore, to see a number of different customary laws operating at the same time in a single society. The following discussions explore the concept of customary law and its position in relation to Western, codified law.

The Discourse of Customary Law in Modern Society

Legal anthropologist Norbert Rouland (1994) argued that the functions of law are the same regardless of the type of legal system, namely to promote social interchange, preserve the social order, and mediate disputes. Legal scholar Lon Fuller (1985, 911) noted that although the term customary law "prejudges its subject; it asserts that the force and meaning of what we call 'customary law' lie in mere habit or usage", it is nonetheless impossible to understand our current common law and legal system without obtaining an understanding of customary law and its evolution. Fuller stated that:

> the phenomenon called customary law can best be described as a language of interaction. To interact meaningfully men require a social setting in which the moves of the participating players will fall generally within some predictable pattern. To engage in effective social behavior men need the support of intermeshing anticipations that will let them know what their opposite numbers will do, or that will at least enable them to gauge the general scope of the repertory from which responses to their actions will be drawn (in Lloyd and Freeman, 1985, 911).

Canadian anthropologist Joan Ryan (1995) agreed with both Fuller (1985) and Rouland (1994). She offered the notion that all laws, no matter how simple or complex, are simply rules for living together in a group. Every human group has both rules and one or more mechanisms for their making and remaking over time (Falk-Moore, 1978). The function of these rules has been to control social behavior through informal or formal means. *Informal social control* is the collection of methods employed by individuals or small groups, such as family or kin groups, to ensure that the behavior of its members comply with the rules of the group. We can find examples of informal social control in almost any small group, such as those portrayed in films such as *Grease* or *West Side Story* or in legal scholar Lawrence Friedman's (2002) account of the people of Tristan da Cunha where conformity was ensured more through gossip, apologies, and restitution than by relying on outside authority figures. *Formal social control* is the collection of methods employed by the larger group, such as a tribal group, community, or state to ensure that the behavior of an individual or group complies with the rules of the larger culture or society. Examples of formal methods of social control include the use of group or community meetings wherein the behavior is discussed, a group consensus concerning corrective action is determined, and conformity ensured through public shaming, restitution, or ostracism. Examples of formal social control may be seen throughout the film *Witness* starring Harrison Ford as a police officer hiding a witness in one of Pennsylvania's Amish communities. Within nation-states, such as the U.S., governments practice formal social control through the use of specialists (e.g., police, courts, and corrections) to enforce compliance with those norms of behavior and the application of sanctions (or punishments) such as fines, imprisonment, etc., upon those whose behavior does not comply with accepted norms.

In order to adequately discuss customary law from a contemporary legal perspective, a heuristic model was employed that positioned customary law as part of a *primitive-transitional-modern law* continuum. Legal anthropologist Norbert Rouland (1994) argued that the functions of law in each of these three legal systems is the same, namely to promote social interchange, preserve the social order, and mediate disputes.

Customary law and legal systems are generally relegated by legally trained scholars (i.e., law school graduates) as primitive law because of their form rather than their function. The use of councils of elders, religious leaders, or chiefs to enact and change laws, promote harmony, and settle disputes is often regarded as primitive by legal scholars in much the same way as early explorers regarded indigenous peoples (such as Native Americans) as primitive, as the form of the society did not match their own political or economic structures.

Transitional law and legal systems are usually found within advanced agrarian and early industrial societies. With the development of surplus food and other materials, rules for land use and ownership as well as the trading of surplus goods begin to evolve as a result of the development of permanent settlements and changes in the dominant mode of production. Legal anthropologist Leopold Pospisil (1978) notes that this type of law is marked by the adoption of authoritarian law based upon the societal acceptance of external persuasion rather than customary law with its internal acceptance by individual members of that society. Transitional legal systems are marked by steps to remove the influence of kinship and religion from the dispute settlement process.

Modern law and legal systems are typically found in industrial and postindustrial societies. The development of a production-based economy among a sedentary and heterogeneous society is usually accompanied by a complex, codified system of authoritarian law that distinguishes between civil and criminal laws (crimes are now regarded as offences against the larger community and state with private wrongs regarded as civil torts viewed as from social disputes). These systems of laws are typically supported by full- and part-time legal specialists.

Customary law has evolved in line with the society that practiced it and was tied to the dominant mode of economic production within the society. Hunter-gatherer, pastoralist (nomadic animal herding), and early agrarian societies each developed different systems of customary law to deal with social relations under the different modes of production. Customary law is not usually found within industrialized societies although it may be practiced among distinct cultures and subcultures within such pluralized societies (e.g., Native American reservations, Amish settlements, outlaw biker gangs, and so forth).

Customary Law in Action

Native American tribal nations have a unique fiduciary relationship with the American and Canadian nation-states and have struggled to maintain their traditional practices. This has included customary law, traditional means of social control, and other methods to keep their respective cultures alive. Although the U.S. federal government, for example, has sought to develop western-style policing and judicial systems on tribal lands and reservations, these methods of social control are often seen as foreign and the Native American justice practitioners as coopted because of the vast differences between traditional and modern laws. An example of the differences between one Native American people (the Arctic-dwelling Inuit) and the modern Euro-Canadian legal system is offered in Table 1. Customary law among the Inuit was based on the concept of law being rules for living. Conflict was to be avoided at all costs and efforts were to be undertaken to resolve individual conflict and restore harmony among the group. Anthropologist E. Adamson Hoebel (1954), having studied the customary law among the Cheyenne, explored the law ways of a branch of the Alaskan Inuit, the Nunamiut. At that time, he was able to identify nine postulates within their society that he felt were juridically significant as the philosophical basis for their common law. These postulates included:

TABLE 1. Comparisons of Euro-Canadian and Inuit (Eskimo) Justice Concepts

Euro-Canadian	Traditional Inuit
Laws formulated by elected representatives.	Laws formulated by community tradition and consensus.
Laws tied to man made economy and therefore complex and numerous.	Laws tied to the natural environment; only a few universally condemned actions in Inuit customary law.
Protestant Ethic and Christianity the moral foundation of the law.	Traditional Inuit religions are the moral foundation of Inuit codes of behavior.
Personal offenses seen as transgressions against the state as represented by the monarch.	Personal offenses seen as transgressions against the victim and his or her family; community involved only when the public peace is threatened.
Law administered by representatives of the state in the form of officially recognized or operated social institutions.	Law usually administered by the offended party, i.e., the family, clan, or tribe through a process of mediation or negotiation.
Force and punishment used as methods of social control.	Arbitration and ostracism usual peace-keeping methods.
Individualistic basis for society and the use of the law to protect private property.	Communal basis for society; no legal protection for private property; land held in trust by an individual and protected by the group.

Source: A.L. Patenaude (1989)

Postulate VIII. The bilateral small family is the basic social and economic unit *and* is autonomous in the direction of its activities.

Postulate IX. For the safety of the person and the local group, individual behavior must be predictable (Hoebel, 1954, 69–70).

These two postulates are the most germane to this discussion as they provide both the rationale and locus for social control in any society.

The approach of American and Canadian criminal courts toward customary law, however, has been based upon total rejection since the early 19th century. This judicial tradition may have its origins in the ethnocentricity of the Anglo-American or Anglo-Canadian criminal justice systems as well as the power relations between the two federal governments and their respective indigenous peoples. Indeed, the insertion of Native American customary law into Canadian common law and legal practices *may* occur *if* it can be shown that such customary law complies with certain judicial prerequisites as detailed by the dominant society (Yabsley, 1984).

Contemporary Applications of Customary Law

In the contemporary U.S., customary law continues to be practiced, albeit on a reduced scale, despite the effects of urbanization and industrialization. The Navajo Tribal Council in the southwest and the Tanana Tribal Council in Alaska have incorporated traditional dispute resolution and the restorative principles of their customary law into the modern judicial processes. Similarly, Canadian native peoples such as the Dogrib (an *Athapaskan*-speaking tribe in the Dene Nation) in the subarctic Northwest Territories have found a way of incorporating traditional and modern legal practices to deal with persons who have broken the Queen's law.

Although the customary law of the Dogrib:

1. had a system of rules for making sure society worked in an orderly way at all times;
2. passed down these rules from generation to generation orally;
3. had ways of enforcing the rules;
4. had ways of dealing with individuals who did not follow the rules or who broke them (Ryan, 1995, xxvi),

these laws and legal practices were often in conflict with the Anglo-Canadian law and legal processes. This discontinuity resulted in local communities and the Canadian criminal justice system becoming irrelevant to one another and, at times, a source of irritation.

To reduce this discontinuity, a Territorial Court judge met with community leaders and elders to see if a new method could be found to make the courts more responsive to the needs of the community while remaining attuned to the criminal justice system. The result was the introduction of circle sentencing with a relaxed court process and the involvement of the community. The court officers, accused, police, victims, elders, witnesses, and interested community members now sit in a large circle in the local community hall where they hear the charges, pleas, and evidence. The determination of guilt and burden of proof remains the same as in other Anglo-Canadian courts, but the determination and imposition of sentence involves the community. The judge, in conjunction with a panel of respected members of the community (usually elders), determines which sanction would be the most effective for the individual offender and requires the offender to apologize for whatever he or she has done and to listen to the voices of the community. Many offenders, including those with lengthy prison records, have been reduced to tears as a result of the harsh words from elderly grandmothers and grandfathers who spoke of the shame that their behavior brought upon the offender, his or her family, and the community as well as ways in which the offender could replace bad behavior with good and shame with pride. Sentence is then imposed with restoration of harmony rather than punitiveness as the guiding principles, and the offender is required to return to the court upon completion of sentence and is welcomed back into the community.

Another example is found in Nigeria, where mixed legal and judicial systems coexist alongside one another; native customary law exists alongside English common and Islamic religious laws. As a result of the unique colonial history of that part of Africa, Nigeria developed a system whereby village law (common law) was given full constitutional recognition and equality with the two systems of law and legal beliefs that arrived during the 11th and 19th centuries, Islamic religious law and English common law, respectively. Today, depending on the nature of the offense and the tribal or religious affiliations of the offender, his or her crime could be heard in a tribal trial court (for customary law offenses), a Sha'ria court (crimes against Islam), or a state court (English common law offenses). Appeals from tribal, religious, and state trial courts are determined in a respective appeal court of the same legal family. Appellate court appeals are determined in the Supreme Court of Nigeria.

Conclusion

Customary law and legal systems typically focus on the resolution of interpersonal conflict and restoration of order through (1) a strong focus on individual rights, (2) collective decision making, (3) the use of corrective rather than punitive sanctions, and (4) the acceptance of sanctions as prerequisite for continued group membership. Often unwritten and uncodified, these laws are passed from generation to generation as rules for living together in a group. For the most part, customary law has been rejected by the dominant group and superseded by common law, as seen in the legal histories of Australia, Canada, New Zealand, and the U.S. There remains the *possibility* that customary law could return in the U.S. although this would most likely be limited to those Native American tribal nations who petition the federal government for that right on tribal lands.

It remains ironic, however, that many Western-trained jurists and legal scholars continue to denigrate customary law, as mere custom or norms of behavior, when customary law is the foundation upon which our modern Anglo-American common law is built. The movements toward alternative dispute resolution, restorative justice, reintegrative shaming, and therapeutic jurisprudence (in the form of drug courts) seek to resolve the conflict between the individual and the community while also seeking to restore harmony in the community may be seen as customary law practices.

Allan L. Patenaude

References and Further Reading

Allott, A. and Woodman, G.R. (Eds.). 1985. *People's Law and State Law: The Bellagio Papers*. Cinnaminson, NJ: Foris Publications.

Bell, D. 1986. The character of aboriginal customary laws in Australian Law Reform Commission Report No. 31, *The Recognition of Aboriginal Customary Laws*. Canberra, Australia: Australian Government Printing Service. pp. 21–22.

Falk-Moore, S. 1978. *Law as Process: An Anthropological Approach*. London, UK: Routledge and Kegan Paul.

Friedman, L. 2002. *American Law in the Twentieth Century*. New Haven, CT: Yale University Press.

Fuller, L.L. 1985. Human interaction and the law. in Lord Lloyd of Hampstead and M.D.A. Freeman. London, UK: Stevens and Sons. pp. 911–921. (reprint: 1969, *American Journal of Jurisprudence*, Vol. 14)

Hoebel, E.A. 1954. *The Law of Primitive Man: A Study in Comparative Legal Dynamics*. Cambridge, MA: Harvard University Press.

Holmes, Chief Justice Oliver Wendell, Jr. 1897. The path of law. in *Harvard Law Review*, Vol. 10. pp. 457–478.

Keon-Cohen, B.S. 1982. Native justice in Australia, Canada and the USA: A comparative analysis in *Canadian Legal Aid Bulletin*, Vol. 5. pp. 187–250.

Maine, H.S. 1883. *Early Law and Custom*. New York City, NY: Holt, Rinehart and Winston.

Maine, H.S. 1861. *Ancient Law*. Boston, MA: Beacon Press.

Patenaude, A.L. 1989. *Whose Law? Whose Justice? Two Conflicting Systems of Law in Canada's Northwest Territories*. Burnaby, British Columbia: Northern Justice Society.

Pospisil, L. 1978. *The Ethnography of Law: A Comparative Theory*. 2nd ed. Menlo Park, CA: Cummings Publishing Company.

Rasing, W. 1984. *On Conflict Management with Nomadic Inuit: An Ethnological Essay*. Unpublished Doctoral Dissertation. Department of Cultural Anthropology, Catholic University of Nijmegan. Nijmegan, Holland

Rouland, N. 1994. *Legal Anthropology* (translated by Planel, P.G.). Stanford, CA: Stanford University Press.

Rouland, N. 1979. Les modes juridiques de solution des conflicts chex les inuits. *Études Inuit Studies*, Vol. 3 (hors-serie). pp. 1–171.

Ryan, J. 1995. *Doing Things the Right Way: Dene Traditional Justice in Lac La Martre, N.W.T.* Dene Cultural Institute. Calgary, Alberta: University of Calgary Press and Arctic Institute of North America, 1995.

Tylor, K.J. 1985. *The Recognition of Aboriginal Customary Law by the Canadian Courts*. Regina, Sask.: Saskatchewan—Justice. Working paper presented to joint Canada-Saskatchewan-Federation of Saskatchewan Indian Nations Project on Aboriginal Customary Law.

van den Steenhoven, G. 1955. Study of Legal Concepts among the Eskimos in Some Parts of the Keewatin District, N.W.T. in the Summer of 1955. Ottawa, Ontario, CA: Department of Northern Affairs and National Resources.

van den Steenhoven, Geert. 1959. *Legal Concepts Among the Netsilik Eskimos of Pelly Bay, N.W.T.* Ottawa, Ontario, CA: Northern Co-ordination and Research Centre, Department of Northern Affairs and National Resources.

Yabsley, G.R. 1984. *Nunavut and Inuit Customary Law. Report to the Nunavut Constitutional Forum*. Yellowknife, N.W.T. Available from the Northern Conference Resource Centre, Simon Fraser University, Burnaby, British Columbia.

Yago, S. 2003. *Law and Society*. 7th ed. Upper Saddle River, NJ: Prentice Hall.

See also **Crime and Justice in Colonial America**

Customs Service, U.S.

The U.S. Customs Service was originally established in 1789 to collect taxes and increase revenues for the newly established government, making it the nation's oldest law enforcement agency. Over the years, its responsibilities have evolved and changed to meet the needs of the nation.

Since its inception, Customs has been responsible for enforcing a variety of laws covering a variety of areas, depending upon the circumstances and needs of the country. In the early days, Customs officials were responsible for enforcing the Embargo Act of 1807 that prohibited the export of American goods to Europe. Other laws that fell to Customs agents to enforce were an 1808 law that placed a ban on the importation of slaves, and the Tariff Acts of 1828 and 1832, which put a tax on manufactured goods. In 1842, Customs was given the task of enforcing the first federal pornography law. During the Civil War, Customs officials blocked cargo traveling from northern to southern ports, as well as foreign goods being sent to southern states. During the 1880s until the early 1900s, Customs officials were assigned to watch border crossings (as there was no Immigration and Naturalization Service yet). This became a more difficult task when Congress passed the Chinese Exclusion Act of 1882 to stop the flow of illegal Chinese immigrants into the country. During WWI (1914–1919), the Customs Intelligence Bureau searched ships for aliens, jewels, and unpaid income tax. They also had to issue war zone passes to protect piers from unauthorized visitors, and filed reports for the War Trade Board, the Shipping Board, and the War Risk Insurance Board. In 1949, Customs was charged with enforcing the Export Control Act of 1949. To do this, Customs began searching luggage, checking passports, and generally looking for prohibited and restricted items.

Today, the primary mission of the U.S. Customs Service is to collect duty and taxes on all imported goods. It ensures that all taxes and tariffs are paid on imported goods and products brought into the U.S. However, Customs agents are also responsible for protecting the country against the smuggling of contraband into the U.S. This can include drugs, cars, electronics, beer, weapons, child pornography, Cuban cigars, or anything else deemed illegal or unsafe. To do this, the Customs Service protects points of entry into the U.S., including airports, where Customs agents are recognized as the people who go through the luggage of travelers looking for drugs, food, and other products. They watch over more than 17,000 miles of borders with Canada and Mexico, and 10,000 miles of coastline. They also inspect cargo shipments with the help of mobile x-ray vans that allow agents to check shipments without opening them. Agents also use atomizers, which are hand-held electronic vacuums that pick up trace scents of drugs, explosives, and weapons from outside the box.

Despite the many changes that have occurred in the agency, Customs continues to be the first line of defense in the nation's war against drugs and illegal narcotics. Fighting the importation of illicit drugs is one of the agency's top priorities, and they have developed many weapons to do that. One of those weapons, specially trained dogs, can detect the presence of five drug odors: heroin, cocaine, marijuana, methamphetamines, and hash. At border crossings, customs agents often use density readers to assist in looking for packages of drugs in cars and trucks, and x-ray machines to examine the internal compartments of an entire truck. They also use hightech snooping devices such as fiber optic cameras that look into gas tanks, handheld devices called "busters" that look for any irregularities that might indicate hidden compartments, and laser range finders that check the dimensions of trucks to look for hidden walls. At airports, Customs agents can legally open and inspect anyone's luggage any time for any reason, and can even order a body search that passengers may not refuse. This can include a traditional body pat-down or a full body scan. Agents can also take a suspected passenger to a medical facility for x-rays.

In 1969, Congress passed the Customs Aviation Program in response to an increase in drug smuggling with light, private aircraft. In 1971, Customs' Interdiction Program began operations with a small fleet of confiscated aircraft. In 1973, the Customs Marine Program was established. These two divisions were merged in 1999, and became the Air and Marine Interdiction Branch of U.S. Customs. This is now the nation's premier air and marine law enforcement interdiction organization. Agents working in this division have special clearances, including "air speed restriction lifted" (so they can fly faster than other planes). These agents are also allowed to fly below 10,000 feet, can fly lights-out at night, and can fly in formation closer than other planes are allowed. Additionally, they have a complex radar network that includes information from Airborne Warning and Control System (AWACS), air traffic control (both military and domestic air traffic information), military radar, and aerostat balloons (giant tethered radar balloons that collect data). The Air and Marine Interdiction Coordination Center (AMIC) is located in Riverside California, and has advanced technology to catch smugglers trying to enter the country by air.

Customs is also on the lookout for contraband other than drugs. It is responsible for enforcing the 1976 Arms Export Control Act. With this responsibility, Customs has to detect, interdict, or investigate illegal international trafficking in arms and munitions. Customs is also fighting the illegal trafficking and distribution of child pornography. In the early 1990s, Customs investigations expanded to include child pornography transmitted through the Internet. The U.S. Customs Service International Child Pornography Investigation and Coordination Center was created in 1996 to expand and coordinate Customs Internet child pornography investigation. In August 1997, Customs expanded its internet investigations to include all forms of criminal activity under its jurisdiction that takes place over the internet. Today, they have the Customs Cyber Smuggling Center that includes high-speed lines, a forensics lab that can find images hidden deep in a computer's memory, and a "war room" to plan sophisticated multicountry activities.

The terrorist attacks of September 11, 2001, have altered the U.S. Customs Service in many ways. New agreements include:

The Smart Border Declaration: signed between the U.S. and Canada in December 2002 to improve security and expedite trade along the U.S-Canadian border; will allow U.S. customs officers to be posted at different Canadian ports to prescreen products intended for the U.S.;

The Container Security Initiative: an attempt to prevent shipped goods from being used by terrorists; agreements were made with all major and mid-sized ports around the world to post customs agents and inspectors to prevent deadly cargo from reaching America; also creates new security measures in an attempt to stop crime and fraud in world trade;

The Customs-Trade Partnership against Terrorism: a way to assist shippers to create ways to prevent their vessels from being used for smuggling contraband; allows customs, major importers, and other members of the trade community to work together to develop security measures; and,

The Advance Passenger Information System: allows commercial airliners to gather information on passengers and crew members and provide it to customs; includes items such as flight itineraries.

As of March 1, 2003, the responsibilities of the U.S. Customs Service were transferred to the newly established Department of Homeland Security. There, agents will continue to be concerned with protecting the nation but with increased responsibilities. After September 11, 2001, agents are concerned with the potential for smuggling nuclear, chemical, and biological materials into the country to be used in terrorist attacks against the public. As our nation continues to grow and prosper, the U.S. Customs Service will continue to evolve and protect all citizens.

NANCY MARION

References and Further Reading

Green, M. 1998. *Customs Service* (New York, NY: Riverfront Books).

Prince, C.E. 1989. *The U.S. Customs Service: A Bicentennial History* (Washington, DC: Department of Treasury).

U.S. Customs Service. 1995. *Customs From A to Z*, Customs Publication No. 567 (Washington, DC: Department of Treasury).

U.S. Customs Service. 1998. *Exceptional Careers, U.S. Customs Service*, Customs Publication No. 502 (Washington, DC: Department of Treasury).

U.S. Customs Service. 1998. U.S Customs Service, Protectors of Independence Since 1789 Customs Publication No. 534 (Washington, D.C.: Department of Treasury).

U.S. Customs Service. 1997. "An Old American Custom", Customs Publication No. 545 (Washington, D.C.: Department of Treasury).

U.S. Customs Website: http://www.customs.gov

See also **Terrorism: Enforcement and Prevention Strategies**

Cybercrime

See **Computer Offenses; Hackers: History, Motivations, and Activities**

Day Release Programs *See* **Work Release**

See **Work Release**

Death Penalty *See* **Capital Punishment**

Defense Attorneys

Sometimes reviled by the public as the root cause of the problems with the criminal justice system, the criminal defense attorney nevertheless serves the valuable function of protecting the constitutional rights of the accused in our adversarial system. The defense attorney performs the often-thankless job of zealously representing the interests of a client accused of a crime. Defense attorneys suffer the same public perception problem of other lawyers, as evidenced by recent public opinion polls that rank the honesty of lawyers very low. But it is always helpful to examine the realities behind the public perception. As with all professions, the outrageous examples of unethical conduct often grab the headlines, while the vast majority of those practitioners who perform their duties ethically and conscientiously go unreported. In an effort to examine the role of the defense attorney in the American criminal justice system, this essay will explore the history of the right to counsel afforded by the U.S. Constitution, including an examination of the meaning of effective counsel. It will also consider the actual work that defense attorneys perform; the ethical responsibilities of defense attorneys; common defenses that defense attorneys assert on behalf of clients; and recent Bureau of Justice Statistics studies that examine the difference in effectiveness between public defenders and private attorneys. Finally the article will examine the most recent guidelines promulgated by the American Bar Association regarding the performance of defense counsel in death penalty cases.

Brief History of the Right to Counsel

The Sixth Amendment to the U.S. Constitution establishes the importance of the criminal defense attorney in our justice system:

> In all criminal prosecutions, the accused shall enjoy the right to a speedy and public trial, by an impartial jury of the State and district wherein the crime shall have been committed, which district shall have been previously ascertained by law, and to be informed of the nature and cause of the accusation; to be confronted with the witnesses against him; to have compulsory process for obtaining witnesses in his favor, and to have the Assistance of Counsel for his defence (sic).

This constitutionally protected right to counsel has become a vital part of the American criminal justice system. It is now commonly understood that a person accused of a crime, especially a serious crime, should have the opportunity to have an attorney to protect his rights and to help him defend himself against the awesome power and resources of the state. The seemingly limitless resources of the government include the police who investigate and arrest criminal suspects and the prosecutors who rely on public resources to prosecute cases effectively. But during the last century our courts have struggled to interpret the language in this succinct amendment. The words in this amendment have informed the on-going discussion about *when* defense attorneys must be appointed to criminal defendants, and also about how to determine whether a defense attorney has provided *effective* representation.

The Sixth Amendment specifically states that a criminal defendant has the right to counsel in all criminal prosecutions. The U.S. Supreme Court has addressed this issue in some of its most noteworthy cases. Early on, the Supreme Court interpreted the amendment to mean simply that criminal defendants were entitled to hire their own counsel in all criminal prosecutions. This interpretation left out the many cases where defendants were indigent and not able to afford private counsel. As a result, it is widely believed that many unrepresented indigent defendants were convicted even though they were not guilty. Later the U.S. Supreme Court expanded its interpretation of the Sixth Amendment to mean that defendants were entitled to court-appointed attorneys only when facing capital felonies, including rape and murder, like in the case *Betts. v. Brady*, 316 U.S. 455 (1942). This case was followed by many states until the 1960s. Then the U.S. Supreme Court once again expanded its interpretation of the right to counsel in 1963 in a landmark decision. In *Gideon v. Wainwright*, 372 U.S. 335 (1963), the U.S. Supreme Court addressed the issue regarding when the right to counsel for criminal defendants attaches. In *Gideon*, an indigent defendant was charged with a felony, breaking and entering with the intent to commit larceny, and asked the Florida trial court to appoint an attorney to represent him. The court refused his request and explained that defendants were entitled to court-appointed counsel only if they were charged with a capital felony offense. Mr. Gideon had to proceed at trial as a *pro se* defendant, which means he represented himself. The U.S. Supreme Court reversed the Florida trial court's ruling and held that all indigent defendants are entitled to court-appointed counsel when they are charged with any felony offense. Justice Black eloquently delivered the opinion of the Court, and he relied upon the words of Justice Sutherland, a Supreme Court justice who had written the following words in the 1932 U.S. Supreme Court case *Powell v. Alabama* regarding the importance of defense attorneys:

> The right to be heard would be, in many cases, of little avail if it did not comprehend the right to be heard by counsel. Even the intelligent and educated layman has small and sometimes no skill in the science of the law. If charged with crime, he is incapable, generally, of determining for himself whether the indictment is good or bad. He is unfamiliar with the rules of evidence. Left without the aid of counsel he may be put on trial without a proper charge, and convicted upon incompetent evidence, or evidence irrelevant to the issue or otherwise inadmissible. He lacks both the skill and knowledge adequately to prepare his defense, even though he has a perfect one. He requires the guiding hand of counsel at every step in the proceedings against him. Without it, though he may not be guilty, he faces the danger of conviction because he does not know how to establish his innocence (287 U.S. 45 [1932]).

Nine years later, in 1972, the U.S. Supreme Court once again expanded the reach of the Sixth Amendment's right to counsel clause in *Argersinger v. Hamlin*, 407 U.S. 25 (1972). In this case, the criminal defendant was charged with the misdemeanor crime of carrying a concealed weapon. This offense carried a maximum sentence of six months in jail. When the indigent defendant requested court-appointed counsel, the trial court refused, explaining that the defendant did not have a constitutionally protected right to counsel in his case. The Supreme Court once again overruled the trial court and held that the right to counsel attaches when a criminal defendant is facing *possible* imprisonment.

These holdings continue to impact our criminal courtrooms today. As a practical matter, the current interpretation of the right to counsel means that unless a criminal offense cannot by statute result in incarceration, or unless a judge is willing to certify that the defendant will not face any jail time even if convicted of a criminal offense, then the judge must appoint the defendant an attorney if the defendant cannot afford to hire one. The right to an attorney attaches even if the defendant is charged with one of the least serious crimes, like disorderly conduct or public intoxication, as long as the state statutes indicate that the defendant is facing possible jail time. The presiding judge can protect the defendant's rights and yet not appoint counsel, so long as the judge certifies on the record that even if convicted, the defendant will not go to jail. In some jurisdictions, judges employ this tactic as a way to reduce public defender workloads and as a way to expedite cases and to increase judicial efficiency.

The Supreme Court has also interpreted the Sixth Amendment to mean that a defendant has a right to effective counsel. The meaning of "effective" has been debated widely in our common law tradition. The term can be extremely difficult to define in criminal defense work, because trial strategy can vary widely. Additionally, the quality of an attorney's work is directly related to the experience and expertise of the attorney. Some legal scholars have asserted that defense counsel should always be expected to "do their best" when representing clients. Many jurisdictions simply used an objective standard of reasonableness to judge the effectiveness of defense attorneys, and relied on the ethical standards under the American Bar Association's Canons of Ethics that required attorneys to represent clients zealously and competently. The objective standard requires the attorney to provide legal assistance, which a reasonably competent attorney would provide in the same circumstances. The U.S. Supreme Court attempted to clarify this widely used objective standard in *Strickland v. Washington*, 466 U.S. 668 (1984), which is considered to be the leading case regarding the effective assistance of counsel. In this case, the Court instituted a two-prong test that must be applied when a defendant alleges that his counsel was ineffective. The Strickland test requires the defendant to show (1) that his counsel failed to meet a reasonableness standard, and (2) that the actions of his counsel probably affected the outcome of the trial. Some commentators have asserted that *Strickland* basically establishes a "but-for" test for attorney competence; that is, the defendant must successfully show that but for the mistakes made by his counsel, the outcome of the trial would have been different. The *Strickland* decision has been criticized for making it too difficult for criminal defendants to prove that their attorneys were ineffective. The reasonableness standard of attorney conduct can give attorneys some flexibility in their conduct. Clearly, *Strickland* does not require perfect, error-free representation. It also does not require that a defendant be provided the best counsel available to represent him. But practically speaking it sets the bar high for defendants to be able to prove that the conduct of their attorneys was so bad that it altered the outcome of the proceedings. However, defendants post-*Strickland* have been quite successful in asserting that their counsel provided ineffective assistance in a variety of cases. Some common examples of egregious attorney misconduct that have been held to rise to the level of ineffective assistance of counsel have included cases when attorneys have slept during trial, drunk alcohol or used drugs during trials, failed to file motions, and failed to assert legal defenses on behalf of their clients. When appellate courts find that the attorney misconduct resulted in the client receiving ineffective assistance of counsel, the courts generally reverse the defendant's conviction and order a new trial. Additionally, attorneys who provide ineffective assistance of counsel may face sanctions from the state bar association that can range from fines to suspension to disbarment.

Ethical Duties

In order to practice law, defense attorneys must be members of the bar in the state where they practice. After graduating from law school, attorneys must apply to take a bar exam in the state in which they intend to practice. They must also pass an ethics exam. Each state bar serves as the governing body of attorneys, and is charged with regulating the practice of law within the state. The bar organizations establish specific ethical rules that lawyers must follow. Most states have enacted ethical rules that are based on the American Bar Association's Model Rules of Professional Conduct, adopted in 1983 as a model for states to use in enacting a code of ethical conduct for lawyers. Lawyers who fail to follow these rules subject themselves to disciplinary actions from the bar, including the possibility of being disbarred. All licensed attorneys are bound to follow the Rules of Professional Conduct that are in effect in the state in which they are licensed. Criminal defense attorneys must be extremely familiar with these rules, and should seek advice from the bar's ethics hotline in the event that an ethical question arises which the attorney is not sure how to handle. In the practice of criminal defense work, there are ethical dilemmas that face the defense attorney routinely. The list of ethical rules is quite long and detailed, so this section will examine some of the most important ethical duties that govern the work of criminal defense attorneys.

There are numerous categories of the ethical rules that apply to the conduct of criminal defense attorneys. But perhaps one of the most important areas involves the decisions that must be made during the scope of the representation. The ABA Model Rules of Professional Conduct address which decisions should be made by the client and which should be made by the attorney. The ethical rules provide that criminal clients must be the ones to make any decision that affects any substantial legal rights. This means that criminal defendants must decide the following issues during the criminal prosecution: whether to accept or reject any plea offer; whether to waive the right to a jury trial; and whether to testify during a trial. Of course, the defense attorney should counsel and advise the defendant on each of those important decisions, but ultimately those decisions must be made by the client. Clearly, all of these substantive legal rights are personal to the client and it makes sense to allow the client to make these decisions after receiving the advice of counsel. But there are some decisions that defense attorneys must make during the course of the representation of the criminal defendant. Under the ABA Model Rules, the defense attorney must make decisions that relate to strategy and procedure, such as what evidence to present during trial, which witnesses to call, whether to give an opening statement, and how to conduct witness examinations. All of these areas relate to the legal training and experience of the defense counsel. The attorney should discuss the trial strategy with the client, but ultimately these decisions must be made by the attorney and should be based on the attorney's expertise and knowledge about what would best benefit the client's position.

Additionally, under the ABA's Model Rules of Professional Conduct, the criminal defense attorney also has an ethical duty to act in a competent manner. This duty was discussed earlier in the context of the effective assistance of counsel. This is the ethical rule that imposes the reasonableness standard on attorney conduct. The rule specifically defines competence to include legal knowledge, skill, thoroughness, and preparation. This rule requires attorneys to prepare adequately for representing clients, and also requires attorneys to handle cases only when the attorney can do so competently. Additionally, this rule explains that lawyers should continue to update their legal knowledge by taking continuing legal education courses in their practice areas so they stay on top of new legal developments.

One of the hallmarks of the defense attorney and client relationship is the attorney-client privilege. This privilege is the oldest recognized privilege in our legal system. It basically states that defense attorneys must keep all communications made by the client confidential. The defense attorney may not share any of the client's secrets, unless the client waives the privilege, or under certain very specific circumstances. For instance, the attorney-client privilege does not protect communications made when a client seeks the attorney's services to commit a future crime. The purpose of the attorney-client privilege is to foster candid discussions between clients and their attorneys. Defense attorneys need to know all the relevant facts in order to represent the client competently, and clients need to know that their secrets are secure. Privileged communications can also include written materials that are provided to the attorney during the representation. The sanctity of the attorney-client privilege is often questioned by those who believe that attorneys should be forced to disclose information when a client confesses to a crime. The privilege is best understood in the context of the protections afforded to the criminal defendant under our Constitution. Our constitution reflects our belief that the government bears the burden of proving the guilt of the defendant with no assistance from the defendant whatsoever.

One of the most important ethical duties of the defense attorney is the duty to keep the client informed. Many state bar associations report that clients complain most frequently about lawyers failing to return their telephone calls. Lawyers must communicate with their clients and must respond to the client's reasonable requests for information. In the context of criminal defense work, this ethical duty requires attorneys to meet with their clients soon in the process and to explain what the client can expect at each stage of the proceedings. This duty also requires the defense attorney to communicate all plea offers made by the prosecutor. This ethical duty requires attorneys to consider the needs of the client in deciding how to communicate effectively. For instance, juvenile clients or mentally impaired clients may require more of the lawyer's time in order to explain the criminal process completely.

Finally, defense attorneys must be careful to abide by the ethical rule that requires that all lawyers follow their duty to be candid towards the tribunal (the court). This rule recognizes that attorneys must protect the interests of their clients, but that they must not do so at the expense of lying to the court. A criminal defense attorney does not have to volunteer facts that are harmful to the client's case, unless the attorney must do so in order to avoid assisting the client in a crime or a fraud. But the duty of candor prohibits the attorney from offering evidence to the court that the attorney knows to be false. This means that an attorney cannot knowingly allow a client to lie in giving testimony. If a lawyer discovers that the criminal defendant has committed or plans to commit perjury, under the Rules the attorney must urge the client to recant or to avoid giving false testimony. If this fails, it is the lawyer's ethical duty to seek to withdraw from representing the client.

Duties of Defense Attorneys

What duties do defense attorneys perform? The duties of defense attorneys are best understood in the context of the constitutional rights of the criminal defendant and in light of the rules that govern the conduct of defense attorneys, both of which have been discussed. At a minimum, the Rules of Professional Conduct require that defense attorneys must meet with their clients as soon as possible and interview them about the charge. If the criminal defendant is in jail, defense attorneys should meet with them as soon as they are appointed or retained. Defense attorneys should attempt to have a reasonable bond set for their clients, and should begin to participate in the discovery process to find out what information the state has. The discovery process is governed by the local rules of criminal procedure, and criminal defense attorneys should be very familiar with the time limits and procedures under the rules. The discovery process requires the prosecutor to share all the information in its possession with the defense attorney. This includes a list of all witnesses who may testify at trial, a copy of all witness statements, a copy of all reports involved in the case. Additionally, and perhaps most significantly, the prosecutor is also required to disclose all exculpatory evidence to the defense attorney. Exculpatory evidence includes all evidence that could possibly support the exoneration of the defendant, including test results or witness statements.

The defense attorney should begin an investigation into the incident as soon as possible, in order to find witnesses or any other information that might be helpful for the defense. Early investigation by the defense attorney or her staff will help the attorney determine whether there are any viable defenses that should be explored. After reviewing the state's evidence, the defense attorney should be prepared to file any necessary pretrial motions on the client's behalf, such as motions to suppress illegally obtained evidence, or motions to dismiss the charges. Once again, the rules of procedure should be consulted regarding the local requirements for filing all motions. The defense attorney must communicate regularly with the prosecutor to determine what charges the prosecutor intends to file, and to find out about any plea offers the prosecutor is willing to make. The defense attorney has an ethical duty to explain all plea offers to the client. If the case looks like it will result in a trial, the defense attorney must thoroughly prepare the case for trial, by conducting depositions, interviewing all potential defense witnesses, conducting legal research, preparing a defense strategy, discussing the trial with the defendant, and filing all necessary pretrial motions. The defense attorney must have all trial preparation completed before jury selection, so that the questions he asks during jury selection will set the tone for the defense strategy. Generally speaking, the more serious the charge the client is facing, the more time the defense attorney should spend preparing for the case. Experienced defense attorneys will have extensive knowledge about what to expect from certain prosecutors or judges, and the defense attorney should use that knowledge to inform the client and to explain what the client should reasonably expect from the process.

Commonly Used Defenses in Criminal Cases

One of the most important strategic decisions that defense attorneys can make involves whether there is a viable defense to the client's alleged criminal conduct. In many crimes of violence, including murder and battery, a defendant may be able to assert the defense of self-defense. Self-defense is a legal defense that claims that the defendant had no other choice of action under the circumstances. Given the appropriate circumstances, self-defense can be a successful defense because it does not deny the actions of the defendant, but merely justifies the actions.

Another commonly used defense in criminal cases is the alibi defense. An alibi defense asserts that the defendant could not have been the perpetrator of the crime because he was somewhere else when the crime was committed. Most rules of procedure require the defense attorney to provide notice to the prosecutor of the intention to use the alibi defense well in advance of trial so that the prosecutor can interview any alibi witnesses the defense plans to call. Strong alibi witnesses can sometimes help the prosecutor decide not to pursue charges against the defendant. Family members usually do not make strong alibi witnesses because of the assumption that family members will do almost anything to protect the defendant from criminal prosecution.

Defense attorneys should also be prepared to explore the insanity defense. Each state has adopted its own definition of insanity, and defense attorneys must certainly be aware of what constitutes insanity in a certain jurisdiction. Basically the insanity defense allows the defense attorney to argue that the defendant did not possess the required *mens rea* when the crime was committed. Most insanity standards define insanity as the inability to know the difference between right and wrong, acting under an irresistible impulse, or having an inability to conform one's conduct to the requirements of the law. Using the insanity defense requires the defense attorney to employ the services of expert psychological witnesses to interview the client to determine whether the client met the legal definition of insanity at the time the crime was committed.

Finally, defense attorneys often use the entrapment defense. Entrapment occurs when the government, usually in the form of police officers, aggressively steps over the line and encourages defendants to break the law. If entrapment has occurred, the defendant is not guilty of criminal conduct. Entrapment defenses can be used successfully in drug sale cases, where undercover officers may be conducting a sting operation and may lure someone into committing a crime they did not intend to commit. Entrapment defenses are also used in prostitution cases, where officers may pose as prostitutes and attempt to find someone to solicit them. Entrapment defenses can be argued successfully to juries, especially when jurors are selected who are inclined to believe that the police sometimes go too far.

Public v. Private Counsel: Is there a Difference in Effectiveness?

In recent years there has been extensive debate regarding the quality of representation indigent defendants receive. Public defenders nationwide have been criticized for having systems in place that hire young, inexperienced lawyers with little legal training and for throwing them into court with heavy caseloads. In contrast, private lawyers have more training and resources to defend their paying clients. Additionally, private attorneys often have established relationships with judges and prosecutors that lead to the perception that they receive better deals for their clients. Sometimes private attorneys are personal friends or campaign contributors to the judges they practice in front of. The problem with this outlook is that it is a bit too simplistic. There are some public defenders who do not receive adequate training; yet there are other offices that have training programs that serve as models. Many public defenders also work so often with the same judges and prosecutors that they are able to provide better representation to their clients than an attorney who has little dealings with that judge or prosecutor. Additionally, sometimes judges are former public defenders and they may be more sympathetic to defendants and their public defenders.

The most recent national statistics compiled by the Bureau of Justice Statistics sheds some light on the differences between public defender representations and private attorney representation. The Bureau reports that the conviction rates for defendants with private attorneys and for those with public defenders were about the same in both federal and state courts. There were notable differences in the incarceration rates and the sentence lengths for these defendants. Defendants represented by public defenders were sentenced to incarceration more often than defendants represented by private attorneys at both the state and federal levels. Perhaps most interestingly, however, is the difference between sentence lengths for the defendants. In both state and federal courts, when defendants were sentenced to jail or prison, defendants represented by private counsel received slightly longer prison sentences on average than those represented by public defenders. These statistics seems to suggest that though public perception of the gap between private and public counsel is wide, in practice there is not that much difference. There is certainly ample evidence to suggest that public defenders' offices should be given more resources. The ABA has also established some guidelines for acceptable caseloads for these offices. There is a recognition that poor performance in defense of the indigent usually has more to do with huge caseloads than with the ability of individual attorneys.

American Bar Association's Guidelines on the Appointment and Performance of Counsel in Death Penalty Cases

Additionally, there has been a recent trend among legal experts to strengthen the standards for attorneys who perform specialized criminal defense work, such as death penalty defense work. Recent examinations of death penalty cases has shown that since the 1970s, over 100 defendants were wrongly convicted at trial for a variety of reasons, among which is the ineffective assistance of defense counsel during the trial. Citing the compelling words of Justice Sutherland that the person facing serious charges "requires the guiding hand of counsel at every stage in the proceeding against him" the guidelines seek to prove that death penalty work requires specialized skill. Given the extraordinary stakes in death penalty cases, most legal scholars recognize that the conduct of defense counsel must also be extraordinary. As a result, the ABA has recently established strict standards that govern the conduct of criminal defense attorneys who represent clients facing the death penalty. The standards, entitled "American Bar Association Guidelines for the Appointment and Performance of Defense Counsel in Death Penalty Cases," are aspirational and not mandatory, and establish that attorneys who handle death penalty defendants should be attorneys with significant trial experience in serious cases.

These standards are also very specific regarding the actions that attorneys must take in all death penalty defense cases. Basically, the standards recognize that death penalty cases are similar in many respects to other criminal cases, but given the extreme nature of the penalty, defense attorneys must work even more diligently in preparing the case for trial. This additional preparation may include the following: the use of more expert witnesses; the use of a strong defense team that includes supporting services; a highly experienced, qualified, and trained defense attorney; and a manageable workload for any attorney working on a death penalty case. These guidelines also stress the importance of the role of the defense attorney "from the moment the client is taken into custody." This policy recognizes the vital role that defense attorneys can have in the early stages of the death penalty case. Defense attorneys who get involved in the most serious cases at this stage can begin exploring mitigating evidence before the prosecutor even makes a decision about whether or not to seek the death penalty. This evidence could be used to help the prosecutor decide not to seek the death penalty.

Additionally, and perhaps most importantly, these standards call for sufficient funding and allocation of resources to be given to attorneys who are appointed in death penalty cases. Given the recent number of prisoners set free from death row after exonerating evidence was discovered, it is important to ensure that attorneys who defend those facing our severest sanctions have the ability to be competent advocates.

KIMBERLY TATUM

References and Further Reading

American Bar Association, Guidelines for the Appointment and Performance of Defense Counsel in Death Penalty Cases, February 2003.

Carlson, R.L., *Criminal Justice Procedure,* 6th ed., Anderson Co., 1999.

Ferdico, J. N., *Criminal Procedure for the Criminal Justice Professional*, 8th ed., Wadsworth Publishing Co., 2002.

Kamisar, L. and Israel, *Modern Criminal Procedure*, West Publishing, 2000.

U.S. Department of Justice, *Two of Three Felony Defendants Represented by Publicly-Financed Counsel,* Bureau of Justice Statistics, November 2000.

See also **Counsel, Right to; Criminal Courts: Personnel; Due Process**

Defenses to Criminal Liability: Justifications and Excuses

Introduction

A defense is a response made by the defendant to a charge in a criminal trial. It is raised after the prosecution has established its case, and permits the defendant to avoid liability even when the government has met its burden of proof on the elements of the offense. There are two general defenses of justification and excuse—these are the focus of this entry. Justification and excuse defenses are referred to as affirmative defenses, because the defendant must raise them in order for the jury to consider them. This is referred to as the burden of production. Generally, the defendant must also meet the burden of persuasion on an affirmative defense, by a "preponderance of the evidence," although some states impose a greater burden of persuasion on the defendant for certain defenses such as the insanity defense, while other states require the prosecution to disprove an affirmative defense beyond a reasonable doubt (Dressler, 1995).

Justification Defenses

A justification defense is raised when the defendant admits responsibility for the act but claims that under the circumstances the act was not criminal, that what was done was lawful. Justified behavior precludes punishment because the conduct lacks blameworthiness. Examples of common justification defenses include self-defense, defense of others or property, consent, and the execution of public duties.

Self-defense

Self-defense may be successfully claimed if the defendants can demonstrate that they used force to repel an imminent, unprovoked attack that would have caused them serious injury (Fletcher, 1978). In such a situation the defendants may only use as much force as they honestly and reasonably believe is necessary to repel the attack—the defendants cannot use excessive force. Additionally, force may only be used against unprovoked attacks. This means the defendants cannot provoke the attack, or if they did, they must have withdrawn completely from the fight before asserting a right to self-defense. Force may be used only when the victims honestly and reasonably believe they are about to be killed or seriously injured. Threats that cannot be taken seriously do not justify the use of force. Force may be used only when an attack is either in progress or "imminent"—meaning it will occur immediately. It cannot be used to prevent a future attack. One cannot claim self-defense against one who is justified in using force, as during an arrest (Hemmens and Levin, 2000). Self-defense may be asserted only against an aggressor using unlawful force. Self-defense applies to both deadly and nondeadly uses of force. One may use deadly force only if faced with it. Less than deadly attacks authorize resort to less than deadly responses.

There are a number of limitations and exceptions to the general rules of self-defense. The retreat doctrine requires that a person must retreat rather than use deadly force if safe retreat is possible. This doctrine places a premium on human life and discourages the use of deadly force unless absolutely necessary, and is endorsed by the majority of states. The true man doctrine, conversely, states that the victim of an attack need not retreat, and may use whatever force is necessary to repel an attack, even if a safe retreat was possible. It is based on the idea that the criminal law should not force a victim to take a cowardly/humiliating position. Few states follow this doctrine today. The castle doctrine states that a person attacked in the home does not have to retreat, even if retreat is possible. This exception to the retreat doctrine is based on the idea that a person's home is their castle, and that one should never be forced by the criminal law to abandon it (Brown, 1991).

Self-defense may also apply to defense of others and, in some circumstances, to the defense of property. Historically, defense of others was allowed only for family members. Most states have expanded this restriction to include other special relationships, such as lovers and friends, while other states have abandoned the special relationship requirement altogether. The "other" must have the right to defend himself for the defender to claim the defense. Thus if A provokes an attack by B, C could not use force against B and claim defense of B. Most states restrict the use of deadly force to defense of the person or the home, and allow only nondeadly force for defense of property. In contrast, some states, such as Texas, allow deadly force to protect land or certain types of property, such as natural gas.

Consent

Consent is a defense to some crimes. Most jurisdictions provide that persons may consent to suffer what would otherwise be considered a legal harm. The acts a person can consent to suffer are quite limited, however, and it must be demonstrated that the consent was voluntary, knowing and intelligent. There can be no duress, trickery, or incompetence involved in obtaining consent. Additionally, one cannot consent after the fact to injuries already received (Dressler, 1995).

Most jurisdictions allow consent only for minor injuries, or for activities society widely recognizes have a high potential for injury. An example of consent is professional athletes who choose to engage in activity where injury similar to an assault may occur, as when a boxer punches another boxer. One cannot consent to serious injury, as doing so is assumed irrational. Thus, one cannot claim consent as a defense in mercy killing or euthanasia cases.

Execution of Public Duties

The common law allowed a public official to use reasonable force in the execution of his official duties. This defense recognizes the value society places on obeying the law, and in permitting those charged with official duties the necessary authority to carry out those duties. Today an agent of the state, such as a police officer or soldier, is permitted to use reasonable force in the lawful execution of his or her duties. This defense allows the use of deadly force under the proper circumstances, and also allows police to engage in activities that are otherwise criminal if they are doing so as part of their law enforcement efforts, such as posing as a drug dealer.

In the early development of English common law, sheriffs and posses could use deadly force to apprehend any fleeing felon. At this time, felonies were capital offenses, and it was particularly difficult to apprehend fleeing criminals. This was known as the fleeing felon rule. The U.S. Supreme Court, in *Tennessee v. Garner* (471 U.S. 1, 1985), held that police use of deadly force to apprehend fleeing criminal suspects was limited by the Fourth Amendment that requires that all seizures be conducted in a reasonable manner. The ruling limited the use of deadly force against fleeing felons who pose a threat to public safety (e.g., armed, violent offenders).

Excuse Defenses

The second type of affirmative defense is the excuse defense. With an excuse defense the defendant admits what he did was wrong but argues that under the circumstances he is not responsible for the improper conduct. Examples of excuse defenses include duress, intoxication, mistake, age, and insanity.

Duress

Duress may be raised as a defense in a limited number of situations. An example of duress is as follows: A is forced to rob a store by B, who holds a gun to A's head and threatens to kill A unless A does as instructed. In this instance A committed a serious crime, the robbery, but did so only to avoid a more serious crime, being murdered by B. Duress is allowed as a defense under the rationale that those forced to commit a crime in such circumstances do not act voluntarily, and the criminal law, as a practical matter, cannot force people to act irrationally against their own self-interest (Kadish, 1987).

At common law, the defense of duress was permitted only when the defendant was threatened with both imminent and serious harm, and the act committed under duress resulted in less harm than the threatened harm. Most states now allow the defense for all crimes except murder (which is never excused), while some still limit the defense to minor crimes. Some states allow the duress defense only under fear of "instant harm," but most still follow the common law "imminent harm" rule. Threats to harm a third person or property do not constitute duress.

Intoxication

There are two forms of intoxication, voluntary and involuntary. Intoxication here refers to the effects of either alcohol or drugs. The effect of intoxication on criminal liability differs according to whether it was voluntary or involuntary (Ward, 1974). Voluntary intoxication never provides a complete defense, but it may be used to mitigate the punishment. Involuntary intoxication may provide a defense if it can be shown that the actors were unaware that they were being drugged. In such cases the actors are excused because they are not responsible for becoming intoxicated; consequently it would be unfair to hold them liable for the resulting uncontrollable and unintended action. Interestingly, the Supreme Court has held that due process does not require that states allow the defense of intoxication (*Montana v. Egelhoff*, 518 U.S. 37, 1996). Obviously, intoxication is also never recognized as a defense in situations where intoxication is an element of the crime, such as drunk driving or public intoxication.

Mistake

There are two types of mistake defenses—mistake of law and mistake of fact. The cliché "ignorance of the law is no excuse" is actually a misstatement. Mistake of law has always excused some (but very little) criminal responsibility. Ignorance is an excuse if the defendant undertakes reasonable efforts to learn the law, but is still unaware that he has violated some obscure, unusual law (Fletcher, 1978). The constitutional prohibition on vague laws means persons must be provided with reasonable notice of what constitutes criminal conduct before they are punished for such conduct.

Mistake of fact excuses criminal liability when it negates a material element of the crime. The mistake must be both reasonable and honest. An example would be if an airline traveler took another passenger's luggage by mistake, thinking it was theirs. Although they have taken the property of another, as in larceny, they lack the requisite intent to deprive another of their property.

Age

Historically, youth has been treated as a defense to criminal liability on the ground that persons below a certain age lack the requisite mental capability to form *mens rea*, or criminal intent. At common law there was an irrebuttable presumption that children under the age of seven years were incompetent. Children between the ages of seven and fourteen were presumed incapable, but this presumption could be rebutted by the prosecution. Children over the age of fourteen were presumed to have the mental capacity to form *mens rea*, but the defense could rebut this presumption (Feld, 2000). Today the various jurisdictions define the age of maturity differently, ranging from sixteen to twenty-one.

Those classified as juveniles are processed through the juvenile justice system rather than the criminal justice system. The juvenile court was established as an alternate, more forgiving approach to juvenile offenders, and was based on the *parens patriae* doctrine, which hold that the state should act in the best interests of a child. Today the *parens patriae* doctrine of the juvenile court is slowly giving way to an increased desire to treat juveniles similarly to adult offenders; hence a number of states have removed juvenile court jurisdiction for serious crimes or repeat offenders, or have lowered the age at which a juvenile can be transferred to adult criminal court (Fritsch and Hemmens, 1996).

Insanity

Insanity is a legal term that describes mental illness. It is not a medical term. Insanity excuses criminal liability by impairing the *mens rea* of the defendant. If a defendant is determined to be insane, then he is not blameworthy or culpable (Morris, 1982). There are several different legal tests for insanity that have been developed over time, usually in response to a particularly egregious crime. They focus on the reason and willpower of the defendant. These tests include the right-wrong test (also called the M'Naghten rule), the irresistible impulse test, and the substantial capacity test. Each of the tests of insanity is slightly different.

The M'Naghten test for insanity focuses on the defendant's intellectual capacity to know what they are doing and to distinguish right from wrong. It is a two-prong test: (1) the defendant must suffer from a disease or defect of the mind; and (2) this must cause the defendant either to not know the nature and quality of the criminal act or to not know right from wrong. This definition prompts a number of questions. (1) What constitutes a "disease of the mind"? Is it any mental problem, or just a severe psychosis? (2) What does "knowing" mean? Most courts have held that it means intellectual awareness, which nearly everyone has. Other courts say it means being able to grasp an act's true significance. (3) What is "wrong"? Does it refer to what is defined as wrong by the law, or rather what is considered immoral?

The irresistible impulse test for insanity is an excuse for criminal liability when defendants are unable to control their conduct or compelled to commit a crime because they suffer from a mental disease or impairment. This test holds that the defendants may not be responsible for controlling their conduct, even if they know the conduct is wrong. This test is broader than the right-wrong test, but critics have argued that it ignores the ability of the mentally ill to engage in reflection. There is great difficulty in distinguishing between irresistible impulses and mere unresisted impulses (Morse, 1985).

The substantial capacity test is defined as when defendants lack substantial capacity to either control their conduct or appreciate the wrongfulness of the conduct. This test was developed by the American Law Institute, which drafted the *Model Penal Code*, and was adopted widely by the states during the 1960s and 1970s. It is a modified version of the right-wrong and irresistible impulse tests. This test states that defendant is not responsible if he lacks "substantial capacity to appreciate criminality of act or to conform his [sic] conduct." It requires that defendants lack substantial, rather than total, capacity. The right-wrong and irresistible impulse tests are ambiguous on this point.

All of these tests have been criticized as either too difficult or too easy for the defense to prove insanity (Dressler, 1995). Courts and legislatures have limited the use of the insanity defense or shifted the burden of proof. This movement stems from a fear that insane defendants will not be adequately punished, or will be released too soon. An example is the 1984 Federal Comprehensive Crime Control Act, passed shortly after John Hinckley was found not guilty by reason of insanity for attempting to assassinate President Reagan. This legislation shifted the burden of proof from requiring the prosecutor to prove sanity beyond a reasonable doubt to requiring the defense to prove insanity by clear and convincing evidence (a tougher standard than the preponderance of the evidence standard usually applied to affirmative defenses). The *Model Penal Code* rejects this approach, and requires the state to prove sanity beyond a reasonable doubt. Some states allow a verdict of "guilty but mentally ill," but require the state to treat the defendants in a hospital instead of putting them in prison. Some states have abolished the insanity defense altogether.

Conclusion

Affirmative defenses have a long history in the criminal law. Most were developed in English common law, and have been codified subsequently in criminal codes. As with any legal doctrine, these defenses are subject to modification over time. As society changes, so does the criminal law. An example is the insanity defense. First adopted by courts as a means of providing clearly incompetent defendants with the opportunity to avoid criminal liability, the insanity defense has been altered so that it is harder to claim.

Although they differ in their elements, justification and excuse defenses provide an important limit to the application of the criminal law. These defenses represent a recognition that not every person who does something that appears to be a crime should be punished for their actions. Whereas the basic elements of an offense (act, intent, and harm) may be present, the law recognizes that some persons still should not be subject to criminal sanction for their conduct. This is because what they did was in fact appropriate (a justification), or because there is some factor that eliminates their personal culpability (an excuse).

CRAIG HEMMENS

References and Further Reading

Brown, R.M., *No Duty to Retreat: Violence and Values in American History and Society*, Oxford University Press, New York, 1991.

Dressler, J., *Understanding Criminal Law*, Matthew Bender, New York, 1995.

Feld, B.C., *Bad Kids*, Oxford University Press, New York, 1999.

Fletcher, G., *Rethinking Criminal Law*, Little, Brown & Co. Boston, MA, 1978.

Fritsch, E.J. and Hemmens, C., Juvenile Waiver in the United States 1977–1993: A Comparison and Analysis of Waiver Statutes, *Juvenile and Family Court Journal*, 46:43 (1996).

Hemmens, C. and Levin, D., Resistance is Futile: The Right to Resist Unlawful Arrest in an Era of Aggressive Policing, *Crime and Delinquency*, 46:472 (2000).

Kadish, S., Excusing Crime, *California Law Review*, 75:257 (1987).

Morris, N., *Madness and the Criminal Law*, Oxford University Press, New York, 1982.

Morse, S.J., Excusing the Crazy: The Insanity Defense Reconsidered, *Southern California Law Review*, 58:777 (1985).

Ward, P., Judicial Activism in the Law of Criminal Responsibility: Alcohol, Drugs and Criminal Responsibility, *Georgetown Law Journal*, 63:69 (1997).

See also **Accident as a Defense to Criminal Liability; Battered Woman Defense to Criminal Liability; Consent as a Defense to Criminal Liability; Duress as a Defense to Criminal Liability; Entrapment as a Defense to a Criminal Liability; Infancy and Immaturity as Defenses to Criminal Liability; Insanity and Diminished Responsibility as Defenses to Criminal Liability; Intoxication as a Defense to Criminal Liability; Mistake of Fact as a Defense to Criminal Liability; Necessity as a Defense to Criminal Liability; Self-Defense as a Defense to Criminal Liability; Statute of Limitations as a Defense to Criminal Liability; Superior Orders as a Defense to Criminal Liability.**

Demonology

The longest standing belief about the cause of crime is *demonology*—that unclean spirits or demons possess the bodies of humans and take control of their actions. Long before the Renaissance brought belief in naturalism and the free will of humankind, primitives, then ancients, barbarians, Greeks, Romans, Druids, Christians, and Muslims credited or blamed gods or demons for the good and evil men do (Fox, 1985; Mathias, Rescorla, and Stephens, 1980; Vold, 1979).

Demonology predominated until the mid-18th century as the explanation for serious crime, with naturalism—before the development of classical thinking about crime (i.e., Cesare Beccaria's *On Crimes and Punishment* in the 1750s)—only rising briefly among the Greeks (e.g., Plato's admonishment that "man's gold has always been the cause of many crimes" and Aristotle's observation that "poverty engenders rebellion and crime") (Mathias et al., 1980). The remnants of demonology continue in the 21st century with exorcism of demons by the Catholic priests as an example. Indeed fundamental or radical (depending on your point of view) Christians and Muslims have continuously seen the work of the devil in the lifestyles of those who do not share their religious beliefs—from the Christian Crusades of the Middle Ages to convert or destroy the infidels (i.e., demon-possessed enemy) to the "Kill the infidels in the service of Allah" Muslim cries of religious fervor in the 21st century.

In prehistoric times, desperate pagans turned to the heavens in a fervent hope that some being stronger than they would intercede on their behalf and save them from the cold, from starvation, from vicious predators, and even from each other. They created gods for all occasions and to protect them from demons from all directions. The Greeks and then the Romans raised the gods and demons interplay to high art form. Today one cannot understand paintings, tapestry, and sculpture in the Mediterranean world without understanding their mythology.

From the Hebrew Bible of the Jews came a God who protected his "chosen people" from many of the demons he had created when he cast his once beloved archangel out of heaven into hell, setting up the eternal battle between good and evil, angels and devils, and God and Satan. With the coming of Jesus and Christianity came a New Testament filled with demons (Ferguson, 1984). Soon after his baptism, Jesus begins to confront demons, as in the synagogue at Capernaum where Christ drove out "the spirit of an unclean demon" from a possessed man to the astonishment of those gathered for Jesus' Sabbath message (Luke 4:31–37).

Later, Luke (8:26–39) tells the story of Legion of the Gerasenes. When Jesus commanded "the unclean spirit" to depart from Legion, the demons begged Jesus not to send them into the abyss, but instead allow them to enter the bodies of a passing herd of swine. Jesus agreed, but as the demons possessed them, the pigs ran down a steep embankment into a lake and drowned. Jesus told Legion to return to his village and "declare how much God has done for you." The story is also recounted in the Gospels of Matthew and Mark. Shortly before going to the cross, Jesus was confronted by Satan, who tried to tempt him to join the forces of darkness and avoid his mortal death, provoking Jesus to command the demon to "get thyself behind me."

Analyzing the impact of demons on early Christianity, Ferguson (1984) concluded: "Jesus accepted the demons as real. ... The demons were acting under the direction of Satan. ... Jesus had authority over demons. ... Jesus gave his disciplines authority over the demons."

Thus, the belief in demons and *other world forces* as the cause of crime is firmly rooted in history, as is the remedy—to use corporal punishment to drive out the evil spirits or capital punishment to destroy the home of the demons (Mathias et al., 1980; Fox, 1985). Sin and crime have often been intertwined—seen as the same phenomenon. Sin is breaking God's law, and crime is breaking man's divinely inspired law. Thus, God-made or man-made, the law was the law, and to break it was sin, often brought on by possession by demons, sometimes as inherent demons ("original sin") (Mathias et al., 1980).

Punishments logically sought to exorcise the demons from the individual and the community. Witchdoctors, for example, often put on grotesque masks and danced around the deviant tribe member to frighten the demons out, drive away the evil spirits, or literally scare "the hell" out of the hapless victim of possession. "Another approach was to concoct a nauseous potion made of saliva, fingernails, feces, pimple pus, urine, nose-pickings, hair, and other obnoxious items and make the patient eat it, thereby making his or her body intolerable for the demons" (Fox, 1985). Still another favorite of the ancients to more modern times was trephination, or drilling holes in the person's skull (often with a sharp stone), to let the demons out. Often archeological expeditions have found ancient graves and even mummies with trephinated openings in the skull.

Some attribute the 1000-year Dark Ages in Europe to belief in demonology—as the populace looked to fervent religious belief and intercession by priests of Christ to protect them from demons. In these Middle Age years (roughly 500–1500 AD), kings and queens claimed to be agents of God; their reign and succession was divinely inspired and thus their actions were not to be questioned by mere mortals. During this time, it was obviously in the best interest of the rulers to have their subjects—primarily serfs—believe they had no real say in their fate, that they were at the mercy of forces beyond their control, with royalty and the royal court the only protection against the demons that were everywhere. The church, likewise, needed the belief in demons to maintain its power and wealth, as it promised intercession between the possessed and the other world, that through faith they would receive God's protection.

During this period, trials by battle and ordeal were instituted to determine if those accused of crimes (e.g., theft, assault, and blasphemy) were indeed victims of demonic possession. Usually the alleged offender (a serf) was forced to fight a soldier in the local brigade of the king's army. If he won, he wasn't possessed, but if he lost, which was more than likely, he was clearly demon inhabited. If he wasn't killed in the battle, he was to be expelled from the community or worse (e.g., hung, dunked, or branded). Ordeal was often a gauntlet where the accused ran down a path between villagers who beat him with sticks or stoned him. If he made it to the end, either he was not possessed or at least "the devil" had been beaten out of him (Mathias et al., 1980). During this period, fear of witches was heightened by some clergy, and persons accused often underwent torture (e.g., the Spanish Inquisition) and faced burning at the stake (e.g., Joan of Arc) to rid the individual and the community of the demons and their human host.

Vold (1979) concluded that Middle Ages Europe "saw a fusion of the intellectual conceptions of demonism and the political and social organization of feudalism. The Inquisition reflects the resulting theocracy… Ritual and procedure developed to determine guilt or innocence, but the principle of explanation is still the operation of an otherworldly power. Crime, or criminal behavior, in this view is then simply evidence of that which everyone knew and accepted … that the individual had been possessed by the devil."

The zeal carried over into the colonies of the New World with the most famous example being the witch trials in Salem, where in a single year, 1692, 19 women and 6 men were sent to their deaths (most hanged to "choke the devil" out of them) after being found to be demon-inspired or witches. This was primarily the result of the fervent preaching by Rev. Samuel Parrish and others, who pictured life for the pilgrims as a battleground for each individual's body and soul between Christ and Satan (Fox, 1985; Boyer and Nissenhawm, 1974).

The remnants of demonology in modern times have primarily involved exorcism, a ceremony around since the early days of Christianity and greatly increased when about 250 AD, special "exorcist" clergy developed (Blatty, 1971; Oesterreich, 1974). Whereas usually performed by the Catholic Church (as shown in Blatty's 1974 movie, *The Exorcist*), in the 1970s an Episcopal Church minister in Park Ridge, Illinois, used exorcism to eliminate vandalism from his suburban church. American evangelist Oral Roberts discussed demon-possession and exorcism at length in his *Twelve Greatest Miracles of My Ministry* (1974).

As the Renaissance brought the popularity of naturalistic, scientific explanations for human behavior to dominance, new interpretations of demonology began to appear. While some dismissed the supernatural approach as primitive and prescientific superstition, others saw more "method than madness" by the demonology advocates. In his study of *The Crime of Crimes: Demonology and Politics in France 1560–1620*, Pearl (1999) concluded the use of demons and witch hunts in that period were used in a power struggle among Catholics, Protestants, royalists and other elites. Pearl, however, found the tactic was not very successful, as the Inquisitions led to many being condemned as witches, often at the behest of Jesuits, but the professional judiciary in France often overturned the convictions, and the local officials often commuted the trial court death sentences to lesser penalties, often to the fury of the Jesuits and other demonologists.

Pearl held: "The science of demons, in France at least, was developed and disseminated in order to tie the Protestant heresy to the machinations of the Devil, and to convince the learned classes, especially indifferent and incredulous clergy and judges that witchcraft should be take seriously as a pressing danger that had to be addressed energetically. But later Pearl concluded: "Political, religious, and judicial moderation triumphed over extremism. Though the demonologists demanded death for witches, the high courts acquitted them. Demonology did not carry the day in France."

Cynics might also look at the practices under demonological theory in the colonies as well, as for almost any crime, corporal or capital punishment to expel the demons could be avoided by paying a fine. Thus if tribute could be paid to the king, suddenly the person was no longer suspected of harboring demons and endangering the community. The severe tests to uncover demon possession were reserved for the illiterate and poor, or, on occasion, for political enemies of the crown.

The concept of free will—applied to crime and criminality by Beccaria—brought with it the belief that human beings held the power to shape their own destinies and could choose their own behavior, choose their own leaders, and choose and even operate their own government. This powerful paradigm switch from demonology and divinely inspired leaders to individual responsibility and elected leaders came just in time to inspire the American colonies to declare their independence and soon afterwards write their own Constitution—both free will documents—and shortly thereafter to the French Revolution and constitutional government. Codes of laws were enacted throughout the western world—replacing predominantly common law—and penalties often involved imprisonment for penance and reform (penitentiaries and reformatories) or simply for retribution. Demons were replaced by human choice—influenced by environment—as the foundation of crime causation theory.

In probably as objective an analysis as possible, Vold (1979) concluded: "Belief in the supernatural is a matter of faith, not a question of information or fact. It is accepted or rejected in terms of individual preferences, but it can never be either established or disproven by methods of scientific inquiry. The theories of scientific criminology can be only the theories reflecting a naturalistic orientation to be problems of causation."

R. Eugene Stephens

References and Further Reading

Bengt, A. and Henningsen, G., Eds., *Early Modern European Witchcraft*, Oxford University Press, Oxford, 1990.

Bengt, A. and Henningsen, G., Eds., *Early Modern Witchcraft*, Clarendon Press, London, 1990.

Blatty, P.W., *The Exorcist*, Bantam Books, New York,1971.

Ferguson, E., *Demonology of the Early Christian World*, Edwin Mellen Press, Lewiston, Queensland, Australia, 1984.

Fox, V., *Introduction to Criminology*, 2nd ed., Prentice Hall, Englewood Cliffs, NJ, 1985.

Mannheim, H. Ed., *Pioneers in Criminology*, Patterson Smith, Montclair, NJ 1972.

Mathias, W., Rescorla, R.R., and Eugene, S., *Foundations of Criminal Justice*, Prentice Hall, Englewood Cliffs, NJ, 1980.

Oesterreich, T.K., *Possession and Exorcism*, translated by Ibberson, D., from 1921 German edition, Causeway Books, New York, 1974.

Pearl, J.L., *The Crime of Crimes: Demonology and Politics in France 1560–1620*, Wilfrid Laurier University Press, Waterloo, Ontario, Canada, 1999.

Pearl, J.L., French Catholic Demonologists and Their Enemies in the Late Sixteenth and Early Seventeenth Centuries, *Church History* (1983).

Vold, G.E., *Theoretical Criminology*, 2nd ed., prepared by Bernard, T.J., Oxford University Press, New York, 1979.

See also **Religion and Criminal Behavior**

Designer Drugs

The term "designer drugs" first appeared in a 1988 article entitled, "Designer Drugs: Past History and Future Prospects," authored by Dr. Gary L. Henderson, a University of California at Davis pharmacologist, in the *Journal of Forensic Sciences*. Designer drugs are basically chemical derivatives or analogues of legitimately produced and controlled substances as defined by the Controlled Substances Act (CSA). Designer drugs are produced within the illicit manufacturing underground and its regulation lies under the Federal Analogue Act, or the "Designer Drug Law" of 1986.

As a result of increased manufacturing and illegal distribution of amphetamine analogs of mescaline, and several lethal overdoses involving opioid derivatives in California, the Drug Enforcement Administration (DEA) led congressional hearings in May of 1986 that essentially solidified the drafting of this novel yet controversial regulatory scheme. Although the range of designer drugs produced in a sophisticated underground laboratory is endless, the remaining portion of this essay will focus on the top three designer drugs common in the illicit marketplace.

According to national and international incidence and prevalence rates, the top three designer drugs and their corresponding analogues are synthetic opiates such as fentanyl analogues: 3-methyl-fentanyl (TMF), meperidine analogue: 1-methyl-4-propionoxy-4-phenylpyridine (MPPP) illicitly converted to 1-methy-4-phenyl-1,2,3,6-tetrahydropyridine (MPTP), phencyclidine (PCP), and phenethylamines. Synthetic opiates, such as the fentanyl and meperidine analogues, represent the largest and most lethal of the designer drugs.

It was first noticed in the U.S. during the late 1960s and early 1970s among the heroin-using population.

Although very similar to heroin and morphine, these synthetic opiates were marketed as a "new" form of street heroin with increased analgesic properties and a reduction in addictive qualities. Moreover, these designer drugs were undetectable in routine drug screening protocols at the time. Street names associated with these substances are New Heroin, China White, Goodfellas, Tango & Cash, Mexican Brown, Poison, Persian White, and Super Heroin. For the illicit user these analogues were increasingly more potent than heroin but with an increased risk of overdose. The common route of administration is injection, followed by snorting and smoking.

Phencyclidine (PCP) and its derivatives represent a broad category of hallucinogens. Although some substances in this category still have legitimate medical uses as a general anesthetic in surgery, i.e. ketamine, its popularity has been more so for its presence among illicit users. For instance, PCP and ketamine (or Special K) are two very popular "club drugs" in the U.S. Most of the phencyclidine analogues, with the exception of PCP and Special K, are popular in the underground manufacturing network because it is easy to produce, and many of the precursor chemicals are undetectable in many existing drug surveillance mechanisms. Street names associated with this particular category of designer drugs are Angel Dust, Super Weed, Magic Dust, Mint Weed, PCP, PHP, PCE, TCP, Hog, and Crystal. Common routes of administration are smoking, snorting, or injecting. The effects, although they vary according to dosage, can include visual, auditory, and tactile illusions, disorientation, amnesia, and in some cases, general violent behavior.

The third subgroup of designer drugs is phenethylamines. The most popular of this subgroup is 3,4-methylenedioxymethamphetamine—MDMA or Ecstasy. This substance is also the preferred "club drug" of choice. Phenethylamines are known for their limited hallucinogenic and euphoriant-stimulant properties. Its low cost in production and marketability makes it one of the most popular substances among illicit manufacturers of designer drugs. Phenethylamines are essentially central nervous system stimulants with an amphetamine base. They first appeared in the illicit market in 1960s, and by the mid-1980s, became strictly regulated by the federal government. Street names associated with this subgroup are E, XTC, Zen, Love Drug, Slits, Eve, BDB, Eden, PMA, PMMA, and DOM.

The most common routes of administration are oral and snorting. There have been instances were individuals have opted to use it as a suppository or intravenously. The effects of these substances include a heightened sense of empathy, mild visual and auditory hallucinations, increased tactile sensitivity, teeth grinding, jaw clenching, difficulty walking, dilated pupils, headaches, irregular heart rhythms, severe abdominal cramps, urinary retention, and stroke. Such effects are mitigated according to dosage, frequency of use, one's current health status, and concurrent use of other drugs. Although dying from the misuse of MDMA is a rare event, in the last five years, there has been a steady increase in lethal overdose episodes attributed to MDMA analogues such as PMA. Contemporary drug screening protocols have only recently been changed to monitor for such derivatives in standard toxicological investigative procedures.

The epidemiology of designer drug use and abuse is the newest challenge for researchers. This is certainly the case for substances identified as phenethylamines. Of the designer drugs presented, users of phenethylamines have been understudied when compared to individuals who use substances such as cocaine, marijuana, and alcohol. The underground manufacturing of this subgroup is astronomical when compared to other illicit drugs. Moreover, users of these substances are commonly involved in multi-drug-using behavior, thereby increasing their risk of negative short- and long-term health effects, at the very least, or a lethal overdose episode, at the very worst. The use of these substances may also increase one's exposure to other forms of risk behaviors, i.e. criminal victimization, driving under the influence or drugged driving, and unprotected sex. When compared to our European counterparts, American public health resources and the criminal justice system have only recently started to monitor the expansion of the phenethylamine market.

Wilson R. Palacios

References and Further Reading

Henderson, G.L., Designer Drugs: Past History and Future Prospects, *Journal of Forensic Sciences,* 33 (1988).

Karch, S.B., *Drug Abuse Handbook.* CRC Press, Boca Raton FL, 1998.

Klee, H., *Amphetamine Misuse: International Perspectives on Current Trends*, Amsterdam, Academic Publishers, Harwood, the Netherlands, 1997.

Jenkins, P., *Synthetic Panics: The Symbolic Politics of Designer Drugs,* New York University Press, New York, 1999.

Lowinson, J.H., Ruiz, P., Millman, R.B., and Langrod, J.G., *Substance Abuse: A Comprehensive Textbook,* 3rd ed., Baltimore, MD, 1997.

Shulgin, A. and Shulgin, A., *Pihkal: A Chemical Love Story.* Transform Press, Berkeley, CA, 1998.

Thornton, S., *Club Cultures: Music, Media, and Subcultural Capital,* Wesleyan University Press, Hanover, NH, 1996.

Valter, K. and Arrizabalga, P., *Designer Drugs Directory,* Elsevier Science, Oxford, U.K. 1998.

See also **Club Drugs**

Detectives *See* **Police: Detectives**

Determinant Sentences *See* **Sentences and Sentencing**

Deterrence, General

General deterrence is a major justification for prescribing and imposing punishment in response to lawbreaking behavior. When the criminal justice system threatens or inflicts punishment, it is expected that there will be less overall crime than would otherwise occur if no penalties existed. In other words, people in the general population will refrain from committing crime due to a fear of being punished. This belief that individuals will curb or avoid criminal behavior because of the potential adverse consequences is essential to virtually any system of criminal law (Zimring and Hawkins, 1973).

The concept of deterrence usually is traced to the development of the classical school of criminology during the latter half of the 18th century. According to classical criminology, humans are rational beings who are guided by their own free will, and both criminal and law-abiding behavior results from conscious choice. Behavioral decisions are made following a consideration of the costs and benefits associated with various actions, and crime generally is selected when it is deemed more beneficial or less costly than noncriminal behavior. Therefore, in order to deter crime, would-be offenders must be persuaded that likely punishments will outweigh the possible gains achieved through breaking the law.

Based on these underlying beliefs, in 1764 Cesare Beccaria proposed a rational system of punishment in his *Essay on Crimes and Punishment*. In reaction to the often arbitrary and cruel systems of justice that were in place at that time, Beccaria presented a series of criminal justice system reforms. His proposals covered such topics as making laws public and easy to understand, eliminating the torture of suspects, the presumption of innocence until proven guilty, equal treatment under the law, and abolishing the death penalty. Furthermore, he stressed that the central purpose of punishment should be deterrence, and to attain maximum deterrence, punishment should be based on the principles of certainty, severity, and swiftness.

Beccaria specifically argued that to deter crime, punishment must be perceived as a highly probable reaction to criminal behavior. He emphasized the certainty of punishment over its severity, cautioning that overly harsh punishments could actually be counterproductive. In line with classical criminology, Beccaria proposed that deterrence would occur if the harm of a punishment simply exceeded the potential gain from a crime. Finally, he placed great emphasis on swiftness (or celerity), maintaining that punishing offenders as quickly as possible following the commission of a crime would leave a lasting impression. Overall, a strong association between crime and punishment is necessary to ensure that would-be offenders choose not to break the law when deciding on a course of action. Deterrence, then, should occur to the greatest extent when potential offenders believe a punishment will likely and swiftly follow a criminal act, and the sanction will be of adequate strength to outweigh any expected benefits from the crime.

In the later 18th and early 19th centuries, Jeremy Bentham extended the ideas of Beccaria and the classical school of criminology. While maintaining that individual behavior is governed by free will and rational choice, he asserted that humans engage in a process of "hedonistic calculus," whereby they spend much effort weighing the costs and benefits of their behavior and choosing the one that would be expected to maximize pleasure and minimize pain. This, according to Bentham, necessitates a carefully crafted approach to identifying various types of offenders and supplying an exact amount of punishment to be applied to a specific offense. Like Beccaria, he believed that crime could be deterred if punishment was properly provided, and that the criminal justice system should be responsible for ensuring a fair and effective system of punishment. Finally, Bentham was one of the first to suggest that informal sanctions (those coming from outside the criminal justice system) also may be an effective deterrent for criminal behavior.

It is important to note that two separate types of deterrence were inherent in the writings of Beccaria and Bentham. Specific deterrence pertains to the effect of a punishment on the future behavior of an individual who is sanctioned (Andenaes, 1974). This type of deterrence occurs when someone is punished for a crime and subsequently refrains from breaking the law due to a fear of further punishment (e.g., a speeder receives a ticket and drives more slowly in the future to avoid another citation). In contrast, general deterrence refers to the effect of threatened or imposed punishment on other potential offenders (Blumstein, Cohen, and Nagin, 1978). In other words, general deterrence takes place when sanctions are in place and inflicted on law-breakers, and others in the population are thereby discouraged from committing crime (e.g., a vehicle operator sees another driver receiving a ticket and slows down to avoid a similar penalty). Overall, specific deterrence has been thought to impact on offenders who have been caught and punished, whereas general deterrence most often has been applied to those in the general public who have not experienced sanctioning. The discussion that follows is centered on general deterrence.

Although the concept of deterrence is well over 200 years old, it has only been examined through research during the past few decades. Modern scholars have emphasized the certainty and, to a lesser extent, the severity of punishment, although the swiftness of punishment has received little consideration (Blumstein et al., 1978; Paternoster, 1987). Furthermore, deterrence research has progressed in a number of clearly defined stages. The findings produced from these studies have not always been consistent, but overall, the best evidence available suggests that the sanctions provided by the criminal justice system do produce a significant general deterrent effect, at least for some people and under certain conditions.

In the later 1960s and early 1970s, deterrence research was conducted at the "objective level," whereby comparisons were made between jurisdictions in terms of their levels of punishment risk and corresponding levels of crime (Blumstein et al., 1978). For example, it was expected that states with higher levels of punishment certainty (i.e., greater rates of arrest or imprisonment for specific crimes) and severity (i.e., lengthier time served for the offense) would exhibit lower crime rates. These studies by and large found inconsistent support for this hypothesis, but it did appear that the certainty of punishment had a greater general deterrent effect than punishment severity (Zimring and Hawkins, 1973). However, it was hard to determine from this research whether levels of punishment impacted on crime, or whether crime rates actually impacted on punishment levels. It could be that jurisdictions with lower crime rates are better able to arrest and incarcerate those who break the law. It was also suggested that at lower levels, punishment certainty and severity might fail to deter, but at higher levels, a "tipping effect" may occur when punishment does become a credible threat. Finally, it was proposed that deterrence could depend more on individual perceptions of punishment certainty and severity, rather than objective risk levels, meaning that someone's personal beliefs about punishment risk might be much more important in guiding their behavior than the actual risks that exist at the objective level (Paternoster, 1987).

This recognition of the importance of individual perceptions in the process of deterrence guided much research from the mid-1970s through the mid-1980s. Numerous cross-sectional studies were conducted to examine whether those who perceived punishment to be a certain and severe response to crime were less likely to self-report criminal behavior than were those who believed there was little risk (Paternoster, 1987). By the early 1980s, many of these studies appeared to indicate a moderately strong inverse relationship between perceptions of certain punishment and various criminal behaviors, as those who perceived a higher likelihood of receiving some sort of punishment reported less prior criminal behavior than did those who perceived a lower likelihood of punishment. This same research generally failed to find a similar inverse relationship between the perceived severity of punishment and illegal acts, because a belief that harsh punishment would be imposed was not found to be associated with less criminal behavior.

The perceptual studies discussed above were also soon questioned concerning their methodology. In this research, individual perceptions were measured at a given point in time, and then people were asked about their past behavior. Other researchers began to demonstrate with longitudinal (or "panel") data that active participants in crime often do not get caught and that leads them to lower their estimates of punishment risk (Paternoster 1987). Therefore, the earlier, cross-sectional studies were actually measuring an "experiential effect" of prior behavior on current perceptions of risk, rather than a true deterrent effect of perceived risk on behavior. When the experiential and deterrent effects were separated using a longitudinal design, a much weaker deterrent effect from the perceived certainty of punishment was found than had been suggested through the flawed cross-sectional research. Furthermore, better studies that considered a wider variety of factors that potentially impact on criminal behavior (e.g., rewards, informal sanctions, peer influences, moral beliefs, etc.) found the weakest evidence of a general deterrent effect from the perceived risk of formal sanctions.

By the mid-1980s, perceptual deterrence research seemed to indicate little reason to be optimistic about the general deterrent effect of formal punishments. However, the most methodologically rigorous, longitudinal studies also suggested that people's perceptions of punishment risk were unstable, meaning that these perceptions could change from time to time or situation to situation (Paternoster, 1987). This finding led to a major improvement in recent deterrence research, resulting in conclusions that are more in favor of the presence of general deterrence. In the late 1980s and early 1990s, researchers began to use scenarios or detailed descriptions of situations and then ask people about their perceptions of risk and if they would commit a crime in the presented setting (e.g., "given the situation described, how likely is it that the person in the scenario would be arrested, and would you commit the crime under the same circumstances?"). Using this technique, risk perceptions and behavioral intentions were measured at the same time, overcoming the problems of experiential effects and unstable risk perceptions that had plagued earlier research. These studies have found that, while controlling for a variety of other factors that may influence behavior, a more highly perceived sanction risk does have a significant deterrent effect on a variety of criminal behaviors (Nagin, 1998). Moreover, this research shows that perceptions of sanction risk depend greatly on the context of the situation that encompasses such things as relationship to the victim, presence of witnesses, security devices, and so on.

In addition to the recent scenario-based studies that suggest formal sanctions do produce a general deterrent effect (particularly when the perceived certainty of punishment is high), other types of research have also provided evidence that the presence of legal penalties deters crime. Several studies in a variety of countries have used a time-series design to examine the effect of targeted policy interventions, such as police drunk-driving checkpoints and crackdowns on drug markets (Nagin, 1998). The evidence suggests that these efforts are usually successful in producing an initial general deterrent effect, again based mainly on the increase in punishment certainty that occurs as a result of the intervention, rather than any increase in punishment severity (Sherman, 1990). For instance, Ross's (1992) international research on the impact of police crackdowns on drunk-driving consistently reveals significant decreases in automobile fatalities in the aftermath of highly publicized checkpoints. Unfortunately, this deterrent effect typically begins to decay over time, thereby limiting effectiveness. However, the decrease is often slow and gradual, probably due to individual perceptions of elevated risk taking some time to change. Based on this research, it has been argued that general deterrence can be maximized by a regular rotation of police enforcement strategies that can both create initial deterrence and leave behind "residual" deterrence once police move to another location (Sherman, 1990).

In addition to the time-series research discussed above, the general deterrent effect of the police has been examined through other methods. First, a consideration has been made of what would happen if the police ceased to exist. Studies of police strikes have examined the extreme situation where punishment risk has been greatly reduced or eliminated, due to the police not being available to make arrests. The evidence from a variety of jurisdictions, including the U.S., Europe, and Canada, consistently suggests that in times of minimal or no threat of law enforcement, serious crime substantially and suddenly increases (Andenaes, 1974; Sherman 1995). For example, Makinen and Takala's (1980) study of crime in Helsinki before and during a police strike uncovered large increases in violent crime and emergency room admissions for assault related injuries following the initiation of the strike. Furthermore, research also suggests that cities with greater numbers of police on duty have less crime, apparently due to the increase in punishment risk associated with more police (Nagin, 1998). It appears, then, that police are needed for general deterrence purposes, and again the importance of punishment certainty comes to the forefront.

Other police research has sought to clarify the impact of what police do and where and how they do it. In the mid-1970s, a highly publicized study conducted by the Kansas City, Missouri, police department appeared to indicate that varying amounts of police patrol presence had no effect on crime (Sherman, 1995). Many scholars concluded that although some police presence was obviously needed (in light of the evidence from police strikes), it was foolish to think that more specific police practices could substantially reduce crime. Since that time, however, other research has produced contrary findings. In general, this evidence suggests that a proactive approach, targeting specific places, people, and times, can produce a significant general deterrent effect.

To begin, it is known that crime does not occur in random locations, as certain "hot spot" sites (e.g., certain bars, intersections, parking lots, etc.) are much more crime prone than other places (Sherman, 1995). This piece of information conflicts with the traditional approach to law enforcement that seeks to provide even police visibility throughout a jurisdiction. With this in mind, research has demonstrated that when police patrol efforts are concentrated in high crime areas, crime can be reduced (Sherman, 1995). Other studies suggest that aggressive policing of minor crime and disorder (e.g., public drunkenness, prostitution, or disorderly conduct) can produce a more general deterrent effect on serious crime (Nagin, 1998). Finally, similar findings have also been produced when police focus their efforts on confiscating illegally carried weapons and monitoring known offenders (Sherman, 1995).

Research on the impact of the police supports the presence of a baseline general deterrent effect that appears to be enhanced when targeted strategies are used to increase punishment certainty. Other studies have considered whether increasing the severity of punishment generates any crime reduction effect. Over the past 25 years, prison populations have grown rapidly, and recent reforms (e.g., mandatory and determinant sentencing, parole abolition, transferring juveniles to adult court) are often supported on the grounds that they will deter crime. Unfortunately, there is no clear answer to the question of how much general deterrence has been produced from these efforts. Some research suggests that the impact has been negligible, whereas other evidence indicates a significant or dramatic effect (Myers, 2001; Nagin, 1998). These mixed findings are further complicated by the difficulty associated with separating deterrent effects from incapacitating and rehabilitative effects (i.e., crime could be reduced simply by incarcerating offenders, rehabilitating them, or both). Furthermore, there is little support for any general deterrent effect produced by modern and highly popular incarceration policies directed at drug offenders. In fact, these strategies may actually increase the attractiveness of other crimes to potential offenders. All in all, it seems that efforts to increase punishment severity are not nearly as successful in producing general deterrence as those directed at increasing punishment certainty.

In addition to the major areas of research discussed to this point, there have been other efforts to extend the study of general deterrence beyond the restraining effect of the threat or use of formal, legal punishments. Several scholars have suggested that formal sanctions may deter best when they lead to informal sanctions (Andenaes, 1974; Zimring and Hawkins, 1973; Nagin, 1998). Here, people are deterred from crime because they fear such negative consequences as losing a job, being dismissed from school, or receiving disapproval from significant others. Informal sanctions could also be internal or self-inflicted, as in the case of feelings of remorse and shame. When researchers have included these types of punishments in their studies, they have often been found to inhibit crime better than the threat of formal sanctions (Nagin, 1998). It should be noted, though, that for informal sanctions to deter, individuals must have a stake in conformity (i.e., they must have something to lose). Obviously, if someone has few valued social relationships, a lack of commitment to conventional activities, and poor moral values, it would be hard to expect that the threat of informal sanctions would inhibit their criminal behavior.

Another area of interest concerns the importance of formal sanction delivery. First, it is illogical to believe that general deterrence will occur if a sanction threat is not viewed as credible (Nagin, 1998). If policies are not administered as intended or if penalties are rarely imposed (owing to a lack of enforcement of the law, plea bargaining, or some other reason), perceptions of punishment risk are likely to be low. Therefore, general deterrence probably will be weak or nonexistent if the population has knowledge that punishment will not be imposed for certain behavior (e.g., in the case of drug laws not being enforced in certain locations or jurisdictions). Another important and related factor concerns perceptions of the fairness of the sanction. If police officers, prosecutors, judges, or juries believe that a punishment is being unfairly threatened or imposed, they may act to eliminate the sanction or reduce its magnitude. This process likely will impact on punishment credibility, resulting in diminished general deterrence.

Much has been learned about general deterrence over the past 30 years. However, as discussed by Nagin (1998), there is a strong need for further research and theoretical development. Although the weight of the evidence suggests that formal and informal sanctions do produce at least a marginal, short-term, general deterrent effect (i.e., people seem to at least curtail their criminal behavior under certain circumstances because of the fear of punishment), relatively little is known about any longer-term effects. Secondly, although the importance of individual perceptions of punishment risk has been established, it is not yet clear as to how these risk perceptions are formed (e.g., by some overall knowledge of criminal justice system effectiveness, information obtained from others, or by personal experience with sanctioning). Third, recent research suggests that some targeted policy interventions (e.g., drunk driving crackdowns, hot spot policing) can produce a general deterrent effect, but questions remain concerning the significance of how these efforts are implemented in different locations and under various circumstances. Finally, the discrepancy between policies in their intended form and the way they are actually administered should be a central issue in the continued study of general deterrence.

David L. Myers

References and Further Reading

Andenaes, J., *Punishment and Deterrence,* University of Michigan Press, Ann Arbor, MI, 1974.

Beccaria, C., *Die delitti e delle pene,* 1764; as *On Crimes and Punishments*, translated by Young, D., Hackett Publishing, Indianapolis, IN, 1986.

Bentham, J., An Introduction to the Principles of Morals and Legislation, in Browning, J., Ed., *The Works of Jeremy Bentham,* Russell and Russell, New York, 1962.

Blumstein, A., Cohen, J., and Nagin, D., *Deterrence and Incapacitation: Estimating the Effects of Criminal Sanctions on Crime Rates,* National Academy of Sciences, Washington, DC, 1978.

Makinen, T. and Hannu T., The 1976 Police Strike in Finland, *Scandinavian Studies in Criminology,* 7 (1980).

Myers, D.L., *Excluding Violent Youths from Adult Court: The Effectiveness of Legislative Waiver,* LFB Scholarly Publishing, New York, 2001.

Nagin, D.S., Criminal Deterrence Research at the Outset of the Twenty-First Century, in Tonry, M., Ed., *Crime and Justice: A Review of Research,* Vol. 23, University of Chicago Press, Chicago, IL, 1998.

Paternoster, R., The Deterrent Effect of the Perceived Certainty and Severity of Punishment: A Review of the Evidence and Issues, *Justice Quarterly,* 4 (1987).

Ross, L.H., *Deterring the Drinking Driver: Legal Policy and Social Control,* D.C. Heath, Lexington, MA, 1982.

Sherman, L.W., Police Crackdowns: Initial and Residual Deterrence, in Tonry, M. and Morris, N., Eds., *Crime and Justice: A Review of Research,* Vol. 12, University of Chicago Press, Chicago, IL, 1990.

Sherman, L.W., "The Police," in *Crime,* in Wilson, J.Q. and Petersilia, J., Eds., Institute for Contemporary Studies, San Francisco, 1995.

Zimring, F.E. and Hawkins, G.J., *Deterrence: The Legal Threat in Crime Control,* The University of Chicago Press, Chicago, IL, 1973.

See also **Beccaria, Cesare; Bentham, Jeremy; Deterrence, Specific (Special); Punishment Justifications**

Deterrence, Specific

Along with general deterrence, specific or special deterrence is commonly offered as a major reason for punishing criminal offenders. When known lawbreakers are punished for their behavior, there is usually an expectation that they will refrain from committing further crime due to a fear of additional punishment. In other words, it is anticipated that the experience of some unpleasant punishment will inhibit offenders from breaking the law in the future. As first discussed by Gibbs (1975), it may be that for some offenders the experience of punishment will lead to a complete cessation of criminal behavior (i.e., absolute deterrence), whereas others subsequently may exhibit a reduction in the seriousness or frequency of their offense (i.e., restrictive deterrence). In general, the widespread belief in specific deterrence often leads to calls for stricter law enforcement and harsher sentencing, as applying more certain and severe sanctions would seem to enhance the specific deterrent effect.

Specific deterrence, like general deterrence, has its roots in the development of the classical school of criminology during the 1700s. Based on the classical school's notion that humans are rational beings, guided by free will and conscious choice, it seems logical that those who are punished for committing crime would choose not to do so again. Assuming that the administered sanction was of great enough magnitude to outweigh the gains achieved through breaking the law, punished offenders subsequently should decide on a course of action that would not trigger further adverse consequences. These beliefs were inherent in the writings of both Cesare Beccaria and Jeremy Bentham in the latter 18th and early 19th centuries, and the idea that criminals will alter their behavior in response to imposed punishment remains highly popular among politicians and the public alike.

Unfortunately, the question of how legal punishments actually affect future criminal behavior is not an easy one to answer. An enduring debate in the field of criminology concerns whether formal sanctions reduce or amplify future criminal offending. In other words, rather than producing a specific deterrent effect, the experience of legal punishments could increase the future offending of those who are sanctioned. This increase in criminal behavior may be due to diminished opportunities for success in legitimate activities (e.g., school or jobs), or it may arise through a process of self-identification and value development in which the individual who is "labeled" a criminal adopts the norms and behavior patterns that are characteristic of the label (Paternoster and Iovanni, 1989). In any case, in contrast to the notion of specific deterrence, being sanctioned or negatively labeled might actually increase someone's involvement in future criminal behavior that has been referred to as a "deviance amplification" (or "backfire") effect.

While studying the effects of legal sanctions requires recognition of the two contradicting behavioral predictions discussed above, the task of conducting research on this topic is made even more difficult by the potential obstacle of selection bias (Smith and Paternoster, 1990). For example, a simple test of whether formal punishments have any effect on subsequent criminal behavior could involve comparisons of future offending across two or more groups that naturally received different court dispositions (e.g., diversion, probation, boot camp, or incarceration). In this case, the findings could indicate that offenders receiving harsher punishments are more likely to recidivate in the future than are those receiving more lenient sanctions that would appear to suggest that harsher punishments fail to provide specific deterrence. However, the design of this hypothetical study is problematic, as assignment to the groups is the result of a nonrandom process where judges are more likely to sentence high-risk offenders (i.e., those committing more serious crimes and/or having more extensive offending histories) to harsher dispositions. These individuals therefore would be more likely to commit future crime regardless of the punishment imposed. Selection bias, then, is a major concern when groups under study differ in terms of more than just the "treatment" that was received. Therefore, research on the specific deterrent effect of formal sanctions needs to be interpreted with caution.

One area of relevant research involves examining the impact that arresting juveniles has on their future behavior. A few early studies suggested that arresting young offenders might escalate (rather than deter) their future offending, although this research tended to suffer from such methodological problems as small sample sizes and poorly matched treatment and control groups. A study by Smith and Gartin (1989) improved upon those earlier efforts. Using data on police contacts for all males born in Racine, Wisconsin, in 1949 and followed until age 25, the authors examined the influence of arrest on subsequent criminal behavior. Contrary to earlier research, Smith and Gartin uncovered evidence that supported the presence of specific deterrence. While controlling for the seriousness of the current offense and the extent of prior offense, being arrested was found to reduce future criminal behavior among those offenders who were arrested as compared to those who were contacted by police but not arrested. More specifically, being arrested was associated with an increased probability of desistance from crime for novice or new offenders, but as offenders acquired more police contacts, the effect of arrest on future police contacts diminished. Still, for those offenders who persisted in their criminal behavior, being arrested increased the time until next police contact. Overall, arrest was found to have a consistently negative effect on the total number of future police contacts.

Whereas the research discussed above focused on the future offending of juveniles who were apprehended relative to those who were not, other studies have looked at the effects of varying degrees of punishment on known offenders. In the much debated and somewhat controversial "Provo Experiment," delinquent boys in Utah were randomly assigned to experimental and control groups (Empey and Erickson, 1972). The experimental intervention was community based and provided intensive treatment services. Comparisons were made with a randomly selected group that had been placed on regular probation, as well as a matched group that was institutionalized in a training school. The effectiveness of the treatment program was evaluated based on arrests both during program participation and after the treatment had ended.

Empey and Erickson (1972) reported that boys in the community-based program were significantly less delinquent while under supervision than those placed on regular probation, and they were no more delinquent than youths in the training school. Juveniles in the latter group committed as much delinquency while at home on short furloughs or following escape as did the experimental group that was free in the community. An analysis of postprogram recidivism revealed little difference between the experimental and control groups. However, when preprogram arrests were compared to postprogram arrests, the results supported both the community program and institutionalization as an effective deterrent to offending. Compared with probation, lower case arrests were reduced by 25% for those juveniles who were institutionalized and by 70% for those in community-based programs.

In a somewhat similar study, Murray and Cox (1979) examined chronic delinquents in Chicago who were either incarcerated in a state reformatory or were diverted to one of several less-custodial community-based programs. All of the youths had lengthy records of delinquency, although those who were chosen for the community programs were presumed to be somewhat less dangerous and perhaps more amenable to treatment as compared to the incarcerated offenders. However, the study did produce several striking outcomes that would appear to support a deterrent effect from increasingly severe formal sanctions. A comparison of preprogram and postprogram delinquent behavior revealed a larger reduction in offending among youths sent to reformatories relative to those who remained in the community. Additionally, for youths who remained in the community, the greatest reduction in arrests occurred among those who experienced the most restrictive forms of supervision. The authors suggested that the findings indicated evidence of a "suppression effect" of recidivism brought about by restrictive sanctions, and that court mandated intervention is the most effective deterrent to chronic juvenile offending. As with the Provo Experiment, these conclusions can be challenged on the grounds that they could be the product of subject maturation over time and on the issue of whether the decline in official arrests represented a decrease in criminal behavior or an increase in the ability to avoid apprehension.

Subsequent researchers studying the effects of varying levels of formal punishment sought to improve the methodology of earlier works. Klein (1986) randomly assigned 306 juvenile arrestees, all initially considered referable for further processing, to four different conditions: release, referral to a social service program, referral to a social service program with purchase of treatment, and formal petition for prosecution. By the end of a six month follow-up period, a trend had emerged that as the level of case processing increased, so did the chances of rearrest. This trend continued through a 27-month follow-up period, with released offenders rearrested less commonly than all others, and petitioned offenders rearrested most commonly. In the middle, there was a widening gap between the two social service conditions. The purchase of treatment, designed to ensure a greater level of rehabilitation, actually yielded an increasingly greater number of arrests.

In general, Klein's (1986) findings on future rearrests indicated that diversion to a community agency was less harmful than petitioning to juvenile court, but more harmful than outright release. In a more detailed study of the same issue, Wooldredge (1988) examined the relative effectiveness of 12 different juvenile court dispositions on eliminating recidivism among 2038 youthful offenders in Illinois. Court actions ranged from case dismissals to incarceration, with a variety of combinations employed. Recidivism was measured based on future juvenile and adult arrests during a follow-up period of three to seven years. While controlling for a wide range of individual and environmental characteristics (but not eliminating the possibility of selection bias), a combination of probation supervision and community treatment was found to be associated with the least recidivism. Contrary to the findings of Klein (1986), 8 of 11 dispositional options yielded lower recidivism rates than the case dismissal option. Shorter terms of supervision and longer terms of community treatment were found to be effective in eliminating and prolonging recidivism, whereas longer terms of incarceration were found to be counterproductive.

Research by Gottfredson and Barton (1993) would appear, at least at first glance, to contradict the findings of Klein (1986) and Wooldredge (1988). Their study investigated the effects of the 1988 closing of the Montrose Training School in Maryland. A group of 673 youths who had been incarcerated in the institution was compared to a group of 254 youths who had a high statistical probability of being institutionalized, but juveniles in the latter group did not go to Montrose because they were referred to the Department of Juvenile Services after admissions had ceased. These youths spent little or no time in any other institution and were instead placed in community-based programs. The authors found that during a 2.5-year follow-up period, the incarcerated juveniles had significantly fewer arrests than the noninstitutionalized youths, but the difference was less substantial when only serious offenses were considered. Nevertheless, the results indicated that recidivism was greater among youths in the community-based programs than among those who were incarcerated, which would imply a specific deterrent, rehabilitative, or combined effect from the more restrictive sanction. However, this study was conducted immediately after the closing of the institution, when the community programs were at the earliest stages of implementation. It may be that if the less restrictive programs had been operating for a longer period of time, the quality of services provided would have been greater, and different results would have occurred.

To continue with the theme of the effects of varying degrees of punishment, several studies have examined the juvenile court's response to offenders referred for the first time. Brown and his colleagues (Brown, Miller, Jenkins, and Rhodes, 1991) reported on a random sample of 500 juveniles who were adjudicated delinquent in Pennsylvania between 1960 and 1975. Their analyses indicated that whereas the type of disposition (i.e., probation vs. placement facility) was not related to future criminal behavior, adjudication at first court referral was associated with less recidivism than was postponed adjudication. Additionally, juveniles who were not adjudicated on their first referral had a rate of ending up in prison as an adult that was double that of youths who were adjudicated on their first referral. In a similar study, Jacobs (1990) reported slightly different findings. Among first-time juvenile court referrals, youths who were formally processed displayed less recidivism than those who were diverted. However, for those juveniles placed under formal court supervision, youths who received out-of-home placements exhibited greater recidivism than did those who received in-home supervision. Finally, in a recent study from the same mold, Minor, Hartmann, and Terry (1997) found that for first-time juvenile court referrals, there was minimal relationship between type of court action and recidivism. The one exception was that for persons entering adulthood during the follow-up period, those who had been formally petitioned for further processing during the first court action were significantly more likely to be charged in adult court than those who were diverted.

The findings of Brown et al. (1991), Jacobs (1990), and Minor et al. (1997), although varying somewhat, appear consistent with those of Klein (1986) and Wooldredge (1988). None of these studies found support for a specific deterrent effect from the harshest of formal sanctions. Some of the findings indicate better results from outright release relative to more intermediate community-based programs, although the weight of the evidence appears to support formal supervision in a structured community setting. The results of these studies contrast with those of Murray and Cox (1979) and Gottfredson and Barton (1993), who found support for institutionalization over other less restrictive programs. It is important to point out that the research by Murray and Cox (1979) and Gottfredson and Barton (1993) focused on more serious and frequent offenders. It is quite possible that the specific deterrent effect of legal punishments varies with the extent of past involvement in delinquent or criminal activity among those who are sanctioned. In other words, formal sanctions may have a different effect on beginning offenders than on experienced offenders.

As previously discussed, Smith and Gartin (1989) found arrest to be associated with an increased probability of desistance among less experienced offenders more so than among the more experienced. Along these same lines, the literature appears to indicate that youths referred to juvenile court for the first time and offenders referred for relatively minor delinquent behaviors exhibit less recidivism when they are not forced to undergo incarceration (Jacobs, 1990; Klein, 1986; Minor et al., 1997; Wooldredge, 1988). On the other hand, for the most serious and frequent offenders, institutional confinement may be an effective response that reduces the likelihood of recidivism (Gottfredson and Barton, 1993; Murray and Cox, 1979).

The answer to the question of whether imposing formal sanctions provides specific deterrence probably is not as clear-cut as the previous paragraph would indicate. The final conclusion may be closer to the argument of Sherman (1993), who claimed that legal punishments can either reduce, increase, or have no effect on future criminal activity, depending on a variety of factors related to the offender, offense, and social setting. In presenting a theory of "defiance," Sherman further suggested that the future criminal behavior of formally sanctioned individuals will be influenced by such things as the degree to which offenders perceive punishment as legitimate, the strength of the social bonds that offenders have with the sanctioning agent and the community, and the extent to which offenders accept the sanctioning without becoming angry and feeling rejected. According to this perspective, rather than asking if imposing punishment on those who break the law deters future offending, it may be much more useful to consider under what conditions various types of sanctions reduce, increase, or have no significant effect on future crimes.

As reviewed by Sherman (1993), research has shown that people tend to obey the law more when they believe a criminal sanction has been administered fairly. On the other hand, those who perceive that they have experienced unjust sanctioning (e.g., by courts or the police) are less likely to comply with the law in the future. Furthermore, a number of well-designed, randomized experiments that examined the impact of arrest on future domestic violence found that arrest reduced repeat domestic violence among employed men who were married, but increased it among those who were unemployed and unmarried. Finally, there is at least limited evidence that older people, who generally have more of a stake in conformity, are more effectively deterred by formal sanctions than are younger people. These findings also suggest that formal sanctions are more likely to provide specific deterrence for those from "in-groups," while punished individuals from "out-groups" are less likely to reduce (and may even increase) future offending. This might explain, for example, why juveniles who are transferred to adult court for prosecution and sentencing consistently exhibit greater, more serious, and faster recidivism as compared to similar youths who are retained in juvenile court (Myers, 2001). It is likely that on average, transferred offenders are more weakly tied to conventional society, and they reasonably could perceive a greater level of unfair treatment coming from the criminal justice system.

A final area of theory and research relevant to the topic of specific deterrence is that of situational crime prevention. A number of countries, such as England, France, Sweden, and the Netherlands, have devoted much attention and research toward preventing future crime through the use of techniques other than traditional law enforcement and criminal justice system efforts (Tonry and Farrington, 1995). Situational crime prevention is one such approach, which, like the notion of specific deterrence, assumes that offenders assess the risk, effort, and payoff in deciding whether to commit a crime. Along these lines, then, offenders could be deterred from committing future crime by increasing the perceived efforts and risks associated with certain criminal behaviors, reducing the anticipated rewards from these same acts, or inducing guilt or shame on the part of the offender (Clarke and Homel, 1997). The belief that offenders are capable of making choices, and that these choices are shaped by a variety a factors surrounding a specific criminal incident, links situational crime prevention with rational choice theory, a modern version of deterrence theory.

As reviewed by Clarke and Homel (1997) and others, situational techniques have been applied internationally in response to diverse criminal behaviors. Corresponding research suggests that these efforts have been successful in reducing drunk driving, income tax evasion, sexual harassment, and theft, in such places as Australia, Great Britain, and in the U.S. Although many of these efforts would appear to provide both a general and specific deterrent effect, some strategies focus on preventing repeat crime by known offenders. For example, along the lines of inducing guilt or shame on the part of an offender, the use of family or community accountability conferences has spread through many countries, including New Zealand, Australia, Singapore, Ireland, South Africa, Canada, the United Kingdom, and the U.S. (Braithwaite, 1999). The goal of this "restorative justice" approach is for victims, offenders, and family and community members to participate in forming a collective response to a specific offense. A strong emphasis is placed on victim empowerment and offender reintegration into the community, with agreed-upon sanctions often being informal and less punitive in nature than traditional justice system punishments. As discussed by Braithwaite (1999), this approach has been found effective in preventing future crime and delinquency among a variety of juvenile and adult offenders, although further research is needed.

To sum up, research on the specific deterrent effect of formal sanctions has not established that punishing offenders will consistently reduce their future criminal behavior. This suggests that expectations for a uniform effect from various punishment efforts, common among politicians and the public, are unrealistic. It does appear that a more certain and moderate justice system response (e.g., arrest, adjudication, and supervision with treatment) provides more benefit than a more severe response (e.g., incarceration), but even this conclusion is based on mixed evidence. Furthermore, it may be that for the most serious and frequent offenders, specific deterrence will only take place following harsher or lengthier punishment. To add to the complexity of this matter, the way that offenders are affected by punishment may be strongly influenced by a number of factors. To this end, the way that sanctioned offenders perceive the fairness of their punishment, the role that social bonds play in the punishment process, the issue of distinguishing specific deterrence from defiance, and the role of situational crime prevention and restorative justice in deterring future crime all promise to be important areas of continued research.

David L. Myers

References and Further Reading

Beccaria, C., *Die delitti e delle pene,* 1764, as *On Crimes and Punishments*, translated by Young, D., Hackett Publishing, Indianapolis, IN, 1986.

Bentham, J., An Introduction to the Principles of Morals and Legislation, in Browning J., Ed., *The Works of Jeremy Bentham*, Russell and Russell, New York, 1962.

Braithwaite, J., Restorative Justice: Assessing Optimistic and Pessimistic Accounts, in Torny, M., Ed., *Crime and Justice: A Review of Research*, Vol. 25, University of Chicago Press, Chicago, 1999.

Brown, W.K., Miller, T.P., Jenkins, R.L., and Rhodes, W.A. The Human Costs of 'Giving the Kid Another Chance', *International Journal of Offender Therapy and Comparative Criminology,* 35 (1991).

Clarke, R.V., and Homel, R., A Revised Classification of Situational Crime Prevention Techniques, in Lab, S.P., Ed., *Crime Prevention at a Crossroads*, Anderson Publishing Co., Cincinnati, OH, 1997.

Empey, L.T., and Erickson, M.L., *The Provo Experiment: Evaluating Community Control of Delinquency*, D.C. Heath, Lexington, MA, 1972.

Gibbs, J.P., *Crime, Punishment, and Deterrence*, Elsevier, New York, 1975.

Gottfredson, D.C. and Barton, W.H., Deinstitutionalization of Juvenile Offenders, *Criminology,* 31 (1993).

Jacobs, M.D., *Screwing the System and Making It Work,* University of Chicago Press, Chicago, IL, 1990.

Klein, M.W., Labeling Theory and Delinquency Policy: An Experimental Test, *Criminal Justice and Behavior,* 13 (1986).

Minor, K.I., Hartmann, D.J., and Terry, S., Predictors of Juvenile Court Actions and Recidivism, *Crime & Delinquency,* 43 (1997).

Murray, C.A. and Cox, L.A. *Beyond Probation: Juvenile Corrections and the Chronic Delinquent*, Sage Publications, Inc., Beverly Hills, CA, 1979.

Myers, D.L., *Excluding Violent Youths from Adult Court: The Effectiveness of Legislative Waiver,* LFB Scholarly Publishing, New York, 2001.

Paternoster, R. and Iovanni, L.A., The Labeling Perspective and Delinquency: An Elaboration of the Theory and an Assessment of the Evidence, *Justice Quarterly,* 6 (1989).

Sherman, L.W., Defiance, Deterrence, and Irrelevance: A Theory of the Criminal Sanction, *Journal of Research in Crime and Delinquency,* 30 (1993).

Smith, D.A., and Gartin, P.A., Specifying Specific Deterrence: The Influence of Arrest on Future Criminal Activity, *American Sociological Review,* 54 (1989).

Smith, D.A. and Paternoster, R., Formal Processing and Future Delinquency: Deviance Amplification As a Selection Artifact, *Law and Society Review,* 24 (1990).

Tonry, M. and Farrington, D.P., *Building a Safer Society: Strategic Approaches to Crime Prevention,* University of Chicago Press, Chicago, IL, 1995.

Wooldredge, J.D., Differentiating the Effects of Juvenile Court Sentences on Eliminating Recidivism, *Journal of Research in Crime and Delinquency,* 25 (1988).

See also **Deterrence, General; Punishment Justifications**

Differential Association Theory

Edwin Sutherland (1883–1950) is probably best known for his development of *differential association theory.* Sutherland was trained in sociology at the University of Chicago, where he was heavily influenced by George Herbert Mead's work in symbolic interactionism. Sutherland's theoretical work had a major impact on criminology in the years to follow the initial presentation of differential association theory, in that his theory helped to divert academic interest away from biological and psychological causes of crime to a closer, systematic examination of social, environmental influences (Vold and Bernard, 1986).

Sutherland first proposed differential association theory in the 1939 edition of his seminal text *Principles of Criminology.* Following revision to the theory, Sutherland offered the first complete statement of differential association in 1947. Here, he set out nine propositions of differential association. These are:

1. Criminal behavior is learned.
2. Criminal behavior is learned in interaction with other persons in a process of communication.
3. The principal part of the learning of criminal behavior occurs within intimate personal groups.
4. When criminal behavior is learned, the learning includes (a) techniques of committing the crime that are sometimes very complicated, sometimes very simple; (b) the specific direction of motives, drives, rationalisations, and attitudes.
5. The specific direction of motives and drives is learned from definitions of the legal codes as favorable or unfavorable.
6. A person becomes delinquent because of an excess of definitions favorable to violation of law over definitions unfavorable to violation of law.
7. Differential associations may vary in frequency, duration, priority and intensity.
8. The process of learning criminal behavior by association with criminal and anticriminal patterns involves all of the mechanisms that are involved in any other learning.
9. Whereas criminal behavior is an expression of general needs and values, it is not explained by those general needs and values, as noncriminal behavior is an expression of the same needs and values (Sutherland and Cressey, 1974: 75–76).

The theory has remained unmodified since the 1947 version was offered and continues to stimulate theoretical research today. These propositions are elaborated upon below.

Criminal Behavior Is Learned. Differential association theory refers to a process of learning criminal behavior. Sutherland's theory therefore is a micro-level processual theory and is distinguished from other macro-level structural theories, such as strain and social disorganization theories. Differential association theory proposes that criminal behavior is learned like any other behavior. The learning, however, takes place in intimate social groups.

Criminal Behavior Is Learned in Interaction with Other Persons in a Process of Communication. Sutherland argued that criminal behavior develops over time as one engages in symbolic and verbal communication with other criminals. This shows the influence of symbolic interactionism on the development of Sutherland's theory. George Herbert Mead's theory of symbolic interactionism states that the human mind develops through the process of social interaction. For Mead, the human mind is not a physical structure, but rather is a mechanism for perceiving and interpreting social cues (e.g., gestures, symbols, and language). Human action and interaction are guided by how such social cues are interpreted (Ritzer, 1983). For example, Mead described the difference in conversation between humans and lower animals. A dogfight is a "conversation of gestures" where one dog's actions lead to the other dog's reactions. Neither dog deliberates over its actions before responding (Mead, 1934, 43).

Human action, on the other hand, is largely influenced by "significant symbols" or "language" (Mead 1934, 46–47). Two people coming together in interaction must interpret both the verbal and nonverbal symbols of the other. However, these symbols must be interpreted in the *context of the situation*. Thus, a gesture or utterance will have different meanings to different people in different social situations. A raised fist, for example, may take on several meanings, depending upon the social context within which this gesture is made. If made in a vacant street or alley during the middle of the night, the person interpreting the gesture may perceive danger (as in an impending assault). On the other hand, if the gesture is made on a busy city street during working hours, the person interpreting the gesture may perceive the need for transport (as in hailing a taxi). Here, Mead (1934) and other symbolic interactionists note the importance of the social contexts within which symbolic language is communicated, perceived and interpreted.

The Principal Part of the Learning of Criminal Behavior Occurs Within Intimate Personal Groups. Sutherland argued that individuals have the *opportunity* to learn criminal behavior when they come into contact and communicate with other people who commit crimes. Individuals are taught how to commit crimes (e.g., the skills and techniques) by those already engaged in the practice. For Sutherland, this meant that it is unlikely criminal behavior would be learned from vicarious experiences, such as those in movies, books, magazines and newspapers.

This proposition is interesting because it highlights the importance of the social structure or opportunity structure, or the chances one has of coming into contact with criminals, associating with them and learning criminal techniques. Sutherland argued that economic structures in society influence the opportunities one has to associate with criminals, learn criminal behaviors, and perpetrate crimes. For Sutherland, this was determined by social disorganization (what he later termed differential social organization), where persons from culturally heterogeneous, conflict-ridden neighborhoods had more criminal opportunities. Drawing from Sutherland and early strain theories (Merton, 1957), Cloward and Ohlin (1960) argued that criminal opportunities were determined by a combination of social location and learning environments. That is, one cannot assume that because a person's legitimate learning opportunities are blocked that one will rely on illegitimate opportunities. Rather, both legitimate and illegitimate learning opportunities are unequally distributed in society.

When criminal behavior is learned, the learning includes (a) techniques of committing the crime that are sometimes very complicated, sometimes very simple; (b) the specific direction of motives, drives, rationalizations, and attitudes. This proposition establishes precisely what is learned through association—i.e., both how to commit a crime and what to think about it. Sutherland explained that a person must learn the techniques and skills for committing a crime, along with ways of thinking positively about crime. Thus, the likelihood that a person will commit an offense depends on the degree to which he or she has learned the methods for committing the crime and the associated sentiments, beliefs, and attitudes that support its perpetration. The person who has learned how to commit a crime but does not view the behavior favorably will likely not commit the offense.

The Specific Direction of Motives and Drives is Learned from Definitions of the Legal Codes as Favorable or Unfavorable. Here Sutherland established the role of motivation, directed toward or away from crime. A person likely learns the techniques for committing a crime and associated positive views within groups that favor rule violation and that view crime as acceptable. Criminal techniques and motivations are less likely learned in groups that favor conformity and transmit cultural sentiments opposed to rule infractions.

A Person Becomes Delinquent Because of an Excess of Definitions Favorable to Violation of Law Over Definitions Unfavorable to Violation of Law. "This is the principle of differential association" (Sutherland and Cressey, 1974, 75). Whether a person becomes a criminal depends on the ratio of criminal associations to anticriminal associations (Liska and Messner, 1999). Persons with more criminal associations relative to conventional associations will experience more definitions favorable toward violating the law, so they are more likely to commit crime. Conversely, persons with more conventional associations relative to deviant associations will likely not learn delinquent skills nor acquire deviant definitions, and thus are less likely to commit crime.

Differential Associations May Vary in Frequency, Duration, Priority and Intensity. That one is exposed to criminal or conforming definitions does not alone determine one's chances of becoming either criminal or law-abiding. Rather, it is the character of those definitions that is critical. Criminal behavior is more likely the outcome, where exposure to criminal associations or definitions is repeated and lengthy (frequency and duration), where those definitions were acquired early in one's life (priority), and where the associations involve close emotional bonds (intensity). Thus, it is the quantity and the quality of one's associations that determine what is learned and how one behaves.

The Process of Learning Criminal Behavior by Association with Criminal and Anticriminal Patterns Involves all of the Mechanisms that are Involved in Any Other Learning. Here, Sutherland distinguished between behaviors that are simply imitated and behaviors that are learned, where the latter includes associated favorable definitions. As he put it, "... the learning of criminal behavior is not restricted to the process of imitation. A person who is seduced, for instance, learns criminal behavior by association, but this process would not ordinarily be described as imitation" (1978: 76).

Whereas criminal behavior is an expression of general needs and values, it is not explained by those general needs and values, as noncriminal behavior is an expression of the same needs and values. Innate drives and needs alone cannot account for criminal behavior. What must be explained is why one person chooses a criminal method to satisfy general needs and obtain what is valued and another does not. Both the thief and the waged employee value money. However, one has learned techniques and definitions conducive to stealing money, whereas the other has learned definitions that eschew theft.

Sutherland asserted that the theory of differential association was contained in these nine propositions. Others, however, have argued that many of these propositions are redundant or show how differential association is to be distinguished from other theories. Reduced to its core, the theory "asserts that deviant behavior is an expression of definitions favorable to deviant behavior learned in association with others in intimate social relationships" (eg., Liska and Messner 1999, 63).

Some Concerns About Differential Association Theory

While the theory of differential association has attracted a great deal of interest over the past several decades, it also has attracted criticism. Some, especially control theorists, have charged that the theory is "untestable" (e.g., Hirschi, 1969; Kornhouser, 1978). The problem seems to center on the notion of "definitions favourable to violation of law" and how such definitions can be operationalized or measured. The most common way this has been done is to ask people to report how many of their peers engage in various criminal activities, as well as the extent to which their peers would approve of such behavior.

Warr and Stafford (1991) examined the effect of peers' definitions or attitudes on delinquency. They found that attitudes about delinquency are affected by peers' attitudes, and delinquent attitudes affect delinquency. However, they also found that the delinquent behavior of peers promoted delinquency independent of attitudes. Costello and Vowell (1999) also reached a similar conclusion and found that the behavior of delinquent peers had a greater effect on delinquency than peers' attitudes.

Another concern is that differential association theory incorrectly specifies the temporal sequence differential peer association—delinquency. Some maintain that delinquency may give rise to delinquent associations, which then reinforce further delinquency. Thus, the assertion is that "birds of a feather flock together" (Glueck and Glueck, 1950). Glueck and Glueck (1952) observed, for example, that many delinquent gang members were involved in crime before they joined gangs.

Other criticisms center around how the media plays a critical role in the way criminal behaviors are learned. Sutherland theorized that "criminal behavior is learned in interaction with other persons in a process of communication" and that "the principal part of the learning of criminal behavior occurs within intimate personal groups." Thus, the impersonal nature of media plays an unimportant role. The controversy surrounding the potential link between media depictions of crime and violence and criminal and violent behavior has spawned an enormous amount of research, and the bulk of this has established a strong correlation between the two (Curran and Renzetti, 2001). Nevertheless, it remains unclear how media crime and violence is causally linked to criminal and violent behavior.

Finally, differential association theory has been criticized because it fails to specify how deviance is learned. Ronald Akers (1979, 1985, 1998) developed social learning theory to redress these concerns. His theory incorporates concepts from operant psychology to show how "differential reinforcement" features in the learning process. Very briefly, Akers suggested that one's delinquent peer associations are only part of the learning process. One develops delinquent behaviors by observing delinquency, as well as its consequences (e.g., euphoria following drug use or obtained booty following a burglary). If observed consequences are interpreted positively, delinquency is more likely to occur. (More detail about social learning theory is available from the separate entry in this encyclopedia.)

Contemporary Research on Differential Association Theory

Differential association theory has stirred a great deal of empirical research since it was first proposed in the 1940s. Some of the most influential work comes from Matsueda's research program on differential association (e.g., Matsueda, 1982, 1989; Matsueda and Heimer, 1987; Matsueda and Anderson, 1998). Matsueda's most recent work (Matsueda and Anderson, 1998) suggests that the sequence delinquent peer association–delinquency is not unidirectional, but instead reciprocal. That is, associating with delinquent peers gives rise to delinquency, and delinquency reinforces association with delinquent peers. Furthermore, it seems the effect of delinquency on peer associations is stronger than the effect of peer associations on delinquency.

In contrast to Matsueda's conclusions about the influence of "definitions favorable to law violation," Costello and Vowell (1999) found that social bonds and peers' delinquency had the greatest impact on delinquency. They conclude that their findings render more support for social control theory than differential association theory.

Instead of testing differential association theory separately against social control or other theories, Hayes (1997) tested a model of delinquency formation and continuation that draws from social control, differential association and labeling theory. He concluded that weakened social bonds to conventional others increased the chance of meeting delinquent peers, developing friendships, observing and learning delinquent behaviors and engaging in delinquency. Thus social learning and differential association independently explain only part of the delinquency process.

In summary, differential association theory has been the subject of substantial empirical scrutiny since it was first fully explicated in 1947. Since that time the theory has been criticized (eg., Vold, 1958; Costello and Vowell, 1999), as well as praised (eg., Cressey 1960, 1973; Matsueda, 1982). Nevertheless, differential association theory continues to inform theoretical development in criminology, as well as the formation of criminal justice policy.

HENNESSEY HAYES

References and Further Reading

Akers, R., *Deviant Behavior: A Social Learning Approach,* 3rd ed., Wadsworth Publishing Co., Belmont, CA, 1985.

Akers, R., *Social Learning and Social Structure: A General Theory of Crime and Deviance,* Northeastern University Press, Boston, MA, 1998.

Akers, R., Krohn, M., Lanza-Kaduce, L., and Radosevich, M., Social Learning and Deviant Behavior: A Specific Test of a General Theory, *American Sociological Review*, 44, 635–655 (1979).

Akers, R. and Lee, G., Age, Social Learning, and Social Bonding in Adolescent Substance Use, *Deviant Behavior,* 19, 1–25 (1999).

Burgess, R. and Akers, R., A Differential Association-Reinforcement Theory of Criminal Behavior, *Social Forces*, 14, 128–47 (1966).

Cloward, R. and Ohlin, L., *Delinquency and Opportunity,* Free Press, Glencoe, IL, 1966.

Costello, B. and Vowell, P., Testing Control Theory and Differential Association: A Reanalysis of the Richmond Youth Project Data, *Criminology*, 37, 815–842 (1999).

Cressey, D., Epidemiology and Individual Conduct: A Case for Criminology, *Pacific Sociological Review*, 3, 47–58 (1960).

Cressey, D., Other people's Money: A Study in the Social Psychology of Embezzlement, Patterson Smith, Montclair, NJ, 1973.

Curran, D. and Renzetti, C., *Theories of Crime*, 2nd ed., Allyn and Bacon, Boston, MA, 2001.

DeFleur, M. and Quinney, R. A Reformulation of Sutherland's Differential Association Theory and a Strategy for Empirical Verification, *Journal of Research in Crime and Delinquency*, 3, 1–22.

Glueck, S. and Glueck, E., *Unraveling Juvenile Delinquency,* Commonwealth Fund, New York, 1950.

Glueck, S. and Glueck, E., *Delinquents in the Making*. New York: Harper. 1952.

Hayes, H., Using Integrated Theory to Explain the Movement into Juvenile Delinquency, *Deviant Behaviour*, 18, 161–184, (1997).

Liska, A. and Messner, S., *Perspectives on Crime and Deviance,* 3rd ed., Prentice Hall, NJ, 1999.

Matsueda, R. Testing Control Theory and Differential Association: A Causal Modelling Approach, *American Sociological Review,* 47, 489–504 (1982).

Matsueda, R., The Dynamics of Moral Beliefs and Minor Deviance, *Social Forces,* 68, 428–457 (1989).

Matsueda, R., Cultural Deviance Theory: The Remarkable Persistence of a Flawed Term, *Theoretical Criminology,* 1, 429–452. (1997).

Mead, G., Mind, Self and Society: From the Standpoint of a Social Behaviorist, University of Chicago Press, Chicago, IL, 1934.

Merton, R., *Social Theory and Social Structure,* Glencoe, IL, Free Press, 1957.

Ritzer, G., *Sociological Theory,* A Knopf, New York, 1983.

Sutherland, E., *Criminology,* 4th ed., Lippincott Company, Philadelphia, PA, 1947.

Sutherland, E. and Cressey, D., *Criminology,* 9th ed., J. B. Lippincott Company, New York, 1974.

Thornberry, T., Lizotte, A., Krohn, M., Farnworth, M., and Jang, S., Delinquent Peers, Beliefs, and Delinquent Behavior: A Longitudinal Test of Interactional Theory, *Criminology*, 32, 47–83 (1999).

Thornberry, T., Empirical Support for Interactional Theory: A Review of The Literature, in Hawkins, J., Ed., *Delinquency and Crime: Current Theories,* Cambridge University Press, Cambridge, U.K., 1996.

Vold, G., *Theoretical Criminology,* Oxford University Press, New York, 1958.

Vold, G. and Bernard, T., *Theoretical Criminology,* 3rd ed., Oxford University Press, New York, 1986.

Warr, M., and Stafford, M., The Influence of Delinquent Peers: What They Think or What They Do? *Criminology,* 29, 851–866 (1991).

See also **Akers, Ronald L.; Social Learning Theory; Sutherland, Edwin H.**

Differential Oppression Theory

Regoli and Hewitt's (2003) theory of differential oppression in *Delinquency in Societies* argues that children's problem behaviors including crime and delinquency, drug and alcohol abuse, and mental disorders can be understood as adaptive reactions to oppressive social situations that are created by adults. They further argue that oppressive social situations pervade the lives of children: all children are oppressed. Although all children experience oppression, the specific nature and amount of oppression children experience often differs. That is, it falls on a continuum, ranging from simple demands for obedience to rules designed for the convenience of adults to the physical, sexual, and emotional abuse of children.

Because of their social and legal status, children have little power to affect their social world. Compared to adults, children have almost no choice regarding whom they associate with and limited resources available to influence others or to support themselves independently of adults. Therefore, they have the least access to resources that could allow them to negotiate changes in their environment (Finklehor, 1997). From a resource standpoint, adults having superior power in relationship to children are at a considerable advantage in determining and enforcing rules that control the basic lives of children. Compared to parents, teachers, and other adult authority figures, children are relatively powerless and expected to—and are often required to—submit to the power and authority of these adults. When this power is exercised to prevent children from attaining access to valued material and psychological resources, to deny children participation and self-determination, and to impede children from developing a sense of competence and self-efficacy, it becomes oppression.

One consequence of oppression and control is that people are transformed into objects that are acted upon by those in power, as opposed to subjects, who act upon and transform their world. The greater the exercise of control by oppressors over the oppressed, the more they change them into apparently inanimate things or objects, rather than subjects. One group objectifying another allows the dominant group to control the dialogue about the relationship between the two groups, to establish the rules governing the relationship, and even to create the rules for changing the rules (Friere, 1990, 51). Oppression thus restrains, restricts, and prevents people from experiencing the essential attributes of human life—such as sentience, mobility, awareness, growth, autonomy, and will.

Because the identity a person takes on is profoundly shaped by the way others identify and react to her or him (Cooley, 1902; Becker, 1963), these images and labels are likely to have detrimental consequences for children. Children often fully accept the socially constructed notion that they are inferior, incompetent, and irresponsible. In addition, adults' perceptions of children as inferior, subordinate, and troublemakers allow adults to rationalize their oppressive acts. However, the theory of differential oppression asserts that the oppression children experience is much more than a simple label of deviance or delinquency; rather it is the cumulative result of a lifetime of oppression *beginning at conception.*

The theory of differential oppression contends that the behavioral problems children experience are a consequence of the way they are treated by the adults in their lives. It is organized around the following four principles:

1. Because children lack power because of their age, size, and lack of resources they are easy targets for adult oppression.
2. Adult oppression of children occurs in multiple social contexts and falls on a continuum ranging from benign neglect to malignant abuse.
3. Oppression leads to adaptive reactions by children. The oppression of children produces at least four adaptations: passive acceptance; exercise of illegitimate coercive power; manipulation of one's peers; and retaliation.
4. Children's adaptations to oppression create and reinforce adults' view of children as inferior, subordinate beings and as troublemakers. This view enables adults to justify their role as oppressor and further reinforces children's powerlessness.

It is likely that the psychological, emotional, or physical consequences that a child suffers depend on the duration, frequency, intensity, and priority of the oppression, and on the child's stage of development (Sutherland, 1947).

Adaptations to Oppression

The oppression of children has consequence: it leads to adaptive reactions by children. These adaptations minimally include passive acceptance, exercise of illegitimate coercive power, manipulation of one's peers, and retaliation. Each of these adaptations involves a degree of conscious resistance or "fighting back" by children (Rogers and Buffalo, 1974) as they attempt to negotiate or self-maintain their status.

Passive Acceptance

As most people adapt via conformity to strain produced by a disjuncture between culturally defined goals emphasizing success and institutionalized means available to achieve that success (Merton, 1957), most children adapt to oppression through *passive acceptance* of their subordinate and inferior status. This acceptance, or conformity, produces subsequent obedience to their oppressors—an obedience built upon fear that derives from implied threats and intimidation. Due to the higher status generally afforded to males and the low levels of female involvement in delinquency, conformity seems to be a more common adaptation among females (Steffensmeier, 1996; Hannon and Dufour, 1998). As children are inundated by adult domination, they quickly learn that obedience is expected. Such adaptations among children are similar to the passive acceptance of the slave role, adaptations of prison inmates, and immersion in the cycle of violence for battered women.

However, such acquiescence or passive acceptance may be only a facade, presenting to the oppressor the appearance of conformity. Children outwardly appear to accept their inferior positions, but develop a repressed hatred for their oppressors, adapting to the structures of domination in which they are immersed. Once a situation of violence and oppression had been established, it engenders an entire way of life and behavior for those caught up in it—oppressors and oppressed alike. Both are submerged in this situation and both bear marks of oppression. The oppressed are likely to believe they have no purpose in life except those the oppressor prescribes for them.

Passive children do not fully explore personal autonomy. They never become the "authors of their own lives." This repression results in negative self-perceptions that may manifest itself in a wide range of problem behaviors including alcoholism, drug addiction, eating disorders, low self-esteem, and psychiatric disorders (Gecas and Schwalbe, 1986; Tosone, 1998). But passive acceptance by some children may be more than mere expedience, it may be a "weapon" for fighting back. Payment may be demanded for compliance to an inferior status (Rogers and Buffalo, 1974). This might take the form of monetary payment (allowance), occasional privileges or treats (movies, food, or expensive clothes) for continuing conformity. Resistance through passive acceptance may also involve "accidental" failure by a child to complete homework assignments, frequent requests for bathroom passes to get out of class, "forgetting" to be home on time, or feigning illness to avoid school or family responsibilities.

Exercise of Illegitimate Coercive Power

A second adaptation is the *exercise of illegitimate coercive power.* Many adolescents are attracted to delinquency because it helps them to establish a sense of autonomy and control. This anticipatory delinquency is a yearning for adult status (Matza, 1964; Katz, 1988). Delinquent acts can immediately and demonstratively make things happen and provide the child with a sense of restored potency denied him or her by adults and parents. Sexual misbehavior, illicit use of drugs or alcohol, and violations of the criminal law derive greater symbolic importance for the child to the extent they demonstrate resistance to adult attempts to exert control over his or her behavior.

The "sneaky thrill" that accompanies vandalism, joyriding, and shoplifting, for example, is not simply a product of the rush of the act, but a consequence of knowing that "you" are controlling the event. That is, "you" selected the time, the place, and the act. It was not accidental, nor was it done as a result of others' expectations. Eating disorders, especially among female adolescents, are another way of demonstrating a sense of autonomy and control. When a young girl perceives that she has little or no control over her own life, that her parents determine all important activities and goals, she may then choose to exert absolute control over what food is taken into or kept in her body.

Manipulation of One's Peers

A third adaptation is the *manipulation of one's peers.* This is an attempt by the child to become empowered. Through manipulation of others within the peer group, a child who has experienced oppression at the hands of adults may acquire a sense of strength and control or a degree of empowerment not otherwise felt. The potential for social power depends in great part on the opinions of those with whom a child interacts (Marwell, 1966): "If one is thought strong, one, by and large, is strong, or at least, may use 'strength' to manipulate others." Establishing a reputation as being "real bad" or a true "badass," and being willing to back the reputation up with a readiness to hurt others in immediate and extreme ways enables a youth to manipulate both situations and people (Katz, 1988).

Boys who experience adult oppression and resent their imposed inferior status may attempt to gain a sense of power by controlling girls through verbal manipulation. The sexual labeling of girls through the use of such terms as *slut*, *bitch*, or *whore* reinforces the subordinate status of girls relative to boys (Schur, 1984) and contributes to the double oppression of adolescent girls as both children *and* female. Girls also verbally manipulate peers, especially female peers, in an attempt to establish social hierarchies, eliminate competition for attention, release tensions without violence, or define group membership and friendships (Fleisher, 1998).

Retaliation

The fourth adaptation is *retaliation* that may include delinquent acts ranging from property crimes to violent offenses. It is the least common of the adaptations to oppression, and it is often also the most serious. Children may engage in retaliation or "getting back" at the people or the institutions they believe are the source of their oppression. Teachers are often the objects of assaults by students, with an average of about 14,000 serious violent crimes committed against teachers each year (Kaufman et al., 2001). School vandalism sometimes occurs because a student is angry with a teacher or principal (Ianni, 1989).

Some children severely oppressed by parents may retaliate by striking directly at their parents, assaulting or killing them (Post, 1982; Mones, 1985; Paulson et al., 1990; Flowers, 2002). Parents who are excessively demanding or verbally or physically abusive are instrumental in producing a retaliatory or assertively defensive aggressive response by the child. Reprisals by children may even produce an effective challenge against abusive parents.

Finally, some children may retaliate against their parents by turning inward—by becoming chronically depressed and contemplating or committing suicide (Chandy et al., 1996; Plass, 1993). During the early 1990s, nearly 2200 children between the ages of 10 and 19 committed successful suicides annually in the U.S. Although the specific motives for most adolescent suicides are unknown, anecdotal data suggest retaliation against a parent or other significant adult is not uncommon.

Few, if any, delinquency prevention programs attack the root problem of oppression: the need to change adult perceptions of children that reinforce beliefs that children are inferior to adults and must submit to adult legal and social control over their lives. The micro forces that operate to allow individual decisions to abort a fetus, to demean a child, to beat a child for violating adult rules, or to neglect a child's health, education, or general welfare require changing how adults perceive children in the first place. Ameliorating structural deficiencies found in society will not necessarily change what adults believe about the nature of children and proper relationships between adults and children.

Changing adult perceptions of children is essentially similar to approaches taken to change racist and sexist beliefs. These approaches may include legislation (ranging from no spanking laws to greatly strengthening legal protections against abuse and neglect), education (ranging from appropriate future parent training to broadly teaching both children and adults about the valuing of children as persons and citizens), and promoting social pressure to accept children as autonomous persons (Regoli et al., 2003; Gill, 1991). Prohibiting all physically assaultive behaviors (including spanking, whipping, slapping, twisting of ears, and washing mouths with soap) and emotionally assaultive behaviors (including ageist statements, threats of abandonment, and simple intimidation) by punitive parents, teachers, and adults generally will be a beginning. Reduction in racism and sexism has been slow, but change is very evident. Reducing adult oppression of children will likely be an even slower process.

ROBERT M. REGOLI

References and Further Reading

Becker, H., *Outsiders: Studies in the Sociology of Deviance,* Free Press, New York, 1963.

Chandy, J., Blum, R., and Resnick, M., Gender-Specific Outcomes for Sexually Abused Adolescents, *Child Abuse and Neglect,* 20:12, 1219–1231 (1996).

Cooley, C.H., *Human Nature and the Social Order,* Scribner, New York, 1902.

Finklehor, D., The Victimization of Children: A Developmental Perspective, *American Journal of Orthopsychiatry,* 65:2, 177–193 (1997).

Fleisher, M., *Dead End Kids: Gang Girls and the Boys They Know,* University of Wisconsin Press, Madison, WI, 1998.

Flowers, R.B., Family Violence, in Flowers, R.B., Ed., *Kids Who Commit Adult Crimes: Serious Criminality by Juvenile Offenders,* Haworth Press, Binghamton, New York, 2002, pp. 85–89.

Friere, P., *Pedagogy of the Oppressed,* New York, Continuum, 1990.

Gecas, V. and Schwalbe, M., Parental Behavior and Adolescent Self-Esteem, *Journal of Marriage and the Family,* 48:1, 37–46 (1986).

Gill, C., Essay on the Status of the American Child, 2000 A.D., *Ohio Northern University Law Review,* 17:2, 543–580 (1991).

Hannon, L., and Dufour, L., Still Just the Study of Men and Crime? A Content Analysis, *Sex Roles,* 38:1, 63–71 (1998).

Ianni, F., *The Search for Structure,* The Free Press, New York, 1989.

Katz, J., *Seductions of Crime,* Basic Books, New York, 1988.

Kaufman, P., Chen, X., Choy, S., Ruddy, S., Miller, A., Chandler, K., and Rand, M., *Indicators of School Crime and Safety, 2001,* U.S. Department of Education/U.S. Department of Justice, Washington, DC, 2001.

Marwell, G., Adolescent Powerlessness and Delinquent Behavior, *Social Problems,* 14:1 35–47 (1966).

Matza, D, *Delinquency and Drift*, John Wiley & Sons, New York, 1964.

Merton, R., *Social Theory and Social Structure*, Revised Ed., Free Press, New York, 1957.

Mones, P., Relationship between Child Abuse and Parricide—An Overview, in Newberger, E. and Bourne, R., Eds., *Unhappy Families*, Littleton, MA, 1985, pp. 31–38,

Paulson, M., Coombs, R., and Landsverk, J., Youth Who Physically Assault their Parents, *Journal of Family Violence*, 5:2, 121–133 (1990).

Plass, P., African-American Family Homicide: Patterns in Partner, Parent, and Child Victimization, 1985–1987, *Journal of Black Studies*, 23:4, 515–538 (1993).

Post, S., Adolescent Parricide in Abusive Families, *Child Welfare*, 61:7, 445–455 (1982).

Regoli, R. and Hewitt, J.D., *Delinquency in Society*, 5th ed., McGraw-Hill, New York, 2003.

Regoli, R., Hewitt, J.D., and DeLisi, M., A New Direction for Juvenile Justice Policy in the 21st Century, *Pakistan Social Science Journal*, 1:1, 65–69 (2003).

Rogers, J. and Buffalo, M.D., Fighting Back: Nine Modes of Adaptation to a Deviant Label, *Social Problems*, 22:1, 108–118 (1974).

Schur, E., *Labeling Women Deviant: Gender, Stigma, and Social Control*, Random House, New York, 1984.

Sutherland, E., *Principles of Criminology*, Lippincott, Philadelphia, PA, 1947.

Steffensmeier, D., Gender and Crime: Toward a Gendered Theory of Female Offending, *Annual Review of Sociology*, 22:August 459–487 (1996).

Tosone, C., Revisiting the 'Myth' of Feminine Masochism, *Clinical Social Work Journal*, 26:4, 413–426 (1998).

See also **Juvenile Delinquency: Theories of**

Digital Crime

See **Computer Offenses**

Discretion and the Criminal Justice System

What is discretion, and why is it important? In theory, procedural law and criminal justice system rules determine how legal system processes are carried out. But in practice, criminal justice system actors—police, courtroom personnel, and correctional officials—commonly must make decisions requiring them to use their judgment when choosing between possible courses of action—that is, to exercise their powers of discretion. Motorists apprehended for speeding or other traffic violations encounter these powers firsthand when patrol officers choose between issuing verbal warnings and writing citations that result in fines.

Discretion is an integral part of the work of these criminal justice system practitioners, and thus questions about the nature and impact of discretionary decision making are a key part of any analysis of the function of the criminal justice system. The ability to exercise discretion represents a form of power and influence that can be put to various purposes, thus creating ongoing controversy in criminal justice.

Discretion is a necessary aspect of criminal justice decision making, because laws, procedures, and rules designed for universal application must be applied in a variety of situations, each with its own particular circumstances. Thus, criminal justice decision makers must, to some degree, interpret the rules as they apply them to specific cases. The decision maker must consider a wide array of sometimes conflicting considerations, such as how best to use limited criminal justice system resources, agency priorities, the potential impact of a decision on affected parties, and what the interests of justice demand.

For example, consider the problem of determining which crimes the criminal justice system should focus on preventing and sanctioning. Police cannot enforce every law and arrest every lawbreaker, due to a lack of resources, nor would the public support a "total enforcement" approach, given that crimes vary in seriousness and the degree to which they attract public concern. Thus police departments, and individual officers, must prioritize which crimes they will focus on in order to maximize public safety, given the crime problems in their particular jurisdiction. In some counties, for example, police are less likely to arrest offenders who use marijuana compared to other types of drugs. Police officers must frequently exercise discretion in deciding the best course of action to take in a variety of situations. A juvenile who has stolen a small item from the neighborhood store; a speeding driver; a fraternity party fight; all present the officer with decisions about how best to exercise discretion. Because police are the "gatekeepers" of the criminal justice system, the consequences of their discretionary decisions affect not only the specific individuals involved, but the criminal justice system as a whole. Police officers' decisions about how to respond to domestic violence calls, for example, determine whether and how public policies designed to deter domestic violence such as mandatory arrest are actually implemented.

Similarly, other actors in the criminal justice system must weigh many considerations when choosing their actions. Prosecutors arguably possess more discretion than any other criminal justice decision maker, a power that is reflected in the multifaceted nature of the prosecutorial role. Prosecutors review the evidence in a case in order to determine whether charges should be brought, and they may decide not to file charges for a variety of reasons even when the weight of available evidence supports pursuing a case against a particular suspect. For example, prosecutors will often reject cases that they feel are unlikely to result in a conviction, preferring to devote scarce resources to more "winnable" cases. Prosecutors can decide not to file charges "in the interests of justice," for example, by not bringing child endangerment charges against the devastated parents of a child who drowned in the family pool. Prosecutors assess the evidence in a case to determine what types of charges will be filed and then use this as leverage during plea-bargaining. The prosecutor decides the terms of the plea bargain, and can engage in "charge bargaining" in exchange for information from a defendant that will lead to the capture of a more serious criminal thus furthering the pursuit of "bigger fish." Prosecutors make recommendations to the judge on key decisions such as bail and sentencing, and judges typically accept these. These examples illustrate how prosecutorial responsibilities entail the exercise of discretion in the course of setting priorities and making decisions. These decisions, in turn, will influence the work of other legal decision makers, such as the police, the defense attorney, and the judge.

Judges employ their discretion across a wide range of decisions that their work entails. For example, decisions about the admissibility of certain types of evidence at trial. Whereas the rules of evidence specifying the conditions under which certain types of evidence may be admitted are lengthy, each judge must apply these rules in the context of specific circumstances in each particular case. For example, negative evidence of the defendant's character that is "unduly prejudicial" to the defendant's case is generally inadmissible, but it falls to the judge to determine how this applies in the current case. The exercise of judicial discretion came into the public spotlight as never before in the 2000 presidential election, when the nation awaited the decision of the U.S. Supreme Court that would determine who served as the next president.

In the criminal justice system, the process of sentencing is the most publicly visible example of the issues surrounding judicial discretion. The sentencing process traditionally allowed judges great discretion in tailoring the sentence to the circumstances of each particular case. Some judges have created unique sentences for particular defendants; one judge agreed to a plea bargain involving a reduced sentence for a criminal defendant on condition that he write a book report on Homer's *Odyssey.* Other judges have required defendants convicted of drunk driving or spouse abuse to publicly disclose their conviction (on a bumper sticker or a t-shirt) as part of the sentence (Associated Press, 1998). One judge ordered a woman convicted of child abuse to have a contraceptive implant placed in her arm as a condition of probation (*People v Johnson*, 1992).

However, the increasing shift away from indeterminate sentencing in favor of determinate sentencing, and in particular toward mandatory sentencing policies such as "three strikes" laws, has severely constrained judicial discretion in sentencing. The wide latitude previously given judges to determine the appropriate punishment within the ranges specified under the applicable statutes has increasingly been replaced with statutory provisions for punishment that leave judges little discretion in sentencing. Theoretically, this lessening of judicial discretion was supposed to reduce sentencing disparities and promote greater fairness and uniformity in sentencing across jurisdictions. However, it appears that sentencing provisions that reduce judicial discretion may simply shift power from judges to prosecutors (by giving prosecutors even more leverage during plea bargaining) and to legislatures and sentencing commissions (that formulate and interpret the guidelines for determinate sentencing).

Jurors are legal decision makers who possess great discretion in determining the verdict. In theory, a verdict must be based only on the evidence admitted at trial; in reality, jurors can return a verdict that is inconsistent with the evidence in the case—a power known as "jury nullification." For example, jurors may decide to acquit a defendant despite the fact that sufficient evidence to convict exists. A jury may agree with a defendant's claim that a killing occurred in self-defense even when the elements of the claim do not fit the legal definition of self-defense. Although the power of jury nullification is not a legal right, and many jurors may be unaware of this power, it is a reflection of the jury's historic role as the conscience of the community.

The ultimate power of discretion is illustrated in the power of jurors to choose life or death for defendants convicted of a capital crime. In *Furman v Georgia* (1972), the U.S. Supreme Court considered the claim that the death penalty was unconstitutional because of the manner in which it was applied. Opponents of the death penalty argued that it violated the Eighth Amendment ban on cruel and unusual punishment because it was imposed in an "arbitrary and capricious manner." The court agreed, and imposed a moratorium on the use of capital punishment in the U.S. until states could develop ways to provide sentencing guidance to jurors in capital cases. In *Gregg v Georgia* (1976), the Supreme Court examined the jury instructions that Georgia had developed for use by capital jurors. The instructions spelled out the mitigating and aggravating factors that jurors should legally consider in determining the sentence, such as the defendant's emotional state at the time of the crime, the motive for the murder, and the manner in which the victim was killed. Such instructions were accepted by the Supreme Court as evidence that Georgia provided the required "guided discretion" for jurors, and thus Georgia was allowed to reinstate the death penalty. Other states followed suit by developing instructions for capital jurors that would, in theory, help guide jurors' exercise of their sentencing discretion.

In the correctional system, official decision making involves discretion in a variety of ways. Correctional officers exercise their judgment in deciding whether to take disciplinary action against inmates who break the rules, and correctional authorities' assessments of institutional security needs are given deference by most courts during lawsuits challenging the constitutionality of certain correctional practices. For example, inmate lawsuits challenging restrictions on visitors, search and seizure procedures, and monitoring of inmate communications with the outside world have usually failed when correctional authorities presented security arguments in support of such practices.

Parole boards consider recommendations from a variety of interested parties in deciding whether to grant or deny parole to a prisoner, yet ultimately exercise their own judgment in deciding whether the prospective parolee is an appropriate candidate for supervised release. Prisoners who are paroled must comply with specified conditions of parole, such as regular meetings with a parole officer, regular drug testing in some cases, and prompt notification of any change in address. Failure to comply with such conditions is grounds for revocation of parole, and parole officers exercise discretion in deciding whether a violation of one of the conditions for parole is sufficiently serious to merit returning the parolee to prison.

These and other examples of the central role that discretion plays in criminal justice decision making illustrate why controversies about the effectiveness and impact of criminal justice policies and practices frequently involve disagreements over discretion—how it is exercised, by whom, and with what consequences. Discretion is both necessary and dangerous; it can be used appropriately to fine tune justice to the specific situation or case. Or it can become an instrument that promotes injustice, prejudice, and corruption.

The controversy over peremptory challenges is a good illustration of this. In the interests of obtaining fair and unbiased jurors during jury selection, attorneys are allotted a limited number of peremptory challenges that they can use to remove unwanted prospective jurors, with no explanation needed. However, attorneys do not enjoy completely unlimited discretion in this respect; if they appear to be using peremptory challenges to reject jurors solely on the basis of race or gender, they may be required to explain their actions to the court. This limitation on how "peremptories" may be exercised reflects the Supreme Court's determination that use of peremptories to exclude prospective jurors on the basis of race or gender is a violation of the constitutional guarantee of equal protection (*Batson v Kentucky*, 1986; *J.E.B. v Alabama ex rel. T.B.*, 1994). However, critics charge that attorney discretion to use peremptories in an unconstitutional manner remains essentially unchanged.

Discretion can lead to favoritism or prejudice on the part of police officers, prosecutors, judges, and juries; and it can lead to disparities in the way cases are handled by the criminal justice system. The controversy over racial profiling by police officers at its core is a controversy about the manner in which officers can and should be allowed to exercise their discretion. Controversies over judges' power to take case-specific factors into consideration in determining a sentence illustrate the complex nature of the ethical and legal questions that discretion raises. Where judges have complete discretion in choosing the lengths of prison terms for convictees, offenders with similar criminal histories and cases may receive quite different sentences. Such differences may reflect variations in judicial sentencing philosophies, the influence of local courtroom norms, and other factors, but they raise troubling equity questions.

At the other end of the continuum, mandatory sentencing provisions force judges to impose the same sentence on all defendants convicted of the same crime, regardless of substantive differences in the circumstances of the offense and/or the characteristics of the offender. "Three strikes" sentencing provisions, for example, vary by jurisdiction but typically prescribe a long period of incarceration for defendants with prior convictions who are found guilty of a third "serious" crime. As the definition of what constitutes a serious crime can be interpreted to include a wide variety of offenses, this broad-brush approach to sentencing has resulted in sentences of twenty-five years to life for offenders convicted of crimes ranging from theft of food or writing a bad check to murder—raising questions of equity, fairness, and the proportionality of the sentence to the offense. Yet, although the exercise of discretion in the service of tailoring justice may help ensure proportionate sentencing in individual cases, it may conflict with the goal of equality in sentencing across similar cases (Steiker, 1996).

The way in which criminal justice decision makers exercise their discretion is also a critical determinant of whether and how well criminal justice policies are implemented. Criminal justice policies such Miranda warnings or mandatory arrest in domestic violence cases must be implemented by police officers to have some impact; practitioners on the streets and in courtrooms may facilitate or frustrate attempts to reform the criminal justice system depending upon how they choose to interpret and implement policies (Walker, 2001).

Some people argue that fairness and justice require that criminal justice decision makers be allowed—even required—to consider the unique characteristics associated with each case as they consider how to proceed. Other people assert that fairness and justice require constraints on discretion in order to minimize the potential for disparities in the way cases are handled in the justice system, and to reduce the opportunities for unfairness, corruption, and misuse of power that discretion provides. These disagreements about the role that discretion should play in the criminal justice process have led to many laws and policies designed to guide, restrict, or monitor how criminal justice decision makers employ discretion.

Measures intended to regulate the exercise of discretion vary according to the nature of the criminal justice process in a particular location. For example, in the U.S., the decision about whether to treat a juvenile suspect as an adult may rest with the prosecutor, or a judge, or it may be contingent on factors specified by statute (e.g., the nature of the crime and the age of the accused).

In each country, the opportunities for criminal justice officials to exercise discretion vary with the structure and functions of its criminal justice system. Adversarial criminal justice systems, such as those of the U.S. and the United Kingdom, are characterized by different legal philosophies and procedures than inquisitorial criminal justice systems such as those of France and many other countries. The variations among legal systems are further illustrated by looking at tribal justice systems and those based on religious principles (e.g., countries that use Shariah law). Many nations have justice systems that are a blend of statutory and common law, or a blend of secular and religious law, or some other combination. The roles of criminal justice officials in each type of legal system vary greatly in terms of power and responsibilities, and thus the officials' opportunities to exercise discretion.

However discretion is manifested within a particular criminal justice system, the fundamental dilemma underlying discretionary decision making remains: It is an integral characteristic of legal systems, with both the potential to enhance and to undermine the interests of justice.

DIANA GRANT

References and Further Readings

Associated Press, *Judge wants to stick DUI's with 'scarlet letter.'* Reprinted in the Tri-Valley Herald, December 6, 1998, p. 3.

Fionda, J., *Public Prosecutors and Discretion: A Comparative Study*, Oxford University Press, New York, 1995.

Gottfredson, M.R. and Gottfredson, D.M., *Decision Making in Criminal Justice: Toward the Rational Exercise of Discretion,* Perseus Publishing, Cambridge, U.K., 1987.

Miller, J.L. and Sloan, J.J., III, A Study of Criminal Justice Discretion, *Journal of Criminal Justice,* 22:2, (March–April 1994).

Ohlin, L.E. and Remington, F.J., *Discretion in Criminal Justice: The Tension Between Individualization and Uniformity,* State University of New York Press, Albany, 1993.

Steiker, J.M. The Limits of Legal Language: Decision making in Capital Cases. *Michigan Law Review,* 94:8 (August 1996).

Symposium: Discretion in Law Enforcement, *Law and Contemporary Problems*, 47:4, (Autumn 1984). See entire issue devoted to symposium proceedings.

Walker, S., *Taming the System: The Control of Discretion in Criminal Justice, 1950–1990*, Oxford University Press, New York, 1993.

Walker, S., *Sense and Nonsense About Crime and Drugs: A Policy Guide,* 5th ed., Wadsworth/Thomson Learning, Belmont, CA, 2001.

See also **Sentences and Sentencing: Disparities**

Discrimination in Justice

Discrimination on the basis of gender has long been associated with justice issues. Discrimination refers to the differential treatment of individuals or groups based on factors that are unrelated to their behavior or qualifications (Walker et al. 2000). Gender is posited to affect police, court, and correction outcomes, the development and application of criminal and common laws, and criminal and juvenile justice employment opportunities. The role of gender in criminal and juvenile justice practices has been explored independently, and in more recent analyses, in conjunction with race and social class. In short, it is argued that females hold multiple statuses that independently and collectively affect how they are perceived and treated by justice agencies. Analyses that address the intersections of gender, race, and social class highlight this diversity and its impact on experiences.

Discrimination in justice can be systematic, institutionalized, contextual, or individual. Discrimination is systematic when it occurs at all stages of the justice systems, in all jurisdictions, and at all times. Institutionalized discrimination refers to disparities that result from established criminal and juvenile justice policies, whereas contextual discrimination suggests that discriminatory practices and behaviors only take place in certain situations or contexts. Individual discrimination refers to the discriminatory actions of specific persons rather than the entire agency or the criminal or juvenile justice system as a whole. Systematic discrimination best describes the experiences of females in justice historically, although contextual discrimination better characterizes today's justice systems (Belknap, 2001; Martin and Jurik, 1996; Walker et al., 2000).

Gender, Race, Class, and the Justice Process

Gender biases in the criminal and juvenile justice systems are linked to ascribed differences between males and females that relate to expected social roles. These differences that include acceptable forms of behaviors, social status, and occupations, are posited to affect interactions with justice agencies. The chivalry and paternalism hypotheses suggest that female offenders are treated more leniently by the criminal and juvenile justice systems because they are physically weaker and must be protected or because they are less dangerous, less culpable or less likely to recidivate and deserve less punitive treatment (Spohn and Spears, 1997). The evil women hypothesis, on the other hand, argues that females are treated more harshly than males because they have violated gendered roles and laws (Belknap, 2001). Research provides support for both hypotheses, although this support is dependent on the stage of the justice system. Most support for the evil women hypothesis, for example, has been found at the earliest stages of justice decision making. For offenses that violate gender norms, females are more likely to be treated harshly by the police than other criminal or juvenile justice officials. This is particularly true for status offenders (or those who have committed offenses illegal for youth but not adults), especially for females who are suspected of sexual activity. Female status offenders are more likely to be deferred to juvenile court, to be subjected to pelvic exams to determine virginity, and to be removed from the home and institutionalized. Similar gender biases have been found among male and female youths in countries such as England and France. British girls are more harshly sanctioned for sexual activity than British boys; girls in France, England, and Wales are more likely to be removed from home and placed in institutions for status offenses than their male counterparts (Gelsthorpe, 1989; Hudson, 1989).

The differential handling of male and female youths by the juvenile justice system is further related to race and parents' perceptions of acceptable behavior. Official intervention is more likely for White girls who, unlike other female youths of color, fit the stereotypical images of femininity, fragility, and being in need of protection (Datesman and Aickin, 1984). Parents also tend to be less tolerant of the delinquent and criminal behaviors of their daughters and are more likely to report these problems to juvenile justice officials (Chesney-Lind and Shelden, 1992). The Juvenile Justice and Delinquency Prevention (JJDP) Act of 1974 that removed status offenders from secure institutions did not result in equal treatment for youths by race or gender. White girls who had been previously institutionalized were placed in private correctional facilities for inappropriate behavior while African American youths were warehoused in juvenile institutions (Federle and Chesney-Lind, 1992). Unlike the U.S., the abolishment of status offenses in Australia has resulted in more equal treatment for male and female youths as well as a decreasing concern for girls' sexuality (Naffine, 1989).

Most support for the chivalry and paternalism hypotheses has been found in the latter stages of crime processing. There is evidence that females are more likely than males to be placed in diversion programs, to be given pretrial release, and less likely to be incarcerated in felony offense cases and in cases prosecuted in urban courts (Alozie and Johnston, 2000; Daly and Bordt, 1995; Farnworth and Teske, 1995; Maxwell and Davis, 1999; Spohn and Beicher, 2000). The evidence further suggests that differential treatment is reserved for majority females who hold middle-class status (Farnworth and Teske, 1995). Some, however, argue that gender differences in crime processing are not the result of chivalry and paternalism but differences in family and child-care responsibilities, the belief that women are less blameworthy, and the fact that women are subjected to other types of informal social control in their daily lives (Daly, 1994). As a result, it has been suggested that the chivalry or paternalism argument as an explanation of gender differences in crime processing outcomes be abandoned.

Punishment

In addition to crime processing, ascribed differences between males and females have influenced the punishment of offenders both in terms of the types of punishment that they receive and the facilities in which they are incarcerated. Punishment for men and women have historically differed for sexual offenses and offenses against a spouse. During the middle ages, women were burned at the stake for the crime of adultery; during colonial times in the U.S., they were hanged (Belknap, 2001). Half of the women in U.S. prisons in 1923 were convicted of sex offenses (e.g., prostitution, fornication, and adultery); women convicted of sex outside of marriage were charged with fornication and sentenced to prison until 1950 in Massachusetts (Belknap, 2001).

Women and men were incarcerated in the same institutions in the U.S. until 1850, although they were not treated equally. The prison system was designed to respond to the needs of male inmates who represented the majority of the prison population. The creation of female reformatories in 1874 and female prisons in 1930 did little to reduce gender inequality in that these institutions often reinforced stereotypes and limited the opportunities of women inmates through prison programming and practices.

Contemporary women's prisons continue to be quantitatively and qualitatively different from male prisons. Because women represent approximately 6% of the U.S. prison population, women's prisons are smaller and fewer in number. Treatment and training programs for women prisoners in general are distinctively poorer in quantity, quality, and variety, and are considerably different in nature from those for male offenders (Belknap, 2001; van Wormer, and Bartollas, 2000). Frequently women prisoners have less access to or are simply excluded from educational and vocational opportunities, work release programs, halfway houses, and furloughs, and are unlikely to participate in prison industries that teach lucrative work skills. Prison programming for women follow gender norms with training in cosmetology, office skills, typing, sewing, hairdressing, and homemaking. Women prisoners have more restricted access to legal libraries, medical and dental care, and poorer recreational programs and facilities (Rafter, 1989). For example, in 1990, only about half of the U.S. women's prisons had law libraries for prisoners use (Belknap, 2001). Arguments that women prisoners are not major breadwinners or in need of remunerative employment, are in prison for a relatively short period of time, and represent a small proportion of the overall prison population have been used to justify these discriminatory practices (Belknap, 2001). Although correctional programming for females has improved in recent years, it still reflects society's bias that the most acceptable role for females is wife and mother.

Gender, Race, Class, and Criminal and Common Laws

The law has historically treated women as the property of their fathers or husbands. In fact, it was not until 1971 in *Reed v Reed* that women were interpreted as persons under the U.S. Constitution (Price and Sokoloff, 1995). Until this time, courts determined a woman's rights and responsibilities by her status as a wife and mother.

Gender bias in criminal laws occurs as the result of (1) implementing and applying gender-specific laws, (2) applying gender-neutral laws differently to male and female defendants, and (3) applying gender-neutral laws differently in male and female victimizations (Belknap, 2001). The history of statutory rape laws in the U.S. is an excellent example of a gender-specific statute that promoted gender inequality. Statutory rape laws developed out of concern over the age of sexual consent for females, in particular, that of White girls. These laws paid no attention to the age of sexual consent for males and largely ignored the well-being of female youths of color. They also disproportionately affected African American men, who were more likely than White men to be charged with having sex with underage girls (Belknap, 2001). Although most contemporary laws are written to be gender neutral, they often are not enforced equally. An attempt by New York state in 1978 to make the severity of prostitution and patronization equal resulted in nonenforcement by police who failed to penalize male patrons (Belknap, 2001).

Evidence further suggests that criminal laws are often enforced more harshly depending on the gender of the victim. Males accused of rape and battering are often sanctioned more leniently if it is believed that the female precipitated the violence or is not deserving of protection. In 1993, an Ohio judge, for example, sentenced a man with a criminal record to shock probation who had severely beaten his estranged wife and her daughter (from another relationship) with a crow bar because the woman had allegedly been in bed with another man when her estranged husband barged into her home (Belknap, 2001). A female's culpability also varies with race. Because African American women have historically been characterized as loose, hot natured, and aggressive, these women are often not viewed as being the victims of rape and battering (van Wormer and Bartollas, 2000). Distrust of justice authorities has led to the reluctance on the part of African American women to report these assaults.

Although woman battering has existed historically, it was not recognized as a social problem until the 1970s. Traditionally, the law and the justice systems have responded to woman battering as a private issue. Early British Common Law allowed husbands to beat their wives with rods no larger than the thickness of their thumbs. In 1864, a court in North Carolina ruled that the state would not invade the domestic forum or go behind the curtain except in cases of permanent injury or an excess of violence (Dobash and Dobash, 1979). Since the 1970s, there has been the demand that domestic violence be treated as a crime. Many police departments have responded by initiating mandatory arrest policies for batterers. Criminal justice officials' reactions to these policies and laws are often lax. Only about 15–30% of the dispatched police calls for battering result in an arrest (Belknap, 2001). It is not uncommon for judges to do nothing to first time violators of protection orders, perhaps because of their beliefs in a man's right to privacy, or desire to keep families intact. Battered women who kill their husbands have received little leniency in the courts. Women who are released from charges of killing their batterers have typically had to plead insanity or temporary insanity; those who have been convicted often received life imprisonment with no appeals in spite of otherwise clean records.

One of the most infamous examples of gender disparities in sentencing laws is the 1913 Muncy Act of Pennsylvania. The Muncy Act required judges to sentence women who were convicted of felonies to an indeterminate sentence in the Muncy State Industrial Home for Women. The act was discriminatory in that it gave judges much less discretion for sentencing female than male offenders, especially with regard to parole eligibility. Even after it was overturned, an amendment to the act that ordered courts not to fix a minimum sentence for women continued to deny equal treatment for women in the Pennsylvania courts. Unlike Pennsylvania, other states imposed shorter sentences on women offenders, arguing that they had a greater amenability to custodial rehabilitation or a lesser ability to withstand punishment (Rhode, 1994).

Early common laws prohibited women from jury service except in certain capital punishment cases. Even in these situations, all-male juries had the authority to decide whether their female counterparts had reached the correct result (Belknap, 2001). Reasons for excluding women from jury service ranged from homemaker exemptions, the need to shield women from indecent conduct and language, and the lack of suitable lavatory facilities. Although *Taylor v. Louisiana* (1975) stopped the exclusion of women from jury service on the basis of gender, gender disparities may still occur through biased questioning of possible jury members by lawyers. In *Bobb v. Municipal Court* (1983) attorney Carolyn Bobb refused to answer questions regarding her marital status and spouse's occupation during the *voir dire* process, was held in contempt of court and taken into custody. She was sentenced to one day in jail with credit for time served.

Gender, Race, Class, and Justice Employment

Employment in the criminal and juvenile justice system has historically been male dominated. Up until 1972, women were largely excluded from justice occupations; those who did work in the field were relegated to positions that were consistent with gender roles. The passage of the Equal Employment Act in 1972 made it illegal for state and civil service bodies to discriminate in employment on the basis of gender. As a result, criminal and juvenile justice agencies were forced to change hiring practices that greatly increased the number of women working in all parts of the justice systems.

Women in Law

Up until the mid-1800s, women were formally or informally excluded from the practice of law. Law was viewed as a hard-nosed, "male" profession that could impugn the "delicacy" of a female's biological character (Martin and Jurik, 1996; Belknap, 2001). Men could receive legal training either by attending law school or serving as an apprentice or clerk. Both of these avenues were primarily closed to women. Most early female attorneys studied under husbands or brothers who were lawyers. Many women who completed legal training were denied admission to state bars. The westward expansion of the U.S. and the Civil War increased women's access to legal training. It was in the West that the first law schools were open to women. The Civil War afforded women the opportunity to fill vacant clerkships and law school positions. Admission to law schools and other forms of legal training did not mean equal treatment. Male law students often refused to associate with women students and stamped their feet in protest when women tried to recite their lessons. In 1869, Iowa became the first state to formally admit a woman to the bar. By the 1900s, thirty-four states had admitted women to the bar; all states admitted women to the bar by 1920. In comparison, Canada admitted the first woman lawyer in 1897 and England in 1922. The first African American woman lawyer in the U.S., Charlotte E. Ray, gained entry to Howard Law School in the 1880s by using her first and second names in her application. She was never permitted to join the ranks of practicing lawyers and eventually resumed teaching in Brooklyn public schools. Many of the first women practicing law were dedicated to fighting different aspects of discrimination and serving as an advocate for the poor.

Women in law faced other discriminatory barriers including eligibility for judgeships and teaching opportunities in law schools. Women lawyers were not eligible for elective judgeships in most states until the Nineteenth Amendment that was passed in 1920. Although the first woman appointed to a judgeship occurred in 1870, it wasn't until 1922 that a woman was appointed to a state Supreme Court and 1949 when a woman was appointed to the federal bench.

Women's representation as law faculty members further suggests unequal treatment in the profession. Women are poorly represented at the administration and senior faculty levels; only 8% of the law school deans and 16% of full professors are women. Women law faculty are disproportionately in nontenure track slots or are part of legal writing programs that are considered lower status positions in law schools. Because of their roles as mothers and the nature of the profession, women law faculty members often have more trouble gaining tenure. Women spend more time counseling students and those with small children have difficulty meeting the 60–70 hour workweek demand. Female law professors commonly have their legitimacy questioned by male law professors and have their authority challenged by male students. As for female law students, research shows that the Socratic method of learning and competition and conflict may present obstacles for women who generally perform better in cooperative learning atmospheres. Male students are more likely to called on by faculty in class and to have their opinions taken more seriously.

Women lawyers are still less likely to be made partners and are not highly represented in judge positions. When elected or appointed as judges, it is frequently to judgeships consistent with stereotyped gender roles such as family law, divorce courts, juvenile courts, and the lower municipal courts (Martin and Jurik, 1996). Fewer women make the rank of partner: 8% of partners at the top 250 law firms were women. The median income of women is 40% lower than it is for men ten years after graduation from law school (Belknap, 2001). Women tend to have less participation in management decisions and less desirable work assignments. Women are more likely to be in small offices or in solo practices. Women lawyers are more likely to enter government agencies whereas men cluster in prestigious, highly-paid corporate firms.

In the courtroom, women lawyers are sometimes subjected to demeaning forms of address, comments on their physical appearance and clothing, sexist rmarks and jokes, unwanted touching and verbal and physical sexual harassment. Male lawyers are cited for refusing to take direction from female court employees and for treating them like their personal secretaries (Belknap, 2001). Women seeking judgeships experience biased questioning from bar selection committees and unwarranted low marks from lawyers on these committees and in the community who are hostile to the increasing number of women on the bench. Women of color experience particular disrespect in the courts. Today approximately 25% of the U.S. judges are women; 77 women are seated as state supreme court justices. Women are often assigned to jurisdictions based on gendered stereotypes of their expertise such as municipal or domestic court. Approximately 49.4% of the students who began law school in Fall 2000 were women (American Bar Association, 2001).

Despite the generally favorable climate and the unprecedented opportunities for women in law today, a legacy of discrimination remains. Although more women hold faculty and administrative positions in law schools, they are still accorded relatively low prestige, and their main focus is on women's issues rather than business or corporate law. Female law students study case law from the male point of view; only men's opinions are cited. Legal issues that are important to women such as marital rape and wife beating are only dealt with superficially.

For African American women the racism may be rampant. They are excluded from student study groups and commonly viewed as having lower academic ability. Opportunities to practice in high status, powerful, and financially remunerative sectors of the profession were found to be few and far between. Movement from the first to second job was likely to be unilateral.

Women in Policing

Although women first became police officers in 1910, they were restricted to working with women and children. Policewomen were not intended to displace policemen in any way. Their work was merely supplementary. Even though policewomen had the same authority as policemen (they could arrest people), catching criminals was viewed as men's work. It wasn't until the 1970s that the number of women in policing increased and women began to move into less specialized lines of police work. Many police departments were sued for discriminating on the basis of gender, race or both. These lawsuits contested departmental entrance requirements related to education, age, height, weight, and arrest records, selection criteria (including written examinations, agility tests, and veterans preferences), and discriminatory assignments and promotion procedures.

The culture of policing makes the integration of women into the profession difficult. Many men officers continue to believe that women cannot handle the job physically or emotionally and therefore should not be allowed to exercise the moral authority of the state or be integrated into policing. Men's most vocal concerns about women as police usually are stated in terms of physical capabilities. Men express their opposition to women officers through interactional patterns that marginalize and exclude them. Women's social isolation denies them mobility opportunities by limiting information, mentors, informal training, and a sense of comfort on the job. The resistance faced by the first women on patrol was blatant, malicious, widespread, organized, and sometimes life threatening. Many men refused to teach these women skills routinely imparted to new men. They failed to respond quickly or assist women seeking backup. Supervisors often assigned women to dangerous foot beats alone, overzealously enforced rules, depressed women's performance evaluations, sexually harassed them, and ignored women's mistreatment by fellow officers. Beyond individual attitudes is a work culture that is characterized by drinking, crude jokes, racism and demands that women who enter it assume male characteristics to achieve even a limited social acceptability.

Because they comprise only a small proportion of police officers, policewomen are often subjected to higher performance standards than men. Their higher visibility leads to little margin for error. At the same time, women are treated paternalistically, expected to do less than the men, extravagantly praised for doing an average job, denied opportunities to take initiative, and criticized for doing so. They are also pressured to conform to gendered stereotypes of mother, little sister or seductress. The errors of an individual woman are exaggerated and generalized to all women as a class. Double standards also persist regarding language, sexuality, appearance, and demeanor. Women face language dilemmas in deciding whether to curse (and use male language), whether to tolerate men's use of gross language, and how to deal with being called "honey" or "sweetheart" by colleagues. Women supervisors also must deal with the refusal of male subordinates to acknowledge their rank. Socializing off duty also poses interactional dilemmas for women officers. The men often drink together after work and participate in team sports or other shared recreational activities. Women's limited participation in this informal socializing deprives them of an important source of information and feedback, as well as the opportunity to make contacts, cultivate sponsors, and build alliances that contribute to occupational success. Many women choose not to participate in informal police activities because of family obligations and gossip. This protects their reputation but further isolates them.

Because cultural images or stereotypes of White and Black women differ, Black women often are treated according to separate norms and images. They are less frequently put on a pedestal or treated as ladies or little sisters to be protected by White men. Rather, they are treated as jezebels or welfare mothers. White women, particularly those who are physically attractive, are more likely to get inside assignments and protection on street patrol. Black women are less likely than White women to believe that they are recognized when they do a good job.

Research shows that women are more likely to be assigned to staff support and less likely to be assigned to patrol. The prevailing images of women assume that they have office skills and that inside work is feminized and not real policing. Many of the men encourage women officers to reduce the burdens of tokenism encountered on patrol by transferring to assignments viewed as gender-appropriate. In addition, staff assignments tend to have fixed daytime hours that are attractive to many of the women with primary childcare responsibilities.

Officer performance-rating systems and their outcomes are gendered in several ways. Often evaluation forms use sexist language. Evaluation criteria such as personal relations and quantity of work that appear to be gender-neutral, in fact, may be based on performance standards for men. For example, arrests, traffic enforcement, and court attendance are often weighted to the neglect of crime prevention activities and public service. Women are also rated low for assertiveness.

Policewomen and women working in prisons and jails continue to be subjected to insufficient training, gendered work assignments, and performance evaluations that are based on male gender norms (Martin and Jurik, 1996).

Women in Corrections

Women have been employed in the field of corrections since 1793. As with other criminal justice occupations, early women correctional officers were concerned with the welfare of female prisoners. Between 1860 and 1900, middle class women took on the task of reforming women and girls from the lower, more dangerous classes who were incarcerated in male facilities. From the 1930s to the 1970s women worked as administrators, security officers, and counselors in juvenile and women's detention facilities and as probation and parole officers for women and juvenile offenders. Correctional work for women differed greatly from the work environments of males, especially in girls' juvenile facilities where there were long hours and low pay.

In 1977, the U.S. Supreme Court allowed Alabama to exclude women from correctional officers' positions in men's facilites because they represented a threat to security (*Dothard v. Rawlinson* 1977). Many men supervisors and coworkers are fearful that women guards will become too friendly with inmates. They scrutinize and sexualize women's interactions with men inmates, watching for situations in which women get too close. Female guards complain that male guards' interactions with inmates are rarely monitored. This disadvantage is magnified for women guards of color who know inmates as neighbors or relatives. In such cases, the women guards have been transferred to other institutions. The few women in supervisory positions report that men subordinates use both subtle and blatant forms of resistance. If a woman supervisor complains, she appears to be paranoid and a poor manager. Subordinates can undermine authority by going over the head of the woman supervisor and complaining to her superior. Administrators' failure to monitor gender allocation patterns leads to inconsistencies within the same institution. Assignments reflect supervisor discretion and the view of women guards' proper place in the prison. Evaluations can also be biased against women when security is emphasized over service responsibilities. Concern for women's safety often leads men to be more protective of women than of men coworkers. Evidence suggests that women correctional officer suffer significantly fewer assaults than men; when they are assaulted, they are no more likely to be injured than men.

It was not until the 1970s that women supervised male inmates. In all of these occupations, discriminatory practices and behaviors prevented women from achieving equal status, income, and power with their male counterparts. Although the Equal Employment Opportunities Act of 1972 improved the working conditions of women in criminal and juvenile justice and increased their numbers, women continue to face occupational barriers.

Women in Criminal Justice Education

Little research has been conducted on women in criminal justice education, in comparison to other occupations. Flanagan (1990) found that the proportions of women criminal justice faculty members at doctoral degree granting institutions range from 0 to 35% with a mean of 18%. Only 12% of the Directors of Criminal Justice Programs in institutions of higher learning were women in 1990. Eigenberg and Baro (1992) note that 22% of the membership of American Society of Criminology were females in the early 1990s. Women members of the Society had a lower publication rate than men both in terms of articles and books; 16.5% of journal authors were females. Women's lower publication rate may be explained by their low representation on editorial boards; 17% of the editors, associate editors and editorial board members of leading journals were women.

The number of people of color who are faculty members in criminal justice is minimal. The 1993 African American Directory of Criminology and Criminal Justice listed a total of 40 African Americans with completed Ph.D.s in 1987. Gilbert and Tatum (1999) found 52 African American women teaching in criminology and criminal justice programs in 1994. African American scholars have lower publication levels in mainstream journals and are less likely to have published or worked on major grants during their doctoral training.

BECKY TATUM

References and Further Reading

Belknap, J., *The Invisible Woman: Gender, Crime, and Justice*, Wadsworth Publishing Co., Belmont, CA, 2001.

Chesney-Lind, M. and Sheldon, R., *Girls, Delinquency, and Juvenile Justice*, Brooks/Cole, Pacific Grove, CA, 1992.

Daly, K., *Gender, Crime and Punishment*, Yale University Press, New Haven, CT, 1994.

Dobash, R. and Dobash, R., *Violence Against Wives*, Free Press, New York, 1979.

Farnworth, M. and Teske, R., Gender Differences in Felony Court Processing, *Women and Criminal Justice*, 6:2 (1995).

Flanagan, T., Criminal Justice Doctoral Programs in the U.S. and Canada: Findings from a National Survey, *Journal of Criminal Justice Education,* 1:2, 1990.

Heard, C. and Penn, E., *Directory of Minority Ph.D. Criminologists*, Prairie View A and M University, Prairie View, TX, 2000.

Martin, S. and Jurik, N., *Doing Justice, Doing Gender: Women in Law and Criminal Justice Occupations,* Sage Publications, Thousand Oaks, CA, 1996.
Merlo, A. and Pollock, J., *Women, Law, and Social Control,* MASS: Allyn and Bacon, Boston, MA, 1995.
Naffine, N., *Female Crime,* Allen and Unwin, Sydney, Australia, 1989.
National Center for Women in Policing, *The Status of Women in Policing: 1998,* U.S. Government Printing Office, Washington, DC, 1999.
Price, B. and Sokoloff, N., *The Criminal Justice System and Women: Offenders, Victims, and Workers*, Mc-Graw Hill, New York, 1995.
Rafter, N., *Partial Justice: Women in State Prisons 1800–1935,* MASS: Northeaster Press, Boston, MA,.
Spohn, C. and Beicher, D., Is Preferential Treatment of Female Offenders a Thing of the Past? A Multistate Study of Gender, Race, and Imprisonment, *Criminal Justice Policy Review,* 11:2, 2000.
Spohn, C. and Spears, J., The Effect of Offender and Victim Characteristics on Sexual Assault Case Processing Decisions, *Justice Quarterly,* 13:4, 1996.
Walker, S., Spohn, C. and DeLone, M., *The Color of Justice: Race, Ethnicity, and Crime in America*, Wadsworth Publishing Co., Belmont, CA, 2000.
Wilson, N. and Moyer, I., Affirmative Action, Multiculturalism, and Criminology, in Price, B. and Sokoloff, N., Eds., *The Criminal Justice System and Women: Offenders, Victims, and Workers*, Mc-Graw Hill, New York, 1995.
Wormer, K. and Bartollas, C., *Women and the Criminal Justice System*, MASS: Allyn and Bacon, Boston, 2000.

See also **Gender and Criminal Behavior; Police: Race and Racial Profiling; Race and Ethnicity and Criminal Behavior; Social Class and Criminal Behavior; White-Collar Crimes, Definitions of; Women as Offenders and Victims Throughout History**

Disorderly Conduct and Disturbing the Peace

Without specific statute or ordinance, "disorderly conduct" and "disturbing the peace" are synonymous terms of indefinite meaning. At different times in different places, statutes and ordinances have varied considerably in defining what constitutes disorderly conduct. Despite such variations, however, the offense inherently embraces the notion that certain behaviors are of such little social worth that they have no place in an orderly society, and hence will not be tolerated.

Though disorderly conduct was not an offense under English common law, it is akin to the common law offense of breaching the peace. The latter offense, however, allowed for the prosecution of a host of public disturbances including those triggered by private, silent, or covert behavior. In contrast, the enactment of laws making disorderly conduct an offense focused on public behaviors deemed to be either a public annoyance or detrimental to public health, safety, and morals. Because such laws were potentially unlimited in scope, disorderly conduct has at various times in history, such as periods of economic hardship, been utilized to control the movement of disenfranchised people, including the homeless and unemployed. During these periods, the offenses of disorderly conduct and vagrancy become intertwined. Equally important, disorderly conduct has in the past been a means of prosecuting other people considered "socially undesirable" (e.g., known prostitutes, gamblers, thieves, drug dealers, drug addicts, and alcoholics).

Two major events have significantly impacted our contemporary understanding of disorderly conduct. First, court decisions began to reflect that although protecting citizens from potential criminality was clearly a legitimate state interest, the over-breadth of many disorderly conduct laws were utilized to enforce social norms in ways that conflicted with other constitutional principles. In a series of key cases utilizing the void for vagueness doctrine, the U.S. Supreme Court held that: (1) "state regulations may not be achieved by means that sweep unnecessarily broadly and thereby invade the areas of protected freedoms" (*Zwicker v. Kootai*, 389 U.S. 241 88 S.Ct. 391, 1967); (2) such laws must provide law-abiding citizens fair notice of what is prohibited (*Papachristou v. City of Jacksonville*, 405 U.S. 56, 92 S.Ct. 839, 1971); (3) laws may not be drafted in an imprecise manner that allows arbitrary and discriminatory enforcement (*Coates v. City of Cincinnati*, 402 U.S. 611, 91 S.Ct. 1686, 1972); and (4) laws must be stated in a manner that gives a person of ordinary intelligence a reasonable opportunity to know what conduct is prohibited (*Grayned v. City of Rockford*, 408 U.S. 104, 92 S.Ct. 2994, 1972). Second, most state disorderly conduct laws were substantially influenced by the American Law Institutes *Model Penal Code*. Under Section 250.2 of the *Model Penal Code*, a person is guilty of disorderly conduct if with purpose to cause public inconvenience, annoyance or alarm, or recklessly creating a risk thereof, he or she: (a) engages in fighting or threatening, or in violent or tumultuous behavior; or (b) makes unreasonable noise or offensively coarse utterance, gesture or display, or addresses abusive language to any person present; or (c) creates a hazardous or physically offensive condition by any act that serves no legitimate purpose of the actor.

The definition of disorderly conduct provided by the *Model Penal Code* had many positive ramifications. First, whereas decisions such as *Papachristou* led many jurisdictions to revise their criminal laws, the *Model Penal Code* provided states with a prototype that gave more specific definitions of the types of behaviors that constitute criminal acts. The *Model Penal Code* also offered separate descriptions of related offenses, such as loitering (that replaced vagrancy), riot and failure to disperse, false public alarms, harassment, obstructing public ways, disrupting meetings, lewdness, and obscenity, distinct from disorderly conduct. Consequently, states began abandoning earlier, vague disorderly conduct laws that were based on a person's condition or status.

Most disorderly conduct statutes embrace the *Model Penal Code*'s prohibition of general disruptive behaviors (e.g., fighting in public; threatening, violent and tumultuous behaviors). These laws remind us that in addition to the individual victims of offenses like assault, society is presumed collectively harmed and offended by the conduct of the perpetrator.

Disorderly conduct statutes prohibiting unreasonable noises and offensive utterances, gestures, or displays have historically been the most controversial and are undoubtedly the most difficult to draft from the policymakers' perspective. As stated in the commentary of the *Model Penal Code*, "this provision implicates one of the most difficult questions of constitutional law: when may the state prohibit speech in order to protect public tranquility?"

As explained in *Schneck v. U.S.* (249 U.S. 47, 39 S.Ct. 247, 1919), the right to freedom of speech in public is not absolute. In *Schneck*, the U.S. Supreme Court created the "clear and present danger" test. Under this test, the government cannot suppress or prohibit speech or punish the speaker unless the nexus between the speech and consequential illegal outcome is so close that the speech presents a "clear and present danger." Hence, the right to free speech does not protect a man causing a panic by falsely shouting "fire" in a crowded theater.

Stemming from the recognition that there are limitations on the freedom of speech, the high court created the "fighting word" test. (*Chaplinsky v. New Hampshire*, 315 U.S. 568, 62 S.Ct. 766, 1942). Under *Chaplinsky,* the prosecution would have to prove that a valid statute or ordinance clearly prohibits language likely to cause a breach of the peace, and that such language has a direct tendency to cause acts of violence by the person to whom the language is addressed.

Although many disorderly conduct statutes encompass the "fighting words" doctrine, the Supreme Court has imposed two significant limitations on its application. First, in *Cohen v. California* the Court ruled that the prohibition of fighting words cannot be utilized to prohibit vulgar language, because "one man's vulgarity is another's lyric" (403 U.S. 15, 25, 91 S.Ct. 1780, 1788, 1970). The second limitation on the doctrine was presented in the case of *Gooding v. Wilson* (405 U.S. 518, 92 S.Ct. 1103, 1972), where the Court ruled that words could be rude, impolite, or insulting but fall short of a "fighting word" violation. Furthermore, if the person to whom the words are addressed is not likely to make an immediate response, there is no "fighting word" violation.

Disorderly conduct statutes prohibiting hazardous or offensive conditions and actions serving no legitimate purpose generally act as a broad catch-all provision encompassing a wide host of situations and behaviors deemed irritating or without socially redeeming value. Although definitions vary among jurisdictions, many states now define disorderly conduct to prohibit noxious chemical odors. States such as Texas have built upon the *Model Penal Code*'s open-ended definition of disorderly conduct to maintain public safety and decency by prohibiting the discharge or display of firearms and deadly weapons, certain forms of public nudity (exposure of the anus or genitals), and "peeping tom" offenses.

Ryan Kellus Turner

References and Further Reading

American Law Institute, *Model Penal Code and Commentaries: Official Draft and Revised Comments*. 3 vols. Philadelphia, PA, ALI, 1980.

Hall, D.E., *Survey of Criminal Law,* 2nd ed., Delmar Publishers, Albany, New York, 1997.

Klotter, J.C. and Edwards, T.D., *Criminal Law,* 5th ed., Anderson Press, Cincinnati, OH, 1998.

Lacey, F.W., Vagrancy and Other Crimes of Personal Condition, *Harvard Law Review,* 66 (1953).

Reamey, G., *Criminal Offenses and Defenses in Texas,* 3rd ed., The Harrison Company, Suwanee, GA, 2000.

Samaha, J., *Criminal Law*, 5th ed., West Publishing, St. Paul, MN, 1996.

See also **Public Drunkenness**

Diversion and Diversion Programs

Definition

Diversion programs, broadly defined, are any authorized activity that result in the nonentry of an offender into the criminal justice system or the discontinuation of formal case proceedings against that offender and their replacement with informal, often less punitive, proceedings. Thus, diversion may occur at time of arrest with discretion to arrest exercised by the police patrolman, continue through the arraignment, trial, and sentencing phases in the criminal justice process whereby prosecutors, defense attorneys, and judges may seek alternative methods to break the cycle of crime, and finish within the correctional processes wherein diversion may be seen in the application of parole as correctional professionals seek ways to reduce the negative impacts of imprisonment and provide opportunities for change. Diversion programs are commonly operated, however, as pretrial and preconviction remedies to deal with first time offenders who appear amenable to less formal interventions and to reduce overcrowded court dockets. Diversion programs ideally strive for a balance between having the offenders make amends to their victim and the community (offender accountability), protecting the community by monitoring his or her behavior (community safety), and providing the offenders with opportunities to develop skills and change their behavior (competency development) (Bazemore and Umbreit, 1998).

This discussion explores: (1) the concept and history of diversion within the criminal justice system in the U.S.; (2) its appropriateness as a practice; (3) those points within the criminal justice process at which diversion might occur; and, (4) any possible lessons that we might learn from national and international experiences with diversion. As described here, it is possible to see that diversion strategies (within which individual programs are categorized) have the potential to reduce those costs associated with judicial case proceedings, prevent initial and subsequent stigmatization of the offender, and to bring the administration of justice back to the community level. Although it possible to see these goals and practices in action in the adult criminal justice system, they are most easily observed throughout the juvenile justice system in the U.S. (which itself may be interpreted as the systematic diversion of juveniles from the adult criminal justice system).

A Brief History of Diversion

A discussion of diversion requires the examination of two interrelated themes. The first theme focuses on diversion *from outside* the criminal justice system and the second theme focuses on diversion *from within* the criminal justice process. The former is concerned with those practices that divert a person from the formal criminal system to a community-based system. The latter is concerned with reducing the impact of existing sanctions and programs by diverting the individual to programs and sanctions that are both less formal and less punitive in nature.

The early history of the American system of criminal justice may itself be regarded as a history of diversion. Transportation to colonial America was an alternative to the gallows and prison hulks of Great Britain with large numbers of convicted felons being transported and banished to the American colonies for a specified number of years (usually 7 years for noncapital crimes and 14 years for commuter capital crimes). A lengthy prison term or the death penalty awaited the transported criminal who returned early to England (Branch-Johnson, 1957; Campbell, 2001). With this tradition in mind, but with no place to which they could transport their own felons, it was not surprising that legislators in the new U.S. of America sought less formal and less punitive alternatives to the use of capital punishment. The evolution of the penitentiary during the first half of the nineteenth century was one such alternative (Blomberg and Lucken, 2000; McGowen, 1995; Rothman, 1995;). The negative effects (insanity, sharing of criminal techniques, and so forth) and high costs of the early penitentiaries, however, were believed by the reformers of the day to outweigh the pains of imprisonment and the length of time served.

Nineteenth century reformer John Augustus, the father of American probation, asked Boston magistrates to release offenders to his custody on the promise that he would teach the individual a trade, instill sobriety, and reduce the threat to society that the individual currently posed and might pose as the result of being imprisoned with other felons (Blomberg and Lucken, 2000). This "diversion" from incarceration would eventually become formalized as probation.

During the latter half of the nineteenth and first half of the twentieth centuries, probation became a traditional judicial sanction for first-time and youthful offenders across the U.S. However, critics have argued that it provided neither the reformation of the individual nor the necessary measures of community safety and offender accountability. These same critics, however, were far from unanimous concerning whether the alternatives to probation should be more or less severe.

During the latter three decades of the twentieth century, reformers sought alternatives that were both more and less severe than the probation practices they were intended to replace. During the 1970s, many first-time and youthful offenders were diverted from the formal probation system and placed into programs that sought to help the offender to make better life choices and avoid further criminal behavior. One such program was the use of wilderness challenge programs that were operated along similar lines as the successful Outward Bound programs. Both programs sought to instill in participants a sense of accomplishment by pushing them beyond their previous limits through the use of the gradual successes in new and stressful experiences in a wilderness environment (Klein, 1997). A related type of diversion from both regular probation and incarceration, the youth ranch, had been successful for many years in a number of western U.S. states. Like probation before them, both youth ranches and wilderness challenge programs became formal judicial sanctions in many states although the latter have fallen into disuse.

During the decade of the 1980s, the diversion pendulum continued to swing in both directions and has yet to find a balance between offender accountability and competency building. The Koch Crime Institute (Koch, 1998) noted that one of the reasons for this was the much discussed Martinson report (1976) that proclaimed that "nothing works" and, in turn, set the stage for public opinion and, therefore, sentencing and correctional policies to shift from a rehabilitative focus to an offense-based, punitive focus. Yet, diversion from either within or outside of the criminal justice system would continue to swing the pendulum in the other direction due, in part, to economic and moral concerns. Recognition of the gap between probation and imprisonment being too great led to more punitive measures that emphasized more offender accountability than was believed to occur within probation while still allowing offenders to be diverted from prison. These "intermediate sanctions" (as they became known) included a broad range of sanctions to divert offenders who would otherwise be prison-bound. They included: electronic monitoring, home incarceration, military-style boot camps, intensive probation supervision, and day reporting centers (Clear and Dammer, 2003; Koch, 1998).

Military-style boot camps emerged during the 1980s as a response to cries for increased law and order throughout the U.S., especially in view of increased crime among young people (Mackenzie, 1994; Osborne, 1994). Although Ohio had passed legislation authorizing shock incarceration for first-time, nonviolent juvenile offenders during 1965, correctional boot camp programs that operated along military lines would not emerge until the early 1980s. Correctional boot camps offer offenders reduced sentences in return for successfully completing the 90–105 day program. Correctional boot camps seek to build upon the stress of their programs to promote behavioral changes in their participants. Although such programs employ military discipline with negative as opposed to positive reinforcement, hard work, and other authoritarian techniques, there is no proof that they reduce recidivism, the size of prison populations, or costs of imprisonment (Atkinson, 1995; Parent, 1993).

While these alternatives were being developed *within* the system, a number of alternatives were emerging *outside* of the criminal justice system that involved the community to a far greater extent than had been traditional in the U.S. Much of the impetus for this was found within the restorative justice movements in Australia, Canada, Great Britain, and New Zealand and within Native American cultures (Bazemore and Umbreit, 1998; Daly and Hayes, 2001).

During the decade of the 1990s, criminal justice policymakers and practitioners continued to search for innovative ways to reduce prison crowding, the associated costs of incarceration, and recidivism. Although the concepts are difficult to define due to the broad range of programs and activities that they cover, balanced and restorative justice programs have attempted to hold the offender accountable for his or her actions while addressing the need for competency development and community safety. Daly and Hayes (2001) noted that these activities can occur at different stages in the criminal justice process, "including diversion from court prosecution, actions taken in parallel with court decisions, and meetings between victims and offenders at any stage of the criminal process (for example, arrest, presentencing, and prison release)." This change in focus emphasizes a rejection of the state and its replacement by the community (through appointed community groups) as the primary change agent coupled with the beliefs that justice should resolve existing conflict and restore harmony to the community. Whenever it is practical to do so, apologies to the victim are an integral component of restorative justice activities (Bazemore and Umbreit, 1998; Braithwaite, 1989). From an international perspective, the Canadian youth and criminal justice systems have incorporated restorative justice principles and diversion practices with both systems being required to attempt alternative measures to judicial processing whenever possible.

The point of the discussion, thus far, has been that most diversionary practices that emerged during the past two centuries have been incorporated gradually into the mainstream of criminal justice policies and practices. Yet, is diversion appropriate for every offender?

The Appropriateness of Diversion

Simply put, the answer to the previous question is "no". Diversion is not appropriate for every offender, just as incarceration is not appropriate for most offenders charged with property, drug, or even minor violent offenses. Today, the use of formal judicial proceedings continues to be the norm within both the adult criminal justice and juvenile justice systems across the U.S. even though anecdotal information from corrections practitioners indicate that only about 20% of the current prison populations need to be there to either protect society from them or them from society (because of the heinous nature of their offense).

The use of formal rather than informal processes continues to be the norm within both the adult criminal and juvenile justice systems. The following discussions of the juvenile justice system and the use of drug courts in the adult criminal justice system illustrate this point.

Pretrial Diversion in Practice—Juvenile Diversion

Broadly stated, diversion is what the juvenile justice system is all about. Although the American juvenile justice system began in New York City during 1825 as a method of diverting children and juveniles from the harshness of the criminal justice system of the day, its year of origin is usually linked to 1899 and the establishment of the first juvenile court in Chicago, Illinois (Eggleston, 1999; Mennel, 1973; Platt, 1969). The focus of the new juvenile courts was on "offenders and not offenses, on rehabilitation and not punishment," according to Snider and Sickmund (1999) who noted that such a focus "had substantial procedural impact." With the development of this doctrine, the state could approach the processing of juveniles in a less formal manner than was possible within the adult system of criminal justice. Since the juvenile court was seeking rehabilitation and personalized justice for juveniles in a manner akin to a benevolent parent, it was believed that the formal, adversarial processes and sanctions employed in the criminal justice system were inappropriate for juvenile offenders.

As the result of these philosophical underpinnings, the juvenile justice system has favored a broad range of community sanctions (warnings, unconditional discharges, suspended sentences, fines, conditional discharges, etc.) and employed custodial dispositions as a last resort (Torbet, 1996). Probation supervision remains the workhorse of the juvenile justice system in the U.S. (Torbet, 1996). Juvenile probation departments, or specialized juvenile sections within existing probation agencies, have been established as a method of further diverting juvenile offenders from a custodial disposition. These specialized agencies have developed expertise in dealing with the unique needs and risks posed by juvenile offenders (Snider and Sickmund, 1999; Torbet, 1996).

Interestingly, the juvenile justice system has established a number of *diversion points,* whereby juvenile offenders may be diverted out of the formal judicial processes. Juvenile accountability and rehabilitation are stressed (with some moral elements of punishment) in activities at each of these diversion points. At the present time, the application and success of diversion activities depend on the efforts of well-meaning police officers, intake officers, prosecutors, and judges.

Individual police officers continue to serve as the gatekeepers for the juvenile justice system in the U.S. Police officers generally have personal contact with the juvenile, his or her peer group, and family situation and are, possibly, in the best position to refer a young person in conflict with law to social agencies because of the knowledge gained through such contacts. Diversion at this stage should be preferable to formal judicial activities as police officers may informally (or formally in some countries) act as conflict mediators or conference facilitators when they bring juveniles, victims, and families together to resolve a conflict or seek out repayment for a broken window or similar loss. Unfortunately, the history of police abuse of power, corruption, and lack of training has generated as many opponents as supporters of police diversion.

In the formal sense, according to the federal Office of Juvenile Justice and Delinquency Programs (OJJDP), intake officers divert more juveniles than any other justice practitioner. Employing departmental regulations for guidance, intake officers examine the age, prior offenses, attitude and amenability to treatment when deciding to divert or process a juvenile offender. Exercising their professional judgment, intake officers divert nearly half (43%) of the juvenile cases brought before them nationwide (OJJDP, 1999).

Prosecutorial discretion provides another opportunity for diversion from within the juvenile justice system. In the first instance, prosecutors may decide not to prosecute cases where the interests of the juvenile and justice coincide. Indeed, these interests might be served better through alternative measures such as victim-offender mediation, counseling, and other less stigmatizing options. In the second instance, prosecutors determine which delinquencies (charges) should be brought forth to the juvenile court. Prosecutors rely on information from police officers, social workers, teachers and others in making their decisions as well as the local political situation.

Interestingly, justice for juveniles diverted from the juvenile court process at these two stages does not merely end here. Many states have embraced balanced and restorative justice (BARJ) programs at the community level that seek to make the offender accountable, promote change, and improve community safety through offering the offender an opportunity to accept responsibility for his or her actions. In so doing, the juvenile is required to make a personal commitment to change through a number of activities, including: writing an essay that describes the offense, making an apology to the victim, paying restitution, or performing a number of community service hours or similar hours of personal service to the victim (raking leaves, painting over vandalized walls, etc.)

The juvenile justice system has also been supportive of judicial diversion for juvenile offenders perceived as amenable to nonformal intervention. During the late 1990s, for example, juvenile court judges diverted nearly 42% of the young people who appeared before them without delinquency adjudication (OJJDP, 1999).

Pretrial and Postsentencing Diversion in Practice—Drug Courts

Although a growing number of diversion strategies have and continue to be instituted across the U.S., they may be categorized as either reintegrative or therapeutic in nature. Such diversion strategies have tended to operate at either the pretrial, preconviction, or postsentencing stages of the criminal justice process.

During the last decade, however, there were renewed calls for programs that increased public safety and offender accountability (while avoiding the costs of imprisonment for the taxpayer) in the belief that such intermediate sanctions were too soft on violent and drug crime. Specialty treatment courts for drug offenders were established that diverted offenders either pre- or postadjudication. Preadjudication drug courts divert offenders to treatment once indictments have been filed, but prior to trial. The offender enters a substance abuse treatment program and a program of drug-testing and supervision in addition to regular appearances in the drug court to review his or her progress. If he or she is successful, then the prosecutor does not proceed with the charges that remain on the individual's record. The original charges are prosecuted if the offender fails or leaves the program.

In postadjudication drug courts, however, the court accepts a guilty plea and imposes a substantial prison sentence that would be held in abeyance until the drug offender completes a treatment program and period of drug-free living. At that time, the guilty plea would be dismissed with prejudice and both the record of conviction and warrant of incarceration are shredded in open court. Failure to complete the treatment and clean living phases results in the immediate commencement of the prison sentence. An interesting carrot and stick approach to offender accountability, competency building, and public safety!

Conclusion

Diversion programs are those authorized programs that seek to promote the nonentry or discontinuation of formal judicial proceedings against an offender. They are based on the notion that less formal proceedings are more likely to increase opportunities for change in the offender and reduce labeling and stigmatization by the state. The general effects of diversion are less-crowded court dockets and the avoidance of high costs associated with prosecution, conviction, and correctional supervision (both institutional and community based) of offenders. As mentioned throughout these discussions, many diversion efforts of the past have become accepted as mainstream activities within the adult criminal and juvenile justice systems.

Diversion programs are not appropriate for every adult or juvenile offender nor does every community desire them. Although the seriousness of the offense and the offender's criminal record are often the primary screening foci, diversion is also dependent upon the amenability of both the offender to accept responsibility for his or her actions and the victim to accept this alternative to prosecution coupled with the desire of justice practitioners to devote additional time and nonjudicial resources to be effective. The operation of diversion programs, however, continues to be a localized effort within the American criminal justice system with the public oscillating between a discontent with diversion and less punitive sanctions and enthusiastically adopting them depending upon recent crime in the local area. Alas, history may repeat itself when current diversion practices gain acceptance and become accepted practices within the mainstream criminal and juvenile justice systems.

Allan L. Patenaude and Marc A. Patenaude

References and Further Reading

Atkinson, L. *Boot Camps and Justice: A Contradiction in Terms*? Australian Institute of Criminology, Canberra, Australia, 1995.

Bazemore, G. and Umbreit, M., *A Guide for Implementing the Balanced and Restorative Justice Model,* U.S. Department of Justice, Office of Juvenile Justice and Delinquency Programs, Washington, DC, 1998.

Blomberg, T.G. and Lucken, K., *American Penology: A History of Control,* Aldine De Gruyter, New York, 2000.

Branch-Johnson, W., *The English Prison Hulks,* C. Johnson Publishing, London, 1957.

Braithwaite, J., *Crime, Shame, and Reintegration,* Cambridge, Cambridge University Press, U.K., 1989.

Campbell, C., *The Intolerable Hulks: British Shipboard Confinement, 1776–1857,* 3rd ed., Fenestra Books, Tucson, AZ, 2001.

Clear, T. and Dammer, H., *The Offender in the Community.* 2nd ed., Wadsworth Publishing Co., Belmont, CA, 2003.

Daly, K. and Hayes, H., *Restorative Justice and Conferencing in Australia,* Australian Institute of Criminology, Canberra, Australia, 2001.

Eggleston, C., Locking Up Kids: Learning From Our Historic Legacy, *Reclaiming Children and Youth,* 8:3, 137–139 (1999).

Klein, A.R., *Alternative Sentencing, Intermediate Sanctions and Probation,* 2nd ed., Anderson Publishing, Cincinnati, OH, 1997.

Koch Crime Institute, *Innovative Practices in the Criminal and Juvenile Justice Systems: Sentencing, Corrections, Diversion,* New York, 1998.

Mackenzie, D.L., Boot Camps: A National Assessment, *Overcrowded Times,* 5:4, (1994).

Martinson, R. What Works?—Questions and Answers About Prison Reform, *The Public Interest,* 35, 22–54 (1974).

McGowen, R., The Well-Ordered Prison: England 1780–1865, in Morris, N. and Rothman D.J., Eds., *The Oxford History of the Prison: The Practice of Punishment in Western Society,* Oxford University Press, Oxford, U.K., 1995, pp. 71–99.

Mennel, R.M., *Thorns and Thistles,* University of New Hampshire Press Hanover, New Hampshire, U.K., 1973.

Office of Juvenile Justice and Delinquency Programs, *Statistical Briefing Book, 1999.* Available at: http://ojjdp.ncjrs.org/ojstatbb/delinquencytotal.html. Retrieved on May 21, 2003.

Osborne, W.N., Shock Incarceration and the Boot Camp Model: Theory and Practice, *American Jails,* July/August.

Parent, D.G., Boot Camps Failing to Achieve Goals, *Overcrowded Times,* 4:4, August

Platt, A., *The Child Savers: The Invention of Delinquency,* Chicago, University of Chicago Press, IL, 1969.

Rothman, D.J., Perfecting the Prison: U.S., 1879–1965, in Morris, N., and Rothman D.J., Eds., *The Oxford History of the Prison: The Practice of Punishment in Western Society,* Oxford University Press, Oxford, U.K., 1995, pp. 100–116.

Snyder, H., Finnegan, T., Kang, W., Poole, R., Stahl, A., and Wan, Y., *Easy Access to Juvenile Court Statistics: 1989–1998,* 2001. Available at: http://ojjdp.ncjrs.org/ojstatbb/ezajcs98. Retrieved on May 21, 2003.

Torbet, T.M., *Juvenile Probation: The Workhorse of the Juvenile Justice System,* Office of Juvenile Justice and Delinquency Programs, Washington, DC, 1996.

See also **Boot Camps and Shock Incarceration; Community Service and Restitution Programs; Work Release**

Domestic Assault: Extent and Correlates

There are many forms of behavior that constitute domestic assault. Definitions range from legal classifications to discipline-specific descriptions provided by criminal justice practitioners, victims' advocates and medical personnel. Domestic assault is generally defined as any type of assault, battery (including sexual) or other behavior that warrants criminal justice intervention and results in the injury or death of one family member by another. Included in this description would be spousal/intimate assault, child abuse and neglect, as well as elder abuse. This entry will focus exclusively on spousal/intimate assault. Domestic abuse can be either physical or mental. Physical assault includes behaviors ranging from slapping, hitting, and pushing to serious injury, rape, or death. Domestic assault may also include psychological or emotional abuse, such as threats of physical harm, intimidation, degradation, or extreme jealousy and possessiveness. These types of behaviors, however, rarely come to the attention of authorities.

Domestic assault differs from other forms of violence in two important ways. First, most domestic assault occurs within the privacy of the home, making it harder to detect than assaults that occur in public. Second, the abuse often occurs between individuals who are emotionally tied to one another. Victims may also be financially dependant upon their abusers and to end the relationship may result in significant economic hardship.

The true extent of domestic assault in the U.S. is unknown. What is known is that domestic assault is the most common form of violence encountered by the police and is the leading cause of violence against women. According to data collected by the FBI, the U.S. Department of Justice's Bureau of Justice Statistics, and by the American Medical Association, between two and five million women in the U.S. are physically abused annually by their partners. Every 15 seconds a woman in this country is battered. Twenty-five percent of all rapes occur between married or intimate partners.

Six to ten women are killed by their partners every day. Women are most likely to be killed when trying to break off an abusive relationship.

The difficulty in determining how frequently domestic assault occurs stems from a reluctance of many women to report the abuse. There are three primary sources for estimating the extent of domestic assault in the U.S.: police reports, victimization surveys, and information from the medical community. Police reports and victimization surveys are problematic because they rely upon the victim to report the abuse. Only one fourth of all incidents of domestic assault are reported to the police. Victims are often reluctant to report abuse for reasons that include embarrassment, fear or retaliation, economic concerns, or the belief that no purpose would be served by bringing the abuse to the attention of authorities.

A second source used to measure the extent of domestic assault involves the use of victimization surveys. In 1992, the Bureau of Justice Statistics redesigned the National Crime Victimization Survey in an effort to improve estimates of domestic assault. The National Crime Victimization Survey (NCVS) is a self-report victimization survey involving over 100,000 individuals. Figures from the NCVS reveal that the incidence of domestic assault is two to four times greater than figures reported to the police. Reports from the medical community disclose even higher estimates. Physicians report four times the number of cases discovered by the NCVS. One out of every four women seen by physicians was battered during the past year and 39% of female patients have been battered in their lifetime.

Domestic assault is not only an American problem. Complete information on the extent of domestic assault across the globe does not exist; however, research suggests that in many countries outside of the U.S. one fourth to more than one half of women report physical and psychological abuse at the hands of their partners (Gosselin, 2000). Rates of domestic assault are particularly high in societies where patriarchal social inequality is great. For example, over 5000 women in India are killed annually by their in-laws because their dowries are considered insufficient and in many Chinese provences there are no legal protections available for domestic assault victims.

According to official reports, domestic assault is an offense committed primarily by men. Male batterers share many similar characteristics. First, men who batter tend to be young. The average age for abusers is 32 years old and two thirds are between their mid-20s and early 40s. Second, male batterers usually have a history of substance abuse. Over one half of offenders have prior records for alcohol or other drug charges. Third, male abusers are typically unmarried or separated and have children by their victims. Fourth, male offenders tend to have extensive criminal histories with a generalized pattern of violent behavior. Other common characteristics include having a history of child abuse or witnessing abuse between parents, poor family ties, a lack of stable residence or employment, and having traditional patriarchal views toward women's role in society. It is important to note that all male batterers may not share all of the aforementioned characteristics.

Holtzworth-Munroe and Stuart (1994) provide a useful typology of male batterers that takes into account the severity of violence, whether violence was against strangers in addition to partners, as well as the presence of any personality or psychopathology disorders. Three distinct categories of offenders exist: family only, dysphoric or borderline personality, and the generally violent or antisocial. Offenders falling into each category differ in terms of their attitudes toward women, levels of impulsivity, social skills, and childhood home environment. Differentiating between types of male batterers is useful in determining how offenders will respond to legal sanctions or treatment.

Victims of domestic assault also share similar characteristics. Women aged 19 to 29 and women in families with incomes below $10,000 are the most likely victims of domestic assault. The rate of victimization by a female who is separated from her partner is three times higher than that of divorced women and 25 times higher than that of married women. Race also plays a factor. African American and American Indian or Alaska Native women are more likely than women of other races to be domestic assault victims (Tjaden and Thoennes, 2000). In addition, many female victims tend to blame themselves for the abuse, exhibit low self-esteem, lack any social support system, and often believe they can change their partner's behavior.

Recently, the numbers of domestic assault cases involving female batterers and male victims has started to increase. The idea that males could be victims of domestic assault is still a controversial issue. There is a growing body of research that suggests the incidence of male battering may be as high as female battering. Part of the increase stems from proarrest policies that require the police to arrest one, if not both, parties involved in a domestic dispute. There still appears to be a difference in the severity of abuse encountered by males and females. Three percent of male murder victims are killed by their wives or girlfriends annually, whereas 29% of female murder victims are slain by their husbands or boyfriends. Self-defense is often cited as the reason why females engage in violence against their male partners.

Research on gay and lesbian violence is sparse. Society has been reluctant to accept that women could be violent with one another and that males could be the victims of domestic assault. According to Coleman (1996), the incidence of gay and lesbian domestic assault is comparable to that of heterosexual relationships. Other research finds that gays may actually have higher rates of domestic assault compared to heterosexual couples (Tjaden and Thoennes, 2000).

The consequences of domestic assault are numerous. Domestic assault results in almost 100,000 days of hospitalizations, almost 30,000 emergency department visits, and almost 40,000 visits to a physician annually. Domestic assault is the leading cause of birth defects and infant mortality and children who grow up in an abusive household are more likely to become violent as adults. A significant percentage of the homeless population in this country are women fleeing abusive households (Gosselin, 2000).

Historically, there was a lack of governmental or public interest in domestic assault. Under British common law, husbands were permitted to beat their wives provided the stick they used was not bigger in circumference than the husband's thumb (hence the popular phrase "the rule of thumb"). In the American colonies, initial efforts to criminalize domestic assault date back to 1641 when the Puritans of Massachusetts included in their *Body of Laws and Liberties* provisions against it (Pleck, 1989). Interest in family violence was limited to the New England colonies primarily because they were founded by religious dissenters. Early laws reflected Puritan religious principles in which family violence was viewed as amoral and a sin against God. Despite criminalization, laws were seldom enforced. Enforcement took a back seat to efforts to keep families united and to maintain respect for family privacy. Inhabitants of Plymouth Colony were the last to pass a law against domestic assault in the 17th century, but by the end of the century, limited enforcement turned into nonenforcement.

Attention to domestic assault was virtually nonexistent throughout the 18th and the first half of the 19th century. Family violence once again became a private matter, no longer subject to state interference. The few cases brought before the courts met with opposition. If a wife tried to leave her abusive husband, she could be tried for abandonment. If she dismissed a complaint, she could be held in contempt of court. Although two states passed laws against domestic assault during the 1850s (Tennessee and Georgia), enforcement was still rare. Convicted offenders could choose between jail time and a fine. Too poor to pay, the majority went to jail leaving families unable to take care of themselves. Fearing impoverishment, many wives dismissed their complaints, resulting in an unwillingness of the police to continue making the arrests (Friedman and Percival, 1981). Interest in domestic assault was renewed during the last quarter of the 19th century. Three groups emerged as advocates for protecting females from domestic assault. Lawyers and judges campaigned for stricter penalties for offenders. Laws allowing corporal punishment were passed in three states: Maryland, Delaware, and Oregon. Early feminists supported these laws, but were more interested in protecting and assisting female victims. Despite their efforts, legislation to increase access to legal remedies never passed, resulting in feminists joining forces with supporters of corporal punishment.

A third group of advocates belonged to various women's temperance organizations. These women believed that the cause of domestic assault was alcohol. The solution lay in prohibition and stricter penalties for offenders. As a result of their efforts, several jurisdictions passed civil laws permitting a wife to sue saloon owners for injuries resulting from intoxication provided the wife had requested the owner not to serve her husband (Pleck, 1989).

The response to domestic assault changed during the first part of the 20th century. Rehabilitation became the dominant approach to criminality so the state embraced a social service approach, as opposed to punitive penalties. The solution to domestic assault lay in policies designed to improve social conditions and provide psychological treatment to offenders. Maintaining the family unit was still the goal of intervention.

The social service response to domestic assault endured for the next 80 years. Public attention remained low until the 1960s when domestic assault finally became a social problem of national concern. Several factors were responsible for the increasing interest. The public became more aware of the true extent of domestic assault. More women are injured at the hands of a spouse or partner than any other source. Battered women's advocates and victims' rights groups were organized to provide shelters, telephone hotlines and legal assistance to the victims of domestic assault. These groups were also responsible for calling attention to the lack of police response to the problem, particularly for misdemeanor domestic assault in which no apparent serious injury is present. Research suggests that during this time the police were apathetic toward domestic assault and it was considered a low priority. Most police departments had explicit nonarrest policies. Such inaction by the police often appeared to make matters worse. According to a study on spousal homicides conducted by the Police Foundation in 1977, 85% of the sample had called for police assistance at least once in the preceding two years and 54% had called five or more times.

The increased attention given to domestic assault during the 1960s for the most part did not extend to the problem of marital or intimate partner rape. The belief that once married, a women lost her right to refuse to have sex with her husband was firmly established in the legal system. All states had "marital exception laws" making it impossible for husbands to be charged with raping their wives. It was not until the 1970s that members of the women's movement began campaigning for the elimination of these laws. Today, all states recognize marital rape as a crime, however, many states still have marital exemption statutes in place for nonconsensual sex in which no force is used (Russell, 1990).

During the past thirty years, three approaches to the problem of domestic assault have prevailed: increasing the certainty and severity of punishment for domestic assault offenders, providing protection and assistance to domestic assault victims, and offering batterers treatment. Efforts to increase the certainty and severity of punishment for offenders are based upon a deterrence strategy. Most of these efforts have been focused exclusively on the police. In the early 1980s, an experiment was conducted by Lawrence Sherman and Richard Berk with the Minneapolis Police Department. The purpose of the experiment was to determine which police response—arrest, counseling, or separation—would produce the lowest recidivism rates for misdemeanor domestic violence offenders. Official arrest records and victim interview data revealed that arrested offenders were less likely to recidivate compared to offenders that were counseled or separated. It was believed that because arrest constitutes a more severe sanction than counseling or separation, offenders were being deterred by the arrest from future acts of violence.

Dramatic changes in police policies occurred following the release of the experiment's results. By 1989, 84% of police agencies in large urban areas adopted policies favoring arrest. Further, Chapter 3 (under Title IV) of the 1994 Federal Crime Control Bill advocated the adoption of mandatory arrest policies for domestic assault offenders throughout the U.S.

The Minneapolis Domestic Violence Experiment was replicated six times in five different cities, but only three studies confirmed the results. Findings from three studies revealed that arrested offenders were actually more likely to recidivate. The inconsistent findings question whether arrest is actually preventing future abuse. What appears to be clear from the replication studies that examined interactions between particular types of offenders and the effectiveness of arrest is that arrest does in fact "work" for offenders who are married or employed. Offenders who are married or employed are believed to have a "stake in conformity" (Sherman et al., 1992). Arrest serves as a deterrent for these offenders because they have something to lose if caught engaging in crime. Offenders who have nothing to lose are not going to be deterred and will likely continue their behavior.

The inconsistent findings have led many to question the ability of the criminal justice system to prevent domestic assault. Any deterrent effect of arrest is usually undermined by a lack of prosecution for domestic assault offenders. As many as 90% of all misdemeanor domestic assault cases are dismissed by prosecutors. Of those cases where charges are filed against the suspect, most receive no jail time.

Given the criminal justice system's apparent inability to deter domestic assault offenders through punishment, two other approaches have dominated policy agendas. Several jurisdictions have implemented "specialized" courts for processing domestic assault offenders and to provide assistance to victims. Emphasis is given to improving the speed and efficiency of case processing and increasing the use of civil protection orders. Research suggests that reducing case processing time results in less pretrial violence and increases the likelihood of a conviction (Fagan, 1996). Special attention is also focused upon the victims of domestic assault. For years, victims of abuse had no voice in the criminal justice system. Many victims were discouraged from pursuing formal charges against their partners or became disillusioned with the criminal justice system when prosecutors would reduce charges. Victims' advocates groups have been successful in significantly increasing the role and participation of domestic assault victims in the process and for providing assistance to victims trying to escape their batterers. The number of domestic assault shelters has increased to over 2000, but there are still too few shelters to meet the demand.

Civil protection orders are increasingly being used as an alternative to, or in conjunction with, criminal charges as a way for victims to seek protection from subsequent violence. Civil protection orders (commonly referred to as restraining orders) offer protection to a domestic assault victim by making it a criminal offense for an offender to come to close proximity with the victim. Civil protection orders are now available in all 50 states and the District of Columbia.

Treatment interventions for batterers are typically based upon the three dominant theories used to explain domestic assault today: the feminist approach, family systems model, and the psychotherapeutic approach (Healey and Smith, 1998). Feminists were the first to develop batterer treatment programs in the 1970s. The approach is based upon a gender analysis of power in which domestic assault reflects the patriarchal nature of society. Men who batter are asserting their power through violence. Domestic assault occurs in all types of homes and among all socioeconomic classes, but its occurrence is over-represented among the lower classes, and most particularly among lower class households in which the patriarchal division of labor and power is most pronounced. Males with low incomes, less education, and who are employed in low-status jobs are significantly more likely than their counterparts to engage in domestic assault and to subscribe to conventional patriarchal beliefs. These types of males are not likely to be in a position to assert their power and authority at work, and so may be more likely to assert their power and authority through violence within the home. The goal of intervention is to offer males insight into their patriarchal sex-role conditioning and to impart an egalitarian relationship structure emphasizing trust and mutual respect.

The family systems model views domestic assault as a symptom of larger familial problems. Both partners in a relationship may be contributing to situations that result in violence. Interventions seek to improve communication skills often lacking in families where violence is present.

Finally, psychotherapeutic approaches focus exclusively on the individual batterer. Domestic assault stems from early childhood trauma or personality disorders that may predispose some individuals to become violent adults. Two treatment strategies are utilized. Psychodynamic counseling attempts to bring unconscious motivations out into the open so that they can be resolved consciously. Cognitive-behavioral therapy is used in an attempt to change violent patterns of thought and behavior.

The different approaches discussed above demonstrate the complexity of understanding the extent, correlates, and causes of domestic assault. Furthermore, there is the recognition that efforts to prevent domestic assault cannot lie solely with the criminal justice system. Only through the combined efforts of the police, courts, treatment providers, victims' advocates, social service agencies, and medical community can a systematic course of action be taken to identify and stop domestic assault.

Amy Thistlethwaite

References and Further Reading

Coleman, V.E., Lesbian Battering: The Relationship Between Personality and Perpetration of Violence, in Hamberger, K.L. and Renzetti, C., Eds., *Domestic Partner Abuse*, Springer Publishing Company, New York, 1996.

Fagan, J., The Criminalization of Domestic Violence: Promises and Limits, *Research Report,* National Institute of Justice, Washington, DC, 1996.

Friedman, L.M. and Percival, R.V., *The Roots of Justice: Crime and Punishment in Alameda County, California, 1870–1910*, University of North Carolina Press, Chapel Hill, NC, 1981.

Gosselin, D.K., *Heavy Hands: An Introduction to the Crimes of Domestic Violence*, Princeton University Press, Upper Saddle River, NJ, 2000.

Hamberger, L.K., Ambuel, B., Marbella, A., and Donze, J., Physician Interaction with Battered Women, *The Journal of the American Medical Association*, 7 (1998).

Haley, K.M., and Smith, C., Batterer Programs: What Criminal Justice Agencies Need to Know, *Research in Action*, National Institute of Justice, Washington, DC, 1998.

Holzworth-Munroe, A. and Stuart, G.L., Typologies of Male Batterers: Three Subtypes and Differences Among Them, *Psychological Bulletin,* 116 (1994).

Pleck, E.H., Criminal Approaches to Family Violence, 1640–1980, in Ohlin, L. and Torny M., Eds., *Family Violence: Crime and Justice a Review of Research,* University of Chicago Press, Chicago, IL, 1989.

Russell, D.E.H., *Rape in Marriage*, Macmillan Press, New York, 1990.

Sherman, L.W., Schmidt, J.D., and Rogan, D.P., *Policing Domestic Violence: Experiments and Dilemmas*, Free Press, New York, 1992.

Straus, M.A., Gelles, R.J., and Steinmetz, S.K., *Behind Closed Doors: Physical Violence in the American Family,* Doubleday/Anchor, New York, 1980.

Tjaden, P. and Thoennes, N., Extent, Nature, and Consequences of Intimate Partner Violence: Findings from the National Violence Against Women Survey, *Research Report*, National Institute of Justice, Washington, DC, (2000).

See also **Assault and Battery: Extent and Correlates; Child Abuse: Extent and Correlates; Domestic Assault: Law; Domestic Assault: Prevention and Treatment; Family Relationships and Criminal Behavior; Victimization, Repeated**

Domestic Assault: Prevention and Treatment

Prevention and treatment programs for domestic assault victims and offenders first began to emerge in the 1970s. The women's movement in the 1960s helped to heighten public awareness about the problem and generate public concern for victims. Public interest for the safety of victims ultimately led to the development of domestic abuse focused prevention and treatment services. The first prevention strategies primarily focused on protecting and supporting the female victim. The shelter movement, established in the early 1970s, provided the oldest type of support services created for battered women and their children. Shelters provide a variety of support services and a safe haven to which women could flee with their children. In addition to shelters, other victim focused prevention and treatment services included 24-hour hotlines, legal advocacy, social and economic services, and other support services. As most victims' programs encouraged battered women to leave their abusers, batterers were seldom held accountable for their behavior, and there were few offender-based treatment programs. However, shortly after the creation of victim services, professionals discovered that again and again, women return to their abusive partner and the abuse continues and often escalates into more serious forms of violence. The growing number of repeat victimizations among women entering domestic violence shelters and other services, indicated a strong need for separate batterer treatment programs.

The first batterer treatment program to be developed in the U.S. was the EMERGE Project established in 1977 in Boston, Massachusetts. The EMERGE Project is a twelve-month program that provides peer group counseling for batterers on a weekly basis. According to the goals of the program, a participant's success is defined as "the total elimination of violence." The EMERGE Project is a collaborative effort among the criminal justice system, the treatment program, and the victim. Project staff have regular contact with the victim to monitor any further abuse, and report to the probation department when a participant neglects to self-report abuse, misses more than two sessions, or fails to participate in group discussion. The most common consequence is revocation of probation for the batterer.

In 1980 the city of Duluth, Minnesota established one of the first integrated community responses to domestic assault, the Duluth Domestic Abuse Intervention Project. The Duluth Project offers a variety of treatment and prevention services to offenders, victims, and the community. The Duluth batterer program provides comprehensive 26-week treatment built on the theory that a man's need to gain power and control over a woman is the primary cause of domestic violence. The goals of the program are designed to help men change their authoritative and destructive behavior, teach batterers to take responsibility for their actions, and to end the cycle of abuse. The program is an educational treatment strategy using group counseling to challenge the batterer's right to empower and control their partner and teaches alternative nonabusive behaviors. The Project has since expanded to include educational and treatment services for all family members, training for other service providers, community-wide educational services and resources, and antiviolence campaigns. The Duluth Project was one of the first coordinated efforts to integrate the police, prosecutors, judges, shelters, advocates, victims, and treatment providers. Both the EMERGE and Duluth Projects have been models for other communities to duplicate across the country. By the early 1980s more than 200 conventional individual and group counseling treatment programs for batterers were established across the U.S. The assumption for many programs is that domestic assault is a learned behavior resistant to change, and that abuse follows a cyclical pattern ("the cycle of violence"). Hence, the goal for most batterer programs is to change and control the violent behavior through comprehensive intervention and treatment. Typically, the batterer is encouraged to take responsibility for his behavior and learn alternative methods for expressing anger. Although some agencies offer diverse batterer services, most early programs were developed by community mental health agencies and were designed as peer support groups. Agencies relied on former batterers who graduated from the program to run the groups and provide peer support. Other programs attempt to help men through individual counseling to unlearn violent behavior by teaching communication and interpersonal skill building and anger management techniques as alternatives to violence. Although both individual and group counseling are widely used, group counseling methods have been repeatedly shown to be the most effective in changing assaultive behavior. The research indicates a much higher drop out rate among participants who receive individual counseling versus participants who receive group counseling. Oftentimes, group counseling programs have greater success in retention because participants learn from their peers, the group helps to reinforce positive behavior, and participants develop supportive relationships with one another.

At the same time that group support programs were spreading, family therapy programs emerged for the less serious batterer. Family therapy programs focus on family and couple counseling that may involve the batterer and his victim, and other family members. Recently, couple's therapy has been viewed as very controversial in its effect on future battering. Typically, the goals of couple counseling encourage preservation of the relationship, counter indicative of serious domestic violence that is more conducive to separation. Many professionals believe that couples' therapy is not appropriate or safe for domestic assault; some believe that the victim is placed at risk because of the therapy. Yet, others believe that there are some situations where couple's therapy may be an appropriate and successful form of treatment. For example, it may be appropriate for couples who have not yet experienced actual physical abuse, or when the batterer is willing to take responsibility for his behavior and is motivated to change. The research is limited in determining the effectiveness of couples' therapy. The few available studies show only a slight decline in the amount of abuse after participating in this sort of treatment.

Numerous programs have adopted the major premise of the Duluth model and combined the educational components with a cognitive behavioral approach. A combined approach focuses on violence as the primary focus of treatment. Many times programs will include three primary goals; the first addresses the issue of power and control, and the denial of responsibility. The second focuses on skill building techniques to change behavior, and the final goal addresses the psychological issues of each participant. A combined program provides more individualized case management and can more aptly address the needs of a diverse population. Multicomponent programs have demonstrated a greater likelihood of changing violent behavior and ending violence. Experts will often agree that there are three basic components to a successful program, the first is that a batterer accepts responsibility for his behavior and is willing to change, the second is that mandated treatment increases participation rates, and the third is ongoing accountability through monitoring by the criminal justice system.

Although treatment strategies are a primary means for changing violent behavior, we should not overlook the fact that treatment programs alone often have little impact on ending the violence. Treatment completion and the level of overall success are often reliant on court-mandated services, and developing an integrated community response. The primary goal for programs, whether servicing batterers or victims is to ensure victim safety. With the main focus on victim safety, batterer prevention and treatment approaches are typically integrated with a criminal justice response. Between 1975 and 1980, 44 states enacted legislation on domestic violence to encourage a legal response to help protect the victim, and to hold the abuser accountable for their behavior. The primary means for states to ensure batterer accountability is through court-mandated treatment programs. Court-mandated pretrial diversion programs emerged as an alternative to incarceration. Because few batterers will seek help on their own, we continue to rely on criminal justice interventions as a way to both mandate services and to monitor a participant's completion of the program. Recent studies have shown that criminal justice interventions may increase the completion rate for participants because there is a consequence if they do not attend services. However, research also indicates that criminal justice interventions have little affect if there are no clear and consistent sanctions when a participant drops out of the program. Recidivism research shows that a combination of court-mandated treatment and consistent legal responses to those who are noncompliant is necessary for reducing recidivism. The key to program success is closely associated with the level of collaboration between criminal justice agencies and treatment programs, and the level of social control implemented by the criminal justice system.

Comprehensive evaluation research on the effectiveness of batterer treatment programs began to emerge in the 1990s. In 1994, the Violence Crime Control and Law Enforcement Act, Title IV which is called the Violence Against Women Act (VAWA) was enacted by Congress. The VAWA Act mandated that all agencies dealing with issues of domestic violence form partnerships and work together to respond to violence against women. The Act provided funding for research to study the problem and to help develop comprehensive prevention and treatment responses to violence against women.

An expanding body of literature is now available to support various models of interventions and to guide future policy and practices. Although not all treatment models have been studied, those that have show promising results. The growing body of knowledge has also provided us with areas of program deficiency. For example, the early evaluation research discovered that many batterer treatment programs used a single treatment strategy that provided only a basic form of therapy. We have little research to support that any one type of treatment has an affect on reducing domestic assault. In addition, repeated studies have shown that many programs do not address the specific cultural needs of clients. Traditionally, treatment methods do not address a culturally diverse population, suggesting that programs will not be successful in changing behavior that is derived from one's culture. Cultural diversity in program components and treatment methods is critical for changing behavior.

Although many advocates believe that the development of treatment strategies has been slow in coming, treatment for batterers continues to evolve as we learn more about the batterer and why they behave in violent ways, and how they respond to change. Today, victims' safety continues to be the number one priority for all treatment programs. More often, programs address the domestic violence problem in a comprehensive manner, providing treatment for batterers and also working with victim advocates to ensure victim safety. Most programs have a victim safety plan built into their program that requires program staff to maintain contact with victims or victim advocates assisting in establishing a safety net for the victim. Frequently, programs today address a combination of concerns—stress and anger management, coping and communication skills, parenting skills, building self-esteem, and setting boundaries. Programs combine a variety of techniques—group and individual counseling, education, and cognitive and behavioral conditioning. At present, there is a vast array of treatment and prevention strategies used to help both victims and batterers break the cycle of abuse. Some newer approaches to prevention and treatment include educational programs for children to teach them alternative nonabusive behaviors before they learn to become violent, and to provide skill-building techniques such as stress management, conflict resolution, and assertion skills.

Much can be learned from 25 years of experimenting with different types of treatment strategies. We now know that an effective program design requires comprehensive client assessment at intake and ongoing case management to ensure that changing treatment needs are addressed. We also know that clients' completion of a program, strategies for developing a cooperative relationship between criminal justice agents and treatment programs, collaboration with victims, and a victim safety plan are critical to program success. However, what treatment strategies work best is still in question, especially given that the domestic assault rates continue to be a serious problem. Encouraging professionals to measure program effectiveness using rigorous methodologies will lead to promising results for future development, and the hope that the frequency and seriousness of domestic assault will be reduced.

DEBRA L. STANLEY

Reference and Further Reading

Buzawa, E. and Buzawa, C., *Domestic Violence: The Criminal Justice Response,* 2nd ed., Sage Publications, Thousand Oaks, CA, 1996.

Crowell, N.A. and Burgess, A.W., Eds., *Understanding Violence Against Women,* National Research Council, Panel on Research on Violence Against Women, National Academy Press, Washington, DC, 1996.

Edleson, J.L. and Tolman, R.M., *Intervention for Men Who Batter: An Ecological Approach,* Sage Publications, Newbury Park, CA, 1992.

Gondolf, E.W., The Effect of Batterer Counseling on Shelter Outcome, *Journal of Interpersonal Violence,* 3, 275–283, 1988.

Gondolf, E.W., Changing Men Who Batter: A Developmental Model for Integrated Interventions. *Journal of Family Violence*, 2(4), 335–349, 1987.

Pence, E. and Paymar, M., *Education Groups for Men Who Batter: The Duluth Model.* New York, NY Springer, 1993.

Vincent, John P. and Jouriles, E.N., editors, *Domestic Violence: Guidelines for Research-Informed Practice.* Philadelphia, PA: Jessica Kingsley Publishers, 2000.

See also **Domestic Assault: Extent and Correlates; Domestic Assault: The Law; Family Relationships and Criminal Behavior**

Domestic Assault: The Law

No universal definition of domestic assault exists. Although many equate domestic assault with the term "domestic violence," in reality domestic assault falls within the broader concept of domestic violence, particularly because domestic violence can extend beyond the narrower legalistic definition of assault. Depending on the expert or jurisdiction, domestic assault has a variety of definitions that can include child abuse, sibling abuse, or spousal abuse. For the purposes of this essay the definition will be narrowed to any intentional act (or acts) between two individuals who share a domestic relationship (those who are married, cohabitating, involved in a serious relationship, or previously shared a domestic relationship) that results in physical, sexual, or emotional injury. Domestic violence knows no absolute cultural or racial boundaries, yet approximately 95% of the abusers are males. Thus, this essay will address the prototypical situation of the male as the abuser and the woman as the victim.

Domestic assault has existed in most civilizations since the beginning of recorded history. Until recent years domestic assault was viewed to be an acceptable and sometimes an expected means of controlling and punishing women. As such, it was perceived by society as a private, family matter and was not recognized as a legal problem. Societies typically gave the patriarch of the family the right to use force against women in the family. In Rome, civil law mandated that when a woman married, her legal guardianship was transferred from her father (or brother) to her husband. As her legal guardian he had the right to beat her, sell her into slavery, or in some cases order her death. These laws were often supported by religious orthodoxy, and as such were given even more credibility.

The 16th and 17th century common law (that served as the foundation for the laws and practices in the U.S.) also embraced similar perceptions of men's and women's roles in society with the exception that men were expected to *restrain* their physical control of their wives. In reality husbands continued to use violence to punish their wives and few men were punished for failing to restrain themselves. The common law "rule of thumb" was the requirement that husbands were not allowed to beat their wives with an object larger than the circumference of the husband's thumb.

Later, in the eighteenth century, another English law was enacted addressing the often visible signs of abuse that women exhibited. The law provided that a husband had the right to physically abuse his wife as long as the abuse only involved "blows, thumps, kicks or punches in the back which did not leave marks." Essentially, early English law considered married women the property of their husbands; they did not have the legal right to retain their inherited title or wealth, or own property. In fact, it was not until the mid-1800s that the legal status of women began to change, particularly in England and in the U.S. The Married Women's Property Acts (New York State, 1848, 1860) were significant pieces of legislation passed in America that provided women with the legal right to retain their inheritances and to own property. Shortly after, some states passed laws prohibiting husbands from assaulting their wives. These laws, however, were rarely enforced against husbands who violated them, particularly if permanent physical injury did not occur. Thus, domestic assault continued to be a hidden societal reality that was not considered a proper topic for social discussions let alone legal discourse (or recourse). Interestingly, when domestic assault was finally acknowledged, it was typically associated among the poor and minority groups, and rarely in the white, middle, and upper classes.

Intervention of domestic assaults did not occur until the early 1900s by the development of family courts whose primary agenda was to address family problems such as child abuse and juvenile delinquency. Although family courts did not perceive domestic assault as a criminal problem, it did consider it to be a social problem that should at least be dealt with by social workers. Social workers used a rehabilitation model seeking to rehabilitate the batterer and the reconciliation of family members. Domestic assault incidents soon became the most frequently heard cases in the family court system.

Most societies continued to deal with domestic assault either through informal systems (the family or church) or through more formal systems (family courts) without the assault as a criminal act (despite the technical application of laws prohibiting *all* forms of assault). In the U.S., it was not until the 1970s that states began enacting laws specifically related to domestic assault; by 1980, 44 states had passed legislation making domestic assault a crime.

Despite domestic assault legislation, police remained slow to respond to reports and often failed to intervene for three reasons. First, police departments continued to perceive domestic assault as a family problem and not a criminal matter. As a result, the police gave domestic assault calls low priority, which in turn meant a slower response time. In addition, when the police eventually arrived at the scene they would not arrest the batterer if the injury to the victim was not severe or if the victim requested that the batterer not be arrested.

In addition, police officers often perceived domestic assault calls as more dangerous than other situations, which again resulted in delayed response times, or failing to respond until a backup unit arrived on the scene.

Police officers also were bound by statutory limitations when making arrests. Until recently, most state statutes that outlawed domestic assault have classified the act as a misdemeanor. Unlike felonies, police officers must witness the alleged misdemeanor conduct to make an immediate arrest. In most cases, the domestic assault occurred without the officer's presence.

Today most states have *mandatory arrest laws* to correct these deficiencies. Mandatory arrest laws require police officers to respond in a reasonable time and to make an arrest if there is any evidence of domestic violence regardless of whether the victim requests the batterer to be arrested. Two significant events occurred to spur this legislation. The first was the well-known Minneapolis Experiment conducted in 1984 (that was modeled on an earlier mandatory arrest policy in Duluth, Minnesota). The experiment was conducted by the Minneapolis Police Department to determine the effectiveness of arresting batterers. Essentially police officers called to domestic assault situations were required to choose one of the following three options: (1) arrest (with the batterer spending one night in jail), (2) ordering the offender to leave the scene (batterers who refused would spend one night in jail), and (3) provide the batterer and victim with advice and referral information.

The results of the experiment suggested that the arrest and jail response was the most effective in terms of reducing recidivism. However, researchers who have replicated this experiment in other cities found that arrest and jail time are not necessarily a deterrent in preventing future violence. Some experts have even suggested that in certain cases arrest results in a backfire effect, leading to additional assaults. Regardless, the experiment brought domestic assault into the forefront as a criminal problem, causing debate among scholars and other professionals in the field on the efficacy of arrest policies.

The second significant event that spurred legislation in this area was litigation against police departments. During the 1970s and 1980s, a number of cases were filed against police departments and individual officers on behalf of the victims of domestic assaults. These suits led to the development and enforcement of mandatory arrest policies. One case that clearly demonstrated police officer's apathy toward domestic assault was *Thurman v. The City of Torrington, Connecticut*, 595 F.Supp. 1521 (D.Conn.1984).

In the Thurman case, Tracy Thurman had contacted the Torrington police department numerous times between October 1982 and June 1983 requesting police protection from her estranged husband, Buck. The police department failed to protect her, citing numerous excuses (e.g., she had no restraining order, the only officer who could arrest Buck was on vacation, or that arrests were not made on holidays or weekends.) On the day of the final assault, Tracy once again called the police telling them that Buck was at her door making verbal threats. A police officer eventually arrived on the scene, but not before he stopped to use the toilet. Buck had already attacked Tracy by the time the officer arrived, and in the police officer's presence, Buck repeatedly stabbed Tracy. At one point Buck stomped and kicked Tracy in the head. Buck was not restrained by the police officer until he attempted once again to attack Tracy as she was being placed in the ambulance. Tracy survived the attack but was permanently disfigured and partially paralyzed as a result. She filed a civil law suit against the police officers on the scene and every officer who had previously failed to intervene. The court awarded her $2.3 million in damages. The court found that the Torrington Police Department and 24 police officers were negligent in failing to respond in an appropriate time, and failed to provide her with equal protection under the law as guaranteed by the fourteenth amendment to the U.S. Constitution. In other words, the court found that the police officers provided differential treatment to an assault by a stranger versus an assault by a man on his wife.

Today, the U.S., England, and other industrialized nations recognize that domestic assault is a legal and a social problem, and not simply a family matter. Victims are afforded legal rights and protections including the legal protection of obtaining restraining orders against batterers. Protection orders prohibit batterers from having any type of contact with victims. Batterers may be jailed and fined if they fail to comply with the restraining order. However, research is presently inconclusive in terms of how effective restraining orders are as a prevention or a deterrent. In addition, victims also have a variety of services and resources available to them such as legal aid, shelters, and counseling.

Despite these changes, it is currently estimated that the U.S. has approximately two to eight million domestic assaults annually. Other indicators suggest that one half of all the women in the U.S. will become victims of battering sometime in their lifetimes. In 1994, Congress passed federal legislation referred to as the Violence Against Women Act (VAWA). This act has a number of objectives, including: (1) providing hotline services for women, (2) funding for domestic violence programs and shelters, (3) funding to improve investigation and prosecution, and (4) funding for programs to educate school-aged children about domestic violence.

Domestic assault is a complex and far-reaching problem that can have devastating consequences. Some countries have taken substantial steps to alleviate this problem, but many others still adhere to traditional societal norms and religious doctrines that relegate women to subservient roles. Nations have yet to discover means that are effective in deterring such conduct and reducing recidivism.

LANETTE P. DALLEY

References and Further Readings

Buzawa, E.S. and Buzawa, C.G., *Domestic Violence: The Criminal Justice Response,* 2nd ed., Sage Publications, Thousand Oaks, CA, 1996.

Dobash, R.E. and Dobash, R., *Violence Against Wives: A Case Against the Patriarchy,* Free Press, New York.

Domestic Violence: The Law and Criminal Prosecution, 2nd ed., The Family Violence Project, San Francisco, CA, 1990.

Eppler, A., Battered Women and the Equal Protection Clause: Will the Constitution Help Them When the Police Won't? *Yale Law Journal*, 95, 1986, pp. 788–789.

Gundle, R., Civil Liability for Police Failure to Arrest: *Nearing v. Weaver, Women's Rights Law Reporter*, 3 & 4, 1986.

Martin, D., Domestic Violence: A Sociological Perspective, in Sonkin, D.J., Martin, D., and Walker, L.E., Eds., *Male Batterer*, Springer, New York.

Merlo, A.V. and Pollock, J.M., Ed., *Women, Law and Social Control*, Allyn and Bacon, Boston, MA, 1995.

Straus, M.A. and Gelles, R.J., *Physical Violence in American Families*, New Brunswick, N.J., Transaction Publishers, 1990.

Walker, L.E., *The Battered Women*, Harper and Row, New York, 1979.

Wallace, H., *Family Violence,* 2nd ed., Allyn and Bacon, Boston, 1999.

See also **Assault and Battery: Law; Child Abuse: Law; Domestic Assault: Extent and Correlates; Domestic Assault: Prevention and Treatment; Family Relationships and Criminal Behavior**

Double Jeopardy, Protection Against

In the U.S., the constitutionally guaranteed protection against double jeopardy is designed to ensure that a person who has been convicted or acquitted of a crime is not tried or punished for the same offense twice. Double jeopardy occurs when, for the same offense, a person is (1) reprosecuted after acquittal, (2) reprosecuted after conviction, or (3) subjected to separate punishments for the same offense. Double jeopardy does not apply to prosecutions brought by separate sovereigns. The federal government, each state government, and each Indian tribe is considered a separate sovereign.

Early English common law contains the foundations of the modern day protection against double jeopardy. The rule of *autrefois acquit* prohibited the retrial of a defendant who was found not guilty. *Autrefois convict*, on the other hand, prohibited the retrial of a defendant who *was* found guilty. These rules were adopted by the American colonies. Today, every state provides double jeopardy protection because of the Supreme Court's decision in *Benton v. Maryland* (395 U.S. 784, 1969), where the Court declared that the Fifth Amendment's protection against double jeopardy is a fundamental right.

The Fifth Amendment suggests that double jeopardy occurs when a person's "life or limb" is threatened. This language has been taken to mean that double jeopardy applies in all criminal proceedings. Determining whether a proceeding is criminal, however, is not always easy. Accordingly, courts will often look to the legislature's intent in writing the statute that is the basis for prosecution. For example, in *Kansas v. Hendricks* (521 U.S. 346, 1997), the Supreme Court found that a statute providing for a "sexual predator" proceeding, in addition to a criminal proceeding, did not place the defendant in double jeopardy because it provided for *civil* confinement. Courts will also examine the punitiveness of the sanctions involved in determining whether a proceeding is criminal. In *Helvering v. Mitchell* (1938) the Supreme Court upheld the constitutionality of a tax proceeding that was used to recover back taxes from a person *after* the person was acquitted on criminal charges. The Court declared that the proceeding was designed as a "remedial sanction" designed to reimburse the government. Thus, it was not considered punitive, so double jeopardy did not apply.

A rather complicated issue in double jeopardy jurisprudence concerns the definition of "same offense." In *Blockburger v. U.S.* (1932), the Supreme Court developed a test that states that "[w]here the same act or transaction constitutes a violation of two distinct statutory provisions, the test to be applied to determine whether there are two offenses or only one, is whether each requires proof of an additional fact that the other does not." This test came to be known as the Blockburger rule.

According to the Blockburger rule, an offense is considered the same offense if two separate statutes contain elements A, B, and C. Likewise, if one crime contains elements A, B, and C and the other has elements A and B, both are considered the same offense because each statute does *not* require proof of a fact that the other does not. For example, assume the offense of first degree murder contains elements A (premeditated), B (deliberate), and C (killing) and second degree murder contains elements B (deliberate) and C (killing). Both offenses are considered the same for double jeopardy purposes because second degree murder does not require proof of another element that first degree murder does. If a person is convicted of first degree murder, then, according to this example, the person cannot be charged with second degree murder.

Separate offenses can be identified where, for example, one crime contains elements A, B, and C and the other contains elements A, B, and D. Both crimes require proof of an additional element that the other does not. For example, assume the offense of joyriding contains elements A (unlawful taking), B (of an automobile), with C (the intent to temporarily deprive the owner of possession). Assume also that the offense of car theft contains elements A (unlawful taking), B (of an automobile) with D (the intent to *permanently* deprive the owner of possession). These are considered separate offenses because each offense requires proof of an element that the other does not. Thus, a person who is found guilty of joyriding can also be charged with the crime of car theft.

There are four exceptions to the Blockburger rule. First, double jeopardy does not apply if the second prosecution is based on conduct committed after the first prosecution. Second, if the defendant is responsible for the second prosecution, double jeopardy does not apply. Third, double jeopardy does not apply when the court hearing the first offense lacked jurisdiction to try the second offense. Fourth, if the defense plea bargains over the prosecution's objection, double jeopardy protections do not apply.

There are still other exceptions where reprosecution for the same offense is permissible. First, if a defendant successfully appeals a criminal conviction or otherwise succeeds in overturning a conviction, he or she may be reprosecuted. Second, if a case is dismissed, but the defendant is not acquitted, the defendant may be reprosecuted. Finally, reprosecution is permissible if a mistrial occurs (1) over the defendant's objections and is a "manifest necessity" or (2) with the defendant's consent or by the defendant's motion, provided that the prosecution does not agree to the defendant's consent or motion in bad faith (e.g., by intending to pursue subsequent retrials for the purpose of subjecting the defendant to the harassment of multiple trials).

Double jeopardy protections also extend to sentencing increases. Again, however, there are exceptions. Increasing the sentence for the same charge (as opposed to increasing the sentence for separate charges, as in the case of multiple sentences for multiple separate offenses) after it has been imposed is permissible when: (1) a conviction is reversed by an appeal; (2) after the prosecution appeals a sentence, provided there is legal authorization to do so (a rare occurrence); and (3) after discovery of a defect in the first sentence, subject to certain limitations.

JOHN L. WORRALL

References and Further Reading

Amar, A., Double Jeopardy Law Made Simple, *Yale Law Journal,* 106 (1997).

Double Jeopardy and Multiple Punishment: An Historical Analysis, *S. Tex. L. J.* 24 (1983).

McAninch, W., Unfolding the Law of Double Jeopardy, *S.C.L. Rev,* 44 (1993).

See also **Appeals and Posttrial Motions; Guilty Pleas and Plea Bargaining; Sentences and Sentencing: Guidelines**

Driving Under the Influence (DUI)

For a criminologist, drinking and driving is a particularly interesting phenomenon. Large numbers of people admit to doing it, yet it arouses emotions of a similar intensity to crimes against children. Even the terminology we use betrays the contradictions inherent in our thinking. In the U.S. the most common term is *drunken driving,* which suggests that the real problem is, in the words of the American sociologist Joseph Gusfield, "the killer drunk," the grossly inebriated reprobate who recklessly disregards the welfare of others to indulge his own pleasures. In many other countries, however, the problem is construed more in terms of driving after drinking, with even the consumption of small amounts of alcohol—perhaps one or two drinks—constituting an offense if it is combined with driving. In these countries the most common term used is *drinking and driving*.

The debate over whether *all* motorists who drink should be the target of drinking-driving countermeasures, or whether only *high risk* offenders should be of concern, underlies much of the thinking in this field. The "punishment response" dominated public policy in most countries for much of the last century, although in practice this response was not as rigorous as its proponents might have wished. From the 1920s punishments ranged from the frequent, even mandatory use of imprisonment in Scandinavian countries like Sweden, Norway and Finland with a history of strong alcohol prohibitions, to small fines or no punishment at all for a minority of lucky offenders in societies such as Australia and the U.S. where alcohol is widely valued as a social lubricant. Nevertheless, what these penalties all reflected, despite their widely varying severity, was a reliance on criminal law as a satisfactory societal response to a problem that was generally viewed as being confined to a small minority of drivers.

What gradually changed thinking was a new technology. Just before the middle of the twentieth century the means became available to measure the quantity of alcohol in a person's blood (the blood alcohol concentration, or BAC, measured in terms of grams of alcohol per milliliter of blood). Laboratory research showed that at BAC levels much lower than those normally associated with intoxication, tasks related to driving performance (such as divided attention tasks) were noticeably affected. Although the effects of BAC depend on such factors as an individual's weight, rate of drinking, and presence of food in the stomach, deterioration in performance becomes quite marked between BACs of 0.05 and 0.08.

In a further application of standard scientific method, the alcohol–crash link was confirmed in a series of case-control studies that compared the BACs of drivers experiencing crashes with those of matched non-crash-involved drivers. These studies found that relative crash risks increase exponentially with BAC: at 0.05 the risk is double that for a zero-BAC driver, at 0.08 the risk is multiplied by ten, and at 0.15 or higher (the levels typically attained by drivers arrested for drink-driving) the relative risk is in the hundreds.

The Scandinavian countries, led by Norway in 1936, were the first to introduce so called *per se* laws, making it an offense to drive when over a legislatively prescribed BAC, usually 0.05 or 0.08. The United Kingdom followed in 1967 with a 0.08 law, introducing on a large scale the hand-held balloon-type breath testing devices that permitted police to determine quickly whether a motorist should be held for evidential testing using either blood tests or the photometric 'Breathalyzer' device developed by Borkenstein. The invention of the Breathalyzer and the portable devices for preliminary breath tests, combined with *per se* legislation, revolutionized law enforcement and greatly increased the number of drivers who were at risk of detection for driving after drinking.

However, old thinking was combined with the new technology. Although many more drivers could be detected, the primary aim remained punishment rather than *general deterrence*. However, deterrence is at heart a communication process, depending primarily on increasing the perceived probability of apprehension in the target population. A further revolution in enforcement occurred in several countries in the 1970s and 1980s with the introduction of *random breath testing* of millions of motorists who had not committed any offense or been involved in an accident. These methods, used most intensively in Australia and Scandinavia, are designed to increase markedly the perceived risk of detection. Scientific evaluations have found a median decline of 22% in fatal crashes as a result of random breath testing. However, constitutional protections against unreasonable search and seizure have prevented the use of these methods in the U.S., where sobriety checkpoints are used instead. In these checkpoints motorists can only be asked to take a breath test if police can produce evidence that they may have committed an offense. This reduces their deterrent impact.

A very important lesson emerges from experience with random testing. This is that major reductions in accidents can be achieved if the *whole population* is the target, not just heavy drinking offenders. The same principle is illustrated by the surprisingly large effects of simply reducing the *per se* BAC from (say) 0.08 to 0.05. It seems that such laws do not simply influence the small number of drivers between 0.05 and 0.08 but the whole spectrum of offenders, particularly those at the high alcohol end. This demonstrates a fundamental principle of population health, which is that small behavior changes by a large number of people exposed to a small risk may yield better aggregate results than large changes by a small number of high-risk individuals.

In 1992 this public health approach was described by Laurence Ross, the well-known American scholar, as "the challenging paradigm." He used this term because in that country there has been a greater resistance to population strategies than in many other countries. One reason for the difficulties is that this way of thinking leads not only to radical laws but to a questioning of two key institutions, recreation and transportation. The problem from this perspective is to change institutional practices that encourage the combination of drinking and driving. As Ross (1992, 138) wryly notes, "... America's love affair with the automobile knows few bounds." For this reason, programs that attempt to influence driving practices—like those based in alcohol policy—generally target very specific groups: the young or newly licensed drivers (who are generally agreed to have more limited rights to drive anyway), drivers at particular risk of driving impaired (such as those drinking in licensed venues), and convicted drinking drivers (through licensing suspension and other restrictions such as ignition interlocks that prevent a vehicle from starting if the driver fails a breath test using a device built into the ignition system). All these strategies have been shown to reduce accidents.

The challenging paradigm applied to drinking and driving, based on the principles of population health, is continuing to score successes through these strategies and others, such as reducing the legal blood alcohol concentration, limiting alcohol availability, improving emergency medical response times, and increasing the age at which young people can obtain a full driving license. However unlike most other forms of crime drinking and driving can also be effectively deterred through the criminal justice system, although not through the heavy penalties beloved of citizen groups. Thus the field of drinking-driving research has demonstrated that an old institution (the criminal justice system) can achieve major public benefits if used correctly. It all depends on how you think about the problem.

Ross Homel

References and Further Reading

Babor, T., Caetano, R., Casswell, S., Edwards, G., Giesbrecht, N., Graham, K., Grube, J., Gruenewald, P., Hill, L., Holder, H., Homel, R., Österberg, E., Rehm, J., Room, R., and Rossow, I., *Alcohol: No Ordinary Commodity. Research and Public Policy,* Oxford University Press, Oxford, 2003.

Gusfield, J.R., *The Culture of Public Problems: Drinking-Driving and the Symbolic Order,* The University of Chicago Press, Chicago, IL, 1981.

Homel, R., *Policing and Punishing the Drinking Driver: A Study of General and Specific Deterrence. New York,* Springer-Verlag, Heidelberg, Germany, 1988.

Ross, H.L., *Confronting Drunk Driving: Social Policy for Saving Lives,* Yale University Press, New Haven, CT, 1992.

See also **Alcohol Use and Criminal Behavior; Alcohol Use: The Law; Traffic Offenses**

Drug Control Policy: Enforcement, Interdiction, and the War on Drugs

Illegal drug use in America is a serious threat to public health and has a wide range of deleterious effects on individuals, families, and communities. Illegal drug use can lead to life-altering and often fatal consequences, including overdoses, infectious diseases (e.g., HIV/AIDS, hepatitis, and tuberculosis), premature aging, accidents, and crippling addictions. Illegal drug use also places tremendous strains on the nation's health care system and increases the costs of health care services for all Americans. The distribution and sale of illegal drugs can often lead to violent episodes arising from competition over illicit drug markets and from disputes between drug dealers and customers. Furthermore, illegal drug sales and use are associated with numerous other crimes that disrupt the social order and stability of neighborhoods.

Since the beginning of the last century, the government has regulated drug production and distribution and has enforced drug laws. Many of these efforts have been driven by prevailing notions that illegal drug use is related to a host of social maladies, especially violent and predatory crimes. Since the early 1970s, public officials at every level (federal, state, and local) have attempted to curtail illegal drug sales and use by implementing a series of programmatic and legislative initiatives known collectively as the "war on drugs."

Illegal Drug Users and Crime

There are an estimated 4.4 million hard-core, chronic, illegal drug users in the U.S. Although these individuals represent only 20% of all persons who use illegal drugs, they use three fourths of the heroin and cocaine in this country. Chronic illegal drug users are highly likely to become involved in the criminal justice system.

Rates of illegal drug use, especially heroin and cocaine, are many times greater among criminal justice populations than within the general population. In fact, illegal drug use has been declining or holding steady within the general population during the past few years, with only slight increases in marijuana use in the early 1990s, but it has been increasing within various populations involved in the criminal justice system over the same time period.

Among crime-prone persons, illegal drug use encourages other types of criminal activities, such as income-generating property crimes (e.g., burglary) and violent crimes (e.g., robbery). As illegal drug use increases in frequency and amount, so does criminal behavior. People who are criminally inclined tend to commit more crimes and more serious crimes after they become drug dependent. Conversely, as their illegal drug use decreases so do the numbers of other crimes they commit. In addition, illegal drug use and criminal activity often occur together as part of a deviant lifestyle.

History of Antidrug Legislation

The federal government's regulation of drugs began with the passage of the Pure Food and Drug Act of 1906, bringing under federal control the manufacture, sales, and distribution of all foods and drugs. Cocaine, heroin, and morphine—then legal drugs sold as patent medicines—could be purchased in pharmacies or through mail order catalogs as long as the ingredients were clearly displayed on the packaging. The 1906 law also required that certain drugs be sold by prescription only and that patent medicines be tested before being released for human consumption.

The Harrison Act of 1914 was the first criminal law to regulate drugs and is the legal forerunner of the nation's drug control policies. The Harrison Act was a revenue-enhancing measure enacted to make narcotic transfers a matter of record. The Act criminalized the manufacture, prescription, transfer, and possession of narcotics by persons failing to register with the federal government or neglecting to pay the government taxes on opium derivatives and cocaine. Whereas physicians and other medical professionals were required to pay an annual tax of only $1.00, nonmedical professionals, who wished to distribute or sell these drugs, were charged exorbitant cash amounts many times more expensive than the drugs themselves. Hence, no one other than medical professionals ever paid the taxes or registered as legitimate sellers or dispensers of the drugs. A nonphysician found in possession of cocaine could therefore be charged with tax evasion, instead of drug possession, and could be sentenced to spend a maximum of five years in prison or to pay a fine of up to $2,000.

The federal drug legislation that followed the Harrison Act grew increasingly restrictive and punitive. The Jones-Miller Act of 1922, for example, criminalized the possession of illegally obtained narcotics. The Marijuana Tax Act of 1937 classified marijuana in the same category as opiates and cocaine, ordering physicians who prescribed marijuana and druggists who sold it to register with the Internal Revenue Service and to pay annual fees or taxes.

In 1956, the federal government passed the Narcotic Drug Act, the most punitive law to date. For example, the Act rendered the sale of heroin to minors a federal offense punishable by death and mandated prison sentences for persons convicted of two or more drug crimes. Throughout the years, similar drug laws were enacted at the state level, so that the federal government played a relatively minor role in combating illegal drug sales and use until the 1970s.

Drug laws and penalties for drug law violations were consolidated under the Comprehensive Drug Abuse and Control Act of 1970. Title II of the law, known as the Controlled Substances Act, classified drugs into one of five schedules based on their authorized medical use and their addictive potential. Schedule-I drugs are controlled substances with no accepted medical use and a high potential for abuse or physical dependence (e.g., LSD, cocaine, and PCP). At the other end of the spectrum, Schedule-V drugs have a low potential for abuse and an accepted medical use (e.g., antidiarrheal agents that contain small amounts of narcotics).

The Controlled Substances Act also provided penalties for manufacturing, distributing, selling, or possessing the drugs in each schedule, ranging from Schedule-I, with the most severe (e.g., life imprisonment) punishments, to Schedule-V, with the least severe (e.g., fines). In 1978, the Comprehensive Drug Abuse and Control Act was amended to allow law enforcement agents to seize all monies, properties, and other proceeds traceable to drug transactions.

Overview of the War on Drugs

The war on drugs was first instituted in the 1970s and generally refers to federal policies and programs aimed at curbing the availability, sales, and use of illicit substances in the U.S. The war on drugs has pursued two general strategies. The first, supply reduction strategies, consists of law enforcement activities undertaken to disrupt the growth, manufacture, importation, distribution, and sale of drugs. Examples include crop eradication in other countries to reduce the production and harvesting of illegal substances, interdiction to stem the influx of illegal drugs across this country's vast borders, and local enforcement and prosecution practices that involve arresting and convicting persons for drug law violations.

The second, demand reduction strategies, consists of several types of programs. Drug education or primary prevention programs are designed to discourage people from using drugs in the first place. Drug treatment or secondary prevention programs are designed to help users recover from drug abuse and dependence disorders and to keep them from using more serious drugs or from escalating their current drug use. Harm reduction or tertiary prevention programs are designed to mitigate the harmful effects of drug use among persons already addicted to illicit substances.

White House Policies

The war on drugs was officially declared in 1971 by President Richard Nixon, who designated drug abuse as "public enemy number one in the U.S." As a tangible demonstration of the White House's serious commitment to reduce illegal drug use, Nixon created the Special Action Office for Drug Abuse Prevention. He appointed Dr. Jerome Jaffe, a physician and leading methadone treatment specialist, to head the office and to spearhead several demand reduction projects.

Under Dr. Jaffe's leadership, the federal government, for the only time in the history of the nation's drug war, allocated and spent twice as much money on treatment and prevention programs than on law enforcement strategies. In 1973, Nixon consolidated all federal agencies participating in drug enforcement efforts under the auspices of the Drug Enforcement Agency.

The most liberal stance in the federal war on drugs was adopted by the Carter Administration. President Jimmy Carter supported the decriminalization of marijuana, and his drug policy leader, Dr. Peter Bourne, viewed marijuana and cocaine as minor threats to public health and safety. The federal government's movement to decriminalize marijuana fell quickly into political disfavor with the establishment of the parents' antidrug movement, epitomized and led by an organization known as Families in Action. The Reagan Administration's controversial antidrug campaign, "Just Say No," focused on white middle class youth and was funded by corporate and private donations. In his second term, President Ronald Reagan signed the Omnibus Anti-Drug Abuse Acts of 1986 and 1988 that stiffened penalties for drug law violations, and he established the position of "drug czar" to oversee and coordinate all federal government activities for combating illegal drug sales and use. The 1986 bill specified mandatory minimum prison sentences for violations of heroin and cocaine statutes and created marked disparities between powder and crack cocaine in terms of legal penalties for their possession and sales. According to federal law and some state laws, conviction for selling 5 grams of crack cocaine carried the same penalty of five years imprisonment as the selling of 50 grams of powdered cocaine.

In 1989, President George H. W. Bush established the Office of National Drug Control Policy, and he appointed William Bennett as the country's new drug czar. Bennett's approach, referred to as "denormalization," attempted to discourage illegal drug use by making it a socially unacceptable behavior. Federal spending on antidrug programs increased during Bennett's tenure, but treatment dollars remained less than one-third of the total amount of antidrug expenditures.

During President William Clinton's tenure in office, the importance of drug treatment gained greater recognition, but supply-reduction strategies continued to eclipse drug treatment in spending and resources. In 1995, the U.S. Sentencing Commission recommended reducing the sentencing disparity between crack and powder cocaine. For the first time in history, Congress rejected the commission's recommendations. In 1996, President Clinton appointed General Barry McCaffrey, a veteran of the Vietnam and Gulf Wars, as the nation's drug czar. As part of the administration's international drug law enforcement initiatives, Clinton authorized more than $1.3 billion to finance the Columbian government's efforts to combat drug trafficking. The money was used to purchase combat helicopters and to train the military in antidrug tactics. Despite these and other international operations against illicit drugs, the worldwide production and importation of cocaine, opiates, and other illicit substances into the U.S. remains rampant.

Consequences of the War on Drugs

Since the Reagan administration, the overwhelming emphasis on law enforcement efforts to combat drugs has resulted in a massive increase in the nation's arrest and incarceration rates for drug crimes and has affected all components of the criminal justice system. General population surveys have found some declines in illicit drug consumption in the U.S. during the 1990s, although the rates of arrests and imprisonments for violations of drug laws continued at a record pace into the 21st century. In 2000 alone, more than 1.5 million persons were arrested for drug offenses. From 1979 to 1988, arrests for drug charges nearly doubled from 400,000 to 750,000. In 1998 and 1999, a combined total of more than 3 million arrests were made for drug crimes—more than three fourth for drug possession.

The federal system and every state system in the country have laws that mandate imprisonment for drug law violations. Between 1980 and 1992, the chances of persons being sentenced to prison for drug crimes increased 447%. From 1980 to 1996, the prison population in America tripled, owing mostly to mandatory incarcerations and increased incarceration times for drug offenders. In 1998 and 1999, nearly 600,000 new offenders were sentenced to state prisons for drug convictions, more than 10 times as many imprisonments for drug crimes than there were in 1980 and 1981. The incarceration of drug offenders accounts for 25% of the growth in state prison populations and more than 70% of the growth in the federal prison population since 1990.

Most drug offenders sentenced to prison are low-level dealers instead of so-called drug kingpins. A Department of Justice study, for example, found that more than one third of federal prison inmates serving sentences for drug crimes were low-level offenders. Long sentences for low-level, nonviolent drug offenders have done little to reduce the price or availability of illegal drugs.

The war on drugs has been extremely costly. Estimates suggest that federal and state governments spent in 2000 more than $38 billion on efforts to combat illegal drug use and sales. Moreover, the costs of building and maintaining prisons have increased fourfold since 1982; this growth in expenditures is largely attributable to the enforcement of drug laws.

The nation's drug policies have disproportionately affected persons of color, especially African Americans who are significantly more likely than other racial groups to be arrested, prosecuted, convicted, and sentenced to prison for drug possession. Law enforcement tactics, such as buy-and-bust operations, are concentrated in poorer neighborhoods where drug sales are more likely to occur in public places, trapping more African Americans in the criminal justice net.

According to the Sentencing Project, African Americans constitute 13% of the population in America, but account for 35% of those arrested, 55% of those convicted, and 75% of those sentenced to prison for drug possession. Furthermore, the sentencing disparities attached to crack cocaine, a cheaper form of cocaine readily available in inner-city neighborhoods, resulted in more African Americans being sentenced to mandatory prison terms. Almost 90% of the defendants sentenced for crack cocaine sales, at the federal level, have been African American. The dearth of drug treatment options in poorer communities has encouraged the view that drug use is a criminal justice rather than a public health problem.

The war on drugs has also exacted a toll on women of color. Women in prison are significantly more likely than men in prison to have been convicted of drug crimes. More than two thirds of the women imprisoned for drug crimes have children under 18 years old. These women are usually single parents and the sole source of support for their children. In 1996, federal welfare legislation was enacted to prohibit persons convicted of felony crimes from ever receiving welfare benefits. This provision that is being enforced in 24 states makes it even more difficult for drug offenders, especially women, to reintegrate into the community.

Drug Policy Outside the U.S.

The U.S. War on Drugs has extended well beyond its continental borders. Under the auspices of the Office of National Drug Control Policy, the country has launched numerous initiatives designed to control drug trafficking between source countries and the U.S. One major strategy involves interdicting the flow of illegal drugs into the country from overseas markets. The Drug Enforcement Administration and local law enforcement agencies seize millions of dollars of illegal drugs each year through interdiction efforts that take place in the air and on the sea. In addition, the U.S. has supported foreign governments in their attempts to eradicate opium and cocaine crops by spraying or burning them. Farmers are discouraged from cultivating illegal crops by serious punishments and encouraged to grow legal crops by farm subsidies that reduce the monetary incentives of the illegal drug trade. In Colombia and other countries, the U.S. has also provided substantial military aid and technical assistance to supplement local drug enforcement efforts to arrest drug traffickers and sellers.

The problem of illicit drug use is much less serious in European countries than it is in the U.S. Nonetheless, European countries prohibit the sales and consumption of many of the same drugs that are prohibited in the U.S. Unlike the drug control policies of the U.S. that are governed by nationwide and highly similar state policies, the drug control policies of European countries are varied and generally less punitive than those of the U.S. Italy and France, for example, impose no criminal sanctions for possession of small amounts of any drugs for personal use. Germany's policies are similar to Italy's and France's with respect to marijuana use. In addition, Germany allows its individual states to define the terms: "small quantities" and "occasional private use."

The Netherlands' drug control polices are among the most liberal in the world, especially with respect to marijuana. The country has adopted a formal policy of nonenforcement (de facto legalization) for the possession and sales of small quantities of marijuana. Furthermore, the country allows the sale of marijuana in coffee shops. Switzerland adopted a policy of containment in the late 1980s by permitting the open use and sales of drugs in a public area known as "needle park." The park attracted a large influx of drug users from throughout Europe. Several violent acts occurred in the park—including the murders of drug sellers—that eventually led to its demise. Other European countries as well as Great Britain have adopted harm reduction policies that focus on diminishing the costs of illicit drug use for individual users and the larger society. For example, British physicians are authorized to administer heroin to addicts that protects users from infected needles and alleviates the deleterious health consequences that are related to use. Such harm reduction programs also protect the community from the crimes that heroin addicts would be forced to commit to order to finance their purchases of the drug.

Importance of Treatment

Throughout the world, prevention and education programs for nonusers of drugs and treatment programs for users are widely recognized as the most effective interventions for diminishing the demand for drugs. However, throughout the 30-year history of the drug war, approximately two thirds of government expenditures have been on efforts to reduce the supply of drugs.

Numerous experts acknowledge that supply-side interventions have done little to curtail drug use or the violence attendant with the sale and distribution of illegal drugs in the U.S. Moreover, as noted above, prohibition and strict penalties for drug possession and sales have spawned many unanticipated problems. Nonetheless, few government officials are willing to shift the emphasis of the war on drugs away from punitive measures and toward treatment and rehabilitation programs for drug users. Most politicians are particularly reluctant to decry punitive drug policies out of fear of being labeled as "soft on crime" and losing the support of constituents.

Offenders with drug problems are a diverse group, and the relationship between drugs and crime is complicated. Offenders become addicted to drugs and commit crimes as a result of various events in their lives. Whatever the road to addiction and criminality, drug control policies must begin to recognize fully what research has consistently demonstrated: drug addiction is a chronic relapsing brain disorder with biological, psychological, social, and behavioral concomitants. Therefore, programs for drug-abusing offenders must be comprehensive and should include a wide range of treatment and adjunctive social services.

Much data show the crime-reducing benefits and cost effectiveness of treatment relative to other anti-drug measures (e.g., interdiction) and support a greater investment in drug treatment. Unfortunately, the treatment infrastructure in the criminal justice system has eroded farther over the past few years, a disheartening development that bodes ill for future efforts to control crime and to reduce illegal drug use. For example, despite burgeoning numbers of drug offenders behind bars, the proportion of drug offenders who received drug treatment in prison declined throughout the 1990s.

The lengthy debate in the U.S. about the best means to reduce illegal drug use in this country continues to be fueled by ideological fervor instead of sound research. However, there is no debate over the fact that illegal drug use is a significant and complex social problem that will continue to challenge policy makers, criminal justice professionals, and drug treatment providers for many years.

Arthur J. Lurigio and Melody M. Heaps

References and Further Reading

Anglin, M.D. and Hser, Y., Treatment of Drug Abuse, in Torny, M. and Wilson, J.Q., *Drugs and Crime*, University of Chicago Press, Chicago, 1990, pp. 393–460.

Bureau of Justice Statistics, *Drugs and Crime Data. Fact Sheet: Drug Data Summary*, Washington, DC, 1991.

Gerstein, D.R. and Harwood, H.J., Eds., *Treating Drug Problems: A Study of the Evolution, Effectiveness, and Financing of Public and Private Drug Treatment Systems,* National Academy Press, Washington, DC, 1990.

Hamid, A., *Drugs in America*, Aspen Publishers, Gaithersburg, MD, 1998.

Inciardi, J.A., *A Corrections-Based Continuum of Effective Drug Abuse Treatment*, National Institute of Justice, Washington, DC, 1996.

Kleiman, M.A.R., *Against Excess: Drug Policy for Results*, Basic Books, New York, 1992.

Lipton, D.S., *The Effectiveness of Treatment for Drug Abusers Under Criminal Justice Supervision,* National Institute of Justice, Washington, DC, 1995.

Lurigio, A.J. and Swartz, J.A., The Nexus Between Drugs and Crime: Theory, Research, and Practice, *Federal Probation*, 63, 67–72 (1999).

MacCoun, R.J. and Reuter, P., Drug control, in Torny, M., Ed., *The Handbook of Crime and Punishment*, Oxford University Press, New York, 1998, pp. 207–240.

Massing, M., *The Fix*, Simon & Schuster, New York, 1998.

Musto, D.F., *The American Disease: Origins of Narcotic Control*, Oxford University Press, New York, 1999.

Nadelmann, E., Drug Prohibition in the United States: Costs, Consequences, and Alternatives, *Science*, 245, 939–947 (1989).

Office of National Drug Control Policy, *The National Drug Control Strategy, 1998: A Ten Year Plan*, Washington, DC, 1998.

See also **Drug Control Policy: Decriminalization and Legalization; Drug Use: The Law**

Drug Control Policy: Legalization and Decriminalization

Drug control policy in the U.S. has long been and remains a source of debate and controversy. Relevant to and intertwined with a plethora of other social issues, such as medical access, civil liberties, and prison overcrowding, the focus of the debate centers on the current legal status of the prohibition of various illicit substances, especially marijuana. The policy alternatives of legalization and decriminalization combine with prohibition to comprise a drug control policy continuum from liberal to conservative perspectives that are defined and considered below.

Legalization

Legalization refers to the removal of criminal penalties associated with the use and possession personal use quantities of drugs. This policy position generally advocates for a government-regulated market where taxed drugs are available to consumers through prescriptions or licensed state-controlled retailers. Because of the high demand for illegal drugs and the limited deterrent effect of prohibitive laws and sanctions, legalization would provide safe and regulated substances to users while reducing the burden on law enforcement and the criminal justice system (Inciardi, 1999).

Legalization advocates focus on advantages for social issues where current prohibition has apparently failed. Economically, the prohibition of drugs is very costly, approximately 16 billion dollars annually, yet it has not produced drastic decreases in the supply of and the demand for illegal drugs. Legalizing and regulating substances allows for increased government revenue through taxes, licenses, and fees for the manufacture and distribution of legalized drugs, which in turn, could generate resources for drug education, research, and treatment programs (Faupel, Horowitz, and Weaver, 2004). Also, legalizing drugs would theoretically decrease crime associated with illegal drug activity, subsequently reducing the number of people incarcerated (currently over 1.5 million inmates) in state and local prisons (Rosenthal and Kubby, 1996).

Legalization also has numerous medical and public health implications. Theoretically, the regulation of legalized drugs removes toxic adulterants used to "cut" illegal drugs to increase profits, thus eliminating many adverse reactions drug users experience. Legalization would enable patients with glaucoma, asthma, chronic depression, and cancer easier access to marijuana, which is a proven effective treatment for reducing symptoms and discomfort experienced with these ailments. Furthermore, the distribution of clean needles or other paraphernalia to drug users helps to decrease the spread of HIV or AIDS (Rosenthal and Kubby, 1996).

Opponents to legalization criticize underdeveloped policy details, such as which drugs to legalize, setting an age limit, distribution guidelines, production responsibility, and advertising restrictions. It is also possible that legalization could spur a new black market offering "harder" drugs than publicly available. These issues have slowed legalization efforts spearheaded by marijuana legal reform organizations, most notably the National Organization for the Reform of Marijuana Laws (NORML) and the Marijuana Policy Foundation. Whereas prohibition controls and slightly decreases drug availability and the number of users, legalization would increase use and the potential for some health risks, as well as addiction and treatment expenses. Opponents believe that increased use and availability would result in various unintended consequences, ranging from police corruption to violence and property crime by addicts (Inciardi, 1999).

Legalization policies generally focus on marijuana, typically for personal recreational or medicinal use. California and Arizona have partial legalization allowing individuals to possess small amounts of the drug without consequences. Medical marijuana legalization allows patients who could benefit from the effects to obtain marijuana through a prescription from a physician. Britain legalized drugs, specifically heroin, for the medical maintenance of addicts in 1914 and illegal drug use and drug trafficking remained extremely low for about fifty years. Britain eventually abandoned this model due to the overwhelming amount of addiction and recreational use that developed (Faupel, Horowitz, and Weaver, 2004).

Recently, partial legalization proposals have been passed in the U.S. Medicinal marijuana use, by prescription only, was legalized in California and Arizona in 1996, however, laws concerning buying or selling marijuana remained the same (Inciardi, 1999). One of the primary organizations involved in initiating legalization legislation is NORML, whose "mission is to move public opinion sufficiently to achieve the repeal of marijuana prohibition so that the responsible use of cannabis by adults is no longer subject to penalty" (NORML, 2002). The Marijuana Policy Foundation is a similar Organization whose agenda is focused on a range of cannabis-specific initiatives, most notably reducing the harm associated with marijuana through consumption and current laws (MPP, 2004).

Decriminalization

Decriminalization is the removal of criminal sanctions associated with a particular aspect of drug behavior. The policy focuses on removing consequences for the possession of small amounts of an illegal drug, most notably marijuana. Although the drug activity remains illegal, the offender is subject to lesser sanctions such as fines rather than imprisonment and users are treated as patients as opposed to criminals (Faupel, Horowitz, and Weaver, 2004). Supporters of this policy believe that drug prohibition is eroding civil liberties and stripping individuals of basic freedoms. As a liberal drug policy position, supporters advocate for limited government involvement in regulating one's personal decisions and actions, positing that individuals can exhibit self control and make rational choices concerning issues of personal health care, including drug use (Inciardi, 1991).

This policy typically focuses on marijuana decriminalization because it is easily obtainable, widely used and accepted, whereas harsher drug decriminalization is less considered. The decriminalization of drugs like heroin and cocaine is more controversial because of concerns for increased addiction potential, even at experimental stages, the high amounts of substances needed because of rapid tolerance increases, and negative public opinion associated with illicit drugs, generally, and concerning the propensity for violent behavior, specifically (Inciardi, 1999). There have been several attempts at marijuana decriminalization in the past that have decreased criminal penalties for use or possession, but most have realized only minimal success in altering social attitudes about the drug.

In the 1960s eleven states began to reduce penalties for marijuana possession and in 1973 Oregon became the first state to decriminalize possession, declaring that it was punishable by no more than a $100 fine. This initiative motivated several states to decriminalize possession to a misdemeanor and a fine. Now, all fifty states have reduced the sanctions associated with marijuana possession. Twelve states allow individuals to possess up to an ounce of marijuana (up to 3 ounces for Ohio and Maine) with an average nominal fine of $100. In Alaska, possession has been decriminalized for small amounts for personal use (up to eight ounces) and harvesting up to 25 marijuana plants is permissible (Faupel, Horowitz, and Weaver, 2004).

Despite the widespread popularity of recreational drug use in the U.S., particularly marijuana, many Americans endorse a seemingly contradictory stance of personal use while opposing legalization. Sociologists have attributed this outlook to the "symbolic significance" of drug use wherein substances' prohibited status ensures certain social functions, such as engaging in deviant rites of passage, group bonding and solidification, and, for teenagers, experimentation and rebellion (Miller, 2001). Other common beliefs about drug use, especially the "drug use escalation effect," also frustrate legalization efforts, but the prospects for reform are promising with the aging of a younger, more informed cohort of voters.

J. Mitchell Miller and Jessica McGowan

References and Further Reading

Faupel, C.E., Horowitz, A.M., and Weaver, G.S., *The Sociology of American Drug Use,* McGraw Hill, New York, 2004.

Inciardi, J.A., *The Drug Legalization Debate*, Sage, CA, 1991.

Inciardi, J.A., *The Drug Legalization Debate*, Sage, CA, 1999.

Marijuana Policy Foundation. 2004. http://www.mpp.org/about.html.

Miller, J.M., Marijuana as social common denominator: Reconsidering the use and academic success relationship, *Humanity and Society,* 24:4, 338–347 (2001).

National Organization for the Reform of Marijuana Laws, 2002. Available at: http://www.norml.com/index.cfm? Group_ID=3414.

Rosenthal, E. and Kubby, S., *Why Marijuana Should be Legal,* Thunder's Mouth Press, New York, 1996.

See also **Drug Control Policy: Prevention, Treatment and the War on Drugs; Drug Use: The Law**

Drug Control Policy: Prevention and Treatment

Introduction

According to the National Household Survey on Drug Abuse, over 15 million Americans aged 12 or older (7% of the total population) used an illicit drug in the previous month (Epstein, 2002). Among individuals, the most common illicit drug used was marijuana, followed by cocaine and hallucinogens. Recent surveys reveal conflicting reports on the level of substance abuse among American youth. Some national surveys even show a leveling off or decrease in substance use in specific subpopulations of adolescents and young adults. In the past decade, use of inhalants and LSD have decreased, while the use of heroin and "club drugs" such as Ecstasy (MDMA) have increased among high school students. More than $60 billion dollars was spent on illicit drugs last year, and the estimated costs to society from drug abuse was projected at over $160 billion during the same year.

Drug Policy

According to the 2003 U.S. National Drug Control Strategy, the majority of federal drug spending ($11.7 billion total) will be for domestic law enforcement, drug treatment, interdiction, and drug prevention. The National Drug Control Strategy targeted a 2-year goal of a 10% reduction in current use of illegal drugs for 8th, 10th, and 12th grade students as well as those adults age 18 and older. The 5-year goals of the strategy seek for a 25% reduction in current illicit drug use for the same groups. This most recent national drug control policy is based on three priorities: (1) stopping drug use before it starts; (2) healing America's drug users; and (3) disrupting the market.

History has shown that drug laws do not always serve as an effective deterrent to illicit drug use. Indeed, there is evidence that indicates that stricter policies may increase the prevalence of addiction problems. Should we identify those arrested for drug offenses as criminals, or as those afflicted with a disease in need of treatment? This is a difficult question to answer because illicit drug abuse is both an illness and a crime. It is important to distinguish those criminals who use drugs from those criminals who are involved with the selling of drugs. Who should be more harshly punished, those who create the demand, or those who satisfy the demand for illicit drugs? When developing, enacting, and enforcing drug policies, it is necessary to take these factors into consideration.

In a response to the widespread use of illicit drugs and the ongoing efforts of drug smugglers and dealers to distribute illegal substances, governments typically focus their efforts on reducing supply as well as demand. Supply reduction policies are aimed at reducing the supply of illegal drugs and controlling therapeutic drugs. One element of supply reduction, interdiction, refers to the policy of cutting off supplies of illicit drugs coming into the country. Despite the enormous resources devoted to supply reduction, there is a legitimate concern that even if the supply of a particular substance is successfully reduced, the demand for drugs will persist and be replaced by another (Hanson et al., 2002).

Demand reduction policies attempt to decrease an individual's intention to use drugs and are often focused on adolescents and young adults. Demand reduction prevention strategies appeal to values, attitudes, and skills to resist the urge to try or continue the use of illicit drugs. Typically, two thirds of the budget for drug abuse in America is devoted to supply reduction, while the remainder is spent on reducing the demand for such drugs. However, a new U.S. substance abuse treatment initiative, *Access to Recovery*, enables those seeking drug treatment to receive vouchers to pay for appropriate community-based services. This initiative is backed by $600 million in new funds and is designed to make treatment services more accessible to those without private treatment coverage.

Substance Use, Crime, and Violence

Although there is a clear association between drug use and crime, the determinants of such relationships differ by type of drug, user, and criminal offense. One explanation for this association is that crime and violence are pharmacologically induced, in that criminal acts are committed by individuals under the influence of psychoactive drugs. Another theory postulates that an individual often commits criminal acts in order to purchase drugs. Finally, there is also drug-defined crime, referring to acts associated with the possession, use, trafficking or distribution of illicit drugs. Numerous substances of abuse, including alcohol, amphetamines, cocaine, and LSD have been shown to increase aggression and may also precipitate violence in certain individuals. According to the FBI's Uniform Crime Reporting program, 4.5% of the 12,658 homicides in 1999 were narcotics-related (FBI, 2000). In that same year, over 13% of all convicted jail inmates reported that they committed their offenses to obtain money to purchase drugs and one third of state prisoners admitted that they had committed their offenses while under the influence of drugs.

Drug use is disproportionately prevalent among arrestees compared to the general population, with over 63% testing positive for an illicit drug. In 1998, drug offenders accounted for 21% of the state prison population and over half (59%) of the federal prison population (Federal Bureau of Prisons, 2000). Estimates from the Bureau of Justice Statistics (BJS) and the National Center on Addiction and Substance Abuse (CASA) show that from 60% to 83% of the prison population have used drugs in their lifetime, nearly twice the national average (CASA, 1998). Of the $38 billion spent on corrections in 1996, it is estimated that over $30 billion was spent on prisoners who either had a history of drug or alcohol problems, were convicted of alcohol or drug related crimes, were using drugs or alcohol at the time of their offenses, or committed crimes for money to purchase drugs (CASA, 1998).

Drug Testing

The negative consequences associated with drug abuse affecting all segments of society have increased the range and demand for drug testing in a variety of settings. In the workplace, drug testing is often utilized for those professions that focus on public safety, such as medical care, law enforcement, or transportation. Numerous private businesses have also adopted drug testing policies for employees. Drug testing is also used for athletes on all levels of sports, from high school to college and professional governing bodies. The criminal justice system also uses drug testing to assist in the prosecution of those individuals engaging in drug-related crimes. The increase in drug testing has led some to scrutinize its effectiveness as a deterrent to drug abuse, suggesting that such negative consequences of a drug test can lead to more serious problems for an individual. Others point to such advantages of drug testing as identifying those in need of treatment and allowing them to gain access to rehabilitation services that they may not have sought themselves.

Prevention

Substance abuse is a problem that often develops from a myriad of influences on an individual. In the prevention literature, these influences have been grouped into the domains of the individual, family, peers, school, community, and the environment (SAMHSA, 2001). The level of influence each of these factors has on a person varies with each individual as they develop. Especially among youth, both risk factors (factors that increase likelihood of substance use) and protective factors (those that counter risk factors) become a necessary component of all prevention programming.

The term "prevention," even when limited to the field of drug abuse, is a broad concept that includes a range of approaches applied to a variety of groups at different levels of drug use. Prevention can be broken down into three main levels, *primary*, *secondary*, and *tertiary* prevention. Primary prevention strategies are aimed at preventing a problem before it gets a chance to manifest itself, such as preventing a child from ever trying marijuana. Secondary prevention is a type of early intervention in that it attempts to treat those individuals with drug problems early to reduce or minimize the severity of the substance abuse. Tertiary prevention is often viewed as rehabilitation in that its goal is to reduce the degree of suffering and minimize long-term consequences of substance abuse.

A large portion of funding for primary prevention activities in the U.S. is earmarked for two programs aimed towards reducing illicit drug use, the *National Youth Anti-Drug Media Campaign* and the *Drug-Free Communities Program*. The National Youth Anti-Drug Media Campaign utilizes advertising and grassroots public outreach to educate families, parents, and youths about drug use and associated negative consequences. This campaign includes media messages at both the national and local levels targeting youths ages 14–16, years during which there is a greater risk for the initiation of illicit drug use. The Drug-Free Communities program serves community groups through assistance with the formation of effective community and antidrug coalitions that work to reduce substance abuse among youths through collaboration among both private and public organizations and increased citizen participation.

There are a wide variety of approaches to drug abuse prevention, and the Center for Substance Abuse Prevention (CSAP) has identified six strategies often used for substance abuse prevention programs to reduce risk factors and increase protective factors: Information Dissemination, Prevention Education, Alternative Activities, Community-Based Processes, Environmental Approaches, and Problem Identification and Referral.

Drug Abuse Treatment

The provision of adequate drug treatment is a priority for the U.S. to address the growing need for such services as evidenced by recent estimates that almost 4 million people are in need of treatment services (Epstein, 2002). The discrepancy between those who are in need of drug treatment and those who actually receive such services, or treatment gap, has been revealed in surveys and reinforced by professionals in the addictions field, suggesting only 1 in 10 people receive the treatment they need (Epstein, 2002). Although the underlying goal of most drug treatment programs is abstinence, the types of treatment modalities vary widely.

Providing treatment services can reduce drug-related costs to society by reducing crime, medical care, enrollment in social welfare programs, and lost work productivity from those abusing drugs. For the most part, however, treatment programs lack the funding they need to provide adequate services to accommodate those in need. Because drug addiction is a disease that does not discriminate based on age, gender, race, or income, there is a need for culturally sensitive treatment options reflecting the vast differences among those with substance abuse problems.

Cost-Effectiveness of Drug Treatment

Numerous studies have found that treatment of drug abuse is much less expensive than letting addiction problems persist. For every dollar spent on drug treatment, there is a $4 to $7 return in reduced drug-related crime and criminal justice costs (NIDA, 1999). Although long-term residential care may cost as much as $16,000 per year, it costs society over $40,000 to let one drug addict remain untreated (Hanson et al., 2002). It is also more expensive to incarcerate individuals than to send them to a drug treatment facility.

Drug Treatment and the Criminal Justice System

There is a growing trend for nonviolent drug offenders to be diverted into treatment as a cost-effective and humane alternative to incarceration. Prison drug treatment programs have been associated with decreased rates of recidivism among drug offenders. In another attempt recognizing the relationship between criminal activity and substance abuse, many correctional facilities offer drug treatment services. Under the *Violent Crime Control and Law Enforcement Act* of 1994, the Federal Bureau of Prisons provides drug treatment to all eligible inmates before they are released. However, treatment varies widely by facility, and the problem of drug abuse in the prison system persists. In 1997, approximately 40% of all correctional facilities offered drug and alcohol counseling, serving over 170,000 adults and juveniles (SAMHSA, 2000). However, those inmates who received treatment represented only 11% of the incarcerated population, whereas estimates of those inmates in need of treatment are between 70% and 85% (U.S. General Accounting Office, 1991).

Drug Courts

As many court officials have become increasingly frustrated with repeat drug offenders and the association between criminal activity and drug use, many have replaced traditional sentences with drug treatment. There are currently over 1400 drug courts in the U.S., and over 140,000 drug offenders have participated in these programs since 1989. With success rates as high as 70% for some drug courts, these programs offer an important step to move nonviolent drug offenders into treatment. Drug courts are increasingly used as a means to utilize the coercive authority of a judge and the criminal justice system to change behavior by requiring abstinence for the drug offender. Typically, drug courts differ from criminal courts in that both sides are working toward the common goal of treatment. Drug courts often enforce a combination of sanctions such as mandatory drug testing, supervised treatment, case management, and aftercare programs.

Addiction Treatment Modalities

There are a variety of approaches currently being used to treat drug addiction. Behavioral therapies often employed include counseling, psychotherapy, support groups, and family therapy for addicted persons. Other forms of treatment include prescribed medications to help prevent withdrawal symptoms and craving. The most successful drug treatment options typically are those that involve a combination of treatment services to best meet the client's needs (Hanson et al., 2002). For example, drug treatment for a heroin addict may consist of the use of methadone replacement combined with behavioral therapy to decrease use to the point of abstinence.

The type and setting of treatment deemed appropriate for an individual depends on such factors as extent of social support, family participation, socioeconomic status, legal history, and education level. The long-term goal of all drug abuse treatment is to achieve sustained abstinence, but more immediate goals are to reduce drug use, improve the individuals' level of functioning, and minimize adverse consequences of their drug abuse. Research has shown that the length of treatment is an important factor in successful outcome for drug treatment programs (Hanson et al., 2002). Short-term treatment programs may last less than 6 months and include residential, medication, or outpatient therapy. Residential therapeutic communities and methadone maintenance outpatient services are more common forms of long-term treatment programs.

Therapeutic communities (TCs) are residential treatment programs that typically last for 6 to 12 months. These programs attempt to "resocialize" the drug addict through a community of individuals with histories of drug dependence. The primary goal of TCs is to change an overall lifestyle that includes personal responsibility and elimination of criminal behavior in addition to abstinence from drugs (NIDA, 1999).

Pharmaceutical Treatments

Pharmaceutical treatments involve the long-term administration of a medication to either replace an illicit drug, or block the actions of such a drug. One such pharmacological replacement is methadone, which is a narcotic analgesic often used as a substitute for heroin, morphine, codeine, and other opiates. Methadone maintenance programs have been found to be cost-effective in terms of both reduced criminal activity and medical care. Also, those programs that provide additional services, such as counseling, therapy, or medical care, in addition to methadone generally achieve more positive outcomes. Methadone maintenance and other such programs are a form of harm reduction that attempts to lessen the dangers of drug abuse through practical solutions. There is some debate as to whether the substitution of a less harmful drug for a more harmful substance is an appropriate treatment method.

Drug Abuse Treatment for Women

As the etiology of drug abuse differs between genders, treatment approaches must take such differences into consideration as well. For example, the majority of drug abusing women report histories of physical and sexual abuse. Many drug-using women do not seek treatment because of legitimate fears such as not being able to keep their children, reprisal from spouses or boyfriends, or punishment from authorities in the community. In addition, research indicates that drug-dependent women have even greater difficulty resisting drugs if their male partners engage in drug use.

Drug treatment programs have traditionally been developed to meet the needs of male clients, not taking the unique circumstances of women drug abusers into consideration. In an effort to meet the needs of females, drug abuse treatment services have been developed that focus on those services that could improve the chances for effective, sustained change in drug abuse. More specifically, drug abuse treatment programs targeting women are more effective when they include such services as job counseling and training, literacy training and educational opportunities, parenting training, child care, social services, and psychological assessment.

Future Directions

There are conflicting findings on whether or not laws serve as effective deterrents against drug abuse. With increasing numbers of drug courts across the country, there are many who feel that it is more productive and cost-effective to treat nonviolent drug offenders as those suffering from the disease of addiction rather than criminals. Studies have shown several promising approaches to drug abuse treatment, but more research is necessary to explore the potential of delivering effective treatment to meet the needs of various subpopulations such as women, youth, and minorities. It is imperative that those who are in need of and actively seeking out treatment have access to such services. This remains a difficult task for the U.S., with only one-third of the budget devoted to demand reduction, and the majority used to reduce the supply of illicit drugs. With limited funding, it is imperative to develop practical drug policies that are consistent with the needs and interests of the general population, focus on reducing the demand for drugs, and increase the availability of services for those in need of drug treatment. Finally, as the severity of penalties associated with drug-related offenses varies by state, it is the responsibility of each individual state to ensure that adequate treatment services are provided in accordance with such laws.

STUART L. USDAN

References and Further Reading

National Center on Addiction and Substance Abuse, *Behind Bars: Substance Abuse and America's Prison Population,* Columbia University, New York, 1998.

Drug Courts Program Office, *Summary of All Drug Court Activities by State*, The American University, Washington, DC, 2000.

Epstein, J.F., Substance Dependence, Abuse and Treatment: Findings From the 2000 National Household Survey on Drug Abuse, NHSDA Series A-16, DHHS Pub. No. (SMA) 02-3642, SAMHSA, Rockville, MD, 2002.

Federal Bureau of Investigation (FBI), *Crime in the United States 1980 Through 1999,* Uniform Crime Reporting Program, U.S. Department of Justice, Washington, DC, 2000.

Federal Bureau of Prisons, *Federal Bureau of Prisons Quick Facts,* U.S. Department of Justice, Washington, DC, 2000.

Hanson, G. R., Venturelli, P. J., and Fleckenstein, A. E., *Drugs and Society,* 7th ed., Jones and Bartlett Publishers, Sudbury, MA, 2002.

National Center on Addiction and Substance Abuse, *Behind Bars: Substance Abuse and America's Prison Population,* Columbia University, New York, 1998.

National Institute on Drug Abuse (NIDA), *Principles of Drug Addiction Treatment: A Research Based Guide,* NIDA, Rockville, MD, 1999.

Substance Abuse and Mental Health Services Administration (SAMHSA). Substance Abuse Treatment in Adult and Juvenile Correctional Facilities: Findings from the Uniform Facility Data Set 1997 Survey of Correctional Facilities, U.S. Department of Health and Human Services, Washington, DC, 2000.

Substance Abuse and Mental Health Services Administration (SAMHSA). *Principles of Substance Abuse Prevention.* DHHS Pub. No. (SMA) 01-3507, U.S. Department of Health and Human Services, Rockville, MD, 2001.

U.S. General Accounting Office, Drug Treatment: State Prisons Face Challenges in Providing Services (PDF), Report to the Committee on Government Operations, House of Representatives, U.S. Congress, Washington, DC, 1991.

See also **Alcohol Use: Prevention and Treatment; Rehabilitation/Treatment**

Drug Enforcement Administration, The (DEA)

The Drug Enforcement Administration (DEA) has a fairly short yet rich history as the nation's primary drug law enforcement agency. The primary mission of the DEA is to enforce federal laws and regulations germane to controlled substances in the U.S. The DEA actively pursues, apprehends, and prosecutes individuals and groups involved in growing, manufacturing, or distributing controlled substances. Additionally, the DEA is responsible for recommending and advocating drug awareness and prevention programs targeted toward reducing the availability and the demand for drugs in the domestic and international markets.

The DEA's origins are traceable to the Harrison Narcotic Act of 1914, and its enforcement efforts began the following year. Originally classified as a "Miscellaneous Division" of the Bureau of Internal Revenue, the agency's first year successes included seizures of 44 pounds of heroin and 106 convictions. The DEA underwent a time of significant expansion and reorganization over the next several decades with the passage of: (1) the Narcotics Drugs Import and Export Act of 1922, legislation that established the Federal Narcotics Control Board and prohibited importation of narcotics except for medicinal purposes, (2) the Marijuana Tax Act of 1937 which placed $100 per ounce fine on nontax paid marijuana, and (3) the Boggs Act of 1956 that made heroin use illegal (Machette, 1995).

The DEA's immediate predecessor, the Bureau of Narcotics and Dangerous Drugs (BNDD), was created in 1968 through a Congressional approved merger of the Bureau of Narcotics and the Bureau of Drug Abuse Control (BDAC). Immediately following the formation of the BNDD, Congress passed the Controlled Substances Act (CSA), known as Title II of the Comprehensive Drug Abuse Prevention and Control Act of 1970. This pioneering legislation established a single system of control for both narcotic and psychotropic drugs. The rapid growth in the BNDD's personnel, domestic and international enforcement efforts, and the emerging social problems presented by illicit drugs, particularly LSD and other "designer drugs," confirmed the need for the creation of a separate agency in 1973, the Drug Enforcement Administration (Drug Enforcement Administration, 1999).

The Senate Committee on Government Operations outlined six anticipated benefits of creating the DEA:

1. Ending interagency rivalries between the BNDD and the U.S. Customs Service,
2. Giving FBI its first role in drug enforcement through cooperative efforts with DEA in combating organized crime,
3. Providing a centralized agency for coordinating foreign, federal, state, and local drug enforcement efforts,
4. Placing a single administrator in charge of federal drug law enforcement to ensure accountability and buffer against corruption and enforcement abuses,
5. Consolidating DEA drug enforcement operations to maximize coordination between federal investigations and prosecution efforts,
6. Establishing DEA as a "superagency" to coordinate all drug enforcement efforts and the gathering of intelligence on international drug trafficking (Drug Enforcement Administration, 1999).

Upon its creation in 1973, the DEA was comprised of 2775 total employees (1470 special agents/1305 support staff) and operated with an annual budget of $65.2 million. Today, the DEA commands a budget of $1.9 billion and has 9629 total employees (4680 special agents/4949 support staff). Since 1986, the DEA is responsible for making approximately 443,600 domestic drug arrests. Additionally, the DEA seized 61,594 kilograms of cocaine, 705 kilograms of heroine, 195,644 kilograms of marijuana, 118,049,279 dosage units of methamphetamine, and 11,532,704 dosage units of hallucinogens in 2002 alone. The DEA currently operates 237 domestic field offices throughout the U.S. and 80 foreign field offices located in 58 different countries (Drug Enforcement Administration, 2004).

In as little as three decades, the DEA has established a significant worldwide presence and is the world's premier drug law enforcement agency. The DEA has realized continued success in the fight against the "War on Drugs" and has evolved into an agency responsible for far more than the six envisioned benefits first outlined in the aforementioned Senate Committee's final report of 1973. The DEA controls the investigation and preparation for the prosecution of major violators of federal controlled substance laws and engages in operations focused on disrupting and dissolving violent drug trafficking organizations. The agency also is responsible for the maintenance of a national drug intelligence program that involves collecting, analyzing, and disseminating drug intelligence information. Also, the DEA serves as the U.S. liaison to the United Nations and Interpol and is responsible for the seizure and forfeiture of assets that are either directly or indirectly associated with the criminal drug enterprise.

Despite the DEA's expansion and rapid evolution, its primary mission and operational goals remain concrete. The majority of the DEA's efforts are still devoted to its designed functions: (1) to coordinate and cooperate with federal, state, and local law enforcement on mutual drug enforcement efforts and nonenforcement methods such as crop eradication, crop substitution, and relevant training (supply reduction); and (2) to continue to recommend and promote drug resistance education and foster awareness of the adverse effects and current trends in drug use, essentially demand-reduction.

The DEA, as the nation's foremost drug enforcement mechanism, has come to symbolize law enforcement's drug suppression and intervention efforts, generally. Accordingly, the DEA does not enjoy consensus endorsement throughout American society and is especially disliked by critical criminologists whose objections to its operations are based on both intended and unintended consequences. Strategies of foreign drug crop eradication are argued to exacerbate poverty and disdain of the U.S. in third world countries, especially nations whose moralistic or normative outlook embraces or condones drugs either legally or in popular culture regarding manufacture as a cash crop or for personal use (Miller & Selva, 1994). Unintended consequences of a harsh zero tolerance approach to minimizing drug use and problems may be the solidification of the symbolic significance of drug use as a form of social deviance and the question of the proportionality of sanctions for drug offenses relative to seemingly more threatening property and violent crime. Some scholars have contended that large-scale operational successes by the DEA ensure higher profitability by the principles of supply and demand. Thus, success by the DEA may yield the unintended consequences of greater illicit drug sales profits and higher levels of associated street violence (Miller, 2001). Whereas these contentions may or may not prove valid by empirical standards, it is unlikely that the DEA would be responsive, as its agenda is rooted in conservative, if not monolithic, and strictly legalistic ideology.

J. Mitchell Miller and Wesley G. Jennings

References and Further Reading

Drug Enforcement Administration, *Tradition of Excellence: The History of the DEA from 1973–1998*. U.S. Department of Justice, Washington, DC, 1999.

Drug Enforcement Administration, *Statistics*, 2004. Retrieved January 23, 2004 from www.dea.gov/statistics.html.

Machette, R.B., *Guide to Federal Records in the National Archives of the United States*, National Archive and Records Administration, Washington, DC, 1995.

Miller, J.M. and Selva, L.H., Drug enforcement's double-edged sword: An assessment of asset forfeiture programs, *Justice Quarterly* 11:4, 313–335 (1994).

Miller, J.M., Marijuana as social common denominator: Reconsidering the use and academic success relationship, *Humanity and Society*, 24:4 (2001).

Additional information and references available at: www.dea.gov.

See also **Drug Control Policy: Enforcement, Interdiction and the War on Drugs; Drug Use: The Law**

Drug Trafficking as an Occupation

Drug dealing is not just a crime, but a form of business as well. Cocaine, methamphetamines, heroin, marijuana, as well as diverted pharmaceutical drugs, and a variety of designer drugs, such as ecstasy and LSD, are drugs that are commonly sold by drug dealers. This business employs all the structure and assets that make them almost identical to the operation of a legitimate business. They have a sales force, distributors, an import and export division, and a product that is in high demand to sell. Figure 1 depicts the structure and operation of a former Colombian drug cartel. In this case the product is a very addictive drug, often produced and distributed by "drug lords" or cartels. The structural aspects generally include three major levels of drug dealers, the street dealer, the distributors, and the cartels that are classified as organized crime by U.S. federal agencies such as the Drug Enforcement Administration and the Federal Bureau of Investigation. Other major drug trafficking groups are often given the status of organized crime. Some of these are the Yakuza, based in Japan; the Triads, based in China; Russian organized crime; outlaw biker gangs such as the Bandidos, Hell's Angels, Outlaws, and Pagans; street gangs such as the Disciple Nation and the Vice Lord Nation, and black organizations such as the Jamaican posses or the Nigerians. Almost every country has its brand of organized drug traffickers.

The drug traffic is controlled by such organized crime groups who have formed alliances to become more effective and efficient in their goal of producing enormous profits. Thus drug trafficking has become both a transnational and international phenomenon. Drug trafficking is the primary means of acquiring large sums of money and power, and is a major cause of both human and financial suffering world wide. This globalization of drug trafficking is a major concern for the governments of most countries, and it has resulted in many debates of how to deal with this problem as

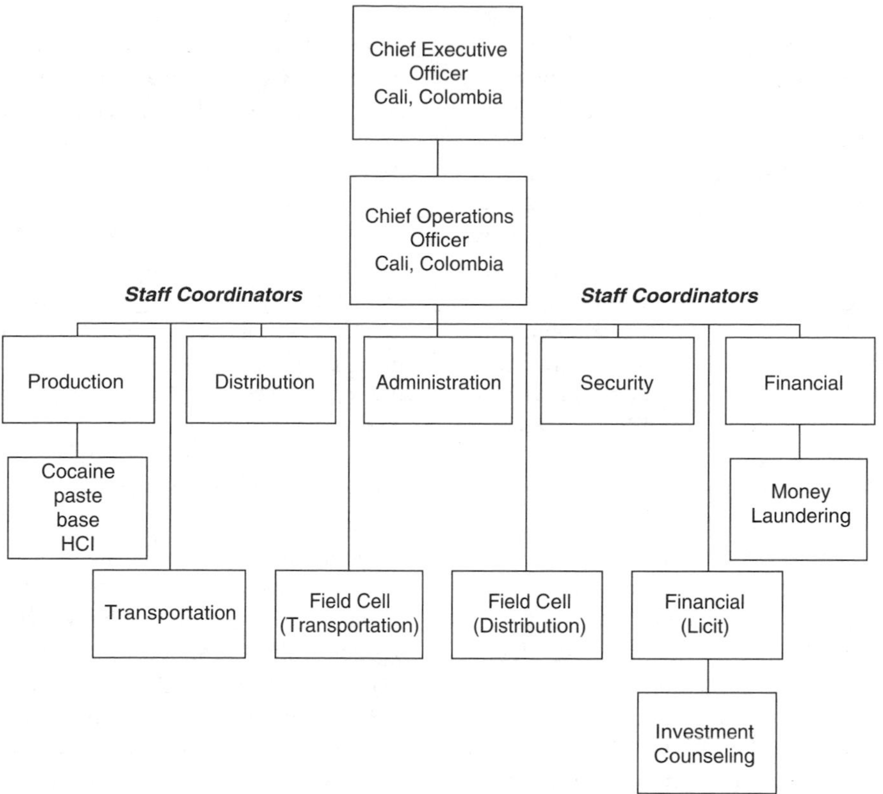

FIGURE 1 Organizational Structure

well as massive expenditures of resources to address drug trafficking (Einstein and Amiv, 1999).

> Globalization has dramatically changed the face of both legitimate and illegitimate enterprise. Criminals, by exploiting advances in technology, finance, communications, and transportation in pursuit of their illegal endeavors, have become criminal entrepreneurs. Perhaps the most alarming aspect of this "entrepreneurial" style of crime is the intricate manner in which drugs and terrorism may be intermingled (Casteel, 2003).

The Drug Enforcement Administration (DEA) has identified 14 of the 36 designated foreign terrorist organizations that have been involved in drug trafficking activities. The profits from these activities have been used to fund the causes of the various terrorist organizations. Both organized crime and terrorist organizations have used the proceeds of drug sales as a source of funding for many of their other criminal activity. The DEA has defined narcoterrorism as an organized group that is complicit in the activities of drug trafficking in order to further or to fund premeditated and politically motivated violence perpetrated against noncombatant targets with the intention to influence a government or people (Casteel, 2003).

The characterization of drug dealers is often equated to what the public has seen in a movie or on a TV show. This portrayal is more one of traffickers that are well within the hierarchy of the drug cartels. Drug trafficking may also be divided into two general categories; the dealer for profit and the person that must deal to support their own habit. Profit dealers are classified as wholesalers, suppliers or producers, mid level distributors, and street level or retail distributors. The profit dealers are the people who are in the profession of the distribution of illicit drugs. The profit dealer obtains large quantities of drugs that are classified as controlled substances by law or statutes. They then distribute these drugs to either the smaller profit drug dealers or to the habitual drug user. They can make anywhere from $400 up to $700 on an average day. This can produce a profit of $3000 to $4200 a week. This money results in the drug dealer having the ability to indulge in an extravagant lifestyle. These indulgences may be anything from luxury cars and gambling to providing for their family. Major dealers may not use drugs themselves, and often do nothing other than supply the drugs and employ others to sell drugs for them. In 1960 the Medellin Drug Cartel of Colombia, South America, had an estimated network of 55 billion dollars with a membership of 75,000. The leader of this cartel, Pablo Escobar, had an estimated net worth of two to four billion dollars. He began as a petty thief, became a gang member and was employed as a murderer for hire before becoming the leader of the Medellin Cartel. The path that Pablo Escobar took is a path frequently taken by leaders of major drug trafficking organizations. The Carrillo–Fuentes organization based in Ciudad Juarez, Mexico is another major drug trafficking organization. Its leader became known as the "Lord of the Skies," based on his transporting tons of cocaine by air into North America from Mexico. Both organizations expended millions on corruption of police and government officials to maintain and protect their operations.

On the other side of the drug-dealing spectrum are the people who become drug dealers to support their own habits. These dealers do not make as much money as the profit dealers (generally only around three hundred dollars a day), but they receive other benefits. These benefits are usually in the form of drugs. They can receive over two hundred dollars a day in free drugs that they value more than money itself. This amount can range from two hundred to three hundred dollars in of drugs, and some drug users say that they can easily use more drugs than the amount that they receive for free (Knowles, 1996). This results in the dealer or user actually paying to buy drugs from the money that they earned while selling drugs. This is what makes these dealers such a good asset for major drug distributors or profit dealers. The distributors do not have to pay the drug dealer or user as much money. It is cheaper to give away their product at "retail value" than to pay them cash for selling the drugs. The distributors may be viewed as over achieving drug dealers, but they over achieve on a grand scale. The distributor may move anywhere from one kilogram of cocaine a day to multiple kilogram quantities. This level of movement is more than one drug dealer alone would be able to move on the street in one day (Ringwald, 1996). This results in the distributor becoming a major player, who employs many other smaller scale drug dealers. To put it more in perspective, think of the distributor as the owner of a chain of gas stations, and each gas station represents a drug dealer. The distributor moves more of his or her product by being more visible, and by having more places where the product can be purchased. By being more visible and by having more drug dealers out selling their drugs, the distributors make profit and remain in the background with less exposure to law enforcement efforts.

The people who reside in elaborate mansions are frequently depicted in the movies and on TV shows as being involved in the import or export of illegal drugs that results in the forming of cartels or syndicates. These cartels are the primary source of drugs worldwide that are sold by the mid-level street dealer. The mid-level dealers often form units referred to as cells, and are responsible for returning a large part of the money to the cartels from the drug cells. Money laundering has become a major part of the illicit drug industry. Money laundering can be defined as "the process by which one conceals the existence, illegal source, or illegal application of income, and then disguises that income to make it appear legitimate" (President's Commission on Organized Crime, 1984). The process of money laundering is a major concern for law enforcement. Not only does it clean the money that is gained illegally by drug dealers, but it also results in unpaid taxes. With the growing number of transactions that are being done electronically between countries, it can be very difficult for governments to track money once it leaves their borders. This has caused the international community to develop the Locus Regit Actum Principle. This principle allows agencies of separate countries to act together to identify and apprehend money launderers. Up until the Locus Regit Actum Principle was created, whenever a country tried to track money that went out of the country, they had to stop when they reached the border of another country. This principle allowed for alliances between countries making it easier to track money, and harder for the money launderer to hide illicit income.

The drug cartels are major organizations that grow, process, and import drugs into other countries. The Cali Cartel of Colombia, South America, is yet another example of the magnitude and complexity of drug trafficking. The Cali cartel produces profits approaching three hundred billion dollars a year. All of this is from illegal drug trafficking with most of the profit from illegal drug sales in the U.S. At the height of the Cali cartel's power they were providing an estimated 85% of the world's cocaine (Bunker, 2003). The Cali cartel has many strengths and weaknesses. Some of their strengths are as follows: (1) Their distribution network is second to none; they do not have any problem in finding people who are willing to risk their lives to move the drugs from Colombia, South America, to the U.S. and other countries. (2) They have one of the best money laundering schemes around, and seem to be able to move their money without foreign governments being able to detect their efforts. (3) Their wealth is another of their great assets; they are able to use the money to buy the fastest boats, the best equipment, and are able to pay government officials, members of Colombia's armies, and guerrillas to act as their guards and to fight for them. (4) The land that they use to grow their cocaine is very fertile and able to grow the coca in a very efficient manner. Some of their weaknesses are: (1) They operate a business that almost the entire world sees as illegal. This causes the operating costs of doing business to grow, but this is counteracted by the fact that they do not pay any taxes on the money they receive from doing business. (2) The product that they are selling is one that is sold based on how pure the product is, and they cannot reduce the purity of the cocaine for fear of a reduced share of the market. (3) When some of their product is captured by law enforcement they may lose some of the market that they currently hold. (4) The fact that they are such a major player in the drug trade causes them to become the focus of law enforcement rather than some of the smaller organizations (Kwan, 2003).

The Cali cartel has many things that allow it to combat these threats to their organization. They are able to get their product to many other countries because Colombia's border is not very secure, and they are able to move the drugs out relatively easily. Some dealers attempt to increase the number of new users of their drugs by influencing people who use softer drugs like marijuana to get addicted to cocaine. These are examples from the Cali cartel, but they can be applied to just about every major drug organization around the world.

The U.S. government has made significant seizures over the years, but that has not seemed to decrease the availability of illicit drugs. The government has seized over fifteen million dollars in cash in just two raids (House of Representatives, Subcommittee on General Oversight and Investigations, 1997). However, the cartels make billions, and a loss of a few millions does not even seem to be much of a ripple in their grand scheme. The cartels amass great quantities of money that they expend on methods to get their drugs into a county. They often have greater resources than the people who are trying to stop them. The cartels employ observation posts to observe the police and other government agents. They corrupt people in government agencies to give them information much like an informant would for a government agency. They also set up elaborate posts to intercept phone calls and computer transmissions just as the government uses electronic intercepts to intercept their phone calls and computer transmissions. In one of the most famous hightech raids in Colombia, South America, government agents seized a 1.5 million dollar IBM Main Frame computer. This computer was one of the largest and fastest of its time, and the computer was being used to scan calls to and from all of the Cali cartel's members and associates to identify any possible undercover government agents or government informants. The computer had custom software, and was linked directly to the phone network in Colombia. This is indicative of the complexity to which the cartels have evolved. Cartels have used computers to inform their pilots when to land and take off, or when they need to dump their cargo due to detection by law enforcement. Computer systems also keep records of shipments of illicit drugs, financial records of transactions, and are used for online bidding for their drugs (Everhart, 2002). This allowed drug dealers across the world to bid on and hopefully get the price they wanted to pay for the drugs. The system was not very different from the system that is in use today on web auctions such as eBay.

Drug trafficking as an occupation can be as simple as street transactions of illegal drugs or as complex as the operations of hightech drug cartels. Motives for traffickers can range from drug use and peer pressure to huge profits. Demand drives the supply of drugs with greed and human weakness assuring that someone will always be in the business of drug trafficking. The problem has risen to the level of a national threat for many countries and will likely continue as long as the demand is present. As Al Capone, a notorious Chicago mob boss, once said, "All I ever did was to supply a demand that was pretty popular" (Browning, 1980).

STEPHEN MALLORY

References and Further Reading

Browning, F. and Gerassi, J., *The American Way of Crime,* G.P. Putnam & Sons, New York, 1980.

Bunker, M., *Cocaine Kingpins Stick to their Guns,* MSNBC, available at: http://www.msnbc.com/news/165141.asp?cp1=1, retrieved on July 23, 2003.

Casteel, S.W., *Assistant Administrator for Intelligence Before the Senate Committee on Judiciary May 20, 2003,* available at: http://www.usdoj.gov/dea/pubs/cngrtest/ct052003p.html, retrieved on July 20, 2003.

Everhart, D., *Colombian Cartels Hum With High Tech,* available at: http://www.newsmax.com/archives/articles/2002/6/30/65538.shtml, retrieved on July 28, 2003.

House of Representatives, *Subcommittee on General Oversight and Investigations,* Committee on banking and Financial Services, Washington, DC, March 11, 1997.

Knowles, G.J., *Dealing Crack Cocaine: A View from the Streets of Honolulu,* 1996, available at: http://www.fbi.gov/publications/leb/1996/july961.txt on July 23, 2003.

Kwan, M., *Cali Drug Cartel Marketing Analysis,* 2003, available at: http://www.darkside.com.au/mba/cali.html on August 3.

President's Commission on Organized Crime, Interim Report to the President and the Attorney General, *The Cash Connection: Organized Crime, Financial Institutions, and Money Laundering,* 1984.

Ringwald, C.G., *A Case Study Under New Management: Using Federal Forfeiture Statutes to Attack the Drug Trade,* available at: http://www.fbi.gov/publications/leb/1996/june965.txt, retrieved on July 23, 2003.

Drug Use and Criminal Behavior

There is an association between drug use and crime. Many assume that drug use causes crime. However, the association is more complex than that. When social scientists speak of an association between two factors, like drug use and crime, they mean that the factors often occur together. There are several ways that this association could be explained without drug use directly causing criminal behavior. For example, prior delinquency and criminal lifestyle could make later drug use more likely. Drug use and criminal behavior could develop independently. Early risk taking attitudes, early problem behaviors, chronic poverty, parental neglect or abuse, the presence of juvenile gangs, and high levels of street crime could influence both drug use and criminality. Alternatively, drug users may have certain expectations about how they will feel or behave when they take the drug that increase the odds of criminal behavior. Perhaps drug users choose high crime areas in which to use their drug of choice. It could be that drug prohibition laws and drug enforcement activities foster both high levels of drug use and high crime rates similar to the 1920s and early 1930s in the U.S. with alcohol prohibition. Finally, any association could be conditional, operating under certain circumstances and not others (Goode, 1999).

This picture becomes even more complex when different types of crime and drugs are considered. There is a much stronger association between drug use and common street crimes (homicide, assault, rape, robbery, burglary, larceny or theft, and motor vehicle theft) than with white-collar and corporate crimes. Yet, these elite crimes cause greater property loss, more personal injuries and more deaths annually than all street crimes combined (Albanese, 1995; Friedrichs, 1996). If drug use causes street crime, what causes crime by professional, social, political, business, and corporate elites? Of all psychoactive drugs used alcohol is the one most frequently associated with street crimes, including homicide, yet alcohol is legal. By comparison, illegal drugs have a much weaker association with crime and violence (Bureau of Justice Statistics, 1998). Some illegal drugs, most notably marijuana, appear to have little relationship to either crime or violence apart from that associated with black market distribution of illegal goods and services (Goode, 1999; Maisto, Galizio, and Connors, 1999).

Before the drug-crime relationship can be explored further a few terms need to be clarified. A "drug" is a naturally occurring or manufactured chemical substance that when consumed alters bodily function (physically or psychologically) and excludes nutrients related to normal functioning. Nicotine in tobacco, caffeine in coffee, alcohol in wine, over the counter and prescription medicines (e.g., cough syrups, antacids, Viagra, and the contraceptive pill) are drugs along with cocaine, marijuana, heroin, and ecstasy. Some drugs alter the functioning of the body in ways that are undetectable to the user without medical tests (e.g., antibiotics and anticholesterol medicines). "Psychoactive drugs" affect the chemistry of the brain and alter perceptions and consciousness in detectable, unusual, and often pleasurable ways. Human beings have sought periodically to alter their mental state with chemical substances for thousands of years out of a desire for pleasure, curiosity, enlightenment, personal discovery, and religious experience (Weil, 1995). The desire to experience an altered mental state is why people smoke tobacco, drink coffee or alcohol, snort powder cocaine, inhale cocaine vapors, swallow ecstasy, or inject heroin (Levinthal, 1999). All of these acts of substance use are fundamentally the same, the only differences are the substance used and whether they are legal or illegal.

"Substance abuse" usually refers to the use of illegal drugs, misuse of prescribed drugs or excessive use of legal drugs to the point where users are physically, psychologically or functionally impaired. Initially, users of psychoactive drugs achieve the desired effect with relatively small doses. However, as their pattern of use progresses they often find that to achieve a satisfactory high they must use larger doses. This is because they have developed a "tolerance" for the drug and require higher dosages to produce the same sensations. A user's tolerance level can be lowered by detoxification through self-disciplined abstinence, voluntary commitment for treatment or confinement. An "addict" is a drug user who has developed a compulsive need to continue taking the drug and has become physically or psychologically dependent on their drug of choice. Addicts must maintain a minimal level of the drugs in their systems to function normally and take larger doses to attain the highs they crave. Additionally, they feel a compulsive need to continue taking the drug. Physically dependent addicts suffer severe physical symptoms of withdrawal as their bodies compensate for the absence of the drug when regular drug use is interrupted. Alcoholics and heroin addicts are physically dependent. Some addictive drugs do not produce physical dependency. Cocaine addicts, as well as heavy marijuana users, do not suffer physical withdrawal symptoms. Instead, they experience strong urges to continue using their drug of choice because of the pleasurable and reinforcing effects they produce. They are psychologically dependent because they have great difficulty controlling their urge to use the drug again and again. Both physically and psychologically dependent users are likely to use their preferred drugs whenever there is an opportunity to do so.

Finally, the subjective effects felt by the user or objective effects observed are strongly dependent on four other factors: set, setting, method of administration, and dosage. Set refers to the user's mood, personality, imagination, experience, and expectations about the effects of the drug (Goode, 1999, 40–41). A number of studies have shown that people who expect to be given a drug but instead are given a placebo will report feeling high and act inebriated as if they had actually taken the drug (Mendelson and Mello, 1995). Setting refers to the social and physical environment in which the drug is taken. Setting encompasses the immediate surroundings, the local drug subculture, whether friends or strangers are present, whether the user feels safe or threatened, the legal status of the drug used, local drug enforcement practices, and whether the user's activities are compatible with intoxication (Goode, 1995, 41). Set and setting are interactive (one can influence the other) and exert a profound influence on the effects of any psychoactive drug on the user.

Method of administration refers to the means by which the drug is introduced into the user's blood stream. There are several ways drugs may be taken—orally, injected under the skin, injected into a vein, injected into a muscle, snorted and absorbed through the mucous membranes of the nose, inhaled into the lungs, dissolved in saliva by chewing, digested, or absorbed directly through the skin. Different methods of administration with the same drug will produce different effects. Drugs that are swallowed or chewed take a much longer time to enter the blood system and reach the brain. Consequently, the effects are often subtle and take longer to be recognized. When drugs are injected intravenously or inhaled the effects are felt almost instantly. The sudden intense sensation produced by psychoactive drugs administered in these ways is strongly pleasurable. This sensation is called the "rush" and has been described as a "full body orgasm" (Goode, 1999).

Finally, dosage is the amount of active ingredient administered. All drugs, legal or illegal, have different subjective and objective effects depending on the dosage. Psychoactive drugs administered in very small amounts typically have no objective or subjective effects. Conversely, at some dosage nearly every drug can be harmful or fatal. The blood alcohol concentration (BAC) level used to distinguish criminal from noncriminal driving behavior is a dosage indicator correlated to the severity of driving impairment. Perhaps the safest psychoactive drug is delta-9-tetrahydracanabinol (THC), the active ingredient in marijuana. There is no known dosage at which THC is acutely harmful or fatal (Goode, 1999). However, chronic exposure to marijuana smoke, as with tobacco smoke, has many deleterious health consequences (Levinthal, 1999).

Official crime data are based on arrests of street criminals or victimization reports from street crimes. These sources of data create the appearance of a causal drug-crime relationship. First, the failure to distinguish between causality and an association in the mass media presents a distorted image of drug users, the drug problem and the relationship between drug use and crime (Beckett and Sasson, 1998; Brownstein, 1997). These data exclude the use of legal drugs. Consequently, the association between crime and alcohol or tobacco use is largely ignored. Second, common street criminals, dealers, and drug users are easily spotted by police, arrested and convicted. However, these offenders are not representative of the drug using population. Burglars, thieves, prostitutes, armed robbers, corner drug dealers, and street drug users are common street criminals. Most of these offenders are young, minorities, and male. They are poorly educated and often raised in impoverished neighborhoods with high levels of both street crime and drug use. The appearance of a strong relationship between drug use and crime is largely a function of the arrest of common street criminals. Simply stated, most drug-crime offenders are found to have committed other street crimes and most common street criminals are found to have used illegal drugs (Beckett and Sasson, 2000; Huizinga and Jakob-Chien, 1998; Nurco, Kinlock and Hanlon, 1995). Among prison inmates, 80% report using illegal drugs at some point in their lives and 60% report having used illegal drugs during the month before their most recent arrest. Among arrestees, 50–60% test positive for marijuana or cocaine when booked into the local jail (National Institute of Justice, 2000; Office of National Drug Control Policy, 2001).

What is missing from these data are millions of hidden users who commit no crimes, other than drug-defined crimes—buying, selling and using controlled substances. Most hidden users buy drugs with legally earned money. They are mostly White, middle or upper class and employed. The Substance Abuse and Mental Health Services Administration (2000) estimated that

14.8 million Americans were current users who had used an illegal drug once or more in the 30 days prior to their interview. Of these, 77% were employed full-time or part-time. During 1999 there were 1.5 million arrests (10% of all arrests) for use, possession, sale or distribution of controlled substances. Most of those arrested for drug violations were street users and dealers (Office of National Drug Control Policy, 2001). Many, perhaps most, drug users are neither street criminals nor street drug users and do not show up in the official statistics. Middle and upper class users buy much less frequently than street users, often purchasing enough to last a month or more with intermittent personal use. This is similar to the way someone might buy a monthly bottle of expensive scotch to savor slowly. Furthermore, drug purchases are often arranged by phone through a series of contacts or through a beeper service. The drugs are discreetly delivered to the user, like pizza. This pattern of buying and using illegal drugs sharply reduces the risks of discovery by police. As a result they are able to maintain the appearance of a drug free lifestyle—earning good grades, an active school life, paying the bills on time, managing a household, taking care of a family, working hard and maintaining steady employment for an extensive period while discreetly buying and using illegal drugs. In some cases, hidden users take illegal drugs for prosocial reasons such as advancing their careers by working longer hours. This type of illegal drug user is essentially noncriminal (Waldorf, Reinarman and Murphy, 1991; Goode, 1999). This distinction between the street user and the upscale hidden user is rarely noted in the public, political or policy discourse about drugs, crime or drug policy (Zinberg, 1995).

The disconnect between the reality and rhetoric about the drug problem and the association between drug use and crime points out a definitional issue. The appearance of a causal relationship between drugs and crime is partly a function of the laws that criminalized use, possession, sale and distribution of controlled substances. Circular or tautological reasoning is often used to define the drug-crime relationship. The logical process is that self-fulfilling drug users buy and use drugs, the drugs they use are illegal, therefore drugs cause crime because drug users buy and use drugs. Violations of drug laws are "drug-defined crimes" (Walker, 2001). Drug-defined crimes should not be used to measure the drug-crime relationship because these types of crimes cannot meaningfully contribute to an understanding of the drug-crime relationship. Goode (1999, 149) captures the essence of this issue succinctly:

> … it must be emphasized in the strongest possible terms that this powerful correlation between drug use and crime does not mean that all individuals who use drugs commit criminal or delinquent acts. Or that all individuals who commit such acts use drugs. Or that no one who does not use drugs does not commit crimes. Or that no one who does not commit crimes does not use drugs.

Siegel (1995) identified four patterns of cocaine use: experimental, social-recreational, circumstantial-situational, and intensive-compulsive users. Faupel and Klockars' (1997) identify four patterns among heroin users: occasional, stabilized, free-wheeling, and destabilized street users. The descriptions of cocaine and heroin users presented in these two works are similar in many ways, suggesting that these models may have general application to other addictive substances. Although both models describe relationships between drug use patterns and street crime, the one proposed by Faupel and Klockars (1997) has the strongest theoretical foundation and is discussed below.

The "occasional user" is an initial or experimental drug user who has a structured lifestyle focused mostly on conventional, drug free, activities. These users either establish strict rules governing when, where and how they use drugs or they have not established (or cannot afford) a reliable drug supply. As a result, occasional users have not become drug dependent and have not built up a tolerance to the drug. Under circumstances where set, setting, method of administration, and dosage are highly structured or constricted, an occasional user could maintain the appearance of a drug free lifestyle indefinitely. An occasional user could be anyone willing to use an illegal substance and self-disciplined enough to use the drug in a very limited way.

A "stabilized addict" is a regular user who has become physically or psychologically dependent on the drug. These types of users have established a reliable and affordable supply of drugs and maintain highly structured lives involving family, work, or school but reorganize their lifestyles to facilitate and hide regular drug use. As long as stabilized addicts limit their drug use so that it is affordable with legally earned income and does not interfere with occupational performance or family responsibilities, this pattern of use could be maintained indefinitely. However, it is a difficult drug use pattern to maintain without progressively using higher doses to compensate for increasing drug tolerance. Periodic detoxification can help there users maintain their addictions by lowering their drug tolerance and level of chemical dependency.

"Free-wheeling addicts" have access to a reliable and easily accessible supply of drugs but the physical or psychological effects of increasingly frequent drug use erodes or eliminates the structured lifestyle that they previously enjoyed. A number of famous music, movie, and television personalities have had their drug use revealed when their addiction began to escalate out of control. Robert Downey, a well-known actor, struggled with an addiction for many years in the 1990s and was incarcerated as a result of relapses. Many other celebrities have died from an overdose during a "run" of heavy drug use (Levinthal, 1999). During a "run" the free-wheeling addict will typically use drugs as often as possible. Over time they may deplete checking accounts, savings accounts, and retirement plans. They may also borrow against credit cards and sell valuable personal possessions to buy more drugs. As they become increasingly less able to afford drugs with legal sources of income, they may become more desperate and begin to steal from relatives and friends. They may also join the black market as drug dealers or couriers to ensure a reliable drug supply and provide an income.

If the free-wheeling addict cannot reestablish a structured lifestyle he or she may become a "destabilized street addict" (i.e., common street drug user). This type of addict is most directly associated with street crime because they no longer have a structured lifestyle, support system or the resources to maintain the outward appearance of sobriety and stability. Their unreliable behavior makes it difficult to maintain trust among those within the drug subculture. Once they have lost the trust of dealers and users, the destabilized addict no longer has the credibility to maintain a regular drug supply and has to "hustle" all day, every day, to find enough money to keep from suffering symptoms of physical withdrawal or strong psychological cravings. Thus, the strongest association between drug use and criminal behavior is found among destabilized street addicts and desperate free-wheeling addicts who no longer have access to legal money and have exhausted trust among others in the drug subculture. Occasional users, stabilized addicts, and many free-wheeling addicts who have legal sources of money, structured lifestyles and support systems are rarely involved in common street crimes. As long as they are able to limit their use and are able to afford a regular supply of drugs with legal earned income, they could use drugs indefinitely. The most direct cause of common street crime among drug addicts is economic desperation brought on by loss of legal income sources rather than something inherent in the substances they use. The only crimes committed by all illegal drug users are drug-defined crimes—buying, using, and selling illegal drugs.

A model of drug violence developed by Goldstein (1995) identified three distinct categories of violence. One of these is economic compulsive violence, although it is not motivated primarily out of violent impulses but rather economic desperation. As violence does not guarantee money, few addicts use violence as an end in itself; they are primarily interested in obtaining money that can be used directly to purchase drugs or stolen property that can be exchanged for cash in the black market. When violence does occur it is usually because something went wrong. This is directly analogous to economic desperation among free-wheeling and destabilized street addicts that often leads to increased property crime.

"Psychopharmacological violence" is directly influenced by the chemical properties of the drug consumed—alcohol, PCP, LSD, crack, heroin. The research literature is quite consistent in finding that this type of violence is rare among drug users. However, when psychopharmacological violence does occur it is associated with the absence, rather than the presence, of the drug. That is, it is associated with the irritability and desperation of dependent users suffering physical withdrawal or intense cravings without a reliable supply of drugs and who are forced to "hustle" to obtain cash daily. Robbery, assault, prostitution, theft, or burglary may all be part of a destabilized addict's hustle to obtain money when they are "sick" and are physically or psychologically desperate for another dose of cocaine. Studies of the effects of tranquilizers, pain-killers, and marijuana suggest that these drugs reduce the likelihood of violence or other criminal behaviors. Drugs produce different subjective effects with different people. Some people become sleepy when drunk while others become angry and belligerent. The precise psychoactive and behavioral effects of any drug depend on a number of variables. These include the person's weight, stomach context, type of drug, the dosage, method of administration, the user's past drug experience, and the social context in which the drug is used (Goode, 1999; Levinthal, 1999).

The third type of drug related violence identified by Goldstein (1995) is "systemic violence." This type has little to do with the drug or the user but is an intrinsic aspect of any black market system involved in the distribution or sale of illegal goods and services. Under black market conditions, individuals settle disputes and conflicts by self-defense or vendetta. Conflicts between rival syndicates are settled by warfare. The court of last resort is found in the streets and not before judges. Drug cartels, crime syndicates, and local street gangs involved in illegal drug production, distribution and sales are notoriously willing to use violence. Violence becomes the means by which drug supplies are protected from police and rival organizations, informers are punished, debts are settled, threats by rival groups are repelled, and the normative standards of drug trafficking are enforced. Systemic drug crime and violence accounts for most drug related crime. This situation is directly parallel to violence and crime during the Prohibition era in the U.S. During that period, millions of Americans were forced to either give up alcohol or associate with "gangsters" and "bootleggers" to buy liquor or socialize at secret clubs and taverns called "speakeasies" (Lyman and Potter, 1998). Overnight, the Eighteenth Amendment to the U.S. Constitution and the Volstead Act turned millions of Americans into lawbreakers when they bought or sold black market alcohol. Since marijuana remained legal to use, marijuana use increased sharply. Opiate and cocaine products had been effectively criminalized since 1914 with the passage of the Harrison Act. This was followed by a series of U.S. Supreme Court decisions that closed all medical use loopholes by 1924. When Prohibition was repealed in 1933, alcohol could once again be manufactured, distributed, sold, and used legally but the prohibition of opiates and cocaine remained in place. In 1937 the Marijuana Tax Act became law, adding the second most popular drug (after alcohol) to the list of prohibited substances (Musto, 1987). Alcohol and marijuana simply traded places as legal drugs. As Faupel and Klockars (1995, 124) note, "... criminalization ... has profoundly affected the dynamics of the drug-crime nexus."

The organizations that produce, distribute, and sell illegal drugs are highly structured, well-equipped, and ruthless enterprises with economic resources that exceed the gross national product of many nations. For example, the Office of National Drug Control Policy (2001) estimates that between 1988 and the end of 2000 American drug users spent $1.014 trillion dollars on illegal drugs. It is likely that the annual worldwide profit from illegal drug sales far exceeds the resources available to governments, like the U.S., intent on waging a "war on drugs." From 1988 to 2000 the U.S., the wealthiest country in the world, spent roughly $200 billion on all federal drug control programs during that period. The power and wealth of modern criminal syndicates is derived directly from black market opportunities, created by prohibition laws, to provide illegal goods and services demanded by a large segment of the population. Perhaps the lesson from alcohol prohibition in the 1920s and 1930s is that prohibition strategies often create serious social problems that are worse than the original drug problem. In 1933 the Volstead Act and the 18th Amendment to the U.S. Constitution were repealed largely because alcohol was extremely popular and the unintended consequences of Prohibition were more harmful than alcohol consumption itself.

The view that the drug–crime association is largely a product of prohibition is reinforced by the history of drug use. Natural and synthetic substances have been used to alter moods and mental states for many thousands of years (Levinthal, 1999). Some researchers argue that the ubiquitous human desire to alter perception and consciousness reflects a basic human appetite (Weil, 1995). In most societies the use of psychoactive substances was accepted within cultural norms. The Incan people of South America regularly chewed coca leaves for religious, medicinal and work-related purposes for thousands of years. The low cocaine dosages from chewed coca leaves were sufficient to alleviate pains and increase both stamina and strength among workers. In this context drug use served a prosocial rather than antisocial purpose. It was considered a gift from the gods and is still widely used among people living in the Peruvian Andes. When coca leaves are chewed cocaine is dissolved in saliva, swallowed and absorbed by the digestive system. Thus, a small dose of cocaine reaches the brain slowly and produces few adverse, toxic or addictive effects. Users continue to be seen as normal members of the society. In the early to mid-1700s gin was introduced to Europe. In London, there was broad public drunkenness when gin first appeared. This "gin epidemic" was analogous to the "crack cocaine epidemic" in the U.S. during the late 1980s and early 1990s. Yet, in the 1700s manufacturers, distributors, sellers, and users (including alcohol addicts) were not seen as criminal and the product was not banned (Levinthal, 1999).

British citizens, of all classes, in England and the American colonies, used opiates in the form of patent medicines for relief of symptomatic pains. As long as a dependent user carried out his or her social role, the use of patent medicines was neither deviant nor criminal. Social stigma was attached to the users only when the became debilitated by drug use and could not function within established gender and occupational roles as wives, mothers, husbands, fathers, farmers, professionals, employers, and employees. The rate of morphine addiction (i.e., the "soldiers' disease") was very high among American males following the Civil War (Courtwright, 1982). Patent medicines containing opiates, cocaine, and alcohol were widely used and abused by all classes of people. Addiction rates among women and older citizens were high because patent medicines provided reliable alleviation of pain and symptoms from untreatable health conditions related to aging or childbearing. Despite high levels of opiate use and addiction within the general population, there is little historical evidence of crime being consistently associated with the users of these drugs. Street addicts and users who were unable to function within socially established roles were seen as weak rather than criminal (Courtwright, 1982; Lusane, 1997; Musto, 1997).

The association between drug use and criminal behavior emerged in the U.S. during the early 1870s in San Francisco, California. The Federation of Organized Trades and Labor Unions, under the leadership of Samuel Gompers, sought to protect American workers from low wage competition of Chinese laborers (Helmer, 1975). Between the 1840s and 1850s, the British won two wars with China over the opium trade and forced China to allow opium imports to offset the trade imbalance from British demand for Chinese tea (Owen, 1934). As a result, many of the Chinese laborers recruited to build the transcontinental railroads and excavate gold and silver mines in the U.S. were opium users. Railroad and mining companies used opium as a monthly bonus for good Chinese workers. In demonizing the Chinese for their opium use, Samuel Gompers ignored the way companies had used opium as a work incentive for Chinese laborers. His labor movement also ignored the widespread use of liquid opiates in patent medicines among the American population while portraying Chinese opium smokers as deviant and criminally dangerous to women and children. His campaign was successful. In 1875 the San Francisco Ordinances against smokable opium passed and the first policy link between drug use and criminal behavior was established. After this success in San Francisco, Gompers was appointed to head the national American Federation of Labor and lobbied for several national laws aimed at limiting Chinese labor using the same drug-crime rhetoric that had worked in San Francisco. The Chinese Exclusion Act (1882), the Tariff on Smokable Opium (1883), and the Ban on Importation of Opium by Chinese Persons (1887) were passed largely as a result of Gomper's influence. Each law targeted Chinese use of opium while protecting American use of opiates and American production of opiate-based products sold by the patent medicine industry. Thus, the drug-crime association first appeared in the U.S. as part of a racist political strategy by unions designed to protect American workers from low wage Chinese labor. The use of opium by the Chinese provided a vehicle for the demonization of a vulnerable population and political or economic advantage to others (Helmer, 1975).

Similarly, the Harrison Act of 1914 and the Marijuana Tax Act of 1937 were passed for reasons unrelated to the objective harms or criminal behavior associated with the substances targeted by these laws. The Harrison Act fulfilled an earlier trade concession to China in exchange for access to Chinese markets by American business. The Marijuana Tax Act was patterned after the Harrison Act and passed in the middle of the Great Depression. Its passage reassured American workers who feared the competition of low wage laborers from Mexico and the Caribbean who also happened to use an unfamiliar substance—marijuana. Broad, unsubstantiated, policy arguments linking marijuana users with extremely violent behavior were used despite medical testimony refuting such claims (Helmer, 1975; Lusane 1997; Musto, 1987). This was precisely the same pattern used successfully by Gompers in 1875. Much of the argument that drug use causes criminal behavior is rooted in the political agendas of those who had the power to demonize others for their use of unfamiliar substances.

Finally, there is the question of temporal order—does drug use occur before or after delinquent or criminal behavior? If drug use occurs after delinquent behavior begins, drug use cannot be a primary cause of criminality. The research evidence on temporal order is mixed. Many early cross-sectional studies (measuring behavior at one time period) focused on drug use as an independent variable with delinquency or criminal behavior as the dependent variable. Significant associations with criminal behavior were consistently found. Researchers interpreted these findings as being consistent with their original conceptualization that drug use increased criminal behavior. Additionally, they frequently included drug-defined crimes as an indicator of criminal behavior. However, more recent longitudinal studies (with multiple measurements over time) raise questions about these early findings. Recent studies have found that early risk taking attitudes and behavioral problems are identifiable in young children between ages six and ten, and are quite predictive of teenage delinquency and subsequent adult criminality (Farrington, 1997). Additionally, recent research on drug use suggests that early onset of alcohol and tobacco use typically occurs before age 12, and early onset of marijuana use occurs sometime between age 12 and 14. Among those willing to take the highest risks, early use of harder drug (e.g., cocaine, LSD, heroin, PCP, ecstasy, etc.) follows marijuana use (Goode, 1999; Vega and Gil, 1998).

These findings suggest that the path to delinquency starts well before the use of illegal drugs. This implies that criminal behavior and drug use are either independent phenomena influenced by unidentified or unmeasured factors; or that delinquency predisposes youths to subsequent drug use; or that the relationship between drug use and criminal behavior is interactive once either factor occurs. A likely scenario is that early risk taking attitudes and problem behaviors lead to contacts with other children who have similar attitudes and behaviors. Some of these new friends are older children who are willing to take greater risks, including minor delinquent or criminal acts. Social learning and peer pressure encourage modeling of behavior observed in older children by younger children. Older children probably introduce younger children to alcohol and tobacco use as well as early sexual activity. Once again social learning and peer pressure encourage younger children to model the behaviors of older peers. As the circle of risk taking friends and acquaintances expands, children progressively encounter more young people whose risk taking behaviors include using illegal drugs—usually marijuana. Again, younger children learn from older peers how to use the drug and recognize its effects. Regular marijuana users will eventually meet juveniles who have access to other illegal drugs. Those youths willing to take greater risks may begin using inhalants, cocaine, ecstasy or heroin. Increasing drug use leads to greater drug tolerance, dependency and escalating needs for cash to purchase illegal drugs. Some of these users will exhaust legally available funds and commit property or vice crimes out of economic necessity. Others may become involved in systemic crime as a victim of a drug deal "gone bad" or as a drug courier or dealer (Goldstein, 1995).

Early use of legal drugs is most predictive of later use of illegal substances. Early risk taking attitudes and problem behaviors are most predictive of later delinquency and criminal behavior (Farrington, 1997; Vega and Gil, 1998). To the extent that one factor influences the other, it appears that early delinquent or criminal behavior influences early drug use. Drug users suffering physical or psychological symptoms of withdrawal may resort to crime or participation in the black market system out of economic necessity. Economic compulsive street crime and violence is a function of laws that make users criminals for buying and using drugs. Systemic street crime and violence is a function of drug prohibition, similar to that experienced in the 1920s and 1930s when alcohol was prohibited. Criminal behavior is more strongly associated with alcohol than any illegal drug. There is little empirical evidence that psychopharmacological crime and violence is consistently produced by the use of illegal drugs. The effects of any drug are determined by the user's set (expectations and experience), drug use setting (the physical and social context), dosage, method of administration, pattern of use, and drug tolerance. Alcohol and tobacco use accounts for more deaths and injuries annually than all illegal drugs combined. Finally, drug control laws created black market conditions that made systemic crime and violence necessary as a business tool, turned noncriminal users into criminals and created the appearance of a causal relationship between drug use and crime. The laws were largely an outgrowth of political agendas unrelated to either the drugs or drug use problems. Drug use and criminal behavior are associated because they co-occur but they are not causally related in any inherent way that is not a function of other individual and social factors. As Goode (1999, 147) states: "The correlation is real: the causal connection is not."

MICHAEL J. GILBERT

References and Further Reading

Albanese, J., *White Collar Crime in America,* Prentice Hall, Englewood Cliffs, NJ, 1995.

Albanese, J. and Pursley, R., *Crime in America: Some Existing and Emerging Issues,* Regents/Prentice Hall, Englewood Cliffs, NJ, 1993.

Beckett, K. and Sasson, T., The Media and the Construction of the Drug Crisis in America, in Jensen, E.L. and Gerger, J., Eds., *The New War on Drugs: Symbolic Politics and Criminal Justice Policy,* Anderson Publishing, Cincinnati, OH, 1998.

Beckett, K. and Sasson, T., *The Politics of Injustice: Crime and Punishment in America,* Pine Forge Press, Thousand Oaks, CA, 2000.

Brownstein, H.H., The Media and the Construction of Random Drug Violence, in Gaines, L.K. and Kraska, P.B., Eds., *Drugs, Crime, and Justice: Contemporary Perspectives,* Waveland Press, Prospect Heights, IL, 1997.

Bureau of Justice Statistics, *Alcohol and Crime: An Analysis of National Data on the Prevalence of Alcohol Involvement in Crime,* Washington, DC, Bureau of Justice Statistics, Office of Justice Programs, U.S. Department of Justice, 1998.

Courtwright, D.T., *Dark Paradise: Opiate Addiction in American Before 1940,* Harvard University Press, Cambridge, MA, 1982.

Farrington, D.P., Early Prediction of Violent and Nonviolent Youthful Offending, *European Journal on Criminal Policy and Research,* 5, 1997.

Faupel, C.E. and Klockars, C.B., Drugs-Crime Connections: Elaborations from the Life Histories of Hard-Core Heroin Addicts, in Gaines L.K. and Kraska, P.B., Eds., *Drugs, Crime, and Justice: Contemporary Perspectives,* Waveland Press, Prospect Heights, IL, 1997.

Friedrichs, D.O., *Trusted Criminals: White Collar Crime in Contemporary Society,* Wadsworth Publishing Co., Belmont, CA, 1996.

Goldstein, P.J., The Drugs/Violence Nexus: A Tripartite Conceptual Framework. in Inciardi, J.A. and McElrath K., Eds., *The American Drug Scene: An Anthology,* Roxbury Publishing Company, Los Angeles, CA, 1995.

Goode, E., *Drugs in American Society,* 5th ed., McGraw-Hill College, New York, 1999.

Helmer, J., *Drugs and Minority Oppression,* The Seabury Press, New York, 1975.

Huizinga, D. and Jakob-Chien, C., The Contemporaneous Co-Occurrence of Serious And Violent Juvenile Offending and Other Problem Behaviors, in Loeber, R. and Farrington, D.P., Eds., *Serious & Violent Juvenile Offenders: Risk Factors and Successful Interventions,* Sage Publications, Thousand Oaks, CA, 1998.

Lusane, C., Racism and the Drug Crisis, in Gaines, L.K. and Kraska, P.B., Eds., *Drugs, Crime, and Justice: Contemporary Perspectives.* Waveland Press, Prospect Heights, IL, 1997.

Lyman, M.D. and Potter, G.W., *Drugs in Society: Causes, Concepts and Control,* 3rd ed., Anderson Publishing Company, Cincinnati, OH,

Maisto, S.A., Galizio M., and Connors, G.J., *Drug Use and Abuse,* 3rd ed., Harcourt Brace College Publishers, New York, 1999.

Mendleson, J.H. and Mello, N.K., Alcohol, Sex and Agression, in Inciardi, J.A. and McElrath, K., Eds., *The American Drug Scene: An Anthology,* Roxbury Publishing Company, Los Angeles, CA, 1995.

Musto, D.F., *The American Disease: Origins of Narcotic Control,* Expanded Edition, Oxford University Press, New York, 1987.

Musto, D.F., Opium, Cocaine and Marijuana in American History, in Gaines, L.K. and Kraska, P.B., Eds., *Drugs, Crime, and Justice: Contemporary Perspectives,* Waveland Press, Prospect Heights, IL, 1997.

National Institute of Justice, *1999 Annual Report on Drug Use Among Adult and Juvenile Arrestees,* National Institute of Justice, U.S. Department of Justice, Washington, DC, 2000.

Nurco, D.N., Kinlock, T.W., and Hanlon, T.E., The Drug-Crime Connection, in Inciardi, J.A., and McElrath, K., Eds., *The American Drug Scene: An Anthology,* Roxbury Publishing Company, Los Angeles, CA, 1995.

Office of National Drug Control Policy, *The National Drug Control Strategy: 2001 Annual Report,* Washington, DC, Office of National Drug Control Policy, The White House, 2001.

Owen, D.E., *British Opium Policy in China and India.* Yale University Press, *New Haven,* CT, 1934.

Russell, S. and Gilbert, M.J., Truman's Revenge: Social Control and Corporate Crime, *Crime, Law and Social Change,* 32, (1999).

Substance Abuse and Mental Health Services Administration, *Summary of Findings from the 1999 National Household Survey on Drug Abuse,* Substance Abuse and Mental Health Services Administration, U.S. Department of Health and Human Services, Washington, DC, 2000. Available at http://www.samhsa.gov/oas/NHSDA/1999. Retrieved on March 16, 2001.

Vega, W.A., Andres Gill and Associates, *Drug Use and Ethnicity in Early Adolescence,* Plenum Press, New York, 1998.

Waldorf, D., Reinarman, C., and Murphy, S., *Cocaine Changes: The Experience of Using and Quitting,* Temple University Press, Philadelphia, PA, 1991.

Walker, S., *Sense and Nonsense About Crime and Drugs: A Policy Guide,* Wadsworth/Thomson Learning, Belmont, CA, 2001.

Weil, A., Why People Take Drugs, in Inciardi, J.A., and McElrath, K., Eds., *The American Drug Scene: An Anthology,* Roxbury Publishing Company, Los Angeles, CA, 1995.

Zinberg, N.E., Nonaddictive Opiate Use, in Inciardi, J.A., and McElrath, K., Eds., *The American Drug Scene: An Anthology,* Roxbury Publishing Company, Los Angeles, CA, 1995.

See also **Drug Enforcement Administration (DEA); Drug Policy: Enforcement, Interdiction, and the War on Drugs; Drug Policy: Prevention and Treatment; Drug Policy: The Decriminalization/Legalization Argument; Drug Trafficking as an Occupation; Drug Use: Extent and Correlates; Drug Use: Law**

Drug Use: Extent and Correlates

Human beings have used psychoactive substances for literally thousands of years. As sensory beings we first begin our lives by exploring the world orally. Infants and toddlers put almost everything they grasp into their mouths and in the process sort out the features of their world into things that they like or dislike—"good stuff" and "bad stuff." The culinary history of our species has largely been one of trial and error as we reliably learned to separate nutritional foods from inedible or poisonous plants and animals. We learned not to eat certain kinds of mushrooms because some people died when these mushrooms were eaten. Some substances had unusual and powerful effects to alleviate pain, cure disease, heal wounds and infections, increase endurance, heighten alertness, alter moods, create visions, calm the nerves, engender a sense of well being, and provide pleasurable sensations.

There is evidence of Chinese use of the herbs *Ephedra vulgaris* (ephedrine) and *Cannabis sativa* (marijuana) between 3000 and 2000 BC. The Babylonians, Egyptians and Greeks recorded the use of alcohol and opium as early as 1700 BC. The chewing of coca leaves was part of Incan culture and economy as early as 1000 BC. There is archeological evidence that Aztecs used hallucinogens—peyote buttons (mescaline), mushrooms (psilocybin), and morning glory seeds (lysergic acid) as early as 100 BC. American Indians and other indigenous peoples in the "new world" were smoking or chewing tobacco (nicotine) when discovered by the first European explorers.

The earliest man-made substances that affected brain chemistry were alcoholic. Evidence of alcohol use has been traced back over 7000 years. Even the book of Genesis in the Bible discusses drunkenness by two early biblical figures—Noah and Lot. Nearly every human culture made some type of alcoholic beverage. The earliest forms were fermented honey (mead), grapes (wine), and grains—barley, corn, rice and hops (beer). Sometime during the Middle Ages (1100–1400 AD) boiling fermented mixtures and condensing the alcohol vapors became popular. This distillation process increased the alcohol content to produce brandy, gin, rum, and whiskey (i.e., distilled spirits). Without question, the use of psychoactive substances ("drugs") for medical, cultural, and recreational purposes has been a ubiquitous part of human history (Abadinsky, 2001; Levinthal, 1999).

The use of drugs is still ubiquitous. What has changed is the number and types of substances used, availability, price, and whether the substance used is considered legal or illegal. In modern societies, mixed messages about drug use are everywhere. Race cars are sponsored by tobacco and beer companies, movies glamorize smoking and illicit drug use, popular television programs are sponsored by pharmaceutical companies to mass market their latest drug—a new sleeping pill, antianxiety drug, or treatment for some physical malady. It often seems that there is a drug for everything. Modern culture can be characterized as one of self-medication.

The term "drug" typically refers to a naturally occurring or manufactured chemical substance that when taken into the body alters the functioning of the body (physically or psychologically) and excludes nutrients related to normal functioning (adapted from Levinthal, 1999). Under this definition, nicotine in tobacco, caffeine in coffee, alcohol in wine, over the counter antihistamines, antibiotics, and Viagra are all drugs along with cocaine, marijuana, heroin, and ecstacy. A "psychoactive drug" alters perception and consciousness by affecting the chemistry of the brain.

"Substance abuse" usually refers to the use of illegal drugs, misuse of prescribed drugs or the excessive use of legal, over-the-counter or prescribed drugs that leads to individual impairment—physically, psychologically, and functionally (Levinthal, 1999). The term "addiction" refers to drug cravings and physical or psychological dependence where the user feels compulsive urges to use the drug repeatedly. In the process they develop a tolerance to the drug and require higher doses to attain the desired high. In the U.S., the White House Office of National Drug Control Policy (ONDCP) and the Department of Health and Human Services through the National Institute of Drug Abuse (NIDA) and the Substance Abuse and Mental Health Services Administration (SAMHSA) track substance abuse and addiction trends.

In 1997, the National Household Survey on Drug Abuse found that 35.6% of Americans (77 million), age 12 or older, reported that they had used illegal drugs at some point in their lifetime. When asked about use during the past year and past month, 11.2% and 6.4% of Americans responded that they used illegal drugs. That is, in 1997 roughly 24 million people used illegal drugs within the past 12 months and 14 million were current users who used one or more illegal drugs within the last 30 days. In the same year, 177 million people (82% of the population) reported they had used alcohol at some time in their life. Furthermore, 138 million people (64%) used alcohol within the last 12 months and 110 million used it within the last 30 days. The numbers of users of tobacco products are roughly similar to those for alcohol use. Of these, about 27 million people are heavy smokers who smoke a pack or more of cigarettes daily (Substance Abuse and Mental Health Services Administration, 1998). Legal and illegal psychoactive substances are widely used throughout American society, along with most of the developed and developing nations of the world (Killias and Aebi, 2000).

In 1999, the proportion of current users (i.e., use within the last 30 days) of illicit drugs among Americans increased from 6.4% to 6.7% (from less than 14 million to 14.8 million people). Despite this slight increase the proportion of current users of illegal drugs has remained essentially stable for more than a decade, fluctuating between 5.8% and 7.7% of the population, age 12 or older, since 1988. However, depending on the substances used and user characteristics, there is considerable variation within this overall picture. For example, The National Drug Control Strategy: 2001 Annual Report (Office of National Drug Control Policy, 2001) shows that the number of occasional cocaine users (two or three times per month) declined by 66% from six million to two million between 1998 and 2000. Yet, the number of frequent cocaine users (one or more times a week) remained relatively stable, between three and four million users per year. The number of occasional heroin users increased steadily from an estimated 140,000 in 1990 to 514,000 in 2000. This is a 367% increase in a decade. The number of frequent heroin users remained stable.

The trends are somewhat different for American juveniles. The "gateway" substances that introduce most children to drug use are alcohol and tobacco. Marijuana is a distant third. The proportion of juveniles who use other substances one or more times a month is a tiny proportion compared to those who currently use alcohol or tobacco. Table 1 shows the five-year trends for current users in the 8th and 12th grades.

Alcohol and tobacco use is substantially higher among American Indian or Alaskan Native youths than all other racial or ethnic groups. However, White youths use alcohol and tobacco more than African Americans or Hispanics between age 12 and 20. Of the 10.4 million underage current drinkers in 1998 approximately 65% or 6.8 million engaged in binge drinking of five or more drinks on one occasion during the last 30 days (Substance Abuse and Mental Health Services Administration, 2000). The most common reasons given by 12th graders for underage use of alcohol are to have a good time with friends (73%), see what it is like (52%), get high or feel good (46%),

TABLE 1. Five Year Trends in 30-Day Prevalence of Selected Drugs Among 8th and 12th Graders, 1996–2000

	30-Day Prevalence (Percent)				
Grade/Selected Drug	**1996**	**1997**	**1998**	**1999**	**2000**
8th Grade					
Alcohol	26.2	24.5	23.0	24.0	22.4
Tobacco	21.0	19.4	19.1	17.5	14.6
Marijuana	11.3	10.2	9.7	9.7	9.1
Inhalants	5.8	5.6	4.8	5	4.5
Hallucinogens	1.9	1.8	1.4	1.3	1.2
Cocaine	1.3	1.1	1.4	1.3	1.2
12th Grade					
Alcohol	50.8	52.7	52.0	51.0	50.0
Tobacco	34.0	36.5	35.1	34.6	31.4
Marijuana	21.9	23.7	22.8	23.1	21.6
Inhalants	2.5	2.5	2.3	2.0	2.2
Hallucinogens	3.5	3.9	2.8	3.5	3.5
Cocaine	2.0	2.3	2.4	2.6	2.1

Source: Office of National Drug Control Policy, *The National Drug Control Strategy: 2001 Annual Report*, 2001, p. 144.

enjoy the taste (46%), relax or relieve tension (46%), alleviate boredom (25%), get away from problems or troubles (23%), and alleviate anger or frustration (17%). Eight percent or less report using alcohol to heighten or decrease the effects of other drugs, fit in with a particular group, get to sleep, get through the day, gain insights, or because they are "hooked" and need to satisfy cravings for alcohol (O'Malley, Johnston, and Bachman, 1998, 92).

The rate of illegal drug use is eight to ten times higher among youths currently using cigarettes and alcohol and is highest among the heaviest smokers and drinkers. The highest rate of illegal drug use is among persons aged 18–20. These data suggest that the primary gateway to illegal drug use is early use of tobacco and alcohol between 10 and 17 years of age (Vega and Gill, 1998).

Marijuana is, by far, the most commonly used illicit drug. The 1999 National Survey on Drug Abuse estimates that there were 2.3 million new marijuana users in 1998. That same year it is estimated that there were:

- 1.6 million new users of nonprescription pain relievers,
- 1.2 million new users of hallucinogens,
- 991,000 new inhalant users,
- 934,000 new cocaine users,
- 823,000 new users of tranquilizers,
- 682,000 new stimulant users,
- 186,000 of new users of sedatives, and
- 149,000 new heroin users.

Each of these categories increased sharply between 1990 and 1998, from 37% to 181% (Substance Abuse and Mental Health Services Administration, 2000).

The most popular new "designer drug" or "club drug" to emerge in the last decade is MDMA (3,4-methylenedioxymethamphetamine). The most common street names for MDMA are "Ecstasy," "XTC," "Hug Drug" or simply "X." It is a synthetic stimulant that may also have mild hallucinogenic effects. Many of the 682,000 new users of stimulants were probably using Ecstasy. The recently published *Monitoring the Future: National Results on Adolescent Drug Use: Overview of Key Findings, 2000* found that Ecstasy use by American teenagers in the 8th, 10th, and 12th grades exceeded their use of cocaine (Johnston, O'Malley and Bachman, 2001). The prevalence of Ecstasy use by 8th graders was 3.1% and 8.2% for 12th graders (compare these rates to those presented in Table 1 above). Ecstasy is most commonly sold and used by young people at all-night dance parties and concerts called "raves" (Office of National Drug Control Policy, 2001). The primary risk associated with the use of Ecstasy purchased on the street or at a rave is that unscrupulous dealers "cut" the MDMA with many other chemicals to increase their profits. Unless each tablet is tested the users cannot be certain about what they are actually consuming. Ecstasy users commonly report a mild euphoric sensation, a feeling of well being, increased self-confidence, heightened affection for others, and increased stamina while dancing. The most hazardous side effect associated with Ecstasy is that users may overheat while dancing in a hot, crowded club and suffer heat stroke. Ecstasy use has been associated with a sharp increase in hospital emergency room visits (Office of National Drug Control Policy, 2001). Recently, tablet-testing services have become available at many raves to help users assess whether the drug they purchased has been mixed with other substances and whether it contains MDMA. Between 1970 and 1985, MDMA was used clinically by psychiatrists to treat mental and emotional disorders before it was initially classified in 1985 and officially classified in 1986 as an illegal, Schedule I drug. Under clinical conditions (125mg/dose and medical supervision) few negative side effects were documented. However, recent medical studies suggest that continued exposure to MDMA, without time to heal cell damage, may result in long lasting damage to the areas of brain neurons associated with serotonin transport and reception (McCann, Szabo, Sheffel, Dannals and Ricaute, 1998).

Recently, other designer drugs have begun to emerge, including ketamine, gamma-hydroxybutrate (GHB), gamma-butyrolactone (GBL) and rohypnol. Although each of these drugs has gained a reputation for dangerousness because lethal doses can easily be reached, it is rohypnol that has become the most infamous. It is known as the "date rape drug" because of the ease with which it can be slipped into drinks and render victims unconscious so that they may be sexually assaulted without memory of the assault. At this time there are no reliable data on the extent to which these drugs are used.

Early, occasional, and chronic use of legal and illegal psychoactive substances is associated with many other factors. These factors are called correlates because they often occur with drug use. Precisely how these factors are linked to drug use is often unclear. Some factors appear to influence drug use, others appear to be a result of drug use, and some may be interactive effects produced by other variables. Among the factors that appear to influence drug use are those thought to decrease use (protective factors) and those thought to increase drug use (risk factors). Risk factors have a positive association with drug use in that as they increase in frequency or severity, drug use also increases. Protective factors have a negative association with drug use in that as they increase in frequency or intensity, drug use decreases. In many cases protective factors are the logical opposite of the risk factor. Risk and protective factors can be clustered into categories. Table 2 shows one way to cluster these factors and displays a number of correlates, identified by research, that increase or decrease drug use.

There are also demographic correlates of drug use. The patterns of drug use vary by age, gender, race or ethnicity, and other correlates. The age distribution for current drug users (one or more times a month) in the U.S. reveals steady increases in use between ages 12–13 and 18–20. After the peak at 18–20 years of age, the distribution demonstrates a fairly steady decline until age 65 or above. Current drug use among males is nearly double that for women (8.7% compared to 4.9% in 1999); however, among teenagers age 12–17 illegal drug use is almost equally distributed (11.3% for boys and 10.5% for girls in 1999). Substance abuse by women seems especially damaging to their health. As a result of their smaller body mass, women tend to become acutely intoxicated on lesser amounts of any substance and their health deteriorates more quickly compared to men. In part, this is because woman appear much more likely to have unprotected sex and have multiple partners than males. Women are also more likely to be dependent on males economically and therefore trade sex for drugs or money (Inciardi, Lockwood and Pottieger, 1993; McCoy, Miles, and Inciardi, 1995).

American Indians or Alaskan Natives have the highest overall rates of illegal drug use (10.6%) followed by African Americans (7.7%), Hispanics (6.8%), Whites (6.6%) and Asians (3.2%). However, among youths aged between 12 and 17 the pattern is somewhat different, with American Indians or Alaskan Natives at 19.6% followed by Whites (10.9%), African Americans (10.7%) and Asians (8.4%). The current use rate among adult college graduates in 1999 was 4.8% compared to 7.1% for those who had dropped out before completing high school. Interestingly, college graduates were much more likely to have tried illicit drugs in their lifetime than those who had not completed high school (45.6% compared to 30%). The rate of illegal drug use is about 2.5 times higher among the unemployed compared to employed people (16.5% of the unemployed, 6.5% of the employed). However, more than 77% of current drug users are employed full or part-time and purchase their drug supply primarily with legally earned income. Geographically, use of illegal drugs is slightly more concentrated in the western and northeastern areas of the U.S. and predominantly within metropolitan and suburban areas (Substance Abuse and Mental Health Services Administration, 2000; Office of National Drug Control Policy, 2001).

Beyond the correlated risk, protective, and demographic factors, there are factors that may be produced as a result of drug use. These correlates include black market expenditures for drugs diverted from the legal economy, drug related deaths, sexually transmitted diseases including HIV or AIDS, drug related medical emergencies, homelessness, mental illness, neglect of children, deterioration of neighborhoods and urban areas, crime rates, arrest rates, incarceration rates, criminal justice and health costs. The Office of National Drug Control Policy estimates that the total expenditure

TABLE 2. Drug Use Correlates: Risk and Protective Factors

	Documented Drug Use Correlates	
Correlate Category	**Risk Factors**	**Protective Factors**
1. Individual Factors	a. Anxious/withdrawn	a. Self-confident/outgoing
	b. Mental/emotional problem	b. Mental/emotional stability
	c. Sensation/risk seeking	c. Inhibited/self-disciplined
	d. Adolescent smoking	d. First tobacco use in later teens
	e. Adolescent use of alcohol	e. First alcohol use in later teens
	f. Impulsive/attention deficit	f. Patience/delays gratification
	g. Early problem behaviors	g. Conventional behaviors
	h. Lack of goals/ambition	h. Goal/achievement oriented
	i. Delinquent/criminal activities	i. Enjoys conventional activities
	j. Lacks empathy for others	j. Empathetic toward others
	k. Feelings of hopelessness	k. Aspirations for the future/hope
	l. Illness/pains/failing health	l. Good health/no pains
	m. Pregnancy/birth complications	m. Routine pregnancy/birth
	n. Antisocial beliefs/attitudes	n. Prosocial beliefs/attitudes
	o. Early onset of sexual activity	o. Late onset of sexual activity
2. Family Factors	a. Parent(s) tolerate deviancy	a. Parent(s) intolerant of deviancy
	b. Alcoholic parent(s)	b. Nonalcoholic parents
	c. Parent(s) use illicit drugs	c. Parents do not use illicit drugs
	d. Father's criminality	d. Noncriminal father
	e. Parental arrests (before age 10 y)	e. Neither parent arrested
	f. High parental conflict	f. Low parental conflict
	g. High parent-child conflict	g. Low parent-child conflict
	h. Low family achievement	h. High family achievement
	i. Living in poverty	i. Not living in poverty
	j. Maltreatment/abuse/neglect	j. Parental care/support/monitoring
	k. Parental rejection	k. Parental acceptance
	l. Lax/punitive/harsh discipline	l. Consistent/reasonable discipline
	m. Family breakup (before age 10)	m. Family remains intact
3. Peer Factors	a. Friends antisocial	a. Friends prosocial
	b. Sensation/risk seeking friends	b. Few sensation/risk seeking friends
	c. Friends in gangs/delinquent	c. Few delinquent/gang friends
	d. Friends smoke	d. Few friends smoke
	e. Friends use alcohol	e. Few friends use alcohol
	f. Friends use marijuana	f. Few friends use marijuana
	g. Friends use other illicit drugs	g. Few friends use other illicit drugs
	h. Low peer achievement	h. High peer achievement
	i. Sibling delinquency/drug use	i. Nondelinquent/drug using sibling
4. Community Factors	a. High drug use in school	a. Low drug use in school
	b. Disorganized neighborhoods	b. Well maintained neighborhoods
	c. High levels of street crime	c. Low levels of street crime
	d. High levels of drug use	d. Low levels of drug use
	e. Unsupervised activities	e. Mostly supervised activities
	f. Prevalent street gangs	f. None/few street gangs
	g. Frequent victimization	g. Never/rarely victimized
	h. Poor grades/failure/dropout	h. Good grades/graduation
	i. Frequently truant from school	i. Not truant from school
5. Acculturation Factors	a. Negative race/ethnic identity	a. Positive race/ethnic identity
	b. Weak family cohesion/pride	b. Strong family cohesion/pride
	c. Low/no church attendance	c. Regular church attendance
	d. Perceived discrimination	d. No perceived discrimination
	e. Few prevention messages	e. Many prevention messages
	f. Difficulty with the language	f. Little difficulty with the language

by American users for illegal drugs from 1988 and 2000 to be $1,014 billion (i.e., $1 trillion and 14 billion). Since 1988 the annual expenditure by users for drugs has declined steadily, from $115.7 billion in 1988 to $62.4 billion in 2000. To put this in perspective, the entire federal drug control budget for 2000 was $18.8 billion, the highest funding level since 1988. As noted earlier, the estimated number of drug users in the U.S. has remained relatively stable since 1988. However, during that same period the price for most illegal drugs has fallen consistently while the purity has increased (Office of National Drug Control Policy, 2001, 140, 171). The most likely explanation for the reduction in expenditures by drug users is the reduced or lowered costs of some drugs (e.g., from powdered to cheaper "crack" cocaine) rather than drug policy.

There is a consistent increase in both the number and rate of drug-related deaths from 1988 to 1998. A similar pattern is seen for the number of cocaine and heroin related emergency room episodes (Office of National Drug Control Policy, 2001). One plausible explanation for these patterns is the increases in purity of both cocaine and heroin during this same period. Increased purity brings the effective and the lethal dose limits closer together so that it is easier to accidentally overdose. This is especially true for intravenous drug users. Both inexperienced and long time drug users can easily overdose when the drug is of higher purity than expected. The closer the drug comes to absolute purity, the more likely a self-administered dose will be lethal. Most current users have no idea of the purity of the drug they are using. Furthermore, if the drug has been "cut" with other substances they do not know what those substances are. Whether an intravenous drug user overdoses is a gamble each time they shoot up unless they have the ability to test the drug for adulterants and purity (to make an informed decision about whether to use the drug and how much of the drug to use; Goode, 1999).

Drug use, regardless of the drug or the method of administration, has been strongly associated with sexually transmitted diseases. HIV or AIDS is the most serious disease and most directly associated with drug use because unprotected heterosexual and homosexual encounters are often accompanied by drug use. Casual, unprotected sexual contact is especially prevalent among powder cocaine and crack users. Cocaine and heroin users also frequently inject these drugs and share needles, syringes, and equipment or supplies with friends or strangers (Hser, Boyle, and Anglin, 1998; Inciardi, et al., 1995). The Office of National Drug Control Policy (2001, 164–165) reports that 30–40% of the males who have died of AIDS or are currently living with AIDS were also intravenous drug users. The rates for women are higher; 40–50% of those who have died from or are living with AIDS also injected drugs.

The homeless often have multiple health problems that contribute to their homelessness either as one of the primary reasons for their situation or as a barrier to stabilizing their lives. A survey of homeless people revealed that nearly 90% had at some point in their life had an alcohol, drug or mental health problem. Of those homeless in the past month, 66% were found to have one or more of these problems. Roughly, two thirds had used alcohol three or more times a week or had started using illegal drugs before their eighteenth birthday. The major barriers preventing most homeless people from reestablishing a home were insufficient income or lack of a job rather than addiction to alcohol or drugs. Among the estimated 250,000 homeless veterans, approximately 70% have substance abuse problems and 45% have a dual diagnosis for an addictive disorder and mental illness. Roughly 10 million Americans have a similar dual diagnosis. Among frequent drug users (i.e., addicts) more than 40% also have a mental disorder. However, in all but 20% of the cases, the onset of mental illness preceded the onset of drug use by several years (Office of National Drug Control Policy, 2001, 67, 161).

More than 500,000 children were in foster care at the end of 2000. Of these, roughly 66% have parents with substance abuse problems that contributed to these children being removed from parental custody for abuse or neglect. Among adults receiving welfare it is estimated that 15–20% have substance abuse problems that prevent them from working or make them sufficiently unemployable that they are unlikely to be able to support themselves or their family without public assistance (Office of National Drug Control Policy, 2001, 58).

Finally, there is a clear association among drug use, public policy responses to drug users or dealers, and the rapid expansion in the capacity and cost of criminal justice system since 1974. Annually, there are about 15 million arrests in the U.S. Approximately 1.5 million of these arrests are for drug abuse violations and 80% of these are for possession (i.e, distribution/sales account for only 20% of these arrests). Drug arrests are an increasingly large proportion of felony arrests and often result in long prison sentences upon conviction. Mandatory sentencing, longer sentences, and reduced opportunities for early release caused a sharp increase in the proportion of inmates in prison because of a drug conviction. In state prisons about 20% of the inmate population are confined because of a drug conviction. In U.S. federal prisons, roughly 60% of the inmate population was convicted of a drug crime. In both cases, the proportions of drug related offenders confined are understated. Inmates with a "lesser-included" drug offense are not counted in these data because only the most serious conviction is reported for these statistics. Between 1990 and 2000 about 1800 confinement beds per week were built. As a result, there are now over 2 million people confined in the U.S. Most of the growth in the rate of confinement can be attributed to convictions for possession or distribution and sales of illegal drugs (Austin and Irwin, 2001).

No one seriously questions that there is an association between drug use and crime. However, there are vigorous debates over whether such crime is a direct effect of drug use, a byproduct of black-market drug trafficking, a result of economic necessity to support a drug habit, or a consequence of drug prohibition laws.

MICHAEL J. GILBERT

References and Further Reading

Abadinsky, H., *Drugs: An Introduction,* 4th ed., Wadsworth/Thomson Learning, Belmont, CA, 2001.

Austin, J. and Irwin, J., *It's About Time: America's Imprisonment Binge,* 3rd ed. Wadsworth/Thomson Learning, Belmont, CA.

Hser, Y.-I., Boyle, K., and Anglin, M.D., Drug Use and Correlates Among Sexually Transmitted Disease Patients, Emergency Room Patients and Arrestees, Journal of Drug Issues 28:2, (1998).

Goode, E., *Drugs in American Society,* 5th ed. McGraw-Hill College, New York.

Inciardi, J.A., Lockwood D., and Pottieger, A.E., *Women and Crack-Cocaine,* Macmillan Publishing Company, New York, 1993.

Inciardi, J.A., Page, J.B., McBride, D.C., Chitwood, D.D., McCoy, C.B., McCoy H.V., and Trapido, E., The Risk of Exposure to HIV-Contaminated Needles and Syringes in Shooting Galleries, in Inciardi, J.A. and McElrath K., Eds., *The American Drug Scene,* Roxbury Publishing Company, Los Angeles, CA, 1995.

Johnston, Lloyd D., Patrick M. O'Malley, Jerald G. Bachman, *Monitoring the Future—National Results on Adolescent Drug Use: Overview of Key Findings, 2000.* Bethesda, MD, National Institute of Drug Abuse, U.S. Department of Health and Human Services, 2001.

Killias, M., and Aebi, M.F., Crime Trends in Europe from 1990 to 1996: How Europe Illustrates the Limits of the American Experience, *European Journal on Criminal Policy and Research,* 8, 2000.

Levinthal, C.F., Drugs, Behavior, and Modern Society, 2nd ed., Ally and Bacon, Boston, MA, 1999.

McCann, U.D., Szabo, Z., Scheffel, U., Dannals, R.F., and Ricaute, G.A., Positron Emission Tomographic Evidence of Toxic Effect of MDMA ("Ecstasy") on Brain Serotonin Neurons in Human Beings, *The Lancet* 352:9138 (1998).

McCoy, H.V., Miles C., and Inciardi, J.A., Survival Sex: Inner-City Women and Crack Cocaine, in Inciardi J.A. and McElrath, K., Eds., *The American Drug Scene,* Roxbury Publishing Company, Los Angeles, CA, 1995.

Office of National Drug Control Policy, *The National Drug Control Strategy: 2001 Annual Report,* Office of National Drug Control Policy, The White House, Washington, DC, 2001.

O'Malley, P., Johnson, L.D., and Bachman, J.G., Alcohol Use Among Adolescents, *Alcohol, Health & Research World,* 22:2, (1998).

Substance Abuse and Mental Health Services Administration, *1997 National Household Survey on Drug Abuse,* Substance Abuse and Mental Health Services Administration, U.S. Department of Health and Human Services, Washington, DC, 1998.

Substance Abuse and Mental Health Services Administration, *Summary of Findings from the 1999 National Household Survey on Drug Abuse,* U.S. Department of Health and Human Services, Washington, DC, 2000. Available at: http://www.samhsa.gov/oas/NHSDA/1999. Retrieved on March 16, 2001.

Vega, W.A., Andres Gill and Associates, *Drug Use and Ethnicity in Early Adolescence,* New York, Plenum Press, 1998.

See also **Acquired Immune Deficiency Syndrome (AIDS) and the Law; Club Drugs; Designer Drugs; Drug Use and Criminal Behavior; Drug Use: Law; Rape Acquaintance and Date**

Drug Use: The Law

Before 1912, there were no international laws that sought to control the traffic, regulation, and use of psychoactive substances. Nearly 100 years later, it is common to speak of a *War on Drugs*, as though illicit substances think and act for themselves. In this sociological sense, illegal drugs have become *reified*: it is not recognized that people take drugs, but instead the media—shaped by criminal justice and political leaders—project the image that drugs take people.

The current U.S. War on Drugs, waged domestically and across international borders, can be traced to an unprecedented White House ceremony on June 24, 1982, when President Ronald Reagan launched the war's first volley (Trebach, 1987):

> We're rejecting the helpless attitude that drug use is so rampant that we're defenseless to do anything about it. We're taking down the surrender flag that has flown over so many drug efforts. We're running up the battle flag. We can fight the drug problem, and we can win.

One Law: Three Methods of Treating Drug Use

The origin of drug control laws and policies in the U.S. is rooted in the Hague Opium Convention of 1912, a treaty promulgated for the purpose of solving the opium problems of China and the Far East. The Hague Convention of 1912 attempted to provide for effective international control of opium, morphine, cocaine, and their derivatives. Its aims were to gradually suppress the abuse of these drugs and to prevent their use for other than "medical and legitimate purposes." The Convention specifically targeted the production, manufacture, export, trade, and distribution of opium. It also sought to classify the illegal possession of opium, morphine, and cocaine as penal offenses (Renborg, 1947). Until then, antidrug legislation was virtually nonexistent throughout the nations of the globe. In 1914, the U.S. passed the Harrison Narcotic Act and spearheaded an international effort to assure compliance with the Convention. Thereafter, a prohibitionist model of law came to be applied to users of illegal drugs in the U.S.

Although bound by the same international treaty obligations as was (and is) the U.S., Great Britain and the Netherlands have developed much different strategies of applying problems of drug use to the law. The drug control policies of each nation have been shaped within the context of distinct nationalistic and cultural factors.

Today, in the U.S., "the British system" and the Dutch policy of *normalization* have largely been ignored, misunderstood or misrepresented by proponents of the War on Drugs. In England, heroin and cocaine have been dispensed legally through a medical framework ever since their discovery and acceptance as medicines. (The cocaine alkaloid within the leaf of the coca plant, or the "active ingredient" within cocaine, was first isolated between 1844 and 1860, depending on which of the numerous sources on the subject is to be believed. Heroin, essentially an extract of morphine that is derived from the dried flowers of the poppy plant, was "discovered" in 1874 and popularized as a medicine in 1898. Cannabis refers to marijuana, hashish, and other products of the hemp plant, such as hashish oil, bhang, and ganja. The term marijuana is not used in England and the Netherlands. Thus, all references to marijuana and hashish within this text are encompassed by the term cannabis.) In the Netherlands, these substances and cannabis remain strictly illegal but they are available to users through a system of decriminalization (*normalization*). Both systems of drug control, however, have rarely been the subjects of objective academic study.

Whereas the concepts of drug decriminalization and legalization are quite distinct, they are often confused and inappropriately interchanged with one another. In today's U.S., the thought of decriminalizing or legalizing illicit substances is generally met with disdain by the U.S. law enforcement community. This sentiment is perhaps best evidenced by Jerald Vaughn, who testified before the U.S. House of Representatives (1988) as the Executive Director of the International Association of Chiefs of Police:

> Drugs are diabolical and destructive not only to the human system, but to the democratic way of life and a responsible citizenry.

This notion of drug users as evil beings contrasts sharply with the British "harm reduction" and the Dutch "normalization" model of drug control that are outlined below.

Historical Foundations of Drug Control

In 1863, during the U.S. Civil War and twenty years after the hypodermic needle had been invented, drug addiction in the U.S. was pervasive (Lindesmith, 1947):

> Addiction spread throughout all socioeconomic strata, and there was no significant link between drug addiction and criminality. The habit was neither approved nor regarded as criminal or monstrous, it was usually looked upon as a vice or personal misfortune. Narcotics users were pitied, rather than loathed as criminals or degenerates.

A "twin campaign" in the U.S. provided the impetus for the eventual passage of both the Harrison Narcotic Act and the 18th Amendment to the U.S. Constitution. Ratified in 1919 and repealed in 1933, the 18th Amendment prohibited the manufacture, sale and transportation of alcohol. The Harrison Act, championed by U.S. Secretary of State William Jennings Bryan, known for his deep prohibitionist and missionary beliefs and convictions, outlawed cocaine and heroin for nonmedicinal uses. The U.S. thereby fulfilled its new international treaty obligation, and it thereafter led an international movement whereby other nations would comply with the Hague Convention. Thus, domestic and international drug law enforcement was born.

The Anti-Drug Campaign became manifested first through the League of Nations and then through the United Nations. In the aftermath of the Hague Convention and prior to World War II, international treaties came about through drug control conventions that took place in Geneva, Switzerland in 1925, 1931 and 1936 (Renborg, 1947).

In 1948, the U.S. launched a United Nations campaign, with Harry Anslinger at the helm as the U.S.

Commissioner of Narcotics at the U.N., "to consolidate all international drug agreements into a new Single Convention." In 1964, through "the remarkable phenomenon of direct international manipulation" by the U.S., the Single Convention finally came into force (King, 1972). In drug control matters, largely through the efforts of Harry Anslinger, the international community succumbed to the will of the U.S. As well, Anslinger was equally effective in formulating, executing and instituting U.S. domestic drug control policies.

The U.S. System of Drug Control

From 1912–1925, clinics were established in over forty U.S. cities to dispense low-cost narcotics to addicts.(Cocaine was misclassified as a narcotic by the Harrison Act. Narcotics are analgesics, or pain killers that slow the respiratory rate. Cocaine is a stimulant, which is still inappropriately referred to as a narcotic.) Most clinics were established in the 1920s, when physicians feared prescribing such drugs to addict-patients after the Harrison Narcotic Act was ruled on in a number of cases by the U.S. Supreme Court. The judicial interpretation of the Harrison Narcotic Act, in which the right of physicians to prescribe narcotics to addicts in "good faith" came under scrutiny, has been called the "narcotization of the high court" (King, 1953). The possibility of facing criminal charges, imprisonment, and losing one's medical license effectively deterred most physicians from prescribing narcotics to addict-patients because the "good faith" of adherence to medical standards could only be proved after a trial (Ploscowe, 1961). Images of colonial U.S. witchcraft trials thus come to mind.

Eventually, all the U.S. narcotic clinics were closed down. "While no one would maintain that the clinics were an unqualified success, a good argument can be made that they were never really given a fair chance to demonstrate their worth" (Schur, 1962).

Following the Harrison Narcotic Act Era, the chief architect of drug laws in the U.S. was the aforementioned Harry Anslinger. Appointed by President Herbert Hoover in 1930 as the first Commissioner of the Federal Bureau of Narcotics (FBN), the forerunner of today's Drug Enforcement Administration, Anslinger was elevated to his post after having served as Assistant Commissioner of Prohibition. Until the formation of the FBN, federal narcotics laws were first enforced by the Bureau of Internal Revenue (today's I.R.S.) and then by the Narcotic Division of the U.S. Treasury Department's Prohibition Unit. Anslinger served as Commissioner of the FBN until 1962, and he greatly influenced Congress in constructing national drug laws and policies: laws and policies that are still largely in place today. As the spiritual ancestor of Gerald Vaughn, the "Anslinger philosophy" (Schur, 1962) was rooted in the view that drugs were essentially a police problem:

> At the core of the Commissioner's outlook [was] a belief that basically the addict is a wrongdoer ... that almost all addicts are parasites and that "this parasitic drug addict is a tremendous burden on the community."

Anslinger consistently both fought and sought: he fought the concept of treating addiction as a medical problem, and he sought harsher prison sentences for those convicted of violating U.S. drug laws. He opposed the reestablishment of narcotic clinics, saying that "legalized clinics have never worked since they were opened in 1919" (Jeffee, 1966), and he equated the concept with "bar rooms for addicts" and "morphine feeding stations" (Musto, 1973). Throughout the 1930s, 1940s, and 1950s, Anslinger succeeded in greatly lengthening prison sentences for offenders convicted of federal violations of opiate, cocaine, and marijuana laws. These sentencing laws were a precursor of the *mandatory* and *mandatory minimum* sentences for drug offenses that were later initiated, on the federal level, through the U.S. Anti-Drug Abuse Acts of 1986 and 1988. These and similar laws, that came to adopted by virtually all the U.S. states, are in large part responsible for the dramatic increase in the U.S. prison population, which essentially doubled from 1980 to 1990, and doubled again from 1990 to 2000.

Dr. Lawrence Kolb, a contemporary of Anslinger who from 1909 to 1944 headed the U.S. Public Health Service's Mental Hygiene Division, the predecessor of today's National Institutes of Mental Health, described Anslinger's role in the creation of U.S. drug policies this way (1961):

> People with only a police training have secured commanding positions in the formulation of narcotics policies; sound medical opinion based on careful research is cried down or ignored.

Commissioner Anslinger not only was opposed to the clinic concept, but he viewed the less punitive, medical approach of other nations, such as England, as constituting surrender in the battle to cure addicts (Schur, 1962). How he would have reacted to the idea of methadone maintenance programs that were implemented during the Nixon administration is, of course, unknown. In 1956, Anslinger falsely claimed that the British system "actually ... is one of compulsory hospitalization because they force that addict into a nursing home until he is cured" (Schur, 1962). Anslinger either did not understand or purposely misrepresented the "British system" of addition treatment.

By 1940, after cannabis was outlawed in the U.S. through the Marihuana Tax Act of 1937, two objectives of U.S. drug control policy can be traced in the historical record:

1. It enabled a repressive form of domestic social control, enforced against racial, ethnic, and cultural minorities, to remain unchallenged within the borders of the U.S., and
2. It enabled U.S. foreign policy objectives to be formulated and executed in conjunction with its drug control policy, thereby extending and solidifying U.S. political hegemony or dominance abroad.

The British System of Drug Control

Whereas the U.S. Harrison Narcotic Act was paralleled by the British Dangerous Drugs Act of 1920, physicians in England remained empowered to prescribe heroin and cocaine to addicts and other patients as they saw fit. The so-called British system, described by Fazey (Elsner, 1993) as "a patchwork of treatment responses where nothing is standardized," is philosophically rooted in Great Britain's 1924 Rolleston Committee report. This report recognized two facts: (1) that drug addiction is a "chronic, relapsing disease"; and (2) that "the indefinitely prolonged administration of morphine or heroin may be necessary" for a segment of the addict population.

Treating drug addicts through traditional medical practice as part of Britain's National Health Service (NHS), which is commonly referred to as "socialized medicine," has been called a "state rationing system" or "controlled availability" by John Marks (Elsner, 1993). Under the "British system," which Anslinger criticized, patients addicted to heroin or other drugs could be prescribed drugs by their doctor (known as a general practitioner, or a GP). However, the commonly construed idea of anyone walking into a local British pharmacy to purchase heroin simply was, and is, a falsehood.

In 1968, British drug control policy changed drastically, in large part because of abuse of the system by foreigners. A "clinic system," managed by psychiatrists, was then instituted. Thereafter, for an addict to be maintained on heroin or cocaine through the NHS, he or she had to enroll as a patient in a drug dependence clinic. "[T]he power of general practitioners to dispense heroin and cocaine addicts ceased... on April 16, 1968" (Trebach, 1982).

Gradually, the psychiatrists developed a philosophy of "less is better," and although they were empowered to prescribe drugs to patients as was medically needed, they saw it fit to reduce the amount prescribed to addicts. Additionally, rather than prescribing intravenous opiates, the British psychiatrists followed the lead of the U.S. treatment community by prescribing oral methadone (Terrence Tanner, as quoted in Trebach, 1982):

> Those wretched doctors! ... About 1972 they started moving off heroin to physeptone [methadone]. Then off i.v. [injectable] to oral. The result: the addicts go back to the black market, lose their jobs, and stop paying taxes.

Although GPs in England are still lawfully permitted to prescribe heroin substitutes to their addict patients, they are reluctant to do so. In many ways, this fear to prescribe narcotics to addicts parallels the fear of U.S. physicians in the early 1920s. In the 1980s, for example, convictions were twice obtained against an English physician, Ann Dally, who was charged with prescribing in "bad faith," and came to incur the wrath of certain British authorities when she insisted on maintaining approximately 140 long-term addict patients on heroin substitutes. The new British system, with which Dr. Dally was said to be *out of sync*, has been referred to as the *Short, Sharp, Cure*: *the most mystical belief that if you abruptly deprive someone of what they most crave they will cease to crave it* (Tyler, as quoted in Elsner, 1993).

Over the years, the new British system has styled itself on a U.S. law enforcement approach. Despite this conservative trend, an innovative alternative, the *harm reduction model*, emerged in England in the 1980s.

The Harm Reduction Model

Developed in Liverpool's Merseyside region, the "harm reduction model" is comprised of five essential components:

1. Committed drug addicts are prescribed and maintained on drugs.
2. Through counseling, addicts are encouraged to "kick" their habits and lead drug free lives.
3. Intravenous drug users are provided with clean syringes and hypodermic needles so as to prevent the spread of HIV or AIDS.
4. Drug users are educated about how the AIDS virus is contracted and spread.
5. Drug users are empowered to act and think for themselves.

The Merseyside harm reduction strategy breaks new ground by not treating drug users as "empty vessels, waiting to be filled with the wisdom of experts," but rather as human beings who play an important role in their own drug treatment (O'Hare, as cited in Trebach and Zeese, 1990a). From the aspect of the drug dependent person, Parry has described the harm reduction model in terms of "relief" (cited in Trebach and Zeese, 1990b): relief that not all is lost.

There are still places where drug users are not only treated humanely, but offered the widest range of options from traditional drug free programs to safer drug programs that may involve the legal supply of injectable or smokable forms of heroin, cocaine, amphetamine, etc. Relief that there are services in existence where staff will not only help you stop using drugs, but will offer advice to committed users and the equipment to achieve the desired drug experience in the safest possible way.

The Liverpool experience demonstrates that drug maintenance for addicts can be synonymous with drug treatment. While critics of the medical distribution of drugs, such as criminologist J.Q. Wilson, equate it with running up the white flag of surrender, Dr. John Marks of the Mersey Drug Dependency Service defends England's *state rationing system* (Elsner, 1993):

> Controlled availability [of drugs] produces controlled use, whereas prohibition or promotion produces uncontrolled use. Currently we have the former with drugs and the latter with alcohol, and society suffers at both these extremes.

"Controlled availability," concludes Marks, "is a happy medium between total prohibition and irresponsible pressured advertising."

Normalization: The Dutch System of Drug Control

In response to the same pressures that brought forth the U.S. Harrison Narcotic Act and the British Dangerous Drugs Act, the first criminal drug legislation was introduced in the Netherlands in 1919. This Act remained virtually unchanged until 1976, when maximum penalties for "hard drugs" were, in keeping pace with the trend set by the international community, significantly increased.

The Amended Opium Act of 1976 draws a distinction between "drugs presenting unacceptable risks," such as cocaine, opiates, LSD, and amphetamines, and "hemp products" that include marijuana and hashish. In keeping in line with their international commitment through treaties, the Dutch have tried to steer a course that has been described as a compromise between a "war on drugs" and "legalization."

The Dutch view drug use and abuse as a public health problem, not one of the police or the criminal justice system. Although law enforcement concentrates on reducing the supply of drugs, it does not seek to criminalize and punish drug users.

The Dutch consider their policy of "normalization" to be both pragmatic and conservative. It is based on the realization that a nation surrounded by water, such as the Netherlands, cannot conquer the sea. Rather, by building dikes and locks, the Dutch have adapted and learned to control the sea to the best of their ability. The policy of normalization that aims to integrate drug users into Dutch society rather than stigmatize them, utilizes this philosophy in regards to illicit drug use.

In 1976, when the Amended Opium Act was adopted, so was a set of guidelines that set a national policy regarding the investigation and prosecution of drug offenses. It is under these guidelines that priorities are set and "prosecutorial discretion" is employed:

1. Sale of cannabis in small quantities by a "reliable person" (known as a "house dealer") in a "youth centre" results in no prosecution unless a dealer trades provocatively or openly advertises.
2. Possession of a small quantity of "hard" drugs for personal consumption results, as a rule, in no police investigation, no pretrial detention, and no prosecution.
3. Dealing, possessing, and producing a maximum of thirty grams of marijuana results, as a rule, in no police investigation, no pretrial detention, and no prosecution.
4. When confronted with users who deal in "hard" drugs to provide for their own needs, or those found in possession of more than a small quantity, the public prosecutor employs discretion in determining the prison sentence that must be demanded.

Dutch Cannabis Policy

Although "hemp products" (i.e., marijuana and hashish) remain illegal in the Netherlands, their use and small-scale sales are permitted. In other words, through a policy of prosecutorial discretion, marijuana and hashish laws remain on the books but are not enforced by the Dutch authorities. In fact, cannabis may be purchased in numerous coffeehouses throughout Holland, and it is also available through "youth centres."

The underlying philosophy by which the Dutch have shaped their cannabis policy is this: by *separating the markets*, Dutch cannabis-seeking youths do not need a *pusher*. The Dutch have been successful in creating two markets: above-ground, where cannabis may be purchased and used by youths (sixteen years and older) without fear; and underground, where the Dutch authorities do not want their youths to venture.

Summary of How Three Systems Apply Law to Drug Use

Although the U.S., the Netherlands and England are bound by the same international drug control treaties, aspects of each nation's drug policies are quite distinct from one another. Whereas the British have a "state rationing system" of "controlled availability" in place through a medical framework, and the Netherlands' policy of "normalization" has effectively decriminalized both "hard" and "soft" drug use, the U.S. is content to tell drug users to "just say no." Although the British and the Dutch have adopted innovative strategies to cope with illicit drug use and related social harms, the prohibitionist stance remains firmly entrenched in the body politic of the USA.

Since 1914, despite the failure of alcohol prohibition, the prohibition model has been dominant in the U.S. "war" that has been waged against heroin, cocaine, and cannabis. Although Presidents Nixon, Reagan, and George H.W. Bush each declared their own war on drugs, and their policies were continued by Presidents Clinton and George W. Bush, the objectives of U.S. drug control policies have remained virtually unchanged since Franklin Delano Roosevelt occupied the White House.

MICHAEL C. ELSNER

References and Further Reading

Elsner, M.C., A Transnational Comparison of Drug Control Policies in the U.S., England and the Netherlands, in Kraska, P., Ed., *Altered States of Mind: Critical Observations on the Drug War,* Garland, New York, 1993, pp. 207–228.

Jeffee, S., *Narcotics: An American Plan,* Paul S. Eriksson, Inc., New York, 1966.

King, R., *The Drug Hang-Up: America's Fifty-Year Folly,* Charles C. Thomas, Springfield, IL, 1972.

King, R., The Narcotics Bureau and the Harrison Act: Jailing the Healers and the Sick, *Yale Law Journal,* 62 (1953).

Kolb, L., Drug Addiction: Crime or Disease? *The Nation*, May 20, 1961.

Lindesmith, A.R., *Opiate Addiction,* Principia Press, Bloomington, IN, 1947.

Musto, D.F., *The American Disease,* Yale University Press, New Haven, CT, 1973.

Ploscowe, M., Interim and Final Reports of the Joint Committee of the American Bar Association and the American Medical Association on Narcotic Drugs, *Drug Addiction: Crime or Disease?,* Indiana University Press, Bloomington, IN, 1961.

Renborg, B.A., International Drug Control: A Study of International Administration By and Through the League of Nations, Carnegie Endowment for International Peace, Washington, DC, 1947.

Schur, E.M., *Narcotic Addiction, Britain and America,* Greenwood Press, Westport, CT, 1962.

Trebach, A., *The Great Drug War,* MacMillan, New York, 1987.

Trebach, A., *The Heroin Solution*, Yale University Press, New Haven, CT, 1982.

Trebach, A. and Zeese, K., *Drug Prohibition and the Conscience of Nations,* Drug Policy Foundation, Washington, DC, 1990.

Trebach, A. and Zeese, K., *The Great Issues of Drug Policy,* Drug Policy Foundation, Washington, DC, 1990.

U.S. House of Representatives Select Committee on Narcotics Abuse and Control, *Legalization of Illicit Drugs: Impact and Feasibility, Part I,* Government Printing Office, Washington, DC, September 29, 1988.

See also **Drug Policy: The Decriminalization/Legalization Argument**

Due Process

The fundamental principles of due process have shaped the scope and nature of individual rights in the U.S. The interpretation and application of the Constitutional provisions delineating a citizen's rights with respect to the state and federal governments by American courts, most notably the U.S. Supreme Court, have led to numerous landmark decisions in U.S. history. These decisions, combined with statutory provisions implemented by the federal government and individual state governments, have defined the types of rights conferred upon individuals and the processes by which such rights are enforced.

Historical Background

The basic principle of due process finds its theoretical basis in Article 39 of the Magna Carta. In 1215, King John of England pledged that "[n]o free man shall be taken, or imprisoned, or disseized, or outlawed, or exiled, or any wise destroyed... but by the lawful judgment of his peers, or by the law of the land." The term "law of the land" eventually evolved into a synonym for "due process" when, in 1344, the British Parliament obliged King Edward III to assent to a statute that provided: "no man... shall be put out of land or tenement, nor taken nor imprisoned, nor disinherited, nor put to death without being brought in answer by due process of law." It is upon these basic tenets that the due process clauses found in the Fifth Amendment of the American Bill of Rights and the Fourteenth Amendment to the U.S. Constitution were developed. These protections have been interpreted to mandate fair and lawful procedures by law enforcement officials and the courts, as well as affording the judiciary the power to review legislative acts bearing upon the deprivation of a citizen's life, liberty or property.

The evolution of American jurisprudence and the applicability of those rights enumerated in the Bill of Rights to the states was a lengthy and arduous process. Prior to the turn of the twentieth century, the U.S. Supreme Court refused to apply the protections afforded to citizens by the Bill of Rights to state governments in order to make those Constitutional protections binding on the states, as well as the federal government. With such restrictions absent, state governments were—at one time—free to implement their own initiatives and protections for violations of an individual's rights under state law. However, through a process of selective incorporation, the U.S. Supreme Court slowly began to hold that various rights enumerated in the Bill of Rights were applicable to the states via the Due Process Clause of the Fourteenth Amendment. Prior to the 1960s, the provisions of the First Amendment (that entails the rights of freedom of religion, freedom of speech, freedom of the press, the right to assembly, the right to petition the government, and the prohibition against the establishment of religion) and the Fourth Amendment protection against unreasonable search and seizure, were held to apply to state governments. In later years, the Sixth Amendment's provisions regarding notice and public trial, as well as the rights to speedy trial, trial by jury, to confront witnesses, to compel witnesses for the defense, and the right to assistance of counsel were incorporated, as well as the Eighth Amendment's prohibitions against cruel and unusual punishment and excessive bail. Eventually, those provisions of the Bill of Rights deemed essential to individual liberty had been incorporated, thereby making them binding upon the states, with the exception of the Second Amendment, the grand jury clause of the Fifth Amendment, and the Seventh Amendment.

The U.S. Constitution contains two due process clauses—one found in the text of the Fifth Amendment that operates as a restraint upon the power of the federal government, and the other in the text of the Fourteenth Amendment that limits the power of the states. These provisions provide that neither the federal government nor the states may deprive a person of "life, liberty, or property, without due process of law." The limitations prescribed by these provisions are of two discrete types: substantive and procedural. Substantive due process provides that a law itself be fair and reasonable, with an appropriate justification independent of the procedures necessary for enforcing it. Thus, a substantive due process argument alleging that a particular law violates an individual's rights claims that the law is invalid because it lacks a sufficient rationalization to warrant government interference with the individual's liberty or property. In contrast, procedural due process requires that, when the government seeks to deprive a person of life, liberty or property, the procedures designed to enforce the law at issue are fair. A due process argument premised upon an alleged violation of an individual's procedural rights is based upon the notion that the law itself is otherwise valid; however, the procedures used in enforcing the law are inequitably applied.

The Fifth and Fourteenth Amendment Due Process Clauses

The Fifth Amendment to the U.S. Constitution contains several provisions affecting various rights of those accused of criminal offenses. The Fifth Amendment provides that, "no person shall be held to answer for a capital, or otherwise infamous crime, unless on a presentment or indictment of a Grand Jury, except in cases arising in the land or naval forces, or in the Militia, when in actual service in time of War or public danger; nor shall any person be subject for the same offense to be twice put in jeopardy of life or limb; nor shall be compelled in any criminal case to be a witness against himself, nor be deprived of life, liberty, or property, without due process of law..." The protections afforded citizens under this amendment have been the subject of much debate and criticism. Judicial scrutiny of these rights and their application to individuals accused of state law crimes has led to some of the most notable legal decisions in modern legal history.

In considering the Fifth Amendment and its relevance to criminal law and criminal procedure, it is noteworthy to review the other provisions contained in this amendment, aside from the Due Process Clause, as applied in our modern system of justice.

The Indictment Clause

The Indictment Clause of the Fifth Amendment states that, "no person shall be held to answer for a capital, or otherwise infamous crime, unless on a presentment or indictment of a Grand Jury…"

The foundation for the grand jury system, like many of the other fundamental principles now embodied in the American system of criminal justice, is found in the Magna Carta. By the late seventeenth century, the grand jury had evolved into an independent body charged with both investigative and protective functions. As the legal system of the American colonies began to take shape in the early 1600s, the institution of the grand jury was incorporated into early colonial law and was ultimately adopted by the drafters of the Bill of Rights as a fundamental component of the Fifth Amendment.

The Indictment Clause serves as a procedural safeguard to prevent the abuse of power of a prosecutor in charging an individual with a crime. It is designed to protect individuals accused of federal offenses or, in those states employing a grand jury system, those accused of violating state law, from being wrongfully prosecuted. A grand jury is charged with the task of evaluating the strength of a prosecutor's case and determining whether, on the basis of the government's evidence, a sufficient factual basis exists to support formal criminal charges. If a grand jury concludes that such a factual predicate exists, an indictment will be returned and a person will be formally charged and ordered to stand trial for his offenses.

It is important to note that, whereas many of the rights afforded to citizens in the Bill of Rights have been incorporated to be applicable to the states, the Indictment Clause of the Fifth Amendment still remains unincorporated. As such, this provision is only binding on the federal government and thus, an indictment is not required in state criminal proceedings in order to pass Constitutional muster.

The Self-Incrimination Clause

The privilege against self-incrimination is perhaps one of the most well known provisions of the Fifth Amendment. This clause provides that, "no person…shall be compelled in any criminal case to be a witness against himself." This premise is essential to the adversarial system of justice in the U.S. Under the auspices of this protection are the fundamental notions that a defendant is presumed innocent until proven guilty, that the burden of proving guilt lies with government, and that a defendant need not testify or present evidence against himself.

This concept is particularly applicable in the context of police interrogations. The U.S. Supreme Court addressed the issue of police coercion in extracting confessions and has held that the principles of due process are violated when confessions are coerced from criminal suspects. In the case of *Brown v. Mississippi* (297 U.S. 278 , 1936), law enforcement officers, with the assistance of other citizens, physically tortured African American suspects in order to force them into confessing to a murder. The Supreme Court held that such physical abuse and police tactics were violative of the defendants' due process rights. Later, in *Spano v. New York* (360 U.S. 315, 1959), the Supreme Court unanimously held that police are also prohibited from using psychological coercion to obtain a confession. Perhaps the most well known case in this area of criminal law is that of *Miranda v. Arizona*, (384 U.S. 436, 1966). In *Miranda*, the Supreme Court was faced with the question of how to enforce a person's rights against self-incrimination under the Fifth Amendment. The Court held that the prosecution may not use statements derived from a custodial interrogation by law enforcement unless it can be shown that procedural safeguards designed to protect an individual's right against self-incrimination are employed. These safeguards provide that, prior to questioning, a person must be warned that he has the right to remain silent, that any statement he makes may be used against him in a court of law, and that he has the right to have an attorney present during questioning.

The Double Jeopardy Clause

The Double Jeopardy Clause states, "…nor shall any person be subject for the same offense to be twice put in jeopardy of life or limb." This provision of the Fifth Amendment is designed to prevent the government from making repeated attempts to convict an individual for an alleged offense. As a general proposition, the Double Jeopardy Clause provides protection against a second prosecution for the same offense after an acquittal; it protects against a second prosecution for the same offense after a conviction; and it protects against multiple punishments for the same offense.

The Fourteenth Amendment to the U.S. Constitution prohibits any state from depriving an individual of life, liberty or property without due process of law. By its terms, the Fourteenth Amendment is implicated only in instances where there is "state action." In order for a particular action to be subjected to constitutional analysis under this provision, the action at issue must be attributable to the state, to one of its agencies, or to one of its employees acting under color of state law. The state action requirement can also be satisfied where private individuals engage in activities that are generally the exclusive prerogative of the state or where a state affirmatively authorizes or facilitates discriminatory conduct by a private individual.

Pursuant to Article VI, the Constitution of the U.S. is the supreme law of the land. As such, states may not deprive their citizens of any of those rights guaranteed by through the Due Process Clause of the Fourteenth Amendment. This does not mean, however, that states are prevented from providing their citizens with supplementary rights that provide greater protection beyond that afforded to them by the Constitution. In this regard, those rights conferred by the federal Constitution serve as a floor rather than a ceiling. That is, states may grant their citizens greater protections than those provided by the Constitution, but they may not undercut those protections through their own constitutions or statutes.

Substantive Due Process

Substantive due process evaluates the fundamental fairness and reasonableness of a law. Whether analyzing a particular law under the Due Process Clause of the Fifth Amendment or the Fourteenth Amendment, the same standard of analysis is employed. The specific test that will be applied to evaluate a particular law is determined by the type of right the law impacts and the classification of persons to whom it affects. The three levels of analysis used to determine a law's constitutionality are strict scrutiny, intermediate scrutiny, and rational basis.

In cases where the law or action at issue impinges upon a "fundamental" right or involves a "suspect" classification, a court will evaluate the constitutionality of the law using the standard of strict scrutiny. Under strict scrutiny, the law or action will be upheld only if it is found to be necessary to achieve a compelling governmental interest. This is a difficult test to satisfy and, as a result, many laws examined under the standard are found to be unconstitutional, especially in cases where a less burdensome alternative to the challenged law is available. Among those rights deemed to be "fundamental" are the right to privacy, free speech, freedom of religion, the right to travel, and the right to vote. The three "suspect" classifications examined under this level of scrutiny are those of race, alienage and national origin.

The second level of scrutiny used in evaluating the constitutionality of a particular law is that of intermediate scrutiny. Intermediate scrutiny is used in analyzing regulations affecting the "quasi-suspect" classifications of gender and legitimacy. Under this standard, a law will be deemed valid if it bears a substantial relationship to an important governmental interest.

Finally, the least stringent test used by courts to scrutinize laws challenged under the Due Process Clause is the rational basis test. This test is used in evaluating all other regulations or actions that do not bear upon a fundamental right or affect a suspect or quasi-suspect class. Under this standard, a law will be upheld if it is rationally related to a legitimate governmental interest. As this is the least strict standard of review and, if it cannot be shown that the law is irrational or arbitrary, the law will be upheld. Examples of laws evaluated under this standard include those dealing with age and disability.

Procedural Due Process

In order to comport with the requirements of procedural due process, a state must provide an individual with notice and an opportunity to be heard prior to exacting any infringement upon that individual's life, liberty or property interests. To understand when such procedural protections are required, it is necessary to define what "liberty" and "property" mean in the context of due process jurisprudence.

Liberty interests that are subject to procedural due process protection are derived from a host of sources, including the United States Constitution, federal and state statutes, federal and state regulations, and official custom and practice. For purposes of procedural due process, those rights that are considered "liberties" under substantive due process are also protected under the Constitutional principle of procedural due process. Among these liberties are rights such as the liberty to contract, freedom to engage in an occupation of one's own choosing, the right to privacy, and freedom from physical restraint.

In contrast to "liberties," "property" interests as considered with respect to due process are not derived from the text of the Constitution; rather they have their foundation in other sources, including federal and state law. For constitutional purposes, "property" encompasses real and personal property, as well as other benefits including social security and welfare benefits, tax exemptions and trade licenses. In determining whether a particular government-conferred benefit is considered a protected property interest for procedural due process purposes, the appropriate analysis is whether the benefit in question can be denied or withheld only for cause. If such nonconstitutionally based interests can only be impinged upon for specific reasons, then any deprivation of such benefits may only be imposed after the individual is provided with notice and an opportunity to be heard. The concept of "notice" is an essential component of the right to procedural due process. In order to meet the constitutional standard of adequacy, a notice must reasonably apprise the interested parties of the nature of the pending proceedings and provide them with an opportunity to present objections. The issue of whether a particular type of notice is adequate to satisfy the requirements of procedural due process is resolved by a court weighing the interest of the government versus the interest of the individual.

In considering when a hearing is required and the level of formality that is appropriate in a given case, a court generally requires the evaluation of three distinct factors: (1) the private interest that will be impacted by official government action; (2) the risk of an erroneous deprivation of the interest at issue and the extent, if any, to which additional or substitute procedural safeguards would minimize such risk; and (3) the government's interest, including the fiscal and administrative burdens that additional or substitute safeguards would entail. As to the timing of the hearing, the Supreme Court has set forth a requirement that a hearing be held *prior* to the deprivation of any liberty or property interest. This requirement is designed to comport with the fundamental notion that individuals should not be subjected to an unauthorized deprivation of liberty or property "without due process of law."

There are, however, exceptions to the general requirement of having a hearing prior to any deprivation. Such situations arise where, under the given circumstances, it is either impossible or impracticable for a court to hold a hearing prior to a potential deprivation of a liberty or property interest. In such cases, the existence of adequate postdeprivation remedies, such as monetary damages and injunctive relief, has been deemed to satisfy the requirements of procedural due process. For example, in the case of *Hudson v. Palmer*, (468 U.S. 517, 1984), a prisoner alleged that his due process rights were violated when a prison guard intentionally destroyed some of his personal property, including letters and legal materials, during the course of a search of his cell. The Supreme Court held that such a *random and unauthorized* deprivation by a state agent did not amount to a due process violation because a predeprivation hearing was impossible given that the state could not have anticipated such an unauthorized act, and because an adequate postdeprivation remedy existed.

Applications of Due Process in Criminal Law and Procedure

Judicial decisions addressing substantive due process in the context of criminal law are few. Rather, it is the procedural due process arena where the Supreme Court has closely examined the procedures used by law enforcement and the rights afforded to those suspected of criminal offenses. Of the first eight amendments to the Constitution, four of them deal with the rights of the criminally accused—the Fourth Amendment, the Fifth Amendment (as previously noted), the Sixth Amendment, and the Eighth Amendment. These requirements have been instrumental in shaping American criminal law and criminal procedural. Thus, the application of those constitutional provisions, as incorporated by the Fourteenth Amendment, bearing upon the rights of the accused have made procedural due process an area ripe for constitutional litigation.

The Fourth Amendment is comprised of two clauses applicable to criminal procedure. First, the "reasonableness clause" provides for the "right of the people to be secure in their persons, houses, papers, and effects, against unreasonable searches and seizures." Second, the "warrant clause" delineates the conditions required for the issuance of a valid warrant. Specifically, this clause requires that there be probable cause, supported by an oath or affirmation by the affiant, and a description, embodying some modicum of particularity, of the place to be searched or the person or things to be seized in order to secure a valid warrant. In practice, this means a law enforcement officer must appear before a magistrate or judge and swear under oath that there is justifiable reason to believe that a crime has been committed and that evidence relating to that crime can be found in a particular location. The magistrate or judge then makes a determination as to whether probable cause exists to support the issuance of a warrant. If such a determination is made, a warrant will issue authorizing the seizure of the described evidence.

By its own terms, the Fourth Amendment holds that reasonable searches and seizures are constitutional. It is the protection from "unreasonable" searches and seizures that has been the subject of continuing litigation in this area of constitutional law. Among the issues raised under the Fourth Amendment that have shaped modern criminal procedure are the scope and nature of searches, exceptions to the warrant requirement, the extent of privacy that individuals can expect to enjoy in their homes and persons, the utility of improperly seized evidence, use of deadly force by law enforcement officers, and the constitutionality of such practices as random searches, roadblocks, sobriety checkpoints, and mandatory drug testing.

The Sixth Amendment provides constitutional protection to individuals in the course of criminal proceedings. It affords defendants the right to a speedy and public trial, the right to the assistance of counsel, the right to call witnesses on their behalf, and the right to confront their accusers. Because the American criminal justice system is adversarial in nature, the Sixth Amendment is paramount in ensuring fundamental fairness in the trial process. Among the constitutional issues considered by courts in this area are the utility of coerced confessions, questions regarding the admissibility of evidence, the imposition of bail, impartiality of jurors, guilty pleas, plea bargains, and the application of the exclusionary rule as a matter of due process.

The Eighth Amendment prohibition against the imposition of excessive bail, in conjunction with the Fifth and Fourteenth Amendments, restricts the government's power to detain persons accused of criminal offenses. Bail is a measure exacted to secure a person's appearance in court. It enables an accused person to secure release from detention prior to trial or during the pendency of an appeal. Another matter considered under the Eighth Amendment is the issue of preventative detention. Preventive detention is employed to prevent a person from fleeing the jurisdiction where he stands accused or to prevent further danger to the community. This is another area of constitutional law that has been the subject of much litigation and debate on both substantive and procedural due process grounds. Issues arising under the Eighth Amendment provision prohibiting excessive bail and the Fourteenth Amendment Due Process Clause include the nature of preventative detention (i.e., "regulatory" rather than "punitive"), the procedural protections implemented to prevent unjust deprivations of liberty, and the constitutionality of imposing monetary bail upon indigent persons in light of alternative, nonmonetary alternatives.

Finally, another area in which due process challenges come into play in the context of criminal law and procedure is the appeals process. Once a defendant has been convicted, a direct appeal serves as the final step in the adjudication of one's guilt or innocence. Although there is no constitutional guarantee to an appeal as a matter of right, where the government has created and implemented an appellate process, it must comport with those safeguards provided by the Constitution. Thus, pursuant to the Due Process Clause of the Fourteenth Amendment, the state must resolve the appeal in a manner that is not arbitrary and affords an appellant an opportunity to fairly present his claims. In jurisdictions where a first appeal is afforded a person as a matter of right, due process guarantees that such person has the right to the assistance of counsel. Furthermore, in cases where a transcript of trial proceedings is necessary for meaningful appellate review of the issues presented, the Due Process Clause guarantees an appellant a copy of the transcript or an alternative means that will facilitate adequate appellant review.

Due Process and Prison Inmates

Another context in which due process rights are implicated in the criminal justice system is found in the implementation and application of the rights of convicted inmates. Whereas those convicted of criminal offenses are subject to the forfeiture of some civil liberties, inmates do retain some constitutional rights and protections while being confined to a correctional facility. However, the standard of review to determine the constitutionality of a prison regulation or action taken by a prison official is less stringent than that which would be applied to the same regulation or conduct outside of an institutional setting. In evaluating a challenged regulation in this context, the standard of review is the rational basis test. Thus, in the prison context, a regulation that constrains an inmate's constitutional rights will be upheld so long as it is rationally related to a legitimate penological interest.

The U.S. Supreme Court has set forth several factors that are generally considered when evaluating the reasonableness of a prison regulation. First, there must exist a valid, rational nexus between the regulation and the proposed legitimate governmental interest to justify it. Second, it should be considered whether or not there is an alternative means of exercising the right that is available to inmates. Third, the court should consider the impact the accommodation of a particular right would have on prison staff, other inmates and prison resources. Finally, the court should consider the absence of a readily available alternative as evidence that the regulation at issue is reasonable.

In recent years, prisoner's rights litigation has expanded and the scope and nature of the rights afforded convicted criminals has become the subject of much debate. The Supreme Court has examined several areas of law affecting the rights and privileges of prison inmates, as well as pretrial detainees and those subject to involuntary commitment to mental health facilities.

In the case of *Wolff v. McDonell*, (418 U.S. 539, 1974), the Supreme Court addressed the issue of the applicability of due process in the context of institutional disciplinary proceedings. The underlying purpose of the Court's holding in this case was to prevent arbitrary decision making by prison officials in cases where inmates were charged with infractions of institutional rules. The Supreme Court held that, in cases where an inmate is subject to a loss of statutory good time credits, the inmate has a right to some minimal due process protections before such a liberty interest can be withheld or forfeited. *Wolff* delineates several procedural requirements that must be adhered to by institutional officials, including: (1) the inmate must be provided with written notice of the charges he is facing in order to inform him of the nature of the charges and enable him to marshal a defense; (2) this written notice must be given to an inmate at least 24 hours prior to a disciplinary hearing to allow him to prepare to appear before the institutional hearing officer or committee; (3) an inmate has a limited entitlement to call witnesses and present documentary evidence in his defense when such measures do not pose a safety hazard or threaten the orderly running of the institution; (4) the hearing shall be conducted by an impartial fact finder; and (5) the fact finder must provide a written statement documenting the evidence relied upon and the reasons supporting any disciplinary action taken.

Whereas the Supreme Court held that inmates are entitled to the aforementioned rights, it refused to go so far as to hold that inmates are entitled to the full panoply of rights afforded to criminal defendants at trial. The majority of the Court held that inmates do not have a right to retained or appointed counsel in prison disciplinary proceedings. However, in cases where an inmate is illiterate or the complexity of the case is such that it is unlikely that the inmate will have the ability to collect and present evidence sufficient for an adequate presentation of the case, the inmate should be permitted to seek the assistance of a fellow inmate, or, in the alternative, to have assistance from a staff member or sufficiently competent inmate designated by the institution. With respect to an inmate's privilege against self-incrimination, the Supreme Court has held that, unlike in criminal cases, in prison disciplinary hearings, an inmate's failure to testify on his own behalf can be used to draw an adverse inference of guilt for the purpose of the imposition of prison disciplinary measures. Other areas of prisoners' rights litigation in which claims of due process claims are raised include involuntary commitment to mental health facilities, inmate work assignments, deprivations of property within correctional institutions, inmate privacy rights, and other civil rights violations brought by inmates pursuant to federal statutes.

Due Process and the Death Penalty

One of the most significant areas of criminal justice where the notion of due process and constitutional protections is considered is in the application of the death penalty. The Fifth and Fourteenth Amendments prohibit the government from depriving a person of "life" without appropriate procedural protections (i.e., due process). This protection prevents federal and state governments from acting in an arbitrary and capricious manner in applying this most severe form of punishment. The death penalty has remained a viable punishment for the most egregious of offenders in several states. The question of the constitutionality of the death penalty has been challenged under several constitutional provisions, including the equal protection clause of the Fourteenth Amendment and under the Eighth Amendment as violation of that provision's prohibition against cruel and unusual punishment. In addition, numerous due process challenges to the death penalty have been brought before the Supreme Court. Among these challenges are questions surrounding the types of crimes for which this punishment is prescribed, the role of juries in sentencing, the disparate application of the death penalty, the validity of state death penalty statutes, and the constitutionality of the death penalty itself as a viable form of punishment in the American criminal justice system. This area remains ripe for constitutional litigation in interpreting the applicability of the Eighth Amendment and the rights of convicted criminals facing the ultimate sentence.

KRISTINE A. BROWN

References and Further Reading

Epstein, L. and Walker, T.G., *Constitutional Law for a Changing America: Rights, Liberties and Justice,* 2nd ed., Congressional Quarterly, Inc., Washington, DC, 1995.

Gora, J.M., *Due Process of Law,* National Textbook Co., Skokie, IL, 1982.

Israel, J.H., Kamisar, Y., and LaFave, W.R., *Criminal Procedure and the Constitution: Leading Criminal Procedure Cases and Introductory Text,* West Group, St. Paul, MN, 1998.

Ides, A. and May, C.N., *Constitutional Law: Individual Rights,* Aspen Law & Business, New York, 1998.

Jupiter, S.H., Constitution Notwithstanding: The Political Illegitimacy of the Death Penalty in American Democracy, *Fordham Urban Law Journal*, 23, 437–481 (1996).

Kramer, D.T., American Jurisprudence: Constitutional Law, 2nd ed. Available: www.westlaw.com. (as 16B A. Jur. 2d Constitutional Law '934).

Nowak, J.E., Criminal procedure: Constitutional aspects, in Kadish, S.H., Ed., *The Encyclopedia of Crime and Justice,* Vol. 1 and 2, The Free Press, New York, 1983, pp. 527–537.

Prendergast, N., No Instructions Required: Due Process and Post Deprivation Remedies for Property Seized in Criminal Investigations, *Journal of Criminal Law and Criminology,* 90, 1013–1045 (2000).

Stoel, C.P. and Clarke, A.B., *Magna Carta to the Constitution: Liberty under law,* Magna Carta in America & Graphic Arts Center Publishing Co., Portland, OR, 1986.

Tomkovicz, J.J., *Criminal procedure*, Aspen Law and Business, New York, 1997.

See also **Arraignment and Arrest; Bail: Right to; Trial, Right to**

Duress as a Defense to Criminal Liability

Among the many criminal law defenses, duress is perhaps the most understandable in human terms: it bars criminal liability when one is forced, by some unlawful threat or coercion, to commit an illegal act. By way of illustration, if A points a gun at B and credibly threatens to shoot B if B does not hit C with his fist, and B in fact hits C, it would appear unjust to hold B criminally liable for battery. Also, in deterrence terms, it would appear arbitrary and illogical to make B criminally liable if the threat of punishment is, in ultimate terms, likely without practical effect given the immediate harm faced by B.

Despite this intuitive appeal, the duress defense has not always met with approval. For instance, esteemed nineteenth century criminal law scholar Sir James Fitzjames Stephen opined that in "no case" should the defense be available. To Stephen, "surely it is at the moment when temptation to [commit a crime] is strongest... that the law should speak most clearly and emphatically to the contrary" (Stephen, 1883).

Over the years, however, the duress defense has enjoyed increasing acceptance within the U.S. and throughout the world. Although the particularities of the substantive law of duress can vary, to raise a duress defense generally it must be established that: (1) another person threatens to kill or cause serious bodily harm to the actor or a third party unless the actor performs specified illegal conduct; (2) the actor reasonably believes that the threat is real; (3) the threat is imminent; (4) the actor cannot avoid the threatened harm except by committing the illegal behavior that is the subject of coercion; and (5) the actor is not at fault in making himself subject to the threat.

Several of the aforementioned requirements warrant some elaboration. First, duress arises only with threats emanating from human actors. For example, although an angry dog or a tornado might threaten one's safety, neither constitutes a recognized threat for purposes of the duress defense. Also, only threats of serious bodily harm or death are taken into account; harm to property, financial interests, or something else of value, such as reputation, do not suffice. Even more specifically, in many jurisdictions the person threatened must either be the actor herself or a family member. Second, although in most U.S. jurisdictions the threatened harm must be imminent, this requirement has been relaxed, of late, with the Model Penal Code and several jurisdictions allowing consideration of threats involving nonimminent harms (*State v. Toscano*). Third, jurisdictions can differ on the requisite mental state of the actor. Many subscribe to the position of the Model Penal Code, an objective standard that asks whether the threatened harm was one that a "person of reasonable firmness in [the actor's] position would have been able to resist" (Model Penal Code, 1980). Others, however, use a subjective approach that asks whether the particular actor's will was overborne.

Another area of disagreement relates to whether the duress defense should be permitted in homicide prosecutions. The question has arisen in several high-profile twentieth century cases, including unsuccessful efforts by those accused of Nazi war-time atrocities, where individuals claimed that they acted under specific threat of punishment from superiors or were "following orders" (Andenaes, 1965; Green, 1976). More recently, the defense was rejected in the prosecution in the International Criminal Tribunal for the Former Yugoslavia of an individual who admitted killing civilians in the town of Srebrenica, but asserted that he did so under threat of being killed himself if he did not comply (*Prosecutor v. Erdemovic*).

Courts have been similarly hesitant to invoke the duress defense outside the context of mass killings. In Britain, after briefly making the defense available to homicide accomplices—but not principals—the courts bar duress altogether with regard to killings (*Regina v. Howe*). In the U.S., a significant majority of jurisdictions prohibit duress in homicide prosecutions; the Model Penal Code and a handful of jurisdictions, however, allow duress to be raised in the defense of all crimes, including homicides.

It is important to recognize that duress is distinct from the related defense of necessity (discussed *infra*), which if successful, also serves to exculpate a criminal defendant. Necessity ("choice of evils") is available when an actor reasonably and consciously decides to commit an illegal act in order to avoid the occurrence of an immediate, greater harm. Duress, on the other hand, is available when an actor's deliberative capacity is overwhelmed, and exculpates the actor regardless of whether the "evil" avoided is greater, lesser, or the same as that associated with the coerced illegal behavior. Another distinction often drawn between the two defenses is that duress involves an intervening human force that compels the illegal behavior in question; necessity, on the other hand, typically involves natural forces, such as when one illegally enters another's cabin to seek refuge from a dangerous snowstorm at the risk of facing burglary or trespass charges.

Another important distinction lies between duress and instances of so-called "brainwashing" or "coercive persuasion." The defense was raised, unsuccessfully, by U.S. prisoners in the Korean conflict of the 1950s who sought to defend against charges of collaboration (*U.S. v. Olsen*). Even more recently, newspaper heiress Patricia Hearst, who was kidnapped and held for roughly two months by the Symbionese Liberation Army, raised a similar defense when she was prosecuted, along with her abductors, for bank robbery (*U.S. v. Hearst*). Again, the defense proved unsuccessful, on the reasoning that Hearst's participation was "voluntarily," and not the result of threat of physical harm.

Finally, some disagreement exists over whether duress should be classified as a justification or an excuse, the two primary species of criminal law defenses. A behavior is justified when on balance it is not thought to be socially blameworthy under the circumstances (e.g., self-defense or necessity). Behavior is excused when the actor's will is overborne for some reason that does not make the illegal act itself any less repugnant in moral terms but somehow renders it more understandable (e.g., insanity or intoxication). A handful of scholars categorize duress as a justification (e.g., LaFave & Scott), on the rationale that those under duress act with justification when they commit illegalities in the face of threatened greater harm (choosing the "lesser evil"). However, duress is generally thought an excuse because the act is not justified but rather remains morally wrong. It is legally excused because the act is deemed understandable and nonculpable because of the coercive circumstances experienced by the actor (Dressler).

WAYNE A. LOGAN

References and Further Reading

American Law Institute, *Model Penal Code and Commentaries,* Philadelphia, PA, American Law Institute, 1980.

Andenaes, J., *The General Part of the Criminal Law of Norway,* Sweet & Maxwell, London, and Fred B. Rothman, South Hackensack, NJ, 1965.

Carr, C.L., Duress and Criminal Responsibility, *Law and Philosophy* 161:10 (1991).

Dressler, J., *Understanding Criminal Law,* 2nd ed., LexisNexis, New York, 2001.

Fletcher, G.P., *Rethinking Criminal Law,* Little Brown, Boston, MA, 1978.

Green, L.C., *Superior Orders in National and International Law,* A.W. Sijhoff, Leiden, the Netherlands, 1976.

LaFave, W.R. and Scott, A.W., Jr., *Criminal Law,* 2nd ed., West Publishing, St. Paul, MN, 1986.

Stephen, J.F., *A History of the Criminal Law of England,* Vol. 2, Macmillan, London, 1883.

Wertheimer, A., *Coercion*, Princeton University Press, Princeton, NJ, 1987.

Yeo, S.M.H., *Compulsion in the Criminal Law,* Law Book, North Ryde, New South Wales, 1990.

See also **Self-Defense as a Defense to Criminal Liability**

Durkheim, Emile

French Sociologist

For over 100 years, Emile Durkheim has occupied the position as the preeminent theorist in the sociological treatment of deviance, especially criminal behavior. Beginning with his discussion of crime and punishment in the *Division of Labor in Society* (1893), followed by his careful elaboration of the scientific study of social pathology and crime in the *Rules of Sociological Method* (1895), and then by offering his brilliant treatise *Suicide* (1897) illustrating the social roots of deviance as well as the blending of theory and research, Durkheim established the social basis for the study of crime, leaving an impressive legacy in modern criminology both in Europe and the U.S.

Questions such as, how do we come to know what is criminal or noncriminal, what is normal or abnormal, and what is moral or immoral, have interested human beings since antiquity. Durkheim departed from explanations rooted in biological or psychological defects by claiming that labels such as "criminal," "deviant," and "lunatic" are fundamentally developed by social consensus. Accordingly, behavior is neither criminal nor noncriminal in and of itself. It is made criminal by the collective decision and definition of a group. He wrote: "We must not say that an action shocks the common consciousness because it is criminal, but rather that it is criminal because it shocks common conscience" (1893, 81). Responses to crime depend on the social milieu, making crime culturally and socially relative.

Although the definitions and responses to crime vary according to social context and culture, no known society is exempt from crime. Trying to imagine a society in which criminal acts are no longer committed, Durkheim argued that: "Assuming that this condition could actually be realized, crime would not thereby disappear. It would only change its form, for the very cause that would thus dry up the source of criminality would immediately open up new ones" (1895, 67). Even in a society of saints, crime would not be unknown, because crime, like beauty, is in the eyes of the beholder. Durkheim believed that in such a society, "faults which appear venial to the layman will create there the same scandal that the ordinary offense does in ordinary consciousness" (1895, 69).

Impressed by Adolphe Quetelet's (1831) analysis of French national crime statistics, Durkheim believed that the study of the rates of occurrences of suicide and crime rather than the study of their incidence allowed comparative analysis of various social structures. Noting the same precision with which crime statistics make their appearance every year, he proposed that certain levels are culturally "normal" (i.e., crime occurs with regularity in all societies). Indeed, he insisted that crime is an inherent element of social life with both integrative and divisive potential and, therefore, not necessarily something evil that required eradication. As long as society exists, so too will crime.

He argued that crime has four basic functions:

1. Crime or deviation from norms is a primary source of change. Society is not a straight jacket; total consensus or conformity is impossible. When deviations exceed conformity, new norms may be in the process of emergence. Durkheim's argument also left room for deviance of the conscientious objector or genius such as Socrates and Galileo who departed from the norms of their day as a result of their insights and discoveries.
2. Crime or deviation from norms serves to clarify social boundaries. Punishment of law violators, for example, is not carried out to deter or rehabilitate the transgressor, but to establish the boundaries of permissive conduct for the rest of the members of society.
3. Crime or deviation from norms may result in social outrage bringing upright consciousnesses together. A community's condemnation of the law-violating minority reaffirms the social solidarity.
4. Whereas some level of crime or deviance is normal, too much is dysfunctional. Analysis of varying rates of crime in connection with social structures offers insights into the root causes. For example, Durkheim observed that crime rates and suicide rates rise when social norms change too rapidly creating what he referred to as a state of anomie or relative normlessness.

In his study of suicide, Durkheim addressed the question of "how do we account for variable suicide rates?" Through his statistical analysis of different social structures he posited a description of four types of suicides: egoistic, altruistic, anomic, and fatalistic. Durkheim claimed that when individuals are "detached from society" they become vulnerable to egoistic suicide. Altruistic suicide results from an excessive attachment or hyper-identification with the social group. When the external norms surrounding individual conduct are relaxed or fail to regulate behavior or propensities, individuals may succumb to anomic suicide. Fatalistic suicide stems from excessive regulation. Whitney Pope (1976, 12–13) interrelated low and high integration with egoistic and altruistic suicide, respectively; and low and high social regulation with anomic and fatalistic suicide, respectively. Each type of suicide has been associated with a unique set of social dynamics and theoretical explanation.

The typology presented in *Suicide* has provided a rich seed bed of explanations for criminologists. For example, Clifford Shaw and Henry McKay's (1942) ecological theory of crime was greatly inspired by Durkheim's concepts of anomie and its connection with urban decay and disorganization. Robert K. Merton (1949) also focused on the concept of anomie when he developed his theory of delinquency and social strain arising from the dislocation of cultural goals and means. Travis Hirschi (1969) in his social control theory elaborated upon Durkheim's notion of egoistic suicide. Each of these theorists inspired the development of different applications of Durkheim's theory. Currently, there are few mainstream sociological theories of crime that do not draw some influence from Durkheim.

In his effort to establish a legitimate role of the sociological analysis of deviance and crime, he is both credited and criticized for underplaying the role of the individual's free will. Durkheim's emphasis on the constraining effects of society, with little to say regarding individual consciousness, for example, has led to the criticism that the principal weakness of his theory is his "failure to consider active moral judgment" (Ernest Wallwork, 1972, 65). In the field of criminology, Durkheim is usually associated with the development of a consensus theory of crime and the law that takes the status quo for granted, minimizing the conflicting relations between the dominant and subjugated classes in society. In recent years scholars have distinguished Durkheim's earlier structural emphasis with his later more cultural emphasis. George Ritzer noted that "while the early work played a key role in the rise of mainstream sociological theories like structural functionalism, the later work has been instrumental in the development of theoretical perspectives (especially poststructuralism and postmodernism) that pose a profound threat to that mainstream" (1996, 108).

There is every reason to believe, however, that Durkheim's influence upon the field of criminology will continue. Durkheim's insights appear to be particularly illuminating today. As Robert Nisbet pointed out, "The test of a classic in any field is that it continue to speak meaningfully and pertinently and that it continue to serve as an exemplar of what is important" (1974:vii). By this definition Durkheim has become even more relevant in contemporary society.

Biography

Born in Epinal, France, April 15, 1858; son of a rabbi and descending from a long line of rabbis. Educated at Ecole Normale Superieure in Paris, graduating in 1882. Taught in several Lycees in Paris, 1882–1887. Lecturer to full professor in social science, University of Bordeaux in 1887–1906. Charge de cours to professor of the science of education and sociology, 1902–1917. Founded and edited the journal, *L'Annee Sociologique*, 1898–1917. Died in Paris, November 15, 1917.

LYDIA VOIGT

Selected Works

Montesquieu and Rousseau: Forerunners of Sociology, 1892/1960
The Division of Labor in Society, 1893/1964
The Rules of Sociological Method, 1895/1964
Suicide, 1897/1951
Primitive Classification 1903/1963, co-authored with Marcel Mauss
The Elementary Forms of Religious Life, 1912/1965
Sociology and Philosophy, 1924/1974
Education and Sociology, 1922/1956
Socialism, 1928/1962
Professional Ethics and Civic Morals, 1950/1957
Moral Education: A Study in the Theory and Application of the Sociology of Education, 1925/1973
(Note: years = original publication/English translation)

References and Further Reading

Coser, L.A., *Masters of Sociological Thought*, Harcourt Brace Jovanovich, New York, 1977.
Fenton, S., *Durkheim and Modern Sociology*, Cambridge University Press, Cambridge, U.K., 1984.
Giddens, A., *Durkheim*, Fontana, London, 1978.
Hirschi, T., *Causes of Delinquency*, University of California Press, Berkeley, CA, 1969.
Lehmann, J.M., Durkheim's Theories of Deviance and Suicide: A Feminist Reconsideration, *American Journal of Sociology*, 100, 904–930, 1995.
Lukes, S., *Durkheim, Emile, His Life and Work*, Penguin Press, Allen Lane, London, 1973.
Martin, R., Mutchnick, R., and Austin, W.T., *Criminological Thought: Pioneers Past and Present*, Macmillan, New York, 1990.
Merton, R.K., *Social Theory and Social Structure*, London, Glencoe, 1949.
Nisbet, R.A., *The Sociology of Emile Durkheim*, Oxford University Press, New York, 1974.
Parsons, T., Emile Durkheim, in Lisills, D., Ed., *International Encyclopedia of the Social Sciences*, Macmillan, New York, 1968.
Pope, W., *Durkheim's Suicide: A Classic Analyzed*, University of Chicago Press, Chicago, IL, 1976.
Quetelet, A., *Research on the Propensity for Crime at Different Ages*, Anderson, Cincinnati, OH, 1831/1994.
Ritzer, G., *Sociological Theory*, 4th ed., McGraw Hill, New York, 1996.
Shaw, C.R. and McKay, H.D., *Juvenile Delinquency in Urban Areas*, University of Chicago Press, Chicago, IL, 1942.
Turner, B.S., Preface, in Durkheim, E., Ed., *Professional Ethics and Civic Morals*, Routledge, London, 1992.
Voigt, L., Durkheimian Justice: With a View Toward the Future of Sociology, in Altschuler, R., Ed., *The Living Legacy of Marx, Durkheim, and Weber*, Vol. 2, Gordian Knot Books, New York, 2000.
Voigt, L., Thornton, W., Barrile, L., and Seaman, J., *Criminology and Justice*, McGraw-Hill, New York, 1994.
Wallwork, E., *Durkheim: Morality and Milieu*, Harvard University Press, Cambridge, MA, 1972.
Zeitlin, I., *Ideology and the Development of Sociological Theory*, Prentice Hall, Englewood Cliffs, NJ, 1997.

See also **Sociological Theories of Criminal Behavior; Strain Theories: From Durkheim to Merton; Suicide: Extent and Correlates**

E

Eastern and Central Europe, Crime and Justice in

Introduction: Diversity in Central and Eastern Europe

The 27 countries of Central and Eastern Europe (Albania, Armenia, Azerbaijan, Belarus, Bosnia-Herzegovina, Bulgaria, Croatia, the Czech Republic, Estonia, Georgia, Hungary, Kazakhstan, Kyrgyzstan, Latvia, Lithuania, the former Yugoslav Republic of Macedonia, Moldova, Poland, Romania, the Russian Federation, Slovakia, Slovenia, Tajikistan, Turkmenistan, Ukraine, Uzbekistan, and the Federal Republic of Yugoslavia) share a common heritage in having belonged to the so-called Communist bloc for most of the post-World War II period. Today, perhaps the most dominant feature of crime and criminal justice in these countries is the rate of change brought about by the collapse of the Soviet Union; there is scarcely any other comparable group of countries where both crime and criminal justice systems have changed so extensively in such a short time.

There are considerable differences among the Central and Eastern European countries in this respect. Even during the long period of Soviet dominance, the criminal justice systems of countries such as Poland, Hungary, and especially Yugoslavia retained many of their distinctive features. For example, although some countries such as the Democratic Republic of Germany made wide use of so-called "comrades' courts" to deal with many petty offences, attempts to introduce similar courts in other countries failed. Because of differences in social and political development, crime and the definition of crime also evolved differently.

Structure and Trends in Crime

According to crime statistics and the little criminological research that is available, the crime rate in the region as a whole prior to the 1990s was somewhat lower than in Western Europe or in North America. The end of the 1980s and the beginning of the 1990s brought a very sharp increase in crime. In many categories and countries, the rates increased two, three, or even four times. This increase was because of a number of factors, ranging from the increase in the opportunity for crime (such as the greater availability of goods to steal), widespread unemployment, the impoverishment of large sectors of the population as a result of the sudden shift to a market economy, the weakening of informal social controls, and the lack of resources available to the police.

Subsequently, the increase in crime slowed, and the rates tended to stabilize in 1992 and 1993. It is presumably not a coincidence that at about the same time, the economy and the political and social situation stabilized in many of these countries.

Today, personal victimization in the region as a whole (as measured by victimization surveys carried out in urban areas) appears to be somewhat above the level of victimization in Western Europe, below the level in North America and considerably below the level in Africa or Latin America. In particular, violent crimes such as assaults, homicides, and robberies are more prevalent in Central and Eastern Europe than in Western Europe. This is apparently connected with socioeconomic deprivation, and with widespread unemployment and alcohol abuse. Furthermore, in most Central and Eastern European countries violence against women is relatively high. In addition to economic strain and alcohol abuse, this specific crime problem is probably related to the low social status of women. Within the region, serious violent crimes tend to be more prevalent in the countries of the former Soviet Union (such as the Russian Federation, Estonia, Kyrgyzstan, and Kazakhstan). Other nations, such as Hungary and Macedonia, have relatively low levels of violence.

Property crime in the region appears to be somewhat more prevalent than in Western Europe. Moreover, the increase in the level of affluence (especially in Hungary, Poland, and the Baltic republics) and the limited availability of antitheft protective devices suggest that the situation may worsen further.

Corruption is reportedly much more common in many Central and Eastern European countries than in Western Europe and North America. The level of corruption appears to be lower in the countries where economic restructuring is relatively advanced, for example, in Estonia and Hungary. Such countries as Armenia, Azerbaijan, Moldova, the Russian Federation, Ukraine, Uzbekistan, and Yugoslavia, in turn, appear to have among the highest rates of corruption in the world.

Worldwide, police statistics reflect a considerably lower crime rate than do victimization surveys. However, this appears to be even more so for Central and Eastern Europe. Victims in the Central and Eastern European countries appear to be less likely to report crime to the police, and the police appear less likely to record a reported offense than is the case in Western Europe and North America.

Neither crime statistics nor victimization surveys are useful in showing the extent of economic crime, drug trafficking, organized crime, and environmental crime. According to largely anecdotal evidence, petty economic crime was largely built into certain facets of the Soviet model. Prior to the end of the 1980s, drug trafficking and organized crime appear to have been minimal, with the exception of the Central Asian republics and of drug trafficking through the Balkans into Western Europe. As for environmental crime, most of the considerable despoliation of such regions as the Czech Republic, Poland, and the Russian Federation has occurred with the permission of the authorities; this seems "criminal" only in retrospect.

Today, drug trafficking has increased throughout the region, and the Central Asian republics are major sources of drugs for all of Europe. Trafficking in persons, especially for the purpose of prostitution, has expanded considerably, in particular through the Balkans into Italy and Austria and on to other Western European countries. The economic transition brought with it an enormous potential for economic crime that criminal groups have been quick to seize. The large-scale transfer and demobilization of Soviet troops have fed the growth in the trafficking of firearms. Car thefts have been increasing, and indeed many cars stolen from Western Europe have been driven across the borders into Central and Eastern Europe. All of these forms of crime have resulted in considerable illegal profits and an expansion in money laundering.

Evolution of Criminal Justice

Before the economic and political transformation, the criminal codes of all of the Central and Eastern European countries emphasized to varying degrees the seriousness of such crimes against the State as anti-State agitation and propaganda, along with crimes against socialist ownership (e.g., those involving black market "profiteering"). In addition, the criminal law was used to deal with certain behavior that elsewhere would normally be dealt with administratively, if at all; examples are laws prohibiting monetary "speculation" and a "parasitic way of life." A special element of the criminal justice system of several Central and Eastern European countries, in particular the former USSR, was the "*prokuratuura*," all-powerful officials who not only acted as prosecutors but also sought to ensure that all government officials—including the judges—towed the ideologically and legally "correct" line. These special features should be balanced against the fact that much of the run-of-the-mill crime in Central and Eastern Europe—such as thefts, assaults, damage to property—was dealt with, in practice, in much the same way as elsewhere in Europe or in North America.

A fundamental shift in the ideology and practice of criminal justice took place at the end of the 1980s. The principle that the criminal law and the entire criminal justice system were developed to protect the State (and not the citizen) was rejected. This principle has been replaced by greater recognition of the diversity of interests, of the need to achieve a system of checks and balances also in the administration of criminal justice, and of the importance of the protection of basic human rights. This has several corollaries, involving for example a redefinition of what constitutes a crime, and in some cases a shift from an inquisitorial to an adversarial system of justice.

The reform of criminal laws and criminal procedure in Central and Eastern Europe has forced the police, the prosecutors, and the courts to change their modes of operation. The police have to relearn police or community relations, and how to use hard evidence (as opposed to confessions) in investigations. Rejection of a relatively strict principle of mandatory prosecution and the increasing workload of the prosecutors are forcing prosecutors to exercise discretion to a far wider extent. As for the courts, releasing the judicial system from the all-powerful control of the *prokuratuura* and adopting an adversarial approach forces judges to learn new roles. Judges now have the primary responsibility for ensuring the "equality of arms" between the prosecutor and the defense counsel.

The speed of reform in Central and Eastern Europe, and the manner in which it is being carried out, has varied from country to country. Some criminal justice systems, such as those in Hungary and Poland, were highly developed at the time that the restructuring process began at the end of the 1980s. All Central and Eastern European countries, however, have relied heavily on outside expertise, and on financial, technical, and material support from other countries in further reforming their systems. New criminal codes have been adopted in Croatia (1997), Estonia (1992), Poland (1997), Macedonia (1996), and the Russian Federation (1996). All other countries have carried out extensive partial reforms. (It should be added that, in many countries, the practical impact of many of the new criminalizations has been small, because the law enforcement machinery has difficulties in detecting and investigating offenses, or necessary supplemental legislation is not yet in place.)

To some extent, the reforms are evolving along similar lines. For example, following ratification of the 1988 United Nations Convention against Illicit Traffic in Narcotic Drugs and Psychotropic Substances as well as the 1990 European Convention on Laundering, Search, Seizure and Confiscation of the Proceeds from Crime, most Central and Eastern European countries have criminalized money laundering. These countries include Bulgaria, Croatia, Estonia, Hungary, Lithuania, Macedonia, Poland, the Russian Federation, Slovakia, and Slovenia. Although there are considerable differences between the nations in the scope of this criminalization and in how the laws are enforced, the international pressure from the Financial Action Task Force, the United Nations, the Council of Europe, the European Union and other entities is likely to lead to more uniform implementation in the future.

Another example is that of financial disclosure requirements as a means for detecting corruption among public officials. Legislation requiring all or at least the more senior civil servants to report their assets and income at regular intervals has been adopted in short order in several countries, such as Albania, Estonia, Latvia, Lithuania, Moldova, Slovenia, and the Russian Federation.

In other respects, the Central and Eastern European countries are evolving along different lines. Most Central and Eastern European countries are considerably more punitive than most Western European countries. For example, at the end of 1999, the Russian Federation had an estimated 730 prisoners per 100,000 in population, a prisoner rate that surpasses even that of the U.S. (680). Also, Belarus (575 per 100,000), Latvia (360), Lithuania (385), and Ukraine (430) rank high on the list. At the other extreme are Slovenia and Croatia. Both have 50 prisoners per 100,000, and in this respect are among the least punitive countries in the world. In between are some countries that have succeeded in lowering their prisoner rate closer to a "European average" even during the period of transformation. Examples are Hungary (from 220 per 100,000 in 1985 to 150 in 1999), Poland (correspondingly, from 270 to 145), and Slovakia (from 225 to 125).

Another example of diverging trends is community involvement in the control of behavior. "Community involvement" is widely associated in many Central and Eastern European countries with citizen militias and comrades' courts that existed under the Soviet regime, and the concept thus carries considerable negative cultural baggage. Nonetheless, some Central and Eastern countries (such as the Czech Republic, Hungary, and Poland) are considering introducing Western-oriented community policing, as well as mediation schemes in particular for offenses committed by juveniles.

Overall, the Central and Eastern European countries are reforming their criminal justice systems quite rapidly, and in doing so they have received considerable support from the Council of Europe and the European Union (as well as other organizations and governments). Almost all of these countries, furthermore, are already members of the Council of Europe, and ten Central and Eastern European countries are candidate countries to the European Union. It is thus not surprising that many features of the criminal justice systems that are emerging as the result of this transformation are distinctly "Western."

The rapid pace of reform and the growing integration of Central and Eastern Europe will increase the number of common denominators with Western nations. Criminal law in almost every country will increasingly contain more or less uniform definitions of many offenses that have international ramifications, such as money laundering and drug trafficking. Criminal procedure will bow to the dictates of the European Convention on Human Rights and to recommendations of the Council of Europe, and to the day-to-day necessities of informal police cooperation. Criminal law and criminal procedure in the ten countries that are candidates for membership in the European Union (Bulgaria, the Czech Republic, Estonia, Hungary, Latvia, Lithuania, Poland, Romania, Slovakia, and Slovenia) will be reformed considerably along "Western" lines.

Nonetheless, each of the criminal justice systems will continue to retain many distinctive features, just as has been done in the Western European countries. Diversity will be the rule rather than the exception.

MATTI JOUTSEN

References and Further Reading

Kangaspunta, K., Joutsen, M., and Ollus, N. (Ed.), *Crime and Criminal Justice Systems in Europe and North America 1990–1994*, European Institute for Crime Prevention and Control, affiliated with the United Nations, Helsinki 1998.

Newman, G. (Ed.), *Global Report on Crime and Justice*, New York, NY and Oxford, UK: Oxford University Press, 1998.

Zvekic, U., *Criminal Victimisation in Countries in Transition*, United Nations Interregional Crime and Justice Research Institute, publication no. 61, Rome 1998.

See also **Soviet Union, Crime and Justice in**

Ecclesiastical Law

Ecclesiastical or canon law is defined, essentially, as church law (Rush, 1994). It was developed by the ecclesiastical (i.e., church) courts of the 12th and 13th centuries and is influenced by Roman law (Rush, 1994). The mark of canon law on the common law is well-documented especially with the consensual crimes. Adultery, fornication, incest, sodomy, laws regulating marriage, and probate are all historically rooted in canon law. Even such crimes as perjury and defamation have their roots in the ecclesiastical foundation.

The ultimate source for canonical law is God. Each denomination has its own constitution and interpretations thereof, but the authority for action stems from natural and divine law. Within, for example, the Catholic Church there exists a rather extensive bureaucratic organization from God to the Pope, to the Archbishops, Bishops, and then finally the parish priest. All have authority for their particular sphere, of course to be administered within the laws of God. The Catholic Encyclopedia, for example, indicates that,

> Modern law has only a restricted and local influence on canon law, and that particularly on two points. On the one hand, the Church conforms to the civil laws on mixed matters, especially with regard to the administration of its property; on some occasions even it has finally adopted as its own measures passed by the civil powers acting independently; a notable case is the French decree of 1809 on the "Fabriques d'église." On the other hand, modern legislation is indebted to the canon law for certain beneficial measures: part of the procedure in criminal, civil, and matrimonial cases, and to some extent, the organization of courts and tribunals (online, Section 3, para. 7)

Property disputes, issues of marriage and divorce, and really anything that the Church might choose to take action against can result in ecclesiastical charges. For example, Episcopal priest John Shelby Spong appeared on the show *Politically Incorrect*. His appearance raised "the hue and cry urging the House of Bishops of the Episcopal Church to act with dispatch in bringing ecclesiastic charges against Mr. Spong for heresy, apostasy, and a variety of other transgressions" (North, 1999).

As an example of the thrust of canonical law, one need look no further than the Canon Law Institute (http://www.canonlaw.org/about_the_institute.htm). On its opening page, the following description appears:

> The Canon Law Institute is a not-for-profit corporation organized as a scholarly resource center, think tank, and support organization for Christian denominations throughout the world. The Institute's primary mission is to educate Christian churches and denominations on the importance of establishing and maintaining just and righteous systems of internal justice which include governance, disciplinary matters, and personal conflict resolution within the Body of Christ. As an interrelated component of this mission, the Institute is engaged in providing information, education and training for canonists and attorneys throughout the Christian community.

If one then goes to "Church Discipline" one finds three biblical verses, "which give some guidance as to the appropriate process for dealing with conflict within the Body and among Believers" (http://www.canonlaw.org/church%20discipline.htm). This, then, is the essence of ecclesiastical law, the regulation of disputes, and the enforcement of the law as emanates from God.

Ecclesiastical law exists whether the secular law does or not, and in many cases in spite of what the secular law might say. Take, for example, devout Catholic who get divorced. Even though in the eyes of the state they are no longer married, within the Catholic Church there are rituals in which they cannot participate (e.g., Communion) without being divorced (i.e., the marriage being annulled) within the Church. In addition, it should be noted that in many instances the Church refuses to do so. In addition, the Pope has issued a decree that indicates that politicians (e.g., legislators) who indicate that they are "good Catholics" must oppose abortion. There have even been calls for excommunication of "good Catholics" who support abortion. That has not yet happened.

The last two sections of the Code of (Catholic) Canon Law (http://www.vatican.va/archive/ENG1104/__PU.htm) perhaps best summarize this entry:

> Can. 223. §1. In exercising their rights, the Christian faithful, both as individuals and gathered together in associations, must take into account the common good of the Church, the rights of others, and their own duties toward others.
>
> §2. In view of the common good, ecclesiastical authority can direct the exercise of rights which are proper to the Christian faithful.

Jeffrey P. Rush

References and Further Reading

Canon Law. Catholic Encyclopedia. Available at http://www.newadvent.org/cathen/09056a.htm.

Code of Canon Law. Available at http://www.vatican.va/archive/ENG1104/__PU.htm Book 2, Part 1, Title 2.

North, K. (1999). *Episcopal Justice and Mr. Spong: There IS a Way!* Available at http://www.canonlaw.org/article_spong.htm.

Rush, G. (1994). *The Dictionary of Criminal Justice*, 4th ed. New York, NY: Dushkin.

Ecstasy *See* **Club Drugs**

Economic Theories of Criminal Behavior *See* **Strain Theories**

Edge Ethnography *See* **Qualitative Research**

Educational Attainment and Criminal Behavior

For centuries, criminologists have explored the link between education and delinquency; it has long been thought that educational success leads to lower levels of delinquency among adolescents. Modern empirical studies of the educational attainment or academic performance and delinquency association have consistently found an inverse relationship between the two (for a review of studies see Maguin and Loeber, 1996); children who perform poorly academically are more likely to be delinquent and commit more serious and violent offenses. This association is also stronger for males than for females.

After reviewing the literature, Maguin and Loeber (1996) identified four main findings from the previous research. First, poor academic performance is associated with onset and frequency of delinquency whereas improved academic performance is associated with desistance from delinquency. Second, low intelligence and attention problems are both common causal variables in the educational success–delinquency association; when these two variables are controlled for, the association is greatly reduced. Third, intervention studies show that as academic success increases, delinquency decreases. Finally, a review of the research shows that the effectiveness of intervention studies varies with children of different ages.

Perhaps the first documented natural study of this association occurred in Ireland in the early 1800s. The study followed 7000 children for 20 years. Out of those 7000 children educated in schools that concentrated on religious education with strong moral overtones, only one juvenile had been charged with an offense (Maguin and Loeber, 1996).

Criminologists in the early 19th century studying the link between intelligence and delinquency suggested that people of low intelligence were tricked into offending by people of higher intelligence. They further speculated that lower-intelligence individuals were unable to realize the consequences of their actions. Some criminologists even measured the IQs of offenders but only speculated about the IQs of non-offenders. For more than a decade, "feeblemindedness" was an accepted explanation of delinquency. Although IQ and educational attainment do not measure the same thing, they tended to be synonymous in earlier studies. In the 1920s the U.S. Army began administering IQ tests to draftees and found their average scores to be on the verge of "moronity" thus challenging the feeblemindedness explanation (Regoli and Hewitt, 1997, 319).

In the early 1800s, Andre-Michel Guerry studied the education levels in different sections of France as they related to crime. Using new statistics on reading and writing, Guerry found that areas with the highest levels of education also had the highest levels of violent crime and the areas with the lowest levels of education had the lowest levels of violent crime. He concluded that higher education did not reduce crime. Rather than looking at individuals, Guerry was looking at areas (Vold et al., 2002), and drawing conclusions about individuals from area data is ill-advised (Robinson, 1950).

A few years later, Adolphe Quetelet reanalyzed Guerry's data. He found that men who were young, poor, unemployed, and undereducated were more likely to engage in criminal behavior, but similar to Guerry's finding, the crimes were occurring in the wealthier, higher educated areas of France. This was the case because poor, undereducated individuals were committing crimes in the wealthier educated sections. The data also showed that whereas undereducated individuals committed the most crime, mostly property crime, higher educated individuals engaged in more violent crime. Therefore, Quetelet agreed with Guerry that higher education did not reduce crime (Vold et al., 2002). More studies followed and different results linking education and delinquency were reported.

Contemporary studies of the academic performance–delinquency relationship can be categorized into two types, naturalistic studies and intervention or prevention studies (see Maguin and Loeber, 1996). In naturalistic studies, data are gathered under natural conditions so that no manipulation or lab settings are used. Intervention studies usually involve a control group and a test group that is being manipulated. There are also several ways to measure educational success and delinquency. GPA, achievement tests in reading, writing, or math, teacher ratings, commitment to education, and other such factors have been used as academic measures. Delinquency has been measured using self-report data, police records, parental or teacher reports, convictions, adjudication, and other such factors.

Naturalistic studies of the academic performance–delinquency relationship have attempted to address two important questions: (1) how strong is the association? and (2) does the association remain after controlling for other variables? Maguin and Loeber (1996) reviewed over 1000 studies on the educational attainment–delinquency association. After selecting the studies that met four specific criteria (one or more measures of delinquency, one or more measures of academic performance, an age limit of 18 years, and sufficient data to compute effect sizes), they conducted a meta-analysis to summarize the relationship reported in previous studies.

Cross-sectional studies have consistently found that the lower the academic performance, the higher the delinquency, and this association was higher for males than for females and higher for European Americans than for African Americans. However, meta-analysis indicates no significant difference in the mean effect size for European Americans and African Americans. After controlling for low intelligence and attention problems, Maguin and Loeber found that both were associated with delinquency and academic success, and therefore, they are both likely to be common cause variables. Socioeconomic status (SES) was also found to be associated with delinquency and attitude problems, but after controlling for SES, results imply that it does not account for the academic performance–delinquency relationship.

Cross-sectional studies only measure variables at one single point in time. Most cross-sectional studies on the educational success–delinquency association consisted of self-report questionnaires asking respondents (usually children or adolescents in an institution such as school) about their home life, attitudes toward school or community, involvement in delinquency, and many other topics. Perhaps the best-known cross-sectional study was the Richmond Youth Project, which surveyed adolescents in the seventh through twelfth grades in Richmond, California, schools in 1964. The study found significant associations between educational and delinquency measures.

Longitudinal studies, on the other hand, consist of a selected sample that is followed over time with at least one or more follow-up studies with results reported at each wave. These studies can start at any point in time. For example, the Dunedin Multidisciplinary Health and Development Study followed children born in one hospital in New Zealand in 1972. These children were assessed every 2 years from age 3 to age 18. The Youth in Transition Project studied tenth-grade boys in 1966 and assessed them four separate times throughout their remaining high-school years. Although both studies started at different points in the life course, they both found that academic performance and delinquency were strongly associated during the high-school years (Maguin and Loeber, 1996).

Longitudinal studies report a significant association between academic performance and delinquency, but the association is stronger for official records as opposed to self-reported measures of delinquency. A meta-analysis by Maguin and Loeber (1996) shows that the association is stronger for males than for females; however, unlike cross-sectional studies, longitudinal studies suggest that the association is stronger for European Americans than it is for African Americans. Longitudinal analysis also suggests that the association strengthens with increasing age. Socioeconomic status and conduct problems were not found to be common cause variables; however, once prior delinquency was controlled for, academic performance only weakly predicted future delinquency.

Intervention studies have also attempted to answer two important questions, (1) is poor academic performance related to delinquency? and (2) can intervention programs reduce delinquency and increase academic performance? Intervention studies can be categorized into two types, at-risk intervention studies and prevention studies. A review of at-risk programs found that children in intervention groups improved their academic performance or lowered their delinquency involvement more than those in control groups (see Maguin and Loeber, 1996). Researchers also found that different intervention programs work better for different age groups. Law-related and moral education programs were the most effective in improving academic performance and reducing delinquency for adolescents. Alternative school programs, social skills and self-control training, and behavioral parent training for parents produced significant decreases in delinquency among elementary-school-aged children. Children enrolled in prevention programs did show changes in academic performance; however, no significant effect on delinquency was observed.

Many theories from strain to social control and integrated theories have attempted to explain the educational success–delinquency relationship. They mainly focus on some sort of weak bond to individuals and institutions that leads to stronger bonds to delinquent peers. For example, strain theory suggests that individuals with lower SES lack the necessary resources needed to succeed in school, thus causing frustration that could lead to delinquency. Control theory suggests that social bonds or attachments to individuals (i.e., family, peers, etc.) and institutions (i.e., school) produce a commitment to socially accepted courses of action and a breakdown in these attachments increases the likelihood of delinquency. Social learning theory hypothesizes that children learn behaviors from social interactions with others and take on similar attitudes and values, including delinquency and lack of interest in school. Social development theory suggests that children who perform well academically receive rewards and praise from others. This praise produces positive beliefs and higher levels of interaction skills that ultimately reduce the likelihood of delinquency. Interactional theory suggests that delinquency is affected by the belief that children who perform poorly, academically, have a low commitment to school.

It is also possible that the academic performance–delinquency association is purely spurious. Psychological theories suggest that there are other underlying factors involved in the association. Low intelligence and attention problems are two factors that have been identified as common cause variables. Researchers have found that when low intelligence and attention problems are controlled for, the partial correlations between academic performance and delinquency are greatly reduced (see Maguin and Loeber, 1996).

In criminology, perhaps no other theory attributes as much influence to cognitive abilities (that manifest in educational test scores and attainment) as Moffitt's (1993) developmental taxonomy. Moffitt's theory proposes that there are two primary types of offenders, adolescent-limited and the life-course persisters, each possessing a unique set of factors that contribute to antisocial behavior and delinquency. Adolescent-limited offenders restrict their offending to the adolescent years, from puberty until they attain adult social roles. Factors contributing to their antisocial behavior are the maturity gap and peer influence. Unlike adolescent-limiteds, Moffitt hypothesizes that life-course persisters begin their antisocial behavior in early childhood (preschool or earlier) and continue throughout adulthood. Contributing factors to their antisocial behavior are inadequate parenting, poverty, disrupted family bonds, and so on; peer influence is not necessarily a factor in life-course persisting. It is important to note that these two types of offenders can only be distinguished in longitudinal studies that follow individuals from an early age through adulthood; cross-sectional studies carried out at only one point in time are unable to distinguish between the two types.

In particular, Moffitt hypothesizes that life-course persisters are affected by neurological and neuropsychological impairments. Neuropsychological refers to anatomical and psychological processes within the nervous system that influence temperament, behavioral development, and cognitive abilities. These impairments lead to immaturity, hyperactivity, poor attention, temper tantrums, and poor school performance, which later lead to antisocial behaviors. It has also been shown that children resemble their parents on cognitive ability; therefore, children who are in the most need of cognitive stimulation may have parents who are the least likely to provide it. It is also possible that these particular families may not be able to financially afford intervention programs, such as those mentioned previously, to help their children improve their abilities. Moffitt also discusses how deviant behavior for life-course persisters intensifies with interactions with the social environment, first emerging at home and then later at school. If Moffitt's taxonomy is correct, then it is these neuropsychological impairments that underlie the educational attainment–delinquency relationship.

Similarly, Piquero (2001) used measures of neuropsychological deficits to predict four manifestations of life-course persistent offending, early onset, violent and nonviolent offending, serious offending, and chronic offending. Piquero used the Wechsler Intelligence Scale for Children (WISC), a test that measures verbal and performance factors, to indirectly measure neuropsychological dysfunctions. The verbal component of the WISC measures information, comprehension, vocabulary, and digit span, whereas the performance component measures spatial abilities such as picture arrangement, block design, and coding. Although the WISC indirectly measures neuropsychological factors, Moffitt (1993) suggests that deficits in language and reasoning (what the WISC measures) ultimately manifest as academic failure.

Using data from the Philadelphia biosocial correlates of crime study, Piquero found that neither verbal nor performance subscales were significantly related to early onset. However, verbal subscales were significantly and negatively related to the remaining three manifestations of life-course persistent offending. Individuals who score higher on the verbal subscale are less likely to be involved in violent and nonviolent offending, serious offending, or chronic offending than those individuals who score lower on the verbal subscale. Piquero also found that males are significantly more likely to engage in offending than females. These results support Moffitt's (1993) theory that neuropsychological deficits can predict life-course persistent forms of antisocial behavior and delinquency.

In sum, children with lower academic performance offend more frequently and commit more serious offenses than children who achieve academic success; the poorer the academic performance, the higher the delinquency, and this relationship is consistently stronger for males than for females. Intelligence and attention problems are two factors that have been identified as common cause variables. When these two variables are controlled for, the association between academic performance and delinquency is greatly reduced.

Intervention programs that are age appropriate have been shown to be successful in increasing academic performance or decreasing delinquency among children and adolescents. Results also suggest that intervention programs aimed at increasing intelligence and decreasing attention problems will have the greatest effect on improving academic success and decreasing delinquency. However, as mentioned by Moffitt (1993), the parents of children in most need of these programs may not necessarily be able to afford them.

Although research has brought much data to bear on the relationship between educational attainment and delinquency, they are still unsure about the causal order; does poor educational success lead to delinquency or does delinquency lead to poor educational success? Although it is important to collect test scores early in a child's life, before the onset of antisocial behavior, it is still difficult to determine the causal order between educational attainment and criminal behavior; however, there is consensus that the relationship does indeed exist.

Andrea Schoepfer and Alex R. Piquero

References and Further Reading

Maguin, E. and Loeber, R. (1996). Academic Performance and Delinquency. *Crime & Justice* 20:145–264.

Moffitt, T. (1993). Adolescence-Limited and Life-Course-Persistent Antisocial Behavior: A Developmental Taxonomy. *Psychological Review* 100:674–701.

Piquero, A. (2001). Testing Moffitt's Neuropsychological Variation Hypothesis for the Prediction of Life-Course Persistent Offending. *Psychology, Crime & Law* 7:193–215.

Regoli, R. and Hewitt, J. (1997). *Delinquency in Society.* New York, NY: McGraw-Hill Companies, Inc.

Robinson, E.S. (1950) Ecological Considerations and the Behavior of Individuals. *American Sociological Review* 15:351–357.

Vold, G., Bernard, T., and Snipes, J. (2002). *Theoretical Criminology.* New York, NY: Oxford University Press.

See also **Intelligence (IQ) and Criminal Behavior**

Educational Programs in Criminology and Criminal Justice

It is certainly true that criminology is a somewhat older academic discipline than criminal justice, especially with respect to which discipline was first to have an educational program. Throughout most of the 20th century, criminology was taught as a subdivision of sociology in the American college and university system. It has only been since around the mid-1970s that criminology was partially separated from sociology, allowing criminology to draw more fully upon its other influences, such as biology, psychology, economics, and other disciplines that study humans in their environment. It was also during the 1970s that the academic discipline of criminal justice emerged as a formal area of study in colleges and universities. Many contemporary observers regard the further development of criminology and criminal justice educational programs as intertwined.

The History of Criminology and Criminal Justice Education

Criminal justice and criminology as academic disciplines have had a tumultuous past. The area known as "police science" began in the late 1920s when August Vollmer and others convinced the University of California to offer courses on the subject. Vollmer was a police chief in Berkeley, California, and is considered the founder of that discipline. One might refer to these early years (1930–1950) as the "Police Science Era" because policing was the main focus. During the late 1960s until the early 70s, the focus hardened, and criminal justice became one of many programs (along with military science) that students protested against at college campuses across America. Subsequently, courses in criminal justice (as well as whole programs in criminology and criminal justice) fell back into the hands of sociology or political science departments during this period. Around 1974, the federal government started subsidizing colleges and universities to create financial aid programs (LEEP, or Law Enforcement Education Program) and research or evaluation programs (LEAA, or Law Enforcement Assistance Administration) for the study of criminal justice. Baccalaureate criminal justice education expanded quite rapidly during this period, and one piece of research stands out as notable for charting the course of educational program development: *Quest for Quality* (Ward and Webb, 1984), which was part of a set of monographs published by the Joint Commission on Criminology and Criminal Justice Education and Standards.

Quest for Quality presented no less than 19 recommendations concerning curricula issues, and these have been analyzed or interpreted in detail elsewhere (Southerland, 1991). Suffice it to say that ideas about the core curriculum cohered around criminology, criminal law and procedure, policing, judicial process, corrections, research methods, and statistics. Criminology was suggested as an integral part of that core because it imparted a broader understanding of the sociopolitical context in which criminal justice operates, it was interdisciplinary, and it had the advantage of being associated with a liberal arts education. Cognate fields could also be drawn from to accomplish the same objectives, in fields such as sociology, political science, psychology, cultural anthropology, and in some cases, public administration. It was criminology, however, as a field that studied the causes of crime (etiology), the meaning of crime, and societal reaction to crime that brought sociology to criminal justice. It is this unfinished project of integration that is usually referred to when it is said that the futures of criminology and criminal justice are intertwined.

After the 1980s, police-oriented programs continued to grow, and their curricula left out the recommended research methods and statistics courses, substituting criminalistics and investigation courses. Such programs became a standard part of the country's community college system, and debate raged over whether the educational programs were accomplishing training or education (Cullen, 1995). However, several 4-year schools (over 600 of them by 1990) followed the Joint Commission's recommendations for a liberal arts criminal justice curriculum. Today, criminal justice and criminology educational programs are well-established in academic curricula, with over 1500 associate (2-year) degree programs, 900 bachelor's (4-year) degree programs, 90 master's (2-year) degree programs, and 18 Ph.D. (3-year) programs.

Graduate Educational Programs in Criminology and Criminal Justice

Thirty-six credit hours are usually required for a master's in criminology and criminal justice. This includes 15 hours in core courses that are essentially more management-oriented versions of the undergraduate core, 15 hours in an area of concentration (usually policing or corrections), and 6 hours for a thesis or nonthesis option. Elective coursework will consist usually of crime-specific courses, such as violent crime, crime in the workplace, white-collar crime, environmental crime, as well as focused policy and research courses. Fifty-four credit hours beyond the master's are usually required for a doctorate in criminology and criminal justice, and most of this coursework is split between advanced research courses and dissertation research credit, with room for a few electives such as race, gender and crime; policy analysis; and violent behavior.

There is a shortage of doctoral programs. Doctoral programs are harder than master's programs, requiring comprehensive exams, strong quantitative skills (a conceptual and practical understanding of advanced statistics), strong writing skills, strong verbal presentation skills, and in most cases, translation of a foreign language or learning of a computer programming language, and then there is the typical 400-page dissertation that has to be groundbreaking. The following schools offer the Ph.D. in criminology or criminal justice: American University, School of Public Affairs; Arizona State University, School of Justice Studies; University of California–Irvine, Program in Social Ecology; University of Cincinnati, Dept. of Criminal Justice; Claremont Graduate School, Center for Politics and Public Policy; Florida State University, School of Criminology; University of Illinois–Chicago, Dept. of Criminal Justice; Indiana University, Dept. of Criminal Justice; Indiana University of Pennsylvania, Dept. of Criminology; John Jay College of Criminal Justice; University of Delaware, Dept. of Sociology and Criminal Justice; University of Maryland, Dept. of Criminology and Criminal Justice; Michigan State University, School of Criminal Justice; University of Missouri–St. Louis, Dept. of Criminology and Criminal Justice; University of Nebraska, Dept. of Criminal Justice; North Dakota State University, Criminal Justice and Political Science Dept.; Northeastern University, College of Criminal Justice; Pennsylvania State University, Sociology and Administration of Justice Dept.; Portland State University, Criminal Justice Program.; Rutgers University, School of Criminal Justice; Sam Houston St. University, College of Criminal Justice; University of South Florida, Criminology Dept.; University of Southern Mississippi, Administration of Justice Program; State University of New York–Albany, School of Criminal Justice; and Temple University, Criminal Justice Department. An online doctorate can be earned at three schools: Capella University, a Ph.D. in Human Services with a Concentration in Criminal Justice; Northcentral University, a Ph.D. in Business Administration with a Concentration in Criminal Justice; and Walden University, a Ph.D. in Human Services with a Concentration in Criminal Justice.

Thomas O'Connor

References and Further Reading

Clear, T. (2001). Has academic criminal justice come of age? ACJS Presidential Address, Washington, DC, April 2001. *Justice Quarterly* 18(4): 709–726.

Cullen, F. (1995). Fighting back: Criminal justice as an academic discipline. *ACJS Today* 13(4): 1, 3.

Siegel, L. and Zalman, M. (1991). Cultural literacy in criminal justice: A preliminary assessment. *Journal of Criminal Justice Education* 2(1): 15–44.

Southerland, M. (1991). Criminal justice curricula in the United States: An examination of baccalaureate programs, 1988–1989. *Journal of Criminal Justice Education* 2(1): 45–68.

Thornberry, T. (1990). Cultural literacy in criminology. *Journal of Criminal Justice Education* 1(1): 33–50.

Ward, R. and Webb, V. (1984). *Quest for quality.* New York, NY: Joint Commission on Criminology and Criminal Justice Education and Standards.

Elder Abuse

Elder abuse, also referred to as elder mistreatment, encompasses a wide variety of intentional or unintentional acts and omissions that result in harm to an older adult. The acts referred to in this definition include physical, sexual, and psychological abuse, as well as financial exploitation. The word omission refers to neglect or the failure to take some action that results or could result in harm to an older adult.

Many specific acts or omissions are covered by the term elder abuse. These can include, but are not limited to, slapping, hitting, excessively criticizing and ridiculing, negligent or fraudulent taking of property or money, failing to provide necessary food, shelter, or clothing, and failing to provide adequate hygiene. The age one must reach to be considered an elder varies among jurisdictions.

Although the problem of elder abuse likely has been plaguing the world for centuries, it has only been closely scrutinized and included in criminal statutes in the last half century. The criminalization of elder abuse began in the U.S. in 1962 when the Public Welfare Amendments to the Social Security Act were passed. These amendments allowed states to begin receiving federal money to create services to protect people with physical or mental disabilities, people unable to provide for their own care, and those being neglected or exploited. The next important federal legislation came with the passage of Title XX in the 1974 Social Security Act. This legislation compelled states to create some type of adult protective services, or APS as they are now commonly called, for all persons 18 years and older. These services now are provided by agencies that have the power to investigate and intervene in cases of abuse or neglect. However, even with these legislative mandates in place, elder abuse did not become a major public concern until the late 1970s. Media attention and a general public outcry resulted from testimony given on the battering of parents in a hearing before a U.S. Congressional subcommittee on violence in families in 1978. Apart from offering public aid to states that had services for their abused elderly populations and bringing national attention to the problem of elder abuse, the federal government has not established an aggressive elder abuse crime policy. What has resulted from this lack of guidance is a multitude of statutes that differ, sometimes significantly, from state to state.

Currently, all 50 states and the District of Columbia have laws declaring elder abuse a crime, but the definitions of the crime and the punishments proscribed differ from jurisdiction to jurisdiction. Many states have, in addition, chosen to enact statutes dealing with who is legally required to report elder abuse to the proper authorities. Forty-two states have made it a crime for any professional in a health-care setting to fail to report elder abuse. Many of these states also include other categories of professionals deemed to be mandatory reporters. The states that have chosen to include mandatory reporting in their statutes often consider it a misdemeanor punishable by fine, jail time, or revocation of a professional's license. This is, however, where the similarities end. States differ a great deal in other aspects of mandatory reporting, such as how long a person has to report the crime, under what conditions the person should report the crime, and what intent a person must have in the act of not reporting abuse. Also in some states, the remedy for the failure to report elder abuse is not limited to criminal sanctions. In these states, there now is a possibility that the professional, or at times even their employer, could be sued by the victim or the victim's family for a failure to comply with mandatory reporting.

Many states have chosen not to criminalize a failure to comply with mandatory reporting statutes, and, of these states, many have based this decision on the victim's self-determinism. An abused elder is a legally consenting adult who may choose to stay in a potentially harmful situation. The intervening professional then has the difficult task of determining whether or not this decision was made rationally, and, if so, dealing with the fact that the professional cannot force the victimized adult to press charges or leave the situation. In states with mandatory reporting, this may also mean that the professional is not required to report the abuse to the proper authorities. Self-determinism also has been cited as a reason some state criminal laws include only those adults who are thought to be vulnerable or incapacitated physically or mentally.

The great variability of statutes has made it difficult to determine the number of elderly who are abused across jurisdictions. Researchers trying to measure the true extent of elder abuse also have cited other difficulties in measurements. These difficulties include victim denial of abuse, failure to report because of embarrassment or intimidation, and lack of a standard definition of what elder abuse encompasses. Even with these difficulties, some studies have undertaken the task of exploring the nature and extent of victimization and the characteristics and possible causes of this phenomenon. Currently, research suggests that approximately one half million to one million cases of elder abuse are reported annually in the U.S. What is not known, however, is the potentially huge number of cases that continue to go unreported each year. Research has determined that women, and elderly persons over the age of 80, tend to be at a greater risk of elder abuse. Researchers have made progress in identifying the "causes" of elder abuse, leaving states scrambling to find ways to develop prevention programs to attack this serious societal problem.

DENNIS LASTER

References and Furthser Reading

Bergerson, L.R. (2000). Servicing the needs of elder abuse victims. *Policy and Practice of Public Human Services*, 58(3), 40–45.

Cyphers, G.C. (1999). Elder abuse and neglect. *Policy and Practice of Public Human Services*, 57(3), 25–30.

Marshall, C.E., Benton, D., Brazier, J.M. (2000). Elder abuse. *Geriatrics*, 55(2), 42–48.

Mixon, P.M. (1995). An adult protective services perspective. *Journal of Elder Abuse and Neglect*, 7, 69–87.

Moskowitz, S. (1998). Private enforcement of criminal mandatory reporting laws. *Journal of Elder Abuse and Neglect*, 9(3), 1–22.

Peterson, M., Paris, B.E. (1995). Elder abuse and neglect: How to recognize the warning signs and intervene. *Geriatrics*, 50(4), 47–51.

Quinn, M.J. Elder Abuse and Neglect: Causes, Diagnosis, and Intervention Strategies, New York, NY: Springer Publishing, 1997.

Wolf, R.E. (2000). The nature and scope of elder abuse. *Generations*, 24(2), 6–12.

See also **Domestic Assault: Extent and Correlates**

Elderly in Prison, The

In many state and federal prisons of the U.S., the number of elderly prisoners has been steadily rising since the 1980s. This trend, often termed the "graying" of the prisons, has been attributed to the aging of the baby boomers, truth-in-sentencing laws, and mandatory sentencing. *The Corrections Yearbook* reported that as of January 1, 2001, more than 1.3 million inmates populated both the state and federal U.S. prisons. Of this population, 8.2% are 50 years of age or above. The same report indicated that 11%, or 16,066 of a total of 145,416 of the inmates held in the Federal Bureau of Prisons were age 50 or over. It has been estimated that by the year 2010, prisoners who are over the age of 50 years will make up approximately 20% of the total prison population. Others have suggested even higher estimates of up to 33%.

As the large cohort of baby boomers age, the elderly will increasingly be involved in the criminal justice system in some manner. Additionally, a considerable increase of elderly prisoners occurred in the 1990s, as older offenders were sentenced to longer terms of incarceration. Laws in many states, and a general inclination toward stricter sentencing, are keeping inmates in prisons for longer periods of time. For example, truth-in-sentencing laws, where over half of the states in the U.S. require that prisoners serve out 85% of their sentence, increased the average time violent offenders actually spend in prison by 15 months. Mandatory sentencing laws, which are found in many states, have also played a large role in the increase of time served by prisoners, as well as the increase of elderly inmates in prisons. In 2000, *The Corrections Yearbook* indicated that inmates who were "natural-lifers," "lifers," those serving 20 years or more, and those inmates on death row made up 24% of all prisoners in both state and federal prisons. In fact, between the years 1995 and 2000, there was an overall growth of 38% of inmates who were 50 years of age or older.

Unlike younger inmates, the elderly in prison have additional needs and concerns. Prison personnel are now faced with having to be knowledgeable of the aging process, as the populations of inmates they work with are both growing in numbers and aging in years. Elderly inmates in prisons tend to have poorer health than individuals in the general population, owing to their low socioeconomic status, their lack of access to preventative medical and dental services, and elderly inmates' tendency to be physiologically older than their given age. Older inmates, like the elderly in the general population, are faced with more chronic conditions, disabilities, need for assistance, etc. Aging is often accompanied by increased risks for major diseases, such as cancer and cardiac failure, a decline in health that may include the development of chronic conditions such as arthritis and hypertension, and an increased need for assistance with activities of daily living. Inmates, in general, have higher frequencies of tuberculosis, mental health needs, and sexually transmitted diseases. Elderly prisoners are, therefore, prone to both the medical needs associated with aging as well as the health concerns related to being an inmate.

The cost of housing and caring for elderly inmates is higher than the cost of caring for a younger prisoner, in part because of their medical needs. As the population of elderly inmates continues to increase, the cost of caring for these inmates will persistently rise. Currently, prison health-care costs are roughly $3.3 billion dollars a year, and researchers have noted that health-care expenditures are one of the most critical problems for correctional administrators.

However, longer sentencing has also increased the costs of housing elderly inmates. According to the

National Council on Crime and Delinquency, housing a single inmate for 30 years costs over $1 million dollars, and the costs for housing an inmate for 50 years can surpass $2 million dollars. These estimations do not include the cost of medical treatments, which, as previously discussed, are higher for elderly inmates. It has been estimated that it costs $70,000 dollars a year to incarcerate and care for an inmate who is 60 years of age or older. In comparison, a younger adult prisoner costs an estimated $22,000 dollars a year.

Currently, the majority of elderly inmates are housed with the general population of prisoners. However, special housing and programs designed to meet the needs of the elderly can be found across the nation. Traditionally, prisons have been designed to house younger adult inmates. This can pose a problem for elderly inmates in a variety of ways. The lack of temperature control, insufficient lighting, lack of privacy, and the noise levels in prisons can produce discomfort and anxiety in some elderly inmates. Elderly inmates with decreased mobility can find it difficult to climb stairs and maneuver distances to prison facilities. Research has indicated that elderly inmates often feel unsafe, and afraid that younger prisoners will victimize them. Whereas some critics of having specialized units for elderly inmates have argued that these prisoners will experience boredom and isolation if separated from the general prison population, other research has indicated that elderly prisoners prefer to be separated and placed in specialized housing or programs.

Faced with these concerns, many states have been building specialized facilities for geriatric prisoners. The practice of housing elderly inmates apart from the general prison population, and providing special services, is becoming increasingly popular across correctional systems. Currently, about half the states in the U.S. have some form of specialized facilities, programs, or services for elderly inmates. Some states are creating nursing homes and assisted living facilities for prisoners, which are intended to provide elderly inmates with more specialized accommodation and services. Also, many states have implemented hospice services for qualified inmates with terminal conditions.

As the graying of the prison system continues, the challenges related to incarcerating elderly inmates will become increasingly important for correctional administrators and policymakers. Elderly inmates are the fastest growing population in U.S. and Canadian prisons, and accommodations in the criminal justice system in order to meet the challenges and concerns associated with elderly prisoners are likely to continue and gain relevance into the foreseeable future.

ZENTA GOMEZ-SMITH

References and Further Reading

Aday, R.H. (2003). *Aging Prisoners: Crisis in American Corrections.* Westport, CT: Praeger.

Dubler, N.N. (1998). The collision of confinement and care: End-of-life care in prisons and jails. *Journal of Law, Medicine & Ethics* 26: 149–156.

Knapp, J.L. and Elder, K.B. (1998). Assessing prison personnel's knowledge of the aging process. *Journal of the Oklahoma Criminal Justice Research Consortium* 4. Available at www.doc.state.ok.us/Research%20Docs/Assessing%20Prison%20Personnel's.PDF.

Neeley, C.L., Addison. L., and Craig-Moreland, D. (1997). Addressing the needs of elderly offenders. *Corrections Today* 59(5): 120–123.

Wall, J. (1998). Elder care: Louisiana initiates program to meet needs of aging population. *Corrections Today* 60(2): 136–138.

See also **Prisons, Problems, and Recent Developments in; Prisons: Inmate Populations and Subcultures**

Electronic Surveillance and Wiretapping

Even prior to the age of electricity, the practice of eavesdropping was a problem. The main difference was that eavesdropping only occurred within earshot. At the time, listening in on another's conversation was considered rude and bothersome, yet not criminal or threatening to privacy. Intercepting conversations could be done with minimal planning or effort.

Electronic surveillance and wiretaps are now very advanced, allowing conversations to be overheard quite easily. Yet individual privacy is protected to some degree by the Fourth Amendment to the U.S. Constitution. It is the law rather than technology that imposes boundaries on the use of these mechanisms. Evidently the founding fathers in the U.S. were looking out for individual citizens, but by allowing searches at all, they were also protecting the powers of government (Diffie and Landau, 1998).

Legislation had been developed in more than half of the states in the U.S. by 1927 making it illegal to use a wiretap device. This legislation was created to protect the government and their communications throughout World War I. When the war ended, government was not nearly as concerned with legislating wiretapping and ended most of their policies prohibiting it, although most states retained some aspects of the initial legislation (Regan, 1995). The attorney general specifically prohibited the use of wiretaps, yet the Department of Treasury relied heavily on wiretaps throughout Prohibition to thwart the bootlegging business. The constitutionality of these actions was brought before the Supreme Court in *Olmstead v. U.S.* (277 U.S. 438, 1928). Roy Olmstead was involved in bootlegging and was charged with violating federal Prohibition laws. The evidence against him was largely derived from the wiretapping efforts of federal agents. The basic issue in *Olmstead* was whether allowing this evidence to be used in court would be a violation of Olmstead's Fourth and Fifth Amendment rights. The Court determined that they would base their decision on their interpretation of the Fourth Amendment, holding that because there had been no searching, and there had been no seizure, the Fourth Amendment had not been violated. Still, the Court recognized the potential abuses that may arise in the arena of electronic surveillance, acknowledging the need to uphold individual privacy rights and to protect citizens from the actions of the government.

In 1933, Congress passed legislation that forbade the government from spending money on wiretaps except in Prohibition cases in which the evidence was to be used in court (Regan, 1995). Prohibition was later repealed and Congress decided to review their policies concerning communication. Shortly after, the Communication Act of 1934 was passed and read as follows: "no person not being authorized by the sender shall intercept any communication and divulge … the contents" (Federal Government, 1985, 18). Despite the Act's language prohibiting communication interception, the use of wiretaps increased after 1934 (Regan, 1995).

With the onset of World War II, the focus of the wiretapping debate shifted from constitutional issues and law enforcement interests to national security concerns. President Franklin D. Roosevelt permitted the use of wiretaps in 1940 for investigations into persons who were suspected of "engaging in subversive activities" (Regan, 1995, 3). Still, these cases required the approval of the attorney general on a case-by-case basis.

Pressure on Congress to pass wiretapping legislation increased in the 1960s. Depending upon the circumstances, legislation was passed that either permitted or banned wiretapping. It was not until the President's Commission on Law Enforcement and the Administration of Justice appeared in 1967 that the focus shifted from privacy concerns to the value of electronic surveillance in combating organized crime (Regan, 1995).

In *Katz v. U.S.* (389 U.S. 88, 1967) the Supreme Court held that wiretapping was to be considered a search, and thus overturned the decision in *Olmstead.* Katz had been convicted for transmitting betting information over telephone lines and across state lines. The main evidence against Katz was his end of telephone conversations that FBI agents had overheard by attaching a recording device to the outside of a telephone booth. The Court determined that Katz had a reasonable expectation of privacy in the phone booth, and therefore, the actions of the FBI agents constituted a search and seizure, which is protected by the Fourth Amendment.

Subsequently, the Court focused on the constitutionality of this search and seizure. They found that although a warrant should have been issued in light of the circumstances surrounding this case, the fact that the agents acted without such a warrant violated Katz' constitutional rights. Justice Harlan, in a concurring opinion, created a standard formula to be used to determine if an investigation is in violation of the Fourth Amendment. There are two conditions to this test. "First, that a person have exhibited an actual (subjective) expectation of privacy and, second, that the expectation be one that society is prepared to recognize as 'reasonable'" (Katz, 1967). Even with the development of this standard, there are still some ambiguities with regard to defining terms such as "reasonable" and "expectation of privacy." Still, having a standard at minimum gives the Court some guidelines for future cases that until this time were virtually nonexistent.

Until *Katz v. U.S.* (1967), wiretapping and electronic eavesdropping were not considered to be a violation of a defendant's Fourth Amendment rights. The Court held that "unless there has been an official search and seizure of his person, or such a seizure of his papers or his tangible material effects, or an actual physical invasion of his house 'or curtilage' for the purpose of making the seizure" there was no privacy violation. The Court's decision in *Katz* did away with the notion that a physical intrusion must occur in order for search and seizure, as protected by the Constitution, to have taken place.

In 1968, pursuant to *Katz*, the first major congressional action concerning surveillance was enacted in the Omnibus Crime Control and Safe Streets Act. Title III of the Act authorized the use of court-ordered wiretapping and electronic surveillance, prohibited private wiretapping completely, and eliminated most private electronic eavesdropping. The Act also outlawed the making and selling of any devices used to intercept communication.

Title III essentially served two purposes. First, it protected the privacy of both wire and oral communications. Second, the Act set forth explicit guidelines detailing the circumstances and conditions under which wiretapping would be authorized (Federal Government, 1985). Title III filled the gap where law was lacking in the domain of electronic surveillance, and it regulated the use of wiretapping so as to eliminate abuses on the part of the government. Title III was limited in scope in that it only applied to telephone taps and bugs (Federal Government, 1985), yet at the time it was enacted, these were basically the only two types of electronic surveillance mechanisms in use.

The Act also provided that if a state passes wiretapping legislation that is modeled after the Federal Act, officials of that state are authorized to employ wiretapping techniques (Federal Government, 1985). As a rule, states must be only less permissive or as permissive in their use of wiretaps (Fishman, 1994). The federal government wanted to be sure they had overall control in matters that would potentially be abused and possibly infringe on the rights of individual citizens.

The years following the passage of Title III (1970–1984) saw an easing in the stringency of legal restrictions pertaining to wiretaps. The rights or desires of the government continually trumped an individual's right to privacy. Law enforcement actually doubled the number of annual wires and bugs nationwide from 1969 to 1980 (Albanese, 1984).

There are specific requirements and procedures for law enforcement officials who are conducting electronic surveillance and wiretapping investigations. Although wiretaps can be one of the most effective forms of investigation, they are also very time-consuming and costly. In addition, wiretaps are very tedious; when an agency is considering the use of a wiretap in their investigation, they need to ask themselves what they expect to find in these efforts and if their findings will hold up in court. The court will often require that an agency document their previous investigation efforts in the application for a court ordered wiretap to be sure all other investigatory options have been exhausted.

It is important to understand the large scope of electronic surveillance, because it encompasses an array of technological systems including landline telephones, cellular telephones, facsimile machines, computer modems, oral communications, videotape, mobile tracking devices, and more. No matter what the mechanism or the transmission that is being intercepted, law enforcement must be able to show probable cause for carrying out the interception in order to obtain a court order.

If the state's attorney authorizes the application, and the judge issues a court order, the process of setting up for the wiretap begins. Minimization is one important aspect of electronic surveillance, and it is required by law. All personnel who will be listening to the interception must first attend a meeting where they are made aware of their responsibilities and limitations. If nothing relevant is mentioned in a wiretapped conversation, the officer is required to minimize, meaning they must temporarily stop recording and listening. If the conversation is between a client and an attorney, the officers are not allowed to tape or listen to any of that communication. Basically, wiretaps do not give free reign to intercept all conversations for any length of time. Some conversations are protected by attorney or client privilege; others are simply not relevant to the investigation. Recording is closely monitored to be sure all guidelines are followed and any seizures of communication do not violate a subject's rights.

All recordings are subsequently transcribed onto transcripts. If conversations are occurring in a foreign language, they are recorded in full and an interpreter later listens to them and is then held to the same minimization requirements. This provision is possible because of the Electronic Surveillance Privacy Act of 1986 that amended minimization laws. It also provided for the use of roving wiretaps, as well as the interception of electronic mail and other computer transmissions (Fishman, 1994). Wiretaps are like searches, and law enforcement is still limited in their search to what has been approved in that warrant. Violating these rules will lead to an invalid search so that evidence will be thrown out of court.

Wiretapping is by no means a speedy process. Remember that all other investigatory techniques must first be exhausted. Next, the application is made and then goes to the judge. It then takes a great deal of time to actually find incriminating evidence. After the initial time period of authorized surveillance has expired, an extension can be applied for. All evidence must then be reviewed and sorted so the prosecutor can prepare the documentation for presentation in court.

At the international level, many countries take their cue from the U.S. Countries such as England and Canada have developed legislation to regulate wiretapping and electronic surveillance and continue to create new legislation as technology advances (Sharpe, 2000). However, both England and Canada take a unique approach to issues concerning privacy and must turn to their own rules of law to keep in step with the constitutionality of their laws. Other countries such as Israel, Argentina, Italy, and Russia also have laws governing the legality of electronic surveillance and its admissibility in court (Bradley, 1999). These countries too, face the challenge of balancing rights to privacy with the rights of governing bodies. Not unlike the U.S. today, laws often favor one side of the coin for a period and then shift to the other side over time, in an attempt to create a fair balance.

With advances in the world of technology, criminals are using more modern equipment, including cellular phones, digital phones, pagers, and the Internet. In response to these advancements, legislation has been drafted to be certain that the law covers different means of wiretapping and eavesdropping, so that law enforcement officials can use the latest technologies.

We have come a long way from eavesdropping solely through the power of our own ears. Still, the balancing of rights is no easier today than it was 100 years ago. Because interception is such a sensitive issue, law enforcement must be cautious in their actions. As advancements in technology are made, it is imperative that legislation keeps in step with current communications systems. At the same time, laws pertaining to electronic surveillance must continue to be heavily regulated and closely monitored to ensure abuses are not occurring, and that individual rights are still being protected.

KELLY E. FITZ

References and Further Reading

Albanese, J.S., *Justice, Privacy, and Crime Control*, New York University Press of America, 1984.

Alberti, A.A., *Wiretaps: A Complete Guide for the Law and Criminal Justice Professional*, San Francisco, CA: Austin & Winfield, 1999.

Bradley, C.M., *Criminal Procedure: A Worldwide Study*, Durham, NC: Carolina Academic Press, 1999.

Cederbaums, J., *Wiretapping and Electronic Eavesdropping: The Law and its Implications*. New York, NY: New York University, 1969.

Diffie, W. and Landau, S., *Privacy on the Line: The Politics of Wiretapping and Encryption*, Cambridge, MA: The MIT Press, 1998.

Federal Government, *Information Technology: Electronic Surveillance and Civil Liberties*, Washington, DC: U.S. Congress, Office of Technology Assessment, 1985.

Fishman, C.S., *Wiretapping and Eavesdropping*, Deerfield, IL: Clark Boardman, Callaghan, 1994.

National Commission for the Review of Federal and State Laws Relating to Wiretapping and Electronic Surveillance, *Law Enforcement Effectiveness Conference*, Washington, DC: U.S. Government Printing Office, 1976.

Paulsen, M.G., *The Problems of Electronic Eavesdropping*, Philadelphia, PA: The American Law Institute, 1977.

Regan, P.M., *Legislating Privacy: Technology, Values, and Public Policy*, Chapel Hill, NC: University of North Carolina Press, 1995.

Sharpe, S., *Search and Surveillance: The Movement from Evidence to Information*, Burlington, VT: Ashgate, 2000.

Title III of the Omnibus Crime Control and Safe Streets Act of 1968, Pub. L. No. 90-351, H.R. 5037, 90th Cong., 1968.

See also **Search and Seizure**

Elements of Crime

Introduction

The elements common to every criminal offense are referred to as the *corpus delecti*, or "body of the crime" (Black, 1983). Although every crime has different specific components, all share the same five basic elements. Each of these five elements must be proven by the prosecution beyond a reasonable doubt in order for a criminal defendant to be found guilty.

The criminal law has developed as society has developed. Definitions of crimes have changed, and new offenses have been created in an effort to maintain a rational set of rules whereby society can function and individuals within society are protected from others (Hart, 1958). The criminal law in the U.S. is derived from a variety of sources including constitutions, state and federal statutes, and the common law. The bulk of the criminal law is located in state statutes, variously referred to as penal or criminal codes. Many of these state criminal codes were derived originally from the English common law of crimes. The common law is based on the practice of using judicial opinions both to create and define the law (Dressler, 1995). During the middle of the 19th century, states began to codify the common law, enacting criminal codes that set forth in one location the law of crimes. Some states still recognize as crimes acts defined as such under common law but not codified; other states do not.

Criminal liability exists, or in legal parlance "attaches," in most instances only when there is both a criminal act and intent, which together are the cause of a harm to another. Act, intent, concurrence, causation, and harm are the five common elements for criminal liability. These five elements of criminal liability are required in both countries whose legal system are based on the common law (such as England and the U.S.), as well as countries with a civil law system (such as France and Germany).

Criminal Act

Without a criminal act, or *actus reus* (Black, 1983), meaning guilty act, no criminal liability exists. The law does not punish evil thoughts alone. It is only when such thoughts are acted upon that liability may attach. There are three forms of the criminal act: voluntary bodily movements, an omission in the face of a duty to act, and possession (Katz, Moore, and Morse, 1999). Omission and possession are treated as acts for the purpose of the criminal law, although they are not acts in the normal sense of the word.

Voluntary movements are those occurring by virtue of the actor's free will, without coercion and with awareness of conduct. This definition excludes involuntary bodily movements such as reflexive actions or unconscious activity such as sleepwalking. A voluntary act is indicative of free will, an essential component of the criminal law (Fletcher, 1978). Words can also constitute acts, in some cases, such as solicitation to commit a crime, a threat, or inciting panic by yelling "fire" in a crowded theater. The Supreme Court has held that a state may not punish someone on the basis of status, or what the person is. For instance, the Supreme Court has said that it is unconstitutional to punish someone for simply being an alcoholic, but lawful to punish someone for being drunk in a public place, on the grounds that being an alcoholic is a status whereas being drunk in public is an action (*Powell v. Texas,* 392 U.S. 514, 1968).

An omission is generally not subject to sanction, even if morally reprehensible. The general rule is that there is no legal duty to aid another, or be a Good Samaritan. However, there are two narrow circumstances where failure to act may result in criminal liability. One is a failure to perform a legally imposed duty, such as failing to register a handgun when the law requires registration. Another is a failure to intervene to prevent a serious harm when there exists a special relationship between the parties, as in the case of parents and children or a doctor and patient.

Possession may itself constitute a criminal act if a person has some knowledge of what they possess. This is sometimes referred to as "conscious possession," to distinguish it from the case where a person is unaware that what they possess is illegal. Although possession is passive, the act of acquiring possession requires action, and retaining possession in the face of an awareness that it is unlawful to possess the item is similar to an omission.

Criminal Intent

Criminal liability is not based on action alone. There must also be some sort of guilty mind or *mens rea* (Black, 1983). *Mens rea* is the degree or level of awareness of one's conduct and its repercussions. The rationale for this requirement is that society does not wish to punish unavoidable accidents or unintended conduct. It is important to note that motive and intent are different. Intent is the mental purpose to commit a specific act. Motive is the cause, the reason why, an act is committed. Some degree of intent is generally required for criminal liability to exist; there is no requirement that the prosecution prove motive, although it is commonly done as a means of explaining the act to the jury (Gardner, 1993).

Modern criminal law recognizes several levels of intent, with varying levels of punishment associated with each. Although the language varies by jurisdiction, many states use the language of the Model Penal Code, published by the American Law Institute in 1962.

The *Model Penal Code* sets forth four levels of intent: purposeful, knowing, reckless, and negligent. A person acting purposefully intends to produce a certain result. He or she has both the intent to commit the act and the knowledge of the harm that will result. A person acts knowingly when he or she is virtually certain of the result of conduct. A person acts recklessly when they possess an awareness of the risk involved but lack the certainty of knowledge that harm will follow. Negligence is the unconscious creation of a risk of harm. Negligent actors are those who should have been aware that they were creating a substantial and unjustifiable risk of harm, but for some reason they were not aware (Dressler, 1995).

There is one other form of intent. This is the doctrine of transferred intent, applying to situations where a person intended to harm A, but in error harmed B. The intent to harm A is transferred to B, to allow imposition of punishment. This prevents wrongdoers from escaping liability by claiming they did not intend to hurt B and that the element of intent is therefore missing.

Concurrence

Concurrence is simply the union of the criminal act and criminal intent. The criminal intent must exist prior to the criminal act, and set the criminal act in motion. Acts not generated by criminal intent do not constitute criminal conduct. The criminal state of mind and the criminal act must coincide, with the intent developing prior to the act.

Causation

Causation is the legal principle that the criminal act is that which is the cause of the harm. There are two types of causation: factual and legal. Factual cause refers to the idea that "but for" the actor's conduct, the harm would not have occurred. The factual cause is the event that sets in motion a chain of events that eventually leads to the harmful result. It is a necessary, but not sufficient, element for the imposition of criminal liability. There must also exist legal cause (Schulhofer, 1974).

Legal cause, also referred to as "proximate cause" is the legal principle defining the criminal act as the most significant act in the chain of events leading to harm. Consequences of an act that are not reasonably foreseeable by the actor are referred to as intervening causes, and serve to relieve the actor of criminal liability. There can be multiple causes of harm. The prosecution must prove the defendant's act was both the factual and legal cause of the harm.

Harm

Harm is simply the result of the act, the injury to another. This harm may be physical, as in murder, or mental, as in threatening someone with some form of harm. There can be no liability without harm, although this harm may be to society in general rather than to a specific individual. The state may even criminalize acts that harm only the actor, such as suicide or drug abuse.

Liability without Fault

In a few instances, criminal liability may exist without proof of criminal intent. These include strict liability and vicarious liability. Strict liability, an important tort law concept, is also used in the criminal law. It imposes liability without proof of criminal intent in situations where society deems it fair, such as violations of drug and alcohol sales laws. The rationale for liability without fault for this narrow class of crimes is that the actor has chosen to engage in a business or activity that poses a high risk to society, and he or she therefore, assumes the risk of liability for the foreseeable consequences of his actions (Katz, Moore, and Morse, 1995).

Vicarious liability refers to the imputation of liability from one person to another, usually a person in a superior position. It is similar to the tort law concept of *respondeat superior* (Black, 1983). Here, liability is based not on a person's act but on his relationship to the person who committed an illegal act. It eliminates the criminal act requirement for the second actor by imputing the first actor's intent to him. Thus A may be held criminally liable for the conduct of B if A is responsible for B's conduct or supervises B. Liability generally attaches only if B's conduct was reasonably foreseeable to A and A benefits in some way from B's conduct. This is done to prevent employers from insulating themselves from blame for the criminal acts committed on their behalf (Fletcher, 1978).

Conclusion

Scholars, judges, and juries continue to struggle over the proper limits of the criminal sanction. The criminal law is expanding at a rapid rate, as legislatures add new crimes to the penal code. Victimless crimes, drug-related offenses, and weapons offenses are examples of the burgeoning criminal law. Punishments for violation of the criminal law are being increased, as well. How much can society expect the criminal law to accomplish? When is it fair and just to hold persons accountable for their conduct, and to subject such persons to punishment? Determining not only when liability should exist, but also the appropriate level of punishment is difficult. The choices involve a combination of policy considerations, legal doctrine, and morality.

CRAIG HEMMENS

References and Further Reading

Dressler, J. (1995). *Understanding Criminal Law.* New York, NY: Matthew Bender.

Fletcher, G. (1978). *Rethinking Criminal Law.* Boston, MA: Little, Brown.

Gardner, M.R. (1993). The *mens rea* enigma: Observations on the role of motive in the criminal law past and present. *Utah Law Review* 1993: 635.

Hart, H.M. (1958). The aims of the criminal law. *Law and Contemporary Problems* 23: 401.

Katz, L., Moore, M.S., and Morse, S.J. (1999). *Foundations of Criminal Law.* New York, NY: Foundation Press.

Schulhofer, S.J. (1974). Harm and punishment: A critique of emphasis on the results of conduct in the criminal law. *University of Pennsylvania Law Review* 122: 1497.

See also ***Corpus Delicti***; ***Mens Rea*** **(Criminal Intent)**

Employee Theft and Inventory Shrinkage

The theft of money, goods, intellectual property, and services by employees is a growing concern for companies of every size. Employee theft is classified by criminologists as a white collar, occupational crime that is committed by an individual or individuals for personal gain within the scope of their normal employment. What most people do not realize is that employee theft can have a more devastating effect on a business than victimization by burglars, robbers, or shoplifters. In retail businesses, the majority of inventory shrinkage—or merchandise unaccounted for—results from employee theft. Employee theft costs U.S. businesses \$15–\$25 billion annually, and affects every type of business operation. Some estimates suggest that nearly one third of all businesses that go bankrupt do so because of employee theft whereas countless others experience continuing losses. A survey of 20,000 job applicants revealed that about 30% of the respondents said that they could be tempted to steal from their employer; 18% admitted to stealing money in the last 3 years, and 22% stated they had frequently associated with fellow employees who admitted they were stealing merchandise from the company (Doyle, 2000). Other research reports conclude that as many as 50% of the U.S. workforce may steal from their employers (Friedrichs, 1996).

Results from foreign retail crime surveys report that employee theft is also a serious problem in many countries. These surveys generally report that employee or staff thieves are responsible for increasing amounts of retail dollar losses. In almost all instances, employees per incident losses are substantially greater than customer incident losses. For example, the Canadian Retail Security Report conducted by the Retail Council of Canada for the year 2000 reported that even though employee theft accounted for 31% compared to 40% for customer theft, the actual loss per employee theft was \$450.00 per incident compared to \$116.00 per customer theft per incident. A study conducted in New Zealand by the Centre for Retail Research and Studies in 1999 found that theft by employees was about 26% of total retail losses compared to theft by customers accounting for 56% of total retail losses. Average incidents of employee theft were \$280 whereas average per incident loss was \$59 for customer theft.

Many employees steal for personal use. Some might view the stealing of equipment or other expensive items as reprehensible by fellow employees, but classify their own taking home of pencils, stationary, envelopes, and other "minor" items as perfectly acceptable. Similarly, the stealing of company "time," such as false certification of hours worked or conducting personal business on company time, accounts for huge losses to businesses, and may not be seen as particularly harmful to an employer. However, research shows that employee theft is ubiquitous, occurring perhaps in 95% of all businesses, and can involve the stealing of virtually anything of value in business environments as varied as retail stores, hospitals, warehouses, food-processing plants, mines, factories, offices, and banks. More elaborate employee theft schemes, often occurring over a period of years, and involving an organized group of employees, some in trusted management positions, result in huge monetary losses to businesses. Commonly, such activities are hidden through various fraudulent documents, including falsified accounting records.

Employee theft falls in the category of a larceny or theft offense. Other larceny offenses include shoplifting and pickpocketing. Under common law, larceny is defined as the taking and carrying away of the personal property of another with intent to steal. Larceny requires the *wrongful taking* of property from another's possession. The acquisition is not obtained by force or threats to the victim (as in robbery) or by breaking into the victim's business (as in burglary). Wrongful taking also can include possession by fraud or deceit, often referred to as "larceny by trick." The early common law interpretation of larceny was originally limited to property that had a value and was tangible. All states now have expanded larceny to include intangible items such as stocks, bonds, checks, trade secrets, data, and other valuable proprietary information that can be sold. A great deal of a company's valuable knowledge is reduced to data stored on company computers, much of which is classified as "intellectual property." An employee's unauthorized access and copying of trade secrets and other proprietary information such as sales strategies, manufacturing plans and processes, research and development, customer lists, formulas or security codes can be devastating for a company's bottom line but a valuable commodity for a dishonest employee on the open market. It is estimated, for example, that 70% of the market value of a typical U.S. company resides in intellectual property. Today, virtually all property is included within the scope of modern larceny statutes. States usually separate larceny into *petty larceny* and *grand larceny.* Petty larceny is theft of small amounts of property or money, usually less than $100. The crime is classified as a misdemeanor and is punishable by a small fine or short period of incarceration. Grand larceny, on the other hand, is the stealing of larger sums of money or costly property. This crime is a felony subject to a longer term of incarceration. Employee theft can also be referred to in terms of embezzlement. Embezzlement is the misappropriation of property voluntarily and temporarily given to another such as a trusted employee (referred to as *constructive possession*). A bank teller who falsifies accounts and takes money from the bank to purchase a new car committed the crime of embezzlement.

Employee theft is one of the most underreported crimes in the U.S. as well as in other countries. Official crime statistics maintained by law enforcement agencies are virtually nonexistent. Much of what we know about the crime comes from surveys of a diverse spectrum of businesses in which researchers ask owners about their known sources of inventory shrinkage. For example, the National Retail Security Survey conducted by Richard Hollander of the University of Florida analyzes theft incidents submitted by major retail companies on an annual basis in the U.S. According to the most recent survey (2000), employee theft is the main source of inventory shrinkage. Responding retailers attributed 44.5% of their losses to employee theft, 32.7% to shoplifting, 17.5% to administrative error and 5.1% to vendor fraud. In dollar losses, employee theft cost American retailers $13.2 billion in 1999, substantially surpassing the amount lost to shoplifting, $9.7 billion. The amount of financial loss caused by a "typical" dishonest employee was $1,023, whereas the amount of merchandise taken by the "typical" shoplifter was $128. Hollander found that employee theft was up 2% from the previous survey (1998), and suggested that a possible reason for the increase was the low unemployment rate in the nation forcing employers in a tight labor market possibly to hire more dishonest and uncommitted persons. It was also reported that the length of time worked by the dishonest employees prior to their apprehension was less than 1 year.

A 1999 survey conducted by the Centre for Retail Research in the United Kingdom based on interviews with 30 retailers responsible for more that 50% of UK retail sales reported that staff-related crime accounted for about 51% of total store theft. This amounted to a yearly loss of 640 million pounds or 50.8% of total retail theft, roughly equivalent to customer theft. The typical staff thief was usually someone who had been employed for less than a year and who was sometimes taught to steal by a coworker. Of particular interest in the study was the finding that as much as 16% of customer theft may be the result of collusion between retail employees and customers. The main forms of collusion included refund fraud, false markdowns, and sweethearting ("discounts" for friends and family). Supermarkets, department stores, pharmacies, variety chains, clothing, stores, and record shops were particularly susceptible to collusion between employees and customers.

Results from other industry-specific surveys such as those conducted by the Food Marketing Institute and the Retail Institute at Purdue University in their Annual Reports on Employee Theft in the Supermarket Industry likewise report that employee theft is a serious and costly problem. Although their 1999 survey found that losses per episode of self-reported theft were at an all time low ($43 per incident) for a supermarket chain of 50 stores, with 150 employees per store, the total loss per year would be $291,383 in employee theft, a substantial loss to a company. It was found, however, that supermarket chains with "winning" cultures, or work environments that stressed employee training on company policies and procedures regarding theft, conveying antitheft sentiments to employees, open communication, flexibility, career advancement, fairness, and above-average compensation, had significantly less employee theft than other companies which did not incorporate these things into their workplace. Another national employee theft survey, the Annual Survey of Restaurant and Fast Food Employees administered by National Computer Systems, Inc., found that the average annual theft per restaurant employee in 1998 was $218. This estimate of employee theft translates into $2,453,700 in lost revenue per year for a 300-restaurant chain with 30 employees per store. The researchers also found that employee theft could be reduced through a "positive corporate culture" as well as through various preemployment screening practices that could possibly identify employees likely to engage in counterproductive activities in the workplace.

What prompts employees to steal? Other than stealing from an employer, employee thefts are not all the same. Individuals have different reasons, rationalizations, and justifications for their crimes. A classic study of bank embezzlers by Donald Cressey, *Other People's Money* (1953), indicated that embezzlement by trusted employees usually began as the result of a nonsharable financial problem. This condition was the result of individuals who were living beyond their means, possibly as a result of gambling debts or an extravagant lifestyle. The solution to their financial difficulty was to steal money from the bank, and then rationalize that they were only temporarily borrowing the money, which they would eventually pay back. This rationalization of "borrowing" eventually breaks down as embezzlers realize that they cannot pay the money back in time and caught. Financial need on the part of employees is a common excuse offered by individuals who are caught stealing from their workplaces. The social meanings that employees give to their stealing is a topic that criminologists have studied for decades. Various rationalizations related to employee's perceptions regarding, for example, undercompensation, overwork, perceived mistreatment, and dissatisfaction with their job are often used to justify the theft of money, merchandise, or information from their employers. In essence, stealing becomes a "symbol of personal control" over conditions in their work environment that they otherwise would have no control over (Altheide et al., 1978). Another common motivation to steal evolves from the culture of the work organization. If employees observe top management taking advantage of the business for their personal benefit, lower level employees will see this as an invitation to do likewise. Businesses need to create a culture where all personnel are actively encouraged to be honest and productive and actively discouraged from being dishonest and unproductive.

Many, if not most, employee thefts begin with opportunities made available to employees in the workplace. If supervision is lax or indifferent, the temptation to steal money, items or information that is improperly secured or unaccountable may be too great a temptation for some employees. Measures to prevent and control employee theft include several behavioral and procedural measures:

Morale of Employees. It is important that each employee in an organization feels that he or she is an integral part of the operation, both as a contributor and as an individual. Clear statements of company policy should be consistently and fairly administered with procedures for airing grievances and personal problems. There is no substitute for a good work environment in which employees are valued and rewarded for their productivity.

Preemployment Screening. Companies should verify all information on employment applications, follow up on references and former employers, and check for criminal convictions.

Money Controls. Business owners should make sure that bank accounts are reconciled by someone other than those who handle deposits and withdrawals. All cash receipts should be deposited intact daily. Prenumbered invoices should be used that require cash to be posted by invoice number.

Proprietary Information Protection. A well-executed safeguarding proprietary information (SPI) protection program should begin with an inventory of the key intellectual assets of the organization. The organization should then perform a risk assessment and determine which assets are adequately protected and which may be at risk (*Trends in Proprietary Information Loss*, 1999).

Auditing Assets. Periodic audits by outside auditors are essential to any well-run business. Although audits will discover thefts only after the fact, they also uncover regular schemes of embezzlement in time to prevent serious damage. Audits normally cover an examination of inventory schedules, prices, footings, and extensions. They should also verify company assets by physical inventory samplings, accounts receivable, accounts payable, deposits, and outstanding liabilities through an ongoing financial audit (Fischer, 1989).

Shrinkage Investigations. Proper management means paying attention to all the details in retailing as well as recognizing and pinpointing the location of shrinkage. Shrinkage investigations should track inventory from the stocks until sales. Especially important is the use of point-of-sales systems that can monitor price overrides, returns without receipts, under-ring keyed items, and multiple charge voids before and after closing.

Physical Security. Warehouses, stockrooms, and other storage spaces must be equipped with adequate physical protection to secure goods and merchandise. Only authorized employees should have access to these areas. Special attention should be given to the cargo receiving facilities of a business. Without the proper means of securing merchandise during every phase of its handling, internal thefts by employees cannot be controlled.

High Tech Security Measures. When properly used, techniques such as video observation, checkpoint alarm stickers, and electronic transaction processing systems can be effective in preventing employee thefts.

Exit Interviews. Corporations should conduct exit interviews with employees who have been privy to proprietary information and stress to them their confidential obligations, putting them on legal notice not to divulge trade secrets or other vital information to competitors. Employers who hire employees from other companies must prove that new employees are not using trade secrets on a new product, project, or service.

Unfortunately, many business owners become concerned about employee theft only after it reaches serious levels, usually in the form of a huge inventory shrinkage or other monetary losses. The *modus operandi* for work related theft may be as simple as a lone employee occasionally pilfering merchandise for his or her own use, or as complicated as an elaborate embezzlement scheme using the skills of several employees in an organization to steal large sums of money daily over time. As is often the case in the field of criminology, more attention has been focused on lower-level types of work-related theft as opposed to higher or executive level stealing. However, irrespective of the source of employee theft, research suggests that the normative structure and values of an organization set the tone for employee honesty. Organizations that emphasize mutual respect, honesty, and fairness, as well as clearly defined behavioral expectations, are least likely to experience employee thefts.

William E. Thornton

References and Further Reading

Altheide, D.L., Adler, P.A., Adler, P., and Altheide, D.A. The social meanings of employee theft, in *Crime at The Top*, Johnson, J.M. and Douglas, J.D. (Eds.), New York, NY: J.B. Lippincott, 1978.

Bamfield, J. A breach of trust: Employee collusion and theft from major retailers, in *Crime at Work*, Gill, M. (Ed.), Leicester, UK: Perpetuity Press, 1998.

Beck, A. and Willis, A. *Crime and Security: Managing the Risk to Safe Shopping*. London, UK: Perpetuity Press, 1995.

Clarke, J. and Hollinger, R.C. *Theft by Employees in Work Organizations*. Lexington, MA: Lexington Books, 1983.

Cressey, D.R. *Other People's Money: A Study in the Social Psychology of Embezzlement*, Belmont, CA: Wadsworth, 1971.

Doyle, M.R. *Admissions of Dishonesty—Ask and They Will Tell*, Fruitland Park, FL: CHC Forecast, Inc., 2000.

Etheridge-Longman, A. Stop insiders from eating profits, *Security Management*, November, 1999.

Felson, M. and Clarke, R.V. *Business and Crime Prevention*, Monsey, NY: Criminal Justice Press/Willow Press, 1997.

Fishcher, R.J. Internal theft controls, in *Handbook of Loss Prevention and Crime Prevention*, Fennelly, L.J. (Ed.), Boston, MA: Butterworth-Heinemann, 1989.

Fourth Annual Survey of Restaurant and Fast Food Employees, National Computer Systems, Inc., 1999.

Friedrichs, D.O. *Trusted Criminals: White-Collar Crime in Contemporary Society*. Belmont, CA: Wadsworth, 1996.

Harold, V. Loss prevention checklist, in *Handbook of Loss Prevention and Crime Prevention*, Fennelly, L.J. (Ed.), Boston, MA: Butterworth-Heinemann, 1989.

Harman, A. Restricting computer theft, *Law and Order* 48, 1, 2000.

Henry, S. and Mars, G. Crime at work: The social construction of amateur property theft, *Sociology* 12, 1978.

Hollinger, R.C. *National Retail Security Survey*. Gainesville, FL: University of Florida, 2000.

Hollinger, R.C. *National Retail Security Survey*. Gainesville, FL: University of Florida, 1998.

Hollander, R.C. Measuring crime and its impact in the business environment, in *Business and Crime Prevention*, Felson, M. and Clarke, R.V. (Eds.), Monsey, NJ: Criminal Justice Press, 1997.

Le Stradic, H. Étude Sur La Démarque Inconnue et Les Mesures de Sécurité des Commerces de Détail, Group ESC: Rennes, 1995.

Trends in Proprietary Information Loss Survey Report, American Society of Industrial Security and Price Waterhouse Cooper, 1999.

Voigt, L., Thornton, W.E., Barrile, L., and Seaman, J.M. *Criminology and Justice*. New York, NY: McGraw-Hill, 1994.

See also **Larceny or Theft: Extent and Correlates; Occupational Crime; White-Collar Crime: Enforcement Strategies; White-Collar Crime: Theories**

English Legal Traditions

The English Common Law arose gradually from the judicial uses and customs of English judges between the 12th and 14th centuries, rather than from written statute. Its basic features include trial by jury (grand and petty), the adjudication of civil and criminal cases in "common law" courts, and the institution of royal justices on circuit to try defendants accused of grave crimes. Increasingly, after the proclamation of Magna Carta in 1215, the Common Law came to represent the sacred rights of Englishmen to be exempt from arbitrary government action, symbolized by the rights to trial by a jury of one's peers after a grand jury's determination of probable cause and a speedy trial in accordance with established procedure. After Magna Carta, English kings who ran afoul of the Common Law were obliged to yield or abdicate their throne. By the 17th century, the Common Law had become a hedge against royal absolutism, challenging the claims of absolute monarchs with principles of legal equality and natural rights that transcended the decrees of civil authority. In this fashion, the ancient Common Law became imbricated in the early modern movement toward constitutional governance, culminating in the Glorious Revolution of 1688 and the subsequent English Bill of Rights.

Historical Antecedents of the English Common Law

The Common Law was an institution that evolved at an almost geological rate of development, and thus should be viewed in the context of English Medieval history. With the destruction of the Western Roman Empire in 426, the western territory fell under the control of Germanic kings. Germanic tribes from modern-day Scandinavia, the Angles, Saxons, and Jutes, invaded Britain in the years after the fall of the Empire, establishing their control of the island by the year 500. Historians call the next 566 years of British history "Anglo-Saxon" after the two most prominent of the invading tribes. The Germans replaced Roman law and culture in Britain with their own tribal customs, including Germanic legal practices. Until the beginning of the 7th century, German law was oral and to a significant degree clan based. Because of the primacy of kinship groups and "blood ties" among the Germans, an offense committed by one person on another was punished chiefly through the "blood feud"—a practice whereby the clan group of a murder victim would exact revenge by taking the killer's life. This "eye for an eye" approach to vengeance against the wrongdoer could also be satisfied through payment of compensation to the victim or the victim's family, a sum called the *wergeld*. The Salic Law of the Franks, for example, stipulated that *wergeld* be paid for offenses like theft, rape, arson, assault, and murder.

From the 7th century onward, the payment of *wergeld* displaced the blood feud as the most common form of punishment in Anglo-Saxon Britain. Between 601 and 604 Aethelbert of Kent promulgated the first in a series of Anglo-Saxon laws called "dooms," which prescribed monetary fines for different kinds of criminal offense. The dooms of Aethelbert and his successors marked a clear effort by the Anglo-Saxon kings to quell tribal resort to the blood feud. After the 9th century, crime victims and their families largely sought redress from royal officials rather than personal vengeance, a trend perpetuated by the dooms of Edgar (946) and Canute (1020–1034). By the 11th century the blood feud had all but vanished from English criminal justice.

As the number of aggrieved parties seeking redress from the king grew, the need for a procedure to determine the merits of individual cases emerged—the system of trial. The latter began as a proceeding in which the parties to the dispute swore to the truth of their respective claims (an oath called "compurgation"). If the outcome was inconclusive, an "ordeal" often followed, designed to invite divine intervention in the matter. Ordeal could take as many as three forms: trial by hot water, cold water, and red-hot iron. The guilt or innocence of the defendant depended on the outcomes of these trials. With the Norman invasion of 1066, William of Normandy introduced a fourth kind of ordeal, trial by battle, in which the result of a duel between the disputants determined guilt or innocence (the assumption being that God would ensure that the party with the just cause won).

William's invasion of Britain in 1066 was an important paving stone on the historical road to the English Common Law. After he had subjugated all of England, William rewarded his Norman countrymen with grants of land in exchange for oaths of allegiance to himself as king. He also replaced Anglo-Saxon sheriffs with his own handpicked followers, and substituted the *curia regis* (royal council) for the main Anglo-Saxon council, the *witenagemot*. William was the first ruler of Britain to introduce subinfeudation, a complex skein of relationships between lords, vassals, and subvassals, which he imported from his kingdom in Normandy. At the top of this convoluted structure was the English king, supreme ruler of his realm. William's successors would continue his centralization of royal power, especially his grandson Henry II, the official founder of English Common Law.

Henry II and the Rise of the English Common Law

Henry II (reign: 1154–1189) is generally credited with laying the foundation for the Common Law through his reforms of the English legal system. Under Henry's reign, the English king for the first time asserted exclusive jurisdiction over civil and criminal cases. Emulating the centralizing tendencies of his grandfather, Henry emerged as both the prime guarantor of property and the holder of sole jurisdiction over criminal matters. He projected his power over the latter sphere by dispatching itinerant judges called "justices in eyre"—circuit judges who traveled throughout England hearing civil and criminal cases on behalf of the king. Following earlier precedent, Henry's judges summoned knowledgeable citizens of the locales they visited to provide information about the case and furnish their opinions about who the perpetrator might be. The royal justices thereby solidified a practice with roots in Germanic tribal society, the Anglo-Saxon period, and Norman England, an institution that became known as the "grand jury." Over time, what we today recognize as a "petty jury" developed from Henry's grand jury system to decide issues of guilt and innocence in local criminal cases.

In 1166, Henry published the Assize of Clarendon (an "assize" being either a decree of law by the king, or new judicial procedures derived from such a decree), requiring that the 12 heads of family of every "hundred" (a group of villages) be placed under oath and compelled to report the identities of notorious criminals and their accomplices to the royal justices. The convicted were typically banished after a trial by ordeal, usually the ordeal of cold water. Even if the trial resulted in the acquittal of the accused, he or she could still be punished through exile if his or her reputation was sufficiently unsavory. A system of royal writs enforced this extension of the king's power over the crimes of his subjects. These writs represent a significant innovation introduced by Henry II. Often addressed to the sheriff regarding a case within his county, the writs were peremptory in tone, enjoining the recipient to substitute, for example, a jury trial for trial by battle. Regardless of the subject matter, the expectation was that the writs would be obeyed to the letter. As M.T. Clanchy, a scholar of Medieval England, has noted, the effect of reducing the king's commands to standardized written form served to stabilize English criminal procedure and to promote enforcement of the substantive criminal law, thereby lending to English justice an air of permanence. For Clanchy, the technology of writing was Henry II's main contribution to the Common Law.

Through his innovative use of writs, Henry directed that specific types of civil and criminal matters be resolved through trial by jury. He ordered that a body of 12 local men resolve such matters as disputes over title to land, possession of weapons, and malicious abuse of process ("appeals of felony"). Superintended by Henry's justices in Eyre, these proceedings generated a body of legal principles that became the nucleus of the English Common Law. In 1215, the Fourth Lateran Council banned participation by clergy in trial by ordeal, a prohibition that virtually ended the practice in much of Western Europe, including England. Consequently, in the ensuing decades the trial (or petty) jury became a common means of adjudicating criminal cases, modeled on Henry II's grand jury of 12 local men. By 1275, it was rare that a juror sitting on a grand jury would serve on a petty jury in the same case. In 1352, such double service was banned by law.

Magna Carta and Parliament

At the same time as the Vatican banned trial by ordeal in 1215, an epoch in the history of English law was dawning: the signing of the Magna Carta. Weakened by bruising struggles with the pope over appointment of the new archbishop of Canterbury and with Philip Augustus over his French territories, King John (reign: 1199–1216) was vulnerable to domestic encroachments on his royal power. English barons exploited his disadvantage by forcing him to sign the Magna Carta, whereby the king pledged not to levy excessive financial contributions on his noble vassals or to prosecute them contrary to law. Under the Charter, the king was further obliged to acknowledge the Church's freedom to select its own bishops and the rights of the towns to exercise their customary liberties. From King John's time forward, every English king had to respect the law and traditions of his realm. Those kings who did not—like Edward II (reign: 1311–1327) and Richard II (reign: 1377–1358)—were deposed or forced to abdicate. In the modern age, Magna Carta, which had originally only restrained the actions of the king in dealing with his noble vassals, was broadly interpreted to protect *all* citizens against royal usurpation.

As the principles of Magna Carta settled into the bedrock of English legal history, the forerunner of the English Parliament came into being. It began as a meeting of the primary "estates" in English society (the clergy, nobility, and wealthy commoners) to confer with the king, particularly when he wished to raise taxes from them. The term "parliament" was attached to these meetings of the estates, meaning "discussions." Edward I summoned the first parliament (the so-called "Model Parliament") in 1295; this meeting established the precedent for subsequent parliaments of nobles and prelates to meet in the House of Lords and knights and eminent commoners in the House of Commons. As the Middle Ages waned into the early modern period, English kings recognized the growing power of parliament: Henry VII secured from parliament an act of succession to legitimate his claim to the throne, achieved by his victory on Bosworth Field in 1485; similarly, Henry VIII engineered his break with the Catholic Church through parliamentary statutes abrogating appeals to the papal court and instituting royal dominance of the Anglican church (1533 and 1534, respectively). Clearly, at the onset of the modern age, the notion of the king's accountability to longstanding tradition and precedent had converged with the Common Law to prepare the way for constitutional polity in England.

The Development of the Common Law: The Early Modern Period

Between the 12th and 14th centuries, three main Common Law courts emerged: Common Pleas (1187), which presided over misdemeanors and civil cases; Exchequer (ca. 1179), which heard financial cases; and Chancery (ca. 1320), which enjoyed equity jurisdiction and resolved matters involving orphans and incompetents. These Medieval common law courts, in other words, had jurisdiction over a limited range of cases—an inadequacy only compounded as social and economic modernization in England created new crimes beyond the scope of their mandate. In part to fill the jurisdictional gaps, in part to expand royal power, the Tudors established new judicial institutions like the Court of High Commission (1534), which heard criminal appeals from Archbishops' Courts, and the Courts of Star Chamber (1470), devoted to trying crimes involving ecclesiastical matters (church doctrine and discipline). Additionally, the Tudors enlarged the jurisdiction of the Privy Council, which, after 1470, flexed its new judicial muscle through the Star Chamber.

Prosecution in these royal forums stood in stark contrast with the legal forms of the Common Law. Subject to interrogation by court members, defendants were not informed of the charges against them, the names of the accusing witnesses, or the gist of witness statements. Neither the Court of High Commission nor of Star Chamber sat with a jury. Accordingly, rates of conviction before the royal courts were high. Defendants tried for heresy and other deviations from religious orthodoxy faced possible death sentences if convicted. In 1538, John Lambert was prosecuted before the Privy Council for denying the doctrine of transubstantiation (the Catholic dogma that the substance of the bread and wine in the Eucharist was transformed into the body and blood of Jesus), found guilty of heresy, and burned at the stake. In the aftermath of Lambert's trial, Parliament passed the Act of Six Articles, which criminalized all speech critical of the dogma of transubstantiation. This interfusing of theological correctness and political authority was characteristic of Tudor England. It eventually galvanized opposition in the 17th century—an opposition that would define itself, with growing vehemence, in terms of the ancient Common Law rights of Englishmen.

If royal prerogative and religious orthodoxy were the dominant themes of Tudor jurisprudence, the tumultuous era of the Stuart kings was notable for the struggle to limit the authority of the monarch. An early manifestation of this struggle was the campaign waged in the early 1600s by the Chief Justice of the Court of King's Bench, Sir Edward Coke, to combat the authority of the royal courts. Coke and his Common Law adherents employed writs as weapons against these courts: the writ of habeas corpus to obtain release of defendants convicted and sentenced to jail terms and the writ of prohibition to discontinue trials in the Star Chamber and Court of High Commission. When in 1641 the parliamentary party gained control of the government, it promptly abolished the courts of Star Chamber and High Commission.

The abolition of the two leading royal courts presaged the ultimate victory of the Common Law over political absolutism in England. The Stuart kings—particularly James I and his son, Charles I—insisted on their divine right as monarchs to rule without consent from their subjects, beholden only to God for their actions. Between 1603 and 1640, the royal absolutism of James and Charles envenomed the Crown's relations with the House of Commons. In 1629, Charles refused to consult with Parliament in his government of the country, arbitrarily levying taxes without parliamentary input. When Charles finally summoned Parliament in 1640 to finance an army to crush a rebellion in Scotland, the House of Commons abolished the royal courts, passed an act requiring the King to summon Parliament every 3 years, and impeached the unpopular Archbishop Laud (an ally of Charles). This much Charles could stomach. What he could not tolerate, however, was Parliament's refusal to finance another army to quell an uprising in Ireland, a refusal that drove Charles to take military action against Parliament. At the center of the English Civil War (1642–1649) that followed was the issue of where sovereign power resided in England: with the king or with Parliament. When parliamentary forces defeated the king's army in 1649, Charles was convicted of high treason and executed. For the next 11 years, England was governed by a military dictatorship. When its leader, Oliver Cromwell, died in 1658, the English had tired of military rule, and hankered after a return to civil government and stability. In 1660 Charles II, oldest son of Charles I, was restored to the throne.

In confirming the abolition of the Courts of Star Chamber and High Commission, Charles II reaffirmed the vitality of the common law courts and the tradition of trial by jury. Yet, restrictions on common law courts compromised their ability to ensure due process protections in criminal trials. Judges held their positions at the pleasure of the king, thus opening the criminal trial process to political influence. Furthermore, sanctions could be imposed on jurors who returned verdicts at odds with the wishes of the chief judge, including fines and even imprisonment. In *Bushell's Case* (1670) jurors were jailed for refusing to convict William Penn (who later founded Pennsylvania) as the judge desired. On appeal to the King's Bench, the Court found in favor of the imprisoned jurors, holding that their verdict was not incommensurable with the evidence. Although the decision in *Bushell's Case* scored a victory for the integrity of the common law jury, Charles II and his successor, James II, were not deterred. Their agents browbeat jurors who defied the will of royalist judges, especially in the trials of nonconforming Protestant defendants. In his "bloody assizes," the Chief Justice of the King's Bench, Sir George Jeffreys, became the loyal executor of the king's demands that the criminal law punish religious dissent, even at the cost of overriding the findings of the jury. Political trials during the Restoration, like the "Popish Plot" (1678–1680), likewise renounced any semblance of due process. The defendants were charged with plotting to depose Charles II and replace him with James II. Not only were the accused held in close confinement without access to legal counsel or opportunity to confront adverse witnesses, but they also lacked knowledge of the charges against them. The later Stuart kings, in their willful disregard for the spirit of the English Common Law, provoked a backlash from English commoners.

That backlash came in the form of the "Glorious Revolution" of 1688, a velvet revolution that peacefully deposed James II and elevated William of Orange, a grandson of Charles I, to the throne. William's accession supplied the occasion for a renewal of the Common Law and adoption of a constitutional monarchy that would decisively circumscribe the power of the English monarch. William recognized the political supremacy of Parliament (as symbolized in William's instauration by Parliament). The divine right of kings in England had expired; henceforth, the king would acknowledge that he ruled with the consent of his English subjects. The Glorious Revolution produced an English Bill of Rights, a blend of both traditional and novel legal protections and privileges. Judges would hold their offices as long as they preserved "good behavior," rather than at the pleasure of the king, thereby minimizing royal interference in criminal trials. New laws guaranteed freedom of religion to Protestant nonconformists and dissenters, requiring that the English king could not be Catholic. After 1688, no standing army could exist without parliamentary approval, nor could the rights of Protestant subjects to carry weapons for their self-defense be infringed. As for criminal law, the English Bill of Rights immunized debates in Parliament from criminal prosecution, banned exorbitant fines or bail, restricted the king's ability to grant immunity from prosecution, prohibited cruel punishment, and mandated that jurors be returned and empaneled in accordance with accepted procedure. It required that defendants in trials for treason be given a copy of the indictment and access to defense counsel. In such trials, conviction was allowed only on the testimony of two or more witnesses (or by an uncoerced, in-court confession by the accused).

The Glorious Revolution should not be viewed as a triumph of democracy as we understand the word today. Instead, it shifted the site of power from the English monarch to Parliament, a body that represented the interests of the English elite. The Revolution thus established a constitutional monarchy and an aristocracy that would endure at least until the first Franchise Act of 1832, and even beyond to the outbreak of world war in 1914. This being said, Common Law courts emerged from the Revolution as vehicles for protecting the rights of English citizens against despotic power. The independence of judges, the autonomy of jurors to reach verdicts based on the evidence, and the rights of due process (e.g., freedom from self-incrimination, access to counsel) were all undeniable gains made possible by the Revolution. These were fundamental tenets of an ancient tradition of law, given new life in 1688, which dated back to the era of Henry II and the primogenitors of the Common Law.

The Legacy and Influence of the English Common Law

After 1688, England's Common Law courts functioned as the prime guarantor of constitutional rights until 1873, when they were placed under the control of Parliament. The old wine of the English Common Law was decanted into the new wineskins of Britain's overseas colonies and their legal systems. In the colonial U.S., for example, the colonists imported the substantive and procedural criminal principles imbedded in the English Common Law. Over time, many state legislatures codified these Common Law principles. In the late 1800s, the American jurist David Dudley Field published his "Field Code," a collection of uniform criminal and civil statutes and procedures based on the Common Law that was later adopted in whole or in part by states throughout the country, including New York. Today, the majority of states have abolished Common Law crimes, which have been assimilated into and statutorily defined by state penal codes. This trend notwithstanding, some U.S. states continue to acknowledge the legal efficacy of the Common Law. The Florida Criminal Code states: "The common law of England in relation to crimes, except so far as the same relates to the modes and degrees of punishment, shall be of full force in this state where there is no existing provision by statute on the subject." Arizona Revised Statutes echoes this language: "The common law only so far as it is consistent with … the natural and physical conditions of this state … is adopted and shall be the rule of decision in all courts of this state."

Periodically, defendants in state courts are charged with violations of the common law rather than a statutory provision. In 1996, Michigan prosecuted Dr. Jack Kevorkian under the state's common law against suicide. The jury acquitted Kevorkian on the ground that the common law was vague on the issue of assisted suicide. (Kevorkian was later convicted after Michigan passed a law making doctor-assisted suicide illegal.)

In other cases, resort to common law principles has met with greater success: where state law fails to define with specificity crimes like "manslaughter" or an element of murder like "malice," the common law often serves as a gapfiller to clarify the statute. Most U.S. states today, including those that have codified the Common Law, are "Common Law states"—i.e., Common Law principles are still in effect, although typically as sources for elucidating statutory provisions. Some states, on the other hand, are "code jurisdictions"; they have dispensed with all resort to Common Law precepts, declining to regard as a criminal offense actions that do not violate the statutory law of the state. Whether identified with Common Law states or Code Jurisdictions, the penal code of nearly every U.S. state embodies the principles and prohibitions of the Common Law, including defenses traditionally recognized under it.

The Common Law as it exists in the contemporary U.S. legal system is an artifact of Medieval and early modern England. The core of the Common Law in the U.S. today—*stare decisis*, due process, the rule of law, and trial by jury—all have archaic pedigrees. With its roots in ancient soil, shaped by centuries of conflict, struggle, and reform, modern American criminal law demonstrates, as a repository of a still vibrant Common Law tradition, its surprising continuity with the past.

MICHAEL BRYANT

References and Further Reading

Brewer, J. and Styles, J., *An Ungovernable People: The English and their Law in the Seventeenth and Eighteenth Centuries*, London, UK: Hutchinson, 1980.

Clanchy, M.T., *Early Medieval England*, London, UK: The Folio Society, 1996.

Holdsworth, *A History of English Law*, London, UK: Methuen & Co., 1937.

Hudson, J., *The Formation of the English Common Law*, London, UK: Longman, 1996.

Milsom, S.F.C., *The Legal Framework of English Feudalism*, Cambridge, UK: Cambridge University Press, 1976.

Milsom, S.F.C., *Historical Foundations of the Common Law*, Toronto, Canada: Butterworths, 1981.

Prall, S.E., *The Agitation for Law Reform during the Puritan Revolution*, 1640–1660, The Hague, the Netherlands: Martinus Nijhoff, 1966.

Stephens, Sir J.F., *A History of Criminal Law of England*, 3 Vols., London, UK: Macmillan & Co., 1883.

See also **United Kingdom, Crime and Justice in the**

Entrapment as a Defense to Criminal Liability

The entrapment defense is based on the belief that people should not be convicted of crimes that the government instigated. In its simplest form, the entrapment defense arises when government officials "plant the seeds" of criminal intent. That is, if a person commits a crime that he or she would not have otherwise committed but for the government's conduct, such a person might succeed with an entrapment defense. Entrapment is a frequent topic in both criminal law and criminal procedure. In the legal sense, it is a defense; in the procedural sense, it places restrictions on government actors by discouraging them from encouraging people to violate the law.

The first Supreme Court case recognizing the entrapment defense was *Sorrells v. U.S.* (287 U.S. 435, 1932). In that case, Justice Hughes stated: "We are unable to conclude that … [the] … processes of detection or enforcement should be abused by the instigation by government officials of an act on the part of persons otherwise innocent in order to lure them to its commission and punish them." This reasoning underlies the treatment of the entrapment defense in our nation's courts to this day.

Despite its apparent simplicity, the entrapment defense has been a contentious one. In particular, there has been some disagreement in the courts over what role the offender's predisposition plays and how far the government can go in order to lure a person into criminal activity. When entrapment decisions are based on the offender's predisposition, this is known as a "subjective" inquiry. By contrast, a focus on the governmental conduct presumably responsible for someone's decision to commit a crime is known as an "objective" inquiry.

The American Law Institute's Model Penal Code takes an objective approach with regard to the entrapment defense: if the government "employ[ed] methods of persuasion or inducement which create a substantial risk that such an offense will be committed by persons other than those who are ready to commit it," then the defense is available regardless of the offender's initial willingness to offend. The Supreme Court, however, has opted to focus on the (subjective) predisposition of the offender instead of the government's role in instigating the crime in question (e.g., *Hampton v. U.S.*, 425 U.S. 484, 1976).

In *Sorrells*, the defendant was charged with violating the National Prohibition Act. After two unsuccessful attempts, a law enforcement agent convinced the defendant to sell him whiskey. Chief Justice Hughes noted that "artifice and stratagem" are permissible methods of catching criminals, so entrapment did not occur. Instead, it was the defendant's predisposition to offend that was important.

In the next leading entrapment case, *Sherman v. U.S.* (356 U.S. 369, 1958), the Supreme Court reached the opposite conclusion but still adhered to the predisposition test. In that case, a government informant met the defendant at a doctor's office where both were being treated for narcotics addiction. After repeated requests by the informant, the defendant provided him with illegal narcotics. The Supreme Court reversed Sherman's conviction, noting that entrapment was "patently clear" as a matter of law, but the Court also pointed out that it is difficult to judge the conduct of informants without knowing how predisposed the offender was before the crime was committed.

In *U.S. v. Russell* (411 U.S. 423, 1973), the Court continued to focus on the defendant's predisposition. In *Russell*, a narcotics agent posed as a narcotics manufacturer and offered the defendant a difficult-to-obtain ingredient used to manufacture the drug. The defendant accepted and was convicted. Justice Rehnquist, author of the majority opinion, observed that there was sufficient predisposition on the part of the defendant, so the entrapment defense did not apply.

In *Hampton v. U.S.* (425 U.S. 484, 1976), the Supreme Court focused again on the defendant's predisposition. In that case, the defendant was convicted of distributing heroin supplied to the defendant by a government informant. The Court stated that "[i]f the police engage in illegal activity in concert with a defendant beyond the scope of their duties the remedy lies, not in freeing the equally culpable defendant, but in prosecuting the police under the applicable provisions of state or federal law." In other words, it is the defendant's predisposition that matters in the context of the entrapment defense, not the government conduct.

To suggest that the Supreme Court has ignored the role of government conduct is not entirely true. In a concurring opinion in *Hampton*, Justices Powell and Blackmun argued that government behavior that "shocks the conscience" conceivably violated due process. In their words, "there is certainly a limit to allowing governmental involvement in crime. … It would be unthinkable … to permit government agents to instigate robberies and beatings merely to gather evidence to convict other members of a gang of hoodlums."

The Supreme Court has yet to recognize affirmatively a due process-based defense to government entrapment, but some lower courts have. Generally, if government officials use violence, supply contraband that is wholly unobtainable, or engage in a "criminal enterprise," then defendants in such cases will often succeed with the entrapment defense based on a due process argument.

In *U.S. v. Twigg* (588 F.2d 373, 3rd Cir. 1978), the Court of Appeals for the Third Circuit found entrapment on due process grounds. In that case, Drug Enforcement Administration agents sought out a convicted felon, Kubica, and offered to reduce the severity of his sentence if he agreed to cooperate with them. At the request of the DEA, Kubica contacted another man, Neville, and suggested that they set up a laboratory to manufacture speed. Neville agreed, and the government supplied Kubica with glassware and a difficult-to-obtain ingredient used in the manufacture of speed. The government also made arrangements for purchasing the chemicals and even supplied an isolated farmhouse to serve as the laboratory. The court concluded that the government's conduct reached a "demonstrable level of outrageousness."

Thus, even though the Supreme Court has chosen to focus on the predisposition of the defendant, it is possible in certain situations that the government's conduct rises to such a level of "outrageousness" that a due process violation occurs. It is conceivable, then, that a predisposed defendant could succeed with an entrapment defense so long as the government conduct is sufficiently outrageous.

JOHN L. WORRALL

References and Further Reading

Daniels, R. 1988. Outrageousness! What does it really mean—An examination of the outrageous conduct defense. *Southwestern University Law Review*, 18, 105.

Gershman, B.L. 1982. Entrapment, shocked consciences, and staged arrest. *Minnesota Law Review*, 66, 567.

Marcus, P. 1986. The development of entrapment law. *Wayne Law Review*, 33, 5.

Park, R. 1976. The entrapment controversy. *Minnesota Law Review*, 60, 163.

Seidman, L.M. 1981. The Supreme Court, entrapment, and our criminal justice dilemma. *Superme Court Review*, 111.

Whelan, M.F.J. 1985. Lead us not into (unwarranted) temptation: A proposal to replace the entrapment defense with a reasonable suspicion requirement. *University of Pennsylvania Law Review*, 133, 1193.

See also **Defenses to Criminal Liability: Justifications and Excuses; Due Process**

Environmental Crimes

Global warming, acid rain, air pollution, and water pollution are all part of industrialized societies and are becoming increasingly dangerous to our health. Miscarriages, birth defects, cancers, skin rashes, and headaches have all been linked to environmental crimes. These dangers have been depicted in the media and the public has witnessed more cases of environmental catastrophes over the past several decades. Most Americans are familiar with Love Canal (August, 1978), which was one of the first known of these catastrophes in the U.S. Globally, the nuclear meltdown at Chernobyl (April, 1986) also ranks high among environmental tragedies. Recognizing an environmental crime may be obvious, but defining environmental crime is no easy matter. No single definition of environmental crime prevails.

According to Clifford (1998), an environmental crime is an act committed with the intent to harm or with a potential to cause harm to ecological and biological systems and for the purpose of securing business or personal advantage. Situ and Emmons (2000) define an environmental crime as an unauthorized act or omission that violates the law and is therefore subject to criminal prosecution and criminal sanctions. This offense harms or endangers people's physical safety or health as well as the environment itself.

Generally speaking, environmental crime violates existing environmental laws. Environmental crime victimizes people and the environment. Their victimization may be gradual and silent, going undetected for years. Although corporations are the chief environmental offenders, other organizations as well as individuals can also commit environmental crimes. For example, organized crime has infiltrated the waste disposal industry and illegally dumped hazardous contaminants. Local governments have shipped solid waste to prohibited sites. Individuals have contributed to the destruction of protected forests and wildlife. Vendors have sold contaminated meat and seafood to the public.

The public recognizes the severity of environmental crimes. More than a decade ago, a Bureau of Justice Statistics survey found that Americans believed environmental crimes to be more serious than a number of "traditional" crimes such as burglary or bank robbery. Similarly, a 1991 survey revealed that 84% of Americans believed that damaging the environment is a serious crime, and 75% believed that corporate officials should be held personally responsible for environmental offenses. But despite increased public concern, pollution still threatens public health and jeopardizes the ecological balance on a global scale.

The first serious threat to the environment and public health arose during the Industrial Revolution. Until the 1970s in the U.S., the prevailing view held that the environmental harm from industrial production was the unavoidable price for economic progress. A significant attempt to coordinate environmental protection efforts did not happen in the U.S. until 1970, when President Nixon created the U.S. Environmental Protection Agency (EPA) by executive order. Congress approved the creation of the agency and outlined as its objective the enforcement of all environmental laws in the U.S. During the succeeding years, between 1972 and 1982, Congress passed several major pieces of environmental protection legislation still in place today.

Hazardous waste enforcement probably constitutes the bulk of environmental investigation and prosecution. The Resource Conservation and Recovery Act of 1976 (RCRA), 42 U.S.C. 6901, established a framework for regulating hazardous waste from generation to disposal ("from cradle to grave"). The RCRA defines hazardous waste based on such characteristics as toxicity, reactivity, corrosivity, and flammability. The RCRA gives the EPA power to regulate hazardous waste labeling, containment, transportation and record keeping. The primary regulatory vehicles provided under RCRA include record keeping and reporting requirements for hazardous waste generators, and a complex permitting system for hazardous waste treatment, storage, and disposal facilities (TSDFs). All TSDFs must obtain permits requiring them to meet certain standards in the handling of hazardous waste.

Other components of the U.S. Federal environmental statutory and regulatory scheme include the Clean Air Act (CAA), 42 U.S.C. 7401, the Clean Water Act (CWA), 33 U.S.C. 1251, the Toxic Substances Control Act (TSCA), 15 U.S.C. 2601, the Federal Insecticide, Fungicide, and Rodenticide Act (FIFRA), 7 U.S.C. 136, the Comprehensive Environmental Resource Compensation and Liability Act (CERCLA), 42 U.S.C. 9601, and the Noise Control Act of 1972, 42 U.S.C. 4901. Each of these statutory schemes criminalizes certain acts as well as the falsification and in some instances the omission of information that is required by the government.

Overall responsibility for environmental compliance and enforcement rests with the EPA, although several other federal agencies also have responsibility for protecting the natural environment or managing environmental resources. States desiring to implement their own regulatory program are required to meet the minimum standards and procedures contained in RCRA. Most states have been delegated this authority.

Environmental crime is a serious global problem. Environmental crimes do have victims. The cumulative costs in environmental damage and the long-range toll in illness, injury, and death may be considerable. Estimating the extent of environmental crime is conceptually and practically very difficult. The problem is exacerbated because it may be years before the crimes, and their often devastating effects, are discovered.

Environmental crime may be divided into three basic categories. The first involves violation of permit conditions or other illegal acts committed by individuals or firms who are legally a part of the regulatory scheme. An example of this would be a business that bypasses its wastewater treatment plant in violation of its Clean Water Act permit and discharges untreated waste into a river. Another example is a waste-hauling firm that is permitted under TSCA but improperly disposes of hazardous waste while invoicing the generators as if legal disposal procedures had been followed. The second category involves acts committed by individuals or firms operating outside of the regulatory scheme—for example, the storage or disposal of hazardous waste without a RCRA permit. The third category of environmental crimes involves acts that would be illegal regardless of whether the actor was within the regulatory scheme. This category is exemplified by the classic "midnight dumper" who discharges hazardous waste at random alongside the highway.

A look at the illegal disposal of hazardous waste, probably the largest component of environmental crime, offers a glimpse of not only the potential immensity but also the difficulty in quantifying the problem. Estimates of the number of hazardous waste sites in the U.S. range from 4,000 to 50,000. Consensus is also lacking on the amount of hazardous waste generated annually. Although several widely cited studies from the mid-1980s claimed that the U.S. produces 245–275 million metric tons per year, these figures are subject to dispute.

Several factors account for the difficulty of developing precise figures regarding hazardous waste generation. First, hazardous waste is heterogeneous, including both liquids and solids and a large set of diverse chemicals. Because nonhazardous waste that is mixed with hazardous waste becomes legally hazardous waste itself, total quantities of hazardous waste generated are sensitive to changes in industrial practices and processes. For example, water used to flush out a container of hazardous waste may become legally hazardous. If firms use less water to clean these containers, the quantity of hazardous waste they generate will be smaller.

Estimation is also hampered by regulatory agencies' employment of conflicting definitions of hazardous waste. Moreover, both Federal and State definitions have changed over time as wastes are added to or removed from the list. The distinction between legally hazardous and nonhazardous waste can be subtle, and can vary from country to country, state to state, and county to county.

A third obstacle to obtaining an accurate estimate of hazardous waste generation is the difficulty in identifying the universe of hazardous waste generators and treatment, storage, and disposal facilities. As of 1990, the EPA reported that there were 211,000 generators of hazardous waste in the U.S. subject to RCRA regulation. The number had increased nine fold since 1980, due primarily to the addition of 118,000 small quantity generators to the regulated universe by the Hazardous and Solid Waste Amendments that took effect in 1985. In 1990, there were reported to be 4700 transportation, storage, and disposal facilities subject to RCRA. However, this list of firms that initially notified the EPA that they were generators included many that are not actually subject to RCRA regulation (many of these companies notified the EPA either mistakenly or protectively, to avoid any possible sanctions for failure to notify).

Although it is hard to estimate the number of environmental crimes occurring in the U.S., the picture becomes even bleaker when looking globally. Over the past 20 years environmental laws covering hazardous waste, toxic substances, and air and water pollution across the globe have become more complex and stringent. But paradoxically, the very laws and regulations designed to protect the environment may have contributed in several ways to increasing the incidence of environmental violations. Pervasive statutory inconsistencies, both within and across jurisdictions, and the scarcity of uniform codification of State environmental laws pose difficulties for prosecutors and offer environmental criminals opportunities to evade prosecution by moving their operations across jurisdictional lines. Thus, although the precise extent of illegal handling and disposal of hazardous waste is unknown, it is probably very large.

Because regulated businesses have found it increasingly expensive to comply with the new statutes, more and more are avoiding these costs, even if it means violating the law. Although there are still numerous instances of "midnight dumping," increasing numbers of businesses are consciously and systematically violating environmental laws to save money and increase profit margins (DeCicco and Bonanno, 1989). As the costs of legal disposal rise, the financial incentive for illegal disposal also increases, leading to more disposal in sewers or storm drains, evaporation, burial, abandonment on land, or transportation to other countries with less stringent regulations.

Explanations for inappropriate waste disposal by industry range from ignorance to conscious disregard for the harmful consequences in an attempt to reduce disposal costs. The availability of legal disposal facilities plays an important role in waste generator compliance with legal methods of disposal. Availability varies widely from country to country and state to state. In 1988, there was only one legally operating hazardous-waste land-disposal site in highly developed southern California and there were none in Florida.

Whereas some commentators allege that a combination of corporate naivete regarding environmental damage, corruption, and regulatory inefficiencies are the chief causes of illegal waste disposal (Rebovich, 1992), others take a less charitable view of generators. Because hazardous waste management generally receives a small share of a firm's resources and attention, a suspect generator may claim to be unaware of disposal regulations, its responsibility to comply, or even how to comply with known regulations. As new chemicals are being developed rapidly, the law may not be able to keep up with these changes. If the legislators have trouble keeping up with the law, then the employees may have even more difficulty in knowing that a new law has been passed and how to comply with it. The Code of Federal Regulations (CFR) for hazardous waste and environmental issues is vast and may not be understandable to everyone. Some executives have even stated that the review of regulations so complex is "like learning the Koran." On the other side are critics who view industry as disingenuously attempting to exonerate itself by claiming ignorance of the law and of the possible damage caused by what are today recognized as grossly substandard disposal methods.

Although the debate goes on, the public increasingly views these explanations of improper activity as questionable. The emerging view holds that toleration is declining for individuals or businesses that may consciously disregard potentially harmful consequences simply to reduce their waste disposal costs. Globally, the creation of new and more stringent laws and increased enforcement of environmental crimes has been the trend. Some environmental criminal law has already been adopted by an overwhelming majority of the nations of the world. Criminal environmental enforcement and prosecution are practiced in some measure by every industrialized nation. At the moment, environmental law remains the responsibility of each individual nation as no international environmental law or agency exists.

DEBRA E. ROSS

Further Reading

Celebrezze, A.J. et al., Criminal enforcement of state environmental laws: The Ohio solution, *Harvard Environmental Law Review* 14:217–218 (1990).

Clifford, M., *Environmental Crime: Enforcement, Policy and Social Responsibility*, Gaithersburg, MD: Aspen Publications, 1998.

Cohen, M.A., Environmental crime and punishment: Legal/economic theory and empirical evidence on enforcement of federal environmental statutes, *The Journal of Criminal Law and Criminology* 82(4):1054–1108 (1992).

DeCicco, J. and Bonanno, E., A comparative analysis of the criminal environmental laws of the fifty states: The need for statutory uniformity as a catalyst for effective enforcement of existing and proposed laws, *Florida State University Journal on Land Use and Environmental Laws* 5:1 (Summer 1989).

Edwards, S.M., Edwards, T.D., and Fields, C.B. (Eds.), *Environmental Crime and Criminality: Theoretical and Practical Issues*, Garland Publications, 1996.

Hammett, T.M. and Epstein, J., *Prosecuting Environmental Crime: Los Angeles County,* Washington, DC: U.S. Department of Justice, August 1993.

Hammett, T.M. and Epstein, J., *Local Prosecution of Environmental Crime,* Washington, DC: U.S. Department of Justice, June 1993.

Hammett, J.K. and Reuter, P., *Measuring and Deterring Illegal Disposal of Hazardous Waste: A Preliminary Assessment*, Santa Monica, CA: Rand Corporation, 1988.

McCarthy, J.E. and Reisch, M.E.A., *Hazardous Waste Fact Book*, Washington, DC: Congressional Research Service, 1987.

Rebovich, D.J., *Dangerous Ground: The World of Hazardous Waste Crime*, New Brunswick, NJ: Transaction Press, 1992.

Ross, D.E., Explanations of the factors related to hazardous waste crimes using the organizational field as the level of analysis, Ph.D. dissertation, Rutgers University, New Jersey, 1999.

Situ, Y. and Emmons, D., *Environmental Crime: The Criminal Justice System's Role in Protecting the Environment*, Thousand Oaks, CA: Sage Publications, 2000.

See also **Environmental Theory**

Environmental Theory

Crime does not occur randomly within the urban landscape. In cities, certain neighborhoods and certain streets have more crimes than others. Environmental criminology is a generic term that includes many different types of research centering on the analysis of the spatial distribution of crime within metropolitan regions, cities, or neighborhoods. The oldest tradition of research is the ecological approach that is derived mainly from a sociological perspective. The second tradition, much more recent and derived from urban geography, focuses on the spatial distribution of incidents or persons throughout the urban space. We will briefly present both traditions of research as well as their major theoretical foundations.

Social Disorganization and the Ecology of Crime

Adolphe Quetelet (1796–1874) and André Michel Guerry (1802–1866) were the first scholars to draw maps representing the quantity of known crimes across a given territory. By comparing maps of the different "moral statistics" (i.e., suicide, poverty, alcoholism, etc.), they could assess the possible causal connections between them. The term *social ecology*, pertaining to crime, was later applied to the work of early American urban sociologists Robert Park and Ernest Burgess (1928), and subsequently to that of Clifford Shaw and Henry McKay (1942). The work of the scholars from the University of Chicago sociology department, who mainly wrote in the first half of the 20th century, is now referred to as the Chicago School of criminology.

In their research, Shaw and McKay (1942) divided the city of Chicago into 1-square-mile sectors, measured the number of known juvenile delinquents in each sector, and then ran statistical analyses comparing those measures and various measures applied to the general population in those sectors. The geographic pattern of delinquency was found to fit a concentric model, or a pattern of declining rates of delinquency from the inner city neighborhoods to the outer city suburbs. The Chicago School is now known for innovations in both theory and research methods that led to a better understanding of the social causes or correlates of crime. The main concept developed to explain crime is social disorganization, which is a breakdown or weakness in a community's formal and informal social control mechanisms. Studying Chicago, Shaw and McKay (1942) found that areas of the city with abnormally high delinquency rates had three characteristics in common: poverty, ethnic heterogeneity, and residential mobility. These three variables might be viewed in two ways, i.e., as causes of social disorganization, or as indicators of social disorganization. Social disorganization "exists in the first instance when the structure and the culture of a community are incapable of implementing and expressing the values of its own residents" (Kornhauser, 1978, 63). Numerous studies have focused on the processes responsible for a social organization that is conducive to juvenile delinquency, but they are beyond the scope of this article (for a review, see Bursik, 1988).

Ecological studies are important in criminology because they provide a better understanding of the social conditions associated with higher rates of crime and violence. Although it is generally accepted that there are areas within cities where there are more crimes, more victims, and also more delinquents, it is not agreed upon whether the neighborhood itself has an independent effect on crime. Wilson and Herrnstein (1985) argue that high-crime areas are the result of a greater concentration of crime-prone individuals. On the contrary, Sampson, Raudenbush, and Earls (1997), using data from a large Chicago survey, show that social cohesion, or what they call neighborhood "collective efficacity," has a direct impact on the level of violence.

The social disorganization approach has been applied in a variety of countries and cities around the world by researchers such as DeFleur (1970) in Argentina, and Eisner and Wikstrom (1999), comparing Stockholm in Sweden and Basel in Switzerland. Although there are differences in the geographic distribution of crime and in offender concentrations (in the U.S., violence is more pronounced in the city core, whereas in Europe, violence is often more pronounced in the housing projects usually located on the outskirts of cities), the same basic ecological pattern is found almost everywhere, i.e., there is more crime and more violence in neighborhoods characterized by poverty and social disorganization.

If there are literally hundreds of ecological studies in criminology, there are also many different types of study designs used by researchers. This often makes it difficult to compare results from one study to another: one theory might work in a given context, whereas another theory might be more meaningful in another situation. There are two important design factors, namely, the aggregation level (how a city is divided into smaller areal units) and the type of dependent variable, namely, crime location or offender residence.

The first important element of the design is the choice of the aggregation level. Cross-sectional ecological studies have been done at different levels of aggregation, namely, census blocks, census tracts, neighborhoods, cities, SMSAs, counties, states, and countries. It is generally agreed that *intraurban*—or neighborhood—research is conceptually different from *intercity* or *interstate* research (Byrne and Sampson, 1986). In their landmark study, Shaw and McKay (1942) used areas of Chicago corresponding to approximately 1 square mile. However, there are two typical aggregation levels used in modern ecological research: neighborhoods (such as wards or police precincts) and census tracts. The choice of one aggregation level over another has an impact on the magnitude and significance of the coefficients that will be obtained (Ouimet, 2000). This is understandable because larger areal units should produce homogenization in the measures (i.e., smaller variance) and therefore, have greater explanatory potential. However, larger areal units will also mean a smaller number of cases, which affects statistical significance tests through a reduction in the degree of freedom.

The second important element of the design is the choice between the use of the crime rate or the offender rate. Shaw and McKay (1942) were analyzing factors that might explain the distribution of the delinquency rate across different sectors of Chicago. Their delinquency measure was a ratio between the number of youths residing in each area appearing before a juvenile court for a given year and the number of youths living in each area. It was believed that social forces play a role in the etiology of delinquency at the individual level, which is reflected in the percentage of youths in each area who are officially identified as delinquent. Social disorganization theories are then usually tested by analyzing the area of residence of the delinquents. However, Turner (1969) suggested that a high-delinquency area could also be one in which many delinquent events occur. Using the place of occurrence of the crime informs us about the proximal causes of the crime. There are areas within each city where youths are more likely to commit their crimes: there might, for example, be more vulnerable targets or less surveillance in certain areas. Thus, the juvenile crime rate should be a better dependent variable than the delinquency rate for testing opportunity level variables. However, Cohen and Felson (1979) hypothesized that changes in opportunity across time or space might very well influence the delinquency level (i.e., the number of motivated offenders). Therefore, the role of opportunities as a cause of crime at the individual level has not been ruled out. In his study of crimes and delinquents in Philadelphia, Turner (1969) found a positive correlation between the juvenile delinquency rate and the juvenile crime rate. Areas with higher delinquency rates also have higher crime rates than others, presumably because delinquents commit most of their offenses close to their homes. Turner also observed that areas with many targets—such as areas with many shops, stores, and theaters—are those most likely to be targeted by delinquents who commit their crimes away from home. Hesseling (1992) compared variables accounting for variations in the property crime rate and the violent crime rate across the city of Utrecht. He found that "violent crimes in neighbourhoods are more often the result of the residence of offenders in these neighbourhoods, while the variation in property crimes is more often the result of differences in opportunity structure."

Opportunity Theory and the Spatial Analysis of Crime

In 1979, Cohen and Felson published an article showing how changes in peoples' daily activity routines account for increases in overall crime rates. It was argued that there has been an increase in criminal opportunities consequent to changes in peoples' daily routines. Although the first-generation opportunity research was typically done at a fairly high level of aggregation (such as at the state or national level), more recent tests have been done at the neighborhood level. A major problem with opportunity studies is that measures of opportunity have often been inferred from census material rather than being measured directly. For example, in Cohen and Felson's original research (1979), the "household activity ratio" includes female labor force participants and the number of nonhusband or nonwife households. These dimensions may be related to opportunities (with more women on the job market and more single-person households, there are more empty houses to burglarize), but they may also be related to economic hardship and poverty in general. Carroll and Jackson (1983) argued that Cohen and Felson's results might be interpreted as giving credit to the role of poverty and inequality in crime. In sum, a major problem with the opportunity theory model is that direct measures of opportunity that are conceptually and empirically different from social disorganization measures have generally not been tested.

Besides macro-level opportunity research, there are a growing number of micro-level opportunity studies. The theory behind spatial analysis or the criminology of place is based on Cohen and Felson's (1979) crime opportunity model. According to the model, there is a crime opportunity when a motivated offender, a suitable target and the absence of a capable guardian converge in time and space. It is interesting to note that technological advances, both in the maintenance of crime databases by police agencies and in the development of sophisticated computer mapping programs (such as Mappoint, Mapinfo, and Arcinfo) that are now relatively cheap and easy to use, have made it possible for researchers and practitioners to analyze spatial data relating to crime. Most studies in that field are based on a careful examination of the distribution of crime plotted against a street map grid. The idea is to look for specific concentrations of crime at different times of the day or on different days of the week. Those studies have shown that crimes are more frequent in areas surrounding subway stations (Block and Davis, 1996), schools (Roncek and Faggiani, 1985), shopping malls (Brantingham, Brantingham, and Wong, 1990) and bars (Roncek and Maier, 1991). Hence, there are some kinds of services that are "crime generators," presumably because they tend to put together would-be offenders and attractive targets. Moreover, malls, subway stations, and bars attract young people who often have nothing to do, thus creating conditions that can lead to conflicts escalating into fights.

One particular application of spatial analysis has been the "journey-to-crime" research, in which the crime trips of offenders are studied. LeBeau (1992) has analyzed the movement patterns of serial rapists. The main finding of this type of research has been that offenders tend to select a victim near their place of residence or their place of work. Areas located in the paths of the home-to-work trip also have a higher probability of being selected by offenders. Advances in the theory and methods of journey-to-crime research have led to a direct application of spatial analysis in the investigation of homicides and sexual aggressions. Rossmo (2000) has written the first book on geographic profiling methods that can be used with serial offenders. The text shows how by studying the spatial clues left by a serial offender (such as where the contacts with the victims were made, where the bodies were dumped, etc.), analysts can map out a "probability surface" where the offender is likely to reside.

A second application of the concepts developed in the spatial analysis of crime is in situational crime prevention. Newman (1972) was among the first to look at micro maps of crime, representing crime locations within one city block or one housing project. He realized that crimes were likely to occur at very specific places on a given housing estate. He then saw that by using simple tools such as small symbolic fences or lighting, it might be possible to reduce the level of crime. There are also important security or anticrime strategies that should be taken into account in the design of new public facilities. For Clarke (1995), situational crime prevention means carefully examining the crime problem in a particular place—such as a shopping mall, a subway station or a car parking lot—and then designing strategies to tackle the problem.

A third application of the spatial analysis of crime is in the development of methods for analyzing the spatial distribution of crime within a city. Mathematical models developed from geography are applied to produce contour maps that show the major concentrations of crime within a city or crime pattern displacements from hour to hour, day to day, or season to season (Brantingham and Brantingham, 1984; Ratcliffe, 2002). Another specific innovation has centered on the use of computer programs to identify the presence of "hot spots" of crime within a city, i.e., small areas in the city that contain a disproportionate number of offenses. The computer programs can generate ellipses onto a map to describe these hot spots. Recent developments in the world of policing, such as the COMPSTAT program adopted in New York City (Silverman, 1999), include the daily or weekly analysis of crime statistics in different precincts by using histograms to detect surges and maps to identify their locations and then attacking those problems in a timely manner. The emergence of a new intelligence-led policing style holds out great promise for the future.

MARC OUIMET

References and Further Reading

Block R. and Davis, S. (1996). Environs of rapid transit stations: A focus for street crime or just another place? Clarke, R.V. (Ed.), *Preventing Mass Transit Crime*, Monsey, NY: Criminal Justice Press/Willow Tree Press, 237–257.

Brantingham, P.J. and Brantingham, P.L. (1984). *Patterns in Crime*. New York, NY: Macmillan.

Brantingham, P.L., Brantingham, P.J., and Wong, P.S. (1990). Malls and Crime. A First Look. *Security Journal*, 1: 175–181.

Bursik, R.J. (1988). Social disorganisation and theories of crime and delinquency: problems and prospects. *Criminology*, 26 (45): 519–552.

Byrne, J.M. and Sampson, R. (1986). Key issues in the social ecology of crime. Byrne and Sampson (Eds.), *The Social Ecology of Crime*, New York, NY: Springer-Verlag.

Carroll, L. and Jackson, P.I. (1983). *Inequality, Opportunity, and Crime Rates in Central Cities. Criminology*, 21 (2): 178–194.

Clarke, R.V. (1995). Situational crime prevention. Tonry and Farrington (Eds.), *Building a Safer Society: Strategic Approaches to Crime Prevention, Crime and Justice*, Vol. 19, Chicago, IL: University of Chicago Press, 91–150.

Cohen, L.E. and Felson, M. (1979). Social change and crime rate trends: A routine activity approach. *American Sociological Review*, 44 (4): 588–608.

DeFleur, L.B. (1970). *Delinquency in Argentina: A Study of Córdoba's Youth*. Pullman, WA: Washington State University.

Eisner, M. and Wikstrom, P.O. (1999). Violent crime in the urban community: A comparison of Stockholm and Basel. *European Journal on Criminal Policy and Research*, 7 (4): 427–442.

Hesseling, R.B.P. (1992). Using data on offender mobility in ecological research. *Journal of Quantitative Criminology*, 8 (1): 95–112.

Kornhauser, R. (1978). *Social Sources of Delinquency.* Chicago, IL: Chicago University Press.

LeBeau, J.L. (1992). Four case studies illustrating the spatial-temporal analysis of serial rapists. *Police Studies*, 15 (3): 124–145.

Newman, O. (1972). *Defensible Space, Crime Prevention through Urban Design.* New York, NY: Macmillan.

Ouimet, M. (2000). Aggregation bias in intracity ecological delinquency research: Testing social disorganization and opportunity theory at three area levels. *Canadian Journal of Criminology*, 42 (2): 135–156.

Park, R.E. and Burgess, E.W. (1928). *The City.* Chicago, IL: University of Chicago Press.

Ratcliffe, J.H. (2002). Aoristic signatures and the temporal analysis of high volume crime patterns. *Journal of Quantitative Criminology*, 18 (1): 23–43.

Roncek, D.W. and Maier, P. (1991). Bars, blocks, and crimes revisited: Linking the theory of routine activities to the empiricism of hot spots. *Criminology*, 29 (4): 725–754.

Roncek, D.W. and Faggiani, D. (1985). High Schools and Crime—A Replication. *Sociological Quarterly*, 26 (4): 491–505.

Rossmo, K.D. (2000). *Geographic Profiling.* Boca Raton, FL: CRC Press.

Sampson, R.J., Raudenbush, S.W., and Earls, F. (1997). Neighborhood and Violent Crime: A multilevel study of collective efficacity. *Science*, 277: 1–7.

Shaw, C.R. and McKay, H.D. (1942). *Juvenile Delinquency in Urban Areas.* Chicago, IL: University of Chicago Press.

Silverman, E.B. (1999). *NYPD Battles Crime: Innovative Strategies in Policing.* Boston, MA: Northeastern University Press.

Turner, S. (1969). The ecology of delinquency. Sellin and Wolfgang (Eds.), *Delinquency: Selected Studies*, New York, NY: John Wiley and Sons.

Wilson, J.Q. and R. Herrnstein (1985). *Crime and Human Nature.* New York, NY: Simon and Schuster.

See also **Social Disorganization Theory**

Equal Protection

Section 1 of the Fourteenth Amendment to the U.S. Constitution provides that a state shall not deny the equal protection of the laws to any person within its jurisdiction. Ratified in the wake of the Civil War and originally designed to protect African Americans from discrimination by state officials, the equal protection clause of the Fourteenth Amendment has been the subject of many Supreme Court and lower court decisions and is frequently invoked by criminal defendants in challenging the constitutionality of their arrests, prosecutions, or detentions. Similarly, the Fifth Amendment's due process clause operates to protect individuals from discrimination by the U.S. government and has been interpreted by the Supreme Court in a fashion nearly identical to the Fourteenth Amendment's equal protection clause (*Johnson v. Robison*, 415 U.S. 361, 1974). Thus, citizens and noncitizens alike are constitutionally guaranteed equal treatment under the law by all governmental entities, including the federal government, state governments, and local governments that derive their authority from the states.

The equal protection clause does not prohibit the government from making legitimate distinctions between persons or groups in adopting laws or policies. Rather, it requires only that similarly situated individuals be treated in a similar manner. Furthermore, the equal protection clause is violated only by purposeful or intentional discrimination. Accidental, unintentional, or even negligent discrimination does not violate the constitution. Generally speaking, the guarantee of equal protection is violated only when governmental actors treat persons or groups differently *because* of their status and not merely *in spite* of any differential impact that a law or policy might have on them. Even then, most laws or policies that treat some people differently than others will withstand constitutional scrutiny so long as they are rational and further a legitimate governmental interest or purpose.

The equal protection clause operates to prevent intentional discrimination in two broad categories of governmental action. First, it prevents intentional discrimination in the passage or adoption of laws or policies that contain express classifications. In other words, policies that by their express language treat persons or groups differently must at least be rational, and as explained below, may be subject to heightened scrutiny under the equal protection clause. Secondly, the equal protection clause prohibits the intentional and unequal enforcement of even facially neutral law or policies. Thus, even if a policy does not, on its face, treat some groups differently from others, it is still subject to scrutiny under equal protection principles if it is intentionally applied in a discriminatory manner.

Constitutional Review of Express Classifications

Statutes that contain express classifications are subject to varying levels of constitutional review, depending upon the nature of the class or right that is treated differently by the statute. Laws are presumed to be constitutional and will usually be upheld if they are rationally related to a legitimate government interest. Laws that regulate social or economic activities, including most criminal laws, are subject only to this low level of review. At the other end of the review spectrum are statutes that make distinctions among groups based on constitutionally suspect criteria. Suspect classifications subject to strict constitutional scrutiny include race, religion, national origin, and alienage. Statutes that classify according to these suspect criteria are closely scrutinized under the equal protection clause and must be narrowly tailored to further a compelling state interest. In between rational basis and strict scrutiny lies intermediate scrutiny, which has been applied by the Supreme Court to classifications based on gender and illegitimacy. Laws that classify by sex or one's status as an illegitimate child must be closely tailored to effectuate an important government interest.

Discriminatory Enforcement of Racially Neutral Statutes

Criminal defendants often allege that they (or members of their class) have been discriminated against by various actors within the criminal justice system. Their complaints lie not with the language embodied in a particular law or policy but in the manner in which the law or policy was enforced. Complaints about racial profiling by police or discriminatory sentencing by judges are examples of these types of claims. The Supreme Court has held that a criminal defendant alleging discriminatory enforcement of a racially neutral policy must demonstrate that the policy both had a discriminatory effect and was motivated by a discriminatory purpose. Purposeful discrimination does not require proof of racial animus but does require evidence that the decision maker chose to enforce the policy against the defendant because of his or her membership in a particular group or class and not merely in spite of any adverse effects the enforcement might have on the group of which the defendant is a member. Moreover, in proving the discriminatory effect prong of the test, the Court has held that defendants (or plaintiffs in civil lawsuits) must show that the policy was not enforced against similarly situated persons of some other group or class (*U.S. v. Armstrong*, 517 U.S. 456, 1996).

Equal Protection and the Criminal Law

Criminal laws classify persons in a myriad of ways, and yet most easily pass muster under a rational basis level of equal protection review. Laws treat misdemeanants differently from felons, murderers differently than shoplifters, and repeat offenders differently from first time offenders. Such classifications are rational and further legitimate state interests in prosecuting and punishing criminals based on justifiable differences among them. Some criminal laws, however, apply only to certain classes of persons, such as men or women, whereas the burdens of others fall disproportionately on certain racial groups. For example, under federal sentencing guidelines, the possession or sale of crack cocaine is treated significantly more harshly than the possession or sale of the same amount of powdered cocaine. Defendants have challenged these provisions on the ground that they are racially discriminatory because crack cocaine convictions fall disproportionately on poor Blacks, whereas powdered cocaine use is more prevalent among wealthier Whites. The cocaine-sentencing provisions contained in the guidelines have been upheld under rational basis review for a variety of race-neutral reasons (*U.S. v. Mathews*, 168 F.3d 1234, 1999).

The Supreme Court has also upheld statutory rape laws that punish males but not females, even though these laws involve a gender classification that ordinarily would subject them to a higher level of equal protection scrutiny. In *Michael M. v. Superior Court of Sonoma County* (1981), a 17-year-old boy was charged under California's statutory rape law, which made it a crime for a male to have consensual sexual intercourse with a female under the age of 18 who was not his wife. The statute did not similarly punish the female involved in the act. The boy challenged his conviction on equal protection grounds, arguing that the statute unconstitutionally discriminated against males. In upholding the constitutionality of the statute, the Court noted that the statute bore a fair and substantial relationship to the legitimate state goal of preventing teenage pregnancies and the harmful effects that they have on women. Because young men and women are not similarly situated when it comes to the physical, psychological, and emotional consequences of pregnancy, the Court held that it was reasonable to punish men for statutory rape and not women.

The intersection between sexuality and the criminal law has long been the subject of heated constitutional debate and equal protection challenges. In 1986, the Supreme Court upheld the conviction of a Georgia man under a state sodomy statute that punished private, homosexual conduct between consenting adults (*Bowers v. Hardwick*, 478 U.S. 186, 1986). The Court held that such conduct was not protected as a fundamental right under the due process clause of the Fourteenth Amendment. In 2003, this issue was again before the Court, which reversed its decision in *Bowers* and struck down a Texas statute that similarly punished private homosexual conduct between adults (*Lawrence v. Texas*, 123 S. Ct. 2472, 2003). Although the four-justice plurality rested its decision on substantive due process grounds (which it had rejected in *Bowers*), Justice O'Connor concurred in the Court's judgment on a different theory. She believed that the Texas sodomy statute violated the equal protection clause. Applying rational basis review, she stated that moral disapproval of homosexual behavior was not a legitimate state interest that could be used to justify the constitutionality of the Texas sodomy statute. Thus, according to Justice O'Connor, the statute failed even rational basis review and must be struck down as unconstitutional.

In the arena of the criminal law, courts give legislatures wide latitude in crafting statutes to punish socially harmful behavior. Criminal statutes start with a presumption of constitutionality, and if challenged on equal protection grounds, most are upheld under rational basis review. Only when criminal laws touch upon suspect classes or impact fundamental rights are they possibly subject to a more searching constitutional analysis. And even then, few judges appear willing to strike down criminal statutes as violative of the equal protection clause.

Equal Protection Challenges to the Administration of Justice

Racial minorities, and particularly Blacks and Hispanics, are overrepresented at most stages of the criminal justice process. As a result, many criminal justice scholars, and perhaps most minority citizens, believe that the criminal justice system is discriminatory. Allegations of discrimination begin at the earliest stages of the criminal process, when citizens first come into contact with the police.

Equal Protection and the Police

The police in America have a long and ignoble history with minority citizens. The Civil Rights movement of the 1960s and the many inner-city clashes between Black citizens and the police served to expose the tension and animosity that has often characterized police–minority relations. Over the last 40 years, sociologists and criminal justice researchers have extensively studied the treatment of minorities by police. Many studies have been conducted on whether minorities are more likely to be arrested than Whites and on whether they are subjected to higher rates of police violence or deadly force. Recently, national attention has focused on the problem of "racial profiling" and whether minority drivers are targeted by police for differential treatment in traffic stops. The common denominator with most of these studies is that evidence of police discrimination is ambiguous and findings of disparity are subject to competing interpretations.

One area where the research is fairly clear is in the identification of disparity in the use of deadly force by police against minority citizens. Compared to their distribution in the population at large, minorities are significantly more likely than Whites to be shot and killed by police (Geller and Scott, 1992). Beyond that, few definitive conclusions can be reached. A variety of explanations have surfaced in the literature for the overrepresentation of minorities in police shootings, most of which do not support a discrimination hypothesis. Researchers have found that police killings of minorities are attributable to factors such as differential involvement in felony arrests, higher rates of violence in inner cities, and a higher incidence of failing to comply with police orders, among others (Locke, 1995).

In contrast, Worden's 1995 reanalysis of older observational data from the 1970s found that police use of nonlethal force was influenced by suspect race, even after controlling for suspect resistance and demeanor. The data analyzed by Worden, however, are 25 years old, and much has changed in policing during the intervening years. More recent studies of nonlethal force have found no relationship between suspect race and the likelihood or severity of force used by police (Alpert and Dunham, 1998; Garner, Maxwell, and Heraux, 2002).

Much of inconsistency in the literature on the effect of suspect race on police behavior is because of the methodological limitations of many of the existing studies. Researchers have been unable to explain much of the variation in police behavior toward minorities or have been unable to rule out nondiscriminatory explanations for the over-involvement of minorities in police contacts, arrests, or shootings. Minority citizens, though, have long been distrustful of the police and beliefs about police discrimination are firmly entrenched in the cultures of most minority groups. These beliefs continue to pose significant challenges to progressive law enforcement administrators who seek to reach out and work closely with minority communities.

Equal Protection and Prosecutorial Discretion

Prosecutors occupy perhaps the most powerful position in the criminal justice system. They have virtually unfettered discretion to charge and bring to trial persons arrested by the police. They, and they alone, decide who to charge, what charges to bring, how many charges to file, whether to offer or accept a plea bargain, and what the terms of a plea bargain should entail. Nonetheless, they are not supposed to base charging decisions on illegitimate criteria such as a defendant's race. Selective prosecution based on a defendant's race is grounds for a lawsuit, although courts are reluctant to interfere with the traditionally broad discretion invested in the office of the prosecutor (*U.S. v Armstrong*, 1996).

Relatively few studies have been done on the effects of race on prosecutorial decision making. Not surprisingly, those few studies have reached different conclusions. Some researchers have found that race had no effect on charging decisions, whereas others have found substantial race effects, even after controlling for the seriousness of the crime, a defendant's prior record, age, gender, and other relevant charging criteria (Walker, Spohn, and DeLone, 2004). Conscious or unconscious bias is most likely to appear at decision-making points that involve a great degree of discretion. As elected officers who operate largely without judicial oversight, prosecutors have greater discretion than other criminal justice officials, all of whom are more constrained by law and policy. Consequently, it would be surprising if race did not influence their charging and plea bargaining decisions, and the weight of the empirical evidence seems to support this conclusion.

Equal Protection and Sentencing

Historically, judges, like prosecutors, have been invested with broad discretion, particularly when it comes to sentencing. The last 20 years has seen a decrease in judicial sentencing discretion as the federal system and now most states have imposed sentencing guidelines designed to minimize disparities in sentencing outcomes. Sentencing guidelines typically constrain judicial discretion by offering a limited range of months or years to which judges must sentence defendants, depending on factors such the severity of the crime committed, a defendant's criminal history, and assistance rendered by the defendant to the police or prosecutor. Theoretically, the application of sentencing guidelines should result in similar sentences for similarly-situated defendants and should minimize the role of inappropriate criteria such as race.

The best available research on racial disparities in sentencing has been conducted on sentences handed out by federal judges under the federal sentencing guidelines. In one of the most comprehensive studies of federal sentencing practices, McDonald and Carlson (1993) analyzed federal sentencing data on those sentenced prior to the implementation of the guidelines and those sentenced after the guidelines went into effect. They found that prior to the full implementation of the guidelines, White, Black, and Hispanic defendants received similar sentences. However, after the guidelines went into effect, Hispanic and Black offenders were more likely than Whites to receive prison terms. Black defendants received longer prison terms than Whites as well, whereas White and Hispanic prison terms were approximately equal. Most, but not all, of the disparity between Blacks and Whites in sentence length was accounted for by the greater proportion of Black defendants convicted of trafficking in crack cocaine, which carried substantially longer average prison terms than trafficking in powdered cocaine.

Research on racial disparities under sentencing guidelines remains inconclusive (Warner, 2001). Guidelines have had the unintended effect of transferring sentencing discretion from judges to prosecutors. By manipulating charges filed and other relevant factors under the guidelines, prosecutors can now largely determine the sentencing range to which a defendant will be sentenced if convicted. The result is that discretion constrained at one point in the criminal justice system reappears at an earlier point in the process, making prosecutorial discretion an even more important focus of research on possible racial bias.

Race and the Death Penalty

Although the influence of race on sentencing outcomes is mixed, its effect on the administration of the death penalty is more clear. The Supreme Court's landmark decision in the case of *McCleskey v. Kemp,* 481 U.S. 279 (1987), served to focus national attention on possible racial discrimination in the imposition of the death penalty in the U.S. The defendant in *McCleskey* challenged his death sentence in Georgia on the ground that Georgia's death penalty system violated the equal protection clause and was cruel and unusual under the Eighth Amendment. In support of his equal protection claim, he relied on a sophisticated statistical study of death penalty outcomes in Georgia, which showed that Black defendants who killed White victims were substantially more likely to receive the death penalty than other defendant–victim racial combinations. Interestingly, the study showed no aggregate effects of defendant race alone on the likelihood of receiving death. Acknowledging the statistical disparities, the Supreme

Court nonetheless rejected McCleskey's constitutional challenge and held that he had not proven that criminal justice officials in Georgia intentionally discriminated against him because of his race, which, they stated, was a prerequisite to proving an equal protection violation.

Although public support for the death penalty remains strong, it has come under increasing attack in recent years for being administered in a discriminatory fashion. Additional research from other states has found race-of-victim effects similar to those in Georgia. A recent study from Maryland found that the race of the defendant had no influence on the imposition of a death sentence once relevant case characteristics were controlled for. However, defendants who killed Whites were significantly more likely than others to have prosecutor seek the death penalty, were less likely to have a death-eligible charge withdrawn, and were more likely to actually receive a death sentence following the penalty phase of a capital case (Paternoster and Brame, 2003). Likewise, a 2001 study of North Carolina's death penalty system also revealed that the race of the victim influenced the likelihood of a death sentence; the odds of receiving a death sentence were at least three and half time higher for those who killed White victims compared to minority victims (Unah and Boger, 2001).

Surprisingly, most empirical research studies on the death penalty have not shown overt race-of-defendant effects. By itself, a defendant's race does not usually predict an increased likelihood of receiving a death sentence. Instead, racial influences on the death penalty are more nuanced and center around the race of the victim and defendant–victim race interactions. Clearly, race has no legitimate role to play at any point in the imposition of society's most severe sanction. But perhaps it is the lack of overt discrimination against minority defendants in death penalty cases that has dampened some of the criticism of the death penalty on racial grounds.

Conclusion

The U.S. Constitution guarantees that all persons will be treated equally in the eyes of the law and by those who administer it. In a complex and multicultural society like the U.S., though, benefits and burdens will inevitably fall more heavily on some groups than on others. The Constitution does not require complete equality. It requires only that similarly situated persons be treated the same. Unfortunately, minorities are rarely similarly situated to Whites in American society. By almost every measure of social and economic welfare, Blacks and Hispanics are less well-off than Whites. These disadvantages manifest themselves in disproportionate minority involvement in the criminal justice system. Moreover, the system itself is a microcosm of society and contains all of the prejudices, stereotypes, and unconscious biases of the nation that it serves. Justice in the 21st century, though, demands that criminal justice officials work to identify and eliminate racial bias wherever it may appear.

Michael R. Smith

References and Further Reading

Alpert, G.P. and Dunham, R. *An Analysis of Police Use of Force Data*, Final Report submitted to the National Institute of Justice, 1998.

Garner, J.H., Christopher, D.M., and Cedrick, G.H. Characteristics associated with the prevalence and severity of force used by the police. *Justice Quarterly*, 19, 4, 705–746.

Geller, W.A. and Michael, S.S. *Deadly Force: What We Know—A Practitioner's Desk-Reference on Police-Involved Shootings*, Washington, DC: Police Executive Research Forum, 1992.

Locke, H.G. The color of law and the issue of color: Race and the abuse of police power, in *And Justice for All: Understanding and Controlling Police Abuse of Force*, Washington, DC: Police Executive Research Forum, 1995, 133–150.

McDonald, D.C. and Carlson, K.E. *Sentencing in the Federal Courts: Does Race Matter?* Washington, DC: U.S. Department of Justice, 1993.

Paternoster, R. and Brame, R. *An Empirical Analysis of Maryland's Death Sentencing System with Respect to the Influence of Race and Legal Jurisdiction*. College Park: University of Maryland, 2003.

Unah, I. and Boger, R. *Race and the Death Penalty in North Carolina an Empirical Analysis: 1993–1997*. Raleigh, NC: Common Sense Foundation, 2001.

Walker, S., Spohn, C., and DeLone, M. *The Color of Justice: Race, Ethnicity, and Crime in America*, 3rd ed., Belmont, CA: Wadsworth, 2004.

Warner, D.E. Race and ethnic bias in sentencing decisions: A review and critique of the literature, in *The System in Black and White: Exploring Connections Between Race Crime and Justice*, Markowitz, M.W. and Jones-Brown, D.D. (Eds.), Westport, CT: Praeger, 2001, 171–180.

Worden, R.E. The 'Causes' of police brutality: Theory and evidence on police use of force, in *And Justice for All: Understanding and Controlling Police Abuse of Force*, Washington, DC: Police Executive Research Forum, 1995, 31–60.

See also **Discrimination in Justice; Race and Ethnicity and Criminal Behavior**

Espionage *See* **Treason and Sedition**

Euthanasia and Physician-Assisted Suicide

Euthanasia is an ancient concept as old as the ages, whereas assisted suicide is a New Age concept, which developed primarily in the last decade of the recently ended millennium, and the two are embraced by the term "medical aid in dying." In order to engage in a discussion regarding the criminological implications, especially the criminalization and decriminalization of euthanasia and assisted suicide, it is essential to establish the basic definitional terms. Euthanasia is, at its most basic level, the acceleration, causing or hastening of death, particularly where the patient is incurably or terminally ill. Euthanasia may be active, where there is a positive act by a physician or another, which is intended to bring about the death of a patient, such as the administration of a lethal injection. Alternatively, euthanasia may be passive, denoting an act of omission or commission, whereby a patient's treatment, nutrition, and hydration are discontinued. These acts of another may be with the voluntarily expressed consent of a patient; nonvoluntary, where a patient is in a persistent vegetative state; or involuntary, such as in the notorious Nazi euthanasia program.

Assisted suicide is distinguishable in that it is not the doctor or medical staffer who is the primary actor. Rather, the patient commits the life-shortening act, while the physician provides the means, such as by prescribing lethal doses of barbiturates or painkillers, which the patient then takes at the time and in the manner of his or her own choosing. It is important to note that under Anglo-American law, suicide has been decriminalized; however, in many jurisdictions, assisting in a suicide has been unlawful or even made a crime (as in Michigan, see *People v. Kevorkian*, 2001WL 1474986 [Mich.App.], No. 221758 Ct. App. Mi. 2001). As an aside, though important in criminal justice terminology, mercy killing has been and remains a crime, despite relaxed standards in some jurisdictions regarding medical euthanasia or physician-assisted suicide. This is because mercy killing is generally seen as nonmedical in either intent or cause of death, and as criminally culpable in nature, notwithstanding the fact that there is usually a humanitarian or compassionate motive (such as where someone shoots, suffocates, or administers poison to a terminally ill parent, spouse, partner, child, or friend).

Two central issues in criminal trials regarding euthanasia in the past century are the cause of death of the decedent and the intent of the actor (in assisted suicide cases, intent is, by definition, not in issue). Hence, if a patient is suffering from an imminently terminal illness and a doctor administers a potentially lethal dose of morphine or an injection of potassium chloride, or deliberately injects air bubbles into arteries, there still remains an argument that the patient in fact died in the moments before the drugs would have taken effect. All of the scenarios described above arise from real cases in which the result was either a prosecution for a lesser, related offence or an acquittal at trial or a suspended sentence after trial. Central to presentation of this issue is that the prosecuting attorneys are unable to prove whether the cause of death is from the act of the accused or from the underlying illness, with the result that an essential element of the crime cannot be proven beyond a reasonable doubt.

The issue of the intent of the person accused of euthanasia or physician-assisted suicide is frequently argued, and in fact on both sides of the Atlantic, the defense of double effect has been successfully presented. Essentially, in these cases, the physician acknowledges that there was a treatment (usually the administration of pharmaceuticals) that would have resulted in the inevitable shortening of life or hastening of death; however, the primary intent of administering the drugs was to relieve pain and suffering, with the secondary (and theoretically unintended) effect of hastening death. Another defense that has been used is that of mistake or of accidental overdose.

In the past 25 years, the question of criminal liability for those who might engage in conduct constituting euthanasia has been increasingly challenged. In the seminal case following the tragic events leading to the case brought by the parents of Karen Ann Quinlan (see *In re Quinlan*, 70 N.J. 10, 355A.2d 647, 1976 N.J. LEXIS 181, 79 A.L.R.3d 205, 1976), who sought guardianship so as to remove their daughter from life support, one of the issues was whether and what criminal liability might result. Subsequent to this, both doctors and patients have brought actions to the highest courts of several countries, wherein declarations of nonliability in criminal law have been sought. Indeed, this issue has reached (unsuccessfully thus far) the U.S. Supreme Court, which has, to date, declined to declare a liberty interest in euthanasia or physician-assisted suicide. The Supreme Court similarly refused to declare that physician-assisted suicide should be viewed as akin to withdrawal of life support, by virtue of the Equal Protection Clause of the Fourteenth Amendment and the Court's prior ruling in the path breaking case of Nancy Cruzan, where the Court determined that the withdrawal of life support would be permissible.

That said, as of the time of this writing, physician-assisted suicide has been legislatively decriminalized and legalized in the state of Oregon (see *State of Oregon v. Ashcroft*, 192 F. Supp. 2d 1077, 2002 U.S. Dist. LEXIS 6695 [D. Ct. Oregon 2002]), under very clearly enumerated circumstances. Where legalization and criminalization have taken place in different states in the same country, there is a climate ripe for opportunities in the criminal law and sentencing structures to expand and contract. It is noteworthy that in the paired case writings of the U.S. Supreme Court in 1997, members of that bench appeared to leave open the door to allow for both decriminalization and criminalization by the states, which in turn will ultimately lead to legal and criminological disparities and further examination of this issue.

DEMETRA M. PAPPAS

References and Further Reading

Hillyard, D. and Dombrink, J., *Dying Right: The Death with Dignity Movement*, Routledge (2002).

St. John-Stevas, N., *Life, Death and the Law: Law and Christian Morals in England and the United States*, Beard Books (2002).

Williams, G., *The Sanctity of Life and the Criminal Law*, Faber and Faber Ltd. (1958).

See also **Suicide: Extent and Correlates; Suicide: The Law**

Evaluation and Policy Research

What does the criminal justice system do when there is a need for creating new policies or revising old ones? What does a criminal justice agency do when the current services provided by the agency change? What does a criminal justice manager do when there is an opportunity to improve the quality of life for clients in the system? This essay reviews the basic steps of how to conduct program or policy planning and how to conduct evaluation research to examine the effectiveness of the program or policy.

Program or policy planning should be based on criminological theories and the findings of previous research. The causes of the criminal or delinquent behaviors should be addressed in the new program or policies or revised ones. For example, according to social control theory (Hirschi, 1969), commitment encompasses the time, energy, and effort expended in pursuit of conventional lines of action, and youth who have demonstrated high levels of commitment are less likely to become delinquent. According to the theory, encouraging youth to participate in conventional activities within the family, church, and school is an effective way to prevent juvenile delinquency. As a result, the Police Activity League (PAL), after school programs, and community activity centers have been implemented in various communities throughout the country. After the implementation of such policies or programs, evaluation research is then conducted to measure the desired changes. The goals and objectives that were determined in the implementation of the program or policy, along with the outcome assessment and a cost efficiency analysis, should be included in the evaluation research.

Analyzing the Problem

The first step of the planning process is to analyze the problems before making a decision to create new programs or policies or revise existing ones. This step involves answering such questions as: what is the problem, what is the current condition of the problem, what are the current practices, what is the history of the issue, what needs to change, who is the targeted population, who is affected by the problem, who will benefit from the new policy, what are the resources in the community, and what agencies are involved in the process?

For example, in order to implement a juvenile delinquency program we need to know what the delinquent problems are in the community. How serious are these problems? What is the juvenile arrest rate? What were the arrest rates in past years? What are the psychological backgrounds of delinquents? What were their social backgrounds? Does the community have any prevention or intervention programs or policies? If yes, what are these programs or policies? How are these programs and policies working out for the community? What changes need to be made? Who will benefit from the new program?

A task force is usually established to study these questions. The task force should consist of all community agencies that are related to delinquency prevention and intervention. These agencies should include the public and private sectors and profit and nonprofit organizations, including probation departments, local law enforcement agencies, mental health departments, social service agencies, school districts, and youth representatives in the task force. The purpose of the task force is to evaluate the current problem and make recommendations on the new program or policy.

The task force's duty is to examine the demographic characteristics of the community. Data such as characteristics of youth, juvenile arrest rates, juvenile arrest rates by offenses, recidivism rates, characteristics of the delinquents, and geographical locations of these delinquents and their families need to be collected.

A study on the resources and existing juvenile prevention and intervention programs needs to be conducted. A list of the current resources and existing programs must be included in the report to the task force. Moreover, the report should also consist information on the current practice of the existing programs or policies. Information such as the goals and objectives, the targeted population, and the numbers of the people served by these programs needs to be included.

Upon the completion of the analysis, the task force can either recommend to create a new program or policy, to revise the existing programs or policies, or to maintain the status quo by not making any changes. If the task force recommends creating a new program or policy or revising the existing ones, the second step of the program or policy planning process begins.

Setting Goals and Objectives

A goal is a general, desired value, and an objective is a specific, desired accomplishment. Goals are general philosophies or ideas that have intended objectives. Objectives are the specific and measurable outcomes, and goals can have more than one objective. For example, the goal of the program or policy could be to help youth lead a crime-free life and the objectives are specific things that are used to measure whether or not juveniles are leading a life free of crime. The objectives in this case could be to reduce juvenile arrest rates and to reduce recidivism rates among youth.

An objective should consist of the following four elements:

1. A time frame: date by which objective will be completed. For example, the objectives will be accomplished in a 12-month period.
2. A target population: who will benefit? For example, youth who are currently under probation supervision will be identified as the targeted population.
3. A result: a specific change attributable to the program. For example, the recidivism rates drop from 25–15%.
4. A criterion: a standard for measuring successful achievement of the result. For example, analysis will use official data provided by the probation department and youth self-reported data.

It is essential for evaluation and policy researchers to measure outcome assessment based on the goals and objectives of the program or policy. Specifically, evaluation plans need to meet the goals and objectives set by the legislature, the task force, and the program manager.

Designing the Program or Policy

The first issue is to define the target population of the program or policy (i.e., Who is the intended audience of the program or policy? Who are the people in need? Who is the population that will benefit from the program or policy?). The eligibility of the targeted population and how many clients are to be served need to be defined at the beginning of the planning stage. Often, given scarce resources, many programs and policies initially will set up restrictive client eligibility conditions, and the number of clients to be served is usually low. For example, the Drug Court Program in Stanislaus County, California, started its program by admitting only pregnant, first-time drug offenders with no history of violence, and there were only four female offenders placed in the program at the outset.

When designing a program, a client selection process needs to be established first. The second issue concerns selection and intake procedures for the program and specific provisions and procedures for the policy. Planners must ascertain the referral process and the referral agencies to be used. For example, they must decide if the clients will be referred by the court, the law enforcement agencies, or the school districts.

Moreover, for the purpose of evaluation, an intake process to collect baseline data needs to be established before the implementation of a program.

However, when designing a policy, the focus on the procedures is slightly different than the designing of the program. The emphasis is on how the goods and services will be delivered, who will deliver them, the steps that need to be followed, and the conditions that must be met to apply the policy.

The third issue is to identify the job descriptions of staff and to define the skills and training required in the program. When designing a policy, it is critical to identify who is to carry out the policy and what the responsibilities of these agencies will be.

Developing an Action Plan

The three major items that need to be addressed in the development of an action plan are: (1) needed resources, (2) cost projections, and (3) a time schedule for the program or policy.

All specific resources in the community need to be identified first. A resource plan should be established to discuss issues such as what resources are needed in the program and where and how these resources are going to be obtained. Besides identifying needed resources, the resource plan needs to address issues related to costs. Issues such as staff salaries, benefits, training, supplies, equipment, physical space, and telephone, electrical, and water bills need to be addressed. Lastly, a time schedule needs to be established to monitor the progress of the program or policy. The time needed to hire a director for the program, to negotiate a rental contract with a local realtor company, and to train the staff are things that are considered when setting up a schedule. After completing a budget and a schedule, it is time to implement the program or policy.

Evaluation Plan

The development of a comprehensive evaluation plan is essential to study the effectiveness of a program or a policy. Nowadays, all programs that receive federal grants are required to include a comprehensive evaluation plan, and there are restrictive guidelines set by the federal government for these evaluations. Furthermore, these evaluations often are required to be conducted by an independent third party such as an educational institution or an evaluation firm.

Testing effectiveness is the most important aspect of evaluation research, and there are two major components that are usually included in evaluation research. The first component is the examination of the outcome assessment compared to the goals and objectives established in the beginning of program or policy planning. For example, if reducing recidivism rates among juvenile delinquents were identified as one of the objectives of the program, the evaluator has to develop the means to measure recidivism rates or, if improving school performance among youth was identified as one of the outcome objectives, the evaluation research has to monitor the school performance using such measures as GPA and grade levels among the participating youth. In order to study the effectiveness of the program or policy, comparisons need to be made between the baseline data and outcome data. Therefore, it is critical to first establish the baseline data in an evaluation research. In many cases, follow-up evaluation research is also required to show the effectiveness of the program after the completion of the program. Most follow-up evaluations are 3, 6, 9, and 12 months after the program is completed.

The second step of establishing an evaluation plan is to develop ways to monitor the research. The plan can be monitored daily, weekly, monthly, quarterly, bi-annually, and annually. The data collected at these intervals can be obtained by the evaluators (observational data), by the staff in the program, by the service provider (such as law enforcement, probation, and mental health departments), and by the participants themselves (self-reported data). The main purpose of monitoring is to establish a database for future evaluation; a solid monitoring system is critical to the success of the program.

Most evaluation plans also include a cost efficiency analysis. For example, costs spent on making juvenile arrest and costs spent on the preventive program will be analyzed. More importantly, the difference between these two costs will be calculated. For a program or policy to be cost effective and to be worthy of continuation, the costs of the preventive program or policy have to be lower than the costs of the juvenile arrest.

Usually, an experimental design will be used for evaluation. In order to equalize two different groups according to unknown differences—IQ, prior records, or drug use—eligible clients will be assigned randomly into an experimental group (treatment group) and a control group. This process is known as random assignment. However, in the criminal justice system it is often impossible to assign eligible clients into treatment and control groups randomly; in these cases, eligible clients are asked to participate in the program voluntarily (quasi-experimental design). For example, a county superior court institutes a new drug court program that requires drug-related offenders to participate in a 9-month 12-step treatment program instead of serving time in jail. The official may be reluctant to permit an evaluator to assign some offenders to the drug court program and some to the jail randomly. In this case, the eligible offenders might be asked to participate in the drug court program voluntarily.

Comparisons will then be made between the offenders who chose to participate in the drug court program and offenders serving time in jail.

There are several experimental designs that can be used in evaluation. They are (1) the simple pretest–posttest design, (2) the pretest–posttest design with a control group, (3) the pretest–posttest design with multiple pretests, and (4) the longitudinal design with treatment and control groups.

1. The Simple Pretest–Posttest Design:

   O1 X O2

(O = observation, X = treatment).

This is a one group (treatment group) pretest and posttest experimental design. There is no control group in the design. The evaluation is conducted by comparing the baseline data (O1) and outcome data (O2) in the treatment group (for example, the recidivism rates before and after the implementation of the new policy).

2. The Pretest–Posttest Design with a Control Group:

   O1 (t) X O2 (t) (treatment group)

   O1 (c) O2 (c) (control group)

This is a two-group pretest and posttest experimental design. Both a treatment group and a control group are included in the design. The evaluation is conducted by comparing data collect at O1 (t) and O1 (c), O1 (t) and O2 (t), and O2 (t) and O2 (c).

3. The Pretest–Posttest Design with Multiple Pretests:

   O1 (t) O2 (t) O3 (t) X O4 (t)

   (treatment group)

   O1 (c) O2 (c) O3 (c) O4 (c)

   (control group)

A pretest–posttest design with multiple pretests is to be used when an evaluator intends to study whether any specified behavior is stable or unstable or to study whether the treatment and control groups differ in their baselines. This design warrants a better baseline study.

4. The Longitudinal Design with Treatment and Control Groups:

   O1 (t) O2 (t) O3 (t) X O4 (t) O5 (t) O6 (t) O7 (t)

   O1 (c) O2 (c) O3 (c) O4 (c) O5 (c) O6 (c) O7 (c)

This is the most favorable but most expensive design. Not only does the program require multiple pretests to study the stability of the baseline, it also requires multiple follow-ups after the completion of the program. This design can be used to examine the effectiveness of the program over time.

A Ten-Point Checklist for Program Evaluators

Here is the ten-point checklist for program evaluators. These are the dos and don'ts for program evaluators.

1. Is the program experimental, or is it ongoing? Experimental programs are seeking to test one or another social theory. It is usually more expensive and time consuming. Therefore, the fundamental question to experimental programs is whether they are worthwhile. The central questions are will this approach achieve the desired ends and will it do so at an acceptable cost to the organization or to society?

   Ongoing programs usually enjoy substantial support among decision makers and program executives. The central focuses of ongoing programs are program planning, organization improvement, and accountability to external funding sources. Therefore, unless the continuation of the program is in question, the evaluators usually do not have to ask whether desired outcomes are being achieved and whether operations can be improved.
2. Who is the audience for this evaluation? The audience of the evaluation could include but is not limited to program staff or manager, legislature, and program critics. Involving program staff or manager in the process of program design and implementation will definitely increase the level of staff cooperation and increase the acceptance of the findings.
3. Are the designs, measures, and indicators appropriate for the needs of the audience? Are the outcome indicators and measures appropriate in the specified circumstances? Is the outcome assessment desired by the program? These questions should be discussed between the evaluators and those commissioning the evaluation.
4. Is an outcome evaluation or an impact evaluation desired? If there is a consensus on an agency that is targeting the appropriate service group, then checking levels of service and customer satisfaction may be all that is necessary. A more complex design is needed if the question is whether the intended audience is being reached or whether the return to society is worth the investment.

5. What is the purpose of the evaluation? Evaluators need to understand the purposes of the evaluation either to seek information on how the program is doing or whether the program is in compliance with the overseeing agency or legislature. A well-designed evaluation should be able to assess the effectiveness of program adaptations and their impacts on agency clients.
6. Do we seek decision-oriented data, or are we building a theory about the client population? If the evaluation is to seek decision-oriented data, the primarily focus of the research will be to find out how the program can provide maximum service to clients within the limits of available resources and within legislative guidelines. If the evaluation is to build a theory about client population, then the evaluation research will include more sophisticated research design and the report will be written in clear and concise language.
7. Will the information be used to decide whether or how much to cut program funding or how funding can best be allocated among various components of the program? Agencies that have established databases on the costs of and the services provided by the program will benefit when a decision of budget cuts is handed down by the legislature.
8. Realistically, can a design be developed that conforms to the standards of quality evaluations within the limits of available funding? Program evaluators should design an evaluation that provides program-relevant and decision-oriented data within funding limits.
9. Am I absolutely sure that what I propose to measure is central to the goals of the agency as determined by my discussions with the program staff? The outcome measurement should reflect the goals and objectives set by the program.
10. What are we doing, how are we doing, and who will care if we tell them? Program evaluation must be tied directly to program goals as developed in consultation with the program staff and weighed against the intent of the legislature. The quality of the evaluation must meet professional standards and standards set by the program. The recommendations by the program evaluators will usually be implemented and impacts of the implementation are most significant in the field of criminal justice.

Note: This ten-point checklist for program evaluators is taken from Dwight F. Davis, "Do You Want a Performance Audit or a Program Evaluation?" *Public Administration Review* (January/February, 1990): 35–41.

CHAU-PU CHIANG

References and Further Reading

Davis, D.F., Do you want a performance audit or a program evaluation? *Public Administration Review* (January/February, 1990): 35–41.

Kettner, P.M., Daley, J.M., and Nichols, A.W., *Initiating Change in Organizations and Communities,* 179–182. Monterey, CA: Brooks/Cole, 1985.

Miller, L.S. and Whitehead, J.T., *Introduction to Criminal Justice Research and Statistics,* Anderson Publishing Co., 1996.

Rossi, P.H. and Freeman, H.E., *Evaluation: A Systematic Approach,* 5th ed., Thousand Oaks, CA: Sage, 1993.

Rutman, L., *Planning Useful Evaluations: Evaluability Assessment*, Beverly Hills CA: Sage, 1984.

Sylvia, R.D., Sylvia, K.M., and Gunn, E.M., *Program Planning and Evaluation for the Public Manager,* 2nd ed., Waveland Press, Inc., 1997.

Welsh, W.N. and Harris, P.W., *Criminal Justice Policy & Planning,* Anderson Publishing Co., 1999.

Wholey, J.S., Hatry, H.P., and Newcomer, K.E. (Eds.), *Handbook of Practical Evaluation,* San Francisco: Jossey-Bass, 1994.

Evidentiary Standards: Burden of Proof

Introduction

In the U.S. the criminal courts use the adversary system to establish the guilt of a criminal defendant. Both the prosecution and defense are expected to do everything they can to win the case, while playing by the rules set forth by the court system. In theory, this adversary system is intended to ensure that all relevant evidence will be brought out, and that each side will have an opportunity to present its case fully and adequately. The prosecution has both the burden of production and the burden of persuasion.

Placing the burden of production on the prosecution means that a criminal defendant cannot be found guilty unless the prosecution introduces evidence to show the defendant committed the crime. The defendant is under no obligation to introduce evidence that he is innocent. A failure by the prosecution to introduce evidence of each element of the crime charged will result in a directed verdict for the defendant, without any requirement that the defense introduce evidence or call any witnesses.

The prosecution must not only introduce evidence that indicates that the defendant committed the crime charged, it must also introduce a sufficient amount of evidence. This is the burden of persuasion, or the burden of proof, as it is more commonly called. Every state has a statutory provision, usually found in the penal code, which requires that no defendant shall be found guilty in a criminal case unless guilt is established "beyond a reasonable doubt." Determining that the prosecution has failed to meet its burden of proof is different from determining that the defendant is innocent. That is why the verdict delivered is "not guilty" rather than "innocent." Not guilty is a legal finding that the prosecution has failed to meet its burden of proof, not necessarily a factual description of reality (Bugliosi, 1981).

The requirement of proof beyond a reasonable doubt is derived from the common law, and the Supreme Court has held that it is required by the Due Process Clause of the Constitution (*In re Winship,* 397 U.S. 357, 1970). Precisely what constitutes "reasonable doubt" is less clear. Many courts have attempted to define it for the jury, with varying degrees of success. This entry discusses the definition and development of the concept of proof beyond a reasonable doubt, and compares this burden of proof with other burdens of proof used in criminal and civil trials.

Development of the Reasonable Doubt Standard

The reasonable doubt standard has been traced back as far as the 12th century (DeLoggio, 1986). The phrase of "moral certainty" was used at that time. "Moral certainty" has been equated with "reasonable doubt" or "almost absolute certainty" (Shapiro, 1991). Achieving "moral certainty" meant that a juror was virtually certain of the defendant's guilt. Finding someone guilty on less than a moral certainty was a violation of church doctrine. Because jurors performed a task regarded as tantamount to a sacred duty, the existence of doubt in a juror's mind sufficed to acquit an accused under this standard, so the "burden of persuasion applied in criminal cases closely approximated absolute certainty in that jurors were expected to acquit if they had any doubt" (Morano, 1975, 511). Horne's legal treatise *The Mirror of Justice*, published in 1320, states that jurors in doubt of a verdict "ought to save rather than condemn" (Morano, 1975, 511).

Little was written about jury decision making or the burden of proof between the 13th and 17th centuries, although at least one 16th-century writer, Fortescue, indicates that a high standard of proof was still required. He remarked, "One would rather that twenty guilty persons escape the punishment of death than one innocent person should be condemned" (quoted in DeLoggio, 1986, 23).

Prior to the 17th century, jurors could use any evidence they deemed useful, including their common sense and personal knowledge, to arrive at a verdict. By the 17th century, however, it had become standard practice to use only evidence presented in court, such as eyewitness testimony, to determine the verdict. Jury charges by judges became an integral part of the criminal trial. These instructions served to inform the jury what information they could consider, and how they should conduct their deliberations. Standardization of trial proceedings resulted in a uniform burden of persuasion (Morano, 1975).

The standard of persuasion at this time was often referred to as the "satisfied conscience test," meaning that jurors were to convict only if in their conscience they were sure that the defendant was guilty (Shapiro, 1991). Although the language is different, the "satisfied conscience" standard is similar to the concept of "reasonable doubt," in that jurors were instructed that a guilty verdict should be delivered only if the evidence supporting it was very strong.

The term "conscience" continued to appear in English trials of the 17th and 18th century. The 17th century legal writings of Coke, Hale, and MacKenzie show an awareness of the concept, although none of these writers used the phrase "reasonable doubt." Hale wrote, in a fashion similar to Fortescue a century earlier, "(I)t is better that five guilty persons should escape unpunished, than one innocent person should die" (quoted in DeLoggio, 1986, 23). The requirement that a juror be virtually certain of the guilt of the defendant was also referred to as a "moral certainty" during this time, and "moral certainty" came to be described during this period as "so certain as not to admit of any reasonable doubt" (Shapiro, 1991, 7–8).

The early 18th century saw various jury charges on the standard of persuasion. The most frequent charge used for the burden of proof was that a juror should acquit if "any doubt" existed (Morano, 1975). The "any doubt" test did not require that the doubt had to be reasonable; jurors could acquit a defendant if they had any doubt whatsoever. This indicates a change in the burden of proof in favor of the defendant. This was a high burden of persuasion for the prosecution, higher even than proof beyond a reasonable doubt.

By the late 17th century, it appears that reasonable doubt was becoming a popular concept. A Scottish case from 1705 is credited by several treatise writers with first using the term. Blackstone, in his *Commentaries*, does not mention reasonable doubt specifically, but does follow earlier writers who said a high burden of proof was required for conviction: "(I)t is better that ten guilty persons escape, than one innocent suffer" (quoted in DeLoggio, 1986, 23).

Morano (1975) suggests that the concept was introduced by the prosecution in place of the "any doubt" test to provide less protection to the defendant. Shapiro (1991) contends, however, that the "any doubt" standard did not really increase the burden on the prosecution. Instead, "moral certainty," which was often used in jury instructions as well, was equated with "reasonable doubt." If one did not have a moral certainty of guilt, then a "reasonable doubt" was established. The reasonable doubt test thus served as an extension of the "any doubt" test and a clarification of "moral certainty," not a replacement for these standards.

By the early 18th century, American courts commonly required proof of guilt beyond a reasonable doubt in criminal trials. There were few attempts to define the term more precisely, and courts often failed to cite authority for their definition (DeLoggio, 1986). The most famous attempt at defining reasonable doubt came in *Commonwealth v. Webster* (59 Mass. 295 (1850)). Most current definitions of reasonable doubt are derived from Chief Justice Shaw's oft-cited opinion, which states:

> [W]hat is reasonable doubt? It is a term often used, probably pretty well understood, but not easily defined. It is not mere possible doubt; because every thing relating to human affairs, and depending on moral evidence, is open to some possible or imaginary doubt. It is that state of the case, which, after the entire comparison and consideration of all the evidence, leaves the minds of jurors in that condition that they cannot say they feel an abiding conviction, to a moral certainty, of the truth of the charge.

Current Status of the Definition of Reasonable Doubt

Most states today have case law that provides some definition of reasonable doubt. Whereas some states adhere to only one definition, other states accept multiple definitions. There are a number of commonly used definitions of reasonable doubt. These include "a doubt that would cause one to hesitate to act" (used in some form in at least 20 states), "a doubt based on reason" (used in 17 states), and "an actual and substantial doubt" (used in 10 states). Other less popular definitions include "a doubt that can be articulated" and "moral certainty" (Hemmens, Scarborough, and del Carmen, 1995).

The U.S. Supreme Court has upheld several definitions of reasonable doubt. In *Miles v. U.S.* (103 U.S. 304, 1881) the Court upheld a definition based on the "moral certainty" language of Chief Justice Shaw's opinion in *Webster*. The Court also suggested that attempts to explain the meaning of reasonable doubt did not help, but instead served to confuse the jury. In *Dunbar v. U.S.* (156 U.S. 185, 1895) the Court endorsed a definition equating reasonable doubt with "strong probabilities." Later that same year, in *Coffin v. U.S.* (156 U.S. 433, 1895), the Court expressed approval of the "hesitate to act" formulation. In 1910, in *Holt v. U.S.* (218 U.S. 245, 1910), the Court endorsed a definition of reasonable doubt which equated it with "a real doubt."

More recent cases on reasonable doubt begin with *Leland v. Oregon* (343 U.S. 790, 1952), in which the Court recommended that courts define reasonable doubt, and do so using the "hesitate to act" formulation. *Leland* is significant because it was the first time the Court advocated the use of a specific definition of reasonable doubt. In 1970, the Court in *In re Winship* (394 U.S. 57, 1970) applied the reasonable doubt standard to juvenile adjudications, and significantly stated that the reasonable doubt standard was a constitutionally required protection for a criminal defendant. In *Cage v. Louisiana* (498 U.S. 39, 1990) the Court held that the jury instructions defining reasonable doubt violated the defendant's due process rights. *Cage* is significant because it is the only case decided by the Court where a conviction was reversed because the reasonable doubt jury instruction violated due process standards. The instructions in Cage stated that a reasonable doubt was "such doubt as would give rise to great uncertainty and ... an actual substantial doubt," and that "moral certainty" was required to convict. Justice O'Connor acknowledged in a recent case (*Victor v. Nebraska*, 1994) that although the requirement of proof beyond a reasonable doubt "is an ancient and honored aspect of our criminal justice system, it defies easy explication." She noted, however, in upholding the jury instruction used in this case, that the Constitution does not require that any particular definition of reasonable doubt be used.

Jury Comprehension of the Definition of Reasonable Doubt

The Supreme Court has reason for its concern over the definition of reasonable doubt. There are a number of studies of the abilities of juries to understand jury instructions. These studies have found that juror misunderstanding is created by the instruction's terminology, phrasing, and manner of presentation, and the general unfamiliarity of the jurors with legal terminology

(Kassin and Wrightsman, 1979; Severance and Loftus, 1982).

Although a number of the studies have focused on jury instructions unrelated to the burden of proof, several have focused on the ability of the jury to understand the meaning of "proof beyond a reasonable doubt." A study of Florida jurors found that half of the jurors who were given an instruction on the presumption of innocence and the burden of proof erroneously believed a defendant was required to prove his innocence (Strawn and Buchanan, 1976).

Kerr et al. (1976) conducted an experiment in which mock jurors were read one of three definitions of reasonable doubt, and the impact of the instruction on the jury's verdict was measured. The jury reading the least stringent definition of reasonable doubt ("you need not be absolutely sure that the defendant is guilty to find him guilty") had the highest conviction rate, whereas the jury reading the most stringent definition of reasonable doubt ("if you are not sure and certain of his guilt, you must find him not guilty") had the lowest conviction rate.

Several other studies have attempted to determine how jurors quantify "reasonable doubt." One early study found that jurors quantified it as 87% sure of guilt (Simon and Mahan, 1971), whereas a later study found jurors quantified it as 86% sure of guilt (Kassin and Wrightsman, 1979). Interestingly, this compares with an estimate of 90% or more by judges (McCauliff, 1982). Although these results suggest that jurors understand the phrase "reasonable doubt" to mean something close to absolute certainty, it is unclear how different definitions of reasonable doubt might affect the quantification of the concept.

Other Standards for the Burden of Proof

Although the general rule is that the state has the burden of production and the burden of proof in a criminal trial, there are exceptions to the rule. If a defendant wishes to raise an affirmative defense, such as alibi, self-defense, or insanity, he or she must introduce evidence to support that defense. Thus, the burden of production may be switched to the defense.

In most states, the burden of proof is also switched to the defense when an affirmative defense is raised. However, the general rule is that the burden is proof by "a preponderance of the evidence" rather than "beyond a reasonable doubt." Proof by a preponderance of the evidence is the burden of proof used in civil trials, and it is often quantified as 51% sure, or if the jury believes it is more likely than not. This is a relatively easy burden of persuasion to meet. A few states do not switch the burden of proof to the defense, but instead still require the state to disprove the affirmative defense beyond a reasonable doubt.

Recently, a few states and the federal courts have changed the burden of proof for the affirmative defense of insanity, requiring the defense to prove it by "clear and convincing evidence." This quantum of proof lies somewhere between "a preponderance of the evidence" and "proof beyond a reasonable doubt." This shift in the level of the burden of proof was in response to several "not guilty by reason of insanity" verdicts in high profile cases, such as the trial of John Hinckley for the attempted assassination of President Reagan. There was a feeling that defendants in such cases were finding it too easy to escape criminal liability for their actions.

Conclusion

The requirement that the prosecution establish proof of guilt beyond a reasonable doubt is a relatively ancient legal concept, dating back some 700 years. It imposes a difficult burden on the prosecution, as a means of ensuring that no innocent person is convicted. The result is that, as many a legal commentator has noted, some guilty persons may go free. This is the price that society pays for restricting the ability of the government to take away the liberty of the individual citizen without very strong justification.

Like many legal concepts, the concept of proof beyond a reasonable doubt is difficult to precisely define and subject to misunderstanding. Although all of us may intuitively understand what it means, providing a definition for the jury to apply in its deliberations is difficult, as the cases have repeatedly demonstrated. Courts continue to struggle with the task of definition, but there is no doubt that the concept is here to stay. The requirement that the state prove the guilt of a criminal defendant beyond a reasonable doubt is a bedrock of the criminal law.

Craig Hemmens

References and Future Reading

Bugliosi, V. (1981). Not guilty and innocent: The problem children of reasonable doubt. *Court Review* 20: 16–25.

DeLoggio, L. (1986). Beyond a reasonable doubt—A historic analysis. *New York State Bar Journal* 58(3): 19–25.

Hemmens, C., Scarborough, K., and del Carmen, R. (1997). Grave doubts about reasonable doubt: Confusion in state and federal courts. *Journal of Criminal Justice* 25: 231–254.

Kassin, S. and Wrightsman, L. (1979). On the requirements of proof: The timing of judicial instruction and mock juror verdicts. *Journal of Personality and Social Psychology* 37: 1877–1887.

Kerr, N., Atkin, R., Stasser, G., Meek, D., Holt, R., and Davis, J. (1976). Guilt beyond a reasonable doubt: Effects of concept definition and assigned decision rule on the judgments of mock jurors. *Journal of Personality and Social Psychology* 34: 282–294.

McCauliff, C. (1982). Burden of proof: Degrees of belief, quanta of evidence, or constitutional guarantees? *Vanderbilt Law Review* 35: 1293–1335.

Morano, A. (1975). A reexamination of the development of the reasonable doubt rule. *Boston University Law Review* 55: 507–528.

Severance, L. and Loftus, E. (1982). Improving the ability of jurors to comprehend and apply criminal jury instructions. *Law and Society Review* 17: 153–197.

Shapiro, B. (1991). *Beyond Reasonable Doubt and Probable Cause: Historical Perspectives on the Anglo-American Law of Evidence*. Berkeley, CA: University of California Press.

Simon, R. and Mahan, L. (1971). Quantifying burdens of proof: A view from the bench, the jury, and the classroom. *Law and Society Review* 5: 319–330.

Strawn, D., and R. Buchanan, R. (1976). Jury confusion: A threat to justice. *Judicature* 59: 478–483.

See also **Criminal Courts: Administration and Organization**

Evolutionary Theories of Criminal Behavior

Lombroso (1876) was first to use Darwinian evolutionary principles to explain criminal behavior. He believed that criminals were biological throwbacks (atavistic) to an earlier evolutionary stage. Following Lombroso, criminologists moved from biological explanations to more environmental and social-psychological explanations. In recent years, increasing knowledge of genetics has resulted in new developments in evolutionary theories of human behavior. In this article, developments in evolutionary theory will be outlined, their application to criminal behavior discussed, the criticisms identified, and the current status of these theories reviewed.

Darwin (1859) outlined a process of natural selection by which species changed over generations. He proposed that genetic advantages or adaptations enabled some members of a population to overcome environmental problems and out-survive other members. Darwin also proposed the competitive reproductive advantages of adaptations that shaped evolution through sexual selection. Two mechanisms contribute to sexual selection: competition between members of the same sex for access to mates (intrasexual) and competition for desirable members of the opposite sex (intersexual).

Modern evolutionary psychology (human behavioral ecology, sociobiology, and Darwinian psychology) explores the ancestral advantages of adaptations, including behavior patterns, and their functionality in modern societies. Because of environmental changes in recent evolutionary time (from the African Savannah to modern cities) behaviors that contributed to ancestral fitness may no longer contribute to current fitness and may be maladaptive and harmful. Evolutionary psychology has developed concepts of relative parental investment and altruism (Hamilton, 1964; Trivers, 1972, 1971) to explain human behavior.

Trivers (1972) explained the operation of sexual selection through the concept of relative parental investment. He argued that as consequence of sexual selection women and men developed different adaptations because they have different reproductive functions. Women are more selective than men about potential mates because they invest highly in a limited number of children. For men, only, the number of matings limits the number of children. Consequently, they benefit by competing among themselves for access to females. However, because fertilization occurs within women, men face the additional adaptive problem of paternity uncertainty. Men risk investing resources in children who are not their own (cuckoldry).

Two evolutionary explanations for altruism (behavior that benefits the receiver at the expense of the giver) have been proposed. Inclusive fitness states that reproductive fitness extends to the genetic offspring of kin. Consequently, altruistic behaviors are disproportionately directed toward genetic kin (e.g., siblings, nieces, and nephews). The second explanation, reciprocal altruism, proposes that, over the long run, the benefits received outweigh the average costs of providing benefits. This provides an evolutionary basis for social–psychological phenomena such as cooperation, helping, altruism, and social exchange (Buss and Kenrick, 1998). Unfortunately, it also provides an understanding of antisocial behavior as this strategy can give rise to "cheating"—the acceptance of altruism from others but with the failure to reciprocate in the future.

There have been two approaches to applying evolutionary theory to criminal behavior. The first has focused on developing general theories to explain the development and maintenance of antisocial personality disorder, also called psychopathy or sociopathy. The second approach has been to apply the principles to explain specific criminal behaviors, especially crimes against women and within the family.

At a general level two theories have been proposed, the cheater theory (Raine, 1993) and the *R/K* theory (Ellis and Walsh, 1989). The cheater theory states that there are two subpopulations of males. The first complies with females to make a high investment in their offspring. The second subpopulation mimics the first by using a range of deceptive methods to acquire the resources to attract numerous sex partners. The second theory states that organisms approach reproduction along a theoretical continuum. At the *K* end of the continuum, organisms invest a lot of time in a small number of offspring. Antisocial behavior occurs at the *R* end of the continuum, where organisms reproduce prolifically and provide minimal care.

Daly and Wilson (1998) proposed that spousal violence results from male sexual proprietariness, husbands wishing to control their wives' autonomy, an evolved adaptation to deal with the problem of paternity uncertainty and male-to-male reproduction competition. Husbands kill because of (suspected or actual) adultery or the women's termination of the marriage. In addition, evolutionary theory predicts that there would be an inverse proportionality between genetic relatedness and homicide. Daly and Wilson found that, controlling for opportunity, nongenetic coresidents were 11 times more likely to kill than genetically related coresidents. Furthermore, stepchildren are abused and killed at a very much higher rate than genetic offspring.

The evolutionary theory of rape (or sexual assault) assets that men who are "pushy" with respect to seeking sex with multiple partners will have a reproductive edge over men who are not "pushy" (Smuts, 1992). Consequently, the women most likely to be raped would be those of a fertile age. However, evolutionary theory does not explain rape against males and children, women beyond menopause, and rape involving oral or anal sex.

The first criticism of evolutionary theory stems from the misapprehension that genetic theories are deterministic theories of crime—that is, that there is a direct relationship between the genes and the behavior. Current biological theorists propose that genetics can provide a predisposition for certain behaviors (Plomin, DeFries, and McClearn, 1990). However, these predispositions interact with the environment to determine behavior.

A second concern comes from the potential political uses of scientific information concerning gender, race, and inequality. Specifically, in relation to gender, evolutionary theory has been accused of androcentrism, providing a scientific veneer under which sexism is reinforced. Evolutionary theorists counter with the argument that although the separation of gender roles might have contributed to ancestral fitness this does not necessarily contribute to current fitness.

A third concern is that evolutionary theories are unscientific because they are retrospectively fitted to the data, and are therefore unverifiable. Evolutionary theories cannot be experimentally tested. However, evolutionary theories do appear to be able to generate a range of hypotheses that can then be tested against the available data and are therefore subject to verification.

Despite claims that it justifies the status quo, evolutionary theory has clear policy implications through effective intervention, prevention, and treatment programs. Crime is conditional; under some situations crime appears to pay off, whereas under other situations it does not. The challenge is to identify the situational factors that predispose members of a particular group toward or away from the use of crime.

Evolutionary theories of crime have developed substantially since Lombroso first proposed them. These theories point to a dynamic interplay between biological and environmental factors. They show promise for providing new explanations for why some crimes occur as well as generating new hypotheses concerning these crimes. However, these hypotheses need careful empirical testing to assess their value.

ANNA STEWART

References and Further Reading

Barkow, J., Cosmides, L., and Tooby, J., Eds., *The Adapted Mind: Evolutionary Psychology and the Generation of Culture*. New York, NY: Oxford University Press, 1992.

Bleier, R., *Science and Gender: A Critique of Biology and Its Theories on Women*, New York, NY: Pergamon Press, 1984.

Buss, D.M. and Kenrick, D.T., Evolutionary social psychology. In Gilbert, D.T. and Fiske, S.T., Eds., *The Handbook of Social Psychology.* Boston, MA: McGraw-Hill, 1998.

Crawford, C. and Krebs, D.L., Eds., *Handbook of Evolutionary Psychology. Ideas, Issues and Applications.* Mahwah, NJ: Lawrence Erlbaum, 1998.

Darwin, C., *On the Origin of the Species by Means of Natural Selection or the Preservation of Favored Races in the Struggle for Life*. London, UK: John Murray, 1859.

Ellis, L. and Walsh, A., Gene-based evolutionary theories in criminology. *Criminology, 35*, 1997.

Hamilton, W.D., The genetic evolution of social behavior. *Journal of Theoretical Biology, 7*, 1964.

Lombroso, C., *L'uomo Delinquente*, Torino, Italy: Bocca, 1896.

Plomin, R., DeFries, J.C., and McClearn, J.E., *Behavioral Genetics: A Primer.* New York, NY: W.H. Freeman, 1990.

Raine, A., *The Psychopathology of Crime: Criminal Behavior as a Clinical Disorder.* San Diego: Academic Press, 1993.

Smuts, B., Male aggression against women: An evolutionary perspective. *Human Nature, 3*, 1992.

Trivers, R.T., *Social Evolution*, Menlo Park, CA: Benjamin/Cummings, 1985.

Wilson, M. and Daly, M., Lethal and nonlethal violence against wives and the evolutionary psychology of male sexual proprietariness, in Dobash, R.E. and Dobash, R.P., Eds., *Rethinking Violence Against Women*, Thousand Oaks, CA: Sage, 1998.

See also **Biological Theories of Criminal Behavior; Genetic Theories of Criminal Behavior; Psychological Theories of Criminal Behavior**

Exclusionary Rule, The

When the constable blunders, the criminal shall go free. This phrase, the distillation of Judge Cardozo's criticism of the Exclusionary Rule (Rule) from a 1926 case (*People v. Defore*, 150 N.E. 585 at 587, 1926) does, however, suggest the essence of the Rule. The Rule, judicially created by the Supreme Court in 1914 and applied to the state criminal proceedings years later, created a remedy for persons aggrieved by certain forms of governmental misconduct. The Rule serves to exclude evidence against a defendant in a criminal case under certain circumstances and has certainly generated its share of controversy and detractors in all branches of government. Yet it remains today a vital if somewhat diminished way courts enforce the rule of law in criminal cases.

Actually there is the Rule and then assorted other rules that involve the suppression of evidence in other contexts. The Exclusionary Rule is universally thought of, as announced in both *Weeks v. U.S.* (232 U.S. 383, 1914) and *Mapp v. Ohio* (367 U.S. 643, 1961), as specifically relating to violations of individuals' rights against unreasonable governmental searches and seizures under both the Fourth and Fourteenth Amendments to the U.S. Constitution. The "rules" apply to a variety of statutory and evidentiary standards and decisions that invoke exclusionary principles in other areas of constitutional procedure. For example, most jurisdictions including the federal government exclude evidence of confessions and eyewitness identification procedures obtained in violation of announced constitutional rules. This article will describe the Rule and not the "rules."

The Rule evolves from two major Supreme Court cases. The first of these, *Weeks v. U.S.*, was a 1914 case involving a conviction stemming from a violation of federal statutes banning the use of the mail for the purpose of transporting lottery tickets. The police officers in that case had searched the defendant's house several times without a warrant or his permission and seized various papers and articles that were used as evidence against Weeks in the criminal matter.

The *Weeks* Court, in reversing the conviction and barring for the first time the use of the evidence at trial, established the Rule, and made very clear the basis of its holding.

"If letters and private documents can thus be seized and held and used in evidence against a citizen accused of an offense, the protection of the Fourth Amendment declaring his right to be secure against such searches and seizures is of no value, and, so far as those thus placed are concerned, might as well be stricken from the Constitution. The efforts of the courts and their officials to bring the guilty to punishment, praiseworthy as they are, are not to be aided by the sacrifice of those great principles established by years of endeavor and suffering which have resulted in their embodiment in the fundamental law of the land" (232 U.S. at 393).

In *Mapp v. Ohio*, the U.S. Supreme Court extended the Rule to all state criminal proceedings by making the Rule a part of State Due Process under both the Fourth and Fourteenth Amendments to the U.S. Constitution. Essentially the *Mapp* Court found that the Rule's protections were an integral and necessary component of fundamental fairness and "implicit in the concept of ordered liberty." The extension of the Rule in *Mapp* has been of considerable importance. Because the vast majority of arrests and criminal cases in this country arise and are prosecuted in state courts, the Rule's potential applicability in those courts reaches a substantial range of government conduct.

Mapp involved an obscenity prosecution for certain allegedly obscene materials found in Ms. Mapp and her daughter's Cleveland apartment. The officers originally arriving at her apartment were in fact looking for another person possibly involved in a recent bombing in the city. The officers were initially denied entry by Ms. Mapp. She was acting on advice she had received from her attorney and demanded to be shown a search warrant. Several hours later, additional officers joined the initial group who had remained at the scene. When Ms. Mapp did not open her door, several of the group of officers forcibly entered. When she asked to see the warrant, a piece of paper was produced (there was never any evidence introduced at the hearing on the matter that a warrant had ever been issued), a struggle ensued and she was finally arrested for interfering with police activities. She was forcibly and violently taken from room to room where dressers, closets, drawers, and suitcases were searched. It was during one of these searches in her basement that the "obscene" materials were located.

The *Mapp* Court insisted that it made no sense and, indeed, was nothing but a "form of words" to apply the substance of the Fourth Amendment protections against unreasonable government searches and seizures to citizens of the states without applying the remedy available against those government agents for violations of those constitutional demands. The Court noted the hypocrisy in the notion that a federal prosecutor might be bound by the Rule's prohibitions (the *Weeks* decision limited the Rule to federal proceedings) yet could go "across the street" to the state prosecutor's office where the evidence might be freely admitted in a trial for the same crime. This "ignoble shortcut to conviction tends to destroy the entire system of constitutional restraints on which the liberties of the people rest." After *Mapp*, then, the Rule became part of the "law of the land."

The importance of the Rule and its raison d'etre lies in its deterrent value. The exclusion of evidence and its potential to destroy a criminal case is a severe penalty to enact against the government. By holding that punishment over the head of government agents and actors, there is a great incentive by the police and prosecutors to make certain the price does not have to be paid. At least in theory, these agents will make every effort to learn and abide by constitutional rules and standards.

The Rule expresses other important ideas about the how we want our criminal justice system to function. One idea in the law, generally, is that a party injured by another individual or a governmental entity should have an appropriate remedy for those injuries suffered and should have a legal forum to vent those claims. This seems to have been a central theme behind the *Weeks* decision.

More specific to the interests of the criminal justice system, the Rule serves a more theoretical purpose. That is, it preserves the integrity of the court hearing the case where improper government action is alleged. Courts that determine constitutional violations occur and ignore sanctioning the wrongdoer are essentially complicit in the wrongdoing. As the *Mapp* Court asserted, "Nothing can destroy a government more quickly than its failure to observe its own laws, or worse," or more forcefully, "if the government becomes a lawbreaker, it breeds contempt for law; it invites every man to become a law unto himself; it invites anarchy." (367 U.S. at 659)

The Rule has engendered much controversy and much of that is related to the "windfall" that a possible criminal defendant receives when a court rules that evidence has been improperly obtained. The first criticism centers on the idea that the Rule extracts too high a price from society for the conduct of parties that society has no direct control over. These critics would argue that there are other remedies available to the aggrieved party that do not put society's safety at risk with the possible release of a dangerous person. Civil suits against the police and administrative sanctions by department heads are two of the more frequently mentioned remedies.

Another criticism of the Rule is the argument that it is only the "guilty" person who receives the benefit of the Rule. The drug carrier whose car is improperly searched and who successfully invokes the Rule has the evidence of his criminal behavior suppressed whereas the lawful driver of a car improperly stopped and searched will never be subject to criminal proceedings nor have to invoke the Rule in the first place.

In part because of the continued opposition to the Rule and in part because of the political shift in this country beginning in the early 1980s, the Rule has been limited substantially in the past 20 years. In terms of the political shift, the Supreme Court began to limit the Rule's application beginning with the Court's "good faith" cases in the mid-1980s. *U.S. v. Leon* (468 U.S. 897, 1984) carved out an exception to the Rule's application where police officers were acting in good faith and in reliance upon a warrant even when the warrant subsequently was deemed in violation of the Constitution. The *Leon* Court noted the "substantial costs" exacted by the Rule and expressed concern over those costs. The Court was further concerned that the "unbending" application of the Rule would interfere with the truth-finding function of the judge and jury.

The *Leon* Court further noted that the Rule's original purpose of deterrence would be unsatisfied in the case where the officer had attempted to follow the law and acted reasonably. The whole basis for the Rule is to deter police misconduct, not to unfairly punish the honest officer. The "good faith" limitation has since *Leon* been extended to two additional situations. In 1987, the Court refused to suppress evidence under the Rule where the officer engaged in searching activity in reliance on a state statute later declared unconstitutional (*Illinois v. Krull*, 480 U.S. 340, 1987). Finally, in 1995, the Court again limited the Rule's application where the basis for the officer's unlawful activity was based on erroneous information from a court clerk (*Arizona v. Evans*, 514 U.S. 1, 1995).

Since *Leon*, the Court has restricted the application of the Rule in several other areas. Evidence improperly seized in violation of the Constitution is not always subject to exclusion where used in grand jury as opposed to trial proceedings (*U.S. v. Calandra*, 414 U.S. 338, 1974).

Finding that the deterrent value of the Rule would not be measurably enhanced when applied to the grand jury stage, the Court refused to extend the Rule's application to that stage. Similarly, the Court has refused to extend the Rule to actions by parole officers that might violate the Fourth Amendment rights of a parolee where such evidence may be used to revoke a person's parole status (*Pennsylvania Board of Probation and Parole v. Scott*, 514 U.S. 357, 1998). The language by the Court in that case seems to suggest a general reluctance of the Supreme Court to expand the Rule beyond the "trial context."

Another way the Rule is potentially limited is by restricting the type and amount of evidence that is subject to exclusion by focusing on the link between the violation and the discovery of the evidence. This is a question of what constitutes the "fruits of the poisonous tree." In other words, if the police misconduct and constitutional violation yield a chain of evidence extending both spatially and temporally beyond the initial misconduct, does the Rule bar some or all the evidence and what is the demarcation point? The general notion, easy to state but hard to apply, is that any and all evidence arising from or tainted by the original violation is excluded. To the extent the government can show the taint removed or an independent source for the evidence, the Rule will not apply. This becomes a very specific factual determination with the government arguing that any "link" between the wrongdoing and evidence has been broken and the evidence, then, is untainted.

Finally, the legal concept of standing plays an important role in who actually receives the remedy envisioned by the Rule. Standing is the notion that the party raising a legal issue (any issue though here we are talking about search and seizure problems) must satisfactorily display to the court a personal interest in the legal question raised. For example, a person complaining about a violation of the Fourth Amendment regarding a car search must show the court a legitimate personal or possessory interest in the automobile. The criminal charge itself does not confer automatic standing on the individual without a legitimate personal interest in the place searched or item seized. Standing problems, then, potentially limit the Rule's application to a much smaller class of persons than all those persons charged with a crime based on the evidence seized.

In light of the controversy over the Rule, one can only speculate what the impact of the Rule has been on the criminal justice system. There is some research that indicates that the Rule has not had a major impact on either the manner law enforcement officials go about their jobs or the rate at which criminal defendants are "beating the system" and being released from custody (Kamisar, 2002). There are logical reasons why the Rule might play a smaller role in the administration of justice than its detractors might think.

First, judges, like the rest of us, are citizens of a community first and foremost. It is easy to envision, then, that a judge would have a difficult time in a close application of the Rule (and there are always two versions of the facts) upholding the defendant's request for exclusion when that would effectively mean the release of a dangerous person. Judges typically will credit a police officer over a criminal defendant where there is a conflict of testimony. In other words, defendants seldom win these motions to exclude evidence.

Next, and perhaps more significant, is the fact that even if some evidence is excluded under the Rule, the state in the vast majority of cases will have other evidence that has not been subjected to the Rule. In other words, it is probably not significant to a defendant to have an item suppressed as a result of an illegal search when the state still has access to his confession and the testimony of important eyewitnesses. It is important to note that the Rule operates only to exclude evidence associated with the legal violation and does not operate as a general dismissal of the case.

Controversy over and modification of the Rule notwithstanding, the Exclusionary Rule provides a major tool for courts to use to ensure fairness and consistency in the criminal justice system. And if it is true as it will be from time to time that "the criminal shall go free" then "... it is the law that sets him free" (367 U.S. at 359).

William L. Shulman

References and Further Reading

Kamisar, et al. *Basic Criminal Procedure*, West Publishing Co., 10th ed., 2002.

Modern Criminal Procedure, Cases and Comments, Kamisar, LaFave, Israel, and King (West Group, 10th ed., 2002), Part Two, Chapter 5.

Criminal Procedure, Cases and Comments, Haddad, Meyer, Zagel, Starkman and Bauer (Foundation Press, University Casebook Series, 5th ed., 1998), Part One, Chapter 6.

Constitutional Criminal Procedure, Taslitz and Paris (Foundation Press, University Casebook Series 1997), Chapter 2, Section 8.

See also **Search and Seizures; Warrants and Subpoenas**

Exhibitionism and Voyeurism

Many remember Paul Reuben's (AKA Pee-Wee Herman) high-profile case from the early 1990s. Reuben was charged and convicted of indecent exposure for allegedly exposing himself and masturbating in a movie theater in Sarasota, Florida. This case certainly received a great deal of attention from the media, but it had more to do with the offender's celebrity status than the nature of the offense. Rarely does a case of this nature appear in the news, not because it does not happen, but because it is not considered a serious offense and many instances go unreported.

A young woman at Mardi Gras, in New Orleans, is arrested and charged with indecent exposure for revealing her genitals in public for beads to wear around her neck. A man is arrested and charged with indecent exposure for urinating in public. Both of these examples are different than Paul Reuben's case mentioned above, but all were arrested for the same crime—are they the same? Are all three examples of exhibitionism?

The word exhibitionism conjures up the image of a male in a long black trench coat who exposes himself in public—the stereotypical "flasher." This image fits within the parameters of exhibitionism; however, exhibitionism is not so easily defined.

Exhibitionists are usually arrested for indecent exposure—exposing their genitals in public, but not all people who are arrested for indecent exposure are exhibitionists. Only when the purpose of the act is sexual gratification is it considered exhibitionism.

Exhibitionism is for the most part a male dominated disorder, but females and children do take part in exhibitionism (Schneider, 1982; O'Callaghan and Print, 1994). Exhibitionism is more prevalent than most people are aware. Although exhibitionism often goes unnoticed by law enforcement, it is believed to be as common as many other sex crimes (Flowers, 2001).

Exhibitionsim is one of many sexual deviations or perversions that falls within the paraphilia category. Paraphilias are desires, usualy sexual, that are considered abnormal and in some conditions termed as mental disorders. "The essential features of a paraphilia are recurrent, intense sexually arousing fantasies, sexual urges, or behaviors that generally involve nonhuman objects, children, non-consenting adults, or the suffering and humiliation of oneself or one's partner" (American Psychiatric Association, 2003). According to the American Psychiatric Association the term paraphilia includes pedophilia, fetishism, frotteurism, transvestism, voyeurism, sexual sadism, masochism, as well as exhibitionism.

Exhibitionism is characterized by sexual fantasies or behaviors involving exposure of an individual's genitals to a stranger in public, considered a mental disorder by the American Psychiatric Association standards. A diagnostic catalogue, *Diagnostic and Statistical Manual of Mental Disorders, Fourth Edition Text Revision (DSM-IV-TR)*, lists the following criteria for exhibitionism (302.4):

> A. Over a period of at least 6 months, recurrent, intense sexually arousing fantasies, sexual urges, or behaviors involving the exposure of one's genitals to an unsuspecting stranger.
>
> B. The person has acted on these urges, or the sexual urges or fantasies cause marked distress or interpersonal difficulty" (APA, 2000).

Exhibitionism, furthermore, can be divided into two categories: invitational and shocking. Invitational exhibitionists are considered less dangerous than their shocking counterparts, and they usually expose themselves from a distance. They desire a positive response from their victims and consider this a very intimate form of expression. Shocking exhibitionists are more threatening, more likely to be driven by anger and power, and desperately want to control their victims. According to Flowers (2001, 131), "shocking exhibitionists will sometimes degrade victims, accompanied by threats and possible stalking—all of which increase the possibility of sexual assault or child molestation."

Estimates have indicated that roughly 40 million women a year are victims of exhibitionism and between 20% and 50% of children have been victims of exhibitionism (Flowers, 130). The exact number of incidences a year is unknown for multiple reasons. First, as stated previously, most cases of exhibitionism go unreported. Many people are often too embarrassed to report such an offense to the police or do not perceive it to be an act that warrants serious police attention. In the case of children, many children do not confide in their parents or other adults that they were victims. Also, women are more likely to report male exhibitionism than males are to report female exhibitionism, possibly creating a bias toward male exhibitionism. Another problem is that different cultures have different definitions of exhibitionism, making it extremely difficult to estimate this offense across cultures. In sum, these problems have prevented systematic, accurate, and reliable measurement of the incidence of exhibitionism.

Although it is often difficult to study and is considered more of a nuisance than a serious offense, exhibitionism should not be ignored. Some research has shown that sexual disorders, including exhibitionism, could be the start of more serious sexual offenses (Holmes, 1991). For example, Holmes (1991, 17) stated that, "there is a growing measure of serious literature that suggest that many rapists, lust murders, and sexually motivated serial murders have histories of sexual behaviors that reflect patterns that in the past have been considered only nuisances." Flowers (2001) has suggested that exhibitionists have recidivism rates that are among the highest of all sex offenders.

Although some exhibitionists receive treatment, intervention is typically not sought or received until after being caught and ordered by the court. Treatments that have been used primarily consist of a combination of therapy and pharmacological supplements that target compulsive behaviors. Cognitive, behavior, and psychoanalytic therapies are used to treat paraphilias, whereas prescription medicines, such as hormones, have been used to stunt compulsive thinking associated with paraphilias. Nevertheless, treatment almost always should be long term if it is to be an effective means of decreasing the propensity of exhibitionists, as well as other individuals with paraphilias, toward compulsive behaviors.

In closing, multiple research avenues should be explored to bring us closer to understanding the etiology and treatment of exhibitionism. This review has attempted to document a brief description of exhibitionism. Readers should consult articles in the bibliography for a more detailed review.

Amy Reckdenwald and Chris Gibson

References and Further Reading

American Psychiatric Association. (2000). *Diagnostic and Statistical Manual of Mental Disorders*, 4th ed., Text Revision. Washington, DC: Author.

Flowers, R.B. (2001). *Sex Crimes, Predators, Perpetrators, Prostitutes, and Victims*. Springfield, IL: Charles C Thomas.

Holmes, R.M. (1991). *Sex Crimes*. Newbury, CA: Sage Publications, Inc.

O'Callaghan, D. and Print, B. (1994). Adolescent sexual abusers: Research assessment and treatment. In Morrison, T., Erooga, M., and Beckett, R.C. (Eds.), *Sexual Offending against Children: Assessment and Treatment of Male Abuser*, 146–177. London, UK: Routledge.

Schneider, R.D. (1982). Exhibitionism: An exclusively male deviation? *International Journal of Offender Therapy and Comparative Criminology*, 26, 173–176.

Zolondek, S.C., Abel, G.G., Northey, Jr., W.F., and Jordan, A.D. (2001). The self-reported behaviors of juvenile sexual offenders. *Journal of Interpersonal Violence*, 16 (1), 73–85.

American Psychiatric Association. (2003). *Diagnostic Criteria for Pedophilia*. Release No. 03-28, June 17, 2003.

See also **Obscenity; Pornography: The Law**

Experimental Research and Randomized Experiments

Randomized Experiments (Also Referred to as Classic or True Experiments, Randomized Trials, Randomized Controlled Trials)

A randomized experiment is a type of research design that relies upon random allocation of subjects or other units of analysis in order to gain equivalence between the subjects or units studied. Although randomized experiments may be used to test both theoretical and substantive questions, in criminal justice randomized experiments have been most common in evaluations of treatments and programs. When used outside the laboratory and in an actual field setting such as a prison or community, they are referred to as randomized field experiments or randomized field trials. There is broad agreement among social and behavioral scientists that randomized experiments provide the best method for drawing causal inferences between treatments and programs and their outcomes.

The Strength of Experimental Research

The key to understanding the strength of experimental research designs is found in what scholars define as the "internal validity" of a study. A research design in which the effects of treatment or intervention can be clearly distinguished from other effects is defined as having high "internal validity." A research design in which the effects of treatment are confounded with other factors is one in which there is low "internal validity." For example, suppose a researcher seeks to assess the effects of a specific drug treatment program on recidivism. If at the end of the evaluation the researcher can present study results and confidently assert that the effects of treatment have been isolated from other confounding causes, the internal validity of the study is high. But if the researcher has been unable to ensure that other factors such as the seriousness of prior records or the social status of offenders have been disentangled from the influence of treatment, he or she must note that the effects observed for treatment may be owing to such confounding causes. In this case, internal validity is low.

In randomized experimental studies, internal validity is gained through the process of random allocation of the units of treatment or intervention to experimental and control or comparison groups. This means that the researcher has randomized other factors besides treatment itself, as there is no systematic bias that brings one type of subject into the treatment group and another into the control or comparison group. Although the groups are not necessarily the same on every characteristic—indeed simply by chance, there are likely to be differences—such differences can be assumed to be randomly distributed and are part and parcel of the stochastic processes taken into account in statistical tests.

Random allocation thus allows the researcher to assume that the only systematic differences between the treatment and comparison groups are found in the treatments or interventions that are applied. When the study is complete, the researcher can argue with confidence that if a difference has been observed between treatment and comparison groups it is likely the result of the treatment itself (because randomization has isolated the treatment effect from other possible causes). In nonrandomized studies it is much more difficult to make this claim, and for this reason randomized experiments have often been described as the "gold standard" for evaluation research.

There is considerable debate both among criminologists and across other fields, such as education or medicine, as to the type of bias that results from relying on nonrandomized as opposed to randomized studies to determine treatment or program effects. Some scholars have argued that the differences between well-designed nonrandomized studies and randomized experiments are not large (Lipsey and Wilson, 1993). However, a recent review of a large number of criminal justice evaluations suggests that nonrandomized studies are likely to systematically overestimate program success (Weisburd, Lum, and Petrosino, 2001).

Example. Most experiments in criminal justice involve the random assignment of individuals. When larger entities such as schools, police beats, or prison living units are randomly assigned, they are sometimes referred to as cluster randomized trials. The Minneapolis Hot Spots Experiment (Sherman and Weisburd, 1995) provides a well-known example of a cluster randomized trial. In that study, the investigators wanted to determine in the least equivocal manner whether intensive police patrol in clusters of addresses that produced significant numbers of calls for service to police, also known as "hot spots," would reduce the levels of crime calls or observed disorder at those places.

To conduct the experiment, the investigators established a pool of 110 hot spots that were eligible for random assignment. This pool of eligible hot spots was then randomly assigned to the innovation group receiving intensive police patrol and a control group that received normal police services. In the Minneapolis study, the investigators randomly assigned the hot spots within what are called statistical blocks or groups of cases that are similar on characteristics measured before the experiment. Such "block randomization" is not required in randomized experiments, but is a method for further ensuring the equivalence of treatment and comparison or control groups.

The strength of the randomized experiment, if it is implemented with full integrity, is that it now permits the investigators to make a direct causal claim that the innovation was responsible for the observed results. If the researchers had simply looked at changes over time at the treated hot spots, it would have been difficult to claim that the observed changes were because of treatment rather than a natural change in levels of crime or disorder over time. Similarly, if the researchers had tried to statistically control for other potential causes in order to isolate out the effect of treatment, it could be argued that some unknown or unmeasured factor was not taken into account. In the Minneapolis study, the researchers found a statistically significant difference between the treatment and control hot spots. Random allocation of subjects to treatment and control conditions allowed the authors to assume that other factors had not systematically confounded their results.

History. Ronald Fisher is often credited with the first discussion of using randomization to ensure equivalent groups in his 1935 treatise entitled "Design of Experiments." The first randomized experiment conducted in criminology is commonly believed to be the Cambridge–Somerville Youth Study (Powers and Witmer, 1951). In this experiment, investigators first matched individual participants (youths nominated by teachers or police as "troubled kids") on certain characteristics and then randomly assigned one to the innovation group receiving counseling and the other to a control group receiving no counseling. Investigators have continuously reported that the counseling program, despite the best intentions, actually hurt the program participants over time when compared to doing nothing to them at all. Although the first participant in the Cambridge–Somerville study was randomly assigned in 1937, the first report of results was not completed until 1951. The first report in a professional journal of the results of a randomized experiment in any field was probably the test of streptomycin for pulmonary tuberculosis in 1948.

Experiments were used selectively until the mid-1960s. As Oakley (1998) notes, randomized experiments became an important research design during that time to evaluate the Johnson Administration's "Great Society" programs. She argues that randomized experiments soon fell out of favor, not because of any new acceptance of the methodological criticisms of experiments, but because the results continuously reported no positive effect for the Administration's social policies and programs.

David Farrington, Lloyd Ohlin, and James Q. Wilson (1986) deserve credit for helping to put randomized experiments on the radar screen of criminologists in the mid-1980s. Their influential book entitled *Understanding and Controlling Crime*, recommended the use of randomized experiments whenever possible to test justice innovations. This book had ramifications for the U.S. National Institute of Justice, which under the direction of James Chips Stewart soon thereafter supported over two dozen such experiments (Sherman, 1992). Although the support of funding agencies like the National Institute of Justice continues to ebb and flow, recent reviews suggest that randomized experiments are increasing each year and are now cumulatively growing to impressive numbers in criminology. For example, Petrosino and his colleagues (2000) found over 700 citations to randomized or possibly randomized trials relevant to criminology for a register of social science experiments. In 1998, the Academy of Experimental Criminology was established to recognize investigators who conduct experiments in justice settings by inducting them as Fellows.

Barriers to the Use of Randomized Experiments

Although randomized experiments in criminal justice have become more accepted, they are a small percentage of the total number of impact or outcome evaluations conducted in areas relevant to crime and justice each year. There are a number of possible explanations for why experiments have lagged behind other research methods. One reason may be simply that the origins of criminology can be traced most directly to disciplines in which experimental methods are not common, like sociology. But a number of scholars have argued that ethical or practical concerns make experimentation particularly difficult in crime and justice research. For example, there is concern that the random allocation of criminal justice sanctions or treatments violates basic legal and normative standards.

Over the last two decades criminal justice researchers have illustrated that randomized experiments can be carried out across a wide variety of settings and across a number of different types of criminal justice institutions. Researchers have overcome barriers to randomization of criminal justice innovations in a number of different ways (see Weisburd, 2000). For example, in the area of treatment experiments, it is common that there are not enough resources to provide treatment to all eligible subjects. In such cases, researchers have argued successfully that random allocation provides a fair method for choosing those who will gain treatment.

The most difficult area for experimentation is when criminal justice sanctions such as arrest or imprisonment are examined. Even here a number of studies have been developed. In general, fewer ethical objections are raised in studies in which the innovation proposed involves a less punitive sanction than that conventionally applied. In most criminal justice experiments, existing treatments or sanctions are compared to innovative approaches. It is not common in randomized experiments in criminal justice for a control group to receive a placebo or no treatment at all.

Practical barriers to experimentation have also hindered the development of randomized studies in criminal justice. It is generally assumed that it is more difficult to gain cooperation for randomized experimental approaches than nonrandomized methods. This has led some scholars to argue that the "external validity" of experimental research is often lower than that of nonrandomized studies. External validity refers to the degree to which the sample studied represents the population of interest. If experimental studies are to be carried out only in select criminal justice jurisdictions or institutions, or only among specific subjects, than the external validity of experimental studies can be questioned.

Although the external validity of randomized studies, like nonrandomized studies, will vary from study to study, a number of recent trends have contributed to the expansion of the experimental model in criminal justice evaluation. First, the wide use of randomized experiments in medicine and the public exposure of such studies have led to wide acceptance among the public and policy makers of experimental methods. Second, there is a growing recognition of the importance of evaluating criminal justice treatments and programs as part of a more general movement referred to as evidence-based policy that seeks to track the effectiveness and efficiency of government. Finally, in the U.S., and more recently in Europe, public support for partnerships between criminal justice researchers and criminal justice professionals has grown. Such collaboration has led to a greater understanding of experimental methods among practitioners.

Conclusions

Although randomized experiments are less common in criminal justice than other types of methods, they are often very influential. There are a number examples in which randomized criminal justice studies have led to changes in policy, practice, and programming (Dennis, 1988; Sherman, 1992).

John DiIulio (1991) writes that because of their methodological rigor, they are the only type of design that allows policy makers to overcome entrenched ideological and political positions in sensitive areas like criminal justice.

DAVID WEISBURD AND ANTHONY PETROSINO

References and Further Reading

Boruch, R.F., *Randomized Experiments for Planning and Evaluation: A Practical Guide*, Newbury Park, CA: Sage, 1997.

Campbell, D.T. and Stanley, J., *Experimental and Quasi-Experimental Designs for Research*, Boston, MA: Houghton-Mifflin, 1963.

Dennis, M.L., *Implementing Randomized Field Experiments: An Analysis of Criminal and Civil Justice Research*, Ph.D. Dissertation, Northwestern University. Ann Arbor, MI: University Microforms, 1988.

DiIulio, J. 1991, *No Escape: The Future of American Corrections*, New York, NY: Basic Books, 1991.

Farrington, D.P., Randomized experiments on crime and justice, in *Crime and Justice: An Annual Review of Research*, Vol. IV, Tonry, M. and Morris, N. (Eds.), Chicago, IL: University of Chicago Press, 1983.

Farrington, D.P., Ohlin, L., and Wilson, J.Q. *Understanding and Controlling Crime*, New York, NY: Springer-Verlag, 1986.

Fisher, R.A., *The Design of Experiments*. London, UK: Oliver and Boyd, 1935.

Lipsey, M.W. and Wilson, D.B., The efficacy of psychological, educational, and behavioral treatment: Confirmation from meta-analysis, *American Psychologist* 48 (1993).

Oakley, A., Experimentation and social interventions: A forgotten but important history, *British Medical Journal* 317 (1998).

Petrosino, A., Boruch, R.F., Rounding, C., McDonald, S., and Chalmers, I. (Eds.), The Campbell collaboration social, psychological, educational and criminological trials register (C2-SPECTR) to facilitate the preparation and maintenance of systematic reviews of social and educational interventions, *Evaluation Research in Education* 14 (2000).

Powers, E. and Witmer, H., *An Experiment in the Prevention of Delinquency: The Cambridge–Somerville Youth Study*, New York, NY: Columbia University Press, 1951.

Sherman, L.W. and Weisburd, D.L., General deterrent effects of police patrol in crime 'hot spots': A randomized, controlled trial, *Justice Quarterly* 12 (1995).

Sherman, L.W., *Policing Domestic Violence*, New York, NY: Free Press, 1992.

Weisburd, D., Randomized experiments in criminal justice policy: Prospects and problems, *Crime & Delinquency* 46 (2000).

Weisburd, D., Lum, C., and Petrosino, A., Does research design affect study outcomes in criminal justice?, *The Annals of the American Academy of Political and Social Research* 578 (2000).

Extortion and Blackmail

The crimes of blackmail and extortion are usually associated with deviance in the business world including governmental agencies. Such associations allow these actions to be classified as examples of white-collar crimes or organized crime. The distinction between these classifications is dependent upon the offender's employment. If the offender is committing the illegal acts of blackmail or extortion but is employed in a legal business, then it is considered to be a white-collar crime. This type of behavior would also include government officials who use their office to engage in acts of extortion or blackmail. If, however, the offender is engaged in these acts but is involved in an illegal business, then the acts would be classified as organized crime.

The behaviors encompassed in the terms of extortion and blackmail are important to delineate, as they have changed throughout time. The definitional constructs of extortion have, however, been slightly refined. In common law times, extortion was generally defined as "the obtaining of property from another induced by wrongful use of actual or threatened force, violence, or fear, or under color of official right" (Black's Law, 1990, 585). Behaviors currently classified as extortion include "obtaining property from another by wrongful use of actual or threatened force, fear or violence, *or* the corrupt taking of a fee by a public officer, under color of his or her office, when that fee is not due." The under-color-of-law distinction is defined as the "inappropriate or illegal action taken by government employees … while acting under the authority of their government positions" (Reid, 2003). The current definition enumerates the corrupt behaviors of public officials who engage in acts of extortion as a specific violation under this crime. Although this distinction was generally embedded in the common law definition of extortion, the enumeration of these behaviors by public officials as criminal expanded the scope of extortion.

The defining characteristics of blackmail have remained stable over time. According to Black's Law (1990, 170), blackmail is defined as "the unlawful demand of money or property under threat to do bodily harm, to injure property, to accuse of crime, or to expose disgraceful defects." Today, the definition of blackmail remains relatively unchanged. It is defined as the "unlawful demand of money or property by threatening bodily harm or exposure of information that is disgraceful or criminal" (Reid, 2003).

Extortion and blackmail are similar offenses and often occur in conjunction with one another. However, it is important to distinguish the two acts as separate from one another. The primary distinction between these two crimes is that in blackmail the threat that is being made is not a physical threat, but rather a threat to release embarrassing or criminal information. Extortion, on the other hand, involves violence or the threat of violence.

To fully understand extortion and blackmail it becomes imperative to explore the causal explanations for such behaviors. Perhaps the most widely recognized explanation is found in Sutherland's concept of white-collar crime. Sutherland (1959) defined white-collar crime as behavior committed by a member of society holding high status during the course of his or her occupation. Sutherland's specific theoretical explanation of crime, differential association, states that criminal behavior is the result of a learning process. In the case of white-collar crimes, such as extortion or blackmail, the behaviors are learned through exposure to similar behaviors within the occupational environment. After prolonged and repeated exposure to the commission of these behaviors by colleagues, many individuals become accustomed to their presence. Eventually, these individuals will tend to adopt those behaviors as normal and acceptable, thus favoring the behaviors exhibited within the workplace rather than the laws favorable to society.

Other theories of plausible explanation include opportunity theory as offered by Cloward and Ohlin (1960). Seeking to expound upon Merton's concept of anomie through the addition of differential association principles, these theorists felt that access to illegal opportunities was just as important as access to legitimate opportunities in the causation of crime. According to the differential opportunity theory, a person's reaction to anomie is largely dependent upon the environment. If there are legitimate means of achieving success, then legitimate means will likely be used. If, however, there are illegitimate means available to realize success, then it is likely the individual will engage in the illegal acts. Thus, the opportunities within one's environment become the pivotal influence. If one's environment is inundated with illegal opportunities, then that individual is more likely to engage in such acts. This particular theoretical explanation's recognition of the importance of opportunities for legal and illegal activities is particularly applicable to extortion and blackmail, given their propensity for involvement in white-collar, as well as organized crime.

Many theorists support the rational choice perspective as a viable approach to the explanation of crimes such as extortion and blackmail. Assuming that people have free will and the ability to make decisions regarding their behavior, this perspective allows for the explanation that people make a calculated decision in which they weigh the benefits and the perceived risk. In the case of extortion and blackmail, many offenders often find that the benefits (usually money) often outweigh any risks, as many of the victims will not likely offer any resistance given the delicate nature of the information held by the offender. In keeping with this perspective, routine activities theory is used as an explanation of crime. This theory is premised upon three fundamental beliefs: (1) there are numerous motivated offenders, (2) suitable targets exist, and (3) capable guardians are lacking (Brown, Esbensen, and Geis, 2001). In the application of this theory to extortion and blackmail, it is assumed that the offenders have calculated the risks and determined that the benefits usually outweigh the risks. As previously discussed, the risks associated with such crimes are usually minimal.

In another integrated approach, Coleman (1985) seeks to explain white-collar crime through the combined approach of opportunity theory and motivation, arguing that that crime is caused by a combination of opportunity and motivation, as well as the neutralization of any ethical or moral restraints. The theory contains an appropriate explanation of extortion and blackmail given their link to opportunity, as well as the likelihood that offenders engage in a rational decision to commit such crimes.

Finally, many offenders engage in the use of one or more of the techniques of neutralization set forth by Sykes and Matza (1957) to explain their involvement in extortion or blackmail. Justifications such as the denial of responsibility, denial of injury, as well as denial of the victim, are often used when "explaining" criminal involvement in extortion or blackmail. The use of these techniques or justifications allows individuals to remain committed to the norms of society although violating such norms through the commission of criminal behaviors. This explanation is especially applicable to these crimes as many individuals who engage in these behaviors are considered to be models members of society. By engaging in the act of neutralization, these individuals are able to commit extortion or blackmail, rationalize their involvement, and still adhere to the norms of society at large.

Statistical information regarding extortion and blackmail are not currently captured on a nationwide basis as a part of the Uniform Crime Report. In an effort to provide for more thorough crime statistics, the Department of Justice has offered an alternative form of data collection. The system, the National Incident Based Reporting System (NIBRS), provides for collection of data in expanded crime categories including measures of extortion and blackmail. The ability to accurately provide statistical information regarding the prevalence of extortion and blackmail, however, is far from being realized. Although created in 1989, by 2001 there were only a total of 21 states involved in the submission of NIBRS data, many of which did not have full participation of jurisdictions (Bureau of Justice Statistics, 2001).

Although the exact amount of blackmail and extortion that occur in the U.S. in unknown, there is an awareness that such behaviors occur frequently in our society. These activities are not unique to the U.S. Great Britain has struggled with politically motivated blackmail throughout history (McCalman, 1988). Japan's corporate world is especially vulnerable to the crimes of extortion and blackmail (McGregory, 1994). These crimes have also been linked to terrorism in Ireland (Silke, 1998).

The government has employed several strategies in an effort combat the activities of blackmail and extortion. One strategy has been to encourage businesses and agencies to provide for more oversight and regulation of themselves. In an effort to deter individuals, in 1991, the Sentencing Commission also recommended harsher penalties for white-collar criminals. Finally, law enforcement agencies have focused their efforts on white-collar crimes. In fact, the identification of such crimes is listed as one of the FBI's top priorities. These efforts are often largely symbolic in nature, as many individuals are reluctant to report such crimes. When blackmail and extortion occur at the hands of government officials and are reported to law enforcement, then such agencies, usually the Federal Bureau of Investigation, investigate the crime and seek remedies in the criminal justice system. Again, owing to the intrinsic nature of these crimes, the likelihood of successfully identifying and prosecuting such crime is problematic at best. Furthermore, when these activities are committed under the auspices of organized crime, the very nature of these crimes and the environment in which they are committed makes the likelihood for reporting even more unlikely.

Finally, the classification of blackmail as an illegal activity has received a lot of attention. In fact, there is a formidable debate among criminologists regarding whether blackmail should be criminalized. The primary proponent of the call for decriminalization involves the Libertarian perspective. The most recognized of these advocates, Block (1999), argues that the essential components of the crime of blackmail are in themselves legal acts. For instance, the threat to release damaging information about another, when carried out alone, does not constitute an illegal act. Likewise, if an individual were to offer another money in return for the withholding of damaging information, then that would not constitute an illegal act. Therefore, the criticisms regarding the designation of these two acts as the criminal offense of blackmail is contingent upon the inherently legal nature of its two essential components. These theorists argue that blackmail should be treated akin to a contract and decriminalized. The only instance in which blackmail should be criminalized, they argue, is if force is threatened or used. The opponents of decriminalization argue that the inherently legal components of blackmail do not necessarily legalize the simultaneous commission of these acts. If blackmail were to be decriminalized and relegated to a contract obligation, as suggested by Block and other proponents, then the secrecy for which one strives in the formation of the contract will be compromised (Kipnis, 1999). Simply stated, by allowing individuals to engage in contractual obligations involving exchange of goods for the silence regarding embarrassing or criminal information, the very secrecy expressly sought in the contract is compromised.

LISA HUTCHINSON WALLACE

References and Further Reading

Black, H.C., Ed., *Black's Law Dictionary.* St. Paul, MN: West Publishing (1990).

Berman, M.N. The evidenciary theory of blackmail, *University of Chicago Law Review, 65* (1998).

Block, W. The crime of blackmail: A libertarian critique, *Criminal Justice Ethics, 18* (1999).

Block, W. Replies to Levin and Kipnis, *Criminal Justice Ethics, 18* (1999).

Brown, S., Esbensen, F., and Geis, G. *Criminology: Explaining Crime and Its Content.* Cincinnati, OH: Anderson Publishing, 2001.

Bureau of Justice Statistics, *Criminal Victimization in the U.S.: 2001*. Washington, DC: U.S. Department of Justice (2002).

Cloward, R. and Ohlin, L. *Delinquency and Opportunity: A Theory of Delinquent Gangs*, New York, NY: Free Press, 1960.

Coleman, J.W. *Criminal Elite: The Sociology of White Collar Crime.* New York, NY: St. Martin's Press, 1985.

Feinberg, J. *Harmless Wrongdoing*, Oxford, UK: Oxford University Press (1990).

Katz, L. *Ill-Gotten Gains: Evasion, Blackmail, Fraud, and Kindred Puzzles of the Law*, Chicago, IL: University of Chicago Press (1996).

Kipnis, K. Blackmail as a career choice: A liberal assessment, *Criminal Justice Ethics, 18* (1999).

Levin, M. Blackmail, *Criminal Justice Ethics, 18* (1999).

Lindgren, J. Unraveling the paradox of blackmail, *84 Columbia Law Review 670* (1984).

McCalman, I. Radical rogues and blackmailers, *History Today, 38* (1988).

McGregor, R. Japan Inc.'s dirty little secret, *World Press Review, 41* (1994).

Reid, S.T. *Crime and Criminology.* Boston, MA: McGraw-Hill, 2003.

Silke, A. In defense of the realm: Financing loyalist terrorism in Northern Ireland, *Studies in Conflict and Terrorism, 21* (1998).

Sykes, G. and Matza, D. Techniques of neutralization, *American Sociological Review, 22* (1957).

Sutherland, E.H. Is 'white-collar crime' crime? *American Sociological Review, 10* (1945).

Sutherland, E.H. *White Collar Crime*, New York, NY: Holt, Rinehart and Winston, 1959.

Eyewitness Identification

The identification by an eyewitness may be the most influential piece of evidence presented in the courtroom, especially in the case where little other evidence is available. Jury members frequently accept eyewitness testimony without question, even in cases where other contradictory evidence is admitted. Police officers, attorneys, and others in the criminal justice system are more likely to accept, rather than reject, the testimony of an eyewitness. The significance of an observer's identification may be explained by law enforcement's dependence on common sense generalizations regarding the behavior of individuals. If a witness recalls information and identifies the suspect in a confident manner, eyewitness identification becomes even more powerful. The power of eyewitness identification may also be because of alleged belief in the ultimate accuracy of human memory and observation. Historically, law enforcement has depended on witness statements to determine what occurred during a crime. Before technological advances in forensic science, crime scene reconstruction was almost exclusively dependent on human memory (Loftus, 1979).

Two different mental processes take place when an individual distinguishes and recollects events. Perception is an interpretive process that involves more than simply seeing. What someone perceives may be different from what someone sees and is based, in part, on past experiences. Evidence shows that the processes determining perception are largely unconscious. In addition to unconscious processes, individual differences such as color blindness, depth perception, and lack of visual discrimination can also influence perception.

The second process associated with recollection is memory, which is examined in three phases: acquisition, retention, and retrieval. A failure to remember occurs when any of the three phases functions improperly. Memory is extremely malleable and subject to change and distortion (Yarmey, 1979). The process by which humans store memories is continually altered and changed in relation to present experiences. Like the process of perception, individuals are cognitively unaware of memory processes. Eyewitnesses are not aware of the neurological process of organizing, interpreting, and associating a final memory with a person or event. Their final memory is only of the person or event. There are also chances for witnesses to receive additional information after an event and then unconsciously incorporate it into their original memories. Even witnesses with the best intentions may distort their identification and recall through unconscious processes, which help explain why witnesses may differ totally in their accounts of the same event.

In the courtroom setting, officials are usually concerned with details of events that tend to be jumbled, strange, and threatening to eyewitnesses. In most instances, the experience of an armed robbery or similar event creates a stimulus overload in the individual. Detailed scrutiny does not usually take place when too many things occur too quickly under less than ideal circumstances (Loftus and Loftus, 1980). Time is also a factor in observation and perception. The less time an individual is exposed to an event or person, the less accurate recall and perception will be. Research in cognitive psychology indicates that the reverse is also true. One study found that the longer subjects had to view slides of faces, the more accurate they were at later identifying a selected face from photographs (Laugherty, Alexander, and Lane, 1971). The smaller the number of photographs the subjects viewed, the more likely they were to be accurate. This finding provides a suggestion to law enforcement agencies with regard to presentation of suspect photo spreads.

Significance of various details surrounding a crime also affects eyewitness identification. Certain components of an event may stand out to a witness, owing to their stimulating nature. Weapons, disguises, and blood are more likely to be noticed than facial features, clothing, or background stimuli (Yarmey and Jones, 1983). A gun pointed at a person's head is more likely to be closely studied compared to other nonthreatening situational factors. Referred to as "weapon focus," this occurrence takes place when concentration of some victim's or witness' attention on a threatening weapon forces him or her to pay less attention to other details and events of a crime (Loftus and Ketcham, 1991).

Crimes vary in the degree of emotional arousal invoked in eyewitnesses. Greater levels of violence tend to generate increases in arousal, to the point where additional increases in severe violence no longer increase arousal because the witness decides not to watch any longer. Witness recall and recognition abilities reflect a negative relationship on the violence-arousal continuum (Clifford and Scott, 1978). Greater levels of criminal violence yield a greater level of emotional reaction to an event, resulting in witness identification that is lower in accuracy. Law enforcement must be cautious in its reliance on eyewitness testimony of violent crimes, especially when the level of violence is extremely high.

Memory and confidence may influence eyewitness testimony accuracy more than situational variables. Research has shown that witnesses are less accurate and complete in their description of events after long time periods have elapsed between the event and recall. Eyewitnesses often must recall events several months (or sometimes years) after they occur. During this time period, the person is likely to receive and process new information, which may contribute to greater inaccuracy (Loftus, 1979). The work of Loftus and others indicates that attorneys or law enforcement officers are capable of manipulating the memory of a witness through the process of feeding relevant information. This practice is more likely to occur with evidence that is less noticeable than with more significant details. If possible, police officers should obtain witness information immediately after an event and then have the information relayed as closely as possible in the actual courtroom testimony.

The identification of a suspect by an eyewitness provides compelling evidence for conviction in criminal cases. It is imperative, then, that this evidence be extremely reliable. Standard identification procedures used by law enforcement include mug shot tasks, photo spreads, and police lineups. According to Wells (1988), mug shot tasks are used when the police have no particular suspect in mind. In a mug shot task, witnesses are asked to view a large array of photographs to determine whether they can recognize a perpetrator. As previous research has noted (Laugherty, Alexander, and Lane, 1971), the large numbers of photos presented in a mug shot task can significantly decrease accuracy of identifications. When police do have a suspect in mind, photo spreads may be used for identification purposes. Because this method uses fewer photos of suspects, it is an improvement over the mug shot task and can therefore minimize false identifications. Although the photo-spread method does have its advantages, it may contribute to false identifications as well. Both of these methods are common practices often used prior to police lineups. When a witness selects a suspect from a mug shot task or photo spread, the suspect selected (who may not be guilty) is often included in a subsequent lineup, which increases the chance that he or she will be selected again owing to increased familiarity. Referred to as a "photo-biased lineup" (Loftus, 1996), this procedure can contribute to misidentification. If used properly, police lineups alone can be a valuable way to identify suspects.

Lineups typically consist of one suspect and some number of known nonsuspects, often referred to as foils or distracters. The foils play a critical role in the function of lineup identification procedures. One purpose is to make it unlikely that the witness will identify the suspect through simple or sophisticated guessing strategies. One method for selecting foils is to select people who look like the suspect. A national survey (Wogalter, Malpass, and Berger, 1993) reported that 83% of police officers construct lineups using the suspect-matched method. This method is appealing because it provides a foundation for the prosecution to argue that the witness who has identified the suspect can distinguish between the perpetrator (assuming the suspect is guilty) and several people who look very similar to the perpetrator; and it should protect innocent suspects from false identification by surrounding them with look-alikes.

As straightforward as this method appears, some have argued that it may have potentially serious problems, and an alternative method for selecting lineup foils has been proposed. With this strategy, the foils are matched not to the photograph of the suspect, but rather to the description of the perpetrator given by the witness. This alternative method is referred to as a description-matched method of foil selection (Luus and Wells, 1991). This method has been criticized because it does not give a clear, operational definition of "similarity." Also, it may reduce the likelihood of correctly identifying a guilty suspect, and it may produce a high rate of false identifications when the suspect is innocent. If these criticisms are indeed valid, police officers using the match-to-suspect method may be using a flawed procedure.

If the task is to pick foils that look similar to the suspect, the question witnesses must answer is, "How similar is similar enough?" If the foils are not similar enough to the suspect, the suspect may be identified merely because he stands out in the lineup, or because he is the only person in the lineup who fits the perpetrator's description. At the other end of the scale, if the foils look too much like the suspect, it may be nearly impossible to distinguish among the lineup alternatives, and even witnesses whose memories are reasonably accurate may have difficulty in correctly identifying the guilty suspect. Presumably, there is some appropriate level of similarity between these two extremes, but just what that appropriate level of similarity should be is not clear. Malpass and Lindsay (1999) proposed the Acceptable Foils Index (AFI) as a standard for foil inclusion in lineups. The AFI is based on an arbitrary percentage of chance expectation for suspect and foil identification. A chance percentage is used to determine the level below which a foil must not go without becoming an unacceptable member of a lineup. Malpass and Lindsay (1999) explain, "if chance expectation were 1/6 (=16.67%), then at a 75% criterion, a foil falling below 12.5% mock witness choices would be deemed unacceptable." Further, when this procedure is used, the resulting AFI is equal to number of foils regarded as acceptable. The authors argue that the AFI is simple to calculate and is a valuable tool because it can be understood by jurors.

Luus and Wells (1991) argue that the suspect-matched method may produce lower correct identification rates than the description-matched method. Because there is no clear standard for "similar enough," and if lineup fairness is defined in terms of the similarity of the foils to the suspect, a conscientious police officer, in attempting to create a very good lineup, may select foils that are so similar to the suspect that even a witness with a reasonably good memory might have difficulty distinguishing the suspect. When applied to lineup assessment procedures, Bayes' theorem, a mathematical model, states that the probability of a suspect's guilt depends as much on the relative number of guilty suspects who are chosen as on the number of innocent suspects. In recent research, Bayes' theorem was used to calculate the probability of an innocent suspect being chosen in a lineup (Levi, 1998). This probability was moderately high, which has potentially serious implications for wrongful convictions based on eyewitness identification.

Research indicates that law enforcement identification methods are subject to a wide range of biases, from subtle methods to the very obvious techniques. In their investigation of wrongful imprisonment, Brandon and Davies (1997) found that 70 convictions were the result of mistaken identifications. It appears that juries tend to strongly believe witnesses who choose defendants from lineups, regardless of contradictory evidence. Limiting lineup testimony in cases where additional evidence is available, or only conducting lineups with a standard of probable cause, might reduce wrongful convictions. A legal term related to standards of numerous police procedures, probable cause refers to facts and circumstances of a given case that lead an arresting officer to believe enough evidence exists to merit further police action. In addition to modifying current police methods, Levi (1998) also advocated further education of judges and juries regarding the value of lineups. The National Institute of Justice (1999) recommends practices and procedures for the collection and preservation of eyewitness evidence. Standardized techniques such as these presented here can be extremely beneficial to law enforcement.

It is apparent that evidence obtained through traditional procedures of eyewitness testimony and questioning is abundant with possible misconceptions and inaccuracies, despite a witness' absolute certainty. Memory and perception may be viewed as an elaborate puzzle, where original input is altered, somewhat lost, and translated into a format that best suits the individual's experiences, expectancies, and needs of others. Witness, offender, and situational variables intertwine to create an acceptable output, which may differ significantly from the event that actually took place. Nonetheless, research indicates that eyewitness identification will continue to be a primary source of evidence in both criminal and civil court cases. As such, the criminal justice system should continue exploring assumptions about eyewitnesses and begin to alter some of its criminal identification procedures.

Kristy Holtfreter

References and Further Reading

Brandon, R. and Davies, C., *Wrongful Imprisonment: Mistaken Convictions and Their Consequences*, London, UK: Allen and Unwin, 1973.

Clifford, B.R. and Scott, J., Individual and situational factors in eyewitness testimony, *Journal of Applied Psychology* 63 (1978).

Laughery, K.R., Judith, F.A., and Lane, A.B., Recognition of human faces: Effects of target exposure time target position, pose position, and type of photograph, *Journal of Applied Psychology* 55 (1971).

Levi, A.M., Are defendants guilty if they were chosen in a lineup? *Law and Human Behavior* 22 (4) (1998).

Loftus, E.F., *Eyewitness Testimony*, Cambridge, MA: Harvard University Press, 1979.

Loftus, E. and Ketcham, K., *Witness for the Defense*. New York, NY: St. Martin's Press, 1991.

Loftus, E.F. and Loftus, G.R., On the permanence of stored information in the human brain, *American Psychologist* 35 (1980).

Luus, C.E. and Wells, G. Eyewitness identification and the selection of distracters for lineups, *Law and Human Behavior* 15 (1991).

Malpass, R.S. and Lindsay, R.C.L., Measuring lineup fairness, *Applied Cognitive Psychology* 13 (1999).

Technical Working Group on Eyewitness Evidence, *Eyewitness Evidence: A Guide for Law Enforcement*, Washington, DC: Research Report, National Institute of Justice, October 1999.

Wells, G.L., *Eyewitness Identification*, Ontario, Canada: The Carswell Co. Ltd, 1988.

Wells, G.L., Applied eyewitness testimony research: System variables and estimator variables, *Journal of Personality and Social Psychology* 36 (1978).

Wogalter, M.S., Malpass, R.S., and Berger, M.A., How police officers construct lineups: A national survey, *Proceedings of the Human Factors and Ergonomics Society*, Santa Monica, CA: Human Factors and Ergonomics Society, 1993.

Yarmey, A.D., *The Psychology of Eyewitness Testimony*, New York, NY: The Free Press, 1979.

Yarmey, A.D. and Jones, H.P., Is the psychology of eyewitness identification a matter of common sense? In *Evaluating Witness Evidence: Recent Psychological Research and New Perspectives,* Lloyd-Bostick, S.M. and Clifford, B.R. (Eds.), Chichester, England: Wiley, 1983.

Yuille, J.C., A critical examination of the psychological and practical implications of eyewitness research. *Law and Human Behavior* 4 (1980).

See also **Witnesses, The Right to Confront**

F

Family Relationships and Criminal Behavior

A variety of sociological and psychological theories offer explanations about the initiation and termination of criminal behavior in the context of family relationships (Bowlby, 1947; Hirschi, 1969; Rosen, 1985; Cernkovich and Giordano, 1987; Gottfredson and Hirschi, 1990; McCord, 1991; Agnew, 1992; Brezina, 1996; Sampson and Laub, 1996; Widom, 1996; Moffitt, 1997; Hagan and McCarthy, 1997; Akers, 1998; Katz, 2000). But regardless of the theoretical or disciplinary framework used, a number of specific family factors have been repeatedly shown to lead to the initiation of criminal offending or toward desistance, the termination of criminal offending. This essay will discuss these elements of family relationships, as well as the social structural forces that impinge on the family creating additional stresses and strains that sometimes increase the likelihood of criminal behavior. Finally, this essay will provide some new and important insights with regard to what social scientists are learning about familial gender and racial differences in the initiation of criminal behavior and in desistance from crime.

Attachments

Although sociological criminology has discussed attachments to parents or the social bond between an adolescent and a parent as a means by which youth will be held back from delinquency and later adult criminality, only psychologically based theories have focused more precisely on the early secure attachment of the infant or toddler to a primary caregiver as one that prohibits the later development of delinquency and adult criminality (Bowlby, 1947; Hirschi, 1969). This early secure attachment between a caretaker and an infant has been shown to facilitate the development of empathy (Born, Chevalier, and Humblet, 1997). Empathy, or the emotional and cognitive capacity to put oneself in someone else's shoes, is causally related to conforming behavior or the absence of criminal behavior (Richardson et al., 1994). However, as Sampson and Laub's (1996) and Hagan and McCarthy's recent research on integrative theories of social capital has shown, a number of social structural background factors also influence these early attachments (Hagan and McCarthy, 1997; Barak, 1998; Katz, 2002). For example, youth who grow up in economically deprived areas with few legitimate job opportunities, poor educational institutions, and parents who have also been the victims of such contexts, become embedded in criminal networks rather than in legitimate social networks. Legitimate social networks facilitate their transition to the world of paid conventional labor (Hagan and McCarthy, 1997; Anderson, 1998; McCord, 1998). Thus, the social world in which the family resides clearly affects the parents' ability to form viable attachments to the youth that will prohibit later delinquency and crime. However, within the social context of our predominantly White and patriarchal or male dominated social institutions, other types of constraints also exist that lead to criminal initiation and desistance. These uniquely gendered and raced socialization patterns will be thoroughly discussed within the context of the parents' parenting as it affects the development of delinquency and the social structural effects that impinge on parents' parenting.

Specific parental behaviors increase or decrease the likelihood of later criminal behavior. For example, a classic piece of scientific research illustrates that specific types of parental management techniques work differently, depending on the gender and race of the youth, in prohibiting the development of criminal behavior (Cernkovich and Giordano, 1987).

Additionally, these scholars found that family processes or interactions matter more in terms of predicting delinquency than does whether or not both parents are physically living in the same household with the child or that the family is a blended family. Similarly, more recent research on child well-being, which includes the absence of problem behaviors like delinquency, reveals that divorce or the two parent family model is less important than is the maintenance of ongoing quality relationships between the absent parent and the child (Acock and Demo, 1993). Cernkovich and Giordano's seven family processes are listed below:

1. Control and supervision of the adolescent.
2. Identity support or support for the adolescent's own interests.
3. Caring and trust exhibited by the parent.
4. Intimate communication with the adolescent about problems or feelings.
5. Instrumental communication with the adolescent or talking about tasks.
6. Parental disapproval of adolescent peers.
7. Conflict between the parent or parents and youth.

Within the contexts of two types of family structures (both biological parents and mother only), they found unique processes within each family structure and unique differences among distinctive racial and gendered groups of youth. Specifically, non-White females reported the greatest levels of parental control whereas White males reported the least. Additionally, among the nonoffending youth, females reported higher levels of identity support. However, identity support decreased directly from low-frequency minority group offenders to high-frequency majority group offenders whereas conflict levels similarly were higher in the more frequent offender groups. Among the higher frequency majority group male offenders, family process better explained White youth crime than non-White youth crime. Although they found that Whites were more affected by family structure than family processes, other work has found that the opposite is true (Rosen, 1985). Among non-White males and females, the best predictors of delinquency were lower levels of parental control and supervision. Among the high frequency majority group offenders, both male and females had the lowest levels of identity support. Interestingly, they did briefly examine mother and stepfather families, but were forced to drop this structural group because the sample size was so small. Before eliminating this group from the analysis they found that all seven family processes had the exact opposite effect on delinquency than what was expected. Other research has also found similarly unique relationships in blended families, especially with regard to sons' development and later delinquent behavior. However, much of this research fails to control for the nature of the boy's relationship with his absent birth father. And there is sufficient evidence that the functional absence of a quality father or a mother relationship (not just the physical absence from a household) in a child's life negatively affects children and increases the likelihood of delinquency (Nagin and Farrington, 1992; Katz, 1999).

More recent work has also explored the effect of racial, class and gender differences in parenting practices on levels of delinquency as well as unique gender and racial gender socialization patterns that may explain some of the differences in the gendered nature of criminal behavior and the race and class-biased nature of criminal justice processing. For example, although White males commit most types of crimes, poor and non-White males are more likely to be incarcerated. Furthermore, although we have a great deal of information with regard to family influences on delinquent behavior, many of our theories focus more exclusively on males and appear to better explain male delinquency and crime than female delinquency and crime.

The argument with regard to the gendered nature of crime (boys and men are more likely to commit crime than girls and women) and its significance to theoretical development has been recently put to test by work revealing that White delinquency was better explained by traditional theories of crime, such as social learning theory and revised strain theory (Katz, 2000). In other words, White girls were more likely to be delinquent if they had delinquent friends and if they had been sexually abused as children. However, both sexual abuse and physical abuse explained minority girls' delinquency. Recent work within the prison population also reveals that adult women inmates are more likely to have abuse histories than male inmates (Wolf Harlow, 1999). More importantly, rather than anger predicting female delinquency as it has been shown to do among males, general upset feelings explained White female delinquency whereas feelings of alienation predicted minority girls' delinquency. Moreover, among both groups of women, having been abused by a mate significantly increased female violence against others and against their spouse. Clearly, there are differences in women's pathways toward initial involvement in crime. In addition to these differences, similarly distinctive patterns appear to lead to desistance.

Specifically, although there are findings in the literature that those men who develop strong marital attachments to women (at least men who are not substance abusers) are more likely to desist, the effects on women are quite different. Minority women who are physically abused while remaining emotionally attached to their spouse are more likely to become involved in generalized violence. Additionally, these attachments do not eliminate spousal abuse and, among non-White women, increase it. By extension, White women's marital attachments have no effects on either type of violence. Most importantly, gender discrimination and/or racial discrimination in the workplace created strain on these women that led them to participation in adult crime (Katz, 2000). Similarly, other research reveals that poor inner-city women of color are more likely to desist as the result of receiving drug and alcohol treatment or becoming fearful of repeated incarcerations (Blount, Danner, Vega, and Silverman, 1991; Pettiway, 1997; Baskin and Sommers, 1998). Additionally, it appears that women's desistance has little to do with becoming a parent, whereas among men becoming a father has been shown to decrease offending (Farrington and West, 1995; Baskin and Sommers, 1998).

Therefore, evidence is growing that the family processes that initiate White and non-White female and male entrance into crime and delinquency remain quite unique (Simpson and Ellis, 1995). Similarly, adult processes of desistance reflect that whereas marital attachments facilitate desistance among men, job and marital attachments among women do not (Katz, 2000). In fact, such attachments to abusive men often lead women into crime (Richie, 1996; Pettiway, 1997; Katz, 2000). Clearly, gender and racial differences exist with regard to the initiation of criminal behavior (men are more likely to commit crimes than women) and the causal pathways towards desistance are also quite dissimilar. But how does the social structure influence these processes? Furthermore, how does the precise nature of early infant-parent attachment affect the gendered nature of crime and the gendered nature of the desistance process?

The Social Structure

As mentioned above, family processes predict the initiation of criminal behavior within the context of our unique social structure. Specifically, whereas marital and job attachments facilitate desistance among men, they have virtually no effects on women's desistance. Why are these desistance processes dissimilar? Some scholars believe that these processes of initiation and desistance are unique because not only are gender socialization processes within the family quite distinctive, but so are the effects of the social structure or the institutional pressures and constraints exerted on men versus women and Whites versus non-Whites.

These processes of initiation and desistance are dissimilar because unique socialization experiences of both gendered and racial groups are as dissimilar as are the structural and institutional processes that impinge on these groups. Stated differently, American culture and the American political economy value certain groups over others. That is, in American society men are viewed as more valuable than women; Whites are viewed as more valuable than Blacks, Hispanics, and Native Americans; and the rich are seen as more valuable than the poor. The evidence for this is apparent if readers consider the following social facts. Non-White perpetrators of crimes against Whites serve longer sentences than Whites who victimize Whites or non-Whites. Moreover, most crimes are intraracial, whereas hate crimes are largely perpetrated by working-class alienated Whites against non-Whites. Moreover, White males with the same years of education as non-Whites and females make significantly more money. Additionally, women and non-Whites are socialized in a family, neighborhood and educational context in which their contributions are less valued and their voices are overtly silenced. And if women's voices are not overtly silenced, they are covertly silenced through race and sexual harassment, sexual abuse, rape, or institutionalized White male supremacy. These social structural contexts are not removed from the family but act on the family and create social, emotional, and financial costs that lend themselves to criminal or delinquent acting-out. Similarly, even inappropriate reactive criminal justice polices, such as arrest, function to worsen the stresses, strains and/or the emotional shame of those who have been previously abused or disenfranchised by a privileged White male social hierarchy (Richey, 1996; Hagan and McCarthy, 1997; Collins, 1998). Interestingly, this same male hierarchy that oppresses women and minorities has been linked to male violence against women and against other males (Crossman, Stith, and Bender, 1990; Yllo and Straus, 1990; Messerschmidt, 1993, 1997; Itzin, 1994; Crowell and Burgress, 1996; Bird, 1996; Schwartz and DeKeseredy, 1997; Bennedict and Klein, 1997; Curry, 1998). The dominance of masculinity is also clearly linked not only to our larger cultural ideologies but also to the early infant-parent attachment processes.

Gendered Early Attachment

A variety of scholarly evidence reveals that attachment processes themselves are gendered. First, consider that most of the care taking of infants and young children in American society continues to be performed by women. Second, women and their partners aim to ensure that their child fits into society and so usually attempt to maintain the child's appropriate gender identity. However, in the midst of attempting to do something quite ordinarily accepted in our culture, these primary caretakers, with support from the secondary caretaker, often create different attachment processes and therefore alter the course of female and male development (Cosse, 1992). There is theoretical guidance that suggests that mothers break off the infant-parent bond much earlier to their male children than they do for their female children to ensure identification with the opposite-sex parent. Such early separation then appears to be responsible for differential paths of development as the child ages. For example, in Eric Erikson's model of psychosocial development, Cosse found that males form identity first (as Erickson's model proposed) and then experience intimacy. However, females experience intimacy first and then form an identity. Similarly, other research has found that girls develop empathy or an ethic of care much younger in life than do males (Cosse, 1992; Olweus and Endresen, 1998). Roberts and Strayer found that young girls were more emotionally expressive, insightful and empathetic than same aged boys. However, when boys learn to take the role of the other, they developed empathy skills much earlier. This ability to take the role of the other appears to occur developmentally when boys have their first relationship with a female. But if the formation of this relationship is delayed, clearly a lack of ability to empathize will be present, and a number of studies have found that impairment in the ability to demonstrate empathy is related to the capacity for violent behavior (Ken-Ichi and Mukai, 1993; Richardson et al., 1994; Born, Chevalier, and Humblet, 1997). However, males who are insecurely attached to their primary caretakers may not be capable of such role taking ability, and thus may never develop the capacity for empathy. For example, in a recent review of the literature, researchers found that early infant-parent secure attachment patterns predicted later martial satisfaction, better marital adjustment, and improved awareness of and kindness towards others (Holtzworth, Gregory, and Hutchinson, 1997). And as discussed above, there is evidence that some women's attachments to men may initiate their offending, especially in the context of a history of physical or sexual abuse. Therefore, if a noncriminal or criminal woman with a secure attachment style who has been physically or sexually abused in childhood becomes attached to a criminal man, her chances of becoming criminal are increased. But if a criminal man who was securely attached and who was sexually or physically abused as a child becomes attached to a noncriminal woman, his chances of desisting from crime increase. A criminal or noncriminal woman or man who was insecurely attached to a parent will experience difficulty in developing a marital or partnership attachment. Either pathway for such an insecurely attached individual can lead to crime and delinquency.

Although all these family factors discussed above are predictive of initiation in delinquent behavior, including secure infant-parent attachment, clearly social structural and institutional processes also impinge on the family. The etiology of desistance (and initiation) may have policy implications for not only individual level or family interventions, but also for possible changes within the social structure that will lead towards desistance for many offenders (Uggen and Kruttschnitt, 1998).

Global Issues

Globally, family structures and processes remain unique as men have different expectations according to their specific cultural mores. However, across the world, men remain more violent than women and more likely to engage in violence against women and children in the family. Also similar predictors within families explain delinquency cross-nationally, particularly in Western industrialized societies. More importantly, economic inequality predicts homicide rates cross-nationally as do lower levels of social welfare spending for families (Gartner, 1991; Lee and Blankton, 1999; and Pampel and Williamson, 2001). Families in the U.S. are more likely to suffer from higher levels of economic inequality than Western European nations. In examining homicide rates across eighteen nations, the homicide rate among young males 15–24 increased throughout the 1990s, with the U.S. having the highest rates followed by New Zealand and the United Kingdom. Female homicide rates also are higher in the U.S. than in other countries. Most importantly, changes in the patriarchal social structure of families, specifically an increase in single female heads of household (an indicator of poverty in most cultures as women continue to earn significantly less income than men) also increased the homicide rates across nation-states (Pampel and Williamson, 2001). Speculatively, such an increase is often caused by the lack of significant male attachments to fathers who, following divorce, often fail to maintain ongoing quality relationships with their sons. Most of these comparisons, however, have been made between developed nations or advanced capitalist nations. Little research has examined the relationship between family process and family structure among developing nations or third world nations.

Conclusion

The solutions to these dilemmas appear to be threefold. First, young children should be taught parenting skills in preschool and elementary school. Second, the primary participation of mothers in parenting needs changes so that fathers are involved in active coparenting with their wives or partners in order to change the gendered nature of the attachment process. Finally, social injustices such as racial, sexual, and class-based discrimination should be eliminated so that children can grow up freely to pursue their dreams, unencumbered by parents with no skills and communities with no jobs, poor social services, inadequate welfare and an absence of living wage jobs.

REBECCA S. KATZ

References and Further Reading

Acock, A.C. and Demo, D.H., Family diversity and well-being, *Sage Library of Social Research*, Vol. 195, Sage Publications, 1993.

Agnew, R., Foundation for a general strain theory of crime and delinquency, *Criminology,* 30, 47–87 (1992).

Agnew, R., Rebellon, C., and Thaxton, S., A general strain theory approach to families and delinquency, *The family's role in the production, mediation and prevention of crime, Part II, Contemporary Perspectives in Family Research,* Vol. 2.

Akers, R.L., Social Learning and Social Structure: A General Theory of Crime and Deviance, Northeastern University Press, Boston, MA, 1998.

Anderson, E., Violence and the inner-city street code, in Joan M., Ed., *Violence and Childhood in the Inner City,* Cambridge University Press, London, 1998.

Barak, G., *Integrating Criminologies,* 1998.

Benedict, J. and Klein, A., Arrest and conviction rates for atheletes accused of sexual assault, *Sociology of Sport*, 14, 86–94 (1997).

Baskin, D.R. and Sommers, I.B., Casualities of Community Disorder: Women's careers in Violent Crime, Westview Press, Boulder, CO, 1998.

Bowlby, J., *Forty-four Juvenile Thieves: Their Characters and Home Life,* Bailliere, Tindall and Cox, London, 1947.

Born, M., Chevalier, V., and Humblet, I., Resilience, desistance and delinquent career of adolsecent offenders, *Journal of Adolescence,* 20, 679–694 (1997).

Blount, W.R., Danner, T.A., Vega, M., and Silverman, I.J., The influence of substance abuse among adult female inmates, *Journal of Drug Issues,* 21, 449–467, 1991.

Brezina, T., Adapting to strain: An examination of delinquency coping responses, *Criminology,* 34, 39–60 (1996).

Cernkovich, S.A. and Giordano, P.C., Family relationships and delinquency, *Criminology,* 25, 295–313 (1987).

Collins H.P., *Fighting Words, Black Women and the Search for Justice,* University of Minnesota Press, Minneapolis, MN, 1998.

Crossman, R.K., Sith, S.M., and Bender, M.M., Sex role egalitariansism and marital violence, *Sex Roles*, 22, 293–304 (1990).

Curry, T.J., Beyond the locker room: Campus bars and college athletes, *Sociology of Sport*, 15, 205–215 (1998).

Farrington, D.P. and West, D.J., Effects of marriage, separation, and children on offending by adult males, *Current Perspectives on Aging and the Life Cycle,* 4, 249–281 (1995).

Gartner, R., Family structure, welfare spending and child homicide in developed democratic nations, *Journal of Marriage and the Family,* 53, 231–240 (1991).

Gottfredson, M. and Hirschi, T., *A General Theory of Crime,* Stanford University Press, Stanford, CA, 1990.

Greer L.F. and Michael L.B., Eds., *Families, Crime and Criminal Justice*, JAI Press, An Imprint of Elsevier Science, 2000.

Hagan, J., McCarthy, B., Parker, P., and Climenhage, J., *Mean Streets: Youth Crime and Homelessness*, Cambridge University Press, 1997.

Heimer, K. and De Coster, S., The gendering of violent delinquency, *Criminology,* 37, 277–317, 1999.

Hirschi, T., *Causes of Delinquency,* University of California Press, Berkeley, 1969.

Holtzworth-Munroe, S., Gregory, L., and Hutchinson, G., Violent versus nonviolent husbands: Differences in attachment patterns, dependency and jealousy, *Journal of Family Psychology,* 11, 314–331 (1997).

Katz, R.S., Building the foundation for a side-by-side explanatory model: A genderal theory of crime, the age-graded life course theory and attachment theory, *Western Criminology Review,* 1, 2, 1999. Available at: http://wcr.sonoma.edu/v1n2/katz.html.

Katz, R.S., Re-examining the integrative social capital theory of crime, *Western Criminology Review,* 4, 1, 2002. Available at: http://wcr.sonoma.edu/v4n1/katz.html

Katz, R.S., Explaining girls' and women's crime and desistance in the context of their victimization experiences: A developmental test of revised strain theory and the life course perspective, *Violence against Women,* 6(6), 633–660 (2000).

Ken-Ichi, O.I. and Mukai, H., Empathy and aggression: Effects of self-disclosure and fearful appeal, *The Journal of Social Psychology,* 133, 243–353, 1993.

Messerschmidt, J.W., *Masculinities and Crime Critique and Reconceptualization of Theory,* Rowman and Littlefield Publishers, 1993.

Lee, M.R. and Blankston, W.B., Political structure, economic inequality and homicide: A cross-national analysis, *Deviant Behavior,* 19, 27–55, 1999.

Messerschmidt, J.W., *Crime as Structured Action, Gender, Race, Class, and Crime in the Making*, Sage Publications, 1997.

McCord, J., Placing American urban violence in context, in J. McCord, Ed., *Violence and Childhood in the Inner City,* Cambridge University Press, London, 1997, Chap. 3.

McCord, J., Family relationships, juvenile delinquency, and adult criminality, *Criminology,* 23, 501–518, 1991.

Moffitt, T.E., Neuropsychology, antisocial behavior, and neighborhood context, J. McCord, Ed., *Violence and Childhood in the Inner City,* Cambridge University Press, 1997, Chap. 4.

Olweus, D. and Endresen, I.M., The importance of sex-of-stimulus object: Age trends and sex differences in empathic responsiveness, *Social Development,* 7(3), 370–388 (1998).

Nagin, D.S. and Farrington, D.P., The onset and persistence of offending, *Criminology,* 30, 501–528 (1992).

Pampel, F.C., Williamson, J.B., Age patterns of suicide and homicide rates in high income nations, *Social Forces*, 80(1), (2001).

Pettiway, L., *Workin' It: Women Living Through Drugs and Crime,* Temple University Press, Philadelphia, PA, 1997.

Raine, A., Brennan, P., and Mednick, S.A., Interaction between birth complications and early maternal rejection in predisposing individuals to adult violence: Specificity to serious, early-onset violence, *American Journal of Psychiatry,* 154, 1265–1271, 1997.

Richardson, D.R., Hammock, G.S., Smith, S.M., and Gardner, M., Empathy as a cognitive inhibitor or interpersonal aggression, *Aggressive Behavior,* 20, 275–290, 1994.

Richie, B., Compelled to Crime: The Gender Entrapment of Battered Black Women, Routledge, New York, 1996.

Roberts, W. and Strayer, J., Empathy, emotional expressiveness, and prosocial behavior, *Child Development*, 67, 449–470, 1996.

Sampson, R.J. and Laub, J.H., *Crime in the Making: Pathways and Turning Points Through Life,* Harvard University Press, Cambridge, MA, 1996.

Rosen, L., Family and delinquency: Structure or function? *Criminology,* 23, 553–573, 1985.

Simpson, S.S. and Elis, L., Doing gender: sorting out the caste and crime conundrum, *Criminology,* 33, 47–81, 1995.

Schwartz, M.D. and DeKesredy, W.S., *Sexual Assault on the College Campus: The Role of Male Peer Support*, Sage Publications, Thousand Oaks, CA, 1997.

Uggen, C. and Kruttschnitt, C., Crime in the breaking: Gender differences in desistance, *Law and Society Review,* 32, 339–366, 1998.

Widom, C.C., Childhood sexual abuse and its criminal consequences, *Society,* 33, 47–53, 1996.

Wolf Harlow, C., *Prior Abuse Reported by Inmates and Probationers,* U.S. Department of Justice, Washington, DC, Bureau of Justice Statistics, 1999.

Yllo, K.A. and Straus, M., Patriarchy and violence against wives: the impact of structural and normative factors, in Straus, M.A. and Gelles, R.J., Eds., *Physical Violence in American Families: Risk Factors and Adaptations to Violence in 8145 Families,* Transaction Publishers, New Brusnwick, NJ, 1990, Chap. 22.

See also **Gender and Criminal Behavior; Psychological Theories of Criminal Behavior; Sociological Theories of Criminal Behavior**

Farrington, David P.

In 1998, the American Society of Criminology elected for the first time a president who was neither a resident in nor a citizen of any country in North America. At the same time, David P. Farrington was also serving as the president of the European Association of Psychology and Law. He is a former president of the British Society of Criminology, a fellow of the British Academy, a fellow of the Academy of Medical Sciences, the chair of the British Psychological Society's Board of Examiners in Forensic Psychology, the chair of the U.K. Department of Health's Advisory Committee for the National Programme on Forensic Mental Health, and a member of the Board of Directors of the International Society of Criminology. A complete list of his professional activities in Britain and abroad would fill several pages. In addition to the many thousands of hours he devotes to professional and public service, Farrington is a prolific researcher and writer who has no plans to stop working anytime in the foreseeable future. By 2000 he had published 26 books, 147 journal articles, and 130 book chapters on a wide variety of criminological and psychological topics. In 1984, Farrington received the American Society of Criminology's Sellin-Glueck Award for his international contributions to criminology. His 1986 book *Understanding and Controlling Crime* won the distinguished scholarship prize from the American Sociological Association's Criminology Section.

Farrington is probably best known for his contributions to longitudinal and developmental research of delinquency and crime. He is a director of the Cambridge Study of Delinquent Development, a prospective longitudinal survey of over 400 London males aged between 8 and 46 years originally begun by Donald J. West. He is also a coprincipal investigator of the Pittsburgh Youth Survey, a prospective longitudinal study of over 1500 Pittsburgh males aged between 7 and 25 years directed by Rolf Loeber. These studies have identified risk factors for offending and focused specifically on the prediction of crime and criminality. Today they are considered outstanding models of longitudinal studies by many in the field.

In addition to his longitudinal research, Farrington has made contributions in many different areas of criminology and psychology. He has published articles and book chapters on such wide-ranging topics as family-based crime prevention, cost-benefit analysis of crime prevention and intervention, situational crime prevention, citation analysis in criminology and criminal justice, juvenile bullying, shoplifting, offender profiling, police research, prison research, sentencing research, juvenile justice research, and field experiments on stealing. His published books cover subjects such as crime prevention, the implementation of effective offender rehabilitation programs, citation analysis, and biosocial bases of violence.

Farrington is extremely interested in cross-national comparative research and has worked with a number of researchers throughout the world on a variety of projects. For example, he has worked with Rolf Loeber to compare risk factors for delinquency in London and Pittsburgh and with Per-Olof Wikstrom to compare criminal careers in London and Stockholm. Recently, Farrington, Wikstrom, and Patrick Langan have compared various measures of crime and justice, such as crime and conviction rates, probability of custodial sentences, and average time served, in England, Sweden, and the U.S. These analyses are now being extended up to the year 2000 and expanded to include a total of eight countries.

One could argue that in the 1980s the dominant criminological paradigm was criminal career research. Farrington's contributions to this area of research, along with the work of Alfred Blumstein, Jacqueline Cohen, and others, has served to define and shape the concept of criminal careers and the direction of research and social policy. Farrington published a number of key articles on criminal careers during the 1980s and served on the National Academy of Sciences Panel on Criminal Careers from 1983 to 1986. During this period, Farrington was also involved in a leadership role with Lloyd Ohlin, James Q. Wilson, Michael Tonry and others on the joint National Institute of Justice–MacArthur Foundation initiative that eventually produced the multimillion dollar program on human development and criminal behavior in the 1990s. This program, now called the Project on Human Development in Chicago Neighborhoods, focuses on increasing our understanding of the causes of criminal activity through the use of a prospective longitudinal study of 11,000 individuals (both males and females) from birth to age 32.

In the 1990s, Farrington, Rolf, and Loeber cochaired two study groups for the Office of Juvenile Justice and Delinquency Prevention: one on Serious and Violent Juvenile Offenders and one on Very Young Offenders. In addition, he was vice-chair of the National Academy of Sciences panel on violence.

Farrington is currently the Chair of the International Campbell Collaboration's Crime and Justice Group. The purpose of the Campbell Collaboration, a network of researchers, practitioners, and policy-makers around the world, is to attempt to summarize and upgrade research on the effects of intervention programs designed to reduce crime. Essentially, the program hopes to determine "what works" to reduce crime and delinquency. Farrington was instrumental in obtaining funding from the British Home Office for the committee's first year activities.

Farrington has taught criminology and psychology at Cambridge University since 1971, conducting lectures, seminars, and supervisions for students studying law and social sciences. At the postgraduate level, he has taught M.Phil. and Ph.D students and is in great demand as a supervisor. He is the Director of the Senior Course in Criminology, a summer program conducted for criminal justice professionals in Great Britain.

Ellen G. Cohn

Biography

Born in Ormskirk, Lancashire, England, 7 March 1944. Educated at Clare College, Cambridge University, B.A., 1966, M.A. and Ph.D. in Psychology, 1969. Research Officer, Cambridge University Institute of Criminology, 1969–1970; Senior Research Officer, 1970–1974; Assistant Director of Research, 1974– 1976; University Lecturer in Criminology, 1976–1988; Reader in Psychological Criminology, 1988–1992; Professor of Psychological Criminology, 1992–Present. University of Maryland Jerry Lee Research Professor, 1998–2001; University of Pittsburgh Western Psychiatric Institute and Clinic Adjunct Professor of Psychiatry, 1998–2001. Fellow of the British Academy, the Academy of Medical Sciences, the British Psychological Society, and the American Society of Criminology. President of the American Society of Criminology, 1998–1999; President of the European Association of Psychology and Law, 1997–1999; President of the British Society of Criminology, 1990–1993; Chair of the Division of Forensic Psychology of the British Psychological Society, 1983–1985; Board of Directors of the International Society of Criminology, 2000–2004.

Selected Writings

Who Becomes Delinquent? (with D.J. West) 1973.

Understanding and Controlling Crime: Toward a New Research Strategy (with L.E. Ohlin and J.Q. Wilson) 1986.

The development of offending and antisocial behaviour from childhood: Key findings from the Cambridge Study in Delinquent Development, *Journal of Child Psychology and Psychiatry*, 36, 929–964, 1995.

Human development and criminal careers, in Maguire, M., Morgan, R., and Reiner, R., Eds., *The Oxford Handbook of Criminology*, 2nd ed., Clarendon Press, Oxford, U.K., 1997, pp. 361–408.

Crime and Justice in the United States and in England and Wales, 1981–1996 (with P. A. Langan), Bureau of Justice Statistics, Washington, DC, 1998.

Evaluating Criminology and Criminal Justice (with E.G. Cohn and R. A. Wright), Greenwood Press, Westport, CO, 1998.

Loeber, R., Ed., *Serious and Violent Juvenile Offenders: Risk Factors and Successful Interventions*, Sage, Thousand Oaks, CA, 1998.

The development of male offending: Key findings from the first decade of the Pittsburgh Youth Study (with Loeber, R., Stouthamer-Loeber, M., Moffitt, T.E., and Caspi, A.), *Studies on Crime and Crime Prevention*, 7, 141–171, 1998.

Delinquency prevention using family-based interventions (with Welsh, B.C.), *Children and Society*, 13, 287–303, 1999.

Transatlantic replicability of risk factors in the development of delinquency (with Loeber, R.) in Cohen, P., Slomkowski, C. and Robins, L.N., Eds., *Historical and Geographical Influences on Psychopathology,* Mahwah, NJ, Lawrence Erlbaum, 299–329, 1999.

Explaining and preventing crime: The globalization of knowledge—The American Society of Criminology 1999 Presidential Address, *Criminology*, 38, 1–24, 2000.

See also **Cross-sectional and Longitudinal Research; Juvenile Delinquency, Theories of**

Fear of Crime

Despite recent decreases in crime levels during the 1990s and evidence that the chances of becoming crime victims for most people are small, opinion polls continue to show that fear of crime is widely prevalent among Americans. Evidence also shows Americans reacting to this perception by engaging in "... precautionary behaviors so pervasive and normative that they form a significant and defining element of American culture" (Mark Warr, 2000, 452). Americans are not unique in their fear levels—there is evidence that citizens of other countries report relatively high levels of fear of crime.

In Sweden, for example, 15% of the adult population (ages 16 or older) reported that during 1995, they had decided against venturing out in the evening because they were anxious about becoming a crime victim. Among those surveyed, the elderly, women, and those residing in large cities showed the highest fear levels (Per-Olof and Dolmen, 1996). During the 1990s, a troubling trend in Venezuela was an increase in fear levels among the country's citizens. Polls conducted in the mid-1990s showed that more than two thirds of its citizens (69%) believed it was likely they would become crime victims during the upcoming year; fear levels were especially pronounced among residents of the capital city and among citizens with high incomes (Salas, 1996). Citizens in England and Wales also reported relatively high levels of fear during the 1990s. Results from the 1998 British Crime Survey (BCS) showed 23% of those in the national-level crime victimization survey reported feeling "very" or "fairly" unsafe out alone after dark in their neighborhood. Women were also generally more fearful than men, and those living in inner-city areas had higher fear levels than those living outside core-urban areas (Mirrlees-Black and Allen, 1998). Similar results concerning fear of crime were found in the BCS conducted in 2000, where nearly 13% of a national sample of citizens indicated they were "very worried" about their home being burglarized and nearly 10% of all adults said they "never" or "rarely" walked in their local areas after dark because they feared being attacked (Kershaw et al., 2000).

What is "fear of crime"? What do criminologists know about it? How has its study evolved? What are the most pressing issues concerning the study of fear of crime? What factors are associated with fear of crime? This entry answers these and additional questions based on nearly 30 years of research.

What is "Fear of Crime"?

Despite nearly 30 years of research and hundreds of studies, "for reasons that remain elusive, the study of fear seems to have stalled at a rudimentary phase of development, a situation that is in danger of turning into outright stagnation" (Mark Warr, 2000, 453). Criminologists have conceptualized "fear of crime" variously as an emotional state, an attitude, or a perception (Warr, 2000). The problem is that researchers have neither consistently defined the term, nor used the same measure(s) of it in their studies. The following sections examine these issues in more detail.

Fear of Crime

Fear involves physiological changes in respiration, pulse, and increased levels of adrenalin in people; it is a response to what is happening at the moment rather than general awareness of what is going on around us. Fear is thus not an attitude, nor it is a belief or an evaluation—it is a *reaction*. In the extreme, psychologists and others have documented that physiological changes produced by fear may empower an individual, enabling him or her to do extraordinary things such as lifting an extremely heavy object or jumping much higher than ordinarily possible. On the other hand, these changes can also produce paralysis—being "frozen with fear."

The key to understanding fear of crime is realizing that people actually *fear* two things: becoming a crime victim *and* the magnitude of the victimization (its seriousness). For example, few would argue there is a fundamental difference in the magnitude of a victimization where the offender uses or threatens to use violence against the victim (like in an armed robbery), compared to a victimization where no violence occurs (e.g., theft of property). Fear of crime research has thus tried to assess the emotional responses generated by people imagining what it would be like to experience different kinds of criminal victimizations, ranging from the most serious in magnitude (e.g., murder) to the least serious (e.g., simple theft of property). Then, using responses by subjects, the studies have classified the magnitude of the responses (the person's level of fear) by placing it on a scale or a continuum ranging from "very fearful" to "not afraid at all." Because people differ in their responses to what it is like to suffer a criminal victimization, variation occurs in people's fear levels: some are more fearful than others. The studies have tried to document this variation, explain why it exists, and understand the processes associated with fear.

Although criminologists have used different definitions of "fear of crime," perhaps the best definition is from Kenneth Ferraro who described it as "… an emotional response of *dread* or *anxiety* to crime or symbols that a person associates with crime" (emphasis added) (Ferraro, 1995, 23). Ferraro (1995) also suggested that the emotional response can be either on a *general* level (the person fears that *others* may become a victim) or a *specific* level (the person is *herself* fearful of becoming a victim). In both cases, the response is emotive—the individual is "worrying" about victimization.

Measuring Fear of Crime

Fear of crime has most often been measured using surveys of groups of people in neighborhoods, cities, or across the country (Ferraro, 1995; Warr, 2000). A sample of respondents typically is administered a survey or a structured interview and asked how fearful are they of crime. Although researchers have inconsistently defined fear of crime, they have consistently used questions found in two large-scale surveys, the General Social Survey (GSS) and the National Crime Victimization Survey (NCVS), as their measures of fear of crime. According to Warr (2000), most published studies of fear of crime have used as their measure of fear the following item found in the GSS: "Is there anywhere near where you live—that is, within a mile—where you would be afraid to walk alone at night?" An alternative measure used by some studies is found in the National Crime Victimization Survey (a national-level survey of people's victimization experiences), which asks respondents "How safe do you feel being out alone in your neighborhood at [night] [during the day]?" These questions each ask the respondent "how fearful are *you*?" and thus are directed at the specific level. The questions are also examples of what social scientists call "single-item measures" of fear—a single question is being asked. Finally, responses to the questions are scaled, such that based on his or her responses an individual is placed on a continuum of fear ranging from "more" to "less" fearful.

Problems with the Measures

Social scientists have identified multiple problems with these "traditional" measures of fear of crime. For example, studies of fear of crime that ask about fear in different contexts—at night, alone versus with others, at home versus in the neighborhood—have failed to systematically vary context and evaluate its effects on fear (Warr, 2000). Thus, little is known about how variation in context affects fear, nor about how specific contexts may generate more or less fear among people.

Further, critics of traditional measures of fear have questioned both the validity and the reliability of single-item measures of fear (Ferraro, 1995; Warr, 2000). In social science, validity refers to the extent a measure—in this case the survey question—is actually measuring what it was *intended* to measure (e.g., "fear of crime"). At the heart of the validity issue is this question: "Are the GSS and NCVS questions *actually* measuring fear of crime, or are they measuring *something else*?" Consider the NCVS question "How safe do you feel or would you feel being out alone in your neighborhood at [night] [during the day]?" Critics have argued this question is actually asking the person to estimate what are her chances of *becoming a crime victim* (her *perceived risk* of victimization), rather than asking about how fearful is one of *experiencing* a specific type of victimization (Warr, 2000). Additionally, in many studies "crime" is left undefined by the researcher, leaving it to the respondent to determine what is meant by the term "crime" (Ferraro, 1995). The problem is that when people think about crime, they are likely to be thinking exclusively about *violent* crime (like murder, rape, or assault), rather than thinking about *other* forms of crime such as automobile theft, burglary, or theft of property. Because the item includes a *generic* reference to crime, the item actually may be measuring people's fear of *violent* crime, not *all* forms of crime.

Another problem with many of the fears of crime studies is concern over the *reliability* of the single-item measure that was used. Reliability involves a researcher being able to obtain the same results over time with the same set of individuals, using the same instrument. Fear of crime measures typically used that are based on questions found in the GSS and the NCVS have unknown reliability, in part, *because* they are single-item questions.

Addressing the Reliability Problem

The reliability problem with fear of crime measures has recently been addressed by several researchers (Warr, 1990; Ferraro, 1995; Fisher, Sloan and Wilkins, 1995). Instead of using the traditional, single-item indicator to measure fear, researchers have begun adopting a different method. First, the person is asked to report his or her level of worry or state of fear, rather asked to make judgments about or express concerns over crime. Second, the person is asked about his or her fear levels as they relate to a particular type of crime (e.g., robbery) rather than being asked about "fear of crime" in a generic sense. Third, the respondent is asked about fear of crime in relation to his or her everyday life, and not some hypothetical situation. Fourth, the person is not asked what are called "double-barreled" questions such as "how safe *do you* or *would you* feel walking alone in your neighborhood" at night or during the day. Finally, the respondent is asked about a *set* of victimizations that vary from "low" to "high" in seriousness level.

Table 1 presents an illustration of what several criminologists (e.g., Ferraro, 1995; Fisher, Sloan, and Wilkins, 1995; Warr, 2000) now consider the standard way to measure fear of crime. Developed by Ferraro (1995, 35), the measure repeatedly has been tested by researchers who obtained similar results, making both the validity and the reliability of the items a known quantity. Ferraro suggested that to measure fear of crime, the researcher should first identify *for the respondent* the context in which the questions are applicable (e.g., "in everyday life"), rather than allowing the respondent to guess or assume context. Additionally, Ferraro's method involves presenting to the respondent a list of specific crimes (including violent and other forms of crime) about which the respondent may fear. Finally, the respondent is asked to rank, on a scale from 1 to 10, how fearful is he or she of experiencing a victimization involving each offense. Responses to the items are then summed to form an index of fear of crime. Items dealing with violent crime like rape, robbery, or murder are summed to form in index of fear of violence, whereas items dealing with property crime are summed to form an index of fear of property crime. The higher the totals for each index, the greater is the respondent's fear of crime.

Studies of fear of crime that were conducted during the 1960s, 1970s, and 1980s that using various measures of fear may be seriously flawed. For example, they may be invalid because their measures of "fear" may actually be measuring something else or they may allow the respondent to incorrectly interpret what the researcher meant by "crime." Additionally, because many of the studies used a single item to measure fear, issues with the reliability of the measures have been raised. Finally, many of the studies failed to systematically examine potential variation in the impact of context on fear levels (Warr, 1990). Beyond developing new measures of fear, criminologists have also suggested a strong link occurring between fear of crime and perceived risk of victimization. It is to that issue our attention now turns.

Fear and Perceived Risk

Increasingly, some criminologists have argued that fear of crime cannot adequately be examined (nor understood) without examining a related concept: *risk of victimization* (Ferraro, 1995; Warr, 2000). People may be fearful if they perceive their risk of victimization is great; they may also be fearful, however, even if their risk is low. The problem is that many fear of crime studies have either not separately considered the concept of "risk," or did so implicitly in the measures of fear that they used.

Risk entails the chance or probability that an event is likely to occur. For example, not all people who talk on a cell phone while driving their car will have an accident, but people who talk on cell phones while driving are at a greater risk of having an accident. At the same time, people who drive while talking on the phone may fear having an accident, so they pull to the side of the road while talking on the phone. The question involves one of relationship: is fear a possible *consequence* of perceived risk or is fear *independent* of risk? Additionally, are fearing an event and perceiving the

Table 1. Measuring Fear of Crime

Kenneth Ferraro (1995, 35) developed what is now considered a standard way to measure fear of crime. The questions have been repeatedly tested in studies by Ferraro and by other social scientists, and generally results show that regardless of the group or individual answering the items are good measures:

At one time or another, most of us have experienced fear about becoming a crime victim. Some crimes probably frighten you more than others. We are interested in how afraid are people in everyday life of being a victim of different types of crimes. Please rate your fear on a scale of 1 to 10, where 1 means you are not at all afraid, and 10 means you are very afraid.

First, rate your fear of…

1. Being approached on the street by a beggar or a panhandler.
2. Being cheated, conned, or swindled out of your money.
3. Having someone break into your home while you are away.
4. Having someone break into your home while you are there.
5. Being raped or sexually assaulted.
6. Being murdered.
7. Being attacked by someone with a weapon.
8. Having your car stolen.
9. Being robbed or mugged on the street.
10. Having your property damaged by vandals.

Responses to all of these items are summed to form an overall index of fear of crime. Items 4, 5, 6, and 7 are summed to form what is called an "index" of fear of personal crime, while items 2, 3, 8, 9, and 10 are summed to create an index of fear of property crime. The higher the total, the greater is the person's fear of the crime or the higher the person's overall fear.

risk of the event happening distributed differentially across different events? For example, people may fear the prospect of a burglary occurring in their residence. However, they may express greater fear of a burglar coming into their house *while they are present* than coming home to find their house has been burglarized. At the same time, they may perceive the *risk* of a burglar coming into their house while they are present as being low. Thus, their fear level is high, but their perceived risk is low.

Because risk entails chance, it is not possible to correctly predict whether an event *will* occur. Rather, assessing risk involves a cognitive process of gathering information and making a judgment of the chances the event will occur. Thus, although *fear* involves an emotional response to stimuli, *risk* involves cognitively assessing cues and making a calculation of chance. Further, fear may be one of several possible *reactions* to risk:

> [O]ther [responses to risk] include constrained behavior, community political activism, compensatory defensive actions, and avoidance behaviors, including relocation. (Ferraro, 1995, 12).

Assessing Risk

People assess risk based on cues received from various sources. Some of the cues arise from one's surroundings, from what criminologists call *physical* and *social incivilities* (Wilson and Kelling, 1982). Physical incivilities arise from disorder in the physical environment: abandoned cars, litter strewn about, vacant lots overgrown with weeds, and abandoned boarded-up houses. Social incivilities refer to disruptive social behaviors: groups of youth loitering on a street corner, homeless people wandering the streets, or intoxicated people staggering down the block. Because people associate physical and social incivilities *with crime*, both provide cues that people use to assess their risk of victimization: the higher the perceived level of incivility in an area, the higher is the perceived risk of a victimization occurring.

Beyond visual cues, risk is assessed using other informational sources. For example, if one "knows" that a certain area has a reputation as a "high crime neighborhood," one is likely to estimate his or her risk of victimization as being higher than in a different neighborhood. Media may also contribute to risk assessment by their coverage of crime stories from certain places and not others (Chiricos, Padgett, and Gertz, 2000). Risk is also assessed based on personal experience. People who have been crime victims may be more likely to assess their risk of repeat victimization as being greater than individuals who have not previously been victimized. Additionally, knowing someone who has been victimized may affect one's risk assessment. For example, if one hears that a neighbor who lives two doors down experienced a burglary, one may assess that his or her risk of experiencing a burglary has suddenly increased.

Finally, risk assessment occurs not only in a global manner but also in a specific sense. One may perceive one's *overall* risk of experiencing *any* sort of victimization is low, but one may also perceive that one's risk of experiencing a *specific type* of victimization is very high. It is therefore necessary, when studying perceived risk of victimization, to examine the extent people perceive they are at risk of victimization for *specific types of crime*.

Measuring Risk

If Ferraro (1995) and others are correct in arguing that risk involves a cognitive assessment of the chances of becoming a crime victim, then how the concept of "risk" is measured becomes important. Two possible methods for assessing victimization risk have recently emerged in the fear of crime literature.

One line of research has assessed risk using so-called "objective" assessments. In these studies, researchers have used official crime statistics compiled from police precincts, Census tracts, cities or towns, or counties to link risk with fear. In these studies, the researcher converts the crime statistics to a standardized rate of victimization per 100,000 people and risk (or fear) is assessed in those terms. Thus, an area with a crime rate of 750 offenses known to the police per 100,000 population is "riskier" than is an area with a crime rate of 50 offenses known to the police per 100,000 population. The researcher then compares the fear levels of people living in the higher crime rate area with those living in the lower crime rate area to examine differences.

A second line of research has asked people to estimate their *own* risk of becoming a victim; that is, to assess one's *perceived risk of victimization* (Ferraro, 1995). Using a survey, the respondent is asked to estimate what are the chances of the described event(s) happening to him or her during a certain period and in the respondent's "everyday" life. Table 2 presents a recent example of this method used by Ferraro (1995) in a national level study of fear and risk.

Table 2 shows that Ferraro (1995) replicates his method of measuring fear to measure perceived risk. Note, however, that beyond asking about the same kinds of events as asked in his measure of fear, Ferraro also asks respondents to rate their chances that the specific offense is likely to happen "during the upcoming year." He thus places a "bounding period" on the question, rather than leaving it to the respondent to determine a particular time frame for the question.

In summary, assessing one's risk of victimization involves cognitive processing of various cues and sources of information. This results in one "calculating" the "chances" that he or she will become a crime victim. Unlike fear of crime, which involves an emotional response to actual or imagined stimuli, *risk* involves assessing the chance an event *will* occur. Further, this assessment results in outputs that may include becoming fearful and changing one's lifestyle or routines. The point is simply that being fearful of crime is *not* the same as perceiving that one's chances of becoming a victim are high. In recent studies of fear of crime, researchers have included, along with crime-specific measures of fear, similar crime-specific measures of the risk of criminal victimization. Some studies have used self-reported assessments of risk ("perceived risk") whereas others have used "objective" measures of risk, such as crime data standardized per population size (e.g., per 100,000 persons). Links between fear and risk are then examined.

Fear and Perceived Risk: What Is Known?

Because a great deal of research has been conducted on fear of crime and risk of victimization, our understanding of these concepts and knowledge about the processes related to them has improved. Taken as a whole, it is now possible to differentiate factors that are associated with fear or risk or both, based on a particular study's theoretical focal point. Among the many studies that have been done, several theoretical models have been identified; each describes a different set of factors that are assumed to be related to fear of crime, or perceived risk of victimization.

Major Theoretical Models

Fisher, Sloan, and Wilkins (1995) have classified studies on fear of crime or perceived risk of victimization as fitting into one of five different theoretical models including: "social and physical vulnerability," "victimization," "social and physical disorders," "neighborhood integration," and "formal social control."

Table 2. Measuring Perceived Risk of Crime

Ferraro (1995, 35) also created what has now become a standard method for measuring perceived risk of victimization. Similar to how fear of crime is measured, Ferraro uses the same items and the same scale to determine how much perceived risk the person feels about becoming a victim of a number of different offenses that vary in their seriousness:

You have already rated your fear of different kinds of crime. Now I would like you to rate the chance that a specific thing will happen to you during the coming year. On a scale from 1 to 10, where 1 means the event is not likely at all and 10 means the event is very likely.

Please tell me how likely you think it is that you will…

1. Be approached on the street by a beggar or a panhandler?
2. Be cheated, conned, or swindled out of your money?
3. Having someone attempt to break into your home while you are away?
4. Having someone attempt to break into your home while you are there?
5. Being raped or sexually assaulted?
6. Being murdered?
7. Being attacked by someone with a weapon?
8. Having your car stolen?
9. Being robbed or mugged on the street?
10. Having your property damaged by vandals?

Similar to the fear of crime index, the items are summed to create an overall index of risk of victimization. Items 4, 5, 6, and 7 are summed to create an index of risk of personal crime, while items 2, 3, 8, 9, and 10 are summed to create an index of risk of property crime. The higher the score, the greater is the person's perceived risk of being victimized.

Social and Physical Vulnerability

This model emphasizes the importance of personal characteristics, like age, race, or sex, that may affect perceptions of risk and the onset of fear; that is, factors that may enhance feelings of "vulnerability" (Skogan, 1990). Vulnerability consists of two dimensions: physical and social. *Physical vulnerability* involves such factors as openness to attack, inability to resist attack, and exposure to significant emotional and physical consequences if attacked. Studies in this area conducted both in the U.S. and elsewhere have suggested that age (elderly) and sex (women) were strong predictors of both fear and perceived risk. *Social vulnerability*, on the other hand, encompasses the frequency of exposure to the risk of attack that directly results from who the person is, and when the consequences of victimization (social, economic, or personal) are felt more directly by these individuals. Primary here are such characteristics as race (African American) and being poor (poverty).

Generally, most studies find that age, race, and sex are strongly related to fear of crime and perceived risk, although there is not always consensus among researchers concerning the exact nature of the relationship. Despite the fact that women are less likely than are men to suffer criminal victimization, they have consistently been found to have higher levels of fear and perceived risk of victimization. Ferraro (1995) suggested one possible reason for this finding is women's fear that *any* type of victimization can lead to a sexual assault that "… may 'shadow' other types of victimization among women [and] operate like a 'master offense'" (Ferraro, 1995, 87). In addition to this, although studies consistently report that age is significantly related to fear of crime and perceived risk, the exact nature of the relationship is in dispute. For example, many studies report the elderly have higher fear levels than younger people, although most of these studies have used the traditional, single-item measure of fear. Other studies, using more sophisticated measures, reported that *depending on the specific crime*, younger people (18–24) actually may have *higher* fear levels than the elderly and differ in their perceived risk of becoming a victim. Finally, several studies report that race is significantly related to fear, although the nature of the relationship is in dispute. Many studies indicate that African Americans are more fearful than Whites, although some studies report the opposite relationship; one possible explanation for this finding is that because Whites perceive that most street crimes are committed by African Americans, the fear is really of Blacks and not crime.

Victimization: Direct and Vicarious

The victimization model predicts that prior victimization experience(s) (direct victimization) and the victimization experiences of others (vicarious victimization) will affect fear. The influence of victimization, direct or vicarious, on fear or risk is mixed, with some studies reporting very strong effects of prior victimization on fear or risk, whereas others reporting weak or insignificant effects. Fear may also be related to the *type* of prior victimization suffered. There is evidence, for example, that past victims of property crime may actually have higher fear levels than prior victims of violence. There is also evidence that victims of *both* property and violent crime have higher levels of fear and risk than nonvictims. Finally, recent evidence suggests that vicarious victimization affects fear of crime. Chiricos, Padgett, and Gertz (2000), for example, found that local and national television news consumption was significantly related to fear of crime, regardless of the influences of other factors such as crime rates or prior victimization experiences.

Social and Physical Disorder

This model suggests that social and physical incivilities contribute to fear of crime; this model has also received substantial support. Research consistently shows strong relationships among incivilities, neighborhood disorder, and fear of crime. Individuals are most fearful of neighborhoods with high levels of disorder, although the converse is also true.

Neighborhood Integration

This model has its basis in urban sociology and suggests neighborhood integration is crucial to understanding how people assess their life space and the problems they encounter in their neighborhoods (Fisher, Sloan, and Wilkins, 1995). This model has two dimensions: a *residential* component (commitment to the neighborhood as measured by residential tenure) and a *social* component (measured by how well one knows people in the neighborhood, as well as how well one can differentiate who belongs in the neighborhood from those who do not). The model suggests that as residential and social integration increase, fear of crime and perceived risk of victimization would decrease.

A variety of studies using different measures of fear and neighborhood integration have found mixed results. The difference in results, beyond use of different measures, appears largely a function of the sample size: a sample of people from a specific neighborhood within a city is more likely to indicate neighborhood integration that was related to their fear levels, whereas in samples of people from multiple neighborhoods in multiple cities, no relationship between the two has been reported.

Formal Social Control

Finally, this model suggests that as people's confidence in the police increases, their fear or risk will decrease. In other words, if people *perceive* that the police are effective at identifying and arresting suspects, they are less likely to be fearful. Additionally, recent studies have also considered how a particular "style" of policing (e.g., "community oriented policing") affects fear levels among neighborhood residents. Again, although results are mixed, there is some evidence showing that citizen attitudes toward the police and style of policing may affect fear. People with more positive attitudes toward the police are less likely to express fear, whereas "community oriented policing" has also been shown to reduce fear levels within the community.

Conclusion

Considering that the discipline of criminology has now existed for over 150 years, only since the 1960s has the study of fear of crime become an area of interest for criminologists. Further, during the 1990s criminologists have begun to address many problems that plagued prior studies of fear of crime. Primary among these problems was how fear of crime was conceptualized and measured. These studies, until recently, failed to consider the role of risk of victimization in understanding fear of crime.

Yet, despite these problems, we do know something about fear of crime. For example, criminologists *can* say, with some confidence, that fear of crime and perceived risk of victimization are separate, but not unrelated, concepts: fear appears to be one possible product of perceived risk. Further, it appears that environmental cues like neighborhood characteristics, and personal factors like age, race, and sex, affect both fear and risk. For example, women consistently report higher fear levels than men, despite their significantly lower risk of victimization.

Although questions remain about the exact processes involved in generating fear and risk, criminologists continue to refine their measures of these concepts, explore better methods of assessing fear and risk, and contemplate future research to more fully understand fear and risk as potentially indirect consequences of crime.

John J. Sloan III

References and Further Reading

Chiricos, T., Padgett, K., and Gertz, M., Fear, TV news, and the reality of crime, *Criminology*, 38, 2000.

Ferraro, K.F., *Fear of Crime: Interpreting Victimization Risk*, State University of New York Press, Albany, NY, 1995.

Fisher, B.S., Sloan, J.J., and Wikins, D.L., Fear of crime and perceived risk of victimization in an urban university setting, in Fisher, B.S. and Sloan, J.J. Eds., *Campus Crime: Legal, Social, and Policy Perspectives*, Charles C. Thomas, Springfield, IL, 1995.

Heath, L. and Gilbert, K., Mass media and fear of crime, *American Behavioral Scientist,* 39, 1996.

Kershaw, C., Budd, T., kinshott, G., Mattinson, J., Mayhew, P., and Myhill, A., *The 2000 British Crime Survey*, The Home Office 2000, London. Available at: http://www.homeoffice.gov.uk/ rds/hosbpubs1.html.

LaGrange, R.L., Ferraro, K.P., and Supancic, M., Perceived risk and fear of crime: role of social and physical incivilities, *Journal of Research in Crime and Delinquency,* 29, 1992.

Mirrlees-Black, C. and Allen, J., *Concern About Crime: Findings from the 1998 British Crime Survey*, The Home Office 1998, London. Available at: http://www.homeoffice.gov.uk/ rds/rfpubs1.html.

Wikstrom, P.H. and Dolmen, L., Sweden, in Newman, G.R., Ed., *World Factbook of Criminal Justice Systems*, Office of Justice Programs 1996, Washington, DC. Available at http://www.ojp.usdoj.gov/bjs/abstract/wfcj.htm.

Roundtree, P.W. and Land, K.C., Perceived risk versus fear of crime: empirical evidence of conceptually distinct reactions in survey data, *Social Forces,* 74, 1996.

Salas, L., Venezuela, in Newman, G.R. Ed., *World Factbook of Criminal Justice Systems*, Office of Justice Programs 1996, Washington, DC. Available at: http://www.ojp.usdoj.gov/bjs/ abstract/wfcj.htm.

Skogan, W.G., Disorder and Decline: Crime and the Spiral of Decay in American Neighborhoods, Free Press, New York, 1990.

Warr, M., Fear of crime in the United States: avenues for research and policy, in Dufee, D., Ed., *Crime and Justice 2000: Volume 4, Measurement and Analysis of Crime and Justice*, Office of Justice Programs 2000, Washington, DC. Available at: http://www.ncjrs.org/criminal_justice2000/ vol_4/04front.pdf.

Warr, M., Dangerous situations: Social context and fear of victimization, *Social Forces,* 68, 1990.

Warr, M., Fear of victimization: Why are women and the elderly more afraid? *Social Science Quarterly,* 65, 1984.

Warr, M. and Stafford, M., Fear of victimization: A look at the proximate causes, *Social Forces,* 61, 1983.

Wilson, J.Q. and kelling, G.L., Broken windows, *Atlantic Monthly,* 249, 1982.

See also **National Crime Victimization Survey (NCVS); Victimization, Crime: Characteristics of Victims; Victimization, Crime: Financial Loss and Personal Suffering; Victimization, Repeated**

Federal Bureau of Investigation (FBI)

The history of the Federal Bureau of Investigation (FBI), extending over nearly a century, originated in 1908 from a force of special agents during the presidency of Theodore Roosevelt (Lowenthal, 1950). The agency was designed as the primary investigative arm of the U.S. Department of Justice in response to growing political and business corruption (Schmalleger, 1993). On its inception, there were only 34 agents in the FBI and their investigations centered on a minimal number of federal crimes, including bankruptcy, naturalization, antitrust, and land fraud (Theoharis, Poveda, Rosenfeld, and Powers, 1999). Currently, the FBI is the nation's largest and most diverse federal law enforcement agency with over 11,000 agents, 16,000 support staff, and 56 field offices across the U.S. and an additional 40 posts in foreign countries. Furthermore, the Bureau has since expanded its investigative interests and reorganized its priorities to include cases involving terrorism, espionage, white-collar crime, organized crime, and crimes of bias and violence (Sousa, 2002).

The Mann Act of 1910 (or White Slave Traffic Act) was the first in a series of congressional legislation that rapidly extended the Bureau's law enforcement authority. The Mann Act made it a federal crime to transport women across state lines for "immoral purposes" and symbolized the Bureau's first involvement in combating organized crime (e.g., prostitution). This legislation was followed by the Dyer Act of 1917 (or Motor Vehicle Theft Act) that was passed in response to the booming sale of automobiles. The increased availability and popularity of automobiles created a significant black market demand for stolen vehicles. The Espionage Act of 1917 and the Sedition Act of 1918 were passed in direct response to the U.S. growing internal security concerns stemming from the dawn of World War I. These federal laws strengthened the Bureau's influence and reprioritized the bulk of their investigative resources on members of labor unions, members of the Socialist Party, and pro-Irish and pro-German activists (Theoharis et al., 1999).

The ensuing years after the end of World War I were a time of abuse of power and political scandals within the Bureau. The Bureau's arrest of communists and Communist Labor Party members in the Palmer Raids of 1920, their arrest of prominent radicals including NAACP member Marcus Garvey and Ku Klux Klan leader Edward Clarke, along with the negative publicity they received from the Teapot Dome Scandal of 1923–1924, in which the Bureau's agents tapped the phones, opened the mail, and broke into the homes of noted Senators to uncover damaging information, all contributed to a marked decline in the public's confidence and political support for the Bureau (Theoharis et al., 1999).

Attorney General Harlan F. Stone appointed J. Edgar Hoover as the director in 1924 in an attempt to stifle the then current political scandals and to manage the implementation of a series of ordered reforms, including the dissolving of the General Intelligence Division (GID), banning wiretapping, and drafting new guidelines to restrict any further or future spying on political officials (Theoharis et al., 1999). On his appointment, Hoover immediately began dynamic restructuring in order to impose discipline and accountability on the Bureau. He established six different functional divisions with each division managed by a chief. Additionally, each of the divisions were further partitioned into 53 field offices each managed by a special agent in charge (SAC).

During his 48-year reign as director, Hoover revolutionized the practices, polices, and procedures of the Bureau, some of which are still emphasized and adhered to today. Hoover instituted new standards of training and education and stressed that promotions be based on merit alone. He established an Inspection division to routinely check and evaluate the extent of each office's compliance with regulations. He standardized the work of the Bureau in order to establish uniformity in reporting procedures and to promote and ease information sharing between and among the field offices. Furthermore, perhaps two of Hoover's most long-standing accomplishments while he served as the director was his development of a national registry of fingerprints to enable the sharing of identification records with officers in the cities, counties, and states and his establishment in 1935 of the FBI National Police Academy, which later became known as the FBI National Academy in Quantico, Virginia (Kessler, 2002).

Hoover's success in orchestrating and implementing his desired reforms led to the portrayal of FBI agents as professional and skilled law enforcement officers, most notably referred to as the crime fighting "G-men" (Sousa, 2002). The G-men acquired their initial notoriety because of their success in high-profile and well-publicized cases against infamous gangsters during the Prohibition Era, including "Baby Face" Nelson, Clyde Barrow, Bonnie Parker, "Ma" Barker, John Dillinger, "Pretty Boy" Floyd, "Machine Gun" Kelly, and Alvin Karpis (Schmalleger, 1993).

During World War II, the Cold War, and the Civil Rights Era the Bureau once again revisited its controversial practices of covert surveillance of political leaders, social activists, and private citizens who allegedly posed a threat to national security (Sousa, 2002). During the 1960s, the demands for racial and sexual equality pressured the Bureau into embracing and encouraging diversity in hiring and in the awarding of government contracts. During the years of 1989–1991, the world observed the dismantling of the Soviet Union, the relative end of communist control in Eastern Europe, and the emergence of terrorism as a new internal security concern, which significantly redefined and reorganized the Bureau's domestic security investigations. In response to the Gulf War, the 1993 bombing of the World Trade Center, numerous attacks on abortion clinics, and the attack of September 11, 2001, the Bureau expanded its investigative interests beyond primarily Marxist movements to include Arab and Muslim fundamentalist groups and various domestic militia groups (Theoharis et al., 1999). Despite the Bureau's contentious practices throughout its history, it has evolved into the nation's most well-recognized and well-respected law enforcement agency through illustrating and supporting diversity in its personnel and in its functions.

WESLEY JENNINGS

References and Further Reading

Kessler, R. (2002), *The Bureau: The Secret History of the FBI*, New York, St. Martin's Press.

Lowenthal, M. (1950). *The Federal Bureau of Investigation*. New York, William Sloane Associates, Inc.

Schmalleger, F. (1993), *Criminal Justice Today: An Introductory Text for the Twenty-First Century*, 2nd ed., Englewood Cliffs, NJ, Prentice Hall.

Sousa, W.H. (2002), Federal bureau of investigation, in *Encyclopedia of Crime and Punishment*, Vol. 2, pp. 684–685, Thousand Oaks, CA, Sage Publications.

Theoharis, A.G., Poveda, T.G., Rosenfeld, S., and Powers, R.G. (1999), *The FBI: A Comprehensive Reference Guide*, Phoenix, AZ, The Oryx Press.

See also **Police: History in the U.S.**

Felonies and Misdemeanors

In the American criminal justice system, criminal offenses are classified as either felonies or misdemeanors. This classification system is used at both the federal and state levels. The process of categorizing crimes is a legacy from the common law tradition. Legislatures have continued to use these common law categories when enacting criminal law statutes. However, the trend among legislatures has been to expand the number of felony-level offenses that have been well known in the common law for centuries. Since the U.S. Constitution reserves the right to enact and enforce criminal law to the states, the vast majority of criminal law originates at the state level, where state codes and statutes define crimes and set the penalties for the violations, and where state case law interprets these codes and statutes. However, the U.S. Code that contains the federal criminal law has expanded greatly since the 1970s, due mostly to an increased number of federal drug and weapons laws. Therefore there is a growing body of federal criminal law as well. But according to recent statistics from the Bureau of Justice Statistics, only about 4% of all criminal convictions occur at the federal level. Therefore, most of this discussion will focus on the body of criminal law that is found in state statutes. Although there is some uniformity among states in the criminal law statutes, there are also numerous differences in the definitions of crimes and the requisite elements, the classification of crimes as felonies or misdemeanors, and the range of penalties for crimes. No two states use all of the same classifications or definitions of crimes. Because of the extensive differences in the criminal law in the country, it is helpful to examine the general principles of criminal law that are similar among the states.

Felonies

Felonies are crimes that carry a potential period of incarceration of 12 months or more, which usually must be served in state prison and not in the local jail. Felonies are the most serious crimes in our criminal system, and include the most egregious and commonly recognized crimes such as murder, rape, robbery, arson, and burglary. Felonies are considered to be so serious that most state statutes hold that convicted felons lose many of their civil rights. These rights include the right to vote, the right to serve on a jury, and the right to carry a firearm. Additionally, those who are convicted of certain felonies are precluded from holding some jobs and also may be denied some governmental benefits. This is one of the most important implications for exploring the classifications of crimes and examining the increasing numbers of felonies in criminal statutes.

Most states classify felonies in degrees of seriousness. There are usually four categories for felonies: the most serious felonies are capital felonies, followed by first-degree felonies, second-degree felonies, and third-degree felonies. The difference in the degree or level of the felony determines the maximum prison sentence that crime carries under the state's penal code.

Capital felonies are the most serious felonies and can be punished by the most severe sanction the state administers; in states where the death penalty is legal, this means that capital felonies can result in the imposition of the death penalty. In states where the death penalty is not legal, this means the sentence can be life in prison without the possibility of parole. Most states define a capital felony only as murder, but some states now classify serious sexual battery offenses that victimize young children as capital felonies as well. In fact, in at least one state, Louisiana, a defendant could receive the death penalty for committing rape on a child under the age of 12. In other states that define sexual battery as a capital felony, the crime carries the sentence of life in prison without the possibility of parole. Florida now follows this model and defines capital sexual battery as an offense that carries a twenty-five year mandatory minimum sentence and a maximum sentence of life imprisonment.

First-degree felonies are the next level of felonies. These felonies are extremely serious and generally carry maximum penalties ranging from 40 years to life in prison. Some states have even classified serious drug possession offenses, for instance where the defendant possesses an extremely high amount of cocaine, as a first-degree felony punishable by life in prison. Second-degree felonies are those that generally carry penalties of up to 15 years in prison. The least serious felonies are third-degree felonies, which can result in a maximum prison sentence of 5 years. As states have continued to expand the list of felony offenses, this lower-level felony category has grown considerably in some states. It is up to the legislature in each state to determine the level of the felony offense and to set the maximum penalties for each category. This is certainly an area where there are significant differences in state statutes, and these disparities have received some criticism from those who argue that such levels are quite arbitrary, especially for nonviolent felony offenses.

Misdemeanors

Misdemeanors are those crimes that are not considered to be as serious as felonies. The U.S. Constitution establishes the distinction between misdemeanors and other crimes by contrasting the term with more serious crimes: treason, bribery, and other high crimes. Misdemeanors are crimes that are punishable by up to one year in a local jail. Misdemeanor convictions can also result in the imposition of fines, probation, or other conditions, such as community service, counseling, and restitution. Misdemeanors, like felonies, are also divided into degrees, with the less serious offenses punishable by less incarceration. Some less serious misdemeanors carry a maximum punishment of 60 days in the county jail. Misdemeanors generally consist of crimes like petit theft, simple assaults and batteries, driving under the influence of alcohol, possession of marijuana, and trespass.

In some states, there are certain misdemeanor offenses that could result in much more serious sanctions, depending on the circumstances. It is useful to examine an example of how a misdemeanor crime can be enhanced to a felony, because as state legislatures have participated in the trend to get tough on crime, more and more states have enacted legislation that allows misdemeanors to be handled as felony-level offenses in some cases. Enhancements can occur when a person has already been convicted of prior related offenses. For instance, many states have added provisions in their statutes that hold that offenders who have committed a certain crime in the past, like a battery, will face the possibility of having a subsequent misdemeanor battery charge treated like a felony-level crime because of the past convictions. For example, in Florida, when a defendant has been convicted of two prior misdemeanor battery charges, the third battery charge, even if it would otherwise meet only the definition of a misdemeanor, can be prosecuted as a felony battery charge. These enhancements are common with several substantive offenses such as driving under the influence of alcohol, battery, and theft. Perhaps the most common public policy explanation for this type of enhancement is that states have tried to respond to the growing problem of domestic violence. As most major crime in the 1990s declined, states continued to witness a rise in domestic violence-related offenses. Most domestic violence offenses are classified as misdemeanor offenses like assault, battery, stalking, and trespass, and these crimes are prosecuted as misdemeanors. Under the traditional statutory approach, a person could continue to commit misdemeanor battery or misdemeanor stalking, but he would face a maximum sentence of one year in the county jail for each new offense. Under the new statutory schemes, the repeat offender faces the possibility of a prison sentence even if his crime was only a slap. Most state legislatures have responded to the problem of domestic violence by increasing the possible penalties for what otherwise might be considered a "simple battery" and hope to see a deterrent effect as a result of the tougher laws.

Issues Implicated in Categorizing Crimes

There are some general common-sense principles involved in determining whether a crime should be defined as a felony or a misdemeanor. As an example, in most states, there is a simple battery crime that constitutes a misdemeanor offense. Most states define misdemeanor battery as consisting of the following elements: (1) an intentional (2) touching or striking of a person (3) against the will of that person. But a simple battery can become an aggravated battery, and therefore a felony level offense, in the following situations: (1) when a weapon is involved in the commission of the offense; (2) when serious or permanent bodily injury results from the offense; or (3) when the victim is a specified person, like a law enforcement officer, a child, a pregnant woman, or an elderly person.

These three factors are all considered aggravating factors, and most states use these or similar factors as a way to distinguish serious crime from less serious crime. Each of these identifies common criteria states use to classify most substantive crimes as either misdemeanors or felonies, and they also show the ways in which the level of violence can be examined. In all states, any crime will be considered more serious when the defendant uses a weapon in the commission of that crime, so crimes that involve the use of a weapon generally will be classified as felonies. Additionally, crimes that result in serious bodily harm to victims are much more serious and will be considered felonies as well. Finally, the characteristics of the victim often factor into the consideration of the seriousness of the crime. One of the purposes of the criminal law is to protect interests that society deems important. This purpose explains the reason for establishing the fact that battery offenses, which victimize the most helpless members of civilized society, will result in harsher treatment of the offender. Most states include law enforcement officers in this group as a way to deter offenders from impeding officers in the execution of the important function of protecting the public. Whether this type of statutory scheme actually results in a deterrent effect or not has certainly been widely debated. Some have pointed to anecdotal examples where defendants received prison sentences for spitting on a law enforcement officer as proof that these types of statutes have reached too far.

One of the main purposes of the criminal law is to reflect a community's values and concerns. This is the main reason the U.S. Constitution left most matters of criminal law to the states. Generally, the more important the state considers an interest that needs to be protected, the more likely the state is to define the offense as a felony instead of a misdemeanor. For example, in the state of Florida, the offense of trespass that involves going onto the property of another without permission is usually defined as a misdemeanor. However, if a person commits a trespass on a construction sight, the trespass is then considered a felony. In the state of Texas, thefts which involve oil are also treated as felony offenses, regardless of the value of the oil. In other states, trapping some designated wild animals may constitute a felony. In some states, growing and consuming marijuana is absolutely legal, whereas in other states, the exact same actions could result in felony charges.

Finally, one of the other important considerations in the classification of crimes as felonies or misdemeanors is to consider the most common categories of crimes. Most states categorize criminal law into the following general groups: crimes against people; crimes against property; crimes against habitation; drug crimes; crimes against public order; and crimes against the administration of justice. All of these categories contain both felonies and misdemeanors, but there are some principles worth noting. Once again the more serious the interest to be protected is, the more likely it is that state code will classify the crime as a felony. Crimes against habitation are most often felony offenses, like burglary and arson. This follows the common sense approach that the state should protect the sanctity and safety of the home. Crimes against public order that consist of crimes like disorderly conduct and public intoxication are not considered to be as serious, and therefore most of these offenses are defined as misdemeanors. Drug crimes consist of possession of proscribed drugs; the level of the offense depends completely on the type of the drug and how much of a threat the state deems that particular drug to be to the community. Most possession of marijuana offenses are considered to be misdemeanors, whereas most states define possession of cocaine as felonies. Additionally, drug-possession crimes can be enhanced depending on the amount of illicit drug that the offender possesses, and whether the offender intended to sell the drug or not. For instance, in some states possessing 20 grams of marijuana is a misdemeanor, but possessing 21 grams is a felony. Property crimes, like criminal mischief (destroying another's property) or theft are usually classified as felonies or misdemeanors based on the value of the property that is stolen, damaged, or destroyed. Obviously, the more valuable the property, the more likely it is that the crime will be treated as a felony. These amounts vary considerably from state to state.

Felony versus Misdemeanor: Jury Trials

The distinction between felonies and misdemeanors can also be important as it relates to the size of the jury. Most states continue to require 12-member juries in felony trials, but allow juries of less than 12 members for misdemeanor jury trials. In many states, felony trials require 12 members whereas misdemeanor trials require only 6 members. In the relatively few states that allow less than 12-member juries for felonies, there is often a requirement that capital cases must still be heard by 12-member juries. The U.S. Supreme Court closely examined this English common law tradition of requiring 12-member juries in the 1970s in a series of cases but determined that it does not violate the Constitution to have juries with less than 12 members. According to the Court, the Constitution requires that the jury must provide a fair possibility for representing a cross-section of the community, and must be large enough to promote fair deliberation free from outside influence. Many courts have proposed reducing the size of juries in order to save money. But opponents argue that smaller juries do not save that much money, and in fact are less representative of the community, and therefore may not pass constitutional challenges. As a result of these two positions, legal scholars have examined the differences between 12- and 6-member juries, and have articulated the following findings. Reducing the size of the jury would result in courts saving money, since smaller juries are less costly to "maintain" (for providing meals and lodging, for example) and *voir dire* would take less time. Additionally, this savings would allow the judicial system to hear more cases, which would improve judicial efficiency. Based on empirical research, these scholars also conclude that smaller juries are less representative of the community. In one study, the researchers determined that reducing the size of the jury from 12 members to 6 members would result in the likelihood of minority representation on a jury going from 72% down to 47%. Finally, jury studies suggest that reducing jury size adversely affects the quality of the deliberations.

Habitual Offender Statutes and Three-Strikes

Since the 1970s there has been an effort among states to punish those offenders who continue to commit crimes. This type of legislation, often called habitual offender laws, attempt to punish the most serious criminal defendants by mandating life sentences for those who commit three or more felony offenses. These statutory schemes can enhance the penalties for certain crimes. There is wide consensus that those who continue to commit the most serious crimes pose the most danger to the community and should therefore receive the most severe sanctions. There have been problems with these types of sentencing laws, however, because some state statutes do not require all three felonies to be violent or serious felonies. This results in some defendants receiving grossly disproportionate sentences for nonviolent offenses, such as theft offenses. Additionally, critics have charged that the growth of the prison population as a result of these mandatory sentencing schemes has been too costly and has not been effective in reducing violent crime. Additionally, some studies show that these mandatory sentencing laws disproportionately affect Blacks and other minority groups. As a result of some of these concerns, some states have attempted to narrow the qualifying felony offenses. States have made distinctions among violent and nonviolent felonies as a way to target those persistent felony offenders who pose the most danger. So far, however, the U.S. Supreme Court has upheld the habitual offender and three-strikes legislation, even when these statutes punish those who commit nonviolent felonies like theft.

Recently, many states have also enacted statutes that address the use of guns in the commission of crime. In these states, the legislatures have mandated flat sentences for the use of weapons. In Florida, for example, this popular legislation is known as "10-20-Life," and it basically establishes that a person who carries a gun during the commission of crime, including a qualifying misdemeanor, faces 10 years in prison; a person who fires a gun during the crime faces 20 years; and a person who injures someone with a gun faces life in prison. Once again, these gun use statutes follow the get-tough movement and attempt to send a message that gun use will be punished severely. Again, critics charge that these statutes do little to affect the crime rate. Most also argue that these sentencing schemes are duplicitous, since statutes already consider the use of weapons as aggravating factors and determining the level of the felony offense.

All of these statutory schemes evidence the get-tough movement in the country. Proponents of these mandatory sentencing structures argue that these schemes have worked to reduce the crime rate. Critics suggest that many of these schemes serve as little more than symbolic efforts by lawmakers to show the public they are doing something to reduce the crime rate. The felony offenses identified by most of the mandatory sentencing statutes have already been identified as serious crimes by the state legislature.

Kimberly M. Tatum

References and Further Reading

Amar, A.R., Edward J. Barrett, Jr. Lecture on Constitutional Law: Reinventing Juries: 10 Suggested Reforms, *University of California Davis Law Review*, 28, 1169, Summer, 1995.

Bermant, G. and Coppock, R., Outcome of Six- and Twelve-Member Jury Trials: An Analysis of 128 Civil Cases in the State of Washington, *Washington Law Review*, 48, 593, 1973.

Clark, J., Austin, J., and Henry, D.A., *Three Strikes and You're Out: A Review of State Legislation*, U.S. Department of Justice, Washington, DC, 1997.

Hofer, P.J., Blackwell, K.R., and Ruback, B.R., The effect of the federal sentencing guidelines on inter-judge disparity, *Journal of Criminal Law and Criminology*, 90, 239–321, 1999.

Irwin, J., Schiraldi, V., and Ziedenberg, J., *America's One Million Nonviolent Prisoners,* Justice Policy Institute, Washington, DC, 1999.

LaFave, W.R. and Scott, A.W., Jr., *Criminal Law,* 2nd ed., West Publishing Co., St. Paul, MN, 1986.

Levin, D.J., Langan, P.A., and Brown, J.M., *State Court Sentencing of Convicted Felons, 1996,* U.S. Bureau of Justice Statistics, Washington, DC, 2000.

Maguire, K. and Pastore, A.L., Eds., *Sourcebook of Criminal Justice Statistics, 1998,* U.S. Department of Justice, Washington, D.C., 1999.

See also **Criminal Courts: Felony; Definitions of Crime; Sentences and Sentencing: Types**

Feminist Theories of Criminal Behavior

Definition and Background

There is no one "feminist theory;" neither is there one unified feminist theory of crime. Rather, feminist theories of crime represent a wide range of thinking, with the unifying themes including a focus on gender (as distinct from biological sex) and its social construction and the recognition of gender inequalities in society, though the sources of such inequalities are hypothesized differently in various (feminist) theories. Danner (1989), as quoted in Belknap (2001), asserts that feminist theory is "a woman-centered description and explanation of human experience and the social world. It asserts that gender governs every aspect of personal and social life … Also, feminist theory is activist and seeks social change to end the neglect and subordination of women" (Belknap, 2001, 16). Feminist theorists have positioned themselves as critics of the social order and of the traditionally male-centered theories that have dominated many academic disciplines, including criminology.

With regard to crime, Naffine notes that the assumption is often made that "feminism is about women, whereas criminology is about men" (1996, 2). Although many feminist theories of delinquency and crime do center on the experiences of girls and women, it is not true that feminist theories focus only on their behavior. However, the use of men and boys as the "normal subjects" in the study of crime and deviance is pervasive (Messerschmidt, 1993). Beyond the assumption that criminology is and should be about men, there are also incorrect assumptions made about feminist criminology. Some of these assumptions include:

1. Feminism lacks objectivity
2. Feminism focuses only on girls and women, never boys and men
3. Feminism dictates the choice of analytical techniques (Daly and Chesney-Lind, 1988)

Feminist criminology has emerged in the wake of the women's rights movement of the 1960s and 1970s and has developed in both epistemological and theoretical directions (Flavin, 2001). Feminists have challenged not only the assumptions listed above, but also the neglect of the study of girls and women with regard to juvenile delinquency, crime, and deviance, and the universal assumption of objectivity in the scientific method. In addition, feminist criminologists have challenged the notion that theories of crime and delinquency developed, either explicitly or implicitly, to explain male offending can be generalized to explain female offending. This approach to theorizing the causes of crime, often referred to as "add women and stir," has been roundly criticized. This is not to say that traditional theories of crime and delinquency are not applicable to girls or women, only that the assumption that this can be done universally is dangerous. Although the feminism that emerged more directly from the women's rights movement of the 1970s included a collective sense of "we," today's feminism(s) are more decentered, meaning that the notion of a collective, homogeneous group called "women" is being challenged (Daly and Chesney-Lind, 1988, 498), thus making the universal application of one theory to all female offenders problematic.

Criminological theory has been relatively slow to integrate feminist perspectives, though great strides are being made in the area. Indeed, it is nearly impossible to summarize the work that has been done in the last decade in the area of feminist criminology. Daly (1998) has identified four major areas of inquiry that have been central to feminist scholars studying crime and delinquency:

1. *Gender ratio of crime*: What are the major gender differences in patterns of offending and arrest? What explains these differences?
2. *Gendered crime*: What is the gendered social organization of crime? What are the particular qualities that might distinguish girls' or women's and boys' or men's crime?
3. *Gendered pathways*: What are the differential patterns that girls or women and boys or men follow into lawbreaking behavior? How do factors such as family and home life, work patterns, and incarceration vary by gender?
4. *Gendered lives*: How does gender organize men's and women's survival strategies? How do men and women differentially experience society, including elements such as the juvenile and criminal justice systems? (Daly, 1998, 95–99)

Most of the advancement in the study of girls or women and crime and the development of feminist theories of deviance, delinquency, and crime have come in these four major areas.

Feminist theories in criminology have emerged over the last several decades as critiques of previous theories of offending that did not take gender into account, particularly those that attempted to explain female offending. As such, to understand fully the roots of feminist theories of crime, one must be familiar with the early, nonfeminist explanations of female offending.

The Development of Theory

Pre-Feminist Explanations of Female Offending

The earliest theories of female delinquency and crime (not to be confused with feminist theories of female delinquency and crime) focused on biological and psychological explanations of offending. In the late 1800s, Cesare Lombroso focused on the differing physical and personality characteristics of men and women to explain gender differences in behavior. Although he believed that women, as a class, are childish, jealous, and lack the moral character of men, Lombroso felt that these tendencies are normally tempered by more maternal and "feminine" characteristics. When such feminine characteristics are absent, however, women are prone to criminality. Influenced by Darwin's theory of evolution, Lombroso also asserted that the most serious of female (and male) criminals were characterized by distinct physical features or "atavistic anomalies" that made them throwbacks to an earlier stage of the human evolutionary process. In the 1920s, criminologists such as W. I. Thomas refined Lombroso's work, reconceptualizing female crime as a pathology induced by social situations as opposed to a biologically predetermined fact. However, Thomas still focused on inherent "sex" differences between men and women, particularly with regard to their involvement in crimes such as prostitution, thereby ignoring any elements of gender socialization.

Psychoanalyst Sigmund Freud presented another, very different view of female criminality. Instead of locating the causes of deviant behavior in physical abnormalities, Freud located causation in the subconscious. For girls, he suggested that the root of most deviant or criminal behavior was in "penis envy." To Freud, the penis was the most significant symbol of male dominance in society, which girls and women were lacking. Freud hypothesized that this lack of a phallus could lead to destructive emotions such as envy and jealousy, which might contribute to later deviant behavior. During the process of psychosexual development, which Freud hypothesized happens in distinct stages, some girls may become excessively masculinized, whereas others may become excessively sexually inhibited. Although most girls pass through the Freudian psychosexual developmental stages without problems, those who become either overly inhibited or overly masculine may develop patterns of deviant and criminal behavior later in life (masculinized behavior in girls or women and homosexuality themselves were viewed as deviant behaviors). Although not making explicit links to criminal behavior, Freudian psychoanalytic theory was frequently used to explain various deviant behaviors of girls and women and remained influential through the mid-20th century.

Other criminologists of the late 1800s and early 1900s echoed the works of Lombroso, Thomas, and Freud. However, instead of focusing on the physical appearance, psychosexual development, or pathological nature of the individual, they focused on the sexual behavior of women and girls (Chesney-Lind, 1973; Odem, 1995; Smart, 1976). Crime and juvenile delinquency in girls and women were often reduced to acts of sexual promiscuity; precocious, nonmarital, and/or extramarital sex were all viewed as both criminal acts in and of themselves as well as symptoms or indications of involvement in other deviant or criminal behaviors. Girls' delinquency and women's crime was "sexualized," particularly in the early juvenile courts (Odem, 1995). Girls, especially those of the lower socioeconomic classes or members of immigrant populations, were routinely brought in front of the juvenile courts because of acts of sexual "indiscretion." Historians such as Mary Odem have interpreted such use of the courts to regulate female sexual behavior as overt attempts at social control, particularly of the "undesirable" classes (1995).

This view of the sexual nature of girls' and women's delinquency and crime limited the ways in which such offending behavior was studied. In particular, relatively little theorizing was done before the 1960s on female criminality beyond biological and psychological explanations, as it was deemed both relatively infrequent—with the exception of sexual crimes such as prostitution—as well as uninteresting to the researchers of the time. When research on girls or women was done, it frequently focused on crimes of a sexual nature or less serious status offenses such as running away and shoplifting.

Liberation and Emancipation

The Women's Rights Movement of the 1960s and 1970s had a great impact on the development of both theories of female offending and explicitly feminist theories of crime. The dominant theoretical paradigms before the 1970s focused on the biological, psychological and pathological nature of female offending. While taking into account biological sex, criminologists largely ignored the socially constructed notion of gender. Some theorists constructed theories with origins in social phenomena, such as Otto Pollak's "chivalry hypothesis" of the processes in the juvenile and criminal courts; however, they largely ignored or discounted the effects of patriarchy in the production and enforcement of offending behavior. Because of this, feminists largely discount such theories.

In attempting to move beyond the limitations of a purely biological or psychological criminology, criminologists such as Sutherland (often considered to be the "father" of American criminology) sought to form "gender neutral" theories equally applicable to boys and girls, men and women. Feminist criminologists have contended, however, that early "gender neutral" theories such as Sutherland's differential association theory and Hirschi's social control theory were implicitly developed to explain boys' or men's offending. Such theories were (and continue to be) largely empirically tested on samples of boys and men, making their direct applicability to girls and women questionable.

With the advent of the women's liberation movement, attention was heightened around all issues pertaining to girls and women, including their offending behavior and the official responses of the police and juvenile or criminal justice systems. The 1970s saw the development of some of the first theories that explicitly dealt with female offending from a sociological rather than biological or psychological perspective. These ideas, often referred to as "liberation" or "emancipation" theories, were advanced by such scholars as Freda Adler and Rita Simon. Liberation theories predicted that, as a result of the women's rights movement, women's opportunities outside of the private sphere of the home would grow. As such opportunities in the public sphere expanded, particularly in the workforce, the behavior of women would come to resemble more the behavior of men across many social domains, including offending. An increase in masculine behavior on the part of girls and women would include increasing rates of offending, particularly in traditionally male offenses, such as property crimes, crimes of violence, corporate crimes, and gang activity. Both Adler and Simon hypothesized that as a wider diversity of social roles became more accessible to females, their rates of offending would rise disproportionately to that of males, leading to an eventual "convergence" of male and female offending rates. However, most empirical research has shown that, although there has been a slight increase in female offending since the 1970s, the notion of convergence is largely without support.

A more recent liberation hypothesis, Hagan and colleague's power-control theory, has explored the ways in which parental power in both the workplace and at home condition boys' and girls' delinquency. Power-control theorists hypothesize that egalitarian families, in which mother and father have relatively equal positions of power both at home and at work, will produce children with more equal involvement in juvenile delinquency. In other words, egalitarian families produce girls who are just as likely to become involved in delinquency as boys. Conversely, patriarchal families, in which the father takes the role of primary breadwinner and the mother takes the traditional role of homemaker, will produce boys with substantially greater involvement in juvenile delinquency than their female siblings. While focusing on the important intersection between gender and class, some feminists have dismissed this as simply a modern version of the liberation theories of the 1970s that received little empirical support. In the updated power-control theory, rather than women's emancipation via entry into the public sector leading to increased rates of offending, "mother's emancipation equals daughter's crime."

Many feminist theorists were dissatisfied with theories of emancipation or liberation, noting that they did not address the existence of a patriarchal society and posited that such theories ignored both the valuing of men's ways of behaving as well as the disregard for women's continued responsibilities in the home. "Convergence," some hypothesized, would only happen when men and women were equally involved in both the public and the private spheres.

Three Strains of Feminist Thought as Applied to Crime

Dissatisfied with the theories of offending with which they were presented (whether theories of male offending applied to females or liberation or convergence theories), feminist criminologists sought to develop explanations for crime that took into account the patriarchal structure of society and the notion of gender as a social construction rather than merely biological sex. In creating theories of offending, feminist criminologists relied heavily on the dominant feminist theories of the time that had emerged in the 1960s and 1970s out of the women's rights movement. These theories were themselves "borrowed" from older schools of social thought (e.g., liberalism or Marxism).

As a school of social thought, feminism is one that is both diverse and complex. Although feminists debate each other over the meaning and definition of feminism, there are several qualities that identify feminism as unique relative to other schools of thought.

Daly and Chesney-Lind (1988, 504) identify the following distinctions made in feminist theories:

1. Gender is not a natural fact but a complex social, historical, and cultural product; it is related to, but not simply derived from, biological sex differences and reproductive capacities.
2. Gender and gender relations order social life and social institutions in fundamental ways.
3. Gender relations and constructs of masculinity and femininity are not symmetrical but are based on an organizing principle of men's superiority and social and political-economic dominance over women.
4. Systems of knowledge reflect men's views of the natural and social world; the production of knowledge is gendered.
5. Women should be at the center of intellectual inquiry, not peripheral, invisible, or appendages to men.

These premises address and discount the methodology of "add women and stir" in studying female offending.

The major schools of feminist thought can be divided into three main "camps": liberal feminism, socialist or Marxist feminism, and radical feminism. Each has been influential in the development of feminist theories of offending, yet each also has its limitations.

Liberal Feminism

Liberal feminism has its roots in the first wave of feminism in the mid-1800s that culminated in the Seneca Falls Convention of 1848 and focuses on equal rights and freedom for all people, a hallmark of traditional liberal thought. Liberal feminists have worked for equality in such domains as the workplace, education, the family, and the juvenile or criminal justice system, typically by seeking to counteract the gender-role socialization that shapes boys and girls into "appropriately" behaving men and women and working to remove discriminatory public policies. Within criminology, liberal feminists have focused their attention on the conditions of men and women in prison, the differing and unequal treatment of boys or men and girls or women by the juvenile and criminal justice systems, and women's access to criminal justice occupations such as lawyer, police officer, and prison guard (Moyer, 1992; Belknap, 2001; Chesney-Lind and Faith, 2001). As Chesney-Lind and Faith (2001) note, however, liberal feminism in criminology does have its limitations. In calling for equality between men and women, the unintended result has been to treat women as if they were men, such as enrolling girls in boot camp programs designed for boys and holding women in prisons designed for violent male offenders. Some have referred to this phenomenon as "equality with a vengeance."

Marxist and Socialist Feminism

Instead of focusing on gender roles and the quest for equality between the sexes, Marxist feminists focus on the economic context of the production and reproduction of inequality. Although traditional or nonfeminist Marxists focus on the struggles of the working class in capitalist society, feminist Marxists focus on the role of capitalism in reproducing patriarchy, or the dominance of boys and men over girls and women. Though Marx himself was not concerned with issues of crime, deviance, or gender, his theories on the relations of production can certainly be applied within criminology. Although Marxism has been quite influential in criminology (e.g., Quinney, 1980), Marxist *feminism* has had less of an influence on the study of juvenile delinquency and crime relative to liberal and radical feminism (Chesney-Lind and Faith, 2001).

Socialist feminism, on the other hand, has been quite influential in the development of feminist criminology. Socialist feminists differ from Marxist feminists in that they do not privilege the system of class-based oppression over the system of gender-based oppression. Rather, they see the two as inextricably linked. Socialist feminists have been central in pointing out the traditional nuclear family as a site of gender oppression, particularly in the form of control over women's domestic and paid labor. Together, socialist and Marxist feminist criminologies focus on the ways in which the criminal justice system, as a tool of the elite, serves to oppress women. Issues that focus on the interplay between gender and social class, such as the growing "prison industrial complex" in the U.S. that is serving to incarcerate disproportionate numbers of poor women, the victimization of women by corporations, rape as a result of the class struggles inherent in capitalism, or the economic nature of sex work, are of particular interest (Chesney-Lind and Faith, 2001; Flavin, 2003).

Radical Feminism

Contrary to the political and economic nature of Marxist feminism, radical feminist theory draws on the notion of power and, in particular, the imbalance of power held by men and women. Radical feminists believe that violence is the ultimate expression of men's power over women and that it is reinforced and rewarded in a patriarchal society. As such, they focus on issues surrounding women's sexual oppression and victimization, sexual harassment, and pornography (e.g., MacKinnon, 1987; Millet, 1969). Radical feminist criminologists have been particularly vocal regarding the issue of domestic violence, advocating for the construction of shelters for abused women, the development of legislation to protect women from their batterers, and training for police officers in dealing with domestic violence situations. In addition, radical feminist criminologists have tried to counteract the notion of a high prevalence of "battered husbands" (e.g., Lucal, 1995), noting the skewed nature of interpersonal violence. Radical feminism is not without its pitfalls, however. Some have accused radical feminists (both within and without the discipline of criminology) of portraying women merely as victims, lacking the will or ability to struggle against the oppressiveness of a patriarchal system and act out against male violence.

Dissatisfied with the theoretical forms that emerged out of the first wave of feminism that began in the 1800s and the second wave of feminism that began in the 1960s, modern feminists have moved beyond the confines of traditional theories such as liberalism and Marxism. Feminist criminologists have developed new ways to study the issues surrounding gender and offending.

Modern Feminism(s) and Crime

Modern feminists have sought to overcome the shortcomings associated with the three dominant strands of feminist theory, each of which has been applied, in varying degrees, within criminology. In particular, feminists have been critical of the "adding on" of women and gender to liberal and Marxist theories (Daly, 1997). Cain notes that "criminology must explore the total lives of women, and there are no tools in existing criminological theory with which to do this" (1990, 10).

In reaction to traditional feminist theory, postmodern theories, multicultural or multiracial theories, and theories of masculinity have emerged. Although not completely divorced from previous theoretical developments in feminism, each has sought to challenge the concepts of "women" or "female offenders" as homogeneous groups, as well as conventional notions of femininity and masculinity. These "standpoint feminisms" seek to put women at the center of their inquiry—to view women through their own experiences and to see how they "do gender" or "do masculinity or femininity."

Postmodernist Feminism

Postmodern feminism seeks to deconstruct the racial, class, and gender stratification that has resulted from modern Western civilization. In particular, postmodernists question the notion of "generalizability" that has been assumed in positivist science as well as the process of constructing knowledge and determining "truth." Cain (1990) points to the importance of language in the construction of knowledge, noting that:

> ... it is clear that discourses can be used to authorize and justify painful and even penal practice, and that sometimes the use of language can constitute a pain in itself. It is necessary, therefore, not only to recognize the discourse but also to examine its internal (il)logic, and the ways and sites in which it is deployed. This is the *strategy of deconstruction* (p. 7, emphasis hers).

Chesney-Lind and Faith (2001) note that postmodernism, particularly feminist postmodernism, is crucial in a media-driven age. The U.S. has been experiencing a "media crime wave" (Chesney-Lind and Faith, 2001, 296) that is not reflective of actual levels of crime. In fact, while the media constantly increases its coverage of crime, particularly crimes of violence, levels of crime are decreasing nationally. What has become known as the "truth" about crime among the general population in the U.S. is, in fact, more a construction of the media than a reflection of the actual state of crime. Postmodernism has encouraged the "deconstruction of media knowledge, linking these ideas to those of the privileged and powerful, whose interests they represent" (Chesney-Lind and Faith, 2001, 297).

Multicultural or Multiracial Feminism

Multicultural or multiracial feminism has challenged the notion that women are one homogeneous entity, noting that classical feminist theories reflect a White, middle-class bias just as most traditional criminological theories reflect a White, middle-class, male bias. In such feminism, no single system of privilege can be fully understood without the others: race, class, and gender must be looked at in terms of their intersections rather than as individual characteristics. As such, multiracial feminists explore not only the cultural explanations for behavior, but also the social structural explanations, such as one's place in the systems of economic, racial, and gender stratification.

Multicultural feminist criminologists such as Beth Ritchie (1996) examine how the intersections of race, gender, class, and domestic violence work to create crime among African-American women. Ritchie hypothesizes that these women are "trapped" because of their membership in the stigmatized classes of women and non-Whites, their location in economically marginalized neighborhoods, culturally constructed gender roles of Black womanhood, and their experiences of interpersonal violence, such that common patterns of offending develop among these women. Other multiracial feminists have highlighted how judicial and policy responses, such as the "War on Drugs," have targeted certain classes of people, particularly poor

African-American women, greatly increasing their rates of incarceration. They hypothesize that the "War on Drugs" has, in fact, become a war on Black women. Multiracial and multicultural feminists have expanded the way in which we look at delinquency and crime, extending beyond theories that focus on single characteristics of individuals to look at the existence of multiple inequalities coexisting and interacting in individual's lives. Indeed, aspects of race, class, and gender are not the only intersections in which multicultural feminists are interested: sexual identity, religion, physical ability, and other potential arenas for discrimination are also of interest.

Masculinity and "Doing Gender"

Theories of masculinity have emerged out of both socialist and radical feminist theories, particularly those that focus on men's violence against women. Masculinity theories center on the ways in which individuals act out the behaviors and expectations associated with their gender—how they "do gender"—and particularly how men enact and reinforce their own and others' masculinity. These theories redirected attention away from social class that had been used as the dominant predictor of criminal behavior, to the question of gender. Researchers in this area generally focus on a specific type of masculinity, termed "hegemonic masculinity" by feminist scholars such as R. W. Connell. Hegemonic masculinity historically privileges characteristics such as physical strength and heterosexual prowess, economic success, and whiteness. In other words, White, heterosexual, economically well-off, physically fit men are acting out the favored type of masculinity. Gay, poor, non-White, or disabled men—and all women—are left out of this privileged group. According to feminist criminologists, certain crimes support various elements of hegemonic masculinity. For example, violence against women may exhibit one's dominance over the "weaker" sex, while victimizing homosexuals reinforces the importance of heterosexuality to maintaining one's masculinity. Those who are unsure of their masculinity may use crimes of violence, particularly against women and children, to reinforce notions of their own status as men. This is particularly true in a group or peer context, in which maintaining one's masculinity is important for both self and others. An example of this might be found on college campuses, where fraternities use violence in the form of sexual assault and rape to objectify women and maintain their collective position of masculine power.

Messerschmidt, perhaps the foremost scholar applying masculinity theory to crime, has stated that "critical to understanding crime by men is the gendered nature of social action" (1993, 77). The gendered division of labor, the structure of social and political power, and the structure of sexuality are all arenas in which men work to create and reinforce their masculinity. In particular, crime is one way in which men enact their masculinity, whether through corporate white-collar crimes or street level crimes of violence. Messerschmidt also brings in the elements of race and social class that are so important to multicultural feminists, while maintaining the focus on masculinity as the primary way in which power is exercised, particularly over women. He does so by examining the ways in which various groups of boys and men enact their masculinity, particularly through crime committed by boys in groups (e.g., White middle-class boys versus lower-working-class non-White boys) and crimes committed by men in such domains as the workplace, the family, and the street.

Postmodern and multicultural feminist criminologists, as well as those who focus on masculinity, have sought to move away from the limitations of classical liberal, socialist or Marxist, and radical feminism and their applications to crime and delinquency. They have challenged ideas about the construction of truth and knowledge and the primacy of race, class, or gender over either of the other two, as well as highlighted the importance of hegemonic masculinity in producing crime and violence. Each has also added a layer of complexity to the way in which gender is theorized to affect juvenile delinquency and crime.

The Future of Feminist Criminology

Feminist scholars have argued that continued refinement and development of feminist theory is essential for the progress of criminological theory. Feminism is relevant for criminology, they argue, not only because of the historical lack of interest in studying female delinquency and crime, but also because of the added "sophistication in thinking about gender relations" that feminism brings (Daly and Chesney-Lind, 1988, 505). Modern feminist criminologists challenge the notion that boys or men and girls or women share the same experiences of their social environment. Rather, they argue that gender dynamics differentially shape women's and men's experiences, even when living in identical social environments (Chesney-Lind, 1997). Research that does not take into account gender misses a large piece of the puzzle when attempting to explain the offending behavior of both boys or men and girls or women.

Most traditional theories of juvenile delinquency and crime have, in one way or another, touched upon the idea of social class as a predictor of offending behavior, yet as some feminist criminologists have noted, the class–crime relationship has been found to be tenuous (Chesney-Lind and Faith, 2001). Yet the relationship between gender and crime, however it is theorized, is undoubtedly strong. One of the strongest predictors of involvement in delinquency and crime is sex: boys and men out-offend girls and women by a ratio of approximately 4 to 1, depending on the crime being examined; therefore, theories that take into account gender become essential to explaining such differences.

Feminist criminologists advocate moving in the direction of both theoretical and policy development, suggesting that we move beyond merely describing female crime to providing theoretical explanations in which gender is central rather than peripheral. Such theoretical developments must also have relevant policy applications to the varied situations of female offenders, both in and out of the juvenile and criminal justice systems. Public policies that purport to be "gender neutral" must be critiqued, as feminists have shown that "gender neutral" theories of crime have typically suffered from a male bias, calling into question the neutrality of programs designed for both women and men.

Some feminist criminologists have offered "an invitation" (Flavin forthcoming) to mainstream criminologists to engage in debate and seek an increased understanding of the importance of gender in the study of crime, thereby challenging the male bias that has been endemic in traditional criminological thinking. Daly and Chesney-Lind (1988, 527) suggest that the practice of feminist criminology should be an "encompassing enterprise," not one that merely focuses on those things considered to be "women's issues." In fact, perhaps one of the most important recognitions to which feminists call attention is that it is not just women who have gender—men have gender too, and hence the study of "gender and crime" becomes all encompassing. Finally, feminist criminologists encourage the recognition of the important linkages between women's victimization and women's offending. Accompanying this is the responsibility to advocate on behalf of women, children, and other oppressed groups. Academic feminist criminologists want to move beyond the academy and put feminist theory in action to work for social change.

AMY V. D'UNGER

References and Further Reading

Belknap, J., *The Invisible Woman: Gender, Crime, and Justice,* 2nd ed., Wadsworth, Belmont, CA, 2001.

Cain, M., Towards transgression: directions in feminist criminology, *International Journal of the Sociology of Law,* 18, 1990.

Chesney-Lind, M., Judicial enforcement of the female sex role: The family court and the female delinquent, *Issues in Criminology,* 8, 1973.

Chesney-Lind, M., *The Female Offender,* Sage, Thousand Oaks, CA, 1997.

Chesney-Lind, M. and Faith, K., What about feminism? Engendering theory-making in criminology, in Paternoster, R. and Bachman, R., Eds., *Explaining Crime and Criminals,* Roxbury, Los Angeles, CA, 2001.

Daly, K., Different ways of conceptualizing sex/gender in feminist theory and their implications for criminology, *Theoretical Criminology,* 1, 1997.

Daly, K., Gender, crime, and criminology, in Tonry, M., Ed., *The Handbook of Crime and Punishment,* Oxford University Press, New York, NY, 1998.

Daly, K. and Chesney-Lindm M., Feminism and criminology, *Justice Quarterly,* 5, 1998.

Danner, M.J.E., Socialist feminism: A brief introduction, in MacLean, B.D. and Milovanovic, D., Eds., *New Directions in Critical Criminology,* The Collective Press, Vancouver, British Columbia, Canada, 1989.

Flavin, J., Feminism for the mainstream criminologist: An invitation, *Journal of Criminal Justice*, 2003.

Lucal, B., The problem with "battered husbands," *Deviant Behavior,* 16, 1995.

MacKinnon, C.A., *Feminism Unmodified: Discourse on Life and Law,* Harvard University Press, Cambridge, MA, 1987.

Messerschmidt, J.W., *Masculinities and Crime: Critique and Reconceptualization of Theory,* Rowman and Littlefield, Lanham, MD, 1993.

Millet, K., *Sexual Politics,* Ballantine, New York, 1969.

Moyer, I.L., Ed., *The Changing Roles of Women in the Criminal Justice System: Offenders, Victims, and Professionals*, 2nd ed., Waveland Press, Prospect Heights, IL, 1992.

Naffine, N., *Feminism and Criminology,* Temple University Press, Philadelphia, PA, 1996.

Odem, M.E., *Delinquent Daughters: Protecting and Policing Adolescent Female Sexuality in the United States,* 1885–1920, University of North Carolina Press, Chapel Hill, NC, 1995.

Quinney, R., *Class, State, and Crime: On the Theory and Practice of Criminal Justice,* David McKay, New York, 1977.

Ritchie, B., *Compelled to Crime: The Gender Entrapment of Black Battered Women,* Routledge, New York, 1996.

Smart, C., *Women, Crime, and Criminology,* Routledge and Kegan Paul, London, 1976.

See also **Marxist Theories of Criminal Behavior; Radical Theories of Criminal Behavior**

Fencing *See* **Receiving Stolen Goods**

Fifth Amendment *See* **Due Process**

Fines, Fees, and Forfeiture

There are several types of penalties that the criminal justice system imposes on people convicted of crime. Two categories of such penalties can be identified, monetary penalties and nonmonetary penalties. Nonmonetary penalties include probation, prison, home confinement, electronic monitoring, and similar sanctions. Monetary penalties include fines, fees, and forfeiture.

Fines are the most common punishment used by the criminal justice system today. They are primarily used in cases involving minor offenses. If a fine is imposed, the offender will be ordered to pay a certain amount of money, usually in accordance with the seriousness of the offense. Fines can be imposed in lieu of other punishments or in conjunction with other punishments. A convicted criminal may be forced to pay a certain amount as well as serve a period of time in prison.

Despite the popularity of fines as a form of punishment, the criminal justice system frequently encounters two problems when attempting to fine criminals. First, in most jurisdictions, the fine to be imposed is defined by law, regardless of the offender's financial position. If a poor offender is convicted of a serious crime, the fine is likely to be high, which means he or she will probably have difficulty paying the required amount (Hillsman et al., 1987). The second problem is an extension of the first. When poor offenders are required to pay large fines, it becomes difficult for the state to collect the money. Many fines go uncollected not only because some offenders cannot pay, but also because many of the collection systems in place across the country are inadequate (Cole, 1989).

In light of the difficulty of collecting fines, some jurisdictions across the U.S. have experimented with "day fine" systems. Day fines attach a "unit value" to the seriousness of given offenses. These unit values are then multiplied by a fixed percentage of the offender's income. The result is, ideally, a proportional fine, one that is not unnecessarily burdensome on an offender, but still large enough to serve a punishment purpose. Day fines were introduced in Sweden in the 1920s and were quickly adopted by other Scandinavian countries. The concept was also adopted in West Germany in the 1970s and throughout other European nations more recently.

A study of a day fine program in Maricopa County, Arizona found that day fines were successful in diverting offenders from routine supervision (e.g., probation) and in encouraging greater financial payments (Turner and Greene, 1999). Other research suggests that it is difficult to implement day fine programs and that outcomes may depart from intentions (Turner and Petersilia, 1996). For example, some offenders may not be able to afford their day fine. Also, it can be difficult to assign dollar values to certain crimes as well as rank order their seriousness. Despite some gloomy predictions for the success of day fine programs, they have been implemented in a number of areas across the U.S., including Des Moines, Iowa, Bridgeport, Connecticut, and in Marion, Malheur, Coos, and Josephine counties in Oregon.

Fees are a relatively new sanction imposed by the criminal justice system. Some jurisdictions require that offenders pay fees for services as another way to hold them accountable for their actions. Fees are not used in lieu of prison or other sanctions. Instead, they are used in conjunction with more traditional methods of punishment, such as probation and prison. There are two types of fees currently being used across the U.S., fees for probation and prison fees.

In the presence of inflation and declining support from taxpayers for many criminal justice expenses, it has become necessary for many states to impose probation fees. In fact, some 40 states now impose fees for correctional supervision. In Texas, for example, one half of the cost of probation supervision is paid for by probationers (Finn and Parent, 1992). The logic underlying probation fees is that offenders under community supervision are capable of affording reasonable fees because they are in a position to work for a decent wage.

Critics of fees-for-probation programs cite two arguments (King, 1989). First, they are concerned that probationers may be incarcerated simply for their inability to pay probation fees. In other words, they imply that it would be unfair to send to prison a probationer who cannot afford the fees he or she is required to pay. Second, critics fear that probation fees will compete with or displace restitution or other court-ordered payments. For such programs to be effective, then, it is important that fee collection be systematic and closely monitored to ensure compliance.

With regard to *prison* fees, many states have begun to require inmates to pay for services they receive while serving time. Prisons are anything but cheap to operate, so the logic behind prison fees is that inmates should pay for certain benefits in order to offset costs. Significantly fewer *inmate* fee-for-service programs are in place across the country than probation fee-for-service programs, but they seem to be gaining popularity. Inmates on work release or who work in prison are increasingly being required to pay for such services as postsecondary and college education and medical care.

The Mobile County Metro Jail in Alabama was one of the first to experiment with fees for medical services (Manning, 1993). The program that began in 1991 operates as follows: Inmates are first seen by a nurse, who evaluates the inmate's condition and determines if the inmate should see a doctor or a dentist. There is a $10 charge to see the nurse and a $10 fee to see a doctor or dentist. Free medical services include a medical evaluation on entering the facility, psychiatric services, and emergency services. Inmates pay for all other services. The program in Mobile County has accomplished two goals. First, it has provided substantial revenue to the jail. Second, it has discouraged frivolous claims and unnecessary trips to see a nurse or doctor.

Forfeiture is another monetary sanction used by the criminal justice system. There are two types of forfeiture: civil and criminal. Each will be addressed separately. For now, however, forfeiture needs to be distinguished from seizure. Simply put, the police can seize property (e.g., cash), but forfeiture is a separate action. When something is forfeited, ownership to it (if any) is relinquished. A seizure, on the other hand, implies a temporary action where ownership is not relinquished.

Criminal forfeiture proceedings are referred to as *in personam*. This means they target people. Criminal forfeiture can only follow a criminal conviction. If criminal forfeiture is sought, the prosecutor must prove beyond a reasonable doubt that the offender is guilty *and* that the property is subject to forfeiture. For example, if, in addition to securing a criminal conviction, the prosecutor can prove beyond a reasonable doubt that the defendant bought his house with the proceeds of the offense for which he is charged, the house can be forfeited. Thus, unlike fines and fees, forfeiture is used to minimize the financial gain associated with certain types of crimes, usually drug offenses.

Civil asset forfeiture, in contrast to criminal forfeiture, is *in rem*, meaning that it targets property. Civil asset forfeiture does not require a criminal proceeding. Civil forfeiture proceedings can be understood in much the same way as wrongful death lawsuits that can be pursued independently (or in lieu) of a trial for homicide. Indeed, all varieties of civil litigation can be pursued independently of criminal proceedings.

Because civil forfeiture does not require that formal criminal proceedings be initiated, the property owner's guilt is basically irrelevant. Because property owner's guilt or innocence is irrelevant in civil forfeiture proceedings, many people have criticized this practice, arguing that because property is targeted—as opposed to an actual defendant—forfeiture laws conveniently circumvent important constitutional protections.

Civil asset forfeiture is also controversial because, depending on state law, proceeds can go back to the law enforcement agency that initiated the forfeiture. In some states, local police agencies that are responsible for the seizure of large quantities of cash can receive the cash (to be used for law enforcement purposes) if ownership to it is forfeited. Critics of this practice have argued that civil asset forfeiture creates a conflict of interest between crime control and fiscal management.

What does it mean to suggest that civil forfeiture targets property? In civil forfeiture proceedings, the government essentially sues property. The parties to the typical forfeiture case include the government (e.g., U.S.) and a piece of property (e.g., funds in a bank account at a certain location). The result can be a case such as *U.S. v. One Mercedes 300E*. Property that can be sued includes cars, cash, funds in a bank account, real property or virtually any thing else of value. The only restriction is that the property targeted be used to facilitate or is derived from criminal activity.

The idea that property can somehow be guilty of crime traces its origins to the Bible. Exodus, Chapter 21, Verse 28 states, "When an ox gores a man or woman to death the ox must be stoned; the flesh may not be eaten. The owner of the ox, however, shall go unpunished." Modern day forfeiture statutes can be attributed to this idea that property (even livestock) can manifest the will to inflict harm. As Justice Harlan has observed:

> Traditionally, forfeiture actions have proceeded on the fiction that the inanimate objects themselves can be guilty of wrongdoing. Simply put, the theory has been that if the object is "guilty," it should be held in forfeit.

In the words of a medieval English writer, "Where a man killeth another with the sword of John at Stile, the sword shall be forfeit as deodand, and yet no default is in the owner." The modern forfeiture statutes are direct descendants of this heritage (*U.S. v. U.S. Coin and Currency,* 1971).

There are three varieties of civil asset forfeiture proceedings. The first is *summary forfeiture*. This is where law enforcement officials summarily, or on the spot, seize property. Property to which no one can claim ownership, such as contraband, is subject to summary forfeiture. "Ownership" of the contraband immediately vests with the police because no one can claim legal ownership of property that is not legal.

The second type of forfeiture proceeding is called *administrative forfeiture*. Administrative forfeiture differs from summary forfeiture in that it requires a formal court proceeding. The process usually begins with the property being seized. Next, the property owner is given a certain amount of time in which to challenge the seizure. Finally, a court date is set, but only if the property owner decides to contest the seizure. If the property owner decides *not* to contest the seizure, the property is forfeited.

Administrative forfeiture is a controversial practice because it *begins* with a summary seizure of the property in question. Administrative forfeitures are justified by the "relation-back" doctrine (Jankowski 1990). The relation-back doctrine is embodied in 21 U.S.C. sec. 881(h) and provides that "all right, title, and interest in property [subject to forfeiture] shall vest in the U.S. on commission of the act given rise to forfeiture." Generally, the only burden the police must meet to seize property is probable cause. Whether the property actually facilitated or was derived from crime is determined in court, but, again, only if the property owner contests the seizure.

The third type of forfeiture proceeding is known as a *civil judicial proceeding*. A civil judicial proceeding is not preceded by a seizure. Usually, civil judicial proceedings are reserved for expensive property or real property, such as real estate, that cannot be moved. The prosecutor will bring a civil action against the property. Then, just like in an administrative forfeiture proceeding, the property owner will be given a reasonable amount of time in which to prepare a defense. If the property owner fails to appear in court in order to contest the proposed forfeiture, the property will be forfeited to the government.

Civil asset forfeiture has been criticized extensively by an unlikely coalition of critics (Hyde, 1995; Levy, 1996). House Judiciary Chairman Henry Hyde, a conservative, along with the American Civil Liberties Union, a staunchly liberal organization, have been champions of forfeiture reform. Their hard work contributed to the recent passage of the Civil Asset Forfeiture Reform Act of 2000 (CAFRA) that has minimized a number of the procedural controversies associated with civil asset forfeiture.

Another type of penalty imposed by the criminal justice system that frequently involves payment is restitution. Restitution is geared toward victims. For example, the offender may be required to pay the victim(s) for harms he or she caused. Or, the offender may be required to work off the damages caused by his or her crime. In either case, the *victim* is served by restitution, not the state. Fines, fees, and forfeiture, however, all have in common the single feature that the monetary penalty results in payment to the appropriate state or federal agency.

JOHN L. WORRALL

References and Further Reading

Cole, G.F., *Innovations in Collecting and Enforcing Fines,* National Institute of Justice, Washington, DC, 1989.

Finn, P. and parent, D., *Making the Offender Foot the Bill: A Texas Program*, National Institute of Justice, Washington, DC, 1992.

Hillsman, S.T., Mahoney, B., Cole, G., and Auchter, B., *Fines as Criminal Sanctions*, National Institute of Justice, Washington, DC, 1987.

Hyde, H., *Forfeiting Our Property Rights: Is Your Property Safe from Seizure?* Cato Institute, Washington, DC, 1995.

Kessler, S.F., *Civil and Criminal Forfeiture: Federal and State Practice,* West, St. Paul, MN, 1993.

King, C.R., Probation supervision fees: shifting the costs to the offender, *Federal Probation,* 2, 1989.

Levy, L.W., *A License to Steal: The Forfeiture of Property,* The University of North Carolina Press, Chapel Hill, NC, 1996.

Manning, R., Inmate fee for medical services program one year later, *American Jails,* 3, 1993.

Turner, S. and Greene, J., The FARE probation experiment: implementation and outcomes of day fines for felony offenders in Maricopa County, *Justice System Journal,* 1, 1999.

Turner, S. and Petersilia, J., *Day Fines in Four U.S. Jurisdictions,* National Institute of Justice, Washington, DC, 1996.

Worrall, J.L., Addicted to the drug war: The role of civil asset forfeiture as a budgetary supplement in contemporary law enforcement, *Journal of Criminal Justice*.

See also **Community Service and Restitution Programs; Retribution**

Firearms and Criminal Behavior

The development of firearms was made possible by the discovery of gunpowder. It is thought that, in the 13th century, the Chinese produced the first explosive powder for use in fireworks and rockets, whereas Roger Bacon, the English priest and alchemist, has been credited with the discovery of gunpowder at about the same time. Before long, the medieval era saw the development of the cannon, as people discovered the great force generated by igniting this explosive powder behind a missile from inside a tube sealed at one end. The earliest datable illustration of a personal, portable firearm dates to 1326. Despite the dangerousness and unreliability of the earliest models of these personal firearms, they were more versatile than cannons, useful for hunting as well as for military purposes. Firearms with short barrels that could be fired with one hand (i.e., handguns) first appeared in the 15th century. From that point in history to the present, firearms have evolved from those that were muzzle-loaded, one projectile at a time, to automatic weapons capable of firing several rounds per second and sniper rifles with a range of five miles that can penetrate the steel cover on armored military vehicles.

The different types and capabilities of firearms available today beg the question as to whether some models are inherently more dangerous than others. Studies of the biomechanics of bullet wounds indicate that the damage inflicted by a firearm is a function of its specific properties, as well as of the ammunition used. Arthur Kellermann, a specialist in emergency medicine, and his colleagues have observed that:

> ... the specific capacity of a firearm to cause injury depends on its accuracy, the rate of fire, muzzle velocity, and specific characteristics of the projectile ... Because the kinetic energy of a moving object increases with the square of its velocity, weapons with high muzzle velocities, for example, hunting rifles, generally cause greater tissue damage than weapons with lower muzzle velocities, for example, handguns. However, the size, shape, and nature of the projectile also play a powerful role in determining the severity of the resultant injury. A nonfragmenting bullet travelling at high speed will penetrate and exit a body with little damage outside the bullet path. A slower bullet, designed to mushroom or fragment on impact, may damage a much larger amount of tissue. ... Damage also increases in direct proportion to the mass of the projectile. Gunshot wounds caused by large caliber handguns are more than twice as likely to result in the death of the victim as wounds caused by small caliber guns. The number of projectiles striking the body also influences the expected severity of injury.

If guns vary in their lethality and ability to induce serious injury, it stands to reason that differences in lethality might also exist between distinct categories of weapons. For example, given the same intent to harm, are assailants using firearms more likely to inflict serious injury on victims than those using knives, clubs, or fists? These questions relating to the risks associated with weapons themselves—the instrumentality effect—are at the core of the often rancorous debate between gun rights advocates and those favoring the strict regulation of firearms.

Other questions are of equal importance. If firearms are shown to be intrinsically more harmful than other weapons or means of attack, can they be as effective in the hands of potential victims, in repelling perpetrators and deterring criminal attacks, as they can be in the hands of lawbreakers? The essential issue is whether the type of weapons available to one contemplating an assault or other crime is a factor in either the decision to commit that offense or in its outcome. A related question is whether the potential adverse effects of civilian gun ownership are offset by the benefits, including defensive gun uses. Furthermore, there is the key issue of weapons substitution; the possibility that those lacking access to firearms will continue to commit their crimes using other weapons.

Firearm Availability and Crime

In general, studies have failed to find a statistical association between firearm ownership levels and rates of various forms of violence, such as robbery. The exception, however, is found in the case of homicide. Several international studies, involving European and other western countries, have found that homicide rates tend to be higher in nations with higher levels of gun ownership. Although such a link is noteworthy, it does not demonstrate that gun ownership *per se* is a causal factor in homicide. Rather, high rates of homicide may contribute to the acquisition of guns for self-protection by many residents. Or, it may be that a high level of tolerance of violence in an area may result in both high levels of gun ownership and homicide.

Direct comparisons of nations and cities also suggest a link between gun availability and homicide, although they are susceptible to a number of criticisms. Since records have been maintained, the U.S. has always had a higher level of homicide than Canada. Proponents of gun control have attributed this situation, in part at least, to higher gun ownership levels in the U.S., while opponents of firearm regulation have pointed to social and cultural differences. Between 1985 and 1995, the per capita overall homicide rate in the U.S. was 3.8 times higher than that of Canada. The American rate for homicides not involving firearms was about double Canada's, whereas the U.S. firearm homicide rate was close to ten times that of Canada. Thus, the gap in firearm homicides exceeded the gap in other homicides by a factor of five, suggesting that the higher ownership levels in the U.S. may have played a role. Furthermore, firearms are twice as likely to be the weapon of choice in American as in Canadian homicides, indicating that the greater availability of guns in the U.S. may have influenced this choice.

Such direct comparisons are susceptible to the criticism that just two nations are examined and that social and cultural differences, not gun availability, are responsible for the differences in homicide (especially firearm homicide) rates. A comparison of two west coast cities, Seattle (Washington) and Vancouver (British Columbia), provided a unique opportunity to isolate the effects of gun ownership levels, as the cities are similar in many respects: climate, size, standard of living, and even in cultural tastes. Furthermore, rates of many forms of crime—robbery, burglary, assault, and even murders not involving firearms—has been very similar. The overall homicide rate, however, was 50% higher in Seattle at the time of the study. This was because of the fact that Seattle had five times Vancouver's rate of gun homicides. The authors attributed the large gap in gun homicides to the substantially higher level of gun ownership in Seattle.

The Vancouver–Seattle study marked the entry of emergency room doctors and other medical researchers into the firearms debate and they have played a prominent role ever since. One of the contributions of these researchers has been the application of the *case control* study to the issue of whether firearms are a risk factor in homicide, when other relevant factors are held constant. One study of 388 homicides in the homes revealed that firearms were more likely to be kept in the homes of homicide victims than in similar homes (in terms of violence and drug use in the home, education, income) nearby not experiencing a homicide. The investigators concluded that the presence of firearms increased the risk of homicide in the home significantly.

The apparent link between firearm availability and homicide might be explained by a number of factors. Firearms may facilitate violent attacks as they provide an impersonal and antiseptic means of inflicting harm by those not willing to stab or hit another person. They may also allow frail, physically vulnerable people, otherwise incapable of serious violence, to visit serious harm on others. Firearms can serve as an equalizer, allowing individuals of less strength and stature to assault those with superior size and strength. Firearms are almost a necessity in crimes committed against guarded or armed targets, such as armored truck and large-scale bank robberies or political assassinations. All presidential assassinations were committed with a firearm and nearly all murdered police officers have been shot. Also, firearm availability may support the criminal careers of robbers because guns allow offenders to attack more lucrative targets, with higher success rates, and with a lower risk of injury, as guns increase the likelihood of victim compliance. Furthermore, bystanders are far more likely to be hurt in an attack involving a firearm than one involving other weapons or fists. Moreover, high levels of gun ownership by civilians may contribute to high rates of residential burglary, as offenders strive to steal weapons for their crimes that will not be traced back to them.

The Role of Weapon Lethality

Perhaps the most compelling explanation for the postulated link between firearm availability and serious violence is that attacks with guns are simply more lethal than other means of attack. It is well established that gun attacks are more likely to result in the victim's death or disability than attacks involving other instruments. Studies have found that gun attacks are at least twice as likely to produce death as knife attacks. Some studies indicate that the difference in lethality may be as much as five-fold when guns and knives are compared.

A study of robberies in 43 large U.S. cities revealed a strong relationship between the type of weapon used and the likelihood of a fatal outcome. Although 1 in 250 gun robberies resulted in a death, 1 in every 750 knife robberies produced a fatality. Knife robberies, in turn, were three times as likely to cause a fatality as those involving other weapons. Unarmed robberies posed the lowest risk to life, as just 1 in 5000 had a fatal outcome. The author, Philip Cook of Duke University, concluded that:

> ... the relatively high death rate in gun robbery is the direct consequence of the fact that a loaded gun provides the assailant with the means to kill quickly at a distance and without much skill, strength, or danger of a counterattack. A passing whim or even the accidental twitch of a trigger finger is sufficient.

Thus, a gun is intrinsically more dangerous than other types of weapons.

Studies like this one have faced the criticism that gun robberies are more fatal because individuals using guns in crime are more dangerous than other robbers, not because of the greater lethality of firearms. Research on robbery shows, however, that very few robbers have a prior intention to kill and that many arm themselves with guns to increase victim compliance and, hence, to lessen the need for violence. Also, gun use is related to their accessibility, rather than simply the robber's intent.

Indeed, much of the debate in this area focuses on the issue of whether the outcome of an attack or robbery is related to the means or weapon used or the intent of the perpetrator. One investigator held perpetrator intent somewhat constant by limiting his analysis to serious aggravated assaults and robberies in which injuries occurred. Three times as many assaults and robberies resulted in death when guns rather than knives were used.

A study by Franklin Zimring, then at the University of Chicago, went to great lengths to sort out this issue of the relative importance of intent versus the "technology of violence." His Chicago sample revealed that firearm attacks were five times more likely to result in death than knife attacks. He then sought to determine whether gun assailants were more determined to kill than those using knives. He found that gun and knife assailants were the same kinds of people and that similar altercations and motives were involved in gun and knife attacks. Furthermore, a higher percentage of knife than gun attacks (70/100 vs. 56/100) struck critical regions of the body (e.g., head, chest, abdomen), indicating that most knife attacks were "attacks in earnest." When Zimring compared all gun attacks with only the most serious knife attacks (i.e., those directed at critical regions of the body), he still found that gun attacks had two and one-half times the death rate of knife attacks.

The importance of the weapon used in the outcome of a violent attack appears undeniable. This is not to say, however, that the intent of an assailant is inconsequential.

Even when guns are used, the likelihood of a fatality varies considerably, depending on whether the injury is inflicted intentionally. Suicide attempts and assaults by firearms are much more likely to produce fatal injuries than are accidental shootings. One study found the case-fatality rate—the ratio of nonfatal to fatal injuries—to be 16:1 for unintentional injuries, 5.3:1 for assaults, and 16:1 for suicides. In the recent civil war in Burundi, machete attacks were said to have a 95% mortality rate, demonstrating that intent to kill can result in a high death rate even when less lethal weapons are used.

The "Weapons Effect"

One line of inquiry pursued by behavioral scientists in an experimental setting suggests that the presence of firearms may do more than simply facilitate the commission of violent crimes by those contemplating them. It has been hypothesized that the presence of firearms may actually precipitate aggressive reactions on the part of angered individuals, as they have learned to associate firearms with aggression through the media, literature, or personal victimization. In one set of studies, naive male subjects were given opportunities to administer what they believed were electric shocks to individuals (accomplices of the researcher) who had angered them. In one condition, the angry men saw guns lying on the table next to the "shock" key and, in another condition, there were two badminton rackets or nothing at all on the table. The angered men who saw guns on the table were found to strike back with the simulated shocks more strongly than those who saw neutral objects or no objects at all next to them. There is some, but not unanimous support, for these findings in other research. There are always concerns that such experimental studies elicit behaviors that will not be duplicated in real-life situations because they are conducted in an artificial setting and subjects may act out of character in trying to please the experimenter. If the findings are valid, it means that lethal weapons visible during domestic or other altercations can escalate the dispute in its intensity and lethality. Such a study also points to the relevance of the storage, in addition to the volume, of firearms.

Weapon Substitution

One of the main arguments leveled at gun control laws is that reducing the volume and accessibility of firearms will merely lead criminals, as well as those bent on self-destruction, to substitute other means of committing crimes and suicides. Thus, one cannot conclude that all gun-related crime could have been averted had firearms been completely absent from a jurisdiction. Aside from firearms, humans have killed and maimed their fellows through stabbing, clubbing, beating, poisoning, strangulation, drowning, and countless other means. An individual with sufficient determination to inflict harm on another will likely succeed, given enough attempts, the element of surprise, and an unguarded target.

Weapon substitution, however, does not always occur when the weapon of choice is unavailable. People intent on harming another with a gun may not switch to another means in its absence because they may be too squeamish to use knives, clubs, or other weapons and lack the confidence to achieve their goals with these other instruments. Some studies, in fact, show that jurisdictions with lower levels of gun ownership and lower levels of gun homicides do not tend to have compensating higher levels of homicide using other means.

Weapon substitution is more likely to occur where an assault or homicide is premeditated, as the perpetrator may have considerable time to secure other weapons, or even firearms, through alternative (perhaps illegal) sources. Many violent crimes, however, are more impulsive, involve little planning, and are committed when the perpetrator is angered and intoxicated. In these instances, the absence of their weapon of choice may sometimes lead offenders to abandon their poorly-conceived offense and, perhaps, allow their anger to dissipate. Those committing impulsive crimes will normally use whatever weapons are at hand and it is in these cases that the presence or absence of highly lethal weapons is most likely to shape the outcome. The critical question is the relative number of premeditated versus impulsive violent acts. The larger the proportion of impulsive acts, the lower the expected rate of substitution. Even where weapons substitutions occur, switching from firearms to knives or other weapons should reduce the extent of harm inflicted as guns are more lethal.

A concern has been expressed that initiatives specifically aimed at controlling handguns may be counterproductive, as offenders may switch to more lethal long guns. It has also been noted that in robberies or hold-ups, robbers lacking access to firearms may inflict more injury as resistance by the victim occurs more frequently when robbers do not possess guns. Although scuffles and injuries are more numerous when robbers do not carry guns, fatalities are fewer.

Firearms and Self-Defence

One of the most contentious issues relates to the protective uses of firearms. This debate is especially intense in the U.S., where the constitutional reference to a "right to bear arms" has been interpreted (misinterpreted according to Supreme Court rulings and the American Bar Association) by a segment of the population as guaranteeing each civilian the right to own guns. Many Americans also believe that the use of guns for the protection of self and property is a sovereign right, whereas others view such uses as regressive and dangerous. Intuitively, it is difficult to argue that firearms are the most effective means of harming and gaining the compliance of victims without conceding that these features might be equally effective in dealing with attackers and intruders. The debate over the last 10 years has shifted somewhat from demagoguery on both sides to views recognizing both the harmful and protective properties of firearms. Although the ideological biases of the participants in this debate are still quite evident, the discourse has moved from one involving slogans to empirical studies weighing the net benefits or liabilities posed by firearms. The key question has become: Are there more criminal or defensive uses of firearms?

Research in this area has yielded an unacceptably wide range of findings in terms of the number of defensive uses per year. Estimates of the annual number of defensive gun uses in the U.S. range from under 100,000 to over 3.5 million. Studies differ in terms of how a defensive use is defined, the manner in which survey respondents are selected, in terms of whether they include uses against animals, and whether handguns only or all firearms were covered. At this point, this issue is far from being resolved and publications on each side continue to launch scathing attacks on the research methods used by the other side.

Those focusing on the defensive uses of guns point to some of the following evidence supporting their position. A survey of incarcerated felons in the U.S. found that many offenders have aborted crimes because of the belief that the intended victim was armed. A program in Orlando, Florida that trained 2500 women in the use of firearms to ward off attackers was accompanied by a dramatic decline in the city's rape rate, at least in the short term. It has also been argued that American homes are less vulnerable to burglaries of occupied homes than most countries because Americans are more likely to have firearms in the home. Firearms are also said to serve as an inexpensive means of self-protection relative to other means of security (bodyguards and alarm systems) and they are said to afford their owners a sense of security.

Equally credible arguments are advanced on the other side of the debate. Owning firearms for self-defense means that they are more likely to be carried and stored loaded and in an accessible place. The accessibility of loaded firearms is likely to increase their use by distraught individuals in suicide attempts and their misuse by children and youth. Greater accessibility is also likely to lead to the escalation of disputes (both domestic and other) from assaults to homicides. Athough armed civilians may sometimes serve as a deterrent, it is unrealistic to believe in the corollary that arming all civilians will lead to the elimination of crime. Rather, arming a critical mass of the population may produce an escalation of violence whereby robbers, for example, shoot first to disable victims they assume are armed. Others have made the point that gun owners rarely have the opportunity to use their weapons when under attack and that using guns for protection is a perilous undertaking. One study found that for every fatal shooting of an intruder in a home, there are 43 fatalities (homicides, suicides, and accidents) of residents in that home.

In most western countries, civilians acquire guns for hunting, target shooting, and gun collections, rather than for self-defense. The situation is different in the U.S., where over half the states have enacted laws permitting civilians to carry concealed guns, providing they meet certain basic criteria (e.g., have no history of violent behavior). Professor John Lott of the University of Chicago found that these laws appear to deter violent crimes but may increase certain property crimes and lead to more accidental deaths.

The Effectiveness of Gun Control Measures

The debate about the efficacy of gun control strategies is as contentious as that concerning the inherent dangerousness of firearms. In reality, gun control encompasses a diverse range of initiatives, including outright bans of specific models or types of guns, reducing magazine size, specifying the manner in which firearms ought to be stored, licensing owners, restricting sales to high-risk purchasers, imposing waiting periods for purchases, disrupting illicit markets, and imposing enhanced sentences for the use of firearms in crime. The variety of measures does not permit sweeping generalizations about gun control. Many of these measures have not been subject to rigorous evaluation. Overall, about half the evaluation studies have shown some crime preventive effects of a gun control measure. Impediments to successful gun control efforts include widespread noncompliance with some measures (e.g., the failure to store guns safely), the failure of prosecutors and the courts to cooperate with laws prescribing longer sentences for using firearms in crime, and, in the case of bans of various models, the large inventory of firearms already present in society.

THOMAS GABOR

References and Further Reading

Block, R., *Violent Crime,* Lexington Books, Lexington, MA, 1977.

Cook, P.J., Robbery violence, *Journal of Criminal Law and Criminology,* 78, 1987.

Cook, P.J., The technology of personal violence, in Tonry, M., Ed., *Crime and Justice: A Review of Research,* Vol. 14, University of Chicago Press, Chicago, IL, 1991.

Gabor, T., *The Impact of the Availability of Firearms on Violent Crime, Suicide, and Accidental Death,* Department of Justice Canada, Ottawa, Canada, 1994.

Kellermann, A.L. and Reay, D.T., Protection or peril? An analysis of firearm-related deaths in the home, *The New England Journal of Medicine,* 314, 1986.

Kellermann, A.L., Lee, R.K., Mercy, J.A., and Banton, J., The epidemiologic basis for the prevention of firearm injuries, *Annual Review of Public Health,* 12, 1991.

Kellermann, A.L., Rivara, F.P., Lee, R.K., Banton, J.G., Cummings, P., Hackman, B.B., and Somes, G., Injuries due to firearms in three cities, *The New England Journal of Medicine,* 335, 1996.

Kellermann, A.L., Rivara, F.P., Rushforth, N.B., Banton, J.G., Reay, D.T., Francisco, J., Locci, A.B., Prodzinski, J., Hackman, B.B., and Somes, G., Gun ownership as a risk factor for homicide in the home, *The New England Journal of Medicine,* 329, 1993.

Killias, M., Gun ownership, suicide, and homicide: An international perspective, in del Frate, A., Zvekic, U., and van Dijk, J.J.M., Eds., *Understanding Crime: Experiences of Crime and Crime Control*, UNICRI, Rome, Italy, 1993.

Kleck, G., *Point Blank: Guns and Violence in America,* Aldine de Gruyter, New York, 1991.

Kleck, G., *Targeting Guns,* Aldine de Gruyter, New York, 1997.

Lott, J.R., *More Guns, Less Crime,* University of Chicago Press, Chicago, 1998.

Reiss, A.J. and Ross, J.A., *Understanding and Preventing Violence,* National Academy Press, Washington, DC, 1993.

Sloan, J.H., Kellermann, A.L., Reay, D.T., Ferris, J.A., Koepsell, T., Rivara, F.P., Rice, C., Gray, L., and LoGerfo, J. Handgun regulations, crime, assaults, and homicide: A tale of two cities, *The New England Journal of Medicine,* 319, 1988.

Wright, J.D. and Rossi, P.H. *The Armed Criminal in America: A Survey of Incarcerated Felons,* U.S. Government Printing Office, Washington, DC, 1985.

Zimring, F.E., Is gun control likely to reduce violent killing? *The University of Chicago Law Review,* 35, 1968.

See also **Firearms and the Law; Firearms: Controversies over Policies**

Firearms: Controversies over Policies

Although prominent for the previous two decades, the issue of what to do about "guns and crime" became especially contentious in the late 1980s. "Drive-by" shootings were making news, gang members seemed to be arming themselves with exceptionally powerful weapons, homicide and armed robbery rates were increasing, and crack sales had destabilized social control within the drug market and introduced more violence into it. Perhaps most alarming, youths were shooting other youths with horrifying frequency. The political debate occasioned by these trends centered on the appropriate governmental response to them, especially regarding policies pertinent to gun ownership by private citizens. So intense was the discord, that members of federal, state, and local legislative bodies were truly at risk of concerted efforts to remove them from office, for example, for casting a single vote to ban the sale of certain kinds of firearms.

This essay examines many of the dimensions of the policy debate over the relationship between levels of firearm possession and carrying and crime rates. It briefly reviews the general parameters of policy in this vein. Efforts to reduce rates of firearm-related crime through traditional deterrence, incapacitation, and market-disruption strategies are explored. Attention is then shifted to efforts to control levels of ownership of guns in the general population. The essay concludes with a discussion of the potential gains of a return to policy that centers on changes in the structure and culture of the social environments in which gun-related violence now is concentrated.

In the present instance, policy will refer to organized governmental plans and corresponding activities designed to reduce rates of firearm-related crime through manipulation of social variables thought connected to such crime. To frame the discussion, the essay will focus on firearm-related crimes that are committed predatorily or within disputes. Excluded from the discussion are accidental shootings that may or may not result in criminal charges and that require policy directions (often equally controversial) that differ considerably from those aimed at predatory or dispute-related uses of firearms. Such government plans and activities may be federal, state, or local in nature; at times they may involve multiple jurisdictions. They may be directed toward individuals or society at large or both. They may target directly the criminal use of guns (e.g., "drive-by shootings"), illegal activity thought to spawn gun-related crime (e.g., drug sales), or behavior that is not inherently criminal (e.g., gun ownership or sales). Finally, policy to reduce levels of firearm-related crime may be aimed at changes in elements of social structure (e.g., the distribution of urban poverty) or culture (beliefs about the appropriateness of violent responses to disputes).

The potential number of types and targets of policy, when combined with the potential number of jurisdictions forming and attempting to implement policy, makes abundantly clear the difficulty of assessing the success of efforts to decrease gun-related crime. Complicating the matter is the passionate and politically well-organized opposition of segments of the population to any form of constraint on gun ownership in America; the organization and political clout of advocates of such constraint are increasing, but not yet to a level the equal of that of their opponents. Yet another complicating factor is that gun-related criminal activity and victimization patterns are not distributed evenly throughout the population. Instead, like many forms of social difficulty, they are patterned contemporarily along class, racial, and ethnic lines; and, like many politically crafted responses to social difficulties, "guns and crime" policies easily drift into the waters of larger structural and cultural conflicts.

Targeting the Criminal Use of Guns

Typically, crime problems elicit "get tough" policies from legislators and criminal justice agencies. In short, it is assumed that we can impact crime rates if we raise the stakes for those who contemplate breaking the law through either or both the threat of more severe punishment and more certain risk of apprehension for law violations. In terms of gun-related crime, legislators have explored the possibility of new laws and have found that there is very little in the way of illicit uses of firearms that is not already legally prohibited. They also have turned to increasing the penalties for gun-related offenses. Many states, for example, have attached additional penalties to be exacted when crimes are committed with guns. Perhaps not surprisingly, attached penalties have had little effect on levels of gun-related offenses, in large part because the original, fairly severe penalties for crimes such as armed robbery did not deter in the first place.

More certain apprehension for criminal behavior theoretically can deter once offenders perceive that their chances of getting caught actually have increased significantly. The perception may promote cessation of criminal activity and certainly will occasion more careful criminal behavior and likely altered and sometimes displaced criminal activity patterns. However, it will not produce a conversion to contemporary morality. If criminal justice agents cannot sustain the impression that the chances of apprehension for a gun-related crime are good, then we can expect drift back toward such crime. Research suggests that such drift has been the outcome of most efforts at deterring violent, gun-related crime. In a related fashion, to some extent, the incapacitation (rather than true deterrence) of serious offenders through such devices as "three-strike" laws, combined with general economic prosperity and demographic patterns over the last decade, appears to have had some impact on declining gun-related crimes, especially among younger males (Visher, 2000).

Importantly, some highly coordinated, interagency attempts to address violent crime, especially gang-related and firearm-related criminal activity, have shown signs of success in such cities as Boston (Kennedy and Braga, 1996). These efforts have involved planning among such groups as the police, various social agencies, community organizations, prosecutors, and parole and probation officers across jurisdictions. The efforts have included attempts to work directly with gang members and members of neighborhood associations to identify the sources of problems, large-scale sweeps of areas by police, frequent checks for and seizure of weapons, rapid record checks by the criminal justice system, quick and full prosecution of offenders by district attorneys, and more coordinated and responsive supervision of probationers and parolees. In the short run, these efforts have been linked to reductions in violent crime in the jurisdictions in which they have been tried. Which of their many elements are key to their success regarding the use of guns in particular is not yet determined; their fluidity to adapt to changing patterns of criminality has not yet been tested; and larger scale variable influences, such as the effects of economic prosperity on the jurisdictions in question, have not yet been sorted out.

Also, the extent to which changes in the drug market have reduced gun-related crime is unclear. Research has indicated that involvement in drug sales (and especially such involvement combined with other forms of crime) is related to gun possession, carrying, and use (Sheley, 1994). It is also reasonably hypothesized that the rather drastic rise in youth homicide rates in the late 1980s and early 1990s, most of it gun-related, was tied to the growing and unstable crack cocaine market (Blumstein, 1995). As that market has become more self-regulated and, to a lesser extent, suppressed by law enforcement (Staley, 2000), the rate of gun-related homicides among young males has decreased.

Finally, it is clear that a street market in stolen guns is a major source of the weapons that ultimately fall into the hands of juvenile and adult offenders (Sheley and Wright, 1995; Wright and Rossi, 1986). Evidence also suggests that levels of illegal gun availability influences levels of gun-related crime (Stolzenberg and D'Alessio, 2000). Thus, considerable effort has been aimed at preventing the illegal sale of firearms as the source of weapons used in crime. At the street level, this has involved "market disruption" strategies (harassment in the form of stings, area sweeps, seizures of stashes of guns, deployment of patrols in high-sales areas, and so forth) borrowed from models of suppression of vice-crime. At the level of more organized sales, it has involved much more systematic tracing of weapons and prosecution of those who abuse federal permits to sell guns, generally independent sellers unaffiliated with legitimate sales outlets. The results of implementing such strategies have been mixed, so that it appears that we cannot rely heavily on them to solve the problem of guns and crime. Ultimately they have more to do with denying *easy* access to various types of guns than with denying access more generally. Unlike vice products, guns are not consumed so much as put on shelves for later use or trade. If they are harder to obtain, then those who want them will pay more, buy less frequently, and retain their purchases longer rather than "upgrading." Indeed, to the extent that the street market is quashed, we can expect more organized criminal sales to meet previously less suppressed demand on a scale now greatly surpassing that of less-regulated nonstreet sales. Realistically, the likelihood of impacting the street market significantly is not high given the supply of firearms that has accumulated in this society, generally quite legally, during the past quarter century.

Gun Control Legislation

Experts put the number of guns now in the hands of private citizens at approximately 200 million (Wright and Vail, 2000). About half of all U.S. households possess at least one firearm; the average household with any firearm has at least two (Cook and Ludwig, 1997). Domestically, manufacturers have introduced over 4 million new firearms annually into this country since 1978 (Kleck, 1997). It is difficult to imagine, then, that proposals to do away with private ownership of firearms would meet with easy acceptance. Indeed, they have not.

Public opinion polls find most Americans favoring "some form" of gun control and desirous of protection from criminals. They leave to their legislators how to accomplish this. Legislators are lobbied and pressured by competing, organized groups of citizens. At one extreme are persons who consider guns a necessary condition of high levels of crime- and accident-related injuries. They envision a society of relative peace and safety achieved through the prohibition of ownership of most types of firearms. At the other pole are those who envision a citizenry impotent in the face of foreign military occupation, without recourse to abuses of power by its own government, and unprotected from violent criminals should guns be outlawed in any way.

"Gun control" has come to refer to nearly any form of government regulation of gun sales, ownership, and possession. Some legislators have called for registration of all firearms; others have sought registration of only some types, such as handguns. Laws differ across jurisdictions in the manner in which they regulate the situations under which persons may carry a gun. Lobbies have sought to convince lawmakers to ban private ownership of all firearms or, at least, certain types such as "assault weapons" and automatic and semiautomatic handguns. Some bills have banned the sale of small, cheap, imported handguns often referred to as "Saturday Night Specials." Attempts have been made to exclude categories of citizens (e.g., convicted felons or persons with histories of mental illness) from acquiring guns. In some instances, guns may not be purchased until a check of the potential purchaser's background is completed. More generally, waiting periods have been enacted in some jurisdictions whereby purchase and possession of a gun must be separated by a specified number of days.

The results of studies of most forms of legislated gun control have not been kind to their advocates. The most restrictive of gun laws have produced, at best, marginal changes in violent crime rates. The reasons may vary: poorly conceptualized laws, unenforceable laws, laws that stop at the boundaries of the next jurisdiction, registration laws that are obeyed variably, laws that focus on firearms that are possessed by so few ("assault weapons," for example) that they simply could not impact aggregate levels of crime significantly. Indeed, some researchers have concluded that guns in the hands of citizens actually act significantly to reduce rates of violent crime (Kleck and Gertz, 1995; Lott, 1998), a view not shared by all who have examined the data underpinning this conclusion (Black and Nagin, 1998).

The difficulty in seeking remedies to violent crime rates through gun-control policies has become fairly clear. The vast majority of guns in the hands of private citizens do little or no harm; indeed, they rarely leave the highest shelf in the closet. The vast majority of guns in the hands of criminals are not acquired through legitimate outlets that generally are the focus of gun-control legislation. The average firearm used in a crime likely was stolen during a home or a car burglary and then placed into black-market circulation. Importantly, a major source of the guns carried by youths is family or friends (Sheley and Wright, 1995, 1998). Yet, these stolen and "borrowed" weapons in illegal circulation represent but a fraction of the firearms purchased and possessed legally (Cook, Molliconi, and Cole, 1995). Ultimately, then, we seek to influence the problematic behavior of a relatively small population through regulating the behavior of a very large group whose ownership of guns affects crime rates neutrally at most. And we seek this outcome in an environment in which significant numbers of law-abiding persons could not imagine not owning a gun and let their lawmakers know it.

Other Policy Avenues

To summarize, firearms pervade American society much beyond their use by criminals. The number of guns in the hands of American citizens is enormous. The larger portion of guns that find their way into criminal hands can be traced to one-time ownership by law-abiding citizens. We have tried to address the "guns–crime connection" through efforts directly to deter or incapacitate persons who use guns for criminal activity, and indirectly through suppression of illegal gun sales and vice and gang activity thought to promote firearm-related crime. We have sought as well to address the connection via a very wide range of gun-control measures. Research suggests that, whereas we may influence the relative ease of access to firearms by potential offenders, the store of guns is so large, and access to them ultimately so easy, that there seems little lawmakers can do to address the "guns and crime" problem directly.

In looking for other policy avenues, it is instructive to note that researchers consistently report that a motivating factor in the average citizen's acquisition of guns is protection in what is perceived as a dangerous environment (Cook and Ludwig, 1997). This is true even of persons who carry handguns for criminal purposes; the primary reason for transport is fear of others who might also be carrying (Sheley and Wright, 1995, 1998). It is especially true of youths who arm themselves, no matter their demographic backgrounds. It is also noteworthy that the distribution of gun-related violence in the U.S. is far from random. Instead, it is far more evident among poorer segments of the population, among young males from underrepresented, poorer subpopulations, and among especially poor urban neighborhoods. It is not uncommon to refer to certain, poorer areas of cities as "under siege." The perception that so many people are armed presumably combines with the reality of relatively more frequent victimization and with routine transit through precarious places and involvement in dangerous activities (such as drug sales, gang behavior, and crime) to create what amounts to a culture of fear among persons inhabiting those areas.

If, indeed, guns (handguns, at any rate) are commonly acquired and used as protective devices, then one avenue by which to control their use in confrontations and crimes of passion is to reduce the level of fear that prompts the acquisition and, especially, carrying of guns. Although predatory behavior may not be as easily addressed through such a strategy, neither is predatory behavior as common a source of firearm-related assaults and homicides as are disputes both between strangers and between nonstrangers. In essence, reducing levels of fear translates into addressing the demand rather than the supply of guns, and the social structure and culture rather than the individuals interacting within them. Convincing persons not to own, carry, and use guns requires convincing them that they can survive in their social environments without being armed, that their unarmed state will not put them at serious risk.

There is nothing *novel* in such an approach to reducing crime—in this instance, gun-related crime. In fact, attempts to alter social structure and culture have been core elements of earlier "liberal" agendas of social change. Their "failure," as they were implemented in the 1960s, ultimately placed us on a path whereby policy was aimed at individuals rather than societal variables. As we found in earlier ventures into larger scale reform, policy in this arena is easier formulated than implemented. We do not always understand the key social relationships involved, and we often are not ready to pay the cost of changing those we understand. Further, no matter the population or subpopulation in question, the majority of individuals within it are quite law-abiding. Instructively, whereas one third of the inner-city males—in a major study of youths, guns, and crime—carried guns outside the home, the remaining two thirds did not (Sheley and Wright, 1995). The policy issue before us is how best to influence the behavior of the one third. Is it better accomplished via greater threat of penalty for gun-related offenses? Is it better accomplished via legislation aimed at the gun ownership of society at large (or certainly of populations larger than that of the offenders in question)? Or is it better accomplished via attempts to alter the more immediate structural and cultural environments of those most at risk of both gun-related criminal activity and victimization? Research results offer some, though imperfect, answers to these questions. Whether or not those answers can inform present and future political debate remains to be seen.

JOSEPH F. SHELEY

References and Further Reading

Black, D.A. and Nagin, D.S., Do right-to-carry laws deter violent crime? *Journal of Legal Studies,* 43(1), 1, 1998.

Blumstein, A., Youth violence, guns, and the illicit-drug industry, *Journal of Criminal Law and Criminology,* 86(1), 1, 1995.

Cook, P.J. and Ludwig, J. *Guns in America: National Survey on Private Ownership and Use of Firearms*, U.S. Department of Justice, Washington, DC, 1997.

Cook, P.J., Molliconi, S., and Cole, T.B. Regulating gun markets, *Journal of Criminal Law and Criminology,* 86(1), 1, 1995.

Stolzenberg, L., and D'Alessio, S.J., Gun availability and violent crime: New evidence from the national incident-based reporting system, *Social Forces,* 78(4), 4, 2000.

Kennedy, D., Piehl, A., and Braga, A., Youth violence in Boston: Gun markets, serious youth offenders, and a use-reduction strategy, *Law and Contemporary Problems,* 59(1), 1996.

Kleck, G., *Targeting Crime: Firearms and Their Control,* Aldine de Gruyter, Hawthorne, New York, 1997.

Kleck, G. and Gertz, M., Armed resistance to crime: The prevalence and nature of self defense with a gun, *Journal of Criminal Law and Criminology,* 85(1), 1995.

Lott, J. and More G., *Less Crime: Understanding Crime and Gun Control Laws,* University of Chicago Press, Chicago, 1998.

Sheley, J.F., Drug activity and firearms possession and use by juveniles, *Journal of Drug Issues,* 24(3), 1994.

Sheley, J.F. and Wright, J.D., *In the Line of Fire: Youth, Guns, and Violence in Urban America,* Aldine de Gruyter, Hawthorne, New York, 1995.

Sheley, J.F. and Wright, J.D., High School Youth, Weapons, and Violence, in *National Institute of Justice: Research in Brief,* U.S. Department of Justice, Washington, DC, 1998.

Staley, S.R., Same old, same old: American drug policy in the 1990s, Sheley, J.F., Ed., *Criminology: A Contemporary Handbook,* 3rd ed., Wadsworth, Belmont, California, 2000.

Visher, C.A., Career criminals and crime control, in Sheley, J.F., Ed., *Criminology: A Contemporary Handbook,* 3rd ed., Wadsworth, Belmont, California, 2000.

Wright, J.D. and Rossi, P., *Armed and Considered Dangerous,* Aldine de Gruyter, Hawthorne, New York, 1986.

Wright, J.D. and Vail, T.E., The guns-crime connection, in Sheley, J.F., Ed., *Criminology: A Contemporary Handbook,* 3rd ed., Wadsworth, Belmont, California, 2000.

See also **Firearms and Criminal Behavior; Firearms: The Law**

Firearms: The Law

Few issues generate as much controversy and debate as the issue of firearm legislation. Discussions concerning this topic are often heated, as both sides of the debate are adamant that theirs is the correct position. Even the academic and legal literature concerning firearms legislation is often prejudiced by the author's view of the issue and, as such, there is little consensus about this hotly debated issue.

This lack of agreement about firearms legislation is readily apparent when examining international laws regarding ownership of firearms. A recent UN study determined that, among the 46 countries where data were collected, only 4 countries prohibited all long guns whereas 10 did not have prohibitions against any long guns. Additionally, 7 countries banned all handguns whereas 12 had no prohibitions against handgun ownership. For all the other countries, there were firearms prohibitions relating to certain types of guns and people. Nevertheless, there was universal agreement among those countries that certain personnel could not own handguns and, with the exception of two countries (Burkina Faso and the Republic of Moldova), long guns. Most countries allow handgun ownership among most citizens with some type of licensing requirement. When firearm purchase was prohibited or restricted in a country, it typically was based on one of the following criteria: age, criminal record, mental illness, or domestic violence (United Nations, 1997).

Any discussion of firearm legislation in the U.S. must begin with the Second Amendment to the U.S. Constitution that reads "A well regulated militia, being necessary to the security of a free state, the right of the people to keep and bear arms, shall not be infringed." From its origin, the meaning of this amendment has been a source of debate among members of the judicial and legislative branches of government, as well as among academic and legal scholars, with little consensus emerging. Advocates of gun rights argue that this amendment ensures individuals the right to own firearms, whereas supporters of gun control argue that the amendment guarantees only a collective, state right to sustain militias.

Despite the debate surrounding the interpretation of the Second Amendment, the Supreme Court has directly addressed its meaning only once, in *U.S. v. Miller* (307 U.S. 174, 1939). In that decision, the court ruled that the National Firearms Act did not violate the Second Amendment and appears to argue that the amendment did not guarantee an individual right to keep and bear arms. Nevertheless, gun rights advocates argue that the definition of the militia given by the Supreme Court in their ruling suggests that even if the right to bear arms is limited to the militia, it is still a broad right. All other Supreme Court decisions to date that allude to the Second Amendment (although not dealing with it directly) seem to support the idea that the Supreme Court views the amendment as one that does not pertain to an individual's right to own firearms.

Until 1999, lower federal court decisions mirror the Supreme Court opinion that the Second Amendment does not ensure an individual the right to keep and bear arms. In *U.S. v. Emerson* (46 F. Supp. 2d 598, 1999), however, a federal circuit court held that a Texas statute prohibiting individuals under restraining orders in divorce proceedings to possess a firearm was unconstitutional because it deprived a citizen of his Second Amendment rights. Although the U.S. Court of Appeals for the Fifth Circuit overturned that decision in 2001, they still endorsed the individual rights reading of the amendment in their opinion. Thus, it appears that what little consensus existed in federal courts regarding the meaning of the Second Amendment appears to be withering.

Despite the controversy surrounding the Second Amendment, most legal, judicial, and academic scholars agree that even if the amendment ensures an individual's right to possess firearms, federal, state, and local jurisdictions may regulate that right. The following is a brief review of the existing firearm legislation in the U.S.

Federal Firearms Legislation

The first federal law that regulated the sale of firearms was the mail-order ban of 1927, which banned the delivery of concealable firearms through the mail. The second was the National Firearms Act of 1934 (NFA). The NFA prohibited the private possession of submachine guns, silencers, sawed off rifles and shotguns, and other weapons made popular by "gangsters" during the Prohibition era. The NFA further required anyone purchasing a regulated weapon to undergo an extensive application process that included a background check and a waiting period of four to six months.

In 1938, the Federal Firearms Act (FFA) was enacted in an attempt to regulate interstate and foreign commerce in firearms and ammunition. The FFA required the licensing of firearms manufacturers and dealers and required dealers to maintain records of firearm transactions. Additionally, the FFA prohibited interstate sales to those in proscribed categories such as felons and fugitives from justice. For 30 years afterwards, little federal legislation was enacted in the area of gun control.

As previously mentioned, the issue of firearms legislation is one of the most hotly debated issues. At the center of the debate is the National Rifle Association (NRA). The NRA was formed in 1871 for the purpose of improving marksmanship among its members and grew throughout the 20th century, from a membership of 3500 in 1920 to its current membership of approximately three million members. Its most active growth period was immediately after World War II. Although by no means the largest lobbying group in the country, the NRA has had a very active, motivated, and well-organized membership that effectively shaped a "hands-off" gun control policy in the U.S. from 1938 to 1968. Nevertheless, many argue the passage of the Gun Control Act of 1968, the Brady Bill, and the Federal Violent Crime Control and Law Enforcement Act in 1994 has weakened the hold of the NRA on gun policy in the U.S. (Spitzer, 1998).

Arguably the most important firearm regulation of the 20th century was the Gun Control Act (GCA) of 1968 that resulted from the legislative response to the murders of Martin Luther King, Jr. and Robert Kennedy. The GCA: (1) set new record-keeping standards and licensing fees for manufacturers, importers, and dealers; (2) banned the importation of surplus military firearms, and "Saturday Night Specials" (inexpensive small caliber pistols); (3) prohibited the interstate sale of handguns, rifles and shotguns except through federally licensed dealers; and (4) set minimum ages for gun purchases: 18 for a long gun and 21 for a handgun.

In 1986, after intense Congressional debate, the Firearms Owners Protection Act (FOPA) was passed. FOPA amended the GCA to: (1) limit the number of unannounced dealer inspections by federal officials to one per year; (2) allow the mail-order sale of ammunition and reduce record-keeping requirements for ammunition dealers; (3) forbid the establishment of any system of firearms registration; (4) legalize the interstate sale of rifles and shotguns as long as the transaction took place face to face and the sale complied with the laws of the home jurisdictions of both the buyer and the seller; and (5) ban the production of new machine guns for civilian sale.

The 1990s brought about a relative eruption of federal gun legislation. In 1993, Congress passed the Brady Bill, which implemented a national five-day waiting period for handgun purchases to allow local police time for a background check. Nevertheless, the Supreme Court ruled in *Printz v. U.S.* (521 U.S. 98, 1997) that the provision of the Brady Bill that required local law enforcement personnel to conduct background checks on prospective purchasers of handguns was unconstitutional, as it violated the principles of federalism that prevent the federal government from forcing state and local officials to carry out provisions of federal law. As a result, some smaller agencies no longer conducted background checks on potential buyers. In 1994, the Federal Violent Crime Control and Law Enforcement Act of 1994 were enacted. Title XI, Subtitle A of that act banned the manufacture, transfer, or possession of specific "assault weapons" (weapons with multiple military-style features, such as flash suppressors, folding stocks, detachable magazines, and threaded barrels) and most ammunition magazines capable of holding more than ten rounds. In 1996, the "Lautenberg Amendment" to the GCA became effective, banning the sale of firearms to individuals convicted of a misdemeanor of domestic violence (felons were already prohibited). Finally, in 1998, the five-day waiting period was replaced by the National Instant Criminal Background Check System (NICS) "instant check" that allows dealers to request a presale background check of all potential buyers to ensure that both handguns and long guns are not sold to purchasers in restricted categories. The instant check did not, however, nullify state waiting periods.

State and Local Legislation of Firearms

In addition to the legislation reviewed above, most states (44) have a specific guarantee of the right to keep and bear arms in their constitution (California, Iowa, Maryland, Minnesota, New Jersey, and New York do not). Furthermore, all states have enacted their own firearms legislation, with some being more restrictive than federal legislation. Although some states have no handgun permit system and prohibit carry of a concealed weapon, others have "shall issue" statutes—if an individual applies for a concealed carry permit, and does not fall in one of the categories that disqualify individuals from carrying firearms, the state must issue that individual a concealed carry permit. Finally, numerous local jurisdictions throughout the U.S. have also enacted firearms legislation, to bring the total of laws concerning firearms to over 20,000.

Guns Used in Self-Defense

The Federal Bureau of Investigation Supplementary Homicide Reports indicates that each year, private citizens in the U.S. kill between 150 and 200 people with a firearm during the commission of a felony. Kleck (1997) argues that the actual number of criminals killed each year is probably far greater, as these figures represent only those homicides that occur during the commission of a felony. Further, a number of polls have examined the extent of guns used in self-defense in the U.S. Kleck (1997) reviews a number of studies that find varying amounts of defensive gun use among U.S. citizens, with the vast majority of the studies estimating at least one million uses of guns in self-defense each year (whether the gun was fired or not) and some estimates of over three million uses in self-defense each year. Thus, the evidence does indicate that some number of private citizens use guns in self defense each year in the U.S.—the size of that number appears to be contingent on the source one chooses to believe.

Lawsuits Against Gunmakers

In recent years, a number of municipalities have brought lawsuits against gun manufacturers in the U.S. These suits typically argue that: (1) guns are a public nuisance; (2) gun manufacturers willingly produce more guns than they could expect to sell to law-abiding citizens, thus aiding criminals to obtain firearms; and (3) gun manufacturers employ designs that allow unauthorized persons to use firearms. Additionally, these municipalities also argue that these suits are needed to recoup money to offset the medical and law enforcement resources necessitated by gun violence. Critics of the gun industry and gun control advocates have compared the suits against the gun industry to those against the tobacco industry. Although these suits were historically largely unsuccessful, recent decisions such as *Hamilton v. Accu-Tek* (1999) found 15 gun manufacturers liable for oversupplying the legitimate gun market, thus creating a pool of weapons for illegal purposes. Although the verdict was later overturned on appeal, some legal scholars suggest this outcome has encouraged numerous municipalities to file suit under tort law. It is too soon to tell the outcome of these lawsuits but the trend appears to be a large increase in the number of lawsuits against gun manufacturers with municipalities and private individuals as defendants (McCoskey, 2002).

David C. May

References and Further Reading

Halbrook, S.P., *That Every Man Be Armed,* Independence Institute, Golden, CO, 1994.

Kleck, G., *Targeting Guns: Firearms and Their Control,* Aldine de Gruyter, New York, 1997.

Kopel, D.B., *The Samurai, the Mountie, and the Cowboy,* Prometheus Books, Amherst, NY, 1992.

Levinson, S., The embarrassing second amendment, *Yale Law Journal,* 637, 1989.

Lott, J.R. Jr., *More Guns, Less Crime: Understanding Crime and Gun-Control Laws,* University of Chicago Press, Chicago, IL, 1998.

McClurg, A.J., Kopel, D.B., and Denning, B.P., Eds., *Gun Control and Gun Rights: A Reader and a Guide*, New York University Press, New York, 2002.

McCoskey, W.L., The right of the people to keep and bear arms shall not be litigated away: Constitutional implications of municipal lawsuits against the gun industry, *Indiana Law Journal* 77(4), 2002.

Spitzer, R.J., *The Politics of Gun Control,* 2nd ed., Chatham House Publishers, New York, NY, 1998.

United Nations Commission on Crime Prevention and Criminal Justice, *Criminal Justice Reform and Strengthening of Legal Institutions Measures to Regulate Firearms,* Report of the Secretary General.

See also **Firearms and Criminal Behavior; Firearms: Controversies**

Fires *See* **Arson**

Forensics *See* **Police: Forensic Evidence**

Forgery

Forgery is defined as the act of falsely and fraudulently making or altering a document. Regardless of whether or not a fraudulent scheme is successful, forgery is a crime whenever an alteration or fabrication is done with willful intent to injure the interests of another. Within criminal law, there are both misdemeanor and felony, state and federal charges for various types of forgery. These acts range from the forgery of government obligations, known as counterfeiting, to the forgery of signatures or documents, postal forgery, the forgery of works of art, and even to literary and historical forgery. The majority of forgery cases are subject to state laws unless the case involves the use of the mail system or the reproduction of currency. Forgery most commonly occurs in connection with instruments for the payment of money.

It is generally understood that an act such as endorsing another's signature on the back of a check with the intent of receiving that person's money is considered forgery. However, the crime of forgery actually encompasses much more. Not only is it illegal to add someone else's signature to a document without their permission, but it is also illegal to make or sign an instrument with a fictitious name. Likewise, it is forgery if a true signature is fraudulently applied to a false document or if a copy of a document is altered and passed off as an original.

Even if there is no ascertainable victim being hurt by an act of forgery, such as with a drug addict forging a physician's signature to a prescription that he or she will fully pay for at the pharmacy, intent to defraud still exists, and thus, forgery has been committed.

Forgers are known for being inventive and finding loopholes in forgery laws. Thus, the legal definition of forgery is constantly being reevaluated and redefined so as to protect the economy from the costs levied by these acts. Even with these legal revisions questions often remain about who is to suffer the monetary loss from acts of forgery.

In the art world, for example, it is estimated that 40% of art on the market fits the category of either complete fake or "half-forgery," a truly old piece that has been doctored to fit a more valuable style or artist. Historically, art forgery has been lumped into the category of intellectual property crime, making it only indirectly prosecutable through laws involving copyright infringement, mail and wire fraud, or the Federal Trade Commission. Left unresolved has been the issue of who should bear the punishment and suffer the loss from acts of art forgery: the gallery selling the forged art, the individual producing it, or the gullible buyer.

In 2001, Republic Act No. 9105, also known as the Art Forgery Act, was established to officially recognize art forgery as its own criminal undertaking. The law applies to any "work of fine art" that is altered, imitated or reproduced with intent to deceive the public or potential buyers of the authenticity of the work. The Act implicates both the art forger and the circulator of the phony work as guilty parties, but does not resolve who shoulders the monetary cost from purchasing the fake art that can cost a gallery or private buyer upwards of a million dollars.

Forgery schemes in the art world have become increasingly complex. A recent scam involved not only the painting of fakes, but also the insertion of documents corroborating the false works into the Tate Gallery archives, used by researchers to authenticate art. As fine art buyers are increasingly less able to protect themselves from the loss of money that comes from purchasing a forged piece of art, many are now opting to spend less money on an honest forgery than to spend huge sums on a piece that is likely to be a forged anyway.

Nowhere are the complications associated with forgery more apparent than in the banking world. For decades, check forgery has been a large, expensive problem. At one point forging rings, which would burglarize businesses and industrial firms to obtain their payroll checks, were known to operate in all major cities in the U.S. The forgers would pickpocket identification cards from individuals who looked similar to them and then would make substantial profit with the payroll checks and different pieces of identification. Insiders, as well as outsiders, have also been involved in these and other independent schemes. Frequently, checking fraud is committed by individuals working within the banking system as bookkeepers, treasurers, or computer programmers.

In 1965, it was estimated that the annual loss from forged checks in the U.S. was over $500 million. By 1996, the approximation was that 90% of the $10 to $60 billion dollar annual loss to the economy from forgery was felt by banks' checking account customers. Today, the problem of banking fraud has grown even more substantially as most forgery cases involve some degree of criminal impersonation or identity theft. Forgers get identification information by contacting individuals over the phone or email and pretending to be banks or credit card companies needing personal information, by searching through dumpsters and trash cans late at night, through stealing purses and through intercepting bills, credit cards, and other mail as they sit in the mail box. With the information, forgers can then spend thousands of dollars using the victim's credit cards and checking accounts, often without being discovered for up to one year. The cost to an individual who suffers from this type of identity theft and forgery commonly exceeds $50,000 plus immeasurable emotional distress and time lost while working to rectify the situation.

For the last 50 years, the allocation of losses in check forgery situations has been governed by the Uniform Commercial Code (UCC). Typically with a checking account, the bank is authorized to pay items out of customers' accounts only if the checks have all the necessary endorsing signatures and have not been altered in any way. If the bank pays out an item that is not considered properly payable, it is bound to recredit the customer's account. The Uniform Commercial Code is then designed to provide a defense for banks that unwittingly cash out forged checks. The UCC states that if a bank pays out a forged instrument to an imposter pretending to be a bank customer, the bank has no obligation to reimburse the customer's account on discovery of the fraudulent act. Essentially, it is the responsibility of the customer to protect his or her own bank account from imposters looking for easy check forgery targets. Most courts concur that the rule is justified because the account holder is in a much better position to provide this type of protection or foil a forgery scheme than is the payer bank.

Enforcers of the imposter rule and the UCC have been faced with constant loss allocation dilemmas as forgers relentlessly implement new and different check forgery schemes. One of the first problems confronted by the courts occurred when imposters began using mail and telephone methods to carry out acts of forgery. The wording of the imposter rule had previously referred to only face-to-face interactions, and thus, the rule had to be altered to widen its scope. More uncertainties arose as to whether or not the rule should be applicable if the bank paid out a check to an imposter's confederate, to an impersonated fictitious person, rather than a real person, or to a forger pretending to be the agent of a checking account customer.

The Revised Uniform Commercial Code (RUCC) was devised in 1990 to alleviate some of the problems arising from the comparably narrow range of forgery issues addressed by the UCC. Under the RUCC, it is nearly impossible for banks to be held negligent in cases of check forgery. The RUCC specifies that the imposter rule is applicable regardless of whether the imposter is real or fictitious, an agent, or a confederate. Unfortunately, however, even the RUCC allows for some uncertainties in terms of loss allocation. Recent cases have come up in which the person committing forgery was a legitimate agent of the payee but was misusing his or her authority. One example is a lawyer who was entitled to represent his client to a degree but forged the client's signature on the settlement agreement and settlement check, and then deposited the money in a personal account. The RUCC does not provide guidance as to whether the bank or the client should shoulder the loss from an incident such as this, and the courts disagree as to whether "misrepresentation of agency authority" is adequate for invoking the imposter rule. Thus, it is likely that the statutory language of the RUCC will have to be changed and clarified again in the near future.

Although plots involving bank accounts are the most common form of forgery, some of the most notable fakes have come from the more unusual realm of the forgery of historical documents and artifacts. One of the best-known cases of forgery in anthropological history was the Piltdown hoax of 1912. A woman's skull and ape's jaw were stained and filed to appear ancient and left in a pit where road workers would discover them. Many paleontologists considered the forgery the "missing link" between humans and apes until the 1950s when radiocarbon dating revealed their true age. Another possible forgery case that has gained attention in recent decades is whether or not the Shroud of Turin, originally claimed to be the burial cloth of Jesus, is a fake. In the 1980s radiocarbon dating and different scientific tests exposed the linen as nothing more than a medieval forgery made with red ocher and paint. Some historians, however, refuse to accept the radiocarbon readings and continue to insist that the shroud is the real thing.

Other well-known forgeries have involved the "private diaries" of major historical figures. "Hitler's secret diaries," for example, which made it into *Newsweek* magazine in 1983, turned out to be written by German con artist Konrad Kujau and sold to a German magazine for $4 million. The magazine never checked the authenticity of the diaries, which contained misspellings and factual errors, and distributed some 2 million copies of the forged writings before the hoax was discovered. In the last decade, the diaries of James Maybrick, confessing to be serial killer Jack the Ripper, were found to be forged by a struggling writer, and debate still rages over the legitimacy of the Black Diaries of Roger Casement, a celebrated human rights activist in the Congo in the early 1900s.

Forgery, in general, is typically viewed by most as a victimless crime, but this is far from the case. Each act of forgery, whether involving art, history, bank accounts or other documents, results in higher interest rates, increased merchandise costs, and a common aura of distrust that impacts all spectrums of society and the economy. The crime of forgery has received more attention in recent years, yet many of the laws involving forgery and the methods of protecting society against forgers do not appropriately reflect the problems and costs associated with this crime. It is likely that in the near future many forgery laws will have to be revised to take into account the changing face of the offense and the seriousness of acts of forgery will have to be acknowledged to a greater degree.

LYNN LANGTON AND ALEX R. PIQUERO

References and Further Reading

Bouvier, J., 1865, Forgery, *Bouvier's Law Dictionary,* 6th ed. Available at: www.constitution.org/boug/bouvier.htm. Retrieved on July 23, 2003.

Bundang, A.R., 2003, Rule of law, *Business World.* Available at: http://proquest.umi.com. Retrieved on July 30, 2003.

Doehrman, M., 2003, Identity theft cases rapidly increasing, *The Colorado Springs Business Journal.* Available at: www.proquest.com. Retrieved on August 19, 2003.

Dow, S.B., 2000, The impostor problem and forged endorsements: New risks under the Revised Uniform Commercial Code., *Journal of Security Administration,* 23(2), 13–26.

2002, Forgery, *The Columbia Encyclopedia,* 7th ed. Available at: http://ask.elibrary.com. Retrieved on July, 14, 2003.

Hemraj, M.B., 2002, The crime of forgery, *Journal of Financial Crime,* 9(4), 355–340. Available at: http://proquest.umi.com. Retrieved July 23, 2003.

Levine, S., 2002, Meet the missing link (wink, wink), *U.S. News and World Report,* 138(8).

Mitchell, A., 2001, Forgery or genuine document? *History Today,* 51(3), 16. Available at: http://ask.library.com. Retrieved July 14, 2003.

Sheler, J., July 24, 2000, Cloudy shroud, *U.S. News and World Report,* 129(4).

See also **Counterfeiting; Crimes against Consumers**

Fourth Amendment *See* **Search and Seizure**

See **Search and Seizure**

France, Crime and Justice in

Introduction

To understand contemporary French criminal justice, one must be at least moderately versed on revisions to French criminal law implanted in the Criminal Code of 1992 (Elliott, 2001). The development of this code has its origins as far back as the 1970s when law experts and scholars noted that revisions were needed (Elliott, 2001). However, it was not until the late early 1990s that revision of the criminal code became a true political priority (Elliott, 2001). The main aim of the revised code was to group offenses together so that they would be accessible and more comprehensible to the general public. The main purpose for these revisions was to modernize the drafting and to simplify the language of the criminal code so that it would be clear for both the general layperson and legal expert alike (Elliott, 2001). Despite these changes, the basic principles of French criminal law have remained largely unchanged in current day France.

One important aspect to the French criminal justice system is the cultural desire to limit the amount of power held by individuals in the French criminal justice system as well as the desire to protect citizens from abuses of power by those holding criminal justice positions (Reichel, 2002). With this in mind, the procedural aspects of French criminal law have been divided into three stages with different officials having power in each stage. These three stages consist of (1) the police investigation and the prosecution stage, (2) the judicial investigation stage, and (3) the trial stage (Elliott, 2001). The distinction between the first two stages is somewhat blurred because of the fact that judges give wide discretion to the police, who incidentally, play a primary role in the both of the first two stages (Elliott, 2001; Reichel, 2002).

Philosophical Basis of Criminal Law

Similar to common law based systems, the French system provides that crime commission requires both *actus reus* and *mens rea*. The French have long established that a person should not be punished for their thoughts alone and their penal code reflects this. Though applied in practice before this, it was not until the 1810 Criminal Code that it was officially recognized in written form that thoughts, in and of themselves, should not be held as punishable (Elliott, 2001). However, there is one exception to this philosophy on criminal intent; that of criminal conspiracy. The Criminal Code does however require the existence of some form of "material fact" to this exception, though this material fact is ambiguously defined in the French Code (Elliott, 2001).

With respect to *mens rea*, a basic distinction does exist in French law between those offenses that require intention and those that do not. Where no intention is required, the *mens rea* requirement can be satisfied on three grounds: through proof of negligence, through proving that a person was deliberately put in danger, or through proving that the conduct was, in fact, voluntary (Elliott, 2001). The serious crimes are always held to be intentional; major offenses are in principle intentional except for those legislative provisions that require a fault of negligence or of deliberately putting another in danger. Minor offenses normally only require that the accused behaved voluntarily. Since their social effects and commensurate punishments are so slight *mens rea* is not considered crucial in processing (Elliott, 2001).

Basics on Criminal Procedure

Throughout these three stages, rules on criminal procedure center on the distinction between three classes of offenses: serious, major, and minor offenses (McKee 2001; Borricand, 2002; Elliott, Reichel, 2002). In particular, a judicial investigation only tends to be used when a serious offense has been committed. Since the French system is inquisitorial in nature, its proceedings are not typically open to the public and the parties do not necessarily have a right to be heard (Elliott, 2001; McKee 2001; Reichel, 2002). Importantly, the judges in these inquisitorial proceedings usually play an active role in collecting the evidence with an emphasis on collecting written documentation to prove or disprove a case. This is especially true during the first two stages of French criminal procedure, with particular emphasis being placed on the construction of a written file of the case containing all the statements, expert reports, and records of investigative procedures carried out (Elliott, 2001). Despite the inquisitorial nature of the French system, recent developments in French criminal and trial procedures have integrated some aspects common to the adversarial process, largely as a measure to protect individual rights in the process (Reichel, 2002).

Similarly, all police and judicial investigations, as well as any judicial deliberations, take place in secret (Elliott, 2001; McKee 2001; Borricand, 2002; Reichel, 2002). This leaves the trial hearing as the only point of the process that is considered open to the public. A fundamental concept in this process is that the democratic principles of freedom of the press should be balanced with the equally important need to ensure that justice is equitably served (Elliott, 2001; McKee 2001; Borricand, 2002; Reichel, 2002). The secrecy of early stages of the criminal procedure means that investigations can be carried out without prior communications taking place between accomplices, relevant evidence begin destroyed and pressure being placed on witnesses (Elliott, 2001). This is considered a huge benefit in the process, which is thought to obtain a more objective determination of truth than does an adversarial system such as that found in the U.S. It should be pointed out that in actuality, only a few actors in the criminal justice process are bound to secrecy, these being limited to those who directly participate in the procedure (Elliott, 2001). On the other hand, private claimants and ordinary witnesses are not bound to secrecy since they are not treated as participating in the process.

The French Police

With respect to the police in France, there are two general types. First among these are the national police, who work primarily in urban areas and belong to the Home Office (Elliott, 2001; McKee, 2001; Borricand, 2002; Reichel, 2002). The second section of police is the Gendarmes, who function in the suburbs and in rural areas and are attached to the Ministry of Defense. Much of the rationale for having two police components is that the French desire to avoid placing control of the police under any single authority (Elliott, 2001; McKee, 2001; Reichel, 2002). Though these two components both ultimately answer to the French Central Government, they do so through differing means. The national police (known as the Police Nationale) answer to the Minister of the Interior, who is charged with administrative control over this section of the French Police (Elliott, 2001; McKee, 2001; Reichel, 2002). On the other hand, the Gendarmerie answer to the Minister of Defense, who is more concerned with the broader security and maintenance of French soil.

The Police Nationale consists of eleven directorates that oversee policing activities (Elliott, 2001). These directorates, who are responsible for urban areas whose populations exceed 10,000 citizens, oversee police responsibility for such things as forensic investigation, criminal statistics, banditry (i.e., gang crimes) and white-collar crimes. The Police Nationale directorates also monitor the investigation of complaints about police behavior, the collection and interpretation of information on social, political, and economic trends (including extremist groups such as in the Basque country), counterespionage and antiterrorist duties, as well as the training of various police units (Elliott, 2001; Reichel, 2002).

Of the two police forces, the Gendarmerie is the oldest. The Gendarmerie is responsible for enforcing the law in the rural areas of France and in communities that have less than 10,000 people (Elliott, 2001; McKee, 2001; Reichel, 2002). The fact that there are few densely populated areas in France means that the majority of the geographical terrain of France is under the Gendarmerie's jurisdiction. Over half of all French citizens fall within the jurisdiction of the Gendarmerie since so many live in small towns and villages. Though the Gendarmerie has a strong link to the military, this does not detract from its ability to conduct true professional civilian (as opposed to military) police work (Reichel, 2002). Indeed, this branch of the French police conducts numerous routine civilian policing tasks such as patrol, surveillance, maintenance of public order, and criminal investigations (Elliott, 2001; McKee, 2001; Reichel, 2002). The Gendarmerie is an organization of personnel that meet high recruitment and training standards and these personnel are given equipment that is considered to be state-of-the-art in nature (Reichel, 2002).

It is important to note that even though the French police have two subgroups, they are still considered a centralized police force because the Ministry of Defense and the Ministry of the Interior both are an active part of the overall French Central Government (Elliott, 2001). This centralization creates an enhanced sense of cooperation between the two police forces. For example, the urban police will typically inform the regional crime service, who then transmits relevant intelligence data to the Central Directorate in Paris. This Central Directorate will often then circulate the information throughout the country, allowing for crosschecks and further implementation of the data (Reichel, 2002). Thus, the advantage to this centralized policing style is the fact that communication between both police groups is more easily facilitated and information is more readily disseminated between both branches.

In France, the distinctions in police duties are also typically separated by two broad police missions; those that are administrative and those that are judicial (Elliott, 2001). The administrative police are tasked with crime prevention and ensuring public order, or in other words, general law enforcement. The judiciary police, on the other hand, are under the supervision of the judiciary and are responsible for bringing perpetrators to the judicial system (Elliott, 2001). Because the judiciary police are under the supervision of the judiciary, the prosecutor must be informed of all arrests made by the police and gendarmerie forces (Elliott, 2001). Only qualified police officials can undertake investigations. The judiciary police are tasked to investigate either by the public prosecutor's office (as for the early stages of a case) or by the investigating magistrate (such as with serious crimes).

Regardless of the type of police or their particular function, the placement of suspects into custody is considered an enormously important stage in the criminal process. The process of police custody is under the control of the Public Prosecutor's Office (Elliott, 2001). It should be noted that in France, a person can be placed in police custody for the purposes of interrogation for 24 hours. In certain special circumstances this can be extended to 48 hours by the public prosecutor (Reichel, 2002). An exception to this occurs if the suspect is thought to be involved in a terrorist or major drug offense; in this case he or she may be held in police detention for up to 98 hours (Elliott, 2001). In the past, the suspect was not informed of his or her right to remain silent, and there was no obligation to inform a suspect as to why he or she was being detained in police custody. The rights of the suspects have been improved in recent years to include these and other protections (Elliott, 2001).

Prosecution, Investigation, and Trial

Once the police investigation is completed, prosecution can be brought by a civil servant, who is normally the public prosecutor. This prosecutor has jurisdiction in the locality where the crime was committed, where the suspect lives, where they were arrested, or sometimes the location in which they are detained (Elliott, 2001). It is up to the prosecutor's sole discretion whether or not prosecution will be pursued. Currently, there is little effort to provide any real guidance or direction in the exercise of this discretion. Prosecuting policies are developed at the national, regional, and local level as seems fit at the time for that particular governing body (Elliott, 2001). Thus, the likelihood of a standardized form of prosecutorial discretion is not likely to occur in the near future of France.

After the prosecution, the next phase is that of the judicial investigation. Judicial investigators are given much greater coercive power than are police investigators (Elliott, 2001). The judicial investigation is designed to build on the work undertaken during the police investigation, in an effort to discover the truth and to determine whether the case should be referred for trial (Elliott, 2001). It is compulsory in relation to serious offenses and discretionary for all other offenses. In practice, it is actually used in only about 10% of all cases, with it being used even less often in minor cases. Further, this stage of the procedure is directed by the investigating judge (Elliott, 2001). Note that the investigating judge does not decide the guilt or innocence of the accused since this is done by the trial court. Thus, the investigating judge's investigation does not compromise the justice process. Rather, the role of the investigating judge is primarily to watch over the regularity of investigations, to prevent abuse of the broad coercive powers available at this stage, and to determine whether a case is suitable for trial (Elliott, 2001, Reichel, 2002). Importantly, investigating judge aims to discover the objective truth, rather than the guilt of a particular suspect. This is an important distinction between the French inquisitorial process and the process used among common law nations.

Investigating judges must also conduct social investigations of offenders, examining the personality and culpability of the accused (Elliott, 2001). This social investigation often involves examining the suspect's personality, including a psychological evaluation, as well as examining social factors such as the area in which the offender lives. These judges do have a significant degree of power in cases set before them. They can visit the scene of the crime, carry out a reconstruction of the offense, hear witnesses, search and seize property, arrest the person charged and, even more importantly, they can place the suspect on remand in custody (Elliott, 2001).

At the trial, the judge usually simply certifies that the findings of the pretrial investigation are legitimate. Although the first stage of the criminal procedure takes place outside the court system, both the second and third stages have their own separate hierarchy with the court system. This court system has three courts of general jurisdiction: The Tribunal de Police, the Tribunal Correctionnel, and the Cour d'assises (Elliott, 2001; McKee, 2001). These three courts all have jurisdiction to hear criminal cases that depends largely on the seriousness of the offense concerned.

The Tribunal de Police handles minor offenses and has restricted powers of sentencing (Elliott, 2001;

McKee, 2001). For instance, this court cannot impose a prison sentence at all, and the maximum fine it can impose is 20,000 francs (Elliott, 2001; McKee, 2001). The right to appeal is not afforded to defendants because of the minor nature of the offenses that are processed by this court. The Tribunal Correctionnel, on the other hand, handles major offenses. This court can impose fines of up to 25,000 francs and does have the power to dole out prison sentences (Elliott, 2001; McKee, 2001). When the Tribunal Correctionnel processes sentences, a three-judge panel is usually used to try sentences that are considered particularly serious, whereas less important offenses are normally tried by a single judge. Minor offenses that are usually tried by a single judge often include traffic offenses, credit card or check abuse, and/or the possession (not trafficking) of soft drugs. The next court of general jurisdiction is known as the Cour d'assises, and it is this court that tries the most serious of charges (Elliott, 2001; McKee, 2001). Obviously, this court is empowered with the ability to impose sentences of imprisonment. Further, this is the only court that uses the services of a jury, which interestingly is a common law (as opposed to inquisitorial law) concept derived from the legal system of the United Kingdom.

During the court hearing, the procedural rules that apply to trial proceedings are generally the same for all of the criminal courts. Criminal trials in France are relatively short. Despite their short duration, these cases are generally heard by a minimum of three judges (Elliott, 2001; McKee, 2001). The reason for this is to provide a safeguard to reduce the risk of judicial error, bias, and/or corruption. However, financial constraints in the French court system increasingly preclude the use of multiple judges, resulting in an increasing number of exceptions to the multiple-judge panel. Likewise, though three judges must officially be involved in cases in the Tribunal Correctionnel, it is more common that only one judge will actually study the case in great detail, whereas the others rely on this judge's extensive research and simply provide professional oversight in the final decision that is made.

Still, because of the strong desire of the French cultural to ensure that the criminal justice system does not abuse its power, judges found to be under suspicion of bias can be challenged and transferred from a case when there is a legitimate suspicion that they will not be impartial. It should be noted that the French criminal justice and court system adheres to numerous edicts from the European Convention (Elliott, 2001; McKee, 2001). For example, in an effort to ensure that trials remain fair, it is mandatory that the French court system investigate any accusation of bias that is leveled against those actors involved. Also, according to the European Convention, all parties have a right to be represented by a lawyer. This is especially true for minors and for those suffering from some form of handicap that prevents them from adequately defending themselves in court (Elliott, 2001; McKee, 2001). Thus, much of the French court system contains numerous checks on itself that are designed to comport with the standards of the European Convention, making the French system compatible with other nations throughout Europe (Elliott, 2001; McKee, 2001). This helps to also ensure that the French system avoids capriciousness, though the incentive comes from the external forces of the European Convention rather than the internal forces of the French public.

Lastly, the Supreme Court of Appeals in France should be mentioned. This court oversees the application of law in all courts throughout France. It verifies judicial decisions to ensure that the application of the law and the resulting sentences are sound, but does not actually hear any cases. Rather, judges in this court determine the appropriate application of the law in a case, but do not draw any conclusions as to the facts of the case (Elliott, 2001). Thus, the Supreme Court of Appeals is not a trier of material fact but is instead more concerned with procedural and interpretive elements of lower court decisions. This befits the true purpose of this court—to ensure that the French court system adheres to the rules of procedure to which it is bound.

Sentencing Issues

When sentencing, a judge can order a wide range of sentences on conviction of the accused. When imprisonment is imposed by the trial judge, the convicted person is sometimes allowed to spend part of his or her sentence outside prison, under various schemes aimed at rehabilitating the offender. The maximum sentence that can be imposed for an offense depends on whether it has been classified as a minor, serious, or major offense.

With minor offenses, the French Criminal Code allows for either the imposition of a fine or various derivatives of deprivations that restrict a person's basic rights in society. In addition, complementary punishments such as the confiscation of assets, the removal of civic and family rights, or even banishment from country can be imposed (Elliot, 2001; McKee, 2001; Reichel, 2002). Minor offenses are divided into five different classes, depending on the seriousness of the offense. The maximum fine that can be imposed depends on the class of the minor offense, with these fines ranging anywhere from 50 francs to 10,000 francs (Elliott, 2001; McKee, 2001).

For serious offenses the sentences incurred are stated in the French Criminal Code. It should be noted that the death penalty was abolished in France in 1981. Thus, in

France, there are four levels of sentences for serious offenses. These levels of sentencing options include: imprisonment for 15 years, imprisonment for 20 years, imprisonment for 30 years, and life imprisonment (Borricand, 2002; McKee, 2001). These are the maximum sentences that a court can impose, though a court can always choose to impose a lighter sentence if it so desires. In any case, the minimum sentence that can be imposed for a serious offense is 10 years (McKee, 2001). A person convicted of a serious offense can also be subjected to a fine and the same range of complementary punishments previously discussed with minor offenses.

With major offenses there are six types of sentence levels. The first level is imprisonment that can range greatly from a simple 6 months in prison up to a full 10 years of incarceration. Next is the fine, which is set at a minimum of 25,000 francs (Elliott, 2001; McKee, 2001). When deciding fines, the maximum amount to be imposed is often included in the penal code definition of the individual offense. Another type of sentence used is the Day Fine, in which the judge fixes a daily sum that must be paid for a certain number of days (McKee, 2001). The total amount is not due until the expiration of this period. Those who fails to pay the full sum will spend half the equivalent number of unpaid days in prison to ensure that some form of equitable sanction is given to offenders. Community service is another sanction frequently used with the defendant consenting to work in the community to pay off their debt for the crime that they have committed. This amount of community work must be no less than 40 hours, but no more than 240 hours over an 18-month period can be given (Elliott, 2001; McKee, 2001). Other sentences may include the deprivation or restriction of rights or the use of complementary punishments similar to minor and serious offenses previously discussed.

There has been one noteworthy development in French criminal justice sentencing that has only recently come into vogue. This development is the use of mediation in criminal case processing (Crawford, 2000). Although the use of mediation has become commonplace throughout many European nations, the French have been slow to implement this form of case resolution and sentencing (Crawford, 2000). However, French "Houses of Justice" have emerged as a new alternative that does employ victim or offender mediation (Crawford, 2000). The mediation approaches that are being employed reflect how France increasingly resembles many of its European neighbors, causing a further blurring between criminal justice differences among Western European nations. Further, the use of the less formal systems of resolution demonstrate the labor pains involved with France's attempt to resolve significant contradictions within its own legal culture (Crawford, 2000). Many of these contradictions were supposed to be rectified with the revised criminal code of 1992. However, the use of mediation has become another effective tool in providing justice in cases not appropriately addressed in the revised criminal code of 1992. It is anticipated that France will continue to increase its use of mediation programs in an effort to provide alternative sanctions and to create a sense of consistency with other European nations.

Juveniles in France

With respect to juveniles, French jurisdictions dealing with children are somewhat different from those in other countries. In France, a separate judge deals exclusively with civil matters that concern juveniles whereas another judge is responsible for juvenile criminal cases (Blatier, 1999). French law typically seeks to employ education-based interventions with juveniles rather than prison sentences or other repressive measures (Blatier, 1999). Although this would be expected in civil matters it is fairly unorthodox when considering criminal matters. This mode of processing juvenile offenders has been France's choice for 50 years (Blatier, 1999). In order to reach this goal, special courts have been established outside the regular penal system for juvenile offenders (Blatier, 1999).

However, public concern in France over juvenile crime increased dramatically in the early part of the decade, with a French senate study finding that the number of youths coming into contact with the juvenile justice system had risen by an amazing 79% (Agence France Presse, 2002). This rise in juvenile crime and the resulting media publicity has led many French government officials to propose the use of increasingly punitive measures with juveniles (Hanser, 2002; Tumbull, 2002). But such changes have had their critics, particularly among children's rights advocates and liberal judges in the French judiciary (Tumbull, 2002). Many educators (those personnel typically responsible for providing services to juvenile offenders) have maintained that the proposed changes would likely shift French juvenile corrections from a rehabilitative paradigm to a punitive paradigm based on incapacitation (Tumbull, 2002). Interestingly, such a trend is not only contradictory to traditional French attitudes toward juvenile offenders, but these changes are also at odds with the tendencies among other European nations as well (Hanser, 2002; Tumbull, 2002).

Incarceration After Sentencing

Following the sentencing phase, offenders are given either some form of fine, community sanction, or some form of incarceration. Presuming that the crime is serious enough, then offenders will be incarcerated in one of five types of penal institutions. The first of these is the Stop House, which is a short-term facility, or remand center that receive offenders with less than a one-year sentence (McKee, 2001). The Central House is a bit more secure and receives offenders who have been sentenced to more than 1 year in prison (McKee, 2001). These Central Houses are in charge of long-term and habitual hardened offenders; the emphasis in these prisons is more on security than on rehabilitation measures.

Detention centers, as they are called in France, are different from those in many other countries using a similar designation; these facilities can also receive offenders with long sentences but are orientated toward the resocialization of offenders (McKee, 2001). In these detention centers, discipline is not harshly imposed and there is less of a punitive flavor because the emphasis in these prisons is on social rehabilitation. Penitentiary centers combine elements of both Stop Houses and Central Houses and receive offenders with both long and short sentences (McKee, 2001). Lastly, semiliberty centers contain offenders who can be released for short periods of time during which they may go to work, school, professional training, or undergo medical treatment (McKee, 2001). Inmates in these facilities typically have short prison sentences or have a small amount left to serve on their original prison sentence. It should be noted that the prison central administration service has its headquarters in Paris under the control of the Minister of Justice (Borricand, 2002; Elliott, 2001; McKee, 2001).

One interesting note about the French prisons is that France's policy of intervention in African nations such as Algeria, Morocco, and the Ivory Coast has resulted in both civilian and military related international inmates within many of its prison facilities. Further still, France experiences numerous problems with minority immigrants from the Northern African region. Many of these inmates are over represented within the French prison system as well (Viviano, 2001). Because of this, as well as the increase in North African Muslim extremist group activity in France, the French prison system has had difficulty in maintaining public security when housing these inmates (Viviano, 2001). A case in point is that more than half of France's 45,000 penitentiary inmates are Muslim; this proportion is more than six times the proportion of Muslims in France's overall population (Viviano, 2001).

Early Release from French Prisons

Inmates can apply for early release from the Penalty Application Commission. This reduction, similar to "good behavior time" in some respects, cannot exceed 3 months per year of incarceration. Time reduction is also permitted if the inmate passes an academic exam or completes university or professional studies (Elliott, 2001; McKee, 2001). However, this form of reduction cannot exceed 2 months per year of incarceration. Further, all offenders who show some form of social rehabilitation and who have served at least half (two thirds for habitual offenders) of their term can qualify for conditional release (Elliott, 2001; McKee, 2001). Parole is also likewise used as a mechanism to control prison populations and to prevent problems with overcrowding. Unlike many common law nations, all parole cases are decided after a full judicial hearing held with the applicant's lawyer (McKee, 2001; Borricand, 2002). The paroled offender is subjected to varying obligations listed in the parole order that are often common community supervision requirements in other countries, such as prohibitions against leaving a home address without permission, the restriction of certain places of business such as casinos or race courses, the payment of compensation to the plaintiff, and the payment of fines (McKee, 2001). Parole in France resembles that of community supervision in other European nations and the U.S.

Concluding Remarks

The French criminal justice system is based on an inquisitorial process that seeks to obtain the objective truth as to matters of guilt or innocence. This is different from a common law perspective that rests on a "may the best argument win" mentality. French culture places a strong emphasis on the truth when meting out justice and also places priority on preventing abuses of power within its criminal justice system. The general flavor of the French criminal justice system matches that of most of its European neighbors, somewhat due to necessity and somewhat due to centuries of cultural sharing in Europe. In any case, the French system has many similarities to other criminal justice systems but is largely a centralized organization with the majority of its authority emanating from its well-known cultural capital, Paris.

ROBERT D. HANSER

References and Further Reading

Agence France Presse (2002), French minister presents justice bill, furor over plans to jail youths, *Agence France Presse, International News Section,* p. 1.

Blatier, C. (1999), Juvenile justice in France, the evolution of sentencing for children and minor delinquents, *The British Journal of Criminology,* 39(2), 240–252.

Borricand, J. (2002), *France,* State University of New York, Albany, New York.

Crawford, A. (2000), Justice de Proximite—The growth of 'Houses of Justice' and victim/offender mediation in

France: A very unFrench legal response? *Social and Legal Studies*, 9(1), 29–53.

Elliott, C. (2001), *French Criminal Law,* Willan Publishing, Portland, OR.

Hanser, R. (2002), Comparing juvenile justice trends in the United States and France, *Criminal Justice International,* 18(66), 7–8.

Hodgson, J. (2002), Hierarchy, bureaucracy, and ideology in French criminal justice: Some empirical observations, *Journal of Law and Society,* 29(2), 227–257.

McKee, J.Y. (2001), *Criminal Justice Systems in Europe and North America: France,* HEUNI—European Institute for Crime Prevention and Control, Affiliated with the United Nations, Helsinki, Finland.

Reichel, P.L. (2002), *Comparative Criminal Justice Systems: A Topical Approach,* 3rd ed., Prentice Hall, Upper Saddle River, NJ.

Tumbull, S. (2002), France's presidential candidates are playing on voter's sense of insecurity, with racial undertones. Sound familiar? *The Weekend Australian,* p. 26.

Viviano, F. (2001), *French Prisons are "cradle of Jihad."* Hearst Newspapers, Nov. 2nd ed.

See also **International Criminal Law; Quetelet, Aldolphe**

Fraud *See* **Crimes against Consumers; White-Collar Crime**

G

Gambling, Illegal

Introduction

Gambling—subjecting something of value (consideration) to a risk (chance) in hopes of winning something of greater value (reward)—existed on this continent long before the first foreigners arrived. When Columbus and his crew introduced playing cards into the New World, they found the natives gambling on games, tests of skill, and foot races. On occasion, the natives lost their freedom, gambling themselves into periods of slavery (Chafetz, 1960). A 2000-year-old archeological discovery in Clark County, Nevada (home of Las Vegas) revealed that gambling contests were a significant part of Native American rituals (Martin, 1996). Nevertheless, the definition of what is legal or illegal gambling is a social experiment in the process of making and changing laws. America has a long tradition of changing the definition in the context of time, place, and changing attitudes. The American love–hate relationship regarding gambling began with the arrival of the first English settlers.

Gambling in the Colonies

Not all of the early American settlers were Puritans seeking religious freedoms. Some had been gamblers in England, where cards, dice, and betting on horse races, dog fights, cockfights, and lotteries flourished. These "reformed" gamblers came to the New World to redeem themselves after gambling away their fortunes and lands. Past gambling practices were made illegal. The Massachusetts Bay Colony outlawed the possession of dice, cards, and gambling tables. Gambling, although considered evil by the Puritans, was not prohibited because it was against God's teachings. Gambling, along with dancing and singing, was prohibited because it promoted idleness. The harsh nature of the Puritan's existence—threats of starvation, disease, and Indian attack—did not allow for idleness (Barker & Britz, 2000). However, it wasn't long before the colonists—without an organized tax system—turned to gambling as an economic necessity.

The early Americans were familiar with the frequent English lotteries to finance public works—the first state-sponsored English lottery was held in 1569 to repair and maintain the country's harbors (Blakey, 1976). In fact, the Virginia Company of London financed the 1612–1615 Jamestown settlement through English lotteries (Rosecrance, 1988). In spite of anti-gambling arguments that lotteries unfairly impacted the poor, all thirteen colonies raised funds through lotteries for roads, bridges, jails, churches, libraries, hospitals, and colleges. Lotteries supported the construction of Yale, William and Mary, Union, Columbia, Dartmouth, University of North Carolina, Harvard, Brown, Princeton, and Pennsylvania (Chafetz, 1960; Rosecrance, 1988). The colonists—like present-day Americans—resisted increased taxes. But lotteries were not the only forms of state sanctioned gambling.

Depending on one's status and social class, card playing and horse racing were legal forms of entertainment. Card playing existed in public and private settings and among the elites and the emerging middle class. Local inns, roadhouses, and taverns were the sites of card and dice games and pitching large copper pennies. George Washington, Thomas Jefferson, and Benjamin Franklin, who also manufactured playing cards and sold them at his post office, were avid gamblers. However, playing cards for gambling purposes was not allowed in the homes of the lower classes.

Quarter horse racing—a quarter of a mile long, all-out-sprint on a straight road or level land cleared of trees—was engaged in by all, no matter the status or social class. But when the first American racetrack was built in Salisbury Plains, it was for New York's aristocratic upper class (Chafetz, 1960). The lower classes were excluded from attending or betting.

Nineteenth Century Gambling

The early nineteenth century brought new forms of gambling based on class lines (Barker & Britz, 2000). The wealthy and merchant classes engaged in stock-jobbing (stockbroking) and land speculation. They also engaged in horse racing at specially constructed tracks and played cards in clubs and residences. The working class and poor gambled in public places like inns and taverns; their cockfights and horse races were held in hastily cleared settings. The lower classes also played private lotteries. Antigambling sentiment fueled by evangelical Christian movements pressed for gambling laws directed at public gambling or lotteries—lower class gambling. Responding to pressure from antigambling interest groups, state legislatures declared lotteries—private and state—illegal by 1840.

Gambling as a way of life also appeared in the nineteenth century. The flatboat traffic along the Mississippi River led to gambling as a commercialized business. Banked games—players bet against the house, not the other players—began to spring up in the ports along the Mississippi River. New Orleans, where the flatboats stopped, became the gambling capital of the U.S. Other ports became Hell Holes where suckers where fleeced, winners were murdered, whiskey was free, games were rigged, and women were willing. The emerging middle class in these wide-open cities, fearing the loss of commercial growth, reacted with laws and vigilante action. Whippings and lynchings of gamblers and prostitutes were common, leading to an exodus of professional gamblers from the ports to the newly invented riverboats.

Riverboats operating on the Mississippi carried with them swaggering professional gamblers decked out in undertaker black or gray coats, white ruffled shirts, diamond or pearl stickpins, and gold chains, holding immense pocket watches. These flamboyant gamblers would rule the rivers until the rails were laid to the West and gold was discovered in the California Sierra foothills in 1848.

San Francisco replaced New Orleans as the U.S. gambling capital as the gamblers, and prostitutes followed the miners and prospectors. The State of California and many cities granted licenses to the gambling dens to raise revenues (Dunstan, 1997). But municipal corruption and a depression blamed on the miners created antigambling sentiments in the middle class, and all banked games were declared illegal in 1860. Gambling—illegal but tolerated—continued with slot machines in all of the 3117 saloons in San Francisco in 1895 (Fey, 1997). However, by then the professional gamblers had moved to Nevada's silver mining towns and western cow towns.

In the late 19th century (1865 to mid-1880s), cowboys after long and lonely drives on the cattle trails to the railheads were only interested in three things: whoring, drinking, and gambling (Barker & Britz, 2000). They were joined in these wide-open cities by buffalo hunters, railroad workers, and soldiers. The gamblers, women and saloon workers eagerly waited in CBSs—combined casinos, bordellos, and saloons. When the cattle drives began fading, gold was discovered in the Black Hills of Dakota Territory and once again the gamblers, women and saloon owners followed the miners and prospectors to cities like Deadwood Gulch. Antigambling forces led by farmers with families more interested in the future and statehood brought an end to the CBSs in the railheads and Deadwood, leaving only legal gambling in Nevada.

The 1859 Comstock Load gold discovery near the California border brought the California gold rush veterans and their gambling behavior into Nevada (Martin, 1996). Towns like Gold Hill, Virginia City and Silver City grew to thousands within weeks. CBSs were the first structures in these boomtowns. Antigambling sentiment led by Mormon conservatives convinced the first territorial Governor, James Nye, to persuade the newly elected legislature to ban all forms of gambling in 1861. However, gambling—illegal but tolerated—continued until it was again legalized in 1869. Nevada then made it illegal again in 1910, and finally legalized it again in 1931 when Nevada, responding to the effects of the depression, passed two revenue generating measures—gambling and "quickie" divorces. While the ping-pong efforts against gambling were being played out in Nevada, the battle between progambling and antigambling factions over lotteries was being waged throughout the entire country.

Lotteries: Legal to Illegal

State-supported lotteries as revenue generating devices had a brief resurgence after the Civil War (Barker & Britz, 2000). In 1869 the Louisiana legislature licensed and chartered the Louisiana Lottery Company. The lottery, known as the "Serpent," originally was to operate only in Louisiana; however, by 1877 tickets were being sold in every state and territory in the Union. A series of scandals involving 23 Louisiana Senators led to a governor's veto of the "Serpent's charter. The scandal led to President Benjamin Harrison persuading Congress to pass legislation prohibiting lotteries using the U.S. Postal Service—the 1890 legislation is still in effect today. The lottery was illegal for 70 years.

Organized Crime and Gambling

After 1931, legal gambling only existed in Nevada, except for a few states with legal parimutual betting on horse racing. However, illegal gambling flourished throughout the country with illegal casinos of varying size in 25 states. Cities like Hot Springs, Arkansas, Saratoga Springs, New York, Newport, Kentucky, Galveston, Texas, Hallendale, Florida, Cleveland and Youngstown, Ohio, Chicago, Illinois, Biloxi, Mississippi, and Phenix, City, Alabama were well-known as wide-open cities in the 1930s, 1940s and early 1950s. Newport, Kentucky—Kentucky's Sin City, often called the prototype for modern Las Vegas—operated wide-open until the early 1960s (Barker & Potter, forthcoming). Many of these illegal casinos—known as bust-out joints—were little different from the Hell Holes of the Mississippi River or the CBSs of the West. However, some like the opulent Beverly Hills Country Club and the Lookout House in Newport, Kentucky featured the finest entertainers of the time, good food and honest games.

During this same period, there were national sports books and policy operations—illegal lotteries—in most urban cities. These illegal gambling operations were run by a mixture of organized crime groups—Eastern Syndicates (Myer Lansky and his Italian colleagues), Cleveland Syndicates (Moe Dalitz and his Jewish colleagues), the Chicago Outfit (former Capone organization), regional groups (the Dixie Mafia) and local independents. They were by definition criminals, but they supplied a wanted commodity—gambling—to a willing clientele. A combination of events would soon force a movement of illegal gamblers to Nevada where their behavior was legal.

Las Vegas: Gambling Capital of the World

Benjamin "Bugsy" Siegel, according to popular fiction, is the man who built Las Vegas. Nothing could be farther from the truth. However, his brutal death had a part in building Las Vegas into the Gambling Capital of the World. Bugsy went to the West Coast in 1936 to pursue his favorite illegal pastime: bookmaking (Barker & Britz, 2000). He was sent there by Meyer Lansky and the Eastern Syndicate to solidify their control of the Trans-American horse-racing wire service—a radio transmission service that transmitted racing information nationwide.

Siegel made his first trip to Las Vegas in 1941. Shortly before he arrived, Nevada had legalized betting on horse races coming over the wire. There was a least one luxurious hotel-casino—the El Rancho Vegas—there when he arrived. The next year the even more luxurious Last Frontier opened. Siegel secured the backing of his East Coast buddies to buy the El Cortez Casino in downtown Las Vegas. He sold the El Cortez and invested the profits in a casino under construction—the Flamingo—by a strapped-for-cash builder. The mercurial Siegel took over the construction himself, leading to huge construction overruns and requests for more money from his gangster friends. Proving that money is more important than friendship among gangsters, they had him murdered and took over the project.

The media frenzy surrounding Siegel's murder, revealing the presence of organized crime in Las Vegas, and wide-open gambling, illegal bookmaking, and casinos nationwide led to a resurgence of antigambling sentiment throughout the country. Citizen crime commissions sprang up in many large cities demanding federal intervention. A federal commission—Special Committee to Investigate Organized Crime in Interstate Commerce—headed by Senator Estes Kefauver held televised hearings into gambling throughout the country. The committee's hearings had two effects: Nevada developed a strong licensing and regulatory process for casino gambling, and the nationwide antigambling sentiment increased the movement of gambling and gamblers to Las Vegas.

This movement of gamblers to Las Vegas was a mixed blessing. The former illegal gamblers invested large sums of money into the construction of new casinos. Their investment monies led to the practice of "skimming" profits from the casinos and into the pockets of gangsters in Chicago, Cleveland and New York. Casino gambling would not become a legitimate industry until the reclusive Howard Hughes arrived in Las Vegas in 1966. His four year sojourn in Las Vegas did not by itself clean up Sin City but it helped. The "Hughes effect" on Las Vegas sparked an influx of investors from publicly owned corporations into Las Vegas (Skolnick, 1978). By 1980, the 20 largest publicly owned casinos were generating 50% of the revenues and employing 50% of the employees (Eadington, 1996).

Lotteries: Illegal to Legal

As Las Vegas was undergoing its changes, state sanctioned lotteries were becoming legal again after a 70 year hiatus. In 1963, the New Hampshire legislature, without a sales or income tax, and strapped for additional revenues for public services, particularly education, began debating the benefits of a state lottery. Pro-lottery forces pointed out that a state-run lottery could provide revenues without resorting to a tax increase, or new taxes—revenue generation is the time-honored justification for state-run lotteries. The need for state revenues is almost always behind the change form illegal to legal gambling in any form. The bill was passed by the legislature, signed by the governor, and approved in a 1964 statewide referendum (Clotfelter and Cook, 1989).

New York, seeing the success of the New Hampshire Lottery and realizing how many of its citizens were traveling out of state to buy tickets, passed a lottery in 1967. New Jersey, in response to New York, voted in a lottery in 1970. And to use a time-worn cliché, the rest is history. Today, there are 39 state-run lotteries with two more under consideration. The forms the lottery games take are only limited by the imagination of the marketing bureaucrats in the state's capitol or the firms hired by the states—instant tickets, pick three or four, five-number draws, pull-tabs, single state drawings, multistate drawings.

Casino Gambling: Illegal to Legal

Casino gambling remained legal only in Las Vegas until 1976. Then Atlantic City, New Jersey in an effort to revitalize the decaying resort city legalized "Las Vegas-style" casino gambling. Casino gambling was hailed as a "magic bullet" that would spur growth, lower unemployment, and restore the blighted resort city to its previous glory (Sternlieb and Hughes, 1983). Until the late 1980s casino-style gambling remained illegal throughout the rest of the country—17 states rejected efforts to legalize casino gambling after 1976—and then the dam burst (Barker & Britz, 2000).

Two events in the late 1980s opened the floodgates for the geographic expansion and redefinition of gambling throughout the U.S. The California Cabazon Band of Mission Indians began offering bingo prizes 200 times higher than the legal California limit. California sued in federal court to stop what they said was illegal gambling, claiming that they could enforce state law on Indian lands. The case went all the way to the Supreme Court. The Supreme Court in *California v. Cabazon,* using the criminal-prohibitory or civil-regulatory test to decide the issue, said that California could ban bingo on Indian lands by banning it statewide but since the Indians were sovereign nations the state could not regulate bingo, if it were allowed elsewhere in the state, on Indian land without the tribe's permission. In effect, the ruling said that federally recognized tribes, being sovereign nations, could offer any form of gambling already offered in the state where they are located. The door was open for Indians to open casinos in any state that allowed charities to have limited "Las Vegas" nights—14 states allowed this. The largest change in the definition of illegal gambling in this country's history was on its way.

The Supreme Court also said that Congress, if it wanted to, could limit Indian gambling by legislation. Congress in the *Indian Gaming Regulatory Act, 1988* (IGRA) created three classes of Indian gambling: Class I—social gambling or gambling engaged in as part of tribal ceremonies or celebrations; Class II—bingo and games similar to bingo and non-banked card games; Class III—slots, casinos, card games, banked card games, horse and dog racing, parimutual wagering, and jai-alai. Indians could engage in Class II gambling if they were (1) in a state that permitted these forms of gambling "for any purpose," and (2) the activity was approved by the tribes' governing board and the National Indian Gaming Commission (NIGA). It was to be regulated solely by the tribe. Class III gambling was permitted if the conditions of Class II were met and there was a tribal-state compact. The NIGA lists 562 tribes, 201 engaged in tribal gaming—Class II or III—in 29 states, and 249 tribal-state compacts (available at http://www.indiangaming.org/library/index.html).

In response to the unprecedented redefinition of illegal gambling brought about by the advent of Indian gambling and the possibility of revenue losses to the tribes, many states moved to riverboat gambling—actually riverboat and dockside gambling—to meet the challenge (Barker & Britz, 2000). Iowa, with three Indian casinos, became the first state to legalize riverboat gambling in 1989. A domino effect was created as several states followed Iowa's lead. Illinois and Mississippi legalized riverboat gambling in 1990, with Louisiana and Missouri following in 1991. The Indiana legislature overrode the governor's veto and legalized riverboat gambling in 1993. Six states now have riverboat gambling, although most are stationary and never leave the dock. They are land casinos, technically called riverboats because they are on the water or near the water, or, as one Mississippi gaming regulatory source told me, "the boats have to serve water." It is all a matter of definition.

Conclusion

Legal gambling in some form is the norm in the U.S.; only two states—Utah and Hawaii—have no forms of legal gambling. Nevertheless, illegal gambling still exists. An unknown number of Americans participate in multiple forms of illegal gambling—youth gambling, casinos, Internet gambling, sports betting; gambling machines (slot machines, video poker machines, pinball machines) in bars, restaurants, truck stops, veterans and civic clubs; card and dice games; cock and dog fights; lotteries; punch boards, etc. The difference between the legal and illegal gambling forms is a matter of definition (Becker, 1973).

There is nothing inherent in the behavior that separates illegal and legal gambling. Behavior for legal purposes can be divided into *Mala in se* and *Mala Prohibita* acts. According to *Black's Law Dictionary* (1991) *Mala in se* acts are those that are wrong in themselves such as murder, stealing, rape, perjury and robbery. There is little debate that these behaviors should be illegal. *Mala Prohibita* acts are those that are not inherently evil but are crimes or illegal by statute. They transgress the accepted moral code: abortion, homosexuality, pornography, drug offenses, gambling, tobacco use in public places. Their legality depends on who wins the conflict between competing interest groups. As we have seen, whether or not the gambling behavior is legal or not depends upon the particular time or place, or for identifiable groups is a political question decided by interest groups with the power to persuade the legislature—state or federal—to attach the label—legal or illegal—on the behavior and form in question.

THOMAS BARKER

References and Further Reading

Barker, T. and Britz, M., *Jokers Wild: Legalized Gambling in the Twenty-first Century,* Prager Publishers, Westport, CT, (and London), 2000.

Barker, T. and Potter, G.W., *Newport: Kentucky's Sin City,* 2003.

Becker, H.S., *Outsiders: Studies in the Sociology of Deviance,* The Free Press, New York and London,

Blakey, R.G., *The Development of the Law of Gambling 1776–1976,* GPO, Washington, DC, 1976.

Chafetz, H., *Play the Devil: A History of Gambling in the United States from 1492–1955,* Clarkston N. Potter, New York, 1960.

Clotfelter, C.T. and Cook, P.J., *Selling Hope: State Lotteries in America,* Harvard University Press, Cambridge, MA, 1989.

Dunstan, R., *Gambling in California,* California Research Bureau, California State Library, Sacramento, CA, 1997.

Eadington, W.R., The Evolution of Corporate Gaming in Nevada, in Hashimoto, K. and Kline, S.F., Ed., *Casino Management for the 90s,* Dubuque, Iowa, Kendall Hunt, 1996.

Fey, M., *Slot Machines: A Pictorial History of the First 100 Years,* 5th ed., Liberty Belle Books, Reno, NV, 1997.

Martin, R.J., Historical Background *The Gaming Industry: Introduction and Perspectives,* John Wiley & Sons, New York, 1996.

Rosecrance, J., *Gambling Without Guilt: The Legitimation of an American Pastime,* Brooks/Cole, Pacific Grove, CA, 1988.

Skolnick, J., *House of Cards: Legalization and Control of Casino Gambling,* Little Brown, Boston, MA, 1978.

Sternlieb, G. and Hughes, J.W., *The Atlantic City Gamble: A Twentieth Century Fund Report,* Harvard University Press, Cambridge, MA, 1983.

See also **Gambling, Legal; Organized Crime: Activities and Extent**

Gambling, Legal

From backroom poker games of the Wild West to craps games on big city street corners to glitzy casinos, horse racing tracks, local bingo games and state lotteries, Americans have always been fascinated with gambling. But this fascination has been accompanied by varying degrees of uncertainty and fear. Historically, much of this fear has been fostered by various reformers, religious leaders and politicians who have regularly warned the public about the potential evils of gambling.

Gambling in the U.S. began its move toward social acceptability shortly after World War II when Nevada, which initially legalized gambling in 1931, became the first state to endorse large-scale casino gambling. Over the decades to come, America's interest in commercial casino gambling would slowly grow. In 1976, the Commission on the Review of the National Policy Toward Gambling (CRNPTG) recommended the legalization, regulation and taxation of gambling.

Since the mid 1970s, gambling in general, and casino gambling in particular, has become increasingly popular and more widespread. State sponsored lotteries contributed significantly to gambling's increased visibility and social acceptance. By the end of the 20th century, much of the public stigma that once surrounded gambling had started to weaken. One survey found that over 70% of Americans supported the legalization of gambling (Cosby et al., 1996). Slowly but surely, this general support began to influence the public's attitude toward casino gambling. This was helped by the discovery that Native American communities could house casinos on tribal lands without the specific permission of state law or voter approval. Thus, in recent years the number of American casinos, primarily those on Native reservations and riverboats, has substantially increased.

Today, as casino gambling continues to spread across the U.S., Las Vegas remains the world's gaming leader. Still, the corporate, commercial casino model developed in Las Vegas and popularized throughout North America is not the only casino gambling model.

In his survey of international gambling, Thompson (1998, 14) found European casinos to be much more restrictive than their American counterparts. Although there are some exceptions, they tend to be smaller, government-owned, and heavily taxed (up to 90%) and are most often local/regional monopolies. Other important distinguishing features include their limited hours of operation (mostly evenings), entrance fees, dress codes, restricted alcohol distribution policies and serious efforts to exclude compulsive gamblers. But perhaps the most striking difference identified by Thompson is related to the goal of the casinos. Whereas American casinos are primarily concerned with attracting tourists, creating jobs and making large profits, European casinos are more interested in community enhancement.

There have been attempts to develop casino gambling in Third World countries (e.g., South Africa), but Thompson (1998) notes that high levels of poverty and remote locations have made it difficult to draw enough tourists from wealthy industrial nations to make these casinos successful. Many other countries, including much of Asia (e.g., China, India, Indonesia and Japan), still do not allow casino gambling.

But even when gambling does gain acceptance, it is often accompanied by controversy. Despite the general acceptance of legalized gambling in the U.S., some forms of gambling remain more acceptable than others. There is seemingly little public concern about lotteries, horse and dog tracks, and bingo parlors, but casino gambling remains controversial in many parts of the country. Whereas various forms of casino gambling have been introduced in several states (e.g., Colorado, Illinois, Indiana, Iowa, Louisiana, Mississippi, Missouri, South Dakota and Wisconsin), voters in other states (e.g., Ohio) have rejected referenda that would have legalized casino gambling in their jurisdictions.

Much of this resistance has been fueled by the frequent attacks on casino gambling found in popular American newspaper and magazine articles. These articles forecast a variety of problems for cities that embrace casino gambling. Some of these include moral decay, family dysfunction, increased personal bankruptcy, and the cannibalization of local businesses. Perhaps the most effective attack on casino gambling has been the contention that casinos are linked to increased crime rates. The media has helped to convince a large segment of the public that casinos breed street crime.

The public is not entirely alone in their belief, in that a number of scholarly articles and studies have reached a similar conclusion. Still, for the most part criminologists remain uncertain about the nature of the casino–crime relationship. The main reason for this uncertainty is a lack of evidence that such a relationship exists. The body of research in this area, although growing, is actually quite small. Further, the scope and quality of the research varies greatly.

The first step in any argument supporting a casino–street crime relationship, whether it is made in the popular press or in a scholarly article, is to assume that there is something specific about the nature of casinos that causes people to commit street crime. Most of the literature seems to assume that there is something truly unique about casinos that cause such crime. For example, there are few arguments suggesting that a theme park or a major sporting event will increase crime and tax city services.

Unfortunately, this assumption is too often based on unsophisticated analyses that do little more than compare a city's crime rates before and after the arrival of casinos. The fundamental problem with this approach is mathematical. Take for example a village of 1000 people that has 50 thefts per year. Now assume that this village builds a racetrack that brings in 40,000 visitors each month. It is not hard to imagine an increase in pick-pocketing, purse snatching and theft from cars. If the village's thefts grow from 50 to 100 per year, and the number of residents remains the same (1000), the rate of thefts is now 100 per 1000 residents. In other words, the theft rate has essentially doubled. Although this analysis may be factually true, it fails to take into account close to 500,000 visitors a year. Any single person's chances of being a victim of theft would remain low in this scenario.

Visitor populations should be a consideration when calculating crime rates. As early as 1966, the Federal Bureau of Investigation's (FBI) Uniform Crime Report (UCR) recognized that population stability can affect crime patterns (viii). Accordingly, highly transient populations may affect the volume and type of crime found in a given community. Despite this, Stitt, Giacopassi and Nichols (2000, 3) point out, "few criminologists have included tourism figures into crime rate calculations." When criminologists fail to include tourism figures into crime rate calculations, the results can be misleading. Such a failure obscures the fact that although casinos may increase the total number of crimes in a particular town, it may not increase an individual's risk of victimization.

One of the most influential early studies on tourism and crime was conducted by Chesney-Lind and Lind (1986). Their study of crime and tourism in two Hawaii counties suggested that tourists were the targets of more violent and property crime than permanent residents. Garcia and Nichols (1995) reached similar conclusions about tourism at the Mall of America, a Minnesota tourist attraction. Although much of the public still fears that tourists will bring criminals with them who will victimize a community's permanent residents, the research indicates that these fears may be misplaced.

Chesney-Lind and Lind (1986) maintain that these results are "consistent with the conventional wisdom that travelers are vulnerable to criminal victimization" (169). Their findings confirm what common sense suggests, and what virtually every travel magazine in the world runs as a staple feature: Tourists are particularly vulnerable to criminal victimization and need take extra steps to be careful. Tourists too often are less careful on vacation than they would be in their daily lives. For example, vacationers often fail to secure valuables safely (e.g., leaving a camera on a beach blanket while in the water), stay out late, drink more, travel in dangerous parts of town, and associate with strangers. These behaviors make tourists attractive targets for criminals.

Given this obvious link between tourism and crime, it remains a mystery why so many researchers have ignored it. Take for example the *Wisconsin Policy Research Institute Report* (Thompson, Gazel and Rickman, 1996), an important, comprehensive and influential examination of the relationship between casinos and crime in Wisconsin. The introduction to this report acknowledges that some researchers believe increased "people traffic" can increase crime rates, but the report itself ignores the influence of tourist traffic and makes the mistake of relying only on per capita crime rates throughout the analysis. Not surprisingly, it found that extremely rural areas that built new tourist attractions and housing also had an increased number of property crimes per capita.

The complete reliance on per capita crime rates is a methodological problem that plagues many casino–crime studies. Most of these studies conclude that the introduction of casino gambling into a community results in higher crime rates. Although this is quite true, it can be misleading because these rates are not based on the "population at risk" (Albanese, 1985). Accordingly, these crime rates are artificially high. Miller and Schwartz (1998) note that this methodological flaw permeates the literature.

Fortunately, there are a number of studies that have corrected this problem by including visitor-adjusted crime rates in their analyses. In their study of Atlantic City crime rates, Curran and Scarpitti (1991) found that casino gambling did not appear to place residents at increased risk for victimization. Albanese (1985) concluded that Atlantic City residents' risk of crime victimization was actually lower after the introduction of casino gambling than before.

More recently, Stitt, Giacopassi and Nichols (2000) examined the effects of legalized casino gambling on crime in different locales. Using both per capita and visitor-adjusted rates, they examined crime in seven new casino jurisdictions. The results were mixed. Some communities showed a significant increase in crime, while others showed a significant decrease. One city showed few significant changes. The authors suggest that a casino's effect on a community may be tied to a number of variables including, but not limited to, the economy, population, demographics, casino location, casino regulation and the number of tourists (20). Their analysis shows how difficult it is to locate the effect of a single cause (e.g. casinos) on crime.

The body of research on the casino–crime relationship remains in the beginning stages of development. Still, early studies have taught us at least three important lessons. First, although the inclusion of tourist-adjusted crime rates alone will not completely explain crime rate variations from one casino community to another (Pelfrey 1998), they are an important consideration. Stitt, Giacopassi and Nichols' (2000:21) research "suggests that taking tourism into account does provide a more accurate measure of offense prevalence." Secondly, researchers need to recognize, appreciate and continue to examine the complex nature of the casino–tourism–crime relationship. Ochrym (1988) correctly points out that tourism and crime are so intertwined that it is extremely difficult to isolate the effects of one from the other. Researchers must continue their efforts to identify the variables that influence a casino's potential impact on a community.

Finally, researchers must begin to set aside the common assumption that casinos are fundamentally different from other forms of entertainment. Research suggests that tourist destinations in general have higher crime rates than nontourist destinations. The influence of moral reformers has made it seem logical to worry about the effect of casinos on crime, but to never ask about the effect of major league baseball on crime, or a major theme park, or even an active downtown night life. All of these attractions provide a cost in city services and all result in increased criminal activity. In this regard, the tourism generated by casinos appears to be no different than the tourism generated by other forms of entertainment (Ochrym, 1990).

The final chapter on the relationship between legalized casino gambling and crime has yet to be written. But one thing seems certain: America's fear of crime and its fascination with gambling will likely keep researchers busy studying the casino–crime phenomenon for many years to come.

WILLIAM J. MILLER AND MARTIN D. SCHWARTZ

References and Further Reading

Barker, T. and Britz, M., *Jokers Wild: Legalized Gambling in the Twenty-First Century,* Praeger, New York, 2001.

Chesney-Lind, M. and Lind, I.Y., Visitors Against Victims: Crimes Against Tourists in Hawaii, *Annals of Tourism Research,* 13 (1986).

Commission on the Review of the National Policy Toward Gambling (CRNPTG). *Gambling in America, final report,* Government Printing Office, Washington, DC, 1976

Cosby, A.G., David, C.M., Frese, W., and Dunaway, R.G., Legalization of Crimes Against the Moral Order: Results From the 1995 United States Survey of Gambling and Gaming, *Deviant Behavior,* 17 (1996).

Curran, D. and Scarpitti, F., Crime in Atlantic City: Do Casinos Make A Difference?, *Deviant Behavior,* 12 (1991).

Federal Bureau of Investigation. Uniform Crime Reports. Washington, DC. Government Printing Office, annual.

Garcia, R. and Nicholls, L.L., Crime in New Tourism Destinations: The Mall of America, *Visions in Leisure and Business,* 14 (1995).

Miller, W.J. and Schwartz, M.D., Casino Gambling and Street Crime, *Annals of the American Academy of Political and Social Science,* 556 (1998).

Ochrym, R.G., Street Crime, Tourism and Casinos: An Empirical Comparison, *Journal of Gambling Studies,* 6 (1990).

Ochrym, R.G., Street Crime In Atlantic City, New Jersey: An Empirical Analysis, *Nevada Review of Business and Economics,* 12 (1988).

Pelfrey, W.V., Tourism and Crime: A Preliminary Assessment of the Relationship of Crime to the Number of Visitors at Selected Sites, *International Journal of Comparative and Applied Criminal Justice,* 22 (1998).

Stitt, B.G., Giacopassi, D., and Nichols, M., The Effect of Casino Gambling on Crime in New Casino Jurisdictions, *Journal of Crime and Justice,* 23 (2000).

Thompson, W., Casinos de Juegos del Mundo: A Survey of World Gambling, *Annals of the American Academy of Political and Social Science,* 556 (1998).

Thompson, W.N., Gazel, R., and Rickman, D., The Social Costs of Gambling in Wisconsin, *Wisconsin Policy Research Institute Report 9,* 1996.

See also **Gambling, Illegal.**

Gangs, European Street

Throughout the twentieth century, European nations experienced outbreaks of troublesome youth groups sometimes labeled as gangs. Examples include the Teddy Boys, and Mods and Rockers in England, Blousons Noirs in France, Halbstarke in Germany, and Bezprizornye in Russia. However, most of these groups were closer to youth social movements and protests than they were to street gangs. With few exceptions, street gangs in Europe have appeared only in the 1980s and after. The earliest, full treatment of a European street gang was John Patrick's 1973 volume, *A Glasgow Gang Observed.*

The recency of the gang phenomenon in Europe has direct relevance to our knowledge about such gangs. How many there are and where they are located is only beginning to be known. Their structures and behavior patterns have been little studied. Programs of gang prevention and control have been sporadic, and usually do not take specific forms beyond general crime prevention and control.

Laws that are specific to street gang existence and gang crime are almost nonexistent. No consistent approach to defining street gangs has taken shape. However, for the sake of this article, we accept the consensus definition offered by scholars of the "Eurogang Program" (see Klein, Kerner, Maxson, and Weitekamp, 2001) as follows: "A street gang is any stable, street-oriented youth group whose own identity includes involvement in antisocial activity." This is somewhat better specified than the definition offered by the Brussels, Belgium police: "A group of minors whose behavior disturbs the public order and security," or the Copenhagen police definition: "A group of youngsters who commit crimes and violate the peace by intimidation and aggressive behavior in public areas." Any of these is more useful than has been the British approach, which has actively denied the obvious existence of gangs by any definition.

What we currently know about European street gangs is severely limited by absence of common measurement procedures (including police crime data on gangs) and by the paucity of gang studies. In addition to the Glasgow description, there are two very useful ethnographic case studies, Tertilt's 1995 study of a Turkish gang in Frankfurt and Werdmolder's 1997 work on a primarily Moroccan gang in Amsterdam.

Most other street gang knowledge comes from a collection of shorter gang studies published as part of the Eurogang Program (Klein et al., 2001). Much of what follows in this article is taken from these sources.

Active street gangs were reported during the 1990s in at least 35 cities, almost one third of them in Russia. Other nations with one or more gang-involved cities are England, France, Belgium, Holland, Germany, Switzerland, Spain, Hungary, Greece, Poland, Norway, Sweden, and Finland. Six of the reported cities are in Germany. Although a number of the gangs are reported to be composed mostly of indigenous youth populations, a great majority is made up primarily of refugee and first or second-generation immigrant populations. Prominent among these are Turkish and Moroccan groups, but more than fifteen nationalities have been reported. A number of mixed-ethnicity gangs have been noted in these reports. This broad spectrum of nationalities contrasts sharply with the American gang makeup.

Other contrasts to American gangs include inner-city locations, gender composition, violence patterns, and the prominence of skinhead or other racist gangs. In a number of European cities, gangs form in inner-city deprived areas, as has been more or less true in major American cities. However in other European settings, public housing for minority refugee and immigrant groups has deliberately been located in the outskirts of the city. Thus in places like Stockholm, Stuttgart, Frankfurt, and Zurich, street gangs evolve beyond the central city, and gang members commute by subway to the central area to engage in criminal pursuits.

The role of girls in European street gangs is unclear. On the basis of the American experience one might expect a 25% female membership, but reports to date say little of female gang membership in Europe. Either female involvement is very low, or gang researchers are simply not attentive to the problem (as was often the case in earlier American research). There is a European tradition of attention to "masculinities" in youth research that could well contribute to overlooking female gang involvement.

European delinquency studies generally reveal a lower violence level than is found in the U.S. (Junger-Tas, Terlouw, and Klein, 1994). This is mirrored in most of the depictions of European gangs, although a greater attention to racist gangs complicates the picture. It may be of particular significance that the availability of lethal firearms is quite low throughout Europe, yielding lower lethality and thus perhaps lower attention to violence generally among and between gangs.

Gang location, gender, ethnicity, and violence issues in Europe, as contrasted with the U.S., seem more complex in relation to neo-Nazi and other racist gangs. These have been reported with some regularity in Sweden, Norway, Germany, and England for example, with some ethnic gangs arising as a defense against racist gangs. Intergang clashes involving racist gangs exacerbate ethnic gang formation, but appear only where ethnic "invasions" have some prominence. Female roles among such combatants can be expected to be low, although the resort to violence is clearly increased. In Europe, data on inter-ethnic violence are hard to uncover, as many countries prohibit the recording of ethnicity in crime data. Thus it is only ethnography and youth interviews that can enumerate violence attributed to intergang rivalries.

In further contrast to the U.S. gang situation, the study of street gangs in Europe is complicated by at least three additional contexts (beyond the obvious cross-nationality differences). These are the traditions of youth group studies, the questions of the export of gang culture from the U.S., and the comparability of communities in the various European settings.

In the first instance, European scholars have shared a long tradition of studying youth groups and youth movements. The process of fitting the relatively new street gangs into this broader context has proven to be complex, as the borders between gang and nongang groups can be ambiguous. Within the Eurogang Program, for instance (Klein et al., 2001), attempts to approach these differences are reported by Gruter and Versteegh in Holland, by Huizinga and Schumann and by Kersten in Germany, by Sarnecki and Pettersson in Sweden, by Dekleva in Slovenia, and by Vercaigne in Belgium. In each case, the initial difficulties in defining street gangs is highlighted, and the gang or nongang distinction is further complicated by the use in various studies of different research methods and sources of data. In the studies just cited, these have included police records, police interviews, youth interviews, school surveys, news reports, and historical records. Uniformity and comparability of findings are difficult to achieve under these conditions of definitional ambiguity and methodological diversity.

A related issue is whether street gang developments in Europe are indigenous to the countries involved or are in some sense imported from the U.S., which has a century-old tradition of street gangs. There are some obvious parallels: adolescent ages, versatility of crime patterns in many cases, a preponderance of membership from marginalized populations, and the external cultural trappings of dress, argot, and graffiti are examples of U.S. and European overlaps. Indeed, in the Hague the Dutch gangs call themselves Crips, after the Los Angeles groups. Gang culture is a clearly importable pattern in an era of global communications.

Yet there are other reasons to view the advent of European street gangs as indigenous. One of these is the parallel of this growth with the demonstrable increase in foreign refugee and immigration patterns—local patterns yielding local developments. Second, the comparisons that are currently available suggest some major differences between the countries in gang composition, types of structures and rivalries, and locations in and around the cities involved. These seem to reflect responses to local realities rather than the simple copying of patterns learned from the U.S. Thus, although there may be some copycat cultural aspects to the European groups, it seems more likely that this is more superficial than fundamental to European street gang development.

Another issue, and one requiring a good deal of further study, is whether these European gangs are being spawned by communities that are similarly constructed. Defining "community" is even more problematic than defining gangs; in the case of a dozen or more countries with many centuries of community developments, the likelihood of coming to a common understanding of "community" is not high. This was well demonstrated in the first Eurogang Program workshop (Klein, et al., 2001, Chap. 25). As noted in that chapter, "When the question of community organizations was raised among the European Workshop participants, such varied responses were received that the whole issue of a generic community conceptualization was called into question" (2001, 331). It is as yet unclear whether different forms of community organization can produce recognizable patterns of street gangs, or whether such community variation necessarily prevents such patterns and thus prevents generalization about the nature of street gangs across countries.

Because gang research is relatively new in Europe, the books and articles produced so far have made very little use of the decades of American theory and research that might be relevant. Instead, media stereotypes of American gangs have tended to form European opinions about the existence of street gangs. In the absence of reference to classical or newer American theoretical formulations, no specifically European theories have as yet emerged. In the absence of attention to the more carefully collected American gang data, stereotypical media reports have tended to frame European discussions of the utility of American knowledge.

These trends, lack of attention to available formulations and reliance on stereotypical depictions of American gangs, have led a number of European scholars and especially European policymakers to be trapped in what has been called the "Eurogang Paradox" (Klein et al., 2001). The elements of the paradox are as follows:

1. American gangs are large, well-organized structures with hierarchical leadership, strong cohesiveness, and a good deal of violent behavior.
2. Most European groups—referred to as "gang-like" or "problematic youth groups"—are not well structured with hierarchical leadership, do not seem very cohesive, and do not engage in high levels of violence.
3. Therefore, most European groups that engage in illegal activity are not street gangs.
4. But, most American street gangs *do not* fit the pattern described in point number 1, as given above. Therefore, many of the European groups may, indeed, be street gangs comparable to those in the U.S.

The best way to resolve the paradox is to take a closer look at the structures of American gangs. If such structures can be identified, then they can be applied to the European situation for comparability.

A major step in this direction has been carried out and reported by Klein et al. (2001). The five typical structures of American gangs—traditional, neotraditional, compressed, collective, and specialty—have been described. The traditional gang, the structure stereotypically described in point one above, is seen to be less common than the others, and thus a poor basis for determining the nature of European youth groups. Other forms, especially the most common compressed gangs and the less common specialty gangs, seem to describe not only many American gangs but also a large proportion of European groups that are "stable, street-oriented youth groups whose own identity includes involvement in antisocial activity." Thus there are indeed a number of street gangs in European cities, and they resemble common structural forms of American gangs but seldom resemble the "traditional" American gangs. Traditional gangs to date have been noted only in Glasgow, Berlin, and Kazan; the other forms have been reported in such cities as Manchester, London, Oslo, Stockholm, Copenhagen, Amsterdam, the Hague, Rotterdam, Paris, Brussels, Berlin, Bremen, Frankfurt, Zurich, Athens, and Kazan along with about ten other Volga region cities. However, it should be noted that the cities not reporting street gangs far outnumber those that do.

Because the street gang problem in these cities is so new, there are very few reports of public policies or programs undertaken to deal with it. The most common approach to date seems to be denial of the problem or its seriousness. In some cases this reflects the "Eurogang Paradox" mentioned earlier, and in some, it reflects a desire not to report the problem publicly for fear of exacerbating it by advertising it. At the same time, other public policies may have a direct, if inadvertent, effect. For example, Europe's drug control practices, generally more lenient than those in the U.S., may have lessened street gang involvement in drug trafficking. Strong policies to prohibit ownership and distribution of firearms may have served to keep a cap on gang-related violence. The use of social agencies in lieu of justice agencies in the case of young offenders may have reduced both resentment of authorities and exposure of youth to gang members in correctional settings.

Most of the direct antigang practices seen to date have been initial attempts by police agencies. In Berlin, Frankfurt, and Stockholm, intelligence files on gang members have been maintained. In Copenhagen, the police have introduced their own mentoring programs for gang members and their families. In Berlin, a gang worker program was initiated to work primarily with Turkish youth, but the workers were instructed not to deal with hardcore gang members who were thought to pose physical dangers to the workers.

These examples aside, Europe has not seen the plethora of gang prevention, intervention, and suppression programs developed over many decades in the U.S. Initial steps will have to include locating the groups that can reasonably be considered as street gangs. Information on their structural types will need to be established. Public officials will need to settle on reasonable social philosophies underlying their approaches: prevention, intervention, and suppression each have contrasting philosophical bases and require different sets of practices. Issues of gang to community connections will require clarification. A careful review of tested American practices should lead to provisional priorities for some practices over others. European cities are in a position to develop gang programs early, before gangs become an inherent component of social structure.

Malcolm W. Klein

References and Further Reading

Junger-Tas, J., Gert-Jan, T., and Klein, M.W., Eds., *Delinquent Behavior Among Young People in the Western World*, Kugler Publications, Amsterdam, the Netherlands, 1994.

Klein, M.W., Kerner, H.-J., Maxson, C.L., and Weitekamp, E.G.M., *The Eurogang Paradox: Street Gangs and Youth Groups in the U.S. and Europe,* Kluwer Academic Publishers, Dordrecht, the Netherlands, 2001.

Patrick, J., *A Glasgow Gang Observed,* Eyre Methuen, London, 1973.

Tertilt, H., *Turkish Power Boys: An Ethnography of a Street Gang,* Shurkamp, Frankfurt, 1995.

Werdmölder, H., *A Generation Adrift: An Ethnography of a Criminal Moroccan Gang in the Netherlands,* Kluwer Law International, The Hague, the Netherlands, 1997.

See also **Gangs, Street; Gangs: Race and Ethnicity**

Gangs, Female

Introduction

Much contemporary research has focused on gangs and their relationship to criminal behavior. Although a significant portion of this work has focused on the males' role in this subculture, both social scientists and law enforcement professionals have increasingly observed female participation in gangs. Despite the acknowledgement that female youth are involved in these types of groups, it is unclear how widespread female participation may be.

According to Miller (1992), 10% of the nation's gang membership is female, which is consistent with the 6% that was reported by Snyder and Sickmund in their 1995 report on juvenile offenders and victims, and Curry's (1997) study of female gang members. In Curry's study, data indicated that 57.3% of the female participants described their gangs as mixed (both male and female members), and 36.4% indicated that they were in gangs that had ties to other male gangs (Miller and Brunson, 2000). Similarly, the National Youth Gang Center (2000) reported that female gang membership regardless of affiliation, accounted for approximately 11% of all gang members in 1996, and 6% in 1998.

These and other findings support Miller's (1975) classification of female gangs, which were categorized as: Mixed-gender gangs with both female and male members, female gangs that were affiliated with male gangs, and independent female gangs. It is unclear how many gangs are purely female in their composition, but it does appear that most female involvement in this subculture entails either coexisting with male gang members or serving as members of affiliated female gangs. Despite this involvement, overall participation in gang activity does appear to be relatively low for female youth.

Demographics of Female Gang Members

Increased media attention concerning youth gangs has resulted in the creation of a gang member profile that has persisted throughout the 1990s and into the new millennium. This individual is often characterized as African American, male, and in his teen-age years. However, this view of youth gangs has been met with conflicting research. In a 1989 and 1990 survey of the youth gang problem, Spergel and Curry found that 53% of youth gang members were African American and 28% at them were Hispanic (Spergel, 1995). In a more recent study, only 31% of the nearly 6000 eighth graders at 11 different sites identified themselves as both African American and gang affiliated. Other information in this study revealed that 25% of student gang members were Hispanic, 25% were White, 5% were Asian, and 15% were of other racial and ethnic groups (Esbensen and Osgood, 1997). (Note that the total percentage adds up to 101 due to rounding error in this study.)

In addition to race, Curry and Decker (1998) reported that the average age of youth gang members was about 17 to 18 years of age, but other research has suggested that the age range may be as large as 12 to 24 years (Hagedorn, 1988; Spergel, 1995). Although gangs are primarily composed of male members, the characteristics of female members appear to mirror those of their male counterpart with the exception of age. Harris (1994) reported that girls involved in gang activity are most active between the ages of 13 and 16, but by age 18, their interests have changed and they are likely to abandon the gang lifestyle. These findings are consistent with the research of Spergel et al. (1994) concerning youth gangs, which suggests females are likely to join gangs at a younger age and leave earlier when compared to male gang members.

Research appears to be consistent with the popular view of characteristics gang members typically have, but increased awareness of the migration of gangs across the country and changing social conditions may influence the composition of these groups in the near future. It also appears that despite the similarities between male and female gang members, female members tend to join and leave gangs at a relatively young age when compared to male gang members.

Factors of Female Involvement

Researchers have identified a number of factors that put young people at risk of gang involvement. Unlike male-based theories of crime and delinquency that have been challenged by feminist criminologists, the majority of risk factors that influence gang involvement appear to be gender neutral. Some of the more recognized risk factors include poverty, school failure, substance abuse, family dysfunction, and domestic and societal violence (Spergel, 1995). Other contributing factors that may influence gang involvement include a need or wish for recognition, a search for status, and a need for safety or security, power, and excitement (Spergel, et al., 1994). Additionally, Moore (1991) identified the need for friendship and self-affirmation and economic and family pressures as other reasons why females may join gangs. Although it is unlikely that any one single risk factor will cause a young girl to become affiliated with a gang, it is possible that her chances of affiliation will increase as additional risk factors present themselves or the intensity or frequency of existing risk factors increases.

Females and Gang Activity

Current popularity with the topic of female delinquency has suggested that young girls are increasingly becoming more violent, particularly those who are involved in the youth gang subculture. Snyder and Sickmund (1995) reported that criminal behavior of male and female gang members differed, and that a higher proportion of male crimes were violent offenses (51% compared with 32% for females). When reviewing female criminality with the same data set, Snyder and Sickmund found that females were not responsible for a significant proportion of violent crimes, but did account for a large proportion of property offenses (43% compared with 15% for males) (Snyder and Sickmund, 1995, 55). Howell (1998) reported similar findings and suggests that female violence has generally been limited to the crimes of simple battery or assault, rather than more violent crimes. However, Joe and Chesney-Lind (1995) reported that participation in violent acts is a stronger normative feature of male gang involvement than it is for young females in gangs, but may be witnessed in females who have experienced or been subjected to abuse at home.

Another factor that may influence females' level of activity or behavior in gangs is the perception that other gang members have of them. Early work examining the female gang culture suggests that young women who entered the territory of the gang were perceived to be acting on male terms as girlfriends and sexual partners (Lees, 1986). Hopper and Moore (1990) reported that this labeling of female youth has continued, and that females have been classified depending on their sexual activity with male gang members. These classifications include girls who are expected to have sexual relations with any male gang member on demand, girls who are the property of one male member, and new female recruits who are expected to have sex as part of the initiation process.

Although some females may serve as sexual property to gang members, they may also serve the gang by infiltrating other groups who are considered to be rivals. In these cases, females have used their sexuality to influence rival gangs in order to provide information that may be helpful in learning about opposing groups' plans (Brown, 1977). Although this role may be dangerous, most of the duties assigned to females are neither violent nor risky when compared to the activities carried out by the majority of male gang members. For example, female affiliates often handle weapons or drugs for male gang members (Hopper and Moore, 1990; Crews and Montgomery, 2000), work as strippers or prostitutes to bring in money to the group, and steal or extort money from others.

Research suggests that females who are involved in gang activity engage primarily in nonviolent offenses that can range from concealing guns and drugs for male gang members to prostitution and extortion. But violence may be more commonplace in girls who have been abused in the home when compared to girls who have not been subjected to this treatment. Sexual activity between female and male gang members also appears to be a cultural practice, but is influenced by the female's classification within the group. Although female sexuality is a factor that influences the relationship that young girls have with the gang, sexuality can be used to assist in obtaining information from rival groups. But why do female youth engage in gang activity?

Why Females Join Gangs

One possible explanation of why young girls may affiliate themselves with a gang is rooted in Hirschi's (1969) social control theory, which suggests that individuals conform to societies' norms when they have strong bonds to their community. However, when these ties or bonds are weakened or broken, the individual is more likely to engage in delinquent behavior. Additionally, Hirschi's theory entails four elements that determine the extent to which people are bonded to society: involvement, commitment, belief, and attachment to society's institutions (Hirschi, 1969). It is the attachment to parents, however, that Hirschi viewed as essential to healthy development and conforming behavior (Hirschi, 1969).

Utilizing this theory to help explain female gang involvement, it is possible that if the bond between the child and parent is weak or absent, young girls may be inclined to search for a substitute. In some cases this may be the gang subculture that for many may replace the traditional family unit. According to Crews and Montgomery (2000), gangs express many of the characteristics of the traditional family, which include respect, support, protection, identity, belonging, and recognition. However, it appears that regardless of the bond between parent and child, the buffer against outside influences begins to wane during the early high school years. According to Paternoster (1988), it is during the high school years that youth shift their attachment from the primary caregiver to the peer group, which results in exposure to different experiences and influences.

According to Edwin Sutherland's theory of differential association, criminal or deviant behavior can be learned through persistent and consistent reinforcement by significant others (Crews and Montgomery, 2000) that may include delinquent peers. For youth that have not established a bond with their family, and have not learned conventional norms and values in a healthy, supportive environment, the peer group may serve as the primary classroom for learning. Provided with the same positive reinforcement that is common in connected families, the peer group may reward deviant or delinquent behavior that may assist in the socialization process into the youth gang culture.

It is unclear why females may join a gang. Some theorists suggest that it is the lack of bonding to parents that influences a child to become affiliated with these types of groups. Still others suggest that delinquent behavior is learned through regular and consistent contact with significant others that may include deviant peers. It is possible, however, that these two theories together may help explain why females choose to affiliate themselves with the gang subculture. If a young girl's relationship with her parent(s) is strained or the family unit fails to provide for her basic needs, it is likely that she will search for what she believes to be an appropriate alternative. Taking these variables into consideration, the gang structure may be able to supply all of the things that traditional families provide including love, support, recognition, money, food, and safety, all while teaching her about the gang lifestyle.

Conclusion

The reasons why female youth choose to join or affiliate themselves with the gang subculture are elusive. Some literature suggests that weak family bonds or strained family relationships may contribute to the decision to join. What is clear, however, is that despite popular belief, female involvement in gang activity is relatively low, usually nonviolent, and not as lengthy as the involvement of male gang members. Although this may be true, little research has been conducted with young female offenders or female gangs to fully understand the problem. According to Esbensen and Winfree (1998), the nature and extent of female delinquency and gang membership is poorly understood because of the belief that women's participation and seriousness of offending are too insignificant to warrant serious attention (Esbensen and Winfree, 1998, 507). However, as our society becomes increasingly aware of the female delinquency issue through research with this unique population, there is an increased chance that gender specific intervention will be developed. These services, which may influence future female delinquency rates, will have the potential to make an immediate contribution by building resiliency among this population that will assist in their ability to resist and ultimately avoid gang involvement.

JEFFREY A. TIPTON

References and Further Reading

Bjerregaard, B. and Carolyn, S., Gender Differences in Gang Participation, Delinquency, and Substance Use, *Journal of Quantitative Criminology,* 9:4, 329–355, (1993).

Bowker, L.H. and Malcolm, W.K., The Etiology of Female Juvenile Delinquency and Gang Membership, A Test of Psychological and Social Structural Explanations, *Adolescence,* 18:72, 739–751, (1983).

Brown, W.K., Black Female Gangs in Philadelphia, *International Journal of Offender Therapy and Comparative Criminology,* 21:3, 221–228, 1983.

Crews, G.A. and Montgomery, R.H., Jr., *Chasing Shadows: Confronting Juvenile Violence in America,* Prentice Hall, Upper Saddle River, NJ, 2000.

Curry, G.D. and Decker, S.H., *Confronting Gangs: Crime and Community,* Roxbury, Los Angeles, CA, 1998.

Decker, S.H., Collective and Normative Features of Gang Violence, *Justice Quarterly,* 13:2, 243–264 (1996).

Esbensen, F. and Osgood, D.W., *National Evaluation of G.R.E.A.T. Research in Brief,* U.S. Department of Justice, National Institute of Justice, Washington, DC, 1997.

Esbensen, F. and Winfree, L.T., Race and Gender Differences Between Gang and Nongang Youths: Results from a Multisite Survey, *Justice Quarterly,* 15:3, 505–525.

Fleisher, M.S., *Dead End Kids: Gang Girls and the Boys They Know.* University of Wisconsin Press, Madison, WI, 1998.

Hagedorn, J.M. *People and Folks: Gangs, Crime and the Underclass in a Rustbelt City,* Lakeview Press, Chicago, IL, 1988.

Harris, M.C., Cholas, Mexican-American Girls, and Gangs, *Sex Roles,* 30:3–4, 289–301 (1994).

Hirschi, T., *Causes of Delinquency,* University of California Press, Berkeley, CA, 1969.

Hopper, C.B. and Moore, J., Women in Outlaw Motorcycle Gangs, *Journal of Contemporary Ethnography,* 18:4, 363–387 (1990).

Howell, J.C., Youth Gangs: An Overview, *Juvenile Justice Bulletin,* U.S. Department of Justice, Office of Justice Programs, Office of Juvenile Justice and Delinquency Prevention, Washington, DC (1998).

Joe, K.A. and Chesney-Lind, M., Just Every Mother's Angel: An Analysis of Gender and Ethnic Variations in Youth Gang Membership, *Gender and Society,* 9, 408–430 (1995).

Lees, S., *Losing Out: Sexuality and Adolescent Girls,* Hutchinson, London, 1986.

Miller, J., *One of the Guys: Girls, Gangs, and Gender,* Oxford University Press, New York, 2001.

Miller, J. and Brunson, R.K., Gender Dynamics in Youth Gangs: A Comparison of Males and Females' Accounts, *Justice Quarterly,* 17:3, 419–448 (2000).

Miller, W., *Violence by Youth Gangs and Youth Groups as a Crime Problem in Major American Cities,* U.S. Government Printing Office, Washington, DC, 1975.

Miller, W.B., *Crime by Youth Gangs and Groups in the United States,* U.S. Department of Justice, Office of Justice Programs, Office of Juvenile Justice and Delinquency Prevention, Washington, DC, 1992. (Revised from 1982).

Moore, J.W., *Going Down to the Barrio,* Temple University Press, Philadelphia, PA, 1991.

National Youth Gang Center, *1998 National Youth Gang Survey,* U.S. Department of Justice, Office of Justice Programs, Office of Juvenile Justice and Delinquency Prevention, Washington, DC, 2000.

Paternoster, R., Examining Three-Wave Deterrence Models: A Question of Temporal Order and Specification, *Journal of Criminal Law and Criminology,* 79:1, 135–179 (1988).

Peterson, D., Miller, J. and Esbensen, F., The Impact of Sex Composition on Gangs and Gang Member Delinquency, *Criminology,* 39:2, 411–439 (2001).

Snyder, H.N. and Sickmund, M., *Juvenile Offenders and Victims: A National Report,* U.S. Department of Justice, Office of Justice Programs, Office of Juvenile Justice and Delinquency Prevention, Washington, DC (1995).

Spergel, I., *The Youth Gang Problem: A Community Approach,* Oxford University Press, New York, 1995.

Spergel, I., Curry, D., Chance, R., Kane, C., Ross, R., et al. *Gang Suppression and Intervention. Problem and Response,* U.S. Department of Justice, Office of Justice Programs, Office of Juvenile Justice and Delinquency Prevention, Washington, DC, 1994.

Widom, C.S., Child Abuse, Neglect, and Violent Criminal Behavior. *Criminology,* 27:2, 251–271 (1989).

See also **Gangs: Definitions; Gender and Criminal Behavior**

Gangs, Prison

Information about prison gangs is limited. Due to a strict code of silence maintained by gang members, it has been difficult to obtain concrete information about the formation of the gangs, structural differences in their organization, the codes of conduct, gang symbols, and the extent of gang activity inside and outside the prisons. Most of the information we do know about prison gangs comes from correctional officers and wardens. Criminologists have also contributed to the literature on gangs, but in general, the number of gangs that are in existence within the U.S. prison culture is unknown, as is the number of gang members.

The prison environment is characterized by identity as insiders and outsiders. The inmates are insiders and anyone who is part of the "free" world is an outsider. Prison culture is an environment that is closed to outsiders, in particular to those that control the institution.

Gangs inside the U.S. prisons are characterized by alliances based on ethnicity, race, and region. Gangs are mainly divided according to ethnicity and race. The oldest gangs are the Mexican Mafia, Nuestra Familia, Texas Syndicate, Black Guerilla Family, and Aryan Brotherhood. These prison gangs came out of the California prison system in the late 1950s and 1960s. The Mexican Mafia, Nuestra Familia, and Texas Syndicate are primarily Hispanic organizations. The Black Guerilla Family is composed mainly of African Americans and the Aryan Brotherhood consists of White supremacists and outlaw motorcycle groups. Most gangs have a paramilitary structure, except for the Aryan Brotherhood. The origins of these prison gangs are rooted in the discriminatory practices of our society and the criminal justice system, the growing consciousness of minorities, the continued conflict between ethnic or racial groups, and the need for protection.

The Mexican Mafia, also known as La EME, formed in 1957 at the Deuel Vocational Institution of the California prison system. The Mexican Mafia is considered one of the oldest prison gangs and it has its origins in the streets of Los Angeles, in particular the neighborhood of La Hoya Maravilla. During World War II, many of the Mexican American youth of La Hoya Maravilla were victims of the Zoot Suit Riots. These Mexican American youths were portrayed by the media as predatory juveniles. The sensationalism or racism of the media resulted in an imaginary crime wave attributed to the Mexican American youth. This led to their persecution by servicemen from the Chavez Ravine Naval Base, as well as the Los Angeles Police Department.

The anxieties of World War II, as well as the racist policies of the Los Angeles Police Department, began a persecution against Mexican American youth. This persecution culminated when Mexican American youth dressed in their Zoot Suits were attacked by servicemen from the Chavez Ravine Naval Base. The Zoot Suit Riots raised Mexican American consciousness about racism in the U.S. Prior to the riots, many of these youths were loosely affiliated, but the attack on the Mexican American community prompted them to organize. Those who survived the Zoot Suit Riots shaved their heads to commemorate the race war they had survived. Many of these youths were from the neighborhood La Hoya Maravilla, and many of these youths did their time at Deuel Vocational Institution.

Nuestra Familia formed in response to the Mexican Mafia, which harassed, brutally beat, and raped Hispanic prisoners from the rural communities. It is believed that Nuestra Familia formed in the late sixties and was mainly composed of Hispanics from rural areas outside of Los Angeles, in particular the Central Valley. These Hispanic inmates were mostly sons of farmworkers who had moved to the urban areas, looking for other sources of employment. Nuestra Familia is considered a "Blood in, Blood out" group that requires killing an enemy in order to become a member or to leave the gang.

Texas Syndicate was formed in the sixties by Texans who were serving time in California. The Texas Syndicate has spread from California to the rest of the Southwest and is considered one of the most violent prison gangs. Their archrival is the Mexican Mafia. It is believed that the Texas Syndicate is one of the largest gangs in the U.S.

The Black Guerrilla Family (BGF) is believed to have been founded by former Black Panther George Jackson in 1966 at San Quentin. Other sources link the BGF with the Black Liberation Army, which was also a revolutionary political group found in the Black community. This gang is predominantly composed of African Americans and they established goals of cultural unity, group protection, and the promotion of an armed revolution.

The Aryan Brotherhood was organized in the 1960s, with a Nazi orientation and anti-Black credo. It is believed that the Aryan Brotherhood came about from the motorcycle gang the "Bluebirds," who were serving time in California's state prisons of San Quentin and Folsom. The Aryan Brotherhood uses elections to set up its leadership. The gang has a steering committee of five members, as well as a chairman, a vice-chairman, and a sergeant-at-arms.

In general, membership in prison gangs is for life. The gang becomes your family and your loyalty is required for life. If a gang member chooses to leave their gang, while serving their sentence, their life becomes endangered and they might become the target of a "hit" or contract on their life. Some ex-gang members request to be segregated from the general population, in order to avoid any retribution from gang members.

Each member is committed to protecting their family members from other gangs or predatory inmates. Gangs also provide economic welfare to their members. They are involved in illegal activity, such as loan sharking, gambling, prostitution, and drug dealing. Gang members are also supported economically through their ties to the outside. Family members may provide funds or may help inmates smuggle drugs, jewelry, or tattoo ink. But the main source for drugs comes from prison guards.

The criminal justice system has attempted to identify the number of gang members in the U.S. Gang members are identified through distinguishing tattoos or through their association with confirmed gang members. Phone calls, as well as inmate mail, are monitored by Gang Intelligence to help identify active gang members. Once a gang member has been identified at a penitentiary, this information is placed in their inmate file for the remainder of their sentence.

In the 1970s, California instituted a method to control gang violence. In order to avoid gang wars, penitentiaries were specified to particular gangs. This continues to be a method of control in state and federal prisons. Other methods used by administrators are the removal of problem gang members from the general population to segregation; locking down gang leaders; relocating gang members to prisons controlled by rival gangs; or relocating problem gang members from medium to maximum security facilities.

Rosalva Resendiz

References and Further Reading

Clemmer, D., *The Prison Community,* Rinehart and Co., New York, 1958.

Fong, R.S., The Organizational Structure of Prison Gangs: A Texas Case Study, *Federal Probation*, 54:1 (1990).

Fong, R.S. and Vogel, R.E., A Comparative Analysis of Prison Gang Members, Security Threat Group Inmates and General Population Prisoners in the Texas Department of Corrections, *Journal of Gang Research*, 2:2 (1994–1995).

Fong, R.S., Vogel, R.E. and Buentello, Salvador, Blood-In, Blood-Out: The Rationale Behind Defecting from Prison Gangs, *Journal of Gang Research 2*, no. 4 (1995)

Koehler, R., The Organizational Structure and Function of La Nuestra Familia within Colorado State Correctional Facilities, *Deviant Behavior: An Interdisciplinary Journal*, 21 (2000).

Knox, G.W., A National Assessment of Gangs and Security Threat Groups (STGs) in Adult Correctional Institutions: Results of the 1999 Adult Corrections Survey, *Journal of Gang Research,* 7:3 (2000).

Moore, J.W. and Garcia, R., *Homeboys, Gangs, Drugs, and Prison in the Barrios of Los Angeles*, Temple University Press, Philadelphia, PA, 1978.

Phelan, M.P. and Hunt, S.A., Prison Gang Members' Tattoos as Identity Work: The Visual Communication of Moral Careers, *Symbolic Interaction,* 21:3 (1998).

Silberman, M., *A World of Violence: Corrections in America*, Belmont, Wadsworth, CA, 1995.

Sykes, G.M., *The Society of Captives: A Study of a Maximum Security Prison,* Princeton University Press, Princeton, NJ, 1958.

See also **Gangs: Enforcement, Intervention, and Prevention Strategies; Gangs: Race and Ethnicity**

Gangs, Street

Definitions and Laws

To a considerable extent, the history of describing and understanding street gangs has been complicated by issues of defining gangs. Thus gang laws, gang statistics, theories of gang development and behavior, gang-related social problems, gang control policies, and comparisons of street gangs across time and locations must all be considered in the context of how street gangs are defined. No full consensus on gang definitions has been achieved because gangs are informal groups. Unlike business organizations, professional groups, adult-sponsored clubs and teams, fraternities and sororities, street gangs do not have constitutions and by-laws, organizational charts, membership rosters, mission statements or required products. As informal groups, they must be defined by observation and agreement; that is, they are social constructions.

A corollary of this ambiguous situation is that distinguishing between street gangs and other informal groups can seem arbitrary, as the conceptual borders between such groups are hazy. Still, one cannot specify well what a street gang is without specifying what it is not.

For purposes of this essay, we accept the nominal definition worked out by a cross-national group of scholars engaged in developing comparative studies between European nations and the U.S. A street gang, by consensus of these scholars, is "any stable, street-oriented youth group whose own identity includes involvement in antisocial activity." Here, stable generally means a matter of many months or more; street-oriented means active visibility ("hanging around") in public places such as streets and alleys, house fronts, malls, parks, school grounds and the like; youth refers to average ages up to the mid-twenties or so; identity refers to the group, not individual self-image (we are a gang); antisocial activity refers to the gamut of illegal behaviors from minor (graffiti, loitering, drug or alcohol use, petty theft) to major (robbery, auto theft, assault, murder).

This definition, as described, separates street gangs from prison gangs, most terrorist groups, adult organized crime groups, and from the many youth groups, clubs, teams, and cliques that proliferate in American or other societies. It is, at the same time, at odds with the legal definitions that have evolved since the 1980s and can now be found in the legislative codes of many states.

Laws about street gangs and street gang behavior have evolved since the mid 20th century in two significant ways. First, they have changed from very ambiguous descriptions to quite specific criteria designed to avoid constitutional issues of ambiguity and freedom of association. Second, they have become increasingly punitive by specifying more gang-relevant crimes, placing more constraints on otherwise legal behavior of gang members, and enhancing the lengths of imprisonment for convicted gang members.

Through much of the 20th century, to engage in "gang behaviors," undefined, was an arrestable offense. But as laws of this sort were increasingly judged too vague to meet constitutional standards, and as street gang problems became far more widespread and serious in the 1980s and 1990s, the response of public officials also became more clear and severe. This is well illustrated by three legal developments.

The first of these is the application of civil injunctions against specific gangs and gang members. The process involves gathering information from local residents and businessmen, adding criminal justice data on gang member crime, and presenting these data to a judge. Their purpose is to document the high degree to which the local gang or segment of it is causing unusual harm and fear in the community. The judge, if convinced by the data, can then enjoin specifically named gang members from engaging in specific behaviors, both legal and illegal. These behaviors have included the usual misdemeanors, but also such presumably crime-relevant activities as carrying knives, beepers, or auto entry devices; being in public after early curfew hours, or appearing on rooftops and other observation locations, or public parks and playgrounds; being seen in public places with other members of the enjoined gang. The injunction serves as a court order, so that failure to comply can be treated as a violation leading to fines or incarceration, or both. Originally developed to combat drug-selling gangs, the injunctions soon were applied in a variety of settings where police and prosecutors wished to apply special suppression procedures to criminally active street gangs.

The second legal development was the enactment of the Street Terrorism Enforcement and Prevention (STEP) act in California, since copied or emulated in many states. The basic purpose of these acts is to define street gangs in such a way as to avoid constitutional issues and permit enhanced sentences for gang members. Thus the STEP act defines a "criminal street gang" as any group of three or more persons whose members join with knowledge of the group's pattern of criminal activity and who willfully promote or further the gang goals of the commission of a list of serious felonies (assault, murder, robbery, witness intimidation, and so on). Anyone convicted under provisions of the STEP act could receive an additional three years on his prison sentence.

Many elements of this gang definition are significant. The "criminal street gang" phrase gets one away from the informal youth groups' notion and clearly labels these gangs as pertinent to law enforcement. "Three or more persons" makes the smallest cliques punishable, although normally speaking, there are no three-person street gangs. Prior knowledge of a pattern of crime provides criminal intent, even though many youngsters become gang members without such knowledge. Willful promotion or furtherance of gang goals cannot be proven, and therefore can be inferred by the police and prosecution by mere commission of the crime alleged, negating disproof. The specification of the most serious felonies gives these groups a severe stamp of criminality that is not reflected in their usual behavior, illegal or otherwise. In other words, antigang legislation like the STEP act does not define street gangs in reality, but rather as a prosecutor's construction to enhance gang suppression. But because the general public tends to accept legal definitions as "real," gangs have become demonized by a legislative sleight of hand.

The third illustration of legal developments, equally suppressive in its intent, was Proposition 21, passed by the California electorate and put into effect in March 2000. Under this new law, one can receive up to 10 years of additional prison time for gang-related offenses; gang-related homicide is made eligible for the death penalty; gang recruitment is added to the penal code; indeterminate sentences (no fixed periods) are available upon conviction for certain gang-stereotypical crimes; wiretaps are authorized for gang activities; and finally, persons convicted of gang-related offenses must register with their local police, just as sex offenders are so required.

To sum up, earlier ambiguity about the definitions of gangs and gang behaviors has been supplanted in legislation by prosecution-driven definitions and punitive sanctions. Significantly, there is little in the development of gang laws that reflects interest in gang prevention or the rehabilitation of gang members. It has been gang crime that has defined street gangs rather than gang structures, ages, ethnicities, social status and poverty, group dynamics, or other facets of gang formation or function.

Street Gang Statistics

Although sporadic studies of street gangs have been undertaken since the 1930s, it is only since 1980 that the proliferation of gangs and consequent growth in gang research has allowed an accumulation of reliable data on gang prevalence, structures, and behavior. A principal and continuing issue with both positive and negative implications has been the wide variety of gang data sources and methods of data collection. What we know of gangs comes from case studies, school surveys, community surveys, street observations and ethnographic studies, focused gang member interviews, news reports, and analyses of reports maintained by the police, courts, and corrections agencies.

Most public information, however, comes from the police. A police department is generally the only source of gang information for an entire city or county, and an accumulation of police reports is the only way to achieve a comprehensive national picture of gangs. But police statistics on gangs are problematic. Many, perhaps most, jurisdictions do not maintain adequate gang data. Like antigang legislation, they often reflect only the most serious or stereotypic gang offenses (homicides, assaults, drive-by shootings and the like), thus missing the preponderance of gang-member crime. Most police jurisdictions do not collect adequate data on female gang members, on gang structure and leadership, on gang histories, or (understandably) on noncriminal behavior. With the exception of police estimates of gang prevalence across the nation, most gang knowledge comes from case studies, surveys, ethnographies, and statistical analyses of police data, all carried out by academic researchers in many settings. When these sources and studies are brought together, they yield conclusions such as the following:

- The numbers of localities reporting gang problems rose steadily from about 60 in the 1950s to about 175 in the 1970s. Thereafter, the numbers increased almost geometrically to a peak of almost 4000 cities, counties, and towns at the beginning of the 21st century. In these locations, police estimates place the number of street gangs at close to 29,000 and the number of gang members at approximately 800,000. No state is without gang problems. Most medium-sized to large cities face gang problems, as do a surprising number of smaller cities and towns. The most affected areas are in California, Illinois, Texas, Florida, and Ohio. Los Angeles and Chicago are by far the most active gang areas.
- The great majority of gang members are marginalized minority youth, mostly Hispanic and African American, as well as a smaller number of Asian Americans. There are, however, increasing numbers of White gangs as well. Gender ratios overall are in the range of three to one, male to female. Ages range from ten or so to the 30s, but peak in late adolescence to the very early 20s. Thus, one often hears street gangs referred to as youth gangs. School surveys suggest that the prevalence of gang membership among school attendees is almost 6% for male students and 3% for females.
- There is a variety of gang structures. Some small "specialty" gangs concentrate their efforts on focused crimes such as drug sales, auto theft, or burglary. Others, most prominent in numbers, are larger groups of youth, seldom as large as 100 members, who exist for up to ten years but then disband with maturation. These are called "compressed gangs." Still others, the "traditional" gangs such as Crips and Bloods in the West, or Latin Kings and Black Gangster Disciples in Chicago, may number many hundreds of members with a tradition of decades behind them and an expanded age range with many subgroups based on age or neighborhood. Such gangs are notorious by reputation, but relatively few in number and atypical of most American street gangs.
- Most gang behavior is normal and legal. Gang members, like most young people, eat and sleep and attend school or work (although less than others) and engage in recreation and hang around with their peers. Delinquent and criminal behavior is occasional and often unpatterned.
- Gang members' illegal activity, in most instances, is versatile rather than specialized. Most common offenses are relatively minor and nonviolent: graffiti, alcohol and drug abuse, petty theft, vandalism, minor fighting, and so on. Violent behavior varies widely across gangs, and overall may account for well under 10% of all offenses. As for drug sales, many gang members engage in sporadic sales at low levels; some but not most gangs engage in organized drug trafficking.
- Gang members engage in far more delinquent behavior than do nongang youth, including other

delinquent youth. Youth already engaged in illegal behavior are more likely to join local gangs, and then in response to peer relations and group dynamics they significantly increase their levels of illegality. Leaving the gang results in a decrease in illegality. Following reduction in gang involvement, most but not all former gang members engage in socially acceptable societal roles—school, work, and marriage.

Street Gang Theories

The period from the 1930s through the 1960s produced some pivotal theoretical writings about street gangs, then more commonly referred to as delinquent gangs because of the adolescent status of most gang members. Theories were based mostly on field observations of gang members in ghettoized areas of large urban centers, principally Chicago, New York, and Boston. Because gangs were most often located in Black or Hispanic communities in the inner city, and earlier in transitional immigrant areas as well, these theories emphasized certain roots of gang behavior. These included poverty, culture conflict, lower class culture, and social disorganization. The basic issues were why gangs exist, and why in these minority areas. A secondary concern was with documenting the behaviors of gang members.

However, as gangs proliferated into a wider variety of settings—smaller cities, more working- and middle-class settings—theoretical concerns have broadened in two ways. First, it has become clear that specific ethnic or racial backgrounds are less predictive of gang formation than is a group's status as an alienated or marginalized population. Original immigrant or non-white groups that are successfully absorbed within the American social structure tend to reverse their trend toward gang formation. Those not as well absorbed—Blacks, Hispanics, Asians, and new immigrant groups such as Central Americans—are more likely to spawn street gangs. It is their marginalization that seems most pivotal. White racist or skinhead gangs seem to draw their membership from marginalized and alienated members of their communities.

A second theoretical development, not yet well articulated, has been the widening recognition that different theoretical thrusts are needed to explain different aspects of the street gang phenomenon. Whereas racism, poverty, and community disorganization may help to explain the conditions under which gangs develop, other variables are needed to explain why some youth in a gang-spawning community are drawn to gang membership although their peers, even from the same blocks and families, are not. Thus gang formation and gang member selection require different theoretical formulations. Similarly, the explosive growth in gang prevalence over recent decades requires yet a third explanatory approach, and a fourth may be needed to explain the patterns of gang crime. Finally, the decline of some gangs and the decisions by members to desist from gang activity are changes that seem to call for even additional theoretical perspectives.

Classical theoretical formulations about the reasons and locus of gang formations are found in Frederic Thrasher's *The Gang* (1927), Richard Cloward and Lloyd Ohlin's *Delinquency and Opportunity* (1960), and Albert Cohen's *Delinquent Boys* (1955). More modern theories of gang membership and behavior were provided by Lewis Yablonsky's *The Violent Gang* (1963), James F. Short and Fred L. Strodtbeck's *Group Process and Gang Delinquency* (1965), and Terance Thornberry et al.'s *The Toll of Gang Membership* (2002). Malcolm W. Klein's *The American Street Gang* offers explanation for the proliferation of street gangs toward the end of the 20th century. No integration of the theories of gang formation, behavior, or proliferation has been attempted. For the most part, gang literature has been more concerned with descriptive analyses than with theoretical analyses.

Correlated Problems

Street gangs do not exist in a vacuum; there are two contexts in which they may be better understood. The first is the set of other social problems that can be observed in communities that spawn gangs. These include poverty, racism, inadequate social services, mental health problems, homelessness, family conflicts, absence of jobs, drug use and sales, and political powerlessness. Attempting to reduce gang activity without attention to these correlated problems may not be productive.

The second context has to do with associated gang problems specifically. These include victimization, gang member migration, cycles of gang activity, female involvement, and predictors of gang involvement.

Gang members are the most common victims of gang violence, and gang-involved neighborhoods are the most likely victims of gang vandalism, theft, and other property crimes. Black on Black, Hispanic on Hispanic, Asian on Asian, and White on White are the most common combinations of suspect and victim. Most gang victims are within a few years of age of their gang assailants. The "random," "senseless," "innocent" victims often highlighted in media reports are far more the exception than the rule.

Media reports have also distorted the nature of gang member migration. In the wake of the appearance of "crack" cocaine in the mid-1980s, it was widely reported in the press that street gangs were in control of crack distribution across the country, and that many gang members migrated to new locations to "franchise" the crack sales business. Later research determined that most crack distribution was not gang controlled, and that most gang migration was not related to drug distribution. Rather, gang members move about the country for many of the same reasons other young people do, because their parents move, because they seek employment opportunities, and because they wish to start new lives. Criminal and drug sales activities account for some, but a relatively minor portion, of such residential moves.

Another poorly understood gang problem is the role of female gang members. Until recently, it was widely thought that female gang membership was minor in proportion, and that females were largely dominated by male gang members for purposes of sexual activity and the hiding of weapons. Recent research, such as that reported by Jody Miller (2001) and Mark Fleisher (1998), reveal that female gang membership is quite common, and the female roles serve the purposes of the girls as much as or more than the purposes of the boys. Female gang participation may take the form of unusual all-female gangs, or groups auxiliary to male groups, or some level of integration into male gang structures. In each case, female gang involvement must be addressed from a more gendered viewpoint than has been the case in the past.

An additional problem in understanding street gangs is that their delinquent and criminal involvement, and even their overall activity level, waxes and wanes. Gang behavior shows wide cycles of activity, varying over time by gang, by neighborhood, and by city. The reasons for these activity cycles are a matter of some debate, but recognition of them requires caution in evaluating the causes of gang activity and the effectiveness of gang prevention and control programs. What might seem to be signs of success or failure—increases or decreases in gang activity—may be nothing more than the normal patterns of gang activity cycles.

Finally, there is the problem of predicting who will become engaged in gang activity. Well over one hundred factors have been identified that help to predict which young people will become more and less involved in illegal activity. But beyond this, few factors have been found that specifically predict gang membership. Comparing gang members to nonmembers from the very same neighborhoods—thus controlling for such social factors as race, ethnicity, poverty, and the like—has to date yielded only a dozen or so gang-specific predictors. Research on this topic is very recent, so caution is required in employing these factors, but what has become clear is that predicting gang membership within a cohort of neighborhood youth is very difficult, and delinquency prevention programs or general youth service programs are likely to miss the mark in street gang prevention.

Prevention Policies

If we understand the term prevention rather broadly, to include early prevention and also active intervention with existing gangs and gang members, then the experience with gang prevention policies and programs is rather extensive and varied. Unfortunately, research to evaluate program effectiveness has been far less extensive and, where carried out in a reasonably scientific fashion, has yielded few indications of success.

Three highly touted, broad community-based programs have received much attention. These are the Chicago Area Projects initiated in the 1930s and carried on over several decades; Mobilization for Youth, a comprehensive attempt to reshape New York neighborhoods in the 1960s; and L.A. Bridges in the city of Los Angeles, a 44 million dollar prevention program for middle school children in almost 30 school neighborhoods. The Chicago project emphasized delinquency and gang prevention through local community residents' involvement and empowerment. The New York project stressed community improvement through the mobilization and reform of major social services. The Los Angeles project stressed organization of community agencies to coordinate services to at-risk youths. In all three cases, specific targeting of gangs and gang members was important but secondary. And in all three cases, the absence of adequate research evaluation has prevented learning what does and does not work with gangs.

By way of contrast, three very targeted gang intervention projects in the 1950s and 1960s included major research involvements. Similar in approach, each relied heavily on the use of street workers or gang workers to reduce gang activity and provide counseling, jobs, tutoring, and other services for gang members. Projects in Boston, Chicago, and Los Angeles were intensively administered for several years. Research evaluations (reported in Klein, 1995) revealed either no effect on the gangs, or negative effects in the sense of increased gang membership and gang crime. It is hypothesized that the increased attention to the gangs inadvertently increased gang cohesiveness and gang crime.

With these lessons in mind, the Office of Juvenile Justice and Delinquency Prevention (OJJDP), an arm of the U.S. Department of Justice, launched a new series of projects in the 1990s that has expanded in the new century. The first step was a national survey on ongoing prevention, intervention, and suppression activities across the nation. Led by Chicago's Professor Irving Spergel, this survey (Spergel, 1995) led to the development of a prototype comprehensive gang control model with particular emphases on community agency coordination, outreach (gang) workers, and police suppression activities. Launched in five cities, the project was supervised by Spergel and subjected to intensive (and still ongoing) research evaluation by him and his colleagues.

Even before research results were available, OJJDP expanded the "Spergel Model," as it is known, to various other locations including rural locations with gang problems. The research evaluation design of the original five-site program includes comparable nonproject areas and the collection of preprogram, program, and postprogram data on gang activity and community activation. Although it may be hard to disaggregate components of the program to determine which are more and which are less directly related to program outcome, the sheer size and comprehensiveness of the OJJDP effort may supply a host of new clues about what does and does not work with street gangs.

Beyond the U.S.

Street gangs have been reported for decades to exist on every continent, but in almost all instances with very little information on their numbers, structures, or behaviors. Outside the U.S., it is only in Europe that adequate street gang descriptions have emerged, and only recently there. Major ethnographic studies have been published about gangs in Glasgow (Patrick, 1975), Frankfurt (Tertilt, 1995), and Amsterdam (Werdmölder, 1997). Nine additional reports from England, Holland, Denmark, Germany, Norway, France, and Russia have been published together as part of a new enterprise called the Eurogang Program (Klein, Kerner, Maxson, and Weitekamp, 2001).

The studies of European gangs suggest that these gangs are generally quite similar to the American structures, although few of them resemble the "traditional" structures and more resemble the "compressed" and "specialty" structures. Ethnic patterns are far more varied in the European gangs, although marginalization is a clearly preponderant characteristic. Crime patterns are similar but with less lethal violence than in the U.S. Because the appearance of street gangs in Europe is primarily a phenomenon of the 1980s and later, officials have as yet not developed systematic approaches to gathering gang data and attempting gang prevention and control. In fact, many prefer to deny or downplay their own gang situations for fear of seeming to acknowledge an American-like problem. Successful gang intervention in Europe will benefit from acknowledging the problem and from understanding the mistakes made by American gang intervention programs.

Malcolm W. Klein

References and Further Reading

Cloward, R.A. and Ohlin, L.E., *Delinquency and Opportunity: A Theory of Delinquent Gangs*, The Free Press, New York, 1960.

Cohen, A.K., *Delinquent Boys: The Culture of the Gang*, The Free Press, New York, 1955.

Fleisher, M.S., *Dead End Kids: Gang Girls and the Boys They Know*, The University of Wisconsin Press, Madison, WI, 1998.

Klein, M.W., *The American Street Gangs Its Nature, Prevalence, and Control*, Oxford University Press, New York, 1995.

Klein, M.W., Kerner, H.-J., Maxson, C.L. and Weitekamp, E.G.M., Eds., *The Eurogang Paradox: Street Gangs and Youth Groups in the U.S. and Europe*, Kluwer Academic Publishers, Dordrecht, the Netherlands, 2001.

Miller, J., *One of the Guys: Girls, Gangs, and Gender*, Oxford University Press, New York, 2001.

Patrick, J., *A Glasgow Gang Observed*, Eyre Methuen, London, 1973.

Short, J.F., Jr. and Strodtbeck, F.L., *Group Process and Gang Delinquency*, University of Chicago Press, Chicago, 1965.

Spergel, I.A., *The Youth Gang Problem: A Community Approach*, Oxford University Press, New York, 1995.

Tertilt, H., *Turkish Power Boys: An Ethnography of a Street Gang*, Shurkamp, Frankfurt, 1995.

Thornberry, T.P., Krohn, M.D., Lizotte, A.J., Smith, C.S. and Tobin, K., *The Toll of Gang Membership: Gangs and Delinquency in Developmental Perspective*, Cambridge University Press, New York, 2002.

Thrasher, F.M., *The Gang: A Study of 1,313 Gangs in Chicago*, University of Chicago Press, Chicago, IL, 1927.

Werdmölder, H., *A Generation Adrift: An Ethnography of a Criminal Moroccan Gang in the Netherlands*, Kluwer Law International, The Hague, the Netherlands, 1997.

Yablonsky, L., *The Violent Gang*, MacMillan, New York, 1963.

See also **Gangs, European Street; Gangs: Definitions; Gangs: The Law; Gangs: Theories**

Gangs: Definitions

Within criminal justice there is no consensus on what exactly is a gang or how it is best defined and characterized. While providing insight into the formation of gangs and their functions and activities, Frederic Thrasher's pioneering work on Chicago gangs in the 1920s was the first of many accounts to conclude that no two gangs are alike; they exhibit variation in terms of structure, territoriality, involvement in delinquency or crime, and other dimensions. Gang researchers have since sought to clarify the issue of definitional ambiguity but it remains problematic and researchers, practitioners and policy makers continue to disagree on what constitutes a gang. A variety of definitions are employed, making it difficult to understand what is meant by the terms gang, gang member, and gang activity or gang-related crime, or to compare gang data across cities. Law enforcement variations in gang definitions limit our ability to obtain an accurate estimate of the national or regional scope of gangs and gang-related crime, and may lead to skewed perceptions about the nature and extent of such problems (and misguided policy responses to them). The lack of consensus about how to define a gang also poses problems in the academic arena. Some researchers' accounts of gangs explicitly explain how and why particular groups are considered gangs (and how the researcher distinguished between these and other types of groups), although other authors are less clear in identifying the definitions of gangs and gang membership, allowing readers to decide whether the groups discussed are in fact gangs.

State legislatures vary in both their statutory criteria for defining gangs and their penalties for gang-related crime. Definitions differ (sometimes markedly), although most state statutes describe a "criminal street gang" as a group of individuals (several states specify that the group consists of three or more persons) that individually or collectively engages in criminal activity (some states specify an ongoing pattern of criminal activity). In defining gang membership, some statutes and most police departments make use of a checklist to determine which individuals are to be classified as gang members. These lists vary but they typically include (but are not limited to) the following types of identifying criteria: self-admission; observation of the individual associating with "known" (previously identified) gang members; the individual has tattoos indicative of membership, wears clothing and symbols associated with a gang, is in a photo with "known" gang members, is identified as a gang member by a reliable source, is arrested in the company of "known" gang members, corresponds with "known" gang members, or resides in or frequents a gang's territory. With most definitional checklists, if individuals are deemed to meet two or three (typically out of eight to ten) criteria, they are then classified and labeled as a gang member. In many jurisdictions this results in the individual's name being entered into a local or regional gang intelligence database. Although such checklists may be useful for law enforcement suppression efforts against gangs, the criteria and their application are subject to vast discretion and could easily result in the over-identification of youth as gang members. It is highly plausible that minority youths who live in a neighborhood known for gang activity, dress in the same style as their peers, or have friends or relatives who have previously been identified as gang members, may be mislabeled as gang members. Since being officially labeled as a gang member carries subsequent legal consequences for that individual (e.g., sentencing enhancements for a crime committed after being classified as such), the misidentification of youth is a serious concern.

Whereas law enforcement definitions of gangs typically include some sort of reference to a pattern of criminal activity or the criminal orientation of a group, many gang researchers are resistant to including delinquency or criminality as a defining characteristic of gangs. James Short, a prominent gang expert whose work dates back to the 1950s, argues that researchers study gangs and gang behavior to examine and understand whether, and the extent to which, such groups engage in delinquency or crime. Therefore, delinquent or criminal conduct should not be a definitional criterion of gangs, but rather, one of many factors to be examined and compared across groups (also see Bursik and Grasmick, 2001; Horowitz, 1990). Short (1998) defines gangs as groups whose members meet together regularly, using membership and organizational characteristics as group-identifying criteria. Gangs are self-determining groups that are unsupervised by adults (distinguishing them from the boy scouts or similar such organizations), demonstrating continuity over time. Thrasher similarly defined gangs without any reference to individual or collective criminal activity of members. The opposing viewpoint is best represented by Malcolm Klein, another prominent gang expert whose body of work has spanned nearly a half-century. Klein (1971) maintains that delinquency or criminality should be a defining characteristic of gangs, and he defines a gang as "any denotable adolescent group of youngsters who (a) are generally perceived as a distinct aggregation by others in their neighborhood; (b) recognize themselves as a denotable group (almost invariably with a group name); and (c) have been involved in a sufficient number of delinquent incidents to call forth a consistent negative response from neighborhood residents and/or enforcement agencies." More recently, Klein has suggested a simplified "tipping point" approach, whereby two signposts are used to differentiate gangs from other peer groups; these are (a) "a commitment to a criminal orientation" and (b) "the group's self-recognition of its gang status" (1995, 30). While the theoretical and practical benefits and drawbacks of various definitions continue to be debated, Klein's definition of gangs appears to be widely adopted by law enforcement agencies and criminal justice researchers.

Some sociologists have called attention to the ways in which certain issues, including gangs, come to be defined as social problems. They suggest that gang definitions and attributions are largely socially constructed. In other words, since media and popular accounts of gangs have continually portrayed them as criminally oriented and deviant groups, the definition of such groups as criminal and potentially dangerous may appear natural and accurate due to its historical repetition rather than its essential truth. This is not to say that gangs do not exist, but rather, that they may be misrepresented and stereotyped by the media. This issue is especially problematic in terms of policy responses to gangs. Where does policymakers' knowledge of gangs come from, and to what extent is it based on experts' or researchers' knowledge, firsthand experience, or media accounts of the issue? A study done by Decker and Kempf-Leonard compared the extent and accuracy of policymakers', police officers', and detained juveniles' (many of whom were gang members) knowledge of gangs in the city of St. Louis. Their findings revealed that policymakers were the least informed of the three groups questioned. Not surprisingly, policymakers' knowledge was based primarily on media accounts of gangs. This study highlighted the need to ensure that gang policymakers are knowledgeable about gangs so they can craft well-informed policy responses.

And so the question remains: how does one define a gang? Despite Thrasher's conclusion that no two gangs are alike, and the fact that few can seem to agree on exactly what constitutes one, there are some commonly identified features of gangs, and characteristics that distinguish youth gangs from other types of groups, such as organized crime groups, hate groups (e.g., skinheads), and drug gangs or crews. Some of the primary distinctions between organized crime (such as the Mafia) and youth gangs are age differences (organized crime being comprised largely of adults), the group's purpose or function (whereas organized crime groups are created specifically for criminal purposes, youth gangs fulfill many other functions, and crime may or may not be a primary activity); and structure or organization (whereas organized crime is highly structured, youth gangs are typically loosely and informally organized). Differences are also usually evident when comparing hate groups and youth gangs. Whereas hate groups—such as skinheads—are organized with a specific purpose (to spread their message through literature and actions that reflect their beliefs) and are driven by a specific ideology (racism being at its core), youth gangs typically lack any specific ideology or agenda and are generally less purposive (in terms of activities). Although it is not always easy to differentiate youth gangs from organized crime or hate groups, it is often even more difficult to distinguish between youth gangs and groups of youth who sell drugs (sometimes referred to as drug gangs, drug crews, or posses). Generally speaking, however, drug gangs tend to be smaller, more cohesive and structured groups that are specifically organized around drug sales. Youth gangs, on the other hand, may or may not commit crime, but those that do generally engage in a versatile array of offenses (e.g., theft, assaults, robberies), and, although youth gangs may have individual members who are involved in drug sales, it is usually not a group function. Most youth gangs are simply not organized enough to operate a drug business successfully. Differences have also been noted with regard to prison gangs and youth gangs. Although in many areas of the country there is at least some degree of overlap between institutional and street gangs, for the most part, prison gangs are considered to be more highly organized, cohesive and hierarchical than their counterparts on the street.

Distinguishing youth gangs from other types of deviant or criminal groups helps to clarify some of their unique features, but the fact remains that youth gangs are marked by great variation. Given the variety of gangs uncovered through their studies, many researchers have developed gang typologies to categorize variations in their structure, function, and activity. Several typologies have addressed structural issues such as age of membership and degree of involvement; for instance, Thrasher and other researchers described the gang as a coalition of age-graded groups (or cliques), and Klein distinguished between "core" members who are fully involved in the gang and its activities, and "fringe" members whose involvement and affiliations are more sporadic and tangential. Along these same lines, Vigil discussed "peripheral" "temporary" and "situational" gang membership, reflecting the intensity and duration of members' attachments. Other typologies combine the nature and level of members' gang involvement with structural or organizational characteristics. Researchers have also noted distinctions in the function or purpose of gangs—with some classifying them as being either "entrepreneurial" and focused on profiting through drug sales (or other illicit activities) or "fighting" gangs for whom honor and respect are key features and a primary source of conflict.

Despite their variety, youth gangs have been found to fulfill similar functions for their members, providing protection or security, a sense of family or belonging, status or prestige, recreational opportunities or something to do, and in some cases, economic rewards (e.g., money earned through illicit activities). Although a standard definition may never exist, researchers will continue to study gangs and attempt to better understand what they are, what they do, what function they serve in their members' lives, and what types of prevention, intervention, and suppression techniques are most effective in curbing gang membership and the violence often accompanying it.

DANA M. NURGE

References and Further Reading

Ball, R.A. and Curry, G.D., The Logic of Definition in Criminology: Purposes and Methods for Defining Gangs, *Criminology,* 33:2, 225–246 (1995).

Brotherton, D.C., Socially Constructing the Nomads: Part One, *Humanity and Society,* 21:2, 110–129 (1997).

Bursik, R.J. and Grasmick. G.G., Defining Gangs and Gang Behavior, in Jody Miller, J., Maxson, C.L. and Klein, M., Eds., *The Modern Gang Reader,* Roxbury Publishing Company, Los Angeles, 2001.

Decker, S. and Kempf-Leonard, K., Constructing Gangs: The Social Definition of Youth Activities, *Criminal Justice Policy Review,* 5, 271–291 (1991).

Fagan, J., Gangs, Drugs, and Neighborhood Change, in Huff, C.R., Ed., *Gangs in America,* 2nd ed., Sage, Newbury Park, CA, 1996.

Horowitz, R., Sociological Perspectives on Gangs: Conflicting Definitions and Concepts, in Huff, C.R., Ed., *Gangs in America,* Sage, Newbury Park, CA, 1990.

Klein, M.W., *The American Street Gang–Its Nature, Prevalence, and Control,* Oxford University Press, New York, 1995.

Klein, M.W., *Street Gangs and Street Workers,* Prentice Hall, Englewood Cliffs, NJ, 1971.

Miller, W.B., Gangs, Groups, and Serious Youth Crime, in Schichor, D. and Kelly, D.H., Eds., *Critical Issues in Juvenile Delinquency,* D.C. Heath, Lexington, MA, 1980.

Short, J.F., The Level of Explanation Problem Revisited—The American Society of Criminology 1997 Presidential Address, *Criminology,* 36:1, 3–36 (1998).

Thrasher, F.M., *The Gang: A Study of 1,313 Gangs in Chicago,* University of Chicago Press, Chicago, IL, 1927.

Vigil, J.D., *Barrio gangs: Street life and Identity in Southern California.* University of Texas Press, Austin, TX, 1988.

See also **Gangs: The Law; Gangs: Theories**

Gangs: Enforcement, Intervention, and Prevention Strategies

Gangs continue to be a major problem across the U.S.—so much so that Los Angeles Police Chief William Bratton called for a national conference to address the problem. The conference was held on the 11th and 12th of January 2004 in Los Angeles, California. Though little of substance was accomplished in this first of what will probably be many such conferences, some interesting comments emerged. Those in attendance believe that a national strategy similar to that used against organized crime and in current counter-terrorism efforts must be created to fight street gangs. There was a recognition that gangs are growing, becoming more sophisticated and "migrating" into medium- and small-sized cities, officials said, and law enforcement agencies must find a unified approach to combat them. Perhaps of most interest was the idea that parallels exist between fighting gangs and efforts taken against the Mafia in the 1980s and '90s and against terrorism today. In such efforts, agencies at all levels pool their resources and strategize together (Hernandez, 2004).

While all that is important in the enforcement, intervention, and prevention of gangs and gang banging—and certainly gangs are expanding beyond traditional city, county and state boundaries—at their heart, gangs remain a local problem. Toward that end, two things must happen. The first is an elimination of the DID syndrome (Sliwa, 1987). This is where cities (and the politicos and in some cases the cops as well) engage in, first, *denying* that a problem exists. Despite the signs that are literally everywhere, "we" do not have a gang problem. Second, and following logically, the problem is *ignored*. If we don't acknowledge it, then it either does not exist or will go away. Third, and again in logical order, there is a *delayed* response to the problem. And as noted by Sergeant Wes McBride of the Los Angeles County Sheriff's office, an author, trainer, and one of the foremost gang experts in the country, once you have gangs, it is difficult to eliminate the problem (Sliwa, 1990).

So the first approach to the enforcement, intervention and prevention of gangs is eliminating DID. Second, there must be a recognition that combating gangs is not in the purview of just a single agency. As the Los Angeles conference noted with respect to the "nationalization" of the gang problem, the local gang problem also requires a multiplicity of efforts. Spergel notes that a community problem solving approach to gangs seems to be slowly emerging. This is based, he avers, on the idea that "an arrest and lock-'em-up strategy is not sufficient" (1995, 199). Segeant. Wes McBride notes that a person working with gang members must understand the gang ethic, customs and practices of the gang(s) in their area. The reason to do this is that knowing these things helps the officer develop rapport with the gangsters, making it easier to deal with them. It also allows for more and better communication with the gang and the gangster (Valdez, 2000, 543). McBride notes that when there was "firm but fair law enforcement, [coupled] with personal knowledge of the gang members backed by a demonstrated humanitarian concern for the status of the individual, violence within targeted gangs began to decline" (Valdez, 1993, 413).

Father Greg Boyle, who runs the Delores Mission in Los Angeles, has noted that "gang members need hope to help make it in life" (Valdez, 2000, 543). Father Boyle suggests that many gang members have no hope and "don't want to look in a mirror and accept what they see" (Valdez, 2000, 543). Dealing with gangs and gangsters requires both a Wes McBride and a Father Boyle (and the many other types of people who work with gangs and gangsters). Dealing with gangsters needs what McBride refers to as full service gang units.

A full service gang unit has responsibility for suppression, intervention and prevention. It "kicks butt" and makes arrests when necessary, and it refers gangsters to a wide array of programs based on the need of the gangster. A full service gang unit is a collaborative program, using resources already in existence, while being open to new resources that become available. The key element, the cement, is that all members are working toward the same goal: increasing the quality of life for the people they serve. Each of the members is working collaboratively but independently (based on their specific expertise and perspective) toward the same goal, under the auspices of a program manager.

The program manager(s) would coordinate the efforts of the various agencies involved in the full service gang unit. They would also know what each agency was doing and could ensure that all agencies were "on the same page." What the full service gang unit allows for is immediate action depending on the need. When working with gangs and gangsters, all too often one cannot wait until tomorrow. When a gang crime is committed, immediate action must take place, "when a gangster comes to you and says, 'I want to change,' that is a totally different scenario and should also be acted on **immediately**" (Valdez, 2000, 544). Young children need the tools and information to handle the pressures of living in gang neighborhoods and avoiding gang membership. Plus, they need the tools sooner rather than later! This, of course, would require involving schools in the full service gang unit.

Full service gang units do not reinvent the wheel. They simply take the multitude of agencies working with gangs and gangsters and put them together in a collaborative program, sharing costs, expertise, knowledge and intelligence. The full service gang unit is a model that can be adopted by any agency and one that can be regionalized depending on the city or county. Just as gangs share some characteristics they also regionalize and now nationalize many practices. The full service gang unit has the flexibility to address this. The issues are time, cooperation and commitment. Egos, rivalries, biases and other negative influences or thoughts must be set aside (Valdez, 2000). The goal is simple: improving the quality of life of the communities in which we serve, the "achievement of 'functional communities,' that is, communities in which family life, work, religion, education, law enforcement and other institutional areas reflect and reinforce common values" (Short, 1990, 226).

Gangs and gangsters are a plague on our society. Gangs and gangsters are what they do, and what they do is crime and violence. When the plague descends on a community, the first response must be one of intelligence gathering, accomplished by the department dedicating an officer(s) to gather and analyze the information. Once it has been established that a gang problem (or the possibility of one) exists, the formation of a gang unit is the next step. Whereas it should be kept in mind that the primary responsibility of law enforcement is "hooking and booking," any approach to dealing with a community's gang problem needs to be multifaceted and involve the entire community. The approach crafted should involve intelligence, suppression, prevention and intervention—a full service gang unit. Members of the gang unit must be able to shift from "rapping" with the gangster to kicking his butt; they must be able to communicate effectively with a wide range of community members and criminal justice personnel; and they must be able to see beyond their own agencies, egos, and communities to adequately address the gang problem.

The gang unit is a specialized unit designed to deal with the special and unique problems associated with the plague of gangs. Given the rapidity with which gangs encompass a community, their rapid mobility, their use of the Internet, and their ever-changing face, a specialized unit is necessary to adequately address these and other concerns regarding gangs. That gang unit must adequately understand the gang ethic, customs and practices of the gang(s) in their area. The reason to do this is that knowing these things helps the officer develop rapport with the gangster, thereby making it easier to deal with them, and also allows for more and better communication with the gang and the gangster. Like any specialized unit, the gang unit can lose its way, can go astray, but that is not a reason to disband it (like LAPD and NYPD). We must keep in mind that specialized units must be adequately staffed and supervised and kept on their mission. We must also keep in mind, as Larry Elder says, "cops are hired out of our flawed, human population. The process screens out numerous applicants for every one who makes it through" (http://www.townhall.com/columnists/larryelder/le000525.shtml).

JEFFREY P. RUSH AND GREGORY P. ORVIS

References and Further Reading

Elder, L., *Police Scandal: Overreaction Equals Anarchy,* Townhall.com Columnists, May 25, 2000.

McBride, W., Speech given in Gulf Shores, AL, Summer 1990.

McBride, W., Part II—Police Departments and Gang Intervention: The Operation Safe Streets Concept, in Goldstein, A.P. and Huff, C.R., Eds., *The Gang Intervention Handbook,* Research Press, Champaign, IL, 1993, pp. 411–415.

Short, J.F., *Delinquency and Society,* Prentice Hall, Englewood Cliffs, NJ, 1990.

Sliwa, C., Speech given in Birmingham, AL, October 1987.

Spergel, I., *The Youth Gang Problem,* Oxford University Press, New York, 1995.

Valdez, A., *Gangs: A Guide to Understanding Street Gangs,* 3rd ed., LawTech Publishing, San Clemente, CA, 2000.

See also **Gangs: The Law; Gangs: Theories**

Gangs: Race and Ethnicity

What constitutes a gang or gang member is not clearly defined. The definition of these terms, which are largely provided by law enforcement agencies, vary greatly across jurisdictions and are often political in nature. Researchers generally suggest that gangs have several identifiable characteristics that include, (1) youth status; (2) a formal organizational structure, (3) an identified leader or leadership hierarchy, (4) control of a specific territory or turf, (5) recurrent interaction among group members, and (6) collective involvement in delinquent or criminal behavior (Miller, 1992; Howell, 1997; Flannery et al., 1998; Esbensen et al., 2001). The term gang or gang member, however, is often applied to youths who are not involved in illegal activity but who are viewed by the public and law enforcement agencies as being troublesome. Definitions of these terms also have a tendency to be racialized, especially by the media, who more readily attach them to the behaviors and activities of racial and ethnic minority youths than majority youths (Hagedorn, 1998; Shelden et al., 2001). The lack of definitional consensus calls into question the accuracy of estimates of gang activity and the demographic characteristics of gang members.

Race and ethnicity have historically been associated with the formation of gangs in the U.S. Racial and ethnic minority youths and young adults, however, have no special predisposition to gang membership; rather, they have a higher probability of being subjected to conditions that are most likely to lead to gang activity (Bursik and Grasmick, 1993). To a large extent, American youth gangs have represented disenfranchised groups who are trying to make it in American society. Up until the mid-1900s, the majority of gangs in the U.S. were composed of White immigrant youths from various European backgrounds who lived in marginal conditions in major urban cities. Gang participation for these youths was directly related to weak familial and community controls, poverty, discrimination, and alienation from mainstream society. These gangs had specific names, recognized leadership, specific styles of dress, defined turfs, and frequently engaged in delinquent and criminal activities, some of which was serious in nature. White ethnic youth gangs, however, tended to be one-generation phenomena in that they dissolved as immigrant youths matured out of gangs into adult labor and as immigrant families moved out of ghetto areas (Moore, 1998).

By the 1970s, African American and Hispanic youths made up approximately 80% of American youth gang members (Flannery et al., 1998). This change in the racial composition of gang membership is associated with the large number of Hispanic immigrants and African American migrants in ghetto areas in large urban centers. These youths joined gangs for many of the same reasons as White ethnic youths of earlier decades: poverty, social disorganization, discrimination, and alienation. Early African American, Hispanic and Asian youth gangs, however, were also formed as protective mechanisms against violence and ridicule from White youth groups and American-born Hispanic and Asian youths (Shelden et al., 2001).

Unlike White ethnic youth gangs, African American and Hispanic gangs became institutionalized in their communities (Moore, 1998). Fewer African American and Hispanic gang members were able to find jobs good enough to move out of poor neighborhoods or overcome segregated housing patterns (Hagedorn, 1998). The transition from a manufacturing to a service-based economy in the U.S. during the 1970s further reduced the demand for low-skilled workers and restricted their access to the labor market (Wilson, 1987; Hagedorn, 1998; Moore, 1998). Gangs, in turn, provided African American and Hispanic youths with alternative economic opportunities through participation in profitable street crimes.

The 1999 National Youth Gang Survey estimates that 47% of the youth gangs in the U.S. are Hispanic, 31% are African American, 13% are White, 7% are Asian American, and 2% are comprised of other races and ethnic groups (Egley, 2000). Although most gangs are racially and ethnically homogeneous, multiracial or multiethnic gangs—those that have a significant mixture of two or more racial or ethnic groups—are not uncommon. Multiracial or multiethnic youth gangs represent approximately 54% of all youth gangs in small cities and are most prominent in the Midwestern region of the U.S. These gangs are sometimes formed through alliances among different racial and ethnic gangs either for protection against rival gang attacks or to facilitate narcotics trafficking. For example, some of the Crips and Bloods, two of the most notorious African American gangs, include Hispanic and Asian gang members. Gangs in Chicago have traditionally belonged to one of two alliances: People or Folks. Both alliances contain African American, White, and Hispanic street gang members.

Modern-day race and ethnic minority youth gangs share several characteristics. First, they are comprised predominately of male youths and young adults. Second, as in past years, these gangs primarily consist of immigrants or lower-class disenfranchised youths. Third, because of limited economic opportunities, gang members often continue their gang affiliation until late adulthood.

Salient differences exist among race and ethnic minority gangs in regards to location, background, organizational structure, type of offending, codes of conduct, and styles of dress. Hispanic youth gangs, for example, are predominant in the Southern and Western U.S. These gangs are structured around age-based cohorts, located in specific neighborhood or barrios, and are often involved in violence that is related to the defense of neighborhood turf. In recent years, however, they have become more involved in the selling of narcotics, particularly PCP, Mexican tar heroin, methamphetamine, and marijuana. Hispanic youth gangs have a distinctive street style of dress, speech, gestures, tattoos, and graffiti that is based on the '*cholo*' culture. A wide degree of commitment to gang affiliation is exercised by Hispanic gang members that ranges according to the following statuses: regular (hang out with group on a regular basis), peripheral (strong attachment to gang but participate less often because of outside interest), temporary (marginally committed, remain in gang short period of time), and situational (marginally attached; join gang for certain activities) (Shelden, et al., 2001).

Asian gangs are a relatively new phenomenon, having primarily emerged in the late 1970s and early 1980s as the Asian population in the U.S. increased. Asian gangs are not monolithic; rather they reflect the cultural traditions of their national origin (e.g., Japanese, Vietnamese, or Chinese). Still there are certain similarities in these gangs. For example, they tend to be highly entrepreneurial. Their criminal activity largely centers around property crimes such as extortion, home invasion, prostitution, gambling, and drug trafficking. The violence that they do commit is usually of an instrumental variety (e.g., threats, retaliation, warnings, and paybacks). Asian gangs are usually nameless, have no specific speech or dress, and do not claim specific turfs. In fact, most Asian gang members are clean-cut, polite, and act with respect toward law enforcement officials. Asian gangs generally victimize people from their own culture who, because of language barriers, lack of trust in law enforcement officials, and collective shame, fail to report their victimization to the police. The highly secretive nature of Asian gangs further makes these gangs difficult to penetrate.

Considerable differences exist among Asian gangs by ethnicity. Vietnamese gangs, for example, are very loosely organized, tend to have few ties to adult groups, and generally avoid drug dealing. Chinese youth gangs, on the other hand, are closely associated with powerful community organizations and organized crime (Chin, 1996). They do not operate in poor deteriorated neighborhoods, and tend to invest in and spend a lot of time in pursuit of legitimate businesses. Many Chinese gangs have national and even international networks. The hierarchical structure of Chinese gangs parallels that of the Mafia or other organized crime groups. Because young Chinese gang members are used as muscle by older gang members, they are seen as the first rung on the ladder of Chinese organized crime. There appears to be little variation in the level of commitment of Chinese youths to gang activity with most gang members being described as "hard core."

There is growing evidence, however, that Asian gangs are becoming more similar to the gangs of other racial and ethnic groups. Some Asian gangs have adopted gang names, graffiti and tattoos. Others have modeled themselves after African American gangs, taking on names such as the Asian Westside Crips. Asian gangs are also attempting to consolidate power by forming alliances among gangs of various Asian ethnicities (Le, 1998).

Most African American gang members are concentrated in the mid-western and northeastern regions of the U.S. The characteristics of African American gangs vary considerably depending on location; that is, African American gangs in Los Angeles can differ greatly from African American gangs in Chicago. All, however, tend to have specific turfs, language, codes of conduct, styles of dress, and street names. African American gangs also tend to be heavily involved in drug trafficking with much of the gang violence being drug related. Different levels of commitment to the drug economy occur when gang members move in and out of conventional jobs (Hagedorn, 1998).

It is not uncommon for African American youth gangs to evolve from relatively disorganized street gangs to formal criminal organizations (Spergel, 1995). An example of this transition is the Black Gangsters Disciples Nation (BGDN) that now exhibits a corporate organizational structure with a chairman of the board, two boards of directors, governors and regents. Another characteristic of African American youth gangs is their migration to other metropolitan areas. Law enforcement authorities, for example, estimate that Crips and Bloods gang members are present in 33 states and 123 cities. Some of this migration can be explained by the development of hybrid gangs—gangs that bear the name of original gangs but have little or no real affiliation with them other than by name. Part of the answer also lies in the family migration of gang members to other locations (for example, by moving from Los Angeles to a small mid-western community) and to a lesser extent, the expansion of criminal markets.

White gang members are most prevalent in small cities in the Midwest and Northeast in the U.S. Although the development of modern-day White youth gangs does not appear to be associated with marginal social and economic conditions, their gang membership is related to disintegrated family structures and drug involvement. Rather than form their own gangs, White youths sometimes join the gangs of other racial and ethnic groups.

Three of the most popular White youth gangs include the skinheads, stoners, and taggers. The skinhead movement first appeared in the U.S. in the late 1970s. Two factions of skinheads can be found in the U.S.: nonracist and racist. Nonracist skinheads such as SHARP (Skinheads Against Racial Prejudice) have multiracial memberships. These youths join the group in reaction to the racist views of parents or family members. The racist faction, which is the most violent of White youth gangs, is often described as the kiddie corps of the neo-Nazi movement. Advocating White supremacy, these gang members are often associated with adult hate groups such as the White Aryan Resistance, Aryan Brotherhood or the Ku Klux Klan (KKK). Most of these groups tend to be disorganized, although there is some evidence that a few skinhead gangs have developed an internal gang structure. Some groups, for example, have printed membership applications, collect dues, have established rules and regulations, and conduct meetings with formal minutes (Wooden and Blazak, 2001). Racist skinheads are likely to direct violent acts against those they perceive as the most different or a threat to the White majority—homosexuals, racial and ethnic groups, and religious minorities. Modern skinheads have specific styles of dress, graffiti and tattoos. Hand signs and violent informal initiations for new members are also common.

Stoners are youth gangs that are made up of lower- and middle-class White adolescents of junior and senior high school age. These youths tend to have higher scholastic and economic status than members of other street gangs and make up about 5% of all gangs in California (Shelden et al., 2000). Although their most common criminal activity is burglary, stoners are also heavily involved in the use of various kinds of drugs, with especially high rates of toxic vapor use. Stoners generally do not have any organized leadership, are antiestablishment, and often dabble in Satanism. Stoners have a distinctive style of dress (typically red or black clothing) and also use graffiti to mark territory.

Taggers differ greatly from traditional racial and ethnic youth gangs. Typically comprised of a large number of suburban middle-class White male youths, taggers are primarily involved in the painting of graffiti on private and public property. Tagging started in the 1970s in New York City and is today most popular in California, where an estimated 600 tagger crews exist (Wooden and Blazak, 2001). Younger taggers (age 10 to 15) usually tag around school grounds, whereas older youths will go after bigger targets, such as freeway overpasses or bridges, public transportation, and streetlight poles. Taggers, like regular street gangs, have their own slang and crew names. Taggers generally do not have much of a formal organizational structure and most members do not go through a formal initiation process. It is common for tagging crews to change their names or for members to drift in and out of the group. Conflict between rival crews involves contests to see which can have their name painted more often on public structures. Taggers do not consider their work to be vandalism. Rather, these youth view their activities as forms of art, recreation, and self-expression. The cost of cleaning up graffiti vandalism, however, is estimated to be in the billions of dollars. Because of this, state and community officials have passed ordinances and legislation to give stiff penalties to those with multiple convictions for graffiti and vandalism.

Researchers have drawn parallels between the formation of racial and ethnic minority gangs in other nations and those in the U.S. Klein (1996) notes that delinquent youth groups in Brussels and Berlin are composed of Muslim immigrants who reside in highly segregated neighborhoods. The fact that the Belgian and Berliner gangs form in inner-city ghettos suggest that these gangs may also become quasi-institutionalized and a permanent fixture of the urban landscape (Moore, 1998). Research examining race and ethnic youth gangs in Australia also suggests that strong social reasons and economic forces encourage the development of youth gangs. Many of these factors are similar to those faced by immigrant youths in the U.S.: lack of parents, unemployment, illiteracy and semiliteracy, poor self-esteem, racism, stress and trauma associated with settling into a new country and language difficulties (Perrone and White, 2000).

There are salient differences, however, between American racial and ethnic gangs and gangs in other nations. The criminal behavior of Australian racial and ethnic gangs is generally limited to petty theft, graffiti and vandalism with few gangs engaging in violence. Violent crimes committed by gang members are seldom gang-related. The criminal offending of youths in Australia is also similar across racial and ethnic groups, with most youths participating in property-related crimes such as theft and drug dealing for alternative income sources.

Research findings from the Australian Institute of Criminology (AIC) suggest that most bands of young people in Australia are not gangs but groups that often mirror the image of gangs. Although these gangs have overwhelming male involvement, high public visibility, and outward displays of collective identity, they organize principally for social reasons with criminal activity involving one-on-one fights and substance abuse. The scarcity of youth gangs in Canada has been attributed to the absence of disorganized inner urban areas containing large populations of disenfranchised, dissolute, and desperate youths and young adults, strict gun control laws, and educational and social services apparatus that provide an effective social safety net for disadvantaged youth (Perrone and White, 2000).

Gang researchers both in the U.S. and abroad have argued that intervention strategies for addressing gang problems, especially as they relate to racial and ethnic populations, must encompass economic, familial, and community responses (Howell, 1995; Spergel, 1995; Hagedorn, 1998; Perrone and White, 2000). Disadvantaged and disenfranchised youths and young adults must be provided with meaningful jobs, job training, and educational opportunities that will allow them to participate in the formal economy and connect them to mainstream values and norms. Efforts must also be taken to strengthen families and communities by reducing factors such as social disorganization and the lack of positive parental involvement and role models that put youths at risk for gang involvement. Aimed at deterrence, school-based gang prevention programs such as GREAT (Gang Resistance Education and Training) that educate students as to the consequences of gang involvement have also shown promise. Youths who have completed these programs have shown lower levels of gang affiliation and self-reported delinquency, including drug use, minor offending, property crimes, and crimes against persons. All gang prevention strategies, however, are not equally effective. Spergel and Curry (1990) found that in chronic gang problem cities such as Los Angeles and Chicago, intervention strategies associated with the provision of economic and educational opportunities and organizing and strengthening communities were the most effective and promising gang prevention methods.

BECKY TATUM

References and Further Readings

Bursik, R. and Grasmick, H., *Neighborhoods and Crime: The Dimension of Effective Community Control,* Lexington Books, New York, 1993.

Egley, A., *Highlights of the 1999 National Youth Gang Survey,* Washington, DC, U.S. Department of Justice, Office of Justice Programs, Office of Juvenile Justice and Delinquency Prevention, November 2000.

Chin, K.-L., *Chinatown Gangs*, Oxford University Press, New York, 1996.

Esbensen, F.-A., Winfree, L., He, N. and Terrance, J., Youth Gangs and Definitional Issues: When is a Gang a Gang, and Why Does it Matter?, *Crime and Delinquency,* 47:1, 105–131, 2001.

Flannery, D., Huff, R. and Manos, M., Youth Gangs: A Developmental Perspective, in Gullotta, T., Adams, G., and Montemayor, R., Eds., *Delinquent Violent Youth: Theory and Interventions,* Sage, Thousand Oaks, CA, 1998.

Hagedorn, J., Gang Violence in the Post Industrial Era, in Tonry, M., and Moore, M., *Youth Violence*, University of Chicago Press, Chicago, IL, 1998.

Howell, J., *Youth Gangs: An Overview,* U.S. Department of Justice, Office of Justice Programs, Office of Juvenile Justice and Delinquency Prevention, Washington, DC, 1997.

Klein, M., Gangs in the United States and Europe, *European Journal of Criminal Policy and Research*, 63–80, 1996.

Li, B., *Asian Gangs: A Bibliography,* Pennsylvania State University, College Station, PA, 1998.

Miller, W., *Crime By Youth Gangs and Groups in the United States*, U.S. Department of Justice, Office of Justice Programs, Office of Juvenile Justice and Delinquency Prevention, Washington, DC.

Moore, J., Understanding Youth Street Gangs: Economic Restructuring and the Urban Underclass, in Watts, M., Ed., *Cross-Cultural Perspectives on Youth and Violence,* JAI Press, Stamford, CT, 1998.

Perrone, S. and White, R., *Young People and Gangs*, Australian Institute of Criminology, Canberra ACT, Australia.

Shelden, R., Tracy, S. and Brown, W., *Youth Gangs in American Society,* Wadsworth Publishing, Belmont, CA, 2001.

Spergel, I., *The Youth Gang Problem*, Oxford University Press, New York, 1995.

Spergel, I. and Curry, G., Strategies and Perceived Agency Effectiveness in Dealing With the Youth Gang Problem, in Huff, R., Ed., *Gangs in America,* Sage, Newbury Park, CA, 1990.

Wilson, W., *The Truly Disadvantaged*, University of Chicago Press, Chicago, IL.

Wooden, W. and Blazak, R., *Renegade Kids, Suburban Outlaws: From Youth Culture to Delinquency,* Wadworths Publishing, Belmont, CA, 2001.

See also **Gangs, Street: An Overview; Gangs: The Law**

Gangs: The Law

The development of societies is the result of the human need to unite for socialization and protection. Being social beings, we have, through the course of history, formed groups that provide us with social interaction and protection. These groups that are formed are usually not criminal groups but are bound together by common beliefs, experiences, and needs. Whereas most of the groups that are formed do not turn to criminal activity, some do. Criminal street gangs are American urban phenomena. Sometimes it depends on the definition that is used, but the beginnings of street gangs were the inner cities of urban America in the late 19th century and the opening of the 20th century. There is no one definition that adequately describes what a criminal gang is, and there is no one strategy on how to combat gangs.

Laws are typically enacted by the majority population through their elected representatives, the mainstream of society. They often seek to preserve the status quo and the power distribution. Some laws were enacted to control the behavior of certain classes of people. Since many of these groups had limited or no voice in the enactment of these laws, they feel disenfranchised and often rebel against laws, they feel are suppressive. Early gang laws were suppressive and meant to control illegal behavior.

Gangs tended to form in urban areas where membership recruitment was relatively easy. Gang congregation in urban areas made the suppressive tactics work much more effectively because the target was small and easily located. When we think of street gangs, we think of disenfranchised young people that belong to minority populations. In the U.S. we have a history of people rebelling against oppressive laws or control. When the King of England and Parliament enacted laws and taxes on the colonies, the citizens rose up to protest. The King responded by using force and enacting more restrictive laws to suppress the rebels. If you look at it from the perspective of the King of England, these rebels were a criminal gang that was breaking the laws of England. Throwing government property into Boston Harbor was a criminal act. From the colonists' point of view they were patriots fighting against tyranny. Suppressive tactics were much less effective because of the distance and area involved in the rebellion.

Prior to urbanization criminal gang activity was limited. There were thieves and robbers who may have banded together to prey upon travelers and take advantage of opportunities to steal. It was the community's obligation to protect itself and come to each other's aid in cases of criminal activity. Citizens were required to take a pledge to help others in their community in time of need. The Hue and Cry was a method of suppressing criminal activity. It was effective as long the community was active in deterring criminal activity.

With increased urbanization the loss of community cohesiveness was the cornerstone to the development of an organized police force. This force was to provide the protection that was once provided by the citizens themselves. The inadequacies of the night watch were exposed. Community disorder or incivilities led to the deterioration of social control. This loss of a sense of community and the increasing gap between the social classes led to increased class tensions and groups banding together to improve their social standing, to provide mutual protection, and in some cases to ensure their very survival.

In the early part of the 20th century, the settlement of immigrant populations in cities was seen by some as a threat to the status quo. Laws were enacted to keep these new citizens under control. Laws were particularly locally based and directed at a particular population that needed to be controlled. Early New York and Boston saw the formation of Irish gangs in the inner city. Restricted to living in certain areas of the city the gangs took it upon themselves to protect their territory. Laws controlling their behavior were enforced when their activities spilled out of the confines of their particular area. Most of the early gang laws were regulatory or suppressive laws that restricted and heavily controlled activities. Gang control has long been a social problem that has been criminalized to make it easier to address.

Early gangs were typically formed along ethnic lines with membership restricted to people from the same ethnic background. These gangs were very territorial and confined their illegal actions to within their own community or territory. Going outside their community would attract the attention of the police and cause stricter enforcement action.

In the early part of the 20th century the politicians were a major force in urban areas; they controlled the resources of communities and could grant favors and make deals to remain in power. These politicians depended on the vice operators for financial backing to help them stay in power and the vice operators were rewarded by having the police look the way when it came to vice operations. The gangs were the enforcers of the politicians—they provided the muscle to help politicians get reelected. In return they were rewarded with control and little interference over certain areas of the community. The politicians still retained the power in the communities and the gangs were still suppressed and localized.

This whole power structure changed as a result of the Volstead Act. Prohibition created a whole new dynamic in the structure of gangs. Gangs became much more organized. They used the demand for alcohol to create a whole new industry to provide alcohol to the general population. Gangs became bigger, richer, and more mobile. Because of the increase in revenue and the ability to move across jurisdictions, gang activity became more difficult for local law enforcement to investigate. With the increase in resources gangs were able to escape many of the activities of the inner cities. They had more monetary resources than some of the law enforcement agencies attempting to control them. Suppression laws were difficult to enforce on gangs that had broken out of the inner city.

These new multijurisdictional gangs were best attacked with federal racketeering laws. Their multijurisdictional threat was better handled by federal laws when it crossed state jurisdictions. The inner city areas were repopulated by new populations of poor ethnic groups. Local statutes were still in place that addressed local problems by suppressing illegal gang activity. Many of the same problems that plagued the inner city in the early 20th century were still present. Lack of social control furthered the recruitment and appeal of gang activity. Territorial issues were still important to the control of neighborhoods by the gangs. Violence helped the gangs maintain that control. Targets of prey were plentiful and the fear by citizens suppressed a lot of crime being reported to the police.

Local restrictions continued to regulate gang activity of the next groups of ethnic minorities inhabiting the inner city. These gangs, like the gangs before them, were primarily territorial until the opportunity arose to increase resources through the sale of drugs. The drug culture opened up national networks for sales. This mobility and increase in resources allowed gangs to escape the control of local jurisdictions. New methods of control were important to decrease gang violence and control crime in urban areas.

The Gang Congregation Ordinance of 1997 was an attempt by the City of Chicago to control the gathering of gang members and increasing fear of crime because of the appearance of a lack of control. The idea behind the ordinance was to prevent gang members from congregating and thus prevent criminal activity. In *Chicago v. Morales* the U.S. Supreme Court ruled that the Chicago Congregation Ordinance was unconstitutional. The court felt that the ordinance was too broad and violated individual freedoms. This was an attempt to prevent gang activity.

The distribution of drugs to all areas of the country has contributed to the network of crime gangs in different parts of the country and was only one reason for the spreading of gang activity. Another reason for the spread of gangs to other areas, rural and urban, was families escaping the inner city so their children would not be involved in gang activity. What occurred was the transplanting of young gangsters by their parents into areas of the country that had never experienced any serious gang activity. Fleeing gang activity in the inner city, they took the gang framework with them.

When we examine past gang laws we find primarily laws that are written to locally suppress and deter criminal gang activity. With the proliferation of street gangs since the early 1980s that has occurred in all parts of the country, the need for other methods of dealing with street gangs has become apparent.

Suppression has typically been the major strategy by law enforcement in targeting gangs. The diversity of criminal activity and the ability of criminal gangs to cross jurisdictional lines have proven that it is a problem that cannot be handled on a local jurisdictional level. The need to form task forces of various agencies to address an area's criminal gang problem has come to be recognized as a viable way to carry out gang suppression strategies. Although suppression laws are still a viable strategy, the need to get involved in prevention programs to eliminate or reduce gang criminal activity has been a focus since the increase of gang activity in the mid-1980s.

Prevention strategies may vary from community to community, as they need to address specific problems. Some of the things that prevention programs address are identification of conditions that promote criminal behavior. Elimination of graffiti may be one action a community can take to come that people care about the community. Eliminating easy targets is another way to try eradicate conditions that lead to gang activity. Other prevention goals have been to identify at-risk juveniles and take steps to reduce the likelihood they will become gang members. Once at-risk juveniles have been identified, we must work with them to increase their resistance to gang recruitment. One way to promote this is through educational programs such as the national Gang Resistance Education and Training program. This program addresses specific gang related recruitment arguments and gives the students knowledge of how to resist the pressure. Another prevention program entails the removal of hard-core gang members through prosecution and incarceration. The 1994 Federal Crime Bill allocated significant funding for programs to help youths avoid criminal activity.

Another strategy employed against gangs particularly in Southern California is the use of civil remedies. Some communities are using restraining orders to eliminate certain people from associating with one another. They post restraining orders to prevent certain types of activity that is prohibited in a particular neighborhood. Whereas the American Civil Liberties Union has contested these civil injunctions as violations of certain free rights, court interpretation so far has upheld their use.

Although much work has been done to eliminate or reduce criminal gang activity, it remains a major problem in all areas of the country. Gangs having moved to rural areas from the inner cities created unique problems for areas that do not have resources or training to address a gang problem. The need for interagency cooperation and community resources has never been more critical to effective intervention strategies. Multidisciplinary and multijurisdictional task forces formed to address gang problems in specific areas using an intervention strategy of suppression and deterrence in conjunction with rehabilitation and prevention strategies hold the most promise of long-term success in criminal gang enforcement. Cooperation of all community stakeholders in developing strategies to deal with the gang problem is critical to a broad-based approach to combating the fear, violence, and drug use associated with gang activity. A multijurisdictional task force should encompass areas that are similar and have similar gang related problems. Multidisciplinary members of a task force should contain people from all areas of the community impacted by the gang activity, such as law enforcement, prosecutors, the community itself, doctors, counselors, educators, and religious leaders. Having such a vast pool of expertise will maximize the opportunity for an effective response.

John Boal

References and Further Reading

Abadinsky, H., *Organized Crime,* 7th Ed., Wadsworth/Thomson Learning, Belmont, CA, 2003.

Addressing Community Gang Problems: A Practical Guide, Bureau of Justice Assistance, May, 1998.

Burch, J. and Chemers, B., *A Comprehensive Response to American Youth Gang Problem,* Office of Juvenile Justice and Delinquency Prevention, March, 1997.

Chicago Gang Congregation Ordinance of 1997.

Violent Crime Control and Law Enforcement Act of 1994.

See also **Gangs: Definitions; Gangs: Theories; Gangs, Street: An Overview**

Gangs: Theories

Theories about gangs and the theories that use the gang to address broader social issues have had a tremendous influence beyond their focal topic. Much of theoretical criminology, for example, is actually explication and depiction of delinquent behavior by youth gangs. Subculture, strain, opportunity, and conflict theories of crime and delinquency are supported, to differing bounds, by data derived from observing gang activity and composition. Some of criminology's central premises are gleaned from these gang theories (e.g., delinquency is learned through interaction with others and most often occurs in a group context).

The construction of gang theories has been consequential to paradigmatic shifts in social science research methodology. Early attention to gangs helped make ethnography standard science, as researchers prior to the 1970s generally followed the example of fieldwork set by the "Chicago School" (e.g., Shaw, 1930; Shaw & McKay, 1942). Though fundamentally treated as delinquent, youth gangs were also considered primary groups (Cooley, 1909) and unique types of collectives (Asbury, 1927) to be explored firsthand via observational and interview techniques. Such techniques facilitated understanding of the processes of gang development, behavior, and member desistence.

Gang study today is by no means limited to qualitative research designs. The typical limitations of fieldwork, such as gaining access to subject groups (initial entry), researcher bias, and the generalizability of findings, are considered especially acute in the study of gangs (Hagedorn, 1990; Hamm, 1995). These problems are supposedly offset by survey instruments fashioned to gang-related topics (e.g., Spergel, 1989; Thornberry et al., 1993). Such surveys reflect a renewed interest in previously assessed predictors of gangs and ganging (Topping, 1943; Dumpson, 1949; Glueck & Glueck, 1950) and have produced a wealth of new information on the prevalence, composition and criminality of gangs.

Objections to the application of survey methodologies in gang research is centered aournd the value of the data. Erickson's "group hazard hypothesis" (1971), for example, contended official overrepresentation of gang delinquency due to the increased likelihood of arrest for acts committed in a group context. This position has recently been restated and expanded in the "courthouse criminology" debate that doubts the validity of gang knowledge derived from official data sources such as law enforcement and prison questionnaires (Hagedorn, 1990). Is a crime considered to be gang related only when it occurs in a group context or also when gang members act alone? More fundamentally, how credible are responses by those with a vested interest in minimizing further conflict with authority? The answers to these and similar questions will necessarily affect, and possibly distort, the knowledge base from which theories are formed.

Gang theories have also had remarkable bearing upon criminal justice policy. This is not surprising given that some of the major theories were framed during the 1950s and 1960s in studies sponsored by federal grants specifying social control objectives (Miller, 1974). The theories of this era spoke to what was considered a timely problem of unprecedented proportion: juvenile delinquency. Rebellious youth associated with the emergence of the rock and roll era presented a new, visible threat to authority. In many ways, gangs were the epitome of this threat. Their banding and symbolism made them readily identifiable targets for criminal justice responses. Policing gangs was thus equated with addressing a larger social issue. One noteworthy and lasting consequence of this application of theory is a tendency to define gangs as socially problematic by means of an enforcement rationale. Social control is an important theoretical theme detectable throughout the history of gang research.

The pervasive social control problems presented by gangs have embedded them as primary research foci in criminology and criminal justice science. Gang research in both of these concentrations unquestionably arose out of sociological tradition. Whereas sociology's impression was evident as early as the 1930s (Asbury, 1927), the applied criminological literature overlooked gangs. The 1949 edition of *The Encyclopedia of Criminology*, for instance, contained no entry under the heading "gang."

Although sociologists had previously noted that delinquency habitually occurred in group contexts, Thrasher's *The Gang: A Study of 1303 Gangs in Chicago* (1928) is frequently considered to be the catalyst for several groundbreaking theories. He observed that gangs were interstitial, concentrated in lower-class neighborhoods, responsive to a lack of conventional employment opportunities, composed of young males lacking skills to compete for jobs, and a process by which delinquents were socialized into adult crime.

Thrasher's innovative conceptualization of interstitial merits brief comment. This descriptive term was used plurally in reference to the transitory and peripheral character of gangs who emerged in socially disorganized areas to replace order where there is little, although they seldom lasted more than a few years (Thrasher, 1928, 22). The gang was more than a fleeting gathering of similarly circumstanced individuals, but less than a permanent organization. Members, then usually immigrants, were only marginally incorporated into broader American culture and were typically between childhood and adulthood. Gang process was interstitial as well, wavering along a continuum from planning to spontaneity. Three decades later, instability was stressed again by the labeling of the youth gang as a "near-group," an idea that remains influential in contemporary explications.

Perhaps what is particularly unique about Thrasher's study is its treatment of why and how gangs are formed. Whereas many later theories utilized the gang to describe, interpret, and explain delinquency, particularly its distribution in the social order, Thrasher was more directly concerned with identifying causal variables of gang formation. Weak social controls are often considered Thrasher's primary determinant of gang development, but his combined model also incorporated lower-class culture, status frustration, collective behavior, and social ecology. Recent works cite Thrasher's study as a precursor to diverse theoretical traditions and present striking disagreement concerning his heritage. Hagedorn (1990, 55) refers to "Thrasher and the Subculturists" but then curiously proceeds with an explanation of gang formation as a result of social disorganization. Thrasher's legacy is also apparent in learning/subcultural and opportunity/strain based theories (Merton, 1938; Cohen, 1955; Miller, 1958; Cloward & Ohlin, 1960).

Other early statements addressing gang formation and behavior have received less attention. Furfey (1928) hypothesized that gang cohesiveness was positively correlated with class and confirmed Thrasher's observation that gangs were concentrated in the slum areas. Asbury (1927) focused on ethnicity and culture to describe the diversity of gangs in New York as early as the late 1920s. Quite differently, Bolitho (1930) submitted that ganging was a form of psychosis, an issue recently raised in an integrated model fusing "kind of person" and "kind of group" (Thornberry et al., 1993). Ganging was similarly treated as a vehicle by which sociopaths vented hostility and anger. Psychological explanations of ganging are readily dismissed as passé in spite of repeated testimony by gang members that their acts of violence result from "just losing my head," that is, a temporary inability to reason.

Street Corner Society (Whyte, 1943) addressed lower-class Italian and Puerto Rican lifestyles and is frequently cited in discussions of gang theory. Its lasting relevance is due to the care afforded the relationship between social forces affecting minorities in depressed urban areas and conventionality rather than delinquent behavior by youth gangs per se. Although the racial and ethnic compositions of gangs have changed over time, today they are largely a minority phenomenon, as one gang theorist notes: "To be white is to be an outsider to gang members" (Hagedorn, 1990, 253). Gangs had become such a hot topic in academia by the 1960s that Dale Hardman published an article titled "Historical Perspectives on Gang Research." Surprisingly, this sharp rise of interest in gangs was less affected by racial concerns than by an emerging theoretical order accenting the relationship between culture, class, and delinquency.

Subcultural theories dominated the study of gangs during the 1950s and 1960s. They stress that some environments are characterized by atypical, criminogenic values and normative systems, making deviant behavior more or less normal for those within the subculture. The subculture has been described in relation to the dominant culture with great clarity:

> A subculture implies that there are value judgments or a social value system, which is apart from and a part of a larger or central value system. From the viewpoint of this larger, dominant culture, the values of the subculture set the latter apart and prevent total

integration, occasionally causing open or covert conflicts (Wolfgang & Ferracuti, 1967:99).

Discussion of subcultural theory often begins with *Delinquent Boys: The Culture of the Gang* (Cohen, 1955) wherein a general theory of subcultures is presented through extraction and characterization of the properties of gangs. Observation of the existing literature revealed that boys from the bottom end of the socioeconomic scale shared difficulty in conforming to the dominant society that largely rejected them. This difficulty is explained partially by differing degrees of drive and ambition that affect individual responsibility, but also by social structural constraints largely beyond their control.

Working-class youth experience a socialization process that devalues success in the classroom, deferred pleasure and satisfaction, long-range planning, and the cultivation of etiquette mandatory for survival in business and social arenas. Rather than participate in "wholesome" leisure activity, they opt for activities typified by physical aggression. Overall, the learning experience of lower-class males leaves them ill-prepared to compete in a world gauged by a *middle-class measuring rod* (Cohen, 1955, 129). Deficiencies are most noticeable in the classroom, where working-class youth are frequently overshadowed and belittled by their middle-class counterparts. Turning to membership in a delinquent gang is but a normal adaptation to status frustration resulting from clashing cultures.

Whereas a strict chronological listing of gang-based subcultural theories would move from Cohen (1955) to Miller (1958), Cloward and Ohlin's (1960) theory of delinquency is more similar to Cohen's work. Their major work, *Delinquency and Opportunity: A Theory of Delinquent Gangs* (1960), also acknowledges the relationship between behavior and status frustration (Merton, 1938). Cloward and Ohlin further Cohen's hypothesis through a detailed accounting of both subculture emergence and the traits of defiant out-groups via a typology of gangs. Often termed an "opportunity theory," the basic premises are (1) limited and blocked economic aspirations lead to frustration and negative self-esteem, and (2) these frustrations move youth to form gangs that vary in type. In short, lower-class teenagers realize that they have little chance for future success through the use of conventional standards and consequently resort to membership in one of three gang types. The ratio of conventional and criminal values to which a delinquent is consistently exposed accounts for the differences in the character of the gangs.

The Cloward-Ohlin gang typology is hierarchal in terms of the amount of prestige associated with affiliation. At the top is the criminal gang whose activities revolve around stealing. Theft and other deviant acts serve to positively reinforce the mutual codependence between the juvenile and the group. Not all have the skills and composure to integrate into criminal gangs that screen potential members for certain abilities and willingness to conform to a code of values necessary to the unit's success. Mandatory criteria include self-control, solidarity to the group, and desire to cultivate one's criminal ability. Those strained youth who are precluded from gangs that primarily steal congregate around violent behavior such as fighting, arson and serious vandalism. Termed a conflict subculture (Cloward & Ohlin, 1960, 171), this type of gang results from an absence of adult role models involved in gainful criminal behavior.

Some youth are neither violent nor successful in criminal endeavors. Having failed in both conventional and multiple deviant sectors of society, they retreat into a third type of gang that is characterized by drug use (Cloward & Ohlin, 1960, 183). Members of this relatively unorganized gang resort to drugs as an escape from failure resulting from differential access to both legitimate and illegitimate opportunities, and also deficient familial and community support. A lack of interest by adults in the future success or failure of their sons and other young males in the neighborhood symbolizes rejection, the adaptation to which is "exploration of nonconformist alternatives" (Cloward & Ohlin, 1960, 86).

Unlike Cohen or Cloward and Ohlin, Walter B. Miller developed a theory that concentrated directly on culture. In an article titled "Lower Class Culture as a Generating Milieu of Gang Delinquency" (1958), he argued the existence of a distinct and observable lower-class culture. Unlike the middle-class emphasis on conventional values, the lower class has defining *focal concerns* that include (1) trouble, (2) toughness, (3) smartness, (4) excitement, (5) fate, and (6) autonomy.

These concerns foster the formation of street corner gangs while undermining conventional values. "Smartness," for example, is a skill that warrants respect in the lower-class culture. This refers to the ability to con someone in real-life situations, rather than formal knowledge that is relatively inapplicable and even resented in poorer areas. A belief in "fate" discourages work ethic, undermines prudence, and minimizes hope for self-improvement, all of which encourages risk taking. "Excitement" rationalizes otherwise senseless acts of gang violence.

"Trouble," however, is perhaps the most defining of the focal concerns: you do not decide to do something on the basis of rightness or wrongness, but rather on the basis of expediency, hassles, and practical consequences. Decisions not to commit certain acts center on whether the commission is likely to get you into trouble.

The theory rests on the supposition that deviance is normal and to be expected in segments of the lower class where culturally specified focal concerns make conformity to criminal behavior as natural as acceptance of conventional mores for the middle class. Juveniles accepting a preponderance of these "practices which comprise essential elements of the total life pattern of lower class culture automatically violate legal norms," typically in a gang setting (Miller, 1958, 167).

To sum up, subcultural explanations were pivotal for theoretical criminology, establishing an explanatory framework for subsequent gang analysis. Youth gangs were linked with delinquency to such an extent that in the future they would be considered inherently deviant. Moreover, subculture became a major concept in conservative and centrist ideologies, a convenient comparative device for highlighting normative standards.

By the 1960s a number of closely related social movements were under way. These movements led to a shift to the political left, and labeling theory replaced subculture as the leading theory. The main thrust of labeling theory was that crime and delinquency are definitions and labels assigned to persons and events by operatives of the criminal justice system. Much of the fashionable literature of the period, not only on gangs but social problems generally, was not only indifferent to subcultural theory but also actively opposed to it. This literature included works such as Chambliss' *The Saints and the Roughnecks* (1973) that emphasized a "conflict" perspective that viewed the subcultural theories as conservative. Social control was deemed reactionary because crime and delinquency were direct, reasonable, and even justified adaptations to injustice. Gangs in this view were perceived as victims.

In the last decade, social scientists have produced a plethora of theories and findings about youth gangs. It is fair to say that gang research has reached an all-time high, evident in part by the 1992 creation of *The Gang Journal*. Indeed, the 1990s marked what is the "second era" of gang research in the social sciences. Those currently crafting gang theories look to the earlier subcultural era for comparative purposes. Alleged shortcomings of cultural deviance theories, such as those discussed above, often serve as point of departure for establishing alternative theory. A debate has emerged that centers on whether the underlying causes of gang formation and behavior stem from cultural deficiencies or socioeconomic factors. Accordingly, contemporary gang theory is frequently categorized dichotomously: subculture versus urban underclass.

American gang policy has been set according to what can be categorized as a general "tolerance" theory, wherein the criminal justice system's ideological orientation to gang-derived social problems has vacillated on a conflict continuum. The least conflictual version of tolerance theory can be witnessed in the "positive tolerance" policies employed during the 1960s and 1970s. Gangs were portrayed as manifestations of social inequality in the political arena and consequently received social support afforded other "downtrodden" groups. Funding and resources provided gangs with community enrichment programs, and several gang leaders were put on government and private sector payrolls.

The onset of the crack cocaine epidemic and gangs' heavy participation in it during the 1980s gave rise to a "zero tolerance" philosophy that stressed awareness programs and shifted policy emphasis away from social support to a strategy of gang moderation. Moderation policies, in turn, have been replaced by a "negative tolerance" approach wherein the criminal justice system seeks to eliminate gang activity. Specifically, antigang units have been created within police departments, often from federal funding. These units seek to increase the cost of doing gang business, use civil, administrative, and criminal sanctions to prevent new recruits, and target hardcore members for stiff sentences.

J. Mitchell Miller

References and Further Reading

Asbury, H., *The Gangs of New York,* Alfred A. Knopf, New York, 1927.

Bolitho, W., The Psychosis of the Gang, *Survey,* 1, 501–506 (1930).

Chambliss, W.J., The Saints and the Roughnecks, *Society,* 11, 24–31, 1973.

Cloward, R.A. and Ohlin, L.E., *Delinquency and Opportunity: A Theory of Delinquent Gangs,* The Free Press, New York, 1960.

Cohen, A., *Delinquent Boys: The Culture of the Gang,* The Free Press, Glencoe, IL, 1955.

Cooley, C.H. *Social Organization,* Scribners, New York, 1909.

Dumpson, J.R., An Approach to Antisocial Street Gangs, *Federal Probation,* 1, 22–29 (1949).

Erickson, M., The Group Context of Delinquent Behavior, *Social Problems,* 19, 14–29.

Furfey, P.H., *The Gang Age,* Macmillan, New York, 1928.

Glueck, S. and Glueck, E., *Unraveling Juvenile Delinquency,* Commonwealth Fund, New York, 1950.

Hagedorn, J.M., Back in the Field Again: Gang Research in the Nineties, in Huff, C.R., Ed., *Gangs in America,* Sage, Newbury Park, CA, 1990, pp. 240–259.

Hamm, M.S., Researching Gangs in the 1990s: Pedagogical Implications of the Literature, in Miller J.M., and Rush, J., Eds., *A Criminal Justice Approach to Gangs: From Explanation to Response,* 1995.

Merton, R.K., Social Structure and Anomie, *American Sociological Review* 3, 372–382 (1938).

Miller, W.B., American Youth Gangs: Past and Present, in Blumberg, A., Ed., *Current Perspective on Criminal Behavior,* Knopf, New York, 1974.

Spergel, I.A., Youth Gangs: Continuity and Change, in Morris, N., and Tonry, M., Eds., *Crime and Justice: An Annual Review of Research,* Vol. 12, Chicago University Press, Chicago, IL, 1989.

Thornberry, T., Moore, M., and Christenson, R., The Effect of Dropping Out of High School on Subsequent Criminal Behavior, *Criminology,* 23, 3–18 (1985).

Thrasher, F.M., *The Gang: A Study of 1,313 Gangs in Chicago,* University of Chicago Press, Chicago, IL, 1927.

Topping, R., Treatment of the Pseudo-Social Boy, *American Journal of Orthopsychiatry,* 1, 313–360 (1943).

Shaw, C.R., *The Jack Roller: A Delinquent Boy's Own Story,* University of Chicago Press, Chicago, IL, 1930.

Shaw, C.R. and McKay, H.D., *Juvenile Delinquency in Urban Areas,* University of Chicago Press, Chicago, IL, 1942.

Whyte, W.F., *Street Corner Society: The Social Structure of an Italian Slum,* University of Chicago Press, Chicago, IL, 1943.

Wolfgang, M.E., and Ferracuti, F., *The Subculture of Violence: Towards an Integrated Theory in Criminology,* Tavistock, London, 1967.

See also **Albert Cohen; Gangs, Street: An Overview; Gangs: Definitions; Subcultural Theories of Criminal Behavior; Lloyd Ohlin; Richard Cloward; Marvin E. Wolfgang; Sociological Theories of Criminal Behavior**

Gangsters

See **Gangs; Organized Crime**

Gender and Criminal Behavior

One of the most widely accepted conclusions in criminology is that females are less likely than males to commit crime. The gender difference in crime is universal: throughout history, for all societies, for all groups, and for nearly every crime category, males offend more than females. The robustness of sex as a predictor of criminal involvement is quite remarkable, though many take it for granted.

Since the prototypical offender is a young male, most efforts to understand crime have been directed toward male crime. However, examining female crime and the ways in which female offending is similar to and different from male crime can contribute greatly to our understanding of the underlying causes of criminality and how it might better be controlled.

This discussion of gender and crime first details extant knowledge on levels and types of female offending in relation to males from both a historical and current perspective. After contrasting female and male rates and patterns of offending, we focus on theoretical explanations of female crime and gender differences in crime. Finally, we briefly outline a "gendered" approach to understanding female crime that takes into account the organization of gender—that is, the influence of gender differences in norms, socialization, social control, and criminal opportunities, as well as psychological and physiological differences between men and women.

Although a variety of sources are available that allow for comparisons of criminal behavior between groups—such as men and women—we concentrate primarily on arrest data from the Uniform Crime Reports (UCR) that are collected from the nation's law enforcement agencies and tabulated by the Federal Bureau of Investigation (FBI). Although the UCR arrest data are the richest source of statistics on trends in crime, we also touch upon the insights to be gained from alternative sources of information on offenders including surveys of victimization experiences, such as the National Crime Victimization Survey (NCVS); surveys of self-reported offending behavior, such as the National Youth Survey (NYS); and case studies based on autobiographical accounts or interviews with and observation of individual offenders and gangs.

Similarities and Differences in Male and Female Offending Rates and Patterns

Table 1 helps to illuminate important gender similarities and differences in criminal offending by displaying arrest statistics for several violent and property crimes over the 1965–2000 period. Included are male and female rates of offending, the female percentage of arrests, and both male and female arrest profiles. Each of these measures is defined at the bottom of the table.

Table 1. Male and Female Arrest Rates per 100,000 (All Ages), Female Percentage of Arrests, and Male and Female Arrest Profiles (1965–2000 *Uniform Crime Reports*)[a]

	Male Rates[b]				**Female Rates**[b]				**Female Percentage (of arrests)**[c]			
Offense	**1965**	**1980**	**1990**	**2000**	**1965**	**1980**	**1990**	**2000**	**1965**	**1980**	**1990**	**2000**
Violent												
Homicide	9	16	17	12	2	2	2	1	17	12	10	10
Weapons	78	140	174	141	5	10	13	12	6	7	7	8
Simple assault	279	369	697	817	32	56	127	221	10	13	15	21
Property/Drugs												
Larceny	466	755	894	685	125	298	391	351	21	28	30	34
Fraud	62	145	169	160	15	96	128	126	20	40	43	44
Drug abuse	66	450	800	1010	10	65	150	182	13	13	16	15

[a] The offender profile percentage is the percentage of all arrests within each sex that are arrests for a particular offense; this measure indicates the distribution of arrests by gender.

[b] Rates are calculated based on 3-year averages and are sex-specific rates (e.g., female rate = no. of female arrests/no. of females in the population∗100,000).

[c] The female percentage of arrests adjusts for the sex composition of the population. It is calculated as follows: [female rate/(female rate + male rate)]*100%.

Several important parallels between male and female offending include the following (for reviews, see Steffensmeier and Allan, 1996 and 2000). First, females have relatively high arrest rates in most of the same crime categories for which males have high arrest rates. Both men and women have much lower rates of arrest for serious crimes like homicide or robbery and higher rates of arrest for petty property crimes like larceny-theft or public order offenses such as alcohol and drug offenses or disorderly conduct. For example, rates of homicide are small for both sexes at about 12 offenders for every 100,000 males and about 1.4 offenders per 100,000 females, as compared to larceny rates that measure about 685 offenders per 100,000 males and 350 offenders per 100,000 females.

Second, female and male arrest trends over time or across groups or geographic regions are similar. That is, decades or groups or regions that have high (or low) rates of male crime also tend to have high (or low) rates of female crime. For example, in the second half of the 20th century, the rates of arrest for larceny-theft and fraud increased dramatically for both men and women and declined even more dramatically for both men and women in the category of public drunkenness. Similarly, states or cities or countries that have higher than average arrest rates for men also have higher arrest rates for women (Steffensmeier, Allan, and Streifel 1989; Steffensmeier, 1993).

Third, female and male offenders have similar age-crime distributions—that is, the peak age, median age, and rate of decline of offending are similar for males and females. Although male levels of offending are always higher than female levels at every age and for virtually all offenses, the female-to-male ratio remains fairly constant across the life span (Steffensmeier and Streifel, 1991). The major exception is for prostitution, where there is a younger and more peaked age curve for females compared to a greater concentration of older male offenders. This pattern clearly reflects differing opportunity structures for sexual misbehaviors: Older women become less able to market sexual services, whereas older men have the power to act as pimps and can continue to purchase sexual services from young females or males.

Fourth, as is the case with male offenders, female offenders tend to come from backgrounds marked by poverty, discrimination, poor schooling, and other disadvantages. However, women who commit crime are somewhat more likely than men to have been abused physically, psychologically, or sexually, both in childhood and as adults.

Although substantial similarities between female and male offending exist, any gender comparison of criminality must acknowledge significant differences as well.

First, females have lower arrest rates than males for virtually all crime categories except prostitution. This is true in all countries for which data are available. It is true for all racial and ethnic groups, and for every historical period. In the U.S., women constitute less than 20% of arrests for most crime categories.

Second, the biggest gender difference is the proportionately greater *female* involvement in minor property crimes, and the relatively greater involvement of *males* in more serious person or property crimes. Relative to males, women's representation in serious crime categories is consistently low—since the 1960s in the U.S., the female percentage of arrests has generally been less than 15% for homicide and aggravated assault, and less than 10% for the serious property crimes of burglary and robbery. Aside from prostitution, female representation has been greatest in the realm of minor property crimes such as larceny-theft, fraud, forgery, and embezzlement. The female percentage of arrests for these crime categories has been as high as 30–45%, especially since the mid-1970s. The thefts and frauds committed by women typically involve shoplifting (larceny-theft), "bad checks" (forgery or fraud), and welfare and credit fraud—all compatible with traditional female consumer/domestic roles.

The patterns just described are corroborated by other sources of data. The percentage of female offenders reported by victims interviewed in the National Crime Victimization Survey is very similar to (or lower than) the female percentage of arrests for comparable categories. Self-report studies also confirm the UCR patterns of relatively low female involvement in serious offenses and greater involvement in the less serious categories. These sources also reveal some important gender differences in the *nature* or *context* of offending.

When women do engage in serious offenses, they perpetrate less harm. Women's acts of violence, compared to those of men, result in fewer injuries and less serious injuries. Their property crimes usually involve less monetary loss or less property damage. In other words, there seems to be little truth to the old saw that "when she's bad, she's horrid."

Women are less likely than men to become repeat offenders, and long-term careers in crime are very rare among women. Some pursue relatively brief careers (in relation to male criminal careers) in prostitution, drug offenses, or minor property crimes like shoplifting or check forging.

Women offenders, more often than men, operate solo. When women do become involved with others in offenses, the group is likely to be small and relatively nonpermanent. Furthermore, women in group operations are generally accomplices to males (for a review, see Steffensmeier, 1983). And males are overwhelmingly dominant in the more organized and highly lucrative crimes, whether based in the underworld or the "upperworld."

Concomitant with male dominance of criminal subcultures and the tendency of female criminals to operate alone or in a male–female pairing, delinquent gang involvement is far less common for females than males. At the turn of the century, female gang involvement was described as "auxiliary" to male gangs (e.g., Thrasher, 1927). Although recent gang research has identified some all-female gangs and suggests that female gang involvement has increased somewhat in recent decades, gang involvement among girls remains relatively low (perhaps 15% of gang members). Additionally, female gang violence, although probably greater than in Thrasher's era, remains far less than male gang violence.

Germane to this discussion of rates and patterns of female crime in relation to male crime is whether these differences in offending are becoming more or less pronounced or reduced over time.

Recent Trends in Female-to-Male Offending

Both in the media and within criminology it is debated whether female crime is increasingly approaching male levels of crime and, if so, how this convergence in the gender gap can be explained. Researchers have found that, for the most part, *there has been neither a significant widening nor a significant narrowing of the gender gap in arrests over the past several decades*, though these trends are not easily summarized (for a more in-depth treatment, see Steffensmeier, 1993).

The main exception to this general pattern of stability in female-to-male offending (i.e., much smaller female rates) involves substantial increases in the female share of arrests for the minor property crimes of larceny-theft, forgery, fraud, and embezzlement, where the female percentage of arrests doubled between 1960 and 1975 (from around 15–30% or more), with slight additional increases since then.

Some criminologists (and the media) have attributed these female increases in minor property crimes to gains in gender equality (e.g., increased female labor force participation)—dubbing this phenomenon the "dark side" of female liberation. The longstanding perspective in criminology that gender differences in crime could be explained by differences in male and female social positions has given rise to the "gender equality hypothesis": as social differences between men and women disappear under the influence of the women's movement, so should differences in crime disappear.

However, other criminologists have pointed to the peculiarity of the view that improving girls' and women's economic conditions would lead to disproportionate increases in female crime when almost all the existing criminological literature stresses the role played by poverty, joblessness, and discrimination in the creation of crime (Miller, 1986; Steffensmeier, 1980 and 1993; Chesney-Lind, 1997). In addition, it is generally not the "liberated woman" who is offending; traditional rather than nontraditional gender views are associated with greater criminality (see reviews in Pollock-Byrne, 1990; Chesney-Lind and Shelden 1992; Steffensmeier and Allan, 1995). Furthermore, typical female (and male) offenders are unemployed or marginally employed (Steffensmeier and Allan, 1990).

Instead most students of female crime propose that a combination of factors explain the increases in female-to-male offending over the past several decades. Besides possible changes in gender roles and in mainstream institutions allowing girls and women greater independence from traditional constraints, these factors include the increasing economic marginalization of large segments of women; increased opportunities for traditionally female crime (e.g., shoplifting, check fraud, welfare fraud); bureaucratization of law enforcement such that females are treated less chivalrously; rising levels of drug use that may increase motivational pressures and initiate females into the underworld; and the social and institutional transformation of the inner city toward greater detachment from mainstream social institutions.

The debate over the role of gender equality in explaining female crime is but one issue in current gender and crime research. Another matter receiving much attention is whether traditional, gender-neutral theories of crime are adequate explanations of female criminality or whether gender-specific theories are needed to explain female offending. Next, we trace the development of theoretical perspectives on female criminality and summarize more recent theoretical advances.

Explaining Female Offending

Early Social Science Views

Prior to the first half of the 20th century, most explanations of female crime were ancillary to explanations of male criminality and reflected prevailing views of human behavior. Lombroso, for example, linked both male and female crime to biological predisposition. Individualistic explanations of crime emerged in the 1930s as psychological theories gained prominence in the social sciences.

Theorists emphasizing the causal role of biological and psychological factors in female crime typically postulated that criminal women exhibited masculine biological or psychological orientations. Lombroso (1895) viewed female criminals as having an excess of male characteristics. He argued that biologically, criminal females were more similar to normal or criminal males than to normal females.

Similarly, Freud (1933) argued that female crime results from a "masculinity complex," stemming from unresolved penis envy. He argued that those women who cannot successfully resolve their penis envy, from which all females suffer, over-identify with maleness and are likely to act out in criminal ways. Both Lombroso and Freud, then, viewed the female criminal as biologically or psychologically male in orientation.

While some theorists linked female crime to "masculinity," others saw it as distinctly feminine. Eleanor and Sheldon Glueck (1934), based on their studies of adult and juvenile delinquents, concluded that female crime reflected the inability of certain women—especially those from disadvantaged neighborhood and family contexts—to control their sexual impulses. The Gluecks also subscribed to the theme of the woman offender as a pathetic creature, a view that characterized much of criminological writings in the 1930s.

Early sociological explanations, manifested already in some early 20th century writings (Kellor, 1900; Bonger, 1916), and presented consistently in textbooks published between 1917 and 1960, generally rejected this biological determinism and offered sociocultural interpretations (e.g., differential association, anomie, and social disorganization) of both male and female crime as well as of gender differences in crime (see the review in Steffensmeier and Clark, 1980). Whatever the orientation, biological or sociocultural, most criminologists focused primarily on male criminality, with female offending largely ignored.

Otto Pollak's *The Criminality of Women*, published in 1950, is the most important work on female crime prior to the modern period. The book summarized previous work on women and crime, and it challenged basic assumptions concerning the extent and quality of women's involvement in criminal behavior. Pollack himself explained female crime and the gender gap with reference to a mix of biological, psychological, and sociological factors.

Pollak is the first writer to insist that women's participation in crime approaches that of men and is commensurate with their representation in the population. He argues that the types of crimes women commit—shoplifting, domestic thefts, thefts by prostitutes, abortions, perjury, and the like—are under-represented in crime statistics for a variety of reasons: easy concealment, underreporting, embarrassment on the part of male victims, and male chivalry in the justice system (for a contemporary treatment of gender differences in case processing of criminal offenders, see Steffensmeier, Ulmer, and Kramer, 1998).

A fundamental theme of Pollak's work is the attribution of a biological and physiological basis to female criminality. Pollak stressed the inherently deceitful nature of the female sex, rooted particularly in the passive role assumed by women during sexual intercourse. Also significant are the influences of hormonal and generative phases (e.g., menstruation, pregnancy, and menopause) on female criminality.

Yet Pollak consistently emphasized the importance of social and environmental factors, including poverty, crowded living conditions, broken homes, delinquent companions, and the adverse effects of doing time in reform schools or penitentiaries. Pollak also noted that there is considerable overlap in causative factors for delinquency among girls and boys, and women and men.

To sum up, in comparison to explanations for male offending, some early explanations of female crime placed greater emphasis on biological and psychological factors. Nevertheless, early sociological explanations of female crime stressing sociocultural factors were also commonplace. Criminology textbooks, in particular, offered an interpretation of female offending and the gender gap that took into account gender differences in role expectations, socialization patterns and application of social control, opportunities to commit particular offenses, and access to criminally oriented subcultures—all themes that have been further developed in more recent accounts (see reviews in Steffensmeier and Clark, 1980; Chesney, 1986).

Recent Theoretical Developments

A rich and complex literature on female criminality has emerged over the past few decades. Recent theoretical and empirical work has allowed criminologists to evaluate whether traditional theories of crime, developed by male criminologists to explain male crime, are equally useful in explaining female crime, or whether female crime can only be explained by gender-specific theories.

Causal factors identified by traditional theories of crime such as anomie, social control, differential association, and social learning appear equally applicable to female and male offending (Steffensmeier and Allan, 1996). For both males and females, the likelihood of criminal behavior is increased by weak social bonds and parental controls, low perceptions of risk, delinquent associations, chances to learn criminal motives and techniques, and other access to criminal opportunities. In this sense, traditional criminological theories are as useful in understanding overall female crime as they are in understanding overall male crime. They can also help explain why female crime rates are so much lower than male rates: e.g., females develop stronger bonds and are subject to stricter parental control, and have less access to criminal opportunity.

On the other hand, a *gendered approach* may offer insight into the subtle and profound differences between female and male offending patterns. Recent "middle range" approaches, which typically draw from the expanding literatures on gender roles and feminism, typically link some aspect of female criminality to the "organization of gender" (i.e., identities, roles, and other areas of social life that differ markedly by gender). These approaches, briefly reviewed next, delineate structural and subjective constraints placed on females that limit the *form* and *frequency* of female deviance.

Cloward and Piven, for example, argue that limits on women's opportunities in the paid workforce, in conjunction with their more extensive domestic responsibilities, constrain the deviant adaptations available to women. As a result, "the only models of female deviance which our society encourages or permits women to imagine, emulate and act out are essentially privatized modes of self destruction" (1979:660).

Harris (1977) makes a comparable point when he asserts that "type-scripts," specifications of acceptable and unacceptable forms of deviance for various categories of social actors, serve to limit the types of crimes committed by women. For example, "it is unlikely or 'impossible' for women to attempt assassination, robbery, or rape" (1977:12). Instead, consistent with gendered type-scripts and roles (e.g., consumer and domestic), women are much more heavily involved in minor thefts and hustles such as shoplifting, theft of services, falsification of identification, passing bad checks, credit card forgery, welfare fraud, and employee pilferage.

Steffensmeier argues that underworld sex segregation adds further structural constraints on female levels of offending, particularly in the more lucrative venues. "Compared to their male counterparts, potential female offenders are at a disadvantage in selection and recruitment into criminal groups, in the range of career paths, and access to them, opened by way of participation in these groups, and in opportunities for tutelage, increased skills, and rewards" (Steffensmeier, 1983, 1025). It is hardly surprising, therefore, that female involvement in professional and organized crime, such as large-scale burglary, fencing operations, gambling enterprises, and racketeering, continues to lag far behind male involvement (Commonwealth of Steffensmeier, 1986; Pennsylvania, 1991).

Several authors have speculated that gender dynamics shape both the types of strains males and females are exposed to and the emotional and behavioral responses available to them, thus leading to distinctly different outcomes (Cloward and Piven, 1979; Steffensmeier and Allan, 1986; Broidy and Agnew, 1997). Aggressive, externalizing behavioral responses are acceptable for males in various environments, whereas such responses are less commonly available to females. Thus, female responses to strain are more likely to be nonaggressive or self-destructive.

Chesney-Lind (1997) further clarifies how gender-specific strain differentially impacts similarly situated (e.g., in schools and neighborhoods) boys and girls.

Specifically, gender-based socialization patterns set the stage for the sexual victimization and harassment of girls that may trigger their entry into delinquency as they try to escape abusive environments. These girls often end up in the streets with few legitimate survival options, so they gravitate toward crime, drug use and dealing, and sexual exchange transactions. Interpersonal victimization as a female path to crime often involves a circular dynamic where victimization places some females at high risk for offending, which in turn puts them at risk for further victimization (Gilfus, 1992; Daly, 1994). This dynamic is especially problematic for minority and low-income women whose risks for both crime and victimization are already heightened by limited access to resources (Arnold, 1995; Richie, 1996).

Gendered Paradigm of Female Offending and the Gender Gap

Figure 1 depicts a gendered paradigm developed by Steffensmeier and Allan (1996 and 2000) for explaining female criminality and gender differences in crime. Drawing on and integrating factors suggested by other theorists, their framework recognizes that causal patterns for female crime often overlap those for male crime, but also proposes that continued profound differences between the lives of women and men also produce varying patterns of female and male offending.

At least five areas of life tend not only to inhibit female crime and encourage male crime, but also to shape the patterns of female offending that do occur: gender norms, moral development and affiliative concerns, social control, physical strength and aggression, and sexuality. These five areas overlap and mutually reinforce one another and, in turn, condition gender differences in criminal opportunities, motives, and contexts of offending. Key points are summarized here.

Gender Norms. Female criminality is both constrained and molded by two powerful focal concerns ascribed to women: (1) relational or domestic obligations (daughter, wife, and mother) and the presumption of female nurturance; and (2) expectations of female beauty and sexual virtue. The constraints posed by child-rearing responsibilities and other nurturant obligations are obvious. Moreover, the fact that female

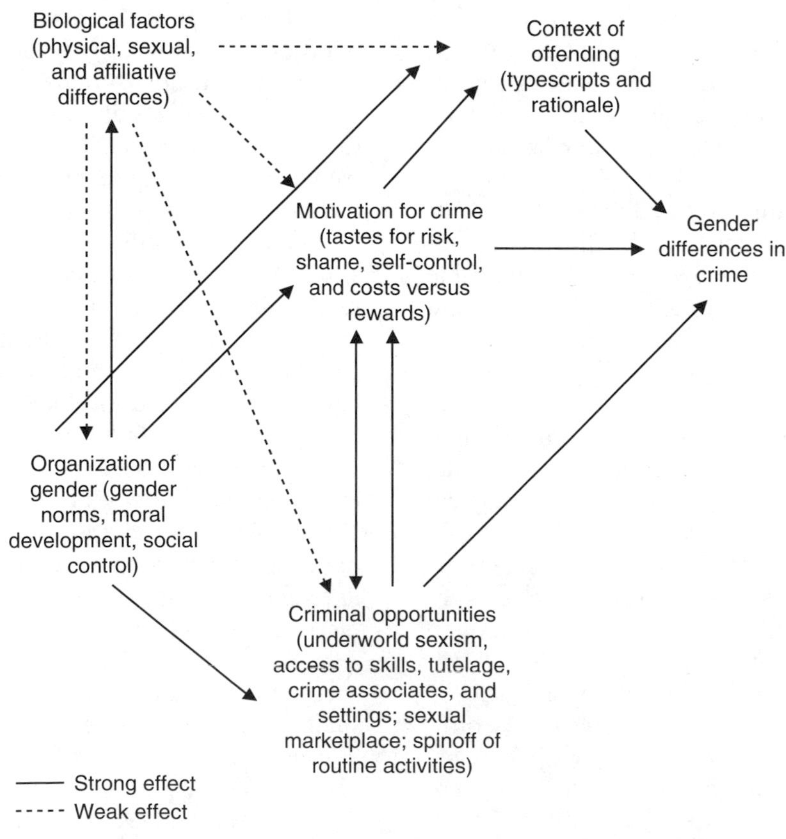

FIGURE 1

identities are often derived from the males in their lives can restrain deviance in women affiliated with conventional males but push wives or girlfriends of male criminals into accomplice roles.

Femininity stereotypes are the antithesis of those qualities valued in the criminal subculture (Steffensmeier, 1986), and crime is almost always more destructive of life chances for females than for males. In contrast, "masculinity" and valued criminal traits share considerable overlap. In addition, expectations of female sexuality may restrict the deviant roles available to women to those of sexual media (pornography) or service roles (prostitution).

Finally, female fear of sexual victimization reduces female exposure to criminal opportunity through avoidance of bars, nighttime streets, and other crime-likely locations.

Moral Development and Affiliative Concerns.
Women are more likely than men to refrain from crime due to concern for others. This predisposition toward an "ethic of care," whether via socialization or differences in moral development (Gilligan, 1982), restrains women from violence and other behavior that may injure others or cause emotional hurt to those they love. Men, on the other hand, are more socialized toward status-seeking behavior and may therefore develop an amoral ethic when they feel those efforts are blocked.

Social Control. The ability and willingness of women to commit crime is powerfully constrained by social control. Particularly during their formative years, females are more closely supervised and discouraged from misbehavior. Risk-taking behavior is rewarded among boys but censured among girls. Careful monitoring of girls' associates reduces the potential for influence by delinquent peers (Giordano et al., 1986). Even as adults, women find their freedom to explore worldly temptations constricted.

Physical Strength and Aggression. Gender differences in strength—whether actual or perceived—puts females at a disadvantage in a criminal underworld where physical violence and power are functional not only for committing crimes, but also for protection, contract enforcement, and recruitment and management of reliable associates.

Sexuality. Reproductive sexual differences and stereotypes of female sexuality both create and hinder certain criminal opportunities for women. The demand for illicit sex generates the opportunity for women to profit from prostitution that may reduce the need for women to seek financial gain through serious property crimes. However, although prostitution is a money-making opportunity that women may exploit, it is a criminal enterprise still largely controlled by men: pimps, clients, police, businessmen. Additionally, stereotypes of female sexuality limit the extent of female involvement in criminal groups, also predominantly controlled by males.

Collectively, the above aspects of the organization of gender serve to condition and shape features of female offending, including criminal opportunity, criminal motives, and contexts of crime.

Access to Criminal Opportunity. Limits on female access to legitimate opportunities put further constraints on their criminal opportunities, since women are less likely to hold jobs such as truck driver, dockworker, or carpenter that would provide opportunities for theft, drug dealing, fencing, and other illegal activities. In contrast, abundant opportunities exist for women to commit and to be caught and arrested for petty forms of theft and fraud, for low-level drug dealing, and sex-for-sale offenses.

Like the upperworld, the underworld has its glass ceiling. The scarcity of women in the top ranks of business and politics limits their chance for involvement in price fixing conspiracies, financial fraud, and corruption. If anything, women face even greater occupational segregation in underworld crime groups, at every stage from selection and recruitment to opportunities for mentoring, skill development, and, especially, rewards (Steffensmeier, 1983; Commonwealth of Pennsylvania, 1991).

Motivation. The organization of gender limits the subjective willingness of women to engage in crime, but inclinations are further constrained by criminal opportunity. Being able tends to make one more willing: Offenders, male or female, tend to be drawn to criminal activities that are easy and within their skill repertoire, and that have a good payoff with low risk. In addition, women's risk-taking preferences differ from those of men (Steffensmeier, 1983; Hagan, 1989; Steffensmeier and Allan, 1996). Men will take risks in order to build status or gain competitive advantage, while women may take greater risks to protect loved ones or to sustain relationships. Criminal motivation is suppressed in women by their greater ability to foresee threats to life chances and by the relative unavailability of female criminal type-scripts that could channel their behavior.

Context of Offending. The often profound differences in the context of female and male offenses is influenced by the organization of gender. Even when the same offense is charged, there may be dramatic differences in the setting, presence of other offenders, the relationship between offender and victim, the offender's role in initiating and committing the offense, weapon (if any), the level of injury or property loss or destruction, and purpose of the offense (Daly, 1994; Steffensmeier, 1983, 1993). Moreover, female to male contextual differences increase with the seriousness of the offense.

Miller's (1998) qualitative study of male and female robbery clarifies how gender shapes the context of robbery, even when motives are the same. Males typically target other males, and their robberies involve direct confrontation, physical violence and guns. Females most often target other females and seldom use guns. When women do rob men, they may carry a gun, but they are more likely to soften the target with sex than with actual violence. Miller concludes that male and female robbery may be triggered by similar social and cultural factors, but that gender shapes the actual manner in which those robberies are enacted.

Spousal murders also illustrate striking male–female differences in context (Dobash et al., 1992). Wives are far more likely to have been victims and turn to murder as a last resort. Husbands who murder wives, however, are more likely to be motivated by rage at suspected infidelity, and the murder often culminates a period of prolonged abuse of their wives. Some patterns of wife-killing are almost never found when wives kill husbands: murder–suicides, family massacres, and stalking.

The various aspects of the organization of gender discussed here—gender norms, moral and relational concerns, social control, lack of strength, and sexual identity—all contribute to gender differences in criminal opportunity, motivation, and context. These factors help explain why women are far less likely than men to be involved in serious crime, regardless of data source, level of involvement, or measure of participation.

Summary

The majority of girls and women involved in the criminal justice system have committed ordinary crimes—mostly minor thefts and frauds, low-level drug dealing, prostitution, and misdemeanor assaults against their mates or children—that are consistent with typical female gender roles. Women are far less likely to be involved in serious crime and rarely would be considered "career criminals." These generalizations are robust regardless of data source or measure of participation.

The gender gap for criminal offending is remarkably persistent across countries, population subgroups within a given country, and historical periods. This persistence can be explained in part by historical durability of the organization of gender and by underlying physical or sexual differences (whether actual or perceived). Human groups, for all their cultural variation, follow basic human forms.

Recent theory and research on female offending have added greatly to our understanding of how the lives of delinquent girls and women continue to be powerfully influenced by gender-related conditions of life. Profound sensitivity to these conditions is essential for understanding gender differences in type and frequency of crime, for explaining differences in the context or "gestalt" of offending, and for developing preventive and remedial programs aimed at female offenders.

Darrell J. Steffensmeier and Jennifer Schwartz

References and Further Reading

Arnold, R., The Processes of Criminalization of Black Women, in Price, B., Sokoloff, N., *The Criminal Justice System and Women,* McGraw-Hill, New York, 1995, pp. 136–146.

Bonger, W., *Criminality and Economic Conditions,* Little Brown, Boston, MA, 1916. This book was first published, in French, in 1905.

Broidy, L. and Agnew, R., Gender and Crime: A General Strain Theory Perspective, *Journal of Research in Crime and Delinquency,* 34, 275–306 (1997).

Campbell, A., *The Girls in the Gang,* Basil Blackwell, Oxford, 1984.

Chesney-Lind, M., Women and Crime: The Female Offender, *Signs,* 12, 78–96 (1986).

Chesney-Lind, M., *The Female Offender,* Sage, Thousand Oaks, CA, 1997.

Cloward, R. and Piven F., Hidden Protest: The Channeling of Female Protest and Resistance, *Signs,* 4, 651–669 (1979).

Commonwealth of Pennsylvania, *Organized Crime in Pennsylvania: The 1990 Report,* Pennsylvania Crime Commission, Conshohocken, PA, 1991.

Daly, K., *Gender, Crime, and Punishment,* Yale University Press, New Haven, CT, 1994.

Dobash, R., Dobash R.E., Wilson, M., and Daly, M., The Myth of Sexual Symmetry in Marital Violence, *Social Problems,* 39, 71–91 (1992).

Denno, D., Gender, Crime and the Criminal Law Defenses, *Journal of Criminal Law and Criminology,* 85:1 80–180 (1994).

Freud, S., *New Introductory Lectures,* Norton, New York, 1933.

Gilfus, M., From Victims to Survivors to Offenders: Women's Routes to Entry and Immersion into Street Crime, *Women and Criminal Justice,* 4, 63–89 (1992).

Gilligan, C., *In a Different Voice: Psychological Theory and Women's Development,* Harvard University Press, Cambridge, MA, 1982.

Giordano, P., Cernkovich, S., and Pugh, M., Friendships and Delinquency, *American Journal of Sociology,* 91, 1170–1203 (1986).

Glueck, S. and Glueck, E., *Five Hundred Delinquent Women,* A.A. Knopf, New York, 1934.

Hagan, J., *Structural Criminology,* Rutgers University Press, New Brunswick, NJ, 1989.

Harris, A., Sex and Theories of Deviance: Toward a Functional Theory of Deviant Type-Scripts, *American Sociological Review,* 42, 3–16 (1977).
James, J., Prostitutes and Prostitution, in Sagarin, E. and Montanino, F., Eds., *Deviants: Voluntary Action in a Hostile World,* Scott Foresman, New York, 1977.
Kellor, F., Psychological and Environmental Study of Women Criminals, *The American Journal of Sociology,* 5, 671–682 (1900).
Lombroso, C. and Ferraro, W., *The Female Offender,* Fisher Unwin, London, 1895.
Miller, E., *Street Women,* Temple University Press, Philadelphia, PA, 1986.
Miller, J., Up It Up: Gender and the Accomplishment of Street Robbery, *Criminology,* 36, 37–65 (1998).
Pollak, O., *The Criminality of Women,* University of Pennsylvania Press, Philadelphia, PA, 1950.
Richie, B., *The Gendered Entrapment of Battered, Black Women,* Routledge, London, 1996.
Steffensmeier, D., Sex Differences in Patterns of Adult Crime, 1965–1977, A Review and Assessment, *Social Forces,* 58, 1080–1108 (1980).
Steffensmeier, D., Sex-Segregation in the Underworld: Building a Sociological Explanation of Sex Differences in Crime, *Social Forces,* 61, 1080–1108. (1983).
Steffensmeier, D., *The Fence: In the Shadow of Two Worlds,* Rowman and Littlefield, Totowa, NJ, 1986.
Steffensmeier, D., National Trends in Female Arrests, 1960–1990: Assessment and Recommendations for Research, *Journal of Quantitative Criminology,* 9, 413–441 (1993).
Steffensmeier, D. and Allan, E., Gender, Age, and Crime, in Sheley, J., *Handbook of Contemporary Criminology,* 3rd ed., Wadsworth, New York, 2000.
Steffensmeier, D. and Allan, E., Gender and Crime: Toward a Gendered Theory of Female Offending, *Annual Review of Sociology,* 22, 459–487 (1996).
Steffensmeier, D., Allan, E., and Streifel, C., Development and Female Crime: A Cross-National Test of Alternative Explanations, *Social Forces,* 68, 262–283 (1989).
Steffensmeier, D. and Clark, R., Sociocultural vs. Biological/Sexist Explanations of Sex Differences in Crime: A Survey of American Criminology Textbooks, 1919–1965, *American Sociologist,* 15, 246–255 (1980).
Steffensmeier, D. and Terry, R., Institutional Sexism in the Underworld: A View from the Inside, *Sociological Inquiry,* 56, 304–323 (1986).
Steffensmeier, D. and Streifel, C., The Distribution of Crime by Age and Gender Across Three Historical Periods–1935, 1960, 1985, *Social Forces,* 69, 869–894 (1991).
Steffensmeier, D., Ulmer, J., and Kramer, J., The Interaction of Race, Gender, and Age in Criminal Sentencing: The Punishment Cost of Being Young, Black, and Male, *Criminology,* 36, 763–798 (1998).
Straus, M. and Gelles, R., *Physical Violence in American Families,* Transaction, New Brunswick, NJ, 1990.

***See also* Gangs: Female; Women and Addictions; Women as Offenders and Victims throughout History**

Genealogical Studies of Crime

Introduction

Crime and its underlying causal factors and explanatory characteristics have been the focus of numerous studies and research. However, little attention has been directed towards the role of genetic factors and their subsequent influence upon criminal behavior (Rutter, 1996).

Despite the relative neglect of genealogical explanations of crime in research, there exist specific biological characteristics that are believed to have an effect on resultant criminal behavior. These definitive biological characteristics are further categorized as either genetic and inherited (i.e., result of genes passed from parent to child at the time of conception), genetic mutations that transpire during conception or in fetal development, or a consequence of the individual's environment (Shah & Roth, 1974).

Family Studies

A review of the research on the relationship between heredity and crime reveals four fundamental research methodologies: family studies, twin studies, adoption studies, and gene–environment interaction studies (Walters & White, 1989). Dugdale (1877) conducted one of the first family studies on the inheritability of crime and found an arrest history along several generations of blood relatives. Goring (1913), using new statistical techniques devised by Francis Galton and his students, concluded that "crime is inherited in much the same way as are ordinary physical traits and features" (Vold, Bernard, and Snipes, 1998, 69). Guze, Wolfgram, McKinney, and Cantwell (1967) found more relatives with a sociopathic diagnosis in the families of 93 convicted male felons than what would be found in the general community. Likewise, Cloniger and Guze (1973) found a significant existence of a cross-generational link of criminality based on a diagnosis of sociopathy and prior arrest record between 86 female felons and 288 of their first-degree relatives. Despite the significant findings of these studies, Walters and White (1989) summarize several methodological limitations offered by Weissman et al. (1986) that are inherent in the design of the studies: lack of appropriate control groups, the existence of differential mortality, and the use of inadequate statistical procedures (465).

Although family studies have established that criminality tends to follow along family lines, because of the difficulty of disentangling the effects of nature and nurture, twin and adoption studies have subsequently received more recent attention in research due to their potential ability to control for the factor of heredity (Vold et al., 1998).

Twin Studies

Twin studies allow researchers to control for the heredity factor, instead of attempting to remove or reduce environmental factors. This is possible because of the explicit distinction between monozygotic (i.e., identical) and dizygotic (i.e., fraternal) twins. Monozygotic (MZ) twins have identical heredity because they are the product of a single fertilized ovum (egg), whereas dizygotic (DZ) twins share the same heredity as common siblings because they are the product of two eggs simultaneously fertilized by two sperm (Vold et al., 1998). Lange (1930), a pioneer in this field of study, found that in a group of 13 pairs of adult male identical twins, 77% of the pairs both had a record of imprisonment, as opposed to only 12% of the 17 pairs of fraternal twins studied.

Walters and White (1989) identify a substantial procedural flaw within twin study designs that predate 1965, drawing on observations of Christiansen (1970 and 1974) that "differential base rates may have still played a role in producing significant MZ/DZ differences in several of these studies." However, recent twin studies have yielded comparable findings to Lange (1930), where Rowe (1983) mailed out questionnaires to a substantial number of twins in the eighth through the twelfth grade and found a higher concordance for delinquent behavior in the MZ twins than among the DZ twins. A significant limitation of this study was that only approximately half of the questionnaires were returned (Walters & White, 1989). Christiansen (1977), in an attempt to control for possible similarity of training and environment, studied eight pairs of MZ twins reared apart and found a concordance for delinquent behavior in four of the cases. In summary of twin studies research, according to Walter and White (1989), "research on criminality in twins suggests the possibility of at least a qualified relationship between crime and certain genetic characteristics, but it is still difficult to unravel fully the effects of heredity and the environment using a twin methodology" (Walter and White, 1989, 468). Therefore, some researchers have alternatively selected to employ the adoption studies methodology.

Adoption Studies

According to Brennan, Mednick, and Jacobsen (1996) "adoptions provide a natural experiment, which can inform us regarding the existence and strength of inherited predispositions" (Brennan, Mednick, and Jacobsen, 1996, 15). Schulsinger (1972) conducted one of the most widely known adoption studies where he matched 57 psychopathic adoptees with 57 nonpsychopathic adoptees on various demographic variables and environmental characteristics. He found that psychopathy was more frequently discovered in the relatives of the psychopathic adoptees, as opposed to their nonpsychopathic counterparts. A second study conducted by Hutchings and Mednick (1975) found that the biological fathers of criminally convicted adoptees had a greater history of criminal convictions than the fathers of the noncriminal control adoptees. Moreover, they found the highest concordance of criminality for those adoptees (36.2%) who had at least one biological parent and at least one adoptive parent previously convicted. Despite the significant findings utilizing adoptions studies to investigate the relationship of heredity and crime, two limitations are worth noting. First, in some of the studies, the adoptive parents engaged in criminal activity at rates lower than that of the normal population, thus making generalization of the effects of the family environment difficult. Secondly, several of the studies found hereditary effects for minor and property offenses, but not for serious and violent offenses (Vold et al., 1998). Thus, Williams and White (1989) identify what they characterize as "a new trend in genetic research on crime" to consider the possibility of an interaction between genetic predisposition and the environment (Vold et al., 1998, 475).

Gene–Environment Interaction Studies

The interaction of biological characteristics and the social environment has increasingly become the focus of biological criminologists in their attempt to explain the roots of criminality (Vold et al., 1998). Gabrielli and Mednick (1984) conducted a study where they found that having both an antisocial biological parent and an antisocial home environment correlated with the adoptee's subsequent criminal behavior. Additionally, Van Dusen and colleagues (1983) examined the interrelationship of social class and adoptee's criminality. They found that both of the sets, biological and adoptive, of the criminal adoptee's parents originated from a lower social class. Despite the study's results, Williams and White (1989) discovered a considerable flaw in Van Dusen et al.'s (1983) design, "because the adoption agency in Denmark had a policy of attempting to match biological and adoptive family environments…[there was] no way of knowing conclusively whether environmental factors alone accounted for these results" (Williams and White, 1989, 475). Alternatively, Rowe and Osgood (1984) conducted a study that further indicated that both genetic (i.e. identical and fraternal twin comparisons) and environmental (i.e. delinquent peer association) factors contributed to an individual's criminal behavior.

Silberg and colleagues (1996) summarize the overall explanation for the relative inattention to genealogical explanations in criminological research in that "there is skepticism about finding a gene for crime, given that criminal behavior is defined by societal and cultural mores and encompasses a large and diverse range of behaviors" (Silberg et al., 1996, 76); nevertheless, Wilson and Herrnstein (1985) emphasize its importance as a viable research issue by emphasizing that "crime cannot be understood without taking into account individual predispositions and their biological roots" (Wilson and Herrnstein, 1985, 103).

According to Williams and White (1989) in order "to clarify genetic research on crime, greater precision is necessary, starting with the use of criterion measures that are more meaningful, replicable, and substantially narrower than the ones currently employed." Future utilization of more rigorous designs, such as a longitudinal or cross-situation model to study cross-situational consistency and the change in genetically influenced personality characteristics might prove to be beneficial (Rowe, 1987). In conclusion, studying the genealogical factors that influence, explain, and may even predict criminal behavior is a feasible prospective research endeavor, although it is essential that future researchers are not only cognizant of the previous methodological limitations evident in past research, but actively pursue innovative designs that employ more exhaustive methods.

Wesley Jennings

References and Further Reading

Breenan, P.A., Mednick, S.A., and Jacobsen, B., Assessing the Role of Genetics in Crime Using Adoption Cohorts, in Bock G.R., and Goode, J.A., Eds., *Genetics of Criminal and Antisocial Behavior,* John Wiley & Sons, Ltd., West Sussex, U.K., 1996.

Christiansen, K.O., Crime in a Danish Twin Population, *Acta Geneticae Medicae Gemellologiae: Twin Research,* 19, 323–326 (1970).

Christiansen, K.O., Seriousness of Criminality and Concordance Among Danish Twins, in Hood, R., Ed., *Crime, Criminology, and Public Policy,* Heinemann, London, 1974.

Christiansen, K.O., A review of Studies of Criminality Among Twins, in Mednick S.A. and Christiansen, K.O., Eds., *Biosocial Bases of Criminal Behavior,* Gardner Press, New York, 1977.

Cloniniger, R.C. and Guze, S.B., Psychiatric Illness in the Families of Female Criminals: A study of 288 First-Degree Relatives, *British Journal of Psychiatry,* 122, 697–703 (1973).

Gabrielli, W. and Mednick, S.A., Urban Environment, Genetics, and Crime, *Criminology,* 22, 645–652 (1984).

Goring, C., *The English Convict,* His Majesty's Stationary Office, London. Reprinted by Patterson Smith, Montclair, NJ, 1972.

Guze, S.B., Wolfgram, E.D., McKinney, J.K., and Cantwell, D.P., Psychiatric Illness in the Families of Convicted Criminals: A Study of 519 First-Degree Relatives, *Diseases of the Nervous System,* 28, 651–659 (1967).

Hutchings, B. and Mednick, S.A., Registered Criminality in the Adoptive and Biological Parents of Registered Male Criminal Adoptees, in Fieve, R.R., Rosenthal, D., and Brill, H., Eds., *Genetic Research in Psychiatry,* John Hopkins University Press, Baltimore, MD, 1975.

Lange, J., *Crime and Destiny,* Charles Boni, New York: 1929.

Lyons, M.J., A Twin Study of Self-Reported Criminal Behaviour, in Bock, G.R., and Goode, J.A., Eds., *Genetics of Criminal and Antisocial Behaviour,* John Wiley & Sons, Ltd., West Sussex, U.K., 1930 (1996).

Rowe, D.C., Biometrical Genetic Models of Self-Reported Delinquent Behavior: A Twin Study, *Behavior Genetics,* 13, 473–489 (1983).

Rowe, D.C., and Osgood, D.W., Heredity and Sociological Theories of Delinquency: A Reconsideration, *American Sociological Review,* 49, 526–540 (1984).

Rowe, D.C., Biometrical Genetic Models of Self-Reported Delinquent Behavior: A Twin Study, *Behavior Genetics,* 13, 473–489 (1987).

Rutter, M., Introduction: Concepts of Antisocial Behaviour, of Cause, and of Genetic Influences, in Bock, G.R., and Goode, G.R., Eds., *Genetics of Criminal and Antisocial Behaviour,* West Sussex, John Wiley & Sons, Ltd., 1996.

Schulsinger, F., Psychopathy: Heredity and Environment, *International Journal of Mental Health,* 1, 190–206 (1972).

Silberg, J., Meyer, J., Pickles, A., Simonoff, E., Eaves, L., Hewitt, J., Maes, H., and Rutter, M., Heterogeneity Among Juvenile Antisocial Behaviours: Findings from the Virginia Twin Study of Adolescent Behavioural Development, in Bock, G.R. and Goode, J.A., Eds., *Genetics of Criminal and Antisocial Behavior,* John Wiley & Sons, Ltd., West Sussex, U.K., 1996.

Shah, S.A. and Roth, L.H., Biological and Psychophysiological Factors in Criminality, in Glasier, D., Ed., *Handbook of Criminology,* Rand McNally, Chicago, IL, 1974.

Van Dusen, K.T., Mednick, S.A., Gabrielli, W.F., and Hutchings, B., Social Class and Crime in an Adoption Cohort, *Journal of Criminal Law and Criminology,* 74, 249–269 (1983).

Vold, G.B., Bernard, T.J., and Snipes, J.B., *Theoretical Criminology,* 4th ed., Oxford University Press, New York, 1998.

Walters, G.D. and White, T.W., Heredity and Crime: Bad Genes or Bad Research? *Criminology,* 27:3, 455–485, 1989.

Weissman, M.M., Merikangas, K.R., John, K., Wickramaratne, P., Prusoff, B.A., and Kidd, K.K., Family-Genetic Studies of Psychiatric Disorder: Developing Technologies, *Archives of General Psychiatry,* 43, 1104–1116 (1986).

Wilson, J.Q. and Hernnstein, R.J., *Crime and Human Nature,* Simon & Schuster, New York, 1985.

See also **Biological Theories of Crime; Genetic Theories of Crime; Wilson, James Q.**

Genetic Theories of Criminal Behavior

Behavior genetics is a discipline that studies the relative contributions of heredity and environment to variation in behavioral, cognitive, and personality traits. Many concepts and methods utilized by behavioral geneticists have been applied in recent decades to the field of criminology. Whereas no specific genetic theory of criminal behavior has come from research in behavioral genetics, strong support has emerged for what is called the genetic influence hypothesis. This hypothesis states that genetic factors substantially influence criminal behavior (as well as a closely related clinical condition known as *antisocial personality disorder*). The genetic influence hypothesis needs to be clearly distinguished from a genetic determination hypothesis that erroneously implies that genetics is all-important, and that environmental factors have no significant role to play in causing criminal behavior.

In recent years, scientists have located genes for specific human diseases, such as cystic fibrosis, using genetic mapping techniques developed as part of the genome project. The purpose of the genome project is to name and identify the functions of all genes in the human population. So far, no specific genes for criminal behavior have been identified. The reason is analogous to finding a gene for height, which has also not yet been successful. In both cases, if there are genetic contributions, they are likely to involve innumerable genes, making the identification of any one gene much more difficult than if there were truly just one gene involved.

Fortunately, there are several ways of detecting impact of genes on traits even when the specific genes are too numerous to identify with the current state of genetic knowledge. A number of these methods have been applied in the field of criminology, and as we will show, they have collectively provided strong support for the genetic influence hypothesis.

The nature of the evidence bearing on the genetic influence hypothesis can be subsumed under seven categories: family studies, twin studies, adoption studies, karyotype studies, biochemical marker studies, studies of genetic influences on correlates of criminality, and studies based on animal models. Each line of evidence is briefly discussed below (detailed evidence is provided in Ellis and Walsh, 2000).

Family Studies

Numerous studies have shown that criminality runs in families. This means that families in which one or more parents have been involved in at least one serious crime (according to either arrest records or self reports) are more likely than families in general to have a child with a serious offending history. Of course, this well documented pattern can only be considered consistent with the genetic influence hypothesis; it does not prove it, because family similarities in offending could reflect the effects of bad example or other "poor parenting" influences.

Twin Studies

Twin studies have been employed frequently to look for evidence of genetic influences on criminal or antisocial behavior. These studies take advantage of the fact that same-sex fraternal twins share an average of 50% of their genes, and identical twins share 100%.

A review of twin studies of criminal or antisocial behavior conducted since the 1930s revealed that nearly all of the studies found identical twins to be significantly more concordant (similar) in their offending tendencies than were fraternal twins. The average degree to which this was true was roughly two-to-one, mirroring the fact that identical twins are twice as similar as fraternal twins are in the number of genes they share in common.

As with family studies, the greater concordance in offending probabilities among identical twins relative to fraternal twins could be due to environmental influences, as identical twins may elicit more similar treatment by parents, teachers, and peers. Once again, we have evidence consistent with the genetic influence hypothesis, but it is not sufficiently strong to rule out other possibilities.

Adoption Studies

Unlike most people, adopted children have two sets of parents: One set gave them their genes, and the other set provided the family environment. Studying adoptees has been a gold mine for scientists interested in probing nature–nurture questions, including those who study criminal and antisocial behavior. If a sample of adoptees ends up more closely resembling their rearing parents for a trait, this favors the view that the adoptive environment is paramount. If they more closely resemble their genetic parents for the trait, this implies that genetic influences are more important.

Nearly all adoption studies conducted to date have been limited to male offspring (since their involvement in serious crime is much greater than that for females). Findings from these studies have been consistent with the genetic influence hypothesis. They indicate that one can better predict a male's involvement in serious criminality by knowing if one or both of his genetic parents had a criminal history than by knowing if one or both of his rearing parents did.

Karyotype Studies

Another method scientists have used to test the genetic influence hypothesis has been to examine chromosomal anomalies. The anomaly that has been most frequently examined is the XYY karyotype, in which males have two Y-chromosomes, instead of the usual one. Although the relationship between the XYY anomaly and criminal behavior was exaggerated in some of the initial studies carried out in the 1960s and 1970s, recent work has continued to suggest that criminality is more than five times as prevalent among XYY males as among XY males. Nevertheless, the fact that only about 1 male out of every 2000 is born with the XYY karyotype means that this genetic abnormality is of little consequence for the overall incidence of crime.

Another karyotype anomaly involves a clinical condition known as the Fragile X syndrome. There are one or more locations on the X-chromosome that appear to be unusually prone to mutate among persons with this genetic condition. Several studies have shown that individuals with Fragile X exhibit high rates of conduct disorders, learning disabilities, and below average IQ scores. These findings raise the possibility that persons with Fragile X will exhibit higher than normal offending rates, but this possibility has not yet been directly tested.

Genetic Influences on Various Correlates of Crime

The next line of evidence pertaining to the genetic influence hypothesis involves evidence that genes influence traits that are strongly associated with criminal behavior. In other words, if Trait A and Trait B are both strongly predictive of criminal behavior, and twin and adoption studies indicate that both of these traits are genetically influenced, it becomes probable that criminal behavior is genetically influenced (and that some of the same genes are responsible).

Here are examples of behavioral and mental health traits that have been found to be substantially correlated with involvement in criminal behavior that also appeared to be genetically influenced: alcoholism, attention deficit hyperactivity disorder, low intelligence, impulsiveness, negative emotionality, lack of empathy, and schizophrenia. Whereas one can argue that genes influence all of these traits without affecting criminal behavior itself, it is much more likely that some of the genes contributing to these traits are also somehow affecting the probability of offending. The evidence in this regard is especially strong in the case of alcoholism.

Biological Markers

A biological marker is a biochemical that is entirely, or almost entirely, under genetic control. Two biological markers have so far been linked to criminal or antisocial behavior. One is an enzyme known as monoamine oxidase (MAO), and the other is a brain receptor for dopamine known as the D_2 receptor.

In the brain, MAO appears to help break down neurotransmitters after they have performed their excitatory tasks. Unfortunately, for research purposes, it is virtually impossible to study MAO activity in a living brain. Therefore, researchers have had to study MAO activity in the blood, which is called platelet MAO activity. Several studies have linked low platelet MAO activity to criminal and antisocial behavior. Low platelet MAO activity is also associated with a number of correlates of crime such as impulsiveness, childhood ADHD, poor academic performance relative to ability, sensation seeking, recreational drug use, and especially alcoholism. Other interesting facts about MAO are that following puberty, its activity is substantially lower in males than in females, and that puberty roughly marks the beginning of a major elevation in the probability of males becoming involved in delinquent and criminal behavior.

D_2 receptors form on the outer walls of nerve cells (neurons), and have a special affinity for dopamine. Dopamine is the major behavioral motivating neurotransmitter and is found most profusely in the brain's "pleasure centers." The number and location of these receptors are determined almost entirely by genes. Since the early 1990s, several studies have found relationships between the prevalence of D_2 receptors in the brain and conduct disorders, official delinquency, and drug abuse. In addition, D_2 receptors have been linked to three correlates of crime: ADHD, gambling addiction, and alcoholism.

Overall, although, much remains to be learned about how platelet MAO and D_2 receptors might be related to offending probabilities, both of these biological markers appear to provide promising leads into the neurochemistry of criminal or antisocial behavior. It is all but impossible to explain why either of these two biological markers would be associated with criminal or antisocial behavior without first accepting the genetic influence hypothesis.

Animal Model for Aggressive Offending

The last line of evidence bearing on the hypothesis that genes influence criminal or antisocial behavior comes from studying nonhuman animals. This evidence is based on what is known as an animal model of human aggression. Nonhuman species exhibit within-species aggression that is strikingly similar to human assaults, murders, and rapes. In fact, a number of these acts have been photographed and published (Ellis, 1998). An animal model for human aggression does not prove that there is a genetic foundation for human criminal or antisocial behavior, but it provides another line of evidence consistent with such a conclusion. It is also interesting to note that the perpetrators of these "nonhuman equivalents of criminal behavior" are by and large males, just as in all known human societies.

Overall, seven lines of evidence pertaining to the genetic influence hypothesis have all converged to suggest that genes substantially influence (but do not determine) variations in criminal behavior. Nevertheless, a great deal needs to be learned about the location of the genes involved, and exactly how they interact with environmental factors to affect brain chemistry. The question is no longer whether genes affect antisocial behavior, but how and under what circumstances.

LEE ELLIS AND ANTHONY WALSH

References and Further Reading

Bock, G. and Goode, J., Eds., *Genetics of Criminal and Antisocial Behavior,* Wiley, Chichester, U.K., 1996.

Ellis, L., NeoDarwinian Theories of Violent Criminality and Antisocial Behavior: Photographic Evidence from Nonhuman Animals and a Review of the Literature, *Aggression and Violent Behavior,* 3, 61–110 (1998).

Ellis, L. and Walsh, A., *Criminology: A Global Perspective,* Allyn & Bacon, Boston, MA, 2000.

Fishbein, D., *Biobehavioral Perspectives in Criminology,* Belmont, CA, Wadsworth, 2001.

Rowe, D., *Biology and Crime: A Primer,* Los Angeles, Roxbury, 2002.

Walsh, A., *Biosocial Criminology: An Introduction and Integration,* Anderson Publishing, Cincinnati, OH, 2002.

See also **Biological Theories of Criminal Behavior; Evolutionary Theories of Criminal Behavior**

Genocide

Coined by the Polish-born jurist Raphael Lemkin in 1933, the word "genocide" consists of the Greek word "genos," meaning "race" or "tribe," and the Latin suffix "cide," meaning "to kill." Lemkin defined "genocide" as the intentional destruction of a nation or an ethnic enclave, the members of which are targeted because they belong to the group. As defined by Lemkin, genocide presupposed deliberate state action calculated to annihilate such groups, a level of meaning that has largely restricted the term to states and their agents until the present day.

Although the "Martens Clause" of the 1907 Hague Convention had left the door open to international prosecution for crimes "against the law of nations," genocide, as an actionable category of criminal behavior, did not come into being until the post World War II era. Decades before the international community recognized the crime of genocide, however, genocidal acts had been inflicted on civilian populations. One of the first genocides in the modern era was the slaughter of as many as 1 million Armenians by the Turkish government during World War I. (Arguably, the annihilation of the Armenians does not meet the legal definition of genocide, because the Young Turks may have been motivated not by the desire to eradicate the Armenians as a people, but by fears the Armenians were saboteurs in league with the Russians.) Whether or not the Armenian massacre qualifies as genocide, international jurists during the Great War referred to the Turks' mass homicide with a new phrase in international law, "crimes against civilization and humanity." For a brief time there was serious discussion within diplomatic circles after World War I of trying the perpetrators before an international court for the murder of their Armenian compatriots. These discussions never ripened into an international trial of the Turkish killers, but they established an early framework for dealing with governmental efforts to destroy civilian populations as such, a precedent that the designers of the International Military Tribunal (IMT) at Nuremberg would later draw upon.

The crimes of the National Socialist government against European Jews, Gypsies, Poles, Soviet P.O.W.s, and many others furnished the occasion for exposing defendants for the first time to prosecution for "crimes against humanity," of which genocide is a subcategory. In mid-1942 stories of frightful German atrocities—particularly the mass annihilation of European Jewry—began to trickle out of occupied Europe, prompting Churchill and Roosevelt to warn that the perpetrators would be accountable to an international tribunal for their crimes once the war was over. Two years later, in November 1944, Raphael Lemkin published a legal study of Nazi criminality entitled *Axis Rule in Occupied Europe*, in which he applied the term he had invented in 1933, "genocide," to the mass slaughter of civilian populations by the Germans. In December 1944, "genocide" appeared for the first time in Webster's New International Dictionary.

A singular feature of the Allies' approach to Nazi criminality was their insistence that only atrocities associated with the waging of war could be prosecuted by an international court. According to U.S. and British policymakers, the persecution or destruction by a state of its own citizens was a domestic affair, and thus not subject to international criminal jurisdiction. For this reason, the three main charges against the 24 "major war criminals" at the IMT in Nuremberg—namely, crimes against peace, war crimes, and crimes against humanity—were dependent on the charge of conspiring to wage aggressive war. Conspiracy to wage a war of aggression (count one of the indictment against the major German war criminals) was the glue that held the other charges together. In the absence of a connection to the war, a novel charge like crimes against humanity could not stand, since it would relate to a purely internal state matter—a matter that international law could adjudicate only on pain of violating the offending nation's sovereignty.

The limitation of the Anglo-Americans' approach is clear: it effectively barred prosecution of crimes committed by the Nazi government on its own citizens. German victims and citizens of the enlarged Reich who had suffered at the Nazis' hands understood this, and pressed the Allies to craft an indictment that would punish German perpetrators for crimes not easily categorized as "war crimes." Article 6(c) of the London Charter (the document that later served as the basis for the indictment) reflected these concerns by charging the 24 Nazi defendants with "crimes against humanity," defined as "murder, extermination, enslavement, deportation, and other inhumane acts committed against any civilian population, before or during the war, or persecutions on political, racial, or religious grounds. . . ." The phrase "before or during the war," however, effectively bound "crimes against humanity" to "war crimes," signifying the Allies' intention that the former remain an offense dependent on the Nazis' act of waging aggressive war.

The subsidiary status of crimes against humanity was finally abolished in the American "successor" trials, a series consisting of 12 proceedings against lesser Nazi war criminals that ensued after the IMT had concluded. Control Council Law #10, the jurisdictional basis of the successor trials, adopted language reminiscent of the London Charter's Article 6(c), but omitted the clause "before or during the war." The omission dissolved the subordinate position of crimes against humanity relative to war crimes, transforming crimes against humanity into a self-contained, independently chargeable offense. The significance of this moment in the history of genocide prosecution must not be overlooked. Prior to 1945, the international community had been loath to prosecute the mass killing of a civilian population carried out by a government if the victims were citizens of that government. In the years after 1945 until the present time, the world's nations shed their earlier reticence and declared their right to prosecute state officials for crimes against humanity, even if these crimes were the pure exercise of domestic sovereignty.

The crime of genocide was not charged against the 24 defendants tried before the IMT, but it did appear in charges leveled at defendants in the subsequent American proceedings. It also surfaced in trials of Nazi war criminals conducted in Poland, e.g., the trials of Amon Goeth (commandant of the Plaszow camp), Rudolf Höss (commandant of the Auschwitz-Birkenau death camp), and Arthur Greiser (Gauleiter of the Warthegau, the annexed portion of Poland). In 1949 the international prosecution of genocidal crimes received an enormous boost when the General Assembly of the UN approved the Convention on the Prevention and Punishment of the Crime of Genocide that became legally operative on January 12, 1951. Since then, at least in theory, perpetrators of genocide would be subject to international prosecution, whether or not their crimes were a purely internal matter. National sovereignty would no longer shield genocidal actors from criminal liability.

The UN Genocide Convention amplified Lemkin's definition of genocide to include the following acts, if performed with the intent to destroy, wholly or partially, a national, ethnic, racial, or religious group: (1) killing members of the group; (2) inflicting serious bodily or mental harm on group members; (3) intentionally imposing on the group "conditions of life" designed to eradicate the group physically, in whole or in part; (4) introducing measures calculated to prevent births within the group; and (5) forcibly removing children from the group to another group. The Convention requires its signatory nations to enact legislation to criminalize genocide within their borders, committed in peacetime or during a state of war, by "rulers, public officials or private individuals." Perpetrators are to be hauled before one of two tribunals: either a national court within the territory in which genocide was committed, or an international tribunal.

Three aspects of the Convention invite comment. First, the Convention suffers from an infirmity implicit in all international criminal law, the absence of mandatory international criminal jurisdiction. Inasmuch as most perpetrators of genocide are nation states, it is highly improbable that national governments will be inclined to conduct trials of their own agents, who commit genocide on behalf of—and frequently on the orders of—the very state that would prosecute them. The establishment in 1998 of the International Criminal Court (ICC) as a permanent tribunal for the investigation and prosecution of genocide, crimes against humanity, and war crimes is a pathbreaking step toward curing this defect in the Genocide Convention. Guided by the "principle of complementarity," the ICC could be an important gap-filler in the punishment of genocide because it prosecutes offenders only when states fail to do so. Second, the Convention tacitly affirms the distinction between genocide and crimes against humanity as defined by the London Charter: genocide applies only to perpetrators acting with the intent to destroy groups based on their national, ethnic, racial, or religious status, whereas crimes against humanity covers "inhumane acts" generally (including "murder" and "extermination") committed on "any civilian population." Presumably, the intentional destruction of political or social groups that do not fit the enumerated victim categories of the Convention, is not punishable as genocide (although it could be prosecuted as a crime against humanity). Third, the *mens rea* requirement of the Convention means that any mass killing without the intent to exterminate all or part of a specified group does not constitute the offense of genocide. As events of the last half-century have borne out, the practical effect of the *mens rea* limitation has been to insulate horrendous mass murders perpetrated by governments from prosecution as genocide. When we consider the victim group and *mens rea* limitations of the Convention in light of this recent history, the restricted utility of the Convention as an instrument of international justice becomes painfully clear. Mass killings in Cambodia (1975–85, 1.5 million victims), Bangladesh (1971–73, 500,000 victims), Vietnam (1945–87, 3.7 million victims), Argentina (1976–83, 25,000 victims), Chile (1973–90, 30,000 victims), Guatemala (1965–96, 60,000 victims), and many other countries have not been—and very likely could not be—tried as genocide. If we bring to mind that two of the most destructive periods of mass slaughter in the 20th century, Stalin's Russia (ca. 30 million killed) and Maoist China (ca. 35 million killed), are beyond the pale of the legal definition of genocide, the power of the Convention consistently to punish true enormities comes into question.

Since 1945 impressive successes and dismal failures have punctuated the record of international prosecution for genocide. Among the successes are the prosecution of war criminals for genocide committed in the Balkans during the 1990s, conducted by the International Criminal Tribunal for Yugoslavia (ICTY) in The Hague, and the prosecution by the International Criminal Tribunal for Rwanda (ICTR) in Arusha, Tanzania of the "machete" genocide of Rwandan Tutsis by Hutu perpetrators. A conspicuous breakthrough in the international prosecution of genocide was the arrest and indictment of former Yugoslavian President Slobodon Milosevic in 2001. At the time of this writing, the trial against Milosevic for human rights abuses (including genocide) is pending, and may not conclude until 2005. (Milosevic is not, contrary to media reports, the first head of state to be indicted for genocide; the former Prime Minister of Rwanda, Jean Kambanda, was convicted of genocide by the ICTR in 1998.) The prosecution of heads of state like Milosevic for genocide is an encouraging sign that the international community will hold high-level political leaders criminally liable for human rights violations. One also has reason for optimism based on the UN military campaign to stop the Serbian genocide of Kossovar Albanians in the late 1990s. Recent successes in combating genocide, however, must be balanced against dispiriting setbacks. The support of a superpower like the U.S. is indispensable to an effective international response to prevent and to punish genocide; yet, domestic and foreign policy considerations sap the will of the U.S. to bolster such efforts. Not until 1986—more than 35 years after the UN Convention on Genocide was passed—did the U.S. finally ratify the

Convention, the 98th country to do so. Political considerations induced the U.S. to overlook Saddam Hussein's resettlement and destruction of the Kurds in northern Iraq in 1987, as they did the refusal of the U.S. government in the 1990s to admit that genocide was being carried out against civilian populations in Bosnia and Rwanda. At the time of this writing, the U.S. has withdrawn its initial support of the ICC, thereby weakening the jurisdictional strength of this historic institution. Notwithstanding these failures, the resolve of the world community to sweep away antiquated notions of sovereign immunity and to hold government officials responsible for acts of genocide is an undeniable triumph of international criminal justice.

MICHAEL BRYANT

References and Further Reading

Alvarez, A., *Governments, Citizens, and Genocide: A Comparative and Interdisciplinary Approach,* Indiana University Press, Bloomington, IN, 2001.

Bassiouni, M.C., *Crimes against Humanity in International Criminal Law,* Kluwer, The Hague, the Netherlands, 1999.

Hinton, A.L., Ed., *Annihilating Difference: The Anthropology of Genocide,* University of California Press, Berkeley, CA, 2002.

Hinton, A.L., Ed., *Genocide: An Anthropological Reader,* Blackwell Publishers Ltd., Oxford, U.K., 2002.

Kuper, L., *The Prevention of Genocide,* Yale University Press, New Haven, CT, 1985.

Weitz, E.D., *A Century of Genocide: Utopias of Race and Nation,* Princeton University Press, Princeton, NJ, 2003.

See also **Homicide: Mass Murder and Serial Killings; War Crimes**

Germany, Crime and Justice in

Crime and its structure, causes and control have to be understood as dimensions of a country that are analyzed in the framework of Comparative Criminology (H.J. Schneider 2001). Crime and its examination and control are seen as phenomena that develop within social, economic and political structures. In this context the term social structure refers to a complex network of social elements (styles of behavior, values, interrelations, and institutions) that interacts with a relative continuity within a superordinate framework.

The scope and structure of crime within a country can be adequately assessed only if it is related to the frequency and severity of crime in other countries. The data sources of the dark-field and light-field are referred to for this purpose. The light-field reflects known, i.e. reported criminality. The term dark-field designates the sum of criminal acts that are actually committed and perceived by the population, but which have not become known to the criminal justice authorities (police, courts). In an international comparison Europe has a low crime rate in the light-field, and Germany—on a European scale—has neither a prominently low nor high position with respect to that crime rate (European Committee on Crime Problems, 1999). In judging the structure and severity of crime, Germany occupies a moderately high mid-field position. In the area of crimes of violence such as homicide, robbery and rape it holds a middle position in a European comparison. The same applies to drug-related crime, assault, burglary and car theft. The proportion of offenses reported to the police is 48% and lies in the upper middle range (van Dijk and Mayhew, 1993). If the dark-field is used as a basis for comparison, crime in Germany turns out to be lower than in North America and Australia (van Dijk, Mayhew, and Killias, 1990), but substantially higher than in Japan (Schneider, 1992). On a global scale—according to dark-field research—Europe occupies a middle position between Latin America and Africa on the one hand, both showing a higher frequency and severity of crime, and Asia with a lower frequency and severity of crime, on the other hand. Within Europe, Germany holds third place behind the Netherlands and Spain in the comparison of crime rates. With one exception, Germany's crime structure shows no conspicuous differences. Physical and sexual violence against women is relatively high in Germany.

The distribution of crime varies in different parts of Germany. Prior to reunification (October 3, 1990) the Eastern part (the former German Democratic Republic) had a lower crime rate than the Western part. This was a result of differences in the social structure. The degree of urbanization and the population density were lower in the East. The population was more homogeneous and the proportion of foreigners not as high as in the West. The social mobility of the population, particularly the possibilities of travelling, were strongly restricted. Material goods, especially cars, were not as widely available as in the West. The population, particularly the younger generation, was strongly controlled by the communist state security forces (Schneider, 1991). After reunification crime in the Eastern part of Germany rose more steeply than in the Western part (Kury, 1992). At present there exists both an East-West gradient and a North-South gradient in the distribution of crime (Kury, Obergfell-Fuchs, and Würger, 1996). More crime is found in the North and the East of the country. This is linked to a defective social structure. In those areas with a higher crime load one also finds more traffic accidents, a higher suicide rate, higher divorce and unemployment figures, more social welfare recipients and lower average wages.

The different groups within the population of Germany are affected to a highly varying degree by the commission of crimes. In the light-field youths and juveniles are over-represented in relation to their contribution to the overall population. In a self-report survey (Sutterer and Karger, 1994) over 80% stated that they had shown delinquent behavior already once in their lives. Over 50% replied that they had committed offenses in the year preceding the survey. Only slightly less than 10% of the legal infractions became known to the police. Childrens' delinquency has been neglected to date in Germany and has remained largely in the dark-field. In the majority of cases this type of delinquency regresses spontaneously, yet a small proportion of delinquent children is at risk of developing into violent, aggravated and recidivist juvenile and adult offenders. Women commit substantially fewer offenses than men. In the dark-field area of crime the sex ratio is 1 to 2 to the disadvantage of men as compared to a ratio of 1 to 3 in the light-field of suspected offenders. The sex-specific dark-field reflects the fact that female criminality is not as frequent and not as severe as male criminality and is therefore considered less dangerous and is consequently reported less.

Since the end of World War II crime and delinquency have increased. The reason for this is the modernization of society (technical progress, mobilization, urbanization, industrialization) that has, over the last few decades, destroyed traditional lifestyles and value concepts, but has not replaced them by new ones. In this way modernization has thus contributed to social developments entailing degradation of values and social disruption.

The increased victimization of various population groups depends on their status, their social position within the economic and power structure of German society. Marginalized and helpless population groups that have been pushed toward the edges of society often become victims. Hate crimes, which are aimed at the victim's being the way he is, against his race, his ethnic origin, his religion, are a part of political crime. Such crimes violate the human and constitutional rights of the victims and undermine the constitutional, democratic, pluralistic public order. They do indeed have social and group-dynamic causes as well. The most important approach in explaining hate crimes is nonetheless the cognitive-social learning process that the offender self-responsibly codetermines. Hate crimes are "message crimes" that inflict considerable physical, psychical and social damage. They convey the message that the population group to which the victim belongs is undesired in German society. Counter-messages by the criminal justice system are therefore indispensable for imposing an effective social control of xenophobic crimes of violence. Criminal justice must unmistakably make clear by its reactions that the offender is responsible for hate crimes and that hate crimes will not be tolerated. Criminal justice must clearly demonstrate—through a learning process—the kind of damage the offender has caused (victim empathy). Through the sanction of cognitive behavior training (cognitive restructuring) criminal justice must strive to make the offender "unlearn" his xenophobic attitude and his racist prejudices. By support signals from the criminal justice system and by therapeutic measures the burden of fear must be removed from the victims and the victim group, as fear often prevents them from reporting their victimization.

The status of women has indeed improved considerably over the past decades. Yet they continue to be frequent victims of male violence, because their improved status has, on the one hand, increased the tensions and conflicts between the sexes and, on the other hand, has led to women more resolutely opposing the use of violence by men and reporting it to the police at an increasing rate. In a special victimization survey 8.6% of the interviewed women reported having become victims of sexual acts of violence. Here 66% of all rape offenses occurred in the social near-field. The reporting rate was merely 18.9% (in view of an average reporting rate of 48% for all offenses in Germany). The low reporting rate demonstrates that male leading figures are predominant in the German criminal justice system and that women have to bear the full burden of exerting social control over their personal victimization.

Children are at great risk of becoming victims of physical abuse in the family (H.J. Schneider, 1993), although the use of violence in child education is prohibited by law in Germany. Violence in the family is the least controlled and most strongly underestimated form of violence in terms of frequency of occurrence and severity. This is because all the participants and confidants, the other family members, relatives, friends and neighbors regard family violence as a "private matter" and tend to keep it concealed. Nevertheless, the social and psychical consequences of family violence for the child victims are by no means harmless; family violence can in fact produce very severe and long-lasting psychical injuries ultimately leading to neurotic and psychosomatic disturbances and may result in repeated victimization at an adult age (victimization propensity). Through the violent model behavior of the parents, children learn—by parental rejection and frequent and hard physical punishment—that violence can apparently serve as an effective means of solving conflicts. In the family the older, stronger children quite often tyrannize their younger and weaker brothers and sisters, and the parents rarely intervene in favor of the victims. The violence interaction continues at school, where aggressive children tyrannize victimization-prone students (bullying at school). The majority of students and teachers fail to protect the victims. In families and schools, offender and victim careers develop in a way that has a negative influence in adult life.

The major part of sexually motivated crime remains in the dark field. Women and children do not report their sexual victimization to the police, because considerable social pressure is imposed on them to ensure that their victimization experience is neither disclosed nor reported. Women who have become rape victims are socially stigmatized when it comes to investigating the crime (the stigma of a "damaged commodity"). They have to bear the largest part of the burden during the criminal proceedings (blaming the victim). Criminal justice has proven to be largely unsuccessful in controlling rape. This is shown by the low indictment and sentencing rates. In a cautious assessment, the victimization rate concerning sexual abuse of children in Germany amounts to about 10–15% for females and 5–10% for males. Less than half of the child victims of sexual abuse ever talk to anyone about their ordeal during the period of their abuse. Even if sexual child abuse is exposed, a mere 10% of cases are reported to the police. Almost three quarters of sexually abused children deny having been sexually victimized, if asked. The child victims who feel helpless and trapped keep their abuse secret, because they fear, with due reason, the dramatic emotional reactions of the adults.

Elderly people constitute a particularly threatened victim group, because they are easily injured on account of their aging process. Elderly persons are fairly often abused or intentionally neglected in their families, especially by their partners, or in nursing homes (Schneider, 1996). They are beaten. They are chastised and threatened by nursing staff. Their money is taken away from them, or the money of elderly people who are no longer mentally able to manage their own affairs is squandered. Abuse of elderly people has increased over the last decades and occurs most frequently in the family, because it is in the family that they are still cared for the most. In general the victims refrain from reporting their victimization and do not disclose their abuse even in interviews on victimization, because they are dependent on the nursing staff abusing them and are afraid of being "dumped" into old age institutions. They often feel shame for the conduct of the persons victimizing them, their partners and children, with whom they live in close personal relationships. The institution, for example, the nursing home or the hospital ward in which elderly persons are subjected to abuse, is often socially isolated. The inmates can become mere work objects, lifeless abstractions for which the staff feels no more personal responsibility. Power is unilaterally distributed. The decision-making and control authority is completely in the hands of the staff members who feel superior and always in the right. Given such a unilateral distribution of power to the disadvantage of the elderly, the group of care personnel—which is basically given unlimited power over the powerless inmate group—is inclined to misuse its superior status to exert authoritarian and violent behavior. During the process of psycho-social degradation the powerless group of elderly victims quickly learns to accept its own depreciation, its growing dependence. Under these circumstances elderly individuals develop a tendency to feel defeated, inferior, weak, reproachable and guilty.

In the 1970s and 1980s, flexible offender interrelationships (dynamically functioning networks of relations) with a loose and variable structure have developed in Germany, and in particular in its densely populated areas. These are complemented by independently operating foreign groups with a more or less rigid hierarchical personnel structure that are active in Germany and operate from abroad, as of recently from Russia and other East European countries. Transnationally organized crime in Germany is centered on drug and weapons trafficking, production and proliferation of forged currency, extortion of protection payments, illicit gambling, prostitution and its promotion, and trade in humans. Asylum seekers and workers for the illegal job market are smuggled into Germany. High-quality cars are systematically stolen and smuggled into foreign countries. Criminal organizations are committing burglaries with central handling of stolen goods and theft of antiques, works of art and cultural objects. Credit cards are misused, nuclear materials are proliferated and toxic waste is illegally disposed of. Although new regulations and laws against organized crime were imposed in the 1990s, the German criminal justice system continues to pursue an offender-oriented instead of an organization-oriented strategy of investigation and control. Therefore, the system's criminal prosecution efforts will have no great success.

Apart from the objective threat of crime, the subjective threat is also a problem in Germany, since the latter results in a loss of quality of life. The term fear of crime implies the psychical anxiety of becoming a victim of crime, in particular of a crime of violence, and holds an affective, emotional dimension. The individual feels at risk of suffering harm, particularly physical or psychical injury. In Germany, fear of crime is more pronounced than the actual extent of victimization. Fear of crime is by no means irrational; it indeed has a real and cognitive basis. The extent of the victimization risk, which is based on everyday knowledge and experience, plays a certain role in determining the scope of fear of crime. In Germany the subjective feeling of insecurity has clearly diverged from the objective security situation. A feeling of insecurity and threat of crime is very widespread in the population, especially in Eastern Germany. Nonetheless, fear of crime in the U.S. is even greater than in Germany.

The intensified and over-emphasized feeling of being threatened by crime in the Eastern part of Germany stems from the general and personal existential fears that were associated with reunification and the resulting changes in lifestyle. Fear of crime is particularly high among foreign residents, women, and the elderly, as they are aware of their increased risk of victimization and also regard themselves as being especially vulnerable because of their insecure social and economic position in German society. Fear of crime is higher in large conurbations than in rural areas, since the signs of incivility are more widespread in big cities and since these signs are rightly viewed as symbols of social decay. They include, for example, signs of buildings falling apart and behavioral signs of social impairment. Moreover, the detachment of the fear of crime from its objective victimization basis draws upon the reality-distorting presentation of crime in the mass media. The dramatized reporting on criminal cases specifically lacks the analysis of the social and psychical causes and consequences of crime. Crimes of violence are often superficially assessed and prematurely explained by the "mental confusion" of the perpetrator.

The structure of the criminal justice system is determined by the social structure and the culture of a country. Culture is the subjective aspect of the social structure: customs, traditions, religious views and the ideology of a society. The economic and the power structure markedly influence attitudes, value concepts and stereotypes of a society. The criminal justice structure has its repercussions and effects on public opinion (interaction process). It is also determined by the scientific insights of a country. In Germany, the dogma of criminal law is predominant; forensic psychiatry has a considerable weight in the implementation of criminal justice. Criminology plays a marginal role within the faculties of law. Its significance in the social sciences is not very prominent either. The dogma of criminal justice is derived primarily from the philosophy and history of law. Crime policy builds on the results of empirical criminological research only to a minor degree. Criminological research itself is poorly funded and understaffed and therefore insufficiently developed. Here the traditional provincial, reality-distant and ideology-susceptible thinking of an influential part of German elites has a negative effect. There exist three directions within German sanctioning theory. They are discussed in the following paragraphs.

The psychopathology of German forensic psychiatry still has (or once again has) the greatest practical influence. A psychopath is understood to be a personality suffering from an abnormity or from whose abnormity society suffers. The term psychopath is extremely unclear, imprecisely defined, and does not constitute a diagnosis, but rather a stigmatization. German psychopathology sees the causes of crime in a personality disturbance and personality disorder of the offender, which is regarded as being beyond his or her control and is viewed as capable of being "therapied"—without the offender's involvement. Psychopathology fosters the opinion that offender therapy within or outside of criminal justice practice offers the best prospects for protecting society.

Reductionism, which represents the crime policy thesis of the least possible amount of intervention, the "do less" policy, has a lower practical significance. It rests on two considerations: Intervention-heavy sanctions inflict unnecessary suffering, as they fail to prevent recidivism to a greater degree than intervention-weak sanctions (exchangeability thesis). The causes of crime derive from a large spectrum of economic, social, personal and situational factors (root causes) that lie beyond the influence of the criminal justice system. The exchangeability thesis exclusively considers the "suffering" of the offender. The thesis of root causes neglects offender responsibility. Both reductionist theses do not give enough consideration to the harm suffered by the victim and to the security interests of society.

The lowest practical significance is given to pragmatically oriented liberal criminology. The latter sees the causes of crime in the social structure as well, but attributes the causation of crime equally to the individual, cognitive-social learning process, which is codetermined by the offender who holds personal responsibility. Crime is not based on a personality disorder, but on a learned behavioral disturbance for which the offender is himself responsible. This pragmatic-liberal direction within German criminology emphasizes the acceptance of responsibility by the offender, as demanded by the victims. This is seen as a prerequisite for a successful offender treatment. This direction recommends cognitive behavior training, which is not based on healing the personality disorder, but on the self-responsible "unlearning" of a behavioral disturbance, a cognitive restructuring of distorted views, and which is aimed at behavior and recidivism control of the offender. Finally, it is the intention of the liberal direction to establish the self-controlled assurance of an external informal control by the offender after his dismissal from the training program.

The sanctioning landscape in Germany looks as follows: Two thirds of adult criminal cases reported to the criminal prosecution authorities are discontinued. The remaining third is processed as follows: Almost 82% of offenders receive a fine. As many as 18% of adult offenders receive prison sentences, of which about two thirds are suspended on probation, so that somewhat less than 6% of all convicted offenders have to serve prison terms immediately. The current German adult criminal law thus essentially rests on two main sanctions: financial penalties (fines) and imprisonment. These are supplemented by suspension of sentences on probation. This leads to a certain sanctioning deficiency and weakness in the domain of minor and medium-severe criminality. The spectrum of penal reactions in this domain is too narrow. The limitations of fines, prison sentences and suspension of sentences on probation are becoming visible:

> Sentencing by way of a fine can lead to an undue financial burden in the case of economically weak offenders. Furthermore, a fine merely exerts a weak reprimanding effect. It is neither adequate for the need to resocialize the offender, nor for maintaining the security interests of society.

Sentencing by imprisonment often has, apart from the high correctional costs, a desocializing effect (prisonization, formation of prison subcultures). As a consequence, the offender quite frequently loses his job and home and his social relations with the members of his family are severely disturbed and disrupted. In a Western European comparison the incidence of prison sentences in Germany lies in the upper middle range. Compared to the U.S. substantially fewer prison sentences are imposed in Germany.

The implementation of suspending sentences on probation is insufficient. Probation represents intensive supervision and treatment in freedom. The German probation system is suffering from a lack of funds and personnel, so that the caseload per probation officer is too high. As a consequence, suspending sentences on probation frequently fails to fulfill the resocialization needs of the offender, the restitution interests of the victims and the security interests of society.

The offender-friendliness and the disinterest in the victim shown by the German criminal justice system became evident in the context of coping with the change in political system after reunification. The unusually high rate of waiving sanctions in prosecuting the use of firearms at the Berlin Wall, at the inner-German border, and in the sentencing of the judges who were responsible for imposing unlawful convictions in the former German Democratic Republic is striking. Merely 0.5% of all those accused were convicted. The discontinuation of proceedings due to illness and old age was frequent. The proportion of suspending punishment on probation, which was in the range of 90%, was distinctly overscaled. Only members of the military and political leadership and excessive offenders had to serve prison sentences. Border guards who had shot fugitives were regularly sentenced to up to two years of imprisonment that were suspended on probation.

The financial penalty (fine) is in many cases a sanctioning option that is too weak, and imprisonment one that is too strong. The costs of the criminal justice system are too high; its success rate (reduction of recidivism) is too low. In the medium term and the long term crime is increasing and fear of crime in the population is on the rise, too. The criminal justice system has to be adapted to societal change. Therefore, the introduction of suitable intermediate sanctions (sanctions with a mid-scale impact) and restitution as an independent sanction has been proposed, welcomed by the population, but rejected by the criminal justice authorities (Sessar, 1995; Kury, Kaiser, and Teske, 1994) on the grounds that these sanctions do not conform to German legal tradition, do not fit in with German sanctioning dogma, and entail a greater burden for the courts. It has been stipulated that the new sanctions are in contradiction to the proven German sanctioning system and that they represent an undesired incursion in that system. Experience gained in foreign countries was rejected on the grounds that this is not transferable to conditions in Germany.

The German Juvenile Justice Act is centered primarily on the rehabilitation of the juvenile offender, and on his education. Indeed, retributive guilt aspects are supposed to be considered as well. Over 50% of all known juvenile and young adult (14 to 21 year old) offenders are informally sanctioned (diversion) (Heinz, 1992). The origination of crime is explained by transient, development-induced personality disturbances of the offender that spontaneously regress. These disturbances are seen to lie outside of the offender's sphere of influence and control. Reaction avoidance or the mildest possible sanctions do not take the possibility into account that the juvenile delinquent action constitutes a phase within a developing offender career that has to be curbed. Reform efforts therefore strive to replace the one-dimensional offender orientation by a three-dimensional "restorative" paradigm. Retributive (retaliation oriented) and rehabilitative (treatment-oriented) paradigms attribute passive roles to the offender; the offenders are objects of punishment and surveillance or of treatment and education. Retributive and rehabilitative paradigms—which are irreconcilable—abstractly regard crime as violation of the law and of legal regulations. Crime, nevertheless, is primarily and above all a specific violation of the victim, community and offender. The restorative (restitution-oriented) paradigm is three-dimensional: it considers damage suffered by the victim, the community and the offender. The rehabilitative concept, which remains restricted to treatment of the offender's personality, only stands a chance if it is expanded and supplemented by the restorative concept, which is: the offender has to actively take on responsibility for his or her action (symbolic restitution) and to actively unlearn the delinquent behavioral sequences of events (scripts) that have led to the offense (cognitive behavior training). Finally, he or she has to learn to actively disrupt the relapse-action-chain (relapse prevention).

Progressive forces in Germany have realized that the reactive criminal justice approach, the reinforcement and professionalization of criminal justice, is insufficient for achieving successful social control. They are calling for the activation of proactive, informal social control by society, its groups and institutions. Since 1995 "German Prevention Days" have taken place every year. These are congresses at which practical crime prevention projects are presented. A "German Forum for Crime Prevention" that is intended to coordinate and take charge of all projects is currently being established. Nonetheless, there is a certain danger of political actionism. There is too little acknowledgement of the facts that prevention projects should be developed on the foundation of a criminologically recognized causative theory, that they should make use of a proven prevention method that has already been successfully implemented abroad, and that the projects will have to be staff- and cost-intensive if they are to be successful.

Hans Joachim Schneider

References and Further Reading

Albrecht, H.-J. and Teske, R., Germany, in Barak, G., Ed., *Crime and Crime Control,* Greenwood Press, Westport/ Conn., London, 2000.

van Dijk, J.J.M., Mayhew, P., and Killias, M., *Experiences of Crime across the World,* Kluwer, Deventer, Boston, MA, 1990.

van Dijk, J.J.M. and Mayhew, P., Criminal Victimisation in the Industrialised World: Key Findings of the 1989 and 1992 International Crime Surveys, in del Frate, A.A., Zvekic, U., van Dijk, J.J.M., Eds., *Understanding Crime: Experiences of Crime and Crime Control,* UNICRI, Rome, 1993.

European Committee on Crime Problems, *European Sourcebook of Crime and Criminal Justice Statistics*, Council of Europe, Strasbourg, France, 1999.

Heinz, W., Diversion in German Juvenile Justice: Its Practice, Impact and Penal Policy Implications, *Studies on Crime and Crime Prevention*, 1:1 (1992).

Kury, H., Crime and Victimization in East and West: Results of the First Comparative Victimological Study, *Studies on Crime and Crime Prevention*, 1:1 (1992).

Kury, H., Kaiser, M., and Teske, R., The Position of the Victim in Criminal Procedure—Results of a German Study, *International Review of Victimology,* 3:1 (1994).

Kury, H., Obergfell-Fuchs, J., and Würger, M., The Regional Distribution of Crime, *Studies on Crime and Crime Prevention*, 5:1 (1996).

Schneider, H.J., Crime, Criminological Research, and Criminal Policy in West and East Germany Before and After Their Unification, *International Journal of Offender Therapy and Comparative Criminology,* 35:4 (1991).

Schneider, H.J., Crime and Its Control in Japan and in the Federal Republic of Germany, *International Journal of Offender Therapy and Comparative Criminology,* 36:4 (1992).

Schneider, H.J., Violence in the Family, *Studies on Crime and Crime Prevention,* 2:1 (1993).

Schneider, H.J., Foreigners as Perpetrators and as Victims in Germany, in Schneider, H.J. and Holyst, B., Eds., *EuroCriminology,* Vol. 8/9, University Press, Lodz, Poland, 1995.

Schneider, H.J., Violence in the Institution, *International Journal of Offender Therapy and Comparative Criminology,* 40:1 (1996).

Schneider, H.J., Comparative Criminology: Purposes, Methods and Research Findings, in Pontell, H.N. and Shichor, D., *Contemporary Issues in Crime and Criminal Justice*, Prentice Hall, Upper Saddle River, 2001.

Sessar, K., Restitution and Punishment. An Empirical Study on Attitudes of the Public and the Justice System in Hamburg, in Schneider, H.J. and Holyst, B., Eds., *EuroCriminology,* Volume 8/9, University Press, Lodz, Poland, 1995.

Sutterer, P. and Karger, T., Self-Reported Juvenile Delinquency in Mannheim, Germany, in Junger-Tas, J., Terlouw, G.-J., and Klein, M.W., Eds., *Delinquent Behavior Among Young People in the Western World,* Kugler, Amsterdam, the Netherlands, 1994.

See also **Organized Crime: Irish, Jewish, and German Mobsters**

Glueck, Sheldon and Eleanor

For some four decades, Sheldon and Eleanor Glueck engaged in studying the lives of delinquents and young-adult criminals. A glance at their principal writings at the end of this encyclopedia entry illustrates how prolific the Gluecks' research is. The Gluecks' research vividly illustrated how complex a phenomena criminality was and continues to be. Whereas the Gluecks enjoy a somewhat diminished status due to critics' assertions about their work and the fact that many of these criticisms have become fact over time (as can be seen in the lackluster attention the Gluecks receive in most theoretical textbooks), their focus on scientific empiricism and many of their conclusions still hold true in the field today. Indeed, a great many of their findings have been replicated in many research studies.

Whereas the majority of criminological research occurring during the early 20th century had a sociologically driven theoretical basis, the Gluecks freely examined ideas pertaining to biology, psychology, psychiatry, public policy, and sociology; this was due to their involvement with Richard C. Cabot and Ernest A. Hooten, who both used ideas inherent to different academic disciplines in their own research. The Gluecks' studies were thus based on a vast array of theoretical perspectives and research methods, some that had been used before and others that had not. Just a small sample of the empirical procedures they used included the examination of official data records, the utilization of control groups, the use of the newest statistical procedures available at the time, and the use of such controversial methods as somatotyping and the Rorschach test. Another pioneering aspect of the Gluecks' work was the incorporation of female samples. At the time they collected their data, most criminological studies had focused predominantly on total male samples or male populations.

The Gluecks are responsible for compiling one of the most detailed and comprehensive longitudinal and cross-sectional studies ever assembled in criminology; this data collection began in 1930 in Boston. The data collected by the Gluecks ranged from official records to field studies, promoting a mixed methodological design. The data represented measures of delinquency, age, race, ethnic background, neighborhood contextual variables, IQ, physique, and family background characteristics. These data would lead the Gluecks to important findings for the field of criminology.

The role of the family as a causal factor for delinquency was critically explored by the Gluecks. Based on their ten-year study of delinquents in Boston, the Gluecks concluded that delinquency appeared to be caused by an interaction between a youth's physique and temperament, a family environment that included an ambivalence or hostility toward the child, and the usage of very harsh or very lax punishment techniques. This held true when factors such as age, race, neighborhood, and intelligence were held constant. The Gluecks also found that a majority of delinquents in their sample came from broken homes. While critics argued that these findings were skewed by the lack of objectivity from observers and that the type of punishment was inferred from statements given by the subjects and their parents, the link between family life and criminality has continued its relationship into the present.

The Gluecks' work also examined the role of a juvenile's somatotype, or physique, on potential delinquency. The Gluecks found that among their delinquent group, delinquents were more likely to have a mesomorphic (athletic) body build. Their study gave strong support for the influence of somatotypes on delinquent behavior; this was so because of their control group. No study prior to the Gluecks' research had a carefully matched control group (studies on somatotyping came from Sheldon's study of youth in a juvenile reformatory).

The Gluecks also explored other correlates of juvenile delinquency in their research. They examined the link between crime and unemployment (delinquents were 10 times as likely to be unemployable). They examined concepts inherent in the social learning approach (98% of delinquents were found to have delinquent friends, whereas only 8% of nondelinquents had delinquent friends). Nondelinquents did better in school than their delinquent counterparts. The Gluecks' research also illustrated that the onset of delinquency often preceded involvement with juvenile gangs. Follow-up studies indicated that individuals who were delinquent as children were more likely to be convicted of criminal behavior as adults between the ages of 17 to 31. This line of research also supported the age–crime curve, since the majority of offenders had desisted from criminal involvement after the age of 31.

In an attempt to put their findings to a more practical use, the Gluecks constructed a table to predict if juveniles would become delinquent. The Gluecks' Social Prediction Tables attempted to identify potential delinquents by the age of six or younger using such criteria as social background characteristics and psychological or character traits. The Gluecks argued that their table could be used by school administrators to identify potential delinquents within public schools. However, since these prediction tables are based on outdated procedures (such as somatotyping and the Rorschach test), the Gluecks' Social Prediction Tables have been generally discredited. It is their attempt to utilize their findings in such a manner that set the Gluecks apart from many earlier criminologists.

In 1972, while in the middle of writing *Of Delinquency and Crime*, Eleanor Glueck passed away, thus ending one of the most influential research partnerships in criminology's brief history. Sheldon Glueck would pass away in 1980, eight years after his beloved wife's death. Even though both Sheldon and Eleanor Glueck had passed away by 1980, part of their legacy would resurface in 1993, when Robert J. Sampson and John Laub found the Gluecks' data in a basement at Harvard. Although this study and these criminologists will be discussed in greater detail in another part of this encyclopedia, it can be mentioned here that Sampson and Laub's work with the Gluecks' data is considered one of the seminal pieces of the life course perspective.

Although it would appear to individuals who are new to the criminological discipline that the Gluecks' greatest contribution to criminology was the collection of their infamous data set on 500 juvenile delinquents and 500 nondelinquents utilized in Sampson and Laub's groundbreaking work on the life course perspective, the Gluecks' commitment to the advancement of knowledge on criminological phenomena through scientific, empirical methods and using their findings to instruct public policy is their true legacy.

SEAN MADDAN

Biographies

Sheldon Glueck: Born in Warsaw, Poland, August 15, 1896; son of a steelworker. Educated at George Washington University, A.B., 1920; Harvard University, A.M., 1922, PhD., 1924; University of Thessaloniki, Greece, LL.D., 1948; Harvard University, S.D., 1958; George Washington University, S.S.D., 1963. Married Eleanor Touroff, 1922. Instructor, Harvard Department of Social Ethics, 1925–1929; assistant professor, Harvard Law School, 1929–1931; professor, Harvard Law School, 1931–1950; Roscoe Pound Professorship of Law, Harvard Law School, 1950–1963. Died in Cambridge, Massachusetts, March 10, 1980. The Sellin-Glueck Award established, 1974.

Eleanor Touroff Glueck: Born in Brooklyn, New York, April 12, 1898; daughter of a real estate salesman. Educated at Barnard College, A.B., 1919; New York School of Social Work, 1921; Harvard School of Education, M.Ed., 1923, Ed.D., 1925; Harvard University, S.D., 1958. Married Sheldon Glueck, 1922. Head worker, Dorchester Welfare Center in Massachusetts, 1921–1922; research criminologist, Harvard Department of Social Ethics, 1923–1928; research assistant, Harvard Law School, 1928–1972; Trustee, Judge Baker Guidance Center in Boston, 1932–1972. Died in Cambridge, Massachusetts, September 25, 1972. The Sellin-Glueck Award established, 1974.

Selected Writings

500 Criminal Careers, New York: A. A. Knopf, 1930
Later Criminal Careers, London, H. Milford: Oxford University Press, 1937
Juvenile Delinquents Grown Up, New York: Commonwealth Fund, 1940
Criminal Careers in Retrospect, New York: The Commonwealth Fund, 1943
Unraveling Juvenile Delinquency, Cambridge, Massachusetts: Harvard University Press, 1950
Crime and Correction: Selected Papers, Cambridge, Massachusetts: Addison-Wesley Press, 1952
Delinquents in the Making: Paths to Prevention, New York: Harper, 1952
Physique and Delinquency, New York: Harper, 1956
Predicting Delinquency and Crime, Cambridge: Harvard University Press, 1959
Family Environment and Delinquency, Boston: Houghton Mifflin, 1962
Ventures in Criminology: Selected Recent Papers, Cambridge: Harvard University Press, 1964
Five Hundred Delinquent Women, New York: Kraus Reprint Corporation, 1934, 1965
One Thousand Juvenile Delinquents: Their Treatment by Court and Clinic, New York: Kraus Reprint Co., 1934, 1965
Delinquents and Nondelinquents in Perspective, Cambridge: Harvard University Press, 1968

References and Further Reading

Glueck, S., *Lives of Labor, Lives of Love, Fragments of Friendly Autobiographies,* New York, Exposition Press, 1977.
Glueck, S. and Glueck, E., *Of Delinquency and Crime: A Panorama of Years of Search and Research,* Charles C. Thomas, Publisher, Springfield, IL, 1974.
Raine, A., *The Pscyhopathology of Crime: Criminal Behavior as a Clinical Disorder,* Academic Press, New York, 1993.
Sampson, R.J. and Laub, J.H., *Crime in the Making: Pathways and Turning Points through Life,* Harvard University Press, Cambridge, MA, 1993.
Vold, G.B., Bernard, T.J., and Snipes, J.B., *Theoretical Criminology,* 5th ed., Oxford University Press, New York, 2002.
Wilson, J.Q. and Herrnstein, R.J., *Crime and Human Nature: The Definitive Study of the Causes of Crime,* Simon and Schuster, New York, 1985.

See also **Biological Theories of Criminal Behavior; Body-Type Theories of Criminal Behavior**

Grand Juries

The grand jury is a group of citizens who come together in secrecy to hear evidence of an alleged crime. Their purpose is to determine if probable cause exists to believe a crime has been committed and the defendant committed that crime. If the grand jury concludes that probable cause exists, a formal charging document, known as an indictment, is filed in the criminal court having jurisdiction.

The modern grand jury evolved from English common law. In 1166, the Assize of Clarendon provided that every six months sixteen men from a particular area were required to come to court and name every person who had a reputation for committing certain serious offenses. The sheriff of that jurisdiction then arrested the accused persons. These early groups of citizens were the predecessors of contemporary grand juries. Over the next fifty years, these original juries were allowed to determine whether the stated accusations were credible. By the early 14th century, English law had again been amended to allow a justice of the peace to bring allegations of wrongdoing to the jury members. If the jurors did not feel the justice of the peace presented sufficient evidence, the accused was allowed to go free. Grand juries thus acquired the power to charge criminals formally.

The grand jury system came to the U.S. with the colonists and was implemented as part of the new British colonial government. By the time of the Declaration of Independence, the grand jury had further developed into an institution that was becoming more powerful as an entity separate from government. In fact, it was seen as a valuable protection for citizens against strong government. The valuable protections afforded by the grand jury system were incorporated in the Constitution. The Fifth Amendment of the U.S. Constitution holds, among other things, that no person will be prosecuted in a felony case without a grand jury hearing. Although the Supreme Court ruled in *Hurtado v. California* (110 U.S. 516, 1884) that this right only applies to federal prosecutions, many states have incorporated this protection into their constitutions as well. Currently, fifteen states and the District of Columbia require grand juries to hear evidence for felony indictments, four require grand jury hearings in all crimes, six require them only in capital cases, twenty-five have the option to use a grand jury, and only one state never uses a grand jury. Although the grand jury was abolished in England in 1933, it still remains a vital component of the criminal justice system in the U.S.

The activities of the modern grand jury differ a great deal from its twelfth-century predecessor. The modern federal grand jury usually consists of twenty-three citizens chosen from the voting rolls. State grand juries vary in size. Depending on the jurisdiction, jurors serve for a period of six months or less. The grand jury meets in secrecy under the direction of the prosecuting attorney. In most cases, the grand jury is used for the sole purpose of hearing evidence presented by the prosecutor and determining if that evidence constitutes probable cause. The grand jury can also be used to investigate crimes, and it is especially useful in those crimes where it is important to keep evidence and the identity of witnesses a secret. Jurors do not hear evidence from defense attorneys, thus giving it the distinction of being the only nonadversarial procedure in an otherwise adversarial justice system.

Grand juries have the power to call witnesses, and in *United States v. Calandra* (414 U.S. 338, 1974), it was determined by the Supreme Court that they could consider hearsay and other evidence that would likely be inadmissible in a criminal trial. In *U.S. v. Mandujano* (425 U.S. 564, 1976), the Supreme Court held that witnesses have no constitutional right to have an attorney present in grand jury proceedings. To remedy this ruling, some states have developed statutes that allow grand jury witnesses to have counsel present. If a person refuses to testify before a grand jury, or refuses to answer a question presented to them by the grand jury, they can be held in contempt and jailed under certain circumstances.

Even if a witness invokes a constitutionally protected right, such as the Fifth Amendment right against self-incrimination, the grand jury can still compel testimony. By granting "prosecutorial" immunity, the government promises that any testimony given by a particular witness that may be incriminating will later be inadmissible in court in the prosecution of that witness. Grand juries can also offer something called "use" immunity. This immunity guarantees that neither the witness's testimony, nor any evidence gathered as a result of that testimony, will be used to prosecute the witness at a later time. If either immunity is granted, the witness can no longer invoke the Fifth Amendment right to be free from self-incrimination. Another protection offered to witnesses and members of a grand jury is the fact that the evidence and testimony presented are kept secret until the expiration of the term of that grand jury.

After the government concludes the presentation of evidence, or the grand jury terminates an investigation, one of two decisions will be reached. The grand jury can issue a "true bill," meaning there has been a finding of probable cause to believe that the accused committed the crime or crimes. They may also issue a no true bill, meaning there was insufficient evidence for a finding probable cause. The issuance of a true bill of indictment results in the formal charge of a crime, and the case is placed on the trial docket. The number of grand jurors required to vote for a true bill in order for a person to be indicted varies from state to state, with most states requiring a two thirds or more vote. The federal government requires that 12 of the 23 members vote for a true bill before an indictment is issued.

In recent years, the grand jury system has been subjected to occasional criticism. Some opponents of the grand jury system assert that the protection once afforded to accused persons has now diminished, since the grand jury is usually under the complete control of the prosecuting attorney. Many grand jury opponents fear that grand juries have the potential to become overzealous in the performance of the investigative function. These concerns focus on fear that a "runaway" grand jury will probe matters that should or need not be investigated. Still other opponents point to the immense cost as a reason for doing away with a grand jury system. Although opponents of this system feel it should be abolished, prosecutors and other government officials are just as quick to point out that the grand jury is a very necessary tool, especially in cases involving organized crime, public corruption, and other cases where secrecy is desirable. Despite criticism, the grand jury system is rich in history and embedded in the U.S. Constitution. It is unlikely that it will be abolished in the foreseeable future.

DENNIS LASTER

References and Further Reading

Abadinsky, H., *Law and Justice: An Introduction to the American Legal System,* 3rd ed., Nelson-Hall Publishers, Chicago, IL, 1995.

Edwards, G.J., The Grand Jury, AMS Press, New York, 1973.

Halstead, J., The American Grand Jury–Due Process of Rights Regress?, *Criminal Justice Policy Review,* 2:2, 103–117 (1987).

Hochstedler-Steury, E. and Frank, N., Criminal Court Process, West Publishing, Minneapolis, MN, 1996.

Sullivan, T.P. and Nachman, R.D., If It Ain't Broke, Don't Fix It: Why the Grand Jury's Accusatory Function Should Not Be Changed, *Journal of Criminal Law and Criminology,* 75:4, 1047–1069 (1984).

See also **Juries and Juror Selection**

Greece, Crime and Justice in

"As early as 1833, the Government Gazette of the Kingdom of Greece published some figures of crime; the first volume of criminal statistics, however, did not appear until 1912" (Spinellis, 1997, 67). Official information about the extent of crime in Greece has been solely drawn from criminal justice system statistics to date. In particular, three sources of information exist: (1) police statistics record crimes known to the police and information on arrested suspects, (2) criminal court statistics record convictions and information on the pretrial procedures, and (3) prison statistics provide information on detainees, length of sentences, prison safety measures, the movement of detainees waiting trial and those on probation or parole. The last two statistics have been published annually since 1957 by the National Statistical Service of Greece in *Statistics of Justice. Civil Justice, Criminal Justice Statistics and Prison Statistics*; since 1971, this volume has included police statistics. Police statistics also have been published by the Ministry of Public Order in the *Statistical Yearbook of Police* since 1984. "Both publications follow the classifications of the Greek Penal Code as well as contain data on violations of other Special Laws" (Spinellis, 1997, 47).

The Greek Penal Code distinguishes three broad categories of crimes according to their seriousness: felonies, misdemeanors and petty offenses. Greek crime statistics cover only the first two. Felonies include crimes such as homicide, rape, and robbery. Misdemeanors refer to crimes such as simple theft and simple assault. According to this classification, the following broad categories of crimes are listed in the *Statistics of Justice. Civil Justice, Criminal Justice Statistics and Prison Statistics*: (1) crimes against the person (e.g., homicide and rape), (2) crimes against honor (e.g., libel

Table 1. Police Recorded Offenses in Greece per 100,000 Population During the Period 1990–1998*

	Year								
Offense	**1990**	**1991**	**1992**	**1993**	**1994**	**1995**	**1996**	**1997****	**1998****
Intentional Homicide	2.0	2.2	2.5	2.4	2.5	2.7	3.0	3.3	3.2
Assault	65	67	66	67	72	65	61	62	65
Rape	1.9	2.4	2.7	2.6	2.5	2.2	1.7	2.0	2.0
Robbery	11	12	15	14	12	15	14	18	21
Theft (Total)	431	502	489	520	548	706	721	801	801
Theft of Motor Vehicles	68	84	82	93	98	121	118	—	—
Burglary	265	309	303	315	325	403	405	—	—
Drug Offenses	19	20	20	15	18	28	40	56	62

*The figures for 1990–1996 are taken from the Council of Europe (1999) *European Sourcebook of Crime and Criminal Justice Statistics*, PC-S-ST (99) 8 DEF, Strasbourg.

**The figures for 1997–1998 are from Nestoras E. Kourakis (1999) Εκθεση για την εξέλιξη τηζ εγκληματικότηταζ στη σημεινή Ελλάσα [Report on the development of criminality in today's Greece] *Ποινική Δικαιοσύνη [Penal Justice]* 10/1999: 1036–1041. The latter source is missing data for theft of motor vehicles and burglary.

and defamation), (3) crimes against property (e.g., theft and embezzlement), (4) crimes against the community (e.g., arson and possession of explosives), (5) all other crimes of the Penal Code, (6) violations of market laws, (7) violations of labor protection laws, (8) violations of laws relating to automobiles, (9) violations of all other Special Penal laws and statutes, and (10) crimes of the Marital Penal Code (Spinellis, 1997, 66–67).

Crime Rates and Trends

Before the 1990s, more than 25% of all criminal convictions concerned violations of traffic laws. The next two largest categories were violations of market laws (16.6%) and crimes against the person (13.9%).

Table 1 presents crime rates per 100,000 population of intentional homicide (total and completed), assault, rape, robbery, theft (total and motor vehicle), burglary, and drug offenses during the period 1990–1998. The data refer to police statistics, and deviations from the common definitions are subnoted. The incidence of most serious crimes has slightly increased, except for assault and rape, which have remained roughly constant, and drug offenses, which more than doubled during the 1990s. Table 2 gives the proportion of suspects per 100,000 population for the same crime types during the same period. These data show that except for drug offenders (whose numbers have sharply increased) the proportion of offending for all crime types has essentially remained stable during the decade. The reader ought to be cautioned that police statistics do not necessarily reflect the true volume of crime. The dark figure of crime unknown to the police in Greece may vary considerably from the official statistics depending on such factors as crime type, offenders' characteristics, victim characteristics, and police effectiveness. (Zarafonitou, 1995, pp. 36–37).

Considering economic correlates of crime there seems to be a significant relationship between car ownership (an index of prosperity) and property crimes in Greece in the period between 1974 and 1986 (Spinellis, 1997). Thus, during this time, availability of targets seemed to be associated with increases in property crimes. Since the mid-1980s Greece has received a relatively large number of economic refugees who arrived from the ex-socialist and some Asian and African countries. This tremendous social change has affected crime trends (Spinellis, 1997). The contribution of migrants to the total crime rate used to be negligible, although it rapidly increased in the late 1990s to roughly 50% for crimes against property (robbery and theft) and organized crime (Kourakis, 1999).

It should be noted that to date in Greece, no official or nationally representative self-report victimization surveys exist. Thus there are no estimates of the prevalence or incidence of crimes that do not come to the attention of the criminal justice system, including tax evasion and domestic violence. Interested readers should see Spinellis (1997), who gives an overview of the sparse data available on such crimes and speculates about the size of the dark figure of crime in Greece.

Greek officials have become very concerned about organized crime due to the potential free movement of individuals and goods within the countries of the European Union (EU) and the strategic position of Greece in drug and gun trafficking. Numbers of small

Table 2. Suspects in Greece per 100,000 Population During the Period 1990–1998*

Offense	Year								
	1990	1991	1992	1993	1994	1995	1996	1997	1998
Intentional Homicide	2	2	3	3	3	3	3	3	3
Assault	73	75	74	75	80	73	69	68	72
Rape	2	2	3	2	2	2	1	2	2
Robbery	6	7	12	12	8	9	5	5	8
Theft (Total)	75	93	97	102	95	97	66	66	76
Theft of Motor Vehicle	11	13	18	19	17	16	7	—	—
Burglary	43	53	52	58	53	48	34	—	—
Drug Offenses	29	29	32	23	28	41	59	—	—

*Sources are the same as those listed in Table 1. Kourakis (1999) is missing data on theft of motor vehicles, burglary, and drug offenses for 1997–1998 for suspects.

criminal groups (3–10 individuals) operate in the country. Albanian, Russian, Bulgarian, Rumanian, Turkish, Iraqi, Pakistani, and Bangladeshi organized criminal groups operate in Greece, apart from native criminal groups. Their criminal activities include drug, gun, cigarette and alcohol trafficking, illegal emigration, motor vehicle and other thefts, robberies, burglaries, prostitution of women and children, abduction for ransom, money laundering, and fraud (Kourakis, 1999; Directorate of Public Safety, Greek Police Headquarters 2000). A number of preventive measures have been undertaken, in many cases in coordination with other countries that are members of the EU (Directorate of Public Safety, Greek Police Headquarters 2000).

Crime Prevention

Despite its status as a Western industrialized country and a large movement of the population from provinces to the cities (predominately Athens) after World War II, Greece has relied on informal social controls. Strong family ties and friendship networks, along with adequate governmental benefits for the poor, the unemployed, and children, have kept crime rates low. Indeed, among 35 European countries, Greece is still rated in the lowest one third in intentional homicide, according to police and health statistics (Council of Europe, 1999).

Until recent times, Greece depended mostly on the criminal justice system (the police and penal system) for crime prevention. With a 1999 law (Law 2713/99), the Ministry of Public Order initiated the constitution of Local Committees of Criminality Prevention (LCCP). These committees are organized by local authorities in communities with a population of at least 3000 and consist of 5 to 11 members who serve on a voluntary basis for a three year period. Members are individuals with relevant expertise, such as judges, criminologists, psychologists, sociologists, police officers, social workers, and doctors, as well as representatives of local businesses and social organizations. Their aims are to (1) create a crime prevention program appropriate for their locality, (2) offer advice on relevant topics to mayors and other interested parties, (3) collaborate with other LCCPs of nearby communities, and (4) organize public conferences and seminars that offer information and crime prevention awareness.

The 1999 law establishing the LCCPs was the first attempt in Greece officially to involve others apart from the criminal justice system in crime prevention. It incorporates the three types of crime prevention (i.e., community, situational and developmental) as noted by Tonry and Farrington (1995). The Minister of Public Order (Police Review, 2000) suggested a number of activities that the LCCPs may undertake. First they could reduce crime opportunities and gains, increase the risks that offenders will be caught, and examine the conditions that facilitate criminal activities in their locality. Second, the LCCPs might help the local community to react immediately to crimes committed by young, first-time offenders in order to stop them from further involvement with crime and keep them out of the criminal justice system. Third, LCCPs could assist known criminals to desist from crime by providing them with the means for a crime-free life, such as education, job training and substance abuse therapy. To these ends, a Group of Experts for Coordinating and Facilitating the LCCPs' Work has been established in the Ministry of Public Order. Other programs implemented by LCCPs may include those seeking to reduce after-school violence, social isolation, the prostitution of women and children, drug abuse, domestic violence, and the fear of crime, as well as programs that promote adequate lighting of public spaces and stronger friendship networks within the neighborhood.

Some academics have expressed concerns that the LCCPs inadvertently might contribute to the crime problem by labeling young people as criminals in their own neighborhood. Others have suggested that, however well-meaning, LCCPs will be unable to control international crimes (including marketing and trafficking) that affect Greece (Panousis, 2000).

ANDROMACHI TSELONI AND CHRISTINA ZARAFONITOU

References and Further Reading

Council of Europe, *European Sourcebook of Crime and Criminal Justice Statistics,* Council of Europe, PC-S-ST (99) 8 DEF, Strasbourg, France, 1999.

Directorate of Public Safety, Greek Police Headquarters, Ετήσιαέκθεση για το οργανωμένο έγκλημα στη Ελλάδα (έτους 1999) [Annual report about the organized crime in Greece (year 1999)] *Αστυομική Επιθεώρηση [Police Review]*, August/September issue, 498–502 (2000).

The Editor, Η εμπλοκή της τοπικής κοινωνίας στην πρόληψη του εγκλήματος [The involvement of the local society in crime prevention] *Αστυνομική Επιθεώρηση [Police Review]*, August/September issue: 482–485 (2000).

Farsedakis, J., *Στοιχεία Εγκληματολγίαζ [Criminology Elements]* Athens, Βιβλιοθηκη [Law Library] (1996).

Kourakis, N.E., Εκθεση για την εξέλιξη της εγκλημα–τικότητας στη σημερινή Ελλάδα [Report on the development of criminality in today's Greece] *Ποινικ΄η Δικαιοσ΄υνη [Penal Justice]*, 10/1999, 1036–1041 (1999).

Kourakis, N.E., Το οργανωμένο έγκλνμα: Φαινομενολογία του προβλήματος και δυνατότητες αντιμετώπισής του στην Ελλάδα [Organized crime: Phenomenology of the problem and possibilities of tackling it in Greece] *Ποινική Δικαιοσύνη [Penal Justice]*, 10/1999, 1017–1026 (1999).

Panousis, I., Τοπικ΄η κοινωνια και ΄εγκλνμα [Local society and crime] *Επιθε΄ωρηση [Police Review]*, August/September issue: 494–497 (2000).

Spinellis, K., *Crime in Greece in Perspective,* Ant. N. Sakkoulas Publishers, Athens-Komotini, 1997.

Tonry, M. and David, P.F., Strategic Approaches to Crime Prevention, *Building a Safer Society, Crime and Justice: A Review of Research,* Vol. 19, The University of Chicago Press, Chicago, IL, 1995, pp. 1–20.

Zarafonitou, C., *Εμπειρικη Εγκληματολογία [Empirical Criminology]* Athens: Νομικη Βιβλιοθήκη [Law Library] (1995).

Guilty Pleas and Plea Bargaining

A person accused of committing a felony is charged in criminal court with the violation of one or more statutes. To these formal charges, the defendant is required to respond with a plea of "not guilty" or "guilty." This response occurs quite early in criminal case processing, usually at the arraignment soon after arrest. In countries following the Anglo-American common law tradition, this procedure is almost universal, though there are a few variations in which defendants may also be allowed to plead *nolo contendere* (not contesting the charges, though not admitting guilt) or "guilty with an explanation." When the plea is "guilty," the judge will ascertain that the plea is voluntary and then officially convict the defendant of the crime. A guilty plea aborts the trial. By contrast, when the plea is "not guilty," proceedings must continue under the legal presumption of innocence, ending eventually with either a guilty plea at a subsequent stage or a verdict of conviction or acquittal decided by a jury after a trial. Sometimes, if the defendant does not plead guilty, a trial may be held solely before a judge if the defendant waives the right to trial by jury; these "bench trials" can comprise a small but significant percentage of the total of case dispositions.

In common law countries (e.g., Australia, Barbados, Canada, Ireland, New Zealand, South Africa, the United Kingdom, and the U.S.), a guilty plea is very often the result of negotiations between attorneys over what the sentence will be, or at the very least the guilty plea is made with the expectation that the resulting sentence will fall into a well-understood norm of typical punishment for that type of crime. If the defendant pleads guilty, the judge will convict and the case will proceed directly to sentencing. Except for finding information relevant to punishment, the investigation ends, so there will be no evidence or witnesses or proof presented and challenged in a public trial.

In civil law countries (e.g., Denmark, France, Germany, Guatemala, Italy, Nicaragua, Norway, Portugal, and Spain), felony defendants may admit guilt at any time, or continue to maintain innocence, but in either event the proceedings must unfold fully based on a complete investigation by a magistrate. A dossier of evidence from the investigation is prepared and presented at trial, and the defendant is not expected to plead guilty beforehand. By contrast, in countries using some variation of the socialist legal system originally instituted in the Soviet Union, defendants are expected first to admit guilt and afterwards testify at trial, though it is possible to claim innocence throughout the entire proceeding. In the socialist system, full disclosure and public presentation of the facts is expected in every case, as in the civil law tradition from which the socialist system evolved. The difference is that investigation continues and trial begins after the defendant admits guilt. The trial becomes, in essence, a sentencing hearing and public explanation of the crime event. That system is used in China today.

The function of the guilty plea can vary even between cases in the same jurisdiction. The guilty plea may be a reluctant acquiescence to state authority, a confession based on true remorse or at least acceptance of responsibility, or a strategic move for which the defendant expects to gain a lower sentence. Any or all of these elements may be at play when defendants plead guilty. Moreover, there are benefits to the state. Convincing a defendant to plead guilty imposes discipline on the criminal, vindicates the victim, and saves the state (the prosecution) the time and money required to take the case to trial. The latter benefit accrues only in common law systems in which the guilty plea aborts the trial; in nations that accept guilty pleas but nevertheless proceed with investigation and prosecution and trial, cost-savings are not an important factor.

Considering all the different reasons that defendants might plead guilty and the variety of court procedures for guilty pleas in different legal systems, it seems that cost-savings would not fully explain why guilty pleas account for approximately 95% of all criminal case dispositions in the U.S. Yet this is the most common and popular explanation for the prevalence of plea bargaining in the U.S. The assumption is that a defendant essentially "purchases" a lower sentence by pleading guilty and thus agreeing to save the state the cost of a trial. If the accused does not plead guilty and instead insists on having a trial, a conviction after trial will carry a heavier sentence. Critics claim that this amounts to unconstitutional coercion, since it punishes a defendant more harshly for exercising constitutional rights (Alschuler, 1968; Brereton and Casper, 1981). Supporters of the system counter with the assertion that guilty people who confess should be rewarded for their acceptance of responsibility (United States Sentencing Commission, 1995). Being rewarded for remorse is different from being rewarded for saving the state money, but judges seldom make the distinction when they accept a plea bargained guilty plea and agree to sentence the defendant according to the terms of the agreement that the prosecutor and defense attorney have made.

Historically, the reasons that plea bargaining and resulting guilty pleas became the predominant method of case disposition in the U.S. did not involve high caseloads or saving the time and expense of trials. Plea bargaining in serious criminal cases began in the mid-nineteenth century (Naheri, 1998; Vogel, 1999) when the number of cases was low and criminal courts could readily accommodate full trials in all cases (Heumann, 1975). Nevertheless, court records show that by the 1920s, plea bargained guilty pleas were the most common method of case disposition in felony cases (Alschuler, 1979) and the practice steadily increased until, by the 1970s, about 90% of all felony cases were concluded through guilty pleas. There are several theories about why this occurred. In the 1860s and subsequent decades, when plea bargaining first appeared, scholars believe that guilty pleas increased because public prosecutors and police became professionalized, serving full-time in those roles instead of their previous "jack-of-all-trades" private practices. Professional interchange between these full-time court professionals, a small private defense bar, and established full-time judges meant that those within the courtroom workgroup became "repeat players" accustomed to the routine disposition of cases and thus able to predict trial outcomes and set sentences based on probabilities of what would happen if the cases went through trials (Alschuler, 1979; Feeley, 1997; Nasheri, 1998). Agreeing to guilty pleas with definite sentences attached eliminated the uncertainty of trial for prosecutors (who feared acquittals) and defenders (who feared high sentences). Sociologists state that once these agreements became common, a typical "going rate" of the expected sentence for a "normal crime" developed, so the system became routine and bureaucratic (Sudnow, 1978). This routinization or explanation of normal crimes is the most widespread among contemporary scholars, and it runs counter to the economic efficiency explanation (which means that plea bargaining is based on the need to save money and the time of trials).

But these explanations do not cleanly contradict each other. Probably, plea bargaining originally arose because of the movement toward court professionalization and bureaucratization of criminal procedure; the newly professional courthouse workgroup developed shared assumptions about typical crimes and normal punishments. But as the practice became embedded in the legal culture, governments began to appropriate only enough money for courts to dispose of the majority of cases through guilty pleas. The pressure to avoid trials increased with urbanization and rising crime rates in the twentieth century. Elite judges and attorneys were reluctant to give full trials to every defendant of the rising urban underclass and immigrant population (Nasheri, 1998, 81). Later, in the 1960s and 1970s, the "due process revolution" expanded the rules of criminal procedure and evidence, and trials therefore become more complex and expensive. Criminal courts in the U.S. became increasingly dependent on plea bargaining as a way of avoiding complicated and costly trials.

How plea bargaining itself is actually conducted has been fully described in the legal and sociological literature (Alschuler, 1968, 1975, and 1976; Mather, 1979; McCoy, 1993) and contrasts with popular notions about plea negotiations and punishment. Whereas, it is true that the system is regarded as providing benefits to all parties involved—-to the prosecutor, because the uncertainty of trial is avoided and the defendant will be punished; to the defendant, because the sentence will be shorter or some charges will be reduced or dropped; to the victim, because the ordeal of testifying at trial is avoided; and to the court and judge, because the expense of trial is avoided—this does not mean that the actual facts of the crime nor defendant culpability or strength of the prosecution evidence are ignored. When prosecutors and defense attorneys negotiate over whether a defendant will plead guilty, they discuss how strong the evidence is. They argue over the meaning of particular case facts, whether the facts probably prove guilt beyond a reasonable doubt and if so, seriousness of the offense (Utz, 1978). They rely on police reports and investigation, and they try to predict how a jury and judge would regard this evidence if the case were to go to trial. If they agree on a plea bargain, it is often because the evidence is not considered strong enough to prove the original charges or because the degree of the defendant's blameworthiness does not warrant a heavy sentence.

But these discussions and agreements are made between the two opposing attorneys, not in a public trial, and therefore the American system has the hint of corruption. Legal scholars in civil law countries condemn this system for its lack of public accountability, and the inevitable sloppiness it encourages may result in inaccurate outcomes. "Inaccurate" dispositions could be convictions and sentences that are either too lenient or too harsh for what the accused person actually did, and it is quite probable that American plea bargaining allows a greater proportion of these mistakes to occur than does the civil law system, in which each case must be fully investigated and sent to trial. But it is important to note that the two systems are not directly comparable. Germany, for instance, is the country most often studied and reported as the "land without plea bargains" (Langbein, 1979). Trial procedure there is less complex since there is no jury, and the role of the judge is more active, involving witness questioning and investigation of the case (Fairchild and Dammer, 2001), so it is possible to say that every defendant can have a trial because they are quicker and less costly. However, although it is true that in Germany all serious felonies (*verbrechen*) such as homicides, rapes, assaults and drug importing are subjected to full investigation and trial, these cases comprise only a very small proportion of the criminal caseload. Felonies of medium seriousness (*vergehen*) such as burglaries, frauds, and thefts are punishable by fines and short jail terms and do not invoke full trial procedure—in fact, they are considered to be misdemeanors and are concluded when a prosecutor applies to the judge for a "penal order" imposing a fine or jail term or both on the defendant, and the defendant does not object. If the defendant objects, a full trial ensures. But in the great majority of cases, the defendant and his attorney review the state's evidence and then do not object to the findings of fact and the established sentence. When defendants do not contest the charges, they are punished with statutorily mandated sentences. In the U.S., this would be regarded as guilty pleas without explicit bargains. Pleading guilty "straight up" to a crime as charged is common for nonserious felonies in the U.S., often with some token reduction in charges, confirming the sociologists' observation that a bureaucratic court can communicate to everyone what a typical punishment for a "normal crime" will be.

Thus, contemporary guilty plea procedures around the world have some features in common. They settle criminal prosecutions before trial when there is a consensus among attorneys and judges that the punishments are just and for reasons of efficiency. They remove the majority of criminal cases from the necessity of going through trials, so that only the most serious cases or the cases with the most ambiguous evidence will be subjected to trials before judges and juries. They also have some features that are different. In the U.S., the guilty plea agreements are made between the two opposing sides in the case, while in civil countries the judge conducts the investigation and is more influential in determining punishment. In the U.S., guilty plea negotiations are conducted privately, while elsewhere the evidence is investigated by a magistrate and then fully aired publicly before a decision may be made. Finally, the American system rests on the assumption—which may be faulty in many cases—that the sentence will be harsher if the defendant is convicted after trial than it would be if the defendant pleaded guilty, an assumption that in other countries is considered to be a violation of statutory sentencing requirements.

Guilty plea and plea bargaining procedures are constantly evolving, especially as the role of the prosecutor and operation of sentencing laws change, but there is no indication in any nation that the procedures are moving towards a greater reliance on trials. Rather, any reforms are likely to concentrate on regulating the conditions of guilty pleas. In Germany, even some serious felony cases now end in guilty pleas with agreed sentences imposed (Herrmann, 1992). These cases are few, but they involve the same circumstances that first gave rise to plea bargaining in the U.S.: the uncertainty of obtaining witness testimony and other difficulties in proof in complex, multidefendant cases. In the U.S., any criticism of the guilty plea system arises from concerns that prosecutors have become too powerful compared to judges when operating under sentencing guidelines and mandatory sentencing systems (Stith and Cabranes, 1998). Recommendations for reform usually involve calls for greater judicial scrutiny of the facts and proof in the plea agreements that prosecutors bring to judges for ratification and conviction, but not calls to eliminate plea bargains themselves. As it has in the past, guilty plea procedure will evolve depending on new historical circumstances, but it is difficult to imagine circumstances that would result in significantly fewer guilty pleas and correspondingly more trials.

CANDACE MCCOY AND SATENIK MARGARYAN

References and Further Readings

Alschuler, A.W., Guilty Plea Bargaining: Compromises by Prosecutors to Secure Guilty Pleas, *University of Pennsylvania Law Review,* 112 (1964).

Alschuler, A.W., The Prosecutor's Role in Plea Bargaining, *University of Chicago Law Review,* 36 (1968).

Alschuler, A.W., The Defense Attorney's Role in Plea Bargaining, *Yale Law Journal,* 84 (1975).

Alschuler, A.W., The Trial Judge's Role in Plea Bargaining, *Columbia Law Review,* 76 (1976).

Alschuler, A.W., Plea Bargaining and its History, *Columbia Law Review,* 79 (1979).

Alschuler, A.W., The Changing Plea Bargaining Debate, *University of California Law Review,* 69 (1981).

Brereton, D. and Casper, J., Does It Pay to Plead Guilty? Differential Sentencing and the Functioning of Criminal Courts, *Law and Society Review,* vol.

Fairchild, E. and Dammer, H., *Comparative Criminal Justice Systems* 2nd ed., Wadsworth Publishing, Belmont, CA, 2001.

Feeley, M.M., Perspectives on Plea Bargaining, *Law and Society Review,* 13 (1979).

——, ——-. Legal Complexity and the Transformation of the Criminal Process: The Origins of Plea Bargaining. *Israel Law Review,* 31 (1997).

Heumann, M., A Note on Plea Bargaining and Case Pressure, *Law & Society Review,* 9, 515 (1975).

Johnson, D.T., The Organization of Prosecution and the Possibility of Order, *Law & Society Review,* 32, 247 (1998).

Herrmann, J., Bargaining Justice: A Bargain for German Criminal Justice? *University of Pittsburgh Law Review,* 53 (1992).

————-, –. Models for the Reform of Criminal Procedure in Eastern Europe: Comparative Remarks on Changes in Trial Structure and European Alternatives to Plea Bargaining, in M. Wise, Ed., *Criminal Science in a Global Society: Essays in Honor of Gerhard O.W. Mueller,* Fred B. Rothman, Littleton, CO, 1994.

Langbein, J.H., *Land Without Plea-Bargaining? How the Germans Do It, Michigan Law Review,* 78 (1979).

Mather, L., *Plea Bargaining or Trial? The Process of Criminal Case Disposition,* Lexington Books, Lexington, MA, 1979.

McCoy, C., Prosecution, in Tonry, M., Ed., *The Handbook of Crime and Punishment*, Oxford University Press, New York, pp. 457–472 (1998).

McCoy, C., *Politics and Plea Bargaining: Victim's Rights in California,* University of Pennsylvania Press, Philadelphia, PA, 1993.

Nasheri, H., *Betrayal of Due Process: A Comparative Assessment of Plea Bargaining in the United States and Canada,* University Press of America, Lanham, MA, 1998.

Stith, K. and Cabranes, J., *Fear of Judging,* University of Chicago Press, Chicago, IL, 1998.

Sudnow, D., Normal Crimes: Sociological Features of the Penal Code in a Public Defender's Office, *Social Problems,* 12, 255–277.

Utz, P.J., *Settling the Facts: Discretion and Negotiation in Criminal Court*, Sage, Thousand Oaks, CA, 1978.

United States Sentencing Commission, *1995 United States Sentencing Guidelines Manual,* amended, Guideline 3E1.1, Chapt. 3: Adjustments.

Vogel, M.E., The Social Origins of Plea Bargaining: Conflict and the Law in the Process of State Formation, 1830–1860, *Law and Society Review,* 33 (1999).

Vorenberg, J., Decent Restraint on Prosecutorial Power, *Harvard Law Review* 94, 1521–1573 (1981).

See also **Trials, Criminal**

Gun Control *See* **Firearms**